INDIA 2017

A REFERENCE ANNUAL

Compiled by

NEW MEDIA WING

PUBLICATIONS DIVISION

MINISTRY OF INFORMATION AND BROADCASTING

GOVERNMENT OF INDIA

2017 (Saka 1938)
61st Edition

ISBN 978-81-230-2328-1
REF-ENG-OP-120-2016-17

Price : ₹ 350.00

Published by

Additional Director General,
Publications Division,
Ministry of Information and Broadcasting,
Government of India,
Soochna Bhawan, CGO Complex,
Lodhi Road, New Delhi-110 003
http :// www.publicationsdivision.nic.in

Compilation and Coordination by New Media Wing
B.Narayanan, Smita Vats Sharma,
Naveen Joshi, Simmi Kumar, Shivanand Pandey

Edited by Publications Division
S.Manjula, A.K.Srivastava, Roma Chatterjee,
Ponnein Selvan M, Ashutosh Mohle

Cover Design by Publications Division
Asha Saxena
Production Coordination by Publications Division
V.K.Meena

Sales Centres : • Soochna Bhavan, C.G.O. Complex, Lodhi Road, **New Delhi**-110003 • Hall No. 196, Old Secretariat, **Delhi**-110054 • 701, B-Wing, Kendriya Sadan, Belapur, **Navi Mumbai**-400614 • 8, Esplanade East, **Kolkata**-700069 • 'A' Wing, Rajaji Bhawan, Besant Nagar, **Chennai**-600090 • Press Road, Near Govt. Press, **Thiruvananthapuram**-695001 • Room No. 204. 2nd Floor CGO Towers, Kavadiguda, **Hyderabad**-500080 • 1st Floor, 'F' Wing, Kendriya Sadan, Koramangala, **Bengaluru**-560034 • Bihar State Co-operative Bank Building, Ashoka Rajpath, **Patna**-800004 • Hall No. 1, 2nd Floor, Kendriya Bhawan, Sector-H, Aliganj, **Lucknow**-226024 • Ambica Complex, 1st Floor, Paldi, **Ahmedabad**-380007 • House No. 7, New Colony, Cheni Kuthi, KKB Road, **Guwahati**-781003.

Typesetter : Quick Prints, Naraina, New Delhi-110 028.
Printed at : International Print-o-Pac Ltd., Noida

Contents

1 Land and the People

"INDIA is the cradle of the human race, the birthplace of human speech, the mother of history, the grandmother of legend and the great grandmother of tradition. Our most valuable and most instructive materials in the history of man are treasured up in India only."—Mark Twain

India has a unique culture and is one of the oldest and greatest civilizations of the world. It stretches from the snow-capped Himalayas in the north to sun drenched coastal villages of the south and the humid tropical forests on the south-west coast, from the fertile Brahmaputra valley on its east to the Thar desert in the west. It covers an area of 32,87,263 sq. km.[1] It has achieved all-round socio-economic progress during the last 66 years of its Independence. India is the seventh largest country in the world and ranks second in population. The country stands apart from the rest of Asia, marked off as it is by mountains and the sea, which give her a distinct geographical entity. Bounded by the Great Himalayas in the north, it stretches southwards and at the Tropic of Cancer tapers off into the Indian Ocean between the Bay of Bengal on the east and the Arabian Sea on the west.

Lying entirely in the northern hemisphere, the mainland extends between latitudes 8°4' and 37°6' north, longitudes 68°7' and 97°25' east and measures about 3,214 km from north to south between the extreme latitudes and about 2,933 km from east to west between the extreme longitudes. It has a land frontier of about 15,200 km. The total length of the coastline of the mainland, Lakshadweep Islands and Andaman and Nicobar Islands is 7,516.6 km.

Geographical Background

Countries having a common border with India are Afghanistan and Pakistan to the north-west, China, Bhutan and Nepal to the north, Myanmar to the far east and Bangladesh to the east. Sri Lanka is separated from India by a narrow channel of sea formed by the Palk Strait and the Gulf of Mannar. The country can be divided into six zones mainly north, south, east, west, central and north-east zone. It has 29 states and seven union territories.

Physical Features

The mainland comprises four regions, namely, the great mountain zone, plains of the Ganga and the Indus, the desert region and the southern peninsula.

The Himalayas comprise three almost parallel ranges interspersed with large plateaus and valleys, some of which, like the Kashmir and Kullu valleys, are fertile, extensive and of great scenic beauty. Some of the highest

[1] Provisional figures

peaks in the world are found in these ranges. The high altitudes allow travel only through a few passes, notably the Jelep La and Nathu La on the main Indo-Tibet trade route through the Chumbi valley, north-east of Darjeeling and Shipki La in the Satluj valley, north-east of Kalpa (Kinnaur). The mountain wall extends over a distance of about 2,400 km with a varying depth of 240 to 320 km. In the east, between India and Myanmar and India and Bangladesh, hill ranges are much lower. Garo, Khasi, Jaintia and Naga Hills, running almost east-west, join the chain to Mizo and Rakhine Hills running north-south.

The plains of the Ganga and the Indus, about 2,400 km long and 240 to 320 km broad, are formed by basins of three distinct river systems—the Indus, the Ganga and the Brahmaputra. They are one of the world's greatest stretches of flat alluvium and also one of the most densely populated areas on the earth. Between the Yamuna at Delhi and the Bay of Bengal, nearly 1,600 km away, there is a drop of only 200 metres in elevation.

The desert region can be divided into two parts—the 'great desert' and the 'little desert'. The great desert extends from the edge of the Rann of Kutch beyond the Luni river northward. The whole of the Rajasthan-Sind frontier runs through this. The little desert extends from the Luni between Jaisalmer and Jodhpur up to the northern west. Between the great and the little deserts lies a zone of absolutely sterile country, consisting of rocky land, cut up by limestone ridges.

The Peninsular Plateau is marked off from the plains of the Ganga and the Indus by a mass of mountain and hill ranges varying from 460 to 1,220 metres in height. Prominent among these are the Aravali, Vindhya, Satpura, Maikala and Ajanta. The Peninsula is flanked on the one side by the Eastern Ghats where average elevation is about 610 metres and on the other by the Western Ghats where it is generally from 915 to 1,220 metres, rising in places to over 2,440 metres. Between the Western Ghats and the Arabian Sea lies a narrow coastal strip, while between Eastern Ghats and the Bay of Bengal, there is a broader coastal area. The southern point of the plateau is formed by the Nilgiri Hills where the Eastern and the Western Ghats meet. The Cardamom Hills lying beyond may be regarded as a continuation of the Western Ghats.

Geological Structure

The geological regions broadly follow the physical features and may be grouped into three regions: the Himalayas and their associated group of mountains, the Indo-Gangetic Plain and the Peninsular Shield.

The Himalayan mountain belt to the north and the Naga-Lushai mountain in the east, are the regions of mountain-building movement. Most of this area, now presenting some of the most magnificent mountain scenery in the world, was under marine conditions about 60 crore years ago. In a series of mountain-building movements commencing about seven crore years ago, the sediments and the basement rocks rose to great heights. The weathering and erosive elements worked on these to produce the relief seen today. The Indo-Ganga plains are a great alluvial tract that separate the Himalayas in the north from the Peninsula in the south.

The Peninsula is a region of relative stability and occasional seismic disturbances. Highly metamorphosed rocks of the earliest periods, dating back as far as 380 crore years, occur in this area; the rest being covered by the Gondwana formations, lava flows belonging to the Deccan Trap formation and younger sediments.

River Systems

The river systems of India can be classified into four groups viz., (i) Himalayan rivers, (ii) Deccan rivers, (iii) Coastal rivers and (iv) Rivers of the inland drainage basin. The Himalayan rivers are formed by melting snow and glaciers and therefore, continuously flow throughout the year. During the monsoon months, Himalayas receive very heavy rainfall and rivers swell, causing frequent floods. The Deccan rivers on the other hand are rainfed and therefore fluctuate in volume. Many of these are non-perennial. The Coastal streams, especially on the west coast are short in length and have limited catchment areas. Most of them are non-perennial. The streams of inland drainage basin of western Rajasthan are few and far apart. Most of them are of an ephemeral character.

The main Himalayan river systems are those of the Indus and the Ganga-Brahmaputra-Meghna system. The Indus, which is one of the great rivers of the world, rises near Mansarovar in Tibet and flows through India and thereafter through Pakistan and finally falls into the Arabian sea near Karachi. Its important tributaries flowing in Indian territory are the Sutlej (originating in Tibet), the Beas, the Ravi, the Chenab and the Jhelum. The Ganga-Brahmaputra-Meghna is another important system of which the principal sub-basins are those of Bhagirathi and the Alaknanda, which join at Dev Prayag to form the Ganga. It traverses through Uttarakhand, Uttar Pradesh, Bihar and West Bengal. Below Rajmahal Hills, the Bhagirathi, which used to be the main course in the past, takes off, while the Padma continues eastward and enters Bangladesh. The Yamuna, the Ramganga, the Ghaghra, the Gandak, the Kosi, the Mahananda and the Sone are the important tributaries of the Ganga. Rivers Chambal and Betwa are the important sub-tributaries, which join the Yamuna before it meets the Ganga. The Padma and the Brahmaputra join at Bangladesh and continue to flow as the Padma or Ganga. The Brahmaputra rises in Tibet, where it is known as Tsangpo and runs a long distance till it crosses over into India in Arunachal Pradesh under the name of Dihang. Near Passighat, the Debang and Lohit join the river Brahmaputra and the combined river runs all along the Assam valley. It crosses into Bangladesh downstream of Dhubri.

The principal tributaries of Brahmaputra in India are the Subansiri, Jia Bhareli, Dhansiri, Puthimari, Pagladiya and the Manas. The Brahmaputra in Bangladesh fed by Teesta, etc. finally falls into the Ganga. The Barak river, the head stream of Meghna, rises in the hills in Manipur. The important tributaries of the river are Makku, Trang, Tuivai, Jiri, Sonai, Rukni, Katakhal, Dhaleswari, Langachini, Maduva and Jatinga. Barak continues in Bangladesh till the combined Ganga-Brahmaputra join it near Bhairab Bazar.

In the Deccan region, most of the major river systems flowing generally in the east fall into Bay of Bengal. The major east flowing rivers are Godavari, Krishna, Cauvery and Mahanadi. Narmada and Tapti are major west flowing rivers.

The Godavari in the southern Peninsula has the second largest river basin covering 10 per cent of the area of India. Next to it is the Krishna basin in the region and the Mahanadi is another large basin of the region. The basin of the Narmada in the uplands of the Deccan, flowing to the Arabian Sea and of the Cauvery in the south, falling into the Bay of Bengal are about the same size, though with different character and shape.

There are numerous coastal rivers, which are comparatively small. While only handful of such rivers drain into the sea near the delta of east coast, there are as many as 600 such rivers on the west coast.

A few rivers in Rajasthan do not drain into the sea. They drain into salt lakes and get lost in sand with no outlet to sea. Besides these, there are the desert rivers which flow for some distance and are lost in the desert. These are Luni, Machhu, Rupen, Saraswati, Banas, Ghaggar and others.

The entire country has been divided into 20 river basins/group of river basins comprising 12 major basins and eight composite river basins. The 12 major river basins are : (1) Indus, (2) Ganga-Brahmaputra-Meghna, (3) Godavari, (4) Krishna, (5) Cauvery, (6) Mahanadi, (7) Pennar, (8) Brahmani-Baitarani, (9) Sabarmati, (10) Mahi, (11) Narmada and (12) Tapti. Each of these basins has a drainage area exceeding 20,000 sq. km.

The eight composite river basins combining suitably together all the other remaining medium (drainage area of 2,000 to 20,000 sq.km) and small river systems (drainage area less than 2000 sq.km) for the purpose of planning and management are : (1) Subarnarekha—combining Subarnarekha and other small rivers between Subarnarekha and Baitarani; (2) east flowing rivers between Mahanadi and Pennar; (3) east flowing rivers between Pennar and Kanyakumari; (4) area of Inland drainage in Rajasthan desert; (5) west flowing rivers of Kutch and Saurashtra including Luni; (6) west flowing rivers from Tapi to Tadri; (7) west flowing rivers from Tadri to Kanyakumari and (8) minor rivers draining into Myanmar (Burma) and Bangladesh.

Climate/Seasons

The climate of India may be broadly described as tropical monsoon type. The Indian Meteorological Department (IMD) designates four official seasons: (i) Winter, from December to early April. The year's coldest months are December and January, when temperatures average around 10-15 °C (50-59°F) in the north-west; temperatures rise as one proceeds towards the equator, peaking around 20-25 °C (68-77 °F) in mainland India's south-east, (ii) Summer or pre-monsoon season, lasting from April to June (April to July in north-western India). In western and southern regions, the hottest month is April; for northern regions, May is the hottest month. Temperatures average around 32-40 °C (90-104 °F) in most of the interior, (iii) Monsoon or rainy season, lasting from June to September. The season is dominated by the humid south-west summer monsoon, which slowly sweeps across the country beginning in late May or early June. Monsoon rains begin to recede from North India at the beginning of October. South India typically receives more rainfall, and (iv) Post-monsoon season, lasting from October to December. In north-western India, October and November are usually cloudless.

The Himalayan states, being more temperate, experience two additional seasons: autumn and spring. Traditionally, Indians note six seasons, each about two months long. These are the spring *(Sanskrit : vasanta)*, summer *(grishma)*, monsoon *(varsha)*, early autumn *(sharada)*, late autumn *(hemanta)* and winter *(shishira)*. These are based on the astronomical division of the 12 months into six parts. The ancient Hindu calendar also reflects these seasons in its arrangement of months.

India's climate is affected by two seasonal winds—the north-east monsoon and the south-west monsoon. The north-east monsoon commonly known as winter monsoon blows from land to sea whereas south-west monsoon known as summer monsoon blows from sea to land after crossing the Indian ocean, the Arabian sea and the Bay of Bengal. The south-west monsoon brings most of the rainfall during the year in the country.

Flora

India is rich in flora. Available data place India in the tenth position in the world and fourth in Asia in plant diversity. From about 70 per cent geographical area surveyed so far, over 46,000 species of plants have been described by the Botanical Survey of India (BSI), Kolkata. The vascular flora, which forms the conspicuous vegetation cover, comprises 15,000 species.

With a wide range of climatic conditions from the torrid to the arctic, India has a rich and varied vegetation, which only a few countries of comparable size possess. India can be divided into eight distinct floristic regions, namely, the western Himalayas, the eastern Himalayas, Assam, the Indus plain, the Ganga plain, the Deccan, the Malabar and the Andamans.

The western Himalayan region extends from Kashmir to Kumaon. Its temperate zone is rich in forests of chir, pine, other conifers and broad-leaved temperate trees. Higher up, forests of deodar, blue pine, spruce and silver fir occur. The alpine zone extends from the upper limit of the temperate zone of about 4,750 metres or even higher. The characteristic trees of this zone are high-level silver fir, silver birch and junipers. The eastern Himalayan region extends from Sikkim eastwards and embraces Darjeeling, Kurseong and the adjacent tracts. The temperate zone has forests of oaks, laurels, maples, rhododendrons, alder and birch. Many conifers, junipers and dwarf willows also grow here. The Assam region comprises the Brahmaputra and the Surma valleys with evergreen forests, occasional thick clumps of bamboos and tall grasses. The Indus plain region comprises the plains of Punjab, western Rajasthan and northern Gujarat. It is dry, hot and supports natural vegetation. The Ganga plain region covers the area which is alluvial plain and is under cultivation for wheat, sugarcane and rice. Only small areas support forests of widely differing types. The Deccan region comprises the entire table land of the Indian Peninsula and supports vegetation of various kinds from shrub jungles to mixed deciduous forests. The Malabar region covers the excessively humid belt of mountain country parallel to the west coast of the Peninsula. Besides being rich in forest vegetation, this region produces important commercial crops, such as coconut, betelnut, pepper, coffee, tea, rubber and cashewnut. The Andaman region abounds in evergreen, mangrove, beach and diluvial forests. The Himalayan region extending from Kashmir to Arunachal Pradesh through Sikkim, Meghalaya and Nagaland and the Deccan Peninsula is rich in endemic flora, with a large number of plants which are not found elsewhere.

The flora of the country is being studied by BSI and its nine circle/field offices located all over the country along with certain universities and research institutions.

Ethno-botanical study deals with the utilization of plants and plant products by ethnic races. A scientific study of such plants has been done by BSI. A number of detailed ethno-botanical explorations have been conducted in different tribal areas of the country. More than 800 plant species of ethno-botanical interest have been collected and identified at different centres.

Owing to destruction of forests for agricultural, industrial and urban development, several Indian plants are facing threat of extinction. About 1,336 plant species are considered vulnerable and endangered. About 20 species of higher plants are categorized as possibly extinct, as these have not been sighted during the last six to ten decades. BSI brings out an inventory of endangered plants in the form of a publication titled 'Red Data Book.'

Faunal Resources

India is very rich in terms of biological diversity due to its unique biogeographical location, diversified climate conditions and enormous ecodiversity and geodiversity. India's immense biological diversity encompasses ecosystems, populations, species and their genetic make-up. This diversity can be attributed to the vast variety in physiography and climatic situations resulting in a diversity of ecological habitats ranging from tropical, sub-tropical, temperate, alpine to desert. According to world biogeographic classification, India represents two of the major realms (the Palearctic and Indo-Malayan) and three biomes (Tropical Humid Forests, Tropical Dry/Deciduous Forests and Warm Deserts/Semi-Deserts). The Wildlife Institute of India has proposed a modified classification which divides the country into ten biogeographic regions: Trans-Himalayan, Himalayan, Indian Desert, Semi-Arid, Western Ghats, Deccan Peninsula, Gangetic Plain, North-East India, Islands and Coasts. In the light of Biodiversity Convention, India holds a unique position with the priority of conservation of natural resources and sustainable development. Infact, within only about 2 per cent of world's total land surface, India is known to have over 7.50 per cent of the species of animals that the world holds and this percentage accounts nearly for 92,037 species so far known, of which insects alone include 61,375 species. It is estimated that about two times that number of species still remain to be discovered in India alone.

Demographic Background

Census

The Census of India 2001, was historic and epoch making, being the first census of the twenty-first century and the third millennium. It reveals benchmark data on the state of abundant human resources available in the country, their demography, culture and economic structure at a juncture, which marks a centennial and millenial transition.

Census 2011 was the 15th census of its kind since 1872. It was held in two phases:

1. House listing and Housing Census (April to September, 2010) and
2. Population Enumeration (February 9th to 28th 2011 with Revisional round during 1st to 5th March,2011). Reference Date was 0.00 hour of March 1st, 2011. In snow bound areas, the Population Enumeration was conducted from September 11th to 30th, 2010. The Final Population data was released on April 30th, 2013. The general trends of census 2011 are being mentioned as under:

- Population: Persons-1,210.9 million; Males=623.3 million; and Females-587.6 million.
- Density of Population 2001-2011: density in 2001=325 and density in 2011-382, difference being 17.5 per cent (density is defined as the number of persons/sq. km.)
- Gender composition of Population 2011: Overall sex ratio at the national level has increased by 7 points since census 2001 to reach 943 at census 2011. This is the highest sex ratio recorded since census 1991.
- As per the census 2011, literates constituted 73.0 per cent of the total population aged seven and above and illiterates formed 27.0 per cent. Literacy rate has gone up from 64.8 per cent in 2001 to 73.0 per cent showing an increase of 8.2 percentage points. It is encouraging to note that out of a total of 202,951,015 literates added during the decade, females 104,721,109 outnumber males 98,229,906.

Population

The population of India as on March 1, 2011 stood at 1,210.9 million (623.2 million males and 587.5 million females). India accounts for a meagre 2.4 per cent of the world surface area of 135.79 million sq.km. Yet, it supports and sustains a whopping per cent of the world population.

The population of India, which at the turn of the twentieth century was around 238.4 million, increased to reach 1,210.9 million by 2011. The population of India as recorded at each decennial census from 1901 has grown steadily except for a decrease during 1911-21.

Population Density

One of the important indices of population concentration is the density of population. It is defined as the number of persons per sq.km. The population density of India in 2011 was 382 per sq. km-decadal growth 17.72 per cent.

The density of population increased in all states and union territories between 1991 and 2011. Among major states, Bihar is the most thickly populated state with (a population density of) 1,106 persons per sq.km followed by West Bengal 1,028 and Kerala 860.

Sex Ratio

Sex ratio, defined as the number of females per thousand males is an important social indicator to measure the extent of prevailing equality between males and females in a society at a given point of time. The sex ratio in the country has always remained unfavourable to females. It was 972 at the beginning of the twenthieth century and thereafter showed continuous decline until 1941. The sex ratio from 1901-2011 has registered a 10 point increase at census 2011 over 2001; however, child sex ratio has declined to 919 per thousand male.

Literacy

For the purpose of census 2011, a person aged seven and above, who can both read and write with understanding in any language, is treated as literate. A person, who can only read but cannot write, is not literate. In the censuses prior to 1991, children below five years of age were necessarily treated as illiterates.

The results of 2011 census reveal that there has been an increase in literacy in the country. The literacy rate in the country is 73.0 per cent, 80.9 for males and 64.6 for females.

Kerala retained its position by being on top with a 94 per cent literacy rate, closely followed by Lakshadweep (91.9 per cent). Bihar with a literacy rate of 61.8 per cent ranks last in the country. Kerala also occupies the top spot in the country both in male literacy with 96.1 per cent and female literacy with 92.1 per cent. On the contrary, Bihar has recorded the lowest literacy rates both in case of males (71.2 per cent) and females (51.5 per cent).

Table 1.1 : Percentage Decadal Variation in Population: 1901-1911 to 2001-2011

Sl.No.	India State/ Union Territory	1901-1911	1911-1921	1921-1931	1931-1941	1941-1951	1951-1961	1961-1971	1971-1981	1981-1991	1991-2001	2001-2011
1	2	3	4	5	6	7	8	9	10	11	12	13
	India	5.75	-0.31	11.00	14.22	13.31	21.64	24.30	24.66	23.86	21.54	17.72
1.	Jammu and Kashmir	7.16	5.75	10.14	10.36	10.42	9.44	29.65	29.59	30.34	29.43	23.71
2.	Himachal Pradesh	-1.22	1.65	5.28	11.54	5.42	17.87	23.04	23.71	20.79	17.54	12.81
3.	Punjab	-10.78	6.26	12.02	19.82	-4.58	21.56	21.70	23.89	20.81	20.10	13.73
4.	Chandigarh*	-16.07	-1.65	9.10	14.11	7.47	394.13	114.59	75.55	42.16	40.28	17.10
5.	Uttarakhand	8.20	-1.23	8.74	13.63	12.67	22.57	24.42	27.45	24.23	20.41	19.17
6.	Haryana	-9.70	1.95	7.14	15.63	7.60	33.79	32.22	28.75	27.41	24.43	19.90
7.	NCT of Delhi*	1.98	18.03	30.26	44.27	90.00	52.44	52.93	53.00	51.45	47.02	20.96
8.	Rajasthan	6.70	-6.29	14.14	18.01	15.20	26.20	27.83	32.97	28.40	28.40	21.44
9.	Uttar Pradesh	-1.36	-3.16	9.56	13.57	11.78	16.38	19.54	25.39	25.55	25.85	20.09
10.	Bihar	1.52	-0.97	9.74	12.22	10.58	19.79	20.91	24.16	23.38	28.62	25.07
11.	Sikkim	48.98	-7.05	34.37	10.57	13.34	17.76	29.38	50.77	28.47	33.06	12.36
12.	Arunachal Pradesh	N.A	N.A	N.A.	N.A.	N.A	N.A.	38.91	35.15	36.83	27.00	25.92
13.	Nagaland	46.76	6.55	12.62	6.04	12.30	73.35	39.88	50.05	56.08	64.53	-0.47
14.	Manipur	21.71	10.32	16.04	14.92	12.80	35.04	37.53	32.46	29.29	24.85	24.50
15.	Mizoram	10.54	7.90	26.42	22.81	28.42	35.61	24.93	48.55	39.70	28.82	22.78
16.	Tripura	32.48	32.59	25.63	34.14	24.56	78.71	36.28	31.92	34.30	16.03	14.75
17.	Meghalaya	15.71	7.21	13.83	15.59	8.97	27.03	31.50	32.04	32.89	30.65	27.82
18.	Assam	16.99	20.48	19.91	20.40	19.93	34.98	34.95	23.36	24.24	18.92	16.93
19.	West Bengal	6.25	-2.91	8.14	22.93	13.22	32.80	26.87	23.17	24.73	17.77	13.93
20.	Jharkhand	11.19	0.31	16.86	12.13	9.35	19.69	22.58	23.79	24.03	23.36	22.34

Sl.No.	India State/ Union Territory	1901-1911	1911-1921	1921-1931	1931-1941	1941-1951	1951-1961	1961-1971	1971-1981	1981-1991	1991-2001	2001-2011
1	2	3	4	5	6	7	8	9	10	11	12	13
21.	Odisha	10.44	-1.94	11.94	10.22	6.38	19.82	25.06	20.17	20.06	16.25	13.97
22.	Chhattisgarh	24.15	1.41	14.51	13.04	9.42	22.77	27.12	20.39	25.73	18.27	22.59
23.	Madhya Pradesh	12.38	-2.40	10.21	12.06	8.38	24.73	29.28	27.16	27.24	24.26	20.30
24.	Gujarat	7.79	3.79	12.92	19.25	18.69	26.88	29.39	27.67	21.19	22.66	19.17
25.	Daman and Diu	1.45	-3.26	15.98	17.52	13.55	-24.56	70.85	26.07	28.62	55.73	53.54
26.	Dadra and Nagar Haveli*	19.52	6.99	23.23	5.70	2.70	39.56	27.96	39.78	33.57	59.22	55.50
27.	Maharashtra	10.74	-2.91	14.91	11.99	19.27	23.60	27.45	24.54	25.73	22.73	15.99
28.	Andhra Pradesh	12.49	-0.13	12.99	12.75	14.02	15.65	20.90	23.10	24.20	14.59	11.10
29.	Karnataka	3.60	-1.09	9.38	11.09	19.36	21.57	24.22	26.75	21.12	17.51	15.67
30.	Goa	2.36	-3.55	7.62	7.05	1.21	7.77	34.77	26.74	16.08	15.21	8.07
31.	Lakshadweep	4.35	-6.31	17.62	14.43	14.60	14.61	31.92	26.53	28.47	17.30	+6.23
32.	Kerala	11.75	9.16	21.85	16.04	22.82	24.76	26.29	16.24	14.32	9.43	4.85
33.	Tamil Nadu	8.57	3.47	8.52	11.91	14.56	11.85	22.30	17.50	15.39	11.72	15.60
34.	Puducherry	4.39	-5.06	5.93	10.20	11.31	16.34	27.81	28.15	33.64	20.62	27.72
35.	Andaman and Nicobar Islands	7.34	2.37	8.78	14.61	-8.28	105.19	81.17	63.93	48.70	26.90	6.58

Note : ** Provisional Population Totals-India*

Table 1.2 : Total Population Growth during 2001-2011, India/State/Union Territory

	India/State/Union Territory*	Total Population						Population Growth
		2001			2011			(2001-2011)
		Persons	Males	Females	Persons	Males	Females	%
1	2	3	4	5	6	7	8	9
	India	1,02,87,37,436	53,22,23,090	49,65,14,346	1,21,08,54,977	62,32,70,258	58,75,84,719	17.72
1.	Jammu and Kashmir	1,01,43,700	53,60,926	47,82,774	1,25,41,302	66,40,662	59,00,640	23.64
2.	Himachal Pradesh	60,77,900	30,87,940	29,89,960	68,64,602	34,81,873	33,82,729	12.94
3.	Punjab	2,43,58,999	1,29,85,045	1,13,73,754	2,77,43,338	1,46,39,465	1,31,03,873	13.89
4.	Chandigarh*	9,00,635	5,06,938	3,93,697	10,55,450	5,80,663	4,74,787	17.19
5.	Uttarakhand	84,89,349	43,25,924	41,63,425	1,00,86,292	51,37,773	49,48,519	18.81
6.	Haryana	2,11,44,564	1,13,63,953	97,80,611	2,53,51,462	1,64,94,734	1,18,56,728	19.90
7.	NCT of Delhi*	1,38,50,507	76,07,234	62,43,273	1,67,87,941	89,87,326	78,00,615	21.21
8.	Rajasthan	5,65,07,188	2,94,20,011	2,70,87,177	6,85,48,437	3,55,50,997	2,29,97,440	21.31
9.	Uttar Pradesh	16,61,97,921	8,75,65,369	7,86,32,552	19,98,12,441	10,44,80,510	9,53,31,831	20.23
10.	Bihar	8,29,98,509	4,32,43,795	3,97,54,714	10,40,99,452	5,42,78,157	4,98,21,295	25.42
11.	Sikkim	5,40,851	2,88,484	2,52,367	6,10,577	3,30,070	2,87,507	12.89
12.	Arunachal Pradesh	10,97,968	5,79,941	5,18,027	13,83,727	7,13,912	6,69,815	26.03
13.	Nagaland	19,90,036	10,47,141	9,42,895	19,78,502	10,24,649	9,53,853	-0.58
14.	Manipur	22,93,896	11,61,952	11,31,944	28,55,794	14,38,586	14,17,208	24.50
15.	Mizoram	8,88,573	4,59,109	4,29,464	10,97,206	5,55,330	5,41,867	23.48

	India/State/Union Territory*	Total Population						Population Growth
		2001			2011			2001-2011
		Persons	Males	Females	Persons	Males	Females	%
1	2	3	4	5	6	7	8	9
16.	Tripura	31,99,203	16,82,225	15,56,978	36,73,917	18,74,376	17,99,541	14.84
17.	Meghalaya	23,18,822	11,76,087	11,42,735	29,66,889	14,91,832	14,75,057	27.95
18.	Assam	2,66,55,528	1,37,77,037	1,28,78,491	3,12,05,576	1,59,39,443	1,52,66,133	17.07
19.	West Bengal	8,01,76,197	4,14,65,985	3,87,10,212	9,12,76,115	4,68,09,027	4,44,67,088	13.84
20.	Jharkhand	2,69,45,829	1,38,85,037	1,30,60,792	3,29,88,134	1,69,30,315	1,60,57,819	22.42
21.	Odisha	3,68,04,660	1,86,60,570	1,81,44,090	4,19,74,213	2,12,12,136	2,07,62,082	14.05
22.	Chhattisgarh	2,08,33,803	1,04,74,218	1,03,59,585	2,55,45,198	1,28,32,895	1,27,12,303	22.61
23.	Madhya Pradesh	6,03,48,023	3,14,43,652	2,89,04,371	7,26,26,809	3,76,12,306	3,50,14,503	20.35
24.	Gujarat	5,06,71,017	2,63,85,577	2,42,85,440	6,04,39,692	3,14,91,260	2,89,48,432	19.28
25.	Daman and Diu*	1,58,204	92,512	65,692	2,43,247	1,50,301	92,946	53.76
26.	Dadra and Nagar Haveli*	2,20,490	1,21,666	98,824	3,43,709	1,93,760	1,49,949	55.88
27.	Maharashtra	9,68,78,627	5,04,00,596	4,64,78,031	11,23,74,333	5,82,43,056	5,41,31,227	15.99
28.	Andhra Pradesh	7,62,10,007	3,85,27,413	3,76,82,594	8,45,80, 777	4,24,42,146	4,21,38,631	10.98
29.	Karnataka	5,28,50,562	6,68,98,918	2,59,51,644	6,10,95,297	3,09,66,657	3,01,28,640	15.60
30.	Goa	13,47,668	6,87,248	6,60,420	14,58,545	7,39,140	7,19,405	8.23
31.	Lakshadweep*	60,650	31,131	29,519	64,473	33,123	31,350	6.30
32.	Kerala	3,18,41,374	1,54,68,614	1,63,72,707	3,34,06,061	1,60,27,412	1,73,78,649	4.91
33.	Tamil Nadu	6,24,05,679	3,14,00,909	3,10,04,770	7,21,47,030	3,61,37,975	3,60,09,055	15.61
34.	Puducherry*	9,74,345	4,86,961	4,87,384	12,47,953	6,12,511	6,35,442	28.08
35.	Andaman and Nicobar Islands*	3,56,152	1,92,972	1,63,180	3,80,581	2,02,871	1,77,710	6.86

Note : The population figures of India and Manipur includes estimated figures of three sub-divisions, viz., Mao Maram, Paomata and Purul of Senapati district of Manipur state for census 2001 due to administrative reasons.

Table 1.3 : Ranking of states by density 2001-2011

Rank in 2011	States/Union Territory*	Density 2011	Density 2001	Rank in 2001
1	2	3	4	5
	India	382	325	-
1.	NCT of Delhi*	11320	9340	1
2.	Chandigarh*	9528	7900	2
3.	Puducherry*	2547	2034	3
4.	Daman and Diu*	2191	1413	4
5.	Lakshadweep*	2149	1895	5
6.	Bihar	1102	881	6
7.	West Bengal	1028	903	7
8.	Kerala	860	819	8
9.	Uttar Pradesh	829	690	9
10.	Dadra and Nagar Haveli*	700	449	10
11.	Haryana	573	478	11
12.	Tamil Nadu	555	480	12
13.	Punjab	551	484	13
14.	Jharkhand	414	338	14
15.	Assam	398	340	15
16.	Goa	394	364	16
17.	Maharashtra	365	315	17
18.	Tripura	350	305	18
19.	Karnataka	319	276	19
20.	Gujarat	308	258	20
21.	Andhra Pradesh	308	277	21
22.	Odisha	270	236	22
23.	Madhya Pradesh	236	196	23
24.	Rajasthan	200	165	24
25.	Chhattisgarh	189	154	25
26.	Uttarakhand	189	159	26
27.	Meghalaya	132	103	27
28.	Himachal Pradesh	123	109	28
29.	Nagaland	119	120	29
30.	Manipur	128	103	30
31.	Sikkim	86	76	31
32.	Jammu and Kashmir	124	100	32
33.	Mizoram	52	42	33
34.	Andaman and Nicobar Islands*	46	43	34
35.	Arunachal Pradesh	17	13	35

Table 1.4 : Distribution of Population, Sex Ratio, Density and Decadal Growth rate of Population:2011

Sl. No.	India/State/ Union Territory*	Total Population Persons	Males	Females	Sex Ratio- (Females per 100	Density (Per sq. km)	Decadal growth rate
1	2	3	4	5	6	7	8
	India	1,21,08,54,977	62,32,70,258	58,75,84,719	943	382	17.72
1.	Jammu and Kashmir	1,25,41,302	66,40,662	59,00,640	889	124	23.71
2.	Himachal Pradesh	68,64,602	34,81,873	33,82,729	972	123	12.81
3.	Punjab	2,77,43,338	1,46,39,465	1,31,03,873	895	550	13.73
4.	Chandigarh*	10,55,450	5,80,663	4,74,787	818	9,252	17.10
5.	Uttarakhand	1,00,86,292	51,37,773	48,48,519	963	189	19.17
6.	Haryana	2,53,51,462	1,34,94,734	1,18,56,728	879	573	19.90
7.	NCT of Delhi*	1,67,87,941	89,87,326	78,00,615	868	11,297	20.96
8.	Rajasthan	6,85,48,437	3,55,50,997	3,29,97,440	928	201	21.44
9.	Uttar Pradesh	19,98,12,341	10,44,80,510	9,53,31,831	912	828	20.09
10.	Bihar	10,40,99,452	5,42,78,157	4,98,21,295	918	1,102	25.07
11.	Sikkim	6,10,577	3,23,070	2,87,507	890	86	12.36
12.	Arunachal Pradesh	13,83,727	7,13,912	6,69,815	938	17	25.92
13.	Nagaland	19,78,502	10,24,707	9,53,853	931	119	-04.47
14.	Manipur	28,55,794	14,38,586	14,17,208	985	128	24.50
15.	Mizoram	10,97,206	5,55,339	5,41,867	976	52	22.78
16.	Tripura	36,73,917	18,74,376	17,99,541	960	350	14.75
17.	Meghalaya	29,66,889	14,91,832	14,75,057	989	132	27.82
18.	Assam	3,12,05,576	1,59,39,443	1,52,66,133	958	397	16.93
19.	West Bengal	9,12,76,115	4,68,09,027	4,44,67,088	950	1,029	13.93
20.	Jharkhand	3,29,88,134	1,69,30,315	1,60,57,819	948	414	22.34
21.	Odisha	4,19,74,218	2,12,12,136	2,07,62,082	979	269	13.97
22.	Chhattisgarh	2,55,45,198	1,28,32,895	1,27,12,303	991	189	22.59
23.	Madhya Pradesh	7,26,26,809	3,76,12,306	3,50,14,503	931	236	20.30
24.	Gujarat	6,04,39,692	3,14,91,260	2,89,48,432	919	308	19.17
25.	Daman and Diu*	2,43,247	1,50,301	92,946	618	2,169	53.54
26.	Dadra and Nagar Haveli*	3,43,709	1,93,760	1,49,949	774	698	55.50
27.	Maharashtra	11,23,74,333	5,82,43,056	5,41,31,277	929	365	15.99
28.	Andhra Pradesh	8,45,80,777	4,24,42,146	4,21,38,631	993	398	11.10
29.	Karnataka	6,10,95,297	3,09,66,657	3,01,28,640	973	319	15.67
30.	Goa	14,58,545	7,39,140	7,19,405	973	394	8.17
31.	Lakshadweep*	64,473	33,123	31,350	946	2,013	6.23
32.	Kerala	3,34,06,061	1,60,27,412	1,73,78,649	1,084	859	4.86
33.	Tamil Nadu	7,21,47,030	3,61,37,975	3,60,09,055	996	555	15.60
34.	Puducherry*	12,47,953	6,12,511	6,35,442	1,037	2,598	27.72
35.	Andaman and Nicobar Islands*	3,80,581	2,02,871	1,77,710	876	46	6.68

Table 1.5 : Sex Ratio : 1901-2011

Census Year	Sex Ratio (Females per 1,000 males)
1901	972
1911	964
1921	955
1931	950
1941	945
1951	946
1961	941
1971	930
1981	934
1991	927
2001	933
2011	943

Notes:
1. *For 1981, interpolated figures for Assam have been used.*
2. *For 1991, interpolated figures for Jammu and Kashmir have been used.*
3. *The population figures of India and Manipur, includes estimated figures of three sub-divisions, viz., Mao Maram, Paomata and Purul of Senapati district of Manipur state for census 2001 and 2011 due to administrative reasons.*

Table 1.7 : Sex Ratio (Females per 1,000 Males): 1901-2011

State UT Code	India/State/ Union Territory*	Census Year 1901	1911	1921	1931	1941	1951	1961	1971	1981	1991	2001	2011
1	2	3	4	5	6	7	8	9	10	11	12	13	14
	India[1]	972	964	955	950	945	946	941	930	934	927	933	943
1.	Jammu and Kashmir	882	876	870	865	869	873	878	878	892	986	892	889
2.	Himachal Pradesh	884	889	890	897	890	912	938	958	973	976	968	972
3.	Punjab	832	780	799	815	836	844	854	865	879	882	876	895
4.	Chandigarh*	771	720	743	751	763	781	652	749	769	790	777	818
5.	Uttarakhand	918	907	916	913	907	940	947	940	936	936	962	963
6.	Haryana	867	835	844	844	869	871	868	867	870	865	861	879
7.	NCT of Delhi*	862	793	733	722	715	768	785	801	808	827	821	868
8.	Rajasthan	905	908	896	907	906	921	908	911	919	910	921	928
9.	Uttar Pradesh	938	916	908	903	907	908	907	876	882	876	898	912
10.	Bihar	1,061	1,051	1,020	995	1,002	1,000	1,005	957	948	907	919	918
11.	Sikkim	916	951	970	967	920	907	904	863	835	878	875	890
12.	Arunachal Pradesh	N.A	N.A	N.A	N.A	N.A	N.A	894	861	862	859	893	938
13.	Nagaland	973	993	992	997	1,021	999	933	871	863	886	900	931
14.	Manipur[1]	1,037	1,029	1,041	1,065	1,055	1,036	1,105	980	971	958	974	985
15.	Mizoram	1,113	1,120	1,109	1,102	1,069	1,041	1,009	946	919	921	935	976
16.	Tripura	874	885	885	885	886	904	932	943	946	945	948	960
17.	Meghalaya	1,036	1,013	1,000	971	966	994	937	942	954	955	972	989
18.	Assam	919	915	896	874	875	868	869	896	910	923	935	958
19.	West Bengal	945	925	905	890	852	865	878	891	911	917	934	950
20.	Jharkhand	1,032	1,021	1,002	989	978	961	960	945	940	922	941	948
21.	Odisha	1,037	1,056	1,086	1,067	1,053	1,022	1,001	988	981	971	972	979
22.	Chhattisgarh	1,046	1,039	1,041	1,043	1,032	1,024	1,008	998	996	985	989	991
23.	Madhya Pradesh	972	967	949	947	946	945	932	920	921	912	919	931
24.	Gujarat	954	946	944	945	941	952	940	934	942	934	920	919

Table 1.6 : Sex Ratio (Females per 1,000 Males): 1901-2011

State UT Code	India/State/ Union Territory*	Census Year 1901	1911	1921	1931	1941	1951	1961	1971	1981	1991	2001	2011
1	2	3	4	5	6	7	8	9	10	11	12	13	14
25.	Daman and Diu*	995	1,040	1,143	1,088	1,080	1,125	1,169	1,099	1,062	969	710	618
26.	Dadra and Nagar Haveli*	960	967	940	911	925	946	963	1,007	974	952	812	774
27.	Maharashtra	978	966	950	947	949	941	936	930	937	934	922	929
28.	Andhra Pradesh	985	992	993	987	980	986	981	977	975	972	973	993
29.	Karnataka	983	981	969	965	960	966	959	957	963	960	965	973
30.	Goa	1,091	1,108	1,120	1,088	1,084	1,128	1,006	981	975	967	961	973
31.	Lakshadweep*	1,063	987	1,127	994	1,018	1,043	1,020	978	975	943	948	946
32.	Kerala	1,004	1,008	1,011	1,022	1,027	1,028	1,022	1,016	1,032	1,036	1,058	1,084
33.	Tamil Nadu	1,044	1,042	1,029	1,027	1,012	1,007	992	978	977	974	987	996
34.	Puducherry*	N.A.	1,058	1,053	N.A.	N.A.	1,030	1,013	989	985	979	1,001	1,037
35.	Andaman and Nicobar Islands*	318	352	303	495	574	625	617	644	760	818	846	876

Note: 1. *For working out the sex ratio of India and Assam for 1981, interpolated figures for Assam have been used.*

2. *For working out the sex ratio of India and Jammu and Kashmir for 1991, interpolated figures for Jammu and Kashmir have been used.*

3. *The sex ratio for Arunachal Pradesh is not available for the years 1901-1951 and for Puducherry it is not available for the years 1901, 1931 and 1941.*

Table 1.7 : Ranking of States/UTs by Literacy Rate among persons, Males and Females, 2011 Census

	Persons		Males		Females	
	State/Union Territory*	Literacy Rate	State/Union Territory	Literacy Rate	State/Union Territory	Literacy Rate
1	2	3	4	5	6	7
1.	Kerala	94.0	Kerala	96.1	Kerala	92.1
2.	Lakshadweep*	91.8	Lakshadweep*	95.6	Mizoram	89.3
3.	Mizoram	91.3	Mizoram	93.3	Lakshadweep*	87.9
4.	Goa	88.7	Goa	92.6	Goa	84.7
5.	Tripura	87.2	Daman & Diu*	91.5	Tripura	82.7
6.	Daman and Diu*	87.1	Tripura	91.5	Andaman and Nicobar Islands*	82.4
7.	Andaman and Nicobar Islands*	86.6	Puducherry*	91.3	Chandigarh*	81.2
8.	NCT of Delhi*	86.2	NCT of Delhi*	90.9	NCT of Delhi*	80.8
9.	Chandigarh*	86.0	Andaman and Nicobar Islands*	90.3	Puducherry*	80.7
10.	Puducherry*	85.8	Chandigarh*	90.0	Daman and Diu*	79.5
11.	Himachal Pradesh	82.8	Himachal Pradesh	89.5	Nagaland	76.1
12.	Maharashtra	82.3	Maharashtra	88.4	Himachal Pradesh	75.9
13.	Sikkim	81.4	Uttarakhand	87.4	Maharashtra	75.9
14.	Tamil Nadu	80.1	Tamil Nadu	86.8	Sikkim	75.6
15.	Nagaland	79.6	Sikkim	86.6	Tamil Nadu	73.4
16.	Uttarakhand	78.8	Gujarat	85.8	Meghalaya	72.9
17.	Gujarat	78.0	Dadra and Nagar Haveli*	85.2	Punjab	70.7
18.	Manipur	76.9	Haryana	84.1	West Bengal	70.5
19.	West Bengal	76.3	Manipur	83.6	Manipur	70.3
20.	Dadra & Nagar Haveli*	76.2	Nagaland	82.8	Uttarakhand	70.0
21.	Punjab	75.8	Karnataka	82.5	Gujarat	69.7
22.	Haryana	75.6	West Bengal	81.7	Karnataka	68.1
23.	Karnataka	75.4	Odisha	81.6	Assam	66.3

Table 1.8 : Ranking of States/UTs by Literacy Rate among persons, Males and Females, 2011 Census

	Persons		Males		Females	
	State/Union Territory	Literacy Rate	State/Union Territory	Literacy Rate	State/Union Territory	Literacy Rate
1	2	3	4	5	6	7
24.	Meghalaya	74.4	Punjab	80.4	Haryana	65.9
25.	Odisha	72.9	Chhattisgarh	80.3	Dadra and Nagar Haveli*	64.3
26.	Assam	72.2	Rajasthan	79.2	Odisha	64.0
27.	Chhattisgarh	70.3	Madhya Pradesh	78.7	Chhattisgarh	60.2
28.	Madhya Pradesh	69.3	Assam	77.8	Madhya Pradesh	59.2
29.	Uttar Pradesh	67.7	Uttar Pradesh	77.3	Andhra Pradesh	59.1
30.	Jammu and Kashmir	67.2	Jharkhand	76.8	Arunachal Pradesh	57.7
31.	Andhra Pradesh	67.0	Jammu and Kashmir	76.8	Uttar Pradesh	57.2
32.	Jharkhand	66.4	Meghalaya	76.0	Jammu and Kashmir	56.4
33.	Rajasthan	66.1	Andhra Pradesh	74.9	Jharkhand	55.4
34.	Arunachal Pradesh	65.4	Arunachal Pradesh	72.6	Rajasthan	52.1
35.	Bihar	61.8	Bihar	71.2	Bihar	51.5

Table 1.9 : Literacy Rate in India: 1951-2011

Census Year	Persons	Males	Females	Male-Female gap in literacy rate
1	2	3	4	5
1951	18.33	21.16	8.86	12.30
1961	28.3	40.4	15.35	25.05
1971	34.45	45.96	21.97	23.98
1981	43.57	56.38	29.76	26.62
1991	52.21	64.13	39.29	24.84
2001	64.83	75.26	53.67	21.59
2011	72.98	80.88	64.63	16.25

Notes:

1. *Literacy rates for 1951,1961 and 1971 census relate to population aged five years and above. The rates for the 1981, 1991, 2001 and 2011 census relate to the population aged seven years and above.*
2. *The 1981 Literacy rates exclude Assam where the 1981 census could not be conducted. The 1991 census Literacy rates exclude Jammu and Kashmir.*

Table 1.10 : Literates and Literacy Rates by Sex: 2011

State UT	India/State/ Union Territory*	Literate Persons	Males	Females	Literacy Rate (%) Persons	Males	Females
1	2	3	4	5	6	7	8
	India	76,36,38,812	43,47,63,622	32,88,75,190	72.98	80.88	64.63
1.	Jammu and Kashmir	70,67,233	42,64,671	28,02,562	67.16	76.75	56.43
2.	Himachal Pradesh	50,39,736	27,52,590	22,87,146	82.8	89.53	75.93
3.	Punjab	1,87,07,137	1,04,36,056	82,71,081	75.84	80.44	70.73
4.	Chandigarh*	8,05,438	4,65,346	3,40,092	86.05	89.99	81.19
5.	Uttarakhand	68,80,953	38,63,708	30,17,245	78.82	87.40	70.01
6.	Haryana	1,65,98,988	97,94,067	68,04,921	75.554	84.06	65.94
7.	NCT of Delhi*	1,27,37,767	71,94,856	55,42,911	86.21	90.94	80.76
8.	Rajasthan	3,82,75,282	2,36,88,412	1,45,86,870	66.11	79.19	52.12
9.	Uttar Pradesh	11,43,97,555	6,82,34,964	4,61,62,591	67.68	77.28	57.18
10.	Bihar	5,25,04,553	3,16,08,023	2,08,96,530	61.80	71.20	51.50
11.	Sikkim	4,44,952	2,51,269	1,93,683	81.42	86.55	75.61
12.	Arunachal Pradesh	7,66,005	4,39,868	3,26,137	65.38	72.55	57.70
13.	Nagaland	13,42,434	7,23,957	6,18,477	79.55	82.75	76.11
14.	Manipur	19,08,475	10,39,858	8,68,618	76.94	83.58	70.26
15.	Mizoram	8,48,175	4,38,529	4,09,646	91.33	93.35	89.27
16.	Tripura	28,04,783	15,01,369	13,03,414	87.22	91.53	82.73
17.	Meghalaya	17,85,005	9,13,879	8,71,126	74.43	75.95	72.89
18.	Assam	1,91,77,977	1,05,68,639	86,09,338	72.19	77.85	66.27
19.	West Bengal	6,15,38,281	3,38,18,810	2,77,19,4717	76.26	81.69	70.54
20.	Jharkhand	1,83,28,069	1,08,82,519	74,45,550	66.41	76.84	55.42
21.	Odisha	2,67,42,595	1,50,89,681	1,16,52,914	72.87	81.59	64.01
22.	Chhattisgarh	1,53,79,922	88,07,893	65,72,029	70.28	80.27	60.24
23.	Madhya Pradesh	4,28,51,169	2,51,74,328	1,76,76,841	69.32	78.73	59.24
24.	Gujarat	4,10,93,358	2,34,74,873	1,76,18,485	78.03	85.75	69.68
25.	Daman and Diu*	1,88,406	1,24,643	63,763	87.10	91.54	79.55
26.	Dadra and Nagar Haveli*	2,23,320	1,42,521	80,709	76.24	85.17	64.32
27.	Maharashtra	8,15,54,290	4,52,57,584	3,62,96,706	82.34	88.38	75.87
28.	Andhra Pradesh	5,05,56,760	2,82,51,243	2,23,05,517	67.02	74.88	59.15
29.	Karnataka	4,06,47,322	2,25,08,471	1,81,38,851	75.36	82.47	68.08
30.	Goa	11,65,487	6,15,823	5,49,664	88.70	92.65	84.66
31.	Lakshadweep*	52,553	28,023	24,530	91.85	95.56	87.95
32.	Kerala	2,81,35,824	1,37,04,903	1,44,30,921	94.00	96.11	92.07
33.	Tamil Nadu	5,18,37,507	2,80,40,491	2,37,97,016	80.09	86.77	73.44
34.	Puducherry*	9,57,309	4,97,378	4,59,931	85.85	91.26	80.67
35.	Andaman and Nicobar Islands*	2,94,281	1,64,377	1,29,904	86.63	90.27	82.43

Table 1.11 Population of States/Union Territories by Sex and percentage share of Population in Total Population 2011

State UT code	India/State/Union Territory*	Total population Person	Males	Females	Percentage share in total population
1	2	3	4	5	6
	INDIA	1,21,08,54,977	62,32,70,258	58,75,84,719	100.00
1.	Jammu and Kashmir	1,25,41,302	66,40,662	59,00,640	1.04
2.	Himachal Pradesh	68,64,602	34,81,873	33,82,729	0.57
3.	Punjab	2,77,43,338	1,46,39,465	1,31,03,873	2.29
4.	Chandigarh*	10,55,450	5,80,663	4,74,787	0.09
5.	Uttarakhand	1,00,86,292	51,37,773	48,48,519	0.83
6.	Haryana	2,53,51,462	1,34,94,734	1,18,56,728	2.09
7.	NCT of Delhi*	1,67,87,941	89,87,326	78,00,615	1.39
8.	Rajasthan	6,85,48,437	3,55,50,997	3,29,97,440	5.66
9.	Uttar Pradesh	19,98,12,341	10,44,80,510	9,53,31,831	16.50
10.	Bihar	10,40,99,452	5,42,78,157	4,98,21,295	8.60
11.	Sikkim	6,10,577	3,23,070	2,87,507	0.05
12.	Arunachal Pradesh	13,83,727	7,13,912	6,69,815	0.11
13.	Nagaland	19,78,502	10,24,707	9,53,853	0.16
14.	Manipur	28,55,794	14,38,586	14,17,208	0.24
15.	Mizoram	10,97,206	5,55,339	5,41,867	0.09
16.	Tripura	36,73,917	18,74,376	17,99,541	0.30
17.	Meghalaya	29,66,889	14,91,832	14,75,057	0.25
18.	Assam	3,12,05,576	1,59,39,443	1,52,66,133	2.58
19.	West Bengal	9,12,76,115	4,68,09,027	4,44,67,088	7.54
20.	Jharkhand	3,29,88,134	1,69,30,315	1,60,57,819	2.72
21.	Odisha	4,19,74,218	2,12,12,136	2,07,62,082	3.47
22.	Chhattisgarh	2,55,45,198	1,28,32,895	1,27,12,303	2.11
23.	Madhya Pradesh	7,26,26,809	3,76,12,306	3,50,14,503	6.00
24.	Gujarat	6,04,39,692	3,14,91,260	2,89,48,432	4.99
25.	Daman and Diu*	2,43,247	1,50,301	92,946	0.02
26.	Dadra and Nagar Haveli*	3,43,709	1,93,760	1,49,949	0.03
27.	Maharashtra	11,23,74,333	5,82,43,056	5,41,31,277	9.28
28.	Andhra Pradesh	8,45,80,777	4,24,42,146	4,21,38,631	6.99
29.	Karnataka	6,10,95,297	3,09,66,657	3,01,28,640	5.05
30.	Goa	14,58,545	7,39,140	7,19,405	0.12
31.	Lakshadweep*	64,473	33,123	31,350	0.01
32.	Kerala	3,34,06,061	1,60,27,412	1,73,78,649	2.76
33.	Tamil Nadu	7,21,47,030	3,61,37,975	3,60,09,055	5.96
34.	Puducherry*	12,47,953	6,12,511	6,35,442	0.10
35.	Andaman and Nicobar Islands*	3,80,581	2,02,871	1,77,710	0.03

Table 1.12: States and Union Territories by Population in Descending order and Rank in 2001 and 2011 Census

Rank in 2011	State/Union Territory*	Total population 2011	Per cent to Total Population of India 2011	Per cent to Total Population of India 2001	Rank in 2001
1	2	3	4	5	6
1.	Uttar Pradesh	19,98,12,341	16.50	16.16	1
2.	Maharashtra	11,23,74,333	9.28	9.42	2
3.	Bihar	10,40,99,452	8.60	8.07	3
4.	West Bengal	9,12,76,115	7.54	7.79	4
5.	Andhra Pradesh	8,45,80,777	6.99	7.41	5
6.	Madhya Pradesh	7,26,26,809	6.00	5.87	7
7.	Tamil Nadu	7,21,47,030	5.96	6.07	6
8.	Rajasthan	6,85,48,437	5.66	5.49	8
9.	Karnataka	6,10,95,297	5.05	5.14	9
10.	Gujarat	6,04,39,692	4.99	4.93	10
11.	Odisha	4,19,74,218	3.47	3.58	11
12.	Kerala	3,34,06,061	2.76	3.10	12
13.	Jharkhand	3,29,88,134	2.72	2.62	13
14.	Assam	3,12,05,576	2.58	2.59	14
15.	Punjab	2,77,43,338	2.29	2.37	15
16.	Chhattisgarh	2,55,45,198	2.11	2.03	17
17.	Haryana	2,53,51,462	2.09	2.06	16
18.	NCT of Delhi*	1,67,87,941	1.39	1.35	18
19.	Jammu and Kashmir	1,25,41,302	1.04	0.99	19
20.	Uttarakhand	1,00,86,292	0.83	0.83	20
21.	Himachal Pradesh	68,64,602	0.57	0.59	21
22.	Tripura	36,73,917	0.30	0.31	22
23.	Meghalaya	29,66,889	0.25	0.23	23
24.	Manipur	28,55,794	0.24	0.22	24
25.	Nagaland	19,78,502	0.16	0.19	25
26.	Goa	14,58,545	0.12	0.13	26
27.	Arunachal Pradesh	13,83,727	0.11	0.11	27
28.	Puducherry*	12,47,953	0.10	0.09	28
29.	Mizoram	10,97,206	0.09	0.09	30
30.	Chandigarh*	10,55,450	0.09	0.09	29
31.	Sikkim	6,10,577	0.05	0.05	31
32.	Andaman and Nicobar Islands*	3,80,581	0.03	0.03	32
33.	Dadra and Nagar Haveli*	3,43,709	0.03	0.02	33
34.	Daman and Diu*	2,43,247	0.02	0.02	34
35.	Lakshadweep*	64,473	0.01	0.01	35

Table 1.13: Total Population Percentage of Scheduled Castes and Scheduled Tribes : 2011

(in thousand)

Sl No.	State/Union Territory*	Total population			Percentage share in total population	
		Person	Males	Females		
1	2	3	4	5	6	7
	INDIA	12,10,570	2,01,378	10,42,81	16.6	8.6
1.	Jammu and Kashmir	12,541	925	1,493	7.4	11.9
2.	Himachal Pradesh	6,865	1,729	392	25.2	5.7
3.	Punjab	27,743	8,860	NST	31.9	NST
4.	Chandigarh*	1,055	199	NST	18.9	NST
5.	Uttarakhand	10,086	1,893	292	18.8	2.9
6.	Haryana	25,351	5,114	NST	20.2	NST
7.	NCT of Delhi*	16,788	2,812	NST	16.8	NST
8.	Rajasthan	68,548	12,222	9,239	17.8	13.5
9.	Uttar Pradesh	1,99,812	41,358	1,134	20.7	0.6
10.	Bihar	1,04,0999	16,567	1,337	15.9	1.3
11.	Sikkim	611	28	206	4.6	33.8
12.	Arunachal Pradesh	1,384	NSC	952	NSC	68.8
13.	Nagaland	1,979	NSC	1,711	NSC	86.5
14.	Manipur	2,570	97	903	3.4	40.9
15.	Mizoram	1,097	1	1,036	0.1	94.4
16.	Tripura	3,674	655	1,167	17.8	31.8
17.	Meghalaya	2,967	17	2,556	0.6	86.1
18.	Assam	31,206	2,231	3,884	7.2	12.4
19.	West Bengal	91,276	21,463	5,297	23.5	5.8
20.	Jharkhand	32,988	3,986	8,645	12.1	26.2
21.	Odisha	41,974	7,188	9,591	17.1	22.8
22.	Chhattisgarh	25,545	3,274	7,823	12.8	30.6
23.	Madhya Pradesh	72,627	11,342	15,317	15.6	21.1
24.	Gujarat	60,440	4,074	8,917	6.7	14.8
25.	Daman and Diu*	243	6	15	2.5	6.3
26.	Dadra and Nagar Haveli*	344	6	179	1.8	52.0
27.	Maharashtra	1,12,374	13,276	10,510	11.8	9.4
28.	Andhra Pradesh	84,581	13,878	5,918	16.4	7.0
29.	Karnataka	61,095	10,475	4,249	17.1	7.0
30.	Goa	1,459	25	149	1.7	10.2
31.	Lakshadweep*	64	NSC	61	NSC	94.8
32.	Kerala	33,406	3,040	485	9.1	1.5
33.	Tamil Nadu	72,147	14,438	795	20.0	1.1
34.	Puducherry*	1,245	196	NST	15.7	NST
35.	Andaman and Nicobar Islands*	381	NSC	29	NSC	7.5

Note: 1. *India and Manipur figures exclude those of the three sub-divisions viz., Mao Maram, Paomata and Purul of Senapati district of Manipur for census of 2011.*

Table 1.14 : Rural and Urban Population

Census Year	Population (Million)		Percentage of total population	
	Rural	Urban	Rural	Urban
1	2	3	4	5
1901	213	26	89.20	10.80
1911	226	26	89.70	10.30
1921	223	28	88.80	11.20
1931	246	33	88.00	12.00
1941	275	44	86.10	13.90
1951	299	62	82.70	17.30
1961	360	79	82.00	18.00
1971	439	109	80.10	19.90
1981	524	159	76.70	23.30
1991	629	218	74.30	25.70
2001	743	286	72.20	27.80
2011	834	377	68.85	31.14

Notes:

1. *The Population figures of India and Manipur figures include estimated figures of the three sub-divisions viz., Mao Maram, Paomata and Purul of Senapati district of Manipur for census of 2001 and 2011 due to administrative reasons.*
2. *The 1991 census could not be held owing to disturbed conditions prevailing in Jammu and Kashmir, hence the population figures for 1991 of Jammu and Kashmir have been worked out by interpolation.*
3. *The 1981 census could not be held in Assam. The figures for 1981 for Assam have been worked out by interpolation.*

Table 1.15 : Population by Class of Town, India-2011 Census (in '000)

	Class of Town	2011
I	1,00,000 and above	2,27,899
II	50,000-99,999	41,328
III	20,000-49,999	58,174
IV	10,000-19,999	31,866
V	5,000-9,999	15,883
VI	Less than 5,000	1,956
	All Classes	3,77,106
	Urban population as percentage to total population	31.2

Table 1.16: Distribution of Villages According to Population Census 2011 and Total Number of Inhabited Villages

Sl No.	State/UTs*	10,000 and above	5,000-9,999	2,000-4,999	1,000-1,999	500-999	200-499	Less than 200	Total number of inhabited villages
1	2	3	4	5	6	7	8	9	10
1.	Jammu and Kashmir @	23	212	1152	1641	1521	1275	513	6337
2.	Himachal Pradesh	1	12	219	832	2459	5898	8461	17882
3.	Punjab	41	330	2227	3471	3237	1903	959	12168
4.	Chandigarh*	0	3	2	0	0	0	0	5
5.	Uttarakhand	21	96	471	824	1826	4684	7823	15745
6.	Haryana	121	594	2256	1967	1035	437	232	6642
7.	NCT of Delhi*	6	9	55	21	6	2	4	103
8.	Rajasthan	120	832	5802	10530	12421	8869	4690	43264
9.	Uttar Pradesh	545	3432	21013	28020	23381	13591	7832	97814
10.	Bihar	1129	3216	10128	10076	7536	4584	2404	39073
11.	Sikkim	0	4	42	127	150	75	27	425
12.	Arunachal Pradesh	0	1	21	112	325	1026	3773	5258
13.	Nagaland	1	30	158	240	337	423	211	1400
14.	Manipur #	7	39	217	260	417	777	798	2515
15.	Mizoram	0	2	43	105	233	236	85	704
16.	Tripura	18	131	375	196	80	52	11	863
17.	Meghalaya	0	7	82	254	953	2515	2648	6459
18.	Assam	21	309	3304	5718	6076	5649	4295	25372
19.	West Bengal	417	1716	7552	8731	8574	6848	3640	37478
20.	Jharkhand	35	224	2365	5215	7948	8249	5456	29492
21.	Odisha	10	195	3058	7902	11978	13271	11263	47677
22.	Chhattisgarh	2	88	1913	5392	6142	4252	1778	19567
23.	Madhya Pradesh	31	583	5084	12515	16339	11943	5434	51929
24.	Gujarat	166	963	4781	5566	3891	1900	576	17843
25.	Daman and Diu*	0	5	4	5	3	2	0	19
26.	Dadra and Nagar Haveli*	1	6	28	18	6	5	1	65
27.	Maharashtra	310	1175	7170	12154	11144	6426	2582	40961
28.	Andhra Pradesh	482	1923	7158	6397	4245	3243	2838	26286
29.	Karnataka	164	836	4433	6492	7039	5296	3137	27397
30.	Goa	1	14	87	75	57	57	29	320
31.	Lakshadweep*	0	1	2	0	0	1	2	6
32.	Kerala	797	146	58	11	3	1	1	1017
33.	Tamil Nadu	209	1490	5100	4231	2376	1171	472	15049
34.	Puducherry*	3	26	46	13	2	0	0	90
35.	Andaman and Nicobar* Islands	0	2	24	53	61	78	178	396

Notes: @ *India and Jammu & Kashmir state exclude the villages of the areas under unlawful occupation of Pakistan and China where Census could not be taken.*

\# *India and Manipur figures exclude those of the three sub-divisions viz., Mao Maram, Paomata and Purul of Senapati district of Manipur as census results 2011 in these sub-divisions were not included due to technical and administrative reasons.*

2 National Symbols

National Flag

THE National Flag shall be a tricolour panel made up of three rectangular panel or sub-panel of equal widths. The colour of the top panel shall be India saffron *(kesari)* and that of the bottom panel India green. The middle panel shall be white, bearing at its centre the design of Ashoka Chakra in navy blue colour with 24 equally spaced spokes. The Ashoka Chakra shall preferably be screen printed or otherwise printed or stenciled or suitably embroidered and shall be completely visible on both sides of the Flag in the centre of the white panel. The National Flag shall be rectangular in shape. The ratio of the length to the height (width) of the Flag shall be 3:2. The design of the National Flag was adopted by the Constitutent Assembly of India on July 22, 1947.

Apart from non-statutory instructions issued by the government from time to time, display of the National Flag is governed by the provisions of the Emblems and Names (Prevention of Improper Use) Act, 1950 (No. 12 of 1950) and the Prevention of Insults to National Honour Act, 1971 (No. 69 of 1971). The Flag Code of India, 2002 is an attempt to bring together all such laws, conventions, practices and instructions for the guidance of all concerned.

The Flag Code of India, 2002 effective from January 26, 2002 superseded the 'Flag Code-India' as it existed then. As per the provisions of the Flag Code of India, 2002, there is no restriction on the display of the National Flag by members of general public, private organizations, educational institutions, etc., except to the extent provided in the Emblems and Names (Prevention of Improper Use) Act, 1950 and the Prevention of Insults to National Honour Act, 1971 and any other law enacted on the subject.

State Emblem

The State Emblem of India is an adaptation from the Sarnath Lion Capital of Asoka. In the original, the Lion Capital has four lions mounted back to back, on a circular abacus. The frieze of the abacus is adorned with sculptures in high relief of an elephant, a galloping horse, a bull and a lion separated by intervening Dharma Chakras. The abacus rests on a bell shaped lotus.

The profile of the Lion Capital showing three lions mounted on the abacus with a Dharma Chakra in the centre, a bull on the right and a galloping horse on the left, and outlines of Dharma Chakras on the extreme right and left was adopted as the State Emblem of India on January 26, 1950. The bell-shaped lotus was omitted. The motto "*Satyameva Jayate*"-Truth alone triumphs-written in Devanagari script below the profile of the Lion Capital is part of the State Emblem of India.

In the State Emblem lies the official seal of the Government of India. Its use is regulated by the State Emblem of India (Prohibition of Improper Use) Act, 2005 and The State Emblem of India (Regulation of Use) Rules, 2007 [read with State Emblem of India (Regulation of Use) Amendment Rules, 2010].

National Anthem

The song *Jana-gana-mana,* composed originally in Bengali by Rabindranath Tagore, was adopted in its Hindi version by the Constituent Assembly as the Nation Anthem of India on January 24, 1950. It was first sung on December 27, 1911 at the Calcutta Session of the Indian National Congress. The complete song consists of five stanzas. The first stanza contains the full version of the National Anthem:

Jana-gana-mana-adhinayaka, jaya he
Bharata-bhagya-vidhata
Punjaba-Sindhu-Gujarata-Maratha
Dravida-Utkala-Banga
Vindhya-Himachala-Yamuna-Ganga
Uchchala-jaladhi-taranga
Tava shubha name jage,
Tava subha asisa mage,
Gahe tava jaya-gatha.
Jana-gana-mangala-dayaka jaya he
Bharata-bhagya-vidhata.
Jaya he, jaya he, jaya he,
Jaya jaya jaya, jaya he!

The playing time of the full version of the National Anthem is approximately 52 seconds. A short version consisting of the first and last lines of the National Anthem (playing time approximately 20 seconds) is also played on certain occasions. The following is Tagore's English rendering of the anthem:

Thou art the ruler of the minds of all people,
Dispenser of India's destiny.

Thy name rouses the hearts of Punjab, Sind,
Gujarat and Maratha,

Of the Dravida and Orissa and Bengal;

It echoes in the hills of the Vindhyas and Himalayas,
mingles in the music of Jamuna and Ganges and is
chanted by the waves of the Indian Sea.

They pray for thy blessings and sing thy praise.

The saving of all people waits in thy hand,
Thou dispenser of India's destiny.

Victory, victory, victory to thee.

National Flag

सत्यमेव जयते

National Emblem

National Song

The song *Vande Mataram,* composed in Sanskrit by Bankimchandra Chatterji, was a source of inspiration to the people in their struggle for freedom. It has an equal status with *Jana-gana-mana.* The first political occasion when it was sung was the 1896 session of the Indian National Congress. The following is the text of its first stanza :

Vande Mataram!

Sujalam, suphalam, malayaja shitalam,
Shasyashyamalam, Mataram!
Shubhrajyotsna pulakitayamini,
Phullakusumita drumadala shobhini,
Suhasinim sumadhura bhashinim,
Sukhadam varadam, Mataram!
Vande Mataram,
Vande Mataram!

The English translation of the stanza rendered by Sri Aurobindo in prose[1] is :

I bow to thee, Mother,
richly-watered, richly-fruited,
cool with the winds of the south,
dark with the crops of the harvests,
The Mother!
Her nights rejoicing in the glory of the moonlight,
her lands clothed beautifully with her trees in flowering bloom,
sweet of laughter, sweet of speech,
The Mother, giver of boons, giver of bliss.

National Calendar

The National Calendar based on the *Saka Era,* with *Chaitra* as its first month and a normal year of 365 days was adopted from March 22, 1957 along with the Gregorian calendar for the following official purposes : (i) Gazette of India, (ii) news broadcast by All India Radio, (iii) calendars issued by the Government of India and (iv) Government communications addressed to the public.

Dates of the National Calendar have a permanent correspondence with dates of the Gregorian calendar, 1 *Chaitra* falling on March 22 normally and on March 21 in leap year.

---

1. As published in Volume Eight of Sri Aurobindo Birth Centenary Library, Popular Edition 1972.

3 Polity

INDIA, a union of states, is a Sovereign Socialist Secular Democratic Republic with a parliamentary system of government. The Republic is governed in terms of the Constitution, which was adopted by Constituent Assembly on November 26th, 1949 and came into force on January 26th, 1950.

The Constitution which envisages parliamentary form of government is federal in structure with unitary features. The President of India is the constitutional head of executive of the Union. Article 74(1) of the Constitution provides that there shall be a Council of Ministers with the Prime Minister as its head to aid and advise the President who shall in exercise of his functions, act in accordance with such advice. The real executive power thus vests in the Council of Ministers with the Prime Minister as its head. The Council of Ministers is collectively responsible to the House of the People (Lok Sabha). Similarly, in states, the Governor is the head of executive, but it is the Council of Ministers with the Chief Minister as its head in whom real executive power vests. The Council of Ministers of a state is collectively responsible to the Legislative Assembly of the state.

The Constitution distributes legislative power between Parliament and State Legislatures and provides for vesting of residual powers in Parliament. The power to amend the Constitution also vests in Parliament. The Constitution has provision for independence of Judiciary, Comptroller and Auditor-General, Public Service Commissions and Chief Election Commission.

Union and its Territory

India comprises 29 states and seven union territories. The states are: Andhra Pradesh, Assam, Arunachal Pradesh, Bihar, Chhattisgarh, Goa, Gujarat, Haryana, Himachal Pradesh, Jammu and Kashmir, Jharkhand, Karnataka, Kerala, Madhya Pradesh, Maharashtra, Manipur, Meghalaya, Mizoram, Nagaland, Odisha, Punjab, Rajasthan, Sikkim, Tamil Nadu, Telangana, Tripura, Uttarakhand, Uttar Pradesh and West Bengal. Union Territories are : Andaman and Nicobar Islands, Chandigarh, Dadra and Nagar Haveli, Daman and Diu, National Capital Territory of Delhi, Lakshadweep and Puducherry.

Citizenship

The Constitution of India provides for a single citizenship for the whole of India. Every person who was at the commencement of the Constitution (January 26, 1950) domiciled in the territory of India and: (a) who was born in India; or (b) either of whose parents were born in India; or (c) who has been ordinarily resident in India for not less than five years became a citizen of India. The Citizenship Act, 1955, deals with matters relating to acquisition, determination and termination of Indian citizenship after the commencement of the Constitution.

Fundamental Rights

The Constitution offers all citizens, individually and collectively, some basic freedoms. These are guaranteed in the Constitution in the form of six broad categories of Fundamental Rights which are justifiable. Articles 12 to 35 contained in Part III of the Constitution deal with Fundamental Rights. These are : (i) Right to equality including equality before law, prohibition of discrimination on grounds of religion, race, caste, sex or place of birth and equality of opportunity in matters of employment; (ii) Right to freedom of speech and expression, assembly, association or union, movement, residence, and right to practice any profession or occupation (some of these rights are subject to security of the State, friendly relations with foreign countries, public order, decency or morality); (iii) Right against exploitation, prohibiting all forms of forced labour, child labour and traffic in human beings; (iv) Right to freedom of conscience and free profession, practice and propagation of religion; (v) Right of any section of citizens to conserve their culture, language or script and right of minorities to establish and administer educational institutions of their choice; and (vi) Right to constitutional remedies for enforcement of Fundamental Rights.

Fundamental Duties

By the 42nd Amendment of the Constitution, adopted in 1976, Fundamental Duties of the citizens have also been enumerated. Article 51 'A' contained in Part IV A of the Constitution deals with Fundamental Duties. These enjoin upon a citizen among other things, to abide by the Constitution, to cherish and follow noble ideals, which inspired India's struggle for freedom, to defend the country and render national service when called upon to do so and to promote harmony and spirit of common brotherhood transcending religious, linguistic and regional or sectional diversities.

Directive Principles of State Policy

The Constitution lays down certain Directive Principles of State Policy, which though not justifiable, are 'fundamental in governance of the country' and it is the duty of the State to apply these principles in making laws. These have been contained in Part IV from Articles 36 to 51 of the Constitution. These lay down that the State shall strive to promote the welfare of people by securing and protecting as effectively as it may a social order in which justice—social, economic and political—shall form the basis in all institutions of national life. The State shall direct its policy in such a manner so as to secure the right of all men and women to an adequate means of livelihood, equal pay for equal work and within limits of its economic capacity and development, to make effective provision for securing the right to work, education and to public assistance in the event of unemployment, old age, sickness and disablement or other cases of undeserved want. The State shall also endeavour to secure to workers a living wage, humane conditions of work, a decent standard of life and full involvement of workers in management of industries.

In the economic sphere, the State is to direct its policy in such a manner as to secure distribution of ownership and control of material resources of community to subserve the common good and to ensure that operation of economic system does not result in concentration of wealth and means of production to common detriment.

Some of the other important directives relate to provision of opportunities and facilities for children to develop in a healthy manner, free and compulsory education for all children up to the age of 14; promotion of education and economic interests of scheduled castes, scheduled tribes and other weaker sections; organisation of village panchayats; separation of judiciary from executive, promulgation of a uniform civil code for whole country; protection of national monuments; promotion of justice on the basis of equal opportunity; provision of free legal aid; protection and improvement of environment and safeguarding of forests and wildlife of the country and promotion of international peace and security, just and honourable relations between nations, respect for international law, treaty obligations and settlement of international disputes by arbitration.

The Union

Executive

The Union executive consists of the President, the Vice-President and the Council of Ministers with the Prime Minister as the head to aid and advise the President.

President

The President is elected by members of an electoral college consisting of elected members of both Houses of Parliament and Legislative Assemblies of the states in accordance with the system of proportional representation by means of single transferable vote. To secure uniformity among states *inter se* as well as parity between the states, as a whole, and the Union, suitable weightage is given to each vote. The President must be a citizen of India, not less than 35 years of age and qualified for election as a member of the Lok Sabha. His term of office is five years and he is eligible for re-election. His removal from office is to be in accordance with procedure prescribed in Article 61 of the Constitution. He may, by writing under his hand addressed to the Vice-President, resign his office.

The executive power of the Union is vested in the President and is exercised by him either directly or through officers subordinate to him in accordance with the Constitution. The supreme command of defence forces of the Union also vests in him. The President summons, prorogues, addresses, sends messages to Parliament and dissolves the Lok Sabha; promulgates Ordinances at any time, except when both Houses of Parliament are in session; makes recommendations for introducing financial and money bills and gives assent to bills; grants pardons, reprieves, respites or remission of punishment or suspends, remits or commutes sentences in certain cases. When there is a failure of the constitutional machinery in a state, he can assume to himself all or any of the functions of the Government of that state. The President can proclaim emergency in the country if he is satisfied that a grave emergency exists whereby security of India or any part of its territory is threatened whether by war or external aggression or armed rebellion.

Vice-President

The Vice-President is elected by members of an electoral college consisting of members of both Houses of Parliament in accordance with the system of proportional representation by means of single transferable vote. He must be a citizen of India, not less than 35 years of age and eligible for election as a member of the Rajya Sabha. His term of office is five years and he is eligible for re-election. His removal from office is to be in accordance with procedure prescribed in Article 67(b).

The Vice-President is *ex-officio* Chairman of the Rajya Sabha and acts as President when the latter is unable to discharge his functions due to absence, illness or any other cause or till the election of a new President (to be held within six months when a vacancy is caused by death, resignation or removal or otherwise of President). While so acting, he ceases to perform the function of the Chairman of the Rajya Sabha.

Council of Ministers

There is a Council of Ministers, headed by the Prime Minister, to aid and advise the President in exercise of his functions. The Prime Minister is appointed by the President who also appoints other ministers on the advice of Prime Minister. The Council is collectively responsible to the Lok Sabha. It is the duty of the Prime Minister to communicate to the President all decisions of Council of Ministers relating to administration of affairs of the Union and proposals for legislation and information relating to them.

The Council of Ministers comprises Ministers who are members of Cabinet, Ministers of State (independent charge), Ministers of State and Deputy Ministers.

Legislature

Legislature of the Union which is called Parliament, consists of the President and two Houses, known as Council of States (Rajya Sabha) and House of the People (Lok Sabha). Each House has to meet within six months of its previous sitting. A joint sitting of two Houses can be held in certain cases.

Rajya Sabha

The Constitution provides that the Rajya Sabha shall consist of 12 members to be nominated by the President from amongst persons having special knowledge or practical experience in respect of such matters as literature, science, art and social service; and not more than 238 representatives of the states and of the union territories. Details of Rajya Sabha members given in Appendices.

Elections to the Rajya Sabha are indirect; members representing states are elected by the elected members of Legislative Assemblies of the states in accordance with the system of proportional representation by means of the single transferable vote, and those representing union territories are chosen in such a manner as Parliament may by law prescribe. The Rajya Sabha is not subject to dissolution; one-third of its members retire every second year.

Lok Sabha

The Lok Sabha is composed of representatives of people chosen by direct election on the basis of adult suffrage. The maximum strength of the House envisaged by the Constitution is now 552 (530 members to represent the states, 20 members to represent the union territories and not more than two members of the Anglo-Indian community to be nominated by the President, if, in his opinion, that community is not adequately represented in the House). The total elective membership of the Lok Sabha is distributed among the states in such a way that the ratio between the number of seats allotted to each state and the population of the state is, as far as practicable, the same for all states. The Lok Sabha at present consists of 543 members. Of these, 530 members are directly elected from the states and 13 from union territories. Following the 84th amendment to the Constitution in 2001, the total number of existing seats as allocated to various states in the Lok Sabha on the basis of the 1971 census shall remain unaltered till the first census to be taken after the year 2026.

The term of the Lok Sabha, unless dissolved earlier is five years from the date appointed for its first meeting. However, while a Proclamation of Emergency is in operation, this period may be extended by Parliament by law for a period not exceeding one year at a time and not extending in any case, beyond a period of six months after the Proclamation is or has ceased to operate. Sixteen Lok Sabhas have been constituted so far. The term of each Lok Sabha and its Speaker(s) is given in table 3.1.

The names of members of the 16th Lok Sabha, their constituencies and party affiliations are given in Appendices.

Qualification for Membership of Parliament

In order to be chosen a member of Parliament, a person must be a citizen of India and not less than 30 years of age in the case of Rajya Sabha and not less than 25 years of age in the case of Lok Sabha. Additional qualifications may be prescribed by Parliament by law.

Functions and Powers of Parliament

The Parliament in India has the cardinal functions of legislation, overseeing of administration, passing of the budget, ventilation of public grievances and discussing various subjects like development plans, national policies and international relations. The distribution of powers between the Union and the States, followed in the Constitution, emphasizes in many ways the general predominance of Parliament in the legislative field. The Parliament can, under

Table 3.1: Lok Sabha and its Speaker(s) from Time to Time

Lok Sabha	Date of first Meeting	Date of Dissolution	Speaker Name	From	To
First Lok Sabha	13 May 1952	4 April 1957[2]	Ganesh Vasudev Mavalankar	15 May 1952	27 February 1956[3]
			M. Ananthasayanam Ayyangar	8 March 1956	10 May 1957
Second Lok Sabha	10 May 1957	31 March 1962[4]	M. Ananthasayanam Ayyangar	11 May 1957	16 April 1962
Third Lok Sabha	16 April 1962	3 March 1967[5]	Sardar Hukam Singh	17 April 1962	16 March 1967
Fourth Lok Sabha	16 March 1967	27 December 1970[6]	Neelam Sanjiva Reddy	17 March 1967	19 July 1969[7]
			Gurdial Singh Dhillon	8 August 1969	19 March 1971
Fifth Lok Sabha	19 March 1971	18 January 1977[8]	Gurdial Singh Dhillon	22 March 1971	1 December 1975[9]
			Bali Ram Bhagat	5 January 1976	25 March 1977
Sixth Lok Sabha	25 March 1977	22 August 12979[10]	Neelam Sanjiva Reddy	26 March 1977	13 July 1977[11]
			K.S. Hegde	21 July 1977	21 January 1985
Seventh Lok Sabha	21 January 1980	31 December 1984[12]	Balram Jakhar	22 January 1980	15 January 1985
Eighth Lok Sabha	15 January 1985	27 November 1989[13]	Balram Jakhar	16 January 1985	18 December 1989
Ninth Lok Sabha	18 December 1989	13 March 1991[14]	Rabi Ray	19 December 1989	9 July 1991
Tenth Lok Sabha	9 July 1991	10 May 1996	Shivraj V. Patil	10 July 1991	22 May 1996
Eleventh Lok Sabha	22 May 1996	4 December 1997[15]	P. A. Sangma	23 May 1996	23 March 1998 (FN)
Twelfth Lok Sabha	23 March 1998	26 April 1999[16]	G.M.C. Balayogi	24 March 1998	20 October 199 (FN)
Thirteenth Lok Sabha	20 October 1999	6 February 2004[18]	G.M.C. Balayogi	22 October 1999	3 March 2002[17]
			Manohar Gajanan Joshi	10 May 2002	2 June 2004
Fourteenth Lok Sabha	2 June 2004	18 May 2009	Somnath Chatterjee	4 June 2004	1 June 2009
Fifteenth Lok Sabha	1 June 2009	18 May 2014	Meira Kumar	1 June 2009	18 May 2014
Sixteenth Lok Sabha	4 June 2014	-	Sumitra Mahajan	6 June 2014	Till date

1. Under Article 94 of the Constitution, in case of dissolution of the Lok Sabha, the Speaker does not vacate his office until immediately before the first meeting of the House after dissolution.
2. Dissolved thirty eight days before expiry of its term.
3. Died.
4. Dissolved forty days before expiry of its term.
5. Dissolved forty four days before expiry of its term.
6. Dissolved one year and seventy nine days before expiry of its term.
7. Resigned.
8. Term of the Lok Sabha which was to expire on 18 March 1976 was extended by one year upto 18 March 1977 by the House of the People (Extension of Duration) Act, 1976. It was extended for a further period of one year upto 18 March 1978 by the House of the People (Extension of Duration) Amendment Act, 1976. However, the House was dissolved after having been in existence for a period of five years, ten months and six days.
9. Resigned.
10. House was dissolved after having been in existence for a period of two years, four months and twenty eight days.
11. Resigned.
12. Dissolved twenty days before expiry of its term.
13. Dissolved forty eight days before expiry of its term.
14. Dissolved after having been in existence for a period of one year, two months and twenty five days.
15. House was dissolved after having been in existence for a period of one year, six months and thirteen days.
16. House was dissolved after having been in existence for a period of one year, one month and four days.
17. Died.
18. Dissolved two hundred fifty three days before expiry of its term.

certain circumstances, assume legislative power with respect to a subject falling within the sphere exclusively reserved for the states. It can impeach the President and remove the Judges of Supreme Court and High Courts, the Chief Election Commissioner and the Comptroller and Auditor General in accordance with the procedure laid down in the Constitution.

All legislation requires consent of both the Houses of Parliament. In the case of money bills, however, the 'will' of the Lok Sabha prevails. Delegated legislation is also subject to review and control by Parliament. Besides the power to legislate, the Constitution vests in Parliament the power to initiate amendment of the Constitution.

Parliamentary Committees

The functions of Parliament are varied in nature. The time at its disposal is limited. It cannot make very detailed scrutiny of all legislative and other matters that come up before it. A good deal of Parliamentary business is, therefore, transacted in the committees.

Both Houses of Parliament have a similar committee structure, with few exceptions. Their appointment, terms of office, functions and procedure of conducting business are also more or less similar and are regulated as per rules made by the two Houses under Article 118(1) of the Constitution.

Broadly, Parliamentary Committees are of two kinds—*Standing Committees* and *Ad Hoc* Committees. The former are elected or appointed every year or periodically and their work goes on, more or less, on a continuous basis. The latter are appointed on an *ad hoc* basis as need arises and they cease to exist as soon as they complete the task assigned to them.

Standing Committees : Among the Standing Committees, the three Financial Committees—*Committees on Estimates, Public Accounts* and *Public Undertakings*—constitute a distinct group as they keep an unremitting vigil over Government expenditure and performance. While members of the Rajya Sabha are associated with Committees on Public Accounts and Public Undertakings, the members of the Committee on Estimates are drawn from the Lok Sabha.

The *Estimates Committee* reports on what economies, improvements in organization, efficiency or administrative reform consistent with policy underlying the estimates may be effected. It also examines whether the money is well laid out within limits of the policy implied in the estimates and suggests the form in which estimates shall be presented to the Parliament. The *Public Accounts Committee* scrutinizes appropriation and finance accounts of Government and reports of the Comptroller and Auditor-General. It ensures that public money is spent in accordance with the Parliament's decision and calls attention to cases of waste, extravagance, loss or nugatory expenditure. *The Committee on Public Undertakings* examines reports of the Comptroller and Auditor-General, if any. It also examines whether public undertakings are being run efficiently and managed in accordance with sound business principles and prudent commercial practices.

Besides these three Financial Committees, the Rules Committee of the Lok Sabha recommended setting-up of *17 Department Related Standing Committees* (DRSCs). Accordingly, 17 Department Related Standing Committees were set up on April 8, 1993. In July, 2004, rules were amended to provide for the constitution of seven more such committees, thus raising the number of DRSCs from 17 to 24. The functions of these committees are : (a) to consider the Demands for Grants of various ministries/departments of Government of India and make reports to the Houses; (b) to examine such Bills as are referred to the committee by the Chairman, Rajya Sabha or the Speaker, Lok Sabha, and make reports thereon; (c) to consider Annual Reports of ministries/departments and make reports thereon; and (d) to consider policy documents presented to the Houses, if referred to the committee by the Chairman, Rajya Sabha or the Speaker, Lok Sabha, and make reports thereon.

Other *Standing Committees* in each House, divided in terms of their functions, are (i) Committees to Inquire: (a) *Committee on Petitions* examines petitions on bills and on matters of general public interest and also entertains representations on matters concerning subjects in the Union List; and (b) *Committee of Privileges* examines any question of privilege referred to it by the House or Speaker/Chairman; (ii) Committees to Scrutinize : (a) *Committee on Government Assurances* keeps track of all the assurances, promises, undertakings, etc., given by Ministers in the House and pursues them till they are implemented; (b) *Committee on Subordinate Legislation* scrutinizes and reports to the House whether the power to make regulations, rules, sub-rules, bye-laws, etc., conferred by the Constitution or Statutes is being properly exercised by the delegated authorities; and (c) *Committee on Papers Laid on the Table* examines all papers laid on the table of the House by Ministers, other than statutory notifications and orders which come within the purview of the Committee on Subordinate Legislation, to see whether there has been compliance with the provisions of the Constitution, Act, rule or regulation under which the paper has been laid; (iii) Committees relating to the day-to-day business of the House: (a) *Business Advisory Committee* recommends allocation of time for items of Government and other business to be brought before the Houses; (b) *Committee on Private Members' Bills and Resolutions of the Lok Sabha* classifies and allocates time to bills introduced by private members, recommends allocation of time for discussion on private members' resolutions and examines Constitution amendment bills before their introduction by private members in the Lok Sabha. The Rajya Sabha does not have such committee. It is the Business Advisory Committee of that House which recommends allocation of time for discussion on stage or stages of private members' bills and resolutions; (c) *Rules Committee* considers matters of procedure and conduct of business in the House and recommends amendments or additions to the Rules; and (d) *Committee on Absence of Members from the Sittings of the House of the Lok Sabha* considers all applications from members for leave or absence from sittings of the House.

There is no such committee in the Rajya Sabha. Applications from members for leave or absence are considered by the House itself; (iv) *Committee on the Welfare of Scheduled Castes and Scheduled Tribes*, on which members from both Houses serve, considers all matters relating to the welfare of Scheduled Castes and Scheduled Tribes which come within the purview of the Union Government and keeps a watch whether constitutional safeguards in respect of these classes are properly implemented; (v) Committees concerned with the provision of facilities to members : (a) *General Purposes Committee* considers and advises Speaker/Chairman on matters concerning affairs of the House, which do not appropriately fall within the purview of any other Parliamentary Committee; and (b) *House Committee* deals with residential accommodation and other amenities for members; (vi) *Joint Committee on Salaries and Allowances of Members of Parliament*, constituted under the Salary, Allowances and Pension of Members of Parliament Act, 1954, apart from framing rules for regulating payment of salary, allowances and pension to Members of Parliament, also frames rules in respect of amenities like medical, housing, telephone, postal, constituency and secretarial facility; (vii) *Joint Committee on Offices of Profit* examines the composition and character of committees and other bodies appointed by the Central and State governments and union territories administrations and recommends what offices ought to or ought not to disqualify a person from being chosen as a member of either House of Parliament; (viii) *The Library Committee* consisting of members from both Houses, considers matters concerning the Library of Parliament; (ix) On April 29, 1997, a *Committee on Empowerment of Women* with members from both the Houses was constituted, to secure, status, dignity and equality for women in all fields; (x) On March 4, 1997, the *Ethics Committee* of the Rajya Sabha was constituted. The Ethics Committee of the Lok Sabha was constituted on May 16, 2000.

Ad hoc Committees : Such committees may be broadly classified under two heads : (a) committees which are constituted from time to time, either by the two Houses on a motion adopted in that behalf or by Speaker/ Chairman to inquire into and report on specific subjects, *(e.g., Committees on food management in Parliament House Complex, Committee on installation of portraits/statues of National leaders and Parliamentarians in Parliament House Complex, Committee on Security in Parliament Complex, Committee on MPLADS, Committee on Railway convention, etc.) and (b)* Select or Joint Committees on Bills which are appointed to consider and report on a particular bill. These committees are distinguishable from the other *ad hoc* committees as much as they are concerned with bills and the procedure to be followed by them as laid down in the Rules of Procedure and Directions by the Speaker/Chairman.

Leaders of Opposition in Parliament

The Leaders of Opposition in the Rajya Sabha and the Lok Sabha are accorded statutory recognition. Salary and other suitable facilities are extended to them through a separate legislation brought into force on November 1, 1977.

Government Business in Parliament

The task of efficiently handling diverse Parliamentary work on behalf of the Government, in the Parliament, has been assigned to the Ministry of Parliamentary Affairs. The Ministry serves as an important link between the two Houses of Parliament on the one hand and the Government on the other in respect of Government Business in parliament. The Minister of Parliamentary Affairs, being the Government Chief Whips is entrusted with the responsibility of coordinating, planning and arranging Government business in both Houses of Parliament. In discharge of this function, he is assisted by two Ministers of State. The Minister also keeps close and constant contact with the presiding officers, the leaders as well as Chief Whips of various parties and groups in both Houses of Parliament. During the period from June 1, 2015 to May 31, 2016 the two Houses of Parliament passed 36 bills.

Consultative Committees

Functioning of Consultative Committees of Members of Parliament for various ministries is one of the functions allocated to the Ministry of Parliamentary Affairs under the Government of India (Allocation of Business) Rules, 1961. In discharge of this function, the Ministry of Parliamentary Affairs constitutes these committees and arranges their meetings. The main objective of these committees is to provide a forum for informal discussion between Members of Parliament, and Ministers and senior officers of the Government, on the policies, principles and programmes of the Government and their implementation. The Minister/ Minister of State in-charge of the Ministry concerned acts as the Chairman of the Consultative Committee attached to that Ministry.

The minimum membership of a Consultative Committee is ten and the maximum membership is thirty. The Consultative Committee stands dissolved upon dissolution of every Lok Sabha and are re-constituted upon constitution of each Lok Sabha.

35 Consultative Committees attached to various ministries were constituted for 16th Lok Sabha and 108 meetings of Consultative Committees were held from June 1, 2015 to May 31, 2016.

Nomination of Members of Parliament on Government Committees/Bodies

The Minister of Parliamentary Affairs nominates Members of Parliament on Committees, Councils, Boards and Commissions, etc., set-up by the Government of India in various ministries (except in case of statutory or other bodies where the statute or the bye-laws framed thereunder provide that the Members of Parliament to be appointed thereon will be nominated by the Presiding Officer of the respective House or will be elected by the Lok Sabha or the Rajya Sabha, (as the case may be). The Members are nominated on such bodies keeping in view their aptitude and special interest in the subject.

Youth Parliament Competition

In order to develop democratic ethos in the younger generation the Ministry conducts Youth Parliament Competitions in various categories of schools and colleges/universities. The 'Youth Parliament Scheme' was first introduced in the schools in Delhi in 1966-67. Kendriya Vidyalayas located in and around Delhi were incorporated into the ongoing Scheme in 1978. Subsequently, a separate scheme of Youth Parliament for Kendriya Vidyalayas at the national level was launched in 1988. In 1997-98, two new Youth Parliament Schemes at the national level, one for Jawahar Navodaya Vidyalayas and the other for universities/colleges were launched. As per recommendations made by seventh All India Whips Conference, the Ministry provides financial assistance to states/union territories for organizing Youth Parliament Competition in their respective States/UTs.

All India Whips Conference

The Ministry of Parliamentary Affairs, Government of India has been organizing All India Whips' Conference from time to time with the purpose of establishing suitable links among the whips of various political parties at the Centre and the states who are concerned with the practical working of the legislatures to discuss matters of common interest and to evolve high standards to strengthen the institution of Parliamentary Democracy. Seventeen All India Whips' Conferences have been organized so far since 1952. The last one was held on September 29-30, 2015 at Visakhapatam, Andhra Pradesh.

Matters Under Rule 377 and Special Mentions

The Ministry of Parliamentary Affairs takes follow-up action on matters raised under Rule 377 of the Rules of Procedure and Conduct of Business in Lok Sabha and by way of Special Mentions in Rajya Sabha. After 'Question Hour' in Lok Sabha members raise matters of urgent public importance at 12.00 Noon. In Rajya Sabha members raises matters of urgent public importance at 11.00 am. Though it is not mandatory, Ministers often react to the points made by the members. In the absence of concerned Minister, the Minister of Parliamentary Affairs assures the House or the individual Members that their sentiments would be conveyed to the concerned Ministers.

Implementation of Assurances

The Ministry culls out from the printed daily proceedings assurances, promises, undertakings, etc., given by Ministers in both the Houses of Parliament, and forward them to the concerned ministries/departments for implementation. Thereafter, periodic review of the stage of implementation is done by the Ministry and the Ministries are also reminded to expedite the fulfillment of assurances.

Goodwill Delegation

The Parliamentarians of a country play a significant role in determining the policy of the country and strengthening of relations with other countries. More particularly, it is indeed useful and necessary for a democratic and developing country like India to select some members of Parliament and distinguished personalities and utilize their services in projecting our policies, programme and achievement in different fields with their counterparts and other opinion makers in other countries and secure their support in favour of India.

The Ministry of Parliamentary Affairs sponsors Goodwill Delegation of Members of Parliament to other countries and receives similar Government sponsored delegations of parliamentarians under the exchange programme from other countries through the Ministry of External Affairs.

Welfare of Members of Parliament

The Ministry of Parliamentary Affairs looks after the welfare of ailing members of Parliament admitted for treatment in hospitals in Delhi and renders any assistance required by them. In the unfortunate event of passing away of a Member of Parliament in Delhi, the Ministry of Parliamentary Affairs renders all necessary assistance to the bereaved family members in taking the mortal remains of the deceased member for last rites to a place chosen by the family.

Comptroller and Auditor General

The Comptroller and Auditor General (CAG) of India is appointed by the President. The procedure and the grounds for his removal from office are the same as for a Supreme Court judge. He is not eligible for further office under the Union or a state government after he ceases to hold his office.

The accounts of the Union and of the states shall be kept in such form as the President may, on the advice of the CAG, prescribe. The reports of the India relating to the accounts of the Union shall be submitted to the President, who shall cause them to be laid before each House of Parliament. The reports of the CAG of India relating to the accounts of a state shall be submitted to the Governor of the state, who shall cause them to be laid before the legislature of the state.

The duties, powers and conditions of service of the CAG have been specified by the Comptroller and Auditor General's (Duties, Powers and Conditions of Service) Act, 1971.

Administrative Set-up

The Government of India (Allocation of Business) Rules, 1961 are made by the President of India under Article 77 of the Constitution for the allocation of business of the Government of India. The ministries/departments of the Government are created by the President on the advice of the Prime Minister under these Rules. The business of the Government is transacted in the ministries/departments, secretariats and offices as per the distribution of subjects specified in these Rules. Each of the ministry(ies) is assigned to a Minister by the President on the advice of the Prime Minister. Each department is generally under the charge of a Secretary to assist the Minister on policy matters and general administration.

Cabinet Secretariat

The Cabinet Secretariat functions directly under the Prime Minister. The administrative head of the Secretariat is the Cabinet Secretary who is also the ex-officio Chairman of the Civil Services Board.

The business allocated to Cabinet Secretariat is (i) Secretarial assistance to Cabinet and Cabinet Committees; and (ii) Rules of Business.

The Cabinet Secretariat is responsible for the administration of the Government of India (Transaction of Business) Rules, 1961 and the Government of India (Allocation of Business) Rules, 1961, facilitating smooth transaction of business in ministries/departments of the Government by ensuring adherence to these rules. It assists in decision-making by ensuring inter-ministerial coordination, ironing out differences amongst ministries/departments and evolving consensus through the instrumentality of the standing and *ad hoc* Committees of Secretaries.

The Cabinet Secretariat ensures that the President, the Vice-President and Ministers are kept informed of the major activities of all ministries/departments by means of monthly summary of their activities. Management of major crisis situation in the country and coordinating activities of various ministries in such a situation is also one of the functions of the Cabinet Secretariat.

The Secretaries keep the Cabinet Secretary informed of developments from time to time. The Transaction of Business Rules also require them to keep the Cabinet Secretary informed specially if there are any departures from these rules.

A list of Cabinet Secretaries since 1950 is given in **Chapter 32 - General Information.**

Ministries/Departments of the Government

The Government consists of a number of ministries/departments, their number and character varying from time to time based on factors such as volume of work, priorities attached to certain subjects, etc.

List of the Ministries/Departments[1]

1. **Ministry of Agriculture and Farmers Welfare *(Krishi evam Kisan Kalyan Mantralaya)***

   (i) Department of Agriculture, Co-operation and Farmers Welfare
   (Krishi, Sahkarita evam Kisan Kalyan Vibhag)

   (ii) Department of Agricultural Research and Education
   (Krishi Anusandhan aur Shiksha Vibhag)

   (iii) Department of Animal Husbandry, and Fisheries and Dairying
   (Pashupalan, Dairy aur Matsyapalan Vibhag)

---

1. The list of Ministries/Departments is based on the information as given under Allocation of Business Rules, 1961 as amended from time to time and available on Cabinet Secretariat website : http://cabsec.nic.in.

2. **Ministry of Ayurveda, Yoga and Naturopathy, Unani, Siddha and Homoeopathy (AYUSH) (Ayurveda, Yoga aur Prakratik Chikitsa, Unani, Siddha aur Homoeopathy) *(Ayush Mantralaya)***
3. **Ministry of Chemicals and Fertilizers *(Rasayan aur Urvarak Mantralaya)***
   (i) Department of Chemicals and Petro-Chemicals *(Rasayan aur Petro-Rasayan Vibhag)*
   (ii) Department of Fertilizers *(Urvarak Vibhag)*
   (iii) Department of Pharmaceuticals. *(Aushadh Vibhag)*
4. **Ministry of Civil Aviation *(Nagar Vimanan Mantralaya)***
5. **Ministry of Coal *(Koyala Mantralaya)***
6. **Ministry of Commerce and Industry *(Vanijya aur Udyog Mantralaya)***
   (i) Department of Commerce *(Vanijya Vibhag)*
   (ii) Department of Industrial Policy and Promotion *(Audyogik Niti aur Samvardhan Vibhag)*
7. **Ministry of Communications (*Sanchar Mantralaya*)**
   (i) Department of Telecommunications *(Doorsanchar Vibhag)*
   (ii) Department of Posts *(Dak Vibhag)*
8. **Ministry of Consumer Affairs, Food and Public Distribution *(Upbhokta Mamle, Khadya aur Sarvajanik Vitaran Mantralaya)***
   (i) Department of Consumer Affairs *(Upbhokta Mamle Vibhag)*
   (ii) Department of Food and Public Distribution *(Khadya aur Sarvajanik Vitaran Vibhag)*
9. **Ministry of Corporate Affairs *(Korporate Karya Mantralaya)***
10. **Ministry of Culture *(Sanskriti Mantralaya)***
11. **Ministry of Defence *(Raksha Mantralaya)***
   (i) Department of Defence *(Raksha Vibhag)*
   (ii) Department of Defence Production *(Raksha Utpadan Vibhag)*
   (iii) Department of Defence Research and Development *(Raksha Anusandhan tatha Vikas Vibhag)*
   (iv) Department of Ex-servicemen Welfare *(Poorva Senani Kalyan Vibhag)*

12. **Ministry of Development of North-Eastern Region *(Uttar Poorvi Kshetra Vikas Mantralaya)***

13. **Ministry of Drinking Water and Sanitation *(Peya Jal aur Swachchhata Mantralaya)***

14. **Ministry of Earth Sciences *(Prithvi Vigyan Mantralaya)***

15. **Ministry of Electronics and Information Technology *(Electroniki aur Soochana Praudyogiki Mantralaya)***

16. **Ministry of Environment, Forest and Climate Change *(Paryavaran,Van aur Jalvayu Parivartan Mantralaya)***

17. **Ministry of External Affairs *(Videsh Mantralaya)***

18. **Ministry of Finance *(Vitta Mantralaya)***

    (i) Department of Economic Affairs *(Arthik Karya Vibhag)*

    (ii) Department of Expenditure *(Vyaya Vibhag)*

    (iii) Department of Revenue *(Rajaswa Vibhag)*

    (iv) Department of Investment and Public Asset Management (DIPAM) (Nivesh aur Lok Parisampatti Prabandhan *Vibhag)* (DIPAM)

    (v) Department of Financial Services *(Vittiya Sewayen Vibhag)*

19. **Ministry of Food Processing Industries *(Khadya Prasanskaran Udyog Mantralaya)***

20. **Ministry of Health and Family Welfare *(Swasthya aur Parivar Kalyan Mantralaya)***

    (i) Department of Health and Family Welfare *(Swasthya aur Parivar Kalyan Vibhag)*

    (ii) Department of Health Research *(Swasthya Anusandhan Vibhag)*

21. **Ministry of Heavy Industries and Public Enterprises *(Bhari Udyog aur Lok Udyam Mantralaya)***

    (i) Department of Heavy Industries *(Bhari Udyog Vibhag)*

    (ii) Department of Public Enterprises *(Lok Udyam Vibhag)*

22. **Ministry of Home Affairs *(Grih Mantralaya)***

    (i) Department of Internal Security *(Aantarik Suraksha Vibhag)*

    (ii) Department of States *(Rajya Vibhag)*

    (iii) Department of Official Language *(Raj Bhasha Vibhag)*

    (iv) Department of Home *(Grih Vibhag)*

    (v) Department of Jammu and Kashmir Affairs *(Jammu tatha Kashmir Vibhag)*

(vi) Department of Border Management
(Seema Prabandhan Vibhag)

23. Ministry of Human Resource Development
(Manav Sansadhan Vikas Mantralaya)

(i) Department of School Education and Literacy
(School Shiksha aur Saksharta Vibhag)

(ii) Department of Higher Education
(Uchchatar Shiksha Vibhag)

24. Ministry of Information and Broadcasting
(Soochana aur Prasaran Mantralaya)

25. Ministry of Labour and Employment *(Shram aur Rozgar Mantralaya)*

26. Ministry of Law and Justice
(Vidhi aur Nyaya Mantralaya)

(i) Department of Legal Affairs *(Vidhi Karya Vibhag)*

(ii) Legislative Department *(Vidhayee Vibhag)*

(iii) Department of Justice *(Nyaya Vibhag)*

27. Ministry of Micro, Small and Medium Enterprises *(Sukshm, Laghu aur Madhyam Udyam Mantralaya)*

28. Ministry of Mines *(Khan Mantralaya)*

29. Ministry of Minority Affairs
(Alpasankhyak Karya Mantralaya)

30. Ministry of New and Renewable Energy
(Naveen aur Navikarniya Oorja Mantralaya)

31. Ministry of Panchayati Raj *(Panchayati Raj Mantralaya)*

32. Ministry of Parliamentary Affairs *(Sansadiya Karya Mantralaya)*

33. Ministry of Personnel, Public Grievances and Pensions
(Karmik, Lok Shikayat tatha Pension Mantralaya)

(i) Department of Personnel and Training
(Karmik aur Prashikshan Vibhag)

(ii) Department of Administrative Reforms and Public Grievances
(Prashasnik Sudhar aur Lok Shikayat Vibhag)

(iii) Department of Pensions and Pensioners' Welfare
(Pension aur Pension Bhogi Kalyan Vibhag)

34. Ministry of Petroleum and Natural Gas
(Petroleum aur Prakritik Gas Mantralaya)

35. Ministry of Planning *(Yojana Mantralya)*

36. **Ministry of Power** ***(Vidyut Mantralaya)***

37. **Ministry of Railways** ***(Rail Mantralaya)***

38. **Ministry of Road Transport and Highways** ***(Sarak Parivahan aur Raj Marg Mantralaya)***

39. **Ministry of Rural Development** ***(Gramin Vikas Mantralaya)***

    (i) Department of Rural Development *(Gramin Vikas Vibhag)*

    (ii) Department of Land Resources *(Bhumi Sansadhan Vibhag)*

40. **Ministry of Science and Technology** ***(Vigyan aur Praudyogiki Mantralaya)***

    (i) Department of Science and Technology *(Vigyan aur Praudyogiki Vibhag)*

    (ii) Department of Scientific and Industrial Research *(Vigyan aur Audyogik Anusandhan Vibhag)*

    (iii) Department of Bio-technology *(Biotechnology Vibhag)*

41. **Ministry of Shipping** ***(Pot Parivahan Mantralaya)***

42. **Ministry of Skill Development and Entrepreneurship** ***(Kaushal Vikas aur Udyamita Mantralaya)***

43. **Ministry of Social Justice and Empowerment** ***(Samajik Nyaya aur Adhikarita Mantralaya)***

    (i) Department of Social Justice and Empowerment *(Samajik Nyaya aur Adhikarita Vibhag)*

    (ii) Department of Empowerment of Persons with Disabilities *(Viklangjan Sashaktikaran Vibhag)*

44. **Ministry of Statistics and Programme Implementation** ***(Sankhyiki aur Karyakram Kiryanvayan Mantralaya)***

45. **Ministry of Steel** ***(Ispat Mantralaya)***

46. **Ministry of Textiles** ***(Vastra Mantralaya)***

47. **Ministry of Tourism** ***(Paryatan Mantralaya)***

48. **Ministry of Tribal Affairs** ***(Janjatiya Karya Mantralaya)***

49. **Ministry of Urban Development** ***(Shahari Vikas Mantralaya)***

50. **Ministry of Housing and Urban Poverty Alleviation** ***(Awas aur Shahari Garibi Upshaman Mantrayala)***

51. Ministry of Water Resources, River Development and Ganga Rejuvenation *(Jal Sansadhan, Nadi Vikas aur Ganga Sanrakshan Mantralaya)*

52. Ministry of Women and Child Development *(Mahila aur Bal Vikas Mantralaya)*

53. Ministry of Youth Affairs and Sports *(Yuva Karyakram aur Khel Mantralaya)*

(i) Department of Youth Affairs *(Yuva Karyakaram Vibhag)*

(ii) Department of Sports *(Khel Vibhag)*

INDEPENDENT DEPARTMENTS

54. Department of Atomic Energy *(Parmanu Oorja Vibhag)*

55. Department of Space *(Antariksh Vibhag)*

APEX/INDEPENDENT OFFICE

56. NITI Aayog (National Institution for Transforming India)

57. Cabinet Secretariat *(Mantrimandal Sachivalaya)*

58. President's Secretariat *(Rashtrapati Sachivalaya)*

59. Prime Minister's Office *(Pradhan Mantri Karyalaya)*

National Authority, Chemical Weapons Convention

National Authority, Chemical Weapons Convention (NACWC) was set up by a resolution of Cabinet Secretariat dated May 5, 1997 to fulfill the obligations enunciated in the Chemical Weapons Convention. It prohibits the development, production, execution, transfer, use and stockpiling of all chemical weapons by Member-States in a non-discriminatory manner.

The Parliament enacted in 2000 a CWC Act which came into force on July 1, 2015 to give effect to the provisions of the Chemical Weapons Convention in India. In accordance with the provisions of this Act a high-level steering committee under the Chairmanship of the Cabinet Secretary with Secretary (Chemical and Petrochemicals), Foreign Secretary, Secretary, Defence Research and Development, Defence Secretary and Chairman, National Authority as its other members, oversees the functioning of the National Authority.

The National Authority is responsible for implementation of the CWC Act, liaison with Organisation for the Prohibition of Chemical Weapons (OPCW) and other state parties, fulfilling of declaration obligation, negotiating facility agreements, coordinating OPCW inspections, providing appropriate facilities for training national inspectors and industry personnel, ensuring protection of confidential business information, checking declarations for consistency, accuracy and completeness of entities engaged in activities related to the CWC.

Every country within 30 days of becoming a state party to the convention is obligated to submit 'Initial Declaration: India submitted its initial declarations in the year 1977. Every state party is also delegated to make 'Annual Declarations' on relevant chemicals and facilities in accordance with verification carried out in the previous calendar year called the Annual Declaration on Past Activities (ADPA) and the second giving particular of activities proposed to be carried out during the following calendar year called the Annual Declaration of Anticipated Activities (ADAA). India submitted its ADAA for the year 2016 on ADPA for the year 2015 well before the stipulated deadline.

Functions of the National Authority

Project Monitoring Group

Project Monitoring Group (PMG), is an institutional mechanism for resolving a variety of issues including fast tracking of approvals for setting up an expeditious commissioning of large Public, Private and Public-Private Partnership (PPP) project. Project Monitoring Group (PMG) was set up in June 2013 under cabinet secretariat. PMG is presently functioning under Prime Minister's Office (PMO) since September 14, 2015.

Generally, following types of clearances/issues have been raised by the Project Proponents for resolution and expeditious commissioning of Projects:

(a) Issues Pertaining to Union Ministries (i) Environment, forest and wildlife clearances; (ii) Eco Sensitive Zone clearance; (iii) Tree cutting permission; (iv) Grant of working permission by Forest Department; (v) Approval for private railways siding construction; (vi) Industrial Licence Permission; (vii) Grant of right of way/right of use permission; and (ix) Shifting of utilities.

(b) Issues pertaining to State Governments: (i) Land acquisition issues such as Government notifications/ disbursement of compensation, transfer of title and handing over of possession; (ii) Removal of encroachments; (iii) Relief and rehabilitation plan; (iv) Certificate under Forest Rights Act, diversion of forest land and compensation for afforestation; (v) Power and water supply connections/tariff; (vi) Consent to establish and operate from State Pollution Control Board; (vii) Transfer of Government land; (viii) Law and Order issues; and (ix) Right of way and right of use permissions.

PMG facilitates resolution of issues brought out by the Project Proponent through regular meetings involving Central and State Government officials as well as Project Proponents. So far 793 projects (anticipated investment of ₹15.31 lakh crore) have been resolved and issues in 106 projects (anticipated investment of ₹ 7.61 lakh crore) required no further action or intervention by PMG. As on August 1, 2016, 265 projects (anticipated investment of ₹10.81 lakh crore) with 614 issues are under consideration of PMG. Majority of the issues pointed out by the Investors/Project Proponents require intervention/ expeditious action on the part of the state government. Hence, meetings are convened in the State capitals, where pending issues are reviewed with the concerned departments of the state government and Investors/ Projects Proponents.

Public Grievances Mechanism

The Directorate of Public Grievances (DPG) was set up in 1988 to entertain grievances from the public after they fail to get satisfactory redress from the ministry/department concerned within a reasonable time. It is thus, an office of the last resort for redress of grievances relating to sectors in its purview. The sectors in DPG's purview are those with extensive public interface. Certain subjects are outside the purview of DPG.

Organizations under DPG's purview are:- (i) Department of Posts, (ii) Department of Telecommunication, (iii) Ministry of Railways, (iv) Department of Financial Services (Banking and Insurance), (v) National Small Savings Scheme: Department of Economic Affairs, (vi) Ministry of Urban Development (DDA, L&DO, CPWD), (vii) Ministry of Road Transport & Highways, (viii) Ministry of Shipping, Ministry of Civil Aviation, (ix) Regional Passport Authorities (MEA), (x) Ministry of Labour, (xi) Employees' Provident Fund Organization, (xii) Employees' State Insurance Corporation - Hospitals and Dispensaries, (xii) Employees' State Insurance Corporation - Hospitals and Dispensaries, (xiii) CGHS: Ministry of Health and Family Welfare, (xiv) Ministry of Petroleum & Natural Gas, Ministry of HRD, (xv) Central Universities, Kendriya Vidyalaya, (xvi) Navodaya Vidyalaya, (xvii) National Institute of Open Learning, (xviii) Central Board of Secondary Education, (xix) Ministry of Tourism & (xx) Ministry of Youth Affairs.

Subjects outside the purview of DPG are:- Policy matters, (ii) Matters that are subjudice (iii) Grievances disposed of at the level of the concerned Minister (iv) Service matters (except those relating to payment of terminal benefits) (v) Commercial contracts.

Grievance can be lodged with DPG through post, email or by lodging the complaint online on the portal. The cases received offline are entered in the system and, thereafter, all cases are handled using PGRAAMS application.

Each grievance is first scrutinized to see if it relates to a sector in DPG's purview. Those concerning the sectors outside the purview of the DPG are forwarded to the Department of Administrative Reforms and Public Grievances for appropriate disposal, under intimation to the complainants. The remaining grievances are then assessed to ascertain whether the issue involved is grave and whether the concerned ministry/department has been given an opportunity to redress the grievance. The grievances of grave nature which are either long pending or where the redress is not forthcoming from concerned service organisation/ministry are taken up for detailed examination. These cases are followed upto a logical and reasonable conclusion. Other cases are transferred to the concerned ministry for appropriate action.

When DPG seeks comments, the department or organization is expected to examine the matter and give a reply within thirty days. After receipt of comments, DPG may, if considered necessary, seek further information to ensure that the grievance is dealt with in a fair and objective manner by the department or organization and confirmation of satisfactory redress of the grievance is also sought from the complainant before closure.

During 2015-16, 10357 grievances were received in DPG pertaining to sectors in its purview, out of which 595 cases were taken up taking the total number of taken up cases to 1372. Out of the 1372 taken up cases, 846 were disposed with 745 in favour of the complainant. Thus approximately 88 per cent of the taken up cases were resolved. In addition, 1,782 grievances were transferred to the Department of Administrative Reforms and Public Grievances.

Grievance Redress

In the responsibility area of 'Application of ICT for technological upgrading' the online system for grievance redress, called the 'Centralized Public Grievance Redress and Monitoring System' (CPGRAMS) has been evolved since 2007. At present its upgraded version 5.0 is accessible at http://pgportal.gov.in and also through www.darpg.gov.in. The CPGRAMS interlinks 142 central ministries /departments/organizations. There are around 19,000 subordinate users listed on it which includes subordinate and field officers also. The number of field offices /organizations linked to CPGRAMS has increased from about 1500 in 2010-11 to 19000 in 2016-17. CPGRAMS in Hindi has also been made available.

Public grievance mechanism of PMO available on website www.pmindia.gov. in has been integrated with the pgportal.gov.in. Now, the grievances lodged to the PMO is being transferred to the Central Ministries/ Departments and State Governments and monitored through the online CPGRAMS which is part of the pg portal.

The public interface of pg portal has also been duly integrated with the pensioners' portal and now an option has been provided to the users to lodge pension related grievance to the pensioners' portal by clicking the relevant option on the pg portal. This prevents the lodging of same grievance on pg portal and pensioners' portal thus avoiding duplication. For providing grass- root access to the pg portal, the Common Service Centre has been integrated with it so that a person can lodge a grievance on the pg portal through the Common Service Centre located in his area by paying a nominal fee.

A Mobile App has been launched on October 21, 2015 which allows lodging of public grievances on android based mobiles by downloading the App from pg portal. The Action Status can also be viewed on the mobile itself. For proper monitoring, the classification of grievances has been reviewed and fresh categorizaton done in consultation with PMO dividing the grievances into 20 main categories which can be further mapped to specific categories by the ministries/departments concerned as per the subject matter being handled by them. Dashboards have been created for all the heads of the ministries/ departments for accessing the relevant information pertaining to pendency of grievances in the respective ministries/departments and subordinate organizations affiliated to them on CPGRAMS. User-ids and passwords have been duly provided to all concerned. For better monitoring, the format of analytical reports generated online through CPGRAMS have been duly modified and additional reports created for the purpose. The colour coding of the ministries/ departments have been done as per their performance on CPGRAMS. The format now includes receipts, disposals and per cent disposals with reference to cases pending for 2-6 months, 6-12 months and more than one year.

An Award Scheme has been launched for recognising performance on CPGRAMS through issue of Certificate of Appreciation. Certificates have been given to three ministries/departments each for the quarter ending December 31, 2015 and March 31, 2016.

Civil Services Day

The Government of India is celebrating April, 21 every year as 'Civil Services Day' for the civil servants to rededicate themselves to the cause of citizens and renew their commitment to public service and excellence in work. The first such function was held in Vigyan Bhavan, New Delhi on April 21, 2006. On the occasion, Prime Minister conferred "Prime Minister Award for Excellence in Public Administration". This date coincides with the date when the first Home Minister of Independent India Sardar Vallabhbhai Patel addressing the first batch of Indian Administrative Services officers at Metcalf House, New Delhi.

Prime Minister's Award for Excellence in Public Administration

Government of India has instituted 'Prime Minister's Award for Excellence in Public Administration' to acknowledge and recognize the extraordinary and innovative work of District and Organisations of the Central and State Governments.

PM's Awards are given on Civil Services Day held every 21st April of the year. On Civil Services Day 2015 held on 20th-21st April 2015, the Prime Minister presented 17 awards for the year 2012-13 and 2013-14 to the initiatives for excellence in Governance. Beginning 2007, sixty seven awards have so far been conferred in three categories, individual, group, organization. From 2016 the Scheme has been revised and for the first time awards were conferred to the best performing districts in identified priority programmes. On the occasion of Civil Services Day 2016 awards were conferred to the 10 best performing districts for excellence done in implementation of four priority programmes namely *Pradhan Mantri Jan Dhan Yojna, Swachh Bharat Gramin, Swachh Vidyalaya Abhiyan* and *Soil Health Care Scheme.*

As a part of selection process, feedback from citizens with more than 3 lakhs surveys was obtained, analysis of feedback was done, and field visits of 38 shortlisted districts were conducted. For the awards to be presented on Civil Services Day, 2017, the identified priority programmes are "Pradhan Mantri Krishi Sinchayee Yojana", "Deen Dayal Upadhyaya Gram Jyoti Yojana", "Pradhan Mantri Fasal Bima Yojana", "Start up India/ Stand up India" and "e-National Agriculture Market (e-NAM)".

In addition to the above, the award will also be given for the excellence/ innovation work done by the Organisations of Central/State Government in the field of environment conservation, disaster management, water conservation, energy, education, health, women and child centric initiatives etc., of public governance.

The award carries with it i) a Medal ii) a Scroll, iii) an incentive of ₹ 10 lakh to the awarded district/organisation to be utilized for implementation of project/programme or bridging resource gaps in any area of activity of public welfare.

The application for the award is evaluated by three hierarchical committees. The Screening Committee chaired by the Additional Secretary level officer, Expert Committee chaired by Secretary, Department of Administrative Reforms and Public Grievances and the Empowered Committee chaired by the Cabinet Secretary. The Empowered Committee then makes its recommendations for the consideration of the Prime Minister for final selection of the awards.

Replication of PM Award Initiatives of Good Governance in the States and UTs

On Civil Services Day 2015 i.e. April 21, 2015, 17 good governance initiatives were awarded Prime Minister Awards for Excellence in Public Administration. State Governments were also requested to identify the PM awarded good governance initiatives and replicate as per their suitability. 23 States and one UT have identified 14 initiatives for replicating and adopting in their respective States/UT.

International Exchange and Cooperation

The Department of Administrative Reforms and Public Grievances (CPAPG) works as the nodal point in respect of matters relating to international cooperation in the field of Public Administration and Governance, which includes organizing programmes as part of projects/bilateral measures taken up in accordance with the Memorandum of Understandings (MOUs)/ Agreements signed between India and other countries (bilateral or multilateral). The purpose of the international cooperation component is to enable the sharing of information, best practices and personnel across national governments.

As a part of its international collaborative efforts, the Department explored the possibility of sharing and exchanging administrative experiences and has signed MOUs with Britain, France, Singapore, Malaysia and China (under renewal), South Africa and Brazil (under IBSA). This involves exchange of visits and undertaking programmes/projects and activities particularly in the area of public administration and delivery of services, so as to improve upon the current system of governance and instill a greater sense of responsiveness, accountability, transparency, and achieving public service excellence in the context of public service delivery, good governance, public service reform, and capacity building and skills upgradation.

MOU with Government of United Kingdom

A Memorandum of Understanding (MoU) on Cooperation in the field of Public Administration and Governance Reforms was signed with Government of UK on November 11, 2015. First meeting of the India-UK Joint Working Group was held in London, UK during 28-29 January, 2016. Both sides shared their best practices in the area of public administration, governance reforms and online delivery of citizen-centric services and explored the possibilities of adopting suitable best practices in these areas. Also Programme of Action (POA) has been agreed to by both the sides to take forward the new initiatives under the overall ambit of the MoU.

India-France Agreement

An Agreement with Government of France on 'Cooperation on Public Administration and Administrative Reform was signed on January 25, 2016. A three member delegation visited Paris to attend India-France First Joint Working Group meeting. Both sides exchanged/shared views in the area of public administration, governance reforms and online delivery of citizen-centric services and explored the possibilities of adopting suitable best practices in these areas. Also Programme of Action (POA) has been agreed to by both the sides to take forward the new initiatives under the overall ambit of the MoU.

India-Singapore Cooperation

Given the priorities of the India and Singapore which are public service reforms and good governance, a Memorandum of understanding (MoU) between the two countries on cooperation in the field of Personnel Management and Public Administration was signed on November 11, 2011.

The 2nd India-Singapore Joint Working Group meeting under the Memorandum of Understanding (MoU) in the field of Personnel Management and Public Administration was held in Singapore on January 19-20, 2015. Both sides adopted a Plan of Action for exchange and cooperation, which is presently under implementation in the area of interest identified under the MoU.

Government of Singapore organised a 4-day training programme on the theme 'e-Governance' for officers of Government of India and States/UTs during 28 June-July1, 2016. The training programme has proved an ideal forum in which participants gathered and shared best practices and, even, the trials and errors which have been implemented or applied in a real administrative environment. The participating officers were updated with the strategies to achieve excellence in public administration.

India-Malaysia Cooperation

A Memorandum of Understanding on cooperation in the field of Public Administration and Governance with Government of Malaysia was signed on November 25, 2013. India-Malaysia 3rd Joint Working Group meeting was held in Kuala Lumpur, Malaysia during 28-30 September, 2015. During the JWG meeting both the sides agreed to the Programme of Action (PoA).

Under the PoA agreement, the Malaysian side organised Short-term Training Programme for 15 Middle Management level officers of Government of India (Director and below) at National Institute of Public Administration (INTAN), Kuala Lumpur, Malaysia during July18-22, 2016 on the theme 'Citizen-Centric Online Services through e-Governance. The participants were exposed to Malaysian Government's experience and good practices in the field of Public Administration and Governance especially in Delivery of Online Public Services which would help participants to replicate the lessons learnt with suitable modifications in India.

India-China Cooperation

An MoU on cooperation in the field of Civil Services, Personnel Management and Public Administration between the Ministry of Personnel, Public Grievances and Pensions, Government of India and the Ministry of Human Resources and Social Security of the People's Republic of China was signed on 27 May, 2010 during the visit of President of India to China. The MoU expired on May 26, 2015.

Cabinet in its meeting held on May 18, 2016, an approval was given to the signing of Memorandum of Understanding (MoU) on cooperation in the field of Civil services, Personnel Management and Public Administration between Department of Administrative Reforms and Public Grievances, Ministry of Personnel, Public Grievances and Pensions, Government of India and Ministry of Human Resources and Social Security of the People's Republic of China.

India-Brazil-South Africa (IBSA) Forum

Recognizing the emergence and consolidation of India - Brazil - South Africa (IBSA) initiatives and collaboration at regional and global level for promoting good governance and wishing to strengthen South-South cooperation, the three countries acknowledged that joint efforts and collaboration will position them as active players in helping to direct the public administration and governance towards democratic values and social inclusion. The Prime Minister of India, the President of Brazil and the President of South Africa met in Brasilia (Brazil) on September 13, 2006 for the 1st Summit meeting of the India-Brazil-South Africa dialogue forum. Pursuant to the IBSA Summit decision as contained in the Joint Declaration issued on the occasion, an IBSA Working Group on Public

Administration (WGPA) has been set up by the three countries. It has since held seven meetings and adopted the areas of cooperation as (i) integrated monitoring and evaluation, (ii) e-governance, (iii) human resource development, (iv) citizen oriented service delivery, (v) anti-corruption and ethics, and (vi) accountability and transparency. Collaboration in these areas represents the essence of the agreed upon MOU which was signed on October 17, 2007 in South Africa, during the 2nd IBSA Summit.

India taking the lead under IBSA cooperation programme in the field of public administration launched the IBSA web portal on public administration on November 30, 2010 with Brazil and South Africa onboard. The web portal, a virtual centre of excellence in public administration, is a wide ranging web-based resource and an interactive platform for the IBSA partners to facilitate among them an exchange of ideas and knowledge on public administration.

Cooperation with IIAS

The DARPS is an institutional member of the International Institute of Administrative Sciences (IIAS) since 1998. The IIAS with its headquarters at Brussels, Belgium, was established for the purpose of promoting the development of Administrative Sciences, better organization and operation of public administrative agencies, improvement of administrative matters and techniques and for the progress of international administration. Membership enables the Government of India in getting information on the latest development in the field of public administration through participation in international meetings and seminars organized by the IIAS as well as through various journals, documents and study reports prepared/issued by them.

Cooperation with CAPAM

The Commonwealth Association for Public Administration and Management (CAPAM), with its headquarters at Ottawa, Canada, is an organization dedicated to strengthening public management and consolidating democracy and good governance throughout the Commonwealth. It was formed in 1994 as a result of decisions taken at the Commonwealth Heads of Government meeting in Harare in 1991 and in Cyprus in 1993. Since inception, CAPAM has grown to a network of over 1,100 members across the Commonwealth countries. The Ministry of Personnel, Public Grievances and Pensions, Government of India became an institutional member of CAPAM in 1997. The membership enables the Government of India to keep pace with the latest developments in the field of public administration, through participation in various programmes of CAPAM viz; International Innovations Awards Programme, International Innovations Cascading Programme, International Meetings, Seminars and Conferences organized by CAPAM, as well as through various publications, journals and study reports issued by CAPAM.

Since 1998, CAPAM has been announcing its Biennial International Innovations Awards Programme to promote the spirit of innovation in the public service by recognizing those who have made significant contribution to improve governance and services to the public. India has been participating in the CAPAM Award Programme since the beginning and has won gold medals in 1998, 2000, 2002, 2004 2010, 2012, 2014 and in recently concluded 2016 CAPAM Innovation Award Programme, (Cancer Cervix Screening: A Life Saving Initiative, Government of Tamil Nadu) and also silver medals in the year 2002, 2004, 2006 and 2016. The Department organized CAPAM International Awards Programme 2012 from 21-22 October 2012 on the theme 'Innovations in the Public Service' in conjunction with CAPAM Biennial Conference (October 24-16, 2012). The 'Sugarcane Information System' of India won the overall Gold medal of CAPAM International Innovation Award, 2012.

Foreign Training Programme for Senior/Middle Level Management Officers of Government of India/ States

As a part of its international collaborative efforts, the possibility of sharing and exchanging administrative experiences with other countries, particularly in the area of public administration and delivery of services has been expired so as to improve upon the current system of governance and instill a greater sense of responsiveness, accountability and transparency and to bring in fresh insights and new perspectives in these areas.

The Department has nominated public service officials from the Government of India/States/UTs including PM Award winners/National e-Governance winners on: (i) five day training programme for a group comprising 16 officers from Government of India and states/Uts including PM Award winners/National e-Governance winners to the Institute of Public Administration of Canada (IPAC), Toronto, Canada from August 22-26 2016; (ii) five day training programme for a group comprising 21 officers from Government of India and States/UTs including PM Award winners/National e-Governance Award winners visit to the PBLQ, Dutch Institute of Public Administration, the Hague, Netherlands scheduled to be held during September 12-16, 2016.

During the training programme the participants would share administrative experiences and best practices in the area of public administration and delivery of services. The participants would share experiences in these countries in the areas of—Public Service Reforms, including Service Delivery and dissemination; e-Governance initiative/IT enabled service delivery including possibility of replication of best practice; and administrative reforms leading to citizen centric governance.

DARPG-UNDP Project

The Department has signed a Project Document "Strengthening Public Administration and Governance" with UNDP on February 3, 2014 as part of Country Programme Action Plan (CPAP) 2013-17. The following two programmes will be organized in the current financial year. The project aims to achieve (a) improved capabilities of institutions and individuals responsible for public administration and governance; deeper understanding of administrators on factors that contribute to success or failure of service delivery under Government programmes; and increased cooperation in the area of public administration globally including the South-South context. The project is fully funded by UNDP with a commitment of US$ 1 million for activities.

The Department had signed Annual Work Plan 2016 with UNDP for a budget of US$ 1,64, 525. The Annual Work Plan 2016 is aimed at creating a world class, open citizen centric services delivered through best practice National Portal, institutional mechanism and infrastructure. The expenditure towards the activities is being met by UNDP. The Department is Implementeing partner.

National Conference on e-Governance

The DARPG along-with the Department of Electronics and Information Technology in association with one of the State Governments has been organizing the National Conference on e-Governance every year since 1997. This conference provides a platform for the senior officers of the Government including IT Secretaries of State Governments. IT Managers of the Central Government, and resource persons, experts, intellectuals from the industry and academic institutions, etc. to discuss, exchange views and experiences relating to various e-Governance initiatives. So far 19 national conference on e-Governance has been held.

To recognize and promote excellence in implementation of e-Governance initiatives, DARPG presents National Awards every year during National Conference on e-Governance in the following categories : (i) Excellence in Government Process Re-engineering; (ii) Outstanding performance in Citizen-Centric Service Delivery; (iii) Innovative use of technology in e-Governance; (iv)Incremental innovations in existing projects; (v) Best district level initiative in Citizen-Centric Service Delivery through ICT; (iv) Incremental Innovations in existing projects; (v) Best District level initiative in citizen-centric service delivery through ICT; (vi) Innovative use of GIS technology in e-Governance; (vii) Innovative use of mobile technology in e-Governance; (viii) Sectorial Award: 'Skill Development and Employability'; (ix) Innovative Use of ICT by Central Government PSUs; (x)Innovative Use of ICT by State Government PSUs/cooperatives/ federations/societies; (xi) Outstanding e-Governance initiative by academic and research institutions; (xii) Use of ICT for development by non-government institutions.

Each category is given one gold and one silver award. The gold award winning project and its team is given a cash award upto a maximum of ₹ 2 lakh, subject to a ceiling of ₹ 75,000/- per individual and silver winning project and its team is given a cash award upto a maximum of ₹ one lakh, subject to a ceiling of ₹ 50,000/- per individual.

Documentation and Dissemination of Good Governance Practices

The DARPG primarily carries out the following activities of documentation, and dissemination of good governance practices of Centre, State/Union

Territory Governments with a view to share experiences and replication elsewhere. Besides, the Division maintains a repository of reference material concerning public administration, management, information technology, human resource development in the shape of a rich and well equipped library.

Financial Assistance for Professional Documentation of Good Governance Initiatives to State Governments/UTs

The objective of the scheme is to provide financial assistance upto ₹ 3.00 lakh to support professional documentation and dissemination of good governance initiatives by the state/union territory governments with a view to sharing experience with each other and replicate elsewhere. So far seventy-two projects have been sanctioned. As per the revised scheme of providing financial assistance to the state government/UT administrations, the professional documentation report will now be in e-book form instead of paper documentation and a short documentary film shall also be made by the State/UT Govt. with the financial assistance of ₹ 3.00 lakh.

Production of Documentary Films on Best Practices

The Department is engaged in producing documentary films on best practices across the country. These films are useful for the administrations and the dissemination of success stories would facilitate replication of the same elsewhere. Seventy-eight such documentary films have already been produced. These documentary films are available on the website of the Department as well as You Tube. Two panel discussions on excellence in implementation of four priority programme of the Government were organized and telecasted on DD National Channel on May 21-22, 2016. These discussions are also available on Department's website as well as social media accounts such as twitter & facebook.

Research and Evaluation Studies on Good Governance Initiatives

The objective of the initiative is to assess the present status of implementation of select good governance initiatives in view of technical advancements and to suggest changes to be incorporated for improving the initiative. It also provides suggestions on sustainability, scalability and replicability of these initiatives. In 2013-14, study on ten initiatives was conducted by M/s KPMG Advisory Services Pvt. Ltd. The Research and Evaluation Studies report is available at www.darpg.gov.in. In FY 2015-16, Research and Evaluation Study on 12 select good governance initiatives is being conducted through Indian Institute of Development Management, Bhopal.

Regional Conferences

Regional Conferences are organised on specific themes in association with various State/Union Territory Governments with a view to bring National and State level organizations along with other stakeholders including NGOs, intelligentsia, media, etc. on the same platform to share experiences in the formulation and implementation of good governance practices. During 2015-

16, one regional conference on the theme 'Minimum Government-Maximum Governance' As part of Gati: Governance with Accountability, Transparency and Innovation" was held in the month of December, 2015 at Bengaluru, Karnataka. Till date, 23 regional conferences were organized.

Presentations on Best Practices

In order to facilitate replication of the successful good governance initiatives in other states, presentations on best practices are being organised in New Delhi. During 2015-16, the Department of AR&PG organised National Workshop on Best Practices in Citizen Centric Governance on September, 10-11, 2015 in New Delhi.

Book on Best Practices

This Division publishes a book containing articles on select award winning good governance practices. These articles are on the initiatives that have been conferred Prime Minister's Award or National e-Governance Awards. This compilation is immensely useful for the administrators as the dissemination of success stories facilitates replication of the same elsewhere also. The Division has already published a series of books on the subject. These are - *Ideas that have Worked, Vichar Jo Kamyab Huye (Hindi version of Ideas that have Worked,) Learn from them, Inse Seekhe (Hindi version of Learn from Them), Splendour in the Grass, Roofless Towers, Management by Listening, In Search of Light, People First, Some Gems Some Pearls, Thinking out of the Box, Lighted Windows and Tomorrow is Here.* This year, two books namely *The Change Makers* and *Re-creating Excellence* has been published and released on the occasion of Civil Services Day, 2016.

Minimum Government-Maximum Governance

The Departmental quarterly Journal - *Minimum Government Minimum Governance* earlier known as *Management in Government* provides a forum for frank exchange of views and opinions among administrators, academicians, scholars and others interested in public administration and public sector management. The Department has been bringing out this quarterly journal since 1969. Earlier the journal was a priced publication with subscribers from all over the country as well as overseas too. Towing the line of e-Governance, the journal has been transformed in e-Book format which is uploaded on the Department's website and is free for all. Till date, six issues of the journal have been uploaded on the website. The latest being the April-June, 2016.

e-Office Project

e-Office is one of the 31 Mission Mode Projects (MMPs) identified in the erstwhile national e-Governance Plan-2006 NeGP 1.0 and its implementation is being steered by the DAR&PG. The e-Office has been subsumed in the current Digital India Programme (NeGP 2.0). e-Office MMP Programme is being monitored on a regular basis by an apex committee headed by Cabinet Secretary.

Administrative Reforms Commission

The second Administrative Reforms Commission (ARC) was constituted on May 31, 2005, as a Commission of Inquiry, under the Chairmanship of Shri Veerappa Moily for preparing a detailed blueprint for revamping the public administrative system. The Commission was requested to suggest measures to achieve a proactive, responsive, accountable, sustainable and efficient administration for the country at all levels of Government. It has presented 15 reports to the Government for consideration: (i) Right to Information: Master Key to Good Governance; (ii) Unlocking Human Capital: Entitlements and Governance - A Case Study; (iii) Crisis Management: From Despair to Hope; (iv) Ethics in Governance; (v) Public Order : Justice for Each ... Peace for All; (vi) Local Governance; (vii) Capacity Building for Conflict Resolution - Friction to Fusion; (viii) Combating Terrorism; (ix) Social Capital - A Shared Destiny; (x) Refurbishing of Personnel Administration - Scaling New Heights; (xi) Promoting e-Governance - The Smart Way Forward; (xii) Citizen Centric Administration - The Heart of Governance; (xiii) Organisational Structure of Government of India; (xiv) Strengthening Financial Management System; (xv) State and District Administration.

The Central Government has considered 14 out of 15 reports and the decisions on the accepted recommendations of 2nd ARC are at various stages of implementation.

Modernization Scheme

The Modernization Scheme is being implemented by this Department of Administrative Reforms and Public Grievances from 1987-88 in order to give boost to modernization of offices at Branch and Section level in various Central Government offices located in Delhi as an overall process of administrative reforms. As per the scheme, the DARPG extends financial assistance to the extent of 75 per cent of the total cost of the project and the beneficiary has to contribute 25 per cent of the cost. The proposals are considered by a Screening Committee and funds are released with the concurrence of Integrated Finance Division.

Right to Information

The Right to Information Act, 2005 empowers the citizens, promotes transparency and accountability in the working of the Government, combat corruption and make the democracy work for people in real sense. The Act aims at creating an informed citizenry which would be better equipped to keep necessary vigil on the instruments of governance and make the government more accountable to the governed.

The Act gives all the citizens the right to seek information held by any authority or body or institution of self government established or constituted by or under the Constitution; or by any other law made by the Parliament or a State Legislature; or by notification issued or order made by the Central Government or a State Government. Bodies owned, controlled or substantially financed by the Central Government or a State Government and non-Government organizations substantially financed by the Central Government or a State Government also fall within the definition of public authority. The financing of the body or the NGO by the Government may be direct or indirect. The right includes inspection of work, documents and records; taking notes, extracts or certified copies of documents or records, taking certified samples of material held by the public authority or held under the control of the public authority. It also includes information relating to any private body which can be accessed by the public authority under any law for the time being in force. There are some categories of information which each public authority is required to publish *suo motu*.

One has to simply make a request to the Public Information Officer of the office indicating the information sought and the address at which the information is required. The request can be sent either by post or submitted in person in Hindi, English or in the official language of the area and can also be sent through e-mail. If the applicant does not get the information within 30 days or the applicant is not satisfied with the reply given to him, he can make an appeal within 30 days to the appellate authority appointed by the authority who is an officer superior to the Public Information Officer. The appellate authority has to decide the appeal within 30 days of the receipt of appeal. If the applicant is not satisfied even with the decision of the appellate authority, he can file a second appeal with the Central Information Commission or the State Information Commission, as the case may be within 90 days. The Central Information Commission entertains appeals in respect of offices, financial institutions, public sector undertakings, etc. under the Central Government and the union territories and a State Information Commission deals with the appeals pertaining to offices, financial institutions, public sector undertakings, etc. under the concerned State Government.

The Central Information Commission/State Information Commissions are high-powered independent bodies created by the Act, and they can impose penalty on the defaulting Public Information Officers. This comprehensive law covers almost all levels of governance, and are applicable not only to Union, State and Local Governments but also to the recipients of Government grants. Access to information under this Act is extensive with minimum exemptions. The Right to Information Act has converted the prevailing culture of secrecy into culture of openness and transparency in the working of the Government.

Official Language

Article 343 (1) of the Constitution provides that Hindi in Devanagari script shall be the official language of the Union. Article 343 (2) also provides for continuing the use of English in official work of the Union for a period of 15 years (i.e., up to January 25, 1965) from the date of commencement of the Constitution. Article 343 (3) empowered the Parliament to provide by law for continued use of English for official purposes even after January 25, 1965. The Act also lays down under Section 3 (3) that both Hindi and English shall compulsorily be used for certain specified purpose such as Resolutions, General Orders, Rules, Notifications, Administrative and other Reports, Press Communiques; Administrative and other reports and official papers to be laid before a House or the Houses of Parliament; contracts, agreements, licences, permits, tender notices and forms of tender, etc.

In 1976, Official Language Rules were framed under the provisions of section 8 (1) of the Official Languages Act, 1963 as amended in 1967. Salient features of the rules are as under: (i) They apply to all Central Government offices, including any office of a Commission, Committee or Tribunal appointed by the Central Government and Corporation or Company owned or controlled by the Central Govt. except the State of Tamil Nadu; (ii) Communications from a Central Government office to State/Union Territories or to any person in region 'A' comprising the States of Uttar Pradesh, Uttarakhand, Himachal Pradesh, Madhya Pradesh, Chhattisgarh, Bihar, Jharkhand, Rajasthan, Haryana and Union Territories of Andaman and Nicobar Islands and Delhi, shall be in Hindi; (iii) Communications from a Central Government Office to States/Union Territories in region 'B' comprising the States of Punjab, Gujarat, Maharahstra and the Union Territory of Chandigarh, Daman and Diu and Dadra and Nagar Haveli shall ordinarily be in Hindi and if any communication is issued to any of them in English, it shall be accompanied by a Hindi translation thereof; (iv) Communications from a Central Government office to State or Union Territory in Region 'C' or to any office (not being a Central Government Office) or person in such State shall be in English; and (v) Communications between Central Government offices in region 'C' to a state or Union Territory of Region 'A' or Region 'B' or to any office (not being a Central Government office) or persons in such state may be either in Hindi or English.

Features of Official Language Policy

The features of official language policy are : i) All manuals, codes and other procedural literature relating to Central Government offices are required to be prepared both in Hindi and English. All forms, headings of registers, name plates, notice boards and various items of stationery, etc. are also required to be in Hindi and English; ii) Officers should ensure that documents specified in Section 3 (3) of the Act are issued both in Hindi and English; and iii) The administrative head of each Central Government office should ensure that the provisions of the Act, the rules and directions issued under Rule 12 shall be properly complied with, and suitable and effective check-points shall be devised for this purpose.

Annual Programme

In compliance with the Official Language Resolution, 1968, an annual programme is prepared by the Department of Official Language in which targets are set for the offices of the Central Government with regard to originating correspondence, replies in Hindi to letters in Hindi, recruitment of Hindi typists and stenos, websites, inspections and meetings of Hindi Salahakar Samiti and Official Language Implementation Committees, purchase of Hindi books for libraries, and purchase of electronic equipments. A Quarterly Progress Report is submitted by the offices of the Central Government regarding achievements vis-a-vis the said targets. An Annual Assessment Report is prepared on the basis of the Quarterly Progress Reports, which is laid on the tables of both Houses of the Parliament, and its copies are endorsed to State Governments and the ministries/departments of the Central Government.

Subordinate Offices of the Department

The Central Hindi Training Institute (CHTI) and Central Translation Bureau (CTB) are the two leading institutions for capacity-building in learning of Hindi language, typing, shorthand, IT tools and translation-skills. There are also eight regional implementation offices at Bengaluru, Cochin, Mumbai, Kolkata, Guwahati, Bhopal, Delhi and Ghaziabad to monitor the implementation of Official Language Policy of the Union.

Committees/Samitis

The Kendriya Hindi Samiti was constituted in the year 1967. Chaired by Prime Minister it is the apex policy making body which lays the guidelines for the propagation and progressive use of Hindi as official language of the Union. The Committee of Parliament on official language has been constituted in 1976 under Section 4 of the Official Languages Act, 1963 to periodically review the progress in the use of Hindi as the official language of the Union and to submit a report to the President. The Committee consists of 20 Members of the Lok Sabha and 10 of the Rajya Sabha. It has so far submitted nine parts of the reports to the President. The Presidential orders have been issued on eight parts so far and work is in progress on the ninth part.

The Hindi Salahakar Samitis have been constituted in various ministries/ departments with a view to rendering advice for proper implementation of the Official Language Policy of the Government. The Chairman of these Samitis are the Ministers concerned. These Samitis are the required to be constituted in accordance with the guidelines formulated on the basis of recommendations of the Kendriya Hindi Samiti chaired by the Prime Minister. The main function of these Samitis is to render advise for implementation of the principles relating of Official Language Act and Rules and the policy decisions and directions of the Kendriya Hindi Samiti and the Department of Official Language with regard to use of Hindi in official work.

Town Official Languages Implementation Committees (TOLICs) are constituted in different cities and towns having ten or more Central Government offices. Its objective is to promote the use of Hindi in their member-offices, and exchange information on good practices for wider use of Hindi experiences.

Besides the Central Official language Implementation Committee headed by Secretary, Department of Official Language reviews the status of use of

Hindi for official purposes of the Union, of the training of its employees in Hindi, and implementation of instructions issued from time to time by the Department of Official Language. It suggests measures for removing the shortcoming and difficulties noticed in implementation these instructions.

Awards Schemes

The Department has Rajbhasha Keerti Puraskar Yojna for awarding the outstanding achievements in the implementation of Official Language Policy of the Union. Under this Scheme shields are given every year to ministries/departments, banks and financial institutions, public sector undertakings and Town Official Language Implementation Committees for outstanding achievements in the implementation of the Official Language Policy of the Union.

Under the Rajbhasha Gaurav Hindi Book-Writing Scheme, cash awards, shields and certificates are awarded to the working/retired employees of the Central Government, banks, financial institutions, universities, training institutions and autonomous bodies of the Central Government for writing original books in Hindi. Under the same scheme cash awards, shields and certificates are awarded to citizen of India for writing original books in Hindi on knowledge and science based subjects besides this, the Central Govt. employees including retired employees are awarded for writing excellent articles in Hindi.

At zonal level, Zonal Official Language Awards are given every year to the Central Government offices, public sector undertakings, Town Official Language Implementation Committees, banks and financial institutions of the Central Government for outstanding achievements in implementing the Official Language Policy of the Union, and for progressive use of Hindi.

Inter-State Council

The provision for setting up an Inter-State Council is mentioned in Article 263 of the Constitution. In pursuance of the recommendation made by the Sarkaria Commission on Centre-State Relations, the Inter-State Council was set up in 1990 through a Presidential Order dated May 28, 1990.

The Inter-State Council (ISC) is a recommendatory body and has been assigned the duties of investigating and discussing such subjects, in which some or all of the States or the Union Territories and one or more of the states have a common interest, for better coordination of policy and action with respect to that subject. It also deliberates upon such other matters of general interests to the states as may be referred by the Chairman to the Council.

The Prime Minister is the Chairman of the Council. Chief Ministers of all the states and Union Territories having Legislative Assemblies, Administrators of Union Territories not having Legislative Assemblies, Governors of States under President's rule and six ministers of Cabinet rank in the Union Council of

Ministers, nominated by the Chairman of the Council, are members of the Council.

The meetings of the Council are held in camera, and all issues, which come up for consideration of the Council in a meeting, are decided by consensus, and the decision of the Chairman as to the consensus is final.

Based on the recommendation of the ISC, the Standing Committee of the Inter-State Council was first constituted in the year 1996 for continuous consultation and processing of matters for the consideration of the Council.

The Inter-State Council and its Standing Committee have, so far held 10 meetings each and have considered all the recommendations made by the Sarkaria Commission. The Council has also considered other public policy and governance issues, such as: (a) Contract labour and contract appointments; (b) Blueprint of an Action Plan on Good Governance; (c) Disaster Management—Preparedness of States to cope with disasters; and (d) Atrocities on Scheduled Castes and Scheduled Tribes and status of implementation of the Scheduled Castes/Scheduled Tribes (Prevention of Atrocities) Act, 1989.

Zonal Council

Five Zonal Councils viz. Northern Zonal Council, Central Zonal Council, Eastern Zonal Council, Western Zonal Council and Southern Zonal Council were set up vide Part-III of the States Re-organisation Act, 1956 with the objectives of bringing out national integration; arresting the growth of acute State consciousness, regionalism, linguism and particularistic tendencies; enabling the Centre and the States to cooperate and exchange ideas and experiences; and establishing a climate of co-operation amongst the States for successful and speedy execution of development projects. The Zonal Council for each zone consist of: (i) Chairman: The Union Home Minister is the Chairman of each of these Councils; (ii) Vice-Chairman: The Chief Minister of the State included in each zone act as Vice-Chairman of the Zonal Council for that zone by rotation, each holding office for a period of one year at a time; (iii) Members: Chief Minister and two other ministers as nominated by the Governor from each of the States and two members from Union Territories included in the zone; (iv) Advisers: One person nominated by the Planning Commission for each of the zonal councils, chief secretaries and another Officer/ Development Commissioner nominated by each of the States included in the Zone.

Composition of Zonal Councils

Zonal Council	Members States/ Union Territories
Northern Zonal Council	Haryana, Punjab, Himachal Pradesh, Rajasthan, Jammu & Kashmir, National Capital Territory of Delhi and the Union Territory of Chandigarh
Central Zonal Council	Uttarakhand, Uttar Pradesh, Chhattisgarh and Madhya Pradesh

Eastern Zonal Council	Bihar, Jharkhand, West Bengal and Odisha
Western Zonal Council	Gujarat, Maharashtra, Goa and the Union Territories of Dadra & Nagar Haveli and Daman and Diu
Southern Zonal Council	Andhra Pradesh, Tamil Nadu, Karnataka, Kerala, Telangana and the Union Territory of Puducherry

Organizational Structure of Zonal Council

The Union Home Minister is the Chairman of all the Zonal Councils. The Office of the Vice-Chairman is held by the Chief Minister of the Member State of the respective Zonal Council by annual rotation, each holding office for a period of one year at a time. Two other ministers of each member state are also members of each Zonal Council. The Chief Secretary of the Member State function as the Secretary of respective Zonal Council by annual rotation and another officer/ Development Commissioner and one officer nominated by the Planning Commission for each of the Zonal Councils as Adviser for a period of one year.

Committees of Zonal Council

Each Zonal Council has set up a Standing Committee consisting of the Chief Secretaries of the States of the respective zones for monitoring implementation of recommendations of the concerned Council as also for screening and scrutinizing agenda items to be placed before the respective Zonal Council. The Chief Secretaries functioning as the Secretaries of the respective Zonal Councils also preside over the meetings of the respective Standing Committee.

Meeting of the Zonal Councils

Since its creation in 1956, the five Zonal Councils have so far held 114 meetings. The Standing Committees of the Councils have met 51 times. A large number of very important issues of Center-State and Inter-State relations have been discussed and resolved in these meetings.

Office of Zonal Councils

As per Section 20 (1) of the Act, the office of Zonal Council for each zone shall be located at such place within the zone as may be determined by the Council. However, since 1963, a single secretariat is looking after the affairs of all Zonal Councils and is functioning from New Delhi. The Zonal Councils Secretariat explores Centre-State, Inter-State and Zonal issues which are to be deliberated by the Councils or the Standing Committees. The Secretariat also follows up on the recommendations of the Councils/Standing Committees, if necessary drawing the attention of the Chairman and other Central Ministers/Chief Ministers.

Transfer of Work of Zonal Council Secretariat

The second Commission on Centre-State relations deliberated on the functioning of the Zonal Councils and *inter-alia* recommended that the Zonal Councils should meet at least twice a year with an agenda proposed by States concerned to maximize coordination and promote harmonization of policies and action having inter-state ramification. The Secretariat of a strengthened Inter-State Council can function as the Secretariat of the Zonal Councils as well. In accordance to the above recommendation, the work of the Zonal Council Secretariat was transferred to the Inter-State Council Secretariat with effect from April 1, 2011 by the Ministry of Home Affairs.

The States

The system of Government in states closely resembles that of the Union.

Executive

Governor

A state executive consists of Governor and Council of Ministers with Chief Minister as its head. The Governor of a State is appointed by the President for a term of five years office. Only Indian citizens above 35 years of age are eligible for appointment to this office. Executive power of the state is vested in Governor.

The Council of Ministers with the Chief Minister as head, aids and advises Governor in exercise of his functions except in so far as he is by or under the Constitution required to exercise his functions or any of them in his discretion. In respect of Nagaland, the Governor has special responsibility under Article 371 A of the Constitution with respect to law and order and even though it is necessary for him to consult Council of Ministers in matters relating to law and order, he can exercise his individual judgment as to the action to be taken.

Similarly, in respect of Arunachal Pradesh, the Governor has special responsibility under Article 371 H of the Constitution with respect to law and order. Governor shall, after consulting Council of Ministers, exercise his individual judgment as to the actions to be taken. These are, however, temporary provisions. If the President, on receipt of a report from Governor or otherwise is satisfied that it is no longer necessary for Governor to have special responsibility with respect to law and order, he may so direct by an order.

Likewise, in the Sixth Schedule which applies to tribal areas of Assam, Meghalaya, Tripura and Mizoram as specified in para 20 of that schedule, discretionary powers are given to Governor in matters relating to sharing of royalties between District Council and State Government. The Sixth Schedule vests additional discretionary powers in Governors of Mizoram and Tripura in almost all their functions (except approving regulations for levy of taxes and money lending by non-tribals by district councils) since December, 1998. In Sikkim, the Governor has been given special responsibility for peace and social and economic advancement of different sections of population.

All Governors while discharging such constitutional functions as appointment of Chief Minister of a state or sending a report to the President about failure of constitutional machinery in a state or in respect of matters relating to assent to a bill passed by legislature, exercise their own judgment.

Council of Ministers

The Chief Minister is appointed by the Governor who also appoints other ministers on the advice of the Chief Minister. The Council of Ministers is collectively responsible to the Legislative Assembly of the state.

Legislature

For every state, there is a legislature which consists of Governor and one House or, two Houses as the case may be. In Andhra Pradesh, Bihar, Jammu and Kashmir, Karnataka, Maharashtra, Telangana and Uttar Pradesh, there are two Houses known as Legislative Council and Legislative Assembly. In the remaining states, there is only one House known as Legislative Assembly. Parliament may, by law, provide for abolition of an existing Legislative Council or for creation of one where it does not exist, if proposal is supported by a resolution of the Legislative Assembly concerned.

Legislative Council

Legislative Council *(Vidhan Parishad)* of a state comprises not more than one-third of total number of members in Legislative Assembly of the state and in no case less than 40 members (Legislative Council of Jammu and Kashmir has 36 members *vide* Section 50 of the Constitution of Jammu and Kashmir). About one-third of members of the Council are elected by members of Legislative Assembly from amongst persons who are not its members, one-third by electorates consisting of members of municipalities, district boards and other local authorities in the state, one-twelfth by electorate consisting of persons who have been, for at least three years, engaged in teaching in educational institutions within the state not lower in standard than secondary school and a further one-twelfth by registered graduates of more than three years standing. Remaining members are nominated by the Governor from among those who have distinguished themselves in literature, science, art, cooperative movement and social service. Legislative councils are not subject to dissolution but one-third of their members retire every second year.

Legislative Assembly

Legislative Assembly *(Vidhan Sabha)* of a state consists of not more than 500 and not less than 60 members (Legislative Assembly of Sikkim has 32 members vide Article 371 F of the Constitution) chosen by direct election from territorial constituencies in the state. Demarcation of territorial constituencies is to be done in such a manner that the ratio between population of each constituency and number of seats allotted to it, as far as practicable, is the same throughout the state. Term of an assembly is five years unless it is dissolved earlier.

Powers and Functions

State legislature has exclusive powers over subjects enumerated in List II of the Seventh Schedule of the Constitution and concurrent powers over those enumerated in List III. Financial powers of legislature include authorization of all expenditure, taxation and borrowing by the State Government. Legislative Assembly alone has power to originate money bills. Legislative Council can make only recommendations in respect of changes it considers necessary within a period of 14 days of the receipt of money bills from assembly. The assembly can accept or reject these recommendations.

Reservation of Bills

The Governor of a state may reserve any bill for the consideration of the President. Bills relating to subjects like compulsory acquisition of property, measures affecting powers and position of High Courts and imposition of taxes on storage, distribution and sale of water or electricity in inter-state river or river valley development projects should necessarily be so reserved. No bills seeking to impose restrictions on inter-state trade can be introduced in a state legislature without previous sanction of the President.

Control over Executive

State legislatures, apart from exercising the usual power of financial control, use all normal parliamentary devices like questions, discussions, debates, adjournments and no-confidence motions and resolutions to keep a watch over day-to-day work of the executive. They also have their committees on estimates and public accounts to ensure that grants sanctioned by legislature are properly utilized.

Union Territories

Union territories are administrated by the President acting to such extent, as he thinks fit, through an administrator appointed by him. Administrators of Andaman and Nicobar Islands, Delhi and Puducherry are designated as Lieutenant Governors. The Governor of Punjab is concurrently the administrator of Chandigarh. The administrator of Dadra and Nagar Haveli is concurrently the administrator of Daman and Diu. Lakshadweep has a separate administrator.

The National Capital Territory of Delhi and Union Territory of Puducherry each has a Legislative Assembly and Council of Ministers. The Legislative Assembly of the Union Territory of Puducherry may make laws with respect to matters enumerated in List II or List III in the Seventh Schedule of the Constitution in so far as these matters are applicable in relation to the union territory. The Legislative Assembly of National Capital Territory of Delhi has also these powers with the exceptions that Entries 1, 2 and 18 of the List II are not within the legislative competence of the Legislative Assembly. Certain categories of bills, however, require the prior approval of the Central Government for introduction in the Legislative Assembly. Some bills, passed by the Legislative Assembly of the Union Territory of Puducherry and National Capital Territory of Delhi are required to be reserved for consideration and assent of the President.

Local Government

Municipalities

Municipal bodies have a long history in India. The first such Municipal Corporation was set-up in the former Presidency Town of Madras in 1688; and later in Bombay and Calcutta in 1726. The Constitution of India has made detailed provisions for ensuring protection of democracy in Parliament and in the state legislatures. However, the Constitution did not make the local self-government in urban areas a clear-cut constitutional obligation. While the Directive Principles of State Policy refer to Village Panchayats, there is no specific reference to municipalities except the implicity in Entry 5 of the State List, which places the subject of local self-governments as a responsibility of the states.

In order to provide for a common framework for urban local bodies and help to strengthen the functioning of the bodies as effective democratic units of self-government, Parliament enacted the Constitution (74th Amendment) Act, 1992 (known as Nagarpalika Act) relating to municipalities in 1992. It came into force on June 1st, 1993. A new part IX-A relating to the municipalities added to provide for among other things, constitution of three types of municipalities, i.e., *Nagar Panchayats* for areas in transition from a rural area to urban area, Municipal Councils for smaller urban areas and Municipal Corporation for large urban areas, fixed duration of municipalities, appointment of State Election Commission, appointment of State Finance Commission and constitution of metropolitan and district planning committees. All state/union territories administrations have set-up their State Election Commissions and Finance Commissions.

Panchayats

Article 40 of the Constitution which enshrines one of the Directive Principles of State Policy lays down that the state shall take steps to organize village panchayats and endow them with such powers and authority as may be necessary to enable them to function as units of self-government.

A new Part IX relating to the Panchayats has been inserted in the Constitution to provide for among other things, Gram Sabha in a village or group of villages; constitution of Panchayats at village and other level or levels; direct elections to all seats in Panchayats at the village and intermediate level, if any, and to the offices of Chairpersons of Panchayats at such levels; reservation of seats for the Scheduled Castes and Scheduled Tribes in proportion to their population for membership of Panchayats and office of Chairpersons in Panchayats at each level; reservation of not less than one-third of the seats for women; fixing tenure of five years for Panchayats and holding elections within a period of six months in the event of supersession of any Panchayat.

Election Commission

The Election Commission of India (ECI) was constituted on January 25, 1950 with its headquarters at New Delhi. It is a permanent independent constitutional body vested with the powers and responsibility of superintendence, direction and control of the entire process of conduct of elections to Parliament and to legislatures of the states and the union territories and elections to the offices of President and Vice-President held under the Constitution.

The Election Commission decides the election schedules for the conduct of elections —both general elections and bye-elections. It prepares, maintains and periodically updates the electoral rolls, supervises the nomination of candidates, registers political parties, monitors the election campaign, including funding and expenditure of candidates. It also facilitates the coverage of the election process by the media, carries out the voter education and awareness measures, organizes the polling stations/ booths where voting takes place, and oversees the counting of votes and the declaration of results. It conducts polling through EVMs (Electronic Voting Machines) and recently, on pilot basis, introduced VVPAT (Voter Verifiable Paper Audit Trail). The Election Commission has also provided for compulsory identification at the time of voting by means of Electors' Photo Identity Cards (EPICs) and distribution of Photo Slip close to polls.

Elections are conducted according to the constitutional provisions, supplemented by laws made by Parliament. The major laws are the Presidential and Vice-Presidential Elections Act, 1952; the Representation of the People Act, 1950; and the Representation of the People Act, 1951.

All political parties are required to get themselves registered with the Election Commission. Based on performance criteria laid down in the Elections Symbols (reservation & allotment) order 1968, the Commission grants recognition to political parties as national or state parties. It also decides disputes relating to splits/mergers of recognized political parties.

The Commission has a small Secretariat. The work is organized in divisions, branches and sections. There are functional and territorial divisions in the Commission headed by Deputy Election Commissioners and Director Generals. The main functional divisions are Planning, Judicial, Electoral Rolls, Political Parties, Election Expenditure, Communication, Systematic Voters' Education and Electoral Participation (SVEEP), International Cooperation, Training, Statistical and Documentation, Automation and Technology, Administration, Finance and Co-ordination. The territorial work is distributed among separate units responsible for five zones into which the 29 constituent states and 7 union territories of the country are grouped for convenience of management.

At the state level, the election work is supervised, subject to overall control of the Commission, by the Chief Electoral Officer of the State, who is appointed by the Commission by selection from amongst senior civil servants of the State Government. Field administration at the district and sub-divisional levels in India is run by the District Magistrates (Deputy Commissioners/Collectors), Sub-Divisional Magistrates, Revenue Divisional Officers, Tehsildars, etc. The Election Commission utilizes these State Government officers, for election work, by designating them as District Election Officers Electoral Registration Officers, Returning Officers, Assistant Electoral Registration Officers, Assistant Returning Officers, etc. During election time, however, they are available to the Commission, more or less, on a full time basis.

During the last 64 years, the Commission has conducted 16 General Elections to the Lok Sabha and about 365 General Elections to State Legislative Assemblies, thus facilitating peaceful orderly and democratic transfer of power.

Election Commission of India has launched the India International Institute of Democracy and Election Management (IIIDEM) an advanced resource center of learning, research, training and extension for electoral democracy and election management. The Institute presently functions from Nirvachan Sadan in New Delhi, with a capacity for 150 trainees. Courses are conducted in the Institute for ECI's field officials and also for participants from abroad. The Commission is increasingly sharing its expertise and experience with election management bodies of other countries, and providing electoral assistance and training based on bilateral requests and multi-lateral arrangements. ECI has MoUs with 16 countries, besides having MoUs with UNDP, International IDEA and IFES.

4 Agriculture

AGRICULTURE plays a vital role in India's economy. Nearly 55 per cent of the population is engaged in agriculture and allied activities (census 2011) and it contributes 17.4 per cent to the country's Gross Value Added. Given the importance of agriculture sector, Government of India took several steps for its sustainable development. Steps have been taken to improve soil fertility on a sustainable basis through the soil health card scheme, to provide improved access to irrigation and enhanced water efficiency through Pradhan Mantri Gram Sinchai Yojana, to support organic farming through Paramparagat Krishi Vikas Yojana (PKVY) and to support for creation of a unified national agriculture market to boost the incomes of farmers.

Production

Due to the deficient rainfall as well as unseasonal rains and hailstorms, agricultural production in 2014-15 was lower than that in 2013-14, a year of record production. As per the fourth Advance Estimates for 2014- 15, total production of rice in the country is estimated at 104.80 million tonnes which is lower by 1.85 million tonnes than the production of rice during 2013- 14. Production of wheat estimated at 88.94 million tonnes is also lower than its record production of 95.85 million tonnes during 2013-14. The production of coarse cereals is estimated at 41.75 million tonnes which is lower than the production of coarse cereals during 2013-14. Total foodgrains production during 2014-15 is estimated at 252.68 million tonnes which is lower by 12.36 million tonnes than the record production of 265.04 million tonnes of foodgrains achieved during 2013-14. Total production of pulses and oilseeds estimated at 17.20 million tonnes and 26.68 million tonnes respectively are also lower by 2.05 million tonnes and 6.07 million tonnes than their production levels during 2013-14. Table here gives area, production and yield of major crops.

National Policy for Farmers

Government of India approved the National Policy for Farmers (NPF) in 2007. The Policy provisions, inter alia, include asset reforms in respect of land, water, livestock, fisheries, and bio-resources; support services and inputs like application of frontier technologies; agricultural bio-security systems; supply of good quality seeds and disease-free planting material, improving soil fertility and health, and integrated pest management systems; support services for women like crèches, child care centres, nutrition, health and training; timely, adequate, and easy reach of institutional credit at reasonable interest rates,

Agricultural Production

(lakh tonnes)

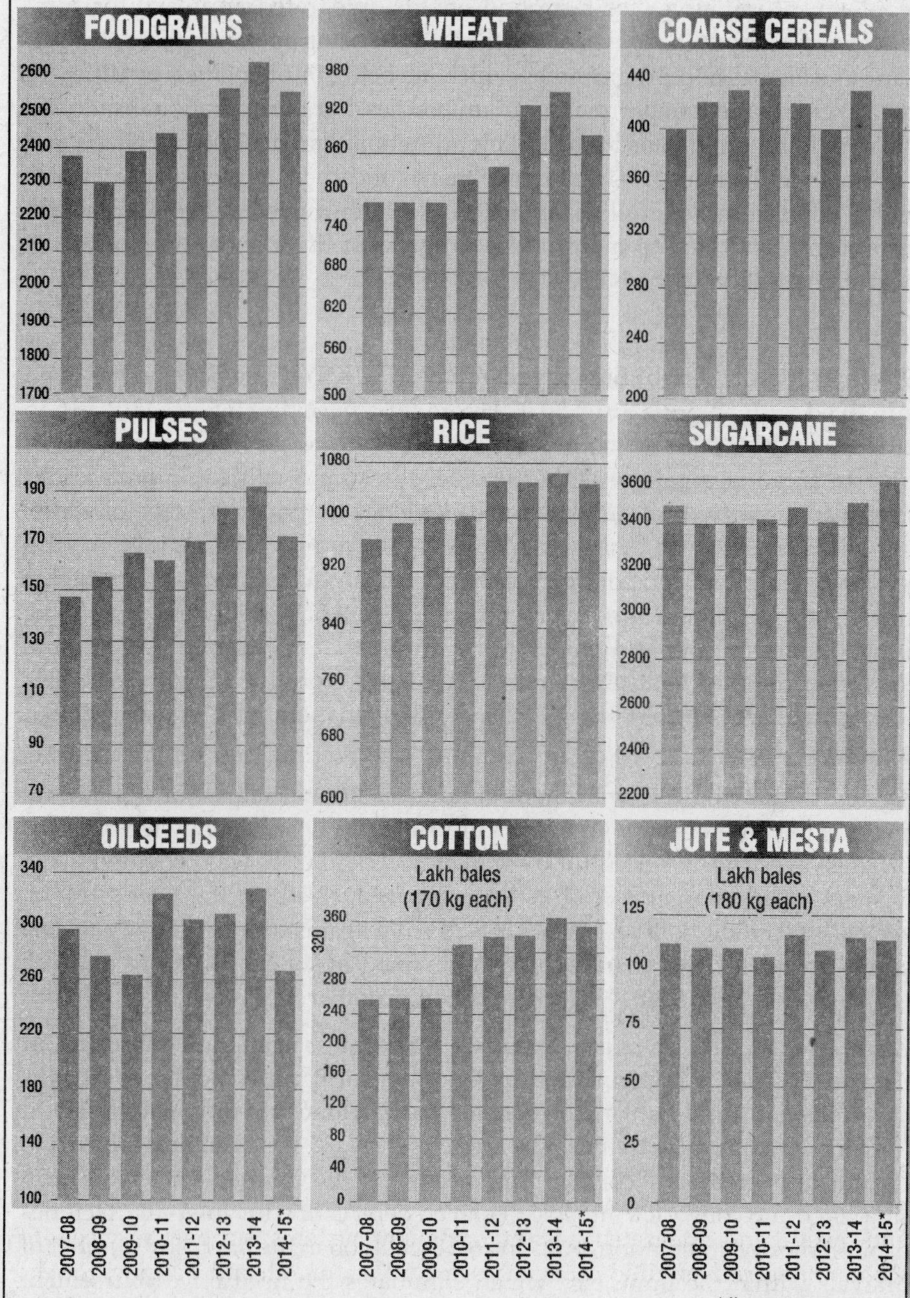

and farmer-friendly insurance instruments; use of Information and Communication Technology (ICT) and setting up of farmers' schools to revitalize agricultural extension; effective implementation of MSP across the country, development of agricultural market infrastructure, and rural non-farm employment initiatives for farm households; integrated approach for rural energy, etc. Many of the provisions of the NPF are being operationalised through various schemes and programmes which are being implemented by different central government departments and ministries. For the operationalisation of the remaining provisions of the Policy, an Action Plan has been finalized and circulated to the ministries and department concerned, as well as to all states and UTs for necessary follow up action. An inter-ministerial committee has also been constituted to monitor the progress of the Plan of Action for the operationalisation of the NPF.

Major Programmes

Pradhan Mantri Krishi Sinchayee Yojana (PMKSY): The Scheme has been approved with an outlay of ₹ 50,000 crore for a period of 5 years (2015-16 to 2019-20). The major objective of PMKSY is to achieve convergence of investments in irrigation at the field level, expand cultivable area under irrigation, improve on-farm water use efficiency to reduce wastage of water, enhance the adoption of precision irrigation and other water saving technologies (more crop per drop), enhance recharge of aquifers and introduce sustainable water conservation practices, etc. A sum of ₹ 5,300 crore, comprising ₹ 1,800 crore for Department of Agriculture & Cooperation, ₹ 1,500 crore for Department of Land Resources and ₹ 2,000 crore for Ministry of Water Resources, River Development & Ganga Rejuvenation has been provisioned in BE 2015-16.

Agricultural Credit: Government announces annual target for agriculture credit in the budget every year. Agricultural credit flow has shown consistent progress every year. Agricultural credit of ₹ 7,11,621 crore was provided to the farmers against target of ₹ 7,00,000 crore in 2013-14. In the year 2014-15, agricultural credit flow was ₹ 8,45,328.23 crore against the target of ₹ 8,00,000 crore. Target for the year 2015-16 was fixed at ₹ 8,50,000 crore and the achievement was ₹ 6,30,243.87 crore upto December 31, 2015.

Kisan Credit Card: The Kisan Credit Card Scheme is in operation throughout the country and is implemented by Commercial Banks, Cooperative Banks and Regional Rural Banks. The Scheme has facilitated in augmenting credit flow for agricultural activities. The scope of the KCC has been broad-based to include term credit and consumption needs. The KCC Scheme has since been simplified and converted into ATM enabled debit card with, inter-alia, facilities of one-time documentation, built-in cost escalation in the limit, any number of drawals within the limit, etc., which eliminates the need for disbursement through camps and mitigates the vulnerability of farmers to middlemen.

Crop Insurance

In order to protect farmers against crop failure due to natural calamities, pests and diseases, weather conditions, Government of India had introduced the National Crop Insurance Programme (NCIP) with component schemes of Modified National Agricultural Scheme (MNAIS), Weather Based Crop Insurance Scheme (WBCIS) and Coconut Palm Insurance Scheme (CPIS). In addition, National Agricultural Insurance Scheme (NAIS) which was to be withdrawn after implementation of NCIP from rabi 2013-14 has been extended further upto 2015-16.

The existing crop insurance schemes have recently been reviewed in consultation with various stakeholders including states/ UTs. As a result of the review, a new scheme Pradhan Mantri Fasal Bima Yojana (PMFBY) has been approved for implementation from kharif 2016 along with pilot Unified Package Insurance Scheme (UPIS) and restructured Weather Based Crop Insurance Scheme (WBCIS). Under the PMFBY, a uniform maximum premium of only 2 per cent will be paid by farmers for all kharif crops and 1.5 per cent for all rabi crops. In case of annual commercial and horticultural crops, the maximum premium to be paid by farmers will be only 5 per cent. The premium rates to be paid by farmers are very low and balance premium will be paid by the Government to provide full insured amount to the farmers against crop loss on account of natural calamities.

Special Rehabilitation Package for Distressed Farmers (i) A Special Rehabilitation Package for 31 suicide prone districts in the four states, namely, Andhra Pradesh, Maharashtra, Karnataka and Kerala was implemented. Against the approved outlay of ₹ 16978.78 crore, ₹ 19,998.70 crore was sanctioned/released under the package to these states. The package has stabilized the conditions of the farmers in the identified districts. (ii) As part of Special Rehabilitation Package meant for suicide districts, two packages were approved by the Government of India for Kerala based on the various programmes/interventions suggested by the M.S. Swaminathan Research Foundation in 2008: (i) development of Kuanad Wetland Ecosystem with financial outlay of ₹ 1,840.75 crore and (ii) mitigation of Agrarian Distress in Idukki district with financial outlay of ₹ 764.65 crore. The Government of Kerala has been adviced to implement sanctioned projects under the ongoing schemes and also to continue the activities for improving the conditions of farmers by taking various initiatives under Rashtriya Krishi Vikas Yojana and other schemes/programmes in order to sustain the gains achieved under these packages.

Commission for Agricultural Costs and Prices: Commission for Agricultural Costs and Prices (CACP), set up with a view to evolving a balanced and integrated price structure, is mandated to advise on the price policy (MSP) of 23 crops. These include seven cereal crops (paddy, wheat, jowar, bajra, maize, ragi and barley), five pulse crops (gram, tur, moong, urad and lentil), seven oilseeds (groundnut, sunflower seed, soyabean, rapeseed—mustard, safflower, niger seed and sesamum), copra (dried coconut), coon, raw jute and sugarcane fair and remunerative prices (FRP) instead of MSPÀ. While recommending MSPs/FRP, CACP is called upon to ensure that the production patterns are broadly in line with the overall needs (demand) of the economy. CACP submits its recommendations to the government in the form of price policy reports every year, separately for five groups of commodities namely kharif crops, rabi crops, sugarcane, raw jute and copra. Before preparing these five pricing policy reports, the Commission seeks views of various state governments, concerned national organizations and ministries.

Determinants of MSP: While recommending price policy of various commodities under its mandate, the Commission keeps in mind demand and supply, cost of production, price trends in the market, both domestic and international, inter-crop price parity, terms of trade between agricultural and non-agricultural sectors, likely implications of MSP on consumers of that product, besides ensuring optimal utilization of natural resources like land and water. It may be noted that cost of production is an important factor that goes as an input in determination of MSP but it is not the only factor. Thus, recommending MSPs of various crops is not a 'cost plus' pricing exercise, though cost is an important determinant.

Indian Council of Agricultural Research

Agricultural research and education in India is spearheaded by the Indian Council of Agricultural Research (ICAR), an autonomous organization under the Department of Agricultural Research and Education (DARE), Ministry of Agriculture and Farmers' Welfare, Government of India. This apex body is mandated for coordinating, guiding and managing research and education in agriculture and allied activities. It has the largest network of agricultural research and education in the world with 109 institutes, 78 all India coordinated projects/networks, 642 *Krishi Vigyan Kendras* (KVKs), 71 state agricultural/ veterinary/horticultural/fishery universities and four general universities with agricultural faculty spread across the country.

Keeping pace with the changing requirements of country's farm sector, ICAR Institutes developed a number of cost-effective technologies, techniques and products, not only to enhance the productivity of various crops and commodities, but also the quality of produce, for enabling remunerative agriculture. The partnerships within the National Agricultural Research and Education System (NARES) as well as outside, with several organizations were the hallmark of R&D efforts during the year. The 87th Foundation Day of ICAR function held at Patna witnessed the launch of several initiatives of ICAR, viz., Farmers FIRST, Student READY, Attracting Retaining Youth in Agriculture (ARYA), Agri-Tech Foresight Centre (ATFC) and Mera Gaon, Mera Gaurav, for building entrepreneurship amongst the agricultural graduates and improving technology delivery as well as knowledge empowerment of farmers. Foundation stone of IARI, Hazaribagh, Jharkhand, was also laid.

Foundation stones of the Indian Institute of Agricultural Biotechnology (IIAB), Ranchi and National Research Centre on Integrated Farming at Motihari, Bihar were also laid. The other initiatives included launching of Consortia Research Programmes and Extra Mural Funding in the Council. The ICAR in a major exercise, formulated the Vision- 2050 documents and revised the mandates of all the institutes keeping in view the changing needs of agricultural research, human resources and technology dissemination vis-à-vis growing population and consequent increase in food demand, changing food consumption pattern, state of natural resources, climate change, commercialization of agriculture, global trade regime and a dynamic policy environment both, domestic as well as global. The nomenclature of several ICAR institutes was also revised. During the year, several areas in the northern states were impacted by hailstorms that caused damage to ready-to-harvest wheat crop; the monsoon was delayed and on an average remained 14 per cent deficient resulting in loss to rainfed farming in some parts of the country. Such unforeseen natural calamities bring out the vulnerability of the agriculture and also look to the agricultural research community to be proactive for building resilience to natural exigencies.

Soil and Water Productivity

Land resource inventory on 1:10,000 scale was prepared taking Landscape Ecological Unit (LEU) consisting of landforms, land use and slope as the base map while bio-climatic map of India was revised. Electronic atlas of water resources developed for Odisha and Himachal Pradesh, is a useful tool for catch assessment and developing GIS based Decision Support System. The information will help planners to concentrate efforts, allocate resources and deploy manpower according to the distribution of fishery resources. Bamboo plantation-based bio-engineering interventions were found promising for reclamation and productive utilization of major ravines namely, Mahi ravines at Vasad (Gujarat), Chambal ravines at Kota (Rajasthan), and Yamuna ravines at Agra (Uttar Pradesh). These interventions could absorb more than 80 per cent of rainfall and reduce the soil and nutrient losses by 90 and 70 per cent, respectively. Foliar sprays with various chemicals were evaluated to mitigate dry spells during crop growing season across diverse rainfed agroecologies. Plant growth promoting Rhizobacteria and Arthrobacter were isolated, characterized and field evaluated in vertisols of Madhya Pradesh; average yield of wheat due to actinomycetes inoculation was 16 per cent higher over control. Shortlisted Arthrobacter isolates effectively improved yield of maize and soyabean. A soil nitrogen test based fertilizer prediction model for targeted yield in Nagpur Mandarin was developed. Integrated farming system (1 ha) model comprising cropping systems (0.52 ha) + horticulture (0.32 ha) + dairy including bio-gas and vermicompost unit (0.08 ha) + fish-cum-poultry (0.1 ha) + mushroom developed in western Himalayas, provided round the year improved production (21.52 tonnes REY (rice equivalent yield)/ year), profit (₹ 3.06 lakh/year) and employment (731 man days/year).

Climate Change

The Cool Farm Tool model used to estimate emission of GHGs, integrates several globally determined empirical GHG quantification models. Using the tool, GHG fluxes (carbon-dioxide and methane), moisture and heat in the soil-plant-atmosphere systems were measured in rice-wheat rotation. Among the cropping systems, maize-wheat cropping registered highest carbon management index. The cumulative seasonal methane emission was reduced by 75 per cent in aerobic rice as compared to continuously flooded rice and the seasonal emissions were lower in slow-release N fertilizer.

Livestock Improvement

India has been holding the position of leading milk producing nation in the world for the last several years with sustainable increase in the annual milk production wherein the research developments played a crucial role. Studies showed that average first lactation 305 day milk yield of cows was 3,703.6±31.3 kg and average age at first calving was 1,036.6±10.2 days. Under Conservation and Genetic Improvement of Indigenous Cattle Breeds, the milk yield showed an increasing trend among the progenies of different sets, and average 305 day milk yield increased from 1,958 kg in first set to 2,604 kg in 10th set. Semen doses of Gir, Kankrej, Sahiwal were produced and utilized for insemination. Cloning of the only alive wild-buffalo of Chhattisgarh has opened up new avenues of cloning technology application in conservation of endangered species. Prolific sheep strain GMM × P (Garole-Malpura-Malpura -Patanwadi) revealed a multiple birth of 50 per cent.

Agricultural Education

For maintaining and upgrading quality and relevance of higher agricultural education, financial and monitoring support was provided for Niche Area of Excellence (28), Experiential Learning Units (21 new), besides refurbishing and maintenance of educational structures, student and faculty amenities, course curricula revision/improvement, strengthening of libraries with ICT and modernization of teaching with multimedia learning resources. HRD programmes/ activities facilitated promotion and execution of ICAR sponsored schemes that include centralized admissions in UG/PG to reduce inbreeding, infuse merit and promote national integration; award and distribution of fellowships to attract talent and promote merit, admission of foreign students for globalization of agriculture education, capacity building of faculty through summer-winter schools and Centre of Advanced Faculty training, National Professorial Chairs and National Fellow Scheme for promotion of excellence, Emeritus Scientist Scheme as a structural method of utilizing skill bank of the outstanding superannuated professionals.

Technology Assessment

The processes of technology assessment and refinement are as important as the technology generation prior to transfer at the field level. During the reported period, 2,652 technology interventions were assessed across 4,003 locations by laying out 27,008 trials on the farmers' fields. Women specific income generation technologies (205) related to technological empowerment of rural women were assessed at 394 locations covering 2,917 trials under the thematic areas. Technological interventions (39) in 43 locations were refined through 398 trials on livestock, poultry and fisheries under the thematic areas, viz., disease management, feed and fodder management, nutrition management and production and management. In all, 228.75 lakh quality planting materials of elite species of different crops were produced and provided to 18.38 lakh farmers. Bio-agents, bio-pesticides, bio-fertilizers, vermin-compost, mineral mixture, etc. were produced and supplied to the extent of 16,406 quintal benefiting 9.39 lakh farmers. Kisan Mobile Advisory (KMA), an initiative by the ICAR, sent 93,949 short text messages, 14,788 voice messages and 1,180 both SMS and voice messages to benefit 223.94 lakh farmers on various aspects of agriculture based on input provided by 557 KVKs.

National Agricultural Science Fund

The National Agricultural Science Fund (NASF), established to support basic and strategic research in agriculture, beside supporting, reviewing, monitoring and evaluation of the ongoing projects also initiated funding of new projects which were in the process of evaluation. During the year 2015-16, the NASF delivered five patents and 38 technologies. Some of the important projects are: Phenomics of moisture deficit and low temperature in rice-double herbicide tolerant transgenic rice for weed management; development of transgenic pigeonpea and chickpea; dominant nuclear male sterility system in rice for hybrid seed production; development of genetically engineered vaccines against poultry viral disease; adaptive mechanism and capture breeding in hilsa; green fishing systems for the tropical seas, defense genes of tiger shrimp against bacteria and white spot syndrome virus besides several others.

Animal Husbandry, Dairying and Fisheries

The Department of Animal Husbandry, Dairying and Fisheries is one of the departments under the Ministry of Agriculture. The department is responsible for matters relating to livestock production, preservation, protection and improvement of stocks, dairy development, matters relating to the Delhi Milk Scheme and the National Dairy Development Board. It also looks after all matters pertaining to fisheries, which includes inland and marine sectors and matters related to the National Fisheries Development Board.

Functions

The Department advises the state governments and union territories in the formulation of policies and programmes in the field of animal husbandry, dairy development and fisheries. The main focus of the activities is on : (a) development of requisite infrastructure in states/union territories for improving animal productivity; (b) promoting infrastructure for handling, processing and marketing of milk and milk products; (c) preservation and protection of livestock through provision of health care; (d) strengthening of central livestock farms (cattle, sheep and poultry) for development of superior germplasm for distribution to states; and (e) expansion of aquaculture in fresh and brackish water, development of marine fisheries infrastructure and post harvest operations and welfare of fisherfolk, etc.

Animal husbandry, dairying and fisheries activities play an important role in national economy and in socio-economic development of the country. These activities have contributed to the food basket, nutrition security, household income of the farmers and play a significant role in generating gainful employment in the rural areas, particularly among the landless, small and marginal farmers and women, besides providing cheap and nutritious food. Livestock are the best insurance for farmers against vagaries of nature like drought and other natural calamities.

Population of Livestock

Livestock census started in the country in the year 1919. So far 19 such censuses have been conducted. It is a complete count of the livestock and poultry at a pre-defined reference date. The livestock species namely cattle, buffaloes, sheep, goats, pigs, horses and ponies, mules, donkeys, camels, mithuns and yaks are covered in the census. The other species covered are dogs, rabbits and elephants. In the census, head count is done for each of these species and recorded in their respective households/household enterprises/non-household enterprises and other institutions. The species-wise population of livestock and poultry in previous two censuses are given in the table here:

Table 4.1: Livestock and Poultry Population

	Species	2007	2012
1	Cattle	199.08	190.90
2	Buffaloes	105.34	108.70
3	Yaks	0.08	0.08
4	Mithuns	0.26	0.30
	Total Bovine	**304.76**	**299.98**
5	Sheep	71.56	65.07
6	Goat	140.54	135.17
7	Horses and Ponies	0.61	0.63
8	Mules	0.14	0.20

9	Donkeys	0.44	0.32
10	Camels	0.52	0.40
11	Pigs	11.13	10.29
	Total Livestock	**529.70**	**512.06**
12	**Total Poultry**	**648.83**	**729.21**

Estimates of Major Livestock Products

The estimation of major livestock products such as milk, egg, meat and wool are based on the results of Integrated Sample Survey. The survey is done on 15 per cent sample of villages every year covering 5 per cent each in every season (summer, rainy and winter). The survey period in the entire year is March to February. The following table shows the estimates of milk, egg, meat and wool during 2007-08 to 2014-15.

Table 4.2: Estimated Production

Year (March-Feb)	Milk (in million tonnes)	Egg (in million nos.)	Meat (in million kg)	Wool (in million kg)
2007-08	107.9	53583	4.0	43.9
2008-09	112.2	55562	4.2	42.8
2009-10	116.4	60267	4.5	43.1
2010-11	121.9	63024	4.9	43.0
2011-12	127.9	66450	5.5	44.7
2012-13	132.4	69731	5.9	46.1
2013-14	137.7	74752	6.2	47.9
2014-15	146.3	78484	6.7	48.1

Based on the estimates, the per-capita availability of milk and egg are also calculated by using the projected human population as per data provided by Office of the Registrar General of India.

Dairy Development

Demand of milk in the country is expected to reach upto 150 million tonnes by the end of year 2016-17 and upto 210 million tonnes by 2021-22. The dairy sector has grown substantially over the years. As a result of prudent policy intervention, India ranks first among the world's milk producing nations, achieving an annual output of 145 million tonnes (Provisional) during the year 2014-15 as compared to 137.68 million tonnes during 2013-14 recording a growth of 5.32 per cent. The anticipated milk production in the country for the year

2015-16 is about 148 million tonnes. This represents a sustained growth in the availability of milk and milk products for growing population.

Dairying has become an important secondary source of income for millions of rural families and has assumed the most important role in providing employment and income generating opportunities particularly for women and marginal farmers. The per capita availability of milk was at a level of 302 grams per day during the year 2013-14, which was more than the world average of 294 grams per day. Most of the milk in the country is produced by small, marginal farmers and landless labours. About 15.46 million farmers have been brought under the ambit of 1,62,186 village level dairy corporative societies upto March 2014. The cooperative milk unions procured an average of 39.2 million kg of milk per day during the year 2014-15 as compared to 34.2 million kg in the previous year recording a growth of 12.5 per cent. The sale of liquid milk by cooperative sector has reached 29.9 million litres per day during the year 2014-15 as compared to 28 million tonnes registering a growth of 6.8 per cent over the previous year.

The efforts of the Department in the dairy sector are concentrated on promotion of dairy activities including non-operation flood areas with emphasis on building up cooperative infrastructure, revitalization of sick dairy cooperative milk unions and creation of infrastructure in the states for production of quality milk and milk products. The National Dairy Development Board (NDDB) continues its activities for overall development of the sector in Operation Flood areas.

National Programme for Bovine Breeding and Dairy Development

A new restructured scheme namely, National Programme for Bovine Breeding and Dairy Development (NPBBDD), was launched in 2014 by merging three Dairy Development schemes of Intensive Dairy Development Programme (IDDP), Strengthening Infrastructure for Quality and Clean Milk Production (SIQ and CMP) and Assistance to Cooperative (A to C) and National Programme for Cattle and Buffalo Breeding. The Scheme has two components: (a) National Programme for Bovine Breeding (NPBB); (b) National Programme for Dairy Development (NPDD). The NPBB will focus on extension of field AI Net work through MAITRI (Multi Purpose AI Technician in Rural India) and to encourage conservation and development of recognized indigenous breeds of the country. The NPDD will focus on creating infrastructure related to production, procurement, processing and marketing of milk and milk products by the State Implementing Agency (SIA), State Milk Marketing Federations/ District Cooperative Milk Producers' Union and manpower development activities including training of milk producers associated to dairy cooperative societies.

The budgetary provision of ₹ 1,800 crore has been provided for implementation of NPBBDD during 12th Plan and an amount of ₹ 150 crore has been allocated for the year 2015-16 under it. Out of it an amount of ₹ 74 crore was allocated for financial year 2015-16 under the component of NPDD.

Under NPDD component, 15 new projects in four states have been approved with total outlay of ₹ 142.84 crore till March 2015. A total sum of ₹ 89.97 crore including ₹ 41.52 crore for new projects were released for implementation of projects approved under the scheme during the year 2014-15.

National Dairy Plan Phase-I

National Dairy Plan was launched in March 2013 with the objective of increasing productivity of milch animals and providing rural producers greater access to organized milk processing sector and is being implemented by National Dairy Development Board (NDDB) focusing on 14 major milk producing states and Chhattisgarh. NDP-I has a total outlay of ₹ 2,242 crore comprising external aid of ₹ 1,584 crore and GoI share of ₹ 176 crore.

Dairy Entrepreneurship Development

Dairy Entrepreneurship Development Scheme (DEDS) was launched in September, 2010 with the objective for promotion of private investment in dairy sector to increase the milk production and helping in poverty reduction through self employment opportunities. This scheme is being implemented through NABARD which provides financial assistance to commercially bankable projects with loans from commercial, cooperative, urban and rural banks with a back ended capital subsidy of 25 per cent of the project cost to the beneficiaries of general category and 33.33 per cent of the project cost to SC and ST beneficiaries. The scheme is being continued with certain modifications and a budget provision of ₹ 1,400 crore during 12th Plan.

Since its inception, an amount of ₹ 842.92 crore has been disbursed by NABARD as back ended capital subsidy to the beneficiaries.

National Livestock Mission

Since 2014-15 and 2015-16, National Livestock Mission (NLM) is being implemented with the objectives of sustainable development of livestock sector, focusing on improving availability of quality feed and fodder, risk coverage, effective extension, skill development, improved flow of credit and organization of livestock farmers/rearers, etc. The other objectives are development of small ruminants, piggery and poultry, there are programmes for strengthening the state farms in terms of modernization, automation and biosecurity to enable production of improved breed of goats, sheep, pigs and stocks of low-input technology chicken. Further, the productivity enhancement component provides for supporting BPL families to encourage rearing of backyard poultry and community-led breed improvement programmes. Similarly, under the Entrepreneurship Development and Employment Generation component there is provision for a number of small ruminants, piggery and poultry farming and allied activities wherein back-ended capital subsidy is provided to the farmers.

Sub-Mission on Livestock Development

Sheep and Goat Development

According to Livestock census 2012, there are about 65.07 million sheep and 135.2 million goats in the country. About five million households in the country are engaged in the rearing of small ruminants (sheep and goats) and other allied activities.

Central Sheep Breeding Farm

Central sheep Breeding Farm, Hisar is mandated to produce acclimatized exotic/ cross bred superior quality rams. The farm supplies rams and bucks to different state agencies and farmers and trains farmers in machine - shearing techniques.

Conservation of Threatened Breeds

The population of purebred animals of some breed of small ruminants, equines, pigs and pack animal has come down considerably; in some cases, even below 10,000 which has brought such breeds to the category of 'threatened breeds' in the country. A Centrally Sponsored Scheme for conservation of such threatened breeds was started during 10th Five Year Plan with a budget outlay of ₹ 15.00 crore. Farms/ farmer's unit in their respective breeding tract are established under the scheme with 100 per cent central assistance. The conservation projects are being implemented by state governments, universities and NGOs. During the 10th Plan period conservation projects for 27 breeds were taken up.

Integrated Development of Small Ruminants and Rabbits

This Central Sector Scheme was approved in 2009 for implementation during 12th Plan with an allocation of ₹ 134.825 crores. Allocation under the scheme during 2012-13 was ₹ 15.00 crore. The scheme envisages setting up of intensive small ruminant development clusters with venture capital through NABARD as well as infrastructure development and institutional restructuring through state implementing agency. During 2014-15, the scheme Integrated Development of Small Ruminants was subsumed under National Livestock Mission (Component [III])—Integrated Development of Small Ruminants and Rabbits under the Sub-Mission on Livestock Development).

Meat and Pig Development

The pig farming constitutes the livelihood of rural poor belonging to the lowest socio-economic strata and they have no means to undertake scientific pig farming with improved foundation stock, proper housing, feeding and management. Therefore, suitable schemes to popularise the scientific pig breeding-cum-rearing of meat producing animals with adequate financial provisions are necessary to modernise the Indian pig industry and to improve the productivity of small sized rural pig farms. The component –

Entrepreneurship Development and Employment Generation of the scheme-National Livestock Mission (NLM) encourages commercial rearing of pigs by adopting scientific methods and creation of infrastructure. The Mission also supports state pig breeding farms for strengthening of existing breeding infrastructure.

Risk Management

The Risk Management as a component of sub-mission on livestock development of NLM is to be implemented in all the districts of the country including those carved out in future, if any. This component aims towards management of risk and uncertainties by providing protection mechanism to the farmers against any eventual loss of their animals due to death; and to demonstrate the benefit of insurance of livestock to the people. The indigenous/crossbred milch animals, pack animals (horses, donkey, mules, camels, ponies and cattle/buffalo male), and other livestock (goat, sheep, pigs, rabbit, yak, mithun, etc.) will be under the purview of this component. Benefit of subsidy is to be restricted to 5 animals per beneficiary per household for all animals except for sheep, goat, pig and rabbit, where the benefit will be restricted to 5 cattle units (1 cattle unit = 10 sheep/goats/pigs/rabbits). Therefore the benefit of subsidy to sheep, goat, pig and rabbit is to be restricted to 5 'Cattle Unit' per beneficiary per house hold.

However, if a beneficiary has less than 5 animals/1 cattle unit can also avail the benefit of subsidy.

Table 4.3 : Funding Pattern under the Sub-Mission on Livestock Development Component of Risk Management

Component of Risk Management

S.No.	Component	Pattern of Assistance
1	Risk Management (CSS) [Premium rates for one year policy in normal areas-3.0 per cent, in NER/ hill areas/ LWE affected areas-3.5 per cent, and in difficult areas–4.0 per cent Premium rates for three year policy in normal areas- 7.5 per cent, in NER/ hill areas- 9.0 per cent, and in difficult areas- 10.5 per cent	Central share 25 per cent, state share 25 per cent and beneficiary share 50 per cent for APL, and Central share 40 per cent, state share 30 per cent and beneficiary share 30 per cent for BPL/ SC/ ST in normal areas Central share 35 per cent, state share 25 per cent and beneficiary share 40 per cent for APL, and Central share 50 per cent, state share 30 per cent and beneficiary share 20 per cent for BPL/ SC/ ST in NER/hill areas/ LWE affected areas Central share 45 per cent, state share 25 per cent and beneficiary share 30 per cent for APL, and Central share 60 per cent, state share 30 per cent and beneficiary share 10 per cent for BPL/ SC/ ST in difficult areas

The risk management and insurance component envisages the following payments from Central funds as grants - in -aid : (a) subsidy as per the following tables; (b) 100 per cent payments of honorarium to the veterinary practitioners; and (c) 100 per cent publicity. However a beneficiary may insure more than 5 animals by paying the full premium without availing the benefit of subsidy for all animals except sheep, goat, pig and rabbit. Similarly, a beneficiary may insure more than five 'Cattle Unit' by paying the full premium without availing the benefit of subsidy for sheep, goat, pig and rabbit.

Implementing Agencies

Department of Animal Husbandry Dairy and Fishers (DADF) is implementing the centrally sponsored 'Risk Management and Insurance' as component of sub-mission on livestock development of NLM is implemented through the SIAs such as state livestock development board/agency which are also implementing national project for cattle and buffalo and breeding. In states/union territories where there are no SIAs, this scheme will be implemented through the state/union territory Animal Husbandry Departments.

Poultry Development

Poultry is one of the fastest growing subsectors of animal husbandry with annual growth rates of eggs of around 6 per cent per annum.

The achievements and growth rates are being sustained despite the ingress of avian influenza which was a severe setback for the industry, showing the resilience of poultry sector, perseverance of the private sector and timely interventions by the government. A general guideline for biosecurity on poultry farms has been compiled and circulated to all states for taking preventive measures against ingress of diseases.

Modernization and Development of Breeding Infrastructure

Central Poultry Development Organizations

The Central Poultry Development Organizations (CPDOs) located at four regions viz., Chandigarh, Bhubaneswar, Mumbai and Hessarghatta have been playing a pivotal role in the implementation of the policies of the Government with respect to poultry. The mandate of these organizations has specially been reoriented to focus on improved birds, which lay on an average 180-200 eggs per annum and have vastly improved feed conversion ratio in terms of feed consumption and weight gain. In these CPDOs, training is also imparted to the farmers to upgrade their technical skills. CPDO and Training Institute, Hessarghatta is also imparting trainers' training to in-service personnel from within the country as well as overseas. Analytical livestock and poultry feed testing is also conducted at the CPDOs. The CPDOs are also promoting diversification with species other than poultry, like ducks, Japanese quail, etc. The Central Poultry Performance Testing Center (CPPTC), located at Gurgaon is entrusted with responsibility of testing the performance of layer and broiler varieties. This centre gives valuable information relating to different genetic stock available in the country.

Strengthening of Breeding Infrastructure

It aims at strengthening existing state poultry farms so as to enable the flow of suitable germplasm from the research institutions/laboratories to the grassroots level along with other technical services through capacity building of state poultry farms; and developing and implementing package of practices at the ground level for different types of poultry system including family poultry system for supplementary income generation and family nutrition. The assistance provided is 75 per cent Central share to all states/union territories. One time operational/revolving fund is provided to these farms for smooth operations maintenance to ensure long term sustainability.

Interventions towards Productivity Enhancement

Rural Backyard Poultry Development

This component is envisaged to cover beneficiaries from Backyard Poultry Development (BPD) families to enable them to gain supplementary income and nutritional support. Under this programme so far funding has been done to cover around 1.45 lakh BPL beneficiaries.

There has been persistent demand from the north-eastern states seeking support for all round development of pigs in the region. Therefore, pig development in the region is being implemented as a sub-mission of NLM. The sub-mission strives to forge synergies of research and development organizations through appropriate interventions, as required for holistic development of pigs in the north-eastern region including genetic improvement and health cover.

Under the scheme cultivation of fodder and preservation of fodder by using post harvest technologies is supported. Further, to improve the seed replacement scenario, this department has taken up production of foundation seeds from breeder seed at its eight regional fodder stations for last two years. For production of certified seeds from the foundation seeds, this department has introduced the component of 'Fodder Seed Procurement and Distribution'. Under the programme, after producing the foundation seeds at all our regional stations, the same is being offered to the states for further multiplication by the state governments preferably through milk federations, dairy co-operatives and progressive farmers, etc., under buy back arrangement for production of certified seeds. For this assistance is provided to the states under the component fodder seed production/ procurement and distribution.

Sub-Mission on Skill Development, Technology Transfer and Extension

The component will provide extension, education, production of livestock, extension literature. The IEC programme for the state would be finalized by factoring in the specific characteristics of each district and block. In knowledge-driven development, there is need for providing extension education keeping in view the diverse needs of the livestock owners not only on production procedures, but also the knowledge about the whole range of livestock—business, production systems, research institutions, programmes and schemes of the development departments, quality certification and reporting procedures, grading, packaging, storage, transportation and other requirements of both domestic and export markets, including interfaces at different levels with unlimited partners. The development of Information Communication Technology (ICT) and telecommunication network have paved the way for creation of information network, knowledge pool and services which can be intensively used for the purpose.

Fisheries

India is the second largest producer of fish in the world contributing 5.68 per cent of global fish production. It is also a major producer of fish through aquaculture and ranks second in the world after China. Fishery is one of the most promising sectors of agriculture and allied activities in India, with an overall growth rate of 6 per cent projected during the 12th Five year Plan.

India is blessed with vast aquatic resources with a rich diversity of fish fauna for sustainable utilization. Our country is recognized to harbour about 2,200 species of fish, which accounted for about 11 per cent of all fish species reported globally. About 24.7 per cent of our fish species live in warm fresh water; 3.3 per cent in cold water; 6.5 per cent in estuaries and the rest 65.5 per cent in the sea.

Inland Fisheries and Aquaculture

Aquaculture is the fastest growing food producing sector in the world with an annual growth of around 7 per cent. India is the second largest producer of fish both in total, and from aquaculture. Increasing demand for fish and fishery products would mostly be sourced from aquaculture and culture based capture fisheries in reservoirs as capture fisheries growth world over is stagnant.

Marine Fisheries

Harvesting of marine fisheries resources in the country warrants stronger emphasis on invoking technological innovations as well as management paradigms that reconcile livelihood issues with concerns on resource conservation. Global production of fish from marine capture fisheries in the last decade has stagnated gradually and many stocks have been either over-exploited or have reached their maximum sustainable yields.

On-going Schemes

i. Development of Inland Fisheries and Aquaculture; ii. Development of Marine Fisheries, Infrastructure and Post Harvest Operations; iii. National Scheme of Welfare of Fishermen; iv. Strengthening of Database and Geographical Information System for the Fisheries Sector; v. Assistance to Fisheries Institutes;

vi. National Fisheries Development Board; and vii. Issuance of Biometric Identity Cards to Coastal Fishermen.

Blue Revolution

All the existing schemes of fisheries sector have been brought under the umbrella of 'Blue Revolution' for growth of fisheries and aquaculture in the country. Blue Revolution refers to an integrated and holistic approach towards the development and management of the fisheries and aquaculture sector in the country for increased production and productivity.

Livestock Health

Livestock sector plays an important role in national economy and socio-economic development of the country. Livestock sector has immense potential for growth. The biggest impediment to growth of this sector, however, is the large-scale prevalence of animal diseases like foot and mouth disease (FMD), Peste des Petits Ruminants, brucellosis, avian influenza, etc., which adversely affect the animal productivity. The disease in livestock results in both morbidity and mortality with consequent production losses. Therefore, to effectively tackle the issue of livestock health, to reduce the losses and thereby enabling livestock owners to derive optimum gains from their animals, Government of India supplements the efforts of State Governments for prevention and control of animal diseases by providing assistance under various components of a Centrally Sponsored Scheme 'Livestock Health and Disease Control (LH andDC)', now renamed as 'Veterinary Services and Animal Health'.

An online system of animal disease reporting in a time bound manner is being implemented for reporting of animal diseases for immediate action to control the disease. Under this each taluka/district and state headquarter is linked with a Central Disease Monitoring Unit in DADF at New Delhi.

Implementations of the Livestock Health and Disease Control scheme have resulted in major achievement for the country.

India was declared Contagious Bovine Pleuro-Pneumonia (CBPP) infection free country by the OIE in May, 2007. The freedom status is being maintained each year thereafter. India has been classified in May, 2010 by the World Animal Health Organization (OIE) as a country having negligible risk for Bovine Spongiform Encephalopathy (BSE). The negligible status for BSE is being maintained each year thereafter. Foot and Mouth Disease Control Programme (FMD-CP) is being implemented in 351 districts as of now. It has been decided that FMD-CP will be extended to whole of India during 12th Plan subject to availability of funds and vaccine. Peste des Petits Ruminants Control Programme (PPR-CP) which was in implementation in the southern states has also been expanded to whole of the country in February, 2014. With the implementation of the planned control programme in all the states, it is expected that the disease will be controlled and ultimately eradicated from the country.

Prevention of ingress of exotic diseases through import of various livestock and livestock products by strengthening quarantine set up in the country is also being ensured. In order to strengthen the veterinary infrastructure for delivering quality veterinary health services by the states/UTs, a programme was launched in August 2010 for establishment new veterinary hospitals and dispensaries and strengthening of the existing ones. The programme has been well accepted by the states and so far 3,419 veterinary hospitals and 4,169 veterinary dispensaries have been supported for construction/renovation under the programme.

To strengthen laboratory infrastructure, the department has established four pre-fabricated Bio-Safety Level-III (BSL-III) laboratories (one each at Kolkata, Jalandhar, Bareilly and Bengaluru). One Mobile BSL-III laboratory is available at NERDDL, Guwahati, Assam. About 23 State Disease Diagnostic Laboratories are being upgraded to BSL-II level, out of which, 18 are functional and remaining are at various stages of completion.

5 Culture and Tourism

THE MANDATE of the Ministry of Culture revolves around the functions like preservation and conservation of ancient cultural heritage and promotion of art and culture both tangible and intangible in the country. Headed by Secretary the administrative set up consists of various bureaux and divisions of the Ministry. The Ministry has two attached, six subordinate offices and thirty five autonomous organisations, which are fully funded by the Government. There are seven Zonal Cultural Centres working mainly on folk and traditional arts of different zones. There are also four missions namely National Mission for Manuscripts, National Mission for Monument and Antiquities, National Mission on Libraries, and Gandhi Heritage Sites Mission.

Broadly, this Ministry is working on the protection, development and promotion of all types of heritage of culture namely, tangible heritage, intangible heritage and knowledge heritage. In addition, the Ministry also harbours the responsibility of Gandhian heritage and commemoration of important historical events and centenaries of great personalities. In tangible heritage, the Ministry takes care of all the centrally protected monuments of national importance, which is achieved through Archeological Survey of India. Similarly, the Ministry is also promoting a museum movement in the country and majority of the museums are under its administrative control. The Ministry also promotes regional museums through grants-in-aid.

In the field of intangible heritage, the Ministry extends financial support to individuals, group of individuals and cultural organizations engaged in performing visual and literary arts. Similarly, the Ministry through its organizations, is engaged in recognizing excellence in the field of art and culture by way of awards given by institutions like Sahitya Akademi and Sangeet Natak Akademi. The National School of Drama is involved in promoting a vibrant theatre movement of contemporary relevance in the context of our traditions and cultural diversity.

In knowledge heritage, the Ministry is the custodian of all the major libraries in the country. It also extends grant-in-aid for library development and is also responsible for all policy matters regarding library development. Through National Archives of India, Ministry is responsible for maintenance of all archival records of the country.

The Ministry is also involved in protection and promotion of Buddhist and Tibetian Culture and is doing this through various institutions located at Sarnath, Varanasi and Leh. This Ministry has a very well-planned capacity-building programme for all those who want to excel in the field of Indian as well as Asian art and culture. Institutions like the School of Archaeology, School of Archives, National Institute of History and Art, Maulana Abul Kalam Azad Institute of Asian Studies are mentionable in this regard. Various courses offered by National School of Drama and Kalakshetra Foundation are also some of the examples of capacity building programmes of the Ministry. Ministry of Culture is also responsible for the implementation of various UNESCO conventions in the field of culture and at present there are 130 agreements/ MoUs. Presently, there are 59 valid/ live CEPs in place out of which 18 CEPs have been signed during the financial year 2015-16 with Mongolia, Algeria, Bangladesh, Uzbekistan, Kyrgyzstan, Tajikistan, Russia, Bulgaria, Indonesia, Malaysia, Singapore, Philippines, Jordan, Israel, France, Austria, United Arab Emirate and Lithuania.

Intangible Cultural Heritage

Lalit Kala Akademi

To promote and propagate understanding of Indian art, both within and outside the country, the Government of India established the Lalit Kala Akademi (National Akademi of Arts) at New Delhi on August 5, 1954. The Akademi has regional centres called Rashtriya Lalit Kala Kendras at Lucknow, Kolkata, Chennai, Garhi in New Delhi, Shimla and Bhubaneshwar with workshop facilities in painting, sculpture, print-making and ceramics.

The Akademi has been organizing national exhibition of contemporary Indian art with 15 National Awards, each of ₹ 50,000. Once in every three years, the Akademi also organizes Triennial India, an international exhibition of contemporary art in New Delhi. Since 1955, the Akademi has organized 52 national exhibitions of art and has presented the National Award to 545 artists.

The Akademi honours eminent artists and art historians every year by electing them as Fellows of the Akademi. To propagate Indian art outside, the Akademi regularly participates in International Biennials and Triennials abroad and also organizes exhibitions of works of art from other countries. In order to foster contacts with artists from outside, it sponsors exchange of artists with other countries under the various Cultural Exchange Programmes and Agreements of the Government.

The Lalit Kala Akademi accords recognition to art institutions/ associations and extends financial assistance to these bodies as well as state academies. It also gives scholarships to deserving young artists belonging to its regional centres. The Akademi brings out monographs on the works of Indian contemporary artists in Hindi and English and books on contemporary, traditional, folk and tribal arts authored by eminent writers and art critics, bi-annual art journals, *Lalit Kala Contemporary* (English), *Lalit Kala Ancient* (English) and *Samkaleen Kala* (Hindi). Apart from these, it brings out large size multi-colour reproductions of contemporary paintings and graphics from time to time. The Akademi has started a regular programme on research and documentation. Scholars are given financial assistance to undertake projects on various contemporary aspects of Indian society and culture.

O. W.: http://www.lalitkala.gov.in

Sangeet Natak Akademi

Sangeet Natak Akademi, India's national academy of music, dance and drama, is a pioneer in creation of modern India . The ephemeral quality of the arts, and the need for their preservation led to the adapting of a democratic system in which the common man had the opportunity to learn, practise and propagate the art.

In 1945, the Asiatic Society of Bengal submitted a proposal for the creation of a National Cultural Trust consisting of three academies—an academy of dance, drama and music; an academy of letters and an academy of art and architecture. It led to the creation of three national academies after Independence. The National Academy named Sangeet Natak Akademi, was the first of these entities to be established by a resolution of the Ministry of Education, headed by Maulana Abul Kalam Azad, signed on May 31, 1952 and inaugurated by the then President of India, Dr Rajendra Prasad. In 1961, the Sangeet Natak Akademi was reconstituted by the Government as a society and registered under the Societies Registration Act, 1860 (as amended in 1957).

The Akademi has worked towards building up a unified structure of support for the practice of music, dance and drama in India encompassing traditional and modern forms, and urban as well as rural environments. The festivals of music, dance and drama presented or promoted by the Akademi are held all over India. The great masters of the performing arts have been elected as Fellows of the Akademi. The Sangeet Natak Akademi Awards conferred annually on eminent artists and scholars are considered the most coveted honours in the field of performing arts. Thousands of institutions across the country, including many in the remote areas, engaged in teaching or promotion of music, dance and theatre have received financial assistance for their work from the Akademi, as do researchers, authors and publishers in relevant disciplines.

It has a large archive of audio and video tapes, 16-mm films, photographs and transparencies and remains the single most important resource for researchers in the field of performing arts of India.

The Akademi's Gallery of Musical Instruments has more than 600 instruments of prominence and has been the source of published documentation over the years.

The Akademi establishes and looks after institutions and projects of national importance in the field of performing arts. The Jawaharlal Nehru Manipuri Dance Academy in Imphal, the premier institution in Manipuri dance and music established in 1954, is the first of these institutions. In 1959, the Akademi established the National School of Drama and in 1964, the Kathak Kendra, both being based in Delhi. The Akademi's other projects of national importance are in *Kutiyattam* theatre of Kerala, commenced in 1991 and recognized by UNESCO as a masterpiece of oral and intangible heritage of humanity in 2001. The project on *Chhau* dance of Odisha, Jharkhand and West Bengal began in 1994. The project support to *Sattriya* music, dance, theatre and allied arts of Assam was started in 2002.

Being the apex body, the Akademi also advises and assists the Government of India in formulating and implementing policies and projects in the field. It fosters cultural contacts nationally and internationally. The Akademi has held exhibitions and major festivals in foreign countries.

O. W.: http://www.sangeetnatak.gov.in

Performing Arts

Music

Two main schools of classical music—*Hindustani* and *Carnatic* continue to survive through oral tradition being passed on by teachers to disciples. This has led to the existence of family traditions called *gharanas* and *sampradayas*.

Dance

Dance in India has an unbroken tradition of over 2,000 years. Its themes are derived from mythology, legends and classical literature, two main divisions being classical and folk. Classical dance forms are based on ancient dance discipline and have rigid rules of presentation. Important among them are *Bharata Natyam, Kathakali, Kathak, Manipuri, Kuchipudi* and *Odissi. Bharata Natyam,* though it derives its roots from Tamil Nadu, has developed into an all India form. *Kathakali* is a dance form of Kerala. *Kathak* is a classical dance form revitalized as a result of Mughal influence on Indian culture. Manipur has contributed to a delicate, lyrical style of dance called *Manipuri,* while *Kuchipudi* is a dance form owing its origin to Andhra Pradesh. *Odissi* from Odisha, once practiced as a temple dance, is today widely exhibited by artistes across the country. Each region limits ethnic folk/tribal dances.

Both classical and folk dances owe their present popularity to institutions like Sangeet Natak Akademi and other training institutes and cultural organizations. The Akademi gives financial assistance to cultural institutions and awards fellowships to scholars, performers and teachers to promote advanced study and training in rare forms of dance and music.

Theatre

Theatre in India is as old as its music and dance. Classical theatre survives only in some places. Folk theatre can be seen in its regional variants practically in every region. There are also professional theatres, mainly city-oriented. Besides, India has a rich tradition of puppet theatre, prevalent forms being puppets, rod puppets, glove puppets and leather puppets (shadow theatre). There are several semi-professional and amateur theatre groups involved in staging plays in both English and Indian languages.

National School of Drama

The National School of Drama (NSD)—one of the foremost theatre institutions in the world and the only one of its kind in India was set up by Sangeet Natak Akademi in 1959. Later in 1975, it became an autonomous organization, totally financed by Department of Culture. The objective of the NSD is to train students in all aspects of theatre, including theatre history, production, scene design, costume design, lighting, make-up, etc. The training course at NSD is of three years duration. The eligible applicants for admission to the course are screened through two stages. The Diploma of NSD is recognized by the Association of Indian Universities as equivalent to M.A. Degree for appointment as teachers in colleges/universities and for purposes of registration for Ph.D.

The School has a performing wing, a *Repertory Company* to establish professional theatre and regular experimental work. The NSD has promoted children's theatre. The *Theatre-in-Education Company* (renamed as Sanskar Rang Toli) was founded in 1989 and has been actively involved in production of plays for children, organizing summer theatre workshops in the schools of Delhi and also promoting children's theatre through Saturday Club. Since 1998, the School has organized National Theatre Festival for Children christened 'Jashne Bachpan' every year. The first ever National Theatre Festival christened *Bharat Rang Mahotsav* was held from March 18 to April 14, 1999 to commemorate the 50th year of India's Independence. *Bharat Rang Mahotsav* has been made an annual feature.

A short-term teaching and training programme titled 'Extension Programme' was started in 1978, under which, the school organizes workshops in collaboration with the local theatre groups/artists and these programmes are invariably held in the local languages. The workshops could be broadly divided under three categories, Production Oriented Workshops, Production Oriented Children's Workshops and Teaching and Training Programmes in Theatre. The School has a Regional Research Centre at Bengaluru to cater to the theatrical needs of the four southern states and Puducherry.

The School also publishes textbooks on theatre and also arranges for translation of important books on theatre from English into Hindi.

O. W.: http://www.nsd.gov.in

Sahitya Akademi

Sahitya Akademi is the Indian National Academy of Letters, to promote Indian literature through publications, translations, seminars, workshops, cultural exchange programmes and literary meets organized all over the country. The Akademi was founded in March 1954 as an autonomous body fully funded by the Department of Culture. It was registered as a Society in 1956 under the Societies Registration Act, 1860. The Akademi has recognized 24 languages. It has an Advisory Board for each of the languages that suggests various programmes and publications in the concerned languages. Besides its head office in New Delhi, it has four offices in Kolkata, Mumbai, Bengaluru and Chennai. The Akademi has two Translation Centres at Bengaluru and Kolkata, besides a Project Office at Shillong for promotion of oral and tribal literature and an Archive of Indian literature in Delhi. It maintains a unique multilingual library in New Delhi and at its regional offices at Bengaluru and Kolkata, having about 1.5 lakh books in over 25 languages.

The three fellowships by Sahitya Akademi are:-

1. Sahitya Akademi Honorary Fellowship
2. Anand Fellowship
3. Premchand Fellowship

The Akademi confers its fellowship, its highest honour to literary figures. Sahitya Akademi also instituted a fellowship named after Premchand during his 125th Birth Anniversary in 2005 for scholars doing research on Indian literature or to creative writers from the countries of the SAARC region other than India. Every year since its inception in 1954, the Sahitya Akademi awards prizes to the most outstanding books of literary merit published in any of the major Indian languages recognized by the Akademi. The award amount, which was ₹ 5,000 at the time of inception, had been enhanced to ₹ 10,000 from 1983, ₹ 25,000 from 1988, ₹ 40, 000 from 2001 and is now ₹ 50,000 since 2003. The first awards were given in 1955.

The Akademi publishes books in 24 languages including translations of award-winning works, monographs on the great pioneers of Indian literature, histories of literature, Indian and foreign classics in translation, anthologies of fiction, poetry and prose, biographies, register of translators, Who's Who of Indian Writers, National Bibliography of Indian Literature and Encyclopedia of Indian Literature. So far, the Akademi has published over 6,000 books in these different categories. It has three journals, *Indian Literature* (bi-monthly in English), *Samkaleena Bharatiya Sahitya* (bi-monthly in Hindi) and *Samskrita Pratibha* (half-yearly in Sanskrit). Every year the Akademi publishes 250-300 books on an average. It has certain special projects like the *Ancient Indian Literature, Medieval Indian Literature* and *Modern Indian Literature* together constituting ten volumes of the best of Indian writing over five millennia. It has also launched a new project *Encyclopedia of Indian Poetics*.

O. W.: http://www.sahitya-akademi.gov.in

Indira Gandhi National Centre for Arts

The Indira Gandhi National Centre for Arts (IGNCA) is an autonomous centre under the Ministry of Culture, Government of India.

The IGNCA's view of the arts encompasses wide areas such as creative and critical literature, written and oral; the visual arts, architecture, sculpture, painting, graphics, photography and film. The Centre aims at exploring, studying and reviving the dialogue between India and her neighbours, in areas pertaining to the arts, and between communities in India and the world.

The IGNCA organizes national seminars, conferences, exhibitions and lecture series. It focuses on schools and educational institutions and complements its research by cross disciplinary landscape studies. During these 25 years, the IGNCA has collaborated with like-minded institutions around the globe, organizing several international seminars and exhibitions, with renowned scholars from world.

The official website www.ignca.nic.in gives complete up-to-date information on the activities of the centre.

O. W.: http://www.ignca.nic.in

Centre for Cultural Resources and Training

The Centre for Cultural Resources and Training (CCRT) is one of the premier institutions working in the field of linking education with culture. The Centre was set up in May, 1979 as an autonomous organization by the Government of India. With headquarters in New Delhi, it has three regional centres at Udaipur, Hyderabad and Guwahati.

The broad objectives of CCRT have been to revitalize the education system by creating an understanding and awareness among students about the plurality of the regional cultures of India and integrating this knowledge with education. The main thrust is on linking education with culture and making students aware of the importance of culture in all development programmes. It conducts a variety of training programmes for in-service teachers drawn from all parts of the country. The training provides an understanding and appreciation of the philosophy, aesthetics and beauty inherent in Indian art and culture and focuses on formulating methodologies for incorporating a cultural component in curriculum teaching. This training also stresses the role of culture in science and technology, housing, agriculture, sports, etc. It creates awareness amongst students and teachers of their role in solving environmental pollution problems and conservation and preservation of the natural and cultural heritage.

It conducts programmes on special request, by organizing workshops on drama, music, narrative art forms, etc., Teachers are encouraged to develop programmes in which the art form can be profitably utilized to teach educational curriculum. The CCRT organizes educational tours to monuments, museums, art galleries, craft centres, zoological parks and gardens, camps on conservation of natural and cultural heritage, camps on learning crafts using low cost locally available resources, lectures and demonstrations by artists and experts on various art forms, demonstrations by artists and craft persons in schools. They emphasize on intellectual and aesthetic development of the students.

Over the years, CCRT has been collecting scripts, colour slides, photographs, audio and video recordings and films. Each year it aims to revive and encourage the art and craft forms of rural India. The Centre also prepares publications, to provide an understanding and appreciation of aspects of Indian art and culture. The Centre implements the Cultural Talent Search Scholarship Scheme, which provides scholarships to outstanding children in the age group of 10 to 14 years, studying either in recognized schools or belonging to families practicing traditional performing or other arts to develop their talent in various cultural fields particularly in rare art forms. The scholarships continues till the age of 20 years or the first year of a University degree.

The Centre has instituted CCRT Teachers Award which is given every year to selected teachers for their outstanding work in education and culture. The award carries with it a citation, a plaque, an *angavastram* and a cash prize of ₹ 10,000.

O. W.: http://www.ccrtindia.gov.in

Zonal Cultural Centres

Zonal Cultural Centres (ZCCs) aim to arouse awareness of the local cultures and to show how these merge into zonal identities and eventually into the rich diversity of India's composite culture. These centres have already established themselves as a premier agency in the field of promotion, preservation and dissemination of culture in the entire country. They promote performing arts by significant contribution in literary and visual arts. The seven zonal cultural centres were established under this scheme during 1985-86 at Patiala, Kolkata, Thanjavur, Udaipur, Allahabad, Dimapur and Nagpur. The participation of states in more than one zonal cultural centre according to their cultural linkage is a special feature of the composition of the zonal centres. The Government of India and the participating State Governments enable the ZCCs to finance their activities from the interest earned on the investment on Corpus Fund. The Government of India has provided a grant of ₹ 5 crore to each ZCC and each constituent state has provided ₹ one crore. From 1993 all the Zonal Cultural Centres have been sending their folk artistes for participation in the Republic Day Folk Dance Festival. This festival is inaugurated by the Hon'ble President of India every year on 24th/25th January at the Talkatora Indoor Stadium in New Delhi. The festival provides a unique opportunity for folk artistes to perform at the national level.

Master craftsmen and artisans from various ZCCs participate in Crafts Fair. Documentation of various rare folk and tribal art forms is one of the main thrust areas of the ZCCs. Under the National Cultural Exchange Programme (NCEP), exchanges of artists, musicologists, performers and scholars between different regions within the country take place. It has been extremely useful in promoting awareness of different tribal/folk art forms in different parts of the country. A scheme of Theatre Rejuvenation provides an opportunity to students, actors, artists, directors and writers to perform on a common platform. Guru Shishya Parampara has been introduced to promote new talents. The ZCCs promote craftsmen through Shilpgrams. The ZCCs identify the different performing/folk art forms in their area and select one or two talented artists in each of the fields.

Tangible Cultural Heritage

Archaeological Survey of India

The Archaeological Survey of India (ASI) was established in 1861. It functions as an attached office of the Department of Culture. The organization is headed by the Director General.

The major activities of the Archaeological Survey of India are :

i) Survey of archaeological remains and excavations;

ii) Maintenance and conservation of centrally protected monuments, sites and remains;

iii) Chemical preservation of monuments and antiquarian remains;

iv) Architectural survey of monuments;

v) Development of epigraphical research and numismatic studies;

vi) Setting up and re-organization of site museums;

vii) Expeditions abroad;

viii) Training in archaeology;

ix) Publication of technical reports and research works.

There are 24 Circles and five Regional Directorates through which the Archaeological Survey of India administers the work of preservation and conservation of monuments under its protection.

Under the Ancient Monuments and Archaeological Sites and Remains Act, 1958, the ASI has declared 3,675 monuments/sites to be of national importance in the country which includes twenty one properties that are inscribed on the World Heritage List by UNESCO.

Three sites, namely, Champaner-Pavagarh Archaeological Park in Gujarat, Chhatrapati Shivaji Terminus (formerly Victoria Terminus) Station in Mumbai and the Brihadisvara temple complex, Gangaikondacholapuram and the Airavatesvara temple complex, Darasuram as an extension to the Brihadisvara temple complex. Thanjavur (now commonly called as the Great Living Chola Temples) have been inscribed on the World Heritage List of UNESCO in 2004.

Nomination dossiers for the following sites have been sent to the World Heritage Centre for inscription on the World Heritage list of UNESCO : (i) Shri Harminder Sahib (Golden Temple) at Amritsar, Punjab, (ii) Majuli Island in Mid-stream of river Brahmaputra in Assam, (iii) Valley of Flowers as an extension to the Nanda Devi National Park in Uttaranchal, (iv) Red Fort, Delhi (a deferred nomination).

The total number of individual structures being maintained by the ASI is over 5,000. The activities of its various wings are as under:

Underwater Archaeology Wing: Search, study and preservation of cultural heritage lying submerged in inland or territorial waters are among the principal functions of the Underwater Archaeology Wing. It carries out exploration and excavation in Arabian Sea as well as in Bay of Bengal.

Science Branch: The Science Branch of the Survey with its headquarters at Dehradun and field laboratories in different parts of the country carries out chemical preservation of monuments, antiquities, manuscripts, paintings, etc.

Laboratories of Science Branch at Dehradun have undertaken the following scientific projects : (1) Evaluation of new materials as preservative coatings and strengthened for stone, terracotta, bricks & adobe structures, (2) Scientific studies related to conservation of ancient lime plaster, (3) Evaluation of physical characteristics of plaster cement with addition of rapid hardening plaster cement in different proportions.

Horticulture Branch : The Horticulture Branch of the ASI maintains gardens in about 287 centrally protected monuments/sites located in different parts of the country. The branch provides periodic plants to be used in gardens by developing base nurseries at Delhi, Agra, Srirangapatnam and Bhubaneswar.

Epigraphy Branch : The Epigraphy Branch at Mysore carries out research work in Sanskrit and Dravidian languages while the one at Nagpur carries out research work in Arabic and Persian.

Expeditions Abroad : The ASI has taken up the conservation project of Ta Prohm, Cambodia under the ITEC programme of Ministry of External Affairs with an outlay of ₹ 19.51 crore. The conservation project has been started on the request of the Royal Government of Cambodia for India's assistance in Conservation and Restoration of Prasat Ta Prohm. The conservation project is for a period of ten years and is to be completed in five phases.

O. W.: http://www.asi.nic.in

National Mission on Monuments and Antiquities

The National Mission on Monuments and Antiquities (NMMA) was launched on March 19, 2007 with a budgetary outlay of ₹ 90 crore. It prepares a National Register for Built Heritage, Sites and Antiques and setting up of a state level database on Built Heritage, Sites and Antiquarian wealth for information and dissemination to planners, researchers, etc., and better management of such cultural resources. The time frame prescribed for the NMMA to accomplish its mandate was five years.

National Mission for Manuscripts

The National Mission for Manuscripts (NMM) was launched by the Government in 2003 with the Indira Gandhi National Centre for Arts (IGNCA) as the nodal agency to reclaim India's inheritance of knowledge contained in the vast treasure of manuscripts. There are 46 Manuscripts Resource Centres, 33 Manuscripts Conservation Centres, 42 Manuscripts Partner Centres and 300 Manuscripts Conservation Partner Centres.

Major activities of the NMM are—documentation of manuscripts through survey, preventive and curative conservation, conducting training courses and workshops on conservation, manuscriptology and paleography, documentation through digitization, research and publication and public outreach programmes to create public consciousness for preserving and dissemination of manuscripts.

National Museum

The National Museum, functions as a subordinate office under the Ministry of Culture since 1960, houses over 2.6 lakh art objects dating from pre-historic era onwards. The main activities of the museum are as follows: Exhibitions, Reorganization/Modernization of Galleries, Educational Activities and Outreach Programmes, Public Relations, Publications, Photo Documentation, Summer Holiday Programmes, Memorial Lectures, Museum Corner, Photo Unit, Modelling Unit, Library, Conservation Laboratory and Workshops.

National Gallery of Modern Art

The National Gallery of Modern Art (NGMA), New Delhi was founded in 1954 to promote and develop contemporary Indian Art. It has 17,858 works of art, representing about 1,748 contemporary Indian artists. The collection has been built up mainly by purchase and also by gift. The NGMA's important collections include paintings, sculptures, graphic arts and photographs. It organizes exhibitions from its collection and under Cultural Exchange Programme periodically. Several colour reproductions have been brought out. The objective of NGMA is to help people look at the works of modern art with understanding and sensitivity.

The other important museums are : Indian Museum, Victoria Memorial Hall, Salarjung Museum and National Council of Science Museum.

O. W.: http://www.ngmaindia.gov.in

National Museum Institute of History of Art, Conservation and Museology

It is an autonomous organization, fully funded by the Ministry of Culture, established and declared as a Deemed University in 1989. This is the only Museum University in India and is presently functioning at the first floor of National Museum, New Delhi. As per its Memorandum of Association, the Director General, National Museum is the ex-officio Vice-Chancellor of this University.

Main objectives : (a) to provide education and training in the specialized areas of art, history, conservation and museology leading to the award of M.A. and Ph.D. Degrees in these three disciplines, (b) a few short-term courses—Indian art and culture, art appreciation and *Bhartiya Kalanidhi* (Hindi Medium) are also conducted to popularize the Indian culture, (c) to organize seminars/ workshops, conferences and special lectures on museum education, art and culture.

National Research Laboratory for Conservation of Cultural Property

National Research Laboratory for Conservation of Cultural Property (NRLC) was established in 1976, as a subordinate office of the Department of Culture, and is recognized by the Department of Science and Technology as a scientific institution of the Government of India. The NRLC aims to develop conservation of cultural property in the country. It provides conservation services and technical advise in matters concerning conservation to museums, archives, archaeology departments and other similar institutions, imparts training in different aspects of conservation, carries out research in methods and materials of conservation, disseminates knowledge in conservation and provides library services to conservators of the country. The headquarters of NRLC is situated at Lucknow. A regional centre of the NRLC, the Regional Conservation Laboratory is functioning at Mysore for conservation.

Ramakrishna Mission Institute of Culture, Kolkata

The Institute was conceived in 1936 as one of the permanent memorials to Sri Ramakrishna (1836-1886) on the occasion of his first birth centenary. It was formally established on January 29, 1938 as a branch centre of the Ramakrishna Mission founded by Swami Vivekananda to propagate the message of Vedanta as propounded by Sri Ramakrishna, whose basic teachings stressed: (i) the equality of all religions; (ii) the potential divinity of man; and (iii) service to man is a way of worshipping God—a new religion for mankind.

Dedicated to promote the ideal of the unity of mankind, the Institute has made people aware of the richness of the cultures of the world and the urgent need for inter-cultural appreciation, understanding and acceptance of each other's points of view. The keynote of everything the Institute does is thus, respect for others' point of view and its assimilation and acceptance for one's own enrichment.

Anthropological Survey of India

The Anthropological Survey of India is a premier research organization under the Ministry of Culture. It has completed 60 years of existence and has carried out anthropological researches in the area of bio-cultural aspects of Indian population in general and on those who are referred to as the 'Weakest of the Weak' in particular. Besides this, the activities include collection, preservation, maintenance, documentation and study of ethnographic materials as well as ancient human skeletal remains. Over the years, the survey has generated information from grass-root level through sustained research by its head office at Kolkata and also its seven regional centres, one sub-regional centre, one permanent field station and eight other field stations located in various parts of the country, besides a Camp Office at New Delhi.

O. W.: http://www.ansi.gov.in

National Archives of India

The National Archives of India (NAI), New Delhi known until Independence as Imperial Record Department, was originally established in Kolkata on March 11, 1891. It is the official custodian of all non-current record of permanent value to the Government of India and its predecessor bodies. It has a regional office at Bhopal and three Record Centres at Bhubaneswar, Jaipur and Puducherry.

Major activities of the Archives include: (i) making public records accessible to various Government agencies and research scholars; (ii) preparation of reference material; (iii) preservation and maintenance of records and conducting of scientific investigations for the said purpose; (iv) evolving records management programmes; (v) rendering technical assistance to individuals and institutions in the field of conservation of records; (vi) imparting training in the field of archives administration, records management, reprography, repair and conservation of records, books and manuscripts at professional and sub-professional levels; and (vii) creation and promotion of archival consciousness in the country by organising thematic exhibitions.

The National Archives of India provides financial assistance to states/ union territories, archives, voluntary organizations and other custodial institutions, so that the documentary heritage is preserved and archival science is promoted.

O. W.: http://www.nationalarchives.nic.in

Libraries

National Library

The National Library, Kolkata was established in 1948 with the passing of the Imperial Library (Change of Name) Act, 1948. It enjoys the status of an institution of national importance, its functions are : (i) acquisition and conservation of all significant printed material (to the exclusion only of ephemera) as well as of manuscripts of national importance; (ii) collection of printed material concerning the country, no matter where this is published; (iii) rendering of bibliographical and documentary services of current and retrospective material, both general and specialized (This implies the responsibility to produce current national bibliographies and retrospective bibliographies on various aspects of the country); (iv) acting as referral centre, surveying full and accurate knowledge of all sources of bibliographical information and participation in international bibliographical activities; and (v) acting as a centre for international book exchange and internal loan.

O. W.: http://www.nationallibrary.gov.in

Central Secretariat Library

The Central Secretariat Library (CSL) originally known as Imperial Secretariat Library, Kolkata was established in 1891. Since 1969 the library has been housed at Shastri Bhawan, New Delhi with a collection of over seven lakh documents mainly on social sciences and humanities. It is a depository of Indian official documents, Central Government and State Government documents.

The collection of Area Studies Division is unique in which books have been arranged according to geographical area. It has an extremely rich rare book collection, with a large biographic collection.

The CSL is mainly responsible for overall collection and development on all subjects useful in policy decision-making process collection on developmental literature. It provides all possible readers' services to Central Government officials and other research scholars visiting the library from all over India. In the recent past, the CSL has digitized the Government of India gazette, committee and commission reports and has also developed the Online Public Access Catalogue (OPAC) system for its collection.

The library has two branches, namely, Hindi and regional languages wing popularly known as Tulsi Sadan Library, Bahawalpur House, New Delhi that houses about 1.9 lakh volumes of Hindi and 13 other constitutionally approved Indian regional language books and a text book Library located at R.K. Puram, New Delhi which caters to the need of the wards of Central Government employees of undergraduate level.

The other important libraries include Raja Rammohan Roy Library Foundation, Delhi Public Library, Rampur Raza Library and Khuda Baksh Oriental Public Library.

Scholarship and Fellowship Division

The Scholarship and Fellowship Division of the Ministry operates the following schemes to provide monetary assistance to individuals/organizations engaged in promoting cultural activities in the country:-

1. **Scheme for Award of Scholarships to Young Artistes in Different Cultural Fields**

   Scholarships are awarded to young artistes of outstanding promise for advanced training in the fields of Indian classical dances, music, theatre, visual arts, folk, and traditional forms of arts, etc. Under the scheme, a total of 400 scholarships of ₹ 5,000/- per month are awarded each year for a period of two years. Artistes in the age group of 18-25 years are eligible to apply. The applicants must have undergone a minimum of five years' training with their gurus/institutes.

2. **Scheme for Award of Fellowships to Outstanding Persons in the Fields of Culture**

   Fellowships are awarded to the outstanding artistes in the fields of literary arts, plastic arts, performing arts, indology, epigraphy, sociology of culture, cultural economics, structural and engineering aspects of monuments, numismatics, scientific and technical aspects of conservation, management aspect of art and heritage, and studies relating to application of science and technology in areas related to culture. These are awarded for a period of two years; out of which 125 are Senior Fellowships having a value of ₹ 15,000/- per month and 125 are Junior Fellowships having a value of ₹ 7,500/- per month. Artistes in the age bracket of 40 years and above are eligible to apply for Senior Fellowships and artistes from 25 to 40 years of age can apply for Junior Fellowships.

The Fellowships are awarded for undertaking research oriented projects. While both academic research and performance related research are encouraged, the applicant is required to provide evidence of his/her capabilities in undertaking the project.

3. **Scheme of Financial Assistance for Seminars, Festivals and Exhibitions on Cultural Subjects by Not-for Profit Organizations (Cultural Functions Grant Scheme)**

   The Ministry of Culture has come up with an enlarged and revised version of 'Seminar Grant Scheme', now called the 'Cultural Functions Grant Scheme'. Formally, it goes under the title 'Scheme of Financial Assistance for Seminars, Festivals and Exhibitions on Cultural Subjects by Not-for-Profit Organizations. Salient features of the Scheme are as under:-

   (i) The new 'Cultural Functions Grant Scheme', covers festivals and exhibitions, along with research projects, seminars, conferences, symposia, etc.

(ii) The new scheme also increases the upper limit of assistance. Assistance in case of any particular project is restricted to 75 per cent of the total project cost, but the Government's contribution can now go up to ₹ 5 lakh.

(iii) University departments and University centres would also be entitled to apply for assistance, along with NGOs, societies, trusts, etc.

(iv) Previously the Seminar Grant Scheme was opened for fresh applications only once during each year, whereas the new 'Cultural Functions Grant Scheme' would remain open for applicants throughout the year.

(v) NGOs/Voluntary Organizations (but not Universities or their Centres) would have to sign up/register with the NGO Partnership National Portal www.ngo.india.gov.in through a simple operation for database purpose.

4. Financial Assistance to Ramakrishna Mission Institute of Culture, Kolkata (a cultural organization with national presence)

The Ramakrishna Mission Institute of Culture, a branch centre of the Ramakrishna Mission, is run by a managing committee comprising of eminent scholars and distinguished persons from different walks of life. The Governor of West Bengal is the President of its managing committee.

Dedicated to promote the ideal of the unity of mankind, the Institute has spread awareness of the richness of the cultures of the world and the need for inter-cultural appreciation, understanding and acceptance of each other's points of view — an approach which is conducive to international understanding at the global level and national integration at home. The key note of everything the institute does is thus to respect other's point of view and its assimilation and acceptance for one's own enrichment.

To support its activities, the Government of India and the Government of West Bengal have been sanctioning grants for the maintenance of the Institute since 1962.

5. Scheme for Visiting Fellows in Art, Culture and Heritage

This Scheme has recently been introduced to invigorate and revitalise the various institutions under the Ministry of Culture which have vast 'treasures' in the form of manuscripts, documents, artifacts, antiquities and paintings. It encourages serious researches into our cultural resources so that the nation gets to benefit from the results. Museums, for instance, can hardly display more than a small fraction of their entire holdings but the schemes like this would encourage research, scholarship and analysis of the objects that are not usually available for public viewing.

At present, it covers 17 institutions or organizations under the Ministry.

The scheme is open to both Indian and foreign academics and researchers.

Scholars and researchers, who have sound academic or professional credentials and experts in their respective fields or are persons with significant creative work in any field of art or culture are eligible. The fellowships are normally awarded for a period of two years.

Fellows will have the benefit of access to national cultural institutions for study and research material and infrastructural support.

The scheme offers the best terms, emoluments and facilities in order to draw the best talent available from academic and research institutes, as well as to attract researchers with domain knowledge.

Professors, who came on two years' lien, would be fully compensated with pay allowance, HRA, etc., and would also be entitled to a sum of upto ₹ 3.5 lakh each year (for two years) by way of project assistance.

Retired academics or researchers, with established credentials, would be entitled to an honorarium of ₹ 80,000 per month, in addition to other financial and logistic support.

Outstation fellows would also be entitled to a 'Settling-in-allowance'.

Tourism

Tourism plays an important role in employment generation and economic growth of the country. It is accepted as the potent engine for inclusive social economic progress at universal level through its forward and backward linkages and ability to create employment in the economy. Tourism sector has a very high employment potential with approximately 90 jobs creation per ₹ 10 lakh of investment. There is high scope for profuse employment generation and related activities in the form of accommodation projects, food oriented projects, amusement parks and water sports, etc.

Visa-on-Arrival

The year 2015 witnessed a growth of 4.5 per cent in Foreign Tourist Arrivals (FTAs) in India, this growth is equivalent to the medium growth rate of 4.5 per cent witnessed in International Tourist Arrivals, globally. FTAs during 2015 were 80.27 lakh as compared to the FTAs of 76.79 lakh during 2014. The Foreign Exchange Earnings (FEEs) from tourism in rupee terms during 2015 were ₹ 1,35,193 crore with a growth of 9.6 per cent.

The Ministry of Tourism supported the initiative regarding the implementation of Tourist Visa on Arrival (VoA) enabled with Electronic Travel Authorisation (ETA) (renamed as e-Tourist Visa) strongly and committed all support to Ministry of Home Affairs and Ministry of External Affairs and Ministry of Civil Aviation for implementing the programme. The Government of India launched the e-Tourist Visa on 27.11.2014. During January- December, 2015 a total of 4,45,300 tourist arrived on e-Tourist Visa. 150 countries are eligible for e-Tourist Visa as on February 26, 2016 . This facility is now available in 16 airports as on February 26, 2016. The Government of India, w.e.f November, 2015, has also revised the e-Tourist Visa (e-TV) fee in four slabs of 0, US$ 25, US$ 48, and US$ 60. Presently e-TV application fee is US$ 60 and bank charge is US$ 2 which is uniform for all the countries. The revision of Visa fee has been done on the principle of reciprocity. Bank charges have also been reduced from US$ 2 to 2.5 per cent of the e-TV fee. There is no bank charge for zero visa fees.

Web based Public Delivery System

Ministry of Tourism has set up a Web based Public Delivery System for recognition of the Travel Trade Service Providers with the objective to ease Travel Trade Service Providers seeking recognition from this Ministry and also to bring in transparency in granting the approvals. This online process has also been integrated with payment gateway with effect from January, 2016.

Niche Tourism Products

The Ministry of Tourism has taken the initiative of identifying, diversifying, developing and promoting niche products of the tourism industry. This is done in order to overcome the aspect of 'seasonality' and to promote India as a 365 days destination, attract tourists with specific interest and to ensure repeat visits for the unique products in which India has a comparative advantage. Identifying niche products is a dynamic process. Thus, new products may be added in due course. The Ministry of Tourism has constituted committees for promotion of Golf Tourism and Wellness Tourism. Guidelines have also been formulated by the Ministry to support golf, polo, medical and wellness tourism. Accordingly, the following niche products have been identified for development and promotion :-

Cruise; Adventure; Medical; Wellness; Golf; Polo; Meetings Incentives Conferences and Exhibitions; Eco-tourism; Film Tourism and Sustainable Tourism.

Medical Tourism

Medical Tourism (also called medical travel, health tourism or global healthcare) is a term used to describe the rapidly growing practice of travelling across international borders to obtain health care. Services typically sought by travellers include elective procedures as well as complex specialized surgeries such as joint replacement (knee/hip), cardiac surgery, dental surgery and cosmetic surgeries. However, virtually every type of healthcare, including psychiatry, alternative treatments and convalescent care is available in India.

The Medical Tourism activity is mainly driven by the private sector. The Ministry of Tourism has only the role of a facilitator in terms of marketing this concept and promoting this in the key markets. The Ministry of Tourism has taken several steps to promote India as a medical and health tourism destination.

India Tourism Development Corporation

India Tourism Development Corporation (ITDC) is a Public Sector Undertaking under administrative control of the Ministry of Tourism. Incorporated on

October 1, 1966, ITDC played a key role in the development of tourism infrastructure in the country. Apart from developing the largest hotel chain in India, the ITDC offers tourism related facilities like transport, duty free shopping, entertainment, production of tourist publicity literature, consultancy, etc. The ITDC has played a committed and pivotal social role in the development of tourism infrastructure in backward areas, thereby trying to promote regional balance. The present network of ITDC consists of eight Ashok Group of Hotels, seven Joint Venture Hotels including one yet to be completed hotel, one Restaurant, 11 Transport Units, one Tourist Service Station, seven Duty Free Shops at airports/seaports, two Sound and Light Shows and three Catering Outlets. Besides, ITDC is also managing a Hotel at Bharatpur and a Tourist Complex at Kosi.

Ek Bharat Shreshtha Bharat

Ek Bharat Shreshtha Bharat was announced by Hon'ble Prime Minister on 31st October, 2015 on the occasion of the 140th birth anniversary of Sardar Vallabhbhai Patel. Subsequently, the Finance Minister announced the initiative in his Budget Speech for 2016-17. Through this innovative measure, the knowledge of the culture, traditions and practices of different states & UTs will lead to an enhanced understanding and bonding between the states, thereby strengthening the unity and integrity of India.

The broad objectives of the initiative are :- (i) To celebrate the unity in diversity of our nation and to maintain and strengthen the fabric of traditionally existing emotional bonds between the people of our country; (ii) To promote the spirit of national integration through a deep and structured engagement between all states and union territories through a year-long planned engagement between states; (iii) To showcase the rich heritage and culture, customs and traditions of either state for enabling people to understand and appreciate the diversity that is India, thus fostering a sense of common identity; (iv) To establish long-term engagements; and (v) To create an environment which promotes learning between states by sharing best practices and experiences.

The key themes of interactions would be:

To celebrate the idea of India as a nation wherein different cultural units across varied geographies coalesce and interact with each other, this glorious manifestation of diverse cuisine, music, dance, theatre, movies & films, handicrafts, sports, literature, festivals, painting, sculpture etc. will enable people to imbibe the innate chord of binding and brotherhood; to make our people aware about the seamless integral hull of the Modern Indian State spread across a vast landmass on whose firm foundations, the geo-political strength of the country is ensured to benefit one and all; to impress upon people at large about the increasing inter-connectedness between the constituents of various cultures and traditions, which is so vital for the spirit of nation building; to induce a sense of responsibility & ownership for the nation as a whole through these close cross-cultural interactions as it intends to build up the inter-dependence matrix unequivocally.

6 Basic Economic Data

THE Ministry of Statistics and Programme Implementation (MoSPI) came into existence as an independent Ministry on October 15, 1999 after the merger of the Department of Statistics and the Department of Programme Implementation. The Ministry has two wings, one relating to Statistics and the other relating to Programme Implementation. The Statistics Wing redesignated as National Statistics Office (NSO), consists of the Central Statistical Office (CSO) and the National Sample Survey Office (NSSO). The Programme Implementation Wing has three divisions, namely : (i) Twenty Point Programme, (ii) Infrastructure and Project Monitoring, and (iii) Members of Parliament Local Area Development Scheme. Besides these three wings, there is National Statistical Commission (NSC) created through a resolution of Government of India and one autonomous institute, viz., Indian Statistical Institute (ISI) declared as an institute of national importance by an Act of Parliament.

O. W.: http://www.mospi.gov.in

National Statistical Commission

The Government of India through a resolution dated June 1, 2005 decided to set up the National Statistical Commission (NSC). The setting up of the NSC followed the decision of the Cabinet to accept the recommendation of the Rangarajan Commission, which reviewed the Indian Statistical System in 2001. The NSC was initially constituted w.e.f. July 12, 2006, to serve as a nodal and empowered body for all core statistical activities of the country, to evolve, monitor and enforce statistical priorities and standards and to ensure statistical coordination. The NSC has, one part-time Chairperson and four part-time members, each having specialization and experience in specified statistical fields. Besides, Secretary, Niti Aayog is an ex-officio member of the Commission. The Chief Statistician of India is the Secretary to the Commission.

Central Statistics Office

The Central Statistics Office (CSO), an attached office of the Ministry, coordinates the statistical activities in the country and evolves statistical standards. Its activities *inter-alia,* include compilation of National Accounts, Index of Industrial Production, Consumer Price Indices (Urban/Rural/Combined), Human Development Statistics, (including Gender Statistics in the states and union territories) and dissemination of Energy Statistics, Social and Environment Statistics and preparation of the National Industrial Classification.

The CSO, Ministry of Statistics and Programme Implementation releases Consumer Price Indices (CPI) for All-India and states/union territories separately for rural, urban and combined (rural plus urban) for the purpose of

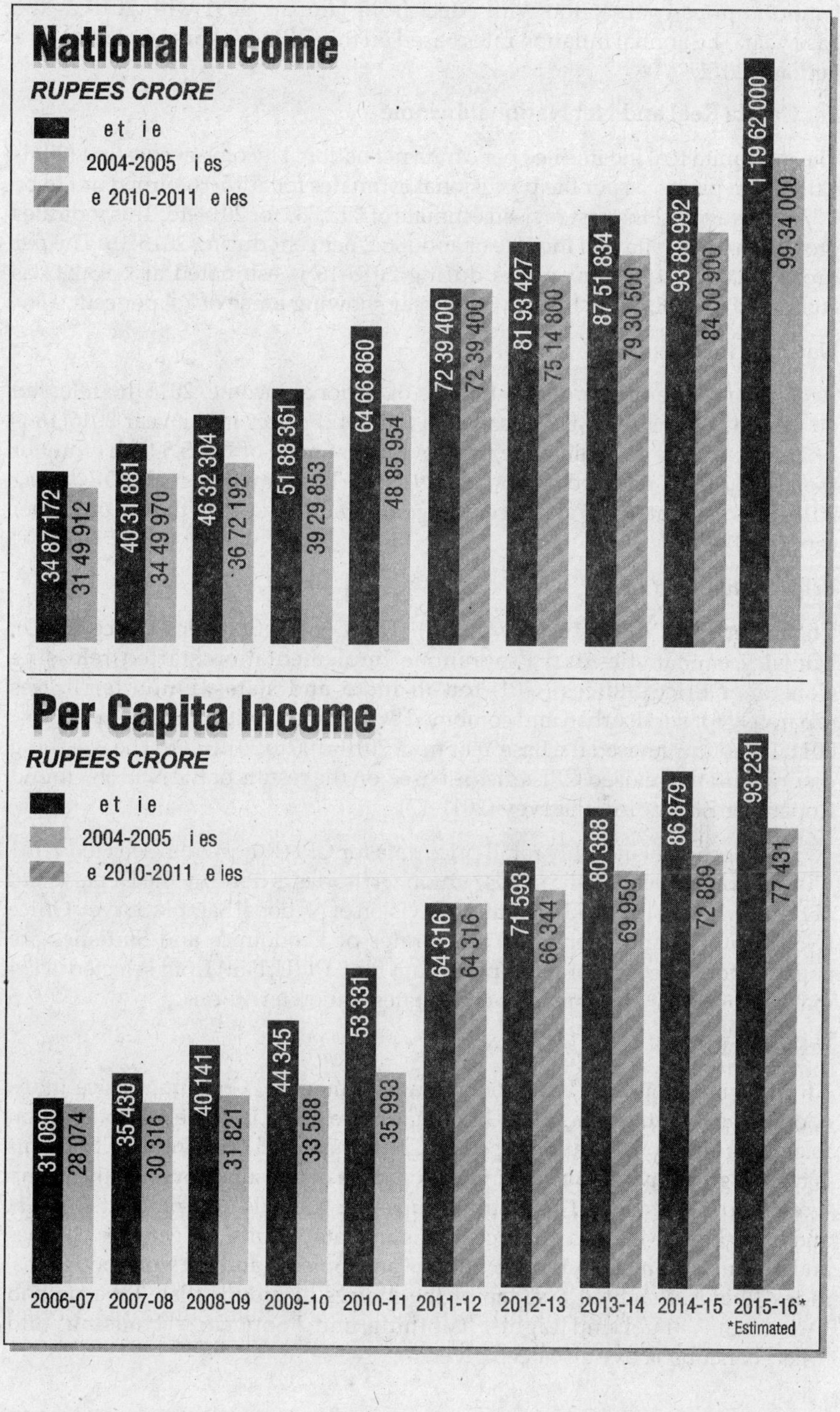
National Income
RUPEES CRORE
et ie
2004-2005 i es
e 2010-2011 e ies
34 87 172
31 49 912
40 31 881
34 49 970
46 32 304
36 72 192
51 88 361
39 29 853
64 66 860
48 85 954
72 39 400
72 39 400
81 93 427
75 14 800
87 51 834
79 30 500
93 88 992
84 00 900
1 19 62 000
99 34 000
Per Capita Income
RUPEES CRORE
et ie
2004-2005 i es
e 2010-2011 e ies
31 080
28 074
35 430
30 316
40 141
31 821
44 345
33 588
53 331
35 993
64 316
64 316
71 593
66 344
80 388
69 959
86 879
72 889
93 231
77 431
2006-07
2007-08
2008-09
2009-10
2010-11
2011-12
2012-13
2013-14
2014-15
2015-16*
*Estimated

temporal price comparison with effect from January, 2011 with 2010 as the base year. The annual inflation rates based on this CPI series are available since January, 2012.

Per Capita Real and Net National Income

The per capita real income i.e., per capita net national income at constant (2011-12) market prices, as per the provisional estimates for 2015-16 turned out to be ₹ 77,435 as against the first revised estimate of ₹ 72,889 for 2014-15. This indicates growth in per capita real income of about 6.2 per cent during 2015-16. The per capita income at current prices during 2015-16 is estimated at ₹ 93,293 as compared to ₹ 86,879 of the previous year showing a rise of 7.4 per cent.

National Income

According to the provisional estimates of national income, 2015-16, released on 31st May 2016, the GDP at constant (2011-12) prices in the year 2015-16 is ₹ 113.5 lakh crore as against the first revised estimate of ₹ 105.5 lakh crore for the year 2014-15, released on January 29, 2016. The growth in real GDP during 2015-16 is estimated at 7.6 per cent as compared to the growth rate of 7.1 per cent in 2014-15.

Price Statistics

Consumer Price Index (Rural/Urban): The Central Statistics Office (CSO), Ministry of Statistics and Programme Implementation started releasing Consumer Price Indices (CPI) for all India and states/union territories separately for rural, urban and combined every month with effect from January 2011. It has now revised the Base Year from 2010=100 to 2012=100. The weighing diagram for the revised CPI series is based on the results of the NSS 68th round Consumer Expenditure Survey (2011-12).

Collection of monthly retail price data for CPI (Rural) from selected 1,181 villages spread over all the states/union territories is done by the Department of Posts, whereas the Field Operation Division of National Sample Survey Office [NSSO (FOD)] and specified Directorates of Economics and Statistics are engaged for collection of retail price data for CPI (Urban) from selected 1,114 markets of 310 towns spread over all states/union territories.

Inflation Rate

All India inflation rate, based on average of monthly Consumer Price Index (Combined), for the years 2012-13 onwards are given in Table 6.1. In addition to general inflation, Inflation based on Consumer Food Price Index (CFPI) (this is the weighted average of the indices of some of the sub-groups of the group 'Food and Beverages'. These sub-groups are: 'Cereals and products', 'Meat and fish', 'Egg', 'Milk and products', 'Oils and fats', 'Fruits', 'Vegetables', 'Pulses and products', 'Sugar and confectionery' and 'Spices') and the Non-food items' index (this is weighted average of the indices of groups 'Pan Tobacoo and Intoxicants', 'Fuel and Light', 'Clothing and Footwear', 'Housing' and 'Miscellaneous') have also been given.

Table.6.1 All India Inflation Rates based on CPI

Period	All	Food (CFPI)	Non Food
2012-13	9.90	11.07	8.88
2013-14	9.44	12.09	7.27
2014-15	5.93	6.36	5.47
2015-16	4.91	4.88	4.64
Apr-16	5.47	6.40	4.66
May-16	5.76	7.47	4.47
Jun-16	5.77	7.79	4.36
Jul-16	6.07	8.35	4.43
Aug-16	5.05	5.91	4.41
Sep-16	4.31	3.88	4.65

Note: Sep16 figures are Provisional.

All India monthly general CPI (Rural/Urban/Combined) and the inflation rates, based thereon, for the last two years, i.e., from January 2015 to September 2016 are given in Table 6.2 and 6.3, respectively.

Table 6.2: Statement of All India General (All Group)

Month	CPI (Rural)	CPI (Urban)	CPI (Combined)
Jan-15	120.3	118.5	119.5
Feb-15	120.6	118.7	119.7
Mar-15	121.1	119.1	120.2
Apr-15	121.5	119.7	120.7
May-15	122.4	120.7	121.6
Jun-15	124.1	121.7	123.0
Jul-15	124.7	122.4	123.6
Aug-15	126.1	123.2	124.8
Sep-15	127.0	123.5	125.4
Oct-15	127.7	124.2	126.1
Nov-15	128.3	124.6	126.6
Dec-15	127.9	124.0	126.1
Jan-16	128.1	124.2	126.3

Feb-16	127.9	123.8	126.0
Mar-16	128.0	123.8	126.0
Apr-16	129.0	125.3	127.3
May-16	130.3	126.6	128.6
Jun-16	131.9	128.1	130.1
Jul-16	133.0	129.0	131.1
Aug-16	133.5	128.4	131.1
Sep-16	133.3	128.0	130.8

**Figures for September 2016 are provisional*

Table 6.3: Statement of All India Annual Inflation Rates Based on CPI

Month	CPI (Rural)	CPI (Urban)	CPI (Combined)
Jan-15	5.34	4.96	5.19
Feb-15	5.79	4.95	5.37
Mar-15	5.67	4.75	5.25
Apr-15	5.29	4.36	4.87
May-15	5.52	4.41	5.01
Jun-15	6.07	4.55	5.40
Jul-15	4.35	2.94	3.69
Aug-15	4.47	2.75	3.74
Sep-15	5.05	3.61	4.41
Oct-15	5.54	4.28	5.00
Nov-15	5.95	4.71	5.41
Dec-15	6.32	4.73	5.61
Jan-16	6.48	4.81	5.69
Feb-16	6.05	4.30	5.26
Mar-16	5.70	3.95	4.83
Apr-16	6.17	4.68	5.47
May-16	6.45	4.89	5.76
Jun-16	6.29	5.26	5.77
Jul-16	6.66	5.39	6.07
Aug-16	5.87	4.22	5.05
Sep-16	4.96	3.64	4.31

** Inflation rates for September 2016 are provisional*

The inflation rate, which was very high in 2012-13 and 2013-14 started declining from 2014-15. During the year 2016-17, the month of September has witnessed the lowest level of inflation. Fall in the overall inflation rate during the period of 2012-13 to 2016-17 has mainly been driven by fall in the prices of food items, which is evident from declining inflation rates, based on CFPI.

Services Sector

The share of services in India's Gross Value Added (GVA) at basic prices (at current prices) increased from 49 per cent in 2011-12 to 53.2 per cent in 2015-16 as per Provisional Estimates (PE). Including construction, the share increased to 61.5 per cent in 2015-16. With a 20.6 per cent share, 'financial, real estate, and professional services' as a group is the largest contributor to GVA among the various services sub-sectors, followed by 'trade, hotels, transport, communication and services related to broadcasting' with a 18.6 per cent share and 'Public Administration, defence and other services' with a share of 14.01 per cent is in third place.

In 2015-16, growth of the services sector dropped to 8.9 per cent as compared to 10.3 per cent in 2014-15. This sector's growth is higher than the overall GVA growth of 7.1 per cent and 7.2 per cent at constant prices in 2014-15 and 2015-16 respectively. This is mainly due to growth deceleration in financial, real estate and professional services to 10.3 per cent in 2015-16 from 10.6 per cent in 2014-15and in trade, repairs, hotels and restaurants at 9 per cent in 2015-16 from 9.80 per cent in 2014-15.

Services Trade

In 2015-16 services exports shrank by -0.73 per cent to US$ 154.3 billion compared to growth of 2.6 per cent in 2014-15 and import of services grew by 6.1 per cent at US$ 84.6 billion compared to growth of 1.6 per cent in 2014-15. This has resulted in deceleration of net services growth to -7.9 per cent in 2015-16 compared to 3.7 per cent growth in 2014-15. In 2015-16, net services financed almost 53.6 per cent of the India's trade deficit on goods.

Infrastructure Supportive Industries

The eight core infrastructure supportive industries, namely, coal, crude oil, natural gas, refinery products, fertilizers, steel, cement and electricity with a total weight of 37.90 per cent in the Index of Industrial Production (IIP) have registered a growth of 3.7 per cent during 2014-15 as compared to 4.2 per cent during 2013-14. During the year 2014-15, the growth in the coal sector was 8.4 per cent, 8.1 per cent in electricity, 5.6 per cent in cement, 1.3 per cent in steel and 0.4 per cent in refinery products sector. Crude oil, natural gas and fertilizers sectors have shown negative growth during 2014-15.

Annual Survey of Industries

The Annual Survey of Industries (ASI) is the principal source of industrial statistics in the country. It provides statistical information to access and evaluate, objectively and realistically, the change in the growth, composition and structure of the organized manufacturing sector comprising activities related to manufacturing processes, repair services, generation, transmission, etc., of electricity, gas and water supply and cold storage.

The ASI extends to the entire country. The survey covers all factories registered under Sections 2m (i) and 2m (ii) of the Factories Act, 1948. The survey also covers *bidi* and *cigar* manufacturing establishments registered under the *Bidi* and *Cigar* Workers (Conditions of Employment) Act, 1966. All the electricity undertakings engaged in the generation, transmission and distribution of electricity registered with the Central Electricity Authority (CEA) were covered under ASI up to 1997-98 irrespective of their employment size. Certain services and activities like cold storage, water supply, repair of motor vehicles and of other consumer durables like watches, etc., are covered under the survey. Defence establishments, oil storage and distribution depots, restaurants, hotels, cafe and computer services and the technical training institutes are excluded from the purview of the survey. The electricity undertakings registered with the CEA are not being covered under ASI with effect from 1998-99. However, captive units not registered with CEA continued to be covered under ASI.

The principal characteristics of the factory sector for the period 2005-06 to 2013-14 as depicted by ASI are given in Table 1. The state-wise principal characteristics of the factory sector from the latest available ASI data, i.e., ASI 2013-14, may be seen in the Table.

Index of Industrial Production

CSO compiles the Index of Industrial Production (IIP) using secondary data received from 15 source agencies in various ministries/ departments or their attached/subordinate offices. The present base year of IIP is 2004-05. IIP is released every month in the form of Quick Estimates with a time-lag of 6 weeks as per the Special Data Dissemination Standard (SDDS) norms of IMF. Apart from breakup of the index for mining, manufacturing and electricity sectors, the estimates are also simultaneously being released as per Use-based classification viz., basic goods, capital goods, intermediate goods, consumer durables and non-durables. These estimates are revised subsequently on receipt of updated production data from the 15 source agencies. The major source of data for IIP is the Department of Industrial Policy and Promotion that supplies data for 268 out of 399 item groups with a weight of 45.6 per cent in overall IIP.

Till October 2016, IIP has been released up to the month of August 2016 as per the actual release calendar. The IIP increased by 2.4 per cent in 2015-16 as compared to a growth of 2.8 per cent in 2014-15. Electricity sector registered a growth of 5.7 per cent during 2015-16 as compared to 8.4 per cent during 2014-15. Mining and manufacturing sectors registered growths of 2.2 per cent and 2.0 per cent respectively during 2015-16 as compared to 1.5 per cent and 2.3 per cent growths in 2013-14.

Table 1: Principal Characteristics

(value figures in ₹ lakhs, mandays in thousands and others in number)

Characteristics	2005-06	2006-07	2007-08	2008-09	2009-10	2010-11	2011-12	2012-13	2013-14
Number of Factories	140160	144710	146385	155321	158877	211660	217554	222120	224576
Fixed Capital	60694028	71513139	84513209	105596614	135218367	160700652	194955088	218026022	237371903
Working Capital	18446260	28218880	31695306	31123298	38774453	62036285	59107859	60341107	66268577
Invested Capital	90157861	107150382	128012553	153517773	193305395	239358002	284114733	314411215	338455535
Outstanding Loans	35150737	42858882	45399645	53641948	66300983	82563795	92438166	107224700	122209355
Number of Workers	7136097	7880536	8198110	8776745	9157802	9901970	10438156	10051626	10444404
Mandays-Workers	2154187	2383707	2477465	2660547	2783026	3035766	3190232	3048628	3163707
Number of Employees	9038523	10252148	10378495	11252793	11722631	12617691	13346243	12873853	13462061
Mandays-Employees	2739729	3034322	3144881	3386622	3574683	3884964	4087324	3910879	4085342
Total Person Engaged	9111680	10328434	10452535	11327485	11792055	12694853	13430483	12950025	13538114
Wages to Workers	3766366	4429135	5103023	5977184	6894071	8564552	10001913	11089620	12649644
Total Emoluments	7400820	8875099	10544284	12944123	14700696	18329574	21509846	23805727	27241503
Funds and Other	857258	1029960	1106509	1284077	1493962	1633875	1813675	2014422	2104617
Workmen & Staff Welfare Expens	612293	753445	851638	1005420	1191381	1326556	1535156	1682187	1849376
Fuels Consumed	9662969	12006706	12956170	15216203	16160001	19542403	24243842	26754523	29850770
Material Consumed	120428441	151177096	175288695	206598245	240909606	302044142	374191914	392949410	423046161

Total Inputs	154365843	194836758	222295282	266148638	303585334	385108361	479846038	501866586	549013952
Products and by- Products	169755185	212863582	247071651	286314842	330614199	408371845	495987634	528558114	570344878
Value of output	190835548	240854764	277570904	327279786	373303593	467621696	570366932	602594536	655525116
Depreciation	5283286	6445480	7116354	8354590	10506872	12055754	14065505	15533081	16976977
Net Value Added	31186419	39572526	48159268	52776558	59211387	70457581	76455389	85194869	89534187
Rent Paid	529948	640399	750549	975778	1200490	1349336	1619529	1642164	1527272
Interest Paid	3339801	4131128	5148688	6868048	7331793	8802079	12065632	13807327	15485061
Net Income	27316670	34800999	42260031	44932732	50679104	60306166	62770228	71928627	75152048
Net Fixed Capital Formation	7324388	7987020	10662743	14240111	16323196	16309792	20316875	20219540	18396832
Gross Fixed Capital Formation	12607674	14432500	17779098	22594701	26830068	28365547	34382380	35752621	35373809
Addition in Stock of									
(I) Material, Fuels, etc.	2178056	2926206	4952720	1974707	5323903	7742594	771176	3323215	3458978
(II) Semi Finished Goods	853964	927755	1060215	909350	1902222	2707800	1794022	1237924	1446002
(iii) Finished Goods	1517008	1646496	2437910	679786	2128264	5774460	3966016	4359554	1905532
(iv) Total	4549027	5500458	8450845	3563843	9354390	16224854	6531214	8920693	6810512
Gross Capital Formation	17156701	19932958	26229942	26158544	36184458	44590400	40913594	44673315	42184321
Profits	18446298	24142496	29757600	29699112	33293065	39016161	37911551	44426292	43956552

Table 2: State-wise Principal Characteristics as per ASI 2013-14

(value figures in ₹ lakhs & others in numbers)

States	Factories	Fixed Capital	Productive Capital	Invested Capital	Workers	Total Persons Engaged	Wages to Workers	Total Emoluments	Total Input	Total Output	Depreciation	Net Value Added	Rent Paid	Interest Paid
Maharashtra	29123	32636160	44677999	48716663	1328688	1886025	2032079	5339045	83739649	106597134	2805836	20051648	343241	2360224
Gujarat	22876	38265385	46817794	54813239	1049725	1372669	1209240	2773399	107510149	123064181	2712028	12842005	97969	2405784
Tamil Nadu	37378	27081648	31918368	38053367	1641460	2046553	1796388	3752027	57019375	67695733	1955090	8721268	211349	1714822
Karnataka	12107	16731050	22115261	23339966	705941	927392	973437	2069905	37702681	44469973	1233936	5533356	154810	868506
Uttar Pradesh	14463	10243627	13110975	16944630	701782	912206	796253	1737049	35044248	41126757	895445	5187064	139172	1027899
Uttarakhand	2936	5479327	6301345	7632858	312131	386654	341534	651128	13485768	17725377	453199	3786410	20539	321327
Haryana	6117	7065108	9102093	11247367	467741	612419	592737	1460800	25179113	29640333	751638	3709582	89725	605521
Telangana	14110	5694436	9525811	9071450	629361	747062	531708	1021006	13631996	17133649	489041	3012612	44734	404573
Rajasthan	8820	7149502	9800522	10287816	356006	470078	418899	878277	18194200	21469179	593835	2681144	44162	512937
Himachal Pradesh	2806	4769133	6237616	6205555	132706	194608	156918	457034	7316952	9954730	361153	2276625	25081	282219
West Bengal	8859	8094660	10489366	12389882	522241	645738	643388	1072868	24854988	27637949	539199	2243761	55030	640845
Odisha	2714	21086599	22188086	24112454	206788	260771	337494	589567	9303658	12237946	800307	2133980	13958	914574
Chhattisgarh	2534	6408052	11443834	8091611	131032	166236	252609	483647	8153091	10599069	320625	2125353	32356	295292
Madhya Pradesh	4047	8608707	10356550	11447244	239212	322833	302055	662013	14648214	17208597	435657	2124725	25570	456949
Punjab	12278	3935562	6478340	7678829	485520	602818	468822	824034	15825805	18210659	378378	2006476	25301	527570
Jharkhand	2688	7134878	8017112	9194872	130450	187877	289564	609658	8335305	10779440	456888	1987246	29720	403160

States	Factories	Fixed Capital	Productive Capital	Invested Capital	Workers	Total Persons Engaged	Wages to Workers	Total Emoluments	Total Input	Total Output	Depreciation	Net Value Added	Rent Paid	Interest Paid
Andhra Pradesh	15719	14862643	17085075	19463961	415127	522057	521945	911322	23558737	26268382	846864	1862780	63077	814131
Kerala	7132	2342965	2931170	3864741	290055	351662	305239	541317	11579148	13105441	180324	1345969	16615	142505
Dadra & Nagar Haveli	1405	3410225	4636432	4755479	83397	148522	94602	200842	8372069	9596018	201750	1022199	7704	234272
Assam	3518	1444632	2158110	2135656	157687	186483	133191	212675	4840084	5761714	119875	801755	5788	92609
Delhi	3918	572580	1638207	1667085	75273	112180	94516	253237	5057130	5901429	56458	787841	32833	110913
Goa	618	793409	1142162	1319622	39618	56684	67967	167754	2539663	3379150	75499	763987	7850	45034
Daman & Diu	1881	1027888	1945751	1769285	89215	109462	93163	186993	3402752	4110609	91198	616659	25566	108908
Bihar	3419	803738	747951	1391746	96122	113594	59895	110631	4945635	5529620	68528	515457	3478	41223
Jammu & Kashmir	943	517712	748745	1008947	52886	66829	47135	91141	1871781	2337180	50477	414922	3299	75958
Sikkim	66	173938	342850	270635	10227	12749	9352	29247	286816	710303	12292	411195	822	3122
Puducherry	857	440126	855065	766764	39751	50108	41900	80518	1557868	2007285	42145	407272	4243	25488
Chandigarh (U.T.)	285	177381	268270	277699	8030	13143	11617	34969	580830	658424	9409	68185	1268	8734
Meghalaya	108	362758	463941	442803	10998	13434	13129	22233	299734	381377	34192	47451	1433	36192
Tripura	552	27221	46484	44251	26524	29121	8048	10925	96571	131623	3390	31661	420	2088
Nagaland	134	17872	33515	27736	3303	3746	1581	2047	31631	39707	447	7629	91	168
Manipur	145	9793	16918	16857	4988	5879	2740	3453	31455	37752	1089	5208	49	818
Andaman & N. Island	20	3185	-1239	4468	421	521	499	742	16853	18397	783	761	19	694
All India	**224576**	**237371903**	**303640480**	**338455535**	**10444404**	**13538114**	**12649644**	**27241503**	**549013952**	**655525116**	**16976977**	**89534187**	**1527272**	**15485061**

In the use-based categories, basic goods registered growth of 3.6 per cent during 2015-16 as compared to 7.0 per cent during 2014-15. Capital goods contracted by 2.9 per cent during 2015-16 as compared to a growth of 6.4 per cent during 2014-15. The growth in the intermediate goods was 2.5 per cent during 2015-16 as compared to 1.7 per cent during 2014-15. Consumer goods registered a growth of 3.0 per cent during 2015-16 as against a decline of 3.4 per cent in 2014-15.

CSO is in the process of revising base year of all-India IIP from 2004-05 to 2011-12 to take into account the changes in the industrial sector. For this purpose, a new basket of items and a panel of factories have already been prepared on the basis of the recommendations of the Working Group headed by Dr. Saumitra Chaudhuri, former Member, Planning Commission (erstwhile). For this purpose production data on the new basket of items have been collected from the chosen factories since April 2011 in collaboration with source agencies. The new series will be introduced soon after the indices and the methodological aspects are approved by the Committee of Secretaries (CoS).

National Sample Survey Office

The National Sample Survey Office (NSSO), in Ministry of Statistics and Programme Implementation, is responsible for conduct of large scale sample surveys, in diverse fields, on all India basis. Primary data is collected regularly through nationwide household surveys on various socio-economic subjects, Annual Survey of Industries (ASI) under the Collection of Statistics Act and Enterprise Surveys, as a follow up of the economic census. Besides these surveys, NSSO collects data on rural and urban prices; plays a significant role in the improvement of crop statistics through supervision of the area enumeration and crop estimation surveys of the state agencies. It also maintains a frame of urban real units for drawing samples for socio-economic surveys in urban areas. The NSSO functions with requisite autonomy, in matters relating to data collection, processing and publication/dissemination of results/data based on its surveys, under overall guidance and supervision of National Statistical Commission (NSC) which appoints Working Groups/Technical Committees comprising both official and non-official members on different subjects for finalization of survey instruments for its surveys and methodologies for the same. The Director General and Chief Executive Officer (DG and CEO) is responsible for overall coordination and supervision of all activities of NSSO and is assisted by four Additional Director Generals, each one being in-charge of separate divisions responsible for four distinct aspects of such large scale surveys relating to their designing and planning, field work, data processing and coordination.

Price Data Collection

Rural Retail Price Collection (RPC): The Field Operations Division (FOD) regularly collects rural price data on monthly basis for the compilation of

Consumer Price Index for agricultural and rural labourers covering 603 villages in 340 districts across the country, on behalf of the Labour Bureau, Ministry of Labour and Employment. Data on wage rates are also collected in respect of 12 agricultural and 13 non agricultural occupations, as part of the scheme. Data on daily wage rates of important agricultural operations are reported by the state governments on monthly basis. For providing an alternative series of wage-rates data, the Data Processing Division of NSSO is compiling and publishing occupation-wise wage rates, based on the data collected in Rural Prices schedule 3.01(R). The RPC bulletin called the 'Prices and Wages in Rural India' which is published for each quarter, provides price data only at national level and wage data at national and state level for 26 major states.

Twenty Point Programme

The Twenty Point Programme (TPP) initiated in the year 1975 was restructured in the years 1982, 1986 and 2006. The thrust of the programme, restructured in 2006, is to eradicate poverty and improve the quality of life of the poor and the underprivileged people all over the country. The programme covers various socio-economic aspects like poverty, employment, education, housing, agriculture, drinking water, afforestation and environment protection, energy to rural areas, welfare of weaker sections of the society, etc.

Twenty Point Programme (TPP)-2006 originally consisted of 20 points and 66 items being monitored individually by Central Nodal Ministries concerned. Out of the 66 items, 25 were for monthly monitoring, while the rest were to be monitored on annual basis by this Ministry. The monthly information in respect of 21 items was collected from various states/union territories and for the remaining four, the information was collected from the concerned Central Nodal Ministries. TPP-2006 has now completed nine years of its operationalization. One of the 66 items viz. 'Sampoorna Grameen Rojgar Yojana (SGRY)' has since been subsumed into another item namely 'National Rural Employment Guarantee Act' with effect from April 1, 2008 and has been renamed as Mahatma Gandhi National Rural Employment Guarantee Act with effect from December 31, 2009. Since September 2014 the data collection is done on quarterly basis and the monthly monitoring has been changed to quarterly monitoring. At present, out of the remaining 65 items, 19 items are being monitored on quarterly basis. The monitoring mechanism for TPP-2006 has also been widened by including block level monitoring in addition to the existing Central, state and district level monitoring.

Monitoring Mechanism

The primary responsibility of implementation and monitoring of the programme lies with the agencies entrusted with the execution of the programme, which in this case are the state governments/union territory administrations and the Central Nodal Ministries. The Ministry of Statistics and Programme Implementation monitors the programmes/schemes covered under TPP-2006 on the basis of performance reports received from state governments/UT administrations and Central Nodal Ministries. The Ministry has developed a web based Management

Information System to expeditiously collect information from the State Governments and the Central Nodal Ministries.

Monitoring Committees at state, district and block level, for monitoring the progress of implementation of all schemes/items covered under the Twenty Point Programme-2006, have been constituted by most of the States/Union Territories as per the provisions of TPP-2006 guidelines.

Quarterly Progress Report (QPR) of TPP-2006 is prepared quarterly on the basis of information provided by state governments /UT administrations on 19 items. QPR provides information on the annual physical targets, cumulative target and achievements upto the period under report. Coverage is based on the data furnished by the State Governments/Union Territory Administrations and by the Central Nodal Ministries. A detailed analysis is made in the QPR to assess the relative performance of quarterly monitored items/parameters and the States/ Union Territories against the set targets. The QPR is sent to all state governments/ UT administrations and Central nodal Ministries for taking appropriate measures in the areas of concern.

The Annual Report on TPP-2006 covers information on all items (except the items which are not yet operational) under the programme. The information on these items is provided by the respective Central Nodal Ministries and states/ UTs.

Monitoring and Impact Assessment of Twenty Point Programme

The Ministry has so far undertaken two impact assessment studies. The first study relates to impact of MGNREGA in three selected districts of north--eastern states and the second study was on rehabilitation of disabled persons under Deendayal Disability Rehabilitation Scheme (DDRS) in the states of Delhi, Karnataka, Madhya Pradesh and West Bengal. The Ministry has also undertaken the task of critically examining the reports of evaluation undertaken by Niti Aayog (erstwhile Planning Commission) and by the Central Nodal Ministries of the schemes implemented by them.

Performance of Quarterly Monitored Items

Based on the data received from the Central Nodal Ministries and state governments/union territory administrations, an analysis of the overall performance of quarterly monitored items for the year 2014-15 and 2015-16 is given in the following paragraphs and in Tables 6.7 and 6.8. The analysis for the year 2014-15 as shown in Table 6.7 indicates that out of 22 targeted parameters of the TPP-2006, the performance under fifteen has been very good (90 per cent or above the targets). These items/parameters are: (i) SC families assisted under SCA to SCSP and NSFDC; (ii) urban poor families assisted under Seven Point Charter, (iii) Number of SHGs provided Community Investment Fund (CIF) during the financial year - NRLM; (iv) pumps sets energized; (v) Road constructed- PMGSY; (vi) Seedlings planted (Public and Forest Lands); (vii) Number of SHGs provided Revolving Fund (RF) during the financial year – NRLM; (viii) habitations covered

Table 6.7 : Performance of Quarterly Monitored Items under Twenty Point Programme-2006 during the Period April, 2014 to March, 2015

Sl. No.	Item Parameters	Units	Target April 2014-March 2015	Achievement April 2014-March 2015	Per cent Achievements w.r.t.the Target
Employment generated under MGNREGA					
1	No. of job cards issued	Number	-	21,10,947	-
2	Employment generated	Mandays	-	157.34 cr	-
3	Wages given	Rupees	-	2,35,22.38 cr	-
National Rural Livelihood Mission (NRLM)					
4	Number of SHGs promoted (New and Revived) during the financial year	Number	2,79,707	2,16,171	77
5	Number of SHGs provided Revolving Fund (RF) during the financial year (NRLM)	Number	1,33,290	1,46,875	110
6	Number of SHGs provided Community Investment Fund (CIF) during the Financial year (NRLM)	Number	75814	2,20,459	291
Distribution of waste land to landless					
7	Total Land distributed	Hectares	-	56,418 hectare	-
Minimum Wages Enforcement Act					
8	Inspections made (MW)	Number	-	3324	-
9	Irregularities datected (MW)	Number	-	1734	-
10	Irregularities rectified(MW)	Number	-	1516	-
11	Claims filed (MW)	Number	-	6	-
12	Claims settled (MW)	Number	-	13	-
13	Prosecution cases pending (MW)	Number	-	3	-

Sl. No.	Item Name	Units	Target April 2014-March 2015	Achievement April 2014-March 2015	Per cent Achievements w.r.t.the Target
14	Prosecution cases filed (MW)	Number	-	212	-
15	Prosecution cases decided (MW)	Number	-	101	-
Food Security:TPDS/NFSA					
16	Food Security: Targeted Public Distribution System (APL+BPL+AAY)	Lakh Tonnes	301.44	257.76	86
17	Food Security: Below Poverty Line (BPL)	Lakh Tonnes	104.93	96.12	92
18	Food Security: Antyodaya Anna Yojana (AAY)	Lakh Tonnes	59.25	56.39	95
19	Food Grains under NFSA - Normal	Lakh Tonnes	213.93	183.5	86
20	Food Grains under NFSA - Tide Over	Lakh Tonnes	4.76	4.61	97
Rural Housing - Indira Awaas Yojana (IAY)					
21	Houses constructed	Number	25,15,108	18,39,490	73
EWS/LIG Houses Constructed					
22	Housed constructed	Number	150000	1,28,559	86
National Rural Drinkng Water Programme(NRDWP)					
23	Partially covered habitations	Number	1,18,671	1,19,933	101
24	Coverage of quality affected hatbitations	Number	23427	15958	68
Sanitation programme in rural areas					
25	No. of Individual household latrines constructed	Number	-	58,54,987	-
Institutinal Delivery					
26	Delivery in institutions	Number	-	1,49,57,060	-
SC Families Assisted					
27	SC families assisted under SCA to SCSP & NSFDC	Number	1,80,000	19,57,119	1087
28	SC Students assisted under post matric scholarship	Number	-	38,83,199	-

Sl. No.	Item Name	Units	Target April 2014- March 2015	Achievement April 2014- March 2015	Per cent Achievements w.r.t.the Target
	Univeraslisation of ICDS Scheme				
29	ICDS Blocks Operational (Cumulative)	Number	6952	7024	101
	Functional Anganwadis				
30	Anganwadis Functional (Cumulative)	Number	13,53,081	13,43,711	99
	No. of urban poor families assisted under seven point charter				
31	Urban poor families assisted under Seven Point Charter	Number	132000	12,88,018	976
	Afforestation				
32	Area Covered under Plantation	Hectares	15,34,923	13,48,412	88
33	Seedlings planted	Number	1,01,88,81,000	1,22,44,06,605	120
	Rural Roads - Pradhan Mantri Grameen Sadak Yojana (PMGSY)				
34	Length of road constructed	Kms	21775	37157	171
	Deendayal Upadhyaya Gram Jyoti Yojana (DDUGJY)				
35	Villages Electrified	Number	14000	13232	95
	Energizing Pump sets				
36	No. of Pump sets energized	Number	3,61,458	6,56,846	182
	Supply of electricity				
37	Electricity supplied	Million Units	1050989	1013285	96

Out of 37 items /parameters, 22 items/parameters are targetable

(Partially covered & Slipped back) – NRDWP; (ix) ICDS Blocks Operational (Cum.); (x) anganwadis functional (Cum.); (xi) Food security-National Food Security Act (Tide Over)-NFSA; (xii) supply of electricity; (xiii) food security-Targeted Public Distribution System (only AAY); (xiv) Villages electrified – DDUGJY; (xv) food security - targeted public distribution system (only BPL).

The performance of four parameters has been 'Good' (80 per cent and above but less than 90 per cent of target).These items/parameters are: (i) area covered under plantation (Public and Forest Lands), (ii) houses constructed - EWS/LIG, (iii)food security-National Food Security Act (Normal)-NFSA, (iv) Food security-Targeted Public Distribution system (APL+BPL+AAY). The performance of three items/parameters viz. (i) Number of SHGs promoted (new and revived) during the financial year – NRLM; (ii) houses constructed – IAY; (iii) coverage of water quality affected habitations – NRDWP has been observed to be 'Poor' (below 80 per cent of target).

In 2015-16, one parameter "Urban poor families assisted under Seven Point Charter" became non-targetable and, therefore, the number of targeted parameters has decreased to 21 from 22. The analysis for the year 2015-16 as shown in Table 6.8 indicates that out of 21 targeted parameters of the TPP-2006, the performance under sixteen parameters of the TPP-2006 has been very good (90 per cent or above the targets). These items/parameters are: (i) SC families assisted under SCA to SCSP and NSFDC; (ii) villages electrified under DDUGJY; (iii) pump sets energized; (iv) seedlings planted (public and forest lands); (v) number of SHGs provided Revolving Fund (RF) during the financial year – NRLM; (vi) area covered under plantation (public and forest lands); (vii) partially covered habitations – NRDWP; (viii) road constructed – PMGSY; (ix) food security: targeted public distribution system only for BPL; (x) food security: targeted public distribution system only for AAY; (xi) houses constructed – IAY; (xii) ICDS blocks operational (Cum.); (xiii) supply of electricity); (xiv) anganwadis functional (Cum.); (xv) food security: targeted public distribution system for (AFL+ BPL+AAY); and (xvi) food security–national food security act (Normal) – NFSA

The performance of one parameter has been 'Good' (80 per cent and above but less than 90 per cent of target); (i) Food Security – National Food Security Act (Tide Over) – NFSA.

The performance of four items/parameters viz. (i) coverage of water quality affected habitations — NRDWP; (ii) number of SHGs promoted (new and revived) during the financial year – NRLM; (iii) houses constructed – EWS/LIG and (iv) number of SHGs provided Community Investment Fund (CIF) during the financial year – NRLM has been observed to be 'Poor' (below 80 per cent of target).

Infrastructure Monitoring

The monitoring of important infrastructure sectors in the country is designed to provide an overview of the performance and highlighting slippages, if any,

Table 6.8 : Performance of Quarterly Monitored Items under Twenty Point Programme-2006 during the period April, 2015 to March, 2016

Sl. No.	Item Name	Units	Target April, 2015 March, 2016	Achievement April, 2015- March, 2016	Per cent Achievements w.r.t. the Target
	Employment genenrated under MGNREGA				
1	No. of job cards issued	Number	-	3224415	-
2	Employment generated	Man days	-	195.79 Cr	-
3	Wages given	Rupees	-	26,445.21 Cr	-
	National Rural Livelihood Mission (NRLM)				
4	Number of SHGs promoted (New and Revived) during the financial year	Number	303086	226536	75
5	Number of SHGs provided Revolving Fund (RF) during the Financial year(NRLM)	Number	157874	188426	119
6	Number of SHGs provided Community Investment Fund (CIF) during the Financial year(NRLM)	Number	188818	101076	54
	Distribution of Waste Land to landless				
7	Total Land Distributed	Hectares	-	3868	-
	Minimum Wages Enforcement Act				
8	Inspections made (MW)	Number	-	190063	-
9	Irregularities datected (MW)	Number	-	23357	-
10	Irregularities rectified(MW)	Number	-	22531	-
11	Claims filed (MW)	Number	-	7052	-
12	Claims settled (MW)	Number	-	6770	-
13	Prosecution cases pending (MW)	Number	-	19369	-

Sl. No.	Item Name	Units	Target April, 2015 March, 2016	Achievement April, 2015- March, 2016	Per cent Achievements w.r.t. the Target
14	Prosecution cases filed (MW)	Number	-	1624	-
15	Prosecution cases decided (MW)	Number	-	707	-
Food Security:TPDS/NFSA					
16	Food Security: Targeted Public Distribution System (APL+BPL+AAY)	Lakh Tonnes	523.4	495.94	95
17	Food Security: Below Poverty Line (BPL)	Lakh Tonnes	83.13	87.59	105
18	Food Security: Antyodaya Anna Yojana (AAY)	Lakh Tonnes	46.16	47.72	103
19	Food Grains under NFSA - Normal	Lakh Tonnes	283.54	254.63	90
20	Food Grains under NFSA - Tide Over	Lakh Tonnes	5.91	5.09	86
Rural Housing - Indira Awaas Yojana (IAY)					
21	Houses constructed	Number	2079146	2080530	100
EWS/LIG Houses Constructed					
22	Housed constructed	Number	149999	109518	73
National Rural Drinkng Water Programme(NRDWP)					
23	Partially Covered Habitations	Number	47080	54979	117
24	Coverage of quality affected hatbitations	Number	10117	7621	75
Sanitation programme in rural areas					
25	No. of Individual household latrines constructed	Number	-	12741367	-
Institutinal Delivery					
26	Delivery in institutions	Number	-	161.17 lakh	-
SC Families Assisted					
27	SC families assisted under SCA to SCSP & NSFDC	Number	177699	388006	218

Sl. No.	Item Name	Units	Target April, 2015 March, 2016	Achievement April, 2015-March, 2016	Per cent Achievements w.r.t. the Target
28	SC Students assisted under post matric scholarship	Number	-	49.15 lakh	-
	Univeraslisation of ICDS Scheme				
29	ICDS Blocks Operational (Cumulative)	Number	7075	7029	99
	Functional Anganwadis				
30	Anganwadis Functional (Cumulative)	Number	1400000	1347312	96
	No. of urban poor families assisted under seven point charter				
31	Urban poor families assisted under Seven Point Charter	Number	-	25.77 lakh	-
	Afforestation				
32	Area Covered under Plantation	Hectares	1166651	1381596	118
33	Seedlings planted	Number	758332000	973843399	128
	Rural Roads - Pradhan Mantri Grameen Sadak Yojana (PMGSY)				
34	Length of road consturcted	Kms.	26000	30187	116
	Deendayal Upadhyaya Gram Jyoti Yojana (DDUGJY)				
35	Villages Electrified	Number	3501	7108	203
	Energizing Pump sets				
36	No. of Pumps sets energized	Number	349954	687248	196
	Supply of electricity				
37	Electricity supplied	Million Units	10,96,258	10,72,848	98

Out of 37 items/parameters, 21 items/parameters are targetable.

before the decision making authorities. This Ministry monitors the performance of the country's eleven key infrastructure sectors viz., power, coal, steel, railways, telecommunications, ports, fertilizers, cement, petroleum and natural gas, roads, and civil aviation. The performance of these sectors is analyzed with reference to the present targets for the month and for the cumulative period and the achievements during the corresponding month and cumulative period of the last year.

Infrastructure performance is regularly reported through the monthly review report on infrastructure performance.

Infrastructure Performance during April-July 2016

The overall infrastructure performance during April-July 2016 has shown positive trend of the growth. All sectors except crude oil, natural gas, goods traffic carried by railways, net addition in switching capacity of telephone exchanges and mobile phone connections recorded a positive growth over the performance for the corresponding period of the previous year. While the growth rate in respect of power generation, production of cement, refinery, upgradation of highways by State PWD and BRO, export cargo handled at airports and passengers handled at both terminals of the airports (domestic & international) were higher than the growth achieved during the corresponding period of the last year (April – July 2015).

However, as compared to the targets set for the period April – July 2016, most of the sectors except production of fertilizers, crude oil, natural gas, upgradation of highways and goods traffic carried by railways have more than their targets for the period. The trend in the overall infrastructure performance during April – July 2016 as compared to the target set for the period and the performance for the year 2015-16.

Members of Parliament Local area Development Scheme

The Members of Parliament Local Area Development Scheme (MPLADS) was launched on 23rd December, 1993 by the then Hon'ble Prime Minister. Initially, Ministry of Rural Development was the Nodal Ministry for this scheme. In October, 1994 this scheme was transferred to the Ministry of Statistics and Programme Implementation. The objective of MPLAD Scheme is enable Hon'ble MPs to recommend works of developmental nature with emphasizes on creation of durable community assets in the areas of national priorities, viz., Drinking water facility; education; electricity facility; health and family welfare; irrigation facility; non-conventional energy severs; railways, roads, pathways and bridges; sanitation and public health, etc. based on the locally felt needs. This Scheme is governed by a set of guidelines. The extant guidelines on MPLAD Scheme were revised and published in June 2016. The year wise funds released under MPLADS are given in Table 6.10.

The salient features of the MPLAD Scheme include: (i) MPLADS is a Central Plan Scheme fully funded by the Government of India under which funds are released in the form of grants-in-aid directly to the district authorities; (ii) The

Table 6.9 : Infrastructure Sector Performance during (April-July, 2016)

(Figures are quick estimates and provisional)

Sl. No.	Sector	Unit	Achievement 2015-16	April-October, 2016 Target	April-October, 2016 Achievement	April- July 2015 Actual	% Variation Over April-July 2016 Target	% Variation Over April-July 2015 Achieve.*
1.	Power Generation	BU	1173.59	389.27	420.86	389.80	8.11	7.97
2.	Coal Production	MT	637.87	191.78	196.89	186.72	2.67	5.45
3.	Finished Steel Production	MT	98.74	NA	35.22	34.37	-	2.46
4.	CementProduction	MT	283.18	NA	99.05	94.58	-	4.73
5.	Fertilizers Production	Lakh Tonne	177.38	62.75	57.01	54.74	-9.14	4.16
6.	Petroleum							
	i) Crude Oil Production	MT	36.95	12.16	12.08	12.45	-9.69	-2.95
	ii) RefineryProduction	MT	231.05	78.66	81.49	74.95	3.60	8.74
	iii) Natural GasProduction	MCM	322.49	107.56	104.49	108.62	-2.85	-3.80
7.	Roads-Upgradation of NH							
	i) NHAI	Km	1,988.00	1,534.00	673.00	617.00	-56.13	9.08
	ii) State PWD & BRO #	Km	1,426.70	833.00	806.74	436.35	-3.15	84.88
8.	Railways							
	Revenue earning goods traffic	MT	1,104.17	385.73	360.42	363.40	-6.56	-0.82

Sl. No.	Sector	Unit	Achievement 2015-16	April-October, 2016		April- July 2015 Actual	% Variation Over	
				Target	Achievement		April-July 2016 Target	April-July 2015 Achieve.*
9.	Shipping & Ports							
	i) Cargo handled at major ports	MT	606.37	NA	212.78	202.11	-	5.28
	ii) Coal handled at major ports	MT	130.05	NA	53.29	52.925	-	0.70
10.	Civil Aviation							
	i) Export Cargo handled at major Airport	Tonne	9,84,666	3,53,097	3,64,941	3,33,820	3.35	9.32
	ii) Import Cargo handled at major Airport	Tonne	6,73,475	2,28,525	2,36,383	2,22,105	3.44	6.43
	iii) Passengers handled at International Terminal	Lakh	546.71	190.21	191.69	175.28	0.78	9.36
	iv) Passengers handled at Domestic Terminal	Lakh	1,684.30	560.42	653.62	532.10	16.63	22.84
11.	Telecommunications							
	i) Addition in switching Capacity (Fixed+wireless)	"000" line	3,603.47	NA	1380.54	1,484.71	-	-7.02
	ii) Provision of net new wire line connections	"000" No.	-1,359.77	NA	-608.47	-490.01	-	-
	iii) Provision of net new Cell phone connections	"000" No.	64,572.79	NA	704.74	14,322.22	-	-95.08

#: Includes widening to four/six/eight lanes & two lanes and strengthening of existing weak pavements. * : Provisional BU : Billion Units
MT: Million Tonnes NA : Not Available MCM: Million cubic metre Km : Kilometer

Table 6.10: The year-wise funds released so far under the MPLADS Scheme

(in ₹ crore)

Year	Funds Released	Cumulative Release
1993-1994	37.80	37.80
1994-1995	771.00	808.80
1995-1996	763.00	1,571.80
1996-1997	778.00	2,349.80
1997-1998	488.00	2,837.80
1998-1999	789.5	3,627.30
1999-2000	1,390.50	5,017.80
2000-2001	2,080.00	7,097.80
2001-2002	1,800.00	8,897.80
2002-2003	1,600.00	10,497.80
2003-2004	1,682.00	12,179.80
2004-2005	1,310.00	13,489.80
2005-2006	1433.90	14923.70
2006-2007	1,451.50	16,375.20
2007-2008	1,470.55	17,845.75
2008-2009	1,580.00	19,425.75
2009-2010	1,531.05	20,957.25
2010-2011	1,533.31	22,490.56
2011-2012	2,507.68	24,998.25
2012-2013	3,722.00	28,720.25
2013-2014	3,937.00	32,657.25
2014-2015	3,350.00	36,007.25
2015-2016	3,502.00	39,509.25
2016-2017 (As on 30.09.2016)	1,668.00	41,177.25
Total	**41,176.79**	**3,83,501.81**

funds released under the Scheme are non-lapsable, i.e. the entitlement of funds not released in a particular year is carried forward to the subsequent years, subject to eligibility. At present, the annual entitlement per MP/constituency is ₹ 5 crore; (iii) under MPLADS, the role of the Members of Parliament is limited to recommend works. Thereafter, it is the responsibility of the district authority to sanction, execute and complete the works recommended by Members of Parliament within the stipulated time period; (v) the elected Lok Sabha Members can recommend works in their respective constituencies. The elected members of the Rajya Sabha can recommend works anywhere in the state from which they are elected. Nominated members of the Lok Sabha and Rajya Sabha can recommend works for implementation, anywhere in the country. (vi) MPLADS works can be implemented in areas affected by natural calamities like floods, cyclone, hailstorm, avalanche, cloudburst, pest attack, landslides, tornado, earthquake, drought, tsunami, fire and biological, chemical, radiological hazards, etc. MPs from the non-affected areas of the state/UT can also recommend permissible works upto a maximum of ₹ 25 lakh per annum in the affected area(s) in that state/UT; (vii) in order to accord special attention to the development of areas inhabited by Scheduled Castes (SCs) and Scheduled Tribes (STs), 15 per cent of MPLADS funds are to be utilized for areas inhabited by SC population and 7.5 per cent for areas inhabited by ST population; (viii) the MP can spend a maximum of ₹ 20 lakh per year for giving assistance to differently abled citizens for purchase of tri-cycles (including motorized tri-cycles), battery operated motorized wheel chair and artificial limbs; and aids for visually and hearing impaired; (ix) funds released by the Government of India are deposited by the District administrations in nationalized banks (including IDBI Banks)/Regional Rural Banks (Gramin Banks) which are on Core Banking Platform with the Nationalized Bank as their sponsor, for each MP for the purpose of MPLAD scheme; and (x) the roles of Central Government, state government, district authorities and implementing agencies have been clearly defined in the guidelines on MPLADS for implementation of MPLAD Scheme.

7 Commerce

THE Department of Commerce formulates, implements and monitors the Foreign Trade Policy (FTP) which provides basic policy and strategy framework to be followed for growth of exports trade. The Policy is periodically reviewed to incorporate changes necessary to take care of emerging economic scenarios both in the domestic and international economy. Besides, the Department is also entrusted with responsibilities to multilateral and bilateral commercial relations, Special Economic Zones, state trading, export promotion and trade facilitation, and development and regulation of certain export oriented industries and commodities.

Current Trade Situation: Global and India

A perusal of the performance of the global economy, since the financial crisis in 2008, indicates that while developed economies have been facing stagnant GDP growth rates, Emerging Market and Developing Economies (EMDEs) have seen recovery with divergent growth. In the current global economic situation, there are elements of risk, challenges and market volatility. This volatility is reflected in the impact of weakening commodity prices and difficult financial conditions, especially of oil exporters. As per the World Economic Outlook update of January, 2016, global growth, currently estimated at 3.1 per cent in 2015, is projected to be 3.4 per cent in 2016 and 3.6 per cent in 2017.

In advanced economies, a modest and uneven recovery is expected to continue, with a gradual further narrowing of output gaps. The picture for emerging market and developing economies is diverse but in many cases challenging. The slowdown and rebalancing of the Chinese economy, lower commodity prices, and strains in some large emerging market economies will continue to weigh growth prospects in 2016-17. The projected pickup in growth in the next two years – despite the ongoing slowdown in China is primarily based on forecasts of a gradual improvement of growth rates of countries such as Brazil, Russia, and some countries in the Middle East, though even this projected partial recovery could be impeded by new economic or political shocks.

World Trade Organization (WTO) lowered their forecast for world trade growth in 2015 to 2.8 per cent, from the 3.3 per cent forecast made in April, and reduced their estimate for 2016 to 3.9 per cent from 4.0 per cent. The projected trade growth of 3.9 per cent in 2016 is still below the average for the last 20 years (1995-2015) of 50 per cent. The downward revision by WTO is due to several factors including falling import demand in China, Brazil and other emerging economies; falling prices for oil and other primary commodities;

significant exchange rate fluctuations, volatility in financial markets and uncertainty regarding monetary policy of the United States.

In the decade of 2000s, China accounted for half of all incremental world demand for commodities. Its rebalancing has caused the global demand for – and price of – commodities to collapse. Oil is now under $ 30/barrel, one-third of its rate in 2014. Commodity exporting economies are in dire straits. Brazil and Russia are in recession. Many Asian manufacturing economies are part of global value chains using China as an assembler, and have also been hard hit by China's slowdown. India has been a resilient exception since it is a net commodity importer, and is not substantially a part of world value chains. But if the world falls into recession, India may also be affected.

Besides, since the global financial crisis, trade has been growing more slowly not only because world income growth is lower but also because trade itself has become much less responsive to income growth. Changes in the structure of trade associated with the expansion or contraction of global supply chains, changes in the composition of world trade, such as the relative importance of goods versus services, changes in the composition of world income, such as the relative importance of investment and consumption and changes in the trade regime, including the rise of protectionism is leading to fragmentation of the global marketplace.

Integration with Global Economy

Global value chains (GVCs) are a prominent feature of the international trade landscape today. Intermediate goods and services from several countries are combined through integrated production networks to produce the final goods and services. India participates in manufacturing GVCs, inter alia, in sectors such as chemicals, electrical equipment and jewellery, in general by way of sourcing intermediates from abroad. India also has a high participation in services sectors, in particular, business services, mainly driven by the use of Indian intermediates in the exports of other countries. The share of imported inputs and intermediate goods in exports is higher in mining, textiles, machinery, and services sectors such as distribution, transport and telecom. In general, inadequate infrastructure, sub-optimal connectivity with global transport networks, low transport capabilities and complicated administrative requirements that cause long delays at ports and customs, are some of the serious obstacles to participation by Indian producers in GVCs. In all these areas, they are at a disadvantage as compared to producers in the ASEAN countries and East Asia.

India to successfully integrate into value chains – regional or global – will need to strengthen trade-related physical infrastructure, implement an appropriate regulatory regime for transport services, improve efficiency and predictability in border procedures, undertake policy reforms in logistics services markets and reduce coordination failures. Also required is an enabling environment for industry to be able to both scale up and scale down their operations in response to demand. Mega-regional trading arrangements are

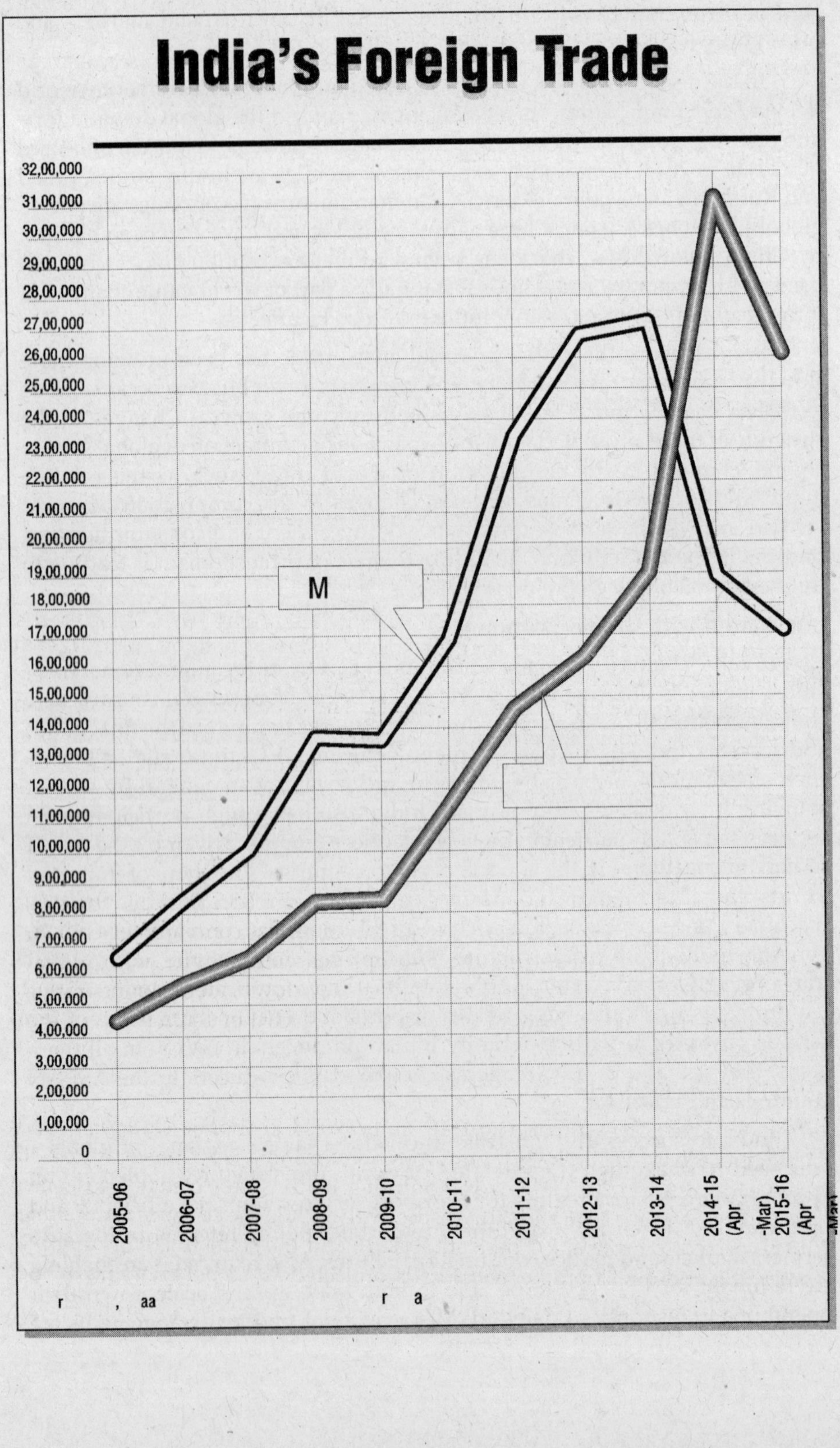
India's Foreign Trade
M
2005-06
2006-07
2007-08
2008-09
2009-10
2010-11
2011-12
2012-13
2013-14
2014-15 (Apr -Mar)
2015-16 (Apr

the other new features of the international trading landscape with the potential to bring about enormous changes in world trade dynamics, given their coverage and scope. They go well beyond trade in goods and services into areas such as investment, competition (including state-owned enterprises), intellectual property, labour, environment, government procurement, transparency, regulatory coherence and dispute settlement and have the capacity to restrict market access for non-members.

In 2015, a group of 12 Pacific Rim nations led by the United States signed the mega Trans Pacific Partnership (TPP), a regional trade agreement which is expected to set higher standards for trade in goods and services. The other two large regional trade agreements being negotiated are the Transatlantic Trade and Investment Partnership (TTIP) between the US and the European Union, and the Regional Comprehensive Economic Partnership (RCEP) between the Association of Southeast Asian Nations and its six partners, including China and India. The TPP, may challenge India's industry in many ways. Firstly, it will erode existing preferences for Indian products in established traditional markets such as the US benefitting those who are partners to these agreements. Secondly, they are likely to develop a rules architecture which will place a greater burden of compliance on India's manufacturing and services standards for access to the markets of the participating countries.

Following the devaluation of yuan by China, there has been a debate regarding whether India also needs to follow a similar path by ensuring that the rupee remains consistently undervalued in the REER index as a concrete measures to support its declining exports. The achievements of East Asian economies like Japan, Korea, Taiwan and more recently China indicate that these economies achieved their remarkable economic performance over three decades or longer with an undervalued exchange rate as one of the essential components of the macro-policy package.

Trade Scenario

India's merchandise exports reached a level of US$ 310.34 billion during 2014-15 registering a negative growth of 1.29 per cent as compared to a positive growth of 4.66 per cent during the previous year. Despite the recent setback faced by India's export sector due to global slowdown, merchandise exports recorded a Compound Annual Growth Rate (CAGR) of 14.02 per cent from 2004-05 to 2014-15.

World Trade Scenario

In their latest forecast made by IMF, in its World Economic Outlook (WEO) Update, January, 2016, the growth projection for India is 7.5 per cent for both the years 2016 and 2017. The world output growth is projected at 3.4 per cent and 3.6 per cent for 2016 and 2017 respectively. While the advanced economies are expected to grow at 2.1 per cent in 2016 and the same in 2017, growth of emerging and developing economies is projected at 4.3 per cent and 4.7 per cent for 2016 and 2017 respectively.

The expected growth in world trade volume has decreased in 2015 to 2.6 per cent from 3.4 per cent in 2014. However it is expected to recover to 3.4 per cent in 2016 and 4.1 per cent in 2017. As per WTO's International Trade Statistics 2015, in merchandise trade, India is the 19th largest exporter in the world with a share of 1.7 per cent and the 12th largest importer with a share of 2.4 per cent in 2014.

Exports

Exports recorded a negative growth of 18.03 per cent during April-Dec 2015-16 (P) over the corresponding period of the previous year in US$ term. The merchandise exports have reached US$ 196.68 billion in April-Dec 2015-16 (P).

Import

Cumulative value of import during Apr-Dec 2015-16 (P) was US$ 295.82 billion as against US $ 351.61 billion during the corresponding period of the previous year registering a negative growth of 15.87 per cent in US$ terms. Oil import were valued at US$ 54.62 billion during Apr-Dec 2015-16 (P) which was 44.59 per cent lower than oil import valued at US$ 98.57 billion in the corresponding period of previous year. Non-oil imports were valued at US$ 241.20 billion during Apr-Dec 2015-16 (P) which was 4.68 per cent lower than nonoil import of US$ 253.05 billion in previous year.

Trade Balance

The Trade deficit in Apr-Dec 2015-16 (P) was estimated at US$ 99.14 billion which was lower than the deficit of US$ 111.69 billion during the corresponding period of the previous year. Performance of exports, import and balance of trade during 2004-05 to 2015-16 (Apr- Dec) (P) is given in the table below:

Table A : Trade Data for Period 2004-05 to 2015-16 (P)

(₹ in crore)

Sl. No.	Year	Exports	Percentage Growth	Imports	Percentage Growth	Trade Balance
1	2004-2005	3,75,340	27.94	5,01.065	39.53	-1,25,725
2	2005-2006	4,56,418	21.6	6,60,409	31.8	-2,03,991
3	2006-2007	5,71,779	25.28	8,40,506	27.27	-2,68,727
4	2007-2008	6,55,864	14.71	10,12,312	20.44	-3,56,448
5	2008-2009	8,40,755	28.19	13,74,436	35.77	-5,33,680
6	2009-2010	8,45,534	0.57	13,63,736	-0.78	-5,18,202
7	2010-2011	11,36,964	34.47	16,83,467	23.45	-5,46,503
8	2011-2012	14,65,959	28.94	23,45,463	39.32	-8,79,504

9	2012-2013	16,34,318	11.48	26,69,162	13.8	-10,34,844
10	2013-2014	19,05,011	16.56	27,15,434	1.73	-8,10,423
11	2014-2015	18,96,348	-0.45	27,37,087	0.8	-8,40,738
12	April-December 2014	14,58,094	-	21,36,855	-	-6,78,761
13	April-December 2015(P)	12,73,734	-12.64	19,15,821	-10.34	-6,42,087

Data Source: DGCIS, Kolkata

Table B : Trade Data for period 2004-05 to 2015-16 (P)

(US$ million)

Sl. No.	Year	Exports	Percentage Growth	Imports	Percentage Growth	Trade Balance
1	2004-2005	83,536	30.85	1,11,517	42.7	-27.981
2	2005-2006	1,03,091	23.41	1,49,166	33.76	-46.075
3	2006-2007	1,26,414	22.62	1,85,735	24.52	-59.321
4	2007-2008	1,63,132	29.05	2,51,654	35.49	-88,522
5	2008-2009	1,85,295	13.59	3,03,696	20.68	-1,18,401
6	2009-2010	1,78,751	-3.53	2,88,373	-5.05	-1,09,621
7	2010-2011	2,49,816	39.76	3,69,769	28.23	-1,19,954
8	2011-2012	3,05,964	22.48	4,89,319	32.33	-1,83,356
9	2012-2013	3,00,401	-1.82	4,90,737	0.29	-1,90,336
10	2013-2014	3,14,405	4.66	4,50,200	-8.26	-1,35,794
11	2014-2015	3,10,338	-1.29	4,48,033	-0.48	-1,37,695
12	April-December 2014	2,39,929	-	3,51,614	-	-1,11,685
13	April-December 2015(P)	1,96,679	-18.09	2,95,821	-15.87	-99,142

Data Source: DGCIS, Kolkata

Exports by Principal Commodities

Disaggregated data on exports of principal commodities, dollar terms available for the period Apr-Dec 2015-16(P) as compared to Apr-Dec 2014-15 are given in appendix I (A). Exports of the top five commodities during the period Apr-Dec 2015-16 (P) registered a share of 32.60 per cent mainly due to significant contribution in the exports of petroleum products; pearl, precious, semi-precious stones; drug formulations biological; gold and other precious metal jewellery; and RMG cotton including accessories.

Table 02 (FA) Export of Principal Commodities

(US$ Million, Growth and Share)

	Commodity	Apr-Mar 2014	Apr-Mar 2015	Apr-Dec 2014	Apr-Dec 2015 (P)	% age Growth	% age Share
1.	**Plantation**	**1,625.05**	**1,502.88**	**1,116.77**	**1,155.25**	**3.45**	**0.59**
	Tea	798.76	681.79	531.01	559.68	5.4	0.28
	Coffee	798.8	814.02	580.65	564.42	-2.8	0.29
	Natural Rubber	27.49	7.06	5.11	31.15	509.58	0.02
2.	**Agri & Allied Products**	**32,953.57**	**30,147.31**	**22,991.80**	**18,047.00**	**-21.51**	**9.18**
	Rice-Basmati	4,864.69	4,516.28	3,370.49	2,717.73	-19.37	1.38
	Rice (other than Basmati)	2,925.05	3,336.84	2,488.98	1,717.70	-30.99	0.87
	Wheat	1,569.03	828.75	778.42	134.6	-82.71	0.07
	Other Cereals	1,204.11	869.11	742.89	193.14	-74	0.1
	Pulses	290.27	199.86	164.18	172.2	4.88	0.09
	Tobacco Unmanufactured	789.04	680.01	493.75	453.05	-8.24	0.23
	Tobacco Manufactured	222.31	278.61	205.64	222.72	8.3	0.11
	Spices	2,497.22	2,430.35	1,845.36	1.853.37	0.43	0.94
	Cashew	842.3	909.26	686.92	593.02	-13.67	0.3
	Cashew Nut Shell Liquid	6.35	9.1	6.02	6.91	14.75	0
	Sesame Seeds	592.14	772.27	640.8	345.86	-46.03	0.18
	Niger Seeds	18.69	17.71	10.69	15.73	47.12	0.01
	Groundnut	525.67	760.37	535.87	421.77	-21.29	0.21
	Other Oil Seeds	155.17	185.03	133.24	116.04	-12.91	0.06
	Vegetable Oils	53.38	94.56	69.15	55.25	-20.11	0.03
	Oil Meals	2,796.34	1,324.17	946.15	441.39	-53.35	0.22
	Guergam Meal	1,979.63	1,551.87	1,292.26	417.87	-67.66	0.21
	Castor Oil	725.68	770.49	554.12	537.02	-3.09	0.27
	Shellac	84.95	43.8	34.4	19.4	-43.61	0.01
	Sugar	1,177.03	871.41	606.05	937.58	54.7	0.48
	Mollases	24.53	31.61	21.34	71.1	233.21	0.04
	Fruits/Vegetable Seeds	68.8	69.96	54.04	50.97	-5.67	0.03
	Fresh Fruits	608.96	516.26	326.44	311.4	-4.61	0.16
	Fresh Vegetables	886.12	763.24	572.76	553.78	-3.31	0.28
	Processed Vegetables	213.04	281.75	203.47	179.83	-11.62	0.09
	Processed Fruits and Juices	547.12	592.26	438.66	419.32	-4.41	0.21
	Cereal Preparatations	471.31	496.41	367.84	376.12	2.25	0.19
	Cocoa Products	93.96	138.87	101.1	142.67	41.11	0.07
	Milled Products	166.15	168.76	134.92	125.8	-6.76	0.06
	Miscellaneous Processed Items	418.03	453.66	342.69	332.31	-3.03	0.17
	Animal Casings	4.73	3.18	2.75	2.37	-13.99	0
	Buffalo Meat	4,350.23	4,781.18	3,769.99	3,171.04	-15.89	1.61
	Sheep/Goat Meat	115.36	135.71	105.29	99.38	-5.61	0.05
	Other Meat	0.55	0.44	0.41	0	-99.46	0
	Processed Meat	1.29	2.29	0.55	0.95	73.48	0

	Dairy Products	727.52	355.83	267.66	196.07	-26.75	0.1
	Poultry Products	93.02	106.38	79.59	89.95	13.02	0.05
	Floriculture Products	75.31	75.4	54.57	52.33	-4.12	0.03
	Alcoholic Beverages	401.51	369.59	271.34	237.09	-12.62	0.12
	Ayush and Herbal Products	366.97	354.68	271.01	262.17	-3.26	0.13
3	**Marine Products**	**5,016.46**	**5,510.49**	**4,432.69**	**3.778.74**	**-14.75**	**1.92**
	Marine Products	5,016.46	5,510.49	4,432.69	3,778.74	-14.75	1.92
4	**Ores & Minerals**	**3,583.86**	**2,410.18**	**1,817.59**	**1,418.02**	**-21.98**	**0.72**
	Iron Ore	1,557.58	526.5	421.11	103.81	-75.35	0.05
	Mica	50.73	56.02	42.38	39.67	-6.39	0.02
	Coal, Coke and Briquities, etc	208.13	136.51	86.68	88.44	2.03	0.04
	Bulk Minerals and Ores	460.56	443.94	334.88	406.06	21.26	0.21
	Processed Minerals	1,003.59	1,034.38	784.35	646.08	-17.63	0.33
	Sulphur, Unroasted Iron Pyrite	66.26	60.57	33.55	62.02	84.87	0.03
	Other Crude Minerals	237.01	152.26	114.63	71.93	-37.25	0.04
5	**Leather & Leather Manufactures**	**5,722.54**	**6,195.21**	**4,754.24**	**4,219.38**	**-11.25**	**2.15**
	Raw Hides and Skins	4.91	2.41	1.69	0.27	-84.03	0
	Finished Leather	1,285.11	1,1331.24	1,014.36	809.87	-22.45	0.41
	Leather Goods	1,350.01	1,453.19	1,100.81	1,048.07	-4.79	0.53
	Leather Garments	591.8	604.58	468.4	430.37	-8.12	0.22
	Footwear of Leather	2,025.65	2,279.00	1,725.48	1,599.81	-7.28	0.81
	Leather Footwear Components	320.01	361.94	287.36	221.02	-23.09	0.11
	Saddlery and Harness	145.05	162.85	126.14	109.97	-12.82	0.06
6	**Gems & Jewellery**	**41,389.07**	**41,266.07**	**31,258.27**	**28,711.17**	**-8.15**	**14.6**
	Pearl, Precious, Semi Precious Stone	27,159.49	24,758.79	18,471.87	16,161.08	-12.51	8.22
	Gold	3,031.84	2,845.15	1,593.79	4,316.53	170.83	2.19
	Silver	18.52	5.68	5.26	5.95	13.28	0
	Other Precious and Base Metals	321.53	414.05	283.03	319.15	12.76	0.16
	Gold and Other Precious Metal Jewellery	10,857.70	13,242.41	10,904.31	7,908.46	-27.47	4.02
7	**Sports Goods**	**236.45**	**274.5**	**215.14**	**179.27**	**-16.68**	**0.09**
	Sports Goods	236.45	274.5	215.14	179.27	-16.68	0.09
8	**Chemicals & Related Products**	**30,793.62**	**31,731.22**	**23,849.90**	**23,932.23**	**0.35**	**12.17**
	Fertilizers Crude	6.42	7.75	5.52	8.72	57.92	0
	Fertilizers Manufactured	75.39	82.54	49	57.9	18.15	0.03
	Bulk Drugs, Drug Intermediates	3,610.70	3,561.39	2,571.53	2,687.53	4.51	1.37
	Dye Intermediates	248.14	239.85	187.27	142.32	-24	0.07
	Dyes	1,904.67	2,129.98	1,646.18	1,401.89	-14.84	0.71
	Drug Formulations, Biologicals	10,669.04	11,215.86	8,466.73	9,480.72	11.98	4.82
	Agro Chemicals	1,923.64	1,951.77	1,447.34	1,423.84	-1.62	0.72
	Inorganic Chemicals	721.25	683.59	519.22	459.64	-11.48	0.23
	Organic Chemicals	5,641.15	5,394.35	4,122.27	3,627.76	-12	1.84
	Other Miscellaneous Chemicals	655.11	742.21	535.88	512.74	-4.32	0.26

	Cosmetics and Toiletries	1,325.86	1,404.01	1,044.50	1,004.44	-3.84	0.51
	Essential Oils	71	90.17	66.77	78.38	17.4	0.04
	Residual Chemical and Allied Products	3,225.27	3,490.25	2,621.38	2,554.00	-2.57	1.3
	Paint, Varnish and Allied Products	645.91	669.06	515.77	441.38	-14.42	0.22
	Graphic Explosive & Accessor	70.07	68.46	50.54	50.97	0.84	0.03
9.	**Plastic & Rubber Articles**	**6,860.02**	**6,615.17**	**5,207.69**	**4,837.23**	**-7.11**	**2.46**
	Other Rubber Product except Footwear	964.16	1,071.11	818.35	685.62	-16.22	0.35
	Footwear of Rubber, Canvas, etc.	201.56	307.2	239.92	242.39	1.03	0.12
	Moulded and Extruded Goods	919.31	988.24	745.4	772.41	3.62	0.39
	Plastic Raw Materials	3,045.64	2,508.66	2,067.83	1,893.78	-8.42	0.96
	Plastic Sheet, Film, Plastic, etc.	1,082.61	1,068.79	819.39	791.19	-3.44	0.4
	Stationry/Office School Supply	226.02	250.07	186.87	181.21	-3.03	0.09
	Other Plastic Items	420.74	421.1	329.94	270.64	-17.97	0.14
10	**Articles of Stone, Plaster, Cement, Asbestos, MICA or Similar Matrials; Carmaic Procuts; Glass and Glassware**	**3,600.58**	**4,042.51**	**3,049.43**	**2,868.79**	**-5.92**	**1.46**
	Granite, Natural Stone and Products	1,996.23	2,019.82	1,524.38	1,356.78	-10.99	0.69
	Cement Clinker and Asbestos Cement	312.26	378.31	282.95	221.27	-21.8	0.11
	Ceramics and Allied Products	633.68	925.89	686.55	731.89	6.6	0.37
	Glass and Glassware	658.41	718.49	555.55	558.84	0.59	0.28
11	**Paper & Related Products**	**2,099.81**	**2,180.66**	**1,647.23**	**1,776.52**	**7.85**	**0.9**
	Books, Publications and Printing	306.19	265.66	203.48	213.72	5.03	0.11
	Newsprint	2.49	8.05	7.57	1.85	-75.6	0
	Paper, Paperboard and Products	1,077.18	1,182.01	893.25	885.5	-0.87	0.45
	Other Wood and Wood Products	709.08	714.81	536.73	584.76	8.95	0.3
	Pulp and Waste Paper	4.32	2.22	2.05	81.74	3,886.53	0.04
12	**Base Metals**	**22,365.63**	**24,742.75**	**18,465.98**	**14,316.45**	**-22.47**	**7.28**
	Iron and Steel	9,223.40	8,684.40	6,665.52	4,363.32	-34.54	2.22
	Products of Iron and Steel	6,780.18	7,562.81	5,668.86	4,613.43	-18.62	2.35
	Aluminium, Products of Aluminium	1,943.18	2,859.37	2,028.33	1,962.69	-3.24	1
	Copper and Products made of Copper	2,855.01	3,420.30	2,603.47	1,979.26	-23.98	1.01
	Lead and Products Made of lead	194.7	173.2	140.35	143.23	2.06	0.07
	Nickel and Products Made of Nickel	437.25	897.58	578.95	437.48	-24.44	0.22
	Tin and Products Made of Tin	80.39	37.73	32.43	41.04	26.55	0.02

	Zinc and Products Made of Zinc	435.38	608.06	369.44	4.55.92	23.41	0.23
	Other Non Ferrous Metal and Products	416.13	499.29	378.53	320.08	-15.44	0.16
13	**Optional, Medical & Surgical Instruments**	**1,562.96**	**1,686.34**	**1,279.02**	**1,196.171**	**-6.48**	**10.61**
	Surgicals	302.35	299.57	229.12	212.73	-7.16	0.11
	Optical Items (Including Lens, etc.)	293.55	306.34	233.9	258.44	10.49	0.13
	Medical and Scientific Instruments	967.06	1,080.43	816.01	725	-11.15	0.37
14	**Electronic Items**	**7,634.85**	**6,009.07**	**4,581.54**	**4,130.82**	**-9.84**	**2.1**
	Computer Hardware, Peripherals	387.45	346.44	267.07	286.8	7.38	0.15
	Consumer Electronics	834.57	808.01	629.39	468.78	-25.52	0.24
	Electronics Components	1,819.39	1,880.45	1,457.67	1,368.79	-6.1	0.7
	Electronics Instruments	1,536.56	1,900.91	1,395.15	1,421.59	1.89	0.72
	Telecom Instruments	3,056.89	1,073.26	832.25	584.88	-29.72	0.3
15	**Machinery**	**17,569.36**	**19,705.35**	**14,723.90**	**14,067.35**	**-4.46**	**7.15**
	Electrodes	37.88	38.6	28.95	31.61	9.2	0.02
	Accumulators and Batteries	170.06	213.06	158.97	142.9	-10.11	0.07
	HND Tool, Cutting Tool of Metals	711.1	755.7	572.91	487.31	-14.94	0.25
	Machine Tools	335.13	376.89	275.06	298.64	8.57	0.15
	AC Refrigeration Machinery, etc.	1,164.08	1,168.33	872.64	778.95	-10.74	0.4
	Cranes, lifts and Winches	309.71	341.79	230.61	285.6	23.84	0.15
	Electric Machinery and Equipment	3,683.19	3,974.08	2,943.96	2,870.39	-2.5	1.46
	IC Engines and Parts	1,170.30	2,397.98	1,881.08	1,443.56	-23.26	0.73
	Industrial Machnery for Dairy, etc.	4,276.13	4,769.28	3,524.97	3,449.05	-2.15	1.75
	ATM, Injecting Molding Machinery, etc	1,244.17	1,344.40	984.34	931.34	-5.38	0.47
	Nuclear Reactor, including boiler, Part	563.08	603.89	450.6	489.49	8.63	0.25
	Other Construction Machinery	1,008.62	1,177.40	892.92	811.54	-9.11	0.41
	Other Miscellanceous Engineering Items	1,585.91	1,751.50	1,318.39	1,501.19	13.86	0.76
	Prime Mica and Mica Prdocuts	19.1	19.51	14.12	13.06	-7.5	0.01
	Pumps of all types	690.89	773.24	574.38	532.73	-7.25	0.27
16	**Office Equipment**	**30.89**	**54.77**	**39.13**	**65.72**	**67.96**	**0.03**
	Office Equipment	30.89	54.77	39.13	65.72	67.96	0.03
17	**Transport Equipment**	**22,164.67**	**26,636.37**	**20,327.83**	**15,928.67**	**-21.64**	**8.1**
	Auto Tyres and Tubes	1,687.47	1,648.11	1,270.70	1,020.89	-19.66	0.52
	Auto Components/Parts	3,971.62	4,438.56	3,329.37	3,110.30	-6.58	1.58
	Bicycle and Parts	348.65	354.16	264.84	214.33	-19.07	0.11

	Aircraft, Spacecraft and Parts	4,584.87	6,159.19	5,121.40	2,742.69	-46.45	1.39
	Motor Vehicle/Cars	6,147.71	6,684.05	5,170.12	5,001.01	-3.27	2.54
	Railway Transport Equipments, Parts	178.17	135.35	109.36	58.62	-46.4	0.03
	Ship, Boat and Floating Structure	3,724.76	5,352.61	3,610.30	2,410.22	-33.24	1.23
	Two and Three Wheelers	1,521.42	1,864.34	1,451.73	1,370.62	-5.59	0.7
18	**Project Goods**	**47.35**	**36.59**	**24.36**	**14.37**	**-41.01**	**0.01**
	Project Goods	47.35	36.59	24.36	14.37	-41.01	0.01
19	**Textiles & Allied Products**	**36,967.56**	**37,140.74**	**27,303.40**	**26,830.46**	**-1.73**	**13.64**
	Manmade Staple Fibre	597.79	551.59	415.06	397.3	-4.28	0.2
	Cotton Yarn	4,550.26	3,937.41	2,906.28	2,755.48	-5.19	1.4
	Cotton Fabrics, Madeups, etc.	5,118.47	5,516.42	4,131.17	3,948.47	-4.42	2.01
	Other Textile Yarn, Fabric Madeup Article	422.09	399.59	302.59	251.45	-16.9	0.13
	Silk, Raw	0.04	0.11	0.06	0.21	287.14	0
	Natural Silk Yarn, Fabrics, Madeup	142.93	124.97	96.87	66.72	-31.12	0.03
	Manmade Yarn, Fabrics, Madeups	5,183.47	5,275.03	3,983.75	3,574.93	-10.26	1.82
	Wool, Raw	0.02	0.04	0.02	0.24	1,323.81	0
	Wollen Yarn, Fabrics, Madeups, etc.	127.07	201.85	147.36	146.74	-0.42	0.07
	RMG Cotton including Accessories	9,106.39	9,282.83	6,733.52	6,566.81	-2.48	3.34
	RMG Silk	236.54	303.97	216.54	197.46	-8.81	0.1
	RMG Manmade Fibres	3,148.83	3,997.13	2,815.94	3,059.26	8.64	1.56
	RMG Wool	307.47	307.75	256.14	225.3	-12.04	0.11
	RMG of other Textile Material	2,190.68	2,941.65	2,116.08	2,376.14	12.29	1.21
	Coir and Coir Manufactures	229,85	285.13	213.69	173.19	-18.95	0.09
	Handloom Products	373.01	369.56	275.06	283.63	3.11	0.14
	Silk Waste	16.25	17.86	13.92	11.22	-19.41	0.01
	Jute, Raw	18.81	19.41	13.85	7.66	-44.69	0
	Jute Yarn	23.46	22.64	15.37	15.6	1.55	0.01
	Jute Hessian	141.7	126	93.32	86.36	-7.46	0.04
	Floor Covering of Jute	63.6	86.3	65.06	52.09	-19.93	0.03
	Other Jute Manufactures	152.82	112.55	91.76	203.42	121.68	0.1
	Carpet (Excluding Silk) Handmade	1,175.73	1,358.17	1,047.06	1,085.19	3.64	0.55
	Silk Carpet	2.57	2.62	2.16	1.7	-21.14	0
	Cotton Raw including Waste	3,637.53	1,900.19	1,350.77	1,343.86	-0.51	0.68

20	**Petroleum Crude & Products**	**63,177.46**	**56,794.15**	**48,569.59**	**23,987.92**	**-50.61**	**12.2**
	Petroleum Crude & Petroleum Products	63,177.46	56,794.15	48,569.59	23,987.92	-50.61	12.2
21.	**Others**	**9,003.52**	**5,656.13**	**4,273.40**	**5,217.96**	**22.1**	**2.65**
	Other Commodities	6,666.75	3,431.80	2,606.80	3,354.83	28.7	1.71
	Human Hair, Products Thereof	384	336.37	238.77	225.17	-5.7	0.11
	Packaging Materials	453.32	509.93	382.41	416.59	8.94	0.21
	Handicrafts (Excluding Handmade Carpets)	1,499.45	1,378.04	1,045.42	1,221.38	16.83	0.62
	Total	**3,14,405.29**	**3,10,338.47**	**2,39,928.90**	**1,96,679.49**	**-18.03**	**100**

Imports by Principal Commodities

Disaggregated data on import by principal commodities, in Dollar terms, available for the period Apr-Dec 2015-16 (P) as compared to Apr-Dec 2014-15 show some progress. Import of the top five commodities during the period Apr-Dec 2015-16 (P) registered a share of 41.15 per cent mainly due to significant import of petroleum crude; gold; pearls, precious and semi-precious stones; petroleum products; and telecom instruments.

Table 03 (TA) : Import of Principal Commodities

(US$ Million, Growth and Share)

	Commodity	Apr-Mar 2014	Apr-Mar 2015	Apr-Dec 2014	Apr-Dec 2015 (P)	% age Growth	% age Share
1.	**Plantation**	**1,075.13**	**1,034.06**	**836.83**	**713.26**	**-14.77**	**0.24**
	Tea	48.54	63.57	47.4	45.47	-4.06	0.02
	Coffee	120.18	152.2	118.5	93.74	-20.9	0.03
	Natural Rubber	906.41	818.29	670.94	574.05	-14.44	0.19
2.	**Agri & Allied Products**	**13,492.25**	**19,004.14**	**14,864.09**	**15,885.04**	**6.87**	**5.37**
	Rice-Basmati	-	-	-	-	-	-
	Rice (other than Basmati)	1.37	1.77	1.35	0.72	-46.56	0
	Wheat	4.42	9.95	6.18	131.04	2,020.76	0.04
	Other Cereals	16.08	10.03	5.09	18.19	257.25	0.01
	Pulses	1,828.16	2,786.11	2,186.18	2,956.30	35.23	1
	Tobacco Unmanufactured	13.09	15.9	12.14	9.18	-24.38	0
	Tobacco Manufactured	27.85	32.76	24.49	23.73	-3.09	0.01
	Spices	571.36	717.78	523.3	593.03	13.33	0.2
	Cashew	773.78	1,087.16	904.66	1,146.66	26.75	0.39
	Cashew Nut Shell Liquid	0.34	1.63	1.11	0.87	-21.52	0
	Sesame Seeds	134.48	62.67	53.64	21.11	-60.64	0.01
	Niger Seeds	0	0.6	0.07	5.36	7,812.09	0
	Groundnut	0.06	0.08	0.02	0.03	21.17	0
	Other Oil Seeds	27.5	26.59	15.96	18.69	17.13	0.01

	Vegetable Oils	7,249.85	10,621.48	8,279.12	8,102.59	-2.13	2.74
	Oil Meals	33.33	44.71	35.62	38.18	7.2	0,01
	Guergam Meal	3.66	0.95	0.87	0.39	-55.5	0
	Castor Oil	0.34	0.3	0.18	0.1	-45.13	0
	Shellac	8.01	9.75	7.08	2.29	-67.62	0
	Sugar	392.18	601.17	527.53	425.35	-19.37	0.14
	Mollases	1.47	4.93	3.6	0.82	-77.26	0
	Fruits/Vegetable Seeds	74.36	100.48	83	87.6	5.54	0.03
	Fresh Fruits	1,273.44	1,565.20	1,205.22	1,335.47	10.81	0.45
	Fresh Vegetables	6.66	1.82	1.57	32.05	1,936.50	0.01
	Processed Vegetables	28.79	17.07	12.62	13.66	8.24	0
	Processed Fruits and Juices	68.28	81.58	61.25	56.92	-7.07	0.02
	Cereal Preparations	69.15	95.44	71.71	67.33	-6.11	0.02
	Cocoa Products	176.89	253.58	205.13	155.91	-24	0.05
	Milled Products	3.64	2.9	2.25	2.23	-1	0
	Miscellaneous Processed Items	244.47	292.05	216.33	197.02	-8.93	0.07
	Animal Casings	0	0	0	0	0	0
	Sheep/Goat Meat	0.86	1.43	1.13	0.51	-54.71	0
	Other Meat	2.61	3.19	2.41	2.17	-10.29	0
	Processed Meat	1.27	0.85	0.74	0.36	-52.15	0
	Dairy Products	38.46	61.49	50.2	43.19	-13.97	0.01
	Poultry Products	3.89	6.18	4,8	3.37	-29.77	0
	Floriculture Products	18.45	18.52	13.4	12.72	-5.06	0
	Alcoholic Beverages	341.26	408.47	300.06	339.3	13.08	0.11
	Ayush and Herbal Products	52.46	57.58	44.07	40.6	-7.86	0.01
3	**Marine Products**	**67.65**	**73.93**	**50.57**	**65.64**	**29.8**	**0.02**
	Marine Products	67.65	73.93	50.57	65.64	29.8	0.02
4	**Ores & Minerals**	**24,603.63**	**26,917.86**	**20,030.04**	**15,820.49**	**-21.02**	**5.35**
	Iron Ore	57.4	1,067.86	675.81	425.28	-37.07	0.14
	Mica	0.6	0,63	0.47	0.56	19.53	0
	Coal, Coke and Briquities, etc.	16,403.03	17,802.56	13,072.90	10,203.50	-21.95	3.45
	Bulk Minerals and Ores	6,813.64	6,622.98	5,193.75	4,233.41	-18.49	1.43
	Processed Minerals	836.6	739.15	559.42	538.19	-3.8	0.18
	Sulpher, Unroasted Iron Pyrite	183.1	286.41	215.75	168.69	-21.81	0.06
	Other Crude Minerals	309.25	398.27	311.94	250.87	-19.58	0.08
5	**Leather & Leather Manufactures**	**901.49**	**1,092.62**	**818.92**	**773.86**	**-5.5**	**0.26**
	Raw Hides and Skins	78.03	87.19	67.53	48.63	-27.98	0.02
	Finished Leather	501.83	646.24	490.29	451.96	-7.82	0.15
	Leather Goods	67.27	76.53	57.54	61.22	6.39	0.02
	Leather Garments	2.23	2.1	1.75	5.79	231.05	0
	Footwear of Leather	229.91	253.87	181.24	184.64	1.88	0.06
	Leather Footwear Component	22.03	26.32	20.31	21.42	5.5	0.01
	Saddlery and Harness	0.02	0.37	0.27	0.19	-29.73	0

6	**Gems & Jewellery**	**58,436.49**	**62,351.34**	**47.722.68**	**45,013.39**	**-5.68**	**15.22**
	Pearl, Precious, Semi-Procious Stone	23,987.59	22,598.25	17,796.24	14,565.49	-18.15	4.92
	Gold	28,704.13	34,407.18	25,868.31	26,478.70	2.36	8.95
	Silver	4,539.88	4,523.51	3,459.40	3,198.77	-7.53	1.08
	Other Precious and Base Metals	239.51	250.48	188.54	172.71	-8.4	0.06
	Gold and other Precious Metal Jewellery	965.39	571.93	410.19	597.72	45.72	0.2
7	**Sports Goods**	**203.05**	**201.29**	**148.99**	**162.21**	**8.87**	**0.05**
	Sports Goods	203.05	201.29	148.99	162.21	8.87	0.05
8	**Chemicals & Related Products**	**35,645.21**	**38,553.65**	**30,356.37**	**29,320.62**	**-3.41**	**9.91**
	Fertilizers Crude	926.07	1,026.79	772.5	812.17	5.14	0.27
	Fertilizers Manufactured	5,337.77	6,371.93	5,171.48	6,284.53	21.52	2.12
	Bulk Drugs, Drug Intermediates	3,146.66	3,245.64	2,457.45	2,510.41	2.16	0.85
	Dye Intermediates	832.97	774.79	612.39	486.6	-20.54	0.16
	Dyes	320.25	328.41	255.47	239.06	-6.42	0.08
	Drug Formulations, Biologicals	1,491.68	1,562.54	1,217.25	1,209.94	-0.6	0.41
	Agro Chemicals	852.2	980.69	792.54	703.21	-11.27	0.24
	Inorganic Chemicals	4,040.29	4,494.25	3,453.70	3,394.82	-1.7	1.15
	Organic Chemicals	11,067.14	11,341.68	9,130.82	7,565.12	-17.15	2.56
	Other Miscellaenious Chemicals	552.16	670.45	520.93	465.25	-10.69	0.16
	Cosmetics and Toiletries	834.35	989.72	781.1	703.33	-9.96	0.24
	Essential Oils	100.14	116.24	90	91.55	1.72	0.03
	Residual Chemical and Allied Products	4,723.54	5,166.22	3,937.95	3,777.30	-4.08	1.28
	Paint, Varnish and Allied Products	1,265.79	1,344.56	1,049.91	1,026.85	-2.2	0.35
	Graphite, Explosives and Accesor	154.2	139.75	112.88	50.47	-55.29	0.02
9.	**Plastic & Rubber Articles**	**12,768.93**	**14,326.69**	**11,265.83**	**10,666.54**	**-5.32**	**3.61**
	Other Rubber Products except Footwear	2,084.11	1,992.76	1,591.09	1,301.40	-18.21	0.44
	Footwear of Rubber, Canvas, etc.	146.02	180.36	132.37	144.51	9.17	0.05
	Moulded and Extruded Goods	1,028.87	1,129.34	852.21	890.89	4.54	0.3
	Plastic Raw Materials	7,839.33	9,223.19	7,317.52	6,896.62	-5.75	2.33
	Plastic Sheet, Film, Plastic, etc.	933.78	1,008.95	775.04	819.74	5.77	0.28
	Stationery/Office School Supply	71.43	81.72	61.91	66.22	6.95	0.02
	Other Plastic Items	665.39	710.36	535.69	547,16	2.14	0.18
10	**Articles of Stone, Plaster, Cement, Asbestos, MICA or Similar Materials; Ceramic Products; Glass and Glassware**	**2,047.01**	**2,373.87**	**1,730.76**	**1,900.71**	**9.82**	**0.64**
	Granite, Natural Stone and Product	438	472.06	329.1	404.9	23.03	0.14
	Cement Clinker and Asbestos Cement	68.34	91.93	68.06	72.82	7	0.02

	Ceramics and Allied Products	769.52	918.65	666.57	703.75	5.58	0.24
	Glass and Glassware	771.15	891.22	667.03	719.24	7.83	0.24
11	**Paper & Related Products**	**7,402.22**	**7,636.46**	**5,842.72**	**5,442.10**	**-6.86**	**1.84**
	Books, Publications and Printing	619.8	382.18	225.72	272.64	20.78	0.09
	Newsprint	887.87	839.25	648.54	601.88	-7.19	0.2
	Paper, Paperboard and Products	2,187.31	2,566.53	2,008.65	1,817.37	-9.52	0.61
	Plywood and Allied Products	867.65	954.46	700.92	826.04	17.85	0.28
	Other Wood and Wood Products	2,072.14	1,950.01	1,532.05	1,215.65	-20.65	0.41
	Pulp and Waste Paper	767.44	944.02	726.85	708.52	-2.52	0.24
12	**Base Metals**	**21,563.13**	**27,046.58**	**20,464.02**	**19,100.31**	**-6.66**	**6.46**
	Iron and Steel	9,109.60	12,342.03	9,314.87	8,704.98	-6.55	2.94
	Products of Iron and Steel	3,576.04	3,959.31	3,059.43	2,831.99	-7.43	0.96
	Aluminium, Products of Aluminium	3,149.38	3,813.40	2,859.70	2,738.55	-4.24	0.93
	Copper and Products made of Copper	3,003.82	3,297.06	2,508.23	2,570.54	2.48	0.87
	Lead and Products Made of Lead	523.07	630.78	499.93	370.23	-25.94	0.13
	Nickel, and Products Made of Nickel	909.94	1,388.66	990.06	791.18	-20.09	0.27
	Tin and Products Made of Tin	244.28	202.91	152.51	142.81	-6.36	0.05
	Zinc and Products Made of Zinc	289.66	560.47	446.95	326.43	-26.97	0.11
	Other Non Ferrous Metal and Products	757.35	851.95	632.33	623.6	-1.38	0.21
13	**Medical & Surgical Instruments**	**4,156.11**	**4,283.47**	**3,245.12**	**3,104.35**	**-4.34**	**1.05**
	Surgicals	554.84	567	436.62	413.62	-5.27	0.14
	Optical Items (including Lens, etc)	309.62	327.74	240.72	248.41	3.2	0.08
	Medical and Scientific Instruments	3,291.65	3,388.72	2,567.78	2,442.32	-4.89	0.83
14	**Electronic Items**	**32,383.80**	**36,857.40**	**27,693.10**	**30,865.77**	**11.46**	**10.43**
	Computer Hardware, Peripherals	6,885.63	7,246.37	5,537.38	5,900.40	6.56	1.99
	Consumer Electronics	3,665.56	4,122.09	3,170.98	3,088.94	-2.59	1.04
	Electronics Components	5,434.39	5,383.29	3,883.94	4,905.14	26.29	1.66
	Electronics Instruments	5,178.04	5,408.32	4,060.60	4,456.33	9.75	1.51
	Telecom Instruments	11,220.17	14,697.34	11,040.21	12,514.95	13.36	4.23
15	**Machinery**	**31,103.36**	**32,023.10**	**23,834.11**	**24,017.55**	**0.77**	**8.12**
	Electrodes	84,71	86.33	64.16	61.67	-3.88	0.02
	Accumulators and Batteries	769,48	596.58	463.9	618.58	33.34	0.21
	HND Tool, Cutting Tool of Metals	881.12	969.7	724.15	632.22	-12.69	0.21
	Machine Tools	2,183.17	2,168.52	1,631.61	1,410.52	-13.55	0.48
	AC Refrigeration Machinery, etc.	2,843.95	3,063.33	2,147.61	2,132.93	-0.68	0.72

	Cranes, Lifts and Winches	1,045.34	1,064.86	778.32	829.94	6.63	0.28
	Electric Machinery and Equipment	5,492.28	6,061.65	4,487.11	4,682.29	4.35	1.58
	IC Engines and Parts	2,270.98	2,190.94	1,672.87	1,578.62	-5.63	0.53
	Industrial Machnery for Dairy, etc.	9,050.01	9,186.54	6,908.46	7,237.72	4.77	2.45
	ATM, Injecting Molding Machinery, etc.	927.99	832.28	624.28	572.39	-8.31	0.19
	Nuclear Reactor, including Boiler, Part	335.51	509.68	368.07	400.72	8.87	0.14
	Other Construction Machinery	1,681.71	1,596.52	1,155.46	1,028.16	-11.02	0.35
	Other Miscellanceous Engineering Items	2,465.07	2,634.54	2,007.69	2,075.69	3.39	0.07
	Prime Mica and Mica Prdocuts	185.61	182.2	136.2	151.8	11.45	0.05
	Pumps of all Types	886.44	879.13	664.23	604.31	-9.02	0.02
16	**Office Equipment**	**129.03**	**161.5**	**115.17**	**94.52**	**-17.92**	**0.03**
	Office Equipment	129.03	161.5	115.17	94.52	-17.92	0.03
17	**Transport Equipment**	**16,167.51**	**15,287.74**	**10,878.44**	**9,511.85**	**-12.56**	**3.22**
	Auto Tyres and Tubes	439.82	442.81	339.69	389.85	14.77	0.13
	Auto Components/Parts	3,824.39	4,225.07	3,243.40	3,329.81	2.66	1.13
	Bicycle and Parts	257.2	219.28	168.33	139.89	-16.9	0.05
	Aircraft, Spacecraft and Parts	4,305.07	4,706.71	3,484.15	2,126.51	-38.97	0.72
	Motor Vehicle/Cars	307.72	300.63	210.64	214.31	1.74	0.07
	Railway Transport Equipments, Parts	278.32	399.32	304.83	375.77	23.27	0.13
	Ship, Boat and Floating Structure	6,723.33	4,959.03	3,105.64	2,901.49	-6.57	0.96
	Two and Three Wheelers	31.65	34.9	21.77	34.22	57.32	0.01
18	**Project Goods**	**4,551.03**	**3,631.43**	**2,758.80**	**2,074.66**	**-24.8**	**0.07**
	Project Goods	4,551.03	3,631.43	2,758.80	2,074.66	-24.8	0.07
19	**Textiles & Allied Products**	**4,835.93**	**5,512.44**	**4,290.96**	**4,118.79**	**-4.01**	**1.39**
	Manmade Staple Fibre	328.29	406.78	317.21	315.3	-0.6	0.11
	Cotton Yarn	54.28	41.33	32.37	32.99	1.91	0.01
	Cotton Fabrics, Madeups, etc.	509.42	506.1	390.79	406.73	4.08	0.14
	Other Textile Yarn, Fabric Madeup Article	614.17	737.33	549.56	575.52	4.72	0.19
	Silk, Raw	148.51	158.93	121.09	115.04	-4.99	0.04
	Natural Silk Yarn, Fabrics, Madeup	65.67	51.72	42	34.67	-17.44	0.01
	Manmade Yarn Fabrics, Madeups	1,659.69	1,885.71	1,451.40	1,326.97	-8.57	0.45
	Wool, Raw	325.22	348.73	277.51	236.45	-14.8	0.08
	Wollen Yarn, Fabrics, Madeups, etc.	52.11	64.46	53.49	48.38	-9.56	0.02
	RMG Cotton including Accessories	217.52	236.49	171.61	187.87	9.47	0.06

	RMG Silk	5.17	6.13	4.5	3.59	-20.21	0
	RMG Manmade Fibres	102.81	142.51	111.05	130.44	17.46	0.04
	RMG Wool	15.19	16.06	13.84	11.68	-15.59	0
	RMG of other Textile Material	93.03	122.72	92.06	95.17	3.38	0.03
	Coir and Coir Manufactures	9.61	5.55	3.98	3.79	-4.76	0
	Handloom Products	18.83	10.2	7.21	8.94	24.01	0
	Silk Waste	4.77	4.24	3.42	2.04	-40.46	0
	Jute, Raw	25.71	23.18	21.92	45.48	107.48	0.02
	Jute Yarn	47.24	49.94	41.64	50.22	20.6	0.02
	Jute Hessian	13.43	29	20.94	19.68	-6.01	0.01
	Floor Covering of Jute	1.29	0.91	0.55	0.92	66.31	0
	Other Jute Manufactures	68.06	81.14	60.23	78.39	30.15	0.03
	Carpet (Excluding Silk) Handmade	61.33	74.42	53.47	58.47	9.36	0.02
	Silk Carpet	0.1	0.07	0.07	0.01	-89.82	0
	Cotton Raw including Waste	394.47	508.8	449.05	330.04	-26.5	0.11
20	**Petroleum Crude & Products**	**1,64,764.69**	**1,38,325.51**	**1,16,559.48**	**68,189.60**	**-41.5**	**23.05**
	Petroleum Crude	1,43,638.53	1,16,442.86	98,567.43	54,617.70	-44.59	48.46
	Petroleum Products	21,126.17	21,882.65	17,992.06	13,571.90	-24.57	4.59
21.	**Others**	**13,902.12**	**11,338.33**	**8,106.91**	**8,980.00**	**10.77**	**3.04**
	Other Commodities	13,177.80	10,515.02	7,505.91	8,308.51	10.69	2.81
	Human Hair, Products Thereof	14.51	13.39	9.77	6.9	-29.39	0
	Packaging Materials	237.74	249.43	188.2	194.11	3.14	0.07
	Handicrafts (Excluding Handmade Carpets)	472.07	560.5	403.03	470.47	16.73	0.16
	Total	**4,50,199.78**	**4,48,033.40**	**3,51,613.93**	**2,95,821.27**	**-15.87**	**100**

Foreign Trade Policy

It is a comprehensive statement on government priorities in the Foreign Trade Sector. Through the statement broad approach on external sector has been articulated. First it spells out government strategy to address some of the structural and institutional mechanism which is of prime importance for foreign trade sector. Secondly, it states the ways government would make trade and economic integration agreement with trade partners and would work better for Indian enterprises. This describes the market and product strategy and measures required for trade promotion infrastructure development and overall enhancement of the trade ecosystem. The FTP statement recognizes 'behind the border' constrains faced while engaging in foreign trade. The statements of intent includes assistance that the Department of Commerce is providing to state and union territory governments to prepare exports strategies and setup 'Export Promotion Mission' to provide an institutional framework to work with state governments to boost India's exports.

The foreign trade policy provides framework for increasing exports of goods and services as well as employment generation and greater value addition in line with the 'Make in India' programme. The policy aims to enable India to respond to the challenges of external environment, keeping pace with rapidly evolving international trading architecture and make trade major contributor to the country's economic growth and development. In this policy, measures have been taken to nudge procurement of capital goods from indigenous manufacturers under the EPCG scheme by reducing specific export obligation to 75 per cent of the normal export obligation. The FTP also boost exports of defense and hi-tech items, e-Commerce exports of handloom products, books/periodicals, leather footwear, toys and customised fashion garments through courier or foreign post office. Under the policy, manufacturers, who are also status holders, will be able to self-certify their manufactured goods in phases, as originating from India with a view to qualifying for preferential treatment under various forms of bilateral and regional trade agreements. Under this policy number of steps have been taken for encouraging manufacturing and exports under cent per cent EOU/EHTP/STPI/BTP schemes. Trade facilitation and enhancing the ease of doing business are the other major focus areas.

The FTP introduces two new schemes, namely "Merchandise Exports from India Schemes (MEIS)" for export of specified goods to specified markets and "Service Exports from India Scheme (SEIS)" for increasing exports of notified services, in place of a plethora of schemes earlier with different conditions for eligibility and usage. There would be no conditionality attached to any scrips issued under these schemes. Duty credit scrips issued under MEIS and SEIS and the goods imported against these scrips are fully transferable.

Merchandise Exports From India Scheme (MEIS)

There were different schemes for rewarding Merchandise Exports with different kinds of duty scrips and with varying conditions attached to their use. These schemes were (i) Focus Product Scheme (FPS), (ii) Focus Market Scheme (FMS), (iii) Market Linked Focus Product Scrip (MLFPS), (iv) Vishesh Krishi and Gram Udyog Yojna (VKGUY), (v) Agri. MEIS Infrastructure Incentive Scrip and (vi) Incremental Export Incentive Scheme. introduced through the Foreign Trade Policy (FTP) 2015-20 in 2015 is a merger of all the schemes. e-Commerce exports of certain specified employment creating sectors, made through courier or foreign post offices, have also been supported under MEIS.

Service Exports From India Scheme (SEIS)

Served From India Scheme (SFIS) has been replaced with Service Exports From India Scheme (SEIS). SEIS is available to 'Service Providers Located in India' instead of 'Indian Service Providers'. Thus SEIS provides for incentives to all service providers of notified services, who are providing services from India, subject to conditions as may be notified, regardless of the condition or profile of the service provider. The notified services and rates of rewards are listed in Appendix 3D of Hand Book of Procedure.

Export through Courier or Foreign Post Offices

The new FTP has introduced a scheme to incentivise exports of goods through courier or foreign post office using e-commerce under MEIS. As the regulatory structure of e-commerce export is still evolving, scope of the scheme was kept limited.

Advance Authorization Scheme

Under this scheme, duty free import of inputs (that are physically incorporated in the export product) are allowed, with minimum 15 per cent value addition. Advance Authorization (AA) is issued for inputs in relation to resultant products as per SION or on the basis of self-declaration, as per procedures of FTP. AA normally has a validity period of 12 months for the purpose of imports and a period of 18 months for fulfilment of Export Obligation (EO) from the date of issue. AA is issued either to a manufacturer exporter or merchant exporter tied to a supporting manufacturer(s).

Duty Free Import Authorization Scheme

Duty Free Import Authorization (DFIA) is issued to allow duty free import of inputs, with a minimum value addition requirement of 20 per cent. DFIA shall be exempted only from the payment of basic customs duty. DFIA shall be issued on post export basis for products for which SION has been notified. Separate schemes exist for gems and jewellery sector.

Export Promotion Capital Goods Scheme

Under this scheme import of capital goods at zero customs duty is allowed for technology upgradation and better services to enhance India's export competitiveness. Import under EPCG is subject to export obligation equivalent to six times of duty saved in six years. It also allows indigenous sourcing of capital goods with 25 per cent less export obligation.

Ease of doing Business and e-Governance Initiatives

Reduction of Documents

The new FTP has brought about reduction in the number of documents required for export and import from 7 and 10 respectively to 3 each. Documents required for export of goods from India are Bill of Lading/Airway Bill, Commercial Invoice cum Packing List and Shipping Bill/Bill of Export. The mandatory documents required for import of goods into India are Bill of Lading/Airway Bill, Commercial Invoice cum Packing List and Bill of Entry. The saving in terms of cost and time associated with the dispensed documents would improve Ease of Doing Business with India. Online filing of documents/applications and paperless trade in 24x7 environment: (i) all the Regional Authorities (RA) of DGFT have been networked with high speed internet. The applications are received and processed electronically; (ii) DGFT has provided the facility of online filing of applications for issuance of Importer Exporter Code and various authorizations/scrips. Applicants can sign applications with a digital signature and submit electronically to the concerned Regional Authority of DGFT. Online filing has minimized the physical interface; (iii) DGFT is one of the first digital signature enabled organisation of the Government of India, which has introduced a higher level of encrypted 2048 bit digital signature; (iv) application fee can be paid through debit/credit cards or online from linked banks; (v) in order to save paper as well as cost and time of the exporters, the requirement of filing hard copies of application forms and supporting documents for advance authorization scheme has been fully dispensed with and beta versions of software to make applications for MEIS and EPCG schemes paperless have been put on the DGFT website. and (vi) online system for expediting issuance of authorisations for dual use items (special chemicals, organisms, materials, equipment and technologies [SCOMET] has been developed.

Importer Exporter Code

A simplified system for issuance of importer exporter code (IEC) online was introduced in February 2015. IEC is mandatory for exporters and is communicated online from DGFT to customs. It allows new entrepreneurs/ exporters/importers to apply online for issue of new IEC and carryout modifications in the details as in the IEC by uploading the documents and paying the required fee through net banking/credit/debit cards. Processing of such applications by Regional Authority of DGFT would be done online and a digitally signed e-IEC would normally be issued/e-mailed to the applicant within two working days.

The e-BRC initiative of DGFT has led to electronic transmission of foreign exchange realisation certificate from the banks to the DGFT's server on a daily basis thereby establishing a seamless electronic data interchange (EDI) connectivity among DGFT, banks and exporters. E-BRC (Electronic Bank Realization Certificate) project launched in 2012 created an integrated platform for receipt, processing and subsequent use of all bank realization related information by exporters, Banks, Central and state government departments. e-BRC was made mandatory in 2012. In a short span of less than three years, it has brought down the cost of doing business for Indian exporters and enhanced the productivity of banks, DGFT and many other organizations. So far, 95 banks have transmitted more than 1.4 crore e-BRCs. 13 state government departments, including Enforcement Directorate of Government of India have signed MoU with DGFT for sharing of e-BRC data.

Complaint Resolution System

A Complaint Resolution System for Resolution of EDI related issues has been set up. It is being actively used by exporters. There is also an online system in place to resolve complaints received through public grievances portal of Department of Administrative Reforms and Public Grievances.

Online Concurrent Audit

System for conducting of online concurrent audit of DGFT schemes was implemented in February, 2015.

ISO 9001-2008 Certification

DGFT HQ, regional offices of Mumbai, Chennai, Delhi and Cochin have obtained ISO 9001-2008 certification. DGCI&S was also awarded ISO 9001-2008 in 2015.

Social Media

Mobile Application

DGFT has developed a mobile application called "DGFT" which allows exporters/importers to access the foreign trade policy and other related documents in an easy-to-use searchable format. The trade community would be able to check the status of transmission of various authorizations and the shipping bills through the dynamic mobile app.

Creating Single Window for Trade

Initiatives have been put in place for creating an electronic single window for trade. India's trade happens through 12 major ports, 187 minor ports and many private notified ports. These are supplemented by 218 functioning and 34 under development Inland Container Depots (ICDs) and Container Freight Stations (CFSs). For clearance of air cargo, there are 36 functional international airports. There are 138 Land Customs Stations (LCSs) along India's international borders, of which 66 are functional LCSs. These interface points need to be connected seamlessly to share information with all stakeholders.

EDI Initiatives

Important EDI Initiatives taken by Customs

The customs EDI system (ICES) and its online interface (ICEGATE) connects customs with importers/exporters, customs house agents, airlines and shipping lines, air and sea custodians, banks, the Reserve Bank of India, and government departments such as the Directorate General of Commercial Intelligence and Statistics, Directorate General of Foreign Trade, and the Directorate of Valuation. A pilot single window project led by customs and including plant quarantine and FSSAI is being implemented at the Inland Container Depot in Tughlakhabad. At present there are 344 ports or customs points through which India's exports and imports take place. But due to infrastructural constraints only 126 of these ports are Electronic Data Interchange (EDI) enabled and the rest of the 218 ports are still operating on manual system or in Non EDI mode. As a result, at present only a part of India's export and import data is captured through EDI mode at customs (for exports, 88.61 per cent transactions accounting for 65.19 per cent of value). However, remaining data (For exports, 11.39 per cent transactions accounting for 34.81 per cent of value) called Non EDI data is still transmitted with a greater time lag (one month).

EDI Initiatives

DGFT endeavors to deliver its services on a transparent and efficient basis using tools like online filing of applications, message exchange with community partners, digital signatures and electronic fee payments. Proposed e-governance initiatives include establishment of message exchange for transmission of scrips from DGFT to customs, integration of e-BRC with CBEC and RBI. Directorate General of Foreign Trade is the first Indian government organization to start web based application processing (1997) using Secured Digital Certificates (2048 Byte Key encryption-2004). Many e-Governance initiatives have been implemented to achieve greater transparency and reduce transaction time and costs for the exporting community: (i) DGFT website is an integrated platform, which performs the following critical functions: it provides information relating to FTP and procedures and all related documents; it allows users' web based electronic filing of applications for DGFT schemes/authorizations to any of the 36 DGFT's regional authorities across the country. The process of applications filing secured with digital signature; it allows users to check and upon information relating to their shipping bills received from customs and electronic Bank Realization Certificates (e-BRCs) receive from banks. (ii) All authorizations are being issued online by DGFT; message exchange with customs has been implemented for advance authorization, EPCG and DFIA. Exporters can track; monitor their application at the DGFT website. (iii) All 36 regional offices of DGFT, across India are computerized and connected through central server. Networking of these offices through high speed broadband/ lease line has enable integration of various applications, message exchange and data bases. (iv) A system has been established to receive Registration-Cum-Membership-Certificate (RCMC) from the Export Promotion Councils, Commodity Boards and FIEO in secured online format. (v) Electronic Fund Transfer Facility is being used by exporters for payment of application fee. So far 21 banks have signed agreement with DGFT for electronic fund transfer. The facility of accepting payments of application fee through credit card is under development and will be launched soon. (vi) Indian Trade Clarification [ITC (HS)] based on internationally acceptable Harmonized System of Coding is compilation of codes for all goods for export/import. Currently the exportability or importability for all goods is indicated in ITC (HS) database available online at DGFT website. Action has been initiated to include information related to online export and import regulatory requirements through an updated online ITC (HS) database.

New Initiatives

(i) Online RTI: DGFT is now integrated with the RTI online system of the Department of Personnel and Training from February, 2015 which will enable the citizen to seek information from DGFT and its regional authorities online; (ii) Online Inter-Ministerial Consultation: For the Policy implementations, different committees have been set up; a few of them are NORM Committees, Committees for SION.

Jawaharlal Nehru Port Trust

DGFT visited Jawaharlal Nehru Port Trust (JNPT). DGFT has identified the following tasks for priority completion: (i) integration/message exchange of port and customs system, in order to dispense with Form e-13/e-11; (ii) integration of Jawaharlal Nehru Port Trust (JNPT) software system with the Customs EDI; (iii) amending JNPT's system to include additional fields to expedite checking by CISF at the port gate; (iv) automating 'Gating' system ; (v) facilitating inter-terminal movement at JNPT through 'virtual gate'; (vi) automating issuance of delivery orders/cargo release order; (vii) development of parking sites; (viii) easing of road congestion and streamlining of traffic movement at JN port; (ix) installation of railway signals at the Hindi CFS; and (x) improving message exchange between custom, CFS, ports and CHA/forwarders.

Niryat Bandhu Scheme

A novel 'Niryat Bandhu' scheme for mentoring first generation entrepreneurs has been conceptualized. The Officer (Niryat Bandhu) would primarily mentor interested individuals in the arena of international business. Such hand-holding by officers of DGFT would help the new exporters/importers by leveraging the knowledge base of officers and by providing timely and appropriate guidance. The objective of the scheme is essentially to reach out to the new and potential exporters and mentoring them through orientation programmes, counselling sessions, individual facilitation, etc., for being able to get into international trade. The implementation of programmes is done through the 36 regional authorities (field offices) of DGFT which directly come into interaction with the new and prospective exporters while sanctioning of IEC, authorizations, incentives, scrips, etc. The funds are allocated to the RAs at the beginning of the year along with a tentative allocation of activities under different components of the scheme, so that they can plan their programmes in advance, in coordination with stakeholders, namely, export councils, industry associations, state governments departments, customs, excise, etc.

As an intervention strategy, considering the strategic significance of small and medium scale enterprises in the manufacturing sector and in employment generation, 108 'MSME clusters' have been identified, based on the export potential of the product and the density of industries in the cluster, for focussed interventions to boost exports. In addition, 35 'Towns of Excellence' have been taken up for outreach interventions under 'Niryat Bandhu' scheme. It is envisaged that the orientation programmes would focus on specific export product with the objective of adding new exporters from that sector and simultaneously boosting the export of the specific product.

An overall allocation of ₹ 23.23 crore has been made for the Plan period (2012-17). While a token allocation of ₹ 2.00 lakh was made in the fourth quarter of FY 2013-14, the implementation of the scheme actually took off with an allocation of ₹ 2 crore in the 2014-15.

India's Engagement in Free Trade Agreements

India has always stood for an open, equitable, predictable, non-discriminatory and rule based international trading system. India views FTAs as 'building blocks' towards the overall objective of trade liberalization as well as complementing the multilateral trading system. India has concluded 11 Free Trade Agreements, 5 limited scope Preferential Trade Agreements and is in the process of negotiating/expanding 19 more agreements, including 3 under review. The list of these agreements is given in Annexures I and II.

The definition of the various terminologies used for trade agreements based on the various parameters like scope of coverage and depth of engagement are: (i) Preferential Trading Agreement (PTA): Tariff liberalization on a limited number of lines e.g. India-Mercosur PTA; (ii) Free Trade Agreement (FTA): Elimination of tariffs on items covering substantial bilateral trade between the partner countries e.g. India - Sri Lanka FTA; and (iii) Comprehensive Economic Cooperation Agreement (CECA)/ Comprehensive Economic Partnership Agreement(CEPA)/Broad Based Trade and Investment Agreement (BTIA): CECA or CEPA or BTIA terms are used to describe agreements which consist of an integrated package of Agreement on Goods, Services, Investment, Mutual Recognition, Intellectual Property, etc., e.g. India Korea CEPA.

Trade with ASEAN

India announced its 'Look East Policy' in 1991 with a view to seeking greater engagement with East Asian countries. In order to address the economic content of the 'Look East Policy', a continuous dialogue is maintained with ASEAN (Association of South East Asian Nations) countries viz., Brunei Darussalam, Cambodia, Indonesia, Laos PDR, Malaysia, Myanmar, Philippines, Singapore, Thailand and Vietnam. Summit level engagements, ministerial meetings and official level discussions are held in order to fulfill the 'Look East Policy' agenda. India's trade with ASEAN countries was US$ 76.5 billion during the year 2014-15 and US$ 26.7 billion during 2015-16 (April-August). India's exports in the region are Singapore, Indonesia, Malaysia, Vietnam and Thailand while the major sources of imports are Indonesia, Malaysia, Singapore, Thailand, Vietnam and Myanmar.

Agreements with ASEAN

India and the ASEAN have signed the agreement on Trade in Goods under the broader framework of Comprehensive Economic Cooperation Agreement (CECA) between India and the ASEAN 2009. The agreement has become fully operational between all the ASEAN member states and India from 2010. India and ASEAN member countries have signed the agreement of Trade in Services and Agreement on Investment.

Trade with North East Asia

India's trade with the North East Asian (hereafter NEA) region comprising People Republic of China, Japan, Republic of Korea, Hong Kong, China, Taiwan China, Democratic People Republic of Korea, Macao and Mongolia stood at US$ 131.60 billion during 2014-15, which is an increase of 5.12 per cent over the previous year. Exports to the NEA region were of the order of US$ 37.81 billion during 2014-15, registering a negative growth of 7.35 per cent over the last year. Imports from the region increased by 11.19 per cent to US$ 93.81 billion during 2014-15. In 2014-15, India's trade deficit with NEA has widened to US$ 55.99 billion from a high level of US$ 43.55 billion in 2013-14, mainly on account of a decline in the export volume and simultaneous increase in the import volume.

Trade with North America Free Trade Agreement

NAFTA consists of United States of America, Canada and Mexico. All the three countries are signatories to the North America Free Trade Agreement (NAFTA) and form one of the largest and the most important trading blocks of the world. In order to resolve issues of concern for these countries the following institutional mechanisms are in place.

Dispute Settlement

Since 1997, WTO members have been negotiating to improve and clarify on various provisions of the Dispute Settlement Understanding (DSU). These negotiations are independent of the single undertaking under DDA and such negotiations are taking place in special sessions of the DSB. India and other developing countries have been reiterating their objectives for a development oriented review of the dispute settlement procedures under the Doha Development Agenda, safeguarding the interest of the developing countries. Some of the issues being stressed by the developing countries include facilitation of cross retaliation, inducement of effective compliance, setting up of Dispute Settlement Fund, etc. After the post Bali Ministerial meeting in December, 2013, DSU reform negotiations picked up momentum. However, on account of divergence of opinion and no consensus on a number of issues, the Chair has expressed willingness to continue discussion post Nairobi Ministerial Meet of December 2015.

Role of Standards in International Trade

In today's markets, both domestic as well as international, standards have assumed tremendous significance. As globally tariffs are going down, the complexities connected with international trade are also increasing. In order to ensure supply of good quality, safe and environmentally-friendly products to our consumers, it is important that our industrial enterprises and business operators also adopt the concept of standards and technical regulations in their respective organisations. To make it possible, Government needs to put in place a complete ecosystem where standards and technical regulations are developed and complied with ease.

The WTO Agreement on 'Technical Barriers to Trade' and the Agreement on the 'Application of Sanitary and Phytosanitary Measures' are the mother agreements on standards and conformity assessment at the international level. These agreements try to balance the competing demands for domestic regulatory autonomy and the global harmonization of products standards in a manner which is trade friendly. Thus, these agreements attempt to prevent standards from becoming a protectionist device; however, in practice we notice the trend otherwise.

Standards in Services

India has export potential in many of the skill based services in several non traditional services exports including professional services such as accountancy, architecture and services such as tourism, medical value travel, etc. Service standardization can be a great enable in this endeavour. The Indian trade portal (www.indiantradeportal.in) was upgraded and launched in December, 2014. It now provides vital information on 42 countries in a user friendly manner in 4 easy steps, which would be of immense help to our exporters. It makes available important data like (i) MFN tariff, (ii) preferential tariff, (iii) rules of origin (RoO) and (iv) non-tariff measures and help our exporters to utilize the FTAs and capture expert opportunities. It is also being used in FTA outreaches. This portal helps businesses to evaluate the competitiveness of their products in a particular market, based on applicable Most Favoured Nation (MFN) tariff and concessional tariff (if any) under any bilateral or regional preferential trade agreement.

Another important feature of the portal is information on 'measures' other than tariff called the Non-tariff Measures (NTMs) like standards, technical regulations, conformity assessment procedures, sanitary and phytosanitary measures which may affect trade adversely. This is important because if Indian manufacturers and enterprises cannot meet mandatory obligations of meeting standards, etc., increasingly we will start losing major export markets in the world.

The portal is in fact a single point for almost all the information required by an exporter in a user friendly manner which will help exporters in accessing markets easily and in comprehensive manner. It also provides information like—How to Export Acts of India, export promotion schemes, banking regulations, Frequently Asked Questions (FAQs) on various topics etc. Free subscription for alerts on the updates on the portal over email and SMS is also available. A small video on the operation of the portal has been made available in the help section of the portal.

India's Duty Free Tariff Preference Scheme

One of the elements of the Hong-Kong Ministerial Declaration of December 2005 was to extend Duty Free Quota Free (DFQF) access to the Least Developed Countries (LDCs). India became the first developing country to extend this facility to LDCs. India announced the Duty Free Tariff Preference (DFTP) Scheme for LDCs in 2008.

Product Strategy

The focus will be on promoting exports of high value products with a strong domestic manufacturing base, including engineering goods, electronics, drugs and pharmaceuticals. Other sectors which require special attention, in the light of India's strengths and their contribution to employment generation, are leather, textiles, gems and jewellery and the sectors based on natural resources, which include agriculture, plantation crops, marine products and iron ore exports. Revitalizing plantations, enabling a less controlled regime for agriculture and aiming at greater value addition and processing would help to increase the value of exports from these sectors. The north-eastern states are a special focus area for organic product exports. A number of steps to address the challenges faced by the plantations sector are on the anvil.

Government aims to encourage and promote exports from the defence sector. The Department of Defence Production has put in place a specific strategy for encouraging defence exports within the overall ambit of the FTP. Various initiatives already taken or to be taken to enhance export of items from the defence sector include modifications in the FDI policy, greater clarity as regards industrial licenses for this sector, fast tracking of applications, listing of munitions, creation of HS codes for items in this sector and setting up promotional institutions for defence exports.

Services Sector

The services sector has emerged as a prominent sector in India in terms of its contribution to national and state incomes, trade flows, employment and FDI inflows. This sector contributes around 58 per cent to the GDP of the country and 28 per cent to employment. Its contribution to total trade is 25 per cent, around 35 per cent to exports and 20 per cent to imports. The sector accounts for more than 50 per cent of FDI into the country. The services sector in India has in general grown at a rate higher than the overall GDP growth rate.

Building the India Brand

A long term branding strategy has been conceptualised to enable India to hold its own in a highly competitive global environment and to ensure that "Brand India" becomes synonymous with high quality. Further, a programme to promote the branding and commercialisation of products registered as Geographical Indications and to promote their exports will be initiated within one year of this policy coming into force.

India Trade Portal

The Indian trade portal (www.indiantradeportal.in) was upgraded and launched in 2014. It now provides vital information on 42 countries in a user friendly manner in four easy steps, which is of immense help to the exporters. It makes available important data like (i) MFN tariff, (ii) Preferential tariff, (iii) Rules of Origin (RoO) and (iv) Non-tariff measures and help our exporters to utilize the FTAs and capture export opportunities. It is also being used in FTA outreaches.

Special Economic Zones

India was one of the first in Asia to recognise the effectiveness of the Export Processing Zone (EPZ) model for export promotion, with Asia's first EPZ set up in Kandla in 1965. To overcome the shortcomings on account of multiplicity of controls and clearances, absence of world-class infrastructure and an unstable fiscal regime and with a view to attract larger foreign investments in India, the Special Economic Zones (SEZs) Policy was announced in April 2000.

This policy intended to make SEZs an engine for economic growth supported by quality infrastructure complemented by an attractive fiscal package, both at the Centre and the state level, with minimum possible regulations. SEZs in India functioned from 2000 to 2006 under the provisions of the Foreign Trade Policy and fiscal incentives were made effective through the provisions of relevant statutes.

Special Economic Zones Act, 2005 and Special Economic Zones Rules, 2006

The Special Economic Zones Act, 2005, was passed in 2005. The SEZ Act, 2005, supported by SEZ Rules, came into effect in 2006, providing simplification of procedures and single window clearance on matters relating to Central and State governments. The main objectives of the SEZ Act are: generation of additional economic activity; promotion of exports of goods and services; promotion of investment from domestic and foreign sources; creation of employment opportunities; and development of infrastructure facilities.

Approvals for Setting Up of Special Economic Zones

Seven Export Processing Zones set up by the Central Government at Kandla (Gujarat), Santa Cruz (Maharashtra), Kochi (Kerala), Noida (U.P.), Chennai (Tamil Nadu), Falta (West Bengal) and Vishakhapatnam (Andhra Pradesh), were converted to SEZs on announcement of the SEZ Policy. Another EPZ set up in the private sector in Surat was also converted to a SEZ. In addition to these, 11 more SEZs were set up by the state governments/private sector during the period 2000-2005 in West Bengal (2), Gujarat (2), Madhya Pradesh (1), Uttar Pradesh (1), Rajasthan (1) and Tamil Nadu (4). After the coming into force of the SEZ Act, 2005, 412 formal approvals have been granted for setting up of Special Economic Zones, out of which 329 SEZs have been notified and are in various stages of operation. A total of 204 SEZs are exporting.

While there is some concentration in certain states, the fact that the approved SEZs are spread over 19 states and 3 union territories indicates that these are not confined to any particular region. State-wise distribution of SEZs as in December 2015 is in Table 7.1. The total land area involved in the formally approved SEZs including notified SEZs is around 51791.62 ha.

Table 7.1 : State-wise Distribution of Approved Special Economic Zone

(As on 14.12.2015)

States/UTs	Formal Approvals	In Principle Exporting Approvals	Notified SEZs	Exporting SEZs (Central Govt.+ State Govt./Pvt. SEZs + Notified SEZs under the SEZ Act, 2005)
Andhra Pradesh	30	4	26	19
Chandigarh	2	0	2	2
Chhattisgarh	2	1	1	1
Delhi	2	0	0	0
Goa	7	0	3	0

Gujarat	31	4	27	18
Haryana	22	3	19	7
Jharkhand	1	0	1	0
Karnataka	59	0	38	26
Kerala	29	0	25	16
Madhya Pradesh	12	1	8	2
Maharashtra	59	9	51	25
Manipur	1	0	1	0
Nagaland	2	0	2	0
Odisha	8	1	4	2
Puducherry	1	1	0	0
Punjab	4	0	2	2
Rajasthan	9	1	8	4
Tamil Nadu	48	4	45	36
Telangana	49	1	42	26
Uttar Pradesh	22	1	19	11
West Bengal	12	2	5	7
GRAND TOTAL	**412**	**33**	**329**	**204**

Source: Department of Commerce (SEZ Division)

Status of RTSs/FTAs:

FTAs in Force

S. No.	Name of the Agreement	Date of Signing of the Agreement	Date of Implementation of the Agreement
1	India - Sri Lanka FTA	28th December, 1998	1st March, 2000
2	Agreement on SAFTA (India, Pakistan, Nepal, Sri Lanka, Bangladesh, Bhutan, the Maldives and Afghanistan)	4th January, 2004	1st January, 2006 (Tariff concessions implemented from 1st July, 2006)
3	Revised Agreement of Cooperation between Government of India and Nepal to control unauthorized trade	27th October, 2009	27th October, 2009
4	India - Bhutan Agreement on Trade, Commerce and Transit	17th January, 1972	Renewed periodically, with mutually agreed modifications
5	India - Thailand FTA - Early Harvest Scheme (EHS)	9th October, 2003	1st September, 2004
6	India-Singapore-CECA	29th June, 2005	1st August, 2005
7	India - ASEAN- CECA - Trade in Goods Agreement (Brunei, Cambodia, Indonesia, Laos, Malaysia, Myanmar, Philippines, Singapore, Thailand and Vietnam)	13th August, 2009	• 1st January, 2010 in respect of India and Malaysia, Singapore, Thailand • 1st June, 2010 in respect of India and Vietnam • 1st September, 2010 in respect of India and Myanmar • 1st October, 2010 in respect of India and Indonesia

			• 1st November, 2010 in respect of India and Brunei • 24 January, 2011 in respect of India and Laos • 1st June, 2011 in respect of India and the Philippines • 1st August, 2011 in respect of India and Cambodia.
8	India - South Korea CEPA	7th August, 2009	1st January, 2010
9	India - Japan CEPA	16th February, 2011	1st August, 2011
10	India - Malaysia CECA	18th February, 2011	1st July, 2011
11	India-ASEAN Services and Investment Agreement (Brunei, Cambodia, Indonesia, Laos, Malaysia; Myanmar, Philippines, Singapore, Thailand and Vietnam)	9th September, 2014	1st July, 2015

Annexure II

PTAs in force

S. No.	Name of the Agreement	Date of Signing of the Agreement	Date of Implementation of the Agreement
1	Asia Pacific Trade Agreement (APTA) (Bangladesh, China, India, Republic of Korea, Sri Lanka)	July, 1975(revised on 2nd November, 2005	1st Nov,1976
2	Global System of Trade Preferences (GSTP)(Algeria, Argentina, Bangladesh, Benin, Bolivia, Brazil, Cameroon, Chile, Colombia, Cuba, Democratic People's Republic of Korea, Ecuador, Egypt, Ghana, Guinea, Guyana, India, Indonesia, Iran, Iraq, Libya, Malaysia, Mexico, Morocco, Mozambique, Myanmar, Nicaragua, Nigeria, Pakistan, Peru, Philippines, Republic of Korea, Romania, Singapore, Sri Lanka, Sudan, Thailand, Trinidad and Tobago, Tunisia, Tanzania, Venezuela, Vietnam, Yugoslavia, Zimbabwe)	13th April, 1988	19th April,1989
3	India-Afghanistan	6th March, 2003	13th May, 2003
4	India-Mercosur	25th January, 2004	1st June, 2009
5	India-Chile	8th March, 2006	11th September, 2007

8 Communications and Information Technology

Communications and information technology in the country are handled by the Ministry of Electronics and Information Technology and Ministry of Communications. The Ministry of Electronics and Technology promotes e-Governance and sustainable growth of the electronics , IT and ITeS industries, enhancing India's role in internet governance while the Ministry of Communications looks after the Department of Posts and Department of Telecommunications. Main activities and initiatives of these departments are given here.

Posts

The modern postal system, the most preferred facilitator of communication, was established in India by Lord Clive in 1766 which was further developed by Warren Hastings in the year 1774. The expansion of its network was made during 1786 to 1793. For the first time, the Post Offices were regulated through an Act of 1837 on a uniform basis to unite all the post office establishments throughout the then existing three Presidencies into one all-India Service. Thereafter, the Post Office Act of 1854 reformed the entire fabric of the postal system and the Post Offices of India were placed on the present administrative footing in 1854, when the first postage stamp valid across the country was issued at an affordable and uniform rate of postage, fixed by weight and not by distance. For the first time the common man could use a facility which included free delivery of letters from door to door—a privilege previously enjoyed only by heads of states and state officials. Since then, the Post Office touched the life of every person of the country. Even though the British established the Post Office for imperial interests, it along with the Railways and Telegraph, became one of the great engines of social development.

The statute presently governing the postal services in the country is the Indian Post Office Act, 1898. In the mid-nineteenth century, the Post Office served as facilitator of travel with its conveyance systems and by maintaining the dak bungalows and dak serais. Mail order services were started with the value payable system introduced in 1877, while fund remittances at the doorstep became possible from 1880 through money order services. With the introduction of the Post Office Savings Bank in 1882 banking facilities were accessible to all and by 1884 all Government employees were covered by the Postal Life Insurance (PLI). Besides providing postal communication facilities, the Post Office network has also provided facilities for remittance of funds, banking and insurance services since the latter half of the nineteenth century.

Organization Overview

The Department of Posts comes under the Ministry of Communications. The Postal Service Board, the apex management body of the department, comprises the Chairman and six Members. The six Members of the Board hold portfolios of personnel, operations, technology, postal life insurance, banking and HRD and planning. The Joint Secretary and Financial Advisor to the department is a permanent invitee to the Board. The Board is assisted by the Secretary (Postal Services Board) who is a senior staff officer at the headquarters of the Department. Deputy Director Generals, Directors and Assistant Director Generals provide the necessary functional support for the Board at the headquarters.

Network

India has the largest postal network in the world with 1,54,939 post offices in 2015, of which 1,39,222 (89.86 per cent) are in the rural areas. At the time of independence, there were 23,344 Post Offices, which were primarily in urban areas. Thus, the network has registered a seven-fold growth since Independence, with the focus of this expansion primarily in rural areas. On an average, a post office serves an area of 21.22 sq.km. and a population of 8,354 people.

The expansion of postal network in the country, especially in rural areas, has taken place mainly through opening of Gramin Dak Sevak Post Offices, and on a smaller scale by opening departmental post offices. The Gramin Dak Sevak Post Offices function for a period of three hours up to a maximum of five hours. These are manned by Gramin Dak Sevaks who are paid time-related continuity allowance for the services they render. On the other hand, the departmental post offices function for a period of eight hours and are manned by regular departmental employees.

Post offices are opened subject to distance, population and income norms fixed for the purpose. In order to fulfill the Universal Service Obligation (USO), subsidy is provided to all Branch Post Offices in rural areas, which ranges from 66.66 per cent in normal rural areas to 85 per cent in hilly, tribal, desert and inaccessible areas.

During the financial year 2015-2016, various targets had been set for the circles. These include - opening of 139 sub-post offices and 92 branch post offices (by relocation/redeployment), 200 franchisee outlets, provision for basic infrastructural equipments to 10,000 Gramin Dak Sevak Post Offices, installation of letter boxes in 2,266 branch post offices in rural areas of the North East region, installation of signages in 62,900 branch post offices and embedding 20,000 cash chests in rural branch post offices.

Rural Business

Department of Posts is concerned with activities relating to various aspects of rural postal operations. This includes technology induction, new business initiatives, leveraging rural postal network of 1.39 lakh Post Offices across the country, marketing of services and monitoring quality of services provided by the rural Post Offices.

Over the years, 'Financial Inclusion' has emerged as the focus of the activities of the Rural Banking (RB) Division, though it is engaged in a few other sectors also. The Division has been entrusted with disbursement activities of various Government sponsored social security schemes like: Mahatma Gandhi National Rural Employment Guarantee Scheme (MGNREGS); Indira Gandhi National Old Age Pension Scheme (IGNOAPS); Indira Gandhi National Widow Pension Scheme (IGNWPS); Indira Gandhi National Disability Pension Scheme (IGNDPS); and; Indira Gandhi Matritva Sahyog Yojana (IGMSY).

Initiatives in Service Quality Improvement

Project Arrow

Project Arrow was conceptualized by the Department of Posts in 2008 with the objective to make a visible difference in the working of post offices by improving and upgrading the core business areas and "Look and Feel". It aims at improving the quality of services offered by post offices in both urban and rural areas. It seeks to provide IT enabled services through post offices and strives to make these "a window to the world" for the common man.

Mail Network Optimization Project

In order to improve the quality of mail processing, transmission and delivery, the department had initiated "Mail Network Optimization Project" (MNOP) in 2010 which involved consolidation and optimization of the erstwhile mail network with a view to streamline core mail operations. It also sought to bring in greater standardization and improvement in the operational processing relating to mail processing, transmission and delivery. The operational networks for Speed Post, First Class and Second Class mail have since been restructured into a hub and spokes network model. Operational processes were redesigned in order to simplify operations and improve efficiency.

Automated Mail Processing Centres

In order to expedite mail processing, department has established Automatic Mail Processing Centres (AMPCs) in Delhi and Kolkata. These centres are equipped with a Letter Sorting Machine (LSM) and a Mixed Mail Sorter (MMS) each with a sorting capacity of 35,000 and 18,000 items respectively per hour. Enhanced sorting capacity and mechanized processing facility have expedited sorting and faster delivery of mail in these cities. The Department has also initiated activities to set up similar centres in Bengaluru, Chennai, Hyderabad and Mumbai for processing packets and parcels in the near future.

National Address Database Management System

The department has initiated a new project named National Address Database Management System which involves creation of a comprehensive address database to expedite delivery of mail.

GPS Equipped Mail Vans

The department has decided to equip its entire fleet of Mail carrying vehicles with Global Positioning System (GPS) device in order to monitor mail transmission and delivery more effectively.

Development of Road Transport Network

In order to ensure safe and secure transmission of Speed Post articles and parcels, particularly e-commerce articles, a Plan Scheme 'Development of Road Transport Network' has been approved for the Department. Under the Scheme, 52 routes have been approved in 17 Circles which will ensure secure transmission of Speed Post articles and e-commerce shipments across 112 cities. Alternate/ additional routes which can be operationally advantageous for transmission of mail are being identified.

Technology Upgradation

The IT Modernization Project was approved by the Government of India in November 2012 as a Mission Mode e-governance Project with an outlay of ₹ 4,909 crore. The project aims at transforming the Department of Posts' operational efficiency and improving service delivery of operational and administrative units through upgraded technology and connectivity. Networking of all 1,55,000 post offices covering the remotest parts of the country will enable track and trace of all kinds of accountable mails and parcels in the country, besides providing real-time information to facilitate customer feedback and management functions. The Primary Data Centre has been commissioned at Navi Mumbai and is operational from 2013 and Disaster Recovery Centre has been powered at Mysore in 2015.

As part of the Network Integrator stream of the project, 27,561 locations have been networked under Wide Area Network (WAN), thereby making it the largest WAN in the country. The Change Management stream of the project aims at preparing all the employees of the Department including Gramin Dak Sevaks to enable them to function effectively in IT environment. The training activities are in progress. Rural ICT Project aims at computerizing approximately 1,30,000 rural branch post offices in the country by supplying computer hardware, other peripherals, solar charging devices and providing network connectivity, development and deployment of software for MNREGS, e-MO, etc., to them.

Premium Services

Speed Post

The flagship product of Department of Posts, Speed Post was started in August 1986 and provides time-bound and express delivery of letters and parcels weighing upto 35 kg across the country. It is the market leader in the domestic express industry with monthly volumes of more than 3 crore articles. Speed Post is booked in almost all the departmental post offices in the country and delivery facility is available across the country.

Speed Post is a value for money product. Under it articles can be booked upto 50 grams for ₹ 35 across the country and local Speed Post upto 50 grams for ₹ 15 (excluding applicable Service Tax). Speed Post articles can also be tracked online by using the 13 digit Speed Post article number through India Post web site (www.indiapost.gov.in) or by sending an SMS, POST TRACK on 166 or to 51969.

Business Post

A number of pre-mailing activities like folding, inserting, franking, addressing and pasting etc., are required to be completed before an article is posted. Large organizations were finding it difficult to carry out these premailing activities. The Department introduced 'Business Post' service in 1996 to offer a comprehensive solution to corporate/ government organizations / PSUs and other corporate houses for their pre-mailing requirements. Besides bringing in additional revenue, this activity is meeting the need of corporate and bulk customers.

Express Parcel and Business Parcel

Increasing e-Commerce market in the country has given a boost to the parcel segment where Business to Customer (B2C) parcels are on rise. There is also a requirement to cater the needs of the Customer to Customer (C2C) category parcels. Considering the market considerations, customer demands and operational feasibility, the Department rationalised parcel services. The Express Parcel / Business Parcel services were introduced from 2013.

Cash on Delivery

Increasing trend for e-tailing (online shopping) has tremendous business opportunities for payment services. In order to cater to these business opportunities and to provide a fast, safe and economical solution of collection of amount of goods at the time of its delivery and its remittance to sender, department introduced Cash on Delivery (COD) facility as value addition to the parcel service from 2013 and is available to the contractual customers of Express Parcel, Business Parcel and Speed Post.

Flat Rate Parcel

In order to provide convenience to its customers and with a view to standardize its parcel size and shape, Flat Rate Parcel service was introduced in 2011. Flat Rate Parcel is an air express parcel service which provides an added convenience to the customers by offering them pre-paid Flat Rate Parcel boxes. These boxes are available in three weight slabs viz. 1 kg, 2.5 kg and 5 kg., Flat Rate Parcel boxes are sold at Head Post Offices and other identified computerized post offices and delivered across India including rural areas. This service is available for international parcels also.

Logistics Post

Logistics Post offers customers a range of integrated logistics and fulfillment service that can be tailor-made to suit the requirements of the customers.

This service includes order processing, warehousing and door-to-door distribution.

e-Post

e-post is an unregistered hybrid mail for both retail and corporate customers providing electronic transmission of messages which may include text messages, scanned images, pictures, etc., and their delivery in hard copies at the destination through postman/delivery staff. Presently, e-post booking facility is available in more than 13,000 post offices and physical delivery through a network of more than 1.54 lakh post offices. e-post is mainly used by individual customers for sending limited number of e-post messages. This service can be availed by the customer by visiting e-post enabled post offices or it can be sent from customer's own premises by registering himself as pre paid user of e-post retail.

e-Payment

When businesses require collection of bills and other payments from customers across the country, the post office offers a simple and convenient solution in the form of e-payment. It is an option for businesses and organizations to collect their bills or other payments through the post office network. It is a many-to-one solution which allows collection of money (telephone bills, electricity bills, examination fee, taxes, university fee, school fee, etc.) on behalf of any organization. The collection is consolidated electronically and the payment is made centrally through a cheque from a specified post office of the biller's choice.

e-Post Office

e-Post Office is an e-commerce portal the Department which provides select postal facility to the common man through the internet. This portal is aimed at providing convenience to the public in availing select services.

Direct Benefit Transfer Through Post Offices

Direct Benefit Transfer (DBT) is a major reform initiative of the Government for re-engineering the existing delivery processes for transparent and simpler flow of funds and benefits to the beneficiaries. It envisages achieving accurate targeting of beneficiaries, deduplication and reduction of fraud, bringing efficiency in the delivery process, elimination of wastage, curbing leakage and thereby controlling expenditure. Department of Posts is functioning for disbursement of various social sector payments under DBT. The depth of our network and expertise in delivery enables unhindered reach of the benefits till last mile.

Philately

Philately is the hobby of collecting stamps as well as the study of postal history and other related items. It is a mode of commemorating, celebrating and promoting national heritage, culture, events and eminent personalities.

It plays a great role as an ambassador, a brand image of the postal administration concerned and a statement of sovereignty of nation.

The philatelic activities of the department include: designing, printing, distribution and sale of special/commemorative postage stamps through philatelic bureaus and counters; designing, printing and distribution of definitive postage stamps and items of postal stationery like envelope, inland letter card, postcard, aerogram, registered cover, etc; promotion of philately and conduct of philatelic exhibitions at the national level, and participation in international and world exhibitions as well as monitoring of exhibitions at state/regional and district levels; maintenance of the National Philatelic Museum, Dak Bhawan.

A total of 24 issues comprising 40 commemorative/special postage stamps were released during April to December 2015 commemorating various personalities, events/occasions. Some of the significant commemorations were, India – France : 50 Years of Space Co-operation (set of two stamps), India – Singapore Joint Issue(set of two stamps), 3rd India – Africa Forum Summit (set of six stamps). A set of four commemorative postage stamps on the theme "Women Empowerment" were also issued.

Financial Services

Department of Posts operates Small Savings Scheme on behalf of Ministry of Finance, Government of India. Post Office Savings Bank (POSB) has a customer base of more than 33.03 crore account holders in 2015. Savings Bank facility is provided through a network of 1.54 lakh post offices across the country. The outstanding balance under all National Savings Schemes and Saving Certificates in Post Offices were over 6,19,317.44 crore by 2015.

Core Banking Solution

The Core Banking Solution (CBS) is part of the India Post IT Modernization project that aims to bring in various IT solutions with the required infrastructure to the post offices. The project aims to implement Core Banking Solution in all the Departmental Post Offices for Small Savings Schemes during current Plan period. By June 2016, 22,395 post offices have been migrated to CBS, and ATMs installed at 946 locations.

Retailing of Mutual Funds

The post office is playing an important role in extending the reach of the capital market of the country and providing the common man easy access to market based investment options. Presently, Mutual Fund products of UTI MF only are being retailed through over 2,000 post Offices.

International Money Transfer Service

International Money Transfer Service is a quick and easy way of transferring personal remittances from abroad to beneficiaries in India. As a result of the collaboration of the Department of Posts, Government of India with the Western Union Financial Services and Money Gram International, a state-of the-art International Money Transfer Service is available through the Post Offices in India, which enables instantaneous remittance of money from around 195 countries to India. Presently the service is available from 9,943 locations across the country.

National Pension System

The Department is a point of presence for the National Pension System (NPS) for Indian citizens. Subscribers (any Indian citizen) in the age group of 18 to 55 can join NPS and contribute till the age of 60. These pension contributions are invested in various schemes of different Pension Fund Managers appointed by Pension Fund Regulatory and Development Authority (PFRDA). The subscriber's contributions will be invested as per the preference of the subscriber. Under this Scheme, any subscriber who intends to open a pension account will be provided the facility at all head post offices in the country.

Jan Suraksha Schemes and Atal Pension Yojana

Jan Suraksha Schemes viz., Pradhan Mantri Suraksha Bima Yojana (PMSBY) and Pradhan Mantri Jeevan Jyoti Bima Yojana (PMJJBY) were launched from 2015 in all CBS post offices. The schemes are available to all post office savings accountholders. By February 2016, 1,06,784 subscribers have been enrolled under PMSBY and 9,140 under PMJJBY. Atal Pension Yojana (APY) was also launched in CBS Head Post Offices from December 2015, and 25,398 subscribers had enrolled in this scheme by February 2016.

Postal Life Insurance and Rural Postal Life Insurance

Postal Life Insurance (PLI) was introduced on February 1884 with the express approval of the Secretary of State (for India) to Her Majesty the Queen Empress of India.

Maximum sum assured limit of PLI was been raised from ₹ 20 lakh to ₹ 50 lakh from December, 2014 and in RPLI from ₹ 5 lakh to ₹ 10 lakh from May, 2015. It now covers employees of Central and state governments, Central and state public sector undertakings, universities, government-aided educational institutions, nationalized banks and local bodies, etc. Of late, contractual employees also are under brought under the umbrella of PLI clientele. Apart from single insurance policies, PLI also manages a Insurance scheme for the Extra Departmental Employees (Gramin Dak Sevaks.

The prime objective of Rural Postal Life Insurance (RPLI) is to provide insurance cover to the rural public in general and to benefit weaker sections and women workers of rural areas in particular and also to spread insurance awareness among the rural population.

PLI is an exempted insurer under Section 118(c) of Insurance Act, 1938. PLI/RPLI is also exempted under Section 44(d) LIC Act, 1956.

With the liberalization of Insurance sector, PLI and RPLI are operating in a very competitive market. Both have the advantage of using the infrastructure of the department and its vast network and hence can offer life insurance cover at a lower cost than the other insurance companies. It has lower premium rate and higher bonus. Therefore various schemes of PLI and RPLI are very popular amongst eligible clients and are doing extremely well. Both the schemes are entirely managed by the employees of the department though the business has been growing substantially, and is being administered without appointing extra staff. All the benefits of such low cost operations are being passed on to the customers by way of low premium and higher bonus.

PLI offers six types of plans: whole life assurance (Suraksha); convertible whole life assurance (Suvidha); endowment assurance (Santosh); anticipated endowment assurance (Sumangal); joint life assurance (Yugal Suraksha); and children policy (Bal Jiwan Bima)

RPLI also offers six types of plans: whole life assurance (Grama Suraksha); convertible whole life assurance (Grama Suvidha); endowment assurance (Grama Santosh); anticipated endowment assurance (Grama Sumangal); 10 years RPLI (Grama Priya); and children policy (Bal Jiwan Bima)

Steps for Betterment of Customer Service

a) Payment of PLI/RPLI premium in any post office across the country. b) Indexing of customers complaints in system for speedy redressal of the complaints. c) Website with all information on PLI/RPLI and downloadable forms (www.postallifeinsurance.gov.in). d) Online transfer of policies from one circle to another. e) Facility for online payment of (www.epostoffice.gov.in) premium and revival amount calculator. f) Decentralization of maturity claims, loan & revival at division level. g) Training to marketing personnel and back office staff in marketing skill and underwriting issues is imparted to improve quality of service.

Training Infrastructure

The department has well established training infrastructure. The following training institutes take care of the training needs of the department: The Rafi Ahmed Kidwai National PostaL Academy (RAKNPA), Ghaziabad is the apex training institute, recognized by the DoP&T as a Central Training Institute. The Academy imparts induction as well as inservice training to the officers of Indian Postal Service and other managerial cadres of the department. It also imparts training to managers of Foreign Postal Administrations and officers of various Central Government Departments and PSUs, in areas of common interest. Postal Training Centres (PTCs) at Darbhanga, Guwahati, Madurai, Mysore, Saharanpur and Vadodara for operative staff and inspectorial cadres.

Information Technology

Ministry of Electronics and information technology (MeitY) deals with policy matters relating to information technology, electronics, internet (other than licensing of ISPs) and cyber security. The aim is to promote e-governance for empowering citizens, promoting the inclusive and sustainable growth of the electronics, IT & ITeS industries, enhancing India's role in internet governance, adopting a multipronged approach that includes development of human resources, promoting R&D and innovation, enhancing efficiency through digital services and ensuring a secure cyber space.

With the unveiling of the 'Digital India Programme' the role of MeitY has enhanced. The overarching vision of the programme is to transform India into a digitally empowered society and knowledge economy. The programme has three vision areas namely, digital infrastructure as a utility for every citizen, governance and services on demand and digital empowerment of citizens by bridging the digital divide in the country. This transformational programme is designed to build holistic capabilities across infrastructure, manufacturing, skills and delivery platforms which in turn will lead to creation of a self-reliant knowledge economy.

Digital infrastructure as a utility to every citizen includes availability of high speed internet for delivery of services to citizens, digital identity for every citizen, mobile phone and bank account enabling citizen participation in digital & financial space, shareable private space on a public cloud and safe and secure cyber-space.

Governance and services on demand includes seamlessly integrated services across departments or jurisdictions, services availability in real time from online & mobile platforms, digitally transformed services for improving ease of doing business, leveraging GIS for decision support systems and development.

The Nine Pillars of growth viz., broadband highways, universal access to mobile connectivity, public internet access programme, e-governance - reforming government through technology, eKranti- electronic delivery of services, information for all, electronics manufacturing, IT for jobs and early harvest programmes, are being promoted under Digital India Programme. The focus of the Government is to implement various components of the programme in an integrated manner. It is coordinated by the ministry of Electronics and Information Technology with the ministries and departments in the central and state governments partnering it in their respective domain areas.

Ministry of Electronics and Information Technology functions around the ambit of two major Acts: The Information Technology Act 2000 which provides legal recognition to the transaction carried out by means of electronic data interchange and other means of electronic communication, commonly referred to as "electronic commerce" which involves the use of alternatives to paper-based methods of communication and storage of information, to facilitate electronic filing of documents with the Government agencies. It gives provisions for the use of electronic records and digital signature with the provision of authentication and security. It also directs the establishment of Cyber Appellate Tribunal.

This Act was amended through the Information Technology (Amendment) Act, 2008 which substituted the word "digital signature" with "electronic signature" with major changes in various sections along with insertion of other sections. In order that various benefits and subsidies reach the targeted beneficiaries, the Government has made all efforts to leverage the Aadhaar platform. Further to give statutory backing to Aadhaar a suitable Bill in the Parliament has been introduced. A statutory backing will help to ensure that the benefits of various subsidies and programmes go to the truly deserving. What is envisaged is that while every resident shall be entitled to obtain an Aadhaar number, it will remain optional and not mandatory.

The Aadhaar (Targeted Delivery of Financial and Other Subsidies, Benefits and Services) Act, 2016 provides for, as a good governance, efficient, transparent and targeted delivery of subsidies, benefits and services, the expenditure for which is incurred from the Consolidated Fund of India, to individuals residing in India through assigning of a unique identity number to such individuals. It covers everything from the enrollment for Aadhaar number, authentication to establishment of UIDAI which has now become a statutory organization. Over 102.60 crore residents have been enrolled.

e-Governance

With the advent of Digital India as an apex programme various new policy initiatives have been taken up by MeitY such as eKranti, policy on adoption of open source software in e-governance systems, email policy, policy on use of IT resources, policy on Collaborative Application Development by Opening the Source Code of Government Applications, Application Development and Re-Engineering Guidelines for Cloud Ready Applications and e-Governance competency framework. Major schemes such as e-Districts, Common Service centres and State Wide Area Network (SWAN) have also been working in this direction.

Policy on Adoption of Open Source Software: It encourages the formal adoption and use of Open Source Software (OSS) in government organizations. As per this policy, all government organizations, while implementing e-governance applications and systems, must ensure compliance of this policy and decide by comparing both OSS and Closed Source Software (CSS) options with respect to capability, strategic control, scalability, security, life-time costs and support requirements.

Policy on Collaborative Application Development by Opening the Source Code of Government Applications: This policy aims to increase the pace of e-Governance application development and rapid roll out/implementation by adopting an open-source code, the Governments want successful, scalable, high quality e-governance applications to be developed in a collaborative manner.

Policy on use of IT Resources: This policy governs the usage of IT resources from an end user's perspective. The objective of this policy is to ensure proper access to and usage of government's IT resources and prevent their misuse by the users. This policy is applicable to all employees of GoI and employees of those of state/UT governments that choose to adopt this policy in future.

e-mail policy: This policy lays down the guidelines with respect to use of email services of GoI and employees of those. State/UT governments that use the e-mail services of GoI and also those that choose to adopt this policy in future. The objective of this policy is to ensure secure access and usage of e-mail services by its users.

Policy on Open Application Programming Interfaces (APIs): This policy is to promote software interoperability for all e-governance applications and systems and provide access to data and services for promoting participation of all stakeholders including citizens.

The 'e-Governance Competency Framework (e-GCF)' toolkit contains a set of end-user knowledge areas required for government employees. The objective of the framework is to strengthen the capacity building scheme to identify and define competencies, through a competency-based system which is required for different job roles under e-Governance.

In order to transform the quality of services and to provide integrated services the "eKranti" initiative aims to utilize emerging technologies such as cloud and mobile platform and focus on integration of services. The principle of this programme is 'Transformation' and not translation, and to provide integrated services and not individual services.

Another important initiative pertains to 'Jeevan Praman' is of providing an Aadhaar based Digital Life Certificate for pensioners. Over 15.96 lakh pensioners have registered on the portal and over 10.81 lakh. Digital life certificates have been successfully processed since its launch. A 'Digital Locker system' has also been envisaged to serve as a platform to enable citizens to securely share their documents with service providers who can directly access them electronically. 'eSign' framework has been released, which would allow citizens to digitally sign a document online using Aadhaar authentication.

National Scholarship Portal provides a centralized platform for application and disbursement of scholarship to students under any scholarship scheme. Over 1 crore applications have been submitted. 21 scholarships from 15 ministries/departments are registered. 54 schemes have been registered. National Scholarship Portal 2.0 Application has been made operational.

In order to integrate the delivery of government services (across various Departments), an initiative called Mobile Seva has been launched. A portal called 'Vikaspedia' to provide information on health, education, agriculture, energy, social welfare and e-governance in more than 10 languages with more languages being added.

MyGov.in is an innovative platform launched to ensure citizens' engagement in decision making by the government so that the ultimate goal of "good governance" for building India is achieved. This initiative is an opportunity for citizens and well-wishers from across the world to share their views on key issues directly with the Prime Minister.

Open Government Data (OGD) is a platform for supporting Open Data initiative of Government of India. The portal is intended to be used by ministries/ departments to publish datasets, documents, services, tools and applications collected by them for public use. It intends to increase transparency in the functioning of government and also open avenues for many more innovative uses of government data to give different perspective.

e-Sampark Database developed to send messages and emails to public representatives and government employees. This database has 98 lakh email addreses and over 12 crore mobile numbers. The count of mailers is over 114 crore for 243 campaigns.

Aadhaar-Enabled Biometric Attendance System (AEBS): In order to bring in efficiency in the Government, an Aadhaar enabled Biometric attendance system was implemented by MeitY.

e-Payment Framework: All payments and receipts to be in electronic mode. The portal payonline.gov.in envisaged as common platform for making physical payments online.

e-Hospital - OPD Registration Framework (ORF) is an initiative to facilitate the patients to take online OPD appointments with government hospitals. This framework also covers patient care, laboratory services and medical record management.

e-Districts: It is one of the 44 Mission Mode Projects (MMPs) under NeGP, with the MeitY, as the nodal Ministry, to be implemented by state government or their designated agencies. This MMP aims at electronic delivery of identified high volume citizen centric services, at district and sub-district level, those are not part of any other MMP. The MMP envisages leveraging and utilizing the four pillars of e-infrastructure namely, State Data Centres (SDC), SWANs, State Service Delivery Gateways (SSDGs) and Common Service Centres (CSCs), optimally to deliver public services electronically to citizens at their door steps. It has been launched in 553 districts and about 890 eServices have also been launched.

Common Services Centre: This Scheme aims at providing ICT enabled front-end service delivery outlets, across rural India covering six lakh villages. These internet enabled centres allow doorstep access to citizens to government, private and social services for skill development, education, digital literacy, health and financial services. New services namely banking, insurance and pension under Prime Minister Jan Dhan Yojna have made CSCs very vibrant. Digital Sakshartha Abhiyan (DISHA) for undertaking digital literacy has enabled active citizen participation through CSCs. Aadhaar Enrolment /

Update has been enabled through CSCs. In all 2,23,307 CSCs have been rolled out till June 2016.

State Wide Area Network (SWAN): SWAN has been identified as an element of the core infrastructure for supporting the e-governance initiatives and the (MeitY) has earmarked a significant outlay for supporting this activity. Under the National e-Governance Action plan, it is proposed to extend connectivity to the block level through NICNET/State Wide Area Network (SWAN). It is operational in 34 states/UTs and average bandwidth utilization is more than 60 per cent. SWAN has been integrated with National Knowledge Network (NKN) in 28 states/UTs.

Capacity Building Scheme II (CB Scheme II): Under the National e-Governance Plan, MeitY, has approved the Capacity Building Scheme Phase II, to give impetus in building capacities within the government by adapting a harmonized and synchronized approach, to ensure the availability of right skills. The core objective of the Capacity Building Scheme Phase II is to build capacities in central line ministries and state/UT line departments for implementation of various e-Governance initiatives. This is to enhance the abilities of the project teams, to have a holistic understanding on visualizing, conceiving and delivering projects.

GI Cloud: In order to utilise and harness the benefits of Cloud Computing, has embarked upon a very ambitious and important initiative – "GI Cloud" which has been coined as "MeghRaj". The focus of this initiative is to evolve a strategy and implement various components including governance mechanism to ensure proliferation of Cloud in government. Formulation of the Cloud Policy is one of the primary steps that will facilitate large scale adoption of Cloud by government.

National Centre for Geo-Informatics (NCoG) provides GIS based services to Government Ministries/ Departments. NCoG is currently involved in rolling out select GIS based Decision Support System for various organizations. Base map layers for administrative boundaries up to village level, major roads, rivers, rail on the scale of 1:10,000 across India have been completed. GIS based Decision Support System (DSS) platforms developed and rolled out for: Government Land Information System (Ministry of Urban Development); Rural Electrification Corporation; Mining Information System (Ministry of Mines); DSS for AICTE; Saltpan Information System (DIPP); PESA and National Asset Directory (MoPR); and e-District services with CSC locations (MeitY)

e-Infrastructure

It comprises tools, facilities and resources that are needed for advanced collaboration and includes integration of various technologies such as internet broadband channels, computing power, bandwidth provisioning, data storage, grid based resource sharing etc. To sustain the growth of Information and Communication Technologies (ICT) and to meet the challenges of globalization leading to highly competitive markets, there is a continuing need to invest in quality infrastructure, promote R&D efforts, create intellectual property in communications.

Information Technology Investment Region (ITIR): The Government has decided to attract major investment by providing a transparent and an investment friendly policy and set up Information Technology investment Regions. These are supposed to be endowed with excellent infrastructure and investor-friendly policy environment. Such ITIR would reap the benefits of co-siting, networking and greater efficiency through the use of common infrastructure and support services. This would boost and augment exports and lead to generation of employment. ITIRs are specifically delineated investment regions with a minimum area of around 40 square kms. It is a combination of production units, public utilities, logistic, environmental protection mechanisms, residential areas and administrative services.

National Policy on Universal Electronic Accessibility: Electronics and ICT can mitigate the barriers faced by differently abled persons as well as help them to participate independently in day-to-day life. National Policy on Universal Electronic Accessibility was formulated by this Ministry. The National Policy on Electronic Accessibility recognizes the need to eliminate discrimination on the basis of disabilities and to facilitate equal access to Electronics and ICT. It recognizes the diversity of differently abled persons and provides for their specific needs.

Promotion of Manufacturing of Electronics and IT-ITES

It is estimated that demand for electronics products and systems in India would grow to about US$ 400 billion by 2020. At the conventional rate of growth of domestic production, it would only be possible to meet demand for about US$ 100 billion by 2020. The Government attaches high priority to electronics and IT hardware manufacturing. It has the potential to generate domestic wealth and employment, apart from enabling a cyber-secure ecosystem. In the area of manufacturing the basic focus in on boosting domestic manufacture in the electronic industry.

Promotion of R&D and Innovation

Technological Incubation and Development of Entrepreneurs (TIDE): It aims to assist Institutions of Higher learning to strengthen their Technology Incubation Centres and thus enable young entrepreneurs to initiate technology startup companies for commercial exploitation of technologies developed by them. The incubation centers provide a host of services to new enterprises and facilitate linkages that are congenial for their survival and growth. The centre also network with Angel Investors and Venture Capitalists who provide mentoring and financial support to the startup companies and enable the tenant companies to mature over a period of 2-3 years and graduate to a commercial place to do the actual business.

Multiplier Grant Scheme (MSG): In order to establish, nurture and strengthen the linkages between the Industry and Institutes and promote industry oriented R&D at institutes; the scheme aims to encourage industry to collaborate with premier Academic and Government R&D institutions for development of products/packages.

National Supercomputing Mission (NSM) has been initiated with an outlay of ₹ 4,500 (crore over 7 years) which will enable India to leapfrog to the league of world class computing power nations.

A new centre of Society for Applied Microwave Electronics Engineering and Research (SAMEER) for Electromagnetic Environmental Effects at Visakhapatnam has been established for highly specialized state-of-the-art EMI/EMC test and measurement facilities including Electromagnetic Pulse (EMP) and Pulse Current Injection (PCI) to meet the strategic and civilian requirements of the country.

Human Resource Development

Scheme for enhancing PhDs in ESDM and IT/ITeS (1500 each in 5 yrs)- Outlay of the scheme is ₹ 466 crore. So far, 1,436 PhD fellowships (1086 full-time and 350 part-time) to 96 academic institutions across 28 States & UTs have been allocated. A total of 872 PhD candidates (738 full-time and 134 parttime) have been enrolled at the institutes.

Graduate level / Niche Area

Scheme for setting up 7 Electronics and ICT Academies for faculty development – Outlay ofthe scheme is ₹ 147.48 crore. The scheme aims at setting up of four Electronics and ICT Academies at IIITDM, Jabalpur (Madhya Pradesh), NIT, Warangal (Telangana) and NIT, Patna (Bihar) and IIT, Guwahati (Assam) has been completed. Three more academies at IIT, Kanpur, IIT, Roorkee & MNIT, Jaipur have been approved.

Information Security Education and Awareness (ISEA) Phase-II: Under this scheme 51 institutions across the country have been identified and MoUs signed.

Digital Literacy

MeitY has approved the following two Schemes for providing Digital Literacy to the masses: Scheme for IT Mass Literacy, National Digital Literacy Mission was approved in March, 2014. The total budget outlay of the Scheme is ₹ 97.02 crore. The duration of the Scheme was initially 18 months, which was later extended up to June 2016. The Scheme aims to train 10 lakh persons. The Scheme was launched in 2014.

Digital Empowerment of citizens by providing Universal Digital Literacy is an integral component of the vision of 'Digital India' initiative. Keeping this in view, a scheme titled 'Digital Saksharta Abhiyan' (DISHA) to make 42.5 lakh persons digitally literate in selected households throughout the country was approved.

Cyber Security

Millions of people in the country (both in rural and urban areas) rely on the services and information available in cyber space. Increasingly, the work of government, business and national infrastructure is becoming highly dependent on cyber space. As the quantity and value of electronic information has increased, so too have the business models and efforts of criminals and other adversaries who have embraced cyber space as a more convenient and profitable way of carrying out their activities anonymously. Hence, security of cyber space has become an important part of the national agenda.

Considering this, the National Cyber Security Policy, 2013 was put in place. It is aimed at building a secure and resilient cyberspace for citizens, businesses and Government, by way of actions to protect information and information infrastructure in cyberspace, build capabilities to prevent and respond to cyber threats, reduce vulnerabilities and minimize damage from cyber incidents through a combination of institutional structures, people, processes, technology and cooperation.

A number of initiatives have been taken towards securing cyber space. These initiatives have focused on issues such as cyber security threat perceptions, threats to critical information infrastructure and national security, protection of critical information infrastructure, adoption of relevant security technologies, enabling legal processes, mechanisms for security compliance and enforcement, information security awareness, training and research.

National Cyber Co-ordination Centre (NCCC) is being set-up with an aim to generate cyber security situational awareness to anticipate and prepare for cyber attacks. NCCC will aggregate cyber threat related information from various identified sources in the country for near real time threat assessment and situational awareness that will help in analysis and generation of timely alerts and periodic reports. This initiative is expected to help in securing the cyber space and strengthening the cyber security posture in the country by leveraging the expertise of people, deploying standard processes and sharing of resources.

Botnet Cleaning and Malware Analysis Centre: Indian Computer Emergency Response Team (CERT-In) is implementing a 'Botnet Cleaning and Malware Analysis Centre' for detection of compromised systems in India and to notify, enable cleaning and securing systems of end users to prevent further malware infections. The project is being implemented in close coordination and collaboration with Internet Service Providers and Industry.

Statutory Organizations

Controller of Certifying Authorities

Digital Signature Certificates (DSC) are issued by Certifying Authorities (CA) who have been licensed by the Controller of Certifying Authorities (CCA). The Office of CCA empanels licensed CAs for offering eSign Services for which the legal framework and guidelines are already in place. So far, three of the eight licensed CAs have been empanelled by the Office of CCA for providing eSign Service. These eSign Service Providers (ESP) are expected to facilitate digital signing for Aadhaar holders only on the basis of their eKYC from UIDAI.

Cyber Appellate Tribunal

In accordance with the provision contained under Section 48(1) of the IT Act 2000, the Cyber Regulations Appellate Tribunal (CRAT) was established in October, 2006. As per the IT Act, any person aggrieved by an order made by the Controller of Certifying Authorities or by an Adjudicating Officer under the Act can appeal before the Cyber Appellate Tribunal (CAT). This Tribunal is headed by a Chairperson who is appointed by the Central Government by notification as provided under Section 49 of the IT Act 2000. In order to carry forward the programmes and schemes there are various Organizations which come under the jurisdiction of MeitY:-

Indian Compuer Emergency Response Team (CERT-IN)

CERT-In is a functional organisation of Ministry of Electronics and Information Technology, Ministry of Communications and Information Technology, Government of India. CERT-In has been designated under Section 70B of the Information Technology (Amendment) Act, 2008 to serve as the national agency to perform the following functions in the area of cyber security: (1) collection, analysis and dissemination of information on cyber security incidents; (2) forecast and alerts of cyber security incidents; (3) emergency measures for handling cyber security incidents; (4) coordination of cyber security incident response activities; (5) issue guidelines, advisories, vulnerability notes and white papers relating to information security practices, procedures, prevention, response and reporting of cyber incidents, and; (6) such other functions relating to cyber security as may be prescribed.

Centre for Development of Advanced Computing

Centre for Development of Advanced Computing (C-DAC) has emerged as a premier R&D organization in IT&E (Information Technologies and Electronics) working on strengthening national technological capabilities in the context of global developments in the field and responding to change in the market need in selected foundation areas.

Society for Applied Microwave Electronics Engineering and Research

Society for Applied Microwave Electronics Engineering and Research (SAMEER) was set up as an autonomous R & D laboratory at Mumbai with a broad mandate to undertake R & D work in the areas of Microwave Engineering and Electromagnetic Engineering Technology. It is an offshoot of the special microwave products unit (SMPU) set up in 1977 at the Tata Institute of Fundamental Research (TIFR), Mumbai. SAMEER, Mumbai was setup in 1984. SAMEER Centres work in high end technology areas of RF/ Microwaves and allied disciplines. It undertakes design, development and delivery of hardware to meet stringent specifications of user agencies in its core areas of expertise including high power RF amplifiers, communication systems, atmospheric radar instrumentation, linear accelerators, RF/ microwave/millimeter wave subsystems and systems, photonics etc.

Centre for Materials for Electronics Technology

Centre for Materials for Electronics Technology (C-MET) was set up as a registered Scientific Society in March 1990 under the Department of Electronics (now Ministry of Electronics & Information Technology) as a unique concept for development of viable technologies in the area of materials mainly for electronics. C-MET is operating through its laboratories situated at Pune, Hyderabad and Thrissur.

ERNET

ERNET India is an Autonomous Scientific Society of Ministry of Electronics and Information Technology, Government of India. ERNET has made significant contribution to the emergence of networking in the country. In addition to providing connectivity, it has been meeting the needs of academic and research institutions by providing IT consultancy, project management and training. ERNET has been providing Domain name services and connectivity services, both terrestrial & via VSAT from its inception.

National e-Governance Division

To meet ever growing demand of e-Governance across the nation, National e-Governance Division (NeGD) was established as amalgamation of experts from the private sector and the Government. NeGD has been playing a pivotal role in discharging the key tasks including programme management and technical support of various components of the Digital India Programme. Some of the major activities of NeGD include monitoring and coordination of the entire Digital India Programme; technical appraisal, assistance to MeitY and other Central ministries/departments on e-Governance Projects.

National Informatics Centre

National Informatics Centre (NIC) was established in 1976, and has since emerged as a "prime builder" of e-Government/e-Governance applications up to the grassroots level as well as a promoter of digital opportunities for sustainable development. NIC, through its ICT Network, "NICNET", has institutional linkages with all the ministries/departments of the Central government, 36 state governments/union territories, and about 650+ district administrations of the country. NIC has been instrumental in steering e-Government/e-Governance applications in government ministries/ departments at the Centre, states, districts and blocks, facilitating improvement in government services, wider transparency, promoting decentralized planning and management, resulting in better efficiency and accountability to the people.

Stantardization, Testing and Quality Certification

Stantardization, Testing and Quality Certification (STQC) Directorate is an attached office of Ministry of Electronics and Information Technology. A network of testing and calibration laboratories has been established across the country including North East region. The laboratories are equipped with state of the art standards and equipment and provide testing, calibration, training and certification services to industry. Currently, STQC services are being utilized by more than 10,000 organizations representing the entire segment of industry, Government departments, R&D organizations etc.

National Internet Exchange of India

National Internet Exchange of India (NIXI) is a not for profit organization set up under Section 25 of the Companies Act, 1956 for peering of ISPs among themselves and routing the domestic traffic within the country. With seed funding from Ministry of Electronics and Information Technology. NIXI is performing the following three activities: 1) internet exchanges 2) IN registry and internationalized domain names (IDNs) 3) national internet registry (NIR).

Unique Identification Authority of India

The Unique Identification Authority of India (UIDAI) was established in January 2009, as an attached office to the Planning Commission now an attached office of Ministry of Electronics & IT with the vision, "To empower residents of India with a unique identity and a digital platform to authenticate anytime, anywhere". A key objective of Aadhaar programme is to provide an 'identity infrastructure' for delivery of various social welfare programs and for effective targeting of welfare services. The potential of Aadhaar can be realized through its use of the infrastructure as an ID proof and as a unique key by various state departments, central ministries, PSUs, and private sector entities to provide service delivery to residents in an integrated fashion.

National Institute of Electronics and Information Technology

National Institute of Electronics and Information Technology (NIELIT), a Scientific Society of the MeitY, is actively engaged in capacity building and skill development in the areas of Information Technology (IT); electronics, communication technologies, hardware, cyber law, cyber security, IPR, GIS, cloud computing; ESDM; e-Waste; ioT; e- governance and related verticals. NIELIT offers courses both in the formal as well as the non-formal sectors and is also one of the national examination bodies which accredit institutes / organizations for the conduct of courses in the non-formal sector. NIELIT is also the preferred agency for many state governments for rolling out IT literacy programmes for its employees and the masses.

Software Technology Parks of India

Software Technology Parks of India (STPI) was set up in 1991 as an autonomous society under the MeitY. It main objective has been the promotion of software exports from the country. It acts as 'single-window' in providing services to the software exporters. The services rendered by It for the software exporting community have been statutory services, data communications services, incubation facilities, training and value added services. It has played a key developmental role in the promotion of software exports with a special focus on SMEs and start up units. STPI is responsible for implementation of the Software Technology Parks (STP) scheme and the Electronics Hardware Technology Parks (EHTP) scheme.

Media Lab Asia

Media Lab Asia has been promoted by Ministry of Electronics and Information technology, as a not for profit company. The objective of the company was set to bring the benefits of ICT to the common man. The functional activity includes application areas such as ICT for healthcare, education, livelihood and empowerment of disabled. The company has a unique way of growth by working with an expanding network of research laboratories for undertaking development work. It started with creating a hub at some of the IITs and the list of such project partners has grown to more than 58. The partners are a combination of academic and Research and Development institutions, industry, NGOs and Govt. agencies. The projects can be sponsored by corporate bodies, govt. (Central/state) and local municipal bodies/ panchayats, etc.

Telecommunication

Communications Sector has assumed the position of an essential infrastructure for socio-economic development in an increasingly knowledge-intensive world. The reach of telecom services to all regions of the country has become an integral part of an innovative and technologically-driven society. Studies have shown a positive correlation of the Internet and Mobile Services on growth of the GDP of a country. As a result of sustainable measures taken by the Government over the years, the Indian Telecom Sector has grown exponentially and has become the second largest network in the world, next only to China.

Present Status

This is the period when the number of telephone connections has crossed the figure of 1 billion. The number of telephones increased from 99.61 crore to 103.6 crore at the end of December, 2015.

Department of Telecommunication

Department of Telecommunication (DOT) is committed to provide secure, reliable, affordable and high quality converged telecommunication services anytime, anywhere for an accelerated inclusive socio-economic development. The department is working towards the objective of maximizing public good by making available affordable, reliable and secure voice and data services across the country.

To serve the nation in its vastness and diversity, modern telecommunication facilities will be facilitated to all remote corners of this country with special focus on underserved areas in North-Eastern Region and backward areas, especially the Left Wing Extremism (LWE) – affected areas. The provision of high speed digital highway to connect the nation and to deliver government services to every citizen will be made for socio-economic development. The telecom sector needs to be strengthened further to ensure rapid growth of the economy and to overcome developmental challenges in other areas like education, health and employment generation. Our present policy with supporting legislative framework and licensing principles has the strong capability to adjust to rapid technological changes and to accelerate the innovation.

Wire Line vs. Wireless

While wireless voice and data services continued to grow, the landline provided remarkable support to high speed data services. The landline telephone connections are now 2.5 crore and the number of wireless telephone connections has grown to 101.1 crore at the end of December, 2015. As a result, the share of wireless telephones increased to 97.54 per cent of total services. The ever-expanding demand for wireless services has propelled the telecom sector to create sustainable resources to meet such requirements.

Public vs. Private

Another noteworthy feature of the Indian Telecom Sector is the continuous rise in the number of telephones of the private sector operators. At the end of December, 2015, the total number of telephone connections provided by the private sector increased to 93.2 crore and number of telephone connections provided by the public sector stood at 10.5 crore. The share of private sector in the total number of connections increased to 89.88 per cent at the end of December, 2015, over public sector share of 10.12 per cent during the same period. In present scenario, the private sector has a dominant position in Telecom Sector.

Table 8.1: Telecom Development Indicators

Sl. No.	Item		March'13	March'14	March'15	December'14	December'15
1	Number of Telephones (In million)	Overall	898.02	933.02	996.13	971.01	1036.57
2		Wire line	30.21	28.50	26.59	27.00	25,52
3		Wireless	867,81	904.52	969.54	944.01	1011.05
4		Rural	349.21	377.78	416.08	398.73	434.23
5		Urban	548,80	555.23	580.05	572.27	602.34
6	Tele-density (Telephones per 100 persons)	Overall	73,32	75.23	79.36	74.03	81.85
7		Rural	41.05	44.01	48,04	42.71	49.82
8		Urban	146.64	145.46	149.04	144.63	152.57
9	Percentage share	Wireless	96.64	96.95	97.33	97.22	97.54
10		Public	14.49	12.87	10,07	10,85	10.12
11		Private	85.51	87.13	89,93	89.15	89.88
12	Percentage growth of Total Telephones - over previous year		(-)5.61	3.90	6.76	6.10	6.75

Percentage growth of Total Telephones in respect of December, 2015-over December, 2014

Tele-Density

Tele-density, which denotes the number of telephones per 100 population, is an important indicator of telecom penetration in any country. Tele-density in India, which was 79.36 per cent in April 2015, increased to 81.85 per cent at the end of December, 2015. The rural tele-density increased from 48.04 per cent to 49.82 per cent per cent during this period. Urban tele-density, maintained its upward trend (higher than the rural tele-density) from 149.04 per cent to 152.57 per cent during this period. Amongst the service areas, Himachal Pradesh (124.54 per cent) had the highest tele-density followed by, Tamil Nadu (117.27 per cent), Punjab (104.15 per cent), Karnataka (102.33 per cent) and Kerala (100.52 per cent). On the other hand, the service areas such as Bihar (52.55 per cent), Assam (55.22 per cent), West Bengal (61.40 per cent), Madhya Pradesh (63.07 per cent), Uttar Pradesh (63.51 per cent) and Odisha (65.69 per cent) have comparatively low tele-density. Amongst the three metros of Delhi, Kolkata and Mumbai, Delhi service area tops in tele-density with 240.93 per cent, followed by Kolkata (160.30 per cent) and Mumbai (149.45 per cent).

Unified Licence

With a view to achieve the objective of NTP-2012 to create one nation – one license across services and service areas, the Department of Telecommunication (DoT) has issued guidelines on Unified Licence. As per these guidelines, the allocation of spectrum is delinked from the licence and has to be obtained separately as per the prescribed procedure, i.e., bidding process. Only one Unified License is required for all telecom services in the entire country. In addition, authorization for various services [like access services, national long distance services, international long distance services, Internet Service Provider (ISP) services will be required separately. Single authorization for Unified License (All services) category would cover all telecom services except ISP (B) and ISP (C) services]. The tenure of such authorization will run concurrently with the Unified License. Also, the entry fee for various telecom services have been reduced substantially.

Foreign Direct Investment (FDI) Policy

To attract the FDI inflow and to make the sector more attractive and investor friendly, the Government raised FDI limit for the telecom services from 74 per cent to 100 per cent. This measure will facilitate telecom licensees to consolidate equity and raise domestic as well as foreign debt from the market. Telecommunication and telecom services have been included under the Harmonized Master list of infrastructure sub-sector and qualify for infrastructure lending. Reserve Bank of India has also expanded the existing definition for infrastructure sector for the purpose of availing External Commercial Borrowing (ECB).

Universal Service Obligation Fund

To give impetus to the rural telephony, the Government in June, 2002, established Universal Service Obligation Fund (USOF). Subsequently, the scope of USOF was widened to provide subsidy support for enabling access to all types of telegraph services including mobile services, broadband connectivity and creation of infrastructure like optical fiber in rural and remote areas. Therefore, various schemes have been launched by USOF for provision of telecom services in rural and remote areas of the country.

Bharatnet

The optical fiber has predominantly reached State capitals, districts and blocks. To connect all 2.5 lakh gram panchayats in the country, the Government approved a project called 'National Optical Fiber Network (NOFN)', now known as BharatNet. Non-discriminatory access to the network will be provided to all the telecom service providers like mobile, Internet and cable TV in rural areas. The project is being executed by a Special Purpose Vehicle (SPV), namely, Bharat Broadband Networks Limited (BBNL). Under this project, up to December 2015, 1,11,645 km of pipes and 82,501 km of optical fibre cables have been laid in the country. Further, the number of gram panchayats which OFC has connected is 34,881.

Mobile Communication Services in Left Wing Extremism Affected Areas

Government, in 2014, approved a project to provide Mobile Services in 2,199 locations in Left Wing Extremism (LWE)-affected areas, identified by Ministry of Home Affairs, in Andhra Pradesh, Bihar, Chhattisgarh, Jharkhand, Maharashtra, Madhya Pradesh, Odisha, Telangana, Uttar Pradesh and West Bengal. The scheme is being executed by Bharat Sanchar Nigam Limited (BSNL). 1,288 sites are connected as on December 31, 2015.

Rural Wire-Line Broadband Scheme

For providing wire-line broadband connectivity up-to village level in rural and remote areas, USOF signed an agreement with BSNL under the Rural Wire-line Broadband Scheme to provide wire-line broadband connectivity to rural and remote areas by leveraging the existing rural exchanges infrastructure and copper wire-line network. The speed of each of the broadband connections shall be at least 512 Kbps. It is estimated that there are about 55,669 villages in the country that do not have mobile coverage. Providing mobile coverage to the 8,621 uncovered villages in the North Eastern Region (NER) has been included as part of Comprehensive Telecom Development Plan for NER.

Regulatory Framework

The Telecom Regulatory Authority of India (TRAI) has always endeavoured to encourage greater competition in the telecom sector together with better quality and affordable prices in order to meet the objectives of National

Telecom Policy (NTP)-2012. A number of recommendations on various telecom issues were made by TRAI during 2015-16. TRAI has also taken steps to ensure the quality of service provided by the service providers by way of monitoring the performance of Basic and Cellular Mobile Telephone Service on quarterly basis and Point of Interconnection (POI) congestion on monthly basis. The regulatory measures taken by TRAI facilitate orderly growth of telecom sector by promoting healthy competition and enhancing investment efficiency besides protecting the interest of consumers.

Research and Development

C-DOT, an autonomous body, is DoT's R&D arm. The organisation is committed to providing a wide range of cost-effective, indigenously developed and state-of-the-art total telecom solutions. C-DOT has grown to the level of a national centre for R&D in communication technology in many areas –Satellite communications, IN, ATM, DWDM, NMS, Wireless Broadband, GPON, NGN and Mobile Cellular systems. C-DOT is also entrusted with the projects of national importance, like Central Monitoring System for telecom security and Secure Network for strategic applications.

DoT has the following PSUs under its administrative control: a) Bharat Sanchar Nigam Limtied (BSNL); b) Mahanagar Telephone Nigam Limited (MTNL); c) ITI Limited; d) Telecommunications Consultants India Limited (TCIL); e) Bharat Broadband Network Limited (BBNL); f) Hemisphere Properties India Limited (HPIL).

Bharat Sanchar Nigam Limited

Bharat Sanchar Nigam Limited (BSNL), fully owned by Government of India, formed in October 2000, provides telecom services across the length and breadth of the country excluding Delhi and Mumbai. BSNL is providing all types of telecom services namely telephone services on landline, WLL and GSM mobile, broadband, internet, leased circuits and long distance telecom services. Rural telephony is one of its focus areas. BSNL also pays special emphasis on development of telecommunication facilities in North-Eastern region and in tribal areas as well as in the LWE affected areas.

Mahanagar Telephone Nigam Limited

Mahanagar Telephone Nigam Limited (MTNL), set up in 1986, is a Navratna PSU and provides telecommunication facilities in India's key metros - Delhi and Mumbai. MTNL is the principal provider of fixed-line telecommunication service in these two metropolitan cities, and for GSM Mobile services in four peripheral towns of Noida, Gurgaon, Faridabad and Ghaziabad along with Delhi city and the areas falling under the Mumbai Municipal Corporation, New Mumbai Corporation and Thane Municipal Corporation along with Mumbai city, also come under the jurisdiction of the company. MTNL is providing triple play services i.e. voice, high speed internet and IPTV on its Broadband network. At present, 56.25 per cent equity shares are held by

Government of India and remaining 43.75 per cent shares are held by FIIs, Financial Institutions, Banks, Mutual Funds and others including individual investors.

ITI Limited

ITI Limited was established in 1948, to supply telecom equipments to the then telecom service provider, DoT. ITI started its operations in Bangalore in 1948, which were further extended to other areas by setting up manufacturing plants at Srinagar in Jammu and Kashmir, Naini, Rae Bareli and Mankapur in Uttar Pradesh, and Palakkad in Kerala. All the manufacturing plants are accreditied with ISO 9001-2000 standards. The establishment of these plants at various locations was aimed not only at the augmentation of manufacturing capacity but also at the development of social infrastructure.

Telecommunications Consultants India Limited

Telecommunications Consultants India Limited (TCIL) was set-up in 1978 with the main objective to provide world class technology in all fields of telecommunications and information technology to excel in its operations in overseas and in the domestic markets by developing proper marketing strategies, to acquire state of the art technology on a continuing basis and to maintain leadership. It has diversified into cyber parks, intelligent buildings, cyber & smart cities and upgradation of legacy networks by focusing on broadband multimedia convergent service networks, entering new areas of IT and IT–enabled services. It is also developing telecom and IT-training infrastructure abroad.

Bharat Broadband Network Limited

Bharat Broadband Network Limited (BBNL) a Special Purpose Vehicle (SPV), namely, Bharat Broadband Networks Limited (BBNL) was incorporated in 2012 under the Indian Companies Act, 1956 for execution of the BharatNet for connecting 2.50 lakh (approximately) Gram Panchayats (GPs).

Hemisphere Properties India Limited (HPIL) is another PSU under DoT. At the time of 25 per cent stake strategic sale in Videsh Sanchar Nigam Limited (now Tata Communications Limited), surplus land measuring 773.13 acres was demarcated out of total 1230.13 acres of land at four stations and it was decided that surplus land will not be a part of disinvestment bid and would be managed by a separate realty company. Rights of the Government in this land were protected through a scheme of arrangement incorporated in the Share Purchase Agreement (SPA) and Share Holders Agreement (SHA). Accordingly, the Government has approved the scheme of demerger of Surplus land of VSNL into a Resulting Company and in March, 2014, 51.12 per cent shares of resulting Company namely Hemisphere Properties India Limited (HPIL) have been acquired by the Government. With this, HPIL has become the Sixth Public Sector Undertaking (PSU) of Department of Telecom.

Vision of Digital India

The vision of Digital India aims to transform the country into a digitally empowered society and knowledge economy. The programme will be implemented in phases till 2018. This programme has been envisaged by Department of Electronics and Information Technology (DeitY). It would also bring in public accountability through mandated delivery of Government's services electronically; a Unique ID and e-Pramaan based on authentic and standard based interoperable and integrated Government applications and data basis. The source of funding for most of the e-Governance projects at present is through budgetary provisions of respective ministries/ departments in the Central or State Governments. Requirements of funds for individual project(s) for Digital India will be worked out by respective nodal ministries/departments.

Scope of Digital India

The overall scope of this programme is: a) to prepare India for a knowledge future; b) on being transformative that is to realize IT (Indian Talent) + IT (Information Technology) = IT (India Tomorrow); c) making technology central to enabling change; and d) on being an Umbrella Programme-covering many departments.

The programme weaves together a large number of ideas and thoughts into a single, comprehensive vision, so that each of them is seen as part of a larger goal. Each individual element stands on its own, but is also part of the larger picture.The weaving together makes the Mission transformative in totality.

It will pull together many existing schemes which would be restructured and re-focused and implemented in a synchronized manner. The common branding of the programmes as Digital India highlights their transformative impact.

Digital India aims to provide the much needed thrust to the nine pillars of growth areas, namely: 1. broadband highways; 2.universal access to mobile connectivity; 3. public internet access programme; 4. e-Governance: reforming government through technology; 5. e-Kranti - electronic delivery of services; 6. information for all; 7. electronics manufacturing; 8.IT for Jobs; and 9. early harvest programmes.

Following initiatives have been taken under the Digital India Programme.

(i) LIMBS (Legal Information and Management Based System)

LIMBS is an easy to access, web-based tool for comprehensive, regulatory and proactive monitoring of court cases.

It is a web-based platform which provides a common access portal to all users having varying needs and cutting across administration pyramids i.e., access is available right from the file dealer to the top management. LIMBS has use friendly data entry screen for capturing the details of court cases. Progress of court cases can be entered. Various MIS reports help to monitor these cases. E-document vault allows user to enter the important judgement. SMS alerts are used to sensitize the users over important issues.

(ii) NDSAP (National Data Sharing and Accessibility Programme)

The objective of this policy is to facilitate the access to Government of India owned shareable data and information in both human readable and machine readable forms through a network all over the country in a proactive updatable manner, within the framework of various related policies. Acts and rules of Government of India, thereby permitting wider accessibility and use of public data and information.

(iii) e-Office

The main objectives of e-office are:- a) to improve efficiency, consistency and effectiveness of government responses; b) to reduce turnaround time and to meet and demands of the citizens charter; c) to provide for effective resource management to improve the quality of administration; d) to reduce processing delays; e) to establish transparency and accountability; f) the system will automate movement of files within government offices, etc.

9 Defence

INDIA'S landmass covers an area of 3.3 million square kilometers and is strategically located vis-a-vis both continental Asia and the Indian Ocean Region (IOR). Land borders extending more than 15,500 kms. and a coastline totalling over 7,500 kilometers make India a continental or maritime neighbour of 11 countries in Asia. The borders that India shares with her neighbours are diverse: Himalayan peaks which rise up to 28,000 feet in the north; deserts and fertile plains in the west; high ranges and dense tropical forests in the east and maritime borders in the Bay of Bengal, Arabian Sea and the Indian Ocean. India is not only centrally located in South Asia, but also abuts West Asia and South East Asia. India's location at the base of continental Asia and at the top of the Indian Ocean provides it a vantage point with respect to both, Central Asia and the Indian Ocean region. The island territories of the Andaman and Nicobar Islands, located 1,300 kms. away from the mainland in the Bay of Bengal, provide India with a strategic presence at the entrance to the Strait of Malacca, through which more than 60,000 shipping vessels transit each year.

The Lakshadweep and Minicoy Islands, located about 450 kms. away from the mainland in the Arabian Sea, sit astride the sea lanes of communication running eastward from the Persian Gulf and the Red Sea. The island territories along with a long coastline extend India's territorial waters to more than 1,60,000 square kilometers and the Exclusive Economic Zone (EEZ) to more than two million square kilometers. India is, thus a maritime as well as a continental entity. India's size, strategic location, trade links and EEZ links its security environment directly with the extended neighbourhood, particularly with neighbouring countries and the regions of West Asia, Central Asia, South-East Asia, East Asia and the Indian Ocean. A stable and peaceful regional and international environment is a critical requirement to create a conducive climate for the overall national development.

The activities of terrorist groups, the menace of drug trafficking, the spread of small arms, the proliferation of weapons of mass destruction and the challenges to maritime security in the immediate and extended neighbourhood are some of the critical factors that affect India's security environment. To deal with these conventional and non-conventional security challenges, India continues to pursue a robust defence strategy that involves both, the strengthening of its own capabilities as well as engagement in regional and global efforts to promote peace and stability.

Regional and Global Security Environment

India's security environment encompasses a complex matrix of regional and global issues and challenges. India's strategic location and its growing global interactions require engagement on a range of issues that impact on national security with a view to securing vital national interests. The need to enhance preparedness to address consequences of instability and volatility in parts of the immediate and extended neighbourhood remains a key priority. At the same time, there are renewed and successful efforts to build stronger defence partnerships with a wide range of friendly foreign countries to enhance international peace and stability.

The security situation in India's immediate South Asian neighbourhood presents a mixed picture. While there was an improvement in the security and political situation in some countries, political developments caused a worsening of the internal security situation in others. Terrorism, insurgency and sectarian conflict increasingly threaten the stability of the region. Amidst ongoing efforts to impart fresh dynamism to strengthening relations with neighbours in a comprehensive manner, cooperative security approaches are of immediate relevance to the region. India is committed to build security cooperation with all partners in the neighbourhood on the basis of equality, mutual benefit and mutual respect.

The Indian Ocean Region (IOR) is central to India's growth and security. By virtue of its geo-physical configuration as well its strategic and economic imperatives, India looks to the seas and oceans surrounding it. India's peninsular projection into the Indian Ocean Region, astride the vital sea-lanes of the world stretching from the Suez Canal and the Persian Gulf to the Malacca Straits, also links India's ability to engage freely in maritime trade and commerce.

India is also impacted by developments beyond its immediate neighbourhood and the Indian Ocean Region. Developments in West Asia, Central Asia and the Asia Pacific have a direct bearing on India's interests. In all these regions, we are witnessing major political and economic shifts with strategic implications. While many of these transitions are marked by growing volatility and violence, at the same time, inter-linkages of globalisation and deepening economic interdependence are also increasingly evident. Consequent re-calibrations and dynamics in the global balance of power, that are also driven by the rise of emerging economies and multipolarity, have created further uncertainties in the strategic outlook.

The continuing economic slowdown in the West, Japan and China, combined with the rapid and sustained fall in energy prices directly affecting major oil producing countries such as Russia, have depressed the global economic outlook. The economies of other regions are also being adversely affected, as manifested through currency fluctuations, decline in exports and lower direct investment flows.

Though the possibility of a full-scale conventional war between states has comparatively receded as compared to the 20th century, the rise of new threats and drivers of conflict, including proxy wars as part of continuing efforts by some states to destabilise other states, have created a regional and global security landscape that in some ways is even more challenging. Rising nationalism, increasing military spending, spiralling migration and refugee flows due to man-made and natural crises, easy availability of weapons and intense competition for natural resources provide added volatility to existing fault lines.

Terrorism and the activities of terrorist organisations are perhaps the most serious threat to peace and security. The use of terrorism as an instrument of policy by a few States has exacerbated intra and inter-state conflicts. Terrorist groups have leveraged new technologies, particularly in cyberspace, for transnational mobilisation and ideological radicalisation, especially of the youth. They also continue to gain logistical and financial support for their activities from disparate sources, including some states, and are increasingly able to threaten regions well beyond their base areas. Notwithstanding the rise of more malevolent terrorist groups, the Af-Pak region in India's neighbourhood continues to be the epicentre of international terrorism. There is continuing concern over terrorist threats emanating from India's neighbourhood and the transnational linkages through which such groups are being sustained.

Peace and stability in various regions of the world are marred by the proliferation of weapons of mass destruction. In particular, the threat of nuclear terrorism continues to be a major international security concern, notwithstanding international efforts to strengthen nuclear security and to prevent non-State actors from acquiring nuclear materials.

Shifts in the global balance of power as reflected in recent developments in the Asia-Pacific region, have introduced new dimensions in military and diplomatic interactions among the major powers and regional states. This has been manifested in renewed maritime disputes, changes in military posture and great power rivalry, all of which have added to complexities of the security situation in the region. In particular, the on-going contestations over island territories in the Asia Pacific have fuelled regional tensions that could seriously strain the cooperative structures that have enabled a rapid growth of the Asia Pacific region as an engine of global growth. With North Korea conducting further nuclear and missile tests, the situation on the Korean peninsula also remains fraught.

India has major strategic interests as well as economic and commercial stakes in continued peace and stability in the Asia Pacific region. India's view is that all countries must exercise restraint and resolve bilateral issues diplomatically and without recourse to the use or threat of use of force. India supports freedom of navigation in international waters and the right of passage, in accordance with international law. India believes that the current regional security landscape calls for a cooperative and inclusive approach. On its part, under the 'Act East' policy which places renewed emphasis on engagement with the Asia Pacific, India has been an active participant in various bilateral as well as multilateral fora with a focus on security matters such as the East Asia Summit, ASEAN Defence Ministers' Meeting (ADMM) and ASEAN Regional Forum (ARF). There is also a need to further improve regional responses to challenges such as transnational crime, terrorism, natural disasters, pandemics, cyber security as well as food and energy security.

Central Asia continues to be of strategic interest, both due to its location and resources as well as in view of recent developments in Eurasia and West Asia. India has focussed on developing its political, economic and security partnerships with all Central Asian Republics. There are indications that the region is being targeted by radical terrorist groups that seek to undermine the secular regimes in these countries. India is also keen to expand its energy basket by deeper engagement in this sector with Central Asian countries that are major energy producers. There is also a mutuality of economic interest in respective markets as a destination of exports and investment, especially given efforts at consolidating the Eurasian economic space. The changes in Iran open up new avenues for establishing regional connectivity between Central Asia and India that would enable access to a wide range of natural resources in the region. Iran occupies a significant place in the economic and security calculus of the region. India has welcomed the nuclear agreement between the E3+3 and Iran.

The West Asian region has progressively become embroiled in violence and instability in the wake of the political transitions ushered in by the Arab Spring which promised to bring about fundamental political and socio-economic transformations in many countries in the region. However, this has been accompanied by the mushrooming of a number of violent Non-State actors, especially terrorist groups. Major sectarian fault-lines have also been thrown open, thereby fracturing the internal cohesion of several countries. India has vital stakes in the region, in terms of diaspora, trade, energy, remittances, and security. Continuing violence and instability in West Asia and the Gulf, which is part of India's extended neighbourhood, could impact India's diverse interests in the region. The situation in Syria has deteriorated into rivalry and competition between great powers and major regional actors. The scenario in Iraq remains of growing concern, especially the rise of Non-State actors that threaten not just regional stability but have shown the capacity to radicalise individuals into carrying out terrorist attacks in other parts of the world. The fusing together of the Syrian conflict and the crisis in Iraq could pose a major challenge, with heightened extremist and sectarian overtones. India has expressed deep concern at the violence and loss of human lives in Syria and has consistently called for an inclusive and comprehensive political solution that takes into account the legitimate aspirations of the Syrian people. India has also expressed firm support to Iraq in its fight against international terrorism and in its efforts to preserve its unity and territorial integrity. Tensions between Israel and Palestine are also a matter of concern. India supports a negotiated solution resulting in a sovereign, independent, viable and United

State of Palestine, living within secure and recognised borders, side by side at peace with Israel as endorsed in the Quartet Roadmap and relevant UNSC resolutions.

Several parts of Africa continue to be in turmoil, as violent insurgencies and terrorist actions have progressively made their presence felt in North, East and West African countries. Of particular concern is the growing influence of terrorist organisations. While, the threat from piracy in the Western Indian Ocean has diminished, the problem has resurfaced in the Gulf of Guinea in which a number of Indian seafarers have been affected. The activities of terrorist outfits in West Africa pose a growing threat to the stability of states in the region. The linkages between local groups and terrorist organisations outside the region are a matter of concern. India has historic ties with several African nations and has sought to deepen its bilateral ties with African countries through the strategic initiative of the India-Africa Forum Summit (IAFS) mechanism that seeks to promote regional and continent-level political and economic cooperation with African countries.

Internal Security Environment

The challenges to internal security in India can be categorised into four broad threats viz. cross border terrorism in Jammu & Kashmir, militancy in the North East, Left Wing Extremism (LWE) in certain states and terrorism in the hinterland. The Government has been making systematic and unrelenting efforts to counter these threats and, as a result, the internal security situation in the country is firmly under control. There is steep decline in terror attacks in the hinterland and the violence perpetrated by LWE. However, developments in Jammu & Kashmir and Punjab have been a cause of concern, especially the cross-border terror attacks and trafficking of arms and narcotics.

The overall security situation in J&K remains stable in spite of the focused efforts of separatists and terrorist *tanzeems* (organisations) to disrupt the prevailing peace. This was primarily due to the protracted operations of the security forces in the hinterland and effectiveness of the counter infiltration grid on the Line of Control/International Border. However, radicalisation and fresh recruitment in South Kashmir is a cause of concern. External factors, including the changing situation in Pakistan and Afghanistan, may also impact the internal situation in Jammu & Kashmir.

The security situation in the North Eastern states has been gradually improving in terms of reduction in number of violent incidents and lower civilian casualties. The number of violent incidents has come down from 1025 in 2012 to 574 in 2015 and the number of civilians killed has come down from 97 to 46 in the same period. The states of Tripura, Mizoram and Sikkim are, by and large, peaceful. In Arunachal Pradesh, barring a few incidents, there is general atmosphere of peace. In Manipur and Nagaland there was increase in violence against security forces by the extremist groups in 2015 in the wake of unilateral abrogation of ceasefire by NSCN/K. In Meghalaya, security forces were able to contain the violent activities of the militant groups. The signing of the Framework for Peace between the Government of India and the National Socialist Council for Nagalim (Issac-Muviah) [NSCN (I-M] in August 2015 was a positive step towards ending the country's oldest insurgency. The extradition of Anup Chetia, a prominent United Liberation of Front of Asom (ULFA) leader, by Bangladesh to India in November 2015 was an encouraging development that may help in the success of peace talks between the Government of India and ULFA (pro talk) leaders. Successful counter insurgency operations against the National Democratic Front of Bodoland – Songjibit [NDFB (S)] and the Garo National Liberation Army (GNLA) by the security forces have dealt a severe blow to the fighting capabilities of these insurgent groups. Talks are continuing with NDFB, Progressive (P) and Ranjan Diamary (RD) factions to resolve Bodo issues.

Left Wing Extremism (LWE) continues to be an area of concern to the internal security of the country. However, LWE violence has been declining over the years due to various efforts of the Government such as greater presence of security forces across the LWE affected states, loss of cadres/ leaders on account of arrests, surrender and desertions, better monitoring of development schemes and insurgency fatigue among Maoist cadres.

Ministry and its Departments

The principal task of the Ministry is to frame policy directions on defence and security related matters and communicate them for implementation to the Services Headquarters, Inter-Service Organisations, Production Establishments and Research and Development Organisations. It is required to ensure effective implementation of the Government's policy directions and the execution of approved programmes within the allocated resources.

The primary functions of the departments are as follows: (i) The Department of Defence deals with the Integrated Defence Staff (IDS) and three Services and various Inter Service Organizations. It is also responsible for the defence budget, establishment matters, defence policy, matters relating to Parliament, defence co-operation with foreign countries and coordination of all defence related activities, (ii) The Department of Defence Production is headed by a Secretary and deals with matters pertaining to defence production, indigenization of imported stores, equipment and spares, planning and control of departmental production units of the Ordnance Factory Board and Defence Public Sector Undertakings (DPSUs), (iii) The Department of Defence Research and Development is headed by a Secretary, who is the Scientific Adviser to the Raksha Mantri. Its function is to advise the Government on scientific aspects of military equipment and logistics and the formulation of research, design and development plans for equipment required by the Services, (iv) The Department of Ex-Servicemen Welfare is headed by a Secretary and deals with all resettlement, welfare and pensionary matters of Ex-Servicemen.

Headquarters Integrated Defence Staff

HQIDS was raised in October 2001 based on the recommendations of Group of Ministers on the Kargil Review Committee (KRC) report. The HQ was raised under the overall command and control of Chairman, Chiefs of Staff Committee (COSC) to foster jointness and synergy amongst the three services. Since its inception, this HQ has achieved several milestones in joint and integrated planning, coordination of intelligence, joint conduct of Human Assistance and Disaster Relief (HADR) operations through Defence Crisis Management Group (DCMG) and prioritising/streamlining procurements.

O. W.: http://www.ids.nic.in

Army

The changing global geo-political dynamics presents the Nation with multiple security challenges. While constantly reviewing its operational preparedness/ postures to meet the perceived security challenges, the Indian Army (IA) is committed to the defence of the country from external and internal threats across the entire spectrum of warfare. Also, in times of disaster/natural calamities, the Indian Army is in the forefront, providing aid and succour to the affected people.

Jammu and Kashmir

The security situation of J&K is at an important cross road of transcending from conflict stabilisation to conflict resolution domain. The relentless efforts put in by security forces helped the 'Awaam' general public gain confidence which led to a high voter turnout in the Parliamentary and Assembly elections. People have entrusted faith in the Indian democratic system, shunned violence and are yearning for peace and stability.

Ceasefire Violations (CFVs)

The ceasefire along the Actual Ground Position Line (AGPL), Line of Control (LoC) and International Border (IB) Sectors in Jammu and Kashmir has generally held. The Indian Army (IA) is committed to the defence of the country from external and internal threats across the entire spectrum of warfare. and effective retaliation, where required, was carried out to the CFVs initiated by Pakistan. The incidents of CFVs are taken up through the established mechanisms of hotlines, Flag Meetings and DGMO's talks. Overall, Pakistan continues to calibrate violence to keep the LoC alive and to showcase issue of unresolved/unsettled borders in J&K.

Infiltration

Pakistan, despite its recent peace overtures, has left no stone unturned to internationalise the Kashmir issue. The terror infrastructure remains intact across the border. However, counter infiltration measures adopted by the Army have been further strengthened to contain the situation.

Situation in the Hinterland

Counter Terrorist Operations: During 2015, relentless and surgical people friendly operations based on a credible intelligence network have resulted in the elimination of 67 terrorists in the hinterland. In 2014, the army had killed 68 terrorists in the hinterland of Jammu and Kashmir.

Terrorists Initiated Incidents : In 2015, there have been 48 terrorists initiated incidents in the hinterland including suicide attacks in Samba and Rajbagh. A number of these terrorist incidents were initiated against the mobile communications infrastructure, surrendered terrorists and Hurriyat affiliates. These incidents, in 2015, have led to the martyrdom of 18 Central Armed Police Forces (CAPF) personnel and 16 civilian fatalities.

Exploitation of Social Media, Local Recruitment and Rise of Radicalisation: Social media and its blatant use by terrorists groups and separatists alike to target impressionable minds is emerging as a challenge from the security point of view. The widespread application of digital media has been able to provide an impetus to local recruitment, radicalisation and has been used extensively by Separatists to mobilise masses for protest.

North East

The overall security situation in North East remained fluid and dynamic. There was spurt in violent activities against Security Forces (SF) post abrogation of ceasefire by NSCN (K) in March 2015. To effectively counter the development, Border Guarding & Counter Insurgency Posture in Nagaland and Manipur were strengthened. In 2015, 1504 terrorists have been neutralised (Killed-103, Apprehended-1359 and Surrendered - 42) along with recovery of 1,111 weapons.

Assam: The security situation in the State remained largely peaceful and under control. Relentless operations by security forces did neutralise important commanders of NDFB (Songbijit), thereby paralysing the Chain of Command of the group. Resultantly, the morale of NDFB (Songbijit) cadres was adversely affected.

Nagaland: The security situation in the State deteriorated post abrogation of Ceasefire (CF) by NSCN (Khaplang) on March 27, 2015. As a result of renewed attacks on Special Forces (SF) by NSCN (K) insurgents in Nagaland, Manipur and Arunachal Pradesh and the outfit was declared 'Unlawful Association' on September 28, 2015. Concerted and relentless operation by SF along India - Myanmar border has severely dented the outfit physically and psychologically forcing the group to move majority of its cadres to Myanmar. Signing of "Framework Agreement for Naga Peace Accord" between Government of India and NSCN-IM (Issac Chishi Swu and Thuingaleng Maivah) on August 3, 2015 was a very significant development and will probably lead towards achievement of a solution to the oldest insurgency in the region having pan

North East effect. There is also a growing public disenchantment against NSCN factions, increasing assertiveness of Against Corruption and Unabated Taxation (ACAUT) and consolidation of Nagas of Nagaland under Naga Tribal Council (NTC) which are positive developments.

Manipur: The State continued to be the most disturbed one in North East region. Majority of the violence has been perpetrated by Valley based groups as they accounted for approximately 61 per cent of the violence in Manipur. Politics of Blockades and Bandhs continued to prevail and led to increasing fissures amongst the three major communities namely; Meiteis-Nagas-Kukis. Inter-tribal rivalry and insider - outsider divide was prominently visible throughout 2015 wherein demands of implementation of Inner Line Permit and its opposition were the main factors for protests.

Arunachal Pradesh: Longding, Tirap and Changlang districts of the State are affected by the presence of Naga insurgents groups which continue their attempts to establish their writ. The State is used as a transit route for illegal movement of weapons, ammunition, narcotics, etc. from Myanmar to Assam and Nagaland. Synergised operations by SF have reduced the operational space of insurgents.

Meghalaya: The violence remained largely confined to Garo hills perpetrated by the Garo groups. Spillover of the activities of these groups was also visible in neighbouring districts of Goalpara and Dhubri in Assam.

Situation along the Border

Bilateral Relations with China: India desires peaceful and cordial relations with all neighbours. To this end, a policy of constructive engagement and maintaining peace and tranquility along the Line of Actual Control (LAC) is ensured along our Northern Borders. Relations between the two nations have improved over the past few years. Constructive engagement at the political, diplomatic and military levels is continuing with regular military exchanges from time to time. Year 2015 has been declared as the 'Visit India Year'. The visit of Indian Prime Minister to China in May 2015 has further strengthened the bonds of friendship and enhanced bilateral cooperation between both the countries.

Situation along the Line of Actual Control: The situation along India-China border continues to be peaceful. There are a few areas along the border where India and China have differing perception of the LAC. Both sides patrol up to their respective perceptions of LAC and due to this, transgressions do occur. Specific cases of transgression by Chinese patrols into such areas across LAC are taken up with relevant Chinese authorities through the established mechanism of Hot Lines, Flag Meetings and Border Personnel Meetings. However, there has been increase in assertiveness during routine patrolling by PLA (People Liberation Army).

Implementation of Border Defence Cooperation Agreement (BDCA): During this year both countries have had wide ranging discussions on implementation of BDCA. Towards this, the scope of the Border Personnel Meetings (BPM) has been increased to include conduct of non contact games and joint celebration of festivals. Recently, two new BPM sites have been made operational.

Fifth Joint Training Exercise: The Fifth Joint Training Exercise was successfully conducted in Kunming (China) in October 2015 aimed at building and promoting positive military relations, inter-operability and undertaking joint operations in Counter Terrorism (CT) environment. These exercises provided valuable opportunity for greater professional military interaction and enhanced confidence in each other.

O. W.: http://www.indianarmy.nic.in

Navy

Indian Navy is the key enabler and guarantor of the country's maritime sovereignty and myriad use-of-the-sea activities. This is discharged by the Indian Navy through its four roles–military, diplomatic, constabulary and benign. The objective of the Navy's military role is deterrence/dissuasion against any intervention or act which is against the national interests, and the ability to inflict a crushing defeat on the adversary in the event of hostilities. A major objective of the Navy's constabulary role is to ensure coastal and offshore security and implement antipiracy measures.

The Indian Navy (IN) has been playing a maritime leadership role in the Indian Ocean Region (IOR) due to its multi-dimensional capabilities and active presence in the region. The environment in India's maritime neighbourhood is dynamic, with increased instabilities, deepening geopolitical and ethnic faultlines, growing military capabilities, and wide range of security challenges. These pose a combination of conventional and sub-conventional threats to India, at and from the seas. Challenges require the Indian Navy to remain effective across the full spectrum of combat operations, and constantly reshape itself to meet future challenges.

India is a maritime nation and the country sits astride a very large number of busy International Shipping Lanes, that criss-cross the Indian Ocean. More than 90 per cent of the trade by volume and 70 per cent by value is transported over the seas. For a rapidly growing economy seeking new markets worldwide, these trade figures will only spiral upwards in the future. The last decade has witnessed India's dependence on maritime environment expanding substantially as her economic, military and technological strength grew, her global interactions widened and her national security imperatives and political interests stretched gradually. It can thus be assumed that the 21st century will be the 'Century of the Seas' for India and that the seas will remain a key enabler in her global resurgence.

The Indian Navy has been actively pursuing activities towards capability building and capacity enhancement of Navies of friendly countries in the IOR.

Towards this end, India has been providing hardware and platforms, which includes ships and aircraft for EEZ surveillance. IN has also been instrumental in maritime infrastructure development of friendly nations. IN initiatives are also geared up for contributing towards developing operational and technical skills of maritime practitioners. Material assistance in terms of providing spares, AIS equipment, ship handling simulators, ammunition, communication equipment, coastal surveillance radars, boats, etc. to the navies/maritime forces in the region has gone a long way in strengthening India's stature and bilateral ties. One frontline fleet ship has been continuously deployed in the Gulf of Aden region since October 2008 to prevent piratical attacks and provide safe escort to merchant ships of Indian and foreign nationalities.

Protection to offshore assets including Offshore Development Areas (ODAs) has been augmented with deployments by the newly inducted Immediate Support Vessels (ISVs). Regular exercises have been conducted at ODAs to validate the safety and security of ODA platforms which are vital to India's energy security.

Overseas Operations

Langkawi International Maritime Aerospace Exhibition: INS Kamorta participated in Langkawi International Maritime Aerospace (LIMA-15) at Langkawi, Malaysia in March 2015.

International Maritime Defence Expo Asia–2015: INS Satpura and Kamorta participated in the 10th Edition of International Maritime Defence Expo (IMDEX) Asia in May 2015 at Singapore. The highlight of the event was the setting up of a 'Make in India' pavilion represented by Indian DPSUs, which included M/s GSL and GRSE.

ARF Disaster Relief Exercise: INS Saryu participated in ASEAN Regional Forum (ARF) Disaster Relief Exercise (DIREx) 2015 at Penang, Malaysia in May 2015.

Eastern Fleet Overseas Deployment : INS Satpura, Kamorta, Ranvir and Shakti as part of Eastern Fleet Overseas Deployment (OSD) were deployed in South China Sea, Sea of Japan and Java Sea in May and June 2015. The Indian Navy participated in SIMBEX-15 in the South China Sea with the Singapore Navy and also carried out PASSEX (passing exercise) with the navies of Indonesia, Australia, Thailand and Cambodia.

International Fleet Review at Sagami Bay, Japan: INS Sahyadri participated in the IFR hosted by Japan at Sagami Bay, Japan in October 2015. The ship also visited Vietnam, Republic of Korea and the Philippines enroute.

Western Fleet Overseas Deployment: INS Delhi, Deepak, Tabar and Trishul were deployed to Persian Gulf as part of Western Fleet Overseas Deployment (OSD) in September 2015.

OSD of Training Squadron: INS 1st Training Squadron (1 TS) visited Indonesia, Singapore, Malaysia, Bangladesh, Sri Lanka in March 2015 and, Mauritius and Seychelles from September–November 2015 as part of sea training of cadets. During the visit of 1 TS to Mauritius, INS Sujata also participated in the *Aprawasi Diwas* held at Mauritius in 2015.

Lokayan 15: INS Tarangini, a Sail Training Ship of the Indian Navy, was deployed overseas for eight months from April-December 2015. Lokayan 2015 signifies Indian Navy's extensive reach across the globe for the sole purpose of a safe and secure maritime environment.

Major Exercises

Tropex 15: The Indian Navy's annual Theatre Level Operational Readiness Exercise (TROPEX) was conducted from end January to February 2015. 42 ships, 3 submarines and 51 aircrafts, including newly inducted (Poseidon Eight India) P8I aircraft participated in the exercise.

Defence of Gujarat Exercise (DGX 15): The Defence of Gujarat Exercise was conducted from end October to November, 2015, on the Western Seaboard. 33 ships, 3 submarines and 29 aircraft from Navy, IAF and ICG participated in the exercise.

Exercises with Foreign Navies

Malabar-15: IN and USN have been regularly participating in bilateral exercise 'MALABAR' since 1992. The 19th edition of MALABAR was held in the Bay of Bengal in October 2015, and also included participation by Japanese Maritime Self Defence Force (JMSDF).

Varuna-15: Indo-French Naval Exercise 'VARUNA' is being conducted since 1993. VARUNA-15 was held in the Arabian Sea in 2015 with the French Navy.

Simbex-15: Singapore India Maritime Bilateral Exercise (SIMBEX) is held each year, alternately in the Bay of Bengal and in South China Sea. SIMBEX-15 was held in the South China Sea in 2015 with Singapore Navy.

Konkan-15: The annual bilateral naval exercise KONKAN with the Royal Navy is an operational interaction being conducted since 2004. KONKAN-15 was held in 2015 off the coast of the UK.

Ausindex-15: The inaugural bilateral maritime exercise AUSINDEX between IN and Royal Australian Navy (RAN) was conducted off Visakhapatnam in 2015.

Slinex-15: The IN-SLN exercise was conducted for the first time in 2005 and in 2010, it was decided to hold the exercise every alternate year. SLINEX-15 was held in 2015 off Sri Lanka.

Indra-15: Indo - Russia naval exercise named 'INDRA' is being conducted since 2003. INDRA-15 was conducted in the Bay of Bengal in December 2015.

O. W.: http://www.indiannavy.nic.in

Indian Coast Guard

Indian Coast Guard (ICG) came into being in 1977 on approval of the Cabinet Committee on Political Affairs to set up an interim Coast Guard Organisation. It was formally established as an independent organisation on August 19, 1978 with the enactment of Coast Guard Act, 1978. The ICG began in 1978 with two frigates seconded from the Indian Navy and five patrol boats from the Department of Customs. Since inception, the ICG has acquired a wide range of capabilities both surface and airborne to undertake the assigned tasks during peace time and to supplement the efforts of Indian Navy during war.

The command and control of the Coast Guard lies with the Director General of Indian Coast Guard, at New Delhi. The organisation has regional headquarters located at Gandhinagar, Mumbai, Chennai, Kolkata and Port Blair. These exercise command and control in the waters adjoining the entire coastline of India through district headquarters located along the coastal states. Air stations, Air Enclaves and an Air Squadron have been set up for the deployment of aircraft for search, rescue and maritime surveillance.

The duties and functions of Coast Guard as enunciated in the Coast Guard Act are as follows: Safety and protection of artificial islands and offshore terminals, installations and devices in maritime zones; protection and assistance to fishermen at sea while in distress; preservation and protection of marine environment; prevention and control of marine pollution; assistance to customs and other authorities in anti-smuggling operations and enforcing of enactments being in force in the maritime zones and other matters, including measures for the safety of life and property at sea and collection of scientific data. In addition to the mandate as laid down under Section 14 of Coast Guard Act, 1978, the Indian Coast Guard has also been entrusted the following additional roles: (i) offshore security coordination authority; (ii) national maritime search and rescue coordinating authority; (iii) lead intelligence agency for coastal and sea border; (iv) coastal security in territorial waters; (v) Chairman, national oil spill disaster committee; and (vi) Indian Governor to Regional Cooperation Agreement on Combating Piracy and Armed Robbery against ships in Asia (ReCAAP).

Air Force

In October, 2015 Indian Air Force (IAF) celebrated the 83rd anniversary of its service to the nation. IAF has been modernising its inventory as per its long-term perspective plan. The focus is on "Make in India" to give impetus to indigenous development and manufacturing, including participation of private sector in defence manufacturing. Modernisation process involves new inductions, as well as upgradation of the existing weapon platforms and support systems as a part of the capability buildup. The on-going modernisation plan spans the entire spectrum of IAF's capability including fighters, transport aircraft, helicopters, combat support assets and air defence network. Net centricity, cyber security and ensuring enhanced visibility of entire battle space for seamless operations are part of this capability build up. To maximise the operational potential, IAF is also creating modern and efficient operational and technical infrastructure. IAF's recently acquired airborne assets have been effectively utilised in Humanitarian Assistance and Disaster Relief (HADR) missions, most noticeably in J&K, Nepal and Yemen.

Operations

Acquisitions and Upgrades

LCA: Light Combat Aircrafts (LCA), Tejas is designed and developed by Aeronautical Development Agency (ADA), Bangalore. The Initial Operational Clearance (IOC) of LCA was achieved in December 2013. The first series production aircraft in IOC configuration was handed over to IAF in January 2015.

Mirage-2000 Upgrade: IAF contracted for the upgrade of Mirage 2000 aircraft to advance standards of improved radar, avionics, electronic suite, weapons and a modern generation glass cockpit. On March 25, 2015, first upgraded aircraft was handed over to the IAF. The induction of the aircraft has added the much needed teeth to air power and keeps the IAF ahead of its adversaries. This multi-role fighter aircraft has achieved enhanced operational life.

MiG-29 Upgrade: The series upgrade of MiG-29 aircraft is currently underway at a Base Repair Depot of IAF.

Rafale Aircraft: Procurement of 36 Rafale Aircraft through Inter Governmental agreement between the Indian and French Government is being progressed.

Additional C-130J: The first C-1307J Squadron has been fully operationalised. Procurement of additional aircraft is also being undertaken. Contract was finalised in December 2013. Procurement of these additional aircrafts would give boost to special operations, airborne assault and air mobility potential of the IAF.

AN-32 Upgrade: AN-32 fleet was inducted into IAF between 1984 and 1991. Total Technical Life Extension (TTLE)/Re Equipment (RE) project is concurrently underway at Kyiv, Ukraine and No.1 Base Repair Depot (BRD) at Kanpur. This project will extend the aircraft's life by 15 years besides enhancing its operational potential and safety.

Helicopters: The rotary wing capabilities of the IAF are poised to undergo a paradigm growth. IAF has already inducted some of the latest machines. Mi-17 V5, is a quantum jump in capability in terms of the avionics, weapon systems as well as its hot and high altitude performance. Process is underway to upgrade existing Mi-17s and Mi-17 IVs with the latest avionics and glass cockpits.

Attack Helicopters: A contract was signed in September 2015 for procurement of state-of-the-art AH-64E Apache attack helicopters. The Attack Helicopters are critical combat assets utilised for employment in Anti-Tank Guided Missile role, Counter Insurgency Operations, Suppression of Enemy Air Defences, Unmanned Aerial Vehicle neutralisation Operations, Combat Search and Rescue Operations and Low Intensity Conflict Operations. Attack helicopters offer unique offensive capability including support to Army Strike Corps and these capabilities are also required at high altitudes in the mountainous terrain on our Northern borders, not available hitherto.

Heavy Lift Helicopters: A contract was signed in September 2015 for procurement of Chinook CH-47F (I) Heavy Lift Helicopters (HLH). The delivery of these helicopters will be in a phased manner. The HLH are required to conduct strategic and tactical airlift missions in support of the armed forces and undertake humanitarian assistance and disaster relief missions during calamities. HLH are critically required to support infrastructure build-up in mountainous regions. Heavy bridging and road construction equipment can be airlifted only by this class of helicopters.

Pilatus Induction: Delivery of all Basic Trainer Aircraft (PC-7 MK II) from M/s Pilatus Aircraft Limited to IAF has been completed in October 2015 as per the procurement contract signed between Government of India and the Swiss company in 2012. Aircraft is currently in use for ab-initio pilot training. However, utilisation of aircraft is further planned to increase to Stage II flying training also. This state-of-the-art aircraft is helping newly recruited pilots to prepare them for exacting requirement of combat flying.

Microlight: A contract was signed in October 2015 with Pipistrel, Slovenia for supply of microlights. It will be used in IAF for enhancement of flight safety by monitoring bird activity in the vicinity of airfields and directing bird controlling measures.

Restoration of Vintage Flight: IAF has several vintage aircrafts of World War II era. These aircrafts represent an important part of world aviation and IAF heritage. In 2008, after undertaking detailed survey of expertise available across the globe on restoration of vintage aircrafts, a decision was taken to restore these aircraft with assistance from vendors within and outside the country. One Tiger Moth and one Harvard aircrafts were sent to UK for Phase-I restoration. These aircrafts have flown on Air Force day displaying the rich heritage of IAF.

O. W.: http://www.indianairforce.nic.in

Commissioned Ranks

The following are the commissioned ranks in the three services; each rank is shown opposite its equivalent in the other service:

Army	Navy	Air Force
General	Admiral	Air Chief Marshal
Lieutenant General	Vice Admiral	Air Marshal
Major General	Rear Admiral	Air Vice Marshal
Brigadier	Commodore	Air Commodore
Colonel	Captain	Group Captain
Lieutenant Colonel	Commander	Wing Commander
Major	Lieutenant Commander	Squadron Leader
Captain	Lieutenant	Flight Lieutenant
Lieutenant	Sub Lieutenant	Flying Officer

Recruitment

The Armed Forces epitomise the ideals of service, sacrifice, patriotism and composite culture of the country. Recruitment to the Armed Forces is voluntary and open to all citizens of the country irrespective of caste, class, religion and community, provided the laid down physical, medical and educational criteria are met.

Recruitment of Commissioned Officers in the Armed Forces is through UPSC: Commissioned Officers in the Armed Forces are recruited through the UPSC which conducts the following two All India Competitive Examinations:

(a) *National Defence Academy and Naval Academy:* The UPSC holds entrance examination twice a year for entry into the National Defence Academy (NDA) and Naval Academy (NA). Candidates on completion of 10+2 examination or while in the 12th standard are eligible to compete.

(b) *Combined Defence Service Examination:* Combined Defence Service Examination (CDSE) is conducted by the UPSC twice a year. University graduates or those in final year of graduation are eligible to appear in the examination. Successful candidates join the Indian Military Academy/ Air Force Academy and Naval Academy for Permanent Commission and Officers Training Academy (OTA) for Short Service Commission.

Recruitment in Army

Recruitment of Commissioned Officers in the Army Through Non-UPSC Entries: Apart from the UPSC entries, the commissioned officers are also recruited in the Army through the following non-UPSC entries:

(a) *University Entry Scheme:* Final/Pre-Final year engineering-degree students in the notified engineering disciplines are eligible to apply for Permanent Commission in the Technical Arms of the Army as

Commissioned Officers under the University Entry Scheme (UES). Eligible candidates are selected through a campus interview by the Screening Teams deputed by the Army Headquarters. These candidates are required to appear before Service Selection Board (SSB) and Medical Board.

(b) *Technical Graduates Course:* Engineering graduates from notified disciplines of engineering/post graduates with minimum second division aggregate marks in notified disciplines for Army Education Corps and M.Sc in Agriculture/Dairy for Military Farms are eligible to apply for Permanent Commission through this entry. After the SSB and the Medical Board, the selected candidates are required to undergo one year precommission training at the IMA, Dehradun, before being commissioned.

(c) *Short Service Commission (Technical) Entry:* The Short Service Commission (Technical) Entry Scheme provides avenues to eligible technical graduates/post graduates for recruitment in Technical Arms. After SSB and Medical Board, the selected candidates are required to undergo approximately 49 weeks pre-commission training at OTA, Chennai.

(d) *10+2 Technical Entry Scheme:* Candidates who have qualified 10+2 CBSE/ICSE/State Board Examination with minimum aggregate of 70 per cent marks in physics, chemistry and mathematics are eligible to apply for commission under the 10+2 Technical Entry Scheme (TES).

(e) *Short Service Commission (Women):* Women are offered Short Service Commission in three streams, viz. Non-Technical Graduate, Technical, Post Graduate/Specialist for a period of ten years, extendable by additional four years purely on voluntary basis. The duration of training is 49 weeks at Officers Training Academy, Chennai. For Short Service Commission (Women) (Technical) Entry, candidates who have passed or are appearing in final year/semester of B.E/B.Tech in notified streams are eligible to apply. Candidates who qualify for the written examination conducted by the UPSC come up for SSB interview.

(f) *NCC (Special Entry Scheme):* Students possessing NCC 'C' certificate with minimum 'B' grade and studying in final year of the three year degree course who have obtained more than 50 per cent aggregate marks in the first two years of the degree course are eligible to apply for Short Service Commission through this entry. If selected in SSB interview, such candidates require to score overall aggregate 50 per cent marks in the three year Bachelor Degree Course failing which the candidate will be rejected. Such cadets are exempted from written examination conducted by UPSC and are directly put through the SSB interview followed by Medical Board.

(g) *Judge Advocate General Entry:* Law graduates with minimum 55 per cent aggregate marks in LLB, who are within the age between 21 to 27 years of age can apply for Judge Advocate General Branch. Eligible candidates are called for direct SSB interview and thereafter, for medical test. It is a Short Service Commission Entry wherein suitable candidates can opt for Permanent Commission.

Recruitment of Personnel Below Officers Rank: In the Army, there are 11 Zonal Recruiting Offices, two Gorkha Recruiting Depots, one Independent Recruiting Office and 59 Army Recruiting Offices in addition to 47 Regimental Centres which carry out recruitment through rallies in their respective areas of jurisdiction. The recruitment of Personnel Below Officers Rank (PBORs) commences with the preliminary screening of aspiring candidates at rally site followed by document checking, physical fitness tests, physical measurements and medical examination. This is followed by a written examination for the candidates who are found eligible in all respects. Finally, selected candidates are dispatched to respective training centres for training.

Recruitment in Indian Navy

Recruitment of officers in Indian Navy: The recruitment system of the Navy is streamlined, transparent, expeditious and candidate friendly. Apart from the UPSC entries the commissioned officers are also recruited through non- UPSC entries.

Non-UPSC Entry: The non-UPSC entries are for both Permanent Commission (PC) and Short Service Commission (SSC) cadres. For such entries, the applications are invited and short-listed at Integrated Headquarters of the Ministry of Defence (Navy) [IHQ of MoD (Navy)]. The short-listed candidates are then sent for SSB interviews for the following Branches/Cadres of the Navy:

(i) *10+2 (Cadet) Entry Scheme:* This scheme provides an avenue for permanent commission in the Executive, Engineering and Electrical branches of the Indian Navy. Under the scheme, candidates with 10 +2 (PCM) qualifications, after selection through the Services Selection Board, are sent to the Indian Naval Academy for the B. Tech Course.

(ii) *Executive:* Short Service Commission for Air Traffic Control/Law/ Logistic/Naval Armament Inspectorate (NAI)/Hydro cadres/Pilot/ Observer and also Permanent Commission for Logistic/Law/NAI Cadres.

(iii) *Engineering (Including Naval Architects):* Short Service Commission through University Entry Scheme (UES), Special Naval Architects Entry Scheme (SNAES) and SSC (E) Schemes. Permanent Commission is through 10+2 (Cadet) Scheme.

(iv) *Electrical Engineering:* SSC entry is through UES and SSC(L) Schemes. Permanent Commission is through 10+2 (Cadet) Scheme.

(v) *Education Branch:* Permanent Commission and Short Service Commission schemes exist for this branch.

(vi) *University Entry Scheme:* Under University Entry Scheme (UES), final and pre-final year engineering students are eligible for induction into the technical Branches/Cadres of the Navy. Naval selection teams from the IHQ of MoD (Navy) and Command Headquarters visit AICTE approved engineering colleges, across the country, to short-list the candidates. The short-listed candidates, based on All India Merit, are called for interview at the Services Selection Board.

(vii) *Recruitment through NCC:* University graduates possessing NCC 'C' certificate, with minimum 'B' grading and 50 per cent marks in the graduation degree examination (physics and maths) are inducted in the Navy as regular commissioned officers. These graduates are exempted from appearing in CDSE conducted by the UPSC and are selected through the SSB interview only.

(viii) *Special Naval Architecture Entry Scheme:* The Government has recently approved the induction of 45 Naval Architect Officers into the Naval Architecture Cadre of the Engineering Branch of the Indian Navy, as Short Service Commission Officers. An empowered Naval team visits IIT Kharagpur, IIT Chennai, Cochin University of Science and Technology (CUSAT) and Andhra University, where B. Tech (Naval Architecture) course is conducted to select candidates through campus interviews. The selected candidates undergo medical examination at the nearest Military Hospital and, if found fit, are selected for training. Recruitment of Sailors: Recruitment into the Navy is carried out on All India basis on State-wise merit of the eligible recruitable male population, as per the number of vacancies available.

Types of Entries of Sailors: The various entries, for recruitment of sailors, are as follows:- (a) Artificer Apprentices (AAs)–10+2 (PCM). (b) Direct Entry (Diploma Holders) [Diploma in Mechanical/Electrical/Electronics/Production/Aeronautical/Metallurgy/Shipbuilding]. (c) Senior Secondary Recruits (SSR)–10+2 (Sc.). (d) Matric Entry Recruits (MR), for recruitment of Cooks, Stewards and Musicians – Matriculation. (e) Non Matric Recruit (NMR), for recruitment of Topass Sailors (Safaiwala)–Class VI. (f) Direct Entry Petty Officer (Outstanding Sportsmen).

Recruitment in Indian Air Force

Induction of officers: Induction to National Defence Academy (NDA) and Combined Defence Service Examination (CDSE) entries are through UPSC. The non-UPSC entries for induction into the officer's cadre are: SSC(Men & Women) Flying, NCC Entry (PC for men), ASC (PC for Men), GDOC (Non Tech) (PC for Men), Airmen Entry (PC for Air Warriors), SSS (Technical) (Men & Women) and SSC (Non Tech) (Men & Women):

(a) *Recruitment through Service Selection:* Recruitment through Service Selection Boards / Air Force Selection Boards is made for the flying (pilot), aeronautical engineering (electronics), aeronautical engineering (mechanical), education, administration, logistics, accounts and meteorology branches of the Air Force.

(b) *University Entry Scheme:* Final/pre-final year students in engineering disciplines are eligible for induction into the technical branches of Air Force as Permanent Commissioned Officers under the University Entry Scheme.

(c) *Recruitment of Women Officers:* Eligible women are recruited as Short Service Commissioned Officers in the flying, aeronautical engineering (electronics), aeronautical engineering (mechanical), education, administration, logistics, accounts and meteorology branches of the IAF.

(d) *Recruitment through National Cadet Corps:* University graduates possessing National Cadet Corps (NCC) 'C' certificate with minimum 'B' grading and 60 per cent marks in graduation are inducted in the IAF as Regular Commissioned Officers by way of selection through the Service Selection Boards. For flying branch cadets should have maths and physics as main subjects in 10+2 level.

Recruitment of Personnel Below Officers Rank: The selection of candidates for Personnel Below Officers Rank (PBORs) is carried out through a centralised selection system on All India basis in which Central Airmen Selection Board (CASB) assisted by 14 Airmen Selection Centres (ASCs) located at different parts of the country, carries out the recruitment.

National Cadet Corps

The National Cadet Corps (NCC) was established under the NCC Act, 1948. It has completed 68 years of existence. The NCC strives to provide the youth of the country opportunities for all round development with a sense of commitment, dedication, self-discipline and moral values, so that they become useful citizens and can take their place in all walks of life in the service of the nation. The motto of NCC is 'Unity and Discipline'.

The total sanctioned strength of NCC cadets is 15 lakh. This includes two lakh NCC cadet strength sanctioned in 2010 that are being absorbed in five phases at 40,000 cadets per year till 2015-16 NCC's presence extends to 642 districts of the country covering 15,749 institutions. The enrolment policy of senior division/senior wing cadets has been changed from two to three years. It would result in improvement in training standards and quality output of cadets. NCC has been made an additional/elective subject in class X and XII from the current year. This would make NCC more attractive and cadets would be able to score credit point in their academic results.

O. W.: http://www.nccindia.nic.in

Training for Defence Services

A large number of training institutions in the Defence Sector work in coordination with one another. The important ones are described in the following paragraphs:

Sainik Schools

The Sainik Schools are established as a joint venture of the Central and State Governments. These are under the overall governance of Sainik Schools Society, Ministry of Defence. At present, there are 25 Sainik Schools located in various parts of the country. There is a growing demand from many States to open new Sainik Schools. As a result, states of Andhra Pradesh, Haryana, Bihar and Karnataka have two Sainik Schools each.

The objectives of Sainik Schools include bringing quality Public School education within the reach of common man, all round development of a child's personality in order to prepare him for entry into National Defence Academy and to remove regional imbalance in the officer's cadre of the Armed Forces. The number of cadets joining the National Defence Academy is on the rise in keeping with the primary aim of establishing of Sainik Schools to prepare boys academically, physically and mentally for entry into NDA. For the 134th NDA/INA Course which commenced in July 2015, a total of 101 Cadets from all Sainik Schools have joined the NDA and Naval Academy.

Sainik Schools admit boys into classes VI and IX. Their age should be 10-11 years for classes VI and 13-14 years for class IX as on 1st July of the year in which admission is sought. Admissions are made strictly as per the order of merit on the basis of an All India Sainik School Entrance Examination held in January each year.

Rashtriya Military Schools

There are five Rashtriya Military Schools in the country at Belgaum and Bangalore in Karnataka, Chail in Himachal Pradesh and Ajmer and Dholpur in Rajasthan. Youngest Rashtriya Military School is at Dholpur established on July 16, 1962. These schools are affiliated to CBSE. These schools aim to provide quality education to the boys and prepare them to join Defence Services.

Rashtriya Military Schools admit boys through a Common Entrance Test. The candidates were tested in four subjects i.e. English, Mathematics, Intelligence and General Knowledge. 67 per cent of the seats in RMS are reserved for the wards of Junior Commissioned Officers/other ranks, 20 per cent seats are reserved for wards of Commissioned Officers and the remaining 13 per cent for the wards of civilians.

O. W.: http://www.rashtriyamilitaryschools.in

National Defence Academy

National Defence Academy (NDA) is a premier Tri-Service institution which trains cadets of all three services before inducting them into their respective pre-commissioning training academies. Keeping in mind the shortage of officers in the Indian Armed Forces and the consequent urgency for making up the deficiency, the intake capacity of NDA was recently enhanced from 1800 cadets to 1920 cadets with the sanction for raising an additional Sqn at NDA i.e. 16th Sqn. Since, the construction of the building will take a few more years, as an interim measure, one set of pre-fabricated shelters to accommodate 120 cadets have been constructed at NDA. The construction for building of 16th Sqn. has commenced. In addition, a proposal for construction of one more set of pre-fabricated shelters and also raising of an additional Battalion (5th Bn) with 4 Sqns at NDA to further enhance the intake capacity of cadets to 2,400 cadets by 2018, has been progressed.

O. W.: http://www.nda.nic.in

Rashtriya Indian Military College

The Rashtriya Indian Military College (RIMC) was founded on March 13, 1922, with the objective of providing the necessary preliminary training for boys of Indian birth or domicile, wishing to become officers in the Armed Forces of India. The institution now serves as a feeder institute to the National Defence Academy. Selection for RIMC is through a written examination-cum-viva voce conducted through the State Governments. Seats for respective States are reserved based on population.

O. W.: http://www.rimc.gov.in

Indian Military Academy, Dehradun

Founded in 1932, Indian Military Academy (IMA), Dehradun aims at the fullest development of intellectual, moral and physical qualities of persons joining the army as officers. The various modes of entry into IMA are:

(a) On graduation from NDA.

(b) On graduation from Army Cadet College, which is a wing of the IMA itself.

(c) Direct Entry graduate cadets, who qualify the Union Public Service Commission Exam and get through the Service Selection Board.

(d) For Technical Graduate's Course (TGC).

(e) Under University Entry Scheme (UES) for engineering college students in Final/ Pre-Final year of studies.

(f) Through 10+2 Technical Entry Scheme (TES).

Officers Training Academy, Chennai

Established in 1963, the Officers Training School (OTS) was re-designated as Officers Training Academy (OTA) from January 01, 1988 on completion of 25 years of its existence. Its main task, before 1965 was to train Gentlemen Cadets for grant of Emergency Commission. From 1965 onwards, the Academy trains cadets for Short Service Commission. With the entry of women officers in the Army since September 21, 1992, around 100 lady officers now get commissioned from OTA every year in Army Service Corps, Army Education Corps, Judge Advocate General's Department, Corps of Engineers, Signals and Electrical and Mechanical Engineers.

Officers Training Academy, Gaya

The Cabinet Committee on Security (CCS), in 2009 approved setting up of second Officers Training Academy (OTA), Gaya. The Academy was commissioned in 2011. The training capacity as of now is around 400 gentlemen cadets. The capacity will be progressively built up to a strength of 750 gentlemen cadets.

College of Military Engineering, Pune

The College of Military Engineering at Pune is a premier technical institution conducting training for personnel of the Corps of Engineers, other Arms and Services, Navy, Air Force, Para Military Forces, Police and Civilians. Besides, personnel from friendly foreign countries are also trained. CME is affiliated to Jawaharlal Nehru University (JNU) for the award of B.Tech.

National Defence College

The National Defence College has established a name for itself as a centre of excellence on matters pertaining to National Security and Strategic Studies. Selected Armed Forces officers of the rank of Brigadier/ equivalent and Civil Services officers of equivalent status of Director and above are nominated for training at the college. The officers undergo an eleven-month programme with focus on National Security, covering all dimensions of domestic, regional and international issues to equip future policy makers with background necessary to get a broad understanding of the multifarious economic, political, military, scientific and organizational aspects that are essential for planning of National Strategy.

College of Defence Management

The College of Defence Management (CDM) is a Armed Forces Training Institution (AFTI) which came into being three decades ago. It is entrusted with the responsibility of instilling contemporary management thoughts, concepts and practices in the senior leadership of the Armed Forces. Osmania University recognizes the core course of CDM, namely the Higher Defence Management Course for the award of the Master of Management Studies (MMS) degree.

Defence Services Staff College

The Defence Services Staff College (DSSC) is one of the oldest military institutions in India. The DSSC imparts training to middle level officers of the three services, besides a few civilian officers and officers from friendly foreign countries. The college conducts a 45-week training programme from June to April every year. After successful completion of the course they are awarded with M.Sc. Degree from Madras University.

Defence Production

The Department of Defence Production was set up in November, 1962 with the objective of developing a comprehensive production infrastructure for the defence of the nation. Over the years, the Department has established wide ranging production facilities for various defence equipment through the Ordnance Factories (OF) and Defence PSUs. The products manufactured include arms and ammunition, tanks, armoured vehicles, heavy vehicles, fighter aircraft and helicopters, warships, submarines, missiles, ammunition, electronic equipment, earth moving equipment, special alloys and special purpose steels.

Ordnance Factories

The Ordnance Factory Board has 39 factories with two more at Nalanda and Korwa. The organisation has over the years progressed from labour intensive manual operations to highly automated computer based manufacturing systems and the emphasis has shifted from production of basic and intermediate inputs to finished stores and the organisation has emerged as the system integrator. Ordnance Factories are divided into five operating groups: (i) ammunition and explosives, (ii) weapons, vehicles and equipments, (iii) materials and components, (iv) armoured vehicles and (v) clothing and equipments, each headed by Additional DGOF.

Defence Undertakings

Hindustan Aeronautics Limited

Hindustan Aeronautics Limited (HAL), is a Navratna Company and a premier aeronautical complex of South Asia. HAL's expertise encompasses design, production, repair, overhaul and upgrade of aircrafts, helicopters, aero-engines, accessories, avionics and systems. HAL has so far designed and developed and manufactured 15 types of aircrafts/helicopters and it has positioned itself as a comprehensive solution provider to the Indian Defence Services in aviation, spanning fighter aircrafts, trainer aircraft and light helicopters. In addition, co-development of Fifth Generation Fighter Aircraft (FGFA) and Multi-role Transport Aircraft, has been taken up with Russian Partners which will enhance the level of contribution of HAL towards self-reliance in defence field. The company has diversified its business into manufactured and repair/overhaul of Industrial and Marine Gas Turbine engines and manufacture of structures for aerospace vehicles. The company has also achieved a foothold in export in more than 20 countries, having demonstrated its quality and price competitiveness.

O. W.: http://www.hal-india.com

Bharat Electronics Limited

Bharat Electronics Limited (BEL), is a Navratna PSU, which was established at Bangalore in the year 1954. BEL ranks 69th among the top 100 companies worldwide in defence revenues, as published by Defence News, USA. BEL has nine operating units spread all over the country. The company has core competencies in areas of radars and fire control systems, weapon systems, sonars, communication, network Centric Systems, Electronic Warfare Systems, Electro Optics and Tank electronics, etc. About 80 per cent turnover of the company comes from these business segments. In the non-defence area, BEL manufactures Electronic Voting Machines (EVMs), Tablet PCs (BEL designed), large variety of components like integrated circuits, hybrid microcircuits, semiconductor devices, solar cells etc. Apart from these, BEL also has presence in the areas of access systems, homeland security systems and select non-defence applications.

O. W.: http://www.bel-india.com

Garden Reach Shipbuilders and Engineers Ltd.

Garden Reach Shipbuilders and Engineers Ltd.(GRSE), a leading shipyard, has expertise of building a wide array of vessels, from world class Frigates to Fast Interceptor Boats. GRSE, Mini Ratna, Category-I, had won the prestigious Raksha Mantri's Award in 2006-07, 2007- 08 and 2010-11. The Institute of Public Enterprises, Hyderabad conferred CSR - Corporate Governance Award on GRSE in 2012. GRSE was conferred with Caring Company Award–2013 at the World CSR Congress in Mumbai in 2013.

O. W.: http://www.grse.nic.in

Goa Shipyard Limited

Goa Shipyard Limited (GSL), is capable of designing and building high technology and sophisticated ships to meet the crucial maritime security needs of the country. For over four decades and more, GSL has designed and built wide range of sophisticated vessels for defence commercial sectors with special expertise in building modern patrol vessels of steel and aluminium hull. GSL product range includes Offshore Patrol Vessels (OPV), fast patrol vessels, missile boats, survey vessels, landing craft utility vessels and other auxiliary vessels. GSL has also successfully ventured into building Glass Reinforced Plastic (GRP) interceptor boats. As on date, GSL has built and delivered 197 ships and 124 GRP boats to various customers.

O. W.: http://www.goashipyard.co.in

Hindustan Shipyard Ltd

Hindustan Shipyard Ltd. (HSL), is located on the east coast of the country and is nation's premium shipbuilding and ship/submarine repair organisation. HSL has been earmarked for undertaking construction of various vessels including IPVs, OPVs, LPDs, SOVs and Submarines.

O. W.: http://www.hsl.gov.in

Mazagaon Dock Limited

Mazagaon Dock Limited (MDL), is the Mini Ratna company and is India's premier shipyard, specialised in construction of warships of various sizes and classes, submarines, other technologically advanced commercial vessels and offshore platforms/drilling rigs. MDL also undertakes repairing of warships, coast guard and submarines. It has the Virtual Reality Centre (VRC) at Design Department which is the first of its kind in the shipbuilding industry. The State-of-the-Art Shore Integration Facility (SIF) which provides complete combat system integration feasible prior installation thereby reducing uncertainties/potential time delays and rework onboard submarine. It is also being used for training of both shipyard and naval sailors. Presently, the yard is constructing scorpene submarines and missile destroyers for the Indian Navy.

O. W.: http://www.mazagondock.gov.in

BEML Limited

BEML Limited established in 1964, is a Mini Ratna Category-I multi-location, multi product engaged in design, manufacturing, marketing and after-sales service of a wide range of equipment to three distinct business segments i.e., Defence, Mining and Construction and Rail and Metro. The international division caters to the global market. The company has a strong base of in-house research, design and development setup.

O. W.: http://www.bemlindia.com

Bharat Dynamics Limited

Bharat Dynamics Limited (BDL), a Mini Ratna Category–I company, was incorporated in the year 1970. A pioneer in the manufacture of Anti-Tank Guided Missiles, BDL is now manufacturing Anti-Tank Guided Missiles (ATGMs) of later generations, surface-to-air weapon systems, strategic weapons, launchers, under water weapons, decoys and test equipment. BDL is producing Konkurs-M and Invar (3BK-20) ATGMs in collaboration with KBP, Tula (Russia) and Rosoboron export (Russia) respectively and Milan-2T with MBDA (France). Recently, BDL has achieved a milestone of producing the wholly indigenous Surface-to-Air Missile – Akash for the Indian Armed Forces. C-303 (Anti-Torpedo Counter Measure Systems) producted by BDL has already been fitted in Indian Navy Submarines and Production of Light Weight Torpedo (TAL) is in progress. In-house developed CMDS (Counter Measure Dispensing System) has been accepted by the Indian Air Force for Jaguar and LCA, BDL is presently working on adaptation of the system for a variety of aircraft platforms and also developing radio frequency controlled ATGM.

O. W.: http://www.bdl.ap.nic.in

Mishra Dhatu Nigam Limited

Mishra Dhatu Nigam Limited (MIDHANI), was established in 1973 at Hyderabad with the main objective of providing the nation self-reliance in strategic materials which are key to sustenance and growth of the critical technologies and products to render support to several programmes of national importance like Light Combat Aircraft, MBT Arjun, PSLV, GSLV power plants, etc. Bestowed as a Category-1 company, it took the leading position in developmental tasks and indigenisation of critical alloys and products needed in the strategic sectors like defence, aerospace, nuclear and other sectors of Indian industry The main product range include super alloys of iron, nickel and cobalt base, titanium and titanium alloys, special steels, soft magnetic materials and molybdenum in various mill forms. With years of engineering experience, MIDHANI has diversified into the manufacturing of biomedical impacts, investment castings, closed die forgings and other value added products.

O. W.: http://www.midhani.gov.in

Production & Turnover of Defence PSUs/Ordnance Factories

The value of production of Defence PSUs/Ordnance Factories and Profit after Tax are indicated in Table 9.1 and Table 9.2, respectively.

Table 9.1 Value of Production of Defence PSUs and OFB

(₹. in crores)

Name of the PSU	2012-13	2013-14	2014-15	2015-16 (up to Dec. 2015)
HAL	14202	15867	16289	10228
BEL	6290	6127	6659	4466
BEML	2879	2814	2599	1840
BDL	1177	1804	2770	2446.70
GRSE	1529	1611	1651.31	1030.95
GSL	507	509	569.55	465.09
HSL	484	453	294.16	340.16
MDL	2291	2865	3592.60	2174.64
MIDHANI	537	572	640.04	477.77
OFB	11975	11123	11364	7526
Total	**41871**	**43745**	**46428.66**	**30995.31**

Table 9.2 : Profit after Tax of DPSUs

(₹. in crores)

Name of the PSU	2012-13	2013-14	2014-15	2015-16* (up to Dec. 2015)
HAL	2997	2693	2388	1005
BEL	890	932	1167	563.16
BEML	-80	5	6.76	-102
BDL	288	346	419	318
GRSE	132	121	43.45	47.22
GSL	16	-61	78.24	32.26
HSL	-55	-46	-202.84	-60.34
MDL	413	398	491.59	388.74
MIDHANI	83	83	102.13	66.26
Total	**4684**	**4471**	**4493.33**	**2258.3**

* *Provisional*

Directorate General of Quality Assurance

Directorate General of Quality Assurance (DGQA) is an Inter-Service Organisation under the Department of Defence Production responsible for quality assurance of all defence equipment and stores for the Army and Navy (excluding Naval Armaments) as well as common use items for the Air Force. DGQA provides technical guidance to manufacturers and users and is also responsible for technical evaluation and final acceptance of specified products. The organisation also acts as the Authority Holding Sealed Particulars (AHSP) and provides technical assistance to the Armed Forces in several areas such as formulation of GSQR and RFPs, technical evaluation of tenders, conduct of defect investigations, assessment of users' satisfaction, etc.

The organisation consists of 11 technical directorates, each of which is responsible for specified range of equipment. Each directorate has three functional tiers (except DQA(N) & DQA (WP) having two functional tiers) at the Headquarters, Controllerates and Quality Assurance Establishments in the field. In addition, DGQA also operates proof establishments for armaments for carrying out proof firing of weapons and ammunition.

O. W.: http://www.dgqadefence.nic.in

Directorate General of Aeronautical Quality Assurance

The Directorate General of Aeronautical Quality Assurance (DGAQA) is an organisation under the Department of Defence Production that is responsible for quality assurance and final acceptance of military aircraft, accessories and other aeronautical stores for use in military aviation. QA coverage is provided through all the stages of design, development, production, overhaul, repairs and upgradation of aeronautical stores.

The DGAQA plays an important role in providing technical guidance to the Service Headquarters during various stages of procurement of aeronautical stores for indigenous as well as imported origin. DGAQA also participated with Service Headquarters and other stakeholders in accident/defect investigations and joint studies for improving the quality and reliability of aeronautical stores. DGAQA headquarters is in New Delhi and has 34 field establishments in different parts of the country. Training of DGAQA officers/ staff in their respective professional domain for competence building and conduct of quality audits in critical areas to improve quality and reliability of aeronautical stores remained the key thrust areas in the year.

O. W.: http://www.dgaeroqa.gov.in

Directorate of Standardisation

The primary objective of the Directorate of Standardisation (DOS) is to establish commonality in equipment and components among the three services so that the overall inventory of the Defence Services is reduced to the minimum. The objective is sought to be achieved through preparation of various standardisation documents, codification of Defence Inventory and through exercising strict entry control.

To formulate the standardisation documents the Directorate coordinates efforts of 13 standardisation sub-committees and 12 inter service working groups. It also maintains constant touch with BIS to ensure defence requirements are catered while national standards are being formulated. Being member of Allied Committee–135 (AC-135), an international body for codification, the directorate also functions as the National Codification Bureau (NCB) and provides training on codification as well as registers Indian manufacturers for inclusion of their products in the central data base maintained by AC-135. This facilitates visibility of Indian products/ manufacturers at international level. The directorate maintains very close liasion with all defence establishments and provides constant guidance for codification of their respective inventory. As of now this directorate has formulated 4,929 Defence Standards and codified 5,41,894 items. The Directorate maintains a website wherein all standards/codified data is made available to all defence registered users.

O. W.: http://www.ddpdos.gov.in

Directorate of Planning and Coordination

The Directorate of Planning & Coordination was set up in 1964 with the primary objective of preparing overall plans for the production of defence equipment in the country. The directorate functions as an attached office of the Department of Defence Production (DDP). It primarily deals with capital acquisition of various weapon systems and platforms of the armed forces of India viz., Air

Force, Army, Navy and Coast Guard. The Directorate also deals with issues relating to defence production policy, formulation of JV guidelines and other policy related issues from DDP's perspective. In addition, the Directorate deals with modernisation of shipyards as well as matters pertaining to international cooperation.

Defence Exhibition Organisation

The main function of Defence Exhibition Organisation (DEO) is to organise and co-ordinate defence exhibitions in India and abroad, primarily with a view to promote the export potential of defence oriented products and services, developed and manufactured by the defence industry. DEO maintains a permanent defence exhibition at the Defence Pavilion, Pragati Maidan, New Delhi. All Defence Public Sector Undertakings (DPSUs), the Ordnance Factory Board (OFB), Defence Research and Development Organisation (DRDO), Directorate General of Quality Assurance (DGQA) and Directorate General of Aeronautical Quality Assurance (DGAQA) have displayed their products, innovations and services in this exhibition.

International Exhibitions Abroad

With a view to provide an impetus to export potential of Indian Defence Industry, DEO organises 'India Pavilion' for major defence products manufactured by them in the international exhibitions abroad.

National Institute for Research and Development in Defence Shipbuilding

The National Institute for Research and Development in Defence Shipbuilding (NIRDESH) set-up as an autonomous society under the aegis of the Ministry of Defence, Department of Defence Production has been envisaged as the nerve centre of India's futuristic shipbuilding programmes. R&D, design, technology development, industry interfacing, training and project management have been identified as the core areas guiding the roles of NIRDESH. This nerve centre will be responsible to collate and consolidate existing capabilities, create new capabilities and cover the gaps that exist.

Research and Development

Defence Research and Development Organisation (DRDO) is the research and development arm of the Ministry of Defence. It was created in 1958 by merging the units of Defence Science Organisation, which was set up in 1948 to advise and assist the Defence Services on scientific problems and to undertake research in areas related to defence, with the then existing Technical Development Establishments of the three Services. Subsequently, a separate Department of Defence Research and Development (DDR&D) was formed in 1980 to improve administrative efficiency. Starting from a cluster of about 10 laboratories in 1958, DRDO today has 46 laboratories which are spread far and wide; from Tezpur in the east to Mumbai in the west, from Leh in the north to Kochi in the south. DRDO's mandate is to provide assessment and advise on scientific aspects of weapons, platforms and surveillance sensors; to carry out research and to develop cutting-edge technologies leading to production of state-of the-art sensors, weapon systems, platforms and allied equipment for our Defence Services.

In the recent past, the mandate has been widened to support national cyber security architecture which includes testing capabilities, security solutions, networking systems and cyber defence tools. In this process, it has also established national infrastructure, enhanced defence industrial capability and developed committed quality human resources.

Organisational Structure

DRDO is headed by the Scientific Adviser to Raksha Mantri (SA to RM) who is also the Secretary, Department of Defence Research and Development and Director General R&D (DGR&D). Based on the R&D work carried out by the 46 laboratories of DRDO, they are grouped into seven technology clusters namely, Armament and Combat Engineering Systems (ACE), Aeronautical Systems (AERO), Missiles and Strategic Systems (MSS), Naval Systems and Materials (NS & M), Electronics and Communication Systems (ECS), Micro Electronic Devices and Computational Systems (MED & CoS) and Life Sciences (LS). Each of these clusters functions under the administrative control of the cluster DGs.

The seven DG offices are located at Pune (ACE), Bengaluru (Aero and ECS), Hyderabad (MSS), Vishakhapatnam (NS & M) and Delhi (MED & CoS and LS). In addition, DDR&D has one autonomous body viz. Aeronautical Development Agency, one joint venture viz. Brahmos Aerospace, four human resource institutions i.e. Centre for Personnel Talent Management (CEPTAM), Institute of Technology Management (ITM), Military Institute of Training (MILIT) and Recruitment and Assessment Centre (RAC), one deemed university viz. Defence Institute of Advance Technology (DIAT) and three certification agencies i.e. Centre for Military Airworthiness and Certification for airworthiness of products, Centre for Fire Explosive and Environment Safety for fire and explosives and Scientific Analysis Group for grading of information security products under its fold. These certification agencies provide services not just for DRDO but other organisations of Government of India as well. Four research boards (Aeronautics, Naval, Armaments and Life Sciences) functioning under DRDO funding, provide thrust to basic research in academia in areas of strategic importance.

Human Resources

Being a mission mode organisation, DRDO follows a dynamic system of manpower planning. Authorisation is reviewed after every two years to meet the contingent requirements on account of workload and new projects undertaken by the laboratories. The organisation optimally utilises manpower through dynamic manpower management system. To keep the organisation young and energetic and also to fill deficiencies created on account of retirement and superannuation, scientists are being inducted every year as required by the laboratories. DRDO follows online receipt of applications under all recruitment and assessment activities thereby discontinuing the offline/ paper application in DRDO. It has a total strength of 25,966 employees, out of which 7,574 are in Defence Research and Development Service (DRDS), 9,643 in Defence Research and Technical Cadre (DRTC) and 8,775 are in Administration and Allied Cadre.

The DRDO ensures training to all cadres of personnel through training institutes, like DIAT, Pune (for technical courses); ITM, Mussoorie (for techno-managerial programmes) and Defence Laboratory, Jodhpur (for technical, administrative and allied cadre). Every year few selected scientists are deputed to undergo ME/ MTech/ PhD at Indian Institute of Technology (IIT), Indian Institute of Science (IISc) and other reputed Indian universities under the sponsorship programme. A Targeted Training Centre has been set up at Dr Raja Ramanna Complex, Bangalore for DRDO scientists. Continuing Education Programme (CEP) are also part of DRDO annual training schedule.

Resettlement of Ex-Servicemen

The Department of Ex-Servicemen Welfare formulates various policies and programmes for the welfare and resettlement of Ex-Servicemen (ESM) in the country. The Department has two divisions viz. Resettlement and Pension, and it has three attached offices namely, Kendriya Sainik Board (KSB Sectt.), Directorate General (Resettlement) (DGR) and Central Organisation, Ex-Servicemen Contributory Health Scheme (ECHS). The KSB is responsible for the welfare of Ex-Servicemen and their dependents and also for the administration of welfare funds. It is assisted in its task by 32 Rajya Sainik Boards (RSBs) and 392 Zila Sainik Boards (ZSBs), which are under the administrative control of respective State governments/Union Territory Administrations. The office of Directorate General of Resettlement implements various Policies/Schemes/Programmes on pre and post retirement training, re-employment and self-employment, etc. The DGR is assisted in its task by five DRZs at each of the five Commands. ECHS takes care of the healthcare and medical needs of Ex-Servicemen and their dependents.

Kendriya Sainik Board Secretariat: KSB Secretariat is the apex body of Government of India responsible for implementing the Central Government policies for rehabilitation and welfare of the war deceased/disabled and retired service personnel and their dependents. The welfare schemes are implemented through Rajya Sainik Boards (RSBs) located in state capitals and Zila Sainik Boards (ZSBs) located at district level. The establishment expenses of these RSBs/ZSBs are shared by the Centre and states. Funding pattern is 75:25 in respect of special category states, namely, Arunachal Pradesh, Assam, Jammu and Kashmir, Meghalaya, Mizoram, Manipur, Nagaland, Sikkim, Tripura, Himachal Pradesh and Uttarakhand, and 60:40 in the case of other states/ UTs. The Central share provided to states/UTs towards establishment/ maintenance of RSBs/ZSBs is reimbursed from the Defence Service Estimate budget allocated to KSB Secretariat for this purpose. ₹ 28.80 crore has been disbursed as Central share upto December, 2015.

Construction of Sainik Rest Houses: In order to provide suitable and cheap accommodation to Ex-Servicemen (ESM) during their short visit to the state capital/district HQs for settlement of their pension cases and other matters like availing facilities of CSD canteen, hospital, etc., KSB Secretariat shares 50 per cent of the cost of construction of Sainik Rest Houses (SRHs) out of DSE. The SRHs are required to be maintained by state governments/UT administration from their own resources/funds.

Armed Forces Flag Day

Armed Forces Flag Day is commemorated on 7th December every year across the country to commemorate the sacrifices made by the armed forces personnel for the country. On this day, token flags are pinned and voluntary contributions collected from public for welfare and rehabilitation of war widows/ disabled, ESM and their dependents.

Armed Forces Flag Day Fund

Apart from the DSE Budget, Armed Forces Flag Day Fund (AFFDF) is the major source of funding for welfare and rehabilitation of war widows, ESM and their dependents. Out of the interest earned on the AFFDF corpus, 7.5 per cent is ploughed back into the corpus and balance is used to fund the welfare and rehabilitation schemes for ESM/dependents. The Fund is administered by KSB Secretariat under the aegis of its Management Committee headed by Raksha Mantri and Executive Committee headed by Secretary, DESW, MoD.

Director General (Resettlement)

The main thrust of the Directorate General Resettlement (DGR) is on resettlement, rehabilitation and welfare of ESM. Nearly 60,000 armed forces personnel retire or are released from active service every year. Most of them are in comparatively younger age bracket of 35 to 45 years and need a second career to support their families. These personnel constitute a valuable, disciplined, well-trained, dedicated and talented pool available for nation building. Resettlement is sought to be achieved through the following: (1) upgrading their skills by imparting necessary training to prepare them to take on new assignment/jobs and assisting them in finding re-employment; (2) constant endeavour to provide employment opportunities in government/ quasi government/public sector organisations; (3) pro-active action to facilitate reemployment of ESM in the corporate sector; (4) providing jobs through schemes on self employment; and (5) assistance in entrepreneurial ventures.

Training Programmes

DGR is entrusted with the responsibility of preparing retiring/retired service personnel for a second career. These resettlement courses are selected with a focus on employability of ESM in Society.

Officers' Training: For training of ESM (Officers), the Resettlement Training Programmes are conducted including 24 Weeks Management Courses at IIMs and other reputed B-Schools, Modular Management courses like Project Finance, Academic Institutions, Supply Chain, Retail, Human Resource,

Facility, Export & Import, Event Six Sigma, Jet Transition and Seafaring, etc. at other reputed institutes. Besides, specially designed six week course on Corporate Security and Safety have been in existence for officers looking to venture into self employment fields such as security agencies. 60 per cent course fee is paid by DGR. Widows of officers are also eligible to undergo these courses.

JCOs/ OR and Equivalent Training: For JCOs/ ORs and equivalent, the training courses are conducted for a duration upto one year in diverse fields, such as Security, Fire & Industrial Safety, Computer & IT including 'O' Level, Hospitality, Tourism, Agri based, Business Management, Modular Management, Vocational & Technical, Medical & Healthcare and Library & Information Science, etc. These courses are also run at reputed institutes of accreditation. Cent per cent course fee is paid by DGR. Widows/one dependent of JCOs/OR are also eligible to undergo any course sponsored by DGR. ESM are now also entitled to apply for regular DGR training which are not fully subscribed by retiring personnel. The move of allowing ESM to attend regular DGR courses is aimed to benefit all those ex-servicemen who have not done any resettlement course in the past and are desirous to do these courses to hone their skill. At least two courses are planned every month at all the Regimental Centres to provide variety of courses to the retirees on pension drill.

ESM Training: Under this scheme, funds are allotted to RSBs for conducting vocational training for ESM in their states. The scheme is primarily meant for those ESM who could not avail the facility of resettlement training while in service.

Employment Opportunities

Reservation in Government Jobs: The Central Government has provided for the following reservation for ESM for vacancies in the posts to be filled by direct recruitment: (a) 10 per cent in Group 'C' posts and 20 per cent in Group 'D' posts. In addition 4.5 per cent reservation in each category is meant for disabled soldiers and widows/dependents. (b) 14.5 per cent in Group 'C' and 24.5 per cent Group 'D' posts in PSUs and nationalised banks. (c) 10 per cent posts up to Assistant Commandants in paramilitary forces. (d) cent per cent in Defence Security Corps.

Implementation of Reservation: The Government has designated Directorate General Resettlement as Nodal agency for the monitoring implementation of reservation policy for ESM. Half yearly report for the period ending June 30, 2015 has been compiled based on data received from various organisations.

Jobs in the Corporate/Private Sector: Substantial employment for ESM can be generated in the Private/Corporate sector. In order to generate awareness and urge these sectors to employ ESM, a National Corporate Conclave was conducted by DGR in August 2014 where the competence of the ESM were presented to Corporate Heads and the Raksha Mantri urged them to open the employment opportunities for ESM. DGR has signed a MoU with Confederation of Indian Industries (CII) towards this end.

Schemes for Self Employment

Coal Transportation Schemes and Tipper Attachment: This scheme has been reenergised by issue of new MoU and guidelines in July 2014.

Company Owned Company Operated Retail Outlets: In accordance with the policy guidelines issued by the Ministry of Petroleum & Natural Gas, DGR sponsors officers for management of Retail Outlets of IOCL, BPCL and HPCL all over India under the Company Owned Company Operated (COCO) Schemes. DGR has sponsored a total of 131 ESM (O) for COCO Scheme during the year.

Gopaljee Dairy and Fresh Farm: The schem aims at providing self-employment to JCOs/ ORs in the National Capital Region (NCR). 11.29 Mother Dairy Milk Booth and Fruit and Vegetable (Safal) Shop: This is a time tested well-paying self-employment scheme for ESM JCOs/ORs equivalent. 284 Mother Dairy Booths and 19 Safal Shops have been allotted to JCOs/ORs Equivalent from this scheme during the year.

Management of CNG Stations by ESM in NCR: The scope of the scheme has been extended to cover entire NCR to include Noida, Faridabad and Gurgaon. 31 ESM (Officers) have benefited from this scheme during the year.

Allotment of Army Surplus Class V 'B' Vehicles: Ex Servicemen and widows of Defence personnel, who died while in service, are eligible to apply for allotment of Army Surplus Class V 'B' Vehicles. 75 ESM were registered with DGR during the year.

Oil Product Agencies Scheme: In accordance with the Policy guidelines issued by the Ministry of Petroleum & Natural Gas/Oil Company, DGR is mandated to issue eligibility certificates for allotment of oil product agencies under the 8 per cent defence quota.

Healthcare

Ex-Servicemen Contributory Health Scheme: Ex-Servicemen Contributory Health Scheme (ECHS) was launched with effect from April 01, 2003. The Scheme was expanded in October 2010. ECHS aims to provide quality healthcare to Ex-Servicemen (ESM) and their dependents through a network of ECHS Polyclinics, Service medical facilities and civil empanelled/ Government hospitals spread across the country. The Scheme has been structured on the lines of Central Government Health Scheme (CGHS) and is financed by the Government of India. Endeavour is to ensure cashless treatment by utilising the empanelled hospitals for the veterans and their dependents.

ECHS Polyclinics are designed to provide 'Out Patient Care' that includes consultations, essential investigation and provision of medicines. Specialised consultations, investigations and 'In Patient Care' (Hospitalisation) is provided through spare capacity available in service hospitals, all Government hospitals and also through civil medical facilities empanelled with ECHS.

Central Organisation: At the apex level is the Central Organisation, ECHS located in Delhi, which functions under the Chiefs of Staff Committee through the Adjutant General in the Integrated Headquarters of Ministry of Defence (Army). The Central Organisation is headed by a serving Major General. Executive control of ECHS is vested with Department of Ex-Servicemen Welfare.

Regional Centres: There are a total of 28 regional centres spread across the country. These regional centres oversee operationalisation and functioning of ECHS Polyclinics placed under them and also take necessary action for empanelment of civil hospitals with ECHS.

Polyclinics: A total of 432 ECHS Polyclinics, including six Polyclinics in Nepal, have been sanctioned by the Government. Out of 426 ECHS Polyclinics in India, 419 have been operationalised.

ECHS Membership: A total of 15,21,563 ESM have enlisted themselves with the Scheme along with 32,02,610 dependents as on May 01, 2015. Total beneficiaries under this scheme are 47,24,173.

Polyclinics and Civil Empanelled Medical Facilities: A total of 177 additional medical facilities have been enlisted with ECHS in last one year. Now the Scheme has 1,445 civil hospitals empanelled with it, for providing cashless treatment to ECHS beneficiaries. However, in case of emergency, members are permitted to avail medical treatment at non-empanelled hospital on payment. Their medical treatment bills are reimbursed at approved (CGHS) rates.

ECHS Toll-Free Helpline: ECHS Toll free Helpline has been made available for all ECHS members at 1800-114-115 for resolving queries on membership, treatment and employment. The service is available from Monday to Friday on all working days from 0900-1700 hours.

ECHS Website: All information regarding ECHS, including list of empanelled facilities, forms for membership and latest policies, etc. are available on www.echs.gov.in.

Pension Reforms

One Rank One Pension to the Defence Forces Personnel: The Government has taken the historic decision to implement One Rank One Pension (OROP) for the Defence Force Personnel from July 01, 2014 and issued notification for its implementation. OROP implies that uniform pension be paid to the Defence Force Personnel retiring in the same rank with the same length of service, regardless of their date of retirement, to bridge the gap between the rates of pension of current and past pensioners at periodic intervals.

There has been revision of 43 per cent and 45 per cent commuted portion of pension of Armed Forces absorbees who had drawn lump sum payment on absorption in public sector undertakings/ autonomous bodies.

Grant of Service element to pre August 30, 2006 released Non Regular Officers in Aggravation-cases: Service element of disability pension in respect of non-regular officers would be calculated after taking into account the full commissioned service rendered by them as calculated in the case of Regular Commissioned Officers. As such, they are also allowed the benefit of revision from August 2006 as allowed to attributable cases. Minimum Guaranteed Pension for Disability/War Injury element as per CSC 2012 recommendation: The Minimum Guaranteed Disability/War Injury Element of Pre-2006 Armed Forces Personnel should be determined with reference to the minimum of the fitment table for the rank in the revised pay structure issued for implementation of recommendations of 6th CPC instead of the minimum of the pay band, subject to the consideration that the rate of disability element/war injury element of lower rank may not exceed that of higher rank.

Payment of Constant Attendance Allowance on Monthly Basis with Disability Pension to Armed Forces personnel: Constant Attendance Allowance (CAA) shall be paid on monthly basis instead of in arrears, during the period of award alongwith disability or war injury pension as the case may be. Grant of Fixed Medical Allowance (FMA) to the Armed Forces pensioners/Family pensioners in such cases where date of retirement is prior to April 01, 2003 and who had opted not to avail medical facilities at OPD of Armed Forces Hospitals/MI rooms and are not member of ECHS. Rate of fixed medical allowance was enhanced from existing rate of ₹ 300/- to ₹ 500/- from November 2014.

Simplification of Pension Process for Permanently Disabled Children/ Siblings and Dependent Parents: To streamline the process of grant of pension to old parents/disabled children, sibling, the employee/pensioner/family pensioner may at any time before or after retirement/death of Armed Force Personnel, may make a request to the Appointing Authority seeking advance approval for grant of family pension for life to a permanently disabled child/sibling.

Simplification of Pension Payment Procedure - Submission of Certificates by Retiring Armed Forces Personnel and Civilian Employees along with Pension Papers: It has been decided that the required undertaking/status of re-employment/employment after retirement may be obtained by the Record Offices/Head of the Offices from the retiring Defence Personnel alongwith other document before his retirement. The undertaking/certificate shall be forwarded to the pension disbursing agencies along with Pension Payment Order (PPO) by the Record Office/Head Office following the usual procedure. The bank shall credit the pensionary awards notified in favour of the pensioner into his/her bank account as and when due if said undertaking/certificate is received along with pension documents. Revision of pension in respect from pre- 2006 retired JCO/ORs pensioners/family pensioners: It has been decided that in respect from January 01, 2006 pension/family pension of pre-2006 JCOs/ORs pensioners/family pensioners shall be determined as 50 per cent and 30 per cent respectively of the minimum of the fitment table for the rank in the revised Pay Band as indicated under fitment tables.

10 Education

THE essence of Human Resource Development is education, which plays a significant and remedial role in balancing the socio-economic fabric of the country. Since citizens of India are its most valuable resource, our billion-strong nation needs the nurture and care in the form of basic education to achieve a better quality of life. This warrants an all-round development of our citizens, which can be achieved by building strong foundations in education. Good quality education is the foundation of new discoveries, new knowledge, innovation and entrepreneurship that trigger growth and prosperity of the individual as well as that of a nation. For this, we need to make our curriculum and pedagogy relevant to the needs of our society and economy and nurture qualities of problem solving and creative thinking, learning-by-doing, greater engagement with the live context, and confident self-expression from a young age.

To lay emphasis on the educational development of students of weaker sections of the society, a number of innovative initiatives have been taken by the ministry such as (i) setting up of national monitoring committee on minorities (ii) setting up of national monitoring committee for education of SCs, STs and persons with disabilities (iii) student support initiatives such as National Means-cum-Merit Scholarship Scheme (NMMSS), National Scheme of Incentive to Girls for Secondary Education (NSIGSE), Special Scholarship Scheme for Jammu and Kashmir, scheme of interest subsidy on educational loans (iv) regulations on prevention of discrimination and establishment of ombudsman and (v) development of an anti-ragging web portal.

Keeping in view the priority of the Government of India, the guidelines for the implementation of the Scheduled Caste Sub-Plan/Tribal Sub-Plan (SCSP/TSP) in the schemes of this Ministry have been prepared and forwarded the same to all within the Ministry and all Organizations/Institutions under this department for implementation. The Ministry's focus has also been on the overall and balanced educational development of all regions of the country including North-Eastern Regions (NER) and Jammu and Kashmir. Currently, the Ministry of Human Resource Development works through two departments - Department of School Education and Literacy and Department of Higher Education.

Ministry of Human Resource Development has adopted a fresh approach to meet its challenges. It is this approach that will define the thrust areas and ensure that all the goals with the right value system, sensitivity and responsibility are achieved. The various policies and programmes of the ministry have successfully enabled the access to quality, inclusive, affordable

Elementary Education in India

Progress of Enrolment

(lakh persons)

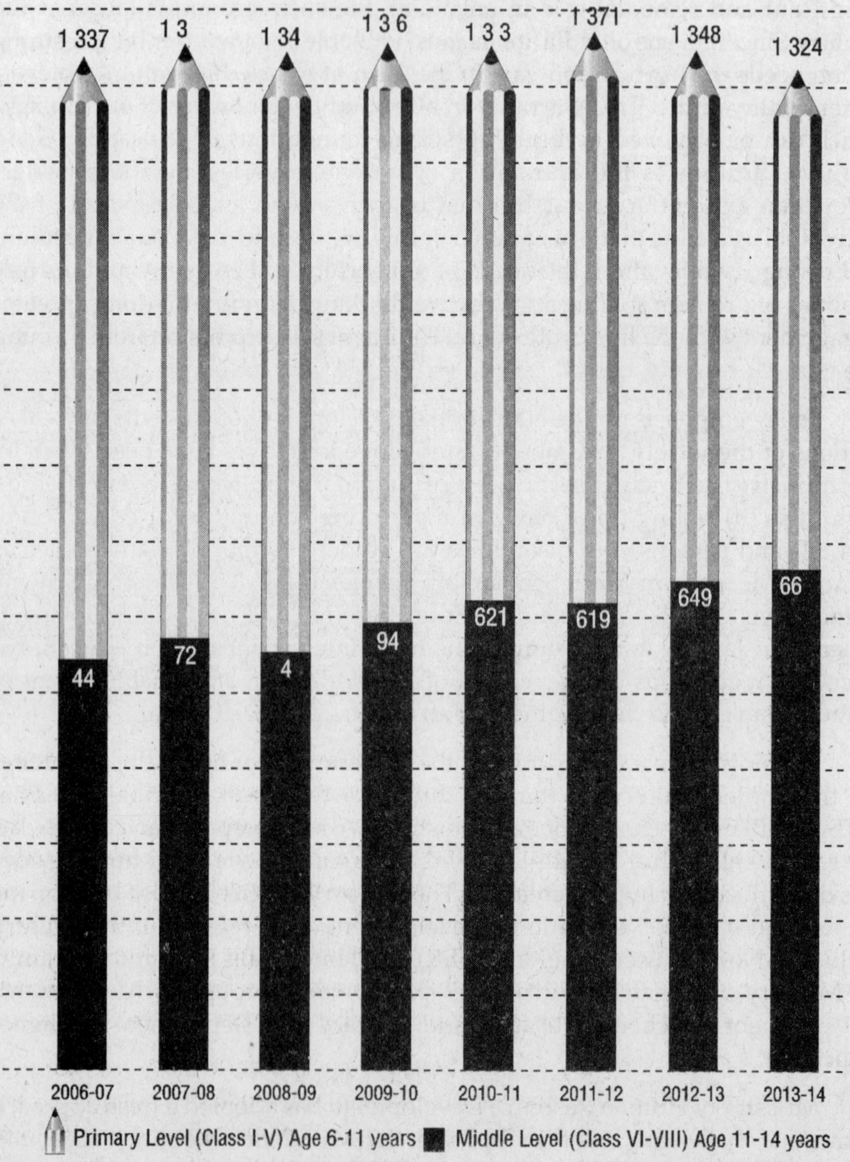

and meaningful education to children and the people across the length and breadth of the country.

Mid day Meal Scheme

The Mid Day Meal Scheme covers children of classes I-VIII studying in government local bodies, government aided schools, special training centres (STC) and madarsas-maqtabs supported under Sarva Shikha Abhiyan (SSA). It is the largest school feeding programme in the world, covering 10.03 crore children in 11.50 lakh institutions across the country. Apart from promoting access and retention, the Mid Day Meal Scheme has also contributed to social and gender equity. It has helped in preventing classroom hunger, promoting school participation and fostering social equality and enhancing gender equality.

Norms for Mid Day Meal Scheme

i) *Calorific Value of Mid Day Meals*: the cooked meal consists of 100 grams of wheat/rice, 20 grams of pulses, 50 grams of vegetables and 5 grams of oil/fat and provides 450 calories of energy and 12 grams of protein at primary stage. For upper primary stage children, it consists of 150 grams of wheat/rice, 30 grams of pulses, 75 grams of vegetables and 7.5 gram of oil/fat and provides 700 calories of energy and 20 grams of proteins and ii) *Cooking cost under MDM Scheme*: The cooking cost covers the expenditure for pulses, vegetables, cooking oils, condiments, fuel, etc. The cooking cost has been increased by 7 per cent from July, 2016 for 2016-17 which comes out to be ₹ 4.13 per cent children per day for primary and 6.18 per child per day for upper primary. The cooking cost is shared between the Centre and the state in the ratio of 60:40 for non-NER states, 100 per cent for UTs and 90:10 for NER states and 3 Himalayan States viz., Himachal Pradesh, Jammu and Kashmir and Uttarakhand.

Tithi Bhojan

Tithi Bhojan is a concept designed to ensure greater public participating under the Mid Day Meal Programme being followed in Gujarat. In order to bring in greater community participation, local communities are encouraged to celebrate important family events viz., birth of a child, success in exams, inauguration of new house, etc., by contributing to the mid day meal served in the local schools. It is voluntarily served by the community/family among school children in several forms like sweets and *namkeen* along with regular MDM, full meals, supplementary nutritive items like sprouted beans, contribution in kind such as cooking ware, utensils, dinner sets or glasses for drinking water.

All the states/UTs have been requested to consider to adopt the practice of Tithi Bhojan with this nomenclature or any nomenclature suitable to the state governments. The concept has been adopted by different states with local nomenclatures like 'Sampriti Bhojan' in Assam, 'Dham' in Himachal Pradesh, 'Sneh Bhojan' in Maharashtra, 'Shalegagi Naavu Neevu' in Karnataka, 'Anna Dhanam' in Puducherry, 'Priti Bhoj' in Punjab and 'Utsav Bhoj' in Rajasthan.

Automated Monitoring System for MDMS

The Department of School Education & Literacy had developed a web based MiS portal for online collection of data on various indicators of the scheme and launched it in June, 2012. Considering the fact that implementation of Mid Day Meal Scheme (MDMS) is primarily with the state governments, which are the primary users of data collected for monitoring the scheme, it has been decided to implement the proposed monitoring project through the state/UT governments. For this purpose, the states/UTs will set up a suitable system of data collection from schools on daily basis and use it for purpose of monitoring and timely follow up action.

Midday Meal Rules 2015

The Mid Day Meal Rules, 2015 have been notified under the National Food Security Act, 2013 and the same are effective from September, 2015. All the states/UTs have been advised to disseminate and enforce the MDM Rules 2015 in all eligible schools. They were also advised to take necessary action to operationalize these rules and lay down set of instructions for their effective implementation in all the schools so as to ensure adherence to the changed norms for serving quality meals to children. The salient features of Mid Day Meal Rules 2015 include: i) strengthen quality by making testing of food samples mandatory; ii) strengthen regularity by allowing temporary use of other funds in case of non-availability of MDM funds in the school and fixing responsibility in case of continued failure to serve meals in schools; iii) enhanced role of school management committees in supervision of MDM in schools; and iv) food security allowance to be paid by the state government, if MDM is not provided in school on any school day due to non-availability of foodgrains, cooking cost, fuel or absence of cook-cum-helper or any other reason.

Testing Food Samples

The Mid Day Meal guidelines for engagement of accredited labs by the state governments is put in place for testing of the meals served in the schools. The meal should contain prescribed nutrients and calorie content and the food served should be hygienic, palatable and attractive to children and therefore provide regular testing of meals has been provided for. Some of the states/UTs have already started the testing of meals:-

Testing of food samples during 2015-16

S.No.	States/UTs	No. of Tests carried out during 2015-16
1	2	3
1	Assam	8
2	Bihar	3
3	Goa	93

4	Gujarat	1060
5	Haryana	3
6	Himachal Pradesh	10
7	Karnataka	51
8	Madhya Pradesh	45
9	Maharashtra	506
10	Mizoram	5
11	Odisha	34
12	Punjab	68
13	Uttar Pradesh	972
14	West Bengal	66
15	Chandigarh	50
16	Delhi	344
17	Puducherry	6
	Total	3324

Source- AWP&B, 2016-17

Social Audit

Social audit means the process in which people collectively monitor and evaluate the planning and implementation of a programme or scheme. The social audit was conducted by Society for Social Audit Accountability and Transparency (SSAAT) in two districts viz., Khammam and Chittoor of Andhra Pradesh during 2012-13. Encouraged by the outcome the Department has issued detailed guidelines for conducting of social audit under Mid Day Meal Scheme. The states/UTs were advised to select the eminent institute available in their respective states for this purpose. So far 10 states viz., Bihar, Maharashtra, Odisha, Karnataka, Punjab, Tamil Nadu, Uttar Pradesh, Telangana, Nagaland and Andhra Pradesh have completed the social audit and it is in progress in Madhya Pradesh, West Bengal and Rajasthan.

National Institutional Ranking Framework Document and Webportal

The National Institutional Ranking Framework (NIRF) for educational institutions was launched to meet a felt need for a framework that would enable parents, students, teachers, educational institutions and other stakeholders to rank institutions on the basis of a set of objective parameters and a transparent process. Developed by a team of experts in education and heads of institutions, the portal and the framework is presently available for engineering and management institutions. Soon, methodologies, parameters and process for ranking universities along with architecture and planning institutions would also be available online. The NIRF will facilitate a level playing field in ranking for institutions which have been working in languages other then English and excelled relatively in the recent past. The ranking framework is designed such that institutions belonging to different sectoral fields such as engineering, management, etc., will be compared separately in their own respective peer groups. The parameters are under the five broad heading (1) teaching learning and resources; (2) research, consulting and collaborative performance; (3) graduation outcomes; (4) outreach and inclusivity and (5) perception.

Sarva Shiksha Abhiyan

The Sarva Shiksha Abhiyan (SSA) is implemented as a centrally sponsored scheme in partnership with state governments for universalizing elementary education across the country. The scheme is implemented from 2010-11 in accordance with the legal framework/provisions of the Right to Children to Free and Compulsory Education (RTE) 2009 which provides for entitlement of all children between the age of 6-14 years for free and compulsory education, attendance and completion of elementary education in a neighbourhood school. The framework for implementation of SSA has been amended to align with the provision of RTE Act, 2009.

The overall goals of SSA include universal access and retention, bridging of gender and social category gaps in education and enhancement of learning levels of children. It provides for a variety of interventions, including opening of new schools, construction of schools and additional classrooms, toilets and drinking water, provisioning for teachers, periodic teacher training and academic resource support, free uniform, textbooks and support for learning achievement. SSA programme has made significant progress in achieving near universal access and equity.

The revised SSA framework for implementation provides a broad outline of approaches and implementation strategies, within which states can frame more detailed guidelines keeping in view their specific social, economic and institutional contexts. The revised SSA framework for implementation is derived from the recommendations of the Committee on Implementation of RTE Act and the Resultant Revamp of SSA, and is intended to demonstrate the harmonization of SSA with the RTE Act. It is also based on child centric assumptions emerging from the National Policy on Education, 1986/92 and the National Curriculum Framework (NCF), 2005.

For implementing SSA, each state/UT has a State Project Office (SPO) and each district has a District Project Office (DPO). At the block level, there are Block Resource Centres (BRC) and within a block there are clusters which have Cluster Resource Centres (CRC). BRC and CRC are responsible for teacher training, academic support and monitoring at the ground level. Each school has a School Management Committee (SMC) which includes Headmaster,

Teachers, Parents and Sarpanch etc. The SMC is responsible for planning, implementation and monitoring of activities at the school level.

Funds are released to states/UTs as per approved Annual Work Plans and Budgets (AWP&B) for each year in two or more installments, depending on the opening balance with the state/UT, release of commensurate state share, pace of expenditure, submission of audit reports and other such criteria laid down in the scheme. The sanction is accorded subject to the terms and conditions contained in the SSA Framework and the Manual for Financial Management and Procurement as well as adherence to financial, administrative and policy norms of the scheme, as amended from time to time. Section 7 of the RTE Act provides that the Central and state governments will have concurrent responsibility for providing funds for carrying out the provisions of the RTE Act. The Planning Commission had conveyed the Gross Budgetary Support (GBS) allocation of ₹ 1,92,726 crore for SSA programme for the XII Plan (2012-13 to 2016-17) in consultation with the Ministry of Finance.

The fund sharing pattern between the Central and state governments for SSA was in the ratio of 65:35 except for the north eastern states for which the ratio is 90:10 from 2010-11 to 2014-15. The fund sharing pattern was revised in 2015-16 to the ratio of 60:40 between centre and states (90:10 for the 8 north-eastern states viz. Arunachal Pradesh, Assam, Manipur, Meghalaya. Mizoram, Nagaland, Sikkim and Tripura and 3 Himalayan states viz., Jammu & Kashmir, Himachal Pradesh and Uttarakhand). The central government funds 100 per cent in case of union territories for SSA with effect from 2015-16.

The Budget allocations for SSA scheme in 2016-17 is ₹ 22500 crore. Allocation & Central share releases for SSA since 2009-10.

(₹ in crore)

Sl.No.	Year	Budget Estimates (BE)	Revised Estimates (RE)	Central share releases
1	2009-2010	13100.00	13100.00	12826.23
2	2010-2011	15000.00	19000.00	19636.53
3	2011-2012	21000.00	21000.00	20866.30
4	2012-2013	25555.00	23875.83	23858.00
5	2013-2014	27258.00	26583.01	24820.92
6	2014-2015	28258.00	24380.00	24122.51
7	2015-2016	22000.00	22015.42	21666.51
8	2016-2017	22500.00	-	5182.52*

* *till June 2016*

Cumulative Progress under SSA

Activity	Cumulative Sanction upto 2015-16	Cumulative Achievement (completed by 31.03.2016)	percentage completed
Primary Schools	199230	183386	92.05
Upper Primary Schools	112392	105943	94.26
Additional Class Rooms	1861336	1740487	93.51
Drinking Water	238973	229742	96.14
Boys Toilets	375976	350888	93.33
Separate Girls Toilets	499946	490779	98.17
CWSN Toilets	138585	114627	82.71

Monitoring of SSA

The central government reviews and monitors implementation of the RTE Act periodically with the states, including the State Education Ministers' Conferences. An concurrent financial review is also undertaken to cover all states within two years. Educational data on outcomes is collected through a Unified District Information System of Education (UDISE) every year. The status of these evaluations and monitoring is placed in the public domain on the Ministry's website.

Impact of SSA and RTE

RTE Act came into force since April 2010. Sarva Shiksha Abhiyaan was started in 2000-01 and the main programme for ensuring universal elementary education, was revised in September 2010 to conform to the RTE mandate. The impact of RTE-SSA may be seen as follows:

Universal Access: 98 per cent habitations have access to primary school and 97 per cent to upper primary school. Since enactment of the Act, 3,67,494 schools have been sanctioned under SSA.

Increased Enrolment: District Information System for Education (DISE) collects annual data as of September of every year on a number of indicators including enrolment across every school in the country. In 2014-15 enrolment in elementary schools was 19.77 crore children as compared to enrolment of 18.79 crore children in 2009-10. As may be seen from the table given here, the enrolment has been increasing over the years at elementary level.

Education Indicators

Educational Indicators	2009-10	2010-11	2011-12	2012-13	2013-14	2014-15
GER at Primary Level	115.63	118.62	104.34	105.98	101.36	100.08
GER at Upper Primary Level	75.80	81.15	80.59	82.50	89.33	19.24
Enrolment at elementary level (number in crore)	18.79	19.30	19.90	19.97	19.89	19.77
Retention Rate at Primary Level	74.01	73.42	75.94	80.07	82.38	83.74
Transition Rate (Primary to Upper Primary)	83.53	85.17	87.09	86.74	89.58	89.74
Average Annual Dropout Rate at Primary Level	6.76	6.50	5.62	4.67	NA	4.34
Number of schools (in lakh)	13.03	13.62	14.12	14.31	14.49	14.46

(Source: UDISE)

The total enrolment in elementary schools has risen from 18.79 crore children in 2009-10 to 19.77 crore children in 2014-15. As per UDISE 2014-15, Gross Enrolment Ratio (GER) is 98.85 per cent for boys and 101.43 per cent for girls, which indicates universal enrolment at primary level. The GER at upper primary level is 87.71 per cent for boys and 95.29 per cent for girls. The Pupil Teacher Ratio (PTR) has improved from 32 in 2009-10 to 25 in 2014-15. 62.65 per cent of the government schools in India have PTR as per the RTE norm (30:1 primary and 35:1 upper primary on an average). Number of out of School children was 134.6 lakh in 2005 which has come down to 81 lakh in 2009 and 61 lakh in 2013. Average Annual Dropout rate at Primary level has come down from 6.76 per cent in 2009-10 to 4.34 per cent in 2013-14. However, average annual dropout rate at upper primary level has increased from 2.65 per cent in 2011-12 to 3.77 per cent in 2013-14. The transition rate from primary to upper primary has gone up from 85.17 in 2009-10 to 89.74 per cent in 2013-14 as per UDISE, 2014-15. The Gender Parity Index (GPI) in 2014-15 has reached to 0.93 for primary level and 0.95 at upper primary level. Percentage of girls' enrolment has gone up from 48.12 in 2009-10 to 48.34 per cent in 2014-15 at elementary level. Enrolment of SC children has gone up from 19.06 in 2010-11 to 19.80 per cent in 2014-15 at elementary level which is more than their share in population. Enrolment of ST children is 10.47 per cent in 2014-15 at elementary level which is more than their share of population. Enrolment of Muslim children has grown up from 12.50 in 2010-11 to 13.77 per cent in 2014-15 at elementary level which is marginally lower than their share of population of 14.2 per cent as per census 2011.

Share of Girls, SC, ST and Muslims in Total Enrolment

Social Group	Primary		Upper Primary	
	2009-10	2014-15	2009-10	2014-15
Girls	48.46 %	48.19%	48.12 %	48.63%
SC	20.07%	19.93%	19.17%	19.55%
ST	11.54%	10.83%	9.4%	9.76%
Muslims	13.48%	14.37%	11.89%	12.60%

Source: DISE

SSA provides assistance to states/UTs for reimbursement of the expenditure incurred towards at least 25 per cent admissions of the children belonging to weaker section and disadvantaged group as notified by respective state government in private unaided schools under Section 12 (1) (c) of the RTE Act, 2009, based on per child cost norms notified by the state government subject to a maximum ceiling of 20 per cent of the size of the SSA Annual Work Plan and Budget with effect from the year 2015-16. States/UTs have reported that a total of 18.10 lakh children were studying in private schools under Section 12(1)(c) during 2014-15.

Inclusive Education

The major interventions under SSA for the education of children with special needs (CWSN) are indentification, functional and formal assessment, provision of aids and appliances, teacher training, engagement of resource persons exclusively for CWSN, support services and barrier free access. SSA also ensures that every CWSN irrespective of the kind, category and degree of disability, is provided quality inclusive education. The number of children with special needs that have been brought into the fold of education (through enrolment in formal schools, school readiness programme and through home-based education) is 23.18 lakh as per the Unified District Information System for Education (UDISE) 2014-15.

Emphasis on Girl Education

(a) *Kasturba Gandhi Balika Vidyalayas*: Kasturba Gandhi Balika Vidyalayas (KGBVs) have been opened in Educationally Backward Blocks (EBBs) where the female rural literacy is below the national average to provide for residential upper primary schools for girls. 3599 KGBVs are operational in the country enrolling 3.64 lakh girls. The KGBV component of SSA scheme targets girl's education for drop out girl children particularly from low literacy habitations, below poverty line and SC/ST minorities population. (b) *Gender Atlas*: The 'Digital Gender Atlas' for advancing girls education was launched on the occasion of International Women's Day in 2015. This helps to identify and ensure equitable education with a focus on vulnerable girls, including girls with disabilities. The Gender Atlas uses geographical representation and numeric data at state, district and block levels and gives information on key indicators for girls education at primary, upper primary and secondary level for three years. (c) '*Swachh Bharat*: Swachh Vidyalaya Initiative: The Department launched Swachh Vidyalaya initiative under the rubric of Swachh Bharat Mission with an objective to provide separate toilets for boys and girls in all government schools within a year. Under Swachh Vidyalaya Initiative, 4,17,796 toilets were constructed in 2,61,400 schools in a period of one year, thus ensuring that every single government school now has separate toilet for girls and boys. This includes schools in the most difficult to reach areas in the country such as districts facing Left Wing Extremism in forests, remote mountainous terrain and in crowded slums. The Initiative was made successful in partnership with all State Governments, Central Public Sector Undertakings, and Private Corporates. With this, about 13.58 crore children in 11.08 lakh government schools all over the country now have access to toilet facilities.

New Initiatives:

(a) *Rashtriya Aavishkar Abhiyan*: Rashtriya Aavishkar Abhiyan was launched in July 2015, to motivate and encourage children of the age-group 6-18 years, in science, mathematics and technology. The programme framework is on a twin track approach (i) systemic improvements in the school system; (ii) initiatives to encourage science, mathematics through alternative strategies. The strategies of the programme targets, teachers, students, effective classroom transaction, school facilities for science and maths, and community engagement. In 2015-16, an amount of ₹ 124.78 crore and ₹ 108.26 crore have been earmarked under SSA and RMSA respectively. In case of collaborative initiatives with Ministry of Science and Technology and Department of Higher Education, funds would be pooled with their schemes and norms. All state governments/ UTs have also been given a funding of ₹ 5 lakh per district under innovation fund of SSA to undertake innovative activities and build awareness around learning of Science and Mathematics.

(b) *Padhe Bharat Badhe Bharat*

A nationwide sub-programme of Sarva Shiksha Abhiyaan named Padhe Bharat Badhe Bharat (PBBB) was launched in 2014 to ensure quality at the foundational years of schooling i.e., classes I and II. Through this programme it will be ensured that all children are able to read with comprehension as well as basic numeracy skills. The programme envisages dedicated teachers for classes I and II. It centers on capacity building of teachers, organizing separate reading periods in daily school time-table, maintaining a print rich environment, for reading through children's literature in school libraries and reading corners in classes I and II; for tribal children special bridge materials have been prepared in states which have a high tribal population.

Saransh

The CBSE Board launched an on-line facility titled 'Saransh' in 2014 for affiliated and CBSE schools. It helps the schools to look at their performance at an aggregate level and at the level of each student. All performance matrices are presented through numbers as well as in charts/ graphs for easy understanding. Saraansh helps schools compare their performance vis-à-vis all CBSE schools at various levels.

Pandit Madan Mohan Malviya National Mission for Teachers' Training

An umbrella scheme to create synergies among the various ongoing initiatives on Teachers and Teaching was launched. The Scheme addresses all issues related to teachers, teaching, teacher preparation, professional development, curriculum design. The scheme also caters to the need to induct qualified teachers, attracting talent into teaching profession and raising the quality of teaching in schools and colleges. Reform in the Teacher Education sector through suitable regulatory changes, to improve quality standard has been initiated. 12 teacher education courses have been revised and the curriculum upgraded and three new programmes have been approved and notified (4 years B.A./ B.Sc. B.Ed., 3 years B.Ed.-M.Ed. and part time B.Ed. in vacations).

Impacting Research Innovation and Technology

To identify the needs of the country in terms of its research and technology requirements, ten goal posts have been identified and research groups are being set up to formulate time-bound plans of action for each. Leading academic institutions like IITs and ISC have been identified to set the process in motion.

Regulator Review

(i) *University Grants Commission* Lots of private institutions have come up in higher education sector with the growing trend of commercialization. They sometimes are not maintaining the laid down standards. UGC's entire functioning continues to be oriented more towards grant giving rather than regulation and enforcement of minimum standards. The Central Government, therefore, recognizing the need for restructuring the University Grants Commission has constituted a UGC Review Committee, in 2014.

(ii) *All India Council for Technical Education*

The MHRD, recognizing the need for restructuring and strengthening the All India Council for Technical Education has constituted Review Committee. The Committee is to conduct a review of the present status of AICTE and suggest restructuring and reorganizing of AICTE for attaining even better performance to meet the desired objectives.

National Ranking Framework

A Committee on National Ranking Framework has been constituted to evolve a ranking framework for universities and institutions. Workshops were organized in coordination with ranking agencies to address various rank parameters.

Mandatory Accreditation

National Assessment and Accreditation Council had submitted a project proposal to MHRD under Rashtriya Ucchatar Shiksha Abhiyan (RUSA) and has been sanctioned ₹ 17 crores. The major features of the National Quality Renaissance Initiative (NQRI) are: (i) awareness building, popularisation and promotion of quality assurance mentoring higher education institutions, (ii) building collegium of assessors and (iii) quality sustenance and enhancement initiatives.

New Higher Educational Institutions

Five IITs - Andhra Pradesh, Jammu and Kashmir, Chhattisgarh, Goa, Kerala, six IIMs -Himachal Pradesh, Andhra Pradesh, Punjab, Maharashtra, Bihar, Odisha, four new central universities – Andhra Pradesh (1 central university & 1 tribal university), Bihar (Mahatma Gandhi Central University), one IISER – Andhra Pradesh, one NIT–Andhra Pradesh, one IIIT – Andhra Pradesh, one Tribal University – Telengana

Bachelor of Vocational Studies

The UGC has introduced the scheme for B.Voc degree with multiple exits at Diploma/ Advanced Diploma under National Skill qualification Framework (NSQF). The objectives are (i) to enhance the employability of youth; (ii) to maintain their competitiveness through provisions of multi-entry multi-exit learning opportunities and vertical mobility; (iii) to fill the gap between educated and employable and (iv) to reduce the dropout rate at the secondary level. Currently, 2035 schools across 25 states are implementing the scheme.

Skills Assessment Matrix for Vocational Advancement of Youth

A credit framework Skills Assessment Matrix for Vocational Advancement of Youth (SAMVAY) is now in place which allows vertical and lateral mobility within vocational education system and between the current education systems. The strength of this framework is the seamless integration of pursuit of academic knowledge and practical vocational skills. Efforts like these will improve the employability of our educated youth.

Education Sector Skill Council

Education Sector Skill Council was constituted in 2014, to consider job roles other than academic faculties and teacher qualifications. The functions of the SSC, include setting up of Labour Market Information System (LMIS) to assist planning and delivery of training Identification of skill development needs and preparing a catalogue of skill types, develop skill development plan and maintain skill inventory developing skill competency standards and qualifications.

Kaushal Kendra

100 Deen Dayal Upadhyay Centres for Knowledge Acquisition and Upgradation of Skilled Human Abilities and Livelihood (KAUSHAL) to be set

up. These Kendras will formulate courses at postgraduate level keeping in mind the need of i) industry in specialized areas; ii) instructional design, curriculum design and contents in the areas of skills development; iii) pedagogy, assessment for skills development education and training. iv) trained faculty in the areas of skill development; and v) entrepreneurship. A Kaushal Kendra will work for coordination between the higher education system and industry to become a Centre of Excellence for skill development in specialized areas.

Unnat Bharat Abhiyaan

IIT, IISER, NIT to adopt villages and develop appropriate rural technologies for sustainable development through peoples' participation. The Abhiyan will enable processes that connect institutes of higher education with local communities. Focus on water management, organic farming, renewable energy, frugal technology, infrastructure, and livelihood.

Yukti - Yogya Kalakriti ki takneek

Yukti aims at skill development and upgradation of design and technologies enhancing the economic prospects of those engaged in traditional crafts and arts as a means of livelihood. It aims at introducing appropriate designs and technology for innovation and pedagogical methods for introducing skills for upgradation.

SAKSHAM - Scholarship for Differently-Abled Children Saksham'

Scheme of AICTE aims at providing encouragement and support to differently-abled children to pursue technical education. Scholarships amounting to ₹ 5 crore per annum as tuition fees and incidentals are to be provided to needy and meritorious students for pursuing technical education at AICTE approved institution. This is to help them to achieve their college goals, despite learning issues, environmental challenges or medical bills.

Ishan Uday-for Students of North East Region

The UGC has launched a special scholarship scheme for students of north east region, Ishan Uday from the academic session 2014-15. The Scheme envisages grant of 10,000 scholarships to students from the region whose parental income is below ₹ 4.5 lakh per annum and would be provided scholarship ranging from ₹ 3,500 to 5,000 per month for studying at under graduate level in colleges/universities of the country.

Ishan Vikas - Academic Exposure for North Eastern Students

The programme has been launched with a plan to bring selected college and school students from the north eastern states into close contact with IITs, NITs and IISERs during their vacation periods for academic exposure. 2112 school students, 528 school teachers from the region will be visiting Premier Institutes every year. From 25 Institutions, about 250 collage students will be visiting 16 IITs and 6 NITs (start with six NITs are being considered) every year.

Women Leader

Women appointed as Chairpersons, Board of Governors of apex technical education institutes and in National Institutes of Technology (NITs). For the first time in the history of IITs, two women scientist nominated on the IIT council.

Udaan

The scheme is dedicated to the development of girl child education, so as to promote the admission of girl students. 951 students have been selected by the CBSE. The aim is to address the teaching gap between school education and engineering entrance examinations. It seeks to enhance the enrolment of girl students in prestigious technical education institutions through incentives & academic support. It offers free online supplementary lessons in physics, chemistry and maths specially prepared in the form of videos, text and practice tests on a tablet.

Saakshar Bharat

Adult Literacy and Pradhan Mantri Jan Dhan Yojna centrally sponsored scheme of Adult Education and Skill Development has a special focus on underprivileged groups. 410 Districts are covered under the programme. Initiatives have been taken under financial literacy to include certified adult literates under Pradhan Mantri Jan Dhan Yojna (PMJDY) and mobilize them to open bank accounts. 82.25 lakh certified adult literates have reportedly opened accounts under the PMJDY.

Pragati

Scholarships for Girl Child for Technical education Pragati aims at providing encouragement and support to girl child to pursue technical education. The scheme envisages providing a scholarship of ₹ 30,000 and tuition fees ₹ 2,000 per month for 10 months until the duration of the course. 4000 girls will be benefited every year with the restriction that only one girl per family with income less than ₹ 6 lakh/annum will be considered. The candidates will be selected on merit through the qualifying examination of the state.

Swami Vivekananda Scholarship for Single Girl Child

The dropout ratio at various levels of education for girls is much higher than that of boys. Keeping Swami Vivekananda's ideas of women education and to promote girls education, UGC has introduced the Swami Vivekananda Scholarship for Single Girl Child for research in social sciences with an aim to compensate direct costs of higher education especially for such girls who happen to be the only girl child in their family.

Shaala Darpan

Shaala Darpan – an ICT programme of the Ministry was launched to provide mobile access to parents of students of government and government aided schools. Using Shaala Darpan parents can view updates on their child's progress. They can view records of attendance, assignments and achievements of their child.

School Report Card

Report cards of schools across the country based on Unified District Information System for Education (UDISE), that is annually updated by states through its schools- covering all aspects of school and its functions. UDISE media campaign was launched for the first time in 2014, to generate awareness amongst stakeholders and also ensure participation of schools specially the private ones. Availability of empirical data and its use in Planning and monitoring under SSA and RMSA has enhanced need based provisioning and utilization of resources.

GIS Mapping

Based on the GIS mapping exercise conducted by the states, Department initiated steps to converge it at the national level with the NICGIS platform, in 2014. The focus has been to test the accuracy of state data and then to create a layer of school information (GIS) system over the platform. Data of 22 states have been made available and has been further linked with the UDISE school level data.

Swachh Vidyalaya

Swachh Vidyalaya Portal, a user-friendly web-portal launched in 2014, has so far facilitated support of more than 200 entities by way of registering online and to enable all process including selection of schools (without toilets), confirmation of their request and to further update the progress of construction with 'geolocation enabled' uploads of actual photographs of the site.

Know Your College

Know Your College is a portal developed for helping a prospective student make a valued judgment for selection of college providing the necessary information about the college. Details like collaborations, mobile education, vocational education, community colleges, use of ICT, model curriculum, and a research portal are available. Details about facilities for specially-abled, facilities for girls, placement facilities and entrepreneurship details are also available. Students can lodge online grievances on the portal for redressal. This application allows a student either in the country or outside to submit an online grievance.

Campus Connect

The National Mission on Education through Information and Communication Technology (NMEICT) Scheme aims to leverage the potential of ICT for teaching and learning processes. The Mission has two major components. (a) content generation, (b) providing connectivity along with provision for access devices to the institutions and learners. Under the NMEICT Mission connectivity to 419 universities/ university level institutions and more than 25000 colleges and polytechnics in the country has been envisaged to be provided.

National e-Library

The National Digital Library of India is envisaged as a National knowledge asset which will provide ubiquitous digital knowledge source. It will support and enhance education, research and innovation catering to the needs of all types of learner groups over the country. Developing and providing efficient access to quality e-content addressed to various learners with different backgrounds, expectations and languages.

Swayam - Study Webs of Active -Learning for Young Aspiring Minds

Swayam is a Massive Open Online Courses (MOOCs) initiative on a national platform with a comprehensive academic structure. The integrated platform will offer courses covering engineering, humanities and social sciences etc., to be used by learners at large. Formation of a Consortium of premier educational institutions and universities to offer flipped online courses instantaneously after due authentication and award of certification.

Global Initiative for Academic Network

Global Initiative for Academic Network (GIAN) aims at tapping the talent pool of scientists and entrepreneurs, internationally to encourage their engagement with the institutes of higher education in India so as to augment the country's existing academic resources, accelerate the pace of quality reform, and elevate India's scientific and technological capacity to global excellence. It is proposed to initiate the program under collaboration with various countries.

Swachh Vidyalaya

The Government has approved 1.70 lakh toilets under SSA and RMSA. In addition, public sector corporations have blocked 91,422 toilets. Private sector corporations have committed to construct 2734 toilets. In addition, PSUs have also undertaken renovation/ re-construction of 67592 dysfunctional toilets. A nodal agency—potentially called the Council for Industry and Higher Education Collaboration (CIHEC) — would be formed to promote and facilitate industry- higher education collaboration.

Research Parks

The objective of the Research Parks is to create a knowledge and innovation ecosystem through collaboration between industry and academia to enable, encourage and develop cutting edge technology and innovation that exceeds the global standard. Phase-I of IITMRP is fully functional. Two more Research Parks apart from IIT Madras have been approved, one each at IIT Bombay and IIT Kharagpur with an allocation of ₹100 crore each.

IIIT Initiative

The IIIT Bill, became a law in 2014. Accordingly it grants statutory status to the four existing Indian Institutes of Information Technology (IIITs) to bring them under a single umbrella; declares them as Institutes of National Importance and so enables them to grant degrees to their students in the academic courses, institutionalize structures such as IIIT Council headed by the Minister of HRD for discussion on policy matters of common interest.

Central Universities Amendment

The Central Universities (Amendment) Bill, 2014 seeking to establish a second Central University in Bihar by the name of "Mahatma Gandhi Central University" and renaming the existing "Central University of Bihar" as "Central University of South Bihar" has been passed in 2014.

Bal Sansad

The Ministry of Parliamentary Affairs, launched Youth Parliament Scheme in order to make the students understand parliamentary procedures and working of parliament, form opinion about public issues, train them in techniques of group discussion, develop abilities to arrive at decision, develop respect and tolerance for views of others, develop leadership and other desirable qualities.

Sanskrit Week

Sanskrit Week focused on enhancing the interest of students in Sanskri language and also on providing channels and platform for the creative potential of the students, teachers and schools was organized.

Swachhata Abhiyaan - Bal Swachhata Mission

The CBSE initiated the Swachh Vidyalaya Abhiyan in its schools in 2014 by asking them to take up a programme for cleanliness. The students, teachers, parents, along with school management committees were encouraged to participate in this programme. 18 out of 2060 schools were selected for award.

Matribhasha Diwas

In order to promote the dissemination of mother tongues and fuller awareness of linguistic and cultural traditions, the CBSE celebrated 'International Mother Language Day' or 'Matribhasha Diwas'.

Growing Aptitude in Numerical Innovations and Training

Growing Aptitude in Numerical Innovations and Training (GANIT) Week in the schools affiliated to CBSE was organized to commemorate the birth anniversary of Srinivasa Ramanujan and to actively promote interest of students in mathematics. Lecture on mathematics by eminent scientists, essay writing competitions, quiz competitions, experience sharing on innovation by teachers and students, screening of films produced by Vigyan Prasar, origami and poster competition followed by a formal culmination function were held.

Shaala Utsav

There are many schools in the country which were established more than 100 years ago. Shaala Utsav is an effort to celebrate the foundation day of such schools. The community participates in celebrating the foundation day. It gives community a sense of ownership and pride in the school in their locality.

Invitation to distinguished retired teachers from the local school and honouring them on such occasions were extended. These Utsavs will engage community to start an education dialogue (Shiksha Samvad) on various issues of improving school functioning and quality of learning.

Copyright

Acquisition of copyright is automatic and it does not require any formality. Copyright comes into existence as soon as a work is created and no formality is required to be completed for acquiring it. However, as per Section 48 of the Act, certificate of registration of copyright and the entries made therein serve as prima facie evidence in a court of law with reference to dispute relating to ownership of copyright.

The Copyright Office was established in 1958 under Section 9(1) of the Copyright Act, 1957. It functions under the administrative control of the Department of Higher Education. It is headed by the Registrar of Copyright, who has quasi-judicial powers in handling cases relating to copyright. The main function of the Copyright Office is to undertake registration of copyright. The Register of Copyrights maintained by the Copyright Office provides information regarding works of copyright to the general public. Now Copyright Office has been separated and is functioning as a separate entity. In addition to registration, facilities like inspection of the Register and taking extracts thereof are also available in the Copyright Office.

As provided under Section 13 of the Copyright Act, 1957, copyright subsists in the following classes or works: (a) original literary, software, musical, and artistic works; (b) cinematographic films; and (c) sound recording. The Copyright Office also registers changes in the particulars of copyright entered in the Register of Copyrights in accordance with Rule 70 of the Copyright Rules, 2013. Section 47 of the Act also provides for inspection of the Register of Copyrights or taking certified copies of the extracts against payment of the prescribed fee. To facilitate this, an index of the works whose particulars have been entered in the Register is also maintained in the Copyright Office. While minor corrections and changes in particulars entered in the Register can be made by the Registrar, only the Copyright Board is empowered to expunge any entries made in the register on an application by the Registrar or any person aggrieved.

As per Section 45 of the Copyright Act, 1957 either the author or publisher or owner of copyright or any other person interested in the copyright of a work can make an application in the prescribed format along with prescribed fee to the Registrar of Copyright for entering particulars of the work in the Register of Copyrights. The Copyright Office provides registration facilities to all types of works and the applications for registration of works can be sent through post to Copyright Office and online applications also be filed. The e-filing facility was started from, 2014 and a new logo of copyright with newly designed certificate has also been issued. Digitization of copyright records is also being started soon.

There is a quasi-judicial body Copyright Board which was constituted in September, 1958 and had been functioning on a part-time basis. The jurisdiction of the Copyright Board extends to the whole of India. The Board is entrusted with the task of adjudication of disputes pertaining to copyright registration and assignment of copyright, rectification of registration, grant of compulsory licences in respect of works withheld from public, unpublished Indian works, for benefit of physically disabled persons, production and publication of translations and works for certain specified purposes. The Copyright Board also determines and fixes rate of royalties for statutory licences for cover versions and broadcasting of literary and musical works and sound recordings. It also hears cases in other miscellaneous matters instituted before it under the Copyright Act, 1957. The Copyright (Amendment) Act, 2012 provides for a three member permanent Copyright Board consisting of a Chairman and two other members.

11 Energy

ENERGY is an essential input for economic development and improving the quality of life. Development of conventional forms of energy for meeting the growing energy needs of society at a reasonable cost is the responsibility of the Government. Development and promotion of non-conventional/alternate/new and renewable sources of energy such as solar, wind and bio-energy, etc., are also getting growing attention. Nuclear energy development is being geared up to contribute significantly to the overall energy availability in the country.

Power

Power development in India commenced at the end of the nineteenth century with the commissioning of electricity supply in Darjeeling during 1897, followed by the commissioning of a hydropower station at Sivasamudram in Karnataka during 1902. In the pre-Independence era, the power supply was mainly in the private sector, that too restricted to the urban areas. With the formation of State Electricity Boards during Five-Year Plans, a significant step was taken in bringing about a systematic growth of power supply industry all over the country. A number of multi-purpose projects came into being, and with the setting up of thermal, hydro and nuclear power stations, power generation started increasing significantly.

The Ministry of Power is primarily responsible for the development of electrical energy in the country. The Ministry is concerned with perspective planning, policy formulation, processing of projects for investment decisions, monitoring of the implementation of power projects, training and manpower development and the administration and enactment of legislation with regard to thermal and hydro power generation, transmission and distribution. In all technical matters, the Ministry of Power is assisted by the Central Electricity Authority (CEA).

The construction and operation of generation and transmission projects in the Central Sector are entrusted to Central Sector Power Corporations, viz., the National Thermal Power Corporation (NTPC), the National Hydroelectric Power Corporation (NHPC), the North-Eastern Electric Power Corporation (NEEPCO), and the Power Grid Corporation of India Limited (PGCIL). The Power Grid is responsible for all the existing and future transmission projects in the Central Sector and also for the formation of the National Power Grid. Two joint-venture power corporations, namely, Satluj Jal Vidyut Nigam (SJVN) (formerly known as NJPC) and Tehri Hydro Development Corporation (THDC) are responsible for the execution of the Nathpa Jhakri Power Project in Himachal Pradesh and projects of Tehri Hydro Power Complex in Uttarakhand respectively. Three statutory bodies, i.e., the Damodar Valley Corporation (DVC), the Bhakra-Beas Management Board (BBMB) and Bureau of Energy

Efficiency (BEE), are also under the administrative control of the Ministry of Power. Programmes of rural electrification are provided financial assistance by the Rural Electrification Corporation (REC). The Power Finance Corporation (PFC) provides term-finance to projects in the power sector. A Power Trading Corporation has also been incorporated primarily to support the Mega Power Projects in private sector by acting as a single entity to enter into Power Purchase Agreements (PPAs).

O. W.: http://www.powermin.nic.in

Capacity Addition

The all India installed power generation capacity by November 2015 is 2,82,023.78 MW comprising 1,96,204.44 MW thermal 42,623.42 MW hydro, 5.780 MW nuclear and 37,415.53 MW R.E.S.

Electricity Generation

The total electricity generation in the country increased from 420.6 billion unit during 1997-98 to 739.92 during April-November, 2015.

Ultra Mega Power Projects

The Government of India had launched an initiative for the development of coal-based Ultra Mega Power Projects (UMPPs), each with a capacity of 4,000 MW. The objective of the initiative is to ensure cheaper tariffs utilising economies of scale, catering to the need of a number of states and to mitigate the risk relating to tie up of land fuel, water and other statutory clearances, etc. The projects are being awarded to the successful developers on the basis of tariff based competitive bidding route employing super critical technology; to tie-up for necessary inputs and clearances such as provision of site, fuel through captive mining blocks, water and in-principle environment and forest clearances, project-specific shell companies (SPVs) are set up as wholly owned subsidiaries of the Power Finance Corporation Ltd. (PFC) - the nodal agency for these projects. These SPVs, along with the various clearances, etc. are subsequently transferred to the successful developer. Four UMPPs namely Sasan in Madhya Pradesh, Mundra in Gujarat, Krishnapatnam in Andhra Pradesh and Tilaiya in Jharkhand have already been awarded to successful bidders and are at different stages of development.

Transmission

Transmission projects continue to be accorded a high priority in the context of the need to evacuate power from generating stations to load centres, system strengthening and augmentation of National Grid.

National Grid

India's natural resources are unevenly distributed as, coal resources are abundant in Bihar/Jharkhand, Odisha, West Bengal and hydro resources are mainly concentrated in northern and North-Eastern Region, etc., far away from the demand centres. Further, acquiring Right-of-Way (ROW) for constructing transmission system is increasingly becoming difficult. These necessitated creation of high capacity 'Transmission Highways', so that, constraints in RoW do not become bottleneck in harnessing natural resources. Power Grid is strengthening its transmission network to establish inter-state and inter-regional links for enhancing the capacity of National Grid in a time-bound manner to ensure optimal utilisation of uneven distribution of energy resources. As on November 30, 2015, National Grid with inter-regional power transfer capacity of about 53,150 MW was established.

Rural Electrification

Rural electrification has been regarded as a vital programme for the development of rural areas. In 1947, only 1,500 villages were electrified in India. The per capital consumption was 14 units.

(i) Rural Electrification under Minimum Needs Programme (MNP): This was started in Fifth Five Year Plan with rural electrification as one of the components of the programme. Under this programme funds were provided as Central assistance to the states in the form of partly grants and partly loans. Since the inception of the MNP, the component that relates to rural electrification has been set off against the loan component. The areas covered under the Programme for the purposes of rural electrification were remote, far flung and difficult villages with low load potential. The scheme has been discontinued from 2004 onwards and has been subsequently merged with the new scheme, Rajiv Gandhi Grameen Vidyutikaran Yojana (RGGVY).

(ii) Pradhan Mantri Gramodaya Yojana (PMGY): This scheme was launched in 2000-01 but rural electrification component was added in the next year. It was being implemented by state electricity boards/electricity developments/power/utilities which were designated as implementing agencies. Funds were being released by state government to the implementing agencies. Funds under the programme were provided to the states as additional central assistance which followed the normal pattern of central assistance i.e., 90 per cent grant and 10 per cent loans for special category states, 30 per cent grant and 70 per cent loan for other states. The scheme has been discontinued from 2005-06 onwards.

(iii) Kutir Jyoti Scheme: This programme was launched in 1988-89 to provide single point light connections to households of rural families below the poverty line including harijans and adivasi families. The allocation amongst the states was based on the size of rural population below the poverty line and level of village electrification in the state, with higher weightage given to states having larger population of rural poor and low electrification levels. This scheme has been now merged with RGGVY.

(iv) Accelerated Rural Electrification Programme (AREP): The scheme was introduced in 2003-04 under which interest subsidy of 4 per cent was to be provided on loans availed by state governments/power utilities from financial institutions for carrying out rural electrification programme. The assistance

was limited to electrification of un-electrified villages, electrification of hamlets/ dalit bastis/tribal village and electrification of households in villages through both conventional and non-conventional sources of energy.

(v) Accelerated Electrification of One lakh villages and One crore households: In 2004-05 a scheme 'Accelerated electrification of One lakh villages and One crore households' was launched by merging the interest subsidy Scheme-AREP and Kutir Jyoti Programme. Under this scheme there was a provision for providing 40 per cent capital subsidy for rural electrification projects and the balance as loan assistance on soft terms from REC. The scheme has now been merged with the new scheme RGGVY.

(vi)Rajiv Gandhi Grameen Vidyutikaran Yojana (RGGVY): This scheme of rural electricity infrastructure and household electrification was introduced in April, 2005 for providing access to electricity to all rural households over a period of four years. Rural Electrification Corporation (REC) is the nodal agency for the programme. An amount of ₹ 5,000 crore was provided for remaining years of X Plan period. Under RGGVY, projects were sanctioned during X and XI Plan, covering electrification of 1,12,027 Un/de-electrified villages (UEV), intensive electrification of 3,815 partially electrified villages (PEV) and released free electricity connections to 2.76 crore BPL households in the country.

Policy on Private Sector

Ministry of Power recognises the fact that private investors have important role to play in the power sector growth map of country. The stipulation under Section 63 of Electricity Act, 2003 has provided impetus to the participation of private sector in generation and transmission provision of open access and tariff framework under tariff policy has been put in place to create an enabling environment for the private investors.

Major Policy Initiatives

To accelerate capacity addition several policy initiatives have been undertaken by the Ministry. Some of the prominent policies which have boosted the private players' confidence in the sector are : National Electricity Policy; Ultra Mega Power Project Policy; Mega Power Policy; Mega Power Policy (since withdrawn) Tariff Policy, New Hydro Policy, 2008.

Captive Power Plants

The Electricity Act, 2003 does away with the requirement of approval/clearance of any authority for setting up a captive generating plant. The new law (as amended) also ensures non-discriminatory open access for transmission of electricity generated from a captive generating plant to the destination of its use, subject to availability of transmission capacity. The surcharge and cross subsidies are being progressively reduced in a manner as may be specified by the State Regulatory Commission. Any person setting up a captive power plant can also establish and maintain dedicated transmission lines.

Automatic approval for FDI

Automatic approval (RBI route) for 100 foreign equity is permitted in generation, transmission and distribution and trading in power sector without any upper ceiling on the quantum of investment. The Government notified revised position for FDI Cap for Power Exchanges registered under CERC Regulations, 2010 as 40 (26 FDI+23 FII) through 'Automatic Route'.

Central Electricity Authority

The Central Electricity Authority (CEA) is a statutory organization constituted under Section 3 (1) of the repealed Electricity (Supply) Act, 1948 and continued under Section 70 of the Electricity Act, 2003. It was established as a part time body in 1951 and made a full time body in the year 1975. As per Section 70 (3) of the Electricity Act, 2003, the authority shall consist of not more than 14 members, including its chairperson of whom not more than eight shall be full time members to be appointed by the Central Government. The CEA is headed by a chairperson who, as the Chief Executive of the authority, oversees largely the development of power sector in the country. A Secretary, appointed by the authority with the approval of the government under Section 72 of Electricity Act, 2003, assists the Chairperson in the discharge of CEA's statutory functions. The Secretary also assists in all matters pertaining to administration and technical matters including Human Resource Development and Techno-Economic Appraisal and concurrence of power projects, etc. Presently, there are six wings namely planning, hydro, thermal, grid operation and distribution, economic and commercial and power system each headed by a member of the authority.

O. W.: http://www.cea.nic.in

UDAY (Ujwal DISCOM Assurance Yojana)

The Union Cabinet approved a new scheme moved by the Ministry - Ujwal DISCOM Assurance Yojna or UDAY. UDAY provides for the financial turnaround and revival of Power Distribution companies (DISCOMs), and importantly also ensures a sustainable permanent solution to the problem.

UDAY is a path breaking reform for affordable and accessible 24x7 Power for All. It is another decisive step furthering the landmark strides made in the power sector over the past one and a half years, with the sector witnessing a series of historic improvements across the entire value chain, from fuel supply (highest coal production growth in over two decades), to generation (highest ever capacity addition), transmission (highest ever increase in transmission lines) and consumption (over 2.3 crore LED bulbs distributed).

UDAY assures the rise of vibrant and efficient DISCOMs through a permanent resolution of past as well as potential future issues of the sector. It empowers DISCOMs with the opportunity to break even in the next 2-3 years. This is through four initiatives (i) improving operational efficiencies of DISCOMs; (ii) reduction of cost of cower; (iii) reduction in interest cost of DISCOMs; (iv) enforcing financial discipline on DISCOMs through alignment with state finances.

Operational efficiency improvements like compulsory smart metering, upgradation of transformers, meters etc., energy efficiency measures like efficient LED bulbs, agricultural pumps, fans and air-conditioners etc., will reduce the average AT&C loss from around 22 per cent to 15 per cent and eliminate the gap between Average Revenue Realised (ARR) & Average Cost of Supply (ACS) by 201 8-19. Reduction in cost of power would be achieved through measures such as increased supply of cheaper domestic coal, coal linkage rationalisation, liberal coal swaps from inefficient to efficient plants, coal price rationalisation based on GCV (Gross Calorific ValueX supply of washed and crushed coal, and faster completion of transmission lines. NTPC alone is expected to save ₹ 0.35/unit through higher supply of domestic coal and rationalisation / swapping of coal which will be passed on to DISCOMs / consumers.

State shall take over the future losses of DISCOMs in a graded manner and shall fund them as follows:

Year	2015-16	2016-17	2017-18	2018-19	2019-20	2020-21
Previous Year's DISCOM loss to be taken over by State	0% of the loss of 2014-15	0% of the loss of 2015-16	5% of the loss of 2016-17	10% of the loss of 2017-18	25% of the loss of 2018-19	50% of the previous year loss

State DISCOMs will comply with the Renewable Purchase Obligation (RPO) outstanding since April, 2012, within a period to be decided in consultation witn the Ministry.

States accepting UDAY and performing as per operational milestones will be given additional / priority funding through Deendayal Upadhyaya Gram Jyoti Yojana (DDUGJY),Integrated Power Development Scheme (IPDS), Power Sector Development Fund (PSDF) or other such schemes.

National Domestic Efficient Lighting Programme

Domestic Efficient Lighting Programme (DELP) was launched in January 2015 urging the people to use LED bulbs in place of incandescent bulbs, tube lights and CFL bulbs as they are more efficient, long lasting and economical in their life cycle duration.

Public Sector Undertakings

National Thermal Power Limited

National Thermal Power Corporation Limited, a Maha Ratna Company of the Government of India, is the largest power generator in India with comprehensive in-house capabilities in building and operating power projects. NTPC has authorised share capital of ₹ 10,000 crore and paid up capital is ₹ 8,245.5 crore 75 per cent of this is held by the Government of India. NTPC has a vision 'to be the world's largest and best power producer, powering India's growth and a mission to develop and provide reliable power and related products and services at competitive prices, integrating multiple energy sources with innovative and eco-friendly technologies and contribute to society'. Over the years, NTPC has attained a global stature. In the top 250 Global Energy Companies for 2014, the company has been ranked No.1 Independent Power Producer in the world. NTPC is ranked 424th largest company in the world among 'Global 2000' list of companies compiled by Forbes for 2014.

O. W.: http://www.ntpc.co.in

National Hydro-electric Power Corporation Limited

National Hydro-electric Power Corporation Limited (earlier known as National Hydroelectric Power Corporation Ltd.) is a Schedule 'A' Mini-Ratna Enterprise of the Government of India with an authorized share capital of ₹ 15,000 crore and an investment base of more than ₹ 40,471 crore. NHPC was set up in 1975 and has now become the largest organisation for hydro power development in the country, with capabilities to undertake all the activities from conceptualization to commissioning of hydro projects. The main objects of NHPC include, to plan, promote and organise an integrated and efficient development of power in all its aspects through conventional and non-conventional sources in India and abroad and also the transmission, distribution, trading and sale of power generated at stations. It is also listed with the Bombay Stock Exchange and National Stock Exchange.

O. W.: http://www.nhpcindia.com

Power Grid Corporation

Power Grid Corporation of India Limited (POWERGRID) was incorporated in 1989 as a public limited company. It is a notified Central Transmission Utility since 1998. The corporation, apart from providing transmission systems assigned to it for evacuation of power from central sector projects, system strengthening scheme, etc., is also responsible for establishment of Regional and National Power Grids and operates through Power System Operation Corporation, a fully owned subsidiary of POWERGRID to facilitate transfer of power within and across the regions with reliability, security and economy on commercial principles.

O. W.: http://www.powergridindia.com

Power Finance Corporation

Power Finance Corporation was incorporated in1986, as a part of Government of India's initiative to enhance funding to power projects, with an objective to provide financial resources and encourage flow of investments to the power and associated sectors. It was declared a Public Financial Institution (PFI), under Section-4A of Companies Act, in 1990. Power Finance Corporation Limited (PFC) is a leading Power Sector Public Financial Institution and a Non-Banking Financial Company, providing fund and non-fund based support for the development of Indian Power Sector. The PFC is a Schedule-A Navratna CPSE in the Financial Services Sector, under the administrative control of the Ministry of Power, with 73.72 per cent shareholding by the Government of India. Its

Registered and Corporate Offices are at New Delhi. The corporation has been conferred with the status of 'Navratna' in 2007.

O. W.: http://www.pfcindia.com

Rural Electrification Corporation

Rural Electrification Corporation Limited (REC) was incorporated as a company under the Companies Act, 1956 in the year 1969 with the main objective of financing rural electrification schemes in the country. Subsequently, the mandate of REC was expanded to include financing of all power projects including generation, transmission and distribution without any restriction. REC is a public financial institution under Section 4A of the Companies Act, 1956. REC is also registered as a Non-Banking Financial Company (NBFC) under Section 45 1A of the RBI Act, 1934 and categorised by RBI as an Infrastructure Finance Company (IFC). REC is a 'Navratna' company and its equity shares are listed since Financial Year 2007-08 with the National Stock Exchange of India Limited (NSE) and BSE Limited (BSE).

O. W.: http://www.recindia.nic.in

Satluj Jal Vidyut Nigam Ltd

Satluj Jal Vidyut Nigam Ltd. (SJVN) was incorporated in 1988 as a joint venture of the Government of India (GoI) and the Government of Himachal Pradesh to plan, investigate, organise, execute, operate and maintain Hydro Electric Power Projects in Satluj basin in Himachal Pradesh and at any other place with equity contribution of GoI and HP as 75:25, respectively. SJVN is 'Schedule-A' Mini Ratna Category-I PSU under the administrative control of Ministry of Power.

After disinvestment by GoI 2010, the present equity contribution between the GoI, GoHP and Public is 64.46 per cent, 25.51 per cent and 10.03 per cent, respectively. Initial authorized share capital of SJVN was ₹ 4,500 crore and present authorized share capital of SJVN is ₹ 7,000 crore. The Nathpa Jhakri Hydro Power Station (1500 MW) was the first project undertaken by SJVN for execution having six units of 250 MW each. All units are under commercial operation since May 2004.

O. W.: http://www.sjvn.nic.in

Bhakra Management Board

Bhakra Management Board (BMB) was constituted under Section 79 of the Punjab Re-Organization Act, 1966 for the administration, maintenance and operation of Bhakra Nangal Project from October, 1967. The Beas Project Works, on completion, were transferred by the Government of India from Beas Construction Board (BCB) to BMB as per Section 80 of the Act and Bhakra Management Board was renamed as Bhakra Beas Management Board (BBMB) with effect from 1976. Bhakra Beas Management Board is responsible for the administration, operation and maintenance of Bhakra Nangal Project, Beas Satluj Link Project and Pong Dam including Power Houses and a network of transmission lines and grid substations.

Beas Management Board is involved in administration, operation and maintenance of Bhakra-Beas Projects. The regulation of supply of power generated at Bhakra-Beas Projects and any other function as the Central Government may assign after consultation with the governments of Haryana, Punjab and Rajasthan. From 1999, additional functions of providing and performing engineering and related technical consultancy services in the field of hydro electric project and irrigation projects were also entrusted to it.

National Power Training Institute

The National Power Training Institute (NPTI), a registered society under the Ministry, is committed to the development of human resources in the power sector for the past four decades. NPTI with its corporate centre at Faridabad operates eight institutes all over the country. It has five regional institutes located at Neyveli (Tamil Nadu), Durgapur (West Bengal), Badarpur (New Delhi), Nagpur (Maharashtra) and Guwahati (Assam) and two specialised centres viz., Power Systems Training Institute (PSTI) and Hot Line Training Centre at Bengaluru, Centre for Advanced Management and Power Studies at Faridabad (Haryana). NPTI (NER) is at present operating from a temporary site at Narangi complex, Guwahati, and the full-fledged training institute, as sanctioned by the Government of India at a cost of ₹ 18.29 crore, is in the advanced stage of completion at Kahilipara, Guwahati. The Government has also sanctioned a scheme for setting up of Hydro Power Training Centre at Nangal at an estimated cost of ₹ 14.75 crore which is under implementation.

The institutes of NPTI are well equipped with hi-tech infrastructural facilities for conducting different courses on technical as well as management subjects covering the needs of thermal, hydro and nuclear power plants, transmission and distribution systems, and energy related fields of the power and allied energy sectors. A Geographical Information System (GIS) Resource Centre for training and consultancy in the areas of GIS based electricity distribution network planning and management has been set up at NPTI.

Several long-term and short-term training programmes in the areas of thermal, hydro, transmission and distribution and management, etc., are being conducted in the various institutes of NPTL. Besides conducting refresher training for working engineers/supervisors, the institute conducts a large number of job-oriented educational programmes also such as MBA in power management, B.Tech (Power) and Post Graduate Diploma in thermal power plant engineering.

O. W.: http://www.npti.in

Central Power Research Institute

The Central Power Research Institute (CPRI), a society registered under the Societies Registration Act under the Ministry of Power, serves as national laboratory to carry out applied research in electrical power engineering. It also functions as an independent national testing and certification authority for electrical equipment for ensuring their reliability.

The institute, with its existence of over four decades has built sophisticated facilities, both in the areas of research and testing. The important facilities include, 2,500 MVA short circuit testing with synthetic testing facility at Bengaluru, ultra high voltage research laboratory at Hyderabad, short circuit testing facility at Bhopal, thermal research centre at Koradi, Nagpur and regional testing laboratory at Noida, Kolkata and Guwahati.

Over the years, the CPRI has built up expertise in the areas of transmission and distribution systems, power quality, energy metering, energy auditing, transmission line, tower design, conductor vibration studies, power systems studies, energy conservation studies, transformer oil reclamation and testing, diagnostic and condition monitoring and estimation of remaining life of equipment, new material for power system application, ultra high voltage testing, short circuit testing, high voltage testing and other related fields. The institute has set up and commissioned the state- of-the-art seismic testing facility and a Real Time Digital Simulation facility.

The CPRI's laboratories are accredited under the National Accreditation Board for Testing and Calibration of Laboratories (NABL), which is the national body for accreditation of laboratories. The research institute has been given the membership status in the group of Short Circuit Testing Liaison of Europe. CPRI laboratories are approved for certain products like communication cables, LT capacitors, etc., by Underwriters Laboratories and Canadian Standard Association. The institute has been accredited by INTERTEKASTA, UK for testing of low voltage and medium voltage equipment, power transformers and power cables.

The research and consultancy activities have been certified for ISO-9001-2000 by NVT, KEMA. The CPRI Laboratories have been recognised as Approved Test House by Electrical Directorate, Kingdom of Bahrain and Saudi Arabia. The certification is widely accepted in the countries of Middle-East, South-East, Far-East Asia and countries of Africa.

The institute works as a nodal agency for national level power system research. Among the new ventures of the CPRI, the Centre for Collaborative and Advanced Research has been established for creating infrastructure for the visiting scientists/technologists to carry out research in the areas related to power sector. A centre has been set up for utilisation of industrial solid wastes to useful value-added products for the benefit of industry.

Regional Testing Laboratories have been established by the institute at Kolkata and Guwahati to cater to testing requirements in the eastern and north-eastern states. The institute has also established the Refrigerator and Air Conditioners testing laboratory under the Standards and Labelling Programme.

The CPRI has served as Advisor-cum-Consultant under APDRP-I for three southern states viz., Karnataka, Kerala and Andhra Pradesh. Pioneering work has been done for a total of nine distribution circles and 256 towns in three states. The institute also offers Third Party Inspection Services and customised training programmes to utilities and industry.

O. W.: http://www.cpri.in

North Eastern Electric Power Corporation Ltd.

With a need to develop the huge power potential, the North Eastern Electric Power Corporation (NEEPCO) was incorporated in 1976 as a wholly owned Government Enterprise under the Ministry of Power to plan, promote, investigate, survey, design, construct, generate, operate and maintain power stations in the north-eastern region. The authorised share capital of the corporation presently stands at ₹ 3,500 crore. The installed capacity of the NEEPCO is 1,130 MW comprising 755 MW of hydro power and 375 MW of gas based power. The corporation currently meets more than 60 per cent of the energy requirement of the North Eastern Region. It is an ISO:9001:2000(Quality) ISO 14001:1996 (Environment) and OHSAS-18001:1999 (Safety) Company at Shillong.

Petroleum and Natural Gas

The Ministry of Petroleum and Natural Gas is concerned with exploration and production of oil and natural gas (including import of liquefied natural Gas), refining, distribution and marketing, import, export and conservation of petroleum products.

Urja Sangam

'Urja Sangam 2015' was held in New Delhi in March 2015. The aim of this biggest global hydrocarbon meet was to showcase India's potential in the hydrocarbon sector to the world and create an investor-friendly atmosphere, besides positioning India's thought leadership by creating a new "Energy Security" platform. On the global level, its aim was to firm up cooperation agreements with key global players.

Ensuring Energy Security

The Ministry of Petroleum and Natural Gas has rolled out an elaborate plan to reassess hydrocarbon resources in Indian's sedimentary basins. Also a project has been approved to carry out survey works of all unappraised sedimentary basins. Reforms have been made in the production sharing contracts to instill confidence among the investors. On 2nd September, 2015, the Cabinet has approved the Discovered Small Fields Policy for development of 69 hydrocarbon discoveries made by national oil companies; Oil & Natural Gas Corporation Ltd. (ONGC) and Oil India Ltd. (OIL) with the objective to augment the domestic production of oil and gas. An attempt has been made to club many reforms including providing marketing and pricing freedom, permitting exploration throughout the contract period, being governed by a single license for exploration and production of all forms of hydrocarbons and adopting a simple and easy to administer revenue sharing model, guided by the vision of Hon'ble Prime Minister on Minimum Government, Maximum Governance and ease of doing business. Recently, Government has approved Hydrocarbon Exploration Licensing Policy (HELP) for Award of Hydrocarbon Acreages with New Contractual System and Fiscal Model along-with the open acreage policy which is designed in such a way that it will usher a new era in the exploration and production of hydrocarbons in India.

Crude Oil and Natural Gas Production

The targeted crude oil production for 2015- 16 is at 37.046 million metric tonnes (MMT) as against production of 37.461 MMT in 2014-15, showing a decrease of about 1.11 per cent. The crude oil production during April-December, 2015 was at 27.952 MMT i.e. marginal decrease of 0.79 per cent over production of 28.174 MMT achieved during the corresponding period last year. Production was affected mainly due to decline in onshore production from old and ageing fields and operational problems particularly in Gujarat, Rajasthan and North East, apart from prolonged bandhs and blockades in Assam. For the year 2015-16, production of natural gas is targeted at 35.280 Billion Cubic Meters (BCM), i.e., 4.83 per cent higher than production of 33.656 BCM in 2014-15. The natural gas production during April-December, 2015 was 24.697 BCM i.e. decrease of 2.76 per cent over production of 25.397 BCM during corresponding period of last year. Shortfall in natural gas production is mainly attributed to lower production from Bassein & Satellite fields, KG-D6, M&S Tapti and Panna-Mukta, restricted production due to repair of pipelines in Gujarat and Andhra Pradesh and lower off-take by potential customers particularly in Assam, Rajasthan and Tamil Nadu.

The trends in the production of crude oil and natural gas for the years 2010-11 to 2015-16 have been depicted here:

Table 11.1: Crude oil and Natural Gas Production

Year	Crude Oil Production (MMT)	% Growth in Crude Oil Prodcution	Natural Gas Production (BCM)	% Growth in Natural Gas Production
2010-11	37.684	11.85	52.219	9.94
2011-12	38.090	1.08	47.559	-8.92
2012-13	37.862	-0.60	40.679	-14.47
2013-14	37.788	-0.19	35.407	-12.96
2014-15	37.461	-0.87	33.656	-4.95
2015-16**	37.046	-1.11	35.280	4.83
2014-15 (Apr.-Dec.)	28.174	-	25.397	-
2015-16 (Apr.-Dec.)*	27.952	-0.79	24.697	-2.76

**Provisional ** Targeted Production*

Oil and Natural Gas Corporation Limited

Oil and Natural Gas Corporation Ltd. (ONGC), engaged in exploration and production of crude oil, natural gas and value added products was incorporated on June 23, 1993 under Companies Act 1956, pursuant to government's decision to transform the statutory commission into a Public Limited Company, through an Act of Parliament [Oil and Natural Gas Commission (Transfer of Undertaking and Repeal Act, 1993)].

Refining Capacity & Refinery Crude Throughput

There has been considerable increase in refining capacity in the country over the years, although there was no capacity expansion during 2015-16, as of December, 2015. The refining capacity stood at 215.066 MMTPA by April, 2015. Refinery Crude Throughput (Crude Oil Processed) for the year 2015-16 is targeted at 224.242 MMT as against 223.242 MMT in 2014-15, showing a marginal increase of about 0.45 per cent. Crude throughput during April-December, 2015 is at 170.711 MMT, marginally higher by 2.41 per cent against 166.688 MMT during April-December, 2014.

Production and Consumption of Petroleum Products

The production of petroleum products is targeted at 220.964 MMT in year 2015-16 as against 221.136 MMT achieved in 2014-15. During April-December, 2015, production of petroleum products was at 170.345 MMT i.e. an increase of 2.98 per cent over 165.412 MMT of production achieved during the corresponding period last year. During the year 2015-16, the consumption of petroleum products in India is estimated at 176.972 MMT with a growth of 6.92 per cent as compared to consumption of 165.520 MMT during 2014-15. The consumption of petroleum product during April-December, 2015 is 134.310 MMT i.e. an increase of 9.50 per cent over 122.659 MMT in April-December, 2014.

Import of Crude Oil

Import of Crude Oil during April-December, 2015 was 149.416 MMT valued at ₹ 3,41,067 crore which marked an increase of 5.05 per cent in quantity terms and 41.37 per cent decrease in value terms over the same period of last year. The decline in value terms is related to reduced crude oil prices by around 70 per cent from June'14 to Dec'15. During 2014-15, the import of crude oil was 189.435 MMT valued at ₹ 6, 87,416 crore. Global prices of crude oil had stayed above US $100 /bbl since February 2010. However, since September 2014 these prices have taken a sharp downturn. From June 2014 when they stood at US $ 111.66 /bbl, they have plummeted and shown a steady decline to US $ 38.21 /bbl in December 2015. This sharp fall can be attributed to weakening of demand in economies of Asia, especially China, and Europe in addition to a production glut. Further, exploration of shale gas by countries like the United States and Canada to reduce their dependence on oil imports has led to lower demand of oil. This has also resulted in reduced retail prices of diesel, domestic LPG and kerosene.

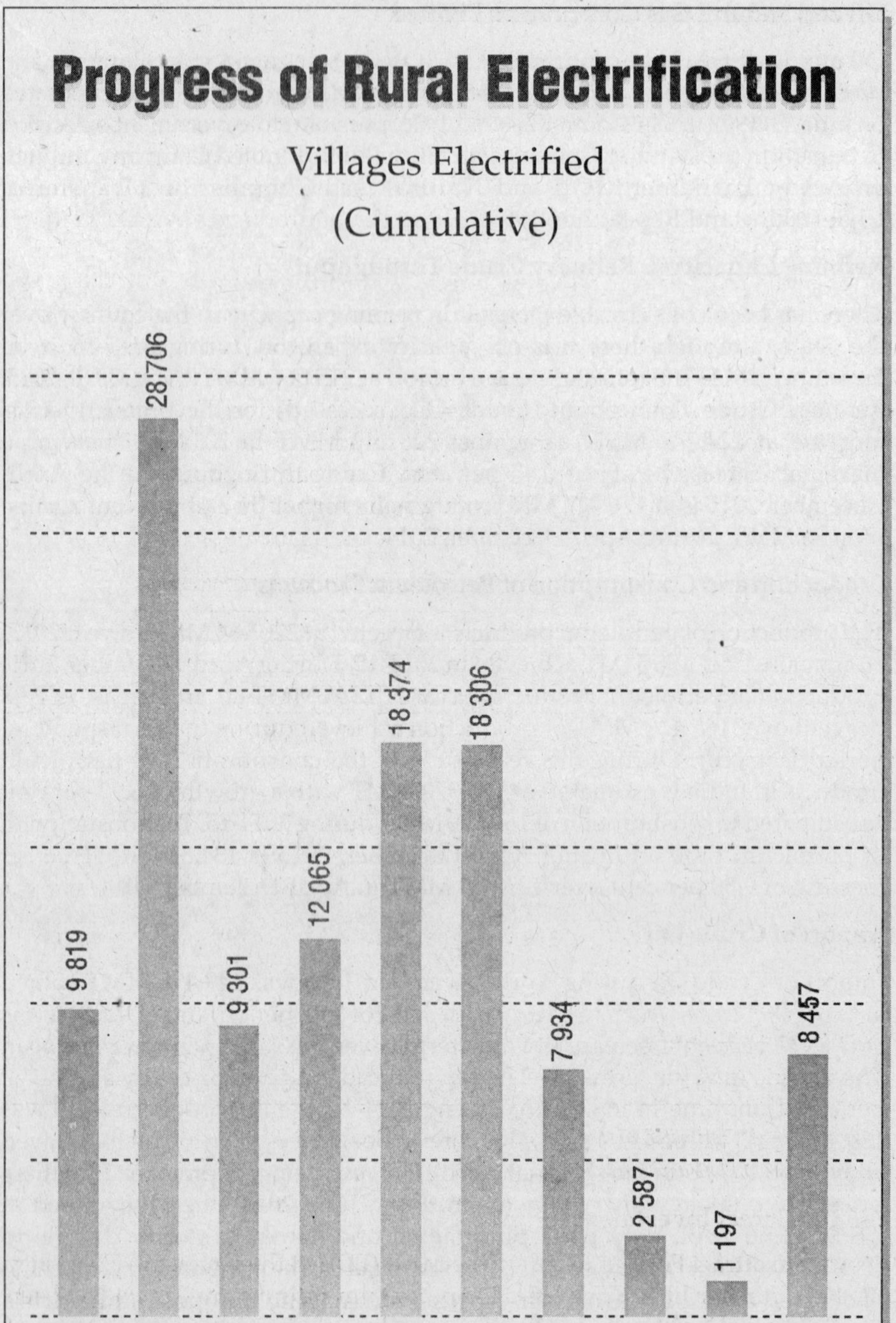
Progress of Rural Electrification
Villages Electrified
(Cumulative)
9 819
28 706
9 301
12 065
18 374
18 306
7 934
2 587
1 197
8 457
2005-06
2006-07
2007-08
2008-09
2009-10
2010-11
2011-12
2012-13
2013-14
2014-15*
* Upto 31.11.2014

Imports and Exports of Petroleum Products

During April-December, 2015-16 imports of petroleum products were 21.175 MMT valued at ₹ 52,224 crore, which shows an increase of 36.01 per cent in quantity terms and 12.52 per cent decrease in value terms, against the corresponding period of previous year. The quantity of petroleum products imported during 2014-15 was 21.301 MMT valued at ₹ 74,644 crore. During April-December, 2015-16 the exports of petroleum products were 43.779 MMT valued at ₹ 1,38,839 crore, which shows a decrease of 10.84 per cent in quantity terms and 42.52 per cent in value terms, against the exports of 49.100 MMT valued at ₹ 2,41,543 crore for the same period of last year. During 2014-15, 63.932 MMT of petroleum products, valued at ₹ 2,88,580 crore were exported. During April-December, 2015-16 the import of LNG was 14.959 MMT valued at ₹ 44,389 crore which marked an increase of 22.87 per cent in quantity terms and 14.07 per cent in value terms, against imports of 12.175 MMT valued at ₹ 51,658 crore for the same period of previous year. During 2014-15, 14.092 MMT of LNG, valued at ₹ 57,384 crore was imported. The trends in quantity of petroleum products and LNG imports & exports are depicted here:

Table 11.2: Imports and Exports of Petroleum Products

Year	Imports of Petroleum Products (MMT)	% Growth in Imports of Petroleum Products	Exports of Petroleum Products (MMT)	% Growth in Export of Petroleum Products	Imports of LNG (MMT)	% Growth in Imports of LNG
2010-11	17.379	18.515	59.077	15.49	9.931	8.56
2011-12	15.849	-8.80	60.837	2.98	13.214	33.06
2012-13	15.774	-0.48	63.408	4.23	13.136	-0.60
2013-14	16.718	5.99	67.864	7.03	13.032	-0.79
2014-15	21.301	27.41	63.932	-5.79	14.092	8.13
2015-16**	28.233	32.54	58.372	-8.70	19.946	41.54
2014-15 (Apr-Dec)	15.569	-	49.100	-	12.175	-
2015-16 (Apr-Dec)	21.175	36.01	43.779	-10.84	14.959	22.87

**Provisional* ** *Estimated on the average of Apr., to Dec., 2015*

Note: *Imports of LNG data available upto Dec' 15*

Foreign Direct Investment Inflows

In order to attract Foreign Direct Investment (FDI) in the sector, the FDI policy has been further liberalised. FDI for petroleum refining by CPSEs has been allowed with 49 per cent foreign equity under the automatic route instead of approval through Foreign Investment Promotion Board. It may be observed that inflow of FDI in petroleum and natural gas has varied considerably over the years that could at least be partly due to the bulkiness of investment in the sector. The highest FDI inflow was received in 2011-12 at ₹ 9,955.17 crore contributing 6.03 per cent of total FDI inflow in the economy. During the year 2014-15, FDI inflow received was ₹ 6495.67 crore contributing almost 3.44 per cent of total FDI inflow in the economy.

O. W.: http://www.ongc-india.com

ONGC Videsh Limited

ONGC Videsh Limited (OVL), is engaged in exploration and production of oil and gas outside India. OVL was incorporated as Hydrocarbons India Limited in 1965 to perform international exploration and production business. The company was rechristened as ONGC Videsh Limited from 1989. It has participated either directly or through its wholly owned subsidiaries/joint venture companies in 30 projects in 15 countries of which nine projects are operated by OVL, 7 projects are jointly operated and 14 projects managed through participating interest. Currently, OVL has oil and gas production from 10 projects in eight countries, namely, Russia (Sakhalin-1 and Imperial Energy), Syria (Al-Furat Petroleum Co.), Vietnam (Block 06.1), Colombia (MECL), Sudan (Greater Nile Petroleum Operating Company), South Sudan (Greater Pioneer Operating Company and Sudd Petroleum Operating (Company), Venezuela (San Cristobal) and Brazil (BC-10). There are five projects where hydrocarbons have been discovered and are at various stages of development and 15 projects are under various stages of exploration.

OVL has drawn an ambitious 'Perspective Plan, 2030' eyeing more than six fold increase in production from about 9 MMTOE during current fiscal to 60 MMTOE per annum by 2030.

Oil India Limited

Oil India Limited (OIL), a Government of India enterprise, is engaged in the business of exploration, production and transportation of crude oil and natural gas. In 1959, Oil India Private Limited was incorporated to expand and develop the newly discovered oil fields of Naharkatiya and Moran in Assam. In 1961, it became a joint venture company between the Indian Government and Burmah Oil Company Limited, UK in 1981, OIL India Pvt. Ltd. became a wholly-owned Government of India enterprise. Authorised share capital of the Company is ₹ 500 crore. The issued, subscribed and paid-up share capital of the company is ₹ 240.45 crore, in which Government holding is 78.43 per cent. OIL has been accorded 'Navaratna' status from first quarter of 2010-11.

In-country operational areas are spread over Assam, Arunachal Pradesh, Mizoram, Bihar, Andhra Pradesh, Puducherry, Andaman and Rajasthan. OIL has presence in nine countries, viz., Venezuela, Libya, Gabon, Iran, Nigeria, Yemen, Sudan, Timor Leste and Egypt, pursuing various activities.

In addition, OIL owns and operates a trunk crude oil pipeline in the north east region of the country for transportation of crude oil to feed Numaligarh, Guwahati and Bongaigaon refineries. OIL also owns and operates a branch line to feed Digboi refinery.

O. W.: http://www.oil-india.com

Gas Authority of India Limited

The setting up of Gas Authority of India Limited (GAIL), formerly known as Gas Authority of India Limited in August 1984 heralded a new era of natural gas in the country. GAIL is now completing 28 glorious years of service to the nation. Starting as a natural gas transmission company, it is today an integrated energy company in the Natural Gas value chain with global footprints. Having started as a gas transmission company during the late 1980s, it grew organically over the years by building a large network of natural gas trunk pipelines covering a length of over 8,700 km.

Further, to strengthen position as India's premier integrated gas company, GAIL has set up LNG import infrastructure and will be focusing on areas like city gas distribution, petrochemicals business, diversifying into high margin downstrem areas in gas value chain and creating a portfolio of renewable business. The expansion of existing petrochemical plant at Pata is ahead of schedule and physical progress of 48 per cent has been achieved.

The company is also expanding its global presence to acquire new expertise and resources through overseas tie-ups in emerging areas such as shale gas. This will allow it to establish a foothold in resource rich countries while complementing the company's core business.

O. W.: http: / /www.gailonline.com

Pricing of Petroleum Products

The Administered Pricing Mechanisam (APM) or cost plus pricing for petroleum products which was introduced in 1976 was abolished from 2002, consequent to the de-regulation of the oil sector in India. The Government notified that pricing of all petroleum products except PDS kerosene and domestic LPG, would be market determined. In June 2006, based on the recommendations of the Rangarajan Committee, the Government changed the pricing mechanism for petrol and diesel from import parity to trade parity (trade parity being the weighted average of import parity and export parity prices in the ratio of 80:20) while the pricing of PDS kerosene and domestic LPG continues on import parity basis. The Government also took a decision 'in principle' on June 25, 2010 to make the price of diesel market determined, both at refinery gate and at retail level. However, in order to insulate the common man from the impact of rise in international oil prices and domestic inflationary conditions, the Government continues to modulate the RSP of diesel. Thus, the RSP of diesel is below the required market price, resulting in incurrence of under-recovery to the OMCs.

The Government is committed to make available the essential fuels, particularly the cooking fuels to the common man at affordable prices. Accordingly, it has been decided to continue subsidizing PDS kerosene and domestic LPG.

Indian Oil Corporation Limited

Indian Oil Corporation (Indian Oil) is India's flagship national oil company with business interests encompassing the entire hydrocarbon value chain—from refining, pipeline transportation and marketing of petroleum products to exploration and production of crude oil and gas, marketing of natural gas, petrochemicals, renewable energy and now into nuclear energy.

The Indian Oil Group of companies own and operate 10 of India's 22 refineries with a combined refining capacity of 213.2 million metric tonnes per annum. Indian Oil's cross-country network of crude oil and product pipeline spans 10,909 km with a capacity of 75.55 MMTPA of crude oil and petroleum products and 96 MMSCMD of gas. This network is the largest in the country and meets the vital energy needs of the consumers in an efficient, economical and environment-friendly manner.

Indian Oil supplies precious petroleum products through an unmatched countrywide network of above 38,000 touch points, which correspond to about 52 per cent of the industry infrastructure. It operates more than 20,000 outlets, the largest and most extensive network of retail outlets. The corporation's Indane cooking gas reaches the doorsteps of about 65 million households through about 5,934 distributors. These efforts are backed by supplies from 139 terminals and depots, 96 aviation fuel stations and 89 Indane bottling plants. About 6,218 bulk consumer pumps are also operational for the convenience of large consumers, ensuring product and inventory at their doorstep.

Over the years, Indian Oil has grown by expanding its own operations, bringing independent refineries like Chennai Petroleum Corporation Ltd (CPCL) and Bongaigaon Refinery and Petrochemicals Ltd. (BRPL) under its fold, by merging Assam Oil Company (AOC) and IBP Co. Ltd with itself, thus synergizing its refining as well as marketing operations. Having set up subsidiaries in Sri Lanka, Mauritius and the United Arab Emirates, Indian Oil is simultaneously scouting for new business opportunities in the energy markets of Asia and Africa.

O. W.: http://www.iocl.com

Hindustan Petroleum Corporation Limited

Hindustan Petroleum Corporation Limited (HPCL) is a mega Public Sector Undertaking (PSU) with 'Navratna' status. It has two refineries; one in Mumbai (west coast) having a capacity of 6.5 MMTPA and the other in Visakhapatnam (east coast) with a capacity of 8.3 MMTPA. These refineries are producing a wide variety of petroleum products-fuels, lubricants and specialty products. HPCL holds an equity stake of 16.95 per cent in Mangalore Refinery and Petrochemicals Limited, a state-of-art refinery at Mangalore with a capacity of 9.69 MMTPA. HPCL, in collaboration with M/s Mittal Energy Investment Pvt. Ltd, has set up a state-of-the-art Green Field Refinery with a capacity of 9 million tonnes at Bathinda in Punjab. The project has been completed and commissioned in 2012.

HPCL owns and operates the largest Lube Refinery in the country producing Lube Base Oils, with a capacity of 3,35,000 metric tonnes. This Lube Refinery accounts for over 40 per cent of the country's total Lube Base Oil production. Besides, the Corporation owns seven Lube Blending Plants (three in Mumbai and one each at Budge Budge, Ramnagar, Chennai and Silvassa) and a Lube oil pipeline for evacuation of base oil from Mumbai Refinery. Presently, HPCL is producing over 300 plus grades of lubes, specialties and greases.

The marketing networking of HPCL consist of 13 zonal offices in major cities and 101 regional offices facilitated by a supply and distribution infrastructure comprising terminals, civiation service facilities, LPG bottling plants, lube filling plants, inland relay depots, etc. HPCL has state-of-art information technology infrastructure to support its core business. The Data Centre is located at Hitech city in Hyderabad.

HPCL has undertaken a path of high growth in keeping with the national priorities. The ambitious plans furthering the synergies and participating in the oil industry's growth by vertically integrating in the upstream and downstream sectors. The policy initiatives undertaken also include growth and diversification ventures in different sectors.

O. W.: http://www.hindustanpetroleum.com

Bharat Petroleum Corporation Limited

Bharat Petroleum Corporation Limited (BPCL) is an integrated oil company, in the downstream sector, engaged in refining of crude oil and marketing of petroleum products. It has also diversified into production and marketing of petrochemical feedstock. BPCL has refineries at Mumbai and Kochi with a combined refining capacity of 21.5 MMTPA. Both the refineries are certified under Integrated Management System (IMS) which aims for a unified approach in processes, interfaces, structures and documentation systems by combining the individual management systems under ISO 9001, ISO 14001 and OHSAS 18001 reflecting the continuing commitment towards quality, environment, health and safety.

BPCL has a robust distribution network comprising major storage installations and depots; LPG bottling plants, 1938 km cross-country pipeline (including 292 km pipeline set up by Joint Venture Company Petronet CCK Ltd) and two lubricant blending plants.

Coal

The Ministry of Coal (MOC) has the overall responsibility of determining policies and strategies in respect of exploration and development of coal and lignite reserves, sanctioning of important projects of high value and for deciding all related issues. These key functions are exercised through its public sector undertakings, namely Coal India Limited (CIL) and Neyveli Lignite

Corporation Limited (NLC) and Singareni Collieries Company Limited (SCCL), a joint sector undertaking of State Government of Telangana and Government of India with equity capital in the ratio of 51:49.

Coal Reserves

Coal reserves have been estimated at 306.595 billion tonnes by the Geological Survey of India. The reserves have been found mainly in the states of Jharkhand, Odisha, Chhattisgarh, West Bengal, Madhya Pradesh, Telangana and Maharashtra.

Lignite Reserves

The Lignite reserves in the country have been estimated at around 44.11 billion tonnes by the Geological Survey of India. The major deposits are located in Tamil Nadu, followed by Rajasthan, Gujarat, Kerala, West Bengal, Jammu & Kashmir and Union Territory of Puducherry. Coal Production: The overall production of coal for 2015-16 was projected at 700 MT. During the period April to December 2015 the actual production was 447.48 Million tonnes compared to 427.278 Million tonnes (MT) during corresponding period of 2014-15 and showing a growth of 9.1 per cent. The Company-wise details for coal production from CIL, SCCL and Others are given below:

Table 11.3

		Production (2015-16) in Mtr.				
Name of Company	2014-15 Actual	Target (BE)	Target (RE)	(Actual) (Apr-Dec. 14)	Achievement (%)	Growth (%) (Apr-Dec. 15)
CIL	494.23	550.00	536.70	373.48	69.6	9.08
SCCL	52.54	56.00	56.00	43.24	77.2	22.70
Captive	52.77	75.50	75.50	21.55	28.2	-46.86
Others	12.90	18.50	18.50	9.21	49.2	1.21
Total	612.44	700.00	686.70	447.48	65.2	4.73

Per cent achievement w.e.f. RE of 2015-16

Coal India Limited

Coal India Limited (CIL) is a 'Maha Ratna' company under the Ministry of Coal, Government of India with headquarters at Kolkata, West Bengal. CIL is the single largest coal producing company in the world and one of the largest corporate employers with a manpower of 3,46,638. CIL operates through 82 mining areas spread over eight provincial states of India. Coal India Limited has 429 mines of which 237 are underground, 166 opencast and 26 mixed mines. CILwith its headquarters at Kolkata is the apex body in coal industry under the administrative control of the Ministry of Coal. Coal India is a holding company with seven wholly owned coal producing subsidiary companies and one mine planning and consultancy company. It encompasses the whole gamut of identification of coal reserves, detailed exploration followed by design and implementation and optimising operations for coal extraction in its mines. The producing companies are: Eastern Coalfields Limited (ECL), Sanctoria, West Bengal; Bharat Coking Coal Limited (BCCL), Dhanbad, Jharkhand; Central Coalfields Limited (CCL), Ranchi, Jharkhand; South Eastern Coalfields Limited (SECL), Bilaspur, Chattisgarh; Western Coalfields Limited (WCL), Nagpur, Maharashtra; Northern Coalfields Limited (NCL), Singrauli, Madhya Pradesh; Mahanadi Coalfields Limtied (MCL), Sambalpur, Odisha. The consultancy company is Central Mine Planning and Design Institute Limited (CMPDIL), Ranchi, Jharkhand.

O. W.: http://www.coalindia.in

Neyveli Lignite Corporation Limited

Neyveli Lignite Corporation Limited (NLC) was registered as a company in November 1956. The mining operations in Mine-I were formally inaugurated in 1957. Neyveli Lignite Corporation has been conferred with 'Navratna' status since April 2011. Its registered office at Chennai and corporate office at Neyveli in Tamil Nadu is a pioneer among the public sector undertakings in the energy sector. NLC operates three Open cast Lignite Mines of total capacity of 28.5 million tonnes per annum at Neyveli and one open cast lignite mine of capacity 2.1 million tonnes per annum at Barsingsar, Rajasthan, three thermal power stations with a total installed capacity of 2,490 mega watt at Neyveli and one thermal power station at Barsingsar, Rajasthan with an installed capacity of 250 mega watt. All the mines of NLC are ISO Certified for Quality Management System, Environmental Management System and Occupational Health and Safety Management System. All the power stations of NLC are also ISO Certified for Quality Management System and Environmental Management System. NLC's growth is sustained and its contribution to India's social and economic development is significant.

O. W'.: http://www.nlcindia.com

New and Renewable Energy

Ministry of New and Renewable Energy (MNRE) is the nodal Ministry at the federal level for all matters relating to new and renewable energy. The ministry has been facilitating the implementation of broad spectrum programmes including harnessing renewable power, renewable energy to rural areas for lighting, cooking and motive power, use of renewable energy in urban, industrial and commercial applications and development of alternate fuels and applications.

Indian Renewable Energy Scenario

Over the years, renewable energy sector in India has emerged as a significant player in the grid connected power generation capacity. It supports the government agenda of sustainable growth, while, emerging as an integral part of the solution to meet the nation's energy needs and an essential player for energy access. It has been realized that renewable energy has to play a much deeper role in achieving energy security in the years ahead and be an integral part of the energy planning process.

There has been a visible impact of renewable energy in the Indian energy scenario during the last five years. Renewable energy sector landscape in India has, during the last few years, witnessed tremendous changes in the policy framework with accelerated and ambitious plans to increase the contribution of solar energy. There is a perception that renewable energy can now play a significant role, as also, there is a confidence in the technologies and capacity to do so. Enlarging the scope of the Jawaharlal Nehru National Solar Mission symbolises both, and indeed encapsulates the vision and ambition for the future. This transformational change is, perhaps, the highlight of the last five years of activities under the Mission. In addition, the launching of Renewable Energy Certificate (REC) mechanism helps in the creation of a Pan-India renewable energy market. The other significant achievements are introduction of solar specific purchase obligations; launching of improved cook-stoves initiatives; initiating coordinated research and development activities in solar PV and thermal; second generation biofuels, hydrogen energy and fuel cells, etc.

Core Drivers for Development

a. Energy security: At present around 69.5 per cent of India's power generation capacity is based on coal. In addition, there is an increasing dependence on imported oil, which is leading to imports of around 33 per cent of India's total energy needs.

b. Electricity shortages: Despite increase in installed capacity by more than 113 times in 65 years, India is still not in a position to meet its peak electricity demand as well as energy requirement. The peak power deficit during financial year 2001-02 was 12.2 per cent, approximately 9252 MW, however, at the end of Financial Year 2014-15, the peak power deficit decreased to the order of 2.4 per cent. As a fallout of this situation, planned and un-planned measures were undertaken by the government and utilities to bridge this demand-supply gap.

c. Energy Access: India faces a challenge to ensure availability of reliable and modern forms of energy for all its citizens. Almost 85 per cent of rural households depend on solid fuel for their cooking needs and only 55 per cent of all rural households have access to electricity. However, even with this low access, most rural households face issues with quality and consistency of energy supply. Lack of rural lighting is leading to large-scale use of kerosene. This usage needs to be reduced, as it leads to increased subsidies and import dependence, and consequent pressure on foreign exchange reserves.

d. Climate change: India has taken a voluntary commitment of reducing emission intensity of its GDP by 33-35 per cent from 2005 levels by 2030. In the recently concluded 21st Conference of the Parties to the United Nations Framework Convention on Climate Change (UNFCCC) held at Paris, France, India committed to achieve about 40 per cent cumulative electric power installed capacity from non-fossil fuel based energy resources by 2030 with the help of transfer of technology and low cost international finance including from Green Climate Fund (GCF).

Renewable Energy Potential

India has an estimated renewable energy potential of about 900 GW from commercially exploitable sources viz. wind – 102 GW (at 80 metre mast height); small hydro – 20 GW; bio-energy – 25 GW; and 750 GW solar power, assuming three per cent wasteland is made available. The Ministry had taken up a new initiative for implementation of wind resource assessment in uncovered / new areas with an aim to assess the realistic potential at 100 m level in 500 new stations across the country under the National Clean Energy Fund (NCEF). The revised wind energy potential in the country extrapolated at 80 metre height has been found to be 102,788 MW. National Institute of Wind Energy has used advanced modelling techniques and revised the estimate the wind power potential at 100 metre at 302 GW. Estimates of offshore wind energy potential indicate potential in Tamil Nadu and Gujarat. Wind energy generators of unit sizes between 250kW and 2.50 MW have been deployed across the country. In addition, there exists significant potential from decentralised distributed applications for meeting hot water requirement for residential, commercial and industrial sector through solar energy and also for meeting cooking energy needs in the rural areas through biogas. Table 11.4 provides details on State wise renewable energy potential in the country.

Table 11.4 : State wise renewable energy potential (in MW)

Sl. No.	States/UTs	Wind Power	Small Hydro Power	Bio-Energy			Solar	Total
				Biomass Power	Bagasse Cogeneration	Waste to Energy		
1	Andhra Pradesh	14497	978	578	300	123	38440	54916
2	Arunachal Pradesh	236	1341	8			8650	10236
3	Assam	112	239	212		8	13760	14330
4	Bihar	144	223	619	300	73	11200	12559
5	Chhattisgarh	314	1107	236		24	18270	19951
6	Goa		7	26			880	912
7	Gujarat	35071	202	1221	350	112	35770	72726
8	Haryana	93	110	1333	350	24	4560	6470
9	Himachal Pradesh	64	2398	142		2	33840	36446
10	Jammu & Kashmir	5685	1431	43			111050	118208
11	Jharkhand	91	209	90		10	18180	18580
12	Karnataka	13593	4141	1131	450		24700	44015

13 Kerala	837	704	1044		36	6110	8732
14 Madhya Pradesh	2931	820	1364		78	61660	66853
15 Maharashtra	5961	794	1887	1250	287	64320	74500
16 Manipur	56	109	13		2	10630	10811
17 Meghalaya	82	230	11		2	5860	6185
18 Mizoram		169	1		2	9090	9261
19 Nagaland	16	197	10			7290	7513
20 Odisha	1384	295	246		22	25780	27728
21 Punjab		441	3172	300	45	2810	6768
22 Rajasthan	5050	57	1039		62	142310	148518
23 Sikkim	98	267	2			4940	5307
24 Tamil Nadu	14152	660	1070	450	151	17670	34152
25 Telangana						20410	20410
26 Tripura		47	3		2	2080	2131
27 Uttar Pradesh	1260	461	1617	1250	176	22830	27593
28 Uttarakhand	534	1708	24		5	16800	19071
29 West Bengal	22	396	396		148	6260	7222
30 Andaman & Nicobar	365	8				0	373
31 Chandigarh					6	0	6
32 Dadra & Nagar Haveli						0	0
33 Daman & Diu	4					0	4
34 Delhi					131	2050	2181
35 Lakshadweep						0	0
36 Puducherry	120				3	0	123
37 Others					1022	790	1812
Total	**102772**	**19749**	**17536**	**5000**	**2554**	**748990**	**896602**

Recent Schemes and Programmes

In continuation of the new initiatives launched in the previous year, the Government has taken up the following new projects/schemes during 2015:

(i) scheme for setting up over 2,000 MW of grid-connected solar PV power projects with Viability Gap Funding (VGF) under Batch-III of Phase II of the NSM. Projects are to be set up by solar power developers on Build-Own-Operate basis, selected through a process of open and transparent competitive reverse bidding on the VGF amount, with a provision of reduction in tariff. These projects would be selected through a process of e-bidding followed by e- reverse auctioning; (ii) conversion of Solar Energy Corporation of India (SECI) from

Section 8 to Section 3 Company under the Companies Act, 2013 (No. 18 Of 2013) and to re-name it as Renewable Energy Corporation Of India (RECI); (iii) creation of intra state transmission system in Andhra Pradesh, Gujarat, Himachal Pradesh, Karnataka, Madhya Pradesh, Maharashtra and Rajasthan at an estimated cost of ₹ 8,548.68 crore with Government of India contribution from National Clean Energy Fund (NCEF) of ₹ 3,419.47 crore. A similar project at a total cost of ₹1,593 crore with contribution from NCEF at ₹ 637 crore was approved earlier by the Government for Tamil Nadu in the previous year; (iv) scaling up of budget from ₹ 600 crore during 12th Five Year Plan to ₹ 5,000 crore for grid connected rooftop and small solar power plants programme over a period of five years upto 2019-20 under National Solar Mission (NSM); and (v) scheme for setting up of over 5,000 MW grid-connected solar PV power projects with viability gap funding under batch-IV of phase-II of the NSM.

National Solar Mission

Twenty six SPV projects of aggregate 330 MW capacity have been commissioned. A 5 MW SPV project by Delhi Mumbai Industrial Corridor Development Corporation Limited (DMICDC) has also been set up under the MNRE bundling scheme. Thus, 523 MW solar PV projects and 202.5 MW solar thermal power projects have been commissioned under the bundling scheme. Under the 100 SPV power plants, 78 projects were selected to set up 98 MW capacity projects from 12 states. Against this, 71 projects of total capacity 90.80 MW have been connected to grid.

Renewable Energy for Rural Applications

More than 37,000 biogas plants of the approved models were installed across the country with financial support of the Ministry, taking the cumulative installation to over 48.34 lakh biogas plants in all the states and union territories of the country. The target of 1.11 lakh during the year is likely to be achieved in full.

Under the National Biomass Cookstoves Initiative, several pilot projects had been taken up during the year for deployment of improved biomass cookstoves for demonstration among domestic and large sized community cooking in Anganwadis, mid-day meal schemes in schools, tribal hostels etc. Projects taken up under Unnat Chulha Abhiyan are now eligible for carbon credits under the CDM mechanism with Sardar Swaran Singh National Institute of Renewable Energy (SSS-NIRE), an autonomous institute of MNRE, located at Jalandhar, Punjab has been designated as coordinating and managing entity (CME). At present 40 models of improved cookstoves have been approved by the Ministry, as per the test reports issued.

Rice husk gasifier based 12 village level projects of 32 kWe each have been installed based on sustainable business model by entrepreneurs in various villages of Bihar. In addition, 10 systems are under various stages of installation / commissioning. Off-grid power capacity from biomass gasifier in 10 rice mills and 12 other industries including bakeries for meeting captive demand of electricity and thermal applications have been added. A grid connected biomass gasifier based project of 1 MW capacity in Haryana has been installed for meeting the captive power needs of the industry.

Renewable Energy for Urban, Industrial and Commercial Applications

During 2015-16, the physical achievement under the programme was 14.1 MWeq. and cumulative achievement in the sector was 265.4 MWeq. As part of the new initiatives the Government has amended the National Tariff Policy to make Distribution Licencees to procure power produced from WTE plants, cent per cent.

A cumulative capacity of 601.87 MW has so far been commissioned mainly to Tamil Nadu, Uttar Pradesh, Haryana, Karnataka, Andhra Pradesh, Uttarakhand, Punjab and Rajasthan. CEA have notified norms for determination of generic tariff for MSW, RDF and Biogas based WTE projects along with generic tariff for FY 2015-16. As a part of new initiative of supporting Bio-CNG production, two MNRE supported projects for cumulative production of 9,538kg/day of Bio-CNG, got commissioned in Ahmedabad, Gujarat and Delawas, Jaipur.

Under Development of solar cities programme the Ministry assists municipal Corporations and urban local bodies in preparation of a Master Plan for increasing energy efficiency and renewable energy supply in the city. Sanction has been accorded for developing three cities as solar city. Under the programme 56 cities have been sanctioned of which master plan of 49 cities has been finalised. Four cities, namely Nagpur, Chandigarh, Mysore and Gandhinagar, are being developed as model solar cities. In addition, 33 solar cities were included under the Smart City programme of Ministry of Urban Development. The proposal of 32 campuses/townships were sanctioned to develop as Green Campuses.

The energy efficient solar/green buildings programme for promoting GRIHA rating system continued under implementation. So far, cumulative sanctions to 97 government building projects have been registered for GRIHA certification-cum-rating. 210 capacity building programmes were conducted for evaluators and trainers on GRIHA Ratings by various technical institutions. 970 GRIHA evaluators and trainers were developed under the programme.

12 Environment

THE Ministry of Environment, Forest and Climate Change (MoEF&CC) started functioning in 1985. The Ministry plans, promotes, coordinates and oversees environmental, ecological, forestry and wildlife programmes. Its main activities include protection of the environment; conservation of existing forests, wildlife, aquatic bodies and water resources, biodiversity and other resources particularly in eco-sensitive areas, adaptation to and mitigation from climate change, and survey of various areas for identification of new species of flora and fauna; afforestation and regeneration of degraded areas; prevention and control of pollution (air, water, noise and industrial pollution), management of hazardous substances and better environmental governance; ensuring welfare of animals; capacity building, training and research in classical and molecular taxonomy; and international cooperation in forestry and environment. The tasks are being fulfilled through Environmental Impact Assessment (EIA), eco-regeneration, assistance to organizations implementing environmental and forestry research, extension, education and training to augment the requisite manpower, collection and dissemination of environmental information and creation of awareness at the national level.

It is nodal agency for United Nations Environment Programme (UNEP). International Centre for Integrated Mountain Development (ICIMOD) and Multilateral Environmental Agreements (MEAs). The Ministry also coordinates with multilateral bodies such as United Nations Convention to Combat Desertification (UNCCD), United Nations Framework Convention on Climate Change (UNFCCC), Convention on Biological Diversity (CBD). It is also focal point of the Global Environment Facility (GEF) and regional bodies such as Economic and Social Council for Asia and Pacific (ESCAP) and South Asian Association for Regional Cooperation (SAARC).

Botanical Survey of India

Botanical Survey of India (BSI) is the apex research organization under MoEF&CC, for carrying out taxonomic and floristic studies on wild plant resources of the country through survey, documentation and conservation. During the successive plan periods, the functional base of BSI was further expanded to include various new areas such as inventorying of endemic, rare and threatened plant species; evolving conservation strategies; studies on fragile ecosystems and protected areas; multiplication and maintenance of EET plant species, wild ornamentals, etc., in Botanic Gardens and Orchidaria; documentation of traditional knowledge of plants and development of National Database on Herbarium (including type specimens) and live collections, plant distribution and nomenclature, botanical paintings/ illustrations, plant uses, etc.

So far BSI undertook 96 field tours under 114 projects (including 27 new projects) were undertaken for collection of plant specimens/materials under floristic, ethnobotanical and pharmacognostical studies on flowering and non-flowering plants covering three biodiversity hotspot, viz., the Himalaya (14 tours), the Indo-Burma (3 tours) and the Western Ghats-Sri Lanka (12 tours). This covers following biogeographical regions: W. Himalaya, E.Himalaya, NE India, arid-semi arid, Genetic Plains, Deccan Peninsula, Western Ghats and Coastal Region covering Kerala coast (for sea weed Survey) and Andaman Islands. This also covers 24 protected areas and 1 fragile ecosystem.

Zoological Survey of India

The Zoological Survey of India (ZSI), is a premier research institution in the country, functioning under the Ministry. ZSI, since its inception in 1916, has been undertaking survey, exploration and research leading to the advancement of our knowledge on the exceptionally rich faunal diversity of the country. Over the successive plan periods, the scientific activities and functions of ZSI have also expanded to the areas like the environmental impact assessment with regard to fauna; survey of conservation areas; status survey of endangered species; computerization of data on faunal resources; environmental information system (ENVIS) on faunal diversity; identification and advisory services; care and management of the national designated repository of 'type' and voucher specimens; supporting enforcement of Wildlife (Protection) Act, 1972; establishment of marine aquaria and acting as the custodian of the National Zoological Collections. ZSI Kolkata and its 16 regional centres.

India Integrated Coastal Zone Management Project

To conserve, project and manage the coastal and marine environment, the Ministry is implementing the India Integrated Coastal Zone Management (ICZM) Project with the World Bank assistance. For the implementation of the project the Ministry has established a Society of Integrated Coastal Management (SICOM) as nodal body under the Society Registration Act, in Delhi.

The ICZM Project is being implemented as pilot investments in the coastal states of Gujarat, Odisha and West Bengal. National activities are implemented through Society of Integrated Coastal Management (SICOM) along with monitoring of activities carried out by three selected states. The project has four implementing agencies—MoEF at the national level with lead responsibilities, and the Departments of Forests and Environment (DoEF) of the three participating states.

Forest Survey of India

Forest Survey of India (FSI), an organization under the Ministry is engaged in the assessment of the country's forest resources on a regular intervals. Established in 1981, the Forest Survey of India succeeded the 'Preinvestment Survey of Forest Resources' (PISFR), a project initiated in 1965 by Government of India with the sponsorship of FAO and UNDP. The main objective of PISFR was to ascertain the availability of raw material for establishment of wood based industries in selected areas of the country.

Major Activities

The major activities of FSI are Biennial Forest Cover Assessment using remote sensing technology, inventory of forest and trees outside forests (rural and urban areas), data processing, methodology design for carrying out various types of survey and inventory, training and extension, and projects and consultancies.

Forests Cover Mapping

FSI is involved in forest cover assessment of the country on biennial basis by interpretation of satellite data on a two-year cycle and presents the information in the form of 'India State of Forest Report'. So far 14 cycles of such assessment have been completed since 1987 till 2015. Work for the 15th cycle is under progress. In addition to forest cover, assessment of tree cover of the country is also being carried out using the trees outside forests (TOF) inventory data. There is an increase of 3,775 sq km in the forest cover and 1,306 sq km in tree cover of the country as compared to 2013 assessment.

TOF inventory

Inventory of forests and Trees Outside Forests (TOF) is the second major activity of FSI. FSI has been following a new sampling design for National Forest Inventory (NFI) since 2002. The country has been divided into 14 physiographic zones and 60 districts randomly selected from these zones on probability proportional to size for detailed inventory in two year cycle. About 7,000 sample plots are laid in forest areas distributed over the country in each cycle for field inventory. The outcome of this inventory is estimation of growing stock according to species and diameter class wise at national levels. In addition to inventory of forests, TOF resources are also inventoried concurrently to provide a national estimate of growing stock of TOF on a two year cycle. About 10,000 sample plots are laid out in TOF areas. India State of Forest Report-2015 (ISFR-2015) was published in December 2015.

Biodiversity Conservation

The Convention on Biological Diversity (CBD) is one of the key agreements adopted during the Earth Summit held in Rio de Janeiro in 1992. The objective of CBD are: conservation of biological diversity, sustainable use of its components, and fair and equitable sharing of benefits arising out of the use of genetic resources. Pursuant to the ratification of the CBD by India in 1994, several steps were initiated to meet the commitments under the Convention, and to realize the opportunities offered by the Convention. These efforts were aimed at bringing the legislative, administrative and policy regimes in tune with the three-fold objectives of the CBD. India enacted the Biological Diversity (BD) Act in 2002 to give effect to the provision of this Convention. India also prepared a National Biodiversity Action Plan (NBAP) in 2008, and an Addendum to NBAP in 2014 with 20 national targets on biodiversity.

The Nagoya Protocol on access and benefit sharing (ABS) adopted under the aegis of CBD in 2010, is aimed at fair and equitable sharing of benefits arising from the utilization of genetic resources. Following the hosting of eleventh Conference of Parties (CoP-11) to the CBD by India in 2012, during India's Presidency of CoP, India facilitated ratifications by requisite number of parties to the CBD's Nagoya Protocol on ABS for its entry into force in 2014. The Nagoya Protocol on ABS is being implemented at the national level inter alia through the Biological Diversity Act.

The BD Act is implemented through a three-tier institutional mechanism: National Biodiversity Authority (NBA), State Biodiversity Boards (SBBs) and Biodiversity Management Committees (BMCs). The NBA is an autonomous body that performs facilitative, regulatory and advisory functions for the Government on biodiversity related issues.

A project proposal was developed on 'Capacity Development of Statutory Institutions for Effective Implementation of the Access and Benefit Sharing (ABS) Mechanism in India' under Indo-German Biodiversity Programme for Euro 3 million, which was approved in the 2015 Indo-German negotiations on development cooperation. The project will be implemented at the national level with NBA and in three pilot states of Maharashtra, Tamil Nadu and Uttarakhand with the respective State Biodiversity Boards.

The Ministry joined UNDP managed global initiative on Biodiversity Finance Initiative (BIOFIN) in 2015. The initiative is hosted by NBA, and technical assistance is being provided by the Wildlife Institute of India and National Institute of Public Finance and Policy in Implementation of BIOFIN. The first National Stakeholder Consultation on BIOFIN-India was held in New Delhi in 2016.

International Day for Biological Diversity (IDB) was celebrated all over the country on 22nd May, 2015. The theme for year 2015-16 was 'Biodiversity for Sustainable Development'.

Conservation and Management of Mangroves and Coral Reefs

The Ministry accords high priority to the conservation and management of mangroves and coral reefs in the country. Cent per cent central assistance extended to all the coastal states/union territories, who so request, for implementation of their approved Management Action Plans (MAPs) which comprise 'Core' and 'Ancillary' activities. Besides, the Ministry also supports R&D activities with emphasis on targeted research on mangrove and coral biodiversity, its management and various aspects of pollution in these areas. The Government has identified 38 mangrove and 4 coral reef sites throughout the country for intensive conservation and management of mangroves and coral reefs.

Table 12.1 List of identified mangrove sites in India

State/Union Territories		Mangrove Sites
West Bengal	1.	Sunderbans
Odisha	1.	Bhaitarkanika
	2.	Mahanadi
	3.	Subernarekha
	4.	Devi
	5.	Dhamra
	6.	Mangrove Genetic Resources Centre
	7.	Chilka
Andhra Pradesh	1.	Coringa
	2.	East Godavari
	3.	Krishna
Tamil Nadu	1.	Pichavaran
	2.	Muthupet
	3.	Ramnad
	4.	Pulicat
	5.	Kazhuveli
Andaman & Nicobar	1.	North Andamans
	2.	Nicobar
Kerala	1.	Vembanad
	2.	Kannur (Northern Kerala)
Karnataka	1.	Coondapur
	2.	Dakshin Kannada/Honnavar
	3.	Karwar
	4.	Mangalore Forest Division
Goa	1.	Goa
Maharashtra	1.	Achra-Ratnagiri
	2.	Devgarj-Vijay Durg
	3.	Veldur

	4.	Kundalika-Revdanda
	5.	Mumbai-Diva
	6.	Vikroli
	7.	Shreevardhan
	8.	Vaitarna
	9.	Vasai-Manori
	10.	Malvan
Gujarat	1.	Gulf of Kutch
	2.	Gulf of Khambhat
	3.	Dumas-Ubhrat
Coral Reef Sites		
Gujarat	1.	Gulf of Kutch
Tamil Nadu	1.	Gulf of Mannar
Andaman & Nicobar	1.	Andaman and Nicobar Coral Reef

Mangroves

The mangroves cover in the country is 4,740 sq.km. Mangroves are plants that survive high salinity, tidal regimes, strong wind velocity, high temperature and muddy anaerobic soil—a combination of conditions hostile for other plants. The mangrove ecosystems constitute a symbiotic link or bridge between terrestrial and marine ecosystems. They are found in the inter-tidal zones of sheltered shores, estuaries, creeks, backwaters, lagoons, marshes and mud-flats. Mangrove vegetation has been reported in all the coastal states/UTs. India is home to some of the best mangroves in the world. West Bengal has the maximum mangrove cover in the country, followed by Gujarat and Andaman and Nicobar Islands. However, not all coastal areas are suitable for mangrove plantation as these plants require an appropriate mix of saline and freshwater, and soft substrate like mudflats to enable it to grow and perpetuate. The Ministry provides financial assistance to the state forest departments for all identified mangrove areas for conservation and management. Besides, the Ministry also supports R&D activities with emphasis on targeted research on mangrove biodiversity, its management and various aspects of pollution in the identified areas.

Coral Reefs

The Indian reef area is estimated to be 2,383.87 sq.km. Coral reefs are the skeletons of stony coral polyps cemented together. They from the most dynamic ecosystem, providing shelter and nourishment to marine flora and fauna. They are the protectors of the coastlines and the coastal populations mostly depend on the coral reef ecosystems wherever they are present. The term 'coral' has been used to describe a variety of invertebrate animals of the Phylum Cnidaria including hard and soft corals. However, 'coral' is most often used as the common name for hard corals of the Order Scleractinia. The four major coral reef areas identified for intensive conservation and management in India are: i) Gulf of Mannar; ii) Gulf of Kutch; iii) Lakshadweep; and iv) Andaman and Nicobar Islands. The emphasis is more on preventive aspects through monitoring and surveillance as the restoration work is both costly and time consuming. The Ministry provides financial assistance to the states for all the four identified coral reef areas for conservation and management of coral and associates. Besides, the Ministry also supports R&D activities with emphasis on targeted research on coral biodiversity, its management and various aspects of pollution in these areas.

Biosphere Reserves

The Indian National Man and Biosphere (MAB) Committee identifies and recommends potential sites for designation as biosphere reserves, following the UNESCO's guidelines and criteria. There are 18 designated Biosphere Reserves (BRs). Out of there 18, 9 have been included in the World Network of Biosphere Reserves of UNESCO. Its main objectives are: to conserve the diversity and integrity of plants animals within natural ecosystems; to safeguard genetic diversity of species on, which their continuing evaluation deplanes; to provide facilities for education and training; to provide areas for multi-faceted research and monitoring and to ensure sustainable use of natural resources through most appropriate technology for improvement of economic well being of the local people.

Biodiversity Conservation Scheme Relating to Biosafety

Genetic Engineering Approval Committee (GEAC)

Under the Biodiversity Conservation scheme, there are two main subcomponents namely biodiversity and biosafety. The biodiversity component includes activities relating to Convention on Biological Diversity (CBD) and support to National Biodiverstiy Authority (NBA). The biosafety component includes activities relating to Genetic Engineering Appraisal Committee/ Cartagena Protocol on Biosafety/ Nagoya Kuala Lumpur Supplementary Protocol on Liability and Redress.

The Ministry under the Environment (Protection) Act, 1986 has notified the "Rules for thee Manufacture, Use, Import, Export and Storage of Hazardous Microorganisms/Genetically Engineered Organisms or Cells, 1989' (Rules, 1989). The rules also cover application of hazardous microorganisms which may not be genetically modified. Hazardous microorganisms include those which are pathogenic to animals as well as plants.

Cartagena Biosafety Protocol

The Cartagena Biosafety Protocol (CBP) was negotiated under the aegis of the Convention on Biological Diversity (CBD) and adopted in 2000. India is a party to the Protocol. The Protocol came into force in 2003. As of date 170 countries are parties to the Protocol.

The main objective of the Protocol is to ensure safe transfer, handling and use of living modified organisms (LMOs) resulting from modern biotechnology that may have adverse effect on the conservation and sustainable use of biological diversity, taking into account risk to human health.

Nagoya COP

The Supplementary Protocol on Liability and Redress is a new international treaty adopted in the fifth meeting of the Conference of the Parties serving as the Meeting of the Parties (COP MOP) to the CPB at Nagoya, Japan in 2010 after six years of intense negotiations. The scheme helps in strenghthening the biosafety management systems and awareness in India.

Genetic Engineering Appraisal Committee

All GMOs and products thereof are regulated under Rules 1989 of EPA, 1986. Activities undertaken for implementation of Rules 1989 since inception till 2015 include: convene monthly Genetic Engineering Appraisal Committee (GEAC) meeting as per schedule for review of applications pertaining to GM technology. So far 126 meetings of the GEAC have been convened.

Status of GEAC approvals is as given here: Bt cotton the first GM crop was approved in 2002. As of date, the GEAC has approved environmental release of Bt cotton expressing six events. Approvals for confined field trials of several GM crops for generation of biosafety data both from the private and public sector institutions. These include transgenic maize, rice, tomato, potato, castor, rubber, cotton, brinjal, mustard, groundnut, sorghum, wheat, watermelon, papaya, sugarcane, banana, pigeonpea, chickpea, artemisia. The biosafety guidelines prescribed by the GEAC include the following; recombinant, DNA safety guidelines, 1990 & 1994; revised guidelines for research in transgenic plants and guidelines for toxicity and allergenicity evaluation, 1998; guidelines and SOPs for the conduct of confined field trials of transgenic plant, 2008. GEAC has adopted the 'event based approval' mechanism wherein a new procedure for commercial release of Bt cotton hybrids expressing approved events has been put in place. Biology document for five crops namely cotton, brinjal, rice, okra and maize have been completed.

Forest Policy

However, Forest Policy Division is Nodal Division for coordination of the USAID/ India Forest PLUS Programme signed under the Partnership Agreement between the Government of India (Department of Economic Affairs) and United States of America for the Sustainable Forests and Climate Adaptation Project in 2010. USAID's contribution is 27 million US$ and Government of India's contribution is 9 m US$. The programme focus is on REDD+ and enhanced carbon sequestration through afforestation, conservation and sustainable management of forests, enhancing climate resilience, capacity building, scientific/technical exchange programmes, etc. The Forest Plus Programme is being implemented in the four states i.e., Madhya Pradesh, Himachal Pradesh, Karnataka and Sikkim.

Brief and Objective

Indian Forest Act, 1927: The Indian Forest Act, 1927 (IAF), provides the legal framework for the protection and management of forest, transit of forest produce and timber, and the duty leviable on timber and other forest produce. IFA is an umbrella Act, which provides the basic architecture for the management of forests in the country including providing mechanism to ensure notification of reserved, protected and village forests, protection of forest resources, forest biodiversity and wildlife of the country.

The National Forest Policy, 1988: National Forest Policy aims to have a minimum of one third of the total land area has been prepared and circulated to the States/UTs for their comments.

Wildlife Conservation

The Protected Area network in India comprises 730 protected areas (103 national parks, 535 wildlife sanctuaries, 66 conservation reserves and 26 community reserves). Apart from providing support to protected areas the Scheme has also the following components—'Protection of Wildlife outside the Protected Areas' and 'Recovery programmes for saving critically endangered species and habitats'.

Objectives

Its objectives include: to assist the states/UTs in the development and management of protected areas networks, protection of wildlife inside and outside protected areas; to create facilities for better protection and management of PAs/High value biodiversity formations; to provide financial and assistance for eco-development, training, capacity building and research studies; and to provide for the voluntary relocation of villages falling within the PAs to outside area and settlement of rights.

Wildlife Crime Control Bureau

Wildlife Crime Control Bureau (WCCB) is a statutory multi-disciplinary body to combat organized wildlife crime in the country. The Bureau has its headquarter in New Delhi and five regional offices at Delhi, Kolkata, Mumbai, Chennai and Jabalpur; three sub-regional offices at Guwahati, Amritsar and Cochin; and five border units at Ramanathapuram, Gorakhpur, Motihari, Nathula and Moreh. It is mandated under Section 38 (Z) of the Wildlife (Protection) Act, 1972, to collect and collate intelligence related to organized wildlife crime activities and to disseminate the same to state and other enforcement agencies for immediate action so as to apprehend the criminals; to establish a centralized wildlife crime data bank; coordinate actions by various agencies in connection with the enforcement of the provisions of the Act; assist foreign authorities and international organization concerned to facilitate co-ordination and universal action for wildlife crime control; capacity building of the wildlife crime enforcement agencies for scientific and professional investigation into wildlife crime and assist State Governments to ensure success in prosecutions related to wildlife crimes; and advise the Government of India on issues relating to wildlife crimes having national and international ramifications, relevant policy and laws.

Central Zoo Authority

The main objective of the Central Zoo Authority is to enforce minimum standards and norms for upkeep and healthcare of animals in the Indian zoos and to control the mushrooming of ill-conceived, ill planned zoos, to monitor and evaluate the existing zoos and to suggest ways and means for the improvement of zoos in the country so that they can be transferred into potent centers for ex-situ conservation of endangered wild fauna.

Endorsement of London Declaration and Kasane Statement on illegal wildlife trade: Hon'ble Prime Minister Narendra Modi and Hon'ble Prime Minister David Cameron met in London on 12-13 November 2015 and issued a joint statement on wildlife conservation. They resolved to work together to combat the illegal wildlife trade and to improve protection for both captive and wild Asian elephants. India endorsed the London Declaration and Kasane Statement on illegal Wildlife Trade.

Project Elephant

Project Elephant (PE) was launched in 1991-92 as a Centrally Sponsored Scheme with following objectives: – to protect elephants, their habitat and corridors; to address issues of man-animal conflict; and welfare of domesticated elephants.

Financial and technical support is being provided to major elephant bearing states in the country. Under the scheme, 100 per cent financial assistance is provided to the concerned state government for undertaking various activities for scientific management of elephant habitats. Presently the project is being mainly implemented in 22 states/UTs , viz. Andhra Pradesh, Arunachal Pradesh, Assam, Chhattisgarh, Jharkhand, Karnataka, Kerala, Maharashtra, Meghalaya, Nagaland, Odhisa, Tamil Nadu, Tripura, Uttarakhand, Uttar Pradesh, West Bengal, Rajasthan, Andaman & Nicobar, Bihar, Punjab, Gujarat and Haryana (where an elephant rescue centre has been set up supported by Project Elephant). There are 29 notified and 2 proposed Elephant Reserve in the country (Khasi Hills Elephant Reserve in Meghalaya and Lemru Elephant Reserve in Chhattisgarh).

Project Tiger/National Tiger Conservation Authority (NTCA)

The Centrally Sponsored Scheme 'Project Tiger' was launched in 1973 with the objective "to ensure maintenance of a viable population of tigers in India for scientific, economic, aesthetic, cultural and ecological values, and to preserve for all times, areas of biological importance as a national heritage for the benefit, education and enjoyment of the people."

Animal Welfare

The Animal Welfare Board of India

The mandate of the Animal Welfare Division is to prevent the infliction of unnecessary pain or suffering on animals, in terms of the provision of the Prevention of Cruelty to Animals (PCA) Act, 1960. General Animal Welfare covers the welfare of individual animals, mainly domesticated animals, as also wild animals in captivity, through Animal Welfare Board of India (AWBI), Chennai, Tamil Nadu.

The following Central Sector schemes are being implemented by the Animal Welfare Board of India: (a) AWBI Plan Scheme; (b) scheme for shelter houses for looking after the animals; (c) scheme for birth control and immunization of stray dogs; (d) scheme for provision of ambulance services to animals in distress; and (e) scheme for relief to animals during natural calamities and unforeseen circumstances.

Committee for Purpose of Control & Supervision of Experiments on Animals

The Committee for Purpose of Control and Supervision of Experiments on Animals (CPCSEA) was established under Chapter 4, Section 15 (1) of the Prevention of Cruelty to Animals Act, 1960. CPCSEA is a statutory committee, which is duty bound to take all such measures as may be necessary to ensure that animals are not subjected to unnecessary pain or suffering before, during or after performance of experiments on them.

National Institute of Animal Welfare

The National Institute of Animal Welfare (NIAW) has been set up as a subordinate office of the Ministry of Environment and Forests. The objective of NIAW is to impart training and education in animal welfare on a diversified basis comprising, among other things, animal management, their behavior and ethics. The aim is to create an enabling environment for fulfilment of the statutory requirements as laid down in the Prevention of Cruelty to Animals Act, 1960. The mandate of NIAW covers the need to improve animal welfare through education, research and public outreach. The institute has been operational since January, 2006.

Environmental Impact Assessment

The Environmental Impact Assessment (EIA), 2006 and CRZ, 2011 have been amended from time to time to further streamline the clearance process. The amendments have also been done to address emerging concerns stemming from the need to integrate environmental concerns into the developmental process for achieving the goal of sustainable development. While according environmental clearance to development project(s), necessary conditions, environmental safeguard and measures are stipulated for their effective implementation during the construction and operation of the project. The safeguard measures are intended to minimize adverse impacts, inter alia, on

(i) air quality, (ii) water quality, (iii) land degradation, (iv) bio-diversity, and (v) wildlife habitat. In addition, measures like rainwater harvesting, water conservation, greenbelt and plantation; wildlife conservation plan, etc., are also required to be implemented in the project.

Environmental Clearance to Developmental Projects

As per the provisions of the EIA Notification 2006, several meetings of various Sectoral Expert Appraisal Committees were convened during the year for appraisal of category 'A' projects from sectors of industry, New Construction and Industrial Estate, infrastructure-II (Miscellaneous projects and CRZ); non-coal mining, coal mining, river valley and hydroelectic projects. As part of appraisal process, wherever required, the Expert Appraisal Committees also visited project sites for obtaining first hand information about the ground level realities and response of people living in the vicinity. Environmental Clearance (EC) has been accorded to 508 projects.

Control of Pollution

Control of Air Pollution

The National Air Quality Index (AQI) has been launched in 2015. AQI is a tool loaded in the web portal of Central Pollution Control Board (CPCB) for public information on the status of ambient air quality of selected cities considering eight Polutants i.e., sulphur, dioxide, nitrogen dioxide, lead, ozone, PM10, PM2.5 carbon monoxide and ammonia for short term (upto 24 hourly) norms as prescribed in the National Ambient Air Quality Standards (NAAQs-2009). The aforesaid air pollutants are monitored by Continuous Ambient Air Quality Monitoring stations (CAAQMs) by CPCB and state pollution air Control Boards. There are six AQI categories, namely good, satisfactory, moderately polluted, poor, very poor, and severe. Each of these categories is decided based on ambient concentration values of air pollutants and their likely health impacts. The National AQI is a significant tool helping the country in decision supporting system as a part of e-Governance measures. CPCB started disseminating the Air Quality Index (AQI) for 10 cities based on the data CAAQM stations. At present, 22 cities are connected to the web-based system of national AQI. They are Agra, Ahmadabad, Bengaluru, Chandrapur, Chennai, Delhi, Faridabad, Jaipur, Jodhpur, Kanpur, Lucknow, Mumbai, Muzaffarpur, Navi Mumbai, Panchkula, Patna, Pune and Varanasi.

Development of Environmental Standards

The Ministry has constituted an Expert Committee (EC) to evolve environmental standards and consequent upon the adoption of the National Environment Policy-2006. The said Committee has been reconstituted. A social scientist, public health expert and environment economist are now on the Committee.

National Ambient Noise Monitoring Network Programme

As per section 5.2.8 (IV) of National Environment Policy (NEP)-2006, Ambient Noise is included as environmental quality parameter and to monitor in specified urban areas regularly. Central Pollution Control Board in association with State Pollution Control Board has laid down National Ambient Noise Monitoring Network (NANMN) in 09 metropolitan cities and installed 35 noise monitoring system in Mumbai, Delhi, Kolkata, Chennai, Bangalore, Lucknow and Hyderabad (five stations in each) during 2010-11. The strengthening of network has been carried out by adding 35 more stations in the same 07 metropolitan cities during 2014-15. Thus the monitoring network has been extended to 70 stations.

Assistance for Abatement of Pollution

The scheme "Assistance for Abatement of Pollution" is being implemented by the Ministry since the Seventh Five Year Plan (1990-1995). The scheme had an allocation of ₹ 45 crore in the XI Five Year Plan (including policy and law and Environmental Health Cell scheme).

Auto Fuel Policy

In order to simplify the procedure, it has been decided by the Ministry to discontinue the joint inspection and grant the recognition to the environmental laboratories subject to fulfilling the criteria which include such as that all environmental laboratories (private/NGOs) government/ autonomous/public sector undertaking/educational institutes/state/central pollution control board laboratories should have either ISO 17025 (NABL Accreditation) or ISO 9001 along with OHSAS 180001 (Occupational Health and Safety Management System) certification before submission of application for consideration of recognition under Environmental (Protection) Act, 1986 duly authenticated by State Pollution Control Board. The applicant is required to submit an undertaking that all activities of laboratory in totality are being carried out as per ISO 17025 (NABL Accreditation) or ISO 9001 along with OHSAS 18001 (Occupational Health and Safety Management System).

Environmental Health

The Ministry had initiated environmental epidemiological studies in different areas of indoor and outdoor pollution so as to identify and develop programmes to create data base and suggest environmental mitigation measures. Continued research in health effects of ambient air pollution is necessary to evaluate changing trends and to suggest corrective measures.

Scheme of Common Effluent Treatment Plants

The concept of the Common Effluent Treatment Plants (CETPs) arose in order to make a cooperative movement for pollution control. The main objective of the CETPs is to reduce the treatment cost to be borne by an individual member unit to a minimum while protecting the environment to a maximum.

Wastewater treatment and water conservation are the prime objectives of the CETP. The concept of CETPs was envisaged to treat the effluent emanating from the clusters of compatible small-scale industries. It was also envisaged that burden of various Government authorities working for controlling pollution and monitoring of water pollution could be reduced once the CETPs are implemented and commissioned.

Taj Protection Mission

In pursuance of the Supreme Court's order, projects for environmental protection of World Heritage Site of Taj Mahal were initiated and funded by the Ministry. The Planning Commission approved ₹ 600 crore on a 50:50 cost sharing basis with the state government to implement various schemes in the Taj Trapezium Zone for environmental protection of the Taj Mahal. In the first phase during the IX Five Year Plan, 10 projects were approved by the Government and implemented by the State Government of Uttar Pradesh.

Central Pollution Control Board

Under the provisions of the Water (Prevention and Control of Pollution) Act, 1974, the Central Government constituted the 'Central Board for the Prevention and Control of Water Pollution' in 1974. The name of the Central Board was amended to Central Pollution Control Board (CPCB) under the Water (Prevention and Control of Pollution) Amendment Act, 1988 (No. 53 of 1988). The enactment of the Environment (Protection) Act, 1986, which is umbrella legislation for enforcement of measures for protection of environment and several notifications of rules under the Act widened the scope of activities of the Central Board.

Ambient Air Quality Monitoring Station

The Ambient Air Quality monitors 8 parameter out of 12 as notified in NAAQS 2009 namely SO_2, NO_2, NH_2, O_3, CO_1 Benzene, PM_{10} & PM_{23}. The Air Quality Index also being generated from 41 stations. The data is live on the website of CPCB.

Categorization of Industrial Sectors under Red, Orange, Green and White Category

A 'Working Group' comprising the members from CPCB, APPCB, TNPCB, WBPCB, PPCB, MPPCB and Maharashtra PCB was constituted to revisit the criteria of categorization of industrial sectors. The Working Group has developed the criteria of the pollution index which is a function of the emissions (air pollutants), effluents (water pollutants), hazardous wastes generated and consumption of resources. For this purpose the references are taken from the Water (Prevention and Control of Pollution) Cess (Amendment) Act, 2003, Standards so far prescribed for various pollutants under Environment (Protection) Act, 1986 and Doon Valley Notification, 1989 issued by MoEF&CC. Accordingly, following criteria on 'Range of Pollution Index 'for the purpose of categorization of industrial sectors is finalized. Industrial sectors having pollution index score of 60 and above—Red category; Industrial sectors having pollution index score of 41 to 59—Orange category; Industrial sectors having pollution index score of 21 to 40—Green category; Industrial sectors having pollution index score incl. and upto 20—white category. The newly introduced White category of industries pertains to those industrial sectors which are practically non-polluting. The salient features of the 'Recategorization' exercise are as follows:

Hazardous Substances Management

The Hazardous Substances Management Division (HSMD) is the nodal point within the Ministry for management of chemical emergencies and hazardous substances. The main objective of the programme is to promote safe management and use of hazardous substances including hazardous chemicals and hazardous wastes, in order to avoid damage to health and environment. The Division is also the nodal point for the following International Conventions/Agreements viz., (a) Basel Convention on Control of Transboundary Movement of Hazardous Waste and their Disposal; (b) Rotterdam Convention on Prior Informed Consent Procedure for certain Chemicals and Pesticides in International Trade; (c) Stockholm Convention on Persistent Organic Pollutants; (d) strategic approach to International Chemicals Management; and (e) Minamata Convention on Mercury.

Chemical Safety

The Ministry notified the Manufacture, Storage and Import of Hazardous Chemicals (MSIHC) Rules, 1989 and the Chemical Accidents (Emergency Planning, Preparedness and Response) (CAEPPR) Rules, 1996 for ensuring chemical safety in the country. These rules delineate the criteria for identification of Major Accident Hazard (MAH) unit. As per the rules, Central crisis group, state crisis groups, district crisis groups and local crisis groups at Central, state, district and local level are required to be set up for the management of accidents due to handling of hazardous chemicals listed in the rules. An off-site emergency plan for a district having MAH unit (s) is required to be in place so as to mitigate the impact of chemical accidents. As per the information received from various States and Union Territories, there are 1,861 MAH units located in 303 districts.

A sub-scheme titled "Industrial Pocket wise Hazard Analysis" has been in operation since the Eighth Five Year Plan.

Hazardous Waste Management

As per information provided by the Central Pollution Control Board (CPCB), there are about 41,523 industries in the country generating about 7.90 million tonnes of hazardous waste annually, out of which landfillable waste is about 3.32 million tonnes (42.02 per cent), incinerable waste is about 0.60 million tonnes (7.60 per cent) and recyclable hazardous waste is about 3.98 million tonnes (50.38 per cent).

The Ministry has also initiated a project on GIS Based National Hazardous Waste Information System. It is a web based system, which has been developed to provide status of hazardous waste management in the country. The database available on the web is required to be regularly updated by all state pollution control boards to ensure updated status at all times. Through NHWIS till now survey of 33,000 hazardous waste industries and MIS Date Entry of about 27,500 Hazardous waste industries has been completed. The system in its present form will provide MIS module for data updation by industries, Regional Offices and SPCBs, Web based GIS tool for analysis of hazardous waste with respect to generation, disposal and recycling; and GIS based disposal vehicle monitoring system for disposal of hazardous waste.

Treatment Storage and Disposal Facilities

At present, 38 Treatment Storage and Disposal Facilities (TSDFs) include 17 Integrated TSDF, 13 exclusive common secure landfills and 8 exclusive common incinerators are available in 10, 9 and 4 states/UT respectively. These states/ UT contribute about 97.8 per cent of total landfillable and 88.19 per cent of total incinerable hazardous wastes generation in the country respectively.

The Ministry notified e-waste (Management and Handling) Rules, 2011. These rules have come into force in 2012. These rules apply to e-waste generated from IT and telecommunication equipment and consumer electrical and electronics namely television sets (including LCD & LED), refrigerators, washing machines and air-conditioners. These rules empower the concerned state agencies to control, supervise and regulate relevant activities connected with e-waste management such as collection, segregation, dismantling and recycling.

The concept of Extended Producer Responsibility (EPR) has been enshrined in these rules. Accordingly, producers are required to set up collection systems and meet the cost involved in the environmentally sound management of e-waste generated from the 'end of life' of their own products. Besides, threshold limits, which are accepted globally, have been prescribed for six hazardous substances used in manufacture of electrical and electronics components. Producers are expected to achieve reduction in use of the hazardous substances (RoHS) to the prescribed limit within a period of two years from the date of commencement of these rules.

These rules are the main instrument to ensure environmentally sound management of e-waste. Under these rules EPR authorizations have been granted to 128 producers which are spread in 11 states. 134 collection centres are set-up in 19 states.

Solid Waste Management

As per information, municipal areas in the country generate 1, 33,760 metric tonnes per day of municipal solid waste (MSW), of which only 91,152 TPD waste is collected and 25,884 TPD treated. The Ministry has notified the Municipal Solid Wastes (Management and Handling) Rules, 2000 for management of the municipal solid waste. These rules, inter-alia, provide for mechanisms to be set up by the municipal authority for management of the waste within their jurisdiction. However, the municipal authorities are facing difficulties in implementation of these rules. The matter was discussed with stakeholders and it has been decided to amend the existing rules on the municipal solid waste. The emphasis is on management of the waste through a sustainable business model which includes segregation of municipal solid waste at source, door to door collection by involving waste collectors, processing of segregated waste into useful products such as methane, compost, etc.

Bio-Medical Waste Management

As per the information received from SPCBs and PCCs of union territories, about 4.16 tonnes of biomedical waste is generated per day. There are 190 Common Bio-Medical Waste Treatment and Disposal Facilities (CBMWTDFs) in operation and 29 CBMWTDFs are under construction. The waste is required to be managed as per the Bio-medical Waste (Management and Handling) Rules, 1998, as amended by the Ministry.

The Ministry initiated the process of amending existing rules in 2011 and notified the draft Bio-Medical Waste (Management & Handling) Rules, 2011 for public comments. The comments/suggestions received in the Ministry were compiled and analyzed in consultation with various stakeholders such as Union Ministry of Health and Family Welfare, SPCBs/PCCs of Union Territories, representatives of health care establishments, operators of common biomedical waste treatment and storage facilitates and civil societies. The activities related to finalization of these rules particularly redefining the categories of bio-medical waste, standards for technologies for bio-medical waste treatment including incineration were undertaken during the year 2014-15.

Plastic Waste Management

The Ministry had notified the Plastic Waste (Management and Handling) Rules, 2011 to regulate the manufacture and usage of plastic carry bags and to manage plastic waste. The quantum of plastic waste generation in the country is estimated to be 15,342.6 tonnes per day. Out of which 9,205 tonnes is recycled and remaining 6,137 tons remains uncollected and littered. The rules are being amended.

Fly Ash Utilization

Electricity generation in the country is and would remain predominantly coal based in the near future. The Indian coal has high ash content of the order of 30-49 per cent generating large quantity of fly ash at coal/lignite based thermal power stations in the country. The management of fly ash has thus been a matter of concern in view of requirement of large area of land for its disposal because of its potential of causing pollution of air and water. To address environmental problem of fly ash disposal, the Ministry issued notification on fly ash untilization in 1999 prescribing therein the targets for fly ash utilization for coal/lignite power based thermal power stations with an aim to achieve 100 per cent utilization in a phased manner.

The objectives of the notification are to protect environment, conserve the top soil, and prevent dumping of fly ash from thermal power stations on land and to promote utilization of ash in the manufacture of building materials and construction activity. The implementation of this notification has resulted in steady increase in the utilization of fly ash. The fly ash utilization in the country has been increased from 13.51 to 57.63 per cent in the year 2013-14. However, the utilization has not reached 100 per cent

Conservation of Water Bodies

The National River Conservation Directorate, functioning under the Ministry is providing financial assistance to the state governments for conservation of river, lakes and wetlands under the Centrally sponsored schemes of 'National River Conservation Plan (NRCP)' and 'National Plan for Conservation of Aquatic Eco-systems (NPCA)'.

National River Conservation Plan

The river conservation programme was initiated with the launching of the Ganga Action Plan (GAP) in 1985. The Ganga Action Plan was expanded to cover other rivers under National River Conservation Plan (NRCP) in the year 1995. The objective of NRCP is to improve the water quality of rivers, which are major water sources in the country, through implementation of pollution abatement works in various towns along identified polluted stretches of rivers on cost sharing basis between the Central and state governments.

The pollution abatement works taken up under the NRCP include: interception and diversion works/laying of sewerage system to capture raw sewage flowing into the rivers through open drains and diverting them for treatment; setting up of Sewage Treatment Plants (STPs) for treating the diverted sewage; construction of low cost sanitation toilets to prevent open defecation on river banks; construction of electric crematoria and improved wood crematoria to conserve the use of wood; river front development works, such as improvement of bathing ghats; public participation and awareness and capacity building, etc.

Presently NRCP (excluding Ganga and its tributaries) has covered polluted stretches of 31 rivers in 75 towns spread over 14 states at a sanctioned cost of ₹ 4517.82 crore. An amount of ₹ 1941.86 crore has been released to various state governments for implementation of various pollution abatement schemes and a treatment capacity of 2,372 million litres per day (mld) has been created so far under NRCP (excluding Ganga and its tributaries). The 31 rivers covered under the programme are given in Table-12.2.

Table-12.2 List of Rivers covered under NRCP Programme

S.No.	River	S.No.	River
1.	Adyar	16.	Narmada
2.	Beas	17.	Pennar
3.	Bhadra	18.	Pamba
4.	Brahmani	19.	Panchganga
5.	Cauvery	20.	Rani Chu
6.	Cooum	21.	Sabarmati
7.	Diphu & Dhansiri	22.	Satluj
8.	Ghaggar	23.	Subarnarekha
9.	Godwari	24.	Tapti
10.	Krishna	25.	Tapi
11.	Mahanadi	26.	Tunga
12.	Mandovi	27.	Tungabadra
13.	Mindhola	28.	Tambarani
14.	Mula Mutha	29.	Vaigai
15	Musi	30.	Vennar
		31.	Wainganga

National Plan for Conservation of Aquatic Eco-Systems

For conservation of lakes and wetlands, the Ministry was earlier implementing two separate Centrally sponsored schemes, namely the 'National Wetlands Conservation Programme' (NWCP) and the 'National Lake Conservation Plan' (NLCP).

To avoid overlap and promote better synergies, NLCP has been merged with the scheme of NWCP, into one integrated scheme of National Plan for Conservation of Aquatic Eco-systems (NPCA). The scheme aims at holistic conservation and restoration of lakes and wetlands for achieving the desired water quality enhancement, besides improvement in biodiversity and ecosystem through an integrated and multidisciplinary approach and a common regulatory framework. The scheme would contribute to reduction of pollution loads in lakes and wise use of wetland resources and their services. NPCA is presently operational on cost sharing between Central and respective state governments.

Conservation of Lakes

So far under NLCP/NPCA, a total of 46 projects for conservation of 63 lakes have been sanctioned in 14 states at a total cost of ₹ 1096.09 crore for undertaking works like providing sewage system and sewage treatment plants, interception and diversion of sewage, desalting, catchment area treatment, storm water management etc. Conservation works for 33 lakes have been completed.

Major projects presently under implementation include Dal lake in Jammu & Kashmir, Shivpuri and Sindh Sagar lakes in Madhya Pradesh, twin lakes at Mokokchung in Nagaland (NE region), Annasagar, Pushkar and Pichola lakes in Rajasthan, Ramgarh Tal and Laxmital in Uttar Pradesh. During 2015-16 an amount of ₹ 34.02 crore has been released for conservation of lakes under NPCA

Conservation of Wetlands

Wetlands are lifeline for a very large number of people and an important source of fresh water to mankind. They provide a host of ecosystem services to humanity, in addition to being host to rich biodiversity. However, due to anthropogenic activities, wetlands are getting degraded. Major pressures on wetlands include fragmentation of hydrological regimes, siltation from degraded catchments, pollution, spread of invasive species and over-harvesting of resources.

To control degradation and conserve wetlands, the National Wetland Conservation Programme (NWCP) was initiated in 1987 and financial assistance is being provided to the State governments for implementing action plans for conservation and management of identified wetlands. So far, ₹ 146.09 crore has been provided to 22 states for conservation and management of the 82 identified wetlands. During the year 2015-16, Management Action Plans of 25 wetlands were approved and financial assistance of ₹ 7.54 crore was provided to the concerned state governments.

Ramsar Convention

As a commitment for conserving potential wetlands, India became a signatory to the Ramsar Convention in 1982. As per this convention, India is committed for international cooperation and to take national action for conservation and wise use of Wetlands. At present there are 26 Ramsar sites in India.

The Wetlands (Conservation and Management) Rules 2010

To implement the objectives of the convention, a regulatory mechanism was put in place through Wetlands (Conservation and Management) Rules in December, 2010.

The Ministry has initiated the process of revising the existing wetland rules for more effective conservation and management of wetlands in the country and to enable a greater role and ownership by state governments in management of wetlands, particularly as water and land are state subjects. The state wetland authorities are envisaged to be entrusted the role of management and regulation of wetlands within their jurisdiction.

World Wetland Day

Each year, World Wetland Day is celebrated on 2nd February for increasing awareness and spreading need for conservation and wise use of wetlands all over the world. This day was celebrated at national level at Nalsarovar wetland, Gujarat during 2015 by the Ministry in collaboration with the Government of Gujarat. The stakeholders of the wetland were invited to participate in the celebration. Prize distribution was held for various competitions held on the eve of WWD on various environmental themes.

Wildlife Institute of India (Dehradun)

Wildlife Institute of India (WII) was established in 1986 as an autonomous institute of the Ministry. The Institute has emerged as a premier training and research institution in the field of wildlife and protected area management in south and south east Asia. Its mandates are to generate quality information and knowledge products in wildlife science through research and mainstream it in capacity building programmes for various target groups and provide advisory on related matter.

Environmental Education, Awareness and Training

The 'Environmental Education, Awareness and Training' is a flagship scheme of the Ministry for enhancing the understanding of people at all level about the relationship between human beings and the environment and to develop capabilities/skills to improve and protect the environment. This scheme was launched in 1983-84 with the following basic objectives: to promote environmental awareness among all sections of the society; to spread environment education, especially in the non-formal system among different sections of the society; to facilitate development of education/training materials and aids in the formal education sector; to promote environment education through existing educational/scientific/research institutions; to ensure training and manpower development for environment education, awareness and training; to encourage non-governmental organizations, mass media and other concerned organizations for promoting awareness about environmental issues among the people at all levels; and to mobilize people's participation for preservation and conservation of environment.

National Green Corps Programme

During financial year 2015-16, due to shortage of funds only 15,500/ eco-clubs were financially supported. Also in order to strengthen monitoring mechanism of NGC programme, MoEFCC is in process to establish Management Information system (MIS) which will open up vistas in sharing and accessing the information on NGC among all stakeholders. The MIS reporting and monitoring would be interactive and creative in ensuring NGC mobility and services.

National Environmental Awareness Campaign

The National Environment Awareness Campaign (NEAC) was hence launched in mid 1986 with the objective of creating environmental awareness at the national level. In this campaign, nominal financial assistance is provided to NGOs, schools, colleges, universities, research institutes, women and youth organisations, army units, government departments, etc., from all over the country for conducting awareness raising and action oriented activities. The awareness activities could be seminars, workshops, training programmes, camps, padyatras, rallies, public meetings, exhibitions, essay/debate/painting/ poster competitions, folk dances and songs, street theatre, puppet shows, preparation and distribution of environmental education resource materials, etc.

The phenomenal response that NEAC has received has made the network of participating agencie more than 16,000 across the country. During financial year 2015-16, 6,760 participating agencies of previous year i.e. 2014-15 were financially supported.

The programme facilitates the transfer of technical know-how to different people including local population. Universities/ professional bodies/technical institutions and other R&D organisations are very responsive to the programme as is evidenced by the increase in the number of proposals being received by the Ministry.

National Nature Camping Programme

National Nature Camping Programme is an initiative of the Ministry in environment education which is aimed at creating greater awareness, understanding and empathy of children with and for the environment. Through this initiative it is hoped that every child who goes through middle school (classes VI-VIII) will get at least one opportunity for a 2-3 day camping experience during these years.

During Financial year 2015-16, only 40 nature camps were financially supported. The financial assistance not exceeding ₹ 2,000/- (rupees two thousand only) per student for a camp of 2 nights - 3 days duration (maximum five number of camps) is provided under this programme.

GLOBE

Global Learning and Observation to Benefit the Environment (GLOBE) is a hands on international environmental science and education programme that brings students, teachers and scientists together to study the global environment. MoEFCC and US Government signed an agreement on 25th day of August 2000 to implement the Globe programme in India. Indian Environmental Society is an implementing agency for Globe in India. The goals of Globe are to enhance the environmental awareness of individuals throughout the world, to contribute to scientific understanding of the Earth and to help all students reach higher levels of achievement in science and mathematics.

National Museum of Natural History

The National Museum of Natural History (NMNH), New Delhi is an institution devoted to environmental education and was opened to the public in 1978, on

June 5, the World Environment Day. The museum undertakes environment education through the means of exhibition programmes and educational activities. Even though the primary target audience of the museum is school students, it has developed programmes for other categories of people as well. The NMNH is the pioneer museum which has initiated several specialized programmes to cater to the needs of persons with disabilities. The museum also undertakes many outreach programmes such as temporary exhibitions, mobile exhibitions and a large number of nature camps. It also arranges many local and national level competitions leading to Young Environmentalist of the Year Award (YEYA).

Centres of Excellence

Enhancement of people's awareness about environment requires capacity building at institutional and individual level for providing adequate support to the efforts in the fields of environment education, research and training. To serve this objective, the Ministry launched the scheme 'Centres of Excellence' (CoE) in 1983 to promote institutions in priority areas of Environmental Sciences and Management.

Ten Centres of Excellence have so far been established in different areas. Out of 108 are in operation. The main objectives of the CoEs include: (i) to create awareness among various sections of the population of the country regarding environmental issues, with a view to encourage and enhance public participation; (ii) to enhance and strengthen the country's human, scientific, technological, organizational, institutional and resource capabilities; (iii) to encourage and support universities/institutions/ NGOs to undertake activities to develop or strengthen the capabilities and capacities of the identified units, so that they may contribute to the process of sustainable development; and (iv) to undertake cutting edge research and to provide inputs for policy decisions in the Ministry.

National Green Tribunal

The National Green Tribunal (NGT) was established in 2010 under the NGT Act, 2010. The NGT has been established for the effective and expeditious disposal of cases relating to environmental protection and conservation of forests and other natural resources. It also hears cases relating to enforcement of any legal rights relating to environment and providing relief and compensation for damages to persons and property and for matters connected therewith or incidental thereto.

It is a specialized body equipped with the necessary expertise to handle environmental disputes involving multi-disciplinary issues. The Tribunal is not bound by the procedure laid down under the Code of Civil Procedure, 1908, but is guided by principles of natural justice. The Tribunal is mandated to make an endeavor for disposal of applications or appeals finally within six months of filing.

Presently, the Tribunal has five places of sitting, including Principal Bench at Delhi. Pune, Kolkata, Bhopal and Chennai are four zonal Benches of sitting of the Tribunal. In addition, the Tribunal holds three circuit Benches at Shimla, Shillong and Jodhpur.

Climate Change

Introduction

The financial year 2015-16 was important for climate change both at domestic and international level. It started with the preparation of the third National Communication (NATCOM) under the United Nations Framework Convention on Climate Change (UNFCCC) and release of the Biennial Update Reports (BURs). Under the Prime Minister's Council on Climate Change (PMCCC) all national missions under the National Action Plan on Climate Change (NAPCC) were asked to revisit their plans. New missions on wind energy, health, waste to energy and coastal areas was also taken up. Also, it redesigned the National Water Mission and National Mission on Sustainable Agriculture. The National Adaptation Fund for Climate Change (NAFCC) was made operational in 2015-16. To develop institutional capacities and implement state level activities to address climate change the State Action Plan on Climate change (SAPCCC) is being prepared. To create and strengthen the scientific and analytical capacity for assessment of climate change in the country different studies under Climate change action programme (CCAP) has been initiated. During this financial year, many important bilateral and multilateral meetings and international negotiations on climate change were held.

India submitted its Intended Nationally Determined Contribution (INDC) to the UNFCCC. During COP21 in Paris, India Pavilion was set up to showcase and share information on India's action on climate change. In addition, a new online Management Information System (MIS) was launched by the National Clean Development Mechanism Authority (NCDMA). Also, the National Designated Entity (NDE) for Reducing Emissions from Deforestation and Forest Degradation (REDD+) has been established in the climate change division along with the National Designated Entity for Climate Technology Centre and Network (CTCN) and Technology Executive Committee (TEC).

National Communication Submitted to the UNFCCC

In pursuance of the reporting obligations under the United Nations Framework Convention on Climate Change (UNFCCC), India has undertaken to communicate information about the implementation of the Convention, taking into account the common but differentiated responsibilities and respective capabilities and specific regional and national development priorities, objectives and circumstances. The elements of information provided in the communication include a national inventory of anthropogenic emissions by sources and removals by sinks of all greenhouse gases, a general description of steps taken to implement the Convention including an assessment of impacts and vulnerability, and any other relevant information. The communication is meant to provide the context and the national circumstances inter alia India's geography, imperative of development needs, climate and economy; based on which India would be addressing and responding to the challenges of climate change.

India has submitted its second National Communication (NATCOM) to the UNFCCC in 2012. The second NATCOM provides information of the emissions of Green House Gases (GHG) for the years 2000 and 2007. The Ministry is currently preparing India's third National Communication (TNC) and in this connection a workshop on National Inventory Management System (NIMS) was organized in July 2015. The purpose of this workshop was to provide inputs for establishment of National Inventory Management System (NIMS) and increased accuracy of Green House Gas Inventory preparation with use of higher tier methods.

The Biennial Update Reports (BURs) are new reporting obligation under the transparency arrangement of sharing information on implementation of the Convention. The BUR is a form of enhanced reporting, containing updates of national greenhouse gas inventories and information on mitigation actions, financial, technical needs and support received and an update to India's second National Communication. The first BUR encompassing information on National Circumstance, GHG Inventories for the year 2010, Mitigation Actions, Analysis of Constraints, Gaps, and related financial, technical and capacity needs and other related information along with information on domestic Monitoring, Reporting and Verification (MRV) arrangements has been released.

National and State Action Plans on Climate Change

India's domestic strategy for addressing climate change is reflected in many of its social and economic development programmes. The National Action Plan on Climate Change (NAPCC) coordinated by the Ministry of Environment, Forest & Climate Change (MoEF & CC) is being implemented through the Nodal Ministries in specific sectors/ areas. Eight national missions in the area of solar energy, enchanced energy efficiency, sustainable agriculture, sustainable habitat, water, Himalayan eco-system, Green India and strategic knowledge for climate change form the core of NAPCC. All National missions were approved by the Prime Minister's Council on Climate change (PMCCC) and are at different stages of implementation. The Missions are under constant review of the Prime Minister's Council on Climate Change. An Executive Committee on Climate Change under the Chairmanship of Principal Secretary to Prime Minister has been set up for assisting the Prime Minister's Council on Climate Change in evolving a coordinating response to issues relating to climate change at national level with regular monitoring of the eight national missions along with other initiatives on climate change and coordinating with various agencies on issues relating to climate change. Prime Minister's office has entrusted the responsibility of convening and servicing the Prime Minister's Council on Climate Change as well as the Executive Committee on Climate Change to MoEF& CC.

The Ministry has also motivated state governments to prepare State Action Plan on Climate Change (SAPCC). These SAPCCs aim to create institutional capacities and implement state level activities to address climate change. So far, 33 states/UTs namely Andaman and Nicobar, Andhra Pradesh including Telangana, Arunachal Pradesh, Assam, Bihar, Chandigarh Chhattisgarh, Delhi, Gujarat, Haryana, Himachal Pradesh, Jammu & Kashmir, Jharkhand, Kerala, Karnataka, Lakshadweep, Madhya Pradesh, Manipur, Meghalaya, Mizoram, Nagaland, Odisha, Puducherry, Punjab, Rajasthan, Sikkim, Tamil Nadu, Tripura, Uttarakhand, West Bengal, Uttar Pradesh, Maharashtra, Goa have prepared and submitted document on SAPCC. MoEF&CC is also closely following up with the remaining two states which have not submitted their SAPCCs.

National Adaptation Fund for Climate Change

The National Adaptation Fund for Climate Change (NAFCC) was operationilised in 2015-16. The fund is meant to assist national and state level activities to meet the cost of adaptation measures in areas that are particularly vulnerable to the adverse effects of climate change. This scheme has been taken as Central Sector Scheme with the National Bank for Agriculture and Rural Development (NABARD) as National Implementing Entity (NIE). The overall aim of the fund is to support concrete adaptation activities which are not covered under on-going schemes of State and National Government that reduce the adverse affects of climate change facing community sector and states.

Climate Change Action Programme

The Ministry is implementing a scheme titled 'Climate Chance Action Programme' (CCAP) since January, 2014, with an objective to create and strengthen the scientific and analytical capacity for assessment of climate change in the country, putting in place appropriate institutional framework for scientific and policy initiatives and implementation of climate change related actions in the context of sustainable development. Total budget for the scheme is ₹ 290 crore for the 12th Plan period.

In order to enhance understanding of climate change the CCAP includes National Corbonaceous Aerosols Programme (NCAP), Long Term Ecological Observatories (LTEO), and Coordinated Studies on Climate Change for North East Region (CSCCNER). The NCAP is a major activity involving multi-institutional and multi-agency study. In this initiative, MoEF & CC will collaborate with the Ministry of Earth Sciences, the Indian Space Research Organization, the Ministry of Science and Technology and other associated agencies to enhance the understanding the role of Black Carbon in climate change through monitoring and assessment of the impacts of Black Carbon using modeling techniques. The work programme envisages three Working Groups namely Long Term Monitoring of Aerosol (Working Group-I), Impact of Aerosol on Himalayan Glaciers (Working Group-II) and Modeling of Black Carbon emissions in India and assessment of its impacts (Working Group-III).

International Negotiations on Climate Change under the United Nations Framework Convention on Climate Change

During the financial year 2015-16 many important bilateral and multilateral meetings and international negotiations on climate change were held. These meetings were crucial in the run up to the 21st Conference of Parties (COP 21). The key contributions envisaged in India's INDCs are as follows: to put forward and further propagate a healthy and sustainable way of living based on traditions and values of conservation and moderation; to adopt a climate friendly and a cleaner path than the one followed hitherto by others at corresponding level of economic development; to reduce the emissions intensity of its GDP by 33 to 35 per cent by 2030 from 2005 level, etc.

India Pavilion at COP-21

An India Pavilion was set up in COP-21 to showcase and share information on India's actions on climate change. Prime Minister of India inaugurated the Indian Pavilion in Paris.

The pavilion hosted 25 sessions, 150 speakers, 130 presentations, over 80 films, 13 book/reports/CDs/films/brochure release. Pavilion was appreciated and viewed by nearly 6,500 visitors from different countries. Information on India's initiatives was also shared in the form of books or brochures and digital material. India Pavilion was one of the centre of attraction in COP-21 due to its water screen, 360 degree film, ipad forest e-book on India's culture and sustainable living.

Reducing Emissions from Deforestation and Forest Degradation

The National Designated Entity (NDE) for Reducing Emissions from Deforestation and Forest Degradation [NDE (REDD+)] has been established in the Climate Change Division of this Ministry. The key function of NDE will include: (i) identification of possible needs and gaps in coordination of support; (ii) improvement for the effectiveness of finance (result-based finance, technology and capacity-building); (iii) sharing of information on knowledge, experiences and good practices; (iv) exchange of information as per the United Nations Framework Convention on Climate Change (UNFCCC) requirements and (v) approval of the national level REDD+ proposal for submission to UNFCCC.

Climate Technology Centre and Network and Technology Executive Committee

The National Designated Entity (NDE) for Climate Technology Centre and Network (CTCN) and Technology Executive Committee (TEC) [NDE (CTCN & TCE)] has been established in the Climate Change Division of this Ministry. The key function will include: (i) leading and coordinating the formulation, selection and submission of requests for tTechnology needs assessment and support; (ii) facilitating and monitoring the implementation of CTCN response assistance; (iii) foster collaboration and access to information and knowledge to accelerate climate technology transfer in the country; (iv) strengthen network, partnership and capacity building for climate technology transfer.

Ozone Layer Protection

Ozone, a tri-atomic molecule of oxygen is formed from oxygen naturally in the upper levels of the earth's atmosphere by high energy Ultraviolet (UV) radiation from the Sun. The UV radiation breaks down oxygen molecules, releasing free atoms, some of which bond with other oxygen molecule to form ozone. About 90 per cent of ozone formed in this way lies between 10 and 50 kilometers above the earth's surface, called the Stratosphere. The ozone found in the part of the atmosphere is called the ozone layer.

The Vienna Convention for the Protection of the Ozone Layer and its Montreal Protocol on Substances that Deplete the Ozone Layer are the international treaties specific for the protection of the Stratospheric Ozone (Ozone layer). The Montreal Protocol has been recognized as the most successful international environmental treaty in history. It has been universally ratified and all the 197 United Nations member countries of the world are the parties to the Vienna Convention and its Montreal Protocol. In the 29 years of operation of the Montreal Protocol, extraordinary international cooperation under this agreement has led to phase-out of production and consumption of several major Ozone Depleting Substances (ODSs) such as Chlorofluorocarbons (CFCs), Carbon tetrachloride (CTC) and halons globally from 1st January, 2010. The production and consumption of methyl chloroform has been phased out globally by 2015, with possible essential use exemptions. The production and consumption of methyl bromide was phased out globally in 2016, except use in quarantine and pre-shipment applications. Global systematic observations have confirmed that atmospheric levels of key ODSs are declining and it is estimated that with continued, full implementation of the Montreal Protocol's provisions, the global ozone layer should return to pre-1980 levels by around the middle of this century and the antarctic ozone around 15 years later. The Montreal Protocol has also delivered substantial climate benefits.

Activities Undertaken

Implementation of phase-out of ODSs

India has completely phased-out production and consumption of CFCs with 50 per cent phase-out by 2005, 85 per cent phase-out by 2007 and complete phase-out in 2008, 17 months ahead of the agreed phase-out schedule. India has successfully implemented the National Strategy for Transition to non-CFC Metered Dose Inhalers (MDIs) and plan for phase-out of CFCs in the manufacture of pharmaceutical MDIs. The implementation of National MDI Transition Strategy has resulted successful phase-out of pharmaceutical grade CFCs in manufacturing of MDIs as of December, 2012, 11 months prior to the schedule approved by the Executive Committee (Ex-Com) of the Multilateral Fund (MLF) for implementation of the Montreal Protocol. The production and consumption of virgin halons in India was phased out as early as in 2002. The use of CFCs and halons was prohibited in manufacturing of new equipment since 2003. India has completely phased-out production and consumption of CTC with 85 per cent phase-out as on January 1, 2010.

International Cooperation and Sustainable Development

International Cooperation and Sustainable Development (IC&SD) Division of the Ministry coordinates matters related to international environmental cooperation and sustainable development including Sustainable Development Goals (SDGs).

International Cooperation - Multilateral Matters

The Division is nodal for United Nations Environment Programme (UNEP), Global Environment Facility (GEF), United Nations Development Programme (UNDP), the World Bank (WB), and regional bodies like Economic & Social Commission for Asia & Pacific (ESCAP), South Asian Association for Regional Cooperation (SAARC), South Asia Cooperative Environment Programme (SACEP), Association of South-East Asian Nations (ASEAN), Asian Development Bank (ADB), European Union (EU), India-Brazil-South Africa (IBSA) Summit on Environment amongst others. The Division supports annual contributions to various UN and other International bodies working on environmental matters. The Division directly contributes USD 31,850 annually to South Asia Cooperative Environment Programme (SACEP).

India is a member of UNEP and provides annual financial contribution of USD 100,000 to UNEP Environment Fund. Three of the thirty three members on UNEP's International Resource Panel (IRP) are currently from India. The Ministry is a member of the IRP Steering Committee. IRP supports UNEP's Resource Efficiency/Sustainable Consumption and Production (SCP) sub-programme and is carrying out assessments of the world's most critical resource issues with a view to developing practical solutions for government policy makers, industry and society.

United Nations Environment Assembly (UNEA) is the governing body of UNEP. The second session of UNEA is scheduled to be held in Nairobi, Kenya from 23 to 27 May, 2016 and the focus will be on 'Delivering on the Environmental Dimension of the Agenda 2030 for Sustainable Development'. The Ministry is actively working with the concerned stakeholders for finalizing the agenda of UNEA-2 by providing inputs and participating in the "Open-ended Meeting of the Committee of Permanent Representative (OECPR) to UNEP" in Feb 2016.

India is a founder member of Global Environment Facility (GEF). Set up in 1991, GEF is the designated multilateral funding mechanism of 183 countries to provide incremental finance for addressing global environmental benefits which are also identified national priorities. The GEF mandate is decided as per the guidance provided by the Conference of the Parties of the multilateral environmental conventions namely Convention on Biological Diversity (CBD), United Nation Framework Convention on Climate Change (UNFCCC), United Nation Convention to Combat Desertification (UNCCD), Stockholm Convention on PoPs and Minamata Convention on Mercury. The GEF grants are available under five focal areas namely, biodiversity, climate change, land degradation, international water and chemicals and waste. The full-sized (> USD 2 m), medium-sized (up to USD 2 m) and small grants (exclusively for NGOs/CBOs up).

Sustainable Development

2015-16 was a landmark year leading to the adoption of 17 Sustainable Development Goals (SDGs) and 169 associated targets by the UN General Assembly in September 2015 by 193 countries including India. The negotiations on SDGs have been ably led by the Ministry of External Affairs (MEA). Though the interministeral consultations were held by MoEFCC, MEA was always kept in loop and comments/reservations furnished by line ministries were duly communicated to MEA. The outcome document known as "Transforming our World: The 2030 Agenda for Sustainable Development" highlights poverty eradication as the overreaching goal of the new development agenda and has at its core the integration of the economic, social and environmental dimensions of sustainable development. The emerging development agenda is unique in that it calls for action by all countries, poor, rich and middle-income. The 'five Ps' people, planet, prosperity, peace, and partnership—capture the broad scope of the agenda. The SDGs are expected to be achieved by 2030.

13 Finance

THE Ministry of Finance is responsible for administration of finances of the government. It is concerned with all economic and financial matters affecting the country as a whole including mobilization of resources for development and other purposes. It regulates expenditure of the government including transfer of resources to the states. This ministry comprises five departments, namely: (i) Economic Affairs; (ii) Expenditure; (iii) Revenue; (iv) Investment & Public Asset Management; and (v) Financial Services.

Department of Economic Affairs

The Department inter alia monitors current economic trends and advises the government on all matters having bearing on internal and external aspects of economic management including, prices, credit, fiscal and monetary policy and investment regulations. All the external, financial and technical assistance received by India, except through specialized international organizations like FAO, ILO, UNIDO and except under international bilateral specific agreement in the field of science and technology, culture and education are also monitored by this Department. The Divisions of the Department of Economic Affairs are: (i) Integrated Finance Division, (ii) Budget Division including Fiscal Responsibility and Budget Management (FRBM), (iii) Financial Market, (iv) Bilateral Cooperation and Administration, (v) Multilateral Institutions, (vi) Multilateral Relations, (vii) Controller of Aid, Accounts and Audit, (viii) Economic Division (ix) Investment & Currency (x) Infrastructure and Energy.

The Department of Economic Affairs is also responsible for preparation and presentation of Union Budget to the Parliament and the budget for the state governments under President's Rule and union territory administrations. The Directorate of Currency has the administrative control of the Security Printing and Minting Corporation of India Limited (SPMCIL), a wholly owned Government of India Corporation that manage Government of India Mints, Currency Presses, Security Presses and Security Paper Mill. In addition to formulating and executing policies and programmes relating to designs/ security feature of bank notes and coins and issue of commemorative coins, the Directorate of Currency has also been mandated to conduct research and development activities in this area and indigenization of all materials required for production of bank note and others security products.

Annual Budget

The Union Budget of India, also called the General Budget, is presented each year on the last working day of February by the Finance Minister of India in Parliament.

Annual Financial Statement

Under Article 112 of the Constitution, a statement of estimated receipts and expenditure of the Government of India has to be laid before Parliament in respect of every financial year. This statement titled 'Annual Financial' Statement is the main budget document. The Annual Financial Statement shows the receipts and payments of government under the three parts in which government accounts are kept: (i) Consolidated Fund, (ii) Contingency Fund and (iii) Public Account.

All revenues received by government, loans raised by it, and also its receipts from recoveries of loans granted by it, form the 'Consolidated Fund'. All expenditure of Government is incurred from the Consolidated Fund and no amount can be withdrawn from the fund without authorisation from Parliament.

Occasions may arise when Government may have to meet urgent unforeseen expenditure pending authorisation from Parliament. The Contingency 'Fund' is an imprest placed at the disposal of the President to incur such expenditure. Parliamentary approval for such expenditure and for withdrawal of an equivalent amount from the Consolidated Fund is subsequently obtained and the amount spent from Contingency Fund is subsequently recouped to the Fund. The corpus of the Fund authorised by the Parliament, at present, is ₹ 500 crore.

Besides the normal receipts and expenditure of government which relate to the Consolidated Fund, certain other transactions enter government accounts, in respect of which, Government acts more as a banker, for example, transactions relating to provident funds, small savings collections and other deposits, etc. The moneys thus received are kept in the Public Account and the connected disbursements are also made from there. Parliamentary authorisation for such payments from the Public Account is, therefore, not required. In a few cases, a part of the revenue of government is set apart in separate funds for expenditure on specific objects like road development, primary education including mid-day meal scheme, etc. These amounts are withdrawn from the Consolidated Fund with the approval of Parliament and kept in the Public Account for expenditure on the specific objects. The actual expenditure proposed on the specific objects is, also submitted for vote of Parliament.

Under the Constitution, Budget has to distinguish expenditure on revenue account from other expenditure. Government Budget, therefore, comprises of (i) Revenue Budget; and (ii) Capital Budget.

Demands for Grants

The estimates of expenditure from the Consolidated Fund included in the Annual Financial Statement and required to be voted by the Lok Sabha are submitted in the form of Demands for Grants in pursuance of Article 113 of the Constitution. Generally, one Demand for Grant is presented in respect of each Ministry or Department. However, in respect of large Ministries or

Departments more than one Demand is presented. Each Demand normally includes the total provisions required for a service, that is, provisions on account of revenue expenditure, capital expenditure, grants to state and union territory governments and also loans and advances relating to the service. In regard to union territories without Legislature, a separate Demand is presented for each of the union territories. Where the provision for a service is entirely for expenditure charged on the Consolidated Fund, for example, interest payments, a separate Appropriation, as distinct from a Demand, is presented for that expenditure and it is not required to be voted by Parliament. Where, however, expenditure on a service includes both 'voted' and 'charged' items of expenditure, the latter are also included in the Demand presented for that service but the 'voted' and 'charged' provisions are shown separately in that Demand. The Demands for Grants are presented to the Lok Sabha along with the Annual Financial Statement.

Finance Bill

At the time of presentation of the Annual Financial Statement before Parliament, a Finance Bill is also presented in fulfilment of the requirement of Article 110(1) (a) of the Constitution, detailing the imposition, abolition, remission, alteration or regulation of taxes proposed in the budget. A Finance Bill is a Money Bill as defined in Article 110 of the Constitution.

Appropriation Bills

After the Demands for Grants are voted by the Lok Sabha, Parliament's approval to the withdrawal from the Consolidated Fund of the amounts so voted and of the amount required to meet the expenditure charged on the Consolidated Fund is sought through the Appropriation Bill. Under Article 114 (3) of the Constitution, no amount can be withdrawn from the Consolidated Fund without the enactment of such a law by Parliament.

Vote-on-Account

The whole process beginning with the presentation of the budget and ending with discussions and voting on the Demands for Grants requires sufficiently long time. The Lok Sabha is, therefore, empowered by the Constitution to make any grant in advance in respect of the estimated expenditure for a part of the financial year pending completion of procedure for the voting of the Demands. The purpose of the 'Vote on Account' is to keep government functioning, pending voting of 'final supply'. The Vote on Account is obtained from Parliament through an Appropriation (Vote on Account) Bill.

Sources of Revenue

In accordance with the Constitution (Eightieth Amendment) Act, 2000, which has been given retrospective effect from 1996, all taxes to in the Union List, except the duties and taxes referred to in Articles 268 and 260, respective surcharge on taxes and duties referred to in Article 27.1 and any cess levied for specific purpose under any law made by Parliament, shall be levied and collected by the Government of India and shall be distributed between the Union and the states in such manner as may be prescribed by the President on the recommendations of the Finance Commission. For the period 2015-2020, the manner of distribution between the Centre and the States has been prescribed in Presidential Orders issued after considering the recommendations of the Fourteenth Finance Commission. The main sources of Union tax revenue are Customs duties, Union excise duties, Service tax, Corporate and Income taxes. Non tax revenues largely comprise interest receipts, dividends/profits, fines and miscellaneous receipts collected in the exercise of sovereign functions, regulatory charges and license fees and user charges for publicly provided goods and services.

Transfer of Resources

In the revised estimates of 2015-16, the devolution of tax receipts from the Union Government to the states as their share of taxes and duties was ₹ 5,06,193 crore. In budget estimates 2016-17, this amount has been increased to ₹ 5,70,337 crore. Besides, total grants and loans to states and union territories has increased from ₹ 3,24,420 crore in revised estimates 2015-16 to ₹ 3,60,337 crore in budget estimates 2016-17.

Public Debt and Other Liabilities

Public Debt of India is classified into three categories of Union Government liabilities into internal debt, external debt and other liabilities.

Internal debt for Government of India largely consists of fixed tenure and fixed rate government papers (dated securities and treasury bills) which are issued through auctions. These include market loans (dated securities), treasury bills (91, 182 and 364 days) and 14 day treasury bills (issued to state governments only), cash management bills, special securities issued to the Reserve Bank of India (RBI), compensation and other bonds, non-negotiable and non-interest bearing rupee securities issued to international financial institutions and securities issued under market stabilization scheme with a view of reduce dependent on physical gold and reduce imports. In 2015-16, Sovereign Gold bond scheme was launched as part of borrowing.

External debt represents loans received from foreign governments and multilateral institutions. The Union Government does not borrow directly for international capital markets. Its foreign currency borrowing takes place from multilateral agencies and bilateral sources, and is a part of official development assistance (ODA). At present, the Government of India does not borrow in the international capital markets.

"Other" liabilities category, not a part of public debt, includes other interest bearing obligations of the government, such as post office saving deposits, deposits under small savings schemes, loans raised through post office cash certificates, provident funds and certain other deposits.

Indian Economic Growth

The growth of the Indian economy accelerated in 2015-16, despite the unfavorable global economic situation. The growth in Gross Domestic Product (GDP) at constant (2011-12) market prices for the year 2015-16 has been estimated at 7.6 per cent as per the provisional estimates of the Central Statistics Office, as against 7.2 per cent in 2014-15. At the sectoral level, the growth rate of GVA at constant (2011-12) basic prices for agriculture and allied sectors, industry and services sectors for the year 2015-16 were estimated to be 1.2 per cent, 7.4 per cent and 8.9 per cent respectively. The corresponding growth rates during the 2014-15 were (-) 0.2 per cent, 5.9 per cent and 10.3 per cent respectively. On the demand side, India's recent growth acceleration has been mainly consumption-driven. The share of final consumption in GDP in 2015-16 was 70.1 per cent, as compared to 68.5 per cent in 2014-15.

Devolution of resources from the Union to the states is a salient feature of the system of federal finance of India. Apart from their share of Central taxes and duties, state governments receive statutory and other grants as well as loans for various development and non-development purposes. The total amount of resources directly transferred to the states during 2004-05 onwards and estimates for 2015-16 and 2016-17 are shown in the following table. In addition, resources are also transferred by Central government to the implementing agencies under various schemes.

Table 13.1 : Resources Transferred to States

(₹ in crore)

Period	Taxes and Duties	Grants	Loans (Gross)	Total
2012-13	2,91,547	1,75,202	10,661	4,77,410
2013-14	3,18,230	1,91,642	11,008	5,20,880
2014-15	3,37,808	3,28,343	11,940	6,78,091
2015-16 (RE)	5,06,193	2,96,483	12,607	8,15,283
2016-17 (BE)	5,70,337	2,69,713	12,610	8,52,660

Source: Central Government Budget Documents

Annual Budget

An estimate of all anticipated receipts and expenditure of the Union for the ensuing financial year is laid before the Parliament. This is known as 'Annual Financial Statement' or 'Budget' and records Central government's transactions of all kinds, in and outside India, during the preceding year, the year in which the statement is prepared as well as ensuing year or the 'Budget Year' as it is known.

The presentation of budget is followed by a general discussion on it in both the Houses of Parliament. Estimates of expenditure from the Consolidated Fund of India are placed before the Lok Sabha in the form of 'Demands for Grants'. All withdrawals of money from the Consolidated Fund are thereafter authorized by an Appropriation Act passed by the Parliament every year. Tax proposals of budget are embodied in a Bill, which is passed as the 'Finance Act' of the year. Estimates of receipts and expenditure are similarly presented by the state governments in their legislatures before the beginning of the financial year and legislative sanction for expenditure is secured through similar procedure. Budgetary position of the Union Government from 2011-12 onwards is shown in Table 13.2.

Table 13.2 : Budgetary Position of the Union Government

(₹ in crore)

	2012-13 Actual	2013-14 Actual	2014-15 Actual	2015-16 Revised Estimates	2016-17 Budget Estimates
1. Revenue receipts	8,79,232	1,014,724	1,101,473	1,206,084	1,377,022
2. Revenue expenditure	1,243,514	1,371,772	1,466,992	1,547,673	1,731,037
3. Revenue deficit	3,64,282	3,57,048	3,65,519	3,41,589	3,54,015
4. Capital receipts	5,31,140	5,44,724	5,62,199	5,79,307	6,01,037
5. Recoveries of loans & other receipts	40,950	41,865	51,475	44,218	67,134
6. Borrowings and other liabilities*	4,90,190	5,02,859	5,10,724	5,35,089	5,33,903
7. Capital expenditure	1,66,858	1,87,675	196,681	2,37,718	2,47,023
8. Total receipts	1,410,372	1,559,448	1,663,672	1,785,391	1,978,059
9. Total expenditure	1,410,372	1,559,447	1,663,673	1,785,391	1,978,060
10.Draw down of cash balance	-51,012	-19,171	77,752	-22,084	13,195
11. Fiscal deficit [(1+5)-9=6]	4,90,190	5,02,858	5,10,725	5,35,089	5,33,904

Source: Central Government Budget Documents

**Includes Draw-down of Cash Balances*

Initiatives in Fiscal Management

Persistent fiscal deficit and concomitant growth in public debt burden have been identified as the most difficult challenges affecting the country's economic growth prospects. To check the potentially damaging impact of the lack of fiscal discipline on macro-economic parameters, the Parliament passed the Fiscal Responsibility and Budget Management (FRBM) Act 2003 which came into force in July 2004. The FRBM Act, *inter alia*, mandated the government to eliminate the revenue deficit by 2007-08.

Keeping in view of the global financial crisis and its adverse impact on the Indian economy, the fiscal targets, mandated by the FRBM Act, got revised from time to time. The budget for 2016-17 estimates the fiscal deficit for 2016-17 at 3.5 per cent of GDP. The Medium Term Fiscal Policy Statement 2016-17 has provided the roadmap for renewed fiscal consolidation with fiscal deficit declining to 3.0 per cent of GDP in 2017-18 and 2018-19. The deficit targets envisaged in the Budget 2016-17 are given in Table 13.3.

Table 13.3: Fiscal Indicators-Rolling Targets as Percentage of GDP (at current market prices)

S.No.	Item	Revised Estimates 2015-16	Budget Estimates 2016-17	Targets for 2017-18	2018-19
1	Revenue deficit	2.5	2.3	1.8	1.3
2	Fiscal deficit	3.9	3.5	3.0	3.0
3	Gross tax revenue	10.8	10.8	10.9	11.1
4	Total outstanding liabilities at the end of the year	47.6	47.1	46.8	44.4

Source: Union Budget Documents, 2016-17

Notes:

1. "GDP" is the Gross Domestic Product at current market prices as per new series from 2011-12.

2. "Total outstanding liabilities" include external public debt at current exchange rates. For projections, constant exchange rates have been assumed. Liabilities do not include part of NSSF and total MSS liabilities which are not used for Central government deficit.

Public Debt

Public debt includes internal debt comprising borrowings inside the country like market loans, compensations and other bonds, treasury bills issued to finance state governments, commercial banks and other parties as well as non-negotiable non-interest bearing rupee securities issued to the international financial institutions and external debt comprising loans from foreign countries, international financial institutions, etc. Table 4 gives the details of public debt and "other liabilities" of the central government. The "other liabilities" include outstanding against the various small saving schemes, provident funds, securities issued to the oil marketing companies, fertilizer companies and Food Corporation of India, reserve funds and deposits and other items.

Table 13.4: Public Debt and other Liabilities of Government of India (As at the end of March)

(₹ in crore)

Item	2012-13	2013-14	2014-15	2015-16 Revised Estimates	2016-17 Budget Estimates
A Public Debt (1+2)	3,920,961	4,425,348	4,935,804	5,520,634	6,029,868
1 Internal Debt (i to xi)	3,764,566	4,240,767	4,738,290	5,311,636	5,801,775
i Market Stablisation Scheme					20,000
ii Market loan	2,984,309	3,441,641	3,891,734	4,296,663	4,723,333
iii Spl. securities converted into marketable securities	76,818	72,818	67,818	64,818	64,818
iv Other special securities issued to RBI	1,489	1,489	1,489	1,489	–
v Compensation, other bonds and securities	13,837	13,628	13,440	9,906	16,210
vii 14 days Treasury Bills	118,380	86,816	85,678	85,678	85,678
vii 91 days Treasury Bills	105,142	125,761	128,961	176,511	193,160
viii 182 days Treasury Bills	64,196	76,417	77,337	87,572	87,572
ix 364 days Treasury Bills	130,467	136,956	143,152	154,033	154,033
x Securities issued to International Financial Institutions	32,226	35,181	46,395	99,262	99,160
xi Securities against	216,808	229,165	261,391	314,809	33,6917
Small Savings	20,894	20,894	20,894	20,894	20,894
2 External Debt*	177,289	184,581	197,514	208,998	228,093
B Other Liabilities @	1,128,737	1,244,081	1,306,716	1,371,579	1,408,613
3 Total Public Debt and Other Liabilities (A+B)	5,049,698	5,669,429	6,242,520	6,892,213	7,438,481

Source: Central Government Budget Documents

* *Balances are according to book value*

@ *Comprises accruals under National Small Savings Fund, Provident Funds, Reserve funds and Deposits Special Securities in lieu of subsidies to oil marketing companies, fertilizer companies and FCI and other items*

Inflation

Headline inflation based on Consumer Price Index (Combined), which remained sticky around 9-10 per cent during 2012–2014, moderated significantly to 5.9 per cent in 2014-15 and further to 4.9 per cent in 2015-16. It averaged 5.8 per cent in 2016-17 (Apr-Jul) and stood at 6.1 per cent in July 2016. Food inflation based on Consumer Food Price Index (CFPI) which was 6.4 per cent in 2014-15 moderated to 4.9 per cent in 2015-16. It averaged 7.5 per cent in 2016-17 (Apr-Jul) and stood at 8.4 percent in July 2016. During the current financial year 2016-17 (Apr-Jul), average food inflation has remained high mainly due to high inflation in pulses, vegetables and sugar. CPI core inflation (non-food non-fuel), remained sticky around 4.7 per cent in the current fiscal. Inflation in terms of other CPI's, viz, Consumer Price Index for industrial workers, agricultural labourers and rural labourers averaged around 6 per cent in the current fiscal.

Headline inflation measured in terms of Wholesale Price Index (WPI) which remained persistently high at around 6-9 per cent during 2011-14 moderated to 2 per cent in 2014-15 and further to (-) 2.5 per cent in 2015-16. It averaged 1.8 per cent in 2016-17 (Apr-Jul) and stood at 3.5 per cent in July 2016. WPI food inflation (food articles + food products) which averaged 9.4 per cent during 2013-14 moderated to 4.9 per cent in 2014-15 and further to 2.6 per cent in 2015-16. It averaged 8.4 per cent in 2016-17 (Apr-Jul) and stood at 11.3 per cent in July 2016.

Table 13.5: Inflation based on WPI and CPI

(in per cent)

	WPI Headline	WPI Food	CPI (Combined) Headline	CPI Food (CFPI*)
2012-13	7.4	9.3	10.2	12.2
2013-14	6.0	9.4	9.5	11.3
2014-15	2.0	4.9	5.9	6.4
2015-16	-2.5	2.6	4.9	4.9
Apr-16	0.8	6.0	5.5	6.4
May-16	1.2	8.1	5.8	7.5
Jun-16	1.6	8.2	5.8	7.8
Jul-16	3.5	11.3	6.1	8.4

Source: *Office of Economic Adviser- DIPP and CSO.* **CFPI: Consumer Food Price Index*

Note: *WPI figures for last two months and CPI figures for last one month are provisional*

Measures to Control Inflation

The government reviews the price situation regularly as price stability remains high on its agenda and has taken a number of measures to control inflation. The steps taken, inter alia, include, (i) increased allocation of ₹ 900 crore for Price Stabilization Fund in the budget 2016-17 to check volatility of prices of essential commodities, in particular of pulses; (ii) decision taken to create buffer stock of pulses through domestic procurement and imports; (iii) announced higher Minimum Support Prices so as to incentivize production; (iv) issued advisory to States/UTs to take strict action against hoarding and black marketing under the Essential Commodities Act 1955 and the Prevention of Black-marketing and Maintenance of Supplies of Essential Commodities Act, 1980; (v) imposed 20 per cent duty on export of sugar and (vi) imposed minimum export price (MEP) of US$ 360 per tonne on potato.

Revised Monetary Policy Framework

As per the revised Monetary Policy Framework, the government has fixed the inflation target of 4 per cent with tolerance level of +/- 2 per cent for the period beginning from August, 2016 to March 2021. If the average inflation is more than or lower than the prescribed tolerance level for three consecutive quarters it would mean a failure to achieve the inflation target. RBI shall set out a report stating the reasons for failure to achieve the inflation target, remedial actions proposed to be taken by it and estimate of the time period with in which the inflation target shall be achieved pursuant to the timely implementation of proposed remedial actions.

The monetary policy stance of the Reserve Bank of India (RBI) has remained accommodative since January 2015. The RBI has cut the repo rate by 150 basis points since January 2015. Consequently, the repo rate has come down from 8 per cent in January 2015 to 6.5 per cent as of August 2016. However, the transmission of monetary policy has remained incomplete. The reduction in average base rate has only been nearly 62 basis points. The base lending rate in July 2016 was 9.30/9.70 per cent as compared to 10.00/10.25 in January 2015.

Agriculture and Food Management

During the South West Monsoon Season of 2016, the cumulative rainfall received for the country as a whole has been 1 per cent above normal. The actual rainfall received during the monsoon 2016, as on 15.08.2016 has been 593.3 mm as against the normal at 589.2 mm. Out of the total 36 meteorological subdivisions, 7 subdivisions received excess season rainfall, 23 subdivisions received normal season rainfall and the remaining 6 subdivisions received deficient season rainfall.

As per the 4th Advance Estimates released by Ministry of Agriculture production of total foodgrains during 2015-16 is estimated at 252.2 million tonnes compared to 252.0 million tonnes in 2014-15 (Final).

Table 13.6: Production of Major Agricultural Crops

Crops	Production (in Million Tonnes)			
	2012-13 (Final)	2013-14 (Final)	2014-15 (Final)	2015-16 (4th AE)
Total foodgrains	257.1	265.0	252.0	252.2
Rice	105.2	106.7	105.5	104.3
Wheat	93.5	95.9	86.5	93.5
Total coarse cereals	40.0	43.3	42.9	37.9
Total pulses	18.3	19.3	17.2	16.5
Total oilseeds	30.9	32.8	27.5	25.3
Sugarcane	341.2	352.1	362.3	352.2
Cotton#	34.2	35.9	34.8	30.1

Source: DES, DAC&FW, M/o Agriculture & Farmers Welfare. # Million bales of 170 kgs each

Foodgrains (rice and wheat) stocks held by Food Corporation of India and state agencies were 54.85 million tonnes as on July 1, 2016 vis-à-vis the buffer stock norm of 41.12 million tonnes as on July 1, 2016.

Price support policies for agricultural commodities are announced with a view to encourage higher investment and production, and to safeguard the interest of consumers by making available supplies at reasonable prices. Substantial hikes in Minimum Support Prices (MSPs) were given in 2011-12 and 2012-13 as compared to the previous years. However, in 2013-14, 2014-15 and 2015-16 MSPs were increased moderately.

Industry & Infrastructure

Indian economy has emerged as fastest growing economy by riding high on the performance of manufacturing sector. As per the provisional estimates of annual national income, 2015-16, the growth of industrial sector comprising mining, manufacturing, electricity and construction was 7.4 per cent in 2015-16 as compared to 5.9 per cent in 2014-15. The manufacturing sector attained 9.3 per cent growth in 2015-16 as against 5.5 per cent in 2014-15. The industrial sector growth has accelerated due to several measures undertaken by the government in the recent years.

(i) Index of Industrial Production

The Index of Industrial Production (IIP) which is quick estimates of the performance of key industrial sectors increased by 2.4 per cent in 2015-16 as compared to growth of 2.8 per cent in 2014-15. Electricity sector registered a growth of 5.7 per cent during 2015-16 as compared to 8.4 per cent during 2014-15. Mining sector increased by 2.2 per cent in 2015-16 as compared to 1.5 per cent in 2014-15. Manufacturing sector registered a growth of 2.0 per cent in 2015-16 as compared to 2.3 per cent in 2014-15.

Basic goods sector registered growth of 3.6 per cent in 2015-16 as compared to 7.0 per cent in 2014-15. The growth in capital goods sector was (-) 2.9 per cent during 2015-16 as compared to 6.4 per cent during 2014-15. The intermediate sector growth was 2.5 per cent in 2015-16 as compared to 1.7 per cent in 2014-15. Consumer durable sector registered tremendous growth of 11.5 per cent in 2015-16 as compared to a decline of 12.6 per cent in 2014-15. The production of consumer non-durable goods fell by 1.8 per cent during 2015-16 as compared to increase in production by 2.8 per cent during 2014-15.

(ii) Eight Core Infrastructure Supportive Industries

The eight core infrastructure supportive industries, namely, coal, crude oil, natural gas, refinery products, fertilizers, steel, cement and electricity with a total weight of 37.90 per cent in the Index of Industrial Production (IIP) have registered a growth of 2.7 per cent in 2015-16 as compared to 4.5 per cent in 2014-15. The growth was 4.6 per cent in the coal sector, 3.8 per cent in refinery products, 11.3 per cent in fertilizers, 4.7 per cent in cement and 5.4 per cent in electricity during 2015-16. Crude oil, natural gas, and steel sectors have shown negative growth in 2015-16.

Social Infrastructure

Social infrastructure like education and health are critical for improving the productivity of the population. Lack of access to affordable and quality health and educational facilities lead to economic impoverishment and lowers potential human capabilities. Economic development needs to be inclusive by involving all sections of society, deprived and marginalized groups like women and children, scheduled tribes, scheduled castes, the differently abled and senior citizens. Thus, India has to address the challenges of not just providing employment but of increasing the employability of the labour force, which is correlated to knowledge and skills developed through quality education and training along with ensuring good quality of health.

Services Sector Performance

Services sector remains the key driver of India's economic growth, contributing almost 65.1 per cent of its gross value added (GVA) growth in 2015-16. Its share in total GVA had risen from 49.0 per cent in 2011-12 to 53.2 per cent in 2015-16 as per Provisional Estimates (PE). With a 20.6 per cent share, 'financial, real estate, and professional services' as a group is the largest contributor to GVA among the various services sub-sectors.

In 2015-16, growth of the services sector decelerated to 8.9 per cent as compared to 10.3 per cent in 2014-15. This sector's growth is much higher than the overall GVA growth of 7.2 per cent and 7.3 per cent GDP growth at market prices in 2014-15. The lower growth in services sector during 2015-16 was mainly due to the high deceleration in combined growth of transport, storage, communication and services related to broadcasting and public administration, defence and other services' despite acceleration in growth of trade, repairs, hotels and restaurants. While the growth of services sector is still higher than industrial and agriculture sectors, the deceleration is due to the slow growth in world output and external trade which is reflected in the fall in growth of transportation services and related sectors.

Services trade

In 2015-16 services exports growth declined by 2.1 per cent to US$ 154.3 billion compared to positive growth of 4.1 per cent in previous year and import of services grew by 4.3 per cent to US$ 84.6 billion compared to growth of 3.3 per cent in previous year. This has resulted in decline in growth of net services growth by 9.0 per cent in 2015-16 compared to 5.0 per cent growth in previous year. In 2015-16, net services financed almost 53.6 per cent of the India's trade deficit.

India's External Sector Performance

(i) Global Economic Environment

In its latest World Economic Outlook (WEO) Update, published in July 2016, the IMF has revised down its global growth estimate for 2016 and 2017 by 0.1 percentage point, to 3.1 per cent and 3.4 per cent respectively. The IMF's growth forecast for India has been revised down by 0.1 per cent to 7.4 per cent in 2016 and 2017 and this surpasses the projection of 6.6 per cent and 6.2 per cent respectively for China. India has overtaken China as the fastest growing major economy in the world, expanding by 7.6 per cent in 2015 compared to China's growth rate of 6.9 per cent due to the slowdown in the Chinese economy.

(ii) India's International Trade Development

India's merchandise exports (customs basis) declined by 1.3 per cent to US$ 310.3 billion in 2014-15. In 2015-16, exports declined by 15.6 per cent (US$ 262.0 billion vis-à-vis US$ 310.3 billion in the previous year). Imports declined by 0.5 per cent in 2014-15. Imports for 2015-16 were at US$ 380.4 billion which is lower by 15.1 per cent as compared to US$ 448.0 billion in the previous year. Petroleum, Oil and Lubricants (POL) imports declined by 40.1 per cent in 2015-16 to US$ 82.9 billion as compared to US$ 138.3 billion in the previous year, mainly due to fall in international crude oil prices. Non-POL imports for 2015-16 decreased by 3.9 per cent compared to the previous year. Gold and silver imports declined by 9.0 per cent in 2015-16 to US$ 35.4 billion as against US$ 38.9 billion in 2014-15. During 2015-16, trade deficit decreased to US$ 118.4 billion as against US$ 137.7 billion in 2013-14. There has been significant market diversification in India's trade from Europe and America to Asia and Africa in recent years—a process that has helped in coping with the sluggish global demand.

(iii) Foreign Exchange Reserves

India's foreign exchange reserves comprise foreign currency assets (FCAs), gold, SDRs and reserve tranche position (RTP) in the IMF. Accretion to foreign exchange reserves is the outcome of absorption of excess of capital flows balance over the current account financing needs and valuation gain/loss. In the recent past, trade deficit witnessed moderation, reflecting the impact of lower crude oil prices, among others. In the fiscal 2015-16, foreign exchange reserves remained in the range of US$ 348.4 billion to US$ 360.2 billion. Foreign exchange reserves stood at US$ 363.5 billion at end June 2016, showing an increase of US$ 3.3 billion over the level of US$ 360.2 billion at end-March 2016.

(iv) Exchange Rate of Rupee

In the fiscal 2015-16, the average monthly exchange rate of rupee (RBI's reference rate) was in the range of ₹ 62-68 per US dollar (₹ 62.75 per US dollar in April 2015 and ₹ 68.24 per US dollar in February 2016). The annual average exchange rate of rupee for 2015-16 was ₹ 65.47 per US dollar, showing a depreciation of 6.6 per cent over ₹ 61.4 per US dollar in 2014-15. During 2016-17, the average monthly exchange rate of rupee was ₹ 66.47 per US dollar in April, 2016, ₹ 66.91 in May 2016, ₹ 67.29 in June 2016, and ₹ 67.21 in July 2016, showing an appreciation of 0.9 per cent and 0.2 per cent for April and May and depreciation of 2.2 per cent and 1.9 per cent for June and July over the level of ₹ 67.06 per US dollar in March 2016.

(v) External Debt

External debt stock stood at US$ 485.6 billion at end-March 2016 recording an increase of 2.2 per cent over the level at end-March 2015. On a quarterly basis, total external debt at end-March 2016 increased by US$ 5.9 billion from the end-December 2015 level. Long-term debt accounted for 82.8 per cent of total external debt at end-March 2016 (82.0 per cent at end-March 2015). Short-term external debt was US$ 83.4 billion at end-March 2016, as compared to US$ 85.5 billion at end-March 2015. The share of commercial borrowings stood highest at 37.3 per cent followed by NRI deposits (26.1 per cent) and short term trade credit (16.5 per cent) at end-March 2016. Sovereign debt stood at US$ 93.4 billion, accounting for 19.2 per cent of the total external debt as compared to 18.9 per cent at end-March 2015. The US dollar denominated debt continued to be the largest component of India's external debt with a share of 57.1 per cent at end-March 2016, followed by Indian rupee (28.9 per cent), SDR (5.8 per cent), Japanese Yen (4.4 per cent) and Euro (2.5 per cent). India's foreign exchange reserves provided a cover of 74.2 per cent to the total external debt stock at the end of March 2016 as compared to 71.9 per cent at end-March 2015.

Infrastructure Financing

Given the enormity of the investment requirements and the limited availability of public resources for investment in physical infrastructure, it is imperative to explore avenues for increasing investment in infrastructure through various sources. In view of this, government has launched the following to mobilize the long term investment in infrastructure:-

i) Bank Financing: Banks continue to be major source of financing infrastructure in India. The outstanding bank credit to the infrastructure sector, which stood at INR 95 billion (US$ 1418 million) in March 2001, has increased gradually to INR 10,074 billion (US$ 150.36 billion) in March 2015, a compound annual growth rate (CAGR) of 39.5 per cent over the last 14 years.

ii) Institutional Finance: The Government has also set up *India Infrastructure Finance Company Limited (IIFCL)* with the specific mandate to play a catalytic role in the infrastructure sector by providing long-term debt for financing infrastructure projects. IIFCL funds viable infrastructure projects through Long Term Debt, Refinance to Banks and Financial Institutions for loans granted by them, with tenor exceeding 10 years or any other mode approved by the Government. PFC, IREDA, REC have also played a critical role in taking the infrastructure agenda forward by way of institutional finance targeting key sectors such as energy both new and renewable energy.

iii) Infrastructure Debt Funds (IDFs): Government has conceptualized the idea of IDF, which is an innovative attempt, for addressing the issue of sourcing long term debt for infrastructure projects. Potential investors under IDFs may include off-shore institutional investors, off-shore high net worth individuals, and other institutional investors (insurance funds, pension funds, sovereign wealth funds, etc.). IDFs can be set up either as a Trust or as a NBFC.

iv) Real Estate Investment Trusts (REITs)/Infrastructure Investment Trust (InvITs) - Government has announced REITs and InvITs – innovative financing instruments for financing real estate and infrastructure projects. The Infrastructure Investment Trust (InvITs) and Real Estate Investment Trusts (REITs) are trust-based structures that maximize returns through efficient tax pass-through and improved governance structures.

v) Municipal Borrowing- Government has initiated a pilot project for developing a framework to build capacities of Urban Local Bodies (ULBs) to raise financing through the capital markets for financing infrastructure projects (normally PPPs). The pilot initiative aims to develop a replicable model and related documents and demonstration of the model through a successful pilot transaction for an ULB. Guidelines for issuance of Municipal Bonds in India have been notified by SEBI. The objective of this exercise is to shortlist four Urban Local Bodies (ULBs) and support them in undertaking a readiness assessment and model development to build preparedness in the ULBs for tapping capital market financing through Municipal Bond issuances, preferably through Corporate Municipal Entity (CME) structures created by the shortlisted ULBs.

vi) Tax Free Bonds: In pursuance of Budget 2015-16, Government of India has allowed the issuance of tax-free bonds of ₹ 43,500 crore (USD 6500 million) during the financial year 2015-16, by Central Public Sector Enterprise (CPSE).

vii) Securitization Trust: In order to get more investment in Asset Reconstruction Companies (ARCs), which play a very important role in resolution of bad debts, Budget 2016-17 provided for a complete pass through of income tax to securitization trusts including trusts of ARCs. This will stimulate the securitization of bank loans and advances and will free substantial banking funds for new infrastructure.

viii) Various norms have been liberalized by respective regulators such as IRDA, RBI, SEBI, and PFRDA to boost the infrastructure investment in India.

ix) Speedy Project Implementation-Facilitation/Debottlenecking of Stalled Projects: With a view to putting in place an institutional mechanism to track stalled investment projects, both in the public and private sectors and to remove implementation bottlenecks in these projects, a cell in the nature of Project Monitoring Group (PMG) has been set up in the Cabinet Secretariat for all large projects, both public and private. Central e-PMS, a web-enabled information system has also been put in place where an entrepreneur can provide the details of projects with investment of over 1000 crore (USD 167 million) each, along with issues inhibiting its smooth implementation.

Public Private Partnerships

Availability of quality infrastructure is a pre-requisite to achieve broad based and inclusive growth on a sustained basis. Infrastructure is also critical for enhancing productivity and export competitiveness. Given the enormity of the investment requirements and the limited availability of public resources for investment in physical infrastructure, the projected infrastructure investments made it imperative to explore avenues for increasing investments in infrastructure through a combination of public investment and Public Private Partnerships (PPPs). PPPs bridge the deficit in financing of infrastructure projects, and also bring in cost effective new technology for operation and maintenance of created asset, thus, extracting long term value for proposition.

India has systematically rolled out a PPP programme for the delivery of high-priority public utilities and infrastructure and, over the last decade or so, developed what is perhaps one of the largest PPP programmes in the world. With close to 1300 PPP projects in various stages of implementation, according to the World Bank, India is one of the leading countries in terms of readiness for PPPs.

The central coordination of PPPs is provided by the PPP Cell within the Department of Economic Affairs (DEA), under the Ministry of Finance. The PPP Cell is responsible for all matters relating to PPPs, including policies, guidelines, schemes, and capacity building initiatives. The PPP Cell also acts as the Secretariat for Private Partnership Appraisal Committee and Empowered Institution (EI)/Empowered Committee (EC) for the projects posed for financial support through DEA's Scheme for financial support to PPPs in infrastructure -Viability Grant Fund (VGF).

Initiatives for Promoting PPPs

a. Institutional Arrangement for Appraisal and Approval of PPP Projects

A major difficulty in building infrastructure through PPPs is the absence of expertise to create and evaluate project proposals. Thus, in order to streamline the appraisal process for PPP projects, the Cabinet Committee on Economic Affairs (CCEA) approved the procedure for approval of PPP projects. Pursuant to this decision, in 2006, the Government of India notified the appraisal mechanism by setting up of the Public Private Partnership Appraisal Committee (PPPAC) responsible for the appraisal of PPP projects in the Central Sector. The appraisal mechanism for the PPP projects was streamlined to ensure speedy appraisal of projects, eliminate delays, adopt international best practices and have uniformity in appraisal mechanisms and guidelines.

b. Standardized Bidding Documents

The Ministry also published standardized bidding documents which include Model Request for Qualification (RFQ) for Pre-Qualification of Bidders for PPP Projects, Model Request for Proposal (RFP) for invitation of Financial Bids for PPP Projects and also a Model RFP for engaging financial consultants and technical advisers for PPP Projects. Standardized contractual documents such as sector specific Model Concession Agreements, which lay down the standard terms relating to allocation of risks, contingent liabilities and guarantees as well as service quality and performance standards have also been developed by various Central ministries such as Ministry of Road Transport and Highways, Ministry of Shipping, etc. These standardized bidding and contractual documents are being adopted by project implementation agencies for developing PPP infrastructure projects in sectors such as ports, roads, airports, food storage (silos), water supply, etc. This has been a defining feature of India's PPP programme.

c. Financial Support to Public Private Partnership in Infrastructure

A scheme to provide financial support (Viability Gap Fund) to PPP projects in Infrastructure in the form of grants with a view to make them commercially viable has also been formulated. Infrastructure projects are often not commercially viable on account of having substantial sunk investment and low returns, however, they continue to be economically essential. Accordingly, the Scheme for Financial support to Public Private Partnership in Infrastructure (Viability Gap Funding Scheme)was formulated to provide financial support in the form of grants, one time or deferred, to infrastructure projects undertaken through PPPs with a view to make them commercially viable. The Scheme provides Viability Gap Funding up to twenty per cent of the Total Project Cost (TPC). The government or statutory entity that owns the project may, if it so decides may provide additional grants out of its budget up to further twenty per cent of the TPC. Viability Gap Funding under the Scheme is normally in the form of a capital grant at the stage of project construction. For the period ending July 2016, 58 projects have been granted final approval of VGF support under the Scheme for a TPC of ₹ 32,764.73 crore and VGF of ₹ 5,797.53 crore.

While quality advisory services are fundamental to developing well-structured, value-for-money PPPs, the costs of procuring PPPs, and particularly the costs of transaction advisors, are significant. Development of robust projects with a sound financial structure and optimal risk allocation is critical for evincing a market response in respect of the projects. The scheme for 'India Infrastructure Project Development Fund' (IIPDF) has been launched to finance the cost incurred towards development of PPP projects. The IIPDF supports up to 75 per cent of the project development expenses.

d. India Infrastructure Finance Company Limited

The Government has also set up India Infrastructure Finance Company Limited (IIFCL) with the specific mandate to play a catalytic role in the infrastructure sector by providing long-term debt for financing infrastructure projects. IIFCL funds viable infrastructure projects through Long Term Debt, Refinance to Banks and Financial Institutions for loans granted by them, with term exceeding 10 years or any other mode approved by the Government.

e. PPP Practitioners Guide

The Government has taken a number of initiatives to promote PPPs in the country and improve the PPP ecosystem in the country. This has resulted in PPPs being implemented in several sectors including, highways, ports and airports. Legislative changes and institutional arrangements have been made to facilitate public authorities to implement PPPs. Financing mechanisms to support PPP have been introduced, including viability gap funding mechanisms. Procurement practices have matured and there are standardized bidding practices. Contract frameworks have been standardized through model concession agreements. Many state governments have set up infrastructure development agencies. Several guidance documents have also been provided to stakeholders to develop capacity and knowledge.

The Department of Economic Affairs (DEA) has developed a comprehensive guidance for practitioners engaged in the PPP development process titled "PPP Guide for Practitioners" intended to provide step-by-step guidance on various processes in the PPP project life cycle including on the pre-award phase. It highlights best practices that could be adopted by practitioners, to ensure transparency, fairness and accountability in the implementation of PPPs. The Guide, available on DEA's PPP Cell website, i.e., pppinindia.gov.in, is divided into 17 modules which discusses a certain stage or concept in the PPP project development process. The Guide is interspersed with examples, key takeaways, web links and case studies.

f. Information Dissemination

i. www.pppinindia.gov.in

DEA, PPP Cell maintains a website dedicated to PPPs, *www.pppinindia.gov.in,* to provide information related to PPP initiatives in India. The website serves as a hub of information on PPP initiatives in India and contains related policy documents, government guidelines issued for mainstreaming such projects. These include information on the institutional mechanisms for speedy appraisal of PPP infrastructure projects and the schemes for financial support to PPP projects. The website also contains various knowledge products developed in the PPP cell, sharing PPP best to enhance the ability of the public officials as well as private developers to implement such projects.

ii. www.infrastructureindia.gov.in

www.infrastructureindia.gov.in is a database of infrastructure projects including PPPs being implemented across the sectors in India. It provides key information on the status of infrastructure projects being executed by government as well as the private sector.

Currency & Coinage

The Currency and Coinage Division deals with policy formulation in respect of currency/bank notes and coins and oversees the production, planning and printing/minting of currency notes and coins. It is responsible for supervision and administrative control of the Security Printing and Minting Corporation of India Ltd. Rules, regulations and approvals of design/security features of bank notes and coins and issue of commemorative coins are also handled by C&C Division.

Security Printing and Minting Corporation of India Ltd. is the only PSU under the Department of Economic Affairs. It was formed after corporatization of nine units, i.e., four mints, four presses (two currency note presses and two security presses) and one paper mill which were earlier functioning under the Ministry of Finance. The Company was incorporated in 2006 under the Companies Act, 1956. It is engaged in the manufacture of security paper, minting of coins, printing of currency and bank notes, non-judicial stamp papers, postage stamps, travel documents, etc. The Company supplies currency/bank notes and coins to RBI, non-judicial stamp papers to various state governments; postal stationery and stamps to postal department; passports, visa stickers and other travel documents to Ministry of External Affairs. Other products include commemorative coins, MICR and non-MICR cheques, etc.

Security Paper Mill, Hoshangabad, a unit of SPMCIL, has successfully commissioned integrated new CWBN paper manufacturing facilities with a state-of-art technology with a capacity of 6000 MT per annum, for commercial production of CWBN paper of denominations ₹ 10, ₹ 20, and ₹ 1000 bank note paper. Commercial production has commenced. In addition, Bank Notes Paper Mill India Private Limited (BNPMIPL) at Mysore, a JV Company between Security Printing and Minting Corporation of India (SPMCIL) and Bharatiya Reserve Bank Note Mudran Private Limited (BRBNMPL), has been set up to increase self-reliance in bank note paper production with a total capacity of around 12000 MT per annum to bring two state of the art technology paper lines. The commercial production has started from both the lines.

Primary Market

Simplified Framework for Capital Raising by Technological Start-ups on Institutional Trading Platform.

Securities Exchange Board of India (SEBI) undertook a review of the extant regulatory framework in the primary market and noted the suggestions of market participants on making the existing avenues for capital raising amenable for accommodating a larger number of start-up companies.

Based on this, the SEBI approved the following proposals to amend the regulations concerning the Institutional Trading Platform (ITP):

i. The platform shall now be called as Institutional Trading Platform (ITP) and shall facilitate capital raising as well.

ii. The said platform will be made accessible to: a) companies which are intensive in their use of technology, information technology, intellectual property, data analytics, bio-technology, nano-technology to provide products, services or business platforms with substantial value addition and with at least 25 per cent of the pre-issue capital being held by Qualified Institutional Buyers (QIBs) (as defined in SEBI [(Issue of Capital and Disclosure Requirements) ICDR] Regulations, 2009), or b). any other company in which at least 50 per cent of the pre-issue capital is held by QIBs.

iii. No person (individually or collectively with persons acting in concert) in such a company shall hold 25 per cent or more of the post-issue share capital.

iv. Considering the nature of business of companies which may list on the said platform, disclosure may contain only broad objects of the issue and there shall be no cap on amount raised for General Corporate Purposes. Further, the lock in of the entire pre-issue capital shall be for a period of six months from the date of allotment uniformly for all shareholders.

v. As the standard valuation parameters such as P/E, EPS, etc., may not be relevant in case of many of such companies, the basis of issue price may include other disclosures, except projections, as deemed fit by the issuers.

vi. Companies intending to list on the proposed ITP, shall be required to file draft offer document with SEBI for observations, as provided in SEBI (ICDR) Regulations, 2009.

vii. Only two categories of investors, i.e., (i) Institutional Investors (QIB as defined in SEBI (ICDR) Regulations, 2009 along with family trusts, systematically important Non-bank financial companies (NBFCs) registered with RBI and the intermediaries registered with SEBI, and (ii) Non-Institutional Investors (NIIs) other than retail individual investors can access the proposed ITP.

viii. In case of public offer, allotment to institutional investors may be on a discretionary basis whereas to NIIs it shall be on proportionate basis. Allocation between the said two categories shall be in the ratio of 75 per cent and 25 per cent, respectively.

ix. In case of discretionary allotment to institutional investors, no institutional investor shall be allotted more than 10 per cent of the issue size. All shares allotted on discretionary basis shall be locked-in in line with requirements for lock in by Anchor Investors i.e., 30 days at present.

x. The minimum application size in case of such issues shall be ₹10 lakh and the minimum trading lot shall be of ₹10 lakh.

xi. The number of allottees in case of a public offer shall be 200 or more.

xii. The company will have the option to migrate to main board after 3 years subject to compliance with eligibility requirements of the stock exchanges.

xiii. For Category I and II Alternative Investment Funds (AIFs), which are required under the SEBI (Alternative Investment Funds) Regulations, 2012 to invest a certain minimum amount in unlisted securities, investment in shares of companies listed on this platform may be treated as investment in 'unlisted securities' for the purpose of calculation of the investment limits.

Streamlining the Process of Public Issues

In order to reduce the post-issue timeline for listing from existing T+12 days to T+6 days, increase the reach of retail investors and reduce the costs involved in public issue of equity shares and convertibles, SEBI took the following decisions:

i. Presently more than 99.5 per cent applications are received from centres where Applications Supported by Blocked Amount (ASBA) facility is available. Based on an analysis of a few public issues, in terms of amount, ASBA applications account for 99.90 per cent of the total bid amount received from all investors. Considering the reach and advantages of ASBA, it shall now be mandatory for all investors to make ASBA applications. Amongst many other significant advantages, ASBA enables investors to give the mandate for payment of application money in the application form itself without suffering loss of interest for the intervening period. It also obviates the hassle of refund of money by the issuer as per the difference in application amount and the amount for which shares are finally allotted.

ii. In order to substantially enhance the points for submission of applications, Registrar and Share Transfer Agents (RTAs) and Depository Participants (DPs) shall also be allowed to accept application forms (both physical as well as online) and make bids on the stock exchange platform. This will be over and above the stock brokers and banks where such facilities are presently available.

iii. To help intermediaries and banks to modify their existing systems and train their staff and also enable the investors to adapt to the new system, there will be a phase-in period of 6 months. Accordingly, a public issue which opens on or after January 01, 2016 will have to follow the new system.

Listing Regulation and Rationalization of Disclosure Norms

SEBI in 2015, issued SEBI (Listing and Disclosure) Regulations, 2015 (hereinafter referred to as 'Regulations') on listing of different segments of the capital market and disclosure norms in relation thereto. These regulations have been structured into one single document consolidating various types of securities listed on the stock exchanges. The latest set of norms provides broad principles for periodic disclosures by listed entities, apart from incorporating corporate governance principles. These regulations shall apply to the listed entity who has listed any of the following designated securities on recognized stock exchange(s): a. specified securities listed on main board or SME Exchange or Institutional trading platform; b. non-convertible debt securities, non-convertible redeemable preference shares, perpetual debt instrument, perpetual non-cumulative preference shares; c. Indian depository receipts; d. securitized debt instruments; e. units issued by mutual funds; and f. any other securities as may be specified by the Board.

These regulations requires every listed entity to disclose events or information (collectively called events) which, in the opinion of the Board of Directors of the Company, are material. The regulations have been structured to provide ease of reference by consolidating into one single document across various types of securities listed on the stock exchanges.

Forfeiture of Partly P[illegible] up Shares—Exemption from SEBI (Takeover Regulations)

a. General Exemption provided for open offer obligations arising due to passive increase in voting rights as a result of expiry of call notice period and forfeiture of shares.

b. SEBI (Takeover Regulations), Regulation 10 provides for instances where exemption would be provided if the total shareholding of a promoter moves above the limits prescribed by SEBI.

Secondary Markets

Reforms in Foreign Investment Policy in Market Infrastructure Institutions

The Government is in process of giving approval for raising foreign shareholding limit from 5 per cent to 15 per cent in Indian Stock Exchanges for a stock exchange. The decision will help enhance global competitiveness of Indian stock exchanges by accelerating/facilitating the adoption of latest technology and global best practices leading to overall growth and development of the Indian Capital Market.

Exclusively Listed Companies of De-recognized/Non-operational/Exited Stock Exchanges

SEBI in the interest of investors of exclusively listed companies of de-recognized/non-operational/exited stock exchanges allowed timeline of eighteen months, within which such companies shall obtain listing upon compliance with the listing requirements of the nation-wide stock exchange. Such listing is permitted only in respect of those classes of securities that were already listed in the non-operational stock exchanges. Also these exclusively listed companies seeking listing on nationwide exchanges shall not undergo any material changes in their shareholding pattern which suggests change of control at the time of listing on nationwide stock exchanges. All the promoters and directors of such companies, who have failed to provide the trading platform or exit to its shareholders, even after the extended time of eighteen months, will have to undergo stricter scrutiny for their any future association with securities market.

Revision of Activity Schedule of Auction Session

In order to facilitate the reduction of time involved in delivering the shares to the buying broker, in case of default by selling broker in a normal settlement, SEBI, provided flexibility to Clearing Corporations to decide the time for conducting the settlement of Auction Session on or before T + 3 day. Earlier the settlement of Auction session i.e. the security delivered short was being delivered to the buying broker on T+3 day.

Exchange Traded Cash Settled Interest Rate Futures

SEBI had prescribed framework for trading of Cash Settled Interest Rate Futures (IRF) on 10-year Government of India Security on Stock Exchanges. To provide hedging instruments for managing interest rate exposure across different maturities of various investments and liabilities of different sets of market participants like corporates and insurance companies and to further enhance depth and liquidity in the underlying bond market, SEBI decided to permit stock exchanges to introduce cash settled IRFs on 6 year and 13 year GoI security. Effectively, exchanges are now permitted to launch IRF contracts on GoI securities with residual maturity between 4 years and 15 years on the day of expiry of IRF contract. Additionally, SEBI permitted stock exchanges to introduce three quarterly contracts of March/June/September/December cycle in addition to three serial monthly contracts of IRFs.

Review of Offer for Sale (OFS) of Shares through Stock Exchange Mechanism

Offer for Sale through Stock Exchange Mechanism (OFS) is one of the mechanism available to the promoters / large shareholders for offloading shares of promoters in listed companies. OFS mechanism has been found to be useful by market participants as it ensures transparency, wider participation and quicker settlement. With the view to encourage retail investors to participate in the OFS and to simplify the bidding process for retail investors, the following modifications to the mechanism were undertaken: a) OFS notice shall continue to be given latest by 5 pm on T-2 days. However, T-2 days shall be reckoned from banking day instead of trading day; b) it would be mandatory for sellers to provide the option to retail investors to place their bids at cut off price in addition to placing price bids.

External Markets

Investment by Foreign Portfolio Investors

With the objective of having a more predictable regime for investment by the foreign portfolio investors (FPI), the medium term framework (MTF) for FPI limits in debt securities has been set out.) The limits for FPI investment in debt securities will henceforth be announced/ fixed in rupee terms. The limits for FPI investment in the Central Government securities will be increased in phases to 5 per cent of the outstanding stock by March 2018. In aggregate terms, this is expected to open up room for additional investment of ₹ 1,200 billion in the limit for central government securities by March 2018 over and above the existing limit of ₹1,535 billion for all government securities (G-sec). Additionally, there will be a separate limit for investment by FPIs in the State Development Loans (SDLs), to be increased in phases to reach 2 per cent of the outstanding stock by March 2018. This would amount to an additional limit of about ₹ 500 billion by March 2018. The increase in limits will be announced every half year in March and September and released every quarter. The existing requirement of investments being made in G-sec (including SDLs) with a minimum residual maturity of three years will continue to apply to all categories of FPIs. Aggregate FPI investments in any Central Government security would be capped at 20 per cent of the outstanding stock of the security. Investments at existing levels in the securities over this limit may continue but not get replenished through fresh purchases by FPIs till these fall below 20 per cent.

Liberalization of External Commercial Borrowings Framework

A new, liberal and revised External Commercial Borrowing (ECB) Framework has been introduced and brought into effect from 2015 by RBI after due consultation with and subsequently being approved by Ministry of Finance. The new ECB framework is more attuned to the current economic and business environment. From regulatory perspective three main clear-cut categories/ track have been created which include Medium term foreign currency denominated ECB (Track-I), Long-term foreign currency denominated ECB (Track-II) and Indian Rupee denominated ECB (Track-III). The new framework has an expanded list of recognized lenders and borrowers comprising overseas regulated financial institutions, SWFs, pension funds, insurance companies, etc., and has an exhaustive list of permissible end-uses with only a small negative list for long-term foreign currency denominated ECB and INR denominated ECB.

Taking into consideration the prevailing external funding sources, particularly for long term lending and the critical needs of infrastructure sector of the country, Government with the objective to promote investments in infrastructure projects, has reviewed the extant ECB guidelines in consultation with the Reserve Bank of India in March, 2016. It has been decided to allow companies in infrastructure sector, Non-Banking Financial Companies-Infrastructure Finance Companies (NBFC-IFCs), NBFCs-Asset Finance

Companies (NBFC-AFCs), Holding Companies and Core Investment Companies (CICs) to raise foreign currency denominated External Commercial Borrowings (ECB) with minimum average maturity period of 5 years subject to 100 per cent hedging. Companies in infrastructure sector have been permitted to utilize the proceeds of ECB so raised for capital expenditure purposes. It is expected that lowering of minimum average maturity period from 10 to 5 years would lead to increase flow of ECBs into India's infrastructure sector and also enable concessional financing from export credit agencies and developmental financial institutions to flow into this sector.

Framework for Overseas Issuance of Rupee Denominated Bonds

In order to facilitate rupee denominated borrowing from overseas, it has been decided to put in place a framework for issuance of rupee denominated bonds overseas within the overarching External Commercial Borrowings policy. Any corporate body, including REITS and InvITs, are eligible to issue rupee denominated bonds overseas and any investor from a FATF compliant jurisdiction is eligible to invest. Only plain vanilla bonds issued in FATF compliant financial centres will be the eligible instrument. The minimum maturity period of these bonds will be 5 years and the all-in-cost of such borrowings should be commensurate with prevailing market conditions. There will be no end-use restrictions except for a negative list which includes investment in real estate and capital markets. Withholding tax of 5 per cent will be applicable on interest income from these bonds and the capital gains arising in case of appreciation of rupee would be exempted from tax.

Approval of GoI has been granted to Government of British Columbia to issue rupee denominated offshore bonds. Further, till May, 2016 it is reported that an amount of INR 1.023 billion in respect of five rupee bonds overseas issuances have been contracted out of which INR 923 million (four issuances) has been contracted to be raised from parent/ group companies. HDFC Bank has also paved way for raising funds through issuance of *Masala Bonds*.

Simplified Procedure for Establishment of Branch Office/Liaison Office / Project Offices

The establishment of BO/LO/PO in India by foreign entities is regulated in terms of FEMA Regulations. Foreign entities can set up their BO/LO/PO in the country without registering themselves as companies/trusts, etc., under Indian Laws. These entities have to seek the approval of Reserve Bank of India before setting up their BO/LO/PO office in India. While Reserve Bank of India generally gives permission in those cases where 100 per cent FDI is allowed under automatic route, all other cases are referred to the Government for approval.

As a measure towards improving the ease of doing business, it has now been decided that except for a few sectors viz. defence, telecom, private security, information and broadcasting and government and Non-government organizations, the power to grant LO/BO/PO approvals would be delegated to the Authorised Dealers Category-I Banks. Further, anyone who has been awarded a contract for a project by a Government authority/PSU should be automatically given approval to open a bank account.

Securities Laws

Merger of SEBI and FMC – Amendment to Securities Contracts (Regulation) Act, 1956

The Securities Contracts (Regulation) Act, 1956 (SCRA)was amended in 2015 in the context of the merger of Forward Markets Commission with SEBI. The Act was amended primarily to incorporate substantive provisions relevant to regulation of commodity derivative markets, which were earlier in the Forward Contracts (Regulation) Act, 1952 which was repealed. The amendment introduced the definition of commodity derivative and included the said term within the definition of derivative thereby bringing commodity derivatives within the ambit of securities. By virtue of the Amendment Act, provisions of the SCRA apply to the erstwhile commodity exchanges and the commodity derivatives market.

New Regulations

The SEBI (Listing Obligations and Disclosure Requirement) Regulation, 2015 was enacted with the objective of consolidating and streamlining the provisions of existing listing agreements for different segments of the capital market viz., Equity (including convertibles) issued by entities listed on the Main Board of the Stock Exchanges, Small and Medium Enterprises listed on SME Exchange and Institutional Trading Platform, Non-Convertible Debt Securities, Non Convertible Redeemable Preference Shares, Indian Depository Receipts, Securitized Debt Instruments and Units issued by Mutual Fund Schemes. The regulations are structured to provide ease of reference by consolidating into one single document across various types of securities listed on the stock exchanges.

SEBI (Issue and Listing of Debt Securities by Municipality) Regulations, 2015 was enacted to provide a regulatory framework for governing issuance of bonds by the Municipalities and listing of the same and enables investors thereof to make an informed investment decision before investing in the municipal bonds by providing for adequate disclosures by the prospective issuers.

Tax Pass through for (Alternative Investment Fund) Category I and II

Under the SEBI Alternative Investment Fund (AIF) Regulations, 2012 various types of Alternative Investment Funds (AIFs) have been classified under three separate categories as Category I, II, and III AIFs. Category I AIFs are funds that invest in start-up or early stage ventures or social ventures or SMEs or infrastructure or other sectors or areas which the government or regulators consider as socially or economically desirable. Category II AIFs are funds including private equity funds or debt funds which do not fall in category I and II and which do not undertake leverage or borrowing other than to meet day-to-day operational requirements. Category III AIFs are funds which employ diverse or complex trading strategies and may employ leverage including through investment in listed or unlisted derivatives.

Resource Mobilization by Mutual Funds and Initial Public Offer

Till July 2016, Mutual Funds mobilized ₹1,93,160 crore. Public sector mobilized ₹ 45,088 crore and the private sector mobilized ₹148,072 crore. The market value of asset under management stood at ₹15,18,097 crore as on July 31, 2016 compared to ₹12,32,823 crore as on March 31, 2016, indicating an increase by 23.13 per cent.

Financial Literacy and Investment Education

SEBI takes various initiatives to spread financial literacy, and investor education with a view to building the capacity of investors in securities market. As part of its financial literacy initiatives, it conducts financial education workshops through its resource persons for seven different target groups, and also invites group of students from educational institutes for a visit. During 2015-16, over 8,700 resource person workshops and over 270 visit to SEBI programmes were conducted across the country.

As part of its initiatives to educate investors, SEBI maintains an updated dedicated website http://investor.sebi.gov.in, conduct various programmes including regional seminars, joint programmes with stock exchanges / depositories, programmes through recognised Investors' Association, campaigns through mass media, etc, across the country specifically in the tier II and tier III cities /locations.

SEBI (Prohibition of Insider Trading) Regulations

The SEBI (Prohibition of Insider Trading) Regulations, 1992 were notified in 1992, which was framed to deter the practice of insider trading in the securities of listed companies. Since then there had been several amendments in the securities of listed companies. Since then there had been several amendments to the regulations. To ensure that the regulatory framework dealing with insider trading in India is further strengthened, SEBI sought review of the extant insider trading regulatory regime. The new regulations strengthen the legal and enforcement framework, align Indian regime with international practices, provide clarity with respect to the definitions and concepts, and facilitate legitimate business transactions. SEBI has notified the SEBI (Prohibition of Insider Trading) Regulations, 2015 in 2015 which has replaced the existing regulations of 1992 with effect from May 2015.

SEBI issued guidelines in 2015 regarding system-driven disclosures wherein the onus of disclosure shifted from individuals/companies to the securities market infrastructure through integration among depositories, exchanges and registrar and transfer agents (RTAs). Initially, the system has been made operational parallel to disclosures by individual entities in respect of certain disclosures under SAST and PIT regulations. Once it stabilises, it will replace manual disclosure obligations. Such a system would aid in eliminating the possibility of inadvertent violations by the entities and would help in providing information to investors on timely basis to take investment decisions and would thus lead to fairness in the markets.

SEBI (Delisting of Equity Shares)(Amendment) Regulations

In order to ensure that small companies proposing to delist their equity shares from recognised stock exchanges are not put to undue hardship due to no trading, the amended regulations state that in case of delisting of small companies, the earlier criteria of shares traded on stock exchanges be replaced by the criteria that the total equity shares traded on the stock exchanges be less than 10 per cent of the total equity shares. Further, the exit price offered to the public shareholders shall not be less than the floor price determined in terms of sub-regulation (2) of regulation 15 of SEBI (Substantial Acquisition of Shares and Takeovers) Regulations, 2011.

Major Policy Developments

Offshore Derivative Instrument (ODI)

The norms relating to issuance and transfer of ODIs have been tightened and instructions have been issued on Know Your Client (KYC) norms for ODI subscribers, transferability of ODIs, reporting of suspicious transactions, periodic review of systems and modified ODI reporting format. A brief detail is as follows:

Applicability of Indian KYC/AML Norms for Client Due Diligence: ODI Issuers shall now be required to identify and verify the beneficial owners (BO) in the subscriber entities, who hold in excess of the threshold as defined under Rule 9 of the Prevention of Money-laundering (Maintenance of Records) Rules, 2005 i.e., 25 per cent in case of a company and 15 per cent in case of partnership firms/ trusts/ unincorporated bodies.

KYC Review: The KYC review shall be done on the basis of the risk criteria as determined by the ODI issuers.

Suspicious Transactions Report: ODI issuers shall be required to file suspicious transaction reports, if any, with the Indian Financial Intelligence Unit, in relation to the ODIs issued by it.

Periodic Operational Evaluation: ODI issuers shall be required to put in place necessary systems and carry out a periodical review and evaluation of its controls, systems and procedures with respect to the ODIs. A certificate in this regard should be submitted on an annual basis to SEBI by the Chief Executive Officer or equivalent of the ODI issuer.

Prior Consent of FPI for Transfer: Prior consent of FPI shall be required to be obtained for transfer of ODI. In this regard, necessary changes in SEBI (FPI) Regulations, 2014 are separately being carried out.

New Depository Receipts Scheme

The New Depository Receipts (DR) Scheme, 2014 formulated on the basis of M.S. Sahoo Committee Recommendations has come into effect from December 2014. Enabling tax amendments pertaining to new DR Scheme have been provided vide Finance Act of 2015. The new DR Scheme allows: i. issuance of Depository Receipts (DRs) against any underlying securities - equity or debt; ii. issuance by any issuer - listed or unlisted; iii. DRs can be issued both for capital raising through new shares or against existing/ secondary shares; iv. issuance may be either sponsored or unsponsored ; and v. DRs will count as public shareholding if they have attached voting rights for holder.

Deepening of Currency Derivatives Market

On the basis of the guidelines issued by RBI and the discussions with stock exchanges, SEBI had permitted stock exchanges to offer currency option contracts in EUR-INR, GBP-INR and USD-INR currency pairs, in addition to the existing USD-INR pair.

Equity Derivatives

The minimum contract size in equity derivatives segment was increased from ₹ 2 lakh to ₹ 5 lakh. Accordingly, the framework for determination of lot size for derivatives contracts were modified.

Interest Rate Derivatives

SEBI permitted stock exchanges to introduce cash settled Interest Rate Futures on six-year and 13-year security. The product specifications, position limits and risk management framework for both IRF products were specified by SEBI.

Currency Derivatives

SEBI revised the transaction limit in exchange traded currency derivatives to $ 15 million, from $10 million previously, for both foreign and domestic investors without having to establish the existence of any underlying exposure. In consultation with RBI, position limits for bank stock brokers, as authorized by RBI, the gross open position across all contracts was revised as 15per cent of the total open interest or USD 1 billion, whichever is higher.

Mutual Funds

Major policy developments in Mutual Funds (MFs) since August 2015 are as follows:

To mitigate risks arising on account of high levels of exposure in the wake of events pertaining to credit downgrades and to put MFs in a better position to handle adverse credit events, SEBI has tightened exposure limits on investments by MFs. Single issuer limits (that have been merged for money market instruments and non-money market instruments) have been reduced to 10 per cent of Net Asset Value (NAV) (extendable to 12 per cent of NAV with the prior approval of the Board of Trustees and the Board of Asset Management Company (AMC)). Single sector exposure limit has been reduced from the 30 per cent of NAV to 25 per cent of NAV. The additional exposure of

10 per cent to Housing Finance Companies remains unchanged. Group level limits have been introduced for debt schemes such that total exposure of debt schemes of MFs in a group (excluding investments in securities issued by Public Sector Units, Public Financial Institutions and Public Sector Banks) shall not exceed 20 per cent of the net assets of the scheme (extendable to 25 per cent of the net assets of the scheme with the prior approval of the Board of Trustees).

Retail Investors

With a view to increase participation, resident individual investors were allowed to open a trading account and demat account by filling up a simplified Saral Account Opening Form. Investor protection has been the pivotal objective of SEBI. Towards this end, during 2014-15, it promptly and vigorously pursued entities raising monies illegally and took punitive and preventive actions against companies found to be falling within its purview. SEBI also issued caution notes to investors informing them not to subscribe to issue/schemes floated by such companies against whom SEBI had taken action and also cautioning the companies not to issue securities/mobilize monies from the public without complying with the relevant provisions of law.

As per the World Bank report on 'Doing Business 2015: Going Beyond Efficiency', India ranks seventh with respect to protection of minority shareholders. SEBI has been taking various regulatory measures to expedite the redressal of investor grievances. SEBI Complaints Redressal System (SCORES) has helped investors in getting real time information about the status of their grievances. Alternatively, investors can also call the SEBI helpline to check the status of their grievances.

Several new powers have been conferred to SEBI via Securities Laws (Amendment) Act, 2014 . The amendments included explicit power to disgorge ill-gotten gains and credit disgorgement amount to Investor Protection and Education Fund and its utilization, power to conduct search and seizure, explicit powers for settlement, special courts and public prosecutors, attachment and recovery, power of review of orders passed by Adjudicating Officers, enhanced powers in respect of Collective Investment Scheme (CIS).

Various new regulations have been put in place by SEBI during 2014-15 which include inter alia, SEBI (Prohibition of Insider trading) Regulations, SEBI (Real Estate Investment Trusts) Regulations, SEBI (Research Analyst) Regulations, SEBI (Infrastructure Investment Trusts) Regulations and SEBI (Share based Employee Benefit) Regulations.

Securities Appellate Tribunal

Securities Appellate Tribunal (SAT) is established under Section 15 K of the Securities and Exchange Board of India Act, 1992, to exercise the jurisdiction, powers and authority conferred on the Tribunal by or under the SEBI Act, 1992, or any other law for the time being in force. The scope and ambit of the jurisdiction of SAT has been widened to include appeals against orders passed by the authorities under PFRDA and IRDA respectively.

SAT comprised one Presiding officer (who has been a sitting/retired judge of the Supreme Court or a sitting retired Chief Justice of a High Court; or a sitting or retired judge of a High Court who has completed not less than seven years of service as a judge of a High Court) and two members who are having ability, integrity and standing and shown capacity in dealing with problems relating to securities law, finance, economics or accountancy. They are appointed by the Central Govt. for a term of five years and are eligible for re-appointment subject of Presiding Officer not exceeding age of 68 years and members of the age of 62 years. The Tribunal is not bound by procedure laid down by Code of Civil Procedure but is guided by principles of natural justice and has powers to regulate its own procedure, including the places at which it shall have its sittings. Appellant may appear in person or authorize chartered accountants, company secretaries, cost accountants and legal practitioners or any of its officers to present his or its case before the Securities Appellate Tribunal.

Civil Courts do not have jurisdiction to entertain any suit or proceeding in respect of any matter which SAT is empowered to determine and no injunction can be granted by any court or any other authority, in respect of any action taken or to be taken, in pursuance to any power conferred upon SAT under the SEBI Act. Any person aggrieved by a decision/order of SAT may file an appeal to Supreme Court. SAT is empowered to review its own decisions.

SAT started functioning in 1997 as a single member Tribunal and thereafter was reconstituted as three members Tribunal in 2003. Mostly cases of following regulations are of SEBI filed before it: stock brokers/sub-brokers and stock exchanges; takeover regulations; prohibition of fraudulent and unfair trade practices; venture capital funds; and appears against orders passed by the authorities under PFRDA and IRDA respectively.

As on 30.6.2016, 394 appeals are pending before SAT and its breakup with time period wise is as given below:

Month & Year	Total Appeals Pending month	Less than 3	Over 3 months	Over 6 months	Over1 year	Over2 years	Over 12 years	Disp. Total	New Institution
June 2016	Pendency of Cases under SEBI Act, 1992								
	389	75	119	84	105	5	1	55	45
	Pendency of Cases under IRDA Act, 1999								
	5	0	5	0	0	0	0	0	0

Note: (i) 45 Misc. Applications filed in the respective Appeals filed under SEBI Act, 1992 have been disposed of during the month of June, 2016

(ii) 1 Review Application filed in the respective appeals filed under SEBI Act 1992 have been disposed of during the month of June, 2016

Financial Stability and Development Council

With a view to strengthening and institutionalizing the mechanism for maintaining financial stability, enhancing inter-regulatory coordination and promoting financial sector development, the Financial Stability and Development Council (FSDC) was set up by the government as the apex level forum in December, 2010. The Chairman of the Council is the Union Finance Minister and its members include the heads of financial sector regulator, Reserve bank of India (RBI), Securities Board of India (SEBI), Pension and Fund Regulatory and Development Authority and Insurance Regulatory and Development Authority of India (IRDAI), Finance Secretary and/ or Secretary, Department of Economic Affairs, Secretary, Department of Financial Services and Chief Economic Adviser. The Council, inter-alia monitors macro prudential supervision of the economy including functioning of large financial sector development issues, including issues relating to financial literacy and financial inclusion. The FSDC Secretariat in Department of Economic Affairs provides secretarial support to the council.

Financial Stability Board

FSB was established in 2009 under the aegis of G 20 by bringing together the national authorities, standard setting bodies and international financial institutions for addressing vulnerabilities and developing and implementing strong regulatory, supervisory and other policies in the interest of financial stability. India is an active member of the FSB having three seats in its Plenary represented by Secretary (EA), Deputy Governor- RBI and Chairman, SEBI. Regular interaction with FSB takes place through meetings and periodic conference call. Information is exchanged with FSB member jurisdictions frequently as per international requirements. The FSDC Secretariat in the Department of Economic Affairs coordinates with the various financial sector regulators and other relevant agencies to represent India's views with the FSB.

Financial Stability Assessment Programme

The Financial Sector Assessment Programme is a joint programme of the International Monetary Fund and the World Bank. In September 2010, IMF made it mandatory for 25 jurisdictions (including India) with systemically important financial sectors, to undergo financial stability assessments under the FSAP every five years based on the size and inter-connectedness of their financial sectors, and is reviewed periodically to make sure it reflects developments in the global financial system. In the G 20 Forum, FSB Members have committed to pursue maintenance of financial stability, enhance the openness and transparency of the financial sector, implement international financial standards and agree to undergo periodic peer reviews, using among other evidence, the IMF World Bank FSAP reports and publishing the results of these assessments.

FSB Peer Review of India, a FSB member jurisdictions have committed to undergo periodic peer reviews focused on the implementation of financial sector standards and policies agreed within the FSB, as well as their effectiveness in achieving the desired outcomes. As part of this commitment, India volunteered to undergo a peer review in 2015. The peer review of India is the seventeenth country peer review conducted by the FSB. Two topics i.e. (i) Macro-prudential policy framework; and (ii) regulation and supervision of non-banking finance companies were identified for the peer review of India. The final report of ongoing FSB Peer Review of India is likely to be ready by August/September, 2016.

Monetary Policy Framework

A Monetary Policy Framework Agreement between the Government and the Reserve Bank of India was signed in 2015, providing for flexible inflation targeting. With a view to maintain price stability, while keeping in mind the objective of growth, the Reserve Bank of India Act, 1934 (RBI Act) has been amended by the Finance Act, 2016, to provide for a statutory and institutionalized framework for a Monetary Policy Committee (MPC).

A Committee-based approach for determining the Monetary Policy will add lot of value and transparency to monetary policy decisions. Out of the six members of MPC, three members will be from the Reserve Bank of India (RBI), including the Governor, RBI, who will be the ex-officio Chairperson, the Deputy Governor, RBI and one officer of RBI. The other three members of MPC will be appointed by the Central Government, on the recommendations of a Search-cum-Selection Committee. These three members of MPC will be experts in the field of economics or banking or finance or monetary policy and will be appointed for a period of four years and shall not be eligible for re-appointment. The meetings of the MPC shall be held at least four times a year and it shall publicise its decisions after each such meeting.

The provisions of the RBI (Amendment) Act, 2016 have been brought into force. The rules governing the procedure for selection of members of monetary policy committee and terms and conditions of their appointment and factors constituting failure to meet inflation target under the MPC Framework have also been notified. The Government, in consultation with the bank, has notified the inflation target beginning from the date of publication of this notification and ending on the March 31, 2021, as under:-

Inflation target : Four per cent

Upper tolerance level : Six per cent

Lower tolerance level : Two per cent

The MPC inter alia would be entrusted with the task of fixing the benchmark policy rate (repo rate) required to contain inflation within the specified target level. The key advantage of a range around a target is that it allows MPC to recognise the short run trade-offs between inflation and growth but enables it to pursue the inflation target in long run over the course of business cycle. The range also accommodates data limitations, projection errors, short-run supply gaps and instability in the agriculture production, an important factor for CPI inflation, as food articles have a major weight in the CPI indices. It also allows to accommodate unanticipated short-term stocks even while nudging public inflation expectations on the centre of the range, to which the monetary policy will return the economy over the medium term, leading to transparency and predictability.

Further, if the average inflation is more than the upper tolerance level of 4 per cent + 2 per cent, that is, 6 per cent, or less than the lower tolerance level of 4 per cent – 2 per cent, that is 2 per cent, for any three consecutive quarters, it would mean a failure to achieve the inflation target. Where RBI fails to meet the inflation target, in terms of the provisions of RBI Act, it shall set out a report to the Central Government stating the reasons for failure to achieve the inflation target; remedial actions proposed to be taken by RBI; and an estimate of the time-period within which the inflation target shall be achieved pursuant to timely implementation of proposed remedial actions.

Fixation of an inflation target while giving due emphasis to the objective of growth and challenges of an increasingly complex economy, is an important monetary policy reform with necessary statutory back-up.

Insolvency and Bankruptcy Code

Insolvency and Bankruptcy Code, 2016 came into force in 2016. The Code aims to promote entrepreneurship, availability of credit, and balance the interests of all the stakeholders by consolidating and amending the laws relating to reorganization and insolvency resolution of corporate persons, partnership firms and individuals in a time bound manner and for maximization of value of the assets of such persons and matters connected therewith or incidental thereto. It proposes a framework to ensure: early detection of stress in a business; initiation of the insolvency resolution process by debtor, financial creditor or operational creditor; timely revival of viable businesses; liquidation of unviable businesses; minimization of losses to all stakeholders; and avoiding destruction of value of failed business.

The administration of the Insolvency and Bankruptcy Code, 2016 has been transferred to the Ministry of Corporate Affairs from July, 2016.

G-20

The G-20 was formed in 1999, as a forum of Finance Ministers and Central Bank Governors, in recognition of the fact that there was a major shift in the global economic weight from the advance economies to emerging market economies. The gradually declining role of G-8 as world's economic coordinator and the increasing clout of EMEs in global deliberations on economic governance resulted in G-20 replacing G-8 in 1999. However, G-20 rose into true prominence in 2008 when it was elevated from a forum of Finance Ministers and Central Bank Governors to that of G-20 Heads of Nations in order to effectively respond to the global financial crisis of 2007-2010. This proved to be a very effective strategy and the G-20 rose to the occasion and helped in ensuring that the world was kept away from a major economic collapse.

The first G-20 Summit was held in November 2008 in Washington DC under the shadow of the greatest financial crisis in the post-war era. This was followed by nine summits held in London (April, 2009), Pittsburgh (September, 2009), Toronto (June, 2010), Seoul (November, 2010), Cannes (November, 2011), Los Cabos (June, 2012), St. Petersburg (September, 2013), Brisbane (November, 2014) and Antalya (November, 2015). The current presidency of G-20 is with China and the Summit under Chinese Presidency is scheduled to be held in Hangzhou, September, 2016.

G-20 Framework Working Group

The G-20 Framework Working Group (FWG) plays a very pivotal role in the functioning of G-20. Established in 2009 during the G-20 Pittsburg Summit, the main task of FWG is to layout the policies to generate strong, sustainable and balanced global growth. In 2016 under the G-20 Chinese Presidency, the main job of the FWG was to deliberate upon the G-20 Enhanced Structural Reform Agenda comprising of two main pillars, namely, the priorities and principles of structural reforms and the G-20 structural reform indicator system. Other issues which the FWG has deliberated extensively in 2016 was the developments in the global economy such as Brexit and its implications, global imbalances, spillover effects of negative interest rates in Japan and Europe as well as the global implications of China's rebalancing efforts.

G-20 Sherpa Track

In 2016, against the backdrop of the Agenda 2030, the Paris Agreement and Nairobi outcomes, the Chinese Presidency has given a huge focus to the traditional agenda items of development, trade and investment, and energy. It has also brought in three new agenda items namely innovation, digital economy and new industrial revolution under the overarching theme "Breaking a New Path of Growth". The Chinese Presidency also focuses on the theme of 'Inclusive and Interconnected Development' encompassing the issues of SDG's, supporting industrialisation in Africa, employment with an emphasis of entrepreneurship, agriculture and food security issues. Apart from the above, other issues such as global health, refugee crisis and terrorism have also been brought on the table this year thus widening the G-20 basket further.

India through the various Sherpa meetings, working groups and ministerial meetings have actively espoused our priority areas such as promoting international mobility of skilled professionals, finance and technology transfers, energy access, clean coal technologies and combating corruption and black money.

Outcomes of Antalya Summit 2015

G 20 Summit 2015 was successfully held in Antalya from November 15-16, 2015.Through intense negotiations in Sherpa meetings, working group meetings, ministerial meetings and pre-summit meetings, India was successfully able to articulate our interests and ensure that our priorities are reflected in the Leaders Communiqué. The following commitments by G 20 countries at the 2015 Summit have been mainly at India's behest:

G 20 commitment to address opportunities and challenges brought into lab our markets by international labour mobility; G 20 commitment to implement all elements of the Bali package including those on agriculture, development and public stockholding; G 20 commitment to prioritise development by aligning with the 2030 agenda; G 20 Leaders endorsed Base Erosion and Profit Shifting (BEPS) Project. India was a member of OECD committee that worked on the BEPS package; Strong traction for a successful outcome of CoP 21; G 20 Technical Platform for measuring food losses and wastes.

To provide a strong impetus to boost investment, particularly through private sector participation, the leaders have developed ambitious country-specific investment strategies, which bring together concrete policies and actions to improve the investment ecosystem, foster efficient and quality infrastructure, including by the public sector, support small and medium sized enterprises (SMEs), and enhance knowledge sharing. Analysis by the OECD indicates that these strategies would contribute to liftingthe aggregate G20 investment to GDP ratio, by an estimated 1 percentage point by 2018. Further, there has been establishment of the private sector-led World SME Forum, a new initiative that will serve as a global body to facilitate the contributions of SMEs to growth and employment. G 20 Leaders agreed on the Antalya Action plan sets out the G 20's plan for decisiveactions to strengthen the global economic recovery and foster strong, sustainable and balanced growth, and complements the Leaders' Communiqué.

To enhance the resilience of the global financial system, G20 have completed further core elements of the financial reform agenda. As a key step towards ending too-big-to- fail, leaders have finalized the common international standard on total-loss absorbing-capacity (TLAC) for global systemically important banks. Leaders also agreed to the first version of higher loss absorbency requirements for global systemically important insurers. To reach a globally fair and modern international tax system, leaders endorsed the package of measures developed under the ambitious G20/OECD Base Erosion and Profit Shifting (BEPS) project at Antalya Summit. Leaders reaffirmed their previous commitments to information exchange on-request as well as to automatic exchange of information by 2017 or end-2018.

Eventually, in December, 2015 the United States Congress approved the 2010 Quota and Governance reforms of the IMF. The reforms significantly increase the IMF's core resources, enabling it to respond to crises more effectively, and also improve the IMF's governance by better reflecting the increasing role of dynamic emerging and developing countries in the global economy. With the implementation of the 14th General Review of Quota (GRQ) reforms, India's quota share will increase from the current 2.44 per cent to 2.75 per cent, making India, the 8th largest quota holding country at the IMF from its previous position of being the 11th largest quota holder.

Achievements of G20 Finance Track in 2016

G 20 Finance Ministers and Central Bank Governors met in February, April and July, 2016. During the deliberations G20 Finance Ministers have, inter alia, achieved the following:

i. It has worked to further enhancing the structural reform agenda, including by developing a set of priorities and guiding principles as a reference for G 20 reform efforts, as well as by creating an indicator system to further improve assessing and monitoring of the progress of structural reforms and their adequacy to address structural challenges, taking into account the diversity of country circumstances. An outcome paper on enhanced structural reforms agenda is prepared and submitted for the endorsement of the leaders in the Hangzhou Summit.

ii. The world body has restored the working group on International Financial Architecture (IFA) to enhance cooperation upon the topics related to international monetary system and international financial architecture.

iii. G 20 proposed measures to mobilize private capital for green investment.

BRICS Finance and Economic Co-operation

India assumed the chairmanship of the BRICS forum in 2016. The theme of India's chairmanship was "Building Responsive, Inclusive and Collective Solution", which resonates with the ethos of the BRICS. During the year, India hosted a number of events under its aegis finance and economic co-operation such as workshop on challenges in the bond markets of BRICS countries, workshop on financial inclusion, seminar on infrastructure financing and PPP best practices, workshop of international arbitration mechanism, workshop on investment flows, etc., with the objective of sharing country-experiences and provide an opportunity for mutual learning on innovative policy instruments among the member nations.

A considerable progress was achieved on existing BRICS initiatives during India's chairmanship – New Development Bank made its first set of loans to the member countries and foundational work related to BRICS Contingent Reserve Arrangement (CRA) was also completed with the member central banks opening the swap accounts in favour of each other. Further, India also mooted idea of setting-up new institutions under the aegis of BRICS viz., New Development Bank Institute and BRICS Rating Agency with the objective of realizing the shared vision of BRICS nations of transforming the global financial architecture to one where there is equity and adequate power balance between developed and developing countries. The discussions on these new initiatives are on-going.

South Asian Association of Regional Cooperation and SAARC Development Fund

The South Asian Association of Regional Cooperation (SAARC), in existence since 1985 (founded in Dhaka), is a regional organisation that aims to promote economic, social, cultural, technical and scientific cooperation in South Asia. Its member states include Afganistan, Bangladesh, Bhutan, India, Nepal, Maldives, Pakistan and Sri Lanka. Its secretariat is based in Kathmandu. It has crafted several regional conventions, agreements and institutions for dealing with issues that affect the citizens of the region. It is a consensus-based forum for exchange of ideas, development of regional programmes and projects India has so far contributed over US$ 530 million to SAARC institutions for socio-economic development. India's trade with South Asia accounts for 5 per cent of its global trade.

The South Asian Free Trade Area (SAFTA) Agreement and the SAARC Agreement on Trade in Services (SATIS) are the two main areas of cooperation among SAARC member states which came into force in 2004 and 2012 respectively. SAFTA envisages eventual zero customs duty on virtually all products traded within the region. Phased reduction of customs duties has been negotiated over time. Negotiations for more reductions under Phase III are on. SATIS provides for expanding intra-regional investments, trade liberalization in the services sector, etc.

The cumulative figure of intra-SAARC trade flows under it has crossed US$ 2.9 per cent during 2013-2014. Currently, trade under SAFTA accounts for only around 10 per cent of the total regional trade because bilateral FTAs offer greater concessions amongst SAARC countries.

SAARC Development Fund (SDF) was established in 2008 by the SAARC countries to improve the livelihood of the people and to accelerate economic growth, social progress and poverty alleviation in the region. SDF is implementing many SAARC projects and programme. Project funding in SDF is to be taken up under three windows (social, economic and infrastructure). Ten projects under the social window have been undertaken in areas such as women empowerment, agriculture, child and maternal health, education and ICT since its formal launching in April 2010. SDF had received approximately USD 441.46 million of funds, which includes capital contribution by member states of USD 289 million and an additional voluntary contribution by India for USD 100 million for the social window. Of the three windows of SDF for project implementation, the latter two are being operationalised.

The currency swap arrangement for the SAARC countries, with a contribution of USD 2 billion by India to address short term foreign exchange liquidity requirements, has been operationalised. Agreements under the arrangement was signed between India and Bhutan (for USD 100 million) and Sri Lanka (USD 400 million).

United Nations Development Programme in India

The United Nations Development Programme (UNDP) is the largest channel for development cooperation in the UN system. The overall mission of the UNDP is to assist the programme countries through capacity development in Sustainable Human Development (SHD) with priority on poverty alleviation, gender equity, women empowerment and environmental protection. All assistance provided by the UNDP is grant assistance. It derives its funds from voluntary contributions from various donor countries. India's annual contribution to the UNDP has been to the extent of US$ 4.5 million, which is one of the largest from developing countries. Over and above its annual contribution, the GOI also pays partly for the expenditure of the Local Office.

The country-specific allocation of UNDP resources is made every five years under the Country Cooperation Framework (CCF) which usually synchronizes with India's five-year plans.

The current Country Programme (2013-17) formulated by the Government in partnership with the UNDP Country Office, flows out of India UN Development Assistance Framework 2013-2017(UNDAF) which encapsulates the entire UN System's Development interaction with Government of India for the period. The present Country Programme (CP) would concentrate on the four UNDAF outcomes namely inclusive growth and poverty eradication, democratic governance, sustainable development, gender equality and inclusion. The present current Country Programme(CP) 2013-17 was signed in 2013 and will remain in force till December 2017. It primarily concentrates on the goals namely, democratic governance, poverty reduction, HIV and development, disaster risk management and energy and environment focusing on nine states that are economically laggard:Bihar, Chhattisgarh, Jharkhand, Madhya Pradesh, Odisha, Rajasthan, Assam, Maharashtra and Uttar Pradesh.

The total resource allocation for the Indian Country Programme 2013-2017 stands at US$ 260 million. During 2015-16, the grant disbursed was USD 51.34 million. The total commitment by March-2016 is USD 199.23 million against which USD 138.96 million has been disbursed.

Bilateral Cooperation

Bilateral Cooperation Division of Department of Economic Affairs deals with bilateral development assistance from G-8 countries, namely, USA, UK, Japan, Germany, Italy, Canada and Russian Federation as well as the European Union. The Division also deals with the work relating to extension of lines of credit to developing countries. It is also the focal point for administering short term foreign training courses of the duration upto four weeks offered by various international agencies/countries.

Bilateral Official Development Assistance Policy

India has been accepting external assistance from bilateral partners in the form of loans, grants and technical assistance for development of infrastructure, social sector and for enhancement of knowledge/skills of Indian nationals at both Centre and states. In terms of the guidelines issued in 2005, bilateral development assistance can be accepted from all G-8 countries, namely, USA, UK, Japan, Germany, France, Italy, Canada and the Russian Federation as well as from European Commission. European Union countries outside the G-8 can also provide bilateral development assistance to India provided they commit a minimum annual development assistance of USD 25 million.

Indo-Japan Bilateral Relations

Japan has been extending Official Development Assistance (ODA) to India since 1958. Japanese ODA in the form of loan assistance, grant-in-aid and technical assistance to India is received through Japan International Cooperation Agency (JICA). Japan is the largest bilateral donor to India.

India has received a commitment from Government of Japan for loan of Yen 389.629 billion ₹ 21446 crore approx.) during the financial year 2015-16. With this, the cumulative ODA loan from Japan has reached yen 4637.746 billion on commitment basis till March 31, 2016.

India-UK Bilateral Development Cooperation Programme

The United Kingdom (UK) has been providing development assistance to India since 1958. Development assistance from UK is received mainly for achieving the Sustainable Development Goals (SDGs) in the areas of health, education, administrative reforms, slum development, etc. The assistance from the UK, through its Department for International Development (DFID), flows to mutually agreed government projects and programmes in the form of financial and technical assistance. Presently, Odisha, Madhya Pradesh and Bihar are the three focus states of DFID.

India-European Union Development Cooperation

The European Union (EU) has been providing development assistance in the form of grants. The EU priority areas include environment, public health and education. EU implements development cooperation programmes through Country Strategy Paper (CSP). EU had committed to provide an amount of Euro 260 million and Euro 105 million to India for Multiannual Indicative programme-I (MIP-I) from 2007-2010 and Multiannual Indicative Programme-II (MIP-II) from 2011-2013 under CSP respectively. The major programmes of Government of India which received EU aid along with other development partners include are Sarva Shiksha Abhiyan (SSA), National Rural Health Mission (NRHM) and Reproductive and Child Health (RCH). In 2012, Government of India has signed an agreement with EU for the project "Sector Policy Support Programme for Elementary and Secondary education", which will receive a grant of Euro 80 million.

European Investment Bank

The European Investment Bank, the Banque Europeenne d'Investissement (EIB) is the European Union's financing institution which was established in 1958 under the Treaty of Rome (1957) to provide financing for capital investment. The members of the EIB are the Member States of the European Union, who have all subscribed to the bank's capital. Outside the European Union, EIB financing operations are conducted principally from the Bank's own resources but also, under mandate, from Union or Member States' budgetary resources.

EIB in India

EIB's activities in India emanate from the Joint Action Plan (JAP) of the Strategic Partnership between the EU and India. EIB intends to increase its lending activities focussing mainly on environmental sustainability and large infrastructure project through FDI, transfer of technology and know-how.

EIB investments in India are governed by the Framework Agreement for Financial Cooperation. This agreement was signed between India and EIB in 1993.

EIB loans

Unlike loans received from sovereign bilateral partners or multilateral institutions, EIB loans are not Official Development Assistance (ODA) loans and therefore, loans from EIB are less concessional in comparison to ODA loans. ODA loan is meant only for Central/state government or PSUs projects, while EIB loans can be availed by both private and public sector entities. It has been decided to provide Government of India's guarantee in respect of EIB loans to PSUs/state entities on case to case basis.

Switzerland

Switzerland has been extending economic and technical assistance to India since 1964 in the form of grants and technical assistance. Switzerland had also provided mix credit comprising 40 per cent grant and 60 per cent loans for power sector project. Bilateral meetings are periodically held between the two countries. The last meeting was held in New Delhi in June 2016.

Indo-German Bilateral Development Cooperation

Germany through their Ministry for Economic Cooperation and Development (BMZ) has been providing both financial and technical assistance to India since 1958. In 2008, German Ministry for the Environment, Nature Conservation and Nuclear Safety (BMU) also initiated assistance under German Government's International Climate Protection Initiative', which is an additional instrument of the Government over above and without undermining the existing sources of Official Development Assistance. Germany implements its financial assistance programmes through KfW, the German Government's Development Bank. The technical assistance programmes are implemented through GIZ (earlier GTZ)—a fully-owned corporation of German Government. Financial assistance is provided as Standard Loan (IDA-pattern loan), Reduced Interest Loan (EURIBOR-based loan) as well as grants. The technical assistance is provided in the form of grant only.

The 'Strategic Framework for Indo German Bilateral Development Cooperation' acts as a guiding framework for bilateral development partnership. The objective is to complement and supplement the efforts of Government of India on issues like poverty eradication, environmental degradation and climate change. In alignment with our plan priorities and development agenda, priority areas to be focused under Indo German bilateral development cooperation are: (i) energy, including energy efficiency, renewable energy, energy sector reforms; (ii) environment, including urban and industrial environment protection, natural resources; and (iii) sustainable economic development, including rural financing, social security systems , SME development and financing.

Indo-French Development Cooperation

The Government of France has been extending development assistance to India since 1968. However, the major drawback of French assistance was that it was tied to supply of goods and services from France. Moreover, French development assistance was not significant in amount. In fact, the average annual disbursement since 2001-02 had been low at ₹ 28 crore only. In 2006, Government of France proposed to provide untied development assistance to India through the French Agency for Development (AFD). The priority areas for AFD financing in India are (i) energy efficiency and renewable energy within the framework of the National Action Plan on Climate Change (NAPCC), (ii) urban infrastructure (public transport, water, etc.) (iii) Preservation of biodiversity.

United States of America

U.S. Agency International Development

The United States of America (USA) bilateral development assistance to India started in 1951. US assistance to India is mainly administered through the US Agency International Development (USAID). USAID is presently partnering with the Government of India to strengthen health systems; food security; accelerate transition to low emissions, and energy secure economy; reduce greenhouse gas emissions through carbon sequestration by forests; and improve the quality of basic education through teachers training and development.

In 2010-2011, USAID had signed six bilateral agreements with Government of India in areas such as food security, health, climate change, and education. These six agreements, along with an agreement in the field of disaster management support (signed in September 2003) and an agreement for the Water, Sanitation and Hygiene (WASH) (signed in October 2015), making it a total of seven ongoing bilateral agreements with USAID.

United States Trade and Development Agency

US Trade and Development Agency (USTDA) promotes economic growth in emerging economies by facilitating the participation of US businesses in the planning and execution of priority development projects in host countries. The

Agency's objectives are to help build the infrastructure for trade, match US technological expertise with overseas development needs, and help create lasting business partnerships between the United States and emerging market economies. Since 1992, the US Trade and Development Agency has been supported over 100 priority development projects in India with public and private sector sponsors. Priorities for USTDA's programme in India include energy and climate change, transportation (especially aviation), and information and communication technology. In 2015-16, four USTDA grants for technical assistance were approved by DEA viz. – (i) provision 2 body scanner system pilot project with Airport Authority of India for US$ 7,12,456 (ii) Technical Assistance project Phase II under US-India Aviation Programme (ACP) with DGCA for US$ 8,08,327 (iii) Technical assistance to Indian Railway to develop PPP and attract private capital for US$ 5,18,100 (iv) Feasibility study of Bottoms Upgrading Project at Mumbai Refinery with BPCL for US$ 8,36,550 (v) Smart City Master Planning and Sector-Specific Smart City Infrastructure Project plans for Vishakhapatnam Grant Agreement.

Canada

Assistance from International Development Research Centre of Canada

International Development Research Centre of Canada (IDRC) extends grant assistance to various government and non-government organizations for projects in the field of agriculture, health and family welfare, etc. During 2015-16, 11 proposals involving grants assistance of CA$ 3.86 million were received by DEA for approval. Out of these 11 proposals, five grants of CA$ 2.06 million have been cleared by DEA.

Canada Fund for Local Initiative (CFLI)

The CFLI is a responsive, flexible programme, directly managed by the High Commission of Canada in New Delhi, to fund small but visible, high impact, results-oriented projects. Through contribution agreements, the CFLI provides monetary assistance that covers all or a portion of the cost of projects that are comparatively modest in scope, scale and cost and that are usually conceived and designed by local authorities or organizations. During 2015, 28 grant proposals amounting to ₹ 3.34 Crore were received by DEA for approval.

Lines of Credit to developing countries

Lines of Credit(LoC) form an important component of India's diplomatic strategy and have been very useful in generating goodwill and building long term partnerships. The scheme also attempts to promote India's strategic political and economic interest abroad by positioning it as an emerging economic power, investor country and partner for developing countries. The Scheme is also expected to boost Indian export of goods and services to hitherto untapped markets and successfully showcase India's expertise in project planning, design and implementation in diverse areas of socio-economic development such as power, irrigation, agriculture, transport, etc. The

Government of India has been extending Lines of Credit to Africa and other developing countries under the Indian Development and Economic Assistance Scheme (IDEAS) since 2005-06. Under the extant Scheme, Ministry of External Affairs selects specific projects keeping in view diplomatic considerations and requests received from various developing countries. On finalization of a specific project proposal, the Line of Credit is issued with the approval of External Affairs Minister and Finance Minister. The LoCs are presently operated through Export-Import Bank of India, which raises resources from the market to finance the LoC and provides concessional loan to the borrowing country on the terms of credit decided by the Government of India as per country classification.

Foreign Investment Unit

A. Brief on FDI policy

The FDI policy, which is presently published by Department of Industrial Policy and Promotion (DIPP), has been liberalized progressively through review of the policy on an ongoing basis and allowing FDI in more industries under the automatic route. As per the extant policy, FDI up to 100 per cent is allowed, under the automatic route, in most of the sectors/activities. FDI under the automatic route does not require prior approval either by the Government of India or the Reserve Bank of India (RBI). Investors are only required to notify and file documents the regional office concerned of RBI. Under the Government approval route, applications for FDI proposals are considered and approved by the Foreign Investment Promotion Board (FIPB). Department of Industrial Policy & Promotion brings out a Consolidated Foreign Direct Investment Policy document. The latest one has been issued on June 7, 2016. It is available at http://dipp.nic.in.

Sectoral guidelines and caps:

(a) The following sectors are prohibited for FDI:- (i) lottery business; (ii) gambling and betting; (iii) business of chit fund; (iv) nidhi company; (v) Trading in Transferable Development Rights (TDRs); and (vi) real estate business or construction of farm houses 'Real estate business' shall not include development of townships, construction of residential /commercial premises, roads or bridges and Real Estate Investment Trusts (REITs) registered and regulated under the SEBI (REITs) Regulations 2014; (vii) manufacturing of cigars, cheroots, cigarillos and cigarettes, of tobacco or of tobacco substitutes and (viii) activity/ sector not opened to private sector investment, e.g: (i) atomic energy and (ii) railway operations.

Sectors having caps and conditionalities can be seen in Consolidated FDI Policy 2016 (available on the website of DIPP www.dipp.gov.in.). In other sectors which is not specified in CFPC-2016, FDI is permitted up to 100 per cent on the automatic route, subject to applicable laws/regulations, security and other conditionalities.

National Investment and Infrastructure Fund

The Government of India has put investment in infrastructure as one of the core elements of its economic programme. The Approach Paper for the Twelfth Plan projected the total investment requirement in infrastructure to be over ₹ 45 lakh crore during the Twelfth Plan period (2012-17). The report of Government of India's High Level Committee on Financing Infrastructure (2014) states that India's average investment in infrastructure was 4.7 per cent of GDP during 1992-2010. The above report also noted that fresh inflows of equity in the infrastructure sectors have slowed down significantly over the past few years, constraining several domestic players from making further investment.

Establishment

Since the above approval, two companies, namely National Investment and Infrastructure Fund Trustee Limited (NIIFTL), the trustee of the fund and National Investment and Infrastructure Fund Limited (NIIFL), the investment management company was incorporated in October 2015 and November, 2015 respectively. Presently both companies are 100 per cent owned by the government, though NIIFTL would have 51 per cent private shareholding in the future. NIIF has also been registered with SEBI as a Category II Alternate Investment Funds (AIF) in December, 2015

Foreign Trade

Gold Monetisation Scheme:- With a view to mobilize the gold lying idle with in the country and putting it into productive use and to reduce the country's reliance on the import of gold to meet the domestic demand, Government of India launched Gold Monetisation Scheme in November, 2015. Under this scheme, 4,539 kilograms of gold have so far been collected from 337 depositors.

International Monetary Fund

India is a founder member of the International Monetary Fund (IMF), which was established to promote a cooperative and stable global monetary framework. At present, 188 nations are members of the IMF. Since it was established, its purposes have remained unchanged but its operations - which involve surveillance, financial assistance and technical assistance - have developed to meet the changing needs of its member countries in an evolving world economy. The Board of Governors of the IMF consists of one Governor and one Alternate Governor from each member country. For India, the Finance Minister is the ex-officio Governor on the Board of Governors of the IMF. There are three other countries in India's constituency at the IMF, viz., Bangladesh, Bhutan and Sri Lanka. Governor, Reserve Bank of India (RBI) is India's Alternate Governor.

Meetings of Board of Governors

The Board of Governors usually meets twice a year to discuss the work of the respective institutions, viz., the Spring meetings and the annual meetings of the IMF and World Bank. At the heart of the gathering are meetings of the IMF's International Monetary and Financial Committee (India is represented by the Finance Minister in IMFC) and the joint World Bank—IMF Development Committee, which discuss progress on the work of the IMF and World Bank.

India's Quota and Ranking

The 2010 IMF Quota and Governance Reforms (including the 14th General Reforms of Quotas) came into effect in January 2016. Consequently, India's quota in the IMF is SDR 13,114.40 million with a shareholding of 2.75 per cent. India ranks eighth in terms of quota holding in IMF. Consequent to this quota increase in IMF, India has provided for the quota increase of SDR 7292.9 million under the 14th General Review of Quotas as SDR 1,823,225,000 through India's SDR holdings for Reserve Asset Portion (25 per cent of quota increase) and SDR 5,469,675,000 for Local Currency Portion (75 per cent of quota increase) through issuance of non-interest bearing, non-negotiable Government of India Rupee Securities.

India's Contribution to Borrowing Arrangements of the IMF

In April 2009, the G-20 agreed to increase the resources available to the IMF by up to $ 500 billion (which would triple the total pre-crisis lending resources of about $ 250 billion) to support growth in emerging market and developing countries, viz. through bilateral financing from IMF member countries; and by incorporating this financing into an expanded and more flexible New Arrangements to Borrow (NAB). As part of efforts to overcome the global financial crisis, in April 2009, G-20 economies agreed to increase the resources available to the IMF by up to $ 500 billion to support growth in emerging market and developing countries. The increase was made through (i) increase in bilateral financing from IMF members and (ii) by incorporation of this financing into an expanded and more flexible NAB. The amended NAB, which became effective in March 2011 increased the maximum amount of resources available under NAB to SDR 370 billion from SDR 34 billion.

International Finance Corporation

International Finance Corporation (IFC), a member of the World Bank Group, focuses exclusively on investing in the private sector in developing countries. Established in 1956, IFC has 184 members. India is founding member of IFC. IFC is an important development partner for India with its operations of financing and advising the private sector in the country. India represents IFC's single-largest country exposure globally. IFC has committed over US$15 billion in India since 1958. The IFC's investments in India are spread across important sectors like infrastructure, manufacturing, financial markets, agribusiness, SMEs and renewable energy. Keeping in alignment with the Country Partnership Strategy (CPS) of the World Bank Group in India, IFC focuses on low-income states in India.

BRICS New Development Bank

The New Development Bank (NDB) has been instituted with a vision to support and foster infrastructure and sustainable development initiatives in emerging economies. The founding members of the NDB - Brazil, Russia, India, China and South Africa (BRICS) - have brought in capital of USD 1 billion as initial contribution. Mr. K.V. Kamath, is the first President of the Bank. The New Development Bank (NDB) has completed one year since its establishment in 2015. Most of the policies and procedures for all functional areas of the Bank were approved at the Board of Directors meeting in January, 2016. So far, six meetings of the Board of Directors (BoD) have been held and most of the operational, HR and finance and control policies of the Bank have been finalized and approved by the BoD. Since commencement of operations, Board of Directors of the NDB have approved its first set of loans for all member countries amounting to USD 911 million and has completed its first bond issuance of RMB 3 billion (approximately USD 450 million).

Asian Infrastructure Investment Bank

Asian Infrastructure Investment Bank (AIIB) is a Multilateral Development Bank (MDB) set up in January, 2016 to foster sustainable economic development, create productive assets and improve infrastructure in Asia through financing of infrastructure projects. India is one of the founding members and the second largest shareholder. The Bank commenced its operation on 16.01.2016 with the inaugural meeting of its Board of Governors.

India along with 20 other countries signed the Inter-Governmental Memorandum of Understanding (MoU) for establishing the AIIB in 2014 in Beijing. Subsequently, 36 other countries endorsed the MOU and became prospective founding members (PFM). India signed the Instrument of Ratification in 2015. India has the largest share in the AIIB (83,673 with a capital subscription of USD 8.37 billion). This has ensured that India has an independent and exclusive seat on the Board of Directors of AIIB.

World Bank

India has been borrowing from the World Bank through International Bank for Reconstruction and Development (IBRD) and International Development Association (IDA) for various development projects in the areas of poverty reduction, infrastructure, rural development, etc. IDA funds are one of the most concessional external loans for Government of India and are used largely in social sector projects that contribute to the achievement of millennium development goals. IBRD funds are relatively costlier but cheaper than commercial external borrowings. The government utilizes IBRD loans primarily for infrastructure projects. However, sometimes a blend of IDA credits and IBRD loans is also used. India's current portfolio of the World Bank projects consists of 96 projects with a commitment of US$ 27.95 billion. The debt disbursed and outstanding (DOD) by March, 2016 for IBRD was US$ 12.67 billion.

After the recent capital increase in IBRD India has been allocated additional 24,092 shares (through General Capital Increase and Selective Capital Increase). As a result India has become the 7th largest shareholder in IBRD with voting power of 2.91 per cent. In 2015-16, India completed the subscription of the total allotted IBRD shares.

India has an Executive Director at the World Bank who is elected from the Indian Constituency consisting of Bangladesh, Bhutan, India and Sri Lanka. The Finance Minister is India's Governor to the World Bank Group, with Secretary in-charge of Department of Economic Affairs being the Alternate Governor.

International Fund for Agricultural Development

International Fund for Agricultural Development (IFAD) was set up in 1977 as the thirteenth specialized agency of the United Nations. It is dedicated to eradicating poverty and hunger in rural areas of developing countries. IFAD provides low interest loans and grants to developing countries to finance innovative agricultural and rural development programmes and projects. 176 countries are members of the IFAD, and these are grouped into three lists: List – A: Developed Countries; List – B: Oil Producing Countries; and List – C: Developing Countries. India is in List – C. Since 1979, IFAD has provided financial support to India through projects in the realm of agriculture, rural development, tribal development, etc. The fund has financed 28 projects with a total portfolio of US$ 926.91 million so far.

The Governing Council is the highest decision-making body of IFAD. The Governing Council meets annually and its meetings are chaired by the Chair of the Governing Council Bureau. The Governing Council Bureau consists of a Chairman and two Vice-Chairmen. The Executive Board of IFAD, headed by the President, is responsible for oversight of the several operations of IFAD. The members and alternate members are elected for three- year team.

Global Environment Facility

The Global Environment Facility (GEF) operates as a mechanism for international cooperation for the purpose of providing new and additional grant and concessional funding to meet the agreed incremental costs of measures to achieve agreed global environmental benefits. GEF provides grants to eligible countries in its five focal areas: biodiversity, climate change, land degradation, international waters, chemicals and waste. It also serves as financial mechanism for the Convention on Biological Diversity (CBD), United Nations Framework Convention on Climate Change (UNFCCC), Stockholm Convention on Persistent Organic Pollutants (POPs), UN Convention to Combat Desertification (UNCCD), Minamata Convention on Mercury and supports implementation of the protocol in countries with economics in transition for the Montreal Protocol on Substances that Deplete the Ozone Layer.

India has been actively involved with GEF process right from its inception. It has been one of the donors to the GEF Trust Fund. The GEF Trust Fund is replenished every four years through a process in which countries that wish to contribute to GEF Trust Fund discuss and come to agreement on a set of policy reforms to be undertaken, the programming of resources and also pledge resources.

Asian Development Bank

India is a founding member of the Asian Development Bank (ADB) which was established in 1966. ADB has 67 members (including 48 regional and 19 non-regional members), with its headquarters at Manila, Philippines. India currently holds 6.331 per cent of shares, totalling 672,030 shares, in ADB as in April, 2016, with 5.363 per cent voting rights. Asian Development Bank has a Board of Governors, a Board of Directors, a President, six Vice Presidents and other necessary officers and staff. All the powers of the Bank are vested in the Board of Governors, which exercises its powers and functions with the assistance of the Board of Directors.

The Union Finance Minister is the designated Governor for India, and Secretary, Department of Economic Affairs is the designated Alternate Governor. India also holds the position of Executive Director on the Board of Directors of the Bank and its constituency comprises Afghanistan, Bangladesh, Bhutan, India, Laos PDR, Tajikistan and Turkmenistan. The Bank is engaged in promoting economic and social progress of its developing member countries (DMCs) in the Asia Pacific Region. The main instruments that it uses to do this are making loans and equity investments, providing technical assistance for the preparation and execution of development projects and programme and other advisory services, guarantees, grants and policy dialogues. India borrows from ADB within overall external debt management policy pursued by the government which focuses on raising funds on concessional terms from less expensive sources with longer maturities. India started borrowing from ADB in 1986.

ADB's India lending programme has matured and expanded significantly under the Country Partnership Strategy (CPS) which is aligned with the Five Year Plans of India. The indicative resource envelope of ADB for sovereign operations in India is around US$ 2 billion per annum. The TA programme is for around $ 8 million a year. Over the past decade, ADB has expanded operations beyond the energy, transport, finance, and urban sectors into areas focusing on generation of sustainable livelihoods; skill development, renewable energy, integrated water resources management with a focus on climate change adaptation (including support for irrigation, coastal zone management, and flood control); agribusiness infrastructure development; and tourism.

ADB assistance has also extended to states such as Assam, Bihar, Chhattisgarh, Jammu & Kashmir, Jharkhand, Odisha , Uttarakhand, and the north eastern region—Assam, Tripura, Mizoram, Nagaland, Sikkim, and Meghalaya, which are experiencing constraints of poverty, low levels of social development, weak capacity, and inadequate infrastructure. ADB's Technical

Assistance (TA) programme for India has also evolved in line with the loan programme. TA support is being used to build capacity, improve project preparedness and implementation, assist the Government's PPP initiative, and undertake scoping studies and knowledge products.

Department of Expenditure

The Department of Expenditure is the nodal department for overseeing the public financial management system in the Central Government and matters connected with state finances. The principal activities of the department include pre-sanction appraisal of major schemes/projects (both Plan and non-Plan expenditure), handling the bulk of the Central budgetary resources transferred to states, implementation of the recommendations of the Finance and central pay commissions, overseeing the expenditure management in the Central ministries/departments through the interface with the Financial Advisors and the administration of the financial rules/regulations/orders through monitoring of audit comments/observations, preparation of Central government accounts, managing the financial aspects of personnel management in the Central government, assisting Central ministries/departments in controlling the costs and prices of public services, assisting organizational re-engineering through review of staffing patterns and O M studies and reviewing systems and procedures to optimize outputs and outcomes of public expenditure. The department is also coordinating matters concerning the Ministry of Finance including Parliament-related work of the Ministry. It has under its administrative control the National Institute of Financial Management (NIFM), Faridabad.

The business allocated to the Department of Expenditure is carried out through its Establishment Division, Plan Finance-Ii and II Divisions, Finance Commission Division, Staff Inspection Unit, Cost Accounts Branch, Controller General of Accounts and the Central Pension Accounting office.

Seventh Central Pay Commission

The Seventh Central Pay Commission which was set up in February, 2014, submitted its recommendations to the government in November 2015. The date of its effect is January 1, 2016 with a minimum basic pay of ₹ 18,000/. The present system of pay bands and grade pay has been replaced by a new pay matrix in respect of both civilians and defence personnel. The additional financial implications as estimated by the Commission is likely to be ₹ 1,02,100-crore in the financial year 2016-17.

Procurement Policy

A Public Procurement Cell (PPC) was set up in this department in June, 2011 to take follow up action on the Report of the Committee on Public Procurement (CoPP) and drafting of the Public Procurement Bill and other related matters such as drafting of rules and setting up of a Central Public Procurement Portal. The Cell was gradually strengthened and a division called Procurement Policy Division (PPD) was created.

Subsequently, the scope of work in PPD was enlarged. The Division now deals with the following items of work (i) public procurement legislation and rules, notifications, orders thereunder; (ii) policies relating to public procurement including administration of general Financial Rules, 2005 on procurement of goods and services and contract management; policies relating to mandatory or preferential procurement; (iii) matters relating to standardization of procurement related documents; (iv) all matters related to Central Public Procurement Portal set up for publishing information relating to public procurement; (v) matters relating to electronic procurement; (vi) professional standards to be achieved by officials dealing with procurement and suitable training and certification requirements for the same; (vii) interface with international bodies on matters relating to public procurement.

Central Public Procurement Portal and e- Procurement

Pursuant to the recommendations of the Committee on Public Procurement (CoPP), a Central Public Procurement Portal (CPP Portal) was set up for providing comprehensive information and data relating to public procurement and is accessible at www.eprocure.gov.in. It is being used at present by various ministries/departments, CPSEs and autonomous/statutory bodies. e-publishing of tender enquiries, corrigenda thereto and details of contracts awarded thereon, on the portal, has been made mandatory in a phased manner from 2012. Further, it has also been decided to implement e-procurement in ministries/departments of the Central Government and instructions have also been issued to all ministries/departments to commence e-procurement in respect of all procurements with estimated value of ₹ 2 lakh or more in a phased manner. Use of e-procurement would enhance transparency and accountability and make procurement more efficient.

Currently, approximately 4,000 tenders are floated per month using this facility. This translates to around 30,000 crore worth procurement per annum through CPP only. Apart from it, many procurement organizations like railways, PSUs like ONGC, BHEL, etc., have their own e-procurement portals.

Swachh Bharat Kosh

The Kosh has been set up to achieve the objective of improving cleanliness levels in rural and urban areas, including in schools. It will also be enabled to bring out innovative/ unique projects and girls toilets will be the priority area to start with. The following broad activities will be financed from the Kosh: a) construction of community/individual toilets in rural areas, urban areas, in elementary, secondary and senior secondary government schools, aanganwaadis (centre that provide support to children below six years and their mothers under the Women and Child Development); b) renovation and repair of dysfunctional community/individual toilets in elementary, secondary and senior secondary government schools, aanganwaadis; c) construction activity for water supply to the constructed toilets; d) training and skill development to facilitate maintenance of constructed toilets and to ensure its inter-linkages with education on hygiene; e) other initiatives of improving sanitation and cleanliness in rural and urban areas including solid and liquid waste management; The donations to the Kosh are covered under 'Corporate Social Responsibility (CSR) under sub-section (5) of Section 135 of the Companies Act, 2013'. Donations other than sums spent for 'Corporate Social Responsibility' are eligible for 100 per cent deductions under Section 80 G of the Income Tax Act, 1961.

Controller General of Accounts

The Controller General of Accounts (CGA) under the Department of Expenditure, of GoI and real time reporting of expenditure at all levels of Programme implementaion. Subsequently (2013), the scope was enlarged to cover direct payment to beneficiaries i.e., Direct benefit Transfers (DBT) under both Plan and non-Plan Schemes. The latest enhancement in the functionalities of PFMS commenced in late 2014, wherein it has been envisaged that digitization of accounts shall be achieved through PFMS. is the principal Accounting Adviser to the Government of India and is responsible for establishing and maintaining a technically sound management accounting system.

The office of CGA prepares monthly and annual analysis of expenditure, revenues, borrowings and various fiscal indicators for the Union Government.

IT Initiatives

The Public Financial Management System (PFMS) is a web-based online software application designed, developed, owned and implemented by the CGA. The primary objective of PFMS is to facilitate sound Public Financial Management System for Government of India by establishing a comprehensive payment, receipt and accounting network. PFMS provides various stakeholders with a real time, reliable and meaningful management information system and an effective decision support system. NIC, DeitY is the technoloy partner.

PFMS was started (in 2009) as a Central Sector Scheme of Planning Commission with the objective of tracking funds released under all Plan schemes.

Expanded Scope of DBT

The mandate of DBT was universalized and extended to cover all Central Sector Schemes and Centrally Sponsored Schemes that have any component of cash benefit transfer to individual beneficiaries. Further, the scope of DBT has been further expanded to include in kind transfers to beneficiaries as well as transfers/honorariums given to various enablers of government schemes like ASHA. Aanganwadi workers, etc., and not limited to cash transfers to beneficiaries only. DBT has shown promising results in schemes like PAHAL (modified DBTL for LPG subsidy), cash subsidy for Public Distribution System (PDS) in Puducherry, Chandigarh, Daman & Diu, Dadra & Nagar Haveli and Mahatma Gandhi National Rural Employment Guarantee Scheme (MGNREGS) across the country. As in June 2016, 74 schemes implemented across 17 ministries/departments are reported to be on DBT. More than

₹ 1,30,000 crores have been transferred to about one fourth of the total population of the country through DBT since inception. The progress of DBT and status of Aadhaar seeding in DBT schemes in current financial year (as of 30.06.2016) is depicted in the table here:

Table 13.7: DBT Progress Report 2016-17 (as of 30.06.2016)

S.No.	Scheme	Total Number of Beneficiaries (in crore)	Amount disbursed (in ₹ cr.)	% of beneficiaries seeded with Aadhaar	% of payment through Aadhaar payment Bridge
1	MGNREGS	10.87	15,403	67.08	18.4
2	PAHAL	16.91	3,481	77.4	65.4
3	NSAP (IGNOAPS, IGNWPS & IGNDPS)	2.94	1,751	37.1	12.04
4	Scholarship schemes	0.38	1,846	1.09	0.82
5	Other Schemes	0.34	296.4	11.9	7.9
	Grand Total	31.4	22,743	68.4	23.57

Direct Benefit Transfer

Direct Benefit Transfer (DBT) is a major reform initiative launched by the Government of India in 2013 to provide on overarching vision and direction to enable direct cash transfer of benefits under various government schemes and programmes to individuals. Leveraging the gains in the Aadhaar Project, DBT was conceived with the objective of accurately targeting the intended beneficiarie and enhancing efficiency, transparency and accountability in delivery of benefits/services under government schemes.

Central Pension Accounting Office

The Central Pension Accounting Office (CPAO) was established in 1990 for payment and accounting of central (civil) pensioners and pension to freedom fighters etc. CPAO is a subordinate office under the Controller General of Accounts, Department of Expenditure. It has been entrusted with the responsibility of administering the scheme of payment of pension to central government (civil) pensioners through authorized banks.

Chief Advisor Cost

The Office of the Chief Advisor Cost (CAC) is responsible for advising the ministries and Government undertakings on cost accounts matters and to undertake cost investigation work on their behalf. Office of Chief Advisor Cost is one of the divisions functioning in the Department of Expenditure. It is a professional body staffed by Cost/Chartered Accountants and deals with matters relating to costing and pricing, industry level studies for determining fair prices, studies on user charges, central excise abatement matters, cost-benefit analysis of projects studies on cost reduction, cost efficiency, appraisal of capital intensive projects, profitability analysis and application of modern management tools evolving cost and commercial financial accounting for ministries/departments.

National Institute of Financial Management

The National Institute of Financial Management (NIFM) was set up in 1993. The Union Cabinet envisaged that NIFM would begin as a training institution for officers recruited by the Union Public Service Commission through the annual Civil Service Examinations and allocated to the various services responsible for managing senior and top management posts dealing with accounts and finance in the Government. NIFM was to develop as a Centre of Excellence in the areas of Financial Management and related disciplines, not only in India but also in Asia.

Currently, the Institute runs five long-term programmes approved by AICTE—Professional Training Course of one year for newly recruited probationers of Accounting Services called Diploma in Public Financial Management; a one year Diploma Course in Government Financial Management; a two-year Post Graduate Diploma in Management (Financial Management) programme for Officers of the Central Government, the State Governments, Public Sector Undertakings and other organizations under Government duly recognized as MBA equivalent by AIU and NBA accredited; and a one-year Post Graduate Diploma in Management (Financial Markets) to produce competent researchers, teachers and consultants.

Department of Revenue

The Department of Revenue exercises control in respect of revenue matters relating to direct and indirect Union taxes. The Department is also entrusted with the administration and enforcement of regulatory measures provided in the enactments concerning Central sales tax, stamp duties and other relevant fiscal statutes. Control over production and disposal of opium and its products is vested in this Department.

The Department is also facilitating taxation reforms in the indirect taxes sector for goods and services in coordination with the states. These cover an extended ambit, encompassing the switch-over from erstwhile state sales tax to value added tax, phasing-out of central sales tax, rationalization of additional excise duties on goods of special importance and eventual evolution of a frame work for dual goods and services tax. Tax policies are formulated in order to mobilize financial resources for nation, achieve sustained growth of the economy, macro-economic stability and promote social welfare by providing fiscal incentives for investments in the social sector.

State Value Added Tax

Under Entry 54 of List II (State List) of the Seventh Schedule of the Constitution of India, tax on sale or purchase of goods within a state is a state subject. Introduction of state Value Added Tax (VAT) to replace the earlier sales tax systems of the states has been one of the important tax reform measures taken on indirect tax side. Sales Tax/VAT being a State subject, the Central government played the role of a facilitator for successful implementation of VAT.

Central Sales Tax

Entry 92A of List-I (Union List) empowers the Central Government to impose tax on inter-state sale of goods. Further, Article 269 (3) empowers the Parliament to formulate principles for determining when a sale or purchase of goods takes place in the course of inter-state trade of commerce. Similarly, Article 286 (2) of Constitution empowers the Parliament to formulate principles for determining when the sale or purchase of goods takes place outside a state or in the course of imports into or exports from India. Besides, Article 286(3) of Constitution authorizes the Parliament to place restrictions on the levy of tax by the states on sale or purchase of goods, declared by the Parliament by law to be goods of special importance in the inter-state trade or commerce.

The Central Sales Tax Act, (CST) 1956 imposes the tax on inter-state sale of goods and formulates the principles and imposes restrictions as per the powers conferred by the Constitution. The Government of India has also framed the Central Sales Tax (Registration and Turnover) Rules, 1957 in exercise of powers conferred by Section 13 (1) of the CST Act, 1956. Though the Central Sales Tax Act 1956 is a Central Act, the states collect and appropriate the proceeds of Central Sales Tax as per Article 269 of the Constitution of India.

The Central Sales Tax, however, being an origin-based non-rebatable tax, is inconsistent with the destination based Goods & Services Tax (GST). Central Sales Tax rate was reduced from 4 per cent to 3 per cent 2007 and from 3 to 2 per cent from June, 2008. A package of compensation to the states for revenue loss on account of phasing out of the Central Sales Tax had been agreed to. The states have been compensated through a combination of revenue enhancing measures and budgetary support. As measures for enhancing revenue and thereby compensating the states for Central Sales Tax revenue loss, the facility of interstate purchases by Government Departments at concessional Central Sales Tax rate against Form-D was withdrawn from April 2007. Also, enabling provisions were made for states to levy Value Added Tax on tobacco and tobacco products without losing any part of the devolution of Central taxes to the states.

Goods and Services Tax

The proposal to introduce a national level Goods and Services Tax (GST) The responsibility of preparing a design and road map for the implementation of GST was assigned to the Empowered Committee of State Finance Ministers. The ratification by at least 50 per cent of the state legislatures will be required before the proposed amendments are brought in effect. Several committees have been formed to look into the various aspects of implementation of GST.

Central Board of Excise and Customs

Central Board of Excise and Customs (CBEC) deals with the tasks of formulation of policy concerning levy and collection of Customs, Central Excise duties and Service Tax, prevention of smuggling and evasion of duties and all administrative matters relating to Customs, Central Excise and Service Tax formations. The Board discharges the various tasks, with the help of its field formations namely, the Zones of Customs, Central Excise and Service Tax, Commissionerates of Customs & Central Excise and various Directorates. It also ensures that applicable taxes on imported & domestically produced goods and services are administrated as per law and the collection agencies deposit the taxes collected to the public exchequer promptly.

Custom, Excise & Service Tax Appellate Tribunal

The Customs, Excise & Service Tax Appellate Tribunal (CESTAT) earlier Customer Excise & Gold (Control) Appellate Tribunal) was created to provide an independent forum to hear the appeal against orders and decisions passed by the Commissioners of Custom & Excise under the Customs Act, 1962, Central Excise Act, 1944 and Gold (Control) Act, 1968. The Gold (Control) Act, 1968 has now been repealed. Presently Service Tax appeals have been included. The Tribunal is also having appellate jurisdiction in anti dumping matters and the special bench headed by the president CESTAT, hears the appeals against the orders passed by the designated authority in the Ministry of Commerce. The headquarter as well as the Principal Bench of the Tribunal is stituated at Delhi and other regional benches are at Mumbai, Kolkata, Chennai, Bengaluru and Ahmedabad. In order to ensure the speedy disposal of appeals and for the benefit of the litigants and the Industry of various regions, the Ministry of Finance, has notified the creation of additional six Benches of Customs Excise and Service tax Appellate Tribunal at Chandigarh, Allahabad and Hyderabad in addition to one each at Delhi, Mumbai and Chennai.

Each Bench consists of a judicial member and a Technical Member. To expedite the disposal of small cases with financial stake involving upto ₹ 50,00,000 wherein no question of rate of duty or valuation issue is involved, a single member Bench is also constituted. The Tribunal is the appellate authority hearing appeals arising against the order of the Commissioner of Customs, Excise, Service Tax and Commissioner (Appeals) order. An appeal against the Tribunal's order lies before the Supreme Court in respect of issues such as classification, valuation, etc.

Customs, Central Excise and Service Tax Settlement Commission

The Central Government constituted the Customs and Central Excise Settlement Commission under Section 32 of the Central Excise Act, 1944. The Commission consists of a Principal Bench presided over by the Chairman at New Delhi and three Additional Benches at Chennai, Mumbai and Kolkata presided over by Vice Chairman with 2 Members in each Bench. The present sanctioned strength of the Commission is 118 officers and staff-30 each for New Delhi. Mumbai and Kolkata and 28 for Chennai. The Commission functions in the Department of Revenue as an Attached office of the Ministry of Finance.

The basic objective in setting up of the Settlement Commission is to expedite payments of customs and excise duties involved in disputes, by avoiding costly and time consuming litigation process and to give an opportunity for tax payers who may have evaded payments of duty to come clean. Settlement Commission is therefore set up as an independent body, manned by experienced tax officers of integrity and outstanding ability, capable of inspiring confidence in the trade and industry and entrusted with the responsibility of defining and safeguarding revenue interest.

Central Board of Direct Taxes

The Central Board of Direct Taxes (CBDT), created by the Central Board of Revenue Act 1963, is the apex body entrusted with the responsibility of administering direct tax laws in India. The CBDT consists of a Chairman and six members, all of whom are ex-officio Special Secretaries to the Government of India, in the apex scale of pay. It is the cadre controlling authority for the Income Tax Department.

Black Money (Undisclosed Foreign Income and Assets) and Imposition of Tax Act

The stringent Black Money (Undisclosed Foreign Income and Assets) and Imposition of Tax Act, 2015 was enacted in 2015. A one-time compliance window under the aforesaid new law was provided from July to September 2015 as an opportunity to declarants to declare their undisclosed foreign assets subject to certain prescribed conditions, before they are subjected to more stringent provisions of the new law.

Department of Financial Services

The Department of Financial Services (DFS) is mainly responsible for policy issues relating to Public Sector Banks (PSBs) and Financial Institutions including their functioning, appointment of Chairman, Managing Director and Chief Executive Officers (MD & CEOs), Executive Directors (EDs), Chairman cum Managing Directors (CMDs), Legislative matters, international banking relations. Appointment of Governor/Deputy Governor of Reserve Bank of India, matters relating to National Bank for Agriculture and Rural Development (NABARD), Agriculture Finance Corporation, Co-operative Banks, Regional

Rural Banks (RRBs) and Rural/Agriculture Credit. The Department also administers the financial inclusion programme of the government, social security schemes and other targeted schemes aimed at facilitating flow of credit, matters relating to insurance sector and performance of public sector insurance companies, administration of various Insurance Acts. Matters relating to Insurance Regulatory and Development Authority of India (IRDAI) and matters relating to pension reforms including the New Pension System (NPS), legislative and other issues regarding the Pension Funds Regulatory and Development Authority (PERDA), etc.

Regional Rural Banks

The Regional Rural Banks (RRBs) were established under Regional Rural Banks Act, 1976 to create an alternative Channel to the cooperative credit structure and to ensure sufficient institutional credit for the rural and agriculture sector. RRBs are jointly owned by Government of India, concerned state government and sponsor banks with the issued capital shared in the proportion of 50 per cent, 15 per cent and 35 per cent, respectively. With a view to bring the CRAR of RRBs to at least 9 per cent, the Dr. K.C. Chakrabarty Committee recommended recapitalisation support to the extent of ₹ 2,200 crore to 40 RRBs in 21 states.

Kisan Credit Card

The Kisan Credit Card (KCC) scheme was introduced in 1998-99, as an innovative credit delivery system aiming at adequate and timely credit support from the banking system to the farmers for their cultivation needs including purchase of inputs in a flexible, convenient and cost effective manner. The scheme is being implemented by all cooperative banks, RRBs and public sector commercial banks throughout the country. KCC is one of the most effective tools for delivering agriculture credit. NABARD monitors the scheme in respect of cooperative banks and RRBs and RBI in respect of commercial banks. A new scheme for KCC has been circulated by RBI and NABARD which provides for KCC as an ATM card which can be used at ATM/Point of Sale (POS) terminal. Position of number of live/operative KCCs in the country is as under:

(No. in lakhs)

Cooperative & RRBs (as on April, 2016)	Commercial Banks (As on March, 2016)	Total
526.10	234.70	760.80

Source: RBI/NABARD

Rural Infrastructure Development Fund

The Central Government established a fund to be operationalised by NABARD namely, the Rural Infrastructure Development Fund (RIDF), which was set-up within NABARD by way of deposits from Scheduled Commercial Banks operating within the country from the shortfall in their agricultural/priority sector/weaker sections lending. The fund has since been continued, with its allocation being announced every year in the Union Budget. Over the years, coverage under the RIDF has been broad based, in each tranche, and at present, a wide range of 34 activities are financed under various sectors.

The annual allocation of funds announced in the Union Budget has gradually increased from ₹ 2,000 crore in 1995-96 (RIDF) to ₹ 25,000 crore in 2016-17.

Life Insurance Corporation of India

Life Insurance Corporation of India (LIC) was established by an Act of Parliament called the Life Insurance Corporation of India Act, 1956. It is governed by the Insurance Act, 1938, LIC Act, 1956, LIC Regulations, 1959 and Insurance Regulatory and Development Authority Act, 1999. As on March 31, 2016, LIC has 08 zonal offices, 113 divisional offices, 2,048 branch offices, 73 customer zones, 1,401 satellite offices and 1,240 mini offices in the country. LIC is present in 14 countries abroad through branch offices/joint ventures companies and wholly owned subsidiary.

Aam Aadmi Bima Yojana

For the benefit of the weaker sections of the society, Government of India has floated a highly subsidized insurance scheme, viz., Aam Aadmi Bima Yojana (AABY) which is administered through Life Insurance Corporation of India. Under this social security scheme below poverty line (BPL) and marginally above poverty line citizens are covered under 48 identified occupations. The scheme provides death cover of ₹ 30,000/- in case of natural death. In case of death of total disability (including loss of two eyes/two limbs) due to accident, a sum of ₹ 75,000/- and in case of partial permanent disability (loss of one eye/limb) due to accident, a sum of ₹ 37,500/- is payable to the nominee/beneficiary. All these benefits are paid for a nominal premium of ₹ 200/- per member per annum, out of which ₹ 100/- is borne by the Central Government through Social Security Fund maintained through LIC of India, and the balance premium of ₹ 100/- is borne by the member and/or nodal agency and/or Central/state government department which acts as the nodal agency. In addition, there is an add on benefit of scholarship at the rate of ₹1,200/- per annum per child for two children per family of the insured members studying from 9th to 12th standard (including ITI courses).

Initiatives

Social Security Schemes

Atal Pension Yojana

The Atal Pension Yojana (APY) was launched in May, 2015, to address the longevity risks among the workers in unorganised sector who are not covered under any statutory social security scheme. The APY is focussed on all citizens in the unorganised sector, who join the National Pension System (NPS) administered by the Pension Fund Regulatory and Development Authority (PFRDA).

Key Features of APY

Any Indian citizen between 18-40 years of age can join through their savings bank account/post office savings account. Minimum pension of ₹ 1,000 or ₹ 2,000 or ₹ 3,000 or ₹ 4,000 or ₹ 5,000 is guaranteed by the Government of India to the subscriber at the age of 60 years, with a minimum monthly contribution (for those joining at age at 18) of ₹ 42 or ₹ 84 or ₹ 126 or ₹ 168 or ₹ 210, respectively. After the subscriber's demise, the spouse of the subscriber shall be entitled to receive the same pension amount as that of the subscriber until the death of the spouse. After the demise of both the subscriber and the spouse, the nominee of the subscriber shall be entitled to receive the pension wealth, as accumulated till age 60 of the subscriber. The subscribers in the eligible age, who are not income-tax payers and who are not covered under any statutory social security scheme, are entitled to receive the co-contribution by Central Government of 50 per cent of the total prescribed contribution, upto ₹ 1,000 per annum, and this will be available for those eligible subscribers, who join APY before March, 2016. The Central Government co-contribution shall be available for a period of 5 years, i.e., from 2015-16 to 2019-20.

Present Status under APY

eNPS

eNPS is an online platform provided by NPS Trust for enabling individuals to open his/her Individual Pension Account under NPS (Tier-I & Tier-II) and also facilitate the new or existing subscribers to make initial or subsequent contributions respectively to their individual pension account under NPS using net banking and debit/credit cards. eNPS does not facilitate enrolment of individuals under Atal Pension Yojana. An individual can open his/her Individual Pension Account under NPS by providing PAN and KYC details as recorded with the bank in which he/she maintains his/her bank account and that bank is empanelled in eNPS or providing Aadhaar details.

Other Functions

With a view to offer quality services to NPS subscribers, new channels have been introduced for interaction with the subscribers.

Mobile App

Mobile App for NPS is now available to the subscribers in 'Google Play Store' as 'NPS by NSDL e-Gov' for installation and use. The features available in Mobile App include: a) transaction statement: using this feature, subscriber will be able to raise the request for transaction statement for a particular financial year. The statement will be sent to the subscriber's registered mail ID at end of the day: b) account details view: subscriber can view his / her NPS account details: c) change in contact details (telephone / mobile no. / email

ID): at present, subscriber can change his/her contact details in CRA system using login credential. The same feature has been extended in Mobile App., etc.

Insurance Sector

Insurance, being an integral part of the financial sector, plays a significant role in India's economy. Apart from protecting against mortality, property and casualty risks and providing a safety net for individuals and enterprises in urban and rural areas, the insurance sector encourages savings and provides long-term funds for infrastructure development and other long gestation projects of the country. The development of the insurance sector is necessary to support its continued economic transformation.

The Public Sector Insurance Companies operating in the sector are: 1. Life Insurance Corporation; 2. National Insurance Company Limited; 3. Oriental Insurance Company Limited; 4. United India Insurance Company Limited; 5. New India Assurance Company Limited: 6. General Insurance Corporation of India Limited (National Re-Insurer) and 7. Agriculture Insurance Company of India Limited (Company floated by Non Life Public Sector insurance.

Reforms in the Insurance Sector

The insurance sector was opened for private participation with the enactment of the Insurance Regulatory and Development Authority Act, 1999. The authority is functioning from its head office in Hyderabad, Andhra Pradesh. The core functions of the authority include (i) licensing of insurers and insurance intermediaries; (ii) financial and regulatory supervision; (iii) regulation of premium rates; and (iv) protection of the interests of the policyholders: With a view to facilitate development of the insurance sector, the authority has issued regulations on protection of the interests of policy holders; obligations towards the rural and social sectors; micro insurance and licensing of agents, corporate agents, brokers and third party administrators. IRDA has also laid down the regulatory framework for registration of insurance companies, maintenance of solvency margin, investments and financial reporting requirements.

Since opening up of the sector, the number of participants in the industry has gone up from seven insurers (including Life Insurance Corporation of India, four public sector general insurers, one specialized insurer viz., Export Credit Guarantee Corporation and General Insurance Corporation as the National Re-insurer) in the year 2000 to fifty five insurers as in March, 2016 operating in the life, non-life and re-insurance segments (including specialized insurers, viz., Export Credit Guarantee Corporation and Agriculture Insurance Company of India Limited (AICIL).

Pradhan Mantri Jeevan Jyoti BimaYojana

Government announced three ambitious social security schemes pertaining to the insurance and pension sectors, namely Pradhan Mantri Jeevan Jyoti BimaYojana (PMJJBY), Pradhan Mantri Suraksha BimaYojana (PMSBY) and the Atal Pension Yojana (APY) to move towards creating a universal social security system, targeted especially for the poor and the under-privileged.

The Pradhan Mantri Jeevan JyotiBimaYojana (PMJJBY) is a one year life insurance scheme, renewable from year to year, offering coverage of two lakhs rupees for death due to any reason and is available to people in the age group of 18 to 50 years (life cover up to 55 years of age) having a bank account who give their consent to join and enable auto-debit. It involves convenient bank account linked enrolment with implementation in IT mode, and premium payment through auto-debit from the bank account of the subscriber. Implementation of this scheme enables affordability and targeting in favour of the poor and the under-privileged and would address the situation of low penetration of life insurance in the country.

Pradhan Mantri Suraksha Bima Yojana

The Pradhan Mantri Suraksha Bima Yojana (PMSBY) is a one year personal accident insurance scheme, renewable from year to year, offering coverage for death/disability due to an accident and is available to people in the age group of 18 to 70 years having a bank account who give their consent to join and enable auto-debit. Under the said scheme, risk coverage available will be ₹ 2 lakh for accidental death and permanent total disability and ₹ 1 lakh for permanent partial disability. It involves convenient bank account linked enrolment with implementation in IT mode, and premium payment through auto-debit from the bank account of the subscriber. Implementation of this scheme enables affordability and targeting in favour of the poor and the under-privileged and would address the situation of low penetration of accident insurance in the country.

Pradhan Mantri Jan Dhan Yojana

With a view to increasing banking penetration and promoting financial inclusion and with the main objective of covering all households with at least one bank account per household across the country, a National Mission on financial inclusion named as *Pradhan Mantri Jan Dhan Yojana* (PMJDY) was announced in 2014.

Objectives of PMJDY include: (i) universal access to banking facilities for all households across the country through a bank branch or a fixed point business correspondent (BC) within a reasonable distance. (ii) to cover all households with atleast one Basic Bank Account with RuPay Debit card having inbuilt accident insurance cover of ₹ 1 lakh, (iii) an overdraft facility upto ₹ 5,000/- after satisfactory operation in the account for 6 months, (iv) a life cover of ₹ 30,000/- to those beneficiaries who open their accounts for the first time from August 2014 to January 2015.

Pension Reforms

National Pension System

With a view to providing adequate retirement income, the National Pension System (NPS) was introduced by the Government. It has been made mandatory for all new recruits to the Government (except armed forces) with effect from January 1, 2004 and has also been rolled out for all citizens with effect from May 1, 2009 on a voluntary basis. The features of the NPS design are: self-sustainability, portability and scalability. Based on individual choice, it is envisaged as a low cost and efficient pension system backed by sound regulation. As a pure 'defined contribution' product, returns would be totally market driven. The NPS provides various investment options and choices to individuals to switch over from one option to another or from one fund manager to another, subject to certain regulatory restrictions.

The NPS architecture is transparent and web enabled. It allows a subscriber to monitor his/ her investments and returns. The facility for seamless portability is designed to enable subscribers to maintain a single pension account (Permanent Retirement Account Number-PRAN) throughout the saving period. Pension Fund Regulatory and Development Authority (PFRDA), set-up as a regulatory body for the pension sector, is engaged in consolidating the initiatives taken so far regarding the full NPS architecture and expanding the reach of NPS distribution network. The process of making NPS available to all citizens entailed the appointment of NPS intermediaries, including institutional entities as Point of Presence (POPs) that serve as pension account opening and collection centers, a Centralized Record Keeping Agency (CRA) and Pension Funds to manage the pension wealth of the investors. The Department of Posts has also been appointed as PoP in addition to other financial institutions which expand the PoP-SP network by more than five times. While Tier-I, the pension account under the NPS has been in operation since May 1, 2009, Tier-II, the withdrawable investment account has been made operational from December 1, 2009. These initiatives are expected to help realize the full potential of the NPS in terms of economics of scale and benefit the subscribers in terms of lower fees and charges and higher returns.

Swavalamban Scheme

To encourage the workers in the unorganized sector to save voluntarily for their old age, an initiative called Swavalamban Scheme was launched in 2010. It is a co-contributory pension scheme whereby the Central Government contributes a sum of ₹ 1,000 per annum in each NPS account opened having a saving of ₹ 1,000 to ₹ 12,000 per annum. Government provides co-contribution for five years to the beneficiaries who registered in the years 2010-11, 2011-12 and 2012-13.Thus Government co-contribution is available to eligible subscribers up to the year 2016-17. The scheme operates through 76 aggregators including some state government(s), Public Sector Banks (PSBs), Regional Rural Banks (RRBs), MFIs, NBFCs and private sector entities. New enrolments under Swavalamban has been stopped with effect from 01-04-2016 consequent upon the launch of the Atal Pension Yojana. Number of subscribers under NPS-Lite/ Swavalamban as on July 2016 was 44.63 lakh.

Rural Housing Fund

The Rural Housing Fund was set up in 2008-09 to enable primary lending institutions to access funds for extending housing finance to targeted groups in rural areas at competitive rates. The corpus of the Fund for 2008-09 was ₹1,778.18 crore, which was enhanced to ₹ 2,000 crore during 2009-10, another ₹ 2,000 crore for 2010-11, another ₹ 3,000 crore for 2011-12, another ₹ 4,000 crore for 2012-13 and another ₹ 6,000 crore for 2013-14 and further by ₹ 8,000 crore in 2014-15. Till June 30, 2016, total amount of ₹ 26,778 crore was received by National Housing Bank under the fund since inception, out of which ₹ 24,927 crore has been deployed towards refinance for rural housing to the target groups.

Pradhan Mantri Mudra Yojana

Micro Units Development and Refinance Agency Limited (MUDRA), is a refinance institution set-up by the Government of India for development of micro units by extending funding support to encourage entrepreneurship in India, mostly from non-corporate small business sector. Under the guidelines of Pradhan Mantri MUDRA Yojana (PMMY), MUDRA has launched three innovative products namely Shishu, Kishor, and Tarun, which signifies the stage of growth and funding needs of the micro units or entrepreneur. MUDRA shall refinance through state level institutions, NBFCs, MFIs, Regional Rural Banks, Nationalized Banks, Private Banks and other intermediaries. Any Indian citizen who is involved in income generating activity such as manufacturing, processing, trading and service sector and whose credit need is less than 10 lakh can approach either banks, MFIs, financial institutions or NBFC for availing of MUDRA loans under PMMY. It has been since decided to extend funding support under PMMY for activities allied to agriculture also.

The lending terms such as margin money, interest rate, security, etc., are as per the RBI stipulations. A separate Credit Guarantee Fund was created for MUDRA loans. Accordingly, Credit Guarantee Fund for Micro Units (CGFMU) was set up. The scheme was notified during April 2016. CGFMU is a portfolio based guarantee. With a view to enable hassle free and flexible credit to the Mudra borrowers, especially those in the Shishu category, whose credit requirement is more in the nature of working capital, MUDRA introduced a scheme called MUDRA card, a debit card on RuPay platform. Many of the banks adopted the scheme and disbursed working capital loan through MUDRA card scheme. There is no subsidy for the loan given under PMMY. However, if the loan proposal is linked to any of the state/Central government schemes, wherein the Government is providing capital subsidy, the same would be extended under PMMY also. Any citizen who is otherwise eligible to take loan and has a business plan for a small business enterprise can avail MUDRA loan upto ₹ 10 lakh. The borrowers need to approach the nearest bank branch and submit the loan application, in the prescribed format along with the required supporting documents for availing of the loan.

Credit Guarantee Fund for Skill Development

To guarantee the loans and advances upto 1.5 lakh (term loan) or any other limit as may be decided by the settler, sanctioned and disbursed by the lending institutions without any collateral security and/or third party guarantees to the eligible borrowers pursuing skill development courses as per the Skill Loan Scheme. Any person (Indian national) taking skill loan having minimum qualification as per National Skill Qualification Framework (NSQF). At present there is no separate dispensation for institutional credit for skill development and most of the loans granted for skill development are subsumed in respective sectors like agriculture, micro and small enterprises, education, etc. The total outstanding in respect of skill loans is not readily available. However, a target of creating 500 million skilled workers by 2022 has been envisaged in the National Skill Development Policy. At an average loan size of ₹ 25,000/- per applicant and approx. 1 million persons to be covered in a year, the total loan requirement of the segment would be in the range of around ₹ 2,500 crore per annum, which is expected to be guaranteed under the Scheme in entirety.

d) Financial and Physical Achievements

S. No.	Type of Achievement	Achievement
1	Financial Achievement	₹490.00 crore received as corpus fund on 31/03/2014.
2	Physical Achievement	74 Member Lending Institutions (MLIs) had been advised for registration.
		17 Member Lending Institutions (MLIs) has been registered for the Guarantee Scheme.
		While the Guarantee Scheme has been notified on November 20, 2015 and the process of guarantee rollout is in progress, the performance is expected to pickup in Financial Year 2016-17 significantly.
		The first guarantee cover of ₹ 1,67,981/- has already been given for skill loan to a PSU bank.

Department of Investment and Public Asset Management

The Department of Disinvestment was set up as a separate Department in 1999 and was later renamed as Ministry of Disinvestment in 2001. From 2004, the Department of Disinvestment is one of the departments under the Ministry of Finance. The Department of Disinvestment has been renamed as Department of investment and Public Asset Management (DIPAM) from 2016.

The mandate of the Department includes all matters related to management of Central Government investments in equity including disinvestment of equity in Central Public Sector Undertakings. Decisions on the recommendations of administrative ministries, NITI Aayog, etc., for disinvestment including strategic disinvestment. All matters related to Independent External Monitor(s) for disinvestment and public asset management. Financial policy in regard to the utilization of the proceeds of disinvestment channelized into the National Investment Fund.

Benefits of Disinvestment

To promote people's ownership of Central Public Sector Enterprises (CPSEs) to share in their prosperity through disinvestment; enables efficient management of public investment in CPSEs for accelerating economic development and augmenting Government's resources for higher expenditure: the process of listing of CPSEs on stock exchanges facilitates development and deepening of capital market and spread of equity culture; helps raise budgetary resources of the Government.

Salient Features of Current Disinvestment Policy

The policy on disinvestment has evolved considerably. The salient features of the policy include: (a) public sector undertakings are the wealth of the Nation and to ensure this wealth rests in the hands of the people, promote public ownership of CPSEs; (b) while pursuing disinvestment through minority stake sale in listed CPSEs, the Government will retain majority shareholding, i.e. at least 51 per cent of the shareholding and management control of the Public Sector Undertakings; and (c) strategic disinvestment by way of sale of substantial portion of Government shareholding in identified CPSEs upto 50 per cent or more, alongwith transfer of management control.

CPSEs Disinvestment (As on 20.07.2016)

Method of Sale	Disinvestment Receipts (₹. crore)
Minority Sales	1,85,715.99
Strategic Sale	6,344.35
Residual Sale	6,398.27
Receipts through sale of majority shareholding of one CPSE to another CPSE	1,317.23
Other transactions like special dividends, control premium, cross-holdings, sale of shares to employees, etc.	12,694.98
Total	2,12,470.82

CPSEs Disinvestment Target and achievements

(Last 5 years)

Sl.No.	Financial year	Target of Disinvestment of CPSE (Minority Stake Sale)	Proceeds from Disinvestment
1.	2011-12	40,000	13,894
2.	2012-13	30,000	23,957

3.	2013-14	40,000	15,819
4	2014-15	43,425	24,349
5.	2015-16	41, 000 (excluding strategic disinvestment of ₹ 28,000 crore)	23,997*

** An additional amount of approx. ₹ 8,152 crore has also been realised through sale of bonus debentures of NTPC to EPFO.*

Reform Measures and Policy Initiatives

(a) Fast Tracking of Approvals & Procedures

Keeping in view the budgeted target of disinvestment, the Department of Disinvestment (DoD) has taken further measures to accelerate the disinvestment process by taking the following measures; replacing annual plan with rolling plans; creating a pipeline of proposals for CPSEs, which at present, are at different stages of approval; fast tracking of approval process. disinvestment programme made more inclusive by following an approach to reserve upto 20 per cent of shares in PSUs-OFS transactions for retail investors on a case to case basis. Based on the suggestion made by the Department, SEBI has reduced the notice period for the OFS transaction from T-2 to T-1 (T being the transaction days). This will help in minimizing the possibility of price hammering between the notice day and transaction day and suitably protecting the interest of retail investors by providing them sufficient time to participate in the OFS transaction.

(b) Disinvestment Programme made more inclusive by Expanding Public Participation

SEBI has expanded the framework of Offer for Sale (OFS) of shares through Stock Exchange Mechanism by reserving a minimum of 10 per cent of the offer size for retail investors. Based on this enabling provision, the Government has made the CPSEs' disinvestment programme more inclusive by following an approach to reserve 20 per cent of shares in CPSEs-OFS transactions for retail investors on a case to case basis.

(c) Restructuring and Re-naming the Department of Disinvestment to implement Government Decisions to Comprehensively Manage Government's investment in PSUs and DIPAM

The re-naming of the Department is in line with focus of the Government on management of its investment in Central Public Sector Enterprises (CPSEs) for accelerating economic development as well as augmenting Government resources for higher expenditure. It underlines Government's recognition of its investment in CPSEs as an important asset for accelerating economic growth and commitment to efficient use of its resources to achieve better return on its investment in CPSEs.

(d) Comprehensive Management of GoI's Investment in CPSEs

Capital Restructuring of CPSEs were issued by this Department in 2016. These guidelines supersede all previously issued guidelines on payment of dividend, but back of shares, issue of bonus shares and splitting of shares. Some of the salient features of the guidelines include: (i) These guidelines shall apply to all 'corporate bodies' where GoI and/or Government controlled one or more body corporates have controlling interest. It will not apply to body corporate which is prohibited from distribution of profits to its members, e.g., companies set up under Section 8 of Companies Act, 2013 or under extant provision of any other Act or which has cumulated losses. (ii) The focus of these guidelines is on optimum utilization of funds by CPSEs/Government to supur economic growth. The CPSEs will have a professional look at the surplus funds available with them and if they do not have plans to deploy them optimally for business purposes, they should explore other options of capital restructuring. (iii) There is emphasis on direct expenditure/Capex by CPSEs for business activities and leveraging their net-worth & assets for higher investment in economic activities. The Guidelines also disincentives parking and sub-optimal investment of funds. (iv) In case any CPSE is not able to comply with any of the above guidelines due to some unforeseen exceptional situation, provisions have been made to ensure that such issues are duly considered upto certain level by the Administrative Ministry in consultation with the Financial Adviser for providing exemptions to CPSEs through a well defined procedure, on a case to case basis.

National Investment Fund

Government constituted the National Investment Fund (NIF) in November, 2005 into which the proceeds from disinvestment of Central Public Sector Enterprises were to be channelized. The corpus of NIF was to be of a permanent nature and NIF was to be professionally managed to provide sustainable returns to the Government, without depleting the corpus. Selected Public Sector Mutual Funds, namely UTI Asset Management Company Ltd., SBI Funds Management Private Ltd. and LIC Mutual Fund Asset Management Company Ltd. were entrusted with the management of the NIF corpus. As per this Scheme, 75 per cent of the annual income of the NIF was to be used for financing selected social sector schemes which promote education, health and employment. The residual 25 Per cent of the annual income of NIF was to be used to meet the capital investment requirements of profitable and revivable PSUs.

In view of the difficult economic situation caused by the global slowdown of 2008-09 and a severe drought in 2009-10, Government approved a change in the policy for utilization of Disinvestment proceeds by granting a one-time exemption to utilize the disinvestment proceeds directly for selected social sector schemes allocated by Department of Expenditure/Planning Commission. In order to align the NIF with the Disinvestment Policy, Government decided that the disinvestment proceeds, with effect from the fiscal year 2013-14, will be credited to the existing NIF which is a public account under the Government

Accounts and the funds would remain there until withdrawn/invested for the approved purposes.

It was also simultaneously decided that the NIF would be utilized for the following purposes: subscribing to the shares being issued by the CPSE on rights basis so as to ensure that 51 per cent ownership of the Government in CPSEs is not diluted; preferential allotment of shares of the CPSE to promoters as per SEBI (Issue of Capital and Disclosure Requirements) Regulations, 2009 so that Government shareholding does not go down below 51 per cent in all cases where the CPSEs desire to raise fresh equity to meet their Capex programme, the Government further approved inclusion of the following purposes to be financed from the NIF. Investment by Government in RRBs/IIFCL/NABRAD/Exim Bank; equity infusion in various Metro projects; investment in Bhartiya Nabhikiya Vidyut Nigam Limited and Uranium Corporation of India Ltd; investment in Indian Railways towards capital expenditure.

Demonetisation of Banknotes

The Government decided to demonetise ₹ 500 and ₹ 1000 banknotes on November 8, 2016. All ₹ 500 and ₹ 1000 banknotes of the Mahatma Gandhi series ceased to be legal tenders in India from November 9, 2016.

Announcing this, Prime Minister Shri Narendra Modi in a live televised address on November 8, 2016 declared that the use of all ₹ 500 and ₹ 1000 banknotes would be invalid from midnight of the same day. He also announced the issuance of new ₹ 500 and ₹ 2000 banknotes of the Mahatma Gandhi New Series in exchange for the old banknotes. However, the banknote denominations of ₹ 100, ₹ 50, ₹ 20, ₹ 10 and ₹ 5 of the Mahatma Gandhi series remained legal tender and were unaffected by the policy.

The government said that the demonetisation move was an effort to stop counterfeiting of the current banknotes allegedly used for funding terrorism, as well as a crackdown on black money in the country.

14 Corporate Affairs

THE Ministry of Corporate Affairs (MCA) administers the following Acts of the Central Government: (i) Companies Act, 2013; (ii) Companies Act, 1956; (iii) Limited Liability Partnership Act, 2008; (iv) The Competition Act, 2002 as amended by Competition (Amendment) Act, 2009; (v) The Insolvency & Bankruptcy Code, 2016; (vi) The Chartered Accountants Act, 1949; (vii) The Cost and Works Accounts Act, 1959; (viii) The Company Secretaries Act, 1980; (ix) Societies Registration Act, 1860; and Indian Partnership Act, 1932 (in Centrally administered areas); (x) The Partnership Act, 1932; and (xi) Companies (Donations to National Funds) Act, 1951.

Administrative Structure

The Ministry has a three tier organizational structure with the headquarters at New Delhi, seven offices of Regional Directors (RDs) at Ahmedabad, Chennai, Hyderabad, Kolkata, Mumbai, New Delhi and Shillong, fifteen Registrars of Companies (RoCs), fourteen Official Liquidators (OLs) and nine RoC-cum-OLs in States and Union Territories.

Registry functions are some of the key activities of the Ministry/ Government Process Re-engineering (GPR) by setting up the Central Registration Centre (CRC) for processing of "Name Availability" (INC-01) and "Incorporation" (INC-02/07/29) e-Forms has been the important change brought out recently. The GPR exercise is in pursuance of the Ministry's objective of providing greater "Ease of Doing Business" to corporate and is expected to result in speedier processing of incorporation related applications, uniformity in application of rules, removing discretion to the extent possible. It is being supplemented by intensive monitoring, aimed at processing of the e-Forms within 1 to 2 working days.

The jurisdictional Registrars of companies, continue to have jurisdiction over the companies incorporated by the Registrar, CRC under the Companies Act, 2013 for all other provisions of the Act and the rules made thereunder, which may be relevant after incorporation. The Official Liquidators function under the overall administrative control of the Ministry, and are attached to corresponding High Courts. They are mainly responsible for implementing court orders regarding liquidation and final dissolution of the companies.

Enactment of Companies Act

The New Companies Act, 2013 (Act) replaced the Companies Act, 1956, by comprehensively revising the law incorporating international best practices as well as in keeping with the needs of the current economic environment. The Ministry has notified 326 Sections out of 470 Sections of the Companies

Act, 2013, which was enacted on August 29, 2013. Remaining 144 Sections are yet to be notified which are related to, inter alia, winding up (100), revival and rehabilitation (17), mergers and arrangements (11), striking off (5) of companies. Bulk of these would become effective with the full implementation of the Insolvency and Bankruptcy Code, 2016.

The Companies Act, 2013 seeks to bring corporate governance and regulation practices in India at par with global best practices. The corporate sector has been given more flexibility in regulating their own affairs, subject to full disclosure and accountability of their actions, with minimal Government interference by the process of approvals. The Act provides more opportunities for new entrepreneurs and enables wide application of information technology in the conduct of affairs by corporates. Key features of the Act are given at Box-I.

KEY FEATURES OF THE COMPANIES ACT, 2013

I. Business Friendly Corporate Regulations/Pro-Business Initiatives

- Provision of self-regulation with disclosures/transparency instead of 'Government approval based regime'.
- Automation of corporate records/meetings – statutory recognition to (i) maintenance of documents by companies in electronic form, (ii) 'video-conferencing' as a mode of conducting Board meetings etc.
- Faster mergers and acquisitions including short form of mergers and cross border mergers.
- Summary liquidation: For companies having net assets of ₹ 1 crore or less, Official Liquidators (OLs) are empowered with adjudicatory powers.
- Setting up of the National Company Law Tribunal (NCLT).
- Concept of 'dormant companies' introduced (companies not engaged in business for two consecutive years can be declared as dormant).
- Concept of One Person Company (OPC) introduced.

II. Good Corporate Governance and Corporate Social Responsibility

- Concept of Independent Directors (IDs) included as a statutory requirement.
- Provision for constitution of several Committees of the Board (Audit Committee, Nomination and Remuneration Committee, Stakeholders Relationship Committee and CSR Committee).

- Woman Director for prescribed class of companies.
- Mandatory provision for constitution of CSR Committee and formulation of CSR Policy, with mandatory disclosure, for prescribed class of companies.

III. Enhancing Accountability of Management

- The term 'Officer in Default' has been reviewed to make it more relevant.
- Terms 'Key Managerial Personnel' (KMP) and 'Promoter' defined to affix responsibility on key functionaries of the company.
- Duties of Directors defined, including to shareholders, employees, the community and environment.
- Cap on number of Directorships: 20 companies, of which 10 can be public companies.

IV. Strengthened Enforcement

- The Central Government to have powers to order investigation, suo-motu, in public interest.
- Statutory recognition of Serious Fraud Investigation Office (SFIO).
- Provision for creation of Special Courts.
- Search and seizure of documents, during investigation, without an order from a Magistrate.
- Freezing of assets or disgorgement of illegal gains of company under investigation.

V. Audit Accountability

- Recognition of accounting and auditing standards.
- Stricter disqualification norms for auditors.
- Auditor not to perform specified non-audit services.
- Tenure or rotation of auditors prescribed.
- Internal audit for bigger companies.
- Substantial civil and criminal liability for an auditor in case of non-compliance.
- Tribunal empowered to direct a change of auditor in case of a fraud detected.
- Cost records and cost audit for prescribed class of companies.
- Secretarial audit for prescribed class of companies.
- National Financial Reporting Authority (NFRA) to be constituted.

- Protection of minority shareholders.
- Exit option provided, if there is dissent to change in object clause, or during compromises, etc.
- Valuation mandated during compromise, arrangements, etc.
- Effect of merger on minority shareholding to be disclosed.
- Listed companies to have one Director representing small shareholders.

VI. Investor Protection

- Stringent norms for acceptance of deposits from the public.
- Strengthened role of Investor Education and Protection Fund (IEPF).
- No time bar on claims of dividends from IEPF.
- Class Action Suits recognized.
- Enhanced powers to tribunal for protection of minority rights.

Companies (Amendment) Act

The Companies Act, 2013 was amended through the Companies (Amendment) Act, 2015 to facilitate business and address certain immediate concerns raised by stakeholders. These amendments along with the relevant rules have been notified under Section 462 of the Companies Act, 2013, which provide exemptions under various provisions of the Act to (i) private companies, (ii) government companies, (iii) section 8 companies and (iv) nidhis.

Companies (Amendment) Bill

On the basis of the recommendations made by Companies Law Committee, 2015, and comments received during public exposure of the report, the Ministry has proposed changes in the Companies Act, 2013 and has introduced Companies (Amendment) Bill, 2016.

The Companies Act, 2013 and rules/notifications/circulars, etc. related to it are available on the official website of Ministry of Corporate Affairs http://www.mca.gov.in.

The Ministry has constituted the National Company Law Tribunal (NCLT) and National Company Law Appellate Tribunal (NCLAT) with benches at ten places.

Justice (Retd.) S. J. Mukhopadhaya has been appointed as Chairperson, NCLAT and Justice (Retd.) M. M. Kumar has been appointed as President, NCLT. On constitution of NCLT and NCLAT, the Company Law Board (CLB) has been dissolved and all the pending cases before the CLB have been transferred to NCLT.

The Ministry has constituted special courts for the purpose of trial of offences punishable under the Companies Act, 2013 with the imprisonment of two years or more having jurisdiction in accordance with Section 435(1) of the Companies Act, 2013.

Number of Companies in the Registry

Total number of companies registered in the country as on March 31, 2016, under Companies Act, 2013, Companies Act, 1956, and previous Company Laws, stood at 15,43,712 of these, 2,85,845 companies were closed; 10,360 companies were under liquidation/dissolve; 29,639 companies were under process of being struck-off, 163 companies were in the process of being re-activated, 594 companies were assigned dormant status under Section 455 of Companies Act, 2013; and 1,38,691 companies were assigned inactive status. Taking these into account, there were 10,88,780 active companies.

Corporate Social Responsibility

Corporate Social Responsibility (CSR) for companies has been mandated through legislation in India through Section 135 of the Companies Act, 2013. Section 135, Schedule VII of the Companies Act, 2013, and the Companies (Corporate Social Responsibility Policy) Rules, 2014 were notified in 2014.

Time to time the Ministry has made amendments to CSR Policy Rules, 2014 and issued clarifications by way of circulars, so as to facilitate effective implementation of CSR and its compliance. Further, the Ministry along with IICA has conducted sensitisation workshops/seminars/conferences with NGO's and corporates for effective implementation.

The extent of compliance and operationalisation of the provision of CSR by the corporates for the Financial Year 2014-15 can be perceived from the CSR expenditure of 4,257 companies that has been analysed in the Ministry.

CSR Expenditure During 2014-15

(₹ in crore)

Sr. No.	Company Type	Total Companies	No. of Companies with CSR Expenditure	No. of Companies with no CSR Expenditure	Actual CSR Expenditure (2014-15)
1.	PSUs	169	116	53	2364
2.	Private Sector Companies	4,088	1,790	2,298	5,665
	Total	**4,257**	**1,906**	**2,351**	**8,029**

Information on CSR expenditure on various developmental sector wise CSR expenditure 2014-15 is as follows:-

Sr. No.	Subject in Schedule VII	CSR Expenditure (in ₹ crore)
1	Health/Eradicating Hunger, Poverty & Malnutrition	2,031.67
2	Education/Differently Abled/Livelihood	2519.92
3	Gender Equality/Women Empowerment / Old Age Homes/Reducing Inequalities	286.81
4	Environment & Animal Welfare	1205.75
5	Heritage Art & Culture	148.09
6	Encouraging Sports	150.07
7	PM National Relief Fund	132.08
8	Rural Development	920.38
9	Slum Development	121.30
10	Swachh Bharat Kosh	115.83
11	Clean Ganga Fund	17.16
12	Others	379.94
Total		**8029**

Limited Liability Partnerships

In India, about 95 per cent of industrial units are Micro Small and Medium Enterprises (MSMEs). As per the survey conducted by MSME over 90 per cent of these MSMEs are registered as proprietorships, about 2 per cent to 3 per cent as partnerships and less than 2 per cent as companies. The corporate form does not appear to be widely prevalent amongst MSMEs. Analysis of the data collected by the Ministry of MSME suggests that high compliance cost under the Companies Act, 1956 deterred the MSMEs from adopting the corporate form.

The functioning of a proprietorship or a partnership firm is too opaque, making assessment of credit-worthiness by bankers difficult, and therefore, the MSME sector is at a comparative disadvantage vis-à-vis corporate bodies in accessing loan/credit facilities from banks and other financial institutions. A need was felt for a new corporate form that would provide an alternative to the traditional partnership with unlimited personal liability on the one hand, and the statute-based governance structure of the limited liability company on the other. In this context, the Limited Liability Partnership (LLP) Act was enacted in 2008 and came to effect in 2009.

LLP is a form of business entity, which allows individual partners to be protected from the joint and several liabilities of partners in a partnership firm. The liability of partners incurred in the normal course of business does not extend to the personal assets of the partners. It is capable of entering into contracts and holding property in its own name. An LLP would be able to fulfil the compliance norms with much greater ease, coupled with limitation of liability. The corporate structure of LLP and the statutory disclosure requirements are expected to enable higher access to credit in the market. As on March 31, 2016, 57,503 LLPs were registered of which 57,496 partnerships were active.

MCA21 e-Governance Project

The Ministry of Corporate Affairs operated an end-to-end e-Governance project called 'MCA21' for registry related services from March 2006 on Build, Own, Operate and Transfer (BOOT) Model under Public-Private Partnership (PPP). The vision is "to introduce a service-oriented approach in the design and delivery of Government Services". The project was undertaken to bring about a Service Centric Approach in the delivery of public services and administration of Companies Act, specifically focusing on (i) starting a business, (ii) doing business. The project has been implemented in field offices (Registrar of Companies (RoCs)/Regional Directorate (RDs) and at the Headquarter, to bring about a service centric approach in the delivery of public services and administration of Companies Act and LLP Act. All functions are provided online without being physically present either at ROCs or at headquarters.

Launch of Single Integrated Incorporation Form

The Ministry has introduced a new form christened INC-29, which provides three services in one single form, which were hitherto available in different forms. With the introduction of this form, stakeholders are able to obtain the name of the company, Director Identification No. (DIN) and incorporate a Company in one single step and single form. This has greatly speeded up and eased the process of incorporation of a new company in the country now.

Cost Audit

The companies engaged in the production of goods or providing services as specified in orders issued by the Central Government under Section 148 of the Companies Act, 2013 are required to include the particulars relating to the utilization of material or labour or to other prescribed items of cost in their books of account. Such companies which are required to maintain cost records, and which have prescribed turnover are also required to get their cost records audited by a cost accountant in practice.

The Central Government has notified the Companies (Cost Records and Audit) Rules, 2014 specifying the class of companies and the threshold limit, which requires to maintain cost records and conduct audit thereof. The aforesaid rules covers 6 regulated sectors and 33 non-regulated sectors which falls under the ambit of Section 148 of the Companies Act, 2013 for maintenance of cost records and conducting of audit thereof subject to the specified threshold limits.

The cost records help the compilation of cost database for the own use of such companies for the purpose of cost management, pricing and other related functions. These records are also used by various Government agencies like price-fixation authorities, regulatory bodies, WTO implementation and monitoring agencies, Competition Commission of India (CCI), Serious Fraud Investigation Office (SFIO), revenue authorities, and other institutions. The Ministry analyses the cost audit reports and monitors compliance to the Act/Rules by the specified companies.

Investor Education and Protection Fund

The Companies Act provides for establishment of Investor Education and Protection Fund (IEPF) for promoting investor awareness and protecting their interests.

The Ministry has been organising Investor Awareness Programmes (IAPs) in association with three professional institutes namely: (a) Institute of Chartered Accountants of India, (b) Institute of Company Secretaries of India and (c) Institute of Cost Accountant of India. CSC e-Governance services of India Ltd; Ministry of Communication & IT (Department of Electronics and Information Technology), New Delhi has been engaged since 2012-2013 for organizing such programmes in the rural areas. In all about 2,291 IAPs were organized across the country during 2015-2016.

Besides organizing IAPs, new initiatives such as crawler messages on Doordarshan news channels and regional kendras, jingles on All India Radio (AIR), etc., were also taken up during 2015-16 for creating awareness amongst investors against unauthorized deposit taking activities.

The Ministry has set up a web page for the companies to file details of unpaid and unclaimed amounts of investors, which have not yet been transferred to Investor Education and Protection Fund (IEPF) (Consolidated Fund of India). A search facility has also been provided on this web page enabling investors to search for unpaid and unclaimed amount due to them and claim the same from concerned company before it is transferred to IEPF.

The amount of dividend, matured deposits, matured debentures, application money, etc., which remained unpaid/unclaimed for a period of seven years from the date they first become due for payment, are transferred to IEPF. Section 205 C of the Companies Act, 1956 does not allow the refund of such amount to individual once it is transferred to IEPF. However, to facilitate refund of unpaid amount transferred to IEPF, a provision has been made in Companies Act, 2013, which provides for establishment of IEPF

Authority. The main objective of this Authority will be to make refund of unpaid amounts to eligible stakeholders and promote investor education, awareness and protection.

Indian Corporate Law Service

Ministry of Corporate Affairs is the Cadre Controlling Authority of the Indian Corporate Law service (ICLS). The erstwhile Indian Company Law Service was rechristened in November, 2008 as the Indian Corporate Law Service.

Serious Fraud Investigation Office

The Serious Fraud Investigation Office (SFIO) was set up by the Government of India in the Ministry of Corporate Affairs. The Companies Act, 2013, inter alia, has accorded statutory status to SFIO and its functions and powers have been enhanced substantially with number of enabling provisions in the Act.

The main function of SFIO is to investigate corporate frauds of serious and complex nature. SFIO takes up investigation of frauds characterized by complexity, and having inter-departmental and multi-disciplinary ramifications, substantial involvement of public interest to be judged by size of either monetary appropriation or the number of persons affected and the possibility of investigations leading to, or contributing towards a clear improvement in systems, laws or procedures. Investigations are carried out by a multidisciplinary team which includes experts from the field of accountancy, forensic auditing, taxation, customs and central excise, information technology, capital market, financial transaction (including banking) and enforcement agencies like Central Bureau of Investigation (CBI), Intelligence Bureau (IB), and Enforcement Directorate.

Indian Institute of Corporate Affairs

The Ministry set up the Indian Institute of Corporate Affairs (IICA), a registered society under Societies Registration Act, 1860 to serve as a 'Holistic Think-Tank', and a 'Capacity Building, Service Delivery Institution' to help corporate growth, reforms through synergized knowledge management, partnerships and problem solving in a one-stop-shop mode. The institute fulfils the training needs of the officers of the Indian Corporate Law Service (ICLS), and other officials working for the Ministry through its network of various schools/centres. The Institute also helps in the continuous improvement of service delivery mechanisms in diverse areas like corporate governance, corporate social responsibility, investor education and protection, etc.

Competition Commission

The Competition Commission of India (CCI) was established in 2003 under the Competition Act, 2002, with the objective of eliminating practices having an adverse effect on competition, promoting and sustaining competition, protecting the interest of consumers and ensuring freedom of trade in India.

The provisions of the Competition Act relating to anti-competitive agreements and abuse of dominant position were brought into force from May, 2009 and the Commission has started dealing with cases under these provisions. The Competition Act, 2002 has been amended twice by the Competition (Amendment) Act, 2007 and the Competition (Amendment) Act, 2009.

As on March 31, 2016, the CCI has received 707 matters relating to anti-competitive agreements and abuse of dominance in diverse sectors such as insurance, travel, transport, cement, automobile manufacture, real estate, pharmaceuticals, financial sector, public procurement and entertainment. It has passed final orders in 576 cases (about 81 per cent). Penalties have also been imposed by CCI in some of the serious cases of infringements.

In respect of Regulation of Combinations, the Commission has received 392 notices for combination till March 2016. Out of them, 372 cases have been disposed off within the stipulated time period, resulting in a disposal rate of 95 per cent of notices filed.

Publications of the Ministry

The Ministry publishes a report on the working and administration of the Companies Act. The Competition Commission of India also publishes an annual report and a quarterly newsletter.

15 Food and Civil Supplies

THE Department of Food and Public Distribution is responsible for the management of the food economy of the nation. To ensure food security for the country, the Department has adopted missions such as efficient procurement at Minimum Support Price (MSP), storage and distribution of food grains; ensuring availability of food grains sugar and edible oils through appropriate policy instruments; including maintenance of Buffer Stocks of food grains; and making food grains accessible at reasonable prices, especially to the weaker and vulnerable sections of society under a Targeted Public Distribution System (TPDS);

The main instruments of the Department's food management policy are procurement, storage and movement of food grains, public distribution and maintenance of buffer stocks.

Procurement of Food Grains

Food Corporation of India (FCI), an autonomous organisation of the Department, with the help of state government agencies, procures wheat, paddy and coarse grains in various states in order to provide price support to the farmers. Before each Rabi / Kharif crop season, Government of India announces the Minimum Support Prices, based on the recommendations of Commission for Agricultural Costs and Prices (CACP), which takes into consideration the cost of various agricultural inputs and the reasonable margin for the farmers for their produce. Before the start of every marketing season, Department of Food and Public Distribution convenes a meeting of State Food Secretaries, FCI and other stake holders to prepare a detailed action plan for making the arrangements of procurement for wheat and barley before Rabi and Paddy, rice and coarse grains before Kharif marketing season. Details of number of procurement centres to be opened and arrangements like purchase of packaging material and storage space are discussed in the meeting. Sufficient numbers of procurement centres are opened by FCI/ State government agencies in mutual consultation before onset of procurement season, keeping in view the procurement potential and geographical spread of the State concerned. Review is made from time to time on the need for additional procurement centres, if any, during the procurement season and required additional procurement centres are also opened. State governments are encouraged to adopt Decentralised procurement (DCP) system of procurement so as to maximise procurement, reduce transportation and increase the reach of MSP operations. Under this system, state governments undertake procurement and distribution of food grains by themselves. Procured quantities in excess of state's requirement are taken in the Central Pool for distribution elsewhere, while shortfall is met from the Central Pool.

With the substantial increase in production of food grains in recent years in the country and with an emphasis on bringing Green Revolution in Eastern-India, the procurement operations have expanded to many states due to which accumulated Central Pool Stock of food grains had reached a record level of 805.16 lakh tonnes in 2012 against the buffer norm of 319 lakh tonnes. Therefore, a balanced policy approach for procurement, distribution and disposal of food grains is now being adopted to provide adequate price support to the farmers, to have optimum level of procurement for meeting TPDS requirement, maintaining buffer stock and to dispose off surpluses without distorting the market in future. Procurement of wheat and rice during last five years is given in Table below:

Table 15.1: Procurement of Wheat and Rice duing last five years

Rabi Marketing Season	Wheat Procurement	Kharif Marketing Season	Rice Procurement
			(in lakh tonnes)
2011-12	283.85	2011-12	350.60
2012-13	381.48	2012-13	340.28
2013-14	250.92	2013-14	315.38
2014-15	280.23	2014-15	320.40
2015-16	280.88	2015-16	338.34*

* *As reported on June 17, 2016*

Foodgrains in Central Pool

The stock of food grains (rice and wheat) in the Central Pool as on July 1, 2016 was 495.95 lakh tonnes (194.14 lakh tonnes of rice and 301.81 lakh tonnes of wheat). The stock as on July 1, 2016 was 9.12 per cent lower than the stock of 545.75 lakh tonnes as on July 1, 2015.

The offtake of food grains (rice and wheat) from the Central Pool by various states/union territories (UTs) under Targeted Public Distribution System and Other Welfare Schemes (OWS), etc., in 2015-16 was 636.55 lakh tonnes as against 559.45 lakh tonnes during 2014-15. The total offtake of food grains (rice and wheat) under TPDS during April, 2015 to March, 2016 is 495.94 lakh MT about (94. per cent) comprising 273.41 lakh tonnes of rice and 222.53 lakh MT of wheat, as against 445.75 lakh tonnes (85.7 per cent) during 2014-15. Under OWS, the offtake is 41.35 lakh tonnes (79.15 per cent) as against 41.24 lakh tonnes (79.12 per cent) during 2014-15.

Allocation of Food Grains

National Food Security Act, 2013

To further strengthen the commitment to food security of the people, Government of India enacted the National Food Security Act, 2013 (NFSA), which came into force in 2013. The Act provides for food and nutritional security in human life cycle approach, by ensuring access to adequate quantity of quality food at affordable prices to people to live a life with dignity. The Act makes a paradigm shift in approach to food security - from welfare to a rights-based one.

The Act provides for coverage of upto 75 per cent of the rural population and upto 50 per cent of the urban population for receiving subsidised food grains under Targeted Public Distribution System (TPDS), thus covering about two-thirds of the population. The eligible persons are entitled to receive 5 kg of food grains per person per month at subsidised prices of ₹ 3, 2 & 1 per kg for rice, wheat and coarse grains, respectively. The existing Antyodaya Anna Yojana (AAY) households, which constitute the poorest of the poor, will continue to receive 35 kg of food grains per household per month at above prices.

The Act also contains provisions for setting up of grievance redressal mechanism at the district and state levels. Separate provisions have also been made for ensuring transparency and accountability.

NFSA is now being implemented in 34 states/UTs covering more than 73 crore beneficiaries, against intended coverage of about 81 crore persons. In Chandigarh, Puducherry and urban areas of Dadra and Nagar Haveli, the Act is being implemented in the cash transfer mode under which food subsidy is being transferred into the bank accounts of beneficiaries who then have a choice to buy food grains from open market.

Antyodaya Anna Yojana

To make TPDS more focused and targeted towards the poorest section of population, the "Antyodaya Anna Yojana" (AAY) was launched in December, 2000 for one crore poor families. AAY contemplates identification of poorest of the poor families from amongst the BPL families covered under TPDS and providing them food grains at a highly subsidied rate of ₹ 2 per kg for wheat and ₹ 3 per kg for rice. Under the Scheme, states/UTs bear the distribution cost, including margin to dealers and retailers as well as the transportation cost, which provides the poorest access to food grains at highly subsidised rates. The scale of issue that was initially 25 kg per family per month increased to 35 kg per family per month with effect from 2002. The AAY Scheme has been expanded in subsequent years so as to cover 2.50 crore households (thus reducing the name of families in BPL by equal number).

The TPDS (Control) Order, 2015 provides that the state-wise number of Antyodaya households shall not exceed the accepted number in that state. Provided that when an Antyodaya household becomes ineligible on account of migration outside the state, improvement in social or economic status, death, etc., no new Antyodaya household shall be identified in that state and the total number of Antyodaya households shall be reduced to that extent. Upon a reduction in the number of Antyodaya households, the states may increase the coverage of the persons to that extent in the priority category, subject to prescribed ceilings.

End-To-End Computerisation of TPDS

Department of Food and Public Distribution is implementing a Plan Scheme on 'End-to-End Computerisation' of TPDS Operations on cost sharing basis with states/UTs with funding requirement of ₹ 884.07 crore, out of which Government of India's share is ₹ 489.37crore and that of states/UTs is ₹ 394.70 crore. It has become more important after coming into force of the National Food Security Act, under which prices of food grains to be distributed through the TPDS are highly subsidised. The key activities and their expected outcomes in the first phase are: (i) digitisation of beneficiary database will enable correct identification of beneficiaries, facilitates helps removal of bogus cards and better targeting of food subsidies; (ii) computerisation of supply chain management timely availability of food grains to intended beneficiaries at FPS and check leakages/diversion; (iii) setting up of grievance redressal mechanism and transparency portal to introduce transparency and public accountability in the implementation of TPDS.

For checking of leakage and diversions, the Department is also pursuing with states/UTs to opt for Direct Benefit Transfer (DBT) in lieu of food grains under which subsidy component will be credited to bank accounts of beneficiaries who are free to buy food grains from anywhere in the market to ensure their food grains entitlement. For taking up this model, pre-requisites for the states/UTs would be to complete digitisation of beneficiary data and seeding of bank account details of beneficiaries. The scheme has been implemented in UTs of Chandigarh and Pucducherry from 2015 and in Dadra & Nagar Haveli from 2016 on pilot basis.

Targeted Public Distribution System

To maintain supplies and securing availability and distribution of essential commodities, PDS (C) Order, 2001 was notified on August 31, 2001. In order to bring the PDS(C) Order, 2001, in consonance with the National Food Security Act, 2013, (NFSA), the Department put in place the Targeted Public Distribution System (Control) Order, 2015 in 2015 in supersession of the PDS (C) Order, 2001 for maintaining supplies and securing availability and distribution of essential commodity, namely, food grains under the TPDS. The provisions of the PDS (C) Order, 2001 shall continue to have effect as against the corresponding provisions of this Order in any state which has not implemented the NFSA, 2013 or is implementing the said Act only in part.

To share the initiatives and best practices as well as the latest development and achievements, the Department has launched the quarterly newsletter namely 'Khadya Suraksha'.

Other Welfare Schemes

Mid-Day Meal Scheme

The Mid-Day Meal Scheme is implemented by the Ministry of Human Resource Development. Up to 2015-16, allocation under the scheme was made at BPL rates. However during the current year food grains for the Scheme are allocated at NFSA rates by the Department of Food & Public Distribution. The Scheme covers students of primary and upper primary classes in the government schools and schools aided by government and the schools run by local bodies. Food grains are supplied free of cost @ 100 grams for primary stage and @ 150 grams for upper primary stage per child per school day where cooked/processed hot meal is being served or 3 kg. per student per month where food grains are distributed in raw form.

Annual allocation and offtake of food grains under the scheme during the last three years & current year are given in Table 15.2:

Table 15.2 : Annual Allocation /Offtake of Foodgrains under Mid-Day Meal Scheme

(In lakh tonnes)

	ALLOCATION			OFFTAKE		
YEAR	RICE	WHEAT	TOTAL	RICE	WHEAT	TOTAL
2013-14	22.79	4.67	27.46	19.86	3.91	23.77
2014-15	23.37	4.09	27.46	20.07	3.63	23.70
2015-16	23.19	4.56	27.75	19.43	3.96	23.39
2016-17	11.35	2.08	13.43 #	1.58	0.31	1.89 *

**offtake upto June, 2016 (Offtake includes backlog quota also.)*

 # for six months i.e. fromApril 01, 2016 to September 30, 2017

Wheat Based Nutrition Programme

This Scheme is implemented by the Ministry of Women & Child Development. Up to 2015-16, allocation under the scheme was made at BPL rates. However during the current year, food grains for the Scheme is allocated at NFSA rates by the Department of Food & Public Distribution The food grains are utilised by the states/UTs under Integrated Child Development Services (ICDS) scheme for providing nutritious/energy food to children in the age group of 0-6 years and expectant/lactating women. During 2016-17, 19.85 lakh lakh tonnes of food grains comprising 9.58 lakh lakh tonnes of rice and 10.27 lakh lakh tonnes of wheat have been allocated under the scheme. Besides, during the 2016-17, a quantity of 24000 lakh tonnes of maize and 21000 lakh tonnes of ragi has been allotted under the scheme.

Annual allocation and offtake of food grains under the scheme during the last three years and current year are given in Table 15.3:

Table 15.3 : Allocation and Offtake under WBNP

(In lakh tonnes)

ALLOCATION				OFFTAKE		
YEAR	RICE	WHEAT	TOTAL	RICE	WHEAT	TOTAL
2013-14	7.15	9.00	16.15	4.49	8.50	12.99
2014-15	8.03	9.72	17.75	4.68	8.23	12.91
2015-16	8.03	9.64	17.67	5.47	8.26	13.73
2016-17 *	9.58	10.27	19.85	0.62	0.78	1.40

**offtake upto June, 2016.*

(Offtake includes backlog quota also)

Rajiv Gandhi Scheme for Empowerment of Adolescent Girls – 'SABLA'

The SABLA Scheme was launched in 2010 by merging two schemes namely Nutrition Programme and Adolescent Girls (NPAG) and Kishori Shakti Yojana (KSY) in to a single scheme and proposed to be implemented in 200 selected districts across the country.

The Ministry of Women and Child Development administers the scheme at the Central level while state/UT governments implement the scheme. However, food grains for the scheme are allotted by the Department of Food & Public Distribution at BPL rates. The Scheme aims at empowering adolescent girls of 11-18 years by improvement of their nutritional and health status and upgrading various skills like home skills, life skills and vocational skills. It also aims at equipping the girls on family welfare, health hygiene etc., and information and guidance on existing public services along with aiming to mainstream out-of-school girls into formal or non-formal education. The requirement of food grains under the scheme for nutrition is @ 100 grams of grains per beneficiary per day for 300 days in a year. During 2015-16 a quantity of 1625 lakh tonnes of maize has been allotted to Government of Tamil Nadu under the scheme. During 2016-17, a quantity of 1750 lakh tonnes of maize and 1100 lakh tonnes of ragi has been allotted to the same states.

Annual allocation and offtake of food grains under the scheme during the last three years and current year are given in Table 15.4:

Table 15.4 : Allocation and Offtake under 'SABLA'

(In lakh tonnes)

	ALLOCATION			OFFTAKE		
YEAR	RICE	WHEAT	TOTAL	RICE	WHEAT	TOTAL
2013-14	0.75	1.28	2.03	0.39	0.73	1.12
2014-15	0.81	1.26	2.07	0.32	1.22	1.54
2015-16	0.81	1.26	2.07	0.27	0.61	0.88
2016-17*	1.25	1.45	2.70	0.04	0.05	0.09

**offtake upto June, 2016*

(Offtake includes backlog quota also)

Scheme for Supply of Foodgrains to Welfare Institutions

With a view to meet the requirement of Welfare Institutions viz., charitable Institutions such as beggar homes, nari niketans and other similar welfare institutions not covered under TPDS or under any other welfare schemes, an additional allocation of food grains (rice and wheat) not exceeding five per cent of the BPL allocation is made to states/UTs at BPL prices.

During the year 2015-16, an allocation of 1.82 lakh tonnes of food grains (wheat/rice) under the scheme has been made. During the 1st half of 2016-17, an allocation of 15,894 lakh tonnes of food grains (wheat/rice) has been made to various States/UT.

Scheme for Supply of Food grains for SC/ST/OBC Hostels

This scheme was introduced in October, 1994. The residents of the hostels having 2/3rd students belonging to SC/ST/OBC are eligible to get 15 kg food grains per resident per month. Allocations of food grains under the scheme are made by the Department of Food and Public Distribution based on the requests received from the state/UT governments.

The total allocation/offtake of food grains under the above two schemes (Welfare Institutions and SC/ST/OBC Hostels) during the last three years is given in Table 15.5:-

Table 15.5 : Allocation Offtake SC/ST/OBC Hostels in Welfare Institution

(In lakh tonnes)

	Total Allocation			Total Offtake	
Year	Welfare Institution	SC/ST/OBC Hostels	TOTAL	Welfare Institution	SC/ST/OBC Hostels
2013-14	2:37	1.66	4.03	3.02	
2014-15	2.11	2.04	4.15	2.86	

2015-16	1.82	2.13	3.95	3.02
2016-17	0.16	0.80	0.96 #	0.16 *

** Offtake figures received from FCI as on June, 2016*

 # for six months i.e. from April 01, 2016 to September 30, 2017.

Offtake figures are combined as reported by FCI.

Annapurna Scheme

This Scheme is implemented by the Ministry of Rural Development. Indigent senior citizens of 65 years of age or above who are not getting pension under the National Old Age Pension Scheme (NOAPS), are provided 10 kgs. of food grains per person per month free of cost under the scheme. Food grains are provided by the Department of Food & Public Distribution under the scheme at BPL prices.

Annual allocation and offtake of food grains under the scheme during the last three years and current year are given in Table 15.6:

Table 15.6

(In lakh tonnes)

	ALLOCATION			OFFTAKE		
YEAR	RICE	WHEAT	TOTAL	RICE	WHEAT	TOTAL
2013-14	0.41	0.17	0.58	0.48	0.09	0.57
2014-15	0.51	0.18	0.69	0.22	0.01	0.23
2015-16	0.61	0.19	0.80	0.26	0.06	0.32
2016-17*	0.00	0.00	0.00	0.17	0.00	0.17

**offtake upto June, 2016 (Offtake includes backlog quota also)*

Open Market Sale Scheme

The Food Corporation of India (FCI), on the instructions from the Government, sells wheat at pre-determined prices in the open market time to time under Open Market Sale Scheme (Domestic) through e-Tender to enhance the supply of wheat, especially during the lean season and, thereby to liquidate excess stock in the Central Pool and moderate the open market prices, especially in the deficit regions.

Sale of Wheat and Rice under OMSS-D

For 2015-16, the Government had approved sale of entire surplus stock of 111 lakh tonnes of wheat available under the Central Pool and 20 lakh tonnes of Grade 'A' rice under Open Market Sale Scheme (Domestic) OMSS (D) to bulk traders/consumers/state governments and separate allocation of small traders as well as to the state governments/national cooperative institutions.

In 2016-17, a target of 65-75 lakh tonnes has been set for sale of wheat by FCI out of Central Pool under the OMSS (D). A target of 20 lakh tonnes of Grade 'A' rice has also been kept for sale during 2016-17.

The reserve price for the bulk sale of wheat under OMSS(D) in 2016-17 to private bulk buyers/traders has been kept as ₹ 1,640 per quintal. For sale from the depots of FCI outside surplus procuring States of Punjab, Haryana and Madhya Pradesh, freight/road transport charges upto the concerned depots of FCI, ex-Ludhiana will be added in this reserve price. For sale under dedicated movement, the handling and transportation charges from FCI depots to the loading in Railway rake will also be added in the reserve price. The overall reserve price for sale of Grade 'A' rice under OMSS (D) has been kept at ₹ 2400 per quintal for 2016-17.

Though special arrangement made for Jammu and Kashmir buyers for purchasing wheat in e-Auction in Punjab at discounted reserve price has been discontinued, FCI has been directed to ensure adequate stock on offer for J&K buyers within the State itself at rail fed depots/railheads at reasonable price after adding ex-Ludhiana freight.

The quantities of wheat and rice sold under the OMSS (D) during the last five years and current year are given in Table 15.7:

Table 15.7 : Quality of Wheat and Rice sold under OMSS (D)

(A-WHEAT)

(In lakh tonnes)

Year	Quantity
2011-12	11.84
2012-13	68.67
2013-14	61.16
2014-15	42.37
2015-16	70.77
2016-17(Upto June, 2016)	04.09

B-RICE

(In lakh tonnes)

Year	Quantity
2011-12	0.19
2012-13	0.99
2013-14	1.68
2014-15	Nil
2015-16	1.11
2016-17 (Upto June, 2016)	0.14

Storage of Food Grains

State-wise capacities of FCI

FCI has its own grid of covered godowns in all states to safely stock the central pool of food grains. In addition, it hires capacity from Central Warehousing Corporation (CWC) and state agencies like state warehousing corporations as well as private parties.

Sufficient storage capacity is available and against 811.94 lakh tonnes capacity available, the Central stock of food grains stood at 534.29 lakh tonnes as in June 2016. The state wise storage capacity is given in Table 15.8.

Augmentation of Storage Capacity

In order to cope with increasing production and procurement of food grains, the Department is implementing Private Entrepreneurs Guarantee (PEG) scheme for augmenting the covered storage capacity in the country.

Under the PEG scheme, which was launched in 2008, godowns are constructed in PPP mode and the land and construction cost is borne by the selected partners. FCI on its part guarantees 10 years usage of storage capacities to the private investors and nine years to CWC and SWCs. Locations for construction of godown are identified by the FCI on the basis of recommendations of State Level Committees (SLCs) to cover the gaps in storage. For consuming areas, the storage gap is assessed on the basis of the four months' requirement of PDS and OWS while for procuring States the storage gap has been assessed based on the highest stock levels in the last three years, and keeping in view the potential of procurement.

Under the scheme, a capacity of 134.45 lakh tonnes has been completed in 20 states out of total sanctioned capacity of 150.80 lakh tonnes in May, 2016.

Warehousing Development and Regulatory Authority

For the growth and development of warehousing sector, to bring reforms in the agricultural marketing and to increase credit flow in the farm sector, the Government of India introduced a negotiable warehouse receipt system by enacting the Warehousing (Development and Regulation) Act, 2007 which has come into force from in 2010. The Central Government constituted the Warehousing Development and Regulatory Authority (WDRA) also in 2010 for implementation of the provisions of the Act.

Warehouses need to be registered with the WDRA for issuing NWRs. The warehouses are accredited by the approved accreditation agencies prior to their registration with the WDRA to ensure that basic requirements of scientific and safe storage of agricultural and other commodities are fully met by these warehouses. The Authority has approved 11 accreditation agencies for accreditation of warehouses.

Table 15.8: State-wise Storage Capacity

(Figures in lakh tonnes)

Sl. No.	State	Total storage capacity with FCI (owned/hired) Covered		CAP		Total		State Agencies State Agencies		Grand Total	
		Owned	Hired	Owned	Hired	Covered	CAP	Covered	CAP	Covered	CAP
1	Bihar	3.66	2.60	1.00	0.00	6.26	1.00	7.85	-	14.11	1.00
2	Jharkhand	0.67	1.81	0.05	0.00	2.48	0.05	-	-	2.48	0.05
3	Odisha	3.12	2.56	0.00	0.00	5.68	-	6.16	-	11.84	-
4	West Bengal	8.50	1.22	0.51	0.00	9.72	0.51	7.82	-	17.54	0.51
5	Assam	3.00	0.96	0.00	0.00	3.96	-	2.27	-	6.23	-
6	Arunachal Pd	0.20	0.03	0.00	0.00	0.23	-	0.01	-	0.24	-
7	Meghalaya	0.14	0.09	0.00	0.00	0.23	-	-	-	0.23	-
8	Mizoram	0.25	0.00	0.00	0.00	0.25	-	0.42	-	0.67	-
9	Tripura	0.29	0.06	0.00	0.00	0.35	-	0.32	-	0.67	-
10	Manipur	0.28	0.04	0.00	0.00	0.32	-	-	-	0.32	-
11	Nagaland	0.29	0.13	0.00	0.00	0.42	-	0.07	-	0.49	-
12	Delhi	3.36	0.00	0.31	0.00	3.36	0.31	-	-	3.36	0.31
13	Haryana	7.68	44.64	3.33	0.00	52.32	3.33	28.66	22.81	80.98	26.14
14	Himachal Pd.	0.19	0.30	0.00	0.00	0.49	-	-	-	0.49	-
15	J & K	1.03	1.34	0.10	0.00	2.37	0.10	-	-	2.37	0.10
16	Punjab	22.24	81.71	7.31	0.00	103.95	7.31	42.42	100.44	146.37	107.75

17	Rajasthan	7.06	11.50	1.85	0.90	18.56	2.75	5.00	0.19	23.56	2.94
18	Uttar Pradesh	14.95	30.57	5.19	0.00	45.52	5.19	14.12	-	59.64	5.19
19	Uttarakhand	0.66	1.01	0.21	0.00	1.67	0.21	1.94	-	3.61	0.21
20	Andhra Pd.	7.36	1.47	1.60	0.00	8.83	1.60	15.61	-	24.44	1.60
21	Telangana	5.37	1.26	1.02	0.00	6.63	1.02	9.74	-	16.37	1.02
22	Kerala	5.29	0.05	0.21	0.00	5.34	0.21	-	-	5.34	0.21
23	Karnataka	3.81	3.58	1.36	0.00	7.39	1.36	20.36	0.41	27.75	1.77
24	Tamil Nadu	6.24	4.90	0.31	0.00	11.14	0.31	16.44	-	27.58	0.31
25	Gujarat	5.00	1.51	0.27	0.00	6.51	0.27	2.29	-	8.80	0.27
26	Maharashtra	8.85	10.45	1.02	0.00	19.30	1.02	11.18	-	30.68	1.02
27	Goa	0.15	0.05	0.00	0.00	0.20	-				
28	Madhya Pd.	3.37	0.03	0.36	0.00	3.40	0.36	103.25	14.28	106.65	14.64
29	Chhattisgarh	5.12	3.55	0.01	0.00	8.67	0.01	15.41	-	24.08	0.01
	Total	**128.13**	**207.42**	**26.02**	**0.90**	**335.55**	**26.92**	**311.34**	**138.13**	**646.89**	**165.05**
	Grand Total	**335.55**		**26.92**		**362.47**		**449.47**		**811.94**	

The Authority has notified 123 agricultural commodities including cereals, pulses, oilseeds, vegetable oils, spices, edible nuts and miscellaneous items like rubber, tobacco, tea coffee and makhana and 26 horticultural commodities such as potato, dehydrated onion, garlic, ginger, turmeric, apple and resins etc. for issuing NWRs. The Primary Agricultural Cooperative Societies (PACSs) warehouses have also been covered under the negotiable warehouse receipt system so that small and marginal farmers may get benefited from this scheme. The Authority, as on mid June, 2016 has registered 1242 warehouses of CWC, SWCs, Private Sector, Cold storages and PACS with a total storage capacity of 54.73 lakh tonnes. These warehouses have issued 58,295 negotiable warehouse receipts against the agricultural commodities valued at ₹ 4543.38 crore. The banks have financed ₹ 1,458.56 crore against NWRs.

To create awareness among stakeholders about the NWR system in the country, the WDRA has been arranging conferences in association with FICCI, ASSOCHAM, PHD Chamber, CAIT and IFC at various locations. Bankers' conferences on pledge financing of negotiable warehouse receipts, training programmes for Warehouse Managers and awareness programmes for farmers are also being organised by the Authority.

Post Harvest Management of Food Grains

Quality Standard for Food Grains

The Government exercises due control over the quality of food grains procured for the Central pool. The Quality Control Cells of the Ministry at New Delhi and the field offices at Bengaluru, Bhopal, Bhubaneshwar, Kolkata, Hyderabad, Lucknow, Pune, Guwahati, Chennai and Patna monitor the quality of food grains procured, stored and issue for distribution by FCI and state governments and their agencies. During 2015-16, 1,096 Food Storage Depots were inspected, 37 trainings for 1,295 officials of state governments and their agencies were conducted by the QCCs.

Indian Grain Storage Management and Research Institute

Indian Grain Storage Management and Research Institute (IGMRI), Hapur and its field stations at Ludhiana (Punjab) and Hyderabad (Andhra Pradesh) are engaged in the training and applied Research and Development (R&D) work relating to grain storage management. The IGMRI also conducts various training courses on storage, inspection of food grains, pest control, etc., for the officers of storages agencies and pest control operator, etc. 16 long/short term training courses on scientific storage of food grains were conducted during 2015-16.

Central Grain Analysis Laboratory

The Central Grain Analysis Laboratory (CGAL) located in New Delhi assists the Department in monitoring the quality of food grains at the time of procurement storage and distribution by analysing samples collected by quality control officers. A total number of 1,201 food grains samples for physical parameters, 501 for protein determination, 104 for presence of uric acid in wheat samples were analysed during 2015-16.

Export Policy of Rice and Wheat

The Government had allowed free export of non-basmati rice by private parties from privately held stocks from 2011. State Trading Enterprises (STEs) including M/s NCCF and NAFED are also permitted to export privately held stocks of non-basmati rice. Export of wheat had also been allowed from 2011.

Export of non-basmati rice and wheat is permitted through Custom EDI ports. Export is also permitted through the non-EDI Land Custom Stations (LCS) on Indo-Bangladesh and Indo-Nepal Border subject to registration of quantity with DGFT. Export of rice of seed quality and other [rice in husk (paddy or rough) other than seed quality] is permitted under licence.

Status of Export of Wheat and Rice on Private Account

A quantity of 63.74 lakh tonnes of non-basmati rice and 6.14 lakh tonnes of wheat has been exported under "free export" category during 2015-16.

Status of Export on Government Account

Non-basmati rice and wheat have not been exported from Central Pool stocks of FCI during 2015-16.

The Government also permits export of wheat and rice to various friendly countries on diplomatic basis/humanitarian aid on the recommendations of the Ministry of External Affairs. A quantity of 100 lakh tonne of rice was made available for flood affected area in Myanmar from Central Pool Stocks during 2015-16.

Import of Rice and Wheat

No import of wheat and rice has been made for Central Pool stock during 2015-16. However, a quantity of 5,16,167 lakh tonnes of wheat and 1,021 lakh tonnes of Non-basmati rice has been imported by private traders/millers during 2015-16.

Sugar

Sugar Production

India is the largest consumer and the second largest producer of sugar in the world. The production of sugar during the current sugar season 2015-16 is estimated to be about 251. 60 lakh tonnes against which 247.19 lakh tonnes (provisional) was achieved upto April 2016. The details of state wise sugar production from 2012-13 to 2014-15 and during the current sugar season 2015-16 (upto April 30, 2016) is as follows:

Table 15.9 : Details of State-wise Sugar Production

(In lakh tonnes)

State	Sugar Season			
	2012-13	2013-14	2014-15	2015-16 (upto 30.04.2016) (Prov.)**
Punjab	4.38	4.73	5.36	6.68
Haryana	5.1	5.37	5.73	5.35
Rajasthan	0.04	0.05	0.06	0.04
Uttarakhand	3.4	2.98	3.28	2.71
Uttar Pradesh	75.01	66.13	71.38	67.76
Madhya Pradesh	2.08	3.51	4.08	3.05
Chhattisgarh	0.49	0.68	0.65	0.57
Gujarat	11.3	11.78	11.46	11.08
Maharashtra	79.87	77.2	105.15	86.10
Bihar	5.1	5.96	5.26	5.03
Odisha	0.64	0.6	0.43	0.48
West Bengal	0.2	0.06	0.05	0.00
Andhra Pradesh	9.84	6.75	5.65	5.49
Telangana		3.32	3.21	2.77
Karnataka	34.43	41.6	49.89	40.00
Tamil Nadu	19.32	14.18	12.56	9.95
Puducherry	0.53	0.52	0.32	0.03
Goa	0.1	0.12	0.11	0.10
Total	251.83*	245.54	284.63	247.19

**Excludes 6.76 lakh lakh tonnes of white sugar produced from imported raw sugar*
***As per on-line P-II/Cane Commissioner (Provisional)*

There are 719 installed sugar mills in the country as on June 15, 2016. The sector-wise break-up is as given below:-

Table 15.10 : Sector-wise break-up of Sugar Factories

S.No	Sector	Number of installed sugar mills
1	Cooperative	327
2	Private	349
3	Public	43
	Total	719*

**Includes one refinery each in the States of West Bengal & Gujarat.*

Sugarcane Pricing Policy

With the amendment of the Sugarcane (Control) Order, 1966 in 2009, the concept of Statutory Minimum Price (SMP) of sugarcane was replaced with the 'Fair and Remunerative Price (FRP)' for 2009-10 and subsequent sugar seasons. The cane price announced by the Central Government is decided on the basis of the recommendations of the Commission for Agricultural Costs and Prices (CACP) after consulting the state governments and associations of sugar industry. The amended provisions of the Sugarcane (Control) Order, 1966 provides for fixation of FRP of sugarcane having regard to the factors:- a) cost of production of sugarcane; b) return to the growers from alternative crops and the general trend of prices of agricultural commodities; c) availability of sugar to consumers at a fair price; d) price at which sugar produced from sugarcane is sold by sugar producers; e) recovery of sugar from sugarcane; f) the realisation made from sale of by-products viz. molasses, bagasse and press mud or their imputed value; and g) reasonable margins for the growers of sugarcane on account of risk and profits.

Under the FRP system, the farmers are not required to wait for the end of the season or for any announcement of the profits by the sugar mills or the Government. The new system also assures the margins on account of profit and risk to farmers, irrespective of the fact whether the sugar mills generate profit or not and is not dependent on the performance of any individual sugar mill.

In order to ensure that higher sugar recoveries are adequately rewarded and considering variations amongst sugar mills, the FRP is linked to a basic recovery rate of sugar, with a premium payable to farmers for higher recoveries of sugar from sugarcane.

The FRP of sugarcane payable by sugar factories for each sugar season for 2009-10 to 2016-17 is tabulated below:-

Table 15.11 : FRP of Sugarcane Payable by Sugar Factories

Sugar Season	FRP (₹ per quintal)	Basic Recovery level	Premium for every increase of 0.1 per cent above basic recovery Level (₹ per quintal)
2009-10	129.84	9.5 per cent	1.37
2010-11	139.12	9.5 per cent	1.46
2011-12	145.00	9.5 per cent	1.53
2012-13	170.00	9.5 per cent	1.79
2013-14	210.00	9.5 per cent	2.21
2014-15	220.00	9.5 per cent	2.32
2015-16	230.00	9.5 per cent	2.42
2016-17	230.00	9.5 per cent	2.42

New System for Distribution of Sugar

Sugar being an essential commodity of mass consumption is supplied under the Public Distribution System (PDS) mainly to Below Poverty Line (BPL) families except in the North Eastern states, hilly states and island territories where universal coverage is allowed, with subsidy support from the Central Government. Prior to de-regulation of sugar sector, the Central Government was following a policy of partial control on sugar under which a part of sugar production was requisitioned from sugar mills as levy for distribution at a uniform Retail Issue Price (RIP) in PDS.

The Central Government, in April 2013 decontrolled the sugar sector by removing the levy obligation on sugar mills and doing away with the regulated release mechanism on open market sale of sugar. Under the new dispensation, to make sugar available in the PDS at the existing Retails Issue Price (RIP) of ₹ 13.50 per kg., the state governments/UT administrations have been asked to procure it from the open market through a transparent system. The Central Government is reimbursing the states/UTs @ ₹18.50 per kg., limited to the quantity based on their existing allocations (about 27 lakh tonnes). The state governments/UT administrations may either absorb the additional cost, if any, on account of handling, transportation and dealer's commission or pass it on the consumers by including it in the Retail Issue Price (RIP).

As of now, 30 states/UTs have participated in the scheme and no disruption in the distribution of sugar through PDS has been reported.

Ethanol Blending Petrol Programme

Ethanol is an agro-based product, basically produced from the by-product of the sugar industry, viz., molasses. In the years of surplus production of sugarcane, when the sugar prices are depressed, the sugar industry is unable to pay cane price to the farmers. The ethanol blended petrol programme, besides lowering pollution levels, is expected to provide another outlet for ethanol use, thus insuring utilization of molasses produced as a by-product during manufacture of sugar.

Ministry of Petroleum & Natural Gas have notified that oil marketing companies shall sell ethanol-blended petrol with percentage of ethanol up to 10 per cent blending across the country as a whole. The Government has modified the policy for procurement of ethanol under the EBP. Under the new arrangement, the ex-depot price of ethanol has been fixed in the range of ₹ 48.50 to ₹ 49.50 per litre and OMC's now call EOI from interested sugar mills and distilleries to supply ethanol at this rate. This price is remunerative and the new process smoothens the entire ethanol supply chain.

Extending Financial Assistance to Sugar Undertakings

A Scheme for Extending Financial Assistance to Sugar Undertakings 2014 (SEFASU-2014) was notified in 2014 envisaging loans of around ₹ 6,600 crore to Sugar Undertakings through participating scheduled commercial banks, regional rural banks and cooperative banks for clearance of cane price arrears.

Incentive Scheme for Marketing and Promotion of Raw Sugar Production

The Government in 2014 notified the scheme allowing incentive for marketing and promotion services for raw sugar production targeted for export market. The incentive available under the scheme shall be utilised by the sugar mills for making payment to the farmers. About ₹ 383.87 crore was reimbursed to concerned sugar mills during FY 2014-15 and 2015-16 for export of 12.87 lakh tonnes of raw sugar.

Sugar Development Fund

Under the Sugar Cess Act, 1982, cess is collected at various rates on all the sugar produced and sold by any sugar factory within India. The present rate of cess is ₹ 124 per quintal from 2016. The Sugar Development Fund Act, 1982, provides that an amount equivalent to the proceeds of the duty of excise levied and collected under the Sugar Cess Act, 1982 reduced by the cost of collection as determined by the Central government, together with any money received by the Central government for purpose of this Act, shall after due appropriation made will be credited to the Sugar Development Fund (SDF).

The Sugar Development Fund Act, 1982, provides for the purposes for which the Fund shall be applied: are a) making loans for facilitating the rehabilitation and modernisation of any sugar factory or any unit thereof, including to a potentially viable sugar undertaking; b) making loans for undertaking any scheme for development of sugarcane in the area in which any sugar factory is situated, including to a potentially viable sugar undertaking; c) making grants for the purpose of carrying out any research project aimed at the promotion and development of any aspect of this industry; d) defraying expenditure to a sugar factory on internal transport and freight charges on export shipment of sugar with a view to promoting its export; e) making loans to any sugar factory having an installed capacity of 2,500 TCD or higher to implement a project of bagasse based cogeneration of power; f) making loans to any sugar factory having an installed capacity of 2,500 TCD or higher for production of anhydrous alcohol or ethanol from alcohol or molasses with a view to improving its viability; g) defraying expenditure to a sugar factory for the purpose of building up and maintenance of buffer stock with a view to stabilising price of sugar; h) defraying expenditure for the purpose of financial assistance to sugar factories towards interest on loans given in terms of any scheme approved by the Central Government from time to time; i) defraying any other expenditure for the purpose of the Act; and j) making loans to any sugar factory for conversion of existing ethanol plant into Zero Liquid Discharge plant.

Imposed Stock Holding and Turn Over Limits on Sugar

To deal with the artificial price rise in market due to hoarding of sugar by traders/dealers, the Government has imposed stock holding and turn over limits on sugar from 2016. The directions have been issued that no dealer of sugar shall hold any stock for a period exceeding thirty days from the date of receipt by him of such stock and shall not keep sugar in stock at any time in excess of the quantities mentioned against each: -

Kolkata and extended area	:	Dealer who bring sugar from outside
West Bengal	:	10000 Qtls.
Other places	:	5000 Qtls.

Fixed Minimum Indicative Export Quota

With a view to reduce the inventory pressure on domestic sugar prices, the Government has fixed indicative export targets for each mill proportionate to their sugar production so as to evacuate 4 m lakh tonnes of sugar stocks. No export subsidy or incentive would be offered. The industry has so far exported 1.64 m lakh tonnes at prevailing international prices. With stock evacuation, domestic sugar prices have improved and reach levels more supportive of cane prices. These are the Minimum Indicative Export Quotas (MIEQ). Since sugar prices have rallied in recent past and current price levels are compatible with FRP of cane (₹ 230/qtl) notified for the current sugar season, it is no longer required to promote export of sugar. Hence, MIEQ was withdrawn from June 2016.

Production Subsidy

The Government has also extended production subsidy @ ₹ 4.50 per quintal to sugar mills to offset the cost of cane and facilitate timely payment of cane price dues of farmers.

After having been satisfied with the assessment that sugar prices are now substantially higher than levels required for operational viability of the sugar industry, the production subsidy scheme has been withdrawnfrom May 2016.

Edible Oils

The efficient management of edible oils in the country involves steps to ensure sufficient availability of edible oils to the consumer at reasonable rates. As per the 3rd Advance Estimates for 2015-16 (Nov.-Oct.) released by Ministry of Agriculture estimated oilseeds production is about 258.99 lakh tonnes as compared to 275.11 lakh tonnes during the previous year, Production of oils from these oilseeds in 2015-16 is likely to be about 61.93 lakh tonnes. The net availability of edible oils from all sources, primary as well as secondary, is estimated to be 87.70 lakh tonnes as against the net availability of 92.06 lakh tonnes in 2014-15. The gap between demand and availability, which is about 60 per cent, is met by imports.

Status of Vegetable Oil Industry

There are about 91 Vanaspati units and 417 solvent extraction plants/ refineries in the country registered in the directorate, with an annual capacity to process around 6,500 lakh tonnes of raw material. Due to various reasons, mainly the seasonal availability of raw material, the total capacity utilisation of the edible oil industry is around 35 per cent.

Ban on Export of Edible oils

Exports of edible oils has been banned from March, 2008 with certain exemptions i.e., coconut oil from all Electronic Data Interchange (EDI) ports and through notified Land Customs Stations (LCS), castor oil, organic edible oils and certain oils produced from minor forest produce. Further, export of edible oil has been permitted in branded consumer packs of up to 5 kg subject to Minimum Export Price of USD 900 per tonnes which was reduced from USD 1100 per tonnes in 2015. Export of rice bran oil in bulk has been allowed from 2015.

Import Duty on Edible Oils

As there is a continuous demand in excess over the domestic supply of edible oils, its import has been resorted to for more than two decades. In order to maintain un-interrupted supply of edible oils at affordable prices to the consumers and at the same time keeping in mind the interest of the farmers as well as the industry, import duty on Crude and Refined edible oils was raised to 12.5 per cent and 20 per cent respectively in 2015.

Import of Edible Oils

The quantity of edible oils imported during the last few years are as under:-

Oil Year (Nov-Oct)	Quantity(In lakh tonnes)
2013-14	109.76
2014-15	138.53
2015-16 (November, 2015 to April, 2016)	76.18

Source: DGCIS (Department of Commerce)

International Cooperation

India is associated with a number of international agencies working in the field of food related matters. These include World Food Programme (WFP), SAARC Food Bank, Food and Agriculture Organisation (FAO), International Grains Council (IGC) and International Sugar Organisation (ISO), etc. Brief details in respect of some of the important International Cooperation activities in the Department of Food and Public Distribution are as follows:

WFP's Country Strategic Plan

The new Country Strategic Plan (CSP) 2015-2018 has been signed between the UN World Food Programme (UNWFP) and Government of India under the Department of Agriculture Cooperation and Farmers' Welfare. Department of Food and Public Distribution has been made the nodal Department for the strategic priority.

SAARC Food Bank

The SAARC Food Bank was established to supplement national efforts to provide food security to the people of the region. As per the agreement, SAARC Food Bank shall have a reserve of food grains to be maintained by each member country consisting of either wheat or rice, or a combination of both as assessed share of the country.

India's initial assessed share in the reserve was 1,53,200 lakh tonnes out of a total share of 2,43,000 lakh tonnes. The assessed share is presently kept as 3,06,400 lakh tonnes out of a total share of 4,86,000 MTs. The quantum of reserve have been kept in different strategic locations in the designated godowns of Food Corporation of India (FCI).

Food and Agricultural Organisation and Committee on World Food Security

Food and Agricultural Organisation (FAO) is one of the largest specialised agencies in the UN system founded in 1945 with a mandate to raise levels of nutrition and standard of living by improving agricultural productivity and living conditions of rural population. The Committee on World Food Security (CFS) serves as a forum for review and follow-up of policies concerning world food security, including food production, physical and economic access to food. India is a member to both FAO and CFS. Committee on World Food Security (CFS) monitors the progress of implementation of the WFS Plan of Action.

G-20 Matters

A Steering Committee has been constituted in the Department of Agriculture and Cooperation to oversee the development, follow-up action on the initiative declared in Ministerial declaration endorsed at G-20 Agriculture Ministers meeting. The Committee is comprised of representatives from different line Ministries. Department of Food and Public Distribution has been made the nodal department for: a) rapid response forum and b) emergency humanitarian food reserves.

International Grains Council

India is a member of the International Grains Council (IGC) an intergovernmental forum of exporting and importing countries for co-operation in wheat and coarse grain matters which was previously known as International Wheat Council up to 1995. It administers the Grains Trade Convention 1995.

The IGC Secretariat, based in London since 1949, also services the Food Aid Committee, established under the Food Aid Convention. International Grains Agreement comprises of Grains Trade Convention (GTC) and Food Aid Convention (FAC). India is a signatory to the International Grains Agreement (IGA) 1995 and its Grain Trade Convention (GTC) 1995 which was effective from 1995. IGC have two types of members-Importing Members and exporting Members. India has been included in the category of Exporting members in July, 2003 and represented in the meetings/session of the Council held from time to time. Besides, this Department also participates in other meetings of IGC like market conditions committee meetings and executive committee meetings.

16 Health and Family Welfare

THE Union Ministry of Health and Family Welfare is instrumental and responsible for implementation of various programmes on the national scale in the areas of health and family welfare, prevention and control of major communicable diseases and promotion of traditional and indigenous systems of medicines. The Ministry also assists states in preventing and controlling the spread of seasonal disease outbreaks and epidemics through technical assistance. Expenditure is incurred by Ministry of Health and Family Welfare either directly under central schemes or by way of grants-in-aids to the autonomous/statutory bodies, etc., and NGOs.

In addition to the centrally sponsored family welfare programmes, the Ministry is implementing several World Bank assisted programmes for control of AIDS, malaria and tuberculosis in designated areas. Besides, state health systems development projects with World Bank assistance are under implementation in various states. The projects are implemented by the respective state governments. The Department of Health and Family Welfare only facilitates the states in availing of external assistance. All these schemes aim at fulfilling the national commitment to improve access to Primary Health Care (PHC) facilities keeping in view the needs of rural areas and where the incidence of disease is high.

Health Policy

The National Health Policy (NHP) of 2002 guides the strategy adopted by the Government for the health sector. The NHP 2002 evolved from the National Health Policy of 1983. Guidance was provided by the Bhore Committee Report (1946) wherein the main underlying principles for future health development of the country, *inter alia,* included that 'No individual should fail to secure adequate medical care because of inability to pay for it. In view of the complexity of modern medical practice, the health services should provide, when fully developed, all the consultant, laboratory and institutional facilities necessary for proper diagnosis and treatment'.

The National Health Policy, 2002 framework envisages, accelerated achievement of public health goals in the backdrop of the socio-economic circumstances prevailing in the country. Some of the salient aspects of the NHP 2002, *inter alia,* include: making good the deficiencies in availability of health facilities, narrowing the gap between various states, the gap across the rural-urban divide in attainment of health goals and reducing the uneven access to and benefits from the public health system between the better endowed and the more vulnerable sections of society.

Accordingly consistent with the primacy given to equity, a marked emphasis has been provided for expanding and improving the primary health facilities. Emphasis has been laid on the implementation of public health programmes through local self-governments. The need to ensure improved standard of medical education, alleviate the shortage of specialists in Public Health and Family Medicine, need for an improvement in the ratio of nurse vis-à-vis doctors/beds, the need for basing treatment regimens on a limited number of essential drugs of a generic nature and progressively strengthening the food and drugs administration are among the various aspects emphasized in the policy.

It also envisages setting up of an organized urban primary care structure, a network of decentralized mental health services and upgrading the physical infrastructure of mental health institutions. It visualizes an Information, Education and Communication Policy which maximizes the dissemination of information to those population groups which cannot be effectively approached by using only the mass media and giving priority to school health programmes with an aim at imparting preventive health education apart from providing regular health check-ups and promotion of health seeking behaviour among children.

The Five Year Plan outline the strategy for implementing the policy, bearing in mind the dynamics of a developing economy. Accordingly, the Twelfth Five Year Plan for the health sector envisages transformation of the National Rural Health Mission into a National Health Mission covering both rural and urban areas. It envisages providing public sector primary care facilities in selected low income urban areas, expansion of teaching and training programmes for healthcare professionals, particularly in the public sector institutions, giving greater attention to public health, strengthening the drug and food regulatory mechanism, regulation of medical practice, human resource development, promoting information technology in health and building an appropriate architecture for Universal Health Care. Government has taken a decision to formulate a new health policy in the light of the changes that have taken place in the country's health sector scenario since the formulation of the National Health Policy, 2002. Accordingly, the Draft New National Health Policy, 2015 has been placed in public domain since 2014 for wider stakeholder consultations.

National Health Mission and National Urban Health Mission

The National Health Mission (NHM) has its two sub-missions, the National Rural Health Mission (NRHM) and the National urban Health Mission (NUHM). The NHM envisages universal access to equitable, affordable & quality healthcare services that are accountable and responsive to people's needs. The main programmatic components include health system strengthening in rural and urban areas, Reproductive-Maternal-Newborn Child and Adolescent Health (RMNCH+A) and control of Communicable and Non-Communicable Diseases. The framework for implementation of National Health Mission was approved in December, 2013. Under NHM, substantial achievements have been made, the details of which are available in the report. The 7th Common Review Mission (CRM) under NHM was conducted from November 2013 in 14 states/UTs namely Bihar, Jharkhand, Odisha, Uttar Pradesh, Jammu & Kashmir, Himachal Pradesh, Arunachal Pradesh, Meghalaya, Nagaland, Andhra Pradesh, Haryana, Karnataka, Maharashtra, and Gujarat. The CRM observed increased child survival, population stabilization and utilization of health services, though the progress across states was not analogous. The Infant Mortality Rate (IMR), the deaths of children before age 1 per 1000 live-births, has fallen steadily every year, with an all India average of 42. While this is short of the 12th Plan target of 25, some states have made remarkable progress with Goa having an IMR of 10, Kerala 12, Nagaland 18, Manipur 10 and Tamil Nadu 21. The Maternal Mortality Ratio (MMR), which measures the number of women of reproductive age (15 to 49) dying due to maternal causes per 1,00,000 live-births, has come down to 178, though this is far short of the 12th Plan target of 100. Some states have registered significant reduction in MMR with Kerala at 66, Maharashtra at 87 and Tamil Nadu at 90.

There has been a significant improvement in creation of new facilities and infrastructure, though adequate staffing of these facilities by qualified health personnel remains a problem. Availability of drugs has improved at all levels and the robust logistic arrangements for procurement and storage of these drugs are being put in place. An important achievement of NHM has been a considerable reduction in out of pocket expenses from 72 per cent to 60 per cent.

Recently, new initiatives have been launched under NHM. Rashtriya Bal Swasthya Karyakram (RBSK) was launched to provide comprehensive healthcare and improve the quality of life of children through early detection of birth defects, diseases, deficiencies, and development delays including disability. Another initiative, viz., Rashtriya Kishore Swasthya Karyakram (RKSK) was launched to comprehensively address the health needs of the 253 million adolescents, who account for over 21 per cent of the country's population, by bringing in several new dimensions like mental health, nutrition, substance misuse, injuries and violence and non-communicable diseases. The programme has introduced community based interventions through peer educators and is underpinned by collaborations with other ministries and state governments and knowledge partners, coupled with operational research. In addition to these initiatives, the Weekly Iron Folic Acid Supplementation Programme (WIFS) was launched to address adolescent anaemia whereunder supervised Iron-Folic Acid (IFA) tablets are given to adolescent population between 10-19 years of age in both rural and urban areas throughout the country. NUHM, a sub-mission under the NHM, caters to the healthcare needs of the urban population with the focus on urban poor and is aimed at reducing out of pocket expenses for treatment. NHM is a step towards realizing the objective of Universal Health Coverage in the country.

National Urban Health Mission

National Urban Health Mission (NUHM) seeks to improve the health status of the urban population particularly urban poor and other vulnerable sections by facilitating their access to quality primary healthcare. NUHM would cover all state capitals, district headquarters and other cities/towns with a population of 50,000 and above (as per census 2011) in a phased manner. Cities and towns with population below 50,000 will continue to be covered under NRHM.

Major Initiatives under NRHM/NHM

ASHA

More than 9.15 lakh Accredited Social Health Activists (ASHAs) are in place across the country and serve as facilitators, mobilizers and providers of community level care. ASHA is the first port of call in the community especially for marginalized sections of the population, with a focus on women and children. Since 2013, when the National Urban Health Mission was launched, ASHAs are being selected in urban areas as well. Several evaluations and successive Common Review Missions show that the ASHA has been a key figure in contributing to the positive outcomes of increases in institutional delivery, immunization, active role in disease control programmes (Malaria, Kala-azar and Lymphatic filariasis, in particular) and improved breastfeeding and nutrition practices. The majority of states have in place an active training and support system for the ASHA to ensure continuing training, on site field mentoring and performance monitoring.

Rogi Kalyan Samiti

Rogi Kalyan Samiti/Hospital Management Society is a simple yet effective management structure. This committee is a registered society whose members act as trustees to manage the affairs of the hospital and is responsible for upkeep of the facilities and ensure provision of better facilities to the patients in the hospital. Financial assistance is provided to these committees through untied fund to undertake activities for patient welfare. 31,763 Rogi Kalyan Samitis (RKS) have been set up involving the community members in almost all District Hospitals (DHs), Sub-District Hospitals (SDHs), Community Health Centres (CHCs) and Primary Health Centres (PHCs).

Janani Suraksha Yojana

Janani Suraksha Yojana (JSY) aims to reduce maternal mortality among pregnant women by encouraging them to deliver in government health facilities. Under the scheme, cash assistance is provided to eligible pregnant women for giving birth in a government health facility. Since the inception of NRHM, 8.55 crore women have benefited under this scheme.

Acceptors of Family Welfare Methods

(in lakhs)

Janani Shishu Suraksha Karyakram

Launched on June 01, 2011, JSSK entitles all pregnant women delivering in public health institutions to absolutely free and no expense delivery, including caesarean section. This marks a shift to an entitlement based approach. The free entitlements include free drugs and consumables, free diagnostics, free diet during stay in the health institutions, free provision of blood, free transport from home to health institution, between health institutions in case of referrals and drop back home and exemption from all kinds of user charges. Similar entitlements are available for all sick infants (up to 1 year of age) accessing public health institutions. All states and union territories are implementing this scheme. As per the latest reports received from the states/UTs, 89 per cent pregnant women availed free drugs, 82 per cent free diagnostics, 75 per cent free diet, 49 per cent free home to facility transport and 56.03 per cent free drop back home. For sick infants, 73 per cent sick infants availed free drugs, 40 per cent free diagnostics, 10 per cent sick infants free home to facility transport and 28 per cent free drop back home.

National Ambulance Services

31 states/UTs have the facility where people can dial 108 or 102 for calling an ambulance. Dial 108 is predominantly an emergency response system, primarily designed to attend to patients of critical care, trauma and accident victims, etc. Dial 102 services essentially consist of basic patient transport aimed at the needs of pregnant women and children though other categories are also taking benefit and are not excluded. JSSK entitlements e.g., free transport from home to facility, inter facility transfer in case of referral and drop back for mother and children are the key focus of 102 service. This service can be accessed through a toll free call to a Call Centre.

Facility Based Newborn Care

A continuum of newborn care has been established with the launch of home based and facility based newborn care components ensuring that every newborn receives essential care right from the time of birth and first 48 hours at the health facility and then at home during the first 42 days of life. Newborn Care Corners (NBCCs) are established at delivery points to provide essential newborn care at birth, while Special Newborn Care Units (SNCUs) at District Hospital/Medical College and Newborn Stabilization Units (NBSUs) at FRUs provide care for sick newborns. As on June 2015, a total of 14,441 NBCCs, 2,020 NBSUs and 575 SNCUs have been made operational across the country.

National Urban Health Mission

National Urban Health Mission (NUHM) was put in place as a sub-mission under an overarching National Health Mission (NHM) for providing equitable and quality Primary Health Care (PHC) services to the urban population with special focus on slum and vulnerable sections of the society. NUHM aims to improve the health status of the urban area with more than 50,000 population particularly the poor and other disadvantaged sections by facilitating equitable access to quality healthcare through a revamped primary healthcare systems, targeted outreach services and involvement of the community and the urban local bodies. The Centre-state funding pattern is 75:25 for all the states except north-eastern states including Sikkim and other special category states of Jammu and Kashmir, Himachal Pradesh and Uttarakhand, for whom the Centre-state funding pattern is 90:10. The progress made on funding status under this scheme has been given in the following tables.

Table 16.1: Financial statement showing Allocation and Release of FY 2014-15 and FY 2015-16 (NUHM)

Sl. No.	Name of the State/UT	2014-15 Alloction	2014-15 Released	2015-16 Allocation	2015-16 Released upto 3rd quarter
1.	Andhra Pradesh	89.96	57.55	92.16	43.14
2.	Bihar	40.86	16.93	32.28	16.14
3.	Chhattisgarh	32.13	24.30	27.98	13.99
4.	Goa	2.70	1.47	0.98	-
5.	Gujarat	110.58	77.30	65.31	48.98
6.	Haryana	51.07	38.63	32.04	24.03
7.	Himachal Pradesh	1.43	1.08	1.08	0.81
8.	Jammu & Kashmir	12.71	8.42	12.02	11.22
9.	Jharkhand	27.97	16.50	17.34	13.01
10.	Karnataka	90.52	64.68	74.80	-
11.	Kerala	30.50	23.07	35.55	26.66
12.	Madhya Pradesh	104.06	78.71	88.17	63.98
13.	Maharashtra	318.52	240.92	214.24	-
14.	Odisha	31.37	23.73	26.41	24.59
15.	Punjab	51.65	39.07	31.96	-
16.	Rajasthan	74.91	56.66	48.70	48.70
17.	Tamil Nadu	156.38	118.28	111.99	111.99
18.	Telangana	64.29	48.63	65.87	49.40
19.	Uttar Pradesh	200.97	152.01	136.55	-

20.	Uttarakhand	12.84	9.71	9.79	4.90
21.	West Bengal	160.69	121.55	115.53	-
22.	Arunachal Pradesh	5.37	0.94	1.61	-
23.	Assam	99.53	33.18	36.34	-
24.	Manipur	9.71	2.11	3.77	-
25.	Meghalaya	17.56	13.17	7.79	-
26.	Mizoram	10.55	4.10	8.85	4.20
27.	Nagaland	8.19	2.53	8.65	4.07
28.	Tripura	10.75	1.84	13.92	1.77
29.	Sikkim	1.34	1.00	3.07	-
30.	Delhi	82.50	62.41	54.03	54.03
31.	Puducherry	3.66	2.21	3.33	1.67
32.	A&N Islands	0.74	0.47	0.38	-
33.	Chandigarh	6.47	2.19	3.10	3.08
34.	Dadra & Nagar Haveli	0.90	0.47	0.21	-
35.	Daman & Diu	0.83	0.00	0.20	0.08
36.	Lakshadweep	0.22	-	-	-
	Total	**1924.43**	**1345.82**	**1386.00**	**570.44**

National Commission on Population

In pursuance of the objectives of the National Population Policy, 2000, the National Commission on Population was constituted in May 2000 to review, monitor and give directions for the implementation of the National Population Policy (NPP) 2000, with a view to meet the goals setout in the Policy, to promote inter-sectoral coordination, involve the civil society in planning and implementation, facilitate initiatives to improve performance in the demographically weaker states in the country and to explore the possibilities of international cooperation in support of the goals setout in the National Population Policy. The National Commission on Population has since been reconstituted in April, 2005 with 40 members. The membership also includes the Chief Ministers of the states of Uttar Pradesh, Madhya Pradesh, Rajasthan, Bihar, Jharkhand, Kerala and Tamil Nadu.

Annual Health Survey

Immunization coverage in India has increased to 65.2 per cent as per Rapid Survey on Children (RSOC), 2013-14 from 35.5 per cent as per National Family

Health Survey (NFHS), 92-93 in the last 21 years. There is a need for further improvement especially in DPT3 and OPV3 coverage and reducing the drop-outs. The following table outlines the achievements as per evaluated coverage. The recent Annual Health Survey (AHS 2012-13) conducted in states documented improvement in immunization coverage.

Table 16.2: Annual Health Survey-3 (2012-2013)

States	BCG	OPV3	DPT3	Measles	FI	Polio (Birth dose)	No Immuni-zation
Uttarakahand	93.3	85.8	85.2	85.2	79.6	76.1	4.9
Chhattisgarh	96.6	83.3	81.8	90.0	749	87.8	2.9
Rajasthan	91.5	80.8	79.6	83.5	74.2	80.9	5.8
Bihar	94.7	82.7	81.6	80.3	69.9	69.0	3.7
Jharkhand	94.8	80.0	80.0	82.9	69.9	77.2	3.1
Assam	93.8	78.1	77.6	80.9	64.4	79.3	3.4
Odisha	98.2	82.0	82.8	89.2	68.8	83.6	0.8
Madhya Pradesh	95.7	77.1	76.3	85.4	66.4	87.1	3.6
Uttar Pradesh	86.3	64.1	63.2	65.8	52.7	70.7	7.6

Jansankhya Sthirata Kosh

Jansankhya Sthirata Kosh (JSK) also known as National Population Stabilisation Fund is an autonomous body under the Ministry of Health and Family Welfare (MoHFW), constituted on the recommendations of the National Commission of Population. It was established in 2003 as an autonomous society under the MoHFW and was reconstituted in 2005 with the addition of a General Body. Its mandate is to promote and undertake schemes, programmes, projects and initiatives to meet the unmet need for contraception, and reproductive and child health. It is aimed at achieving population stabilisation at a level consistent with the needs of sustainable economic growth, social development and environment protection by 2045.

National Helpline

The aim of National Helpline is to provide reliable information on reproductive health, sexual health, contraception, pregnancy, child health and related issues. It is specifically for adolescents, newly married and about to be married persons from the high focus states of Bihar, Uttar Pradesh, Rajasthan, Madhya Pradesh, Jharkhand and Chhattisgarh but anyone of any age can seek help.

Child Health Programme

India is committed to reduce child deaths by two thirds between 1990 and 2015 as pledged in the Millennium Development Goals (MDG). This implies a reduction of Under Five Mortality Rate (U-5MR) from 125/1000 live births in

1990 to 42/1000 live births by 2015. This commitment is also reflected under the National Health Mission (NHM).

Situation of Child Mortality

At present, as per SRS 2013, the Under Five Mortality Rate in India is 49/1000 live births, Infant Mortality Rate (IMR) is 40/1000 live births and Neo-natal Mortality Rate is 28/1000 live births. This translates into an estimated 12.7 lakh under-5 child deaths annually. The U-5MR has declined at a faster pace in the period 2008-2013, registering a compound annual decline of 6.6 per cent per year, compared to 3.3 per cent compound annual decline observed over 1990-2007. However, the efforts need to be intensified to attain the MDG of 42/1000 live births by 2015. Four states together contribute to 58 per cent of all child deaths in the country, namely—Uttar Pradesh (3.5 lakhs), Bihar (1.5 lakhs), Madhya Pradesh (1.3 lakhs) and Rajasthan (1.0 lakh). About 45 per cent of under-five deaths take place within the first 7 days of birth, about 57 per cent of within first one month of birth and approximately 81 per cent within one year of the birth.

Causes of Child Mortality in India

The major causes of child mortality in India (as per WHO, 2012) are—neonatal causes (53 per cent), pneumonia (15 per cent), diarrhoeal diseases (12 per cent), measles (3 per cent) and others. Besides these, malnutrition is a contributory factor in 33 per cent child deaths.

Rashtriya Bal Swasthya Karyakram

Rashtriya Bal Swasthya Karyakram (RBSK) has been launched to provide child health screening and early interventions services by expanding the reach of mobile health teams at block level. These teams will also carry out screening of all the children in the age group 0–6 years enrolled at Anganwadi Centres at least twice a year. RBSK covers 30 common health conditions. States/UTs may incorporate a few more conditions based on high prevalence/endemicity. An estimated 27 crore children in the age group of zero to eighteen (0- 18) years are expected to be covered in a phased manner.

Rashtriya Kishore Swasthya Karyakram

This initiative was launched in January, 2014 to reach out to 253 million adolescents in the country in their own spaces and introduce peer-led interventions at the community level, supported by augmentation of facility based services. This initiative broadens the focus of the adolescent health programme beyond reproductive and sexual health and brings in focus on life skills, nutrition, injuries and violence (including gender based violence), non-communicable diseases, mental health and substance misuse.

Family Planning Programme

With its historic initiation in 1952, the family planning programme has undergone transformation in terms of policy and actual programme implementation. There has been a gradual shift from clinical approach to the reproductive child health approach and further the National Population Policy (NPP), 2000 brought a holistic and a target free approach which helped in reduction of fertility. The target free approach is now reflected in the state project implementation plans based on community needs assessment.

Presently the expected level of achievement is estimated for each state by the indicators reflecting the community needs like contraceptive usage, parity, unmet need and existing fertility. Over the years, the programme has been expanded to reach every nook and corner of the country and has penetrated into PHCs and SCs in rural areas, Urban Family Welfare Centers and Postpartum Centres in the urban areas. Technological advances, improved quality and coverage for healthcare have resulted in a rapid fall in the Crude Birth Rate (CBR) and growth rate.

The objectives, strategies and activities of the Family Planning Division are designed and operated towards achieving the family welfare goals and objectives stated in various policy documents (NPP: National Population Policy 2000; NHP: National Health Policy 2002 and NRHM: National Rural Health Mission) and to honour the commitments of the Government of India (including ICPD: International Conference on Population and Development; MDG: Millennium Development Goals, FP; 2020 Summit and others).

Table 16.3

1.	**Some facts on Family Planning and related matters**	
	Expected increase of population of 15.7% in 15 years	• From 1210 million in 2011 to 1400 million in 2026
	Decline in TFR	• Helps to stabilize India's population growth which in turn spurs the economic and social progress
	Greater investments in family planning	• Helps to mitigate the impact of high population growth by helping women achieve desired family size and avoid unintended and mistimed pregnancioes • Reduce material mortality by 35 % • Reduce infant mortality and abortions significantly
	Govt. of India's commitment by 2017	• Material Mortality Ratio (MMR) to 100/100,000

		• Infant Mortality Rate (IMR) to 30/ 1000 live births • Total Fertility Rate (TFR) to 2.1
2.	**Factors that influence population growth**	
	Unmet need of Family Planning Age of Marriage and first childbirth	• 21.3% as per DLHS-III (2007-08) • 22.1% of the girls get married below the age of 18 years • Out of the total deliveries 5.6% are among teenagers i.e. 15-19 years
	Spacing between Births	• Spacing between two childbirths is less than the recommended period of 3 years in 59.3% of births (SRS 2013)
	15-25 age group (women)	• 52.5% contribution in total fertility • 46% contribution in maternal mortality
3.	**Current demographic scenario in the country (Census 2011)**	
	2.4% of world's land mass	• 17.5% of the world's population
	1.21 billion	• India's population as per Census-2011
	200 million	• Population of Uttar Pradesh-more than the population of Brazil
	Perceptible decline (in last 5 decades)	• Crude Birth Rate—40.8 per 1000 in 1951 to 21.4 in 2013. • Infant Mortality Rate—from 146 in 1951-61 to 40 in 2013 • Total Fertility Rate—from 6.0 in 1951 to 2.3 in 2013. *(Ref. Appendix-I)* • Sleepest decline in growth rate between 2001 and 2011 from 21.54% to 17.64%. • Decline in 0-6 population by 3.08% compared to 2011
	Population added	• Lesser than the previous decade, 18.14 crores added during 2001-2011 compared to 18.23 crores during 1991-2011

	Significant decline	• There is a 4.1 percentage point fall from 24.99% in 2001 to 20.92% in 2011 in the growth rate of population in the EAG States (Uttar Padesh, Bihar, Jharkhand, Madhya Pradesh, Chhattisgarh, Rajasthan, Odisha and Uttarakhand) after decades of stagnation
4.	**Progress in TFR**	
	TFR decline	• From 2.9 in 2005 to 2.3 in 2013 • Decline more signifant in High Focus States
	TFR of 2.1 or less	• 24 States and Union Territories
	TFR 2.1-3.0	• 10 States—Haryana-2.2, Gujarat-2.3, Arunachal Pradesh-2.3, Assam-2.3, Chhattisgarh-2.7, Jharkhand-2.6, Rajasthan-2.8, Madhya Pradesh-2.9, Methalaya-2.9 and Dadara & Nagar Haveli-2.9
	TFR above 3.0	• 2 States—Bihar-3.4, Uttar Pradesh-3.1

Medical Research

Department of Health Research (DHR) aims at bringing modern health technology to people by encouraging innovations related to diagnostics, treatment methods as well as prevention vaccines; translating the innovations into products/processes by facilitating evaluation/testing in synergy with Indian Council of Medical Research (ICMR) which serves as the fulcrum of new department and other departments of Ministry of Health and Family Welfare as well as other science departments. The focus is to introduce these innovations into public health service through health systems research.

Research Schemes

Multidisciplinary Research Units

This scheme aims to establish 80 Multidisciplinary Research Units (MRU) in State Government medical colleges to have a dedicated infrastructure for research in medical colleges to improve the research, clinical care and teaching with special focus on non-communicable diseases (NCDs). ICMR is playing the role of technical support by evaluation and monitoring. In all 62 Government medical colleges have been approved for establishment of MRUs and funds have been released to 42 medical colleges. Research activities have also been initiated in some of the MRUs.

Model Rural Health Research Units

Model Rural Health Research Units (MRHRU) is being launched after the successful experience of ICMR at Ghatampur (UP). This scheme has been launched to establish 15 MRHRUs during the 12th Plan in various states to transfer new technology for early diagnosis and management of various diseases to state health services on a continued basis. 12 MRHRUs units have been established and research activities have also been initiated in five of the MRHRUs including multicentric projects at eight of the MRHRUs.

Network of Viral and other Infectious Diseases Diagnostic Research Laboratories

It is being set up for handling viral diseases and infectious diseases like TB. Under this new scheme this network of Viral and Infectious Diseases Labs will be expanded to 160 laboratories (120 medical colleges; 30 state and 10 regional laboratories) across the country. Some of 30 Viral Research and Diagnostic Laboratories (VRDLs) have been funded (five regional level labs; six state level and 19 medical college level VRDLs). Under ICMR Task Force mode, 12 VRDLs are already ongoing (eight Grade I and four Grade II labs). The DHR and ICMR VRDLs are now spread over 23 states and three Union Territories of the country. In addition, a Resource Centre has been set up at National Institute of Virology, Pune for Quality Control/Quality Assurance and training of various categories of staff working in the VDRLs and an Online Data Mining Centre for VDRLs has been initiated at National Institute of Epidemiology, Chennai.

Scheme for Human Resources Development for Health Research

A major constraint in the current scenario is the lack of adequate and properly trained human resources for the health research. The Department of Health Research plans to strengthen human resource base of the country by organizing focused training programmes within and outside India, for mid-career professionals in medical colleges and other academic establishments.

Activities proposed under this scheme are: fellowships for training: researchers in identified advanced fields; young researcher programme: to encourage young students for research; to engage the qualified women who had break in their career and currently unemployed in the newer areas of health research; special training programmes: in specified areas, this also includes support to selected institutions for training; and mid-career research fellowships: faculty development for medical colleges.

Grants-in-Aid Scheme for Inter-sectoral Convergence

Presently eight science departments are significantly contributing to innovations related to different aspects of biomedical research. The department has planned to provide support in the form of grants-in-aid for carrying out research studies, to identify the existing knowledge gap and to translate the existing health leads into deliverable products. There will be special focus on encouraging innovation, their translation and implementation by collaboration and cooperation with other agencies by laying special stress on implementation research so that there is a better utilization of available knowledge.

Indian Council of Medical Research

The Indian Council of Medical Research (ICMR), New Delhi, working under the Department of Health Research (DHR), Ministry of Health and Family Welfare, Government of India, is the apex body in the country for the formulation, coordination, promotion and conduct of biomedical research. In the context of changing public health scene, the balancing of research efforts between different competing as well as emerging fields, especially when resources are severely limited, is a challenging problem encountered in the management of medical research particularly in the country like India. In addition to tackling the prevailing health problems being faced by our population, in recent years the research has been intensified progressively on emerging health problems. Strengthening of research capabilities as well as definite and robust research strategy are recognised as vital tools for conduct of successful research and the ICMR has strived hard to adopt new strategies from time to time as per need of the situation. For the fulfillment of its goals, the strategies adopted by ICMR includes careful selection of thrust areas as per the national needs, with further refinement in the light of past experiences, undertaking studies to enlarge the scientific basis of preventive medicine and health promotion, development of simplified, cost effective and mass applicable testes which are specific and accurate for early and definitive recognition of diseases/ health problems, establishment of close and effective linkages with social and behavioural scientists, active pursuance of problem oriented and problem solving research.

The ICMR discharges its primary function of promoting biomedical research through intramural as well as extramural research. Apart from 32 permanent research institutes/centres, ICMR has several regional centres, research units, field stations spread across the country. Extramural research is promoted by the ICMR through (i) setting up centres for Advanced Research in different research areas; (ii) task force studies and national multicentric collaborative projects and (iii) open ended ad hoc research projects generated spontaneously by active scientists in biomedical institutions/universities, non-governmental organizations, etc., from different parts of the country.

Affordable Indigenous Medical Technologies

ICMR has significantly contributed towards promoting better health for the Indian public through the development, evaluation and delivery of various public health technologies. Several of the research leads of the various ICMR institutes have been developed into diagnostic kits/devices and vaccine and have been released for the use of common men during the last few years. ICMR has launched seven affordable technologies, which are: vaccine for Japanese

Encephalitis (JE) ; test for molecular diagnosis of thallassemia; magnivisualizer for cervical cancer screening; strips and detection system(s) for diabetes; test for detection of pathogenic bacteria in food; technologies for vitamin A and ferritin estimations; and development of non-invasive diagnosis procedure for visceral leishmaniasis from urine and sputum samples. Efforts are being made to commercialize these technologies through identification of interested/ appropriate industry partners to make them available for the national programmes and public use.

Other Research Activities

AMR Surveillance Network

ICMR has initiated collection of data on Anti Microbial Resistance in four leading hospitals of the country namely AIIMS (New Delhi), PGIMER (Chandigarh), JIPMER (Puducherry) and CMC (Vellore). It is planned to expand this AMR Surveillance Network to include at least five more medical colleges/ hospitals in the network.

Indigenous TB Diagnostics

The ICMR's joint endeavour with Ministry of Health and Family Welfare and DBT to actualize the PM's vision of 'Make in India' and 'Public Private Partnership' has been successful in encouraging researchers and companies to work towards development and commercialization of indigenous technologies for TB/MDR TB detection. Other technologies are being evaluated. This initiative aims to provide a low cost point of care molecular test for DR TB for our country in near future.

RNTCP

A multi-centric study in six districts which are predominantly tribal has been initiated to demonstrate an interventional model to strengthen the RNTCP and reduce the incidence of the disease and improve the outcome of the disease.

Leprosy

A molecular laboratory has been established at Regional Leprosy Training and Research Institute (RLTRI), Raipur, with the help of NJIL and OMD, Agra and is being strengthened further. This would help in early detection of leprosy in nearby endemic areas and also support other institutions in diagnosis.

HIV/AIDS

To encourage development of HIV vaccine, a study has been initiated to validate the immunogenicity of the vaccine constructs in *Macaca mulatta* (Rhesus monkeys) prior to conducting human trials.

Bio-safety

ICMR in association with the DST had established Asia's first Biosafety Level–4 (BSL-4) laboratory within the premises of the Microbial Containment Complex

(MCC), NIV, Pune to cater to scientific studies for safe handling of highly pathogenic/high risk group of pathogens as well as new and re-emerging viruses. In view of the imminent threat of Ebola virus infiltration into the country and to create laboratory preparedness for the EVD two training workshops were conducted by NIV. A total of 16 laboratories have been trained to cover biosafety aspects, work practices of BSL-3 laboratory and molecular diagnosis of Ebola virus.

Poliomyelitis

The roadmap for the Phase IIA laboratory containment activities for wild polio viruses has been chalked out. It is proposed to complete the Phase IIA activities at the earliest.

Influenza

National Institute of Virology (NIV), Pune has strengthened the infrastructure for sustainable development to meet public health challenges from emerging and re-emerging viruses. During the recent outbreak of influenza and influenza like illness in the country 2,545 clinical samples of patients suffering from influenza like illness or severe acute respiratory illness were received by NIV, Pune. These were referred by state health authorities for diagnosis of A (H1N1) pdm09.

NIV also supported and sustained its network of nine influenza surveillance laboratories at NIV itself; SKIMS, Srinagar; NICED, Kolkata; KGMU, Lucknow; KIPM, Chennai; AIIMS, Delhi; RMRC, Dibrugarh; IGGMC, Nagpur; NIV, Kerala Field Unit. Diagnostic kits and reagents were supplied to these labs and the entire network worked in synergy with the diagnostic network of NCDC, MoH&FW to offer timely and accurate diagnosis of H1N1 cases all across the country.

Crimean–Congo Hamorrhagic Fever

NIV has confirmed a number of cases and deaths due to Crimean Congo Hemorrhagic Fever (CCHF) from seven districts of Gujarat (Ahmedabad, Amreli, Patan, Surendranagar, Kutch, Bhuj and Aravalli district) as well as from three districts of Rajasthan (Sirohi, Jodhpur and Jaisalmer districts). Recently cases have also been reported from Moradabad district, Uttar Pradesh.

Outbreak Investigations

Recently, NIV confirmed several outbreaks of CCHF. In the year 2014 CCHF cases were confirmed from Sirohi district in Rajasthan and Aravalli district in Gujarat.

Research Studies

NIV has recently conducted human, animal and tick surveillance studies to understand the prevalence of this disease in Gujarat. These studies were conducted in collaboration with IDSP, local public health authorities, animal husbandry department and National Vector Borne Diseases Control

Programme, Gujarat. Studies revealed that IgG antibody for CCHF was present in domestic animals of 15 districts of Gujarat and also in domestic animals of Sirohi district in Rajasthan. This is indicative of past infection of the animals with the virus. *Hyalomma* species of ticks, which are known to transmit the disease, were also found to be positive in those areas where human CCHF cases were reported and confirmed, thus indicating active transmission of the virus.

Support to the State Governments

NIV has also extended further support to public health system of the states of Gujarat and Rajasthan by conducting several meetings to create awareness of the state government, training and strengthening of diagnostic services of the states and providing essential recommendations to the state government for prevention and control of this disease.

Diagnostics

As no cost effective commercial kit is available in the market for detection of antibodies for CCHF, NIV has developed the following cost effective ELISA kits to screen the CCHF antibodies in humans and animals:

- Anti CCHFV Bovine IgG antibody detection ELISA
- Anti CCHFV Sheep and Goat IgG antibody detection ELISA
- Anti CCHFV Human IgG antibody detection ELISA

ICMR's Flagship Programmes which include Tribal Health Research Forum and Vector Borne Diseases Science Forum continued to work for the health problems of the tribal population as well as studies on the control of malaria, filariais, Japanese Encephalitis (JE), kala-azar, dengue and chikungunya. A research cum intervention project on AES/JE was launched as part of the multipronged strategy developed for prevention, case management and rehabilitation measures for prevention and control of JE/AES in Gorakhpur involving seven ICMR Institutes and will keep on generating new data and support for management of the disease.

ICMR continued to support, coordinate and monitor extramural research in different biomedical subjects viz., anatomy, anthropology, haematology and human genetics through Task Force Projects, adhoc schemes and fellowships in various research institutions, medical colleges and universities of the country. About 20 adhoc projects and 15 fellowships in a variety of topics were completed in 2014-15 including study of surgical anatomy of vasculo-biliary apparatus of human cochlear, ultrastructure of atrioventricular valve apparatus in human hearts, age estimation from teeth, genetic studies in chronic obstructive pulmonary disease, primary congenital glaucoma, Stevens-Johnson Syndrome (SJS), Pediatric Celiac Disease Phase-II, hypospadias, familial hypercholesterolemia, polycystic ovary syndrome, primary nephritic syndrome, mucopolysaccharidosis type II, male infertility, fragile X syndrome, characterization of the Bernard Soulier Syndrome (BSS), thalassemia, molecular characterization of hemoglobin, myelodysplastic syndromes, sickle cell disease gene polymorphism, genetic alterations in disease progression of chronic myeloid leukemia, gene polymorphism in childhood acute lymphoblastic leukemia, etc.

To accreditate, supervise and regulate the Assisted Reproductive Technology (ART) clinics and banks in India, ICMR has developed national guidelines on accreditation, supervision and regulation of ART clinics in India. To implement these guidelines in the country, the ICMR has developed a draft Assisted Reproductive Technology (Regulation) Bill to establish National Board, State Boards and National Registry of Assisted Reproductive Technology clinics and banks in India for accreditation and supervision of ART clinics and banks ensuring that services provided are ethical and that the medical, social and legal rights of all those concerned are protected with maximum benefit to the infertile couples or individuals including surrogate mother, oocyte and sperm donor within a recognized framework of ethics and good medical practice.

Currently more than 1,457 ART clinics and banks have been identified. Out of that around 825 ART clinics and 152 banks have confirmed their contact details (total 977) and remaining 480 ART clinics and banks are in the process of confirmation. Out of 825 ART clinics only 335 ART clinics have been found in compliance with the provisions of the proposed ART (Regulation) Bill, therefore, these 335 ART clinics have been enrolled under the National Registry of ICMR.

ICMR coordinates international collaboration in biomedical research between India and other countries as well as with national and international agencies such as Ministry of Science and Technology, Indian and foreign missions and WHO, etc.

It also supports and coordinates the international travel of Indian scientists engaged in approved bilateral collaborative research projects under various MoUs and joint statements with other countries. In all 28 exchange visits of scientists/officials to and from India were arranged for various international collaborative programmes/projects.

Medicinal Plants

Quality standards on 35 medicinal plants were developed and monographs published as Volume 12 of the series Quality Standards of Indian Medicinal Plants. A MoU between ICMR and Pharmacopoeal Commission of Indian Medicine (PCIM), Ministry of Ayush was signed under which 120 Phytochemical Reference Standards generated through extramural projects of ICMR were transferred to PCIM along with all spectral data for characterization and Quality Assurance of Ayurveda, Siddha and Unani (ASU) drugs. This will lead to wider acceptance of traditional medicines in India and abroad, as quality assurance is the key issue. Currently, Volume 4 of the PRS of selected Indian plants is also being finalized. Earlier 90 PRS compounds have been presented in three volumes and published by ICMR monograph on perspectives of Indian medicinal plants in the management of Diabetes Mellitus. A compendium on the safety aspects of important Indian medicinal plants is also being compiled.

Social and Behavioural Research

ICMR has initiated the 16 new projects on different aspects of gender and health, four new extramural adhoc projects and two fellowships.

A new joint initiative of ICMR-ICSSR was planned to call for projects in the following identified priority areas: (i) issues related to effective delivery and utilization of services by the community focusing on structural factors, health seeking factors and factors influencing effective delivery and utilization; (ii) issue related to service delivery and utilization by marginalized groups/ Dalits; (iii) effective Information, Education and Communication (IEC) and behaviour change strategies; (iv) social and behavioural issues related to diseases like malaria, TB, polio, leprosy, HIV/AIDS, infant mortality, reproductive health, chikungunya, dengue, and the issues of gender and nutrition, etc.

Indian Systems of Medicine and Homoeopathy

Department of Indian Systems of Medicine and Homoeopathy (ISM&H) was created in March,1995 and re-named as Department of Ayurveda, Yoga and Naturopathy, Unani, Siddha and Homoeopathy (AYUSH) in November, 2003. It was elevated to the status of Ministry of AYUSH with a view to providing focused attention to development of education and research in Ayurveda, Yoga and Naturopathy, Unani, Siddha and Homoeopathy systems. The Ministry continued to lay emphasis on upgradation of AYUSH educational standards, quality control and standardization of drugs, improving the availability of medicinal plant material, research and development and awareness generation about the efficacy of the systems domestically and internationally. Sowa Rigpa is the recent addition to the existing family of AYUSH systems.

Encouragement to scientific research and education, laying down pharmacopoeial standards to ensure quality drugs, evolving good laboratory practices, following good manufacturing practices, regulating education standards, supplementing the efforts of state governments in setting up AYUSH in allopathic hospitals and AYUSH units in Primary Health Centres (PHCs) and Community Health Centres (CHCs) and AYUSH wings in District Allopathic hospitals, upgradation of AYUSH hospitals and dispensaries, creating awareness through organization of Health *Melas* and other information, education and communication, are just some of the ways in which the department is helping in the growth and wider reach of Indian systems of medicine and Homoeopathy.

Ayurveda, Siddha, Unani and Homoeopathy drugs are covered under the purview of Drugs and Cosmetics Act, 1940. Since most of the medicines of AYUSH sector are made from medicinal plant materials, the Ministry has set up a National Medicinal Plants Board to promote cultivation of medicinal plants and ensure sustained availability of quality raw material. A separate National Policy on Indian Systems of Medicine and Homoeopathy is in place since 2002.

Pharmacopoeial Laboratory for Indian Medicine

Pharmacopoeial Laboratory for Indian Medicine (PLIM) is a subordinate office of Ministry of AYUSH located at Ghaziabad. The laboratory was established in the year 1970 as a Pharmacopoeial standards setting–cum drugs testing laboratory at national level for Ayurvedic, Siddha and Unani (ASU) medicine. It acts as an appellate laboratory for testing of Ayurvedic, Siddha and Unani (ASU) drugs under Drugs and Cosmetic Act, 1940. The Pharmacopoeial Laboratory for Indian Medicine was established with the objective to develop and validate pharmacopoeial standardization of single drugs and compound formulations for incorporation in Ayurvedic, Siddha and Unani pharmacopoeias and analysis of legal drugs samples received from drugs control authorities and courts.

Homoeopathic Pharmacopoeial Laboratory

Homoeopathic Pharmacopoeial Laboratory, (HPL) Ghaziabad was set up as a national laboratory for the purpose of laying down standards and testing for identity, purity and quality of homoeopathic medicines. The laboratory also functions as Central Drug Laboratory for the testing of homoeopathic medicines under the Rule 3A, Section 6 of the Drugs and Cosmetics Act, 1947. Standards worked out by the laboratory are published in the Homoeopathic Pharmacopoeia of India (HPI). The Department of Science and Technology has recognized HPL as a science and technology institution.

Pharmacopoeia Commission for Indian Medicines and Homoeopathy

Development of quality standards of Ayurveda, Siddha, Unani Medicines and their periodic update to the needs of the consumers is the priority of the department. The popularity and demand of ASU medicines is increasing rapidly. Therefore, it was necessary to upgrade the existing Pharmacopoeia Commission for Indian Medicine. The Pharmacopoeia Commission for Indian Medicine (PCIM) to cater to the needs of ASU Pharmacopoeia Committee and the Pharmacopoeial Laboratory for Indian Medicine (PLIM). Later on the department after taking approval from Cabinet has renamed the earlier Pharmacopoeia Commission for Indian Medicine as Pharmacopoeia Commission of Indian Medicine and Homoeopathy in order to include Homoeopathy also. The Homoeopathic Pharmacopoeia Committee and HPL are also brought under PCIM&H. It is a fully autonomous organization registered under Societies Registration Act, 1860. The main objective of the PCIM&H is to publish and revise the Ayurvedic, Siddha, Unani and Homoeopathic Pharmacopoeias of India as may be deemed necessary to ensure harmonization and development of the ASU&H Pharmacopoeial Standards and to make them acceptable internationally. Till date Pharmacopoeial Standards of 152 Ayurvedic formulations and 100 Unani formulations have been laid down in addition to standards on raw drugs used in ASU medicines.

Public Sector Undertaking

Indian Medicines Pharmaceutical Corporation Limited

Indian Medicines Pharmaceutical Corporation Limited (IMPCL), a Government of India enterprise, having 97.61 per cent shares of Government of India and 2.39 per cent shares of Uttarakhand government through Kumaon Mandal Vikas Nigam Ltd., was incorporated in 1978. The registered office and factory of the company is at Mohan, district Almora, Uttarakhand. IMPCL comes under the administrative control of the Ministry of AYUSH, New Delhi.

The Corporation had acquired 38 acres land on lease at Mohan, a notified backward area, 550 metre above sea level (a valley in thick forest area adjacent to Corbett National Park).

IMPCL is Schedule D, 'Mini-Ratna' Category-II, GMP Certified & ISO 9001-2008 certificated Central Public Sector Undertaking. It has established in-house AYUSH Drug Testing Laboratory (DTL) and obtained approval for testing of raw materials as well as finished goods. The authorized share capital is ₹ 75 crore and paid-up share capital is ₹ 41 crore

The commercial production of the company was started in June, 1983. The production activities are being carried out both manually as well as in mechanized form. The company was set up with the objectives to manufacture and supply the genuine and efficacious Ayurvedic and Unani medicines to the Central Government hospitals, Central Government research units all over India and to state government related departments besides sales in the open market.

IMPCL is supplying Ayurvedic and Unani medicines all over India. As the automation and 3rd phase modernization is under progress, the plant capacity for tablets, vati, capsules, churns, avaleha, etc., will be enhanced at least by eight to ten times on completion of modernization work.

Statutory Regulatory Councils

Central Council of Indian Medicine, New Delhi

The Central Council of Indian Medicine is a statutory body constituted under the Indian Medicine Central Council Act, 1970. The Central Council of Indian Medicine with the previous sanction of the Central Government as required under Section 36 of the Indian Medicine Central Council Act, 1970 and after obtaining the comments of the State Governments as required under Section 22 of the said Act has prescribed courses for Under-graduate and Post-graduate education in Ayurveda, Unani, Siddha and Sowa Rigpa through the Regulations. The Central Council has prescribed 19 Regulations to achieve the goal of the Central Council.

Central Council of Homoeopathy

Central Council of Homoeopathy (CCH), New Delhi is a statutory body constituted under the provisions of the Homoeopathy Central Council Act, 1973, which provides for the maintenance of a Central Register of Homoeopathy and for other matters connected therewith. The Central Government had amended the Homoeopathy Central Council Act, 1973 in 2002, and the amended Act had been enforced from 2003.

Besides these, this Council has also notified the various Regulations as per provisions of said Act. There are: (i) Homoeopathy (Degree Course) B.H.M.S. Regulations, 1983; (ii) Homoeopathy (Graded Degree Course) B.H.M.S. Regulations, 1983; (iii) Homoeopathy (Diploma Course) D.H.M.S. Regulations, 1983; (iv)(a) Homoeopathy (Minimum Standards of Education) Regulations, 1983; (b) Homoeopathy Central Council (Minimum Standards Requirement of Homoeopathic Colleges and attached Hospitals) Regulations 2013; (v) Homoeopathy (Post-graduate Degree Course) M.D. (Hom.) Regulations, 1989; (vi) Establishment of New Medical College (Opening of New or Higher Course of Study or Training and Increase of Admission Capacity by a Medical College) Regulations, 2011; (vii) Homoeopathy Central Council (Inspectors and Visitors) Regulations, 1982; (viii) Homoeopathy Central Council (Registration) Regulations, 1982; (ix) Homoeopathy Practitioners (Professional Conduct, Etiquette and Code of Ethics) Regulations, 1982; (x) Homoeopathy Central Council (Election of the President and Vice-President) Regulations, 1976; and (xi) Central Council of Homoeopathy (General) Regulations, 1984.

Research Councils

There are five apex research councils, namely, Central Council for Research in Ayurvedic Sciences (CCRAS), Central Council for Research in Siddha (CCRS), Central Council for Research in Unani Medicine (CCRUM), Central Council for Research in Homeopathy (CCRH) and Central Council for Research in Yoga and Naturopathy (CCRYN). Research and development activities related to AYUSH are being implemented under intra-mural, extra-mural and collaborative research programmes of these councils. These councils are engaged in conducting clinical research, drug research, survey and cultivation of medicinal plants, toxicology and safety studies, drug standardization and literary research.

Following reform measures/policy initiative were taken:-

- Validation of classical Ayurvedic formulations, to establish clinical safety and efficacy have been undertaken (safety and efficacy).
- Collaborative clinical studies have been undertaken in collaboration with reputed medical institution/universities.
- ISO:9001 certification has been obtained for CCRH, headquarters.

During 2015-16, the research councils have initiated various pilot projects in various states such as Swasthya Rakshan Programme: CCRAS, CCRUM and CCRH and Tribal Health Care Research Project.

CCRH is also engaged in Homoeopathy for Health Child which has been implemented to sensitize target audience including health workers, patients and care-givers about benefits of homoeopathy for common diseases. The project undertaken at Assam (Kamrup district), Delhi (Urban slum Mayapuri), Maharashtra (Palghar district), Odisha(Cuttack district), Uttar Pradesh (Gautam Budh Nagar district) and (Gorakhpur district).

A scheme has been started by Central Council for Research in Yoga and Naturopathy (CCRYN) to conduct one month Yoga camp by administering Common Yoga Protocol in all districts of India to celebrate the International Day of Yoga through Government organizations/NGOs/Voluntary organizations. Provision of grant of ₹ 1 lakh to selected organization from each district has been made under the scheme for conducting Yoga camps for general public, free of cost, for one month.

In accordance with the scheme, Yoga camps were organized for one month across the country which concluded in 2015. Yoga class with Common Yoga Protocol was practiced by the Yoga participants which was followed by one day workshop/seminar on various health related topics.

National Institutes

At present, national institutes to promote the Indian System of Medicine are: National Institute of Ayurveda, Jaipur; National Institute of Homoeopathy, Kolkata; National Institute of Unani Medicine, Bengaluru; National Institute of Siddha, Chennai; Morarji Desai National Institute of Yoga, New Delhi; Rashtriya Ayurveda Vidyapeeth, New Delhi; and National Institute of Naturopathy, Pune.

One institute namely, Institute for Post Graduate Teaching and Research in Ayurveda, Jamnagar is financially assisted by the Ministry though it comes under the administrative control of Gujarat Ayurveda University Act.

Three new Institutes namely, All India Institute of Ayurveda, New Delhi, North-Eastern Institute of Ayurveda and Homoeopathy, Shillong and North-Eastern Institute of Folk Medicine, Passighat are being established and in advance stage of construction.

In addition, an All India Institute of Unani Medicine is to be established at Ghaziabad, Uttar Pradesh and the project consultant has been selected for preparation of DPR. An All India Institute of Homoeopathy is to be established at Delhi for which DDA has allotted 10 acres of land at Narela, Delhi.

National Medicinal Plants Board

National Medicinal Plants Board (NMPB) is an apex national body which co-ordinates all matters relating to medicinal plants in the country. The Board which was established in November 2000, acts as advisory body to the concerned ministries, departments and agencies in strategic planning of medicinal plants related initiatives and to plan and provide financial support to programmes relating to conservation, cultivation and also all round development of medicinal plants sector. The NMPB is presently implementing two schemes namely Central Sector Scheme for 'Conservation, Development and Sustainable Management of Medicinal Plants' and centrally sponsored scheme of National Mission on Medicinal Plants.

AYUSH Service under National AYUSH Mission

Providing cost effective AYUSH services, with a universal access is one of the strategies to improve quality and outreach of healthcare services in the country. Under the National Rural Health Mission (NRHM), a large number of Ayurveda, Siddha, Unani and Homeopathy facilities have been set up on Primary Health Centres, Community Health Centres and District hospitals and physicians in these systems have been posted in these facilities with financial support from the Government of India. Centrally Sponsored Scheme for development of AYUSH hospitals and dispensaries of the Department of AYUSH, provides financial assistance to the State for the creation of such AYUSH facilities and for the supply of essential AYUSH medicines. Under this scheme, financial assistance is also being provided for AYUSH hospitals and dispensaries for upgradation of their infrastructure. Financial assistance for hiring of AYUSH doctors and paramedics and their training is, however, being provided to the states under NRHM Flexi pool. Department of AYUSH proposed a National AYUSH Mission (NAM) for assisting the states/union territories for the overall development of AYUSH Sector.

Drug Quality Control

The Drug Control Cell (DCC) in the Ministry of AYUSH deals with regulatory and quality control matters of Ayurveda, Siddha, Unani and Homoeopathy drugs including amendment in the regulations, introduction of new regulations and examination of other drugs related issues. The cell is made up of Technical Officers and it also administers the Centrally Sponsored Scheme for Quality Control of AYUSH drugs and coordinates with the State Licensing Authorities to achieve uniform administration of the Act, approval of drug testing laboratories and for drugs related matters. The DCC provides secretarial support to the two statuary bodies—Ayurveda, Siddha, Unani Drugs Technical Advisory Board(ASUDTAB) and Ayurveda, Siddha, Unani Drugs Consultative Committee (ASUDCC), which are set up under the provisions of Drugs and Cosmetics Act, 1940. A collaborative mechanism is in place with Central Drugs Standard Control Organization (CDSCO) for WHO GMP certification scheme any other export and import related matters of ASU Drugs.

Information, Education and Communication

With a view to promoting and propagating AYUSH systems, amongst the masses and to give wide publicity to the strengths of the AYUSH systems, the Ministry organised various activities.

International Coooperation

World Health Organization (WHO) is one of the main UN agencies collaborating, in the Health Sector, with the Ministry of Health & Family Welfare, Government of India and providing technical support. Activities under WHO are funded through two sources:- The Country budget, which comes out of contributions made by member countries and Extra Budgetary Resources which comes from (a) donations from various sources for general or specific aspects of health and (b) funds routed through the WHO to countries by other member countries or institutes/agencies. India is the largest beneficiary of the country budget within the South East Asia Region. The budget is operated on a biennium basis, calendar year-wise.

Custom Duty Exemption Certificate

During 2015-16, this Ministry has issued one time Customs Duty Exemption Certificates in favour of:

(i) ESIC Hospital, Sanath Nagar (Telangana), under the control of the Ministry of Labour & Employment, Shram Shakti Bhawan, Rafi Marg, New Delhi - 110001 and

(ii) Jawaharlal Institute of Post-graduate Medical Education and Research (JIPMER), Dhanvantri Nagar, Puducherry–605 006.

17 Housing

URBANIZATION is an important determinant of economic development. As per Census of India 2011, the number of towns is 7,935 comprising 4,041 Statutory Towns and 3,894 Census Towns. Also, proportion of population in urban areas has increased from 27.8 per cent (2001) to 31.2 per cent (2011) and slum population comprises 18 per cent of urban population of 377 million. The Technical Group on Urban Housing Shortage constituted for the Twelfth Five Year Plan estimated that in 2012, total housing shortage comprising obsolescence, congestion and shelter to houseless households was 18.78 million, of which approximately 96 per cent is accounted for by economically weaker section and lower income group categories.

Increased pace of urbanization poses varied challenges for policy primarily in terms of meeting the housing shortage, devising relevant solutions for providing affordable housing, generating appropriate livelihood opportunities and designing effective strategies for alleviating poverty. Key issues and initiatives regarding urban housing and habitat including livelihood, with which Ministry of Housing and Urban Poverty Alleviation is concerned, are detailed here:

Pradhan Mantri Awas Yojana - Housing for All (Urban) Mission

To facilitate housing for all by 2022, the Government of India has launched the PMAY-Housing for All (Urban) Mission in 2015. The Mission targets urban poor, living in slums and others. It envisages Government interventions for different segments of urban poor as follows: a) slum rehabilitation: redevelopment of slums with participation of private developers using land as a resource - slum rehabilitation grant of ₹ 1 lakh per house on an average for all eligible slum dwellers in all such projects; b) promotion of affordable housing for weaker section through credit linked subsidy: the interest rate subvention at 6.5 per cent for both EWS/LIG categories so that interest payable at present is less than 4 per cent. If interest rate varies, even then interest subvention would remain at 6.5 per cent and interest payable after subvention would vary, the subsidy payout on NPV basis would be about ₹ 2.3 lakh per house for both EWS and LIG; c) affordable housing in partnership with public and private sectors: Central assistance at ₹ 1.5 lakh per EWS house in projects where 35 per cent of the houses are mandatorily for EWS category; and d) subsidy for beneficiary-led individual house construction or enhancement: ₹ 1.5 lakh per house for EWS category in slums or otherwise if states/cities make a project.

Houses of up to 30 sq.m. carpet area are to be provided with basic civic infrastructure i.e., water, sanitation, sewerage, road, power, telephone line, etc., and social infrastructure such as community centre, parks and playgrounds, livelihood centre, etc. Flexibility is provided in terms of determining size of house and other facilities at the state level in consultation with the Ministry. Under the Mission, economically weaker sections are defined as urban poor with annual income of ₹ 3 lakh and low income group with annual income between ₹ 3-6 lakh. These limits can be revised by Ministry if required.

All statutory towns as per census 2011 and towns notified subsequently would be eligible for coverage under the Mission. States/UTs will have flexibility to include the planning area as notified with respect to statutory towns and which surrounds the concerned municipal area.

Exact number of houses under the Mission would depend on demand survey for which all states/cities will undertake detailed survey including online registration for assessing actual demand by integrating Jan Dhan Yojana/other bank account number and Aadhaar number/voter ID Card/any other unique identification details of intended beneficiaries or a certificate of house ownership from Revenue Authority of beneficiary's native district. Beneficiaries will be validated by state/ULB. Cities/states will prepare "Housing for All" Action Plan on the basis of available data and survey results.

Following mandatory conditions are envisaged so as to provide an enabling environment facilitating growth of housing especially affordable housing for weaker section in the country by easing the supply side regulations and administrative constraints.

States/UTs to make suitable changes for obviating the need for separate Non Agricultural (NA) permission if land already falls in the residential zone earmarked in Master Plan; states/UTs shall prepare/amend the Master Plans earmarking land for affordable housing employing innovative methods such as land pooling; system would be put in place to ensure single-window; time bound clearance for layout approval and building permissions at ULB level; states/UTs shall adopt the approach of deemed building permission and layout approval on the basis of pre-approved layouts and building plans for EWS/LIG housing or exempt approval for houses below certain area of plot; states/UTs would legislate amendments in existing rental laws on the lines of model tenancy act being prepared by the Ministry; states/UTs shall provide additional FAR/FSI/TDR and relaxed density norms for slum redevelopment and low cost housing.

A beneficiary family will comprise husband, wife, unmarried sons and/or unmarried daughters. The beneficiary family should not own a pucca house either in his/her name or in the name of any member of his/her family in any part of the country.

Technology Sub-Mission

A Technology Sub-mission under PMAY-HFA (Urban) Mission has been set up for adopting modern, innovative, green technologies and building material for faster and quality construction of houses. It would facilitate preparation and adoption of layout designs and building plans suitable for various geo-climatic zones and to also assist states/cities in deploying disaster resistant and environment friendly technologies.

Progress under PMAY-HFA (U) Mission

Under PMAY-HFA (U) Mission, 34 state governments/UT administrations have signed MoA; 2,802 cities have been selected; 1,147 projects involving construction of 8.54 lakh houses have been approved; 1,770 houses have been completed and 8,004 houses have been purchased with loans under Credit Linked Subsidy Scheme of PMAY (U). Also, under on-going Rajiv Awas Yojana projects subsumed in PMAY-HFA (U) Mission, 28,080 houses have been completed.

Deendayal Antyodaya Yojana - National Urban Livelihoods Mission

The National Urban Livelihoods Mission (NULM) and National Rural Livelihoods Mission (NRLM) have been converged and named as Deendayal Antyodaya Yojana (DAY). Also, the scope of NULM has been enhanced to cover all statutory towns and it has been renamed as DAY-NULM. The primary target of DAY-NULM is urban poor, including urban homeless and particular emphasis is laid on mobilisation of vulnerable sections of urban population such as SCs, STs, minorities, female-headed households, persons with disabilities, destitute, migrant labourers, and especially vulnerable occupational groups such as street vendors, rag pickers, domestic workers, beggars, construction workers, etc. Activities under DAY-NULM are directed also at providing shelters equipped with essential services to urban homeless in a phased manner. Moreover, the Mission addresses livelihood concerns of urban street vendors by facilitating access to suitable spaces, institutional credit, social security and skills for accessing emerging market opportunities.

DAY-NULM has following components:

1. Social Mobilization and Institution Development (SM&ID): NULM envisages mobilisation of urban poor households into thrift and credit-based Self-Help Groups (SHGs) and their federations/collectives.

2. Capacity Building and Training (CB&T): A multi-pronged approach is planned under NULM for continuous capacity building of SHGs and their federations/collectives, government functionaries at Central, State and city/town levels, bankers, NGOs, CBOs and other stakeholders. NULM will also create national and state-level mission management units to support the implementation of programme for the poor.

3. Employment through Skills Training and Placement (EST&P): NULM will focus on providing assistance for skill development/upgrading of the urban poor to enhance their capacity for self-employment or better salaried employment.
4. Self-employment Programme (SEP): This component will focus on financial assistance to individuals/groups of urban poor for setting up gainful self-employment ventures/micro-enterprises, suited to their skills, training, aptitude and local conditions.
5. Support to Urban Street Vendors: This component will cover development of vendors market, credit enablement of vendors, socio-economic survey of street vendors, skill development and micro enterprises development and convergence with social assistance under various schemes of the Government.
6. Shelter for Urban Homeless (SUH): Under this component, the construction of permanent shelters for the urban homeless equipped with essential services will be supported.
7. Innovative & Special Projects (I&SP): It will focus on the promotion of novel initiatives in the form of innovative projects. These initiatives may be in the nature of pioneering efforts, aimed at catalysing sustainable approaches to urban livelihoods through Public, Private, Community Partnership (PPCP).

Under DAY-NULM, 6.24 lakh persons have been provided skill training; 1.98 lakh beneficiaries have been placed for wage/self employment and assisted for setting up individual/group micro enterprises; more than 1 lakh Self-Help Groups (SHGs) have been formed and disbursed loans under SHG Bank Linkage programme; 58,437 SHGs have been given Revolving Fund; 815 shelters for urban homeless have been sanctioned, out of which 345 shelters are operational; 7.76 lakh street vendors have been identified in 726 surveyed cities, 1.75 lakh street vendors have been issued ID Cards and street vending plans have started in 70 cities.

Street Vendors (Protection of Livelihood and Regulation of Street Vending) Act, 2014

Street vending is an age old profession in India and it generates livelihood for millions of people. To protect the rights of urban street vendors and to regulate street vending activities, Government of India has enacted the Street Vendors (Protection of Livelihood and Regulation of Street Vending) Act, 2014, provisions of which are aimed at creating a conducive atmosphere where street vendors are able to carryout their business in a fair and transparent manner, without fear of harassment and eviction. Government of India is assisting the State Governments/UT Administrations in preparing relevant rules, schemes, etc., which are mandated under the Act.

The Ministry has notified rules for UTs of Andaman & Nicobar, Chandigarh, Dadra and Nagar Haveli, Diu & Daman and Lakshadweep. Ministry of Home Affairs has delegated the powers and functions to Administrators of UTs without Legislature for framing of further subordinate legislation (Scheme, Bye-laws & Street Vending Plan) under Street Vendors Act, 2014. Assam, Chhattisgarh, NCT of Delhi, Odisha, Punjab, Rajasthan, Tamil Nadu, Jharkhand, Uttarakhand and Tripura have notified Rules. Andhra Pradesh, NCT of Delhi, Odisha, Punjab, Tamil Nadu, Telangana, and Tripura have notified the scheme.

Real Estate (Regulation and Development) Act, 2016

The Real Estate (Regulation and Development) Act, 2016 is aimed at establishing the Real Estate Regulatory Authority for regulation and promotion of the real estate sector and protecting the interest of consumers.

Ministry of Housing and Urban Poverty Alleviation has notified the specific Sections of the Act for implementation with effect from May, 2016, towards making of rules and establishment of regulatory authorities and appellate tribunals. Being the competent authority for preparation of the rules under the Real Estate Act, 2016 for UTs without legislature, the Ministry has drafted the model rules under the Real Estate Act, 2016 and uploaded the same on the Ministry's website for public comments. Separate consultations have also been held with UTs without legislature to discuss the draft rules.

Approval procedures for housing and construction projects have been simplified and streamlined in consultation with other line ministries viz., Environment, Forests and Climate Change, Civil Aviation, Culture, Defence and Consumer Affairs. PMAY guidelines also mandate certain steps in this direction such as setting up of online single window for construction permits, concept of deemed building permission and layout approval in certain circumstances, etc.

Development Agend.. and Sustainable Development Goals

The United Nations General Assembly (UNGA) in its 68th session adopted 17 goals and 169 targets for the proposed Development Agenda Post-2015 (Millennium Development Goals, MDGs) titled 'Sustainable Development Goals, SDGs'. The UN has stated that these goals and targets will be the main basis for integrating SDGs into Post 2015 Development Agenda, while recognizing other inputs will also be considered in the inter-governmental negotiation process.

The Ministry of Housing and Urban Poverty Alleviation is participating in these meetings and dialogues with regard to the negotiations underway on the Proposal of Open Working Group on SDGs especially on the three goals relevant to this Ministry, viz., Goal 1. End poverty in all its forms everywhere, Goal 8. Promote sustained, inclusive and sustainable economic growth, full and productive employment and decent work for all and Goal 11. Make cities and human settlements inclusive, safe, resilient and sustainable.

Asia Pacific Ministerial Conference on Housing and Urban Development

It was established in December, 2006, subsequent to the first Asia Pacific Ministers' Conference on Housing and Urban Development (AMCHUD), held at New Delhi under the aegis of Government of India, Ministry of Housing & Poverty Alleviation and the UN-HABITAT. The objectives of APMCHUD are enshrined in the 'Delhi Declaration' adopted unanimously by the countries participating in the conference from the Asia Pacific Region. India was the first Chair of the APMCHUD.

The Asia Pacific Ministerial Conference on Housing and Urban Development (APMCHUD) envisages regional cooperation for promoting sustainable housing & urban development among Asia Pacific countries, in the context of the region facing similar problems and issues in these areas. This inter-government institutional mechanism facilitates collaboration among the Asia Pacific countries for experience sharing and information exchange of knowledge in the field of housing and urban development. It also enables the Asia Pacific countries to speak with a unified voice at regional and international fora on our common concern and challenges as well as approaches to address the same.

The APMCHUD is third of such bodies created under the aegis of UN-Habitat after the Assembly of Ministers of Housing and Urban Development of Latin American Countries (MINURVI), established in 1992 as the representative body for the Latin American region and African Ministerial Conference for Housing and Urban Development (AMCHUD) established in 2005 to represent the African region.

The APMCHUD's Ministerial Conference is a biennial event. The Conference elects a Bureau which governs the functioning of the body and the implementation of the decisions of the Conference. The Bureau meets regularly, approximately twice in a year. The Bureau is supported by a Secretariat which is established at New Delhi. Currently India is the host of the APMCHUD Permanent Secretariat.

The APMCHUD in 2008 had identified five focal areas for collaborative action among Asia Pacific countries. The broad themes of the working groups and the lead country for each of the working group are as follows: Urban and Rural Planning and Management (lead country Republic of India); slum upgradation aspects (Lead country Islamic Republic of Iran); basic services (to be jointly lead by Sri Lanka and Maldives); financing aspects (lead country Republic of Korea); and urban development with reference to natural disasters, etc. (lead country Republic of Indonesia).

India's Engagement in the APMCHUD

India was the first chair and host of the permanent secretariat of the APMCHUD and thus is a founder member; India has been a member of all the 5 Bureaus since 2006. The Bureau of APMCHUD oversees and guide activities of APMCHUD; India is the lead country for one of the five Working Groups namely Working Group 1 on "Urban & Rural Planning and Management".

National Urban Housing and Habitat Policy

In the backdrop of the recent transformative changes in the urban development sector especially housing and real estate sector, lessons learnt from implementation of the National Urban Housing Habitat Policy (NUHHP), (2007), new programmes/schemes launched by the government, the SDGs and the new Urban Development Agenda, the time is opportune to review/revise the existing NUHHP, 2007. In order to develop a sustainable and implementable Housing and Habitat Policy, Ministry of HUPA has already initiated the process of dialogue with various stakeholders for formulation of NUHHP, 2017.

Template for State Housing Policy for Urban Areas

For addressing the overall challenges faced by the housing sector in the country, the Ministry had come up with the National Urban Housing and Habitat Policy (NUHHP), 2007 which envisaged that the states/UTs would prepare a State Urban Housing and Habitat Policy and also a State Urban Housing & Habitat Action Plan. In order to assist the states in formulating the housing policies to address the current requirements of the sector, Ministry of Housing and Urban Poverty Alleviation has released a 'Template for Preparation of State Housing Policy for Urban Areas'.

Draft Rental Housing Policy

Urban housing shortage in India, estimated to be 18.78 million during the 12th Plan period with consequent increases resulting in increase in urbanization in future years, is an area of concern. Historically housing policy/programmatic interventions have been oriented towards home ownership, nevertheless, providing housing to all on ownership basis has proved challenging. Growing family needs had resulted in overcrowding and slum like situations due to lack of alternatives such as rental housing and absence of rental housing frameworks in the country. In order to address these issues, the Ministry has come up with the Draft National Urban Rental Housing Policy (NURHP), 2015. The vision of the Draft Policy is 'to create a vibrant, sustainable and inclusive rental housing market in India'.

The Draft National Rental Housing Policy is aimed at promoting rental housing as an option for: the destitute, homeless and disabled people, social rental housing for the socially and economically weaker (EWS/LIG) sections, affordable rental housing for specific target groups such as migrant labours, working women, students, etc., rental housing as a stop gap towards aspirant home buyers, institutional rental housing for working class.

The policy will enable: formalization of rental housing through regulatory and legal frameworks; enhance fund flows along with incentives for rental housing; and promote institutions/organisations for constructing, managing, maintenance and operations of rental housing stock – RMCs, Residential REITs, and employee housing, etc.

Model Tenancy Act

Ministry of HUPA has shared with the states and all stakeholders a draft Model Tenancy Act, 2015. The highlights of this model are as follows: framework for the regulation of tenancy for commercial and residential properties; balancing the rights and responsibilities of landlords and tenants through rental contracts; defines period, inheritance, rents payable, obligations of landlord and tenants, etc.; registration of rental contracts with rent authorities outlays process of fast adjudication process for resolution of disputes through rent tribunals; repossession of the premises by the landlord through rent courts; compensation in case of non-vacancy; and not applicable for government/employee housing/charity and religious buildings.

Use of Space Technology Based Tools

To effectively implement and monitor the mission deliverables, Ministry of HUPA through National Remote Sensing Centre (NRSC), Hyderabad, has developed geo-tagging application to track physical progress of houses constructed under the beneficiary-led component of PMAY-HFA(U) Mission, through geo-tagged photographs;

Features of geo-tagging portal for PMAY-HFA(U) include: mobile application on hand held devices for taking geo-tagged photographs of existing houses with beneficiary and monitoring construction by taking periodic photographs. Photographs to be uploaded on Bhuvan Geo-Portal; integration with online MIS being developed for PMAY-HFA (Urban) Mission; it will help in correct identification of beneficiaries, monitoring of construction and timely releases of funds to beneficiary; and using this data, different MIS reports envisaged for use by Centre/state/ULBs.

Management Information System

An online web based Management Information System (MIS) has been designed and developed for monitoring the progress of Deendayal Antyodaya Yojana – National Urban Livelihoods Mission. Training is being imparted to the states for the implementation of MIS. The MIS would include details of beneficiaries, biometric attendance, training and placement details and certificates would be awarded to successful candidates online. This MIS would help the relevant Mission Management Unit to monitor online the progress of the city, ULBs and States on a real-time basis.

In order to streamline the implementation and monitoring of Pradhan Mantri Awas Yojana-Housing for All (Urban) Mission, a centralised web enabled Management Information System has been developed which serves as a bridge between the Ministry, state government, state level nodal agencies (SLNA), urban local bodies (ULBs), central nodal agencies (CNA), beneficiaries and other stakeholders to efficiently manage details of beneficiaries, facilitate project management and generate various monitoring reports. Progress regarding erstwhile RAY and JNNURM projects is captured under Integrated Urban Poverty Management System.

Partners in Progress

Housing and Urban Development Corporation: HUDCO is a techno-financial institution engaged in financing and promotion of housing and urban infrastructure projects. It was established on April 25, 1970 as a wholly owned government company with the objective of providing long term finance and undertaking housing and urban infrastructure development programmes. It has been conferred the status of Mini Ratna. HUDCO has been designated as one of the Central Nodal Agency to channelize the subsidy under CLSS of Pradhan Mantri Awas Yojana (Urban).

Hindustan Prefab Limited: HPL is a Central Public Sector Enterprise under the administrative control of MoHUPA. It is engaged in project management services for execution of civil construction projects through both technologies, conventional and prefab. HPL is focusing to promote adoption of pre-fabricated and pre-engineered technologies through skill upgradation for achieving fast track construction especially for the attainment of the goal of providing "Housing for all by 2022". HPL performed a major role under 'Swachh Bharat Abhiyan' in construction of toilet blocks in schools for various leading PSUs.

Building Materials and Technology Promotion Council: BMTPC, since its inception in 1990, has been promoting innovative and alternate building materials and construction technologies in the field. As the technology promotion council, it is assisting the Ministry in implementation of Pradhan Mantri Awas Yojana (Urban) by anchoring the Technology Sub Mission under it. BMTPC is working as secretariat of the Technology Sub-Mission and it has been designated as one of the agencies for scrutiny of projects from various states.

National Buildings Organisation: NBO is an attached office of Ministry of HUPA and is involved in collection, tabulation and dissemination of statistical information on housing and construction activities in the country. It coordinates and collaborates with state governments/municipal authorities/research and training institutions/statistical institutes and act as the nodal agency catering to data and MIS needs of urban policy-makers, planners and researchers in areas relating to urban poverty, slums, housing, etc.

Central Government Employees Welfare Housing Organisation: CGEWHO is registered under the Societies Registration Act of 1860 in Delhi since 1990. It functions under the aegis of MoHUPA as a 'welfare' organization for construction of dwelling units for the Central Government employees on "No Profit-No Loss" basis. Projects recently undertaken by it include Mohali (Ph-II), Bhubaneswar (Ph-II), Greater Noida and SAS Nagar.

National Cooperative Housing Federation of India is a nation-wide organization of the cooperative housing sector. The primary objective of NCHF is to promote, guide and coordinate activities of housing cooperatives. It undertakes promotional activities in respect of Apex Cooperative Housing Federations (ACHFs) in those states where such organizations do not exist and to strengthen the ACHFs which are comparatively weak. Also, it is involved with education, training, research conferences/seminars, publications, etc. for the benefit of persons and institutions engaged in cooperative housing activities.

18 India and the World

THE primary objective of India's engagement with the world is to ensure a peaceful, stable global environment and create the most propitious climate for India's economic growth and development. The rising profile of India in global affairs and its emergence as a fast growing economy in an otherwise difficult global environment presents a moment of opportunity that can be utilised to diversify India's strategic and economic options. In this context, India's external engagements over the period of April 2015 to June 2016 have sought to simultaneously advance and deepen relations with each bilateral or multilateral partner, in the specific areas where such engagement brings maximum benefit to Indian interests. The common threads that run through the entire gamut of India's international outreach over this period have been put together here.

Greater energy, planning and rigour in India's external outreach, to simultaneously strengthen traditional friendships while expanding India's diplomatic canvas to include new geographic and thematic areas. Revitalising India's engagement with its immediate neighbourhood—at the bilateral level as well as within the framework of SAARC. This also includes enhanced sub-regional cooperation under the BBIN (Bangladesh-Bhutan-India-Nepal) framework, especially with respect to connectivity and power trade, areas that are vital for closer integration within the region. Simultaneously deepening India's ties with all the major powers of the world, by focusing on areas of greatest promise in each relationship and engaging all such partners in an open, transparent and mutually reinforcing manner with the objective of leveraging them to promote India's economic and security interests.

Developing a comprehensive security strategy for India, encompassing both traditional and non-traditional threats (including terrorism and its enabling eco-system across its borders) that can threaten or retard India's developmental aspirations. Giving priority to economic diplomacy in our international outreach, thus strengthening links between diplomacy and domestic development objectives and making foreign policy as an important tool for advancing India's economic and commercial interests. With the developed countries, the focus was on attracting greater investments, easing market access for Indian goods, capacity-building for skill development in India, promoting health service and education and pushing the agenda on services and labour mobility. Specific countries were identified based on their potential for contributing to national objectives, including our flagship programmes, such as, 'Make in India', 'Digital India', 'Skill India', 'Clean Ganga', 'Smart Cities', 'Start-up India'. Similar approach was followed for promoting clean energy, sustainable urban development, and infrastructure development in roads, railways and ports by seeking best practices, promoting public and private sector partnerships, enhancing access to soft loans and grants, attracting investments, setting up joint ventures & institutional linkages for achieving excellence. Areas such as promoting health, education and innovation, and advancing S&T cooperation and high-level R&D by leveraging our relations with developed countries to advance our human resource potential has been another area of focus.

Imparting greater energy, pragmatism and outcome-orientation to the Act East policy based on building security ties, connectivity and stronger economic integration, leveraging the full potential of this policy to accelerate the developmental path of our northeastern states. Promoting linkages with Gulf, West and Central Asian countries to advance energy ties, but also going beyond to seek wider economic cooperation and to leverage relations to promote security objectives. Promoting a strategy towards the Indian Ocean to address issues of maritime security as well as to leverage economic and cultural complementarities between the littoral states, including promotion of blue economy. By virtue of its location and its dependence on maritime linkages for trade and energy supplies, maritime security is an important priority to secure India's economic growth and development.

Making a special outreach towards India's diaspora, to leverage their skills, political influence and human & financial capital as a bridge to their host communities as also offer them an opportunity to contribute to the rise of their ancestral land. The Ministry has taken steps to strengthen administrative and operative measures to enhance the protection and welfare of emigrant workers. The focus is on transforming the emigration system into a simple, efficient, transparent, orderly and humane process geared to benefit of all stakeholders. Leveraging the riches of India's civilisational ethos, such as Yoga, Ayurveda, Buddhist thought, its Islamic traditions or the holistic lifestyle prescribed in our ancient scriptures, to offer solutions to some of the global problems and also to deepen relations at people-to-people level.

India's Neighbourhood

Afghanistan

President Ashraf Ghani's maiden state visit to India in April 2015 and PM's visit to Afghanistan in 2015 underscored the longstanding, growing and deep bilateral ties between the two countries. They were further strengthened with PM and President Ghani, jointly dedicating the Afghan Parliament building, constructed with Indian cooperation, to the Afghan nation, and provision of Mi-25 helicopters by India for strengthening Afghanistan's defensive capabilities. The visits of External Affairs Minister (EAM) to Islamabad in December 2015 to attend the fifth Ministerial Conference of the

Heart of Asia – Istanbul Process for Regional Cooperation on Afghanistan and also, important visits of the Afghan NSA and the Deputy Foreign Minister added to the intense bilateral interactions. The Chief Executive of Afghanistan, Dr. Abdullah Abdullah visited India in 2016 and held discussions on bilateral, regional and global issues of mutual interest including the security situation and peace and reconciliation in Afghanistan.

Bangladesh

India's close relations with Bangladesh were further strengthened through various initiatives. Decisions taken during Prime Minister's visit to Dhaka in June 2015 have drawn the two countries closer together. It is notable that in the last few years, there has been progress on issues that have eluded solution for decades. Both the countries have worked closely to strengthen bilateral cooperation on all issues including settlement of land boundary issues, security, infrastructure development, cooperation in power, trade and investments, connectivity, sub-regional cooperation and people to people exchange. Prime Ministers of the two nations jointly inaugurated through video conferencing the second cross border transmission line between India and Bangladesh to supply 100 MW of power from Palatana Power Plant in Tripura to Bangladesh and international bandwidth for leasing 10 GDPS for broadband internet from Bangladesh to Tripura.

Bhutan

India and Bhutan share close and friendly relations characterized by mutual trust and understanding. The year 2015-16 saw sustained progress in all areas of cooperation, including hydropower, transport, communication, infrastructure, health, education, culture, IT industry and agriculture. The momentum of the bilateral ties was carried forward by high level visits and interactions. Prime Minister of Bhutan Tshering Tobgay met the Indian Prime Minister on the sidelines of the UN Sustainable Development Summit in 2015 in New York. Prime Minister Tobgay visited India in 2015 to attend the 2nd India Ideas Conclave 2015 in Goa. Work on development projects progressed at a healthy pace throughout this period under the Government of India assistance package of ₹ 4,500 crore towards the 11th Five Year Plan of Bhutan (2013-18). India has committed ₹ 2800 crore as Project Tied Assistance (PTA), ₹ 850 crore for Programme Grant and ₹ 850 crore for small Development Projects (SDPs) for Bhutan's 11th Five Year Plan.

China

India-China bilateral relations continued on the high growth trajectory during 2015. There was expanded engagement both in terms of high-level political exchanges and economic interactions. Prime Minister's visit to China in May 2015 was a significant landmark in our bilateral engagement.

India and China agreed that their simultaneous re-emergence as two major powers in the region and the world offers a momentous opportunity for realisation of the Asian century. Both countries agreed to pursue their respective national developmental goals and security interests in a mutually supportive manner and in a spirit of mutual respect and sensitivity to each other's concerns, interests and aspirations.

Closer developmental partnership which is at the core of India-China bilateral relations received a further boost during PM's visit with the signing of an unprecedented 24 agreements/MoUs in areas including railways, trade and commerce, science and technology, space and people to people exchanges along with 26 commercial/business agreements amounting to US$ 22 billion.

Other important visits during the course of the year included visit of Home Minister in November 2015. Visits from the Chinese side include Chairman NPC in June 2015, Vice President of China and Vice-Chairman of Central Military Commission in November 2015.

President paid a state visit to China in 2016. He held bilateral talks with President Xi Jinping and had meetings with Premier Li Keqiang and Chairman of National People's Congress Zhang Dejiang. He witnessed the signing of 10 MoUs for academic collaboration and exchange between universities and educational institutions from India and China.

Myanmar

Relations between India and Myanmar are multi-faceted and rooted in shared historical, ethnic and cultural ties. Bilateral cooperation between India and Myanmar is aimed at promotion of inclusive growth and development and to contribute to peace, prosperity and stability in two countries and in the region.

India-Myanmar relations were further strengthened through exchange of high level visits and setting up of institutionalized mechanisms to carry forward our cooperation in various sectors. Of particular significance was visit to India of the Myanmar Foreign Minister for the first meeting of the newly established India Myanmar Joint Consultative Commission intended to promote all-round development of relations in promising areas for cooperation covering security and defence, trade and investment, development partnership activities, global and multilateral issues, etc.

Nepal

India-Nepal friendship and cooperation has been characterized by open borders, extensive people-to-people ties and multi-faceted socio-economic interaction. India continues to support Nepal in its transition to a prosperous, peaceful, stable and democratic country. Several agreements were signed including MoU on utilization of USD 250 million grant component of India's assistance package for post-earthquake reconstruction assistance in four sectors i.e., housing, health, education and cultural heritage; MoU on strengthening of road infrastructure in the Terai, Letters of Exchange on rail transport and the two Prime Ministers inaugurated the Muzaffarpur-Dhalkebar power transmission line. The third meeting of Pancheshwar Development Authority was held in Kathmandu in March, 2016.

Pakistan

The period 2015-16 was marked by high-level engagements, both formal and informal, focused on normalising relations between the two countries, paving the way towards a meaningful dialogue. A beginning was made in form of agreement of the two countries on a new Comprehensive Bilateral Dialogue to address all outstanding issues through peaceful means. Nevertheless, cross-border terrorism, cease fire violations and infiltrations across the Line of Control (LoC) and International Border (IB) remained our core concerns. In keeping with India's long-standing policy of strengthening relations with Pakistan through peaceful bilateral dialogue, PM met PM of Pakistan on the sidelines of the SCO Summit in July in Ufa (Russia). During his visit to Paris to attend COP 21 Summit in 2015, PM exchanged courtesies with PM Nawaz Sharif. The two leaders had a brief conversation without aides during which they discussed the need for the two countries to find a mutually acceptable way to create an atmosphere for re-engaging with each other. Following PM's conversation with PM Nawaz Sharif in Paris and in line with the Ufa understanding, the NSAs of the two countries met in Bangkok on December 6, 2015. PM stopped over in Lahore in December 2015 on his way back from Kabul where he had arrived for a brief visit the same morning to inaugurate the Afghanistan Parliament building constructed with Indian cooperation. PM's stop over at Lahore at a short notice underscores the vision of India's leadership to build a normal and well connected neighbourhood in South Asia.

Indian Ocean Region

2015 saw a concerted focus by India on securing interests in a safe and secure Indian Ocean and a stable and prosperous Indian Ocean region. The direction was set with Prime Minister's visits to Seychelles, Mauritius and Sri Lanka in March 2015. The process was given form through the creation of a separate division in MEA in January 2016 for the Indian Ocean region, bringing together relationships with key countries in the region such as Sri Lanka, Maldives, Seychelles, Mauritius and the structured Trilateral Maritime Security Dialogue (between India, Sri Lanka and Maldives) to address geo-strategic security, economic and developmental interests in the Indian Ocean region. India's approach to the future track of the Indian Ocean Region Association (IORA) was also made integral to this approach.

Sri Lanka

India-Sri Lanka relations have undergone a significant and qualitative shift during the last year. Bilateral relations reached a new high in 2015 with a number of high level visits. Sri Lankan Prime Minister Ranil Wickremesinghe paid an official visit to India in September 2015. This was his first overseas visit after the Parliamentary elections in August 2015. President of Sri Lanka, made a working visit to India in 2016. Around that time, India extended help and relief to Sri Lanka which was battling torrential rains and landslides that caused significant devastation and loss of life. India's relationship with Sri Lanka has been progressing in keeping with the "neighbourhood first" principle. Since 2005, the Government of India has committed ₹ 2,300 crore as grant assistance and ₹ 12,900 crore under lines of credit for the rehabilitation of internally displaced persons and reconstruction of infrastructure in the northern and eastern provinces of Sri Lanka. India's flagship project of assistance to Sri Lanka – the Housing Project, with an overall commitment of over ₹ 1,372 crore in grants, is progressing well and completion of second phase is expected shortly. Projects completed in 2015 include the Mahatma Gandhi International Centre in Matale, Language Labs in Ampara, Matara, Badulla and Jaffna and a 200 bed ward complex in Vavuniya. Bilateral cooperation has continued to expand in various areas particularly, defence, economic, education, agriculture, development partnership, culture and people to people exchanges. Bilateral trade and investment continued to grow, spurred by growth in both economies. Trade between the two countries has grown rapidly to rise to US$ 7.45 billion in 2014-15. In the investment field, India is one of the major foreign investors in Sri Lanka, with cumulative investments of nearly US$ 1 billion since 2003. India is Sri Lanka's largest trading partner globally, while Sri Lanka is India's second largest trading partner in the SAARC. India continued to be the largest source of tourist arrivals into Sri Lanka in 2015.

Maldives

2015 marked the 50th anniversary of establishment of India-Maldives diplomatic relations. External Affairs Minister visited Maldives in October 2015 for the 5th India-Maldives Joint Commission, which was held after a hiatus of 15 years. President of Maldives visited India in April, 2016. Discussions were held on bilateral and regional issues of mutual interest. Six MoUs/agreements were signed to further strengthen our robust bilateral relationship. In an unprecedented mark of respect, President of Maldives and all his senior Cabinet Ministers visited the Indian High Commission in Male to sign the condolence book and pay homage to late former President Dr. A.P. J. Abdul Kalam. Bilateral defence and security co-operation broadened and deepened further into several areas including defence hardware and capacity building including monthly EEZ surveillance by Indian Navy ships and aircraft was conducted, holding of EKUVERIN 2015, a joint Indian

Army-MNDF Marine Corps training exercise in Trivandrum, participation by India, Sri Lanka and Maldives in the second 2nd Table Top Exercise (TTEX -15), handing over of Phase-I of the Composite Training Centre for Maldives National Defence Force (MNDF)—a project funded by India, etc.

Mauritius

India and Mauritius enjoy close political, economic, cultural and diaspora linkages. 70 per cent of the population of Mauritius is of Indian origin. Mauritius is a hub for financial services and has emerged as the largest route for FDI into India. Mauritius is also an important jurisdiction for Indian investments into Africa. India-Mauritius trade is nearly US$ 2 billion. There is a close defence partnership on issues of maritime security. The India-Mauritius partnership further intensified and broadened in scope in 2015. Prime Minister led the Mauritian delegation at the Third India-Africa Forum Summit held in Delhi in October 2015. The visit followed the visit of Prime Minister to Mauritius in March 2015, when he was the Chief Guest at the National Day of Mauritius and a series of bilateral agreements were finalised. This was followed by an official visit by the President of Mauritius, recently elected as the first woman President of Mauritius, to India in December 2015. The Indian Naval and Coast Guard Ships visited Mauritius during 2015 to undertake joint surveillance and patrolling of the Exclusive Economic Zone (EEZ) in addition to conducting Hydrographic Surveys.

Seychelles

2015 marked a special year in India-Seychelles partnership that encompasses development partnership, capacity building programmes, maritime security cooperation, and cultural exchanges. Blue economy, climate change, renewable energy, tourism and health are the emerging areas of focus. 10 per cent of the population of Seychelles is of India origin. In the field of development assistance, India provided a grant of US$ 4.3 million for procurement of public transportation buses, medicines, ICT equipment and educational items. To facilitate people-to-people contacts and travel, Seychelles has been included in the e-Tourist Visa scheme of the Government of India from August 2015. A Bilateral Air Services agreement was signed in August 2015. The period also witnessed further deepening of the strategic India-Seychelles defence and security cooperation, focusing in particular on maritime safety and surveillance of the extensive Exclusive Economic Zone of Seychelles. There was a significant Indian presence at the Seychelles National Day celebrations on June 29, 2015.

South East Asia and the Asia-Pacific

Australia

The last visit of Prime Minister to Australia in 2014 imparted a strong momentum to the bilateral relationship. Australia is emerging as an important partner in different sectors including development of mineral resources, science and technology, education and skills and water resources management. The bilateral Civil Nuclear Cooperation Agreement was announced in November 2015. This enables Australian companies to commence uranium exports to India. Defence cooperation received a strong boost through the first ever bilateral maritime exercise AUSINDEX that was conducted in the Bay of Bengal in September 2015. The Indian community in Australia continues to grow in size and importance. Australian universities have attracted almost 50,000 students from India and India is now regarded as the largest source of skilled migrants.

Brunei Darussalam

Bilateral relations with Brunei Darussalam continued to be very close and friendly and Brunei remained Country Coordinator for India in ASEAN till June 2015. Likewise previous years, official level visits took place between the two countries including from the National Defence College of India, ISRO, and Deputy Minister of Culture, Youth and Sports of Brunei. Since 2012, officers from Indian Armed Forces have regularly attended the Royal Brunei Armed Forces Command Staff Course at Staff College, Brunei. Vice President visited Brunei in February 2016 during which MoUs on Defence Cooperation, Health and Youth Affairs and Sports were signed.

Cambodia

Bilateral relations between India and Cambodia remained cordial, friendly and continued to grow stronger. India and Cambodia have close civilization and cultural links from ancient times which continues till today. To further strengthen our bilateral relations, Vice President led a high level delegation visit to Cambodia in September 2015. A Memorandum of Understanding on Tourism Cooperation and an agreement on Indian Grant Assistance for implementation of Quick Impact Projects under Mekong Ganga Cooperation initiative were signed during the visit. For the financial year 2015-16, Grant Assistance of US$ 50,000 each for five Quick Impact Projects related to health, women empowerment, and agriculture and skill development was also announced. The first and second phases of conservation and restoration work of Ta Prohm Temple were completed successfully by the Archeological Survey of India in July 2015.

Indonesia

The year 2015 witnessed many high-level political engagements that have helped in reinvigorating our relationship and has provided the necessary momentum to the bilateral relations. Vice President of India visited Indonesia in November 2015. India-Indonesia Defence Cooperation witnessed significant qualitative and quantitative enhancement in 2015. India's trade with Indonesia for the period January-September 2015 was US$ 11 billion which includes import of commodities worth US$ 8.9 billion and export of US$ 2.1 billion worth goods.

Laos PDR

The year saw a continued upward trend in bilateral relations with Laos PDR. Infrastructure projects in areas of irrigation systems, power transmission, capacity building and human resources and cultural cooperation in restoration of heritage monuments and regular high level visits were focus of cooperation. Added to this were 100-150 scholarships given to Lao students and technical personnel for undergoing training programmes and regular courses of study in India under various schemes. The year saw the first ever visit of Indian Vice President to Laos PDR in September 2015.

Malaysia

Bilateral relations with Malaysia, marked by traditional friendship and cordiality, have continued to progress and expand. Prime Minister undertook an official visit to Malaysia in November 2015. Earlier, PM participated in the 13th ASEAN–India Summit and 10th East Asia Summit in November 2015 held in Kuala Lumpur. The PM inaugurated the Torana Gate in Brickfields, Kuala Lumpur, a gift from India. A joint statement for Enhanced Strategic Partnership was issued after the visit.

New Zealand

President of India visited New Zealand in 2016. Several agreements were signed during the visit. India's relations with New Zealand continued to progress in various fields such as economic, scientific, cultural, people-to-people contact and coordination on regional and issues of global importance.

The Philippines

India-Philippines partnership continued to strengthen in the period. The 3rd edition of the bi-annual Joint Commission on Bilateral Cooperation, the highest institutionalized bilateral mechanism, was held in October 2015 in New Delhi. The defence cooperation continued to strengthen with the visit of INS Sahyadri on a goodwill visit to Manila in November 2015. Trade relations between the two countries remained steady at US$ 1.8 billion, despite global downturn, during the first half of 2015-16 with a positive trade balance in India's favour. Indian investment in the Philippines has been characterised by presence of a large number of major Indian IT and pharma firms that continue to do well in the IT enabled services and the generics sector respectively. A new trend of Indian investment is now visible in sectors such as infrastructure, automobiles, renewable energy and agriculture.

Singapore

Bilateral relations with Singapore was elevated to a new level of Strategic Partnership during the visit of Prime Minister in November 2015, on the occasion of the 50th anniversary of the establishment of our diplomatic relations. A Joint Statement was issued which outlined areas of cooperation and mutual interest. Defence cooperation between India and Singapore was strengthened by the signing of the enhanced Defence Cooperation Agreement. Further, the Technical Agreement on sharing White Shipping Information between the Indian Navy and the Republic of Singapore Navy was operationalized during PM's visit. Besides, there were regular exchanges between the three services and the defence establishments of India and Singapore. Both the nations have close economic and commercial ties which has shown some declining trends during the current year (17 per cent decline in the volume of bilateral trade). The total bilateral trade for 2015-16 (April-October) was US$ 8.6 billion with Indian export of US$ 4.2 billion. The outward Indian FDI to Singapore increased from US$ 351 million in 2004-05 to US$ 38.9 billion (October 2015), with Singapore being one of the most favoured destinations for Indian investments abroad. In 2015, Indian investments in Singapore has reached US$ 2.18 billion. Singapore is the second largest source of FDI for India, the total inward FDI from Singapore to India from April 2000 to September 2015 being US$ 38.9 billion. Singapore is the largest investor with FDI inflows from Singapore amounting to US$ 6.69 billion.

Thailand

India's relationship with Thailand continued to deepen and strengthen in 2015 with the exchange of high-level visits and enhanced interactions at all levels. Bilateral trade for the period January–September 2015 was US$ 6.18 billion. The first meetings of the Joint Task Force (JTF) on Maritime Cooperation and Legal and Judicial Cooperation was held in New Delhi in October 2015. Four meetings of Transport Ministry Officials of India, Myanmar and Thailand on the finalization of Motor Vehicles Agreement of the Trilateral Highway were held. In 2015, around 1 million Indian tourists visited Thailand and over 100,000 Thai tourists visited India. The Deputy Prime Minister and Defence Minister of Thailand visited India in March 2016. Prime Minister of Thailand accompanied by his spouse and a high level delegation including several senior ministers and a strong business delegation paid a state visit to India in June 2016. Both the countries agreed to enhance cooperation in the maritime domain, counter terrorism, cyber security, etc. Dual entry e-tourist visas to facilitate Thai pilgrims travel to cities in India and Nepal were announced. It was decided to celebrate 2017, the 70th anniversary of establishment of diplomatic relations between the two countries.

Vietnam

The Strategic Partnership between India and Vietnam was consolidated further during 2015-16. Economic cooperation was accorded strategic priority, even as efforts continued to implement decisions taken at the highest level, encompassing all areas of the bilateral comprehensive cooperation. A Joint Vision Statement for the period 2015-2020 on Defence Cooperation and a MoU on cooperation between the Coast Guards of the two countries was signed. Bilateral trade between India and Vietnam has seen continuous growth over the past few years. India is now among the top ten trading partners of Vietnam. Both sides agreed on a new trade target of US$ 15 billion by 2020. Bilateral defence relation is broadening and deepening into all the areas of defence co-operation including defence production. Vietnam has, over the years, been a large recipient of training programmes under Indian Technical and Economic Cooperation (ITEC) programme.

Countries of Pacific Islands

The 2nd Summit of Forum for India Pacific Islands Cooperation (FIPIC) was held in Jaipur in 2015. Three Heads of States from Marshall Islands, Nauru and Palau; Vice President from Micronesia; six Heads of Governments from Fiji, Niue, Papua New Guinea, Samoa, Tuvalu and Vanuatu; and Deputy Prime Minister/Ministers/Special Envoy from Solomon Islands, Tonga, Cook Islands and Kiribati participated in the Summit.

Association of South-East Asian Nations

The India-ASEAN Strategic Partnership has acquired new momentum, following the enunciation of the "Act-East Policy" by PM at the 12th ASEAN-India Summit and 9th East Asia Summits in November 2014 at Na Pyi Taw, Myanmar. ASEAN is the anchor of India's Act East Policy and India has continued to deepen its political, security, defence and economic ties with ASEAN member states in 2015, including by establishing an Indian Mission to ASEAN. It has also pro-actively engaged with the various ASEAN centric fora shaping the evolving regional architecture, notably the East Asia Summit (EAS), ASEAN Regional Forum (ARF), ASEAN Defence Ministers' Meeting Plus (ADMM+) and Expanded ASEAN Maritime Forum (EAMF). With the entry into force of the ASEAN-India Free Trade Area in July 2015 and the establishment of the ASEAN community in December 2015, India looks forward to greater integration with ASEAN and the wider Asia-Pacific. In 2017, ASEAN and India shall be observing the 25th anniversary of Dialogue Relations, 15 years of Summit level interaction and 5 years of strategic partnership by undertaking wide range of commemorative activities.

East Asia Summit

Prime Minister, Narendra Modi, participated in the 10th East Asia Summit (EAS) in 2015 in Kuala Lumpur. He shared India's perspectives on regional and global issues such as terrorism, maritime security, etc. with his counterparts, while reiterating India's support for strengthening of the East

Asia Summit on its 10th anniversary as the premier leaders-led forum for dialogue on strategic, political and economic issues of common interest and concern in the Asia-Pacific.

India continued to participate actively in EAS activities in 2015 by co-hosting the 4th EAS Workshop on the Regional Security Architecture along with Cambodia in Phnom Penh in July 2015. To further the development agenda under the EAS, India organized an "EAS Roundtable on Nursing and Trauma Care" at the All India Institute of Medical Sciences, New Delhi in October 2015 and an "EAS Conference on Maritime Security and Cooperation" at the ASEAN-India Centre in November 2015.

Asia-Europe Meeting

Vice President, Hamid M Ansari attended the 11th Asia-Europe Meeting (ASEM) Summit, hosted by Mongolia, in July 2016. India is an active participant and contributor in ASEM events, and in order to take forward tangible areas of cooperation, have hosted the 19th Summer University Project on 'Sustainable Urbanization in Heritage Cities' in Pune, in association with the Asia-Europe Foundation (ASEF), in 2015; the 11th meeting of ASEM Directors General/ Commissioners of Customs in Goa in 2015; the 2nd ASEM Roundtable on Green Buildings in Gandhinagar in 2015, and a Youth Dialogue in 2016 in New Delhi, in partnership with the Confederation of Indian Industry.

Mekong-Ganga Cooperation

Minister of State for External Affairs, attended the 7th Mekong-Ganga Cooperation Foreign Minister Meeting held in 2016 in Vientiane, which welcomed the construction by India of the MGC Textiles Museum and appreciated India's contribution to capacity building and human resources development in the Cambodia, Laos PDR, Myanmar and Vietnam (CLMV) countries, including over 900 annual scholarships under the Indian Technical and Economic Cooperation. India's proposal on the establishment of a Common Archival Resource Centre at Nalanda University to facilitate research on the Mekong-Ganga deltaic region was welcomed and the Plan of Action to implement the Mekong Ganga Cooperation (2016-2018) was adopted. 20 projects have also been identified for funding under the India-CLMV Quick Impact Project Fund.

East Asia

East Asia forms part of India's extended neighbourhood. Cultural, trade and people-to-people contacts with the region go back several centuries. Shared values and traditions of peaceful co-existence, pluralism and peace symbolized by Buddhism have provided the glue to this engagement. India's rising political and security stature and its readiness to play a more active role in international relations combined with a growing economic heft is powering closer integration between India and East Asia.

A peaceful and stable East Asia is integral to India's economic development. A substantial volume of India's trade is with the countries of this region. It is important that there is an agreement on the principles of international law and peaceful settlement of disputes; freedom of navigation and overflight; and unimpeded lawful commerce governing the affairs of this region.

Democratic People's Republic of Korea

Diplomatic relations between India and the Democratic People's Republic of Korea (DPRK) were established in December 1973. Relations between India and DPRK are cordial. 2015 saw the visit of Foreign Minister to India in 2015, the first at the Foreign Minister level from DPRK to India. Foreign Minister expressed his country's appreciation for the humanitarian assistance provided by India to DPRK.

Japan

India-Japan relations have witnessed a gradual transformation in recent years and reflect a broad convergence of their long-term political, economic and strategic goals. PM's visit to Japan in 2014, which was his first overseas visit outside the neighbourhood, prepared the ground for a qualitative shift in bilateral relations which elevated the bilateral relationship to a "Special Strategic and Global Partnership". This was further reinforced by Japanese PM visit to India in 2015. The visit resulted in Japan agreeing to provide funding for a slew of key infrastructure projects along with agreements in defence cooperation and civil nuclear energy. The two sides also signed an agreement to implement high speed railways in India.

Japan and India are committed to leverage the synergy between India's "Act East" policy and Japan's "Partnership for Quality Infrastructure" to develop and strengthen reliable, sustainable and resilient infrastructures that augment connectivity within India and between India and other countries in the region. Japanese ODA's contribution to the building of social and physical infrastructure in India was acknowledged. The total commitment of Japanese ODA yen loan to India in FY 2015 may reach around 400 billion yen, the highest ever provided to India.

Indian ships Satpura, Sahyadri, Shakti and Kirch participated in the 20th edition of Exercise Malabar 2016 with the US Navy and Japanese Maritime Self Defence Force (JMSDF) in Japan with harbour phase at Sasebo in June 2016 and the sea phase in the Pacific Ocean in June 2016. The exercise was aimed at increasing interoperability amongst the three navies and develop common understanding of procedures of Maritime Security Operations.

Mongolia

India and Mongolia are democracies, share a common Buddhist legacy and have a history of cultural exchanges spanning centuries. Visit of Prime

Minister Modi to Mongolia in May 2015, the first by an Indian Prime Minister to Mongolia, was a significant milestone in our bilateral relations. During this visit, India and Mongolia elevated their bilateral relationship to a strategic partnership and identified a host of new areas of bilateral cooperation including development of equal and mutually beneficial trade, investment and economic cooperation, which is balanced, sustainable, and leads to prosperity in both countries.

Republic of Korea

The year 2015 marks the sixtieth anniversary of establishment of diplomatic relations between the two countries. Bilateral relations between India and Republic of Korea (RoK) are increasingly becoming multifaceted, spurred by a significant convergence of economic, political and security interests. The year saw adding of new substance, speed and content in the partnership in a wide range of areas including foreign affairs, defence, trade and investment, science and technology, culture and people-to-people exchanges and regional cooperation to take the bilateral relations to a qualitatively higher level. India views the RoK as vital to its "Act East" policy, and the RoK and India recognize the value of the bilateral partnership and its contribution to bringing peace, stability and security in the Asia Pacific Region.

Eurasia

Relations with Russia remain a central pillar of India's foreign policy. Enhancing India's 'special and privileged strategic partnership' with Russia was a key focus this year, with as many as three visits at Head of State/ Government level from India to Russia. President participated in the 70th anniversary commemoration of victory in World War II in Moscow in 2015. Prime Minister visited Russia twice—for the 7th BRICS Summit and SCO Summit in Ufa, Russia and for the 16th India-Russia Annual Summit in Moscow in 2015. India's engagement with its Central Asian partners gained significant momentum with the historic visit by Prime Minister to all five Central Asian countries—Uzbekistan, Kazakhstan, Turkmenistan, Kyrgyz Republic and Tajikistan— in July 2015. Relations with Belarus, Ukraine, and the South Caucasus (Armenia, Azerbaijan, Georgia) also continue to develop well.

Russian Federation

High-level visits as well as ministerial and official interactions in diverse formats contributed to a significant strengthening and deepening of India-Russia relations in diverse fields. Over 25 bilateral agreements and MoUs covering cooperation in areas such as defence, civil nuclear cooperation, education, science and technology, hydrocarbons, railways, solar energy, visa simplification, Ayurveda, satellite navigation, heavy engineering and supercomputing were signed during the year. During the 16th Annual Summit, particular focus was given to enhance trade and economic ties as a strong pillar of the strategic partnership. A wide-ranging joint statement 'Shared Trust, New Horizons' was also issued, which fully reflects the diversity and dynamism in India-Russia relations.

In addition to considerable progress on bilateral relations, India and Russia maintained close consultations on regional and global issues. Russia reaffirmed its strong support for India's candidature for a permanent seat in a reformed UN Security Council, multilateral export control regimes as well as other plurilateral frameworks such as the Shanghai Cooperation Organisation. India and Russia also continued their close cooperation in the framework of Russia's chairmanship of BRICS.

Several measures to promote bilateral trade and investment were implemented, including simplification of visa regime for businessmen, signing of protocol on pre-arrival exchange of information ("Green Corridor"), setting up of a Special Notified Zone for trade in rough diamonds and market access for agricultural exports. Significant investments, particularly in the hydrocarbons sector in both countries, were also announced during the year.

Belarus

Bilateral relations with Belarus received a major fillip with the first ever visit by an Indian President in June 2015. Minister of State for Commerce and Industry also visited Belarus in September 2015 for the Inter-Governmental Commission meeting. Foreign Minister of Belarus visited India in May 2015.

Ukraine and South Caucasus

India's relations with Ukraine continued to develop. Ties with Armenia, Georgia and Azerbaijan were consolidated through active cultural and business exchanges.

Central Asia

The visit of Prime Minister to all the five Central Asian countries, i.e., Kazakhstan, Kyrgyz Republic, Tajikistan, Turkmenistan and Uzbekistan in July 2015 raised the profile of our bilateral relationship with these countries and the region as a whole to an unprecedented high. Visits and interactions at minister and senior official level further consolidated relations with these countries located in India's extended neighbourhood. India continued its significant contributions to capacity building and human resources development in the region. A total of 22 agreements in different fields were signed with the five Central Asian countries.

International North South Transport Corridor

The International North South Transport Corridor (INSTC) made significant progress during the year. Following up on the dry run study conducted by Federation of Freight Forwarders' Association in India on the INSTC route,

India hosted an interactive session on INSTC at Mumbai in June 2015, followed by Expert Level and INSTC Council meetings in Delhi in August 2015 and a conference to popularize the INSTC route in Mumbai in December 2015. Customs officials of India, Russia and Azerbaijan also met in Astrakhan, Russia in November 2015.

Turkmenistan-Afghanistan-Pakistan-India Gas Pipeline Project

Vice President of India attended the ground-breaking ceremony of the Turkmenistan-Afghanistan-Pakistan-India (TAPI) Gas Pipeline Project held in Mary, Turkmenistan in December 2015 along with President of Turkmenistan and Afghanistan and the Prime Minister of Pakistan. Cabinet approved in 2016 India's accession to the Ashgabat Agreement. The transit agreement provides for a transit corridor between Uzbekistan, Turkmenistan, Iran and Oman before reaching the Persian Gulf. India's membership bid now awaits the approval of the original parties to the Agreement. India was invited to join Ashgabat Agreement during the visit of Prime Minister to Turkmenistan in July 2015.

Shanghai Cooperation Organisation

The year heralded a new phase in India's relations with the Shanghai Cooperation Organisation (SCO). During its Council of Heads of State Meeting in Ufa, Russia in July 2015, the SCO announced its decision to initiate India's membership. Prime Minister addressed the SCO Plenary Session. Representatives from India attended various SCO meetings during the year including the health, interior, justice, trade and commerce ministerial meetings and the meeting of SCO Prosecutors General. India signed the Memorandum of Obligation with the Organisation at the Council of Heads of States Summit held in Tashkent, Uzbekistan in June 2016. This initiated India's membership process of SCO, which will be followed by timely accession to various documents under SCO framework.

Gulf, West Asia and North Africa

India enjoys close historical ties with the countries of the Gulf region, which are cemented in age old civilizational links and strong people to people contact. This friendly relationship was further strengthened this year by regular exchange of high-level visits. The Gulf region is India's largest trading partner region with bilateral trade over US$ 97 billion in 2015-16. The region also continues to be a major supplier of crude oil and LNG to India and accounts for over 50 per cent of India's crude oil imports and over 70 per cent of India's natural gas imports, remaining vital to India's energy security needs. Among India's top six oil sourcing countries, four are from the Gulf region – Saudi Arabia, Iraq, UAE and Kuwait. The Gulf countries also host an eight million strong Indian expatriate community which contributes to the development of the host countries and forms an organic link between India and the Gulf states.

Bahraini Minister of Interior paid an official visit to India in December 2015. During the visit, a bilateral agreement on cooperation in combating international terrorism, transnational organized crime and trafficking in illicit, drugs, narcotic and psychotropic substances and precursors chemicals was signed. The year was marked by goodwill visit of two Indian Naval Ships – INS 'Deepak' and 'Talbar' to Bahrain in September 2015.

The continued fragile security situation in Iraq resulting out of ISIS attacks launched in June 2014 has remained a matter of deep concern for India. Despite the volatile security situation there, India continues to maintain its Mission in Baghdad to engage closely with the Government of Iraq and also a controlroom in Erbil, Kurdistan to provide consular assistance to Indian nationals. The Camp Office at Erbil has since been upgraded to the level of a Consulate General. Since the beginning of the crisis in Iraq, the Government of India has provided assistance to over 7,195 Indian nationals to leave Iraq safely.

India sees Islamic Republic of Iran as an important country in India's immediate 'economic and security space'. Interactions between the leadership and senior ministers of the two countries provided thrust to the bilateral relations in 2015, including in economic sphere. India had welcomed the signing of Joint Comprehensive Plan of Action (JCPOA) between Iran and P5+1 (The P5+1 refers to the UN Security Concil's five permanent members (the P5); namely China, France, Russia, the United Kingdom and the United States; plus Germany. The P5+1 is often referred to as the E3+3 by European countries.) in July 2015. The announcement of the Implementation Day in January 2016, as agreed in the JCPOA, is a victory for patient diplomacy and dialogue. This w 'l open a new chapter of peace and prosperity for friendly people of Islamic Republic of Iran and the region. There have been regular bilateral interactions, high level consultations including meeting between PM and President of Iran in Ufa, Russia in July 2015. Minister of Road Transport, Highways and Shipping visited Iran in May 2015 and signed the Inter-Governmental MoU on Chahbahar Port.

After the talks, the two leaders witnessed signing of twelve cooperation documents. The India-Iran-Afghanistan Trilateral Agreement on Establishing Chahbahar Transport and Transit Corridors was signed and a Joint Statement titled, "India - Iran Joint Statement— "Civilisational Connect, Contemporary Context" was also issued during the visit.

During this period, India-Israeli bilateral engagement strengthened in traditional areas of cooperation like defence and agriculture while expanding to new areas such as cyber security and space. The highlight during the period was the first ever visit to Israel by President.

President of India paid a visit to Jordan in October 2015 and had an extensive discussions on entire gamut of bilateral relations, regional and international issues of mutual concern.

The close, multifaceted and friendly relations between India and Kuwait were further cemented during the year. India has consistently been among the top ten trading partners of Kuwait and Kuwait has been a reliable supplier of crude oil and LPG to India and meets about 6 per cent of our energy needs. The Indian community of over 800,000 is the largest expatriate community in Kuwait. Bilaterally with Lebanon, the focus continued on academic and cultural relations.

Oman is India's maritime neighbour and bilateral historical relations with the country have evolved into a strategic partnership. The year 2015 marked the Diamond Jubilee of establishment of diplomatic relations between India and Oman and to commemorate the 60th anniversary, a series of cultural events were organized.

India and Saudi Arabia enjoy cordial and friendly relations reflecting the centuries old economic and socio-cultural ties. Saudi Arabia hosts nearly 3 million Indian expatriates, the largest Indian passport holding community outside India. The two countries have made steady progress in political, economic, defence and security cooperation. The two sides regularly exchange high level visits and remain engaged at various levels. During Haj 2015, around 136,000 Indians visited the Kingdom to perform Haj. Prime Minister visited Saudi Arabia in April 2016. During the visit, the entire gamut of bilateral relations as well as regional and international issues of mutual interest were discussed and several MoUs were signed.

The multi-faceted engagement between India and Qatar further intensified during this period. PM paid an official visit to the State of Qatar, Doha in June 2016 wherein regional and international issues of mutual interest were discussed and 7 MoUs/agreements signed.

In ongoing crisis in Syria, India continues to maintain its consistent position of peaceful resolution of conflicts. India has called upon all sides to the Syrian conflict to abjure violence so that conducive conditions can be created for an inclusive political dialogue leading to a comprehensive political solution, taking into account the legitimate aspirations of the Syrian people. India has maintained that there can be no military solution to this conflict.

The traditionally close and friendly relations between India and UAE were further cemented by exchange of high-level visits during this period. Prime Minister paid a visit to UAE in August 2015. This historic visit of the Prime Minister taking place after a gap of 34 years brought a paradigm shift in our relations with UAE, elevating the relationship to a comprehensive strategic partnership. Shortly after the PM's visit, Crown Prince of Abu Dhabi paid a visit to India in February 2016. Several MoUs were signed during the visit.

India and Yemen enjoy a long history of close and historical people-to-people contacts. Due to the deterioration of political and security situation in Yemen, the Government of India, in coordination with the Indian Missions in Sana and Addis Ababa, undertook a massive evacuation exercise 'Operation Raahat' in April 2015. A total number of 6,710 persons, including 4,748 Indians and 1,962 foreign nationals of 48 countries were assisted in evacuation by air and sea routes from Sana's airport and Aden, Al Hudaydah and Al Mukalla ports.

In Haj 2015, a total of 1,35,868 pilgrims undertook the Haj pilgrimage. For this, the Ministry of External Affairs sent 543 deputationists and supplied medicines and medical equipments worth ₹ 1.76 crore to Consulate General of India, Jeddah. Consulate General of India, Jeddah established main offices in Makkha and Madinah, 13 branch offices in Makkha, 3 branch offices in Madinah, offices with dispensaries at Jeddah and Madinah Haj Terminals, a 40-bedded hospital in Makkha, a 40-beeded hospital in Azizia region of Makkha, 13 branch dispensaries in Makkha, a 10-bedded main dispensary in Madinah and 3 branch dispensaries in Madinah.

Africa

This period marked a very special and a historic year in India-Africa partnership that saw unprecedented interaction at the leadership level. India hosted the Third India Africa Forum Summit in New Delhi in October 2015 with all 54 African countries, with whom India has diplomatic relations, participating in the Summit and a record 41 African countries participating at the level of Heads of State/Government. In the leadup to the Summit, 16 Ministers of State visited 49 African countries as Special Envoys of Prime Minister to personally extend invitations for the Summit. The outreach to Africa was further built upon by President's three-nation tour to Africa in June 2016, beginning with Ghana followed by Cote d'Ivoire and Namibia. Vice-President visited Morocco and Tunisia in 2016. Prime Minister made a four-nation Africa tour to Mozambique, South Africa, Tanzania and Kenya in July 2016.

In addition, there were three incoming visits by the Presidents of Tanzania, Mozambique and Seychelles and an official visit by the President of Mauritius during this period. These engagements helped to cement existing ties, create new linkages and demonstrated India's ability to plan and coordinate its engagement with different parts of the world by integrating interests and coordinating cultural and civilisational ties.

The year 2015 that also marked the 70th anniversary year of the establishment of the United Nations saw two important world conferences take place in Africa – the Third International Conference on Financing for Development (Addis Ababa July 2015) and the WTO Ministerial Conference (Nairobi December 2015). India cooperated closely with the African partners on issues of 2030 Agenda for Sustainable Development that was adopted by the UN General Assembly in September 2015 and on finalization of the post

2020 Agreement on Climate Change that was finalized at the COP 21 of the UNFCCC in Paris in December 2015. The year also saw the adoption of the Agenda 2063 by the African Union in June 2015.

The India Africa engagement intensified the focus on the strengthening of the business linkages of trade and investment and the political interaction that is based on the unique south-south cooperation comprising the multifaceted development partnership that includes education and capacity building, cooperation in agriculture, energy, technology, infrastructure, healthcare among others. The partnership also focused on emerging issues of cooperation in the areas of blue economy, counter-terrorism and maritime security. Longstanding diaspora linkages form an important aspect of India-Africa ties.

There were a number of exchanges of other high level visits and interactions during this period. External Affairs Minister Sushma Swaraj visited Egypt in August 2015 and met President and Arab League Secretary. During this period, the 4th meeting of India Africa Trade Ministers was held in New Delhi in October 2015. 37 delegations comprising Trade Ministers/ officials and 8 Regional Economic Communities participated in the meeting. The 4th India Africa Hydrocarbon Conference was held in New Delhi in January 2016. 25 African countries were invited to participate in the event. The National Treasury of Kenya conveyed acceptance of credit terms offered in EAM's letter conveying GOI's decision to extend a line of credit of US$ 29.95 for upgrading of Rift Valley Textiles Factory Project. A team of Indian agricultural experts visited Mozambique in March 2016 to explore areas of bilateral cooperation in agriculture. The first Joint Hydrography Committee Meeting between India and Tanzania took place in Dar-es-Salaam in March 2016. A 21-member Indian Parliamentary delegation represented India at the 134th Inter Parliamentary Union in Lusaka, Zambia in March. The 11th CII-EXIM Bank Conclave on India Africa Project Partnership was held in March 2016 in New Delhi. Delegations from 37 African countries, including 2 Vice Presidents and 23 Ministers participated. Nigeria was the partner country and Ghana the guest country. Approximately 1000 business delegates, including more than 500 from Africa participated in the event and more than 400 businesses to business meetings were organized. MEA organized a familiarization visit for journalists from 22 African countries in 2016.

The West African region is home to Africa's largest population and fastest growing economies with largest proven reserves of energy resources. Over the past 10 years, many of the economies within the region are outpacing economies anywhere else in the world, and this booming economic growth has helped create the fastest-growing middle class in the world.

A growing population and abundance of natural resources ensure that West Africa offers tremendous investment and economic opportunities for states and businesses alike. Prior to 2000, the combined Gross Domestic Product (GDP) for this region was estimated to be less than $ 250 billion. Yet within the space of a decade GDP had more than doubled to approximately $ 565 billion. Of fundamental importance to economic growth have been a host of economic and political reforms that have stimulated new business opportunities across West Africa. Indeed, the growth in GDP has been mirrored by a substantial rise in Foreign Direct Investment (FDI). Since the mid-1990s, West Africa has seen the historic shift from military regimes to constitutional rule, cessation of civil wars in several countries, and renewed regional economic integration.

The West Africa region continues to gain strategic importance for India. India's bilateral trade with the region has been following a rising trend and currently stands at around US$ 31 billion, having increased 15 times since 2003. India sources about 18 per cent of its crude oil requirements from this region. Capacity building, skills development and strengthening of physical and social infrastructure have remained at the centre of India's expanding development partnership with the region. India has continued to lend its active support to international efforts aimed at restoration of constitutional order, peace, security and stability in the region. Indian troops are involved in several peace keeping operations in countries in West Africa. The Third India Africa Forum Summit provided an opportunity for renewed high level contacts with leaders of West Africa.

As part of our development cooperation with Africa, GoI approved a Line of Credit (LoC) of USD 29.95 mn for upgradation of Rift Valley Textiles Factory (RIVATEX East Africa Limited) of Kenya; another LoC of USD 15 mn was approved for development of SMEs in Kenya; a LoC of USD 23.5 mn was approved for Malawi for construction of a new water supply system from Likhubula river in Mulanje to Blantyre; a LoC of USD 40 mn was approved for Zambia's Agriculture Mechanization Programme. Two MoUs were signed with Madagascar – one on cooperation in agriculture and the other on establishment of a Centre on Geo-Informatics Applications in Rural Development (CGARD). The Namibian Institute of Public Administration and Management signed MoUs with Administrative Staff College of India, Hyderabad and Institute of Public Enterprise, Hyderabad on capacity building and exchanges. From February 2016, the Electronic Tourist Visa (e-TV) facility has been expanded to cover Botswana, Namibia, Swaziland, Zambia, Comoros, Madagascar, Zimbabwe, South Africa, Lesotho, Malawi and Eritrea.

Europe and the European Union

Outreach to Western Europe remained a key focus in this period where high-level visits were instrumental in establishing robust roadmaps for enhanced partnerships with these important countries in priority areas of mutual interest.

India-France relations received a boost in 2015 with the highly successful visit of Prime Minister to France in April 2015. Prime Minister of India and French President met again in Paris in November 2015 at the Leaders' Event of the 21st Session of the Conference of the Parties to the United Nations Framework Convention on Climate Change (CoP-21) in Paris and jointly launched the International Solar Alliance (ISA). The President of France visited India as the Chief Guest of India's 67th Republic Day in January 2016. With this, France became the country with the most number of invitations (five) as the Chief Guest on India's Republic Day. The visit saw concrete progress in bilateral cooperation in the defence, civil, nuclear and space sectors which are the tripod of our Strategic Partnership with France. New emergent areas of counter terrorism, maritime security and renewable energy were added to the strategic agenda.

Prime Minister, accompanied by Minister of State for Commerce & Industry, paid an official visit to Germany in April 2015 to inaugurate the Hannover Messe-2015 where India participated as the Partner Country. Prime Minister and the German Chancellor jointly inaugurated the 'India Pavilion' and an Indo German Business Summit. Prime Minister elaborated on 'Make in India' and other major economic initiatives of the Government in his address to the German industry. The German Chancellor paid an official visit to India in October 2015 for the 3rd Indo-German Inter-Governmental Consultations.

Prime Minister paid a short official visit to Ireland in September 2015 en route to New York for the UN General Assembly. It was the first visit to Ireland. The visit signalled the interest on both sides to take India-Ireland ties to the next level and put in place a forward-looking roadmap for partnerships in priority sectors of mutual interest.

The Dutch Prime Minister paid an official visit to India in 2015. Dutch Prime Minister was accompanied by the Minister for Foreign Trade and Development Cooperation, the Minister for Agriculture, senior officials and a large business delegation representing over 80 Dutch companies.

The year 2015 witnessed an intensification of bilateral relations between India and Spain. This was highlighted by the visit of Spanish Foreign Minister to India in April 2015, the first such visit in 43 years.

India's unique relationship with UK and the 11-year old strategic partnership was substantively upgraded with the Prime Minister's visit to the UK in November 2015. This was the first official bilateral visit by an Indian Prime Minister after 2006. The visit was successful in projecting India's rising profile and forging a deeper strategic partnership in areas such as nuclear, defence, cyber, counter terrorism, maritime security and organized crime; and in India's flagship development projects through fund raising, Smart Cities, Clean India, Skill India and Clean Energy.

Prime Minister paid an official visit to Brussels in March 2016 for the 13th India-EU Summit. The India-EU Summit re-energised our strategic partnership with the European Union and reinforced the EU's position as India's leading trade, investment and technology partner. A key outcome of the Summit was the India-EU Joint Declaration on Migration and Mobility which provides a framework for exploring efficient grant of visas for bonafide travellers and enhanced mobility for highly skilled workers. During the visit, Prime Minister also held bilateral discussions with his Belgian counterpart on areas of mutual interest including cooperation in counter-terrorism, port and maritime sectors, information technology, science and technology, renewable energy, etc.

India continued to share close and cordial relations with the countries in Central Europe. The bilateral relations for the strengthen during the year through a constant exchange of visits, business interactions and cultural exchanges. A special focus during the year was on holding seminars and other such fora to disseminate information about Government of India's policies and flagship projects particularly Make in India, Digital India, Clean Ganga, Skill India, etc. 2nd edition of India-Central Europe Business Forum was held in Bengaluru in 2015 wherein official and business representatives from 18 countries from Central Europe participated. Poland was the partner country in the Forum this year. The first ever International Day of Yoga was also marked by a number of simultaneous yoga classes, lectures and demonstrations in a number of cities throughout the region.

India and countries in Central Europe continued to extend support to each other for including candidates of the two countries for offices in international organizations. Prime Minister visited Switzerland in June 2016 and met the President of Switzerland. PM had a fruitful discussion with the Swiss President on various bilateral, regional and multilateral issues of mutual interest.

The Americas

Canada

India-Canada bilateral relations have seen a transformation in recent years which is underpinned by shared values of democracy, pluralism, expanding economic engagement, regular high-level interactions and long standing people-to-people ties. The relationship witnessed a new momentum with the visit of Prime Minister to Canada in April 2015, and the elevation of bilateral relationship to a strategic partnership. India will continue to engage with the newly elected government in Canada. Canada is home to over 1.2 million Persons of Indian Origin (PIO) who comprise more than 3 per cent of the country's population. In order to expand people-to-people ties, during his visit to Canada, Prime Minister announced the Electronic Travel Authorization for Canadian nationals. Long term visa of ten years for the Canadian nationals was also announced.

Energy has been a primary area of our focus, considering that Canada is an 'energy superpower' with one of the world's largest resources of uranium, natural gas, oil, coal, minerals and advanced technologies in hydropower, mining, renewable energy and nuclear energy. In the hydrocarbon sector, Indian Oil has acquired 10 per cent participating interest in Pacific North West (PNW), LNG Project, British Columbia. During the visit of Prime Minister to Canada, Department of Atomic Energy and M/S CAMECO Inc., Canada signed an agreement for supply of 3000 metric tonnes of uranium ore concentrate to India in 2015-2020. The first shipment of uranium arrived in India in December 2015. Bilateral trade amounted to US$ 4.48 billion in 2014. The cumulative Indian FDI in 2014 was US$ 2781.1 million as against Canadian FDI of US$ 789.6 million in India. To spur bilateral trade and economic ties both sides are actively negotiating CEPA (Comprehensive Economic Partnership Agreement) and BIPPA (Bilateral Investment Protection and Promotion Agreement).

United States of America

Prime Minister visited the US in June 2016. The visit was aimed at consolidation of progress made in various areas and to intensify cooperation for the future. There were significant and concrete outcomes in key areas of cooperation such as civil; nuclear; clean energy; defence and security; politico-strategic engagement; economy and people-to-people ties. A number of documents were also signed/finalized in the run up to the visit. India-US bilateral relations have developed into extensive bilateral strategic and global partnership, based on shared democratic values and increasing convergence of interests on bilateral, regional and global issues. Prime Minister's second visit to the US in September 2015 was aimed at harnessing the US capital and technology and in strengthening existing investment and technology partnerships with the US industry across a range of diversified areas, especially renewable energy; digital economy, innovation and manufacturing. During the year, there were major exchanges at political and functional levels in various sectors, including in trade and economy, health, energy, science and technology, homeland security, counter-terrorism, climate change and others, which culminated in the first Strategic and Commercial Dialogue in September 2015. The year also saw renewed interest on both sides to strengthen bilateral economic engagement. There was robust defence engagement with greater focus on co-development and co-production under the defence technology and trade initiative. Reciprocal visits at the Defence Minister's level this year put the cooperation on a firm footing with the signing of 10 year 'Framework for the India-US Defence Relationship'.

India-US trade and commercial engagement continued to expand in 2015 with healthy growth in trade (in goods and services), investment and technology partnerships. During 2014-15, Indian goods exports to the US amounted to US$ 42.45 billion which accounted for 13.67 per cent of India's global exports. Indian imports amounted to US$ 21.82 billion which accounted for 4.87 per cent of India's total import over the same period. The trade surplus of US$ 20.63 billion is in favour of India. The US is India's second largest trading partner in goods. FDI from the US has increased from $ 806 million in 2013-14 to $ 1.8 billion in 2014-15 marking an increase of 126 per cent making it 6th largest investor in India.

Latin America and Caribbean Countries

Argentina

There has always existed a lot of warmth and mutual respect in bilateral relations between India and Argentina. The relationship between the two countries continued to grow in substance through high-level visits, increased trade and tourism in 2015. Two important developments in India and Argentina´s bilateral commercial relations strengthened bilateral trade relations: Presidential Amendment of Annexe II to include India in the list of countries for pharma imports in Argentina and India´s issuance of phytosanitary clearance on exports of Argentine apples, pears and quinces.

Bolivia

India and Bolivia relations continued to be friendly and intensify during this period particularly after conclusion of 1st Foreign Office Consultation in 2014. Bilateral trade between the two countries substantially increased due to the visit of trade delegations.

Brazil

On the bilateral front, this year has been very important and productive, particularly after the visit of Indian Prime Minister in 2015. The global drop in commodity prices and the economic recession affected Brazil´s overall trade as also our bilateral trade which is approx. US$ 6.63 billion from January-October with Indian exports at US$ 3.73 billion and Brazilian exports at US$ 2.9 billion, giving India a trade surplus of US$ 828 million.

Chile

India and Chile continued to enjoy excellent relations in 2015. During April-October 2015, the bilateral trade between India and Chile reached US$ 1,636.46 million with Indian exports at US$ 404.44 million and imports from Chile at US$ 1,232.02 million.

Colombia

India-Colombia relations continued to grow during the year. Due to fall in crude oil its affected the bilateral trade between the two countries. Colombia's exports to India accounted for US$ 415,38 mn, a fall of 82.41 per cent and India exports to Colombia were US$ 909,72 mn, a fall of 7.15 per cent compared to last year during the same period mainly due to fall in export of crude oil and its price.

Ecuador

Bilateral relations with Ecuador continued to be cordial and strong. Bilateral trade also continued to grow during this period.

Guyana

Bilateral relations between India and Guyana continued to grow during the year. President paid a state visit to India in January 2015 where he attended the Pravasi Bharatiya Divas—2015 as its Chief Guest and was conferred with the Pravasi Bharatiya Samman Award.

Mexico

India's relation with Mexico received a boost when Prime Minister paid a working visit to Mexico in June 2016, with the objective to continue the dialogue held by the two leaders on the margins of the 70th regular session of the United Nations General Assembly in September 2015. The Foreign Minister of Mexico visited India in March 2016 and held bilateral discussions with his counterpart. They undertook a comprehensive review of the entire gamut of bilateral relations including political, commercial, trade, financial, technical and other areas to further broaden and strengthen cooperation. They also discussed important regional and international issues of mutual interest. The year 2015 marked the 65th anniversary of the establishment of diplomatic relations between the two countries. Growth in bilateral trade has been impressive in recent years. In Mexico´s total global exports, India ranks 8th whereas India is Mexico´s 14th largest partner in global market. The total bilateral trade in 2014 was recorded as US$ 6.4 billion. Mexican investments in India too are on the rise.

Peru

As always, bilateral relations between the two countries have been cordial. India's exports were US$ 819.858 million in 2014-15 while imports amounted to US$ 590.395 million in the same year.

Venezuela

India and Venezuela have been maintaining cordial relations. Venezuela has emerged as India´s 3rd largest supplier of crude oil. India imported oil worth US$ 12 billion in 2014-15. Bilateral trade touched US$ 12.3 billion in 2014-15, a steep jump from US$ 6.6 billion in 2011.

Honduras

The bilateral relations between India and Honduras were strengthened with the conclusion of first Foreign Office Consultations (FOC) between India and Honduras. Bilateral trade registered at US$ 213 mn.

Nicaragua

India-Nicaragua bilateral relations strengthened with the holding of the first India-Nicaragua Foreign Office Consultation in 2014. Both side committed to strengthen relations in the political, economic, commercial and consular area. Bilateral Trade registered at US$ 92 million marginal increase during this period.

Barbados

Barbados and India enjoy close and cordial relations and interact actively in the UN, Commonwealth and NAM. The first ever Foreign Office Consultations between India and Barbados was held in Bridgetown, Barbados in 2015. India and Barbados have signed Air Services Agreement in October 2015, for facilitation of travel arrangements for the citizens and the possibility of direct air connectivity and chartered flight operations between the two countries. The electronic travel authorization system (eTVA) for Barbadians have already been implemented from May 2015.

United Nations and International Organisations

United Nations

The 70th session of the United Nations General Assembly (UNGA) commenced in September 2015 in New York. Prime Minister led the Indian delegation at the high-level segment. The G-4 Summit held in September 2015 at New York was the first such meeting in which all G-4 countries were represented at the highest level. In the joint press statement issued at the end of the Summit, the G-4 leaders welcomed the adoption by consensus of the General Assembly Decision 69/560 to use the text presented by the President of the 69th General Assembly as the basis for negotiations within the Inter-Governmental Negotiations. India participated in the 18th Plenary Meeting of the Contact Group on Piracy off the Coast of Somalia in July 2015 in New York. From India's perspective, one of the important issues deliberated was the Piracy High Risk Area and regulation of Private Maritime Security Companies and Privately Contracted Armed Security Personnel on board ships. India continued its active engagement on peacekeeping issues at the UN including with plenary statements and debates within the Special Committee on Peacekeeping (Fourth Committee of the 70th UNGA). India occupies the pole position (in cumulative terms) amongst the countries contributing troops for UN peace-keeping operations with cumulative contributions of more than 180,000 troops in 48 missions out of the 69 UN peacekeeping operations mandated so far. The high standards of performance by the Indian troops and police personnel under the challenging circumstances have won them high regard world-wide. India continued to work closely with the UNSC's Sanctions Committee including the 1267 Al-Qaida Sanctions Committee and also with the Al-Qaeda and Taliban Monitoring Team in order to ensure that there is strict compliance by member states of the sanctions regime. Foreign Minister visited New York in 2015, to preside over the celebration of the First International Day of Yoga at the United Nations on 21 June. The United Nations observed the 9th International Day of Non-

Violence on 2 October 2015 at a special event organized by the Permanent Mission of India at Trusteeship Council of the UN Headquarters in New York.

South Asian Association for Regional Cooperation

India, because of its geography, economy, international stature and commitment to the region, is central to South Asean Association for Regional Cooperation (SAARC). Its contribution to SAARC is also seminal. India has cumulatively contributed over US$ 530 million for socio-economic development. Prime Minister made a number of unilateral offers from India at the 18th SAARC Summit in Kathmandu (November, 2014), such as long term business visas up to 3-5 years being issued to businessmen from SAARC countries, health officials/experts from Afghanistan participated in India's Sub-National Polio Immunisation Day, South Asian University has established partnership with at least one university in each SAARC country, medical visas for patients and accompanying attendants are being issued by our Missions in SAARC countries on priority basis, and the SAARC Framework Agreement on Energy Cooperation (Electricity) was signed. Apart from the above, India organised the South Asian Annual Disaster Management Exercise (SAADMEx) in November 2015 at New Delhi to provide participants with an opportunity to discuss disaster response plans and capabilities of SAARC countries. India's proactive stance in SAARC since 2004 as part of its new approach to the countries in the neighbourhood has been a transformative factor in ensuring the gradual and irreversible transition of the organisation from its declaratory to implementation mode. India's commitment to shoulder more than its assessed responsibilities, in an asymmetric and non-reciprocal manner, has resonated well within the region

The Bay of Bengal Initiative for Multi-Sectoral Technical and Economic Cooperation

During the period April-December 2015, India focussed on themes of common importance to all Member States of BIMSTEC or Bay of Bengal Initiative for Multi-Sectoral Technical and Economic Cooperation namely transportation and communication, trade and investment, technology, energy, agriculture, public health, counter-terrorism and transnational crime and climate change. In 2015, the meeting of the BIMSTEC Sub-group on Combating the Financing of the Terrorism was held in May 2015 in Thimphu, Bhutan. A BIMSTEC Network of National Centres of Coordination in Traditional Medicine has been established. The 3rd BIMSTEC Expert Group Meeting on the Establishment of BIMSTEC- Technology Transfer Facility (TTF) was held in Colombo during August 2015. The 20th meeting of the BIMSTEC Trade Negotiating Committee (TNC) was held in Khon Khaen, Thailand in 2015. Progress has also been achieved in finalising the text of the BIMSTEC Convention on Mutual Legal Assistance in criminal matters and the same is ready for signature in the next BIMSTEC Ministerial Meeting.

Commonwealth of Nations

The Commonwealth Heads of Government Meeting (CHOGM) was held in November 2015 at Malta. External Affairs Minister represented the Prime Minister in various sessions held during the event, where issues like climate action, terrorism, migration, and implementation of sustainable goals were discussed.

Disarmament and International Security Affairs

In 2015-16, India continued to play an active role at various multilateral fora on disarmament and international security affairs in pursuance of its commitment to the goal of universal and non-discriminatory nuclear disarmament, leading towards general and complete disarmament. India's position on these issues was guided by its national security interests and its tradition of close engagement with the international community in promoting cooperative efforts to deal with various traditional and non-traditional security challenges. India was actively at work at the meetings of the UN First Committee in New York, UN Disarmament Commission, Conference on Disarmament in Geneva, Biological and Toxins Weapons Convention (BTWC) in Geneva, Chemical Weapons Convention (CWC) in the Hague, Convention on Certain Conventional Weapons (CCW) in Geneva, UN Programme of Action on Small Arms and Light Weapons (UNPoA on SALW) in New York. Prime Minister led the Indian delegation at Washington D.C. in March 2016 for the 4th Nuclear Security Summit. India submitted its formal application for membership of the Nuclear Suppliers Group (NSG) in 2016. India joined the Hague Code of Conduct against Ballistic Missile Proliferation (HCoC) by notifying the HCoC Central Contact in Vienna through diplomatic channels. The HCoC is a voluntary, legally non-binding international confidence building and transparency measure that seeks to prevent the proliferation of ballistic missiles that are capable of delivering weapons of mass destruction. India's joining the code signals our readiness to further strengthen global non-proliferation objectives. India joined the Missile Technology Control Regime (MTCR) in 2016.

Multilateral Economic Relations

BRICS Summit

Prime Minister led the Indian delegation to the 7th BRICS Summit in July 2015 in Ufa, Russia. The theme of the Summit was "BRICS Partnership – A Powerful Factor of Global Development". The leaders discussed a wide range of issues including UN Reforms, IMF Reforms, WTO, G 20, regional and global political developments, terrorism, New Development Bank (NDB), BRICS Contingent Reserve Arrangement (CRA), cooperation in ICTs and other issues relating to intra-BRICS Cooperation. The leaders adopted the Ufa Declaration and Action Plan at the Summit. The BRICS Strategy for Economic Partnership which was also adopted by the leaders at the Summit includes cooperation in the areas of trade, investment, finance, manufacturing, energy, agriculture, science and technology, connectivity, ICT, etc.

India assumed BRICS Chairmanship in February 2016. The 8th BRICS Summit was hosted by India in Goa in October 2016. People-dimension, youth, and dissemination of BRICS across the country is a priority for our chairmanship. BRICS events are being organized across the cities and provinces of India in order to further enhance their participative and people-centric role. Our objective during India's BRICS Chairmanship is to further consolidate Intra-BRICS cooperation by adopting a five-pronged approach – (i) institution building to further deepen and sustain BRICS cooperation; (ii) implementation of the decisions of previous Summits including Prime Minister's announcements at the Fortaleza and Ufa Summits; (iii) integrating synergies among the existing cooperation mechanisms; (iv) innovation, i.e., new cooperation mechanisms; and (v) continuity, i.e., continuation of mutually agreed existing BRICS cooperation mechanisms. To make BRICS' people-centric, enhancing people-to-people (P2P) contacts is a priority during India's BRICS Chairmanship, including youth.

IBSA Dialogue Forum

The Focal Points (Senior Officials) of IBSA [India, Brazil and South Africa] Dialogue Forum met in New York in September 2015. This was their 25th meeting since inception of IBSA in June 2003. They reaffirmed continued relevance of IBSA in the light of growing importance of South-South cooperation. Brazil and South Africa welcomed new initiatives for IBSA cooperation proposed by India in the fields of micro financing, satellites-based applications, smart cities and joint Antarctica expedition.

G-20 Summit

Prime Minister led the Indian delegation to the 10th G-20 Summit in Antalya, Turkey in November 2015. The agenda of the Summit included terrorism, refugee crisis, climate change, the 10th WTO Ministerial Conference, global economy, growth and employment and investment strategies, enhancing resilience, financial regulation, international tax, anti-corruption, IMF reforms and energy.

Development Cooperation

Development Cooperation is an important constituent of India's foreign policy. India's external development assistance programmes in developing countries have increased significantly in their scope and coverage in the past few years. These include Lines of Credit, grant assistance, technical consultancy, disaster relief, humanitarian aid, educational scholarships and a wide range of capacity-building programmes including short-term civilian and military training courses.

The Development Partnership Administration (DPA) was set up in the Ministry of External Affairs in January 2012 for efficient execution and monitoring of India's development projects through the stages of conceptualization, launch, implementation and commissioning.

Various development projects in infrastructure, hydroelectricity, power transmission, agriculture, education, health, industry and other sectors, as prioritized by the host governments, are under implementation in Afghanistan, Bangladesh, Bhutan, Myanmar, Maldives, Nepal, Sri Lanka and other countries. In addition, a number of projects have been initiated for development and strengthening of cross-border connectivity with India's neighbours and are in various stages of implementation. In South East Asia, Central Asia, Africa and Latin America, bilateral projects in information and computer technology (ICT), small and medium enterprises and archaeological conservation have been undertaken.

The Third India-Africa Forum Summit was held in New Delhi in October 2015 to give a new thrust to the age-old partnership between India and Africa. Heads of State/Heads of Government of 54 African Nations participated in the Summit. The vision document entitled 'Delhi Declaration 2015' and 'India-Africa Framework for Strategic Cooperation' outlined a multi-faceted strategy for dovetailing the India growth story with Africa's Agenda 2063 to spur mutual resurgence.

Extension of Lines of Credit (LoC) on concessional terms to other developing countries has been an important instrument of India's external development assistance. Over the years, 226 LoCs aggregating US$ 16,898.23 million have been allocated to different countries in various sectors, of which US$ 8,705.21 million have been allocated for African countries and US$ 8,193.02 million for non-African countries.

During 2015-16, over 10,400 training slots were offered to 161 partner countries in a wide range of disciplines, including IT and telecommunication, finance and accounts, audit, banking, education, planning and administration, parliamentary affairs, crime records, textiles, rural development, renewable energy, tool design, SMEs and entrepreneurship development, etc., under the Indian Technical and Economic Cooperation (ITEC) Programme. In addition, special courses in a variety of disciplines were also conducted based on requests from partner countries. In order to give thrust for continued engagement with ITEC Alumni as well as in line with the Digital India initiative, a user-friendly ITEC web portal has now been made available.

Humanitarian assistance was provided to Syria, Philippines, Jordan, Lebanon, Yemen and Nepal in 2015-16.

Investment and Technology Promotion

2015-16 has been an exciting year for India's economic diplomacy. MEA's economic engagement worldwide through its Missions/Posts is creating opportunities for the country's investors, entrepreneurs, workers and consumers, while also serving the nation's economic objectives. The Investment and Technology Promotion (ITP) Division, the economic arm of the MEA, provided assistance to Indian Missions/Posts for enhancing their economic outreach; helped resolve trade and investment disputes; facilitated foreign enterprises in identifying business opportunities in India; extended financial assistance to Business Chambers and Think Tanks for organizing seminars and conferences to promote GoI flagship schemes and regional economic cooperation initiatives; supported investment activities of several state governments; commissioned reports and surveys by engaging leading consultancy firms; and worked in close cooperation with other line ministries in the civil aviation, railways, shipping and road transport, energy resources, urban development, agriculture, health, water and sanitation, finance, trade, tourism, culture and information space.

Counter-terrorism

During the year, India continued to hold structured consultations through Joint Working Groups on Counter Terrorism (JWG-CT) with various partner countries. India voiced strong concerns regarding the scourge of terrorism at the BRICS and G-20 Summits held in November 2015. It also emphasized the importance of a united response to address this problem under the umbrella of a Comprehensive Convention on International Terrorism (CCIT) proposed by it in the UN in 1996.

Global Cyber Issues

Global Cyber Issues Division of MEA handles all matters relating to global cyber issues. Keeping in view the vision for achieving 'Digital India' and increasing involvement of India in important global platform on cyber issues, it actively pursued efforts for a leadership role for India on global cyber issues in the period 2015-16.

Cultural diplomacy was one more area that saw remarkable success over the past year. Leveraging India's civilisational values and ethos as a force-multiplier allowed us to project a unique message on issues like sustainable development. The worldwide celebration of the International Day of Yoga on 21 June and the following year was an acknowledgement of the popularity of India's cultural voice and values. Cultural festivals and commemorative weeks were organised in a number of countries including Japan, China and Russia over the course of the year.

In a related vein, the past year saw India reconnect with the 27 million strong NRI and PIO populations across the world in an unprecedented manner. The 10th World Hindi Conference in Bhopal saw the largest ever participation of expatriate Indians and Hindi scholars from all over the world. To re-energise our engagement with the overseas Indian community, Ministry revised the format of the Pravasi Bharatiya Divas Convention, which is organised once in two years. In January 2016, for the first time, Missions celebrated the Pravasi Bharatiya Divas (PBD). For sustained and more productive engagement with the Indian Diaspora, 10 PBD conferences are being organised in 2016 in New Delhi on issues of concern to the Indian Diaspora.

There was a concerted effort by the Ministry of External Affairs to make its public service delivery functions more efficient and user-friendly for citizens as well as foreign visitors. An online grievance redressal system called MADAD was launched to allow Indian citizens abroad to seek assistance from our Missions and Posts. The PIO and OCI schemes were merged to cater to a long-standing demand. Passport applications saw a large jump from the previous year with the organisation of numerous passport seva camps and passport melas, and the opening of new passport seva kendras in the northeastern states. Passport processing time was reduced to 21 days for 96 per cent of the applications. Perhaps the greatest effort mounted by the Ministry to aid its citizens abroad was the evacuation exercise from war-stricken Yemen, where more than 4,700 stranded Indians were successfully rescued. Indian forces also rescued nearly 2,000 foreign citizens from about 50 countries, which won the country much appreciation and established it as a stabilising net-security provider in the region. The Ministry also evacuated Indian citizens from South Sudan in July 2016 as the security situation there deteriorated.

Another unique effort of the Government was to increasingly involve the state governments in the formulation and implementation of foreign policy. Recognising that the states have a critical role to play, particularly in the success of commercial and cultural diplomacy, the newly created States Division of the Ministry of External Affairs proactively reached out to all state governments. It is helping them in identifying their target countries and regions for commercial, cultural, academic, tourism and diaspora outreach, and in fashioning appropriate strategies for maximising the gains from international interaction. The period also saw the signature of a number of twinning agreements between Indian and foreign cities/provinces, to foster closer cooperation for urban development, cultural propagation, heritage conservation and people-to-people links. A Provincial-State Leaders Forum was launched between India and China to encourage sub-national cooperation between the two countries.

External Publicity and Public Diplomacy

This period saw further growth of the Ministry of External Affairs' digital presence on social media platforms. The aggregate following of the Ministry alone, excluding Missions and Posts abroad, is approximately 3.8 million. As a result of this, the average monthly reach of its Posts on Twitter crosses 17.5 million, while on Facebook, the monthly reach goes above 15 million. Around 149 Indian Missions around the world have a Facebook presence. More than 90 Missions and Posts are also active on Twitter.

Nalanda University

The Nalanda University made good progress during the year in its journey as an institution of academic excellence with an international footprint.

Teaching in the School of Historical Studies and School of Ecology and Environment Studies started in September 2014 from leased premises in Rajgir, Bihar and the total number of students reached 62 during the academic year 2015-16. So far, a total number of 17 EAS and non-EAS countries have signed the MoU on the establishment of Nalanda University. The process of notification of Nalanda University laws/regulations was carried forward with the notification of University's first ordinance on June 10, 2015.

The Ministry has a well organised programme for propagation and promotion of Hindi abroad with the involvement of our Missions/Posts. Ministry also extends support to various foreign universities and to the educational institutions through Indian missions abroad for Hindi related activities. 10th World Hindi Conference was organised by the Ministry in September 2015 at Bhopal, Madhya Pradesh. During the Conference, which was attended by a large number of delegates including foreign delegates, extensive discussions were held on twelve themes focusing on the main theme "Hindi Jagat: Vistar evam Sambhavnae". To promote Hindi as an international language, the World Hindi Secretariat has been set-up in Mauritius under a bilateral agreement between India and Mauritius. The Ministry coordinates works relating to grant of scholarships to foreign students to study Hindi at Kendriya Hindi Sansthan, Agra. Implementation of official language policy of the Government of India continued to be accorded a very high priority by the Ministry.

Indian Council for Cultural Relations

In 2015-16, Indian Council for Cultural Relations (ICCR) undertook a wide range of activities to promote better understanding of India abroad. As part of its academic and intellectual activities, ICCR had offered 3,339 scholarship slots for studying in India under its various scholarship schemes. As welfare measures ICCR organized 12 summer camps during May-June 2015 and 11 winter camps during December 2015 and January 2016 and celebrated International Student Day in November 2015 in regional offices as well as some of the Missions abroad. A conference on Higher Education in India for Foreign Students was organized by ICCR in March 2016. ICCR organized 07 conference/ seminars including "International Conference of Indologists 2015". ICCR's 35 full-fledged cultural centres and one sub-centre abroad actively promoted India's soft power abroad through a wide range of activities, including dance, music, yoga, Hindi, talks and exhibitions.

On the occasion of International Yoga Day on 21 June in 2015 and 2016, the Council deputed over 30 India based yoga teachers to various countries to impart knowledge of yoga and also published a special issue of its Hindi journal "Gagnanchal".

ICCR sponsored 121 Indian cultural groups abroad which performed in about 80 countries. "Namaste Russia", a festival of India, was held in May

2015 in Moscow. It also organized performances by 58 foreign groups in India, including at ICCR's various prestigious festivals.

It sent 18 exhibitions out of which 16 were from its own collection for display in various countries and organized the second India-China Women Artists' Residency 'Maitri-II' in Shanghai, China.

ICCR invited distinguished dignitaries (23) and academicians (11) from various countries to visit India for exchange of views. It also supported research of India by some foreign experts.

On the occasion of the 10th World Hindi Conference organised in September 2015 in Bhopal, a special issue of "Gagananchal" and a souvenir entitled "Kavya-Rasdhara" were published. A book on Father Camille Bulcke (Belgian National), Hindi scholar was published entitled "Father Camille Bulcke: Bharatiyata Ke Prakash Punj". ICCR brought out journals in Hindi, English, Arabic, French and Spanish for distribution in various countries.

Indian Council of World Affairs

As mandated under the Indian Council of World Affairs Act, 2001, the Indian Council of World Affairs (ICWA) continued to accord high priority to research, analysis and study of political, security and economic developments in Asia, Africa, Europe, United States, Latin America and Caribbean and wider global geo-strategic environments. ICWA has made a conscious attempt to reach out to the public by disseminating its output in the form of Sapru House Papers, Policy Briefs, Special Reports, Issue Briefs and Viewpoints, which were placed on the ICWA website and Facebook. It has also authorised book projects on topical/important aspects of foreign relations. In order to reach a wider audience, ICWA, besides publishing directly in the Hindi language has also started translating its academic output in Hindi. This too have been posted on its website. The Council has opened its library for general public and membership rules have been eased. It conducted a large number of events, lectures, conferences and outreach activities.

In pursuance of its mandate to create awareness about foreign policy issues among the youth, ICWA undertook two national level essay writing Contests in Hindi and English among school going students and undergraduate and postgraduate students respectively.

Research and Information System for Developing Countries

Research and Information System for Developing Countries (RIS) is a new Delhi–based autonomous policy research institute that specialises in issues related to international economic development, trade, investment and technology. Through its intensive network of think tanks, RIS seeks to strengthen policy coherence on international economic issues and the development partnership canvas. The thrust areas of RIS work programme are organized around four pillars: a) global economic issues and south-south cooperation; b) regional initiatives on trade and investment; c) regional cooperation, trade facilitation and connectivity; and d) new technologies and development issues. With the objective of fostering effective policy dialogue and capacity-building among developing countries on global and regional economic issues, RIS organised several important events during the period which, among others, include: Conference on South-South Cooperation; National Consultation on Road to Sustainable Development Goals; RIS Summer School on International Trade Theory and Practice; India-Africa Partnership: Future Directions, etc. RIS also conducted two capacity building programmes under ITEC with focus on 'Learning South-South Cooperation' and 'Trade Policy and Analysis'. The Institute also brought out a number of publications that include the South-South Cooperation 2016, South Asia Development and Cooperation Report 2015, Prospects of Blue Economy in the Indian Ocean, India-Africa Partnership Towards Sustainable Development, ASEAN-India Development and Cooperation Report 2015, Enhancing India-Myanmar Border Trade: Policy and Implementation Measures 2016, among others.

ASEAN India Centre

ASEAN India Centre (AIC), set up in 2013, serves as a resource centre for ASEAN member states and India for undertaking policy research, advocacy and networking activities with organizations and Think-Tanks in India and ASEAN. It has organised several important events during the period which, inter alia, include the Fourth Roundtable of the ASEAN-India Network of Think Tanks on "ASEAN-India: Strengthening the Ties That Bind"; the 1st International Conference on "ASEAN-India Cultural Links: Historical and Contemporary Dimensions"; a Roundtable on "ASEAN India Air Connectivity"; an EAS Conference on Maritime Security and Cooperation; a Roundtable on "ASEAN-India: Integration and Development" and several lectures under the ASEAN-India Eminent Persons Lecture Series. In addition, it has published reports such as "ASEAN-India Development and Cooperation Report 2015", "ASEAN-India Maritime Connectivity Report", "Dynamics of ASEAN-India Strategic Partnership", "ASEAN-India Economic Relations: Opportunities and Challenges", etc.

The proactive initiatives taken by the government, as described above, showcase an exceptionally energetic period in the area of foreign policy, with many achievements and successes that raised India's profile in the world.

19 Industry

THE quest for industrial development started soon after independence in 1947. The Industrial Policy Resolution of 1948 defined the broad contours of the policy delineating the role of the State in industrial development both as an entrepreneur and authority. This was followed by comprehensive enactment of Industries (Development & Regulation) Act, 1951 (referred as IDR Act) that provides for the necessary framework for implementing the Industrial Policy and enables the Union Government to direct investment into desired channels of industrial activity *inter alia* through the mechanism of licensing keeping with national development objectives and goals.

The main objectives of the Industrial Policy are (i) to maintain a sustained growth in productivity; (ii) to enhance gainful employment;(iii) to achieve optimal utilisation of human resources; (iv) to attain international competitiveness; and (v) to transform India into a major partner and player in the global arena. To achieve these objectives, the Policy focus is on deregulating Indian industry; allowing freedom and flexibility to the industry in responding to market forces; and providing a policy regime that facilitates and fosters growth. Economic reforms initiated since 1991 envisage a significantly bigger role for private initiatives. The Policy has been progressively liberalized over years to at present, as would be evident in subsequent paragraphs.

The Government is continuously taking steps to boost the industrial production and growth. These *inter-alia,* include 'Startup India' initiative as well as 'Make in India' programme under which 25 thrust sectors have been identified to provide a major push to manufacturing in India. The steps have been taken to create ease of doing business, including setting up of an Investor Facilitation Cell, launch of e-biz Portal and liberalizing policy for industrial license for defence industries. National Intellectual Property Rights (IPR) Policy has been approved on 12.5.2016 to stimulate, a dynamic vibrant and balanced IPR system. The Foreign Direct Investment (FDI) policy and procedures have been simplified and liberalized progressively. To further supplement domestic capital, technology and skills, FDI has been further liberalized on 20.6.2016. For creation of state-of-art infrastructure, Government is implementing Delhi Mumbai Industrial Corridor (DMIC) project. In addition, four other industrial corridor projects have been conceptualized.

Industrial Policy

Industrial Policy since 1991 has been more for facilitating the industrial development rather than anchoring it through permits and controls. Industrial licensing has, therefore, been abolished for most of the industries and there are only five industries at present related to security, strategic and environmental concerns, where an industrial license is currently required:

electronic aerospace and defence equipment: all types; industrial explosives including detonating fuses, safety fuses, gunpowder, nitrocellulose and matches; specified hazardous chemicals i.e., (i) hydrocyanic acid and its derivatives; (ii) phosgene and its derivatives; and (iii) isocyanates and disocyanates of hydrocarbon, not elsewhere specified (example Methyl Isocyanate); cigars and cigarettes of tobacco and manufactured tobacco substitutes; and fermentation industry.

During 2014, a list of what constitutes defence equipment were notified, with the stipulation that any item not specifically included in the list, including those for dual use having military as well as civilian applications stand de-licensed. Further, the initial validity of industrial licenses for all sectors (other than Defence Sector) has been extended to three years with a provision to grant two extensions of two years each. Thus, time to commence commercial production is now seven years (3+2+2=7). The initial validity of industrial licence for defence sector were revised to 15 years (Fifteen years), further extendable up to 18 years for existing as well as future licenses.

Policy for Micro, Small & Medium Enterprises Sector

Government has enacted the Micro, Small and Medium Enterprises Development (MSMED) Act, 2006 stepping up the investment limit in plant and machinery to ₹ 5 crore for small enterprises and ₹ 10 crore for medium enterprises, so as to reduce the regulatory interface with the majority of the industrial units. Over the period Government has pruned the list of items reserved for exclusive manufacture by MSE sector. Remaining 20 items which were earlier reserved for exclusive manufacture by MSE Sector have been de-reserved. Presently no item is reserved for exclusive manufacture by MSE Sector.

Sectors Reserved for Public Sector

Consistent with the policy of liberalization of domestic industry, the numbers of industries reserved for public sector have also been reduced. During 2014, private investment in Rail Infrastructure has been permitted. Consequently, at present only two industrial sectors are reserved for public sector: (i) atomic energy (ii) railway operations other than construction, operation and maintenance of the following; a. suburban corridor projects through PPP; b. high speed train project; c. dedicated freight lines; d. rolling stock including train sets, and locomotives/ coaches manufacturing and maintenance facilities; e. railway electrification; f. signaling systems; g. freight terminals; h. passenger terminals; i. infrastructure in industrial park pertaining to railway line/sidings including electrified railway lines and connectivities to main railway line; and j. mass rapid transport systems.

Private investment (domestic as well as foreign) in construction, operation and maintenance of above had been allowed.

Industrial Entrepreneurs' Memorandum

Industries not covered under compulsory licensing and not reserved for public sector are required to file an Industrial Entrepreneurs' Memorandum (IEM)

Production of Selected Industries
(lakh tonnes)

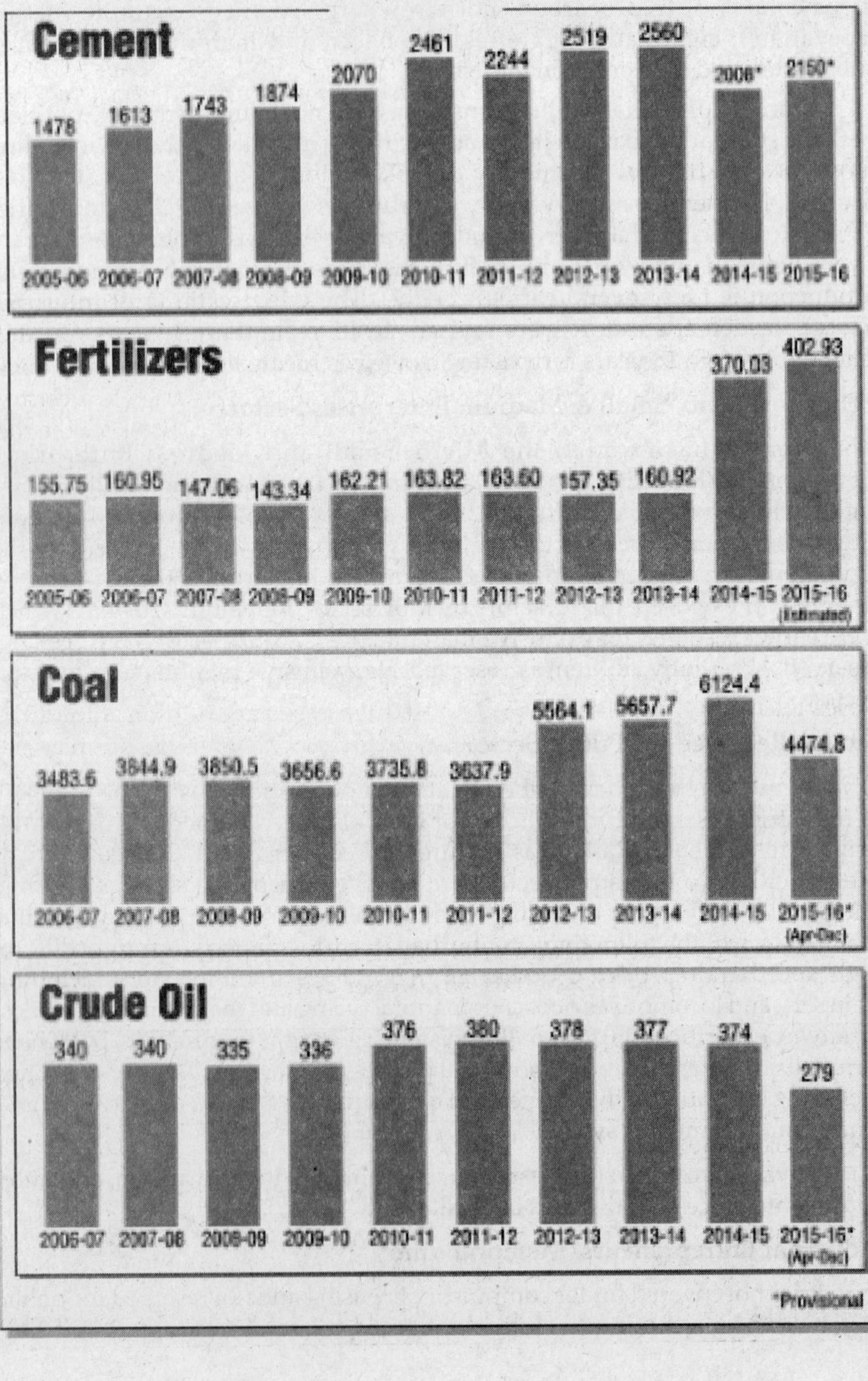

with the Secretariat for Industrial Assistance (SIA), Department of Industrial Policy & Promotion (DIPP). No industrial license is required for such exempted industries. Such memoranda are to be filed by non-MSME category industrial undertakings.

Further, in a paradigm shift in procedural changes, since May 2014, the process of applying for Industrial License and Industrial Entrepreneur Memorandum has been made totally online without human interface on 24x7 basis at the e-Biz website.

I. Trends in Industrial Investment and Production

(i) Investment Intentions

Assessment of investment intentions are based on filing of Industrial Entrepreneurs Memoranda (IEMs) for the delicensed sector and industrial licenses issued for the licensable sector. While figures of Gross Capital Formation (GCF) indicate actualization of investment, investment intentions indicated in IEM filed are early indicators of likely investment flows to industry and of entrepreneurs' perception. The investment intentions also provide the sectoral preferences of investors and shifts in these preferences over time. Information on investment intentions are tabulated in terms of industries included in the First Schedule of the IDR Act, which are referred as scheduled industry.

(ii) Index of Industrial Production

Index of Industrial Production (IIP) is a measure of industrial performance which is compiled and released every month by Central Statistics Office (CSO). It uses fixed weight and base. CSO revised the base year of IIP in June 2011 from 1993-94 to 2004-05. The latest series with base year 2004-05 has an enlarged and more representative basket of the industrial sector. The weighting diagram for this series is drawn using relative importance of the sectors in GDP, which is based on the National Accounts. IIP is categorized in Sectoral and Use-based classifications. The Table-19.1 below indicates the Sectoral and Use-based growth rate for the last five years.

Table 19.1 : Index of Industrial Production (IIP) Growth Rates (Base: 2004-05) (in per cent)

Groups	Annual 2011-12	2012-13	2013-14	2014-15	2015-16	Cumulative (Apr-Jun) 2016-17
Sectoral classification						
Mining	-2.0	-2.3	-0.6	1.5	2.2	2.0
Manufacturing	3.0	1.3	-0.8	2.3	2.0	-1.4
Electricity	8.2	4.0	6.1	8.4	5.7	7.1
General index	2.9	1.1	-0.1	2.8	2.4	-0.2

Use Based classification						
Basic goods	5.5	2.5	2.1	7.0	3.6	4.1
Capital goods	-4.0	-6.0	-3.6	6.4	-2.9	-21.3
Intermediate goods	-0.6	1.6	3.1	1.7	2.5	3.8
Consumer goods	4.4	2.4	-2.8	-3.4	3.0	0.7
i) Consumer Durables	2.6	2.0	-12.2	-12.6	11.3	7.3
ii) Consumer Non - Durables	5.9	2.8	4.8	2.8	-1.8	-3.6

Source: Central Statistics Office

In 2011-12, Index of Industrial Production (IIP) showed growth of 2.9 per cent and during 2012-13, it was only 1.1 per cent. In 2013-14, it further slowed down to (-) 0.1 per cent. However, in 2014-15, growth recovered to some extent and it registered growth of 2.8 per cent. In 2015-16, IIP decelerated to some extent and registered growth of 2.4 per cent owing to growth in electricity generation (5.7 per cent), mining (2.2 per cent) and manufacturing (2.0 per cent).

Table-19.2 gives the growth rate in 22 major industry groups of manufacturing captured by IIP. The growth of manufacturing sector during 2015-16 was primarily driven by the growth in industry groups like furniture (44.4 per cent), motor vehicles, trailers (7.5 per cent), wearing apparel (6.6 per cent) and coke, refined petroleum products and nuclear fuel (6.0 per cent), etc. However, this recovery is not visible so far in the current year with the industrial sector registering a decline of 0.2 per cent during April-July, 2016-17 over the corresponding period of 2015-16 and seven out of the twenty-two industry sub-groups showing negative growth during the period.

Table 19.2 : IIP Growth Rate - by Industry Groups (in per cent)

Industry Group	Weight	2011-12	2012-13	2013-14	2014-15	2015-16	2016-17 (Apr-Jul)
Food products and beverages	72.76	15.4	2.9	-1.1	4.8	-6.2	-8.9
Tobacco products	15.7	5.4	-0.4	0.8	1.0	-0.2	1.1
Textiles	61.64	-1.3	5.9	4.4	2.8	2.6	2.9
Wearing apparel	27.82	-8.5	10.4	19.5	5.1	6.6	-2.7
Luggage, handbags, etc.	5.82	3.7	7.3	5.2	10.4	-1.4	-10.6
Wood & wood products	10.51	1.8	-7.1	-2.2	4.4	3.2	-4.2
Paper & Paper products	9.99	5.0	0.5	-0.1	3.3	2.8	3.5

Publishing, printing & reproduction of recorded media	10.78	29.6	-5.1	0.3	-4.1	-9.0	-3.6
Coke, refined petroleum products & nuclear fuel	67.15	3.5	8.5	5.2	0.8	6.0	10.1
Chemicals and chemical products	100.59	-0.4	3.8	8.9	-0.3	3.8	3.4
Rubber and plastic Products	20.25	-0.3	0.2	-2.1	4.5	0.6	2.5
Other non-metallic mineral products	43.14	4.8	1.9	1.1	2.5	1.6	2.3
Basic metals	113.35	8.7	1.9	0.3	12.7	1.0	2.5
Fabricated metal Products	30.85	11.2	-4.7	-7.0	-0.6	1.5	2.9
Machinery and equipment n.e.c.	37.63	-5.8	-4.7	-4.7	4.0	2.6	8.9
Office, accounting & computing machinery	3.05	1.6	-13.9	-15.7	-38.0	0.8	5.5
Electrical machinery & apparatus	19.8	-22.2	0.6	14.5	21.1	-11.4	-51.3
Radio, TV and communication, equipment	9.89	4.3	5.6	-27.3	-54.4	3.7	12.6
Medical, precision & optical instruments, watches and clocks	5.67	10.9	-2.0	-5.1	-2.3	-2.2	0.7
Motor vehicles, trailers	40.64	10.8	-5.3	-9.6	2.5	7.5	5.9
Other transport n.e.c. equipment	18.25	11.9	-0.1	5.9	6.4	1.3	6.7
Furniture	29.97	-1.8	-5.1	-13.9	7.4	44.4	-0.2
Mining & Quarrying	141.57	-2.0	-2.3	-0.6	1.5	2.2	2.0
Manufacturing	755.27	3.0	1.3	-0.8	2.3	2.0	-1.4
Electricity	103.16	8.2	4.0	6.1	8.4	5.7	7.1
General Index	1000	2.9	1.1	-0.1	2.8	2.4	-0.2

Source: Central Statistics Office (CSO)

Trends in Growth of Eight Core Industries

The Index of Eight Core Industries (ICI) measures the performance of eight core industries i.e., coal, crude oil, natural gas, petroleum refinery products, fertilizers, steel, cement and electricity. It is a monthly production index calculated using base year 2004-05.

The industries included in the ICI roughly comprise 38 per cent weight in the Index of Industrial Production (IIP), although there is no one to one relationship of the item basket in ICI with the item basket in IIP and methodology of computation of the indices also differs.

The details of growth in the production of eight core industries are given in Table-19.3. The overall growth of eight core industries decelerated to 2.7 per cent in 2015-16 as compared to its 4.5 per cent growth in the previous year. During April-July, 2016-17, the growth has paced up and the combined index of eight industries grew by 4.9 per cent over corresponding period of the previous year. The output of crude oil and natural gas registered negative growth while the output of coal, refinery products, fertilizers, steel, cement and electricity registered positive growth during the period April-July, 2016-17.

Table 19.3 : Growth in the Production of Eight Core Industries (in per cent)

Sector	Weight	2011-12	2012-13	2013-14	2014-15	2015-16	2016-17 (Apr-Jun)
Coal	4.379	1.3	4.6	1.3	8.1	4.5	5.3
Crude Oil	5.216	1.0	-0.6	-0.2	-0.9	-1.4	-2.9
Natural Gas	1.708	-8.9	-14.5	-13.0	-4.9	-4.2	-3.8
Refinery Products	5.939	3.1	29.0#	1.5	0.3	3.8	8.7
Fertilizers	1.254	0.4	-3.4	1.5	-0.1	11.3	8.6
Steel	6.684	10.3	4.1	11.5	4.7	-1.5	2.8
Cement	2.406	6.7	7.7	3.1	5.6	4.7	4.6
Electricity	10.316	8.1	4.0	6.0	8.4	5.4	7.1
Overall Index	37.903	5.0	6.5	4.2	4.5	2.7	4.9

Source: Office of the Economic Adviser, DIPP

Refinery Products' yearly growth rates of 2012-13 are not comparable with other years on account of inclusion of RIL (SEZ) production data since April, 2012

National Manufacturing Policy

The Department notified the National Manufacturing Policy (NMP) in 2011 with the objective of enhancing the share of manufacturing in GDP to 25 per cent and creating 100 million jobs by 2022. The policy is based on the principle of industrial growth in partnership with the states. The Central Government will create the enabling policy framework, provide incentives for infrastructure development on a Public Private Partnership (PPP) basis through appropriate financing instruments, and State Governments are encouraged to adopt the instrumentalities provided in the Policy. The proposals in the policy are sector neutral, location neutral and technology neutral except incentivisation of green technology. While the NIMZs are an important instrumentality, the proposals contained in the Policy apply to manufacturing industry throughout the country including wherever industry is able to organize itself into clusters and adopt a model of self-regulation as enunciated therein.

Important instruments/features of the policy are:- National Investment and Manufacturing Zones (NIMZs); rationalization and simplification of business regulations; simple and expeditious exit mechanism for manufacturing units; incentives for SMEs; industrial training and skill upgradation measures; financial and institutional mechanisms for technology development, including green technologies; government procurement; and special focus sectors.

National Investment and Manufacturing Zones

NIMZs have been conceived as large integrated industrial townships with state-of-the-art infrastructure; land use on the basis of zoning; clean and energy efficient technology; necessary social infrastructure; skill development facilities, etc. to provide a conducive environment for manufacturing industries. To enable the zones to function as a self-governing and autonomous body, it will be declared by the state government as a Industrial Township under Article 243 Q (1)(c) of the Constitution. These NIMZs would be managed by a Special Purpose Vehicle (SPV) which would ensure master planning of the zone; pre-clearances for setting up the industrial units to be located within the zone and undertake such other functions as specified in the various sections of the Policy.

The NIMZs would be different from SEZs in terms of size; level of infrastructure planning; governance structures related to regulatory procedures; exit policies; fiscal incentives, etc. The policy mandates that the SPV in a zone will be headed by a senior government official and will include inter-alia an official expert conversant with the work relating to pollution control/environmental protection. There shall be a provision of suitable representation of the allottees and subsequently industrial units.

Make in India

After the launch of 'Make in India' initiative in 2014, ministries/departments concerned with 22 thrust sectors identified under 'Make in India', announced their Action Plans for implementation over one year and three years. Quantifiable and measurable milestones in respect of each activity of the Action Plans have been identified by the ministries/departments concerned with a view to monitoring the implementation of these Action Plans.

This Department has launched an online 'Make in India Dashboard' in April 2016, to enable ministries/departments to view and update the progress of their Action Plans on their own in a timely manner. This Dashboard is being monitored by this Department to evaluate the overall progress of the 'Make in India' related initiatives and address and resolve any issues.

To provide further impetus to 'Make in India' initiative, new Action Plans pertaining to the Ministry of Health & Family Welfare have been identified.

Under the 'Make in India' initiative, a 'Seven Year Strategy' has been adopted which involves redefining the sectors covered by the new initiative, adding new sectors like medical devices while removing sectors that lose relevance in an evolving economy, to maximize job creation potential with evolution of the economy. It should also expand its reach to include service sectors, which have the greatest employment potential. Sectors such as tourism and hospitality are important for their job creation potential. With the objective to generate awareness about the investment opportunities and prospects of the country, to promote India as a preferred investment destination in the markets overseas and to increase Indian share of Global FDI, an interactive portal http://www.makeinindia.com has been created for dissemination of information and interaction with the investors.

Startup India

The 'Startup India' initiative, aims at fostering entrepreneurship and promoting innovation by creating an ecosystem that is conducive to growth. The initiative strives for providing a long due impetus to the entrepreneurial set up in economic landscape of the country. An Action Plan of 19 action items spanning across areas such as simplification and handholding, funding support and incentives and industry-academia partnership and incubation were announced. It is established globally that Startups are driving the economic growth of nations, creating employment and fostering a culture of innovation. It is, therefore, incumbent on the Government to nurture emerging talent and entrepreneurship as part of the larger goal of nation building.

Since the launch of the initiative, a number of forward looking strategic amendments to the existing policy ecology have been introduced, like:

Startup Hub: A Startup India Hub has been set up to address queries of various startups and assist them through their lifecycle. Additionally, a facility for interaction for entrepreneurs on Twitter known as 'Twitter Seva' has also been launched.

Rolling-out of Mobile App and Portal: The Startup India Portal and Mobile App have been made operational. The portal and app provide functionalities such as making application for obtaining real-time Startup recognition, verification of recognition certificate, information availability such as list of incubators, Securities and Exchange Board of India (SEBI) registered funds, notifications issued by various departments, etc.

Fast-tracking Patent Registration and Legal Support: A scheme for Startups IPR Protection (SIPP) for facilitating fast track filing of patents, trademarks and designs by Startups has been introduced. The scheme thus provides for expedited examination of patents filed. This will reduce the time taken in getting patents. The fee for filing of patents has also been reduced up to 80 per cent.

Relaxed Norms in Public Procurement for Startups: Provisions have been introduced in the procurement policy to relax norms pertaining to prior experience / turnover for micro and small enterprises.

Tax Incentives: Tax incentives for Startup companies for a period of three years have been introduced in the Finance Act 2016.

Building Innovation Centres and Setting up of Seven Research Parks: two Research Parks, 16 Technology Business Incubators (TBIs) and 10 Startup Centres have been approved and shall be made operational soon. 25-30 new Innovation Centres have been envisaged to be launched in the current financial year.

Promoting Startups in Biotechnology Sector: Scheme guidelines have been drawn by Department of Bio-Technology (DBT) to scale up existing 15 bio-incubators.

Launching of Innovation Focused Programme: Scheme guidelines for Innovation core and Ucchattar AvishkarYojana (UAY) have been finalized by Ministry of Human Resource Development (MHRD). The guidelines for the National Initiative for Developing and Harnessing Innovations (NIDHI) has been formulated and notified.

Industrial/Economic Corridors

Development of industrial/economic corridors is a very important policy initiative of the Government for boosting industrial development, income and employment. The status of development in this regard is as follows:

Delhi Mumbai Industrial Corridor

The Delhi Mumbai Industrial Corridor (DMIC) project is being developed on both sides of the Western Dedicated Freight Corridor as a global manufacturing and investment destination and has made significant strides since the approval of institutional and financial structure in September, 2011. DMIC industrial cities are being benchmarked against recently established industrial cities in other parts of the world. DMIC Project Implementation Trust Fund was set up as a Trust in September, 2012. The land for the new industrial cities will be the contribution of the state government.

The brief status of projects under implementation is as follows:

Ahmedabad Dholera Special Investment Region

Shareholder's Agreement and State Support Agreement have been executed between Government of Gujarat and DMIC Trust and Node/city level SPV in the name of "Dholera Industrial City Development Ltd." has been incorporated. 1178 hectares of land has already been transferred by the State Government to the SPV. Environment clearance has been obtained for the project and preliminary engineering work has also been completed.

Shendra-Bidkin Industrial Park

Shareholders' Agreement and State Support Agreement have been executed between Government of Maharashtra and DMIC Trust and Node/city level

SPV in the name of "Aurangabad Industrial Township Ltd." has been incorporated. 8.39 sqkms of land has been transferred by Maharashtra Industrial Development Corporation (MIDC) to SPV. Environment clearance has been obtained and preliminary engineering for various trunk infrastructure works has been completed.

Integrated Industrial Township, Vikram Udyogpuri

SPV has been restructured under the name of "Vikram Udyogpuri Ltd." as a joint venture between DMIC Trust and MPTRIFAC and MPAKVN. State government has transferred approximately 1100 acres of land to project SPV. Environment clearance has already been obtained. EPC contractor has been appointed for construction of trunk infrastructure. Work is in progress on ground.

Integrated Industrial Township

SPV has been incorporated with the name of "Integrated Industrial Township Greater Noida Limited" between DMIC Trust and Greater Noida Industrial Development Authority (GNIDA). State Government has transferred approximately 747.5 acres of land to project SPV. EPC contractor for implementation of trunk infrastructure has been appointed and work has started on ground.

Modal Solar Power Project

A company with the name of "DMICDC Neemrana Solar Power Limited" has been incorporated as a wholly owned subsidiary of DMICDC Limited in 2015. Power Purchase Agreement (PPA) between M/s Mikuni India Pvt. Ltd. and M/s DMICDC Neemrana Solar Power Company Limited (DNSPCL) for 1MW has been executed.

Logistic Data Bank

The project of Logistic Data Bank (LOB) was envisaged as service for tracking container cargo movement, integrate the existing IT systems of various stakeholders (ports, customs, trains, ICD, etc.) across the supply chain to provide real time information within a single window.

Foreign Direct Investment

Capital inflows from other countries, particularly in the nature of investment are very important contributor to augmenting availability of capital for funding of infrastructure, industries and other economic ventures. Equity inflows are more stable and bring in new management practices and technology together with investment. For encouraging Foreign Direct Investment (FDI) inflows, the policy is reviewed on an ongoing basis, with a view to make it more investor-friendly. In recent past, the Government has brought policy reforms in a number of sectors. Following are sectors where either sectoral caps have been raised or entry routes changed from Government to automatic, or both:

Table 19.4: Sectors where FDI cap/route has been revised in the last two years

S. No	Sector/Activity	Earlier Cap/Route	Revised Cap/ Route
1.	Tea plantation sector	100 per cent Government	100 per cent automatic
2.	Coffee, rubber, cardamom, palm oil tree and olive oil tree plantations	FDI not allowed	100 per cent automatic
3.	Broadcasting Carriage Services (Teleports, DTH, Cable Networks, Mobile, TV, HITS)	74 per cent automatic up to 49 per cent	100 per cent automatic
4.	Broadcasting Content Service: Up-linking of Non-'News & Current Affairs' TV Channels/ Down-linking of TV Channels	100 per cent government	100 per cent automatic
5.	Broadcasting content service a) FM Radio b) Uplinking of 'News & Current Affairs' TV Channels	26 per cent government	49 per cent government
6.	Airports - Brownfield	100 per cent automatic up to 74 per cent	100 per cent automatic
7.	Air transport service - Non-scheduled	74 per cent automatic up to 49 per cent	100 per cent automatic
8.	Air Transport Service - Scheduled	49 per cent automatic	100 per cent automatic up to 49 per cent
9.	Air Transport service - Regional Air transport services	Not allowed	100 per cent automatic up to 49 per cent
10.	Ground handling services	74 per cent automatic up to 49 per cent	100 per cent automatic
11.	Duty free shops	No such provision	100 per cent automatic
12.	Food product retail Trading	Not allowed	100 per cent government up to 100 per cent
13.	Railway infrastructure*	Not allowed	100 per cent automatic
14.	Asset reconstruction companies	100 per cent automatic up to 49 per cent	100 per cent automatic
15.	Credit information companies	74 per cent automatic	100 per cent automatic
16.	White Label ATM Operations	No such provision	100 per cent automatic
17.	Pharma - medical devices	100 per cent government being part of Pharma	100 per cent automatic
18.	Pharma - brownfield	100 per cent government	100 per cent automatic up to 74 per cent
19.	Defence	26 per cent government	100 per cent automatic up to 49 per cent
20.	Satellites- establishment and operation	74 per cent government	100 per cent government up to 100 per cent

21.	Insurance	26 per cent automatic	49 per cent automatic
22.	Pension	No such provision	49 per cent automatic
23.	Private security agencies	49 per cent government	74 per cent automatic up to 49 per cent

Other measures undertaken to simplify FDI policy and to provide ease of doing business in the country:

(i) Introduction of Composite Caps: Government has introduced composite cap of foreign investment. Sectoral cap i.e., the maximum amount which can be invested by foreign investors in an entity, unless provided otherwise, is composite and includes all types of foreign investments, direct and indirect, regardless of whether the said investments have been made under Schedule 1 (Foreign Direct Investment), 2 (Foreign Institutional Investor), 2A (Foreign Portfolio Investor), 3 (Non Resident Indian), 6 (Foreign Venture Capital Investor), 9 (Limited Liability Partnership), 10 (Depository Receipt) and 11 (Investment Vehicle) of FEMA. The measure provides full fungibility in different types of foreign investments.

(ii) Establishment of Branch, Liaison or Project Office: For establishment of branch, liaison or project office or any other place of business in India if principal business of applicant is defence, telecom, private security or information and broadcasting, it has been provided that approval of Reserve Bank of India is not required in cases where FIPB approval or license/permission by the concerned Ministry/ Regulator has already been granted.

(iii) Guidelines for FDI on E-commerce Sector: The Government has issued guidelines for FDI on e-commerce sector. 100 per cent FDI under automatic route is now permitted in marketplace model of e-commerce. Various terms like e-commerce, e-commerce entity, marketplace, inventory based model have also been defined to bring clarity.

(iv) Investments by NRIs: Investments by Non Resident Indians (NRIs), Persons of Indian Origin (PIOs) and Overseas Citizens of India (OCIs) on non-repatriation basis is now deemed to be domestic investment at par with investment made by residents. As per new definition, NRI would mean an individual resident outside the country who is a citizen of India or is an Overseas Citizen of India cardholder within the meaning of Section 7 (A) of the Citizenship Act, 1955. Such dispensation has also been extended to companies, trusts and partnerships owned by NRIs.

(v) Construction Development: Major reforms have been undertaken in construction development sector. These are - a) removal of conditions of area restriction of floor area of 20,000 sq. mtrs in construction development projects and minimum capitalization of US $ 5 million to be brought in within the period of six months of the commencement of business. b) exit and repatriation of foreign investment is now permitted after a lock-in-period of three years. Transfer of stake from one non-resident to another non-resident, without repatriation of investment is also neither to be subjected to any lock-in period

nor to any government approval. c) exit is permitted at any time if project or trunk infrastructure is completed before lock-in period. d) cent per cent FDI under automatic route is permitted in completed projects for operation and management of townships, malls/ shopping complexes and business centres.

(vi) Banking-Private Sector: Government has introduced full fungibility of foreign investment in banking-private sector. Accordingly, FIIs/FPIs/QFIs, following due procedure, can now invest up to sectoral limit of 74 per cent, provided that there is no change of control and management of the investee company.

(vii) Manufacturing: In order to provide boost to manufacturing sector and give impetus to 'Make in India' initiative, government has permitted a manufacturer to sell its product through wholesale and/or retail, including through e-commerce under automatic route. The term 'manufacturing' has also been defined.

(viii) Trading: In order to encourage investment in the trading sector and provide simplification in the policy, some amendments have been brought in the FDI policy on the sector. Initiatives like Single Brand Retail Trading, Duty Free Shops, Wholesale cash and carry to name a few have been introduced to ease the system.

(ix) Limited Liability Partnerships (LLPs): FDI policy has been amended to provide that investments in LLPs will not require government approval. Cent per cent FDI is now permitted under automatic route in LLPs operating in sectors/activities where 100 per cent FDI is allowed, through automatic route and there are no FDI-linked performance conditions.

(x) Mining: In mining sector, a number of conditions which were not relevant have been removed.

(xi) Companies without operation: Approval requirements in respect of companies without operation have also been relaxed. It has now been decided that for infusion of foreign investment into an Indian company which does not have any operations and also does not have any downstream investments, Government approval would not be required, for undertaking activities which are under automatic route and without FDI-linked performance conditions, regardless of the amount or extent of foreign investment.

(xii) Establishment and Ownership or control of the Indian Company: As per earlier FDI policy establishment and ownership or control of Indian company in sectors/activities with caps required government approval. This provision has now been amended to provide that approval of the government will be required if the company concerned is operating in sectors/ activities which are under government approval route rather than capped sectors. Further no approval of the government is required for investment in automatic route sectors by way of swap of shares.

(xiii) Foreign Investment Promotion Board (FIPB): As per earlier FDI policy Foreign Investment Promotion Board (FIPB) considered proposals having total

foreign equity inflow up to ₹ 1,200 crore and proposals above ₹ 1,200 crore were placed for consideration of Cabinet Committee on Economic Affairs (CCEA). In order to achieve faster approvals of proposals, threshold limit for FIPB approval has been increased to ₹ 5,000 crore.

FDI Inflows

FDI inflows into the country have been quite significant since 2000-01. Its equity inflows have risen from US$ 2.46 billion in 2000-01 to US$ 40.00 billion in 2015-16. Under international practices of reporting, i.e. including equity capital, equity capital of unincorporated bodies, reinvested earnings and other capital, total FDI inflow was US$ 4.03 billion in 2000-01 which increased to US$ 55.46 billion in 2015-16. During 2015-16, US$ 40.00 billion was received as equity inflow. It is the highest ever for a particular financial year. Prior to this, the highest FDI equity inflow of US$ 35.12 billion was reported in 2011-12.

Table 19.5 : Growth FDI Inflows (US$ *billion*)

Amount in US$ million

Financial Year	International Practices	Percentage growth	FDI Equity Inflow(DIPP)	Percentage growth
2000-01	4,029	-	2,463	-
2001-02	6,130	(+) 52 per cent	4,065	(+) 65 per cent
2002-03	5,035	(-) 18 per cent	2,705	(-) 33 per cent
2003-04	4,322	(-) 14 per cent	2,188	(-) 19 per cent
2004-05	6,051	(+) 40 per cent	3,219	(+) 47 per cent
2005-06	8,961	(+) 48 per cent	5,540	(+) 72 per cent
2006-07	22,826	(+) 155 per cent	12,492	(+)125 per cent
2007-08	34,843	(+) 53 per cent	24,575	(+) 97 per cent
2008-09	41,873	(+) 20 per cent	31,396	(+) 28 per cent
2009-10	37,745	(-) 10 per cent	25,834	(-) 18 per cent
2010-11	34,847	(-) 08 per cent	21,383	(-) 17 per cent
2011-12	46,556	(+) 34 per cent	35,121	(+) 64 per cent
2012-13	34,298	(-) 26 per cent	22,423	(-) 36 per cent
2013-14 (P)	36,046	(+) 5 per cent	24,299	(+) 8 per cent
2014-15 (P)	45,148	(+) 25 per cent	30,931	(+) 27 per cent
2015-16 (P)	55,457	(+) 23 per cent	40,001	(+) 29 per cent
Total	4,24,167		2,88,635	

(P) All figures are provisional subject to reconciliation with RBI.

Table 19.6 : Financial Year-wise FDI Equity Inflows

(Amount in US$ million)

S. No	Sector	2010-11	2011-12	2012-13	2013-14	2014-15	2015-16	2016-17 upto May 16	Total
1	Metallurgical industries	1,098.14	1,786.14	1,466.23	567.63	359.34	456.31	79.51	5,813.29
2	Mining	79.51	142.65	57.89	12.73	684.39	520.67	0.77	1,498.62
3	Power	1,271.77	1,652.38	535.68	1,066.08	707.04	868.80	19.01	6,120.76
4	Non-conventional energy	214.40	452.17	1,106.52	414.25	615.95	776.51	126.45	3,706.25
5	Coal Production	0.00	0.00	0.00	2.96	0.00	0.00	0.00	2.96
6	Petroleum & natural gas	556.43	2,029.98	214.80	112.23	1,079.02	103.02	8.23	4,103.72
7	Boilers and Steam Generating plants	0.63	31.79	20.05	0.17	1.33	77.91	4.48	136.37
8	Prime mover (other than electrical generators)	166.44	313.75	184.60	212.78	230.70	159.13	16.60	1,283.99
9	Electrical equipment	153.90	566.39	195.87	134.31	574.83	444.88	43.14	2,113.32
10	Computer Software & Hardware	779.81	796.35	485.96	1,126.27	2,296.04	5,904.36	282.66	11,671.45
11	Electronics	59.72	194.41	38.24	132.58	96.84	208.39	18.07	748.25
12	Telecommunications	1,664.50	1,997.24	303.87	1,306.95	2,894.94	1,324.40	888.62	10,380.53
13	Information & Broadcasting (including print media)	412.11	675.96	404.04	428.52	254.96	1,009.34	39.20	3,224.13
14	Automobile industry	1,299.41	922.99	1,537.28	1,517.28	2,725.64	2,526.82	297.42	10,826.84
15	Air Transport (including Air Freight)	136.60	31.22	15.89	45.95	74.56	361.25	5.65	671.12
16	Sea Transport	300.51	129.36	64.62	20.49	333.22	429.30	9.31	1,286.80
17	Ports	10.92	0.00	0.00	0.31	1.90	0.00	0.00	13.14
18	Railway Related components	70.66	42.27	29.85	236.93	129.73	73.99	0.00	583.44
19	Industrial machinery	467.92	620.66	503.83	477.38	716.79	568.26	48.03	3,402.86
20	Machine Tools	11.63	127.87	101.39	64.52	24.06	126.38	12.03	467.90
21	Agricultural machinery	0.49	2.77	95.41	48.78	72.35	16.44	3.38	239.61
22	Earth-Moving machinery	1.77	16.40	5.10	34.44	30.11	97.66	16.43	201.92
23	Miscellaneous mechanical & engineering industries	108.67	1,295.34	89.45	288.13	186.69	274.57	23.76	2,266.61
24	Commercial, office & Household equipments	25.12	29.04	24.33	21.13	33.39	36.68	0.12	169.81
25	Medical and surgical appliances	32.22	141.61	83.02	173.48	145.93	173.26	0.43	749.95
26	Industrial instruments	25.48	3.99	0.58	0.53	0.85	7.42	0.00	38.86

27	Scientific instruments	2.49	7.08	73.28	45.08	32.34	6.36	0.19	166.81
28	Mathematical, surveying and drawing instruments	0.00	0.00	6.71	0.00	0.00	0.00	0.00	6.71
29	Fertilizers	18.18	32.60	42.55	20.65	225.32	20.93	0.08	360.31
30	Chemicals (other than fertilizers)	2,354.40	4,040.71	292.16	786.76	762.76	1,469.95	92.34	9,799.08
31	Photographic raw film and paper	0.81	0.00	0.00	0.00	0.75	0.00	0.00	1.56
32	Dye-Stuffs	5.37	0.58	0.00	0.00	54.89	3.32	0.00	64.16
33	Drugs & pharmaceuticals	209.38	3,232.28	1,123.46	1,279.34	1,497.74	754.26	452.86	8,549.31
34	Textiles (including dyed, printed)	129.65	164.19	103.89	198.86	197.42	230.13	9.50	1,033.64
35	Paper And Pulp (including paper products)	6.53	407.35	5.09	26.86	116.21	85.21	6.56	653.81
36	Sugar	0.17	4.44	12.26	3.08	27.77	105.85	0.60	154.17
37	Fermentation industries	57.71	69.70	107.21	814.58	225.38	202.36	28.86	1,505.81
38	Food processing industries	188.67	170.21	401.46	3,982.89	515.86	505.88	121.19	5,886.15
39	Vegetable oils and vanaspati	58.07	65.02	108.39	21.55	148.34	34.22	19.65	455.25
40	Soaps, Cosmetics & toilet preparations	102.90	222.08	160.07	108.44	177.22	193.26	0.77	964.74
41	Rubber goods	17.21	187.37	642.18	370.54	284.51	296.15	53.61	1,851.57
42	Leather, leather goods and pickers	9.26	8.30	46.70	6.14	34.21	17.13	0.00	121.74
43	Glue and gelatin	0.01	5.84	0.00	0.97	21.44	0.82	7.08	36.15
44	Glass	7.60	32.22	209.16	43.09	41.82	25.78	0.03	359.70
45	Ceramics	12.00	9.87	4.33	150.09	35.29	51.21	1.22	264.01
46	Cement and Gypsum products	637.68	267.90	12.38	254.01	208.99	19.69	0.10	1,400.75
47	Timber products	1.58	29.60	29.17	6.16	8.97	53.17	0.14	128.80
48	Defence industries	0.00	3.66	0.41	0.82	0.08	0.10	0.00	5.06
49	Consultancy services	274.84	289.89	142.32	285.85	458.13	517.47	61.89	2,030.38
50	Services Sector (Fin., banking, insurance, non Fin/business, outsourcing,R&D, courier, Tech. testing and analysis, other)	3,296.09	5,215.98	4,832.98	2,225.10	4,443.26	6,889.46	1,862.19	28,765.06
51	Hospital & diagnostic Centres	256.00	310.43	256.86	684.58	567.85	742.35	74.28	2,892.35
52	Education	37.94	105.62	172.20	262.09	78.86	230.78	19.86	907.34
53	Hotel & tourism	308.05	992.86	3,259.05	486.38	777.01	1,332.69	119.47	7,275.52
54	Trading	498.04	731.55	717.80	1,343.39	2,727.96	3,845.32	117.71	9,981.77

55	Retail trading	26.27	31.70	22.31	11.30	168.72	262.24	7.94	530.47
56	Agriculture services	43.90	49.02	161.47	91.01	59.95	84.65	1.82	491.82
57	Diamond, gold ornaments	19.59	36.30	52.61	42.56	280.18	58.54	64.27	554.05
58	Tea and coffee (processing & warehousing coffee & rubber)	3.12	5.32	0.27	5.86	1.43	1.12	0.00	17.12
59	Printing of books (including litho printing industry)	36.63	47.39	14.34	113.78	72.58	122.81	4.64	412.18
60	Coir	0.10	0.55	0.15	0.54	1.36	0.00	0.00	2.70
61	Construction (infrastructure) activities	675.07	386.28	283.89	485.37	870.25	4,510.71	196.38	7,407.95
62	Construction Development: townships, housing, built-up infrastructure & construction-development projects	1,663.03	3,140.78	1,332.49	1,226.05	769.14	112.55	16.12	8,260.16
63	Miscellaneous industries	1,475.97	813.38	229.49	468.74	765.88	668.77	60.54	4,482.77
	Grand Total	21,383.05	35,120.80	22,423.58	24,299.33	30,930.50	40,000.98	5,345.21	1,79,503.452

Simplifying the Business Environment

The Department of Industrial Policy and Promotion (DIPP) in collaboration with the Industry Association CII is conducting state workshops with Industry and Industry Associations to make regulations conducive for business including establishment of online single-window, adoption of national and international best practices, simplification of tax-regime, etc.

e-Biz Mission Mode Project

The government has initiated the e-Biz Project, a Mission Mode Project under the National e-Governance Project, to provide online registration, filing payment services to investors and business houses.

Starting a new business in India requires an entrepreneur to register with various regulatory authorities and obtain several licenses, clearances, No Objection Certificates, approvals, etc. Information about these registrations, licenses, clearances and approvals contained in multiple Acts, rules and procedures are difficult to locate and are scattered across a number of Departmental websites. Entrepreneurs are forced to sift through a maze of information to assess their licensing requirements.

An online e-biz Mission Mode Project under the National e-Governance Plan has been conceptualized by the DIPP. The project aims to create an ecosystem by making all business and investment related regulatory services across Central, state and local governments available on a single portal. The project has been designed on a PPP model, and the concessionaire has been awarded the project for a period of 10 years. The first 3 years of the term would be the pilot phase, while the remaining 7 years will be the expansion phase, wherein the project will be expanded to cover the whole country. During the pilot phase, a total of 50 (26 central + 24 state) services are envisaged to be implemented across five pilot states viz., Andhra Pradesh, Delhi, Haryana, Maharashtra and Tamil Nadu. Recently, another five pilot states have been added, namely Odisha, Punjab, Rajasthan, Uttar Pradesh and West Bengal.

The e-Biz portal currently provides 20 Central government services pertaining to pre-registration, registration and filing services. In addition, 14 services of Andhra Pradesh, 14 services of Odisha and two services of NCT of Delhi have been launched. Also, 3 joined-up service (Composite Application Form and one-time payment for multiple services) named INC7 with 7 services, INC29 with 5 services and 5 services under Labour Act has been launched.

Invest India

The Government of India has established "Invest India" as the National Investment Promotion and Facilitation Agency, as a joint venture between the Department of Industrial Policy and Promotion (DIPP), state governments and the Federation of Indian Chamber of Commerce and Industry (FICCI). A full-fledged "Investment Facilitation Cell" has been set-up in 'Invest India', which supports all investment queries apart from handholding and liaisoning with various agencies on behalf of potential investors.

Intellectual Property Rights

The term Intellectual Property (IP) reflects the idea that its subject matter is product of mind or intellect. These could be in the form of patents; trademarks; geographical indications; industrial designs; semiconductor integrated circuits layout-design; plant variety protection and copyright. IP, protected through law, like any other form of property, can be a matter of trade, i.e., it can be owned, bequeathed, sold or bought. Major features that distinguish it from other forms are their intangibility and non-exhaustion by consumption. IP is also foundation of knowledge-based economy. It pervades all sectors of economy and is increasingly becoming important for ensuring competitiveness of enterprises. All aspects of IPRs are administered by DIPP. These are administered through the Office of the Controller General of Patents, Designs and Trade Marks (CGPDTM), a subordinate office, with headquarters at Mumbai.

The details of Controller General of Patents, Designs and Trade Marks are available at http://www.ipindia.nic.in.

Intellectual Property Appellate Board

An Intellectual Property Appellate Board (IPAB) has been set up at Chennai to hear appeals against the decisions of Registrar of Trademarks, Geographical Indications and the Controller of Patents (additional information can be seen at http://www.ipabindia.in).

Other IP Legislations

While DIPP administers laws regarding patents, trade marks, designs and geographical indications, copyright and the semiconductor integrated circuits layout-design, other aspects of IPR are protected as : new varieties of plants are protected through the Protection of Plant Varieties and Farmers' Rights Act, 2001 - administered by the Department of Agriculture and Cooperation. The Patents Office is also bound to follow the scheme of the Patents Act, 1970 and the Patents Rules, 2003 as well as the provisions under the Biological Diversity Act, 2002. Form I of the Patents Rules, 2003 contains an undertaking that is to be signed by applicant to the effect that the invention, as disclosed in specification, uses biological material from India and necessary permission from competent authority shall be submitted by him / them before grant of patent to him / them.

Promotion of IPR Regime

DIPP has taken a multi-pronged strategy to develop an Intellectual Property regime in the country to promote creativity and to develop culture of respect for innovations and creativity. These are: meeting international obligations; safeguarding national interests; modernize administration; and creating awareness.

Patents (Amendment) Rules

The Patents Rules were framed in 2003. These Rules were subsequently amended in 2004, 2006, 2012 and 2014. A fresh amendment of the Rules was considered in 2015.

Trade Mark (Amendment) Act

The Trade Mark (Amendment) Act, 20I0 enabled India to accede to the Madrid Protocol which is a simple, facilitative and cost-effective system for registration of International Trade Marks. India's membership of the Madrid Protocol provides opportunity to Indian companies to register their trade marks in member countries of the Protocol through filing a single application in one language and by paying a one-time fee in one currency. India has acceded to the Protocol in 2013. The Madrid Protocol came into force in India since 2013.

IPR Awareness Programmes

Awareness creation is one of the major planks of the modernization scheme of IP system, as this will educate stakeholders about benefits of registration of their rights as also educate general public, particularly business community, on perils of infringement of IPRs held by others/dealing in pirated and counterfeit products. These programmes are also expected to sensitize enforcement agencies such as state police forces, judiciary, etc. After adoption of National IPR Policy in 2016, the government, in association with various industry associations, has organized 19 awareness programmes on IPRs, including patents, across various states in 2016.

During 2015-16, IPO has conducted many awareness programmes for stakeholders. IPO provided funds for 27 IP awareness programmes and participated in 7 IP related-national conferences/exhibitions. IPO officials participated as Resource Persons in 48 IP awareness programmes/seminars at various places in the country. Besides, Rajiv Gandhi National Institute of Intellectual Property Management conducted 53 training and awareness programmes on IPRs during 2015-16.

National Design Policy

Announced in 2007, this Policy envisages a key role for design in enhancing competitiveness of the industry. Focus is on spread of design education, branding of Indian designs and establishment of a Design Council. This period witnessed both expansion and updation of India's premier design institution i.e., the National Institute of Design (NID) with three campuses at Ahmedabad (main campus), Gandhinagar (PG Campus), and Bengaluru (R&D Campus). India Design Council (IDC), a society under the aegis of DIPP, was constituted on 2.3.2009, a mandate of the policy. The National Institute Design Act, 2014 has been notified in 2014 for declaration of NID, Ahmedabad as an Institution of National Importance.

NID, Vijayawada was set up at its transit campus at Acharya Nagarjuna University and the academic session has already been started for 2015-16 for its four-year Undergraduate programmes. The admission process for 2016-17 has also been completed. NID, Kurukshetra was also set up in temporary accommodation in government polytechnic building for 2016-17.

National IPR Policy

National IPR Policy was framed and approved in 2016. This Policy lays down the following seven objectives: IPR Awareness: outreach and promotion: to create public awareness about the economic, social and cultural benefits of IPRs among all sections of society; generation of IPRs: to stimulate the generation of IPRs; Legal and Legislative Framework: to have strong and effective IPR laws, which balance the interests of rights owners with larger public interest; Administration and Management: to modernize and strengthen service-oriented IPR administration; Commercialization of IPR: get value for IPRs through commercialization; Enforcement and Adjudication: to strengthen enforcement and adjudicatory mechanisms for combating IPR infringements; and Human Capital Development: to strengthen and expand human resources, institutions and capacities for teaching, training, research and skill building in IPRs.

Cell for IPR Promotion and Management

Cell for IPR Promotion and Management (CIPAM) has been constituted to facilitate promotion, creation and commercialization of IP assets. CIPAM shall be a professional body to cater to the need for promotion, creation and commercialization of IP assets in the country. It is not proposed to create any new posts for CIPAM. The tasks shall be undertaken through the existing manpower and outsourcing. CIPAM will also draw on resources of other ministries/ departments. CIPAM will consist of functional units, which will address the seven identified objectives of the IPR Policy.

IPR Initiatives in the International Fora

India has taken a lead role in the discussions in the United Nations specialized agency for intellectual property rights, namely, the World Intellectual Property Organization. It played a proactive role in building consensus for renewal of the mandate of the Inter-Governmental Committee (IGC) on Traditional Knowledge (TK), Genetic Resources (GR) and Traditional Cultural Expressions (TCEs) and was successful in getting the IGC to begin negotiations for an effective international legal instrument aimed at providing protection to TK, GR and TCEs.

Bilateral Negotiations and IPR

India is negotiating an IPR Chapter as part of the proposed India EU Bilateral Trade and Investment Agreement (BTIA), European Free Trade Association (EFTA) and Regional Comprehensive Economic Partnership (RCEP) Agreement keeping in view India's national legislations and also various multilateral agreements.

Modernization and Strengthening of Intellectual Property Offices

During the 11th Five Year Plan, Modernization and Strengthening of Intellectual Property Offices was implemented. The total Plan outlay for it was ₹ 300 crore. The said scheme has been continued in the 12th Five Year Plan with a total outlay of ₹ 258 crore. The Scheme aims at strengthening the capabilities of Intellectual Property Offices in the country and to develop a vibrant Intellectual Property Regime. It also aims to develop the modern infrastructure for the Indian Patent Offices to function as an International Search Authority and International Preliminary Examining Authority under the Patent Cooperation Treaty, for which, the WIPO had recognized Indian Patent Office in October, 2007 to join an exclusive group of 17 countries / organizations.

Rajiv Gandhi National Institute of Intellectual Property Management

The Rajiv Gandhi National Institute of Intellectual Property Management (RGNIIPM) was set up in 2012 at Nagpur as an institute of international importance which would provide training, education, research and function as a think tank on Intellectual Property Rights. In the year 2015-16, it conducted 53 training and awareness programmes on IPRs. This included 20 awareness programmes for various stakeholders and 33 training programmes on IPRs for 1 to 5 days duration.

There has been an increase of 9.7 per cent in filing of Patent Applications in 2015-16 over 2014-15.

Table 19.7 (a): Trend in Patent Applications

Year	2004-05	2005-06	2006-07	2007-08	2008-09	2009-10	2010-11	2011-12	2012-13	2013-14	2014-15	2015-16	2016-17*
Filed	17,466	24,505	28,940	35,218	6,812	34,287	39,400	43,197	43,674	42,950	42,774	46,916	14,564
Examined	14,813	11,569	14,119	11,751	6,069	10,296	11,208	11,031	12,268	18,306	22,631	16,853	3,452
Granted	1,911	4,320	7,539	15,316	6,168	16,061	7,509	4,381	4,126	4,225	5,978	6,322	2,181
Disposals				15,795	17,136	11,339	12,851	8,488	9,027	11,672	14,532	21,350	5,145

* *up to July 2016*

Table 19.7 (b): Trend in Design Applications

There has been an increase of 18.4 per cent in filing of design applications in 2015-16 over 2014-15.

Year	2006-07	2007-08	2008-09	2009-10	2010-11	2011-12	2012-13	2013-14	2014-15	2015-16	2016-17*
Filed	5,521	6,402	6,557	6,092	7,589	8,373	8,337	8,533	9,382	11,108	3,611
Examined	4,976	6,183	6,446	6,266	6,277	6,511	6,771	7,281	7,459	7,545	3,286
Registered	4,250	4,928	4,772	6,025	9,206	6,590	7,250	7,178	7,171	7,904	1,691

* *up to July 2016*

Table 19.7 (c): Trend in Trade marks Applications

There has been increase of 34.5 per cent in filing of trademark applications in 2015-16 over 2014-15.

Year	2006-07	2007-08	2008-09	2009-10	2010-11	2011-12	2012-13	2013-14	2014-15	2015-16	2016-17*
Filed	1,03,419	1,23,514	1,30,172	1,41,943	1,79,317	1,83,588	1,94,216	2,00,005	2,10,501	2,83,060	93,874
Examined	85,185	63,605	1,05,219	25 875	2,05,065	1,16,263	2,02,385	2,03,086	1,68,026	2,67,861	1,36,869
Registered	1,09,361	1,00,857	1,02,257	67 490	1,15,472	51,765	44,361	67,873	41,583	55,045	16,659
Disposal			1,26,540	76 310	1,32,507	57,867	69,736	1,04,753	83,652	1,16,167	24,301

* *up to July 2016*

Table 19.7 (d): Geographical Indications

Year	2006- 07	2007- 08	2008-09	2009-10	2010-11	2011- 12	2012-13	2013 -14	2014-15	2015-16	2016-17*
Filed	33	37	44	40	27	148	24	75	47	17	18
Registered	3	31	45	14	29	23	21	22	20	26	11

** up to July 2016*

Table 19.7 (e): Comparative Trends of IPRs Granted/Registered

Year	2006- 07	2007- 08	2008-09	2009-10	2010-11	2011- 12	2012-13	2013 -14	2014-15	2015-16	2016-17*
Patents	7,539	15,316	16,061	6,168	7,509	4,381	4,126	4,225	5,978	6,322	2,181
Designs	4,250	4,928	4,772	6,025	9,206	6,590	7,250	7,178	7,171	7,904	1,691
Trademarks	1,09,361	1,00,857	1,02,257	67,490	1,15,472	51,765	44,361	67,873	41,583	65,045	16,659
Geographical Indications	3	31	45	14	29	23	21	22	20	26	11

** up to July 2016*

Freight Subsidy Scheme

In order to facilitate the process of industrialization in hilly, remote and inaccessible areas, in terms of subsiding industrial units for transportation of their finished product and raw material Freight Subsidy Scheme (FSS) was introduced in 2013 replacing Transport Subsidy Scheme of 1971. The scheme is applicable to all industrial units (barring plantation, refineries and power generating units both in public and private sectors irrespective of their size). The incentives under the scheme are available for all 8 states of North East, Himachal Pradesh, Uttarakhand, J&K, Darjeeling district of West Bengal, Andaman & Nicobar and Lakshadweep. Subsidy on the transport cost for transportation of raw material and finished goods to and from location of the unit and the designated rail-head is admissible. For North East states, J&K and UTs, subsidy is 90 per cent. For HP, Uttarakhand and Darjeeling districts of West Bengal it is 75 per cent of transport cost. However, for movement of goods within NER, subsidy is 50 per cent on finished goods and 90 per cent on raw material. No subsidy is available for intra state movement of goods. The benefits of subsidy are for five years from commencement of commercial production by units. Salient features include:-subsidy on transportation of fly ash has been disallowed; sunset clause has been introduced so that the scheme terminates after five years from its date of notification; provision for subsidy for an additional period of five years has been made applicable for MSME; and plantations, refineries, power generating units, coke industry and the units producing tobacco and manufactured tobacco substitutes, pan masala and plastic carry bags of less than 20 microns are in the negative list.

North East Industrial and Investment Promotion

The North East Industrial and Investment Promotion Policy(NEIIPP), 2007 is a revised version of the erstwhile North East Industrial Policy, 1997, and has been put in place till 2017. The scheme covers eight north east states recognized under North Eastern Council (NEC) including Sikkim. It provides incentives to all new as well as existing units which go for industrial expansion located anywhere in this region and which commence commercial production within 10 years from the date of notification of NEIIPP, 2007 for a period of 10 years from the date of commercial production. Exceptions are the industries considered hazardous to public health and environment such as tobacco and its substitutes, pan masala, plastic carry bags, refinery products, etc. Incentives are provided in terms of excise duty exemption based on value addition norms specified by the Department of Revenue besides income tax exemption, capital investment subsidy, central interest subsidy and comprehensive insurance. Capital investment subsidy is provided at the rate of 30 per cent of the investment in plant and machinery up to ₹ 1.50 crore through automatic route, ₹ 1.50 crore to ₹ 30 crore with the approval of Empowered Committee and above ₹ 30 crore with the approval of the Union Cabinet. Similarly, under central interest subsidy scheme component, the rate of subsidy provided is 3 per cent of the working capital loan. However, under central comprehensive insurance scheme, industrial units are eligible for reimbursement of cent per cent insurance premium paid for the insurance policy of capital assets.

Modified Industrial Infrastructure Upgradation Scheme

Industrial Infrastructure Upgradation Scheme (IIUS) was launched in 2003 with the objective of enhancing industrial competitiveness of domestic industry by providing quality infrastructure. Modified Industrial Infrastructure Upgradation Scheme (MIIUS) was notified in 2013. Under MIIUS, projects have been undertaken to upgrade infrastructure in existing industrial parks/ estates/ areas. Greenfield projects have also been undertaken in backward areas and North Eastern Region (NER) under the scheme. Projects are being implemented by the State Implementing Agency (SIA) of the state government. Central Grant up to 50 per cent of the project cost with a ceiling of ₹ 50.00 crore is provided under MIIUS with at least 25 per cent contributions of state implementing agency and in case of North Eastern States, the central grant and minimum contribution of the SIA are up to 80 per cent and 10 per cent respectively. A two stage approval mechanism has been retained in the MIIUS. Final approval has been accorded to 24 projects with central grant amounting to ₹ 604.71 crore and 6 projects with central grant of ₹ 129.91 crore are at 'in-principle' approval stage. Central assistance of ₹ 154.35 crore has been released to 18 projects in 2016 under MIIUS.

Table 19.8 : IIUS/MIIUS Projects

(₹ in crore)

FYP	No. of Sanctioned Projects	Total Project Cost	Sanctioned	Released (Up to 03.08.2016)
10th (IIUS)	25 (23 completed and 2 under implementation)	1558.54	893	870.52
11th (IIUS)	12 (4 completed and 8 under implementation)	968.19	633	530.02
Total (IIUS)	37 (27 completed and 10 under implementation)	2526.73	1526	1400.54
12th (MIIUS)	24	1697.42	604.71	154.35
Total	61	4224.15	2130.71	1554.89

Package for Special Category States of Jammu and Kashmir, Himachal Pradesh and Uttarakhand

Jammu and Kashmir

New Industrial policy and other concessions for the State of J&K were introduced by the DIPP in 2002 for a period of ten years. The incentives/ concessions provided for industrial development in the state are (i) central Capital Investment Subsidy Scheme, 2002; (ii) Central Interest Subsidy scheme, 2002; (iii) central Comprehensive Insurance Scheme, 2002; (iv) Cent per cent income tax exemption allowed to all new units for initial period of 5 years and thereafter, 30 per cent for companies and 25 per cent for units other than companies, for a further period of five years, under Section 80- IB of Income Tax Act,1961 and; (v) excise duty exemption. The package of incentives for J&K expired on June 14, 2012. However, the package has been extended for a further period of five years to June 2017 with certain modifications.

Himachal Pradesh and Uttarakhand

New industrial policy and other concessions for Himachal Pradesh and Uttarakhand were introduced by the DIPP in 2003 for a period of ten years. Details of incentives/concessions provided for industrial development in the states are (i) Central Capital Investment Subsidy Scheme, 2003; (ii) Cent per cent income tax exemption for an initial period of five years and thereafter 30 per cent for companies and 25 per cent for other than companies for a further period of five years under Section 80-C of Income Tax Act, 1961 and (iii) Central Excise Duty exemption: 100 per cent exemption on outright basis to the industrial units set up or expanded in these states was available till 2010. The scheme expired in 2013. However, the package has been further extended during the 12th Plan period for a further period up to 2017.

Table 19.9 : Investment made, number of industrial units set-up and employment

S. No.	Name of the State	Investment (₹ in crore)	No. of Industrial Units set up	Employment generated (Persons)
1.	Jammu and Kashmir	4219.501	14778	107541
2.	Himachal Pradesh	15983.45	11404	130633
3.	Uttarakhand	36165.32	33174	263744

Indian Leather Development Programme

Indian Leather Development Programme (ILDP) aims at augmenting raw material base through modernization and technology upgradation of leather units, addressing environmental concerns, human resource development, supporting traditional leather artisans, addressing infrastructure constraints and establishing institutional facilities. Total outlay approved for 12th Plan period is ₹ 990.36 crore for implementation of following six sub-schemes:

Integrated Development of Leather Sector (IDLS): Under this sub-scheme, assistance is provided for technology up-gradation/modernization and/or expansion and setting up of a new unit in leather sector. The sub-scheme provides assistance in form of investment grant to the extent of 30 per cent of cost of new plant and machinery for micro and small enterprises and 20 per cent of cost of new plant and machinery for other units subject to a ceiling of ₹ 2 crore for each product line.

Human Resource Development (HRD): HRD mission targets potential work force for leather sector and lays stress on skill development and technical development. This project is intended to train and prepare individuals to be fit to work in medium to large industrial units. Upgradation of skills of persons already employed in the sector, besides training for trainers/supervisors, is also undertaken. Under Placement Linked Skill Development Training, at least 75 per cent of trained persons are placed in the industry as per the guidelines.

Support to Artisan: There are various clusters in India making traditional footwear and other leather goods. The aim of this scheme is to promote the clusters at various forums as they are an integral part of rural Indian economy and have potential for generating local employment and export. The artisan clusters all over the country would be supported for enhancing their design and product development, capacity building, providing marketing support, establishing common facility center and marketing support/linkage. The broad objective of this component is to ensure better and higher returns to the artisans resulting into socio-economic upliftment.

Establishment of Institutional Facilities: This sub-scheme of ILDP aims at providing institutional facilities by way of establishing new campuses of Fiber Distributed Data Interface to meet the growing demand of the leather industry for footwear technologies, designers, supervisors and mechanics. Two new branches of FDDI in Punjab and Gujarat are being set up.

Leather Technology, Innovation and Environmental Issues: This sub-scheme provides financial support to leather cluster to meet the prescribed pollution control discharge norms and environmental issues. This covers establishment/ expansion/ up gradation of Common Effluent Treatment Plants, Technology benchmarking for implementing cleaner technologies for environment management, utilization of solid waste from tanneries and conducting workshops to educate and train the tanners and tannery workers.

Mega Leather Cluster: Major objective of developing mega leather clusters is to create state of the art infrastructure and to integrate production chain in a manner that caters to business needs of leather industry in the domestic market and exports. These mega clusters will assist entrepreneurs to set up units with modern infrastructure, latest technology, and adequate training and Human Resource Development (HRD) inputs. Mega Leather Clusters (MLC) for development of leather industry will have minimum common facilities. The project cost would cover various infrastructure developments like core infrastructure, special infrastructure, production infrastructure, HRD and social infrastructure, R&D infrastructure and export services related infrastructure.

Performance of Selected Industries

The figures of production are based on estimates made from production returns furnished by industrial units and therefore may not always be true reflection of the entire production of the industry concerned. Trade figures are based on estimates of Department of Commerce.

Cement Industry

Cement is one of the most technologically advanced industries in the country. The industry plays a crucial role in the development of housing and infrastructure sector of the economy. Price and distribution control of cement has been removed since 1989 and cement industry has been de-licensed in 1991 under Industrial (Development & Regulation) Act, 1951. Since then, cement industry has progressed well both in capacity/production and as well as in process technology.

India is producing different varieties of cement like Ordinary Portland Cement (OPC), Portland Pozzolana Cement (PPC), Portland Blast Furnace Slag Cement (PBFS), Oil Well Cement, White Cement, etc. These different varieties of cement are produced as per Bureau of Indian Standard (BIS) specifications and its quality is comparable with the best in the world. Indian cement industry has managed to keep pace with global technological advancement. Induction of advanced technology has helped industry immensely to improve its efficiency by conserving energy, fuel and addressing environmental concerns.

India is the second largest manufacturer of cement after China in the world. Cement industry comprises 190 large cement plants operating under 64 companies with an installed capacity of 324.50 million tonnes. There are approximately 360 mini cement plants with an estimated capacity of 11.10 million tonnes per annum. Total cement production was 256.04 million tonnes and 270.09 million tonnes during 2013-14 and 2014-15 respectively. The Department collects cess on cement @ ₹ 0.75 per metric tonne of cement manufactured/produced from medium and large industries. The cess collected on cement for the years 2013-14 and 2014-15 are ₹ 19.02 cr and ₹ 19.06 cr respectively and deposited in the Consolidated Fund of India. Out of this fund, a sum of ₹ 2.20 cr was given under Development Council for Cement Industry for the year 2014-15 for recurring expenditure on R & D activities for cement industry.

Ceramic Industry

The ceramic industry in the country is about 50 years old. It comprises ceramic tiles, sanitaryware and crockery. Ceramic products are manufactured both in large and small-scale sectors with wide variation in type, size, quality and standard by the national and regional players. Ceramic tile industry is estimated to be ₹ 24,000 crore by 2015 is growing at around 12-13 per cent annually. India continues to rank third in terms of production and consumption of tiles in the world after China and Brazil. The industry gives direct and indirect employment to over 1.5 lakh people across India. With majority of raw materials necessary for production of tiles available, the tile industry has kept pace with the times embracing modern technology in designing and manufacturing and is capable of producing world class tiles. The industry has huge potential to grow at much faster pace at 15-16 per cent per annum. The per capita consumption in India is one of the lowest in the world, so, there is enormous growth potential more particularly in view of Government's thrust on sanitation, housing and urbanization and emphasis on "Make in India".

The tile industry have welcomed the government campaign with great enthusiasm and are fully committed to working hand in hand with the government to make the mission of 'Make in India', 'Housing for All' and 'Swachh Bharat' into a reality. The sector has shown considerable growth in spite of slowdown of the economy and factors leading to increase in production costs. The success of the industry in turn would generate significant employment opportunities, open up the vast export potential earning valuable foreign exchange for the country.

Tyre and Tubes Industry

Tyres play an integral role to ensure mobility including movement of passengers and essential goods across the urban and rural landscape of the country using all types of vehicles ranging from carts, tractors, trucks and buses to the latest generation passenger cars that ply on modern expressways. All types of tyres are manufactured in India. These tyres include moped tyre weighing 1.5 kg to off the road tyres for earthmovers which weigh 1.5 tonnes, bias ply tyres to rugged all steel radial truck tyres to high performance passenger car radial and tubeless tyres, etc. India is one of the few countries worldwide which has attained self-sufficiency in manufacturing a wide range of tyres for all applications. With the objective of ensuring safety of human lives and vehicles and also availability of quality products, a Quality (Control) Order for Pneumatic Tyres and Tubes for Automotive Vehicles was also notified by the Department in 2009. This prohibits import, sale or distribution of pneumatic tyres and tubes which do not conform to specified Bureau of Indian Standard and which do not bear the standard mark. Indian Tyre industry consists of 39 companies with 60 tyre manufacturing plants. The large tyre companies are namely, MRF Ltd., Apollo Tyres, JK Tyres, CEAT, Goodyear, Modi Rubber, etc. Three Indian companies (MRF Ltd., Apollo Tyres and JK Tyres) are in the list of top 25 global tyre companies. Domestic tyre production during 2015-16 was 2,441.37 lakh tyres against 2,605.19 lakh tyres during 2014-15. Domestic tyre production during April-June 2016 was 574.66 lakh. The Indian tyre companies have a consistent track record of exporting tyres to over 75 countries. The export of tyres has fallen to ₹ 9,052.23 crore in 2015-16 as against ₹ 10,070.91 crore during 2014-15. The export of tyres and tubes was to the tune of ₹ 2,381.62 crore during April-June, 2016. The Import of tyres and tubes during April-June, 2016 was for a value of ₹ 901.84 crore. The import has risen to the value of ₹ 3,375.27 crore in 2015-16 as against ₹ 2,707.95 crore during previous year.

Rubber Goods Industry

The rubber goods industry excluding tyre and tubes consists of 4,550 small and tiny units generating about 5.50 lakh direct jobs. Rubber industry manufactures a wide range of products like rubber cots and aprons, contraceptives, footwear, rubber hoses, cables, camelback, battery boxes, latex products, conveyor belts, surgical gloves, balloons, rubber moulded goods, etc. Main raw materials used by the rubber goods manufacturing industry are natural rubber, various types of synthetic rubber, carbon black, rubber chemicals, etc. The turnover of this industry in 2015-16 was ₹ 41,965 crore as against ₹ 32,000 crore in 2014-15. Rubber goods worth ₹ 6,010.18 crore were exported in 2015-16 as against ₹ 6,543.36 crore in 2014-15. Goods worth ₹ 1,451.93 crore were exported during April-June, 2016. Import of rubber goods industry during 2015-16 has fallen to a value of ₹ 11,019.22 crore as against ₹ 12,167.35 crore of the previous year. The import of rubber goods during April-June, 2016 was for a value of ₹ 2,843.73 crore.

Cigarette Industry: The cigarette industry is an agro-based labour intensive industry. Cigarettes are included in the First Schedule to the Industries (Development & Regulations) Act, 1951 and require Industrial License. The production of cigarettes during 2015-16 was 7,93,338.21 lakhs (in numbers). The export and import of tobacco or manufactured tobacco substitutes during 2015-16 has been ₹ 80,423.13 lakhs and ₹ 13,103.01 lakhs respectively.

Paints and Allied Products Industry: The paints and allied industry which has been exempted from compulsory licensing, mainly consists of paints, enamels, varnishes, pigments, printing inks, etc. These play a vital role in the economy by way of protecting national assets from corrosion. These items are manufactured both in the organizer and small scale sector. The production of paints of all kinds and printing ink during 2015-16 was 7,98,715.22tonnes and 2,29,693.88 tonnes respectively. The export and import of these products in the year 2015-16 were ₹ 1,25,543.81 lakhs and ₹ 3,11,624.50 lakhs respectively.

Glass Industry: Glass industry comes under the category of delicensed. Glass industry covers seven items such as sheet and flat glass (including sheet, float, figured, wired, safety, mirror glass), glass fiber and glass wool, hollow glassware, laboratory glassware, table and kitchen glassware, glass bangles and other glassware. There has been growing acceptability of the Indian flat glass products in the global market. The production of glass sheet, toughened glass, fibre glass, glass bottles during 2015-16 was 87,544.08 thousand square metres, 31,17,950.40 square metres, 49,967.40 tonnes, 9,18,969 tonnes respectively. The export and import during the year 2015-16 were ₹ 1,97,231.81 lakhs and ₹ 2,05,725.40 lakhs respectively.

Paper Industry: India continued to rein as one of the fastest growing paper market in the world. The growing knowledge base coupled with synergistic contributions from flagship schemes of the government, namely, Sarva Shiksha Abhiyan (SSA), Rashtriya Madhyamik Shiksha Abhiyan (RMSA), Inclusive Education for the Disabled at Secondary School (IEDSS), Adult Education and Skill Development Scheme, and Right to Education assured a robust demand for paper and paper board. The industry was delicenced in July, 1997. As per the present policy, FDI up to 100 per cent is allowed on the automatic route for the pulp and paper sector. There are around 800 units which manufacture paper, paper board and newsprint, with an installed capacity of nearly 22 million tonnes out of which nearly 3 million tonnes are lying idle. The total operating capacity is around 19 million tonnes. The Indian paper industry is fragmented, consisting of small, medium and large paper mills having capacity ranging from 10 to 1,500 tonnes per day. These units use wood and agro residues as well as recovered paper as raw material. The production share of these units is around 30 per cent, 20 per cent and 60 per cent respectively.

Paper and Paperboard Segment: Indigenous paper and paperboard segment produces all the main varieties of paper that are in demand in the market viz., writing and printing paper (38 per cent), packaging grade paper (54 per cent), newsprint (8 per cent) and specialty paper (1 per cent). However, certain speciality paper such as coated paper, security papers and cheque paper, etc., are being imported in the country. The production of paper in the year 2014-15 stood at 14.78 million tonnes as compared to 14.24 million tonnes in the previous year. During the year 2014-15, 1.36 million tonnes of paper and paperboard was imported whereas in the previous year this figure stood at 1.19 million tonnes. On the other hand about 0.60 million tonnes of paper and paperboard was exported in the year 2014-15, up from a figure of 0.55 million tonnes in the year 2013-14.

Newsprint Segment: The newsprint sector in the country is governed by the Newsprint Control Order (NCO), 2004. The mills listed under the Schedule to this order are exempted from excise duty, subject to actual user condition. At present, there are 121 mills registered under the Schedule to the NCO. However, only 62 are producing newsprint with an operating installed capacity of 2.5 million tonnes per annum. The domestic production of newsprint fell from 1.44 million tonnes in 2013-14 to 1.24 million tons in 2014-15. Nearly half of the newsprint demand in the country is met by imports.

Salt Industry: India continues to hold third position in the production of salt in the world after China and the USA with annual production of 268.87 lakh tonnes and second largest producer of iodized salt, next to China. From an era of shortfall and import at the time of independence, the country has made spectacular progress. In a very short period of time, sufficiency was achieved and made a dent in the export market. Since then, the country has never looked back. Salt production and exports are as follows:

Table 19.10 : Performance of Salt Sector

(Figure in lakh tonnes)

	Production			Export		
Salt Industry	2013-14	2014-15	2015-16	2013-14	2014-15	2015-16
	230.19	268.87	276.44	59.61	56.76	65.67

In 2016-17 (upto May) 92.23 lakh tonnes of salt have been produced. Exports accounted for 12.15 lakh tonnes.

Explosives: There are 67 factories licensed under Explosives Rules in the medium and small scale sector, engaged in the production of explosives. There are 138 site mixed explosive units and 119 licenses issued for manufacture of various class/division of cartridge explosives and accessories. Site mixed explosives (SME) has a consolidated licensed capacity of 1536510.5 MT of explosive production. Gun powder has a consolidated licensed capacity of 855.55 MT while slurry/emulsion explosives 7,04,296 MT, PETN/cast booster/TNT has 21359.67 MT, safety fuse has 261.6 Million metres, detonating fuse has 788 million meters and detonators has 1166.15 million meters of consolidated licensed capacity.

Electrical Wires and Cable Industry

Electrical wires and cable industry is one of the earliest industries established in the country in the field of electrical products. A wide range of wires and cables are manufactured in the country which includes communication cables such as jelly filled telephone cables, optic fibre cables, local area network cables, switchboard cables, co-axial cables, VSAT cables, electrical cables such as electrical wires, winding wires, automotive/battery cables, UPS cables, flexible wires, low voltage power cables and EHT power cables. The power cable industry may be mainly divided into four segments viz: house wiring (up to 440V), LT (1.1 to 3.3 kV), HT (11 to 66 kV), EHV (66 kV and above). Well-established R & D facilities are key factors for development of this industry. In India, renowned laboratories like Central Power Research Institute (CPRI), Electrical Research and Development Association (ERDA) are well equipped with the most advanced product testing facilities to meet international standards. The production of insulated cable and wires of all kinds in 2014-15 was 64.55 lakh core km. and in 2015-16 is 65.85 core km. The export and import of wires and cables in 2014-15 was ₹ 4,306.74 crore and ₹ 5,820.33 crore respectively whereas in 2015-16 the same was ₹ 4,841.66 crore and ₹ 5,461.80 crore respectively.

Transmission Towers

Transmission towers support the high voltage transmission lines which carry electricity over long distance. There is an increasing shift in India to have larger power stations, particularly mega and ultra-mega power projects. Consequently while there would be fewer but larger power generating stations, the demand for transmission of energy would grow substantially. The move to integrate India's transmission networks through a national grid of inter-regional transmission lines will facilitate transfer of power from surplus regions to deficit regions. The industry has facilities for testing transmission towers up to 1000 kV with the objective of catering to future growth of transmission systems in the country as well as to export demand. The export and import of transmission towers in 2014-15 was ₹ 1,929.97 crore and ₹ 31.12 crore respectively whereas in 2015-16 the same was ₹ 2,494.84 crore and ₹ 31.26 crore respectively.

Cranes

Cranes and hoists are an important category of material handling equipment required by almost all sectors across the industry. Wide range of cranes are manufactured in the country and these include Electric Overhead Travelling (EOT) cranes, mobile cranes, ladle cranes, hydraulic decks, crab cranes, floating cranes, controller cranes, etc. There is a good potential for growth of this sector in view of increased industrial activities in various fields as well as construction industry. The production of cranes in 2014-15 was 17,063.63 tonnes and in 2015-16 is 14,597.16 tonnes. The export and import of cranes in 2014-15 was ₹ 689.23 crore and ₹1,852.07 crore respectively whereas in 2015-16 the same was ₹ 1,173.08 crore and ₹ 2,395.92 crore respectively.

Lifts and Escalators

The use of lifts and escalators is increasing rapidly due to substantial investments in construction of multi-storied housing complexes, large malls and supermarkets of international standards, modernization of airports and railway stations apart from industrial sectors. A wide range of lifts and escalators are manufactured in India. These include single speed, double speed, gearless, hydraulic, servo and variable voltage variable frequency (VVVF) elevators. The production of lifts in 2014-15 was of ₹ 1,323.98 crore and in 2015-16 of ₹ 1,126.36 crore. The export and import of lifts, escalators, conveyers etc., in 2014-15 was ₹ 520.15 crore and ₹ 2,329.53 crore respectively whereas in 2015-16 the same was ₹ 556.17 crore and ₹ 2412.05 crore respectively.

Refrigerators

In India, refrigerators have the highest aspiration value of all consumer durables with the exception of television. The refrigerator industry has become highly competitive with a number of brands having entered the market giving the consumers wider choices. There are two basic designs adopted in refrigerators presently being manufactured in the country. These are commonly referred to as Direct Cool (DC) and Frost Free (FF) refrigerators. There has been gradual consumer preference shift towards frost free segment. Increasing number of dual income households are shifting the demand from the conventional 180L refrigerators to the larger 220L and more capacity refrigerators with double doors.The production of refrigerators in 2014-15 was 9,234.10 thousand and in 2015-16 was 9203.13 thousand. The export and import of refrigerators in 2014-15 was ₹ 1,689.67 crore and ₹ 2,379.37 crore respectively whereas in 2015-16 the same was ₹ 1,681.13 crore and ₹ 2,571.44 crore respectively.

Washing Machines

The washing machine market can be divided into semi-automatic and fully-automatic. With rising disposable incomes and higher aspirations, there is a gradual shift towards higher capacity washing machines and also towards fully-automatic washing machines. While providing intelligence, microcontrollers boost reliability, drive down costs and improve energy efficiency. The production of washing machines by the units in the organized sector in 2014-15 was 39.91 lakh and in 2015-16, 43.10 lakh. The export and import of washing machines in 2014-15 was ₹ 2,66.91 crore and ₹ 924.53 crore respectively whereas in 2015-16 the same was ₹ 345.32 crore and ₹ 885.41 crore respectively.

Air Conditioners

Air conditioners (AC) are gradually being treated as necessity in the changed socio-economic environment with changed life style. The air-conditioners' market can be classified into three segments: window AC, split AC and central AC. Split ACs are gaining popularity due to limitation of space and increase in number of people living in flats in multi-storied complexes and also due to less noise. Bureau of Energy Efficiency (BEE), a statutory body under the Ministry of Power has introduced energy efficiency based star rating for air conditioners to help consumers buy the best energy efficient products. The production of air conditioners by the units in organized sector in 2014-15 was 26.50 lakh and in 2015-16, 27.97 lakh. Export and import of air conditioners in

2014-15 was ₹ 799.79 crore and ₹ 5,372.07 crore respectively whereas in 2015-16 the same was ₹ 905.23 crore and ₹ 5,354.04 crore respectively.

Lead Acid Storage Batteries

Lead acid batteries are accumulators of current and power which is discharged over a period of time. They are used in vehicles and also for various industrial uses such as for backup power for UPS application, control rooms, power stations, telecommunications, etc. In addition, it is also used for emergency lights for houses, telephone systems and as power source for mining, etc. A new application of lead acid batteries has emerged in electric vehicles. Average life of battery is approximately 2 years, hence these batteries will be needed as replacement throughout the life of vehicle or machinery in use. In order to ensure safe disposal of lead acid batteries, Ministry of Environment and Forest has issued Batteries (Management and Handling) Rules, 2001 under Environment (Protection) Act 1986. Production of lead acid batteries by units in organized sector in 2014-15 was 86.05 lakh and in 2015-16, 84.96 lakh. Export and import of lead acid batteries in 2014-15 was ₹ 1,231.99 crore and ₹ 3,365.44 crore respectively whereas in 2015-16 the same was ₹ 1,280.41 crore and ₹ 5,038.91 crore respectively.

Dry Cell Batteries

Dry cell batteries are one of the most commonly used items. These are the oldest type of batteries still being used. Performance of dry cell batteries has undergone progressive improvements through technological developments. New types of dry cell batteries with longer shelf life and greater dependability and also rechargeable cells have come up. Nickel cadmium batteries and other rechargeable batteries are manufactured in the country to meet the requirement of defence, telecommunications and electronics. The growing popularity of cellular phones, laptops and imported toys could open the market for a new range of batteries that are not produced. Production of dry cells in 2014-15 was 2,103.62 million and in 2015-16, 1,946.70 million. Export and import of dry cell batteries in 2014-15 was ₹ 93.59 crore and ₹ 672.41 crore respectively whereas in 2015-16 the same was ₹ 70.33 crore and ₹ 728.66 crore respectively.

Electrical Lamps and Tubes

Wide range of lamps and tubes are being manufactured in the country which include general lighting service lamps such as incandescent bulbs, halogen lamps, gas discharge lamps such as fluorescent tube light, compact fluorescent lamp, high pressure mercury vapour lamps, metal halide lamps, low pressure and high pressure sodium vapour lamps and variety of special lamps. Higher energy cost has led to the development of energy efficient lamps consuming less power and giving output as close to daylight. Compact Fluorescent Lamps (CFL) which consume about 20 per cent of the electricity for the same light output and last up to 8 times longer than the General Lighting Service (GLS) are getting more popular. Light emitting diodes have a great potential to provide highly efficient lighting with little environmental pollution in comparison to the incandescent lamps (ICLs) and fluorescent lamps. Penetration of LEDs could significantly reduce lighting load as almost 22-25 per cent of electricity is consumed for lighting, which is also a major contributing factor of peak demand. Due to higher costs, LEDs are not very popular even though its production has started in the country. The production of GLS lamps by the units in the organized sectors and fluorescent tubes in 2014-15 was 736.90 million and 195.45 million respectively. In 2015-16 production of GLS lamps and fluorescent tubes by the units in the organized sectors was 671.44 million and 195.56 million. Export and import of electric lamps and tubes in 2014-15 was ₹ 902.56 crore and ₹ 2,447.20 crore respectively whereas in 2015-16 the same was ₹ 968.92 crore and ₹ 3,839.81 crore respectively.

Light Engineering Industry Sector

Light engineering industry is a diverse industry with a number of distinct sectors. This group also includes industries like bearings, steel pipes and tubes, fasteners, etc. The products covered under the engineering industry are largely used as input to the capital goods industry. Hence the demand of this sector in general depends on the demand of the capital goods industry.

Roller Bearing Industry

Roller bearings are essential components in the rotating parts of virtually all machines such as automobiles, electric motors, diesel engines, industrial machinery and machine tools, etc. Bearings are used in diversified fields. Hence, product range is vast and diversified. Indigenous manufacturers are manufacturing bearings of quality and precision at par with world renowned manufacturers in diversified range of general purpose where demand is large to justify indigenous production on economic consideration. Bearings, generally used for special applications, requiring high technology and / or required in low volumes are still being imported. There is a considerable scope for development of bearings of smaller sizes and lighter weight with improved performance in harsh operating conditions like higher or low temperature. Automobile industry accounts for bulk of total demand of this industry with estimated share of 35 per cent, electrical industry share is 12 per cent, after market (replacement) share is 40 per cent and remaining 13 per cent consumption is by other industries. Production of ball and roller bearings in 2014-15 was 8,907.25 million and in 2015-16 was 8,993.39 million. Export and import of ball and roller bearings in 2014-15 was ₹ 2,674.64 crore and ₹ 5,544.54 crore respectively whereas in 2015-16 the same was ₹ 2,680.91 crore and ₹ 5,716.80 crore respectively.

Ferrous Castings

Ferrous castings are pivotal to growth and development of engineering industries since these constitute essential intermediates for automobiles, industrial machinery, power plants, chemical and fertilizer plants, etc. Indian foundry industry is fifth largest in the world. It is now well established in the country and is spread across a wide spectrum consisting of large, medium, small and tiny sector. Salient feature of the foundry industry is its geographical clustering. Typically, each foundry cluster is known for catering to some specific end use markets. For example, Coimbatore cluster is famous for pump sets castings, Kolhapur and Belgaum cluster for automotive castings, Rajkot cluster for diesel engine castings and Batala and Jalandhar cluster for machinery parts and agricultural implements. Advanced countries like USA, Japan, Germany are unlikely to add much capacity due to stringent pollution control norms there. India can thus have a dominant presence in this field and can become an important casting supplier to the world. Production of steel castings and C.I. castings in 2014-15 was 4,80,129.16 tonnes and in 2015-16, 4,64,375.73 tonnes. Export and import of casting in 2014-15 was ₹ 6,825.76 crore and ₹ 458.73 crore respectively whereas in 2015-16 the same was ₹ 6,305.20 crore and ₹ 609.70 crore respectively.

Process Control Instrument Industry

Process control instruments cover wide range of instruments and systems required for monitoring and measurement of physical, chemical and biological properties. They are used for measurement and control of process variables like pressure, temperature, humidity, liquid level, flow, specific gravity, chemical composition including pH and many forms of spectrometry and spectrophotometry. Process control instruments have become an integral part of the modern industrial activity. This industry is a key industry which provides tools for automation. Their importance is significant in high cost large and sophisticated process industries like fertilizer, steel, power plant, refineries, petrochemicals, cement and other process industries. Present technology is microprocessor based centralised control system. The export and import of process control instruments in 2014-15 was ₹ 1,393.26 crore and ₹ 3,933.31 crore respectively whereas in 2015-16 the same was ₹ 1,598.35 crore and ₹ 4,760.65 crore respectively.

Seamless Steel Pipes & Tubes

Seamless steel pipes and tubes come in all kinds of sizes including thin, small, precise, slender and other special pipes and are used in boilers and pipelines. It is involved in the applications for aircraft, missile and anti-friction bearing, ordinance, etc. Ultra high strength and corrosion-resistant properties make these perfect for oil and gas industry, chemical industry and automobile industry. Bearings and boiler sector contribute around 30 per cent of demand. Industry is able to manufacture tubes up to 14" outer diameter. The export and import of seamless steel pipes and tubes industry in 2014-15 was ₹ 3,274.51 crore and ₹ 5,477.59 crore respectively whereas in 2015-16 the same was ₹ 1,639.72 crore and ₹ 4,216.33 crore respectively.

Electrical Resistance Welded Steel Pipes and Tubes

Based on end-user customers' requirement, Electrical Resistance Welded (ERW) steel pipes and tubes are available in various qualities, wall thickness and diameters of the finished pipes. High performance ERW steel pipes and tubing possess high corrosion resistance, high deformability, high strength and high toughness. These pipes are used in fencing, lining pipes, oil country tubulars, scaffolding, water and gas conveyance, structural, engineering purposes, etc. There has been tremendous increase in production of ERW steel pipes due to higher demand in oil and gas industry, infrastructure and automobile uses. There are large number of units in the MSME sector. Export and import of ERW steel pipes and tubes in 2014-15 was ₹ 293.43 crore and ₹ 16.36 crore respectively whereas in 2015-16 the same was ₹ 172.55 crore and ₹ 1,1.80 crore respectively.

Submerged-Arc Welded Pipes

There are two types of Submerged-Arc Welded (SAW) pipes namely longitudinal and helical welded SAW pipes. Longitudinal SAW pipes are preferred where thickness of pipe is more than 25mm and in high pressure gas pipe line. Helical welded SAW pipes are used for low pressure applications. The cost of helical SAW pipes is less than longitudinal pipes. There is huge demand of SAW pipes in the country due to transportation of oil and gas and transmission of water. The export and import of SAW pipes in 2014-15 was ₹ 4,481.52 crore and ₹ 473.19 crore respectively whereas in 2015-16 the same was ₹ 3,475.97 crore and ₹ 219.57 crore respectively.

Industrial Fasteners

Fastener industry in India may be classified into two segments: high tensile and mild steel fasteners. High tensile and mild steel fasteners broadly include nuts, bolts, studs, rivets and screws. Mild steel fasteners are primarily manufactured by the unorganized sector while high tensile fasteners requiring superior technology are dominated by companies in the organized sector. Automobile industry accounts for bulk of the total demand of this industry. Consumer durables and railways are the other primary users of the high tensile fasteners. Automobile sector is likely to drive growth in fastener industry. Production of nuts and bolts in organized sector in 2014-15 was 1,10,005.00 tonnes and in 2015-16 was 1,08,917.31 tonnes. Export and import of industrial fastener in 2014-15 was ₹ 5,788.46 crore and ₹ 4,309.16 crore respectively whereas in 2015-16 the same was ₹ 3,346.41 crore and ₹ 4,564.10 crore respectively.

Steel Forgings

Forgings are intermediate products used widely by original equipment manufacturers in production of durable goods. Composition of Indian forging industry can be categorized into four sectors - large, medium, small and tiny. A major portion of this industry is made up of small and medium units/ enterprises (SMEs). Industry was previously more labour intensive but now with increasing globalization it is becoming more capital intensive. Among the industries that depend on forgings are automotive; agricultural machinery and equipment; valves, fittings, and petrochemical applications; hand tools and hardware; off-highway and railroad equipment; general industrial equipment; ordnance and marine and aerospace. Key driver of demand of forging is automobile industry. About 65 per cent of the total forging production is used in this sector. Production of stamping and forging in organized sector in 2014-15 was 4,62,766.06 tonnes and in 2015-16 was 4,80,394.61 tonnes. Export and import of forging industry in 2014-15 was ₹ 5,279.87 crore and ₹ 3,767.45 crore respectively whereas in 2015-16 the same was ₹ 6115.68 crore and ₹ 4635.85 crore respectively.

Bicycle Industry

Bicycle industry is one of the most established industries. India is the second largest bicycle producer of the world, next only to China. Most of the manufacturing units are located in Punjab and Tamil Nadu with Ludhiana (Punjab) being a major bicycle production hub. Industry is making endeavour for enhancing export since there is a significant scope for export of Indian bicycles, bicycle spare parts and bicycle accessories. Bicycle companies in India are now focusing on urban markets and are looking to expand their base in professional and adventure categories. Production of all kinds of bicycles in the organized sector in 2014-15 and 2015-16 was 132.46 million and 139.22 million. Export and import of bicycle in 2014-15 was ₹ 360.54 crore and ₹ 194.32 crore respectively whereas in 2015-16 the same was ₹ 285.34 crore and ₹ 205.58 crore respectively.

Light Industrial Machinery Sector

Food Processing Machinery

Indian market for food processing machinery has been growing steadily fuelled by strong domestic demand for processed food and beverage products spurred by increase in income level, increasing number of women joining the work force, rapid urbanization, changing life style and mass media promotion. Most promising areas of growth are fruit and vegetable processing, meat, poultry, dairy and seafood, packaged/convenience food, soft drinks and grain processing. Food processing sector is expected to grow at a healthy pace considering the rapid changes in food habits and consumerist culture developing in the country. Machinery manufacturers have honed their expertise in manufacturing dairy machinery and other core equipment of food processing machinery. The export and import of food processing machinery in 2014-15 was ₹ 1,049.35 crore and ₹ 1,133.76 crore respectively whereas in 2015-16 the same was ₹ 854.85 crore and ₹ 1,201.38 crore respectively.

Packaging Machinery Industry

Packaging of consumer products or industrial products is emerging as the USP in the marketing strategies. Developments in packaging technology have not only contributed to improving aesthetic appeal of the products but also the shelf life. In some cases specialized packaging becomes a technical necessity.

Considering growth prospects in industrial sector and growing consumer awareness of packaging, it is expected that there would be substantial growth in this area. There is a wide range of packaging machinery available in the country covering packaging of vast range of items. Commonly available packag machinery includes machines for coding and on-line printing machines, feeding and labeling machines, strip packaging, form fill and seal machines, carton filling, fully automatic bag making machinery and automatic microprocessor controlled packaging machines. Export and import of packaging machinery industry in 2014-15 was ₹ 798.21 crore and ₹ 1,627.33 crore respectively whereas in 2015-16 the same was ₹ 852.15 crore and ₹ 2,469.37 crore respectively.

Water Pollution Control Equipment

Due to growing awareness of preventing water pollution and stringent environmental control standards being enforced for various uses including process industries, water/waste water treatment industry is poised for huge growth. Various categories of water pollution control equipment include waste water treatment plants, drinking water treatment plants and effluent treatment plants. Primary treatment is the first step in treatment process and involves removal of pollutants that settles or floats. Common industrial equipmentare clarifiers and oil - water separator devises. Secondary treatment is designed to substantially degrade biological content of the sewage. Common equipmentare activated sludge, filters, biological reactors, etc. Tertiary treatment is a polishing step to remove contaminants that missed in primary and secondary treatment and removal of suspended solids, refractory organics and toxic components. Tertiary physical processes are filtration and carbon absorption. Chemical processes are used to remove inorganic and organic, resistant to biodegradation. Chemical process includes precipitation, oxidation and neutralization. Biological processes involve biodegrading. Organisms such as bacteria, fungi, yeasts and algae are commonly used to break down the organic matters. Cell tissues are then removed from the treated water by physical method like clarification. Complete plants are manufactured mostly in organized sector and many of the equipments are manufactured in the small scale sector as well. Export and import of water pollution control equipment in 2014-15 was ₹ 501.00 crore and ₹ 623.15 crore respectively whereas in 2015-16 the same was ₹ 750.16 crore and ₹ 939.56 crore respectively.

Air Pollution Control Equipment

Industrialization and urbanization have resulted in a profound deterioration of India's air quality. Air pollution in the country especially in metropolitan cities and large towns has assumed great significance with adoption of stringent environmental control standards for various industries. Hence pollution control equipment industry has acquired importance. Further judicial pronouncements have given a definite direction and urgency for adoption of air pollution control measures. The choice of control method depends on factors such as nature of pollutant, flow-rate (amount of pollutant emitted), particle size and desired collection efficiency. Air pollution control equipment are classified under the categories such as settling chambers, cyclone and multi-cyclones, bag filters, wet scrubbers, spray tower, venturi scrubber, ionizing scrubber and electrostatic precipitator. Industry is in a position to do basic and detailed engineering and supply of plants on turnkey basis. Export and import of air pollution control equipment in 2014-15 was ₹ 703.49 crore and ₹ 1,440.68 crore respectively whereas in 2015-16 the same was ₹ 680.96 crore and ₹ 1,311.80 crore respectively.

Industrial Gears

Industrial gears comprises mainly gears and gear boxes. Gears are used for two basic purposes: increase or decrease of rotation speed and increase or decrease of power or torque. Gears being an important part of a machine have immense usage within various industries. These industries include automotive industries, coal plants industry, steel plants industry, paper industry, in mining and several others. In these industries they behold a wide area of application. The manufacture of gears and gear boxes involve high precision machining and accurate assembly as mechanical power is to be transmitted noiselessly and with minimum losses. Different types and sizes of gears such as spur gears, helical gears, worm gears, spiral gears and many other kinds are manufactured in the country. Demand for gears and gear boxes predominantly depends on the growth of industrial machinery, machine tools, and consumer and automobile sector. Considering the industrial growth prospects, particularly in automobile sector, demand for gears and gear boxes is expected to grow at a healthy pace. Export and import of gears and gearing in 2014-15 was ₹ 1,028.21 crore and ₹ 1,857.58 crore respectively whereas in 2015-16 the same was ₹ 1,162.67 crore and ₹ 2,027.13 crore respectively. *[Source: Export-Import Data - Export-Import Data Bank, D/o Commerce..Production Data - Industrial Statistics Unit, DIPP.]*

Wholesale Price Index

Current series of index number of wholesale prices (Base: 2004-05=100) was introduced in September, 2010. The series has 676 commodities with 5482 quotations. Table 19.12 gives the index number of wholesale prices (Base: 2004-05) for the period 2005-06 to 2016-17 for all the commodities and selected groups/ sub-groups of three major groups, namely: (i) Primary Articles, (ii) Fuel and Power, and (iii) Manufactured Products.

Wholesale Price Index Based Inflation in Manufacturing Sector

Inflation rate based on Wholesale Price Index (Base: 2004-05 = 100) for manufacturing sector has increased from (-) 1.1 per cent in 2015-16 (April,2015 to March, 2016) to 1.55 per cent in 2016-17 (Provisionally upto August, 2016). The groups which have shown increase in indices in 2016-17 (provisionally from April to August, 2016) as compared to 2015-16 (April to August, 2015) include food products, beverages, tobacco and tobacco products, textiles, wood and wood products, paper and paper products, leather &leather products, non-metallic products, machinery and machine tools and transport, equipment and parts. The groups which have shown decrease in indices in 2016-17 (provisionally from April to August, 2016) as compared to 2015-16 (April to August, 2015) include rubber & plastic products, chemicals & chemical products and basic metals, alloys & metal products. Table 19.13 gives details of inflation based on WPI for Manufacturing Product Groups.

Details of Index Numbers of Wholesale Prices (Base: 2004-05=100) Financial Year Averages and Rate of Inflation in terms of WPI at Table below:

Table 19.11 : Index Numbers of Wholesale Prices (Base: 2004-05=100) Financial Year Averages

Commodities	Weight	2005-06	2006-07	2007-08	2008-09	2009-10	2010-11	2011-12	2012-13	2013-14	2014-15	2015-16	2016-17*
All Commodities	**100.00**	**104.5**	**111.4**	**116.6**	**126.0**	**130.8**	**143.3**	**156.1**	**167.6**	**177.6**	**181.2**	**176.7**	**181.6**
I Primary Articles	**20.12**	**104.3**	**114.3**	**123.9**	**137.5**	**154.9**	**182.4**	**200.3**	**220.0**	**241.6**	**248.8**	**249.6**	**262.7**
(A) Food articles	14.34	105.4	115.5	123.6	134.8	155.4	179.6	192.7	211.8	238.9	253.4	262.1	277.4
(B) Non-Food articles	4.26	96.7	102.3	114.4	129.2	136.2	166.6	182.7	201.9	213.2	212.1	219.5	231.5
(C) Minerals	1.52	115.2	136.6	152.8	186.5	202.9	253.3	320.7	346.9	346.5	308.5	216.2	211.3
II Fuel & Power	**14.91**	**113.6**	**120.9**	**121.0**	**135.0**	**132.1**	**148.3**	**169.0**	**186.5**	**205.4**	**203.5**	**179.8**	**182.9**
A. Coal	2.09	117.6	117.7	121.7	151.3	156.5	165.3	191.0	208.6	190.8	189.8	189.9	190.7
B. Mineral Oils	9.36	116.7	127.4	126.3	141.8	135.8	157.5	184.0	202.5	226.0	219.6	179.5	185.0
C. Electricity	3.45	102.6	105.3	106.2	106.4	107.4	113.2	115.0	129.8	158.7	168.0	174.3	172.3
III Manufactured Products	**64.97**	**102.4**	**108.2**	**113.4**	**120.4**	**123.1**	**130.1**	**139.5**	**147.1**	**151.5**	**155.1**	**153.4**	**156.2**
(A) Food products	9.97	101.2	106.5	110.3	119.9	136.1	141.2	151.2	163.5	168.8	172.9	174.2	187.7
(B) Beverages, Tobacco & tobacco products	1.76	104.7	110.0	117.2	128.3	136.2	146.2	163.3	175.3	186.0	200.8	206.5	220.2
(C) Textiles	7.33	98.9	100.8	101.5	103.2	106.7	119.6	128.5	131.4	139.0	142.6	140.2	141.2
(D) Wood & wood products	0.59	105.7	111.9	119.4	130.7	143.3	149.0	161.0	171.0	179.1	187.8	195.7	197.8
(E) Paper & paper products	2.03	103.6	108.4	111.6	116.3	118.9	125.2	131.9	136.6	143.0	150.7	154.5	156.2
(F) Leather & leather products	0.84	104.3	112.5	116.0	122.3	128.4	127.1	130.0	134.2	143.1	145.0	144.9	146.1
(G) Rubber & plastic products	2.99	101.9	107.6	112.2	117.3	118.2	126.1	133.6	137.5	146.0	149.9	147.2	146.4
(H) Chemicals & Chemical products	12.02	103.8	108.9	112.8	118.1	117.8	124.0	134.7	143.6	148.9	152.8	150.5	150.8
(I) Non-Metallic mineral products	2.56	103.4	115.4	128.3	131.7	140.9	144.6	152.9	163.3	166.2	172.9	177.3	178.4

(J) Basic Metals, Alloys & metal products	10.75	102.2	111.7	123.2	138.0	129.5	140.7	156.3	166.1	164.5	165.6	154.6	153.7
(K) Machinery & machine tools	8.93	103.6	110.1	114.1	117.4	118.0	121.3	125.1	128.4	131.6	134.6	135.0	135.4
(L) Transport, equipment & parts	5.21	102.7	105.0	107.6	113.3	116.8	120.3	124.6	129.8	134.5	136.2	138.1	139.6

**Upto July, 2016. Figures for June and July 2016 are provisional in figures of 2016-17.*

Table 19.12 : Financial Year-wise WPI Inflation With Base Year: 2004-05

Commodities	Weight	2006-07	2007-08	2008-09	2009-10	2010-11	2011-12	2012-13	2013-14	2014-15	2015-16	2016-17*
III Manufactured Products	64.97	5.66	4.78	6.16	2.22	5.70	7.26	5.41	2.99	2.42	-1.10	1.55
(A) Food products	9.97	5.29	3.54	8.69	13.49	3.73	7.12	8.13	3.24	2.42	0.76	9.37
(B) Beverages, tobacco & tobacco products	1.76	5.10	6.52	9.52	6.11	7.37	11.68	7.39	6.08	7.94	2.86	7.18
(C) Textiles	7.33	1.88	0.73	1.62	3.43	12.08	7.46	2.19	5.80	2.63	-1.72	0.36
(D) Wood & wood products	0.59	5.84	6.69	9.49	9.60	3.97	8.10	6.17	4.74	4.86	4.21	1.28
(E) Paper & paper products	2.03	4.60	2.96	4.20	2.20	5.33	5.38	3.55	4.64	5.40	2.57	1.63
(F) Leather & leather products	0.84	7.95	3.06	5.47	4.93	-0.99	2.32	3.21	6.66	1.33	-0.12	1.18
(G) Rubber & plastic products	2.99	5.61	4.28	4.53	0.74	6.68	5.98	2.93	6.17	2.63	-1.79	-1.68
(H) Chemicals & chemical products	12.02	4.96	3.57	4.64	-0.26	5.33	8.61	6.62	3.63	2.64	-1.48	-0.30
(I) Non-Metallic mineral products	2.56	11.58	11.19	2.63	6.97	2.68	5.74	6.77	1.81	3.98	2.60	1.10
(J) Basic metals, Alloys & metal products	10.75	9.28	10.29	11.96	-6.12	8.66	11.06	6.26	-0.93	0.63	-6.63	-2.87
(K) Machinery & machine tools	8.93	6.31	3.65	2.89	0.46	2.82	3.11	2.62	2.56	2.28	0.25	0.25
(L) Transport, equipment & parts	5.21	2.22	2.47	5.36	3.08	3.01	3.52	4.21	3.60	1.28	1.34	1.41

**Up to July, 2016. Figures for June and July 2016 are provisional in figures of 2016-17.*

**Figures for 2016-17 depict year on year percentage change in average of indices from April to July month.*

Scheme for Promoting Innovation Rural Industry and Entrepreneurship

A Scheme for Promoting Innovation, Rural Industry and Entrepreneurship (ASPIRW) was launched in 2015 to promote innovation and rural entrepreneurship through rural livelihood business incubator (LBI), technology business incubator (TBI) and funds for start-up creation in the agro-based industry. During the year 2015-16, 22 LBIs and 2 TBIs have been approved and 2 LBI centres have been operationalized at Deoria (U.P.) and Rajkot (Gujarat). The Ministry of MSME is also implementing various schemes and programmes for promotion and development of MSME sector. The major schemes/ programmes include Prime Minister's Employment Generation Programme (PMEGP), Scheme of fund for Regeneration of Traditional Industries (SFURTI), Credit Guarantee Scheme, Credit Linked Capital Subsidy Scheme (CLCSS), National Manufacturing Competitiveness Programme, Micro & Small Enterprises–Cluster Development Programme (MSE-CDP), Marketing Development Assistance, Skill Development Programmes, International Cooperation Scheme etc.

Prime Minister's Employment Generation Programme

Prime Minister's Employment Generation Programme (PMEGP) is a credit linked subsidy scheme, for setting up of new micro-enterprises and to generate employment opportunities in rural as well as urban areas of the country through KVIC, State Khadi and Village Industries Board (KVIB) and District Industries Centre (DIC). General category beneficiaries can avail of margin money subsidy of 25 per cent of the project cost in rural areas and 15 per cent in urban areas. For beneficiaries belonging to special categories such as SC/ST/Women/PH/ Minorities/Ex-Servicemen/NER, the margin money subsidy is 35 per cent in rural areas and 25 per cent in urban areas. The maximum cost of projects is ₹ 25 lakh in the manufacturing sector and ₹ 10 lakh in the service sector. Since inception and up to January 2016, 3.50 lakh micro enterprises have been set up by utilizing margin money amounting to ₹ 7,004.40 crore. 29.82 lakh jobs have been created from these units.

Indian Textiles

The Indian textile industry represents a rich and diverse spectrum of activities with the hand-woven sector on one end and the capital intensive mill sector on the other. The spectrum includes activities in the decentralized powerlooms, hosiery and knitting sectors, the handicrafts segments and also covers a wide range of fibres which include man-made fibre, cotton, silk, jute and wool. The sector is unique in comparison to that of other countries owing to the close linkage of the industry to agriculture and also due to linkage with the culture and traditions of the country. It has a capacity to produce a versatile spread of products appropriate for varied market segments, both domestic and the export markets. The industry plays a pivotal role through its contribution to industrial output and employment generation and the export earning of the country. It contributes to 10 per cent of manufacturing production, 2 per cent of India's GDP and to 13 per cent of the country's export earnings. With over 45 million people employed directly, textile industry is one of the largest source of employment generation in the country.

India Handloom Brand

With a view to promote handloom industry on a sustainable basis, India Handloom Brand was launched in 2015, the first to endorse the quality of handloom products in terms of raw material, processing, embellishment, weaving, design and other parameters besides social and environment compliance for earning the trust of customers. The main objective of launching the brand is to ensure the production of quality products with new designs for winning the trust and confidence of customers by giving particular attention to the defect free, hand woven, authentic niche products with zero defect and zero impact on environment.

Amended-Technology Upgradation Fund Scheme

With a view to supporting the 'Make in India' initiatives, the 'Amended Technology Upgradation Fund Scheme (A-TUFS) was put in place of the existing Revised Restructured Technology Fund Scheme (RRTUFS), for technology upgradation of the textiles industry with one time capital subsidy for eligible machinery. Segments which have higher employment and export potential such as garmenting and technical textiles will be eligible for capital subsidy at the rate of 15 per cent subject to a cap of ₹1 30 crore. Segments such as weaving for brand new shuttle-less looms (including weaving preparatory and knitting) processing, jute, silk and handlooms will get subsidy at the rate of 10 per cent subject to a cap of ₹ 20 crore. A budget provision of ₹ 17,822 crore has been approved for seven years from 2015-22 to meet the committed liabilities of ₹ 12,671 crore and ₹ 5,151 crore for new cases under ATUFS. A resolution regarding introduction of Amended Technology Upgradation Fund Scheme (A-TUFS) in place of Revised Restructured Technology Upgradation Fund Scheme (FFTUFS) was put in place in 2016.

Protection of cotton Farmers: For the cotton season 2015-16, the Cotton Corporation of India in association with the state governments has made elaborate arrangements for meeting the eventuality of minimum support price in all the cotton growing states. Special initiative has been taken for the cotton growing states to avoid distress sale by cotton farmers. Special initiative has been taken for the cotton season 2015-16 to enable online payment to farmers, provisions of bar coded cards for farmers in Telangana and conduct IEC activities to sensitise the farmers about moisture content and about avoiding contamination.

Infrastructure for Textile Industry

The Scheme for Integrated Textile Park (SITP) addresses infrastructural constraint of the textile sector on cluster basis. Central Government provides assistance up to 40 per cent of the project cost subject to a ceiling of ₹ 40 crore for common infrastructure and common facilities. 24 new parks were sanctioned in 2014-15 and 2015-16. To promote industrialization in backward states, priority has been given to proposals from less industrialized textile states in the selection process.

Skilling in Textile Sector

To bridge the gap of the skilled workforce in sector the Ministry is implementing Integrated Skill Development Scheme (ISDS). Target is to provide 15 lakh additional skilled workers to the textile sector by 2017. The scheme has been revamped with major emphasis on employment. Minimum 70 per cent placement has been made mandatory under the scheme. During the last two years, about 2,60,000 per sons have been provided employment in textile industry after training under the ISDS. Training programmes have been interfaced with an e-platform for ease of implementation and monitoring.

Integrated Processing Development Scheme

Textile processing cluster, dominated by SMEs, and job work units were facing closure under court/NGT order for environmental degradation issues. Prominent textile processing clusters in Tamil Nadu, Rajasthan, Punjab, etc., were closed down rendering lakhs of persons unemployed. The Ministry under Integrated Processing Development Scheme offered help to the industry to provide capital support up to 50 per cent of the project cost subject to a ceiling of ₹ 75 crore for common effluent treatment plants with zero liquid discharge technology. During the year 2015-16 five projects have been sanctioned to Rajasthan (3), Tamil Nadu (1) and Punjab (1).

New initiatives launched in sericulture sector included promotion of imported substitutes by holding silk production, focus on quality silk worm seed production through development of improved breeds, promotion of best cocoon technology innovations and promotion of Vanya silk as an eco-friendly organic silk to boost exports.

Focus Incubation Centres

In order to help the potential entrepreneurs to enter into technical textiles, the Ministry of Textiles is setting up six Focus Incubation Centres (FIC) in Centres of Excellence (CoEs) established under the Technology Mission on Technical Textiles (TMTT) scheme on a plug and play model. An amount of ₹ 17.45 crore has been released to six CoEs namely ATIRA, DKTE, NITRA, PSG College of Tech, SASMIRA and SITRA for setting up of FICs.

Launching of Jute Common Facility Centre Scheme

A new scheme for setting up Common Facility Centres (CFC) for promotion of jute diversified products through Women Self Help Groups (WSHGs) was launched in 2015. The Scheme shall provide avenues for value addition, production in quality assurance by providing infrastructure, integrated design, training and market development through the National Jute Board. The Scheme shall support members of the WSHGs located in the jute cluster. The setting up of 5 CFCs have been sanctioned out of which 3 are located in West Bengal, 1 in Assam and 1 in Bihar.

Block Level Cluster Approach in Handlooms

A new block level cluster approach for supporting the handloom weavers has been initiated in 9 blocks of the Varanasi. In these blocks, 9 Common Facility Centres (CFCs) were set up having yarn depot, office with internet, pre-loom facilities like winding/warping/dyeing and work shed training for the weavers, etc. It is supported by a full time technically qualified staff. Design support is provided by the Weavers' Service Centre, Varanasi and also, through a reputed private designer.

Cotton

Cotton is one of the most important commercial crops cultivated in India. It plays a major role in sustaining the livelihood of an estimated 5.8 million cotton farmers and 40-50 million people engaged in related activities such as cotton processing and trade. The Indian textile industry consumes a diverse range of fibres and yarn. In the raw material consumption of the industry, the ratio of the use of the cotton to man-made fibres and filament yarns is 59:41. Hence, growth and all around development of cotton and cotton industry has a vital bearing on the overall development of the Indian economy. The consumption of cotton is more than 300 lakh bales (170 kg each) per year. To support the cotton industry, Government of India announces Minimum Support Price (MSP) for two basic staple groups viz., medium long staple and long staple cotton. Cotton Corporation of India (CCI) under the Ministry, is one of the nominated agencies for undertaking MSP operations in the event of prevailing *Kapas* price touching the MSP level. As per the mandate and in order to avoid distress selling by cotton farmers, CCI purchases raw cotton directly from the cotton farmers, under the MSP operations at the designated market yards, without quantitative restrictions.

Jute

The jute industry occupies an important place in the national economy. It is one of the major industries in the eastern region, particularly in West Bengal. Jute, the golden fibre, meets all the standards for safe packaging in view of it being a natural, renewable, biodegradable and eco-friendly product. It is estimated that the jute industry provides direct employment of 0.37 million workers in organized mills and in diversified units including tertiary sector and allied activities and supports the livelihood of around 4.0 million farm families. In addition, there are a large number of persons engaged in the trade of jute. The sector is supported by a host of policy initiatives including the statutory mandatory jute packaging norms, the MSP operations, and the promotion of the jute industry.

Silk

India continues to be the second largest producer of silk in the world. Among the four varieties of silk produced, for 2014-15, mulberry accounted for 74.5 per cent (21390 MT), Tasar 8.5 per cent (2434 MT), ERI 16.5 per cent (42726 MT), Tasar 8.5 per cent (2434 MT), Eri 16.5 per cent (4726 MT) and muga 0.5 per cent (158 MT) of the total raw silk production of 28,708 MT. This is against the production of 26480 MT silk during 2013-14 in the country. The Central Silk Board implements a large number of schemes and policy for promotion of sericulture and silk in the country. There has been a significant increase in raw silk production in 2014-15 in spite of drought, unseasonal rain, cyclone, etc. The target set for the year has been fully achieved. The silk production in the country increased to 28,708 MT by the end of 2014-15 from the level of 26,480 MTs during the year 2013-14, registering increase of 8.4 per cent growth. The import substitute bivoltine silk production has increased from 2559 MTs to 3870 MTs registering an increase of 51.0 per cent. Vanya silk production has increased from 7004 MTs to 7318 MT showing an increase of 4.5 per cent. Muga silk has recorded highest ever production of 158 MTs and has set a new momentum of growth.

Wool

The Central Wool Development Board works under overall guidance of Governing Body of Board and under administrative control of the Ministry.

The Board also functions as an Advisory Body to the Ministry of Textiles on the matters relating to growth and development of wool sector. The Ministry is also implementing Pashmina Wool Development Programme (PWDP) through Central Wool Development Board in the Ladakh and Kargil region of J&K for further development of pashmina wool with a budget provision of ₹ 30.00 crore.

Handloom

Handloom weaving is one of the largest economic activities after agriculture providing direct and indirect employment to more than 43 lakh weavers and allied workers. This sector contributes nearly 15 per cent of the cloth production in the country and also contributes to the export earnings of the country. Resultant to the developmental and welfare measures the declining trend in production in the handloom sector has more or less been arrested though number of weavers engaged in handloom sector are declining.

Handicrafts

The handicraft sector plays a significant and important role in the country's economy. It provides employment to a vast segment of craft persons in rural and semi urban areas and generates substantial foreign exchange for the country, while preserving its cultural heritage. Presently, handicrafts contribute substantially to employment generation and exports. The handicraft sector has, however, suffered due to its being unorganized, with the additional constraints of lack of education, low capital, poor exposure to new technologies, absence of market intelligence, and a poor institutional framework. The sector is estimated to employ ₹ 68.86 lakh artisans at present and the export of handicrafts including handmade carpet upto 2015 has been ₹ 22,375 crore.

Powerlooms

The decentralised powerloom sector is one of the most important segments of the textile industry in terms of fabric production and employment generation. It provides employment to 61.72 lakh persons and contributes 60 per cent of total cloth production in the country. More than 60 per cent of fabric meant for export is also sourced from powerloom sector. The readymade garments and home textile sectors are heavily dependent on the powerloom sector to meet their fabric requirement.

There are approximately 24.69 lakh powerlooms as on December, 2015. The technology level of this sector varies from plain loom to high tech shuttleless looms. There are approximately 1.25 lakh shuttleless looms in this sector. It is estimated that more than 75 per cent of the shuttle looms are obsolete and outdated with a vintage of more than 15 years and have virtually no process or quality control devices/attachments.

Mill Sector

The organized textile sector has more than 3400 textile mills both in the small scale industry and the non-small scale industry sectors. The total installed capacity of spindles is the largest in the world with more than 50 million spindle and 8,42.000 rotors. The mill sector produces nearly 2500 million square meters of cloth apart from 2500 million kgs of man made fibre and man made filament yarn.

Apparel and Garmenting

The Indian textile sector includes a large apparel and garment sector which employs 12.3 million persons and produces 3.6 million tonnes of apparel and garments. The readymade garmenting segment contributes to 43 per cent of the Indian textile exports which include cotton garments and accessories, man made fibre garments and other textile clothing.

Export Promotion

India's exports of textiles and clothing have been projected to be US$ 64.41 billion by the end of the 12th Five Year Plan, that is, March, 2017. The textiles industry accounts for 12 per cent share of the country's total exports basket. As per the UN Comtrade database, India is ranked as the 2nd largest textile and clothing exporter globally, after China, with US$ 38.6 bn. worth of exports. In clothing segment, India was ranked 6th largest exporter with US$ 16.5 bn. clothing exports behind China, Bangladesh, Italy, Germany and Vietnam.

Schemes for Promotion of Textiles

Handlooms

National Handloom Development Programme (NHDP) is implemented as a single Centrally sponsored programme for development of handlooms, and includes the Comprehensive Handloom Development Scheme (CHDS). The schemes for promotion of handlooms include:

Institutional Credit/Weaver Credit Card Scheme: To provide subsidized loan to handloom weavers, the government introduced 'Institutional Credit for Handloom Sector' in December, 2012, which was implemented under Integrated Handlooms Development Scheme. The interventions include (i) issuance of weaver credit cards (WCCs) (ii) interest subvention @ 3 per cent for 3 years on loans sanctioned, (iii) margin, money assistance @ ₹ 4200 per individual weaver and (iv) credit guarantee for 3 years.

Block Level Cluster Approach: Block level cluster approach was started in June, 2015. Such an approach is designed to suit the requirements of the cluster with higher scale of funding by GoI. Financial assistance is provided upto ₹ 2.00 crore for various interventions such as setting up of Common Facility Centre (CFC) [including Common Service Centre (CSC)], engagement of textile designer-cum-marketing executive, construction of workshed, appointment of Cluster Development Executive (CDE), technological upgradation, skill upgradation, etc. Financial assistance upto ₹ 50.00 lakh is also available for setting up of dyehouse at district level.

Handicrafts

During 2015, the government implemented seven central sector schemes (Baba Saheb Ambedkar Hastshilp Vikas Yojana, Design and Technology Upgradation Scheme, Marketing Support and Services Scheme, Research and Development Scheme, Human and Resource Development Scheme, Handicrafts Artisans Comprehensive Welfare Scheme, Infrastructure and Technology Development Scheme) for holistic growth and development of handicrafts sector in the country. Recently, the various schemes have been reviewed and rationalized into one umbrella scheme namely, National Handicraft Development Programme [NHDP] to emphasize integrated approach for development of handicraft cluster in a holistic manner. The NHDP has following components: Ambedkar Hastship Vikas Yojna; Dastkar Shashktikaran Yojna; Design and Technology Upgradation; Human Resources Development; Direct Benefit to Artisans; Infrastructure and Technology Support.

Sericulture

The Central Silk Board (CSB) which promotes sericulture has activities relating to research and development, research extension, maintenance of four tier silkworm seed production network, leadership role in commercial silkworm seed production, standardizing and instilling quality parameters in the various production processes, promotion of Indian silk in domestic and international markets and advising the government on all matters concerning sericulture and silk industry. These mandated activities of the Board are being carried out by the 324 units of CSB located in different states under the following Central sector schemes: research and development, training and IT initiatives; seed organizations/coordination and market development; quality certification systems; and export/brand promotion and technology upgradation.

Apart from these, CSB also supported the state governments in implementing the Catalytic Development Programme (CDP) with an aim of synergizing and disseminating improved technology packages, innovations developed by its R&D units and incentivizing investments among the stakeholders to adopt improved technology leading to enhanced production, productivity and improvement in quality of silk so as to enhance the income of primary producers.

Jute

The Jute Technology Mission has been a major component of the National Jute Policy and is the vehicle for implementation of multifarious programmes in the jute sector, both present and future. Pursuant to the National Jute Policy, 2005, the Ministry of Textiles and various organisations under it have been prioritising diversification of jute products part for supporting jute farmers and jute workers.

Schemes of NJB

The schemes for promotion of jute sector are primarily implemented by the National Jute Board.

Powerlooms

The powerloom sector promotion schemes include the Integrated Scheme for Powerloom Sector Development (ISPSD), the Scheme for in situ upgradation of plain powerloom, the Group Workshed Scheme, the Comprehensive Powerloom Mega Cluster Development Scheme, etc. Some of the features of the schemes are outlined here:

Integrated Scheme for Powerloom Sector Development (ISPSD): The components under the scheme include (i) Common Facility Centre (CFC) to provide infrastructure support to the powerloom weavers associated in a group and willing to set up common Facility Centre. (ii) Corpus for Yarn Bank to provide interest free corpus fund to Special Purpose Vehicle (SPV)/Consortium to enable them to purchase the yarn at wholesale rate and give the yarn at reasonable price to the small weavers in the decentralized powerloom sector.

Khadi and Village Industries Commission

Khadi and Village Industries Commission (KVIC) established under the Khadi and Village Industries Commission Act, 1956 (61 of 1956), is a statutory organization under the aegis of the Ministry of MSME, engaged in promoting and developing khadi and village industries for providing employment opportunities in the rural areas, thereby strengthening the rural economy. KVIC has been identified as one of the major organisations in the decentralised sector for generating sustainable non-farm employment opportunities in rural areas at a low per capita investment. It undertakes activities like skill improvement, transfer of technology; research and development; marketing, etc., and helps in generating employment/self-employment opportunities in rural areas. The main objectives of KVIC include:- (i) the social objective of providing employment in rural areas; (ii) the economic objective of producing saleable articles; and (iii) the wider objective of creating self-reliance amongst people and building up a strong rural community spirit.

Workshed Scheme for Khadi Artisans

In order to facilitate and empower khadi spinners and weavers to chart out a sustainable path for growth, income generation and better work environment and to enable them to carry out their spinning and weaving work effectively 'Workshed Scheme for Khadi Artisans' was introduced in 2008-09. Under this Scheme, financial assistance for construction of worksheds is provided to khadi artisans belonging to BPL category through the khadi institutions with which the khadi artisans are associated.

Coir Board

The Coir Board is a statutory body establishment under the Coir Industry Act, 1953 for promoting overall development of the coir industry and improvement of the living conditions of the workers engaged in this traditional industry. The functions of the Board for the development of coir industry inter-alia, include undertaking scientific, technological and economic research and development activities; collection of statistics relating to exports and internal consumption of coir and coir products; development of new products and designs; publicity for promotion of exports and internal sales; marketing of coir and coir products in India and abroad; preventing unfair competition among producers and exporters; assisting in the establishment of units for the manufactures of products; promoting cooperative organisations among producers of husk, coir fibre, coir yarn and manufacturers of coir products; ensuring remunerative returns to producers and manufacturers, etc.

Central Public Sector Enterprises

The Department of Public Enterprises is the nodal department for all the Central Public Sector Enterprises (CPSEs) and it formulates policy pertaining to CPSEs. It lays down, in particular, policy guidelines on performance improvement and evaluation, autonomy and financial delegation and personnel management in CPSEs. It furthermore collects and maintains information on several areas in respect of CPSEs.

Major Activities

In fulfilling its role, the Department coordinates with other ministries, CPSEs and concerned organizations. Some of the important tasks of the Department are listed as follows: coordination of matters of general policy affecting all Public Sector Enterprises; evaluation and monitoring the performance of Public Sector Enterprises, including the Memorandum of Understanding mechanism; matters relating to Permanent Machinery of Arbitration for the Public Sector Enterprises; counselling, training and rehabilitation of employees in Central Public Sector Undertakings under Voluntary Retirement Scheme; measures aimed at improving performance of Central Public Sector Enterprises and other capacity building initiatives of Public Sector enterprises; rendering advice relating to revival, restructuring or closure of Public Sector Enterprises including the mechanisms; and categorisation of Central Public Sector Enterprises including conferring 'Ratna' status.

Public Enterprises Survey

The Department of Public Enterprises (DPE) presents to Parliament every year a comprehensive report known as the Public Enterprises Survey on the financial and physical performance of Central Public Sector Enterprises (CPSEs) in the country.

The Public Enterprises Survey covers the Central Public Sector Enterprises (CPSEs), which have been established either as Government companies under the Companies Act or as Statutory Corporations under specific statutes of Parliament. The Survey, moreover, covers only those Government companies in which Central government's share in paid up capital is more than fifty per cent. This does not, however, include public sector commercial banks and public sector insurance companies.

Highlights of the Performance of CPSEs for the Year 2014-15

Total Number of CPSEs	298
No. of Operating CPSEs	235
Investment (₹ crore)	10960057
Reserves and Surplus (₹ crore)	771672
Total Turnover (₹ crore)	1995902
Overall Profit (₹ crore)	103003
Profit of Profit Making CPSEs (₹ crore)	130363 (157 CPSEs)
Loss of Loss Making CPSEs (₹ crore)	27360 (77 CPSEs)
Dividend Paid by CPSEs (₹ crore)	56527

Contribution to the Central Exchequer (₹ crore)	200585
Foreign Exchange Earnings by CPSEs (₹ crore)	103071
Employment (in numbers)	1291174
Market Capitalization (₹ crore)	1327127

The ratio of total turnover of ₹ 19,95,902 crore to the Gross Domestic Product (GDP) of ₹ 125,41,208 crore at current market price during 2014-15 stood at 15.91 per cent. The major contribution of the production is coming from petroleum, coal, steel, electricity, power generation and marketing of services.

Categorization of CPSEs

CPSEs are categorized into four schedules namely 'A', 'B', 'C', & 'D' based on criteria such as quantitative factors like investment, capital employed, net sales, profit before tax, number of employees and units, capacity addition, revenue per employee, sales/capital employed, capacity utilization, value added per employee and qualitative factors such as national importance, complexities of problems being faced by the company, level of technology, prospects for expansion and diversification of activities and competition from other sectors, etc.

The categorization of CPSE has implications on grant of Ratna status, pay scales of chief executives and full time functional Directors of CPSEs, highest level allowed for below board level posts, etc., By March 2015 there are 64 Schedule 'A', 68 Schedule 'B', 45 Schedule 'C' and 4 Schedule 'D' CPSEs.

Corporate Social Responsibility (CSR) and Sustainability

As per Section-135 of Companies Act, 2013, all profit making Corporates, including Central Public Sector Enterprises (CPSEs) exceeding threshold limits prescribed in the Act regarding net worth of ₹ 500 crore, or turnover of ₹ 1000 crore or net profit of ₹ 5 crore in pursuance of its CSR Policy are mandated to spend at least 2 per cent of the average net profits (Profit Before Tax) of the company made during the three immediately preceding years. As per information in respect of 127 CPSEs, 2 per cent of the average PBT for these 127 CPSEs for 2014-15 was ₹ 3492.29 crore. Against this, total CSR spending in 2014-15 for these 127 CPSEs was ₹ 2450.23 crore.

Steel

The Ministry is responsible for planning and development of iron and steel industry, development of essential inputs such as iron-ore, limestone, dolomite, manganese ore, chromites, ferro-alloys, sponge iron, etc., and other related functions.

Production, Consumption and Growth

The table here shows the trend in production for sale, import, export and real consumption of total finished steel (alloy+non-alloy) in the country for last five years and April-December 2015-16:

Total Finished Steel (alloy+non-alloy) (million tonnes or mt)

Year	Production for sale	Import	Export	Real Comsumption
2010-11	68.62	6.66	3.64	66.42
2011-12	75.69	6.86	4.59	71.02
2012-13	81.68	7.93	5.37	73.48
2013-14	87.67	5.45	5.98	74.09
2014-15	92.16	9.32	5.59	76.99
2015-16*	67.71	8.39	2.91	58.94

**April-December*

*Source: JPC: * provisional*

Crude steel production has shown a sustained rise since 2010-11 along with capacity. Data on crude steel production, capacity and capacity utilization during the last five years and April-December 2015-16 is given in the table here:

Crude Steel

Year	Capacity (mt)	Production (mt)	Capacity Utilization (per cent)
2010-11	80.36	70.67	88
2011-12	90.87	74.29	82
2012-13	97.02	78.42	81
2013-14	101.02	81.69	80
2014-15	109.85	88.98	81
April-December 2015-16*	116.74^	67.08	77#

*Source: JPC: *Provisional; ^ pro-rata, based on annual data, # Pro-rata, based on annual capacity*

Crude steel production grew at a cumulative average growth rate (CAGR) of 6.2 per during the last five completed years ending 2014-15. This growth in production was driven by capacity expansion from 80.36 million tonnes in 2010-11 to 109.85 million tonnes in 2014-15, a growth of 8 per cent (on a CAGR basis). Production for sale of total finished steel stood at 92.16 million tonnes during 2014-15 as against 68.62 million tonnes in 2010-11 growing at average annual growth rate of 8.7 per cent in CAGR terms during this five-year period while real consumption at 76.99 million tonnes during 2014-15 grew by 5.3 per cent on CAGR basis during this period.

India has been a net importer of total finished steel every year since 2007-08 except 2013-14. Exports grew by 11 per cent while imports by 5 per cent during the last five year period, both on a CAGR basis. The above crude steel performance has been contributed largely by the strong trends in growth of the electric route of steel making, particularly the induction furnace route, which accounted for 32 per cent of total crude steel production in the country during 2014-15 and 31 per cent during April-December 2015-16 and has emerged as a key driver of crude steel production.

India is also a leading producer of sponge iron with a large number of coal based units, located in the mineral-rich states of the country. Over the years, the coal based route has emerged as a key contributor and accounted for 90 per cent of total sponge iron production in the country in 2014-15 as well as during April-December 2015-16 (prov.). Capacity in the sponge iron industry has also increased over the years and stood at 46.23 million tonnes in 2014-15. India has been the world's largest sponge iron producer every year since 2003. The table here shows the total production of sponge iron in the country, indicating the break-up of the share of coal and gas based route of production for the last five years and April-December 2015-16:

Production of Sponge Iron (unit: million tonnes)

	2010-11	2011-12	2012-13	2013-14	2014-15	April-December 2015-16*
Coal based	19.27	19.80	19.07	20.19	21.89	14.66
Gas based	6.07	5.17	3.94	2.68	2.35	1.59
Total	25.34	24.97	23.01	22.87	24.24	16.25

*Source : JPC: * provisional*

India is also an important producer of pig iron. Post-liberalisation, with setting up several units in the private sector, not only imports have drastically reduced but also India has turned out to be a net exporter of pig iron. The private sector accounted for 91 per cent of total production for sale of pig iron in the country in 2014-15. The domestic availability situation of pig iron is given in the table below for the last five years and April-December 2015-16.

	Pig Iron Domestic Availability Scenario					('000 tonnes)
	2010-11	2011-12	2012-13	2013-14	2014-15	April-December 2015-16*
Production for Sale	5,683	5,371	6,870	7,950	9,694	7,202
Import	9	8	21	34	23	18
Export	358	491	414	943	540	216
Consumption	5,296	4,975	6,501	7,110	9,057	7,127

*Source : JPC: * provisional*

Global Ranking of Indian Steel

World crude steel production stood at 1622.8 million tonnes during 2015, a decrease of 2.8 per cent over 2014 based on provisional data released by World Steel Association (WSA). During 2015, Chinese crude steel production reached 804 million tonnes, registering a decline of 2.3 per cent over the previous year. China remained the largest crude steel producer in the world, accounting for 73 per cent of Asian and 50 per cent of world crude steel production during 2015. India was the 3rd largest crude steel producer during 2015 and recorded a growth of 2.6 per cent over 2014.

World Crude Steel Production 2014*

Rank	Country	Qty. (mt)	% change over 2014
1	China	803.83	-2.3
2	Japan	105.2	-5.0
3	India	89.60	2.6
4.	United States	78.92	-10.5
5.	Russia	71.11	-0.5
6.	South Korea	69.67	-2.6
7.	Germany	42.67	-0.6
8.	Brazil	33.24	-1.9
9.	Turkey	31.52	-7.4
10.	Ukraine	22.93	-15.6
	World	**1622.08**	**-2.8**

*Source: WSA: * provisional*

Fertilizers

Agriculture which accounts for about one seventh of the GDP, provides sustenance to nearly two-third of our population. Besides, it provides crucial backward and forward linkages to the rest of the economy. Successive five-year plans have laid emphasis on self-sufficiency and self-reliance in foodgrain production and concerted efforts in this direction have resulted in substantial increase in agriculture production and productivity. This is clear from the fact that from a very modest level of 52 million MT in 1951-52, food grain production increased to about 252.68 million MT in 2014-15. In meeting the domestic requirement of foodgrains and also generating exportable surpluses, the significant role played by chemical fertilizers is well recognized.

As of now, the country has achieved 80 per cent self-sufficiency in production capacity of urea. As a result, India could manage its substantial requirement of nitrogenous fertilizers through the indigenous industry besides imports. Similarly, 50 per cent indigenous capacity has developed in respect of phosphatic fertilizers to meet domestic requirements. However, the raw-materials and intermediates for the same are largely imported. For potash (K), since there are no viable sources/reserves in the country, its entire requirement is met through imports.

Growth of Fertilizer Industry

The actual production of all the fertilizers during the year 2014-15 was 370.03 LMT. The production of all the fertilizers during the year 2015-16 was 402.93 LMT showing an increase of more than 8.89 per cent in comparison of the previous year. The installed capacity has reached a level of 207.53 LMT in respect of urea, 83.32 LMT in respect of DAP and 60.72 LMT in respect of complex fertilizers during 2015-16.

At present, there are 30 large size urea plants in the country manufacturing urea, 21 units produce DAP and complex fertilizers and 2 units manufacture ammonium sulphate as a by-product. Besides, there are 105 medium and small-scale units tin operation producing Single Super Phosphate (SSP). The sector-wise installed capacity during the year 2015-16 is given here:

Sector-wise, Installed Capacity of Urea, DAP and Complex Fertilizers during 2015-16

S.No.	Sector	Annual Installed Capacity		
		Urea	DAP	Complex Fertilizers
1.	Public Sector	63.09	-	21.64
2.	Cooperative Sector	54.19	27.00	16.35
3.	Private Sector	90.25	56.32	22.73
	Total	207.53	83.32	60.72

Public Sector Undertakings

Fertilizer Corporation of India Limited

Incorporated on January 1, 1961, FCI was re-organized along with National Fertilizers Corporation Ltd (NFC) from 1978 into five companies namely, FCI, NFL, Hindustan Fertilizer Corporation Ltd. (HFC), Rashtriya Chemicals and Fertilizers Ltd. (RCF) and Projects and Development India Ltd. (PDIL). Following re-organisation, FCI comprised four units located at Sindri (Jharkhand), Gorakhpur (Uttar Pradesh), Ramagundam (Andhra Pradesh) and Talcher (Odisha), with a total annual capacity of 5.87 lakh MT of nitrogen besides and abandoned project at Korbe (Chhattisgarh).

Hindustan Fertilizer Corporation Limited

The Hindustan Fertilizer Corporation Limited (HFCL) was incorporated in 1978 as a result of the reorganization of the erstwhile Fertilizer Corporation of India Limited (FCIL), and NFL Group of Companies. The HFCL comprised Barauni Unit (Bihar), Durgapur Unit and Haldia Project (West Bengal) and Namrup Unit (Assam). The Namrup Unit was hived off from 2002 to form a separate entity with the name of Brahmaputra Valley Fertilizer Corporation Ltd (BVFCL).

Rashtriya Chemicals and Fertilizers Limited

Rashtriya Chemicals and Fertilisers Limited (RCF) was incorporated as a separate company in 1978 as a result of reorganization of the erstwhile Fertilizer Corporation of India Limited. At the time of its formation, the company had only one operating unit at Trombay (near Mumbai) and two major projects under implementation viz. Trombay-IV and Trombay-V expansion. The gas based Thal-Vaishet fertilizer complex about 100 kms from Trombay, was later implemented by RCF and it commenced commercial production in 1985.

National Fertilizers Limited

National Fertilizers Limited (NFL) was incorporated in 1974 for setting up two nitrogenous plants, at Bathinda (Punjab) and Panipat (Haryana) with LSHS as fee stock, each having urea production capacity of 5.11 lakh MT per annum. Consequent upon the reorganization of the FCI, the Nangal Unit (including Nangal Expansion Project) of FCI was also transferred to NFL in 1978.

Projects and Development India Limited

Projects and Development India Limited (PDIL), an erstwhile Division of the Fertilizers Corporation of India (FCIL) was registered as a separate company in 1978. The company has its registered office at Noida, Uttar Pradesh.

Fertilizers and Chemicals Travancore Limited

Fertilizers and Chemicals Travancore Limited (FACT) was incorporated in 1943. In 1947, FACT started production of ammonium sulphate with an installed capacity of 50,000 MT per annum at Udyogamandal, near Cochin (now Kochi). In

1980, FACT became a PSU and towards the end of 1982, the Government became the major shareholder. From a modest beginning, FACT has grown and diversified into a multi-division, multifunction organization with basic interest in manufacture and marketing of fertilisers and petro-chemicals, engineering consultancy and design and in fabrication and erection of industrial equipments.

Madras Fertilizers Limited

Madras Fertilizers Limited (MFL) was incorporated in December 1906 as a joint venture between GOI and AMOCO India Incorporation of USA (AMOCO) with GOI holding 51 per cent of the equity share capital in 1985, AMOCO disinvested their shares, which were purchased by GOI and NIOC in their respective proportions in 1985. The revised share holding pattern was: GOI 67.55 per cent and NIOC 32.45 per cent. The share holding pattern up to 1997 was GOI 69.78 per cent and NIOC 30.22 per cent. From 1997, MFL made its Maiden Public Issue of 2,86,30,000 shares of face value of ₹ 10 at a premium of ₹ 5 per share. Of these, 2,58,09,710 shares were subscribed.

Brahmaputra Valley Fertilizer Corporation Limited

Brahmaputra Valley Fertilizer Corporation Limited (BVFCL) has two operating units at Namrup, Assam. Its corporate office is also situated at Namrup. The other establishments of the company are liaison offices at Noida and Kolkata and marketing offices at Guwahati, Siliguri and Patna. The authorised share capital and paid up capital of the company in 2009 were ₹ 510 crore and ₹ 355.83 crore respectively.

FCI-Aravali Gypsum and Mineral India Limited

FCI-Aravali Gypsum and Mineral India Limited was incorporated under the Companies Act, 1956 as a public sector undertaking in 2003 after being hived off the Jodhpur Mining Organization (JMO) of Fertilizers Corporation of India Limited (FCIL).

Chemicals and Petrochemical Industry

The chemical and petrochemical industry is a knowledge intensive as well as capital intensive industry. It is an integral constituent of the growing industry. It includes basic chemicals and its products, petrochemicals, fertilizers, paints, varnishes, gases, soaps, perfumes and toiletry and pharmaceuticals. The diversification within the chemical industry is large and covers more than eighty thousand commercial products. This industry occupies a pivotal position in meeting basic needs and improving quality of life. The industry is the main stay of industrial and agricultural development of the country and provides building blocks for several downstream industries, such as textiles, papers, paints, soaps, detergents, pharmaceuticals, varnish, etc. India produces a large number of fine and specialty chemicals, which have very specific uses and find wide usage as food additives, pigments, polymer additives and antioxidants in the rubber industry, etc.

In the chemical sector, 100 per cent FDI is permissible. Manufacture of most of the chemical and petrochemical products are delicensed. The entrepreneurs need to submit an Industrial Entrepreneurs' Memorandum (IEM) to the Department of Industrial Policy and Promotion provided no locational angle is applicable. Only the following items are covered in the compulsory licensing list because of their hazardous nature: hydrocyanic acid and its derivatives; phosgene and its derivatives; and isocynates and di-isocynates of hydrocarbons. The production of selected major chemicals and petrochemicals from 2009-10 to 2015-16 is shown in the following Table. The production of major chemicals and petrochemicals in 2015-16 was 24,783 thousand MT, compared to 23,103 thousand MT in 2014-15, implying annual growth of 7.3 per cent.

Production and Growth Rate of Selected Major Chemicals and Petrochemicals

Figures in Thousand Metric Tonnes (MT)

GROUP	PRODUCTION/ GROWTH RATE	2009-2010	2010-2011	2011-2012	2012-2013	2013-2014	2014-2015	2015-2016
Alkali Chemicals	Production	5830	6271	6478	6487	6481	6625	6802
	Growth Rate (%)	5.14	7.57	3.30	0.14	-0.09	2.22	2.67
Inorganic Chemicals	Production	832	911	895	891	906	944	1002
	Growth Rate (%)	5.03	9.49	-1.84	-0.40	1.70	4.18	6.08
Organic Chemicals	Production	1448	1550	1640	1686	1792	1619	1589
	Growth Rate (%)	2.42	7.06	5.80	2.83	6.28	-9.67	-1.87
Pesticides	Production	135	144	156	155	179	186	188
	Growth Rate (%)	3.98	6.59	8.52	-0.48	15.41	3.95	0.57
Dyes& Pigments	Production	220	245	241	240	284	285	304
	Growth Rate (%)	30.63	11.32	-1.63	-0.56	18.40	0.58	6.60
Total Major Chemicals	Production	8465	9121	9409	9459	9643	9660	9884
	Growth Rate (%)	5.16	7.75	3.16	0.53	1.94	0.18	2.32
Synthetic Fibers	Production	2835	3123	3105	3124	3144	3527	3554
	Growth Rate (%}	14.4	10.2	-0.6	0.6	1.3	12.2	0.8
Polymers	Production	5695	6343	7250	7509	7876	7558	8839
	Growth Rate (%)	12.5	11.4	14.3	3.6	8.6	-4.0	17.0
Elastomers (S.Rubber)	Production	106	105	100	96	105	172	242
	Growth Rate (%)	10.4	-0.7	-4.7	-4.2	4.1	64.1	40.8
Synth. Detergent Intermediates	Production	618	638	623	627	597	596	566
	Growth Rate (%)	12.0	3.3	-2.4	0.7	-4.2	-0.1	-5.1

Performance Plastics	Production	1641	1740	1677	1691	1685	1591	1700
	Growth Rate (%)	45.0	6.0	-3.6	0.8	0.5	-5.5	6.9
Total Basic Major Petrochemicals	Production	10895	11950	12755	13047	13406	13443	14900
	Growth Rate (%)	16.9	9.7	6.7	2.3	2.7	3.0	10.8
Total Major Chemicals and Petrochemicals	Production	19360	21071	22165	22507	23048	23103	24783
	Growth Rate (%)	11.5	8.8	5.2	1.5	2.4	0.2	7.3

Index of Industrial Production

In the compilation of Index of Industrial Production (base 2004-05=100) in overall weight of 1000, chemicals and chemical products contribute 100.59. The General Index for 2016 stands at 198.7, which is 0.3 per cent higher as compared to the level in the month of March 2015. The cumulative growth for the period April-Mrch 2015-16 over the corresponding period of the previous year stands at 2.4 per cent. The Index of Industrial Production for the manufacturing sector for the month of March 2016 stands at 208.1, which is 1.0 per cent lower as compared to the level in the month of March 2015, whereas the Index of Industrial Production for the chemical and chemical products for the month of March 2016 stands at 148.8 which is 2.5 per cent higher as compared to the leve in the month of March 2015. The cumulative growth in manufacturing sector during April-March 2015-16 over the corresponding period of 2014-15 has been 2.0 per cent as against the growth 3.8 per cent in respect of chemical and chemical products.

Petroleum, Chemical and Petrochemical Investment Regions (PCPIRs)

The Petroleum, Chemical and Petrochemical Investment Regions (PCPIRs) Policy, a cluster approach to promote the petroleum, chemical and petrochemical sector in an integrated and environmental friendly manner on a large scale, was put in place in 2007. The same is also available on the website of the Department. This policy was an initiative to cater to the evolving needs of the industry. The government has approved setting up four PCPIRs in Andhra Pradesh (Vishakhapatnam - Kakinada), Gujarat (Dahej), Odisha (Paradeep) and Tamil Nadu (Cuddalore - Nagapattinam) which are estimated to attract investment of ₹ 7.63 lakh crore and provide employment to around 34 lakh persons. These PCPIRs are at different stages of implementation. PCPIRs are the projects with long gestation period and may take around 15-20 years to achieve full potential.

Plastic Parks Scheme

The scheme, adopting a cluster approach, aims to set up plastic parks with enabling infrastructure and eco system to boost manufacturing. Government of India provides grant funding up to 50 per cent of the project cost, subject to a ceiling of ₹ 40 crore per project. The remaining project cost is funded by the state government or its agencies, beneficiary industries and loan from financial institutions.

In all 10 plastic parks, at a cost of ₹ 405 crore, have been approved to be set up. Out of these, 4 are under implementation in Jagatsinghpur (Odisha), Raisen (Madhya Pradesh), Tinsukia (Assam) and Thiruvallur (Tamil Nadu). The locations of another 6 parks are identified in Deoghar (Jharkhand), Gwalior (Madhya Pradesh), Rajnandgaon (Chhattisgarh), Udham Singh Nagar (Uttarakhand), Panipat (Haryana) and Bankura (West Bengal). This initiative will boost 'Make in India' programme and will also generate huge employment.

Hindustan Insecticides Limited

Hindustan Insecticides Limited (HIL) was incorporated in 1954 to manufacture and supply of DDT. In 1957, the company set up a factory at Udyogmandal, Kerala and in 1977 at Rasayani, Maharashtra, for manufacture of malathion, an insecticide. The third unit of HIL was set up at Bhatinda, Punjab, in 2003. Rasayani and Udyogmandal plants have both DDT manufacturing and grochemical manufacturing facilities while Bathinda has only formulations manufacturing and packaging facility. The authorised and paid up share capital of HIL is ₹ 100 crore and ₹ 91.33 crore respectively. Cent per cent of its shares are held by the government.

HIL is the sole supplier of DDT to the National Vector Borne Disease Control Programme (NVBDCP) of the Health and Family Welfare. The company also exports DDT to some African countries and other products like malathion and mancozeb to countries like Brazil and Argentina. HIL diversified into agro chemicals in the late 1970s to ensure supply of quality pesticides at reasonable prices to the agricultural sector and has a range of technical and formulation grade pesticides. To further consolidate its position, it has also ventured into the seed business. It has got the status of National Level Seed Agency (NLA) from the Ministry of Agriculture and is producing and supplying seeds under Government sponsored schemes like National Food Security Mission (NFSM), National Mission on Oilseed & Oil Palm (NMOOP) and Mission on Integrated Development Horticulture (MIDH).

With a view to widen the product profile and further reduce the company's dependence on DDT, the company has added buprofezin, chlorpyriphos, acephate, imidacloprid, glyphosate, etc., in the product profile. Facility to manufacture pendimethalin, a weedicide, is under construction at Udyogmandal, Kerala. It has entered into tie-ups with public sector fertilizer companies like RCF, NFL, etc., for marketing of HIL products through their dealer network. HIL has been recently inducted by the Department of Fertilizers as an agency to import fertilizers. With the entry into fertilizer business, the company plans to develop into a 'One Stop' solution provider in the agricultural sector.

Hindustan Organic Chemicals Limited

Hindustan Organic Chemicals Limited (HOCL) was incorporated in December, 1960 with the objective of attaining self-reliance in basic organic chemicals. The company has two manufacturing Units located at Rasayani (Maharashtra) and Kochi (Kerala). The Rasayani unit (Chemical Complex) started production from 1970-71 and the Kochi unit (Phenol Complex) commenced production from 1987-88. Main products manufactured by HOCL include phenol, acetone and hydrogen peroxide at Kochi unit and aniline, nitrobenzene, formaldehyde, concentrated nitric acid and di-nitrogen tetroxide (N_2O_4) at Rasayani Unit. HOCL is the sole manufacturer of N_20_4 in India which is supplied to ISRO for satellites launching programme. HOCL also has a subsidiary company Hindustan Fluorocarbons Limited (HFL) located at Rudraram, Telangana, which manufactures Poly Tetra Fluro Ethylene (PTFE), a high tech engineering plastic, and Chloro Di-fluoro Methane (CFM-22).

HOCL was declared a Mini Ratna company in 1997. This status was however withdrawn in 2005 because of financial problems faced by the company from 1997-98 onwards when it started making losses following globalization and liberalisation of the Indian economy in the early 1990 resulting in competition from international players. Due to negative net worth by 2003-04, the company was referred to BIFR in February, 2005. Government approved a revival package for the company in March, 2006 providing cash infusion of ₹ 270 crore by way of preference share capital (redeemable) for repayment of high interest bonds, bank loans, implementation of VRS, etc. After implementation of the package, the company made profits during 2006-07 and 2007-08 and came out of BIFR.

Hindustan Fluorocarbons Ltd.

Hindustan Fluorocarbons Ltd. (HFL), a subsidiary company of Hindustan Organic Chemicals Ltd. (HOCL), was incorporated in1983. It is located at Rudraram, District Medak, in Telangana. The company started production in 1987 and is engaged in the manufacture of Poly Tetra Fluoro Ethylene (PTFE) and of Chloro Di Fluoro Methane (CFM-22). PTFE is extensively used in chemical, mechanical, electrical and electronic industries and has strategic applications in defence and aerospace sectors. CFM-22 is used as a refrigerant and for production of PTFE.

HFL started making losses from its inception in 1987-88 resulting in erosion of its net worth and reference to BIFR in 1994. A rehabilitation package for HFL was approved by BIFR in 2007.

For revival and growth of HFL, the company has adopted the strategy to develop fluoro specialty chemicals and switching over from single product to multi product facility to reduce dependency on PTFE. A Plan loan of ₹ 16.80 crore was provided to HFL in 2014-15 for plant refurbishment schemes and new initiatives, which includes ₹ 3.60 crore for development of modified PTFE, which has higher profit margins. HFL continues to be under BIFR since the net worth of the company continues to be negative. Issues relating to sick, loss-making and non-performing CPSEs are being examined by the NITI Aayog. Further action on HFL will be taken based on the final decision of the government in the matter.

Assam Gas Cracker Project (Brahmaputra Cracker & Polymers Limited)

The Assam Gas Cracker Project (AGCP) was initiated in pursuance of the Memorandum of Settlement signed between Central Government, All Assam Students Union (AASU) and All Assam Gana Sangram Parishad (AAGSP) in 1985. Subsequently, to implement the project, a Joint Venture Company 'Brahmaputra Cracker and Polymer Limited (BCPL) was incorporated in 2007 as a Central Public Sector Enterprise under the Department of Chemical and Petrochemicals.

Central Institute of Plastics Engineering and Technology

Central Institute of Plastics Engineering and Technology (CIPET) is a premier ISO 9001:2008 QMS, ISO/IEC - 17025, ISO/IEC - 17020 certified plastics institute under the aegis of Department of Chemicals and Petrochemicals, was established in 1968. The diversified activities of CIPET include - 'Skill Development, Technology Support to industry, Academics and Research and Development (STAR)' in all the domains of plastics engineering and technology viz., Design, CAD/CAM/CAE. Horling, plastics processing, testing and quality assurance, etc. for the benefit of plastics and allied industries.

Institute of Pesticide Formulation Technology

Institute of Pesticide Formulation Technology (IPFT) established in 1991, as an autonomous institution under the Department of Chemicals and Petrochemicals (DC&PC), Ministry of Chemicals & Fertilizers. One of the main objectives of the Institute is the development of user and environment friendly pesticide formulation technology. IPFT has established a healthy rapport with the pesticide industries and has been able to successfully transfer more than fifty formulation technologies to Indian and foreign companies. IPFT is significantly contributing towards new generation pesticide formulations through formulation technologies including nanotechnology based nano-emulsion microemulsions. novel gel technology, controlled release formulations (CRF), microencapsulation and tablet formulations.

Pharmaceutical Sector

The Department of Pharmaceuticals was created in 2008 in the Ministry of Chemicals and Fertilizers so as to provide greater focus for the growth of the high potential pharmaceuticals industry.

The Department of Pharmaceuticals notified the National Pharmaceutical Pricing Policy-2012 (NPPP-2012) with the objective to put in place a regulatory framework for pricing of drugs to ensure availability of required medicines - "essential medicines" - at reasonable prices, even while providing sufficient opportunity for innovation and competition to support the growth of industry, thereby meeting the goals of employment and shared economic well being for all. The salient features of this policy are:

All the medicines, as under National List of Essential Medicines (NLEM) -2011, that takes care of the healthcare needs of the majority of the population of the country, will come under price control. Nearly 680 formulations, spread over 27 therapeutic categories including HIV, diabetes, heart diseases, cancer, etc have come under price control.

National Pharmaceutical Pricing Policy

Subsequently, to implement the NPPP-2012, the new Drugs (Prices Control) Order, 2013 to control the prices of specified dosages and strengths as under National List of Essential Medicines-2011(NLEM-2011) was notifided. The medicines of dosages and strengths as specified under the National List of Essential Medicines (NLEM)-2011 have been brought under price control based on a concept of ceiling price by having the simple average price of all the branded and/or generic versions of such medicine having market share more than and equal to 1 per cent of the total domestic market turnover of that medicine. The medicines not listed under NLEM-2011 are under monitoring and no manufacturer can increase the maximum retail price of a drug more than ten per cent of maximum retail price during preceding twelve months.

Medical Devices Industry

Medical devices industry is a multi-product industry, producing wide range of products. Manufacturing and trade in medical devices is also growing quite steadily. Double digit growth rates indicate its importance in health care. Medical devices industry mostly depends on imports. Most hi-tech innovative products and technology originate from a well-developed eco-system and innovative cycle which needs to be developed in India to promote indigenous industry and to reduce our dependence on imports.

Uniform Code for Pharmaceutical Marketing Practices

Uniform code for Pharmaceutical Marketing Practices (UCPMP) for pharmaceutical as well as medical device industry was announced to be implemented voluntarily for a period of six months from 2015.

Indian Drugs and Pharmaceuticals Limited

Indian Drugs and Pharmaceuticals Limited (IDPL) was incorporated in 1961 with the primary objective of creating self-sufficiency in essential life saving drugs and medicines. The company has presently three manufacturing plants, one each at Rishikesh (Uttarakhand), Hyderabad (Andhra Pradesh) and Gurgaon (Haryana). IDPL has two wholly owned subsidiaries, namely, IDPL Ltd., Chennai (Tamil Nadu) and Bihar Drugs and Organic Chemicals Ltd. at Muzaffarpur (Bihar). In addition, IDPL has two joint sector undertakings, promoted in collaboration with the respective state governments. These are

Rajasthan Drugs and Pharmaceuticals Ltd. (RDPL), Jaipur, and Orissa Drugs and Chemicals Ltd. (ODCL), Bhubaneshwar. However, the Government has decided to de-link RDPL from IDPL and the process of delinking is underway.

Bengal Chemicals and Pharmaceuticals Limited

Bengal Chemicals and Pharmaceuticals Limited (BCPL) was a sick company in the private sector in the name and style of Bengal Chemicals and Pharmaceuticals Works. A new public sector company in the name and style of Bengal Chemicals and Pharmaceuticals Limited (BCPL) was incorporated in 1961.The company has four manufacturing units one each at Maniktala at Kolkata, Panihati at North 24 Parganas (West Bengal), one at Mumbai (Maharashtra) and at Kanpur (UP). The company manufactures and markets a wide range of industrial chemicals, a large number of drugs and pharmaceuticals besides cosmetics and home products. In the home products, the well known products include Cantharidine Hair Oil and Lamp Brand Phenol.

Minerals

Ministry of Mines is responsible for survey and exploration of all minerals, other than natural gas, petroleum and atomic minerals, for mining and metallurgy of non-ferrous metals like aluminium, copper, zinc, lead, gold, nickel, etc. and for administration of the Mines and Minerals (Regulation and Development) Act, 1957 and rules made thereunder in respect of all mines and minerals other than coal, natural gas and petroleum as well as Offshore Areas Mineral (Development and Regulation) Act, 2002 and rules made thereunder.

List of Subjects Allocated to the Ministry of Mines include:

(a) Legislation for regulation of mines and development of minerals within the territory of India, including mines and minerals underlying the ocean within the territorial waters or the continental shelf, or the exclusive economic zone and other maritime zones of India as may be specified, from time to time by or under any law made by Parliament.

(b) Regulation of mines and development of minerals other than coal, lignite and sand for stowing and any other mineral declared as prescribed substances for the purpose of the Atomic Energy Act, 1962 under the control of the Union as declared by law, including questions concerning regulation and development of minerals in various states and the matters connected therewith or incidental thereto.

(c) All other metals and minerals not specifically allotted to any other ministry/ department, such as aluminium, zinc, copper, gold, diamonds, lead and nickel.

(d) Planning, development and control of, and assistance to, all industries dealt with by the Ministry.

(e) Administration and management of Geological Survey of India and Indian Bureau of Mines.

(f) Metallurgical-grade silicon.

Important Features of National Mineral Policy, 2008

Sequel to the recommendations of the Hoda Committee which was constituted by the Planning Commission to review the National Mineral Policy, a New National Mineral Policy, 2008 was approved by the Government. The policy advocates: (i) use of state-of-the-art technology for exploration; (ii) zero waste mining; (iii) development of capital market structures to attract risk investment into survey and prospecting; (iv) transparency in allocation of concessions; (v) auction of ore bodies prospected at public response; (vi) independent Mining Administrative Tribunal; and (vii) a framework of sustainable development to take care of biodiversity issues.

Mineral Legislation

India is richly endowed with many minerals. As per the provisions of the Constitution of India, the development and regulation of mines and minerals comes under the control of the Union.

The Central Act to provide for the development and regulation of mines and minerals is the Mines and Minerals (Development and Regulation) (MMDR)Act, 1957. It empowers the Government to formulate rules for regulation of grant of mineral concessions for major minerals; in accordance of which Mineral Concession Rules, 1960 have been framed. It empowers the Government to frame rules for the conservation and systematic development of minerals and for the protection of environment; in accordance of which Mineral Conservation and Development Rules, 1988 were framed. Section 15 of MMDR Act, 1957 permits state governments to frame rules for regulating the grant of quarry leases, mining leases or other mineral concessions in respect of minor minerals; accordingly all state governments and some union territories have framed their own rules in this regard.

The Granite Conservation and Development Rules, 1999 and Marble Development and Conservation Rules, 2002 have also been framed under Section 18 of the MMDR Act, for conservation and systematic development of granite and marble resources in the country, respectively. The MMDR Act, 1957 was amended through the MMDR Amendment Act, 2015 in 2015. The most important feature of the MMDR Amendment Act is the provision for a simple and transparent mechanism for grant of mining lease or prospecting licence through competitive bidding.

The followings rules have been prepared and notified as prescribed under the Amendment Act: (i) Mineral (Evidence of Mineral Contents) Rules, 2015; (ii) Mineral (Auction) Rules, 2015; and (iii) Mineral (No-exclusive Reconnaissance Permit) Rules, 2015. To facilitate the state government the Ministry also issued Model Tender Document containing the Mine Development and production agreement and model district mineral foundation trust deed.

Mineral Resources

The classification of reserves/resources of various minerals based on United Nations Framework Classification (UNFC) in 2010 was done and National

Mineral Inventory is prepared. The UNFC consists of a three dimensional system with the three axes: economic viability; feasibility assessment; and geological assessment.

UNFC is a three-digit code based system, wherein the economic viability axis represent the first digit, the feasibility axis the second and the geological axis represent the third digit. Each of these three axes have further codes in decreasing order.

Total Mineral Resources: Reserve plus remaining resource comprise the total mineral resource.

Mineral Reserves: Economically mineable part of measured and/or indicated mineral resource: (i) proved mineral reserves (111); and (ii) probable mineral reserves (121) and (122).

Mineral Resources: It is the balance of the total mineral resources that have not been identified as a mineral reserve: (i) measured mineral resources - (331); (ii) indicated mineral resources - (332); (iii) inferred mineral resources - (333); (iv) reconnaissance mineral resources - (334); (v) prefeasibility mineral resources - (221) and (222); and (vi) feasibility mineral resources - (211).

Metallic Minerals

The production of iron ore at about 128.91 million tonnes in 2014-15 registered a decrease of 15 per cent over the previous year. About 46 per cent of the total production was shared by public sector companies like NMDC, SAIL and Orissa Mining Corporation, etc. The share of private sector was 54 per cent which includes Tata Steel (TISCO). During the year Odisha was the leading producer of iron ore accounting for 40 per cent of the total production followed by Chhattisgarh (23 per cent), Karnataka (16 per cent), Jharkhand (15 per cent), and remaining (6 per cent) production was reported from Andhra Pradesh, Madhya Pradesh, Maharashtra, Rajasthan and Telangana.

The production of copper concentrate at 108 thousand tonnes in 2014-15 decreased by about 23 per cent as compared to the previous year. The average metal content in copper concentrate was 23.13 per cent Cu.

The production of chromite at 2,164 thousand tonnes in 2014-15 decreased by 25 per cent as compared to the previous year. Odisha reported almost entire output of chromite (99.95 per cent) in the country. A nominal production was reported from Karnataka. Three public sector companies, namely Odisha Mining Corporation (OMC), Mysore Mineral Limited (MML) and Industrial Development Corporation of Odisha Limited (IDCOL) together reported 37 per cent of the total production and the remaining 63 per cent was contributed by private sector mines.

The production of manganese ore at 2,345 thousand tonnes in 2014- 15 decreased by 11 per cent compared to that in the previous year. MOIL continues to be the largest producer of manganese ore with a share of 49 per cent of the total production in 2014-15. Of the total production of manganese ore in 2014-

15, Madhya Pradesh contributed 37.68 per cent, Maharashtra 28.56 per cent, Odisha 13.90 per cent, Andhra Pradesh 10.82 per cent and the remaining production was from Karnataka, Telangana, Jharkhand and Rajasthan.

The production of primary gold at 1,440 kg (excluding by-product gold recovery from imported concentrates) in 2014-15 registered decrease of about 8 per cent as compared to the previous year. Karnataka was the leading producer of gold accounting for 99 per cent of the total production. The remaining production was reported from Jharkhand.

The production of bauxite at 22.23 million tonnes in 2014-15 decreased marginally by 0.4 per cent as compared to the previous year. NALCO, Utkal Alumina Industrial Ltd., HINDALCO and BALCO are the major companies engaged in the mining of bauxite in the country in 2014-15. Odisha accounted for 42 per cent of the total production of bauxite during 2014-15, followed by Gujarat 25 per cent, Maharashtra 12 per cent, Jharkhand 9 per cent Chhattisgarh 7 per cent, and Madhya Pradesh 4 per cent.

During 2014-15, the production of lead concentrate at 198 thousand tonnes increased by 2 per cent and that of zinc concentrate at 1,502 thousand tonnes also increased by 1 per cent over the previous year. Average metal content in lead concentrate was 56.29 per cent Pb and that in zinc concentrate was 51.48 per cent Zn. Rajasthan accounted for the entire production of lead concentrate and zinc concentrate during 2014-15.

Non-Metallic Minerals

The value of production of non metallic minerals at ₹ 7,323.42 crore during 2014-15 decreased by 3 per cent as compared to the previous year. limestone retained its leading position by contributing 68.30 per cent of the total value of non-metallic minerals in 2014-15. The other non-metallic minerals in the order of importance were phosphorite/ rock phosphate (6.33 per cent), barytes (4.74 per cent), dolomite (3.57 per cent), gypsum (2.06 per cent), kaolin (1.65 per cent), garnet (abrasive) (1.48 per cent), ball clay (1.40 per cent), talc/ soapstone/ steatite (1.31 per cent) and silica sand (1.29 per cent). The remaining was from other non metallic minerals.

The production of limestone was at 293 million tonnes in 2014-15 an increase by 4 per cent as compared to that in the previous year. Limestone is widely produced in India. As much as 87.22 per cent of the total output in 2014-15 was contributed by eight principal states; viz, Rajasthan (21.02 per cent), Madhya Pradesh (13.31 per cent), Andhra Pradesh (12.10 per cent), Gujarat (8.79 per cent), Karnataka (8.21 per cent), Telangana (8.18 per cent), Chhattisgarh (8.03 per cent) and Tamil Nadu (7.58 per cent). The remaining 12.78 per cent of the total production was shared by other limestone producing states.

The production of phosphorite/rock phosphate at, 1580 thousand tonnes, increased by 9 per cent in 2014-15, as compared to that of the previous year. The 91 per cent production was from public sector. Jhamarkotra mine of Rajasthan State Mines & Minerals Ltd. (RSMML) alone accounted for 86 per cent of the total production in the country during 2014-15. Rajasthan and Madhya Pradesh contributed 95.09 and 4.91 per cent of the production respectively. The production of dolomite at 6,209 thousand tonnes in 2014-15 registered were the principal producing states of dolomite. The remaining 41 per cent was contributed by eight states during the year, namely, Madhya Pradesh, Telangana, Odisha,Gujarat, Rajasthan, Jharkhand, Maharashtra and Uttarakhand.

The production of kaolin in 2014- 15 at 3,861 thousand tonnes decreased by 20 per cent as compared to that in the previous year. Nearly 63.62 per cent of total output of kaolin in 2014-15 was reported from Gujarat followed by Rajasthan (16.40 per cent), Kerala (14.54 per cent) and West Bengal (2.1 per cent) while remaining (3.33 per cent) was contributed jointly by Andhra Pradesh, Jharkhand, Karnataka and Madhya Pradesh.

Production of gypsum at 2,478 thousand tonnes in 2014-15 registered a decrease of 20 per cent as compared to the previous year. By and large, the entire production of gypsum was reported from Rajasthan (98.84 per cent) and the remaining was from Jammu & Kashmir.

The production of magnesite at 276 thousand tonnes during 2014-15 increased by 40 per cent as compared to the previous year. The production of talc/soapstone/ steatite in 2014-15 at 774 thousand tonnes decreased by about 13 per cent over the previous year. Rajasthan, the principal state accounted for 81.78 per cent of the total production in 2014-15. Five principal producers contributed 60 per cent of the total production of steatite.

Minor Minerals

The value of production of minor minerals was estimated at ₹ 46,678 crore in 2014-15. Andhra Pradesh with share of 29.59 per cent in the value of minor minerals produced in the country occupied the top position. Gujarat was at second place with a share of 20.24 per cent in the value of minor minerals. Next in the order was Rajasthan 16.19 per cent, Maharashtra 12.64 per cent, Uttar Pradesh 8.3 per cent, Karnataka 3.45 per cent, Kerala 2.98 per cent, Jammu & Kashmir 1.13 per cent and Madhya Pradesh 1.03 per cent. The contribution of remaining states and UTs was less than one percent each. Item-wise analysis revealed that building stone had the largest share of 25.7 per cent to the total value of minor minerals followed by road metals 23.9 per cent, brick-earth 15.5 per cent, ordinary sand 14.0 per cent, marble 4.1 per cent, gravel 3.5 per cent, kankar 2.7 per cent, limestone 2.6 per cent, murrum 2.4 per cent, quartzite & sand stone 1.6 per cent, and ordinary earth 1.4 per cent. The individual share of remaining minerals was less than 1.0 per cent which together contributed 2.6 percent of value of minor minerals.

Mineral and Metal Production

Based on the overall trend so far the index of mineral production (base 2004-05) for the year 2015-16 is estimated to be 129.2 as compared to 126.5 for 2014-15 showing a positive growth of 2.1 per cent. The total value of mineral production (excluding atomic minerals) during 2015-16 has been estimated at ₹ 2,68,955 crore, which shows a decrease of about 5.05 per cent over that of the previous year. During 2015-16, estimated value for fuel minerals account for ₹ 1,82,920 crore or 68.01 per cent, metallic minerals, ₹ 31,066 crore or 11.55 per cent of the total value and non-metallic minerals including minor minerals ₹ 54,969 crore or 20.44 per cent of the total value.

Geological Survey of India

Geological Survey of India (GSI), the premier earth science organization of the country, is the principal provider of basic earth science information to the government, industry and the geoscientific sector. Beginning in 1851 as a department engaged primarily in research for coal, GSI in its last 163 years of existence has expanded its activities manifold and has been involved either directly or indirectly in almost all areas of nation building. The vibrant steel, coal, metal, cement and power industries which expanded phenomenally in the post independence era, bear eloquent testimony to GSI's contribution to national development.

GSI is now the custodian of one of the largest and most comprehensive earth science databases developed over the last one and half century. Its Charter of Operation laid down by the Government of India (revised in 21st May 2009) details the scope of activities and responsibilities of GSI that encompasses practically the entire gamut of earth science activities. Creation and updation of national geoscientific information and knowledge base through ground, marine and airborne surveys and their dissemination are the primary goals of GSI.

The present activity domains of GSI include surface mapping, aerial and remote sensing surveys, offshore surveys, exploration for mineral and energy resources, engineering geology, geotechnical investigations, geoenvironmental studies, geology of water resources, geohazard studies, research and development, training and capacity building and information services, etc. GSI now functions as an attached office of the Ministry of Mines. It has its headquarters at Kolkata. The six regional offices of GSI are located at Kolkata, Jaipur, Lucknow, Hyderabad, Nagpur and Shillong. The Training Institute of GSI is located at Hyderabad.

Indian Bureau of Mines

Indian Bureau of Mines (IBM) established in 1948, is a multi-disciplinary scientific and technical organisation under Ministry of Mines with statutory and developmental responsibilities for conservation and systematic exploitation of mineral resources other than coal, petroleum and natural gas, atomic minerals and minor minerals. IBM has its headquarters at Nagpur with 12 regional and 2 sub-regional offices spread all over the country, apart from the Modern Mineral Processing Laboratory Pilot Plant constructed with UNDP assistance at Nagpur. Besides, two regional ore dressing laboratory and pilot plant are in operation at Ajmer and Bengaluru.

The Indian Bureau of Mines (IBM) performs regulatory functions under the relevant provisions of the Mines and Mineral (Development and Regulation) Act, 1957 and rules made thereunder namely enforcement of the Mineral Conservation and Development Rules, 1988, and Mineral Concession Rules, 1960 and Environmental (Protection) Act, 1986 and rules made thereunder. It also undertakes scientific, techno-economic, research oriented studies in various aspects of mining geological studies, ore beneficiation and environmental studies.

IBM provides technical consultancy services to the mining industry for the geological appraisal of mineral resources, and the preparation of feasibility report of mining projects, including beneficiation plants. It prepares mineral maps and countrywide inventory of mineral resources of leasehold and freehold areas. It also promotes and monitors community development activities in mining areas. IBM also functions as data bank of mines and minerals and publishes statistical information. It also brings out technical publications/ monographs/bulletins on mineral commodities. It advises the Central and state governments on all aspects of mineral industry, trade, legislation, etc.

Public Sector Undertakings

The Ministry of Mines has three Public Sector Undertakings (PSUs) under its administrative control. National Aluminium Company Limited (NALCO), Hindustan Copper Limited (HCL) are operating in the field of mining and mineral processing, and Mineral Exploration Corporation Limited (MECL) is operating in the field of mineral exploration.

National Aluminium Company Limited

National Aluminium Company Limited (NALCO) is a Navratna CPSE under Ministry of Steel and Mines. It was established in 1981 in the public sector, with its registered office at Bhubaneswar. The company is a group 'A' CPSE having integrated and diversified operations in mining, metal and power with sales turnover of ₹ 7,024 crore in financial year 2013-14.

The company has a 68.25 lakh TPA bauxite mine and 22.75 lakh TPA alumina refinery located at Damanjodi in Koraput, Odisha, and 4.60 lakh TPA aluminium smelter and 1200 MW captive power plant located at Angul, Odisha. NALCO has bulk shipment facilities at Vizag port for export of alumina/ aluminium and import of caustic soda and also utilises the facilities at Kolkata and Paradeep ports. The company has registered sales offices in Delhi, Kolkata, Mumbai, Chennai and Bengaluru and nine stockyards at various locations in the country to facilitate domestic marketing. The company is one of the low cost producers of metallurgical grade alumina. With sustained quality products, the company's export earnings accounted for about 53 per cent of the sales turnover in the year 2013-14 and the company was rated 3rd highest net export earning CPSE in 2012-13. NALCO is the first public sector company in the country to venture into international market in a big way with London Metal

Exchange (LME) registration since May, 1989. The company is listed at Bombay Stock Exchange (BSE) since 1992. Besides, ISO 9001, ISO 14001, OHSAS 18000 and SA 8000 certification; the company has also adopted ISO 50001 standards for energy management system.

Hindustan Copper Limited

Hindustan Copper Limited (HCL), a Mini Ratna Government of India enterprise under the administrative control of the Ministry of Mines, was incorporated in 1967 under the Companies Act,1956. It was established as a Govt. of India enterprise to take over all plants, projects, schemes and studies pertaining to the exploration and exploitation of copper deposits, including smelting and refining from National Mineral Development Corporation Ltd. It has the distinction of being the nation's only vertically integrated copper producing company as it manufactures copper right from the stage of mining to beneficiation, smelting, refining and casting of refined copper metal into downstream saleable products.

Mineral Exploration Corporation Limited

Mineral Exploration Corporation Limited (MECL) is a premier mineral exploration public sector unit of the country with ISO 9001-2008 certification. Since its inception in 1972, it has completed over 1290 projects of detailed mineral exploration and mine development and has added 150110 million tonnes of mineral reserves to the national mineral inventory.

Autonomous Bodies

National Institute of Rock Mechanics

The Institute is recognized as a Scientific and Industrial Research Organization (SIRO) by the Department of Scientific and Industrial Research, Ministry of S&T, and as a Certified Testing Centre for mining machineries and wire ropes by Directorate General of Mines Safety. The Institute carries out research projects funded by various Government ministries/departments, public sector and private organizations related to excavation in rock.

NIRM is expanding its activities into newer areas, such as oil and gas (for projects related to excavation of large underground caverns for strategic storage of these fuels), metro rails (underground rail tunnels and underground stations) major river-linking projects (irrigation tunnels) and other infrastructure projects.

National Institute of Miners' Health

National Institute of Miners' Health, Nagpur (NIMH) is an autonomous institute established under Ministry of Mines, with the objective of promotion of occupational health and prevention of occupational diseases among the persons employed in mining and mineral based industries. The institute is engaged in research and developmental activities relating to occupational health, work place monitoring, etc. The institute has developed the brand image and reputation of providing quality comprehensive technical support services in the field of occupational health and hygiene.

Jawaharlal Nehru Aluminium Research Development and Design Centre

The Jawaharlal Nehru Aluminium Research Development and Design Centre (JNARDDC), Nagpur is a " Centre of Excellence" set up in 1989 as a joint venture of Ministry of Mines, and UNDP with a view to provide major R&D support system for the emerging modern aluminium industry in India. The Centre has been functional since 1996.

The Centre is recognized as scientific and industrial research organization by the Department of Scientific and Industrial Research, Ministry of S&T. It is the only institute of its kind in India pursuing the cause of R&D from bauxite to finished product under one roof.

20 Law and Justice

MINISTRY of Law and Justice is the oldest limb of the Government of India dating back to 1833 when the Charter Act,1833 was enacted by the British Parliament. The said Act vested for the first time legislative power in a single authority, namely the Governor General of Council. By virtue of this authority and the authority vested under him under section 22 of the Indian Councils Act, 1861 the Governor General in Council enacted laws for the country from 1834 to 1920. After the commencement of the Government of India Act, 1919 the legislative power was exercised by the Indian Legislature constituted there under. The Government of India Act, 1919 was followed by the Government of India Act, 1935. With the passing of the Indian Independence Act, 1947 India became a Dominion and the Dominion Legislature made laws from 1947 to 1949 under the provisions of section 100 of the Government of India Act, 1935 as adapted by the India (Provisional Constitution) Order, 1947. Under the Constitution of India which came into force on the January 26, 1950 the legislative power is vested in Parliament.

Sources of Law

The main sources of law in India are the Constitution, statutes (legislation), customary law and case law. Statutes are enacted by Parliament, State legislatures and Union Territory legislatures. Besides, there is a vast body of laws known as subordinate legislation in the form of rules, regulations as well as bye-laws made by central/state governments and local authorities like municipal corporations, municipalities, gram panchayats and other local bodies. This subordinate legislation is made under the authority conferred or delegated either by Parliament or state or union territory legislatures concerned. Judicial decisions of superior courts like Supreme Court and High Courts are important sources of law. Decisions of the Supreme Court are binding on all courts within the territory of India. Local customs and conventions which are not against statute, morality, etc., are also recognised and taken into account by courts while administering justice in certain spheres.

Enactment of Law

The Parliament is competent to make laws on matters enumerated in the Union List. State legislatures are competent to make laws on matters enumerated in the State List. Parliament alone has power to make laws on matters not included in the State List or Concurrent List. On matters enumerated in the Concurrent List, laws can be made by both Parliament and the state legislature. But in the event of repugnancy, law made by Parliament shall prevail over law made by state legislature, to the extent of repugnancy, be void unless the latter law having been reserved for consideration of President, has received his assent and in that event shall prevail in that state.

Judiciary

At the apex of the entire judicial system exists the Supreme Court of India with a High Court for each state or group of states and under the High Courts there is a hierarchy of subordinate courts. Panchayat Courts also function in some states under various names like Nyaya Panchayat, Panchayat Adalat, Gram Kachehri, etc., to decide civil and criminal disputes of petty and local nature. Different state laws provide for jurisdiction of these courts.

The highest court in each district is that of District and Sessions Judge. This district court is the principal court of civil jurisdiction and can try all offences including those punishable with death. He is the highest judicial authority in a district. Below him, there are courts of civil jurisdiction, known in different states as Munsifs, Sub-Judges, Civil Judges and the like. Similarly, criminal courts comprise Chief Judicial Magistrate and Judicial Magistrate of First and Second class.

Supreme Court

During the British regime, the King in Council, or Privy Council as it was generally called, was the highest forum to entertain appeals from the judgments and orders passed by the courts in India. On enactment of the Judicial Committee Act 1833, it came to be called the Judicial Committee of Privy Council. The decisions of the Judicial Committee used to be couched in advisory form, though, in practice, the Crown always accepted its advice, and it was unthinkable that its report will not be given effect to. The Privy Council acted as a channel, through which English concepts came to be assimilated with Indian laws. It served as a bridge between the Indian and the English legal system, over which legal ideas travelled from England to India. It was through this body, that the common law of England was introduced in India under the British regime, as the base of its legal system. During its career as the highest court of appeals from India for the period of about 200 years, Privy Council rendered over 2,500 judgments, and till today these judgments constitute the fountain-source of law on many points in India.

However, there was a rising demand for establishment of Supreme Court in India, since it was felt that appeal to the Privy Council was very costly and beyond the means of common man. More important was the reason that it detracted from the self respect of the Indian people. Government of India Act, 1935 introduced a federal constitution to India, involving distribution of powers between the Centre and the constituent units. The Federal Court of India began functioning from October 01, 1937. To begin with, Federal Court had a very limited jurisdiction, confined to original jurisdiction in disputes between the centre and constituent units or inter se amongst the latter, advisory jurisdiction and appellate jurisdiction on a certificate from the High Court. Appeals from Federal Court could go to the Privy Council, from the judgments rendered in exercise of original jurisdiction, or by leave of the Federal Court or the Privy Council. In cases involving interpretation of Constitution, the parties had to first go to Federal Court in appeal from the High Court, and in other cases appeals from the High Courts lay directly to the Privy Council. It could give advice on such questions of public importance, as were referred to it by the Governor General, in his discretion. The appellate jurisdiction of the Federal Court was enlarged by enactment of Act No. 1 of 1948 and appeals were provided to Federal Court from the judgment of the High Court in the same circumstances, in which appeals could be brought to the Privy Council, without any special leave and also by special leave of the Federal Court in any other case. However, appeals to the Privy Council were still possible by leave of the Federal Court or of the Council.

After achieving their political aspirations by obtaining independence in August, 1947, there was demand from the Indian polity for enlarging the jurisdiction of Federal Court and granting more powers to it. With effect from October 10, 1949 appeals to the Privy Council were abolished altogether and the entire appellate jurisdiction was vested in the Federal Court. On January 26, 1950, Federal Court gave way to the Supreme Court of India under the new Constitution. Supreme Court of India is located on Tilak Marg, New Delhi.

After its inauguration on January 28, 1950, the Supreme Court commenced its sittings in a part of the Parliament House. The Court moved into the present building on August 4, 1958. The original Constitution of 1950 envisaged a Supreme Court with a Chief Justice and 7 puisne Judges - leaving it to Parliament to increase this number. In the early years, all the Judges of the Supreme Court sat together to hear the cases presented before them. As the work of the Court increased and arrears of cases began to cumulate, Parliament increased the number of Judges from 7 in 1950 to 10 in 1956, 13 in 1960, 17 in 1977, 25 in 1986 and 30 in 2009. As the number of the Judges has increased, they sit in smaller Benches of two and three - coming together in larger Benches of 5 and more only when required to do so or to settle a difference of opinion or controversy.

The Supreme Court of India comprises the Chief Justice and 30 other Judges appointed by the President of India. Supreme Court Judges retire upon attaining the age of 65 years. In order to be appointed as a Judge of the Supreme Court, a person must be a citizen of India and must have been, for at least five years, a Judge of a High Court or of two or more such Courts in succession, or an Advocate of a High Court or of two or more such Courts in succession for at least 10 years or he must be, in the opinion of the President, a distinguished jurist. Provisions exist for the appointment of a Judge of a High Court as an ad hoc Judge of the Supreme Court and for retired Judges of the Supreme Court or High Courts to sit and act as Judges of Supreme Court.

The Constitution seeks to ensure the independence of Supreme Court Judges in various ways. A Judge of the Supreme Court cannot be removed from office except by an order of the President passed after an address in each House of Parliament supported by a majority of the total membership of that House and by a majority of not less than two-thirds of members present and voting, and presented to the President in the same Session for such removal on the ground of proved misbehaviour or incapacity. A person who has been a Judge of the Supreme Court is debarred from practising in any court of law or before any other authority in India.

The proceedings of the Supreme Court are conducted in English only. Supreme Court Rules, 2013 replacing the 1966 Rules, have been framed under Article 145 of the Constitution to regulate the practice and procedure of the Supreme Court.

Hon'ble Justice T.S. Thakur is the 43rd Chief Justice of India.

O. W.: http://www.supremecourtofindia.nic.in

High Courts

High Court stands at the head of the state's judicial administration. There are 24 High Courts in the country, three having jurisdiction over more than one state. Among the union territories, Delhi alone has a High Court of its own. Other six union territories come under the jurisdiction of different state High Courts. Each High Court comprises a Chief Justice and such other Judges as the President may, from time to time, appoint. The Chief Justice of a High Court is appointed by the President in consultation with the Chief Justice of India and the Governor of the state. The procedure for appointing the High Court judges is the same except that the recommendation for the appointment of Judges in the High Court is initiated by the Chief Justice of the High Court concerned.

They hold office up to 62 years of age. To be eligible for appointment as a judge, one must be a citizen of India and should have held a judicial office in India for 10 years or must have practised as an advocate of a High Court or two or more such courts in succession for a similar period.

Jurisdiction and Seat of High Courts

Each High Court has powers of superintendence over all courts and tribunals within its jurisdiction. It can call for returns from such courts, make and issue general rules and prescribed forms to regulate their practices and proceedings and determine the manner and form in which book entries and accounts shall be kept. This table gives the seat and territorial jurisdiction of the high courts.

Name of High Courts, their Principal Seats, Benches and their Jurisdiction

Sl No.	High Court	Principal Seat	Jurisdiction	Permanent Bench and Date from which the Bench began fuctioning
1	Allahabad	Allahabad	Uttar Pradesh	Lucknow (01.07.1948)
2	Andhra Pradesh	Hyderabad	Andhra Pradesh and Telangana,	-
3	Bombay	Mumbai	Maharashtra; Goa; Daman and Diu Dadra and Nagar Haveli	Nagpur (01.05.1960) Panaji (01.07.1948) Aurangabad (27.08.1984)
4	Calcutta	Kolkata	West Bengal and Andaman and Nicobar Islands	Circuit Bench Jalpaiguri (yet to begin functioning)
5	Chhattisgarh	Bilaspur	Chattisgarh	-
6	Delhi	New Delhi	NCT of Delhi	-
7	Gauhati	Guwahati	Assam, Nagaland, Mizoram and Arunachal Pradesh	Kohima (10.02.1990) Aizawl (05.07.1990) Itanagar (12.08.2000)
8	Gujarat	Sola (Ahmedabad)	Gujarat	-
9	Himachal Pradesh	Shimla	Himachal Pradesh	-
10	Jammu and Kashmir	Jammu and Srinagar	Jammu and Kashmir	-
11	Jharkhand	Ranchi	Jharkhand	-
12	Karnataka	Bengaluru	Karnataka	Circuit Benches at Dharwar (07.02.2008) Gulbarga (07.02.2008)
13	Kerala	Kochi	Kerala and Lakshadweep Is.	-
14	Madhya Pradesh	Jabalpur	Madhya Pradesh	Gwalior (01.11.1956) Indore (01.11.1956)
15	Madras	Chennai	Tamil Nadu and Puducherry	Madurai (24.07.2004)
16	Orissa	Cuttack	Odisha	-
17	Patna	Patna	Bihar	-
18	Punjab and Haryana	Chandigarh	Punjab, Haryana and Chandigarh	Chandigarh
19	Rajasthan	Jodhpur	Rajasthan	Jaipur (31.01.1977)
20	Sikkim	Gangtok	Sikkim	-
21	Uttarakhand	Nainital	Uttarakhand	Nainital
22	Manipur	Imphal	Manipur	-
23	Meghalaya	Shillong	Meghalaya	-
24	Tripura	Agartala	Tripura	-

- *There are 24 High Courts in the country*
- *Only 6 High Courts (Allahabad, Bombay, Gauhati, Madhya Pradesh, Madras and Rajasthan) have 11 Permanent Benches amongst themselves*
- *Only Karnataka High Court has two Circuit Benches at Dharwar and Gulbarga.*

Approved and Working Strength of Supreme Court and High Courts

The total approved sanctioned strength, of Judges and Additional Judges in different High Courts and Supreme Court as an 1.4.2016 is given below

Sl. No.	Name of the Court	Approved Strength			Working Strength			Vacancies as per Approved Strength		
A	Supreme Court of India	31			25			06		
B.	High Court	Pmt.	Addl.	Total	Pmt.	Addl.	Total	Pmt.	Addl.	Total
1	Allahabad	76	84	160	63	07	70	13	77	90
2	High Court of Judicature at Hyderabad *	46	15	61	25	0	25	21	15	36
3	Bombay	71	23	94	57	09	66	14	14	28
4	Calcutta	45	13	58	35	09	44	10	04	14
5	Chhattisgarh	17	25	22	09	-	09	08	05	13
6	Delhi	45	15	60	34	05	39	11	10	21
7	Gauhati	18	06	24	07	07	14	11	-01	10
8	Gujarat	39	13	52	27	03	30	12	10	22
9	Himachal Pradesh	10	03	13	07	-	07	03	03	06
10	Jammu & Kashmir	13	04	17	08	01	09	05	03	08
11	Jharkhand	19	06	25	08	04	12	11	02	13
12	Karnataka	47	15	62	27	04	31	20	11	31
13	Kerala	27	11	38	26	09	35	01	02	03
14	Madhya Pradesh	40	13	53	27	04	31	20	11	31
15	Madras	56	19	75	34	0	34	22	19	41
16	Manipur	04	01	05	04	01	05	0	0	0
17	Meghalaya	03	01	04	02	0	02	01	01	02
18	Orissa	20	07	27	15	06	21	05	01	06
19	Patna*	40	13	53	24	05	29	16	08	24
20	Punjab & Haryana*	64	21	85	36	11	47	28	10	38
21	Rajasthan	38	12	50	21	03	24	17	09	26
22	Sikkim	03	0	03	02	0	02	01	0	01
23	Tripura	04	0	04	04	0	04	0	0	0
24	Uttarakhand	09	02	11	06	0	06	03	02	05
	Total	754	302	1056	508	86	594	246	216	462

**Acting Chief Justice*

Power of Supreme Court and High Courts

Supreme Court has power to issue any person or authority and Government within its jurisdiction, direction, order or writs, including writs which are in the nature of *habeas corpur, mandamus, prohibitio, quo warranto and certiorari,* for enforcement of Fundamental Rights and for any other purpose. This power may also be exercised by any high court exercising jurisdiction in relation to territories within which the cause of action, wholly or in part arises for exercise of such power, even if the seat of such government or authority or residence of such person is not within those territorie.

Subordinate Courts

The structure and functions of subordinate courts are more or less uniform throughout the country. Designations of courts connote their functions. These courts deal with all disputes of civil or criminal nature as per the powers conferred on them. These courts follow two important codes prescribing procedures, i.e., the Code of Civil Procedure, 1908 and the Code of Criminal Procedure, Cr. P.C., 1973 and further strengthened by state level amendments. As per direction of Supreme Court in WP (Civil) 1022/1989 in the All India Judges Association case, a uniform designation has been brought about in the subordinate judiciary's judicial officers all over the country, viz., District or Additional District Judge, Civil Judge (Senior Division) and Civil Judge (Junior Division) on the civil side and on criminal side, Sessions Judge, Additional Sessions Judge, Chief Judicial Magistrate and Judicial Magistrate, etc., as laid down in the Cr.P.C. Appropriate adjustment, if any, has been made in existing posts by indicating their equivalent with any of these categories by all state governments/UT administrations. Under Article 235 of the Constitution of India, the administrative control over the members of subordinate judicial service vests with the concerned High Court. Further in exercise of powers conferred under provision to Article 309 read with Articles 233 and 234 of the Constitution, the state government shall frame rules and regulations in consultation with the High Court exercising jurisdiction in relation to such state. The members of the State Judicial Services are governed by these rules and regulations.

National Mission for Justice Delivery and Legal Reforms

The National Mission for Justice Delivery and Legal Reforms was set up in August, 2011 to achieve twin goals of (i) increasing access by reducing delays and arrears; and (ii) enhancing accountability through structural changes and by setting performance standards and capacities. The Mission is pursuing five strategic initiatives: (i) outlining policy and legislative changes, (ii) re-engineering of procedures and court processes, (iii) focussing on human resource development, (iv) leveraging information and communication technology and tools for better justice delivery, and (v) improving infrastructure. The Mission has adopted a coordinated approach for phased liquidation of arrears and pendency in judicial administration which, *inter-alia,* involve better infrastructure for courts including computerisation, increase in strength of subordinate judiciary, policy and legislative measures in the areas prone to excessive litigation, re-engineering of court procedure for quick disposal of cases. The Mission has taken several steps in each of the strategic areas towards fulfilment of its objectives. Judicial Standards and Accountability Bill is being considered by the Parliament. Constitution Amendment Bill for raising the retirement age of High Court Judges is also before the Parliament. A comprehensive proposal has been formulated for constitution of All India Judicial Service (AIJS). All states have formulated their litigation policies with a view to reduce the governmental litigation. State governments have been requested to make an assessment of the impact of the state litigation policies on controlling proliferation of litigation by state agencies. An Inter-Ministerial Group (IMG) constituted to suggest necessary amendments to the Negotiable Instruments (NI) Act along with other policy and administrative measures to check increasing litigation relating to cheque bounce cases, has suggested a number of measures including procedural and legislative changes to reduce number of cheque bounce cases. These measures are being further pursued by Department of Financial Services and Reserve Bank of India.

For limiting the litigation arising out of challan cases under Motor Vehicles Act, 1988, the Ministry of Road Transport and Highways have been requested to take appropriate steps in this regard. They are drawing consolidated guidelines for the Transport Department of states/union territories advising suitable administrative measures to simplify the system of payment of challan without taking recourse to courts. An important aspect of the judicial reforms relates to re-engineering court procedures and court processes for early disposal of cases. A comprehensive scheme of National Court Management Systems (NCMS) has been formulated and notified by the Supreme Court of India. Under the NCMS, a National Framework of Court Excellence (NFCE) has been prepared, which shall set measurable standards of performance for courts addressing the issues of quality, responsiveness and timeliness. A number of suggestions are being received by the National Mission for speedy disposal of court cases. One of the suggestions relates to doing away with the payment of 'Process Fee' to curtail procedural delays. It has been suggested that if needed 'Court Fee' could be suitably modified to include such expenses. This suggestion has been referred to the state governments and high courts for consideration.

Gram Nyayalayas

A Central Sector scheme for providing financial assistance to the state governments / UT administrations for establishment and operationalisation of Gram Nyayalayas was launched in December, 2009. So far 10 states have notified 194 Gram Nyayalayas, out of which 159 are operational. The Conference of Chief Justices of High Courts and Chief Ministers of the states held in April 2013, *inter-alia*, decided that the state governments and High Courts should decide the question of establishment of Gram Nyayalayas wherever feasible, taking into account their local problems. The focus is on covering those talukas under the Gram Nyayalayas scheme where regular courts have not been set up.

Judicial Infrastructure

Judicial Infrastructure Adequacy of Judicial Infrastructure is a pre-requisite for reduction of pendency and backlog of cases in Courts. The primary responsibility of infrastructure development for the subordinate judiciary rests with the State Governments. The Central Government augments the resources of the State Governments by releasing financial assistance under a centrally sponsored scheme for the development of judicial infrastructure. The scheme has been in place since 1993-94, and was revised in 2011. It covers the construction of court buildings and residential accommodation of judicial officers. As of March, 2016, the Central Government had released an amount of ₹ 3,694 crore to the State Governments and UT administrations under the revised funding pattern effective from 2011-2012. This represents a significant increase over the sum of ₹ 1,245 crore that was provided by the Central Government in the initial phase of the scheme from 1993-2011. With higher devolution of funds to the State Governments on the recommendations of Fourteenth Finance Commission, the fund sharing pattern under the Scheme has been further revised to 60 :40 between Central and State Governments with effect from 2015-16. For States in the North Eastern Region and Himalayan States, it has been kept at 90:10.

As per information collected from High Courts as of December 31, 2015, there were 16,513 court halls / court rooms available for District and Subordinate Courts in the country. In addition, 2,447 court halls / court rooms were under construction. Comparing these figures with the working strength of 16,070 judges / judicial officers reported by High Courts as of December, 2015, adequate court rooms / court halls are available for the current strength of judicial manpower. Focus is now to match the availability of court rooms / court halls with the sanctioned strength of judicial officers / judges in District and Subordinate Courts. Considerable progress has also been made with regard to availability of residential units for judicial officers in District and Subordinate Courts. As of December, 2015, 14,420 residential units were available for Subordinate Courts and 1,868 residential units were under construction.

e-Courts Integrated Mission Mode Project Computerisation

The e-Courts Integrated Mission Mode Project is one of the nationa e-Governance projects being implemented in High Courts and District/Subordinate Courts of the Country. The project has been conceptualized on the basis of the "National Policy and Action Plan for Implementation of Information and Communication Technology in the Indian Judiciary-2005" by the e-Committee of the Supreme Court of India. The e-Committee was formed in 2004 to draw up an action plan for the ICT enablement of the Judiciary with the Patron in Chief-cum-Adhoc Chairman as the Chief Justice of India.

The Government approved the computerization of 14,249 District and Subordinate Courts under the project by March, 2014. The objective of the e-Courts project is to provide designated services to litigants, lawyers and the judiciary by universal computerization of district and subordinate courts in the country and enhancement of ICT enablement of the justice system.

Thirteenth Finance Commission Grant

With the objective of improving justice delivery, Thirteenth Finance Commission (FC-XIII) has recommended a grant of ₹ 5000 crore over its award period 2010-15.

Guidelines for release and utilisation of grant-in-aid for improvement in justice delivery system as recommended by the FC-XIII have been finalised and circulated to the state governments. Further, a review committee has been constituted in the Department of Justice to review utilisation of the grants. An amount of ₹ 1,426.46 crore has been released to the states so far under Thirteenth Finance Commission.

Access to Justice for the Marginalised

In partnership with the United Nations Development Programme (UNDP), the Department of Justice (DOJ), Ministry of Law and Justice, is implementing a decade long programme on Access to Justice for Marginalised People (2008-2017). The project extends to the eight UNDAF states of Bihar, Chattisgarh, Jharkhand, Madhya Pradesh, Rajasthan, Uttar Pradesh, Maharashtra and Odisha. This project focuses on strengthening access to justice for marginalised people by developing strategies that address barriers to accessing justice in legal, social and economic domains. The project is presently in the second phase of implementation. The first phase expanding from 2008 to 2012 made significant contributions. Some of the achievements of phase I include: (i) legal literacy initiatives reaching over 20 lakh people from marginalized communities on awareness of their legal rights; (ii) inclusion of legal literacy in the adult literacy programme under the National Literacy Mission Scheme (Sakshar Bharat); (iii) training of over 7,000 paralegals from various backgrounds; and (iv) a first-ever study conducted in India on legal aid clinics run by law schools and needs assessments of several State Legal Services Authorities to enable a better understanding of the barriers faced by marginalized communities in accessing justice.

The second phase of the project extends over five years from 2013 to 2017. In this phase, the project aims to build upon the achievements of previous phase and continues to work on creation of demand for justice and ensuring its supply. Under the project, a technical support team has also been placed with the Department of Justice with the specific purpose of supporting the National Mission for Justice Delivery and Legal Reforms.

The second phase of the project will continue to focus both on the demand and supply side. In terms of geographical coverage, the project will focus efforts in 1-2 selected districts in the eight states of Bihar, Chhattisgarh, Jharkhand, Madhya Pradesh, Maharashtra, Odisha, Rajasthan and Uttar Pradesh for better impact. The project will try to ensure sustainability of results achieved in the previous phase. This project will also provide embedded technical support to the National Mission with a view to assist the Department of Justice in achieving the goals of the Mission. To promote South cooperation, the project will support information sharing and learning exchanges between India and other countries across the globe to create learning opportunities from good practices in terms of strategies, approaches and tools for improved legal aid for the poor.

Appellate Tribunal for Foreign Exchange

The Appellate Tribunal for Foreign Exchange was established in June, 2000 under Section 18 of Foreign Exchange Management Act (FEMA), 1999. Under Section 19 of FEMA, the Central Government or any person aggrieved by an order made by Special Director (Appeals), or made by an Adjudicating Authority other than referred to in sub-section (i) of section 17, may prefer an appeal to the Appellate Tribunal that may be filed within 45 days from the date of receiving the order by the aggrieved person or the Central Government.

Section 20 of FEMA provides that the Appellate Tribunal shall consist of a Chairperson and such number of members as the Central Government may deem fit. The jurisdiction of the Appellate Tribunal may be exercised by the Benches. The Bench may be constituted by the Chairperson, with one or more Members as the Chairperson deems fit. The Benches of the Appellate Tribunal shall ordinarily sit in New Delhi and at such other places as the Central Government may, in consultation with the Chairperson, notify and the Chairperson may transfer a Member from one Bench to another. If at any stage it appears that the matter should be heard by a Bench of two Members the Chairperson may transfer the matter to such Bench as he deems fit. A person who is qualified to be a Judge of a High Court or is or has been a Judge of High Court can be appointed as Chairperson of the Tribunal and a person who has been or is qualified to be a District Judge can be appointed as a Member of the Tribunal. Under Section 49 sub-Section (5) clause (b), all appeals which were pending before PERA Board have been transferred and are at the disposal of the Appellate Tribunal constituted under Foreign Exchange Management Act.

Alternative Dispute Resolution

The International Centre for Alternative Dispute Resolution (ICADR) was registered under the Societies Act, 1860 in 1995. It is an autonomous organization working under the aegis of the Ministry of Law and Justice, Government of India with its headquarters in New Delhi and Regional Centres in Hyderabad and Bengaluru. It has been established to promote, popularize and propagate alternative dispute resolution methods to facilitate earlier resolution of disputes and to reduce the burden of arrears in courts.

Enforcement Agencies

Police

The police force in the country is entrusted with the responsibility of maintenance of public order and prevention and detection of crimes. Public order and police being state subjects under the Constitution, police is maintained and controlled by states.

The police force in a state is headed by the Director General of Police/ Inspector General of Police. State is divided into convenient territorial divisions called ranges and each police range is under the administrative control of a Deputy Inspector General of Police. A number of districts constitute the range. District police is further sub-divided into police divisions, circles and police stations. Besides the civil police, states also maintain their own armed police and have separate intelligence branches, crime branches, etc. Police set up in big cities like Delhi, Kolkata, Mumbai, Chennai, Bengaluru, Hyderabad, Ahmedabad, Nagpur, Pune, etc., is directly under a Commissioner of Police who enjoys magisterial powers. All senior police posts in various states are manned by the Indian Police Service (IPS) cadres, recruitment to which is made on All-India basis.

The central government maintains Central Police forces, Intelligence Bureau (IB), Central Bureau of Investigation (CBI), institutions for training of police officers and forensic science institutions to assist the states in gathering intelligence, in maintaining law and order, in investigating special crime cases and in providing training to the senior police officers of the state governments.

Indo-Tibetan Border Police

The Indo-Tibetan Border Police (ITBP) was raised in 1962 in the wake of Chinese aggression for re-organizing the frontier intelligence and security setup along the Indo-Tibetan border covering 2115 kms from Karakoram pass to Lipulekh pass. Only four battalions were sanctioned to begin with. In view of the additional responsibilities and redefined task in 1976, the force was restructured in 1978 to 09 service battalions with four specialists battalions and two training centres. With additional tasks entrusted to ITBP from time to time on border guarding, counter insurgency and Internal Security Roles, the number of its battalions increased gradually and ITBP presently has 52 service battalions, four specialists battalions and 17 training centres and two logistic centres. Out of 52 service battalions, two battalions have been converted in to DM battalions and transferred to National Disaster Response Force (NDRF). In pursuance of One Border One Force, the entire stretch of Indo-China border comprising 3488 kms, has been assigned to ITBP for Border Guarding duty and accordingly it replaced Assam Rifles in Sikkim and Arunachal Pradesh in 2004-05.

ITBP is basically a mountain trained force and most of the officers and men are professionally trained mountaineers and skiers. They have scaled more than 180 Himalayan peaks including Mt. Everest four times including the recent successful expedition in 2012. ITBP mountaineers have also successfully climbed peaks in Nepal, Iran, Japan and South America. ITBP skiers have been national champions and have taken part in Winter Olympics. It has also participated in adventurous White Water Rafting, through turbulent and mighty waters of the Brahamputra, the Indus and the Ganges and has international achievements to its credit in this field.

O. W.: http://www.itbpolice.nic.in

Border Security Force

International borders of India with Pakistan both east and west were being manned by the respective state police forces till Indo-Pak war in September 1965. Certain inherent shortcomings of this arrangement came to light during the war and it was decided to have one single force under the Union of India for guarding the international borders with Pakistan.

Based on above premise, BSF came into existence in December, 1965 by amalgamation of various state police battalions into BSF. The Force was thus raised with a meagre strength of 25 battalions as against the present size of 175 Battalions. Presently, it is manning 6,623 kms of international borders with Pakistan and Bangladesh. Beside this, BSF plays a crucial role in various internal security duties.

BSF's role during peace time is as : (i) to promote a sense of security among the people living in the border areas; (ii) to prevent trans-border crimes, unauthorized entry into or exit from the territory of India; (iii) to prevent smuggling and any other illegal activities on the border; (iv) anti-infiltraton duties; and (v) to collect trans-border intelligence.

BSF's role during war time is as: (i) holding ground in assigned sectors; (ii) limited aggressive action against central armed police or irregular forces of the enemy; (iii) maintenance of law and order in enemy territory administered under the army's control; (iv) guarding of prisoners of war camps; (v) acting as guides to the army in border areas; (vi) assistance in control of refugees; (vii) provision of sectors; and (viii) performing special tasks connected with intelligence including raids.

O. W.: http://www.bsf.nic.in

Assam Rifles

The Assam Rifles raised as Catchar Levy in 1835 is the oldest Central Para Military Force in India. The Force was raised primarily to guard the alluvial plains of Assam from the wild and unruly tribes inhabiting the surrounding hill tracts. This was the earliest embodied unit of what eventually developed into the Assam Rifles. Gradually more such units were raised and employed for establishing posts in the interior and thus acted as the strong arm of the civil administration in extending the authority of the Britishers. The Force also helped in opening up these inaccessible and isolated areas and in undertaking development activities; earning many accolades from the administration. The Assam Rifles' contribution towards assimilation of the people of the north-east into the national mainstream is truly monumental. Their long association with the region reflects in the force being fondly called "The Sentinel of the North-East" and "Friends of the Hill People" security in the north-eastern region and guarding the Indo-Myanmar border. The Force has 46 battalions and has a dual role of maintaining internal security in the north-eastern region and guarding the Indo-Myanmar border.

At inception, it was essentially a civil force and merely acted as a strong arm of local administration. Gradually, as the 'Forward Policy" was adopted by the British Government, task of the 'Militia' changed from mainly defensive to positively offensive involving expeditions in expanding domain in not only Assam, but also in the tribal areas of the north east region. Changes in roles also brought in nomenclature and character of the Force.

O. W.: http://www.assamrifles.gov.in

National Security Guard

Terrorism, both national and international raised its head in the west during the seventies. It manifested in many forms including hijacking of aircraft, taking of hostages, assassination of dignitaries and others. The normal law and order machinery and the defence forces of the West were found wanting to deal with this menace. Specially equipped and trained forces like SAS of UK, Delta Force of USA and GSG-9 of West Germany were raised abroad. The need for creating a special force for executing surgical operations based on tactical intelligence was felt in India when Operation Blue Star was carried out by the army at the Golden Temple, Amritsar in 1984. This operation not only caused extensive damage to the Golden Temple but also occasioned a large number of casualties, and above all the Sikh psyche was badly hurt. National Security Guard (NSG) was conceptualised and created after studying and analysing Special Force like SAS in the United Kingdom, GIGN in France, GSG-9 in Germany. Shar-et-matkal in Israel and Delta Force in the USA. Accordingly, NSG was raised in October, 1985 as a Federal Contingency Force under the MHA. It consists of selected and highly motivated personnel from the army as well as the central armed police. 53 per cent of the personnel are drawn from the army while the central armed police like BSF, CRPF and ITBP contribute 47 per cent. NSG has a glorious heritage and is held in high esteem by the nation. Since raising, its commandos have been employed in 114 major successful counter terrorist operations, earning numerous awards and rewards including three Ashok Chakras, two Kirti Chakras, three Shaurya Chakras and 10 PPMG. Nine NSG Commandos have also made the supreme sacrifice in living up to the NSG's motto of Sarvatra Sarvotam Suraksha.

O. W.: http://www.nsg.gov.in

Central Reserve Police Force

The Central Reserve Police Force (CRPF) was formed in July 1939 at Neemuch as the Crown Representative's Police. After independence it was renamed as the Central Reserve Police Force and Sardar Vallabh Bhai Patel, the then Home Minister had visualized a multi-dimensional role for it. The CRPF has innumerable achievements to its credit. It was the CRPF which bore the brunt of the first onslaught of the Chinese aggression at Hot Springs in Ladakh in 1959 when a small CRPF patrol was ambushed and heavily out-numbered by the Chinese army. In the ensuing battle, 10 CRPF men laid down their lives. Every year 21st October is observed as the Police Commemoration Day. The force once again proved its mettle in 1965 when a small contingent of Second Bn CRPF, successfully fought and repulsed an attack by a Pakistani Brigade on 9th April at Sardar Post in Gujarat, killing 34 Pakistani soldiers and capturing 4 alive. Never in the history of military battles have a handful policemen fought back a full-fledged infantry brigade in such a manner. In this incident six valiant CRPF men also laid down their lives. As a tribute to the saga of our brave men, 9th April is now befittingly celebrated as "Valour Day" in the Force.

The CRPF has also been deployed internationally at Kosovo, Haiti and Sri Lanka. In Sri Lanka, two CRPF Battalions and one company of Mahila Battalion were a part of the Indian Peace Keeping Force. The first major offensive of the LTTE directed against the CRPF, using unconventional warfare was successfully repelled. Now, for the first time in the history of UN, a fully formed women's unit is posted in Liberia as a part of United Nations Peacekeeping Mission. On December 13, 2001 when the terrorists attacked the Parliament House it was the brave CRPF who successfully foiled the attack. In exchange of fire, all the five militants were eliminated. Mahila Ct Kamlesh Kumari who sacrificed her life during the incident was, for her exemplary bravery, awarded the highest peacetime Gallantry Award 'Ashok Chakra' posthumously. When 5 armed terrorists tried to storm the Ram Janambhoomi/Babri Masjid Complex in Ayodhya in July, 2005 and had penetrated the outer security rings, they were confronted by the CRPF posted at the inner security ring. The CRPF Jawans fought bravely and thwarted the evil designs of the terrorists and successfully eliminated all of them on the spot.

From a single battalion in 1939 the Force has now grown to four zones, 20 Adm. Sectors, 2 Ops Sectors, 36 Adm Ranges, 7 Ops Ranges, 228 Bns, 41 group centers, 15 training institutions and 4 composite hospitals. It is the only Central Armed Police Force in the country which has 3 Mahila Battalions. The bulk of the force is deployed in Jammu and Kashmir; left wing extremism affected states and in north-eastern states to tackle terrorist and insurgent activities. It presently has 10 Cobra units, a specially trained force to fight the naxal means. The Cobra battalions have been deployed strategically in the naxal affected areas. CRPF has always been playing a significant role in times of natural disasters. When the destructive Tsunami had caused an unprecedented damage to lives and property or when the J and K earthquake had devastated large areas disrupting life on a massive scale, CRPF played a significant role in the relief, rescue and rehabilitation efforts. We now have two battalions of CRPF designated as Disaster Management battalions and they have been located in Pune and Ahmedabad.

O. W.: http://www.crpf.nic.in

Rapid Action Force

Presidential colour to Rapid Action Force (RAF) was presented in October, 2003. CRPF is the first central armed police force who have two Presidential colours.

RAF was raised to deal with communal problems and continues to deal with militancy in J and K and Punjab, insurgency in north-east, overseas deployment for UN Peace Keeping in Haiti, Bosnia and Kosovo, rescue and relief (Odisha super cyclone, Gujarat and JandK earthquake). RAF dealt with mammoth human congregations (Amarnath Yatra, Jagannath Yatra, etc.) combating naxalism in LWE affected states guarding of vital shrines in Ayodhya, Kashi, Mathura, Vaishno Devi and Raghunath Temple, Jammu law and order situation on the issue of revocation of transfer of land to Shri Amarnath Shrine Board, dealt with serious law and order problem due to Gujjar agitation in Rajasthan, dealt effectively with serious stone pelting menace in J and K, and monitored successful completion of elections in various states.

Central Industrial Security Force

Raised in 1969, Central Industrial Security Force (CISF) is providing security cover to 303 units including 59 domestic and international airports and fire protection cover to 87 industrial undertakings. With globalization and liberalization of the economy, CISF is no longer a PSU-centric organization. Instead, it has become a premier multi-skilled security agency of the country, mandated to provide security to major critical infrastructure installations of the country in diverse regions including terrorist and naxal affected areas. CISF is currently providing security cover to 308 units which include atomic power plants, space installations, defence production units, mines, oil fields and refineries, major sea ports, heavy engineering steel plants, fertilizer units, airports, hydro electric/thermal power plants, sensitive government buildings and even heritage monuments (including the Taj Mahal and Red Fort) and also iconic private sector units. The Force is also one of the largest fire protection service providers in the country. It provides fire protection cover to 86 industrial undertakings. CISF has been inducted into Ratnagiri Gas and Thermal Power Station Ltd., Rajiv Gandhi Thermal Power Project, Hissar, Haryana. The specialized task of airport security was assigned to CISF in the wake of hijacking of Indian Airlines plane to Kandhar.

The Force has so far taken over security of all major airports in the country, which includes international airports of Mumbai, Delhi, Chennai and Kolkata. Besides, it has taken over security of 45 government buildings, which include North Block, part of South Block and CGO Complex in Delhi. CISF Act was amended to enable the force to provide security, on payment basis, to private/joint venture industrial undertakings, which are vital for the security and economy of the country. After the Mumbai terrorist attack in November, 2008, the mandate of the force has been broadened to provide direct security cover to private sector also. More than 175 private sector installations have already requested for CISF protection and Infosys Technologies Limited - a multinational information technology services company's headquarter in Bengaluru, became the first private sector company to get the CISF security cover in August 2009. CISF is a cost reimbursement force i.e., it is not a burden on the national exchequer. CISF in October, 2009 started a passenger friendly utility on its official website www.cisf.gov.in for the lost and found articles at all airports where CISF has been deployed.

O. W.: http://www.cisf.gov.in

Sashastra Seema Bal

The 'Sashastra Seema Bal" (SSB) is the newest border guarding force of Union of India entrusted with the guarding of Indo-Nepal and Indo-Bhutan borders. "Sashastra Seema Bal" is guarding Indo-Nepal border since 2001 and was also given the additional responsibility of guarding Indo-Bhutan border in 2004. Sashastra Seema Bal came into existence under the name Special Service Bureau in early 1963 in the wake of Indo-China conflict. Its earlier aim was to build people's morale and inculcate a spirit of resistance in border population in the then NEFA, North Assam, North Bengal, hills of Uttar Pradesh, Himachal Pradesh and Jammu and Kashmir (Ladakh). The area of operation was extended to other border areas in Manipur, Tripura, Jammu, Meghalaya, Sikkim, Rajasthan, Gujarat, Mizoram, South Bengal and Nagaland between 1965-1991.

The role of SSB in earlier setup includes : (i) to inculcate a sense of security and spirit of resistance in border population; (ii) promoting national awareness and security consciousness; and (iii) organizing and preparing border population to resist enemy.

Civil Defence

Civil Defence includes any measures not amounting to actual combat, for affording protection to any person, property, place or thing in India or any part of the territory thereof against any hostile attack whether from air, land, sea or other places or for depriving any such attack of the whole or part of its effect, whether such measures are taken before, during or after the time of such attack, or any measures taken for the purpose of disaster management, before during, or after any disaster.

The Amendment Bill to the Civil Defence Act, 1968 passed by the Parliament accorded legal sanction to the additional role of the Civil Defence constituents in the field of disaster mangement. The additional role in Disaster Management will be enacted by the Civil Defence personnel before, during and after emergencies arising out of calamities/disasters, whether natural or manmade. Civil Defence is primarily organized on voluntary basis except for a small nucleus of paid staff and establishment which is augmented during emergencies.

Civil Defence volunteers are in various constructive and nation building activities - including providing assistance to the administration in undertaking social and welfare services and in the prevention, mitigation of natural, man made disasters as well as in post-disaster response and relief operations and law and order situations. The training of its organisation is carried out in three tier levels. The training of master trainers and specialized training is conducted at the National Civil Defence College, Nagpur and team/leadership training is conducted at state civil defence institutes. Training of the volunteers in Civil

Defence Organisation is conducted at local/town levels by trained trainers in the form of short-term training programmes. A centrally sponsored scheme was launched at a cost of ₹ 100 crores in 2009 for revamping the Civil Defence setup in the country during the 11th Plan. The scheme envisages creation of new Civil Defence Training Institutes (CDTIs) in 10 states and renovation of infrastructure of CDTIs in 17 states, in addition 100 multi hazard districts have been selected for creation of civil defence infrastructure. A pilot project has also been launched in 40 selected towns to train and utilize Civil Defence volunteers in internal security tasks.

Home Guards

Home Guards is a voluntary force, first raised in India in December, 1946, to assist the police in controlling civil disturbances and communal riots. Subsequently, the concept of the voluntary citizens force was adopted by several States. In the wake of Chinese aggression in 1962, the Centre advised the states and union territories to merge their existing voluntary organisations into one uniform voluntary force known as Home Guards. The role of Home Guards is to serve as an auxiliary to the police in maintenance of internal security, help the community in any kind of emergency such as an air-raid, fire, cyclone, earthquake, epidemic, etc., help in maintenance of essential services, promote communal harmony and assist the administration in protecting weaker sections, participate in socio-economic and welfare activities and perform civil defence duties. Home Guards are of two types—rural and urban. In border States, Border Wing Home Guard Battalions have also been raised, which serve as an auxiliary to the Border Security Force. The organisation is spread over in all the states and union territories except in Kerala. In seven border states, a total of eighteen (18) Border Wing Home Guards (BWHG) Battalions have also been raised viz., Punjab (6 Bns), Rajasthan (4 Bns), Gujarat (4 Bns) and one each of Bns for Assam, Meghalaya, Tripura and West Bengal to serve as an auxiliary to Border Security Force for preventing infiltration on the international border/ coastal areas, guarding of VVIPs and lines of communication in vulnerable areas at the time of external aggression.

Home Guards are raised under the Home Guards Act and rules of the states/union territories. They are recruited from various cross sections of the people such as doctors, engineers, lawyers, private sector organisations, college and university students, agricultural and industrial workers, etc., who give their spare time to the organisation for betterment of the community. All citizens of India, who are in the age group of 18-50, are eligible to become members of Home Guards. Normal tenure of membership in Home Guards is 3 to 5 years. Home Guard personnel are also awarded President's Medal for gallantry, distinguished and meritorious services. A Home Guard, whenever called out for duty/training, is paid duty/training allowance at prescribed rates to meet out-of-pocket expenses. Members of Home Guards in the organisation are trained to assist police in maintenance of law and order, prevention of crime, anti-dacoity measures, border patrolling, prohibition, flood relief, fire-fighting, election duties and social welfare activities. In the event of national emergency, some portion of Civil Defence work is also entrusted to the Home Guards. The Ministry of Home Affairs formulates the policy in respect of role, target, raising, training, equipping, establishment and other important matters of Home Guards Organisation. Expenditure on Home Guards is generally shared between centre and state governments as per existing financial policy.

Fire Services

"Fire Services" is a state subject and has been included as a municipal function in the XII schedule of the Constitution of India in terms of Article 243-W. As such, it is the primary responsibility of the state governments/municipal bodies to enforce the National Building Code and allocate sufficient resources for strengthening and equipping Fire Services to ensure that safety of life and property of citizens within their jurisdiction. The 13th Finance Commission recognizing the need to restructure Fire and Emergency Services across the country has recommended that a portion of the grants provided to the urban local bodies should be spent on revamping of fire services within their respective jurisdiction. Further the Finance Commission has also recommended that all municipal corporations with a population of more than 1 million (2001 census) must put in place a fire hazard response and mitigation plan for their respective areas. Government of India as a supplemental initiative is also implementing a centrally sponsored scheme at a cost of ₹ 200 crores for strengthening of Fire and Emergency Services in the country. The Scheme attempts to fill the existing gaps in fire fighting and rescue capabilities through introduction of modern technology such as advanced fire tender, high pressure pump with mist technology, quick response team vehicle, combi tools for search and rescue and capacity building of various stakeholders.

Personal Law

The people of India are of different religions and faiths. They are governed by different sets of personal laws in respect of matters relating to family affairs, i.e., marriage, divorce, succession, adoption, wills, etc. The subject matter of personal laws is relatable to entry 5 of List III- Concurrent list in the Seventh Schedule to the Constitution of India and hence the Union Legislature, namely Parliament and subject to the provisions of Article 254 of the Constitution. The state legislatures are also competent to make laws in the field.

Marriage

Law relating to marriage and divorce has been codified in different enactments applicable to people of different religions. These are : (1) The Converts Marriage Dissolution Act, 1866; (2) The Divorce Act, 1869; (3) The Indian Christian Marriage Act, 1872; (4) The Kazis Act, 1180; (5) The Anand Marriage Act, 1909; (6) The Indian Succession Act, 1925; (7) The Parsi Marriage and Divorce Act, 1936; (8) The Dissolution of Muslim Marriage Act, 1939; (9) The Special Marriage Act, 1954; (10) The Hindu Marriage Act, 1955; (11) The Foreign Marriage Act, 1969; and (12) The Muslim Women (Protection of Rights on Divorce) Act, 1986.

The Special Marriage Act, 1954 which provides for a special form of marriage and the registration of such marriages extends to the whole of India except the state of Jammu and Kashmir, but also applies to the citizens of India domiciled in Jammu and Kashmir. Persons governed by this Act can specifically register marriage under the said Act even though they are of different religious faiths. The Act also provides that the marriage celebrated under any other form can also be registered under The Special Marriage Act, if it satisfies the requirements of the Act. The Section 4(b) (iii) of the Act, was amended to omit the words "or epilepsy." Sections 36 and 38 have been amended to provide that an application for alimony *pendente lite* or the maintenance and education of minor children be disposed off within 60 days from the date of service of notice on the respondent. An attempt has been made to codify customary law which is prevalent among Hindus by enacting the Hindu Marriage Act, 1955. This Act, which extends to the whole of India, except the state of Jammu and Kashmir, applies also to Hindus domiciled in territories to which the Act extends and those who are out side the said territories. It applies to Hindus (in any of its forms or development) and also to Buddhists, Sikhs, Jains and also those who are not Muslims, Christians, Parsis or Jews by religion. However, the Act does not apply to members of any scheduled tribes unless the Central Government by notification in the official Gazette otherwise directs. Provisions as regard to divorce are contained in Section 13 of The Hindu Marriage Act and Section 27 of The Special Marriage Act. Common ground on which divorce can be sought by a husband or a wife under these Acts are: adultery, desertion, cruelty, unsoundness of mind, venereal disease, leprosy, mutual consent and being not heard of as alive for seven years.

As regards the Christians, provisions relating to marriage and divorce are contained in The Indian Christian Marriage Act, 1872 and in Section 10 of The Indian Divorce Act, 1869 respectively. Under that Section the husband can seek divorce on grounds of adultery on the part of his wife and the wife can seek divorce on the ground that the husband has become convert to another religion and has gone through marriage with another woman or has been guilty of: (a) incestuous adultery; (b) bigamy with adultery; (c) marriage with another woman with adultery; (d) rape, sodomy or bestiality; (e) adultery coupled with such cruelty as without adultery would have entitled her to a divorce, a *mensa etoro* (a system of divorce created by the Roman Catholic Church equivalent to judicial separation on grounds of adultery, perverse practices, cruelty) and (f) adultery coupled with desertion without reasonable excuse for two years or more.

In The Divorce Act, 1869 comprehensive amendments were made through The Indian Divorce (Amendment) Act, 2001 to remove discriminatory provisions against women in the matter of divorce and to provide for dissolution of marriage by mutual consent. Further, Section 41 of the 1869 Act was amended by The Marriage Laws (Amendment) Act, 2001 to provide that an application for alimony *pendente lite* or the maintenance and education of minor children be disposed off within 60 days from the date of service of notice on the respondent. As regards Muslims, marriages are governed by the Mohammedan Law prevalent in the country. As regards divorce, i.e., *Talaq,* a Muslim wife has a much restricted right to dissolve her marriage. Unwritten and traditional law tried to ameliorate her position by permitting her to see dissolution under the following forms : (a) *Talaq-I-Tafwid:* This is a form of delegated divorce. According to this the husband delegates his right to divorce in a marriage contract which may stipulate, *inter alia,* on his taking another wife, the first wife has a right to divorce him; (b) *Khula* : this is a dissolution of agreement between the parties to marriage on the wife's giving some consideration to the husband for her release from marriage ties. Terms are a matter of bargain and usually take the form of the wife giving up her *mehr* or a portion of it and (c) *Mubarat* : this is divorce by mutual consent.

Further, by The Dissolution of Muslim Marriage Act, 1939, a Muslim wife has been given the right to seek dissolution of her marriage on these grounds; (i) whereabouts of the husband have not been known for a period of four years; (ii) husband is not maintaining her for a period of two years; (iii) imprisonment of husband for a period of seven years or more; (iv) failure on the part of husband to perform his marital obligations, without a reasonable cause, for a period of three years; (v) impotency of husband; (vi) two-year long insanity; (vii) suffering from leprosy or virulent venereal disease; (viii) marriage took place before she attained the age of 15 years and not consummated; and (x) cruelty.

The Parsi Marriage and Divorce Act, 1936 governs the matrimonial relations of Parsis. The word 'Parsi' is defined in the Act as a Parsi Zoroastrian. A Zoroastrian is a person who professes the Zoroastrian religion. It has a racial significance. Every marriage as well as divorce under this Act is required to be registered in accordance with the procedure prescribed in the Act. The provisions of the Parsi Marriage and Divorce Act, 1936 have been enlarged so as to bring them in line with The Hindu Marriage Act, 1955. Sections 39 and 49 of The Parsi Marriage and Divorce Act, 1936 were amended by The Marriage Laws (Amendment) and education of minor children be disposed off within 60 days from the date of service of notice on the wife or the husband as the case may be. As for the matrimonial laws of Jews, there is no codified law in India. Even today, they are governed by their religious laws. Jews do not regard marriage as a civil contract, but as a relation between two persons involving very sacred duties. Marriage can be dissolved through courts on grounds of adultery or cruelty. Marriages are monogamous.

Adoption

Although there is no general law governing adoption, it is permitted by The Hindu Adoption and Maintenance Act, 1956 amongst Hindus and by custom amongst a few numerically insignificant categories of persons. Since adoption is legal affiliation of a child, it forms the subject matter of personal law. Muslims, Christians and Parsis have no adoption laws and have to approach the court under The Guardians and Wards Act, 1890. Muslims, Christians and Parsis can take a child under the said Act only under foster care. Once a child under foster care attaining the age of majority, that is eighteen years old, he is free to break away all these connections. Besides, such a child does not have the legal right of inheritance. Foreigners, who want to adopt Indian children have to approach the court under the aforesaid Act.

The Hindu law relating to adoption has been amended and codified into the Hindu Adoptions and Maintenance Act, 1956, under which a male or female Hindu having legal capacity, can take a son or a daughter in adoption. In dealing with the question of guardianship of a minor child, as in other spheres of family law, there is no uniform law. Hindu law, Muslim Law and the Guardians and Wards Act, 1890 are three distinct legal systems which are prevalent. A guardian may be a natural guardian, testamentary guardian or a guardian appointed by the court. In deciding the question of guardianship two distinct things have to be taken into account - person of the minor and his property. Often the same person is not entrusted with both. Though The Personal Laws (Amendment) Act, 2010, the Hindu adoptions and Maintenance Act, 1956 was amended so as to remove the incapacity of married women to take in adoption of a son or a daughter merely on the basis of her marital status and to provide that the mother with the consent of the father and the father with the consent of the mother shall have equal right to give in adoption of their children.

The Hindu Minority and Guardianship Act, 1956 has codified laws of Hindus relating to minority and guardianship. As in the case of uncodified law, it has upheld the superior right of father. It lays down that a child is a minor till the age of 18 years. Prior right of mother is recognised only for the custody of children below five. In case of illegitimate children, the mother has a better claim than the putative father. The act makes no distinction between the person of the minor and his property and therefore guardianship implies control over both. Under the Muslim Law (Shariat), the father enjoys a dominant position. It also makes a distinction between guardianship and custody. For guardianship, which has usually reference to guardianship of property, according to Sunnis, the father is preferred and in his absence his executor. If no executor has been appointed by the father, the guardianship passes on the paternal grandfather to take over responsibility and not that of the executor. Both schools, however, agree that father while alive is the sole guardian. Mother is not recognised as a natural guardian even after the death of the father. As regards rights of a natural guardian, there is no doubt that father's right extends both to the property and person of the child. Even when mother has the custody of minor child father's general right of supervision and control remains. Father can, however, appoint mother as testamentary guardian. Thus, though mother may not be recognised as natural guardian, there is no objection to her being appointed under the father's will.

The Muslim law recognizes that mother's right to custody of minor children (*Hizanat*) is an absolute right. Even the father cannot deprive her of it. Misconduct is the only condition which can deprive the mother of this right. As regards the age at which the right of mother to custody terminates, the Shia school holds that mother's right to the *Hizanat* is only during the period of rearing which ends when the child completes the age of two, whereas Hanafi school extends the period till the minor son has reached the age of seven. In case of girls, Shia law upholds mother's right till the girl reaches the age of seven and Hanafi school till she attains puberty.

The general law relating to guardians and wards is contained in the Guardians and Wards Act, 1890. It clearly lays down that father's right is primary and no other person can be appointed unless the father is found unfit. This Act also provides that the court must take into consideration the welfare of the child while appointing a guardian under the Act. Though The Personal Laws (Amendment) Act, 2010, the Guardians and Wards Act, 1890 was amended so as to include the mother along with the father as a fit person to be appointed as a guardian of a child so that the courts shall not appoint any other person as a guardian of a minor if either of the parents is fit to be the guardian of such minor.

Maintenance

Obligation of a husband to maintain his wife arises out of the status of the marriage. Right to maintenance forms a part of the personal law. Under the Code of Criminal Procedure, 1973, right of maintenance extends not only to the wife and dependent children, but also to indigent parents and divorced wives. Claims of the wife, etc., however, depends on the husband having sufficient means. Claim of maintenance for all dependent persons was limited to ₹ 500 per month. But, this limit was removed by the Code of Criminal Procedure (Amendment) Act, 2001. Inclusion of the right of maintenance under the Code of Criminal Procedure has the advantage of making the remedy both speedy and cheap. However, divorced wives who have received money payable under the customary personal law are not entitled to claim maintenance under the Code of Criminal Procedure.

Under the Hindu Law, the wife has an absolute right to claim maintenance from her husband. But she loses her right if she deviates from the path of chastity. Her right to maintenance is codified in The Hindu Adoptions and Maintenance Act, 1956. In assessing the amount of maintenance, the court takes into account various factors like position and liabilities of the husband. It also judges whether the wife is justified in living apart from husband. Justifiable reasons are spelt out in the Act. Maintenance *pendente lite* (pending the suit) and even expenses of a matrimonial suit will be borne by either, husband or wife, if the other spouse has no independent income for his or her support. The same principle will govern payment of permanent maintenance.

Under the Muslim Law, The Muslim Women (Protection of Rights on Divorce) Act, 1986 protects rights of Muslim women who have been divorced by or have obtained divorce from their husbands and provides for matters connected therewith or incidental thereto. This Act, *inter alia*, provides that a divorced Muslim woman shall be entitled to (a) reasonable and fair provision and maintenance to be made and paid to her within the *iddat* period by her former husband; (b) where she herself maintains children born to her before or after her former husband for a period of two years from the respective dates of birth of such children; (c) an amount equal to the sum of *mehr* or dower agreed to be paid to her at the time of her marriage or at any time there after according to the Muslim Law; and (d) all property given to her before or at the time of marriage or after her marriage by her relatives or friends or by husband or any relatives of the husband or his friends.

In addition, the Act also provides that where a divorced Muslim woman is unable to maintain herself after the period of *iddat*, the magistrate shall order directing such of her relatives as would been titled to inherit her property on her death according to the Muslim Law and to pay such reasonable and fair maintenance to her as he may determine fit and proper, having regard to the needs of the divorced woman, standard of life enjoyed by her during her marriage and means of such relatives and such maintenance shall be payable by such relatives in proportion to the size of their inheritance of her property and at such periods as he may specify in his order.

Where such divorced woman has children, the magistrate shall order only such children to pay maintenance to her and in the event of any such children being unable to pay such maintenance, the magistrate shall order parents of such divorced woman to pay maintenance to her. In the absence of such relatives or where such relatives are not in a position to maintain her, the magistrate may direct state Wakf Board established under Section 13 of the Wakf Act, 1995 functioning in the area in which the woman resides, to pay such maintenance as determined by him.

The Parsi Marriage and Divorce Act, 1936 recognises the right of wife to maintenance-both alimony *pendente lite* and permanent alimony. The maximum amount that can be decreed by the court as alimony during the time a matrimonial suit is pending in court, is one-fifth of the husband's net income. In fixing the quantum as permanent maintenance, the court will determine what is just, bearing in mind the ability of husband to pay, wife's own assets and conduct of the parties. The order will remain in force as long as wife remains chaste and unmarried. The Divorce Act, 1869, *inter alia,* governs maintenance rights of a Christian wife. The provisions are the same as those under the Parsi Law and the same considerations are applied in granting maintenance, both alimony *pendente lite* and permanent maintenance.

Succession

The Indian Succession Act was enacted in 1925 to consolidate the law applicable to intestate and testamentary succession which was in existence at that time. The Act does not apply to the renoncants of the union territory of Puducherry. While consolidating the law in respect of succession, two schemes, one relating to succession to property of persons like Indian Christians, Jews and persons married under The Special Marriage Act, 1954 and the other relating to succession rights of Parsis, were adopted.

In the first scheme, applying to those other than Parsis, in the case of a person dying intestate leaving behind a widow and lineal descendants, the widow would be entitled to a fixed share of one-third of property and lineal descendants shall be entitled to the remaining two-thirds. This law was amended subsequently with the objective of improving rights of widows and it was provided that where the intestate dies leaving behind his widows and no lineal descendant and the net value of the estate does not exceed ₹ 5,000, the widow would be entitled to the whole of his property. Where the net value of the estate exceeds ₹ 5000, she is entitled to charge a sum of ₹ 5,000 with interest at four per cent payment and in the residue, she is entitled to her share. The Act imposes no restriction on the power of a person to will away his property.

Under the second scheme, the Act provides for Parsi intestate succession. By The Indian Succession (Amendment) Act, 1991, the Act was amended to provide equal shares for both sons and daughters in their parental properties, irrespective of the fact that it was that of the father or that of the mother. It also enables the Parsis to bequeath their property to religious or charitable purposes, etc., without any restrictions. In effect the amended law provides that where a Parsi dies intestate leaving behind a widow or widower as the case may be and children, the property shall be divided so that the widow or widower and each child receives equal share. Further, where a Parsi dies leaving behind one or both parents in addition to children, or widow/widower and children, the property shall be so divided that the parent or each of the parents shall receive a share equal to half the share of each child.

This Act was amended by The Indian Succession (Amendment) Act, 2002. It was felt that Section 32 of the Principal Act is discriminatory to widows and as such the proviso to Section 32 was omitted to remove discrimination in this regard. Section 213 was also amended by this amending Act to make Christians at par with other communities.

The law relating testamentary succession among Hindus, Buddhists, Sikhs or Jains, subject to certain restrictions and modifications is carried in Section 57 of the Indian Succession Act, 1925 read within the Third Schedule. The law relating to intestate succession among Hindus is codified in the Hindu Succession Act, 1956. It extends to the whole of India except the State of Jammu and Kashmir. The remarkable features of the Act are the recognition of the right of women to inherit property of an intestate equally with men and abolition of the life estate of female heirs. Further, (vide The Hindu Succession (Amendment) Act, 2005), the Hindu Succession Act, 1956 was amended so as to provide for the equal share to a coparcener daughter in a joint Hindu property.

A vast majority of Muslims in India follow Hanafi doctrines of Sunni law. Courts presume that Muslims are governed by Hanafi law unless it is established to be the contrary. Though there are many features in common between Shia and Sunni schools, yet there are differences in some respects. Sunni law regards Quranic verses of inheritance as an addendum to pre-Islamic customary law and preserves the superior position of male agnates. Unlike Hindu and Christian laws, Muslim law restricts a persons right of testation. A Muslim can bequeath only one-third of his estate. A bequest to a stranger is valid without the consent of heirs if it does not exceed a third of the estate, but a bequest to an heir with out the consent of other heirs is invalid. Consent of heirs to a bequest must be secured after the succession has opened and any consent given to a bequest during the life time of the testator can be retracted after his death. Shia law allows Muslims the freedom of bequest within the disposable third.

The Anand Marriage (Amendment) Act, 2012

The Anand Marriage Act, 1909 was enacted to remove doubts as to the validity of the marriage rights of the Sikh called "Anand" and it does not provide for the provisions of registration of marriages. The Hindu Marriage Act, 1955 applies to all Hindus, Buddhists, Jains or Sikhs by religion. It also applies to all other persons who are not Muslims, Christians, Parsis or Jews unless they establish that they were not governed by Hindu law, custom or usage prior to the Act. Section 8 of the Hindu Marriage Act, 1955 provides for registration of Hindu marriages and as Sikhs were included in the definition of Hindu, under Section 2 of the Hindu Marriage Act, 1955, a Sikh marriage performed according to the Sikh marriage ceremony called "Anand" or other customary ceremonies could be registered here under the provisions of Section 8 of the Hindu Marriage Act, 1955.

However, vide The Anand Marriage (Amendment), Act, 2012, The Anand Marriage Act, 1909 was amended to provide for registration of Anand marriages commonly known as Anand Karaj.

Election Laws and Electoral Reforms

The Acts in connection with the conduct of elections to Parliament, state legislatures and to the offices of the President and the Vice-President are : (i) The Representation of the People Act, 1950; (ii) The Representation of the People Act, 1951; (iii) The Presidential and Vice-Presidential Elections Act, 1952; (iv) The Delimitation Act, 2002; (v) The Andhra Pradesh Legislative Council Act, 2005; and (vi) The Tamil Nadu Legislative Council Act, 2010. These are administrated by the Legislative Department, Ministry of Law and Justice.

The electoral system of the country, which is also called the first-past-the-post system of elections, has completed sixty six years.

The continuously changing electoral scenario has necessitated reforms of electoral laws on several occasions. In the light of the experience gained during elections, recommendations of the Election Commission, the proposals from different sources including political parties, eminent men in public life and the deliberations in the Legislatures and various public bodies, the successive Governments have taken a number of measures, from time to time, to bring about electoral reforms; though need to effect a comprehensive package of electoral reforms cannot be gainsaid. At present the issue of electoral reforms in its entirety has been referred to the Law Commission of India for its examination and Report. On receipt of the Report of the Law Commission, the matter will be examined in consultation with the stakeholders.

Delimitation of Constituencies

The periodic readjustment of the Lok Sabha and Assembly constituencies is mandatory in a representative system where single-member constituencies are used for electing political representatives. The electoral boundaries are drawn on the basis of the last published census figures and are relatively equal in population. Equally populous constituencies allow voters to have an equally weighted vote in the Legislature. Electoral constituencies that vary greatly in population - a condition called "malapportionment" - violate a central tenet of democracy, namely, that all voters should be able to cast a vote of equal weight. Delimitation and Elections are the two basic pillars of a parliamentary democracy.

The first Delimitation Commission in India was constituted in 1952, the second in 1962 and the third in the year 1973. The third delimitation exercise - based on 1971 census - was completed in the year 1975. The present delimitation, based on 2001 census, has been undertaken after 30 years. The population has increased by almost 87 per cent and the nature of constituencies in the country, by and large, had become malapportioned.

The Government, as part of the National Population Policy strategy, decided to extend the current constitutional freeze on undertaking fresh delimitation up to 2026 as a motivational measure to enable state governments to fearlessly pursue the agenda for population stabilization. It has also been decided, however, to simultaneously undertake readjustment and rationalization of electoral constituencies, including those reserved for the Scheduled Castes and the Scheduled Tribes, based on the population census for the year 1991, without affecting the number of seats allocated to states in the legislative bodies so as to correct the imbalance caused due to uneven growth of population/ electorate in different constituencies. The Constitution (Eighty-fourth Amendment) Act, 2001 enacted in 2002 has effected the aforesaid policy decisions of the Government. Pursuant to the enactment of the Constitution (Eighty-fourth Amendment) Act, 2001 which provided for readjustment of electoral constituencies, including those reserved for the Scheduled Castes and the Scheduled tribes. The Delimitation Act, 2002 was enacted. The Delimitation Commission had accordingly been constituted in 2002 under the provisions of the Delimitation Act, 2002 with Shri Justice Kuldip Singh, a retired judge of the Supreme Court as its Chairperson and Shri B.B. Tandon, Election Commissioner in the Election Commission of India and the State Election Commissioner as its *ex officio* members. The main task of the Commission was to readjust the division of territorial constituencies of the seats in the House of the People allocated to each state and the readjustment of the division of territorial constituencies of the total number of seats in the Legislative assembly of each state. Subsequent to that the Constitution (Eighty-seventh Amendment) Act, 2003 was enacted and by that Act the basis of the delimitation of territorial constituencies was changed based on the 2001 census in place of 1991.

Although the rules for delimitation vary across countries, tasks involved in drawing boundaries are generally similar. In India, the drawing of boundaries, generally, entails: (a) allocating seats to the states and districts within a state; (b) creating a database composed of maps, population figures and the details showing geographic/natural/administrative conditions of the area concerned; (c) associating the statutory representatives from the Lok Sabha and State Assemblies; (d) distributing the states and districts into geographic units called the constituencies; (e) having an extensive exercise for public input into delimitation process; (f) summarizing and evaluating the constituencies; and g) passing and publishing the final order. The procedure for delimiting the constituencies in India stands clearly spelt out in The Delimitation Act, 2002. This legal framework provides for an independent and impartial Delimitation Commission. The final orders of the Commission are not subject to any modification or veto by the Government.

The Delimitation Commission functioned in a transparent manner. The methodology and guidelines were clearly established and published in advance. While framing the constituencies, the Commission - as far as practicable - kept in view the communities of interest such as those sharing a common tribe, race or ethnic background and also those defined geographically or by physical features like mountains, forests, rivers, etc. The Commission drew the boundaries of the constituencies reserved for scheduled castes and scheduled tribes strictly in accordance with the constitutional and statutory provisions. After getting finality of the delimitation exercise, in pursuance of the second proviso to Article 82 and second proviso to clause (3) of Article 170 of the Constitution, a Presidential Order dated February 19, 2008 was issued making new delimitation effective throughout the country. However, Section 10(B) of the Delimitation Act, 2002 deferred the legal effect of the 2007 delimitation order in relation to the state of Jharkhand.

With the issuance of the Presidential Order specifying the date on which the delimitation orders notified by the Delimitation Commission shall take effect, it was necessary to amend the relevant provisions and the First and Second Schedules of the Representation of the People Act, 1950 to reflect the changes made by the delimitation orders notified by the Delimitation Commission. As a consequential requirement, the Representation of the People (Amendment) Act, 2008 amending the Representation of the People Act, 1950 in conformity with the delimitation was enacted and made effective from the April 16, 2008. By this amendment Act, the First Schedule and the Second Schedule to the Representation of the People Act, 1950 were replaced including other amendments. Further, a new Section 8(A) was inserted in the Representation of the People Act, 1950, which, *inter alia*, provided that if the President of India is satisfied that the situation and the conditions prevailing in Arunachal Pradesh, Assam, Manipur or Nagaland are conducive for the conduct of delimitation exercise, he may, by order, rescind the said deferment orders issued under Section 10(A) of The Delimitation Act, 2002 in relation to any of those states and provide for the conduct of delimitation exercise in the states by the Election Commission of India. Further, the Election Commission of India, as per sub-Section (2 of Section 8(A) of The Representation of the People Act, 1950 has now been empowered to under take fresh delimitation in respect to the aforementioned four states as soon as, may be after the deferment orders in respect to these states are rescinded. A fresh delimitation exercise will be initiated as and when conditions prevailing in these states become conducive to the conduct of delimitation exercise.

After the issuance of the Presidential Order of 2008, the Delimitation Commission had issued eight (8) orders/corrigenda amending its earlier orders in respect of Karnataka, West Bengal, Uttar Pradesh, Tamil Nadu, NCT of Delhi, Bihar and Gujarat.

Reservation of Seats for Women

During the years, a consistent demand has been made for giving adequate representation to women in Parliament and state legislatures. Such a demand finds support in the 73 and 74 Amendments to the Constitution made in 1992. There was a proposal to amend the Constitution and to provide for reservation in Parliament and state legislatures.

Electronic Voting Machines

The use of Electronic Voting Machines (EVMs) was started in the country on experiment basis in 1982. It took more than two decades for the universal use of EVMs and during the General Elections to the Lok Sabha in 2004, EVMs were used in all polling stations across the country. Thereafter EVMs are being used in the all elections of the House of the People and state assemblies. The EVMs were developed at the behest of the Election Commission jointly with two Public Sector Undertakings, Bharat Electronics Limited, Bangalore (BEL) and Electronics Corporation of India Limited, Hyderabad (ECIL) in 1989.

Electors' Photo Identity Cards

The use of electors' photo identity cards by the Election Commission was started in 1993 throughout the country to check bogus voting and impersonation of electors at elections. The electoral roll is the basis for issue of EPICs to the registered electors. The electoral rolls are normally revised every year with 1st January of the year as the qualifying date. Every Indian citizen who attains the age of 18 years or above as on that date is eligible for inclusion in the electoral roll and can apply for the same. Once he is registered in the roll, he would be eligible for getting an EPIC. The scheme of issuing the EPICs is, therefore, a continuous and ongoing process for the completion of which no time limit can be fixed.

However, constant efforts are being made to issue EPIC to all such persons whose names have already been enrolled in the electoral roll, as early as possible. Some of them are: (i) special photography campaigns are organised to make

EPIC of all voters; (ii) voters are allowed to give copies of their photographs which are scanned for making EPIC; (iii) booth level officers are appointed by the Commission to collect photographs and make EPIC of all voters; (iv) 25th January has been declared as the National Voters' Day to focus on enrolment of voters and making EPIC; (v) special publicity campaign is undertaken to inform electors of the procedure of preparation of EPIC; and (vi) instruction has been issued that the EPIC number once issued will be valid throughout the elector's life even if address changes.

Voting Rights to the Citizens of India Living Abroad

Section 19 of the Representation of the People Act, 1950 provides that every person who is not less than eighteen years of age on the qualifying date and is ordinarily resident in constituency shall be entitled to be registered in the electoral rolls for that constituency. The meaning of "ordinarily resident" is laid down in Section 20 of the said Act. It has been specified under Chapter-III in the Hand Book for Electoral Registration Officers that a person who has gone out of the country for business or employment should be treated as having moved out of that place. Mere ownership or possession of a building or other immovable property will not bestow on the owner, the residential qualification.

There are a large number of Indian citizens residing outside the country due to various reasons. They have been persistently demanding for conferring them the voting rights.

The Government considered all aspects of the demand and accordingly introduced the Representation of the People (Amendment) Bill, 2006 in Rajya Sabha in 2006 to enable the Indian citizens absenting from their place of ordinarily residence in India owing to their employment, education or otherwise outside India, to get their names registered in the electoral rolls of the concerned constituency of their place of ordinarily residence in India as mentioned in their passport so that they would be in a position to cast their votes in elections to the Lok Sabha and to the state legislatures in case they happen to be in their constituency at the time of polls.

In pursuance of the recommendations of the Standing Committee, the Government have withdrawn, with the leave of the Rajya Sabha, the earlier Bill, namely, The Representation of the People (Amendment) Bill, 2006 introduced on February 27, 2006 in the Rajya Sabha and introduced a fresh Bill, namely, The Representation of the People (Amendment) Bill, 2010 in August, 2010, *inter alia*, to amend the Representation of the People Act, 1950 to : (a) provide that every citizen of India, whose name is not included in the electoral roll and who has not acquired the citizenship of any other country and who is absenting from his place of ordinary residence in India owing to his employment, education, or otherwise outside India, (whether temporarily or not), shall be entitled to have his name registered in the electoral roll in the constituency in which his place of residence in India as mentioned in his passport is located; (b) provide that the Electoral Registration Officer shall make corrections of entries in electoral rolls and inclusion of names in electoral rolls after proper verification; and (c) confer power upon the Central Government to specify, after consulting the Election Commission of India, by rules, the time within which the name of persons referred to in sub-paragraph above shall be registered in the electoral roll and the manner and procedure for registering of such persons in the electoral roll.

The said Bill has been enacted as the Representation of the People (Amendment) Act, 2010. In pursuance of the provisions of the said Act the Central Government, in consultation with the Election Commission prepared and published the Registration of Electors (Amendment) Rules, 2011 on February 3, 2011 and Registration of Electors (Second Amendment) Rules 2011 on February 23, 2011. The Central Government has issued necessary notification bringing the Act into force from February, 2011. The overseas Indians can now furnish the documents self-attested by them and get their name enrolled in the electoral roll of their respective constituency.

Reservation of Seats for Scheduled Castes and Scheduled Tribes

Our Constitution makers were fully conscious of the fact that the Scheduled Castes and Scheduled Tribes had been an oppressed and under-privileged class in our society over the centuries and they deserved a special dispensation so that their condition may be vastly improved. For this purpose, several special provisions were incorporated in our Constitution. One such provision related to the reservation of seats for these communities in Lok Sabha and state legislative assemblies. This provision found place in Articles 330 and 332 of the Constitution. Similarly, they were also sensitive of the difficulties and problems which were likely to be faced by the persons belonging to Anglo Indian community in the country. Consequently, adequate safeguards were provided for them in our Constitution by giving representation to this small section of the society, under Article 331 of the Constitution by way of nomination of two persons of that community in the House of the People by the President.

Likewise, provision for nomination of one member each by the Governor, wherever necessary, belonging to this community in the state legislative assemblies was also incorporated. Initially, the aforesaid provisions were made only for a period of ten years from the commencement of the Constitution. Although several steps have been initiated by the Government from time to time for improving the socio economic status of the Scheduled Castes and Scheduled Tribes, yet they are still far behind other communities. Even in the political field, they are not yet able to come up and get themselves elected to the representative bodies on their own in adequate numbers. Similarly, there are still a small section of Anglo Indians which need representation in the elected bodies. Consequently, the provision initially made for a period of ten years has been extended from time to time. Recently, through the Constitution (One Hundred Ninth Amendment) Bill, 2009 extension of the period for a further ten years has been passed by both the Houses of Parliament and received the assent of the President in January, 2010. The said Bill was enacted as the Constitution (Ninety-fifth Amendment) Act, 2009.

21 Labour, Skill Development and Employment

THE Ministry of Labour and Employment is one of the important and oldest ministries of the Government of India. The main responsibility entrusted to the Ministry is to protect and safeguard the interests of workers in general and the poor, deprived and disadvantaged sections of the society, in particular. Further, the Ministry aims to create a healthy work environment for higher production and productivity and to develop and coordinate vocational skill training and employment services. To keep itself in tandem with the process of liberalisation, the Ministry's attention is focussed on promotion of welfare of labour and providing social security to the labour force both in organised and unorganised sectors. These objectives are sought to be achieved through implementation of various labour laws, which regulate the terms and conditions of service and employment of workers. Labour being the subject in the concurrent list under the Constitution of India the state governments are also empowered to enact legislations.

O. W.: http://www.labour.gov.in

New Initiatives

National Career Service Project

The Ministry is implementing the National Career Service (NCS) Project as a mission mode project for transformation of the national employment service to provide a variety of employment related services like career counseling, vocational guidance, information on apprenticeship, internships etc. The NCS Portal (www.ncs.gov.in) has been made functional. The portal was dedicated to the nation in 2015. The NCSP is supported by a dedicated helpdesk (multi-lingual), available from Tuesday to Sunday (8.00 AM to 8.00 PM) on 18004251514 for assisting users. It has a rich repository of career content of over 3000 occupations.

Aimed at providing better health services, a series of Health Reforms Agenda of Employees' State Insurance Corporation (ESIC) was launched in 2015 which includes: online availability of Electronic Health Record of ESI beneficiaries (Insured Persons and their family members); Abhiyan Indradhanush ensuring the change of bedsheet according to VIBGYOR pattern during the week i.e., bedsheet to be changed everyday; Medical Helpline No. 1800 11 3839 for emergency and seeking guidance from casualty/emergency of ESIC hospitals, and special OPD for senior citizens and differently abled persons in ESIC hospitals.

Shram Suvidha Portal

The Ministry has developed a unified web portal 'Shram Suvidha Portal', to bring transparency and accountability in enforcement of labour laws and ease complexity of compliance. It caters to four major organisations under the Ministry namely; Office of Chief Labour Commissioner (Central); Directorate General of Mines Safety; Employees' Provident Fund Organisation; and Employees' State Insurance Corporation.

Transparent Labour Inspection Scheme

A computerised list of inspections is generated randomly based on risk based objective criteria. Serious matters are to be covered under the mandatory inspection list. Complaints based inspections are determined centrally after examination based on data and evidence. It is mandatory to upload inspection Reports within 72 hours. 1,54,084 inspections have been assigned as in 2016 since the launch of the Labour Inspection Scheme and out of which 1,44,011 have already been uploaded on Shram Suvidha Portal.

Ministry of Labour and Employment has started Single Unified Annual Return for eight Labour Acts. This facilitates filling of simplified Single Online Return by the establishments instead of filing separate Returns, under these Acts. (1) The Payment of wages Act, 1936; (2) The Minimum Wages Act, 1948; (3) The Contract Labour (Regulation and Abolition) Act, 1970; (4) The Maternity Benefit Act, 1961; (5) The Building and Other Construction Workers (Regulation of Employment and Condition of Service) Act, 1996; (6) The Payment of Bonus Act, 1965; (7) The Inter-State Migrant Workmen (Regulation of Employment and conditions of Service) Act, 1979; and (8) The Industrial Disputes Act, 1947.

Common Registration

Facility for Common Registration under five Central Labour Acts has been developed on e-Biz portal of the Department of Industrial Policy & Promotion. The Acts covered under this include: The Employees Provident Fund and Miscellaneous Provisions Act, 1952; The Employees State Insurance Act, 1948. The Building & Other Construction Workers (RECS) Act, 1996; The Contract Labour (Regulation & Abolition) Act, 1970; and The Inter-State Migrant Workmen (RECS) Act, 1979.

Labour Codes

Ministry of Labour and Employment (MoLE) has taken a number of initiatives for bringing transparency and accountability in enforcement of Labour Laws, with the objective of strengthening the safety, health, social security measures for every worker and bringing ease of compliance for running an establishment to catalyse creation of employment opportunities. These initiatives include governance reforms through use of technology and also legislative reforms by simplifying, rationalising and amalgamating the existing labour laws into four labour codes.

Legislative Initiatives

Draft Small Factory Bill

The Bill provides for regulation of working and service conditions of workers in small manufacturing units employing less than 40 workers. The Bill amalgamates, simplifies and rationalises the provisions of six Labour Laws at one place for these small factories. The Bill will ease the operation of small factories. The Bill will ease the operation of small factories. The Bill will ease the operation of small factories and thus catalyse the generation of employment through small factories while ensuring, Inter-alia social security, safety and health of the workers.

The Ministry working on to rationalise the provisions of the 43 labour laws into four Labour Codes.

Social Security

Employees' State Insurance Corporation

To provide medical care and cash benefits in case of sickness, maternity and employment injuries, the Employees' State Insurance Act was enacted in 1948. Employees' State Insurance Corporation (ESIC) is implementing the ESI Scheme introduced since 1952. The achievements are as follows:

The ESIC Scheme has been extended to 101 new areas covering additional 1.28 lakh employees during 2015-16 and the number of beneficiaries covered under the Scheme has gone up to 7.89 crore. The number of claims under Rajiv Gandhi Shramik Kalyan Yojana (Unemployment Allowance) admitted was 1,683 and the expenditure on this scheme was ₹ 7.72 crore. ESI Corporation became the first organisation to integrate its service i.e., registration of employers through e-Biz portal. All PDB/DB payments are being made through ECS.

Social security benefits of ESI Scheme have been extended to Mizoram and Port Blair. ESI Scheme is being implemented in industrial/commercial clusters within districts. Now, the target is to cover whole of the 393 districts of the states where these clusters are located. Opening Health Scheme for selected group of unorganised workers like riskshaw pullers/auto rickshaw drivers in selected urban/metropolitan areas, on pilot basis. Construction workers have been covered to avail benefits under the ESI Scheme from 2015. ESIC has launched independent Public Grievance Module 2.0 for lodging ESIC related Grievance online through its website 'www.esic.in' or 'www.esic. nic.in. Dedicated website www.esichospitals.gov.in was launched in 2015 for ESIC hospitals and dispensaries.

Employees' Provident Fund Organisation

The Employees' Provident Funds (EPF) and Miscellaneous Provisions Act, 1952 provides for Provident Fund, Pension Scheme and Insurance Fund in factories/

establishments employing twenty or more employees in industries mentioned in Schedule-I to the Act. The following three schemes framed are: Employees' Provident funds Scheme, 1952; Employees' Pension Scheme, 1995 and Employees' Deposit-Linked Insurance Scheme, 1976.

The progress achieved by the EPF Organisation under various areas and reforms introduced are given below:

(a) Membership

By 2015, there were 8,61,123 establishments covered under the Act out of which 4,737 were exempted establishments. The total membership (Un-exempted and Exempted) in the Employees' Provident Fund was 1,584.70 lakh with membership in the Pension Fund being 1,325.34 lakh.

(b) Contribution by Members

Total corpus of cumulative contributions received against all three Schemes till 2016 stand at ₹ 7,94,586.67 crore.

(c) Rate of interest

The rate of interest declared on the deposits of members to the EPF was 8.75 per cent (on monthly running balance) for 2014-15. In 2016, 1465.38 lakh annual statements of accounts were issued to members of un-exempted establishments.

Implementation of Minimum Pension

The Government notified in 2014 providing a minimum pension of ₹1000/- per month for member/widow(er)/disabled/nominee/dependent parent pensioners, ₹ 750/- per month for orphan pensioners and ₹ 250/- per month for children pensioners. It was initially for the year 2014-15, which has been continued in perpetuity.

The disbursement of pension is being carried out at present using the core banking system platform of the pension disbursement banks. Instructions were issued to the field offices to ensure that pension was credited to the pensioners' accounts on the first working day of the month.

Online Registration of Establishments

In 2014, the EPFO launched a portal for Online Registration of Establishments for the employers.

Universal Account Number

The facility of Universal Account Number (UAN) for EPF subscribers was formally launched in 2014. Portability is an inherent feature of the UAN programme. UAN provides automatic portability of Provident Fund account on change of employment if the employee has activated his UAN by seeding his Know Your Customer details (through the employer). By February 2016, out of 6.38 crore UAN allotted, 1.09 crore members have activated their UAN.

The present Government has widened the scope of continuous engagement of consultations among the stakeholders for inclusive labour policy formulation at regional and state level. After a gap of 19 years and as a part of fresh initiatives, the regional level conferences of State Labour Ministers and State Labour Secretaries were organised in Eastern, Southern, Northern, Western and North Eastern regions.

Industrial Relations

Maintenance of harmonious industrial relations remains an avowed objective of Ministry of Labour & Employment. Due to constant endeavour of the industrial relations machineries of both the Centre and the states, the overall industrial relations climate has generally remained peaceful and cordial. While the number of incidences of strikes and lockouts reported during 2010 were 371, these figures stood at 104 (Provisional) upto September, 2015 and exhibited a declining trend over the period. Similarly, the figures for mandays lost were 23.13 million in 2010 and 1.66 million (Provisional) upto September, 2015. As regards the spatial/industry wise dispersion of the incidences of strikes and lockouts, there exist wide spread variation among different states/UTs. Wage and allowance, bonus, personnel, retrenchment, indiscipline and violence and others were major reasons for these strikes and lockouts.

Twenty two Industrial tribunal-cum-Labour Courts have been set up under the provisions of the Industrial Disputes Act, 1947 for adjudication of industrial disputes in organisations for which the Central Government is the appropriate Government. These Tribunals are located at Dhanbad (Jharkhand), Mumbai, New Delhi and Chandigarh (two courts each) and one each at Kolkata, Jabalpur, Kanpur, Nagpur, Lucknow, Bengaluru, Jaipur, Chennai, Hyderabad, Bhubaneshwar, Ahmedabad, Ernakulam, Asansol and Guwahati. Further, the two Industrial Tribunals at Mumbai and Kolkata also function as National Tribunals.

In order to reduce pendency of cases Lok Adalats are being organised by the CGIT-cum-Labour Courts as an alternate grievance redressal system. During the period from April, 2015 to December, 2015 eleven (11) Lok Adalats were held wherein ninety-four (94) cases were settled. The process of Lok Adalats provides a platform for settlement of industrial disputes through mutual consent and agreement between the litigant parties and depends on their willingness. Therefore, organisation of Lok Adalats and number of cases settled therein varies, accordingly.

Vulnerable Sections

Child Labour

Elimination of child labour is an area of great concern and Government of India is committed to address the issue. Considering the magnitude and nature of the problem, the government is following a robust multi-pronged strategy to tackle the problem of child labour. It comprises statutory and legislative measures, rescue and rehabilitation, universal elementary eduction along with social protection and poverty alleviation and employment generation schemes. The objective is to create an environment where families are not compelled to send their children to work. The Government has adopted an approach to withdraw and rehabilitate working children, beginning with those working in certain prohibited occupation and processes.

Policy on Child Labour

The National Policy on Child Labour in a comprehensive, holistic and integrated manner. The Action Plan under this policy is multi-pronged and mainly consists of : a legislative action plan; project based action in areas of high concentration of child labour; and focus on general development programmes for the benefit of the families of child labour.

(a) Legislative Action Plan

Under the Legislative Action Plan, the Child Labour (Prohibition and Regulation) Act, was enacted in 1986. The Act prohibits employment of children below the age of 14 years in 18 occupations and 65 processes and regulates the conditions of employment of children in all occupations and processes not prohibited under the Act.

(b) Project Based Action Plan

In pursuance of National Child Labour Policy, the National Child Labour Project (NCLP) Scheme was started in 1988 to rehabilitate children rescued from child labour. Under this Central Scheme, working children are identified through child labour survey, withdrawn from work and put into the special training centres so as to provide them with an environment to subsequently join mainstream education system. In these special training centres, besides formal education, the children are provided stipend, supplementary nutrition, vocational training and regular health check-ups. In addition, efforts are also made to target the families of these children so as to cover them under various developmental and income/employment generating programmes of the Government to raise the economic standard of the family. Further, under the Scheme the Ministry funds awareness generation campaigns against the evils of child labour and enforcement of child labour laws through electronic and print media.

The National Child Labour Project Scheme was initially launched in 12 child labour endemic districts in 1988. At present, NCLP Scheme is sanctioned in 270 districts in the country. About 2860 special training centres are in operation with enrolment of approximately 1.30 lakh children under NCLP scheme. More than 11.77 lakh children have been mainstreamed into the formal education system under the scheme. As poverty is the primary cause of such a social evil, the educational rehabilitation of such children is further complemented by the economic rehabilitation of the families of child labour through the convergence approach so that the children and their families are covered under the benefits of the schemes of various ministries/departments of the Government of India.

Re-alignment of NCLP Scheme

With the enactment of Right to Education (RTE) Act, 2009, there was a need for realignment of the NCLP Scheme with the provisions of RTE Act, 2009.

Ministry of Human Resource Development allowed the NCLP Schools to serve as special training centre for un-enrolled and out of school children in accordance with the provisions of Section 4 of the RTE Act and Rule 5 of the Right of Children for Free and Compulsory Education (RTE) Rules, 2010.

Government is also laying a lot of stress on the enforcement of the Child Labour (Prohibition and Regulation) Act. To make the provision of the Act more stringent, a comprehensive amendment in the Child Labour (Prohibition and Regulation) Act, 1986 has been proposed.

A complaint committee, on sexual harassment at workplace to deal with the complaints of sexual harassment of women employees of Ministry of Labour & Employment and its attached offices, has been reconstituted.

Bonded Labour

Rehabilitation of Bonded Labour

With a view to supplementing the efforts of the state governments; a Centrally Sponsored Plan Scheme for rehabilitation of bonded labour was launched by this Ministry in May, 1978. Under the Scheme, state governments are provided Central assistance on matching grants (50:50) basis for the rehabilitation of bonded labour. The said Plan Scheme has been drastically modified in May 2000 to provide for 100 per cent assistance for conducting district wise surveys for identification of bonded labour, awareness generation activities, and evaluatory studies. The Rehabilitation grant has also been raised from ₹ 10,000/- per identified bonded labour, to ₹ 20,000/- per identified bonded labour. Further, in the case of North-Eastern states, Cent per cent rehabilitation grant is provided in case they fail to provide their matching contribution.

Wages and Bonus

The Minimum Wages Act, 1948

The Minimum Wages Act, 1948 was enacted to safeguard the interests of the workers mostly in the unorganised sector. Under the provision of the Act, both the Central and state governments are the appropriate governments to fix, revise, review and enforce the payment of minimum wages to workers in respect of scheduled employments under their respective jurisdictions. There are 45 scheduled employments in the Central and as many as 1697 in the state sphere. The enforcement of the Minimum Wages Act, 1948 is ensured at two levels. While in the Central sphere, the enforcement is done through the inspecting officers of the Chief Labour Commissioner (Central) commonly designated a Central Industrial Relations Machinery (CIRM), the compliance in the state is ensured through the State Enforcement Machinery.

To protect the minimum wages against inflation, the Central Government has introduced variable Dearness Allowance (VDA) linked to Consumer Price Index. As regards state/UT administrations, 26 of them have made VDA as a component of minimum wages. Both Central and state governments are revising the minimum wages in respect of these scheduled employments from time to time. In the Central sphere, the rates were last revised in 2015.

To have a uniform wage structure and to reduce the disparity in minimum wages across the country, a concept of National Floor Level Minimum Wage (NFLMW) was mooted on the basis of the recommendations of the National Commission on Rural Labour (NCRL) in 1991. NFLMW was revised from time to time. The Central Government has revised the NFLMW from ₹137/- to ₹160/- per day with effect from 2015. It, however, needs to be noted that the National Floor Level Minimum Wage, is a non-statutory measure.

Payment of Wages

The Payment of Wages Act, 1936 ensures timely payment of wages and that no unauthorised deductions are made from the wages of the workers. In exercise of the powers conferred by sub-section (6) of Section 1 of the Act, the Central Government, on the basis of figures of the Consumer Expenditure Survey published by National Sample Survey Office, has enhanced the wage ceiling from ₹ 10,000/- to ₹ 18,000/- per month from 2012.

Payment of Bonus

The Payment of Bonus Act, 1965 has been amended to revise the statutory eligibility limit under Section 2 (13) from ₹ 10,000/- to ₹21,000/- per month and the calculation ceiling under Section 12 from ₹ 3,500/- to ₹ 7,000/- or the minimum wage for the scheduled employment, as fixed by the appropriate Government, whichever is higher. The changes in the Payment of Bonus Act, 1965 are effective retrospectively from 2014.

Occupational Safety and Health

The provisions on Occupational Safety and Health (OSH) of workers as provided for in the Constitution of India are being implemented through the offices of Directorate General of Mines Safety (DGMS) and the Directorate General of Factory Advice Service and Labour Institutes (DGFASLI). The DGMS enforces the safety and health provisions for the workers in the mining industry through its Inspectors appointed under the Mines Act, 1952. The DGFASLI, through its Inspectorate of Dock Safety enforces safety provisions in the docks and also acts as the coordinating agency at the national level for the Inspectorate of Factories functioning under different state governments.

Some of the important events/initiatives in OSH are:- (i) Every year, Ministry of Labour and Employment distributes awards viz., Prime Minister's Shram Awards, National Safety Awards and Vishwakarma Rashtriya Puraskar and National Safety Awards (Mines) to workers. (ii) The Prime Minister's Shram Awards are given to the workers employed in Department/Public Sector Undertakings of the Central and state governments and the manufacturing units employing 500 or more workers in the private sector in recognition of their performance, devotion to duty etc. (iii) The Vishwakarma Rashtriya Puraskars (VRP) are given to individual workers or group of workers for their outstanding suggestions leading to improvement in productivity, safety and health as well as the import substitution resulting in the savings of foreign currency. The National Safety Awards (NSA) are given in recognition of good safety performance on the part of the industrial establishments covered under the factories Act, 1948, the employers covered under the Dock Workers (Safety, Health and Welfare) Act, 1986 and Building and other Construction Workers (Regulation of Employment and Conditions of Service) Act, 1996.

Research and Training

(a) Central Board for Workers' and Education

The Central Board for Workers' Education (CBWE) established in 1958, is a tripartite society which implement the Workers Education Programmes at national, regional and unit/village level. The Board undertakes training programmes, which cover workers from organised unorganised, rural and informal sectors. The main objective of the Board's training programmes is to create awareness among all sections of the working population. Supervisory and managerial cadres are also covered through joint education programmes. With headquarters at Nagpur, the Board has a network of 50 regional and nine sub regional directorates spread throughout the country. The six zonal directorates at Delhi, Guwahati, Kolkata, Chennai, Mumbai and Bhopal monitor the activities of the Regional Directorates of their respective zone. The Board has an apex level training institute - Indian Institute of Workers Education, Mumbai established in 1970 to conduct national level training programmes for the activists of Central Trade Union Organisations/ Federations, Voluntary Organizations besides training programmes for Board's Officials.

Since 1970 till 2015, the Board has conducted 1185 programmes of varied durations, IIWE at national level for 29024 participants. In the organised, unorganised and rural sector, the Board has in all conducted 455435 programmes of varied durations. Besides, the Board has been generating awareness among the informal sector workers about various welfare schemes through its Labour Welfare and Development Programmes. The special programmes for the beneficiaries of Mahatma Gandhi National Rural Employment Guarantee Act (MGNREGA) are being introduced by CBWE from 2012.

(b) V.V. Giri National Labour Institute

V.V. Giri National Labour Institute (VVGNLI), an autonomous body of the Ministry of Labour and Employment, Government of India, set up in July 1974, has grown into a premier institute of labour research and training. Since its inception, the institute has endeavoured through its research, training, education and publications to reach out to diverse groups concerned with various aspects of labour in the organised and unorganised sectors. The focus of such endeavours is the concern to transfer academic insights and understanding for application to policy formulation and action, so as to ensure a just place for labour in an egalitarian and democratic society.

International Cooperation

(a) 104th Session of International Labour Conference of ILO

India is the founder member of ILO and has been contributing to evaluation of global policy on labour welfare. The 104th Session of the international Labour Conference (ILC) of ILO and 324th Session of Governing Body was held during 2015 in Geneva.

(b) G-20 labour and Employment Ministries Meeting

An Indian delegation attended G-20 Labour and Employment Ministers' meeting in September, 2015 in Ankara, Turkey.

Directorate General of Employment

The Directorate General of Employment and Training (DGET) was transferred to the new Ministry of Skill Development and Entrepreneurship to focus all training and skilling activities under the new Ministry. The Ministry is implementing the Nation Career Service (NCS) Project. Employment being concurrent subject, both Central and state governments share the responsibility. Laying down of policies, procedures, standards, norms, guidelines, are the responsibility of the Central Government whereas the administration of Employment exchanges rests with the respective state governments union territories. Most of the states have Directorates of Employment located in the state capitals. In addition to these activities, DGE also runs training institutions to meet the training needs of specific target groups.

Twenty four Coaching-cum-Guidance Centres (CGCs) for SC/STs have been set up in 24 states. Vocational guidance and training in confidence-building is provided to SC/ST job seekers through these centres. Besides, the facilities for practicing typing and shorthand are provided to SC/ST job seekers in 14 coaching-cum-guidance centres. These centres have also been arranging pre-recruitment training programmes for SC/ST candidates to improve their employability through competitive examinations conducted by Staff Selection Commission and other Recruitment Boards for Group 'C' and equivalent posts.

For Central labour Acts please log on to www.labour.gov.in

Skill Development

Skill India

Skill India is an initiative of the Government of India which has been launched to empower the youth of the country with skill sets which make them more employable and more productive in their work environment. India is a country today with 65 per cent of its youth in the working age group. If ever there is a way to reap this demographic advantage, it has to be through skill development of the youth so that they add not only to their personal growth but to the country's economic growth as well. Skill India offers courses across 40 sectors in the country which are aligned to the standards recognised by both, the industry and the Government under the National Skill Qualification Framework. The courses help a person focus on practical delivery of work and help him enhance his technical expertise so that he is ready on day one of his job and companies do not have to invest in training him for his job profile.

The Skill Mission has gathered tremendous steam. The target to train more than a crore fresh entrants into th Indian workforce has been substantially achieved for the first time. 1.04 crore Indian were trained through Central Government Programmes and NSDC associated training partners in the private sector. For the first time in 68 years of India's Independence, a Ministry for Skill Development and Entrepreneurship (MSDE) has been formed to focus on enhancing employability of the youth through skill development. Some reforms and policy interventions are possible because of skill ecosystem in the country which is reinvigorating and re-energising the country's workforce; and is preparing the youth for job and growth opportunities in the international market. The flagship scheme, Pradhan Mantri Kaushal Vikas Yojana (PMKVY) alone has seen close to 20 lakh people getting skilled and prepared for a new successful future.

National Skill Development Mission

The National Skill Development Mission has been developed to create convergence across sectors and States in terms of skill training activities. Further, to achieve the vision of 'Skilled India', the National Skill Development Mission would not only consolidate and coordinate skilling efforts, but also expedite decision making across sectors to achieve skilling at scale with speed and standards. It will be implemented through a streamlined institutional mechanism driven by Ministry of Skill Development and Entrepreneurship. Key institutional mechanisms for achieving the objectives of the Mission have been divided into three tiers, which will consist of a Governing Council for policy guidance at apex level, a Steering Committee and a Mission Directorate (along with an Executive Committee) as the executive arm of the Mission. Mission Directorate will be supported by three other institutions: National Skill Development Agency (NSDA), National Skill Development Corporation (NSDC), and Directorate General of Training (DGT)- all of which are to have horizontal linkages with Mission Directorate to facilitate smooth functioning of the national institutional mechanism. Seven submissions have been proposed initially to act as building blocks for achieving overall objectives of the Mission. They are: (i) institutional training, (ii) infrastructure, (iii) convergence, (iv) trainers, (v) overseas employment, (vi) sustainable livelihoods, and (vii) leveraging public infrastructure.

National Policy on Skill Development and Entrepreneurship

Ministry is an integral part of the government policy on "Sabka Saath, Sabka Vikaas" and its commitment to overall human resource development to take advantage of the demographic profile of the country's population in the coming years. Developing a comprehensive and holistic policy document is an integral part of the process. This requires a fresh look at the already existing National Policy on Skill Development (NPSD). The objective of the National Policy on Skill Development and Entrepreneurship, 2015 will be to meet the challenge of skilling at scale with speed and standard (quality). It will aim to provide an umbrella framework to all skilling activities being carried out within the country, to align them to common standards and link the skilling with demand centres. In addition to laying down the objectives and expected outcomes, the effort will also be to identify the various institutional frameworks which can act as the vehicle to reach the expected outcomes. The national policy will also provide clarity and coherence on how skill development efforts across the country can be aligned within the existing institutional arrangements. This policy will link skill development to improved employability and productivity.

22 Mass Communication

THE Ministry of Information and Broadcasting, through the mass communication media consisting of radio, television, films, press and print publications, advertising and traditional modes of communication such as dance and drama, plays an effective role in helping people to have access to free flow of information. The Ministry is involved in catering to the entertainment needs of various age groups and focusing attention of the people on issues of national integrity, environmental protection, health care and family welfare, eradication of illiteracy and issues relating to women, children, minority and other disadvantaged sections of the society. The Ministry is divided into four wings i.e., the Information Wing, the Broadcasting Wing, the Films Wing and the Integrated Finance Wing. The Ministry functions through its 21 media units/ attached and subordinate offices, autonomous bodies and PSUs.

The Information Wing handles policy matters of the print and press media and publicity requirements of the Government. This Wing also looks after the general administration of the Ministry.

The Broadcasting Wing handles matters relating to the electronic media and the regulation of the content of private TV channels as well as the programme matters of All India Radio and Doordarshan and operation of cable television and community radio, etc. Electronic Media Monitoring Centre (EMMC), which is a subordinate office, functions under the administrative control of this Division.

The Film Wing handles matters relating to the Film Sector. It is involved in the production and distribution of documentary films, development and promotional activities relating to the film industry including training, organization of film festivals, import and export regulations, etc. The Integrated Finance Wing looks after the financial aspects of the Ministry.

Prasar Bharati

o.w. http://prasarbharati.gov.in

Prasar Bharati (Broadcasting Corporation of India) is the public service broadcaster in the country, with Akashvani (All India Radio) and Doordarshan as its two constituents. It came into existence on November 23, 1997, with a mandate to organize and conduct public broadcasting services to inform, educate and entertain the public and to ensure a balanced development of broadcasting on radio and television.

Objectives

The major objectives of the Prasar Bharati Corporation as laid out in the Prasar Bharati Act, 1990 are as follows : (i) to uphold the unity and integrity of the country and the values enshrined in the Constitution; (ii) to promote national integration; (iii) to safeguard citizen's rights to be informed on all matters of public interest and presenting a fair and balanced flow of information; (iv) to pay special attention to the fields of education and spread of literacy, agriculture, rural development, environment, health and family welfare and science and technology; (v) to create awareness about women's issues and to take special steps to protect the interests of children, the aged and other vulnerable sections of the society; (vi) to provide adequate coverage to the diverse cultures, sports and games and youth affairs; (vii) to promote social justice, safeguard the rights of working classes, minorities and tribal communities; and (viii) to promote research and expand broadcasting facilities and development in broadcast technology.

Prasar Bharati Board

The Corporation, is governed by the Prasar Bharati Board, which comprises a Chairman, an Executive Member (also known as Chief Executive Officer), a Member (Finance), a Member (Personnel), six part-time Members, a representative of the Ministry of Information & Broadcasting and Directors General of All India Radio and Doordarshan as ex-officio Members. The Chairman is a part-time member with a three year tenure subject to an age limit of seventy years. The executive Member is a whole time member with a five-year tenure subject to an age limit of sixty five years. The Member (Finance) and the Member (Personnel) are whole time members also with a six-year tenure, subject to the age limit of 62 years. The Prasar Bharati Board meets from time to time and deliberates on important policy issues and gives directions to the executive to implement policy guidelines.

All India Radio

After the invention of Radio and the starting of broadcasting in the western countries, broadcasting by private Radio Clubs started in a few cities in India like Mumbai, Kolkata and Chennai.

The first radio programme was broadcast by the Radio Club of Bombay in June, 1923. It was followed by the setting up of a Broadcasting Service that began broadcasting on July 23, 1927 on an experimental basis at Mumbai and Kolkata simultaneously under an agreement between the Government of India and a private company called the Indian Broadcasting Company Ltd. When this company went into liquidation in 1930, Indian State Broadcasting Service under the Department of "Controller of Broadcasts" was constituted and in 1935 Lionel Fielden was appointed the Controller of Broadcasting in India. The Indian State Broadcasting Service was renamed as All India Radio in January 1936. It remained under Department of Communication, Department of I&B, Department of Information and Arts for periods ranging from 1 to 4 years and finally has been under the Department of Information and Broadcasting since September 10,1946. At the time of partition, India had six radio stations (Delhi, Mumbai, Kolkata, Chennai, Tiruchirapalli and Lucknow) and three radio stations went to Pakistan (Lahore, Peshawar and Dacca, now in Bangladesh).

A 1,000 kw super power medium wave transmitter each was commissioned at Mogra near Kolkata in 1969 and at Rajkot in 1971. Four 500 kw super power short wave transmitters were inaugurated at Bangalore in 1994. This made it one of the biggest transmitting centres in the world. The first ever FM service was started in Madras on July 23, 1977. All AIR stations were provided with 5 channel receiver terminals in 1985. Multitrack recording studio was commissioned at Mumbai in 1994 and in Chennai in 1995.

Infrastructure

All India Radio came to be known as Akashvani from 1957. AIR took over radio stations being run by native states since British days such as Akashvani Mysore, Hyderabad Radio, and Radio Kashmir, etc.

From a meagre 18 transmitters in 1947 AIR acquired 46 by the end of First Plan, 59 by the end of Second Plan, 110 by the end of Third Plan and 433 by the end of 11th Plan and hence forth by March-2015 total number of transmitters went up to 595, consisting of 145 mw, 48 SW and 402 FM transmitters. The number of radio stations went up from six in 1947 to 414 by March, 2015.

Software

AIR has evolved over the years a three-tier system of broadcasting namely national, regional, and local. It caters to the information, education, and entertainment needs of the audience through its stations in this country of continental dimension with plural society. They provide news, music, spoken words, and other programmes in 23 languages and 146 dialects to almost the entire population of the country which crossed 1 billion mark recently.

The entertainment channel of AIR named Vividh Bharati was started on October 3, 1957 and since November 1, 1967, commercials were aired on this channel. The first Radio Sangeet Sammelan was organised in 1954, which has since become annual feature. Akashvani Annual Awards to promote excellence in Programme, Engineering, News and Audience Research were instituted in 1974. Doordarshan was separated from AIR on April 1, 1976. The first broadcast by political parties before Elections went on the air in 1977 from different stations of AIR. The North Eastern Service was commissioned on January 3, 1990 at Shillong in the campus of AIR, Shillong. The public service broadcasting initially in the evening transmission for about five and a half hour daily has since been extended to three transmissions. The programmes are beamed through a 50 kw SW transmitter in Hindi and English besides music programmes in different languages/ dialects of all the states of the North East. Phone-in-Programmes were introduced.

Channels and Programmes

The phenomenal growth achieved by All India Radio through eight decades has made it one of the largest media organisations in the world. Now, it has 407 stations and 578 transmitters. To serve the communication needs of the plural society that India is, the network expanded gradually imbibing new technologies and programme production techniques. All India Radio's services are being digitalized.

Objectives

To provide information, education and entertainment, for promoting the welfare and happiness of the masses (*Bahujana Hitaya Bahujana Sukhaya*), All India Radio strives :- (a) to uphold the unity of the country and the democratic values enshrined in the constitution. (b) to present a fair and balanced flow of information of national, regional, local and international interest, including contrasting views, without advocating any opinion or ideology of its own. (c) to produce and transmit varied programmes designed to awaken, inform, enlighten, educate, entertain, and enrich all sections of the people; (d) to produce and transmit programmes relating to developmental activities in all their facets including extension work in agriculture, education, health and family welfare and science and technology; (e) to serve the rural, illiterate and under-privileged population, keeping in the mind the special needs and interest of the young, social and cultural minorities, the tribal population and those residing in border regions, backward or remote areas; (f) to serve the rural population, minority communities, women, children, illiterate as well as other weaker and vulnerable sections of the society; and (g) to promote national integration.

Three-Tier Broadcasting

To realise its objectives AIR has evolved over the years, a three-tier system of broadcasting namely national, regional, and local. It caters to the information, education, and entertainment needs of the audiences through its stations in this country of continental dimension and with a plural society. They provide news, music, spoken word and other programmes to almost the entire population of the country, 121.0 crore as per the 2011 census. Its vast reach especially in the rural and tribal areas make it the primary and sometimes the only source of information and entertainment.

In National Service the national programmes, which are heard on the Medium Wave in most parts of the country, cater to the first-tier broadcasting. Recently, it has started airing on Short Wave also. The regional and sub-regional stations provide the second-tier of broadcasting giving the programmes in the regional languages and promoting regional cultural facets. In addition, FM Channels at metros cater to the modern needs of the people primarily the youth. The Vividh Bharati has also been shifted to FM broadcasting system at 34 places. The 402 stations on FM mode set up to cater to the needs and tastes of the audiences of small towns in various parts of the country are the Local Radio stations (LRS). Recently, the community radio has become very popular among different electronic media available in the country. All India Radio has also set-up Community Radio Service at five places in the North Eastern India as the voice of the local tribal population.

National Channel

All India Radio offers a 3 tier system of broadcasting, namely national, regional and local. National Channel forms the first stage of it and was started on May 18, 1988. The National Channel of All India Radio works as a night service from 6.50 p.m. to 6.10 a.m. the next morning.

Having the whole area of India as its zone, the programme composition of the Channel has been designed to make it representative of the varied cultural mosaic and ethos of the nation as a whole.

Regional Channels

Regional Channels are located mostly in the state capitals and in the major linguistic-cultural regions of every state. Altogether 127 such channels are spread over 29 states and 6 UTs states and Union territories of the country. The public service broadcasting arm of AIR, the Regional Channels put out infotainment programmes with the objective of enriching the lives of their listeners. The Regional Channels, broadcast largely on the Medium Wave frequency, follow a composite programming mix. They also promote art and culture with a major emphasis on Indian classical music. Around 40 per cent of the total broadcast on primary channels comprises music, which includes classical, light, folk, film and the music of various other languages. News and current affairs programmes constitute 20 to 30 percent of the broadcast time. Radio plays and drama, health and family welfare programmes, programmes for women and children, farm and home programmes aimed at empowering rural masses are the other important segments of the primary channels. These channels being the most accessible of all the AIR channels, strive to reach their audiences in the language most understood by all.

Local Radio Stations

At present 86 Local Radio Stations (LRS) are located across the country.These stations are serving the local population of the area, providing utility services and reaching right into the heart of the community.

Community Radio Stations

Community radio centres were set up at 5 places in the North Eastern India to serve the local tribal population.

FM Rainbow

FM Rainbow channel of All India Radio was launched at a time when radio listening was declining especially in big cities. FM radio filled this gap effectively by ensuring disturbance-free high quality music to its listeners. Even the presentation style of the compere on FM channel was transformed to suit the changing needs of listeners. Inter-personal chatting style of the comperes caught the pulse of youth and allured them to come closer to their radio. In its round-the-clock broadcast, the listeners were served with a recipe of whole new gamut of entertainment. Soon FM radio acquired the status of modern radio because it was speaking in their style and providing them the listening pleasure. The old glory of radio was restored once again at least in terms of listening percentages.

At present AIR has 402 FM transmitters across the country, by which it covers 32.5 per cent of the area and 45 per cent of the population of the country. Out of these, FM Rainbow channel is available at 23 places i.e., Delhi, Mumbai, Chennai, Kolkata, Bengaluru, Lucknow, Panaji, Jalandhar, Kanpur, Kochi, Puducherry, Shillong, Kasauli, Cuttack, Kodaikanal, Tiruchirapalli, Coimbatore, Hyderabad, Vishakhapatnam, Raibareily, Jammu, Srinagar and Vijayawada. Besides this, Delhi Rainbow is also relayed fully from Mussorie, Aligarh, and partly from Dharamshala, and Bhatinda. The FM channel includes pop music, film songs, and classical and devotional music, news headlines, etc.

FM Gold

FM Gold channel was on air in September, 2001 at Delhi as a niche infotainment channel with 30 per cent of news and current affairs component and 70 per cent of entertainment programming. At present, FM Gold channel is available daily round the clock. FM Gold channel is available at five places four metros i.e., Delhi, Mumbai, Kolkata, Chennai and Ludhiana. This additional channel gave its listeners an option to choose between the two, besides listening to other parallel running AIR and private FM stations in the area. This channel is trying to provide information interlinked with entertainment and brings information updates on traffic, airlines, railways, weather, etc.

DTH Service

DTH Radio Channel is a satellite service meant for the listeners, who own a TVset. The Service is available through the DTH platform of Prasar Bharati with uplinking facilities at Todapur, Delhi. It is not a terrestrial broadcast service and its programmes cannot be tuned in through the ordinary radio receiver sets. It is a 24 hour service broadcast digitally. The programming is planned in such a way that the repetitions are kept at a minimum.

Vividh Bharati

The popular Vividh Bharati Service provides entertainment for 15 hours a day from 37 CBS-VB centres. Beside this, Vividh Bharati Service is also relayed through 65 Local Radio Stations and 100 watt FM transmitters located across the country.

External Services

External Services Division of All India Radio ranks high among the external radio networks of the world both in its reach and range covering about 100 countries in 27 languages. The AIR, through its external broadcasts, aims to keep the overseas listeners in touch with the ethos of India. The languages in which AIR reaches its foreign audience are English, French, Russian, Swahili, Arabic, Persian, Pushto, Dari, Baluchi, Sinhalese, Nepali, Tibetan, Chinese, Thai, Burmese, and Bhasha Indonesia. The services in Hindi, Tamil, Telugu, Malayalam and Gujarati are directed at overseas Indians, while those in Urdu, Punjabi, Sindhi, Saraiki, Kannada and Bengali are meant for listeners in the Indian sub-continent.

News Services Division

The News Services Division (NSD) of All India Radio has been expanding its presence across various domains with the aim of reaching diverse cross section of people. Efforts were made to use mobile technology to disseminate news to the public in their own language by launching free AIR News SMS service. During 2014-15 the News Services Division has substantially increased its presence on the social media and has crossed major milestones in reaching out audience far and wide.

NSD broadcasts 651 bulletins daily in 91 languages/ dialects in Home, Regional, External and DTH Services. The total duration of these bulletins is 56 hours. 346 news headlines are put up per hour on FM mode from various AIR stations. News Service Division broadcast 179 news bulletins from headquarter Delhi every day which comes to 21 hours 42 minutes.

NSD's 45 Regional News Units (RNUs) play a vital role to cater to the information needs of the people. RNUs make bulletins and programmes in 76 regional languages/ dialects to make news region specific and people friendly. The RNUs originate 529 bulletins every day for a total duration of about 35 hours that includes regional, external, DTH services, FM headlines and News-on-phone. RNUs also mount 1,076 news- based programmes in a month for a total duration of nearly 140 hours besides broadcasting special programmes when state assemblies are in session.

FM headlines serve immediate needs of information in Indian languages for listeners during their daily busy schedule in cities and towns. At present 252 headline bulletins in 16 languages are being produced by RNUs. Also, 88 hourly update in the form of News on Phone- (NOP) service is available from five RNUs- Mumbai, Bengaluru, Thiruvananthapuram, Jaipur and Raipur in five languages.

Units of NSD

To facilitate the news gathering and broadcasting, NSD has various units viz., the Reporting Unit, Talks and Current Affairs Unit, Reference Unit and the Monitoring Unit. With inputs from these units, NSD is able to cover diverse new events and happenings to present a comprehensive view of developments, flagship programmes and new initiatives of the current government like Swachh Bharat Abhiyan, Pradhan Mantri Jan Dhan Yojana, Adarsh, etc. NSD was able to give wide coverage to Prime Minister's and President's visits/tours abroad.

Mann Ki Baat

For Mann Ki Baat programme, live webcasting is done on website news on air.nic.in. Special window and page is created for the purpose. Fourteen episodes of Prime Minister's radio address to the nation have been done successfully by IT unit. A special window and page is created for the purpose. Live tweeting is done through the NSD's twitter account @airnewsalerts, addresses were being live tweeted in English and Hindi. Near 30 per cent of our tweets were retweeted by the official account of @ PMO India. The audios of programme are uploaded on Soundcloud soon after the broadcast. The links of the programme are provided on both Twitter and Facebook.

Transcription and Programme Exchange Service

AIR also has a Transcription and Programme Exchange Service which includes units like Central Archives, Sound Archives, Digital Sound Archives, Digital Library, Radio Autobiography, Transcription Unit and Refurbishing Unit.

Central Archives

The Transcription Service was started in April, 1954 and entrusted with the main function of preparing transcription of speeches of all dignitaries with a special reference to the Presidents and Prime Ministers of India. This unit was also performing the duty of the processing of vinyl disc labelled "AIR-TS records" for preservation of recordings for future broadcast. The nomenclature of Service was changed to "Transcription and Programme Exchange Service" from 1959. As the processed records eventually proved to be uneconomical, the processing work had to be closed down in 1967 and new modes of preservation like analogue magnetic tapes, etc., came into use.

Sound Archives

The Sound Archives of All India Radio can be called the National Audio Archives of the nation as it is the treasure house of precious recordings of music and spoken word in different categories. It is the largest audio library of Indian Music recordings. The library preserves a separate collection of Mahatma Gandhi's speeches including his first and the last prayer speeches recorded on May 11, 1947 at Sodepur Ashram, Calcutta and January 29, 1948 at Birla House, Delhi respectively. The only broadcast by Gandhiji from AIR Delhi on November 12, 1947 is also preserved. The library contains recordings of all the Presidents and Prime Ministers of India. Voice recordings of eminent personalities like Rabindra Nath Tagore, Netaji Subhas Chandra Bose, Dr. B.R. Ambedkar, Sardar Patel, Sarojini Naidu etc. have also been preserved. Apart from this, award-winning radio dramas, features, documentaries and memorial lectures are available in the library.

Digital Sound Archives

Transcription and Programme Exchange Service (T&PES) has taken up a mega project of digitizing all the analogue content. Major steps have been taken in this direction. A Committee is guiding the Digital Sound Archives in adopting best practices. AIR participated in a big way in the 6-day Annual Conference of IASA (International Association of Sound Archives). International experts visited the Archives. They have appreciated the facilities and given valuable inputs for modernization.

Archives Digital Library

Radio Autobiography

In Radio Autobiography, recordings of eminent personalities from various walks of life are preserved. The Central Archives of All India Radio is a rich repository of priceless recordings of Radio Autobiographies of renowned musicians, public figures, litterateurs etc. Among such eminent persons recorded are Sh. J R D Tata, Ustad Ali Akbar Khan, Sh. Harivansh Rai Bachchan and Dr. Verghese Kurien. With the inputs from different AIR stations, the people of eminence are identified.

Programme Exchange Library

The main purpose of this unit is to exchange good quality programmes among the stations as per their requirements. In PEU Library approx. 8000 tapes containing the recordings of music and spoken word programmes are preserved for this purpose. Besides containing both music and spoken word items in different Indian languages, PEU Library is also preserving the language lessons in Bangla, English, Gujarati, Kannada, Malayalam, Marathi, Odiya, Sanskrit, Tamil and Telugu.

Transcription Unit

One of the important functions of transcription unit is to transcribe the recording of speeches delivered by President and Prime Minister and preserve them in the form of volumes for posterity. Tapes containing the recording of speeches along with transcripts are received from various AIR stations. The bound volumes of all transcriptions are prepared and kept in the archives.

Refurbishing Unit

In order to refurbish the vintage music recordings in archives refurbishing unit was installed some years back with the assistance of United Nations Development Programme. Hundreds of hours of recordings of music and voice of Mahatma Gandhi, Pandit Nehru, etc., were refurbished here. As of now this unit takes care of enhancing the audio quality of the recording being released by AIR and Doordarshan archives.

External Services Division

The cardinal role played by international/external broadcasting as an instrument of foreign policy and public diplomacy needs no elaboration.

Due to its colonial link with England, broadcasting came almost simultaneously in England and India. Similarly, shortly after BBC started its first foreign language broadcast in Arabic in 1938 on All India Radio entered the domain of external broadcast on October 1, 1939 purely as a tool for propaganda for the Allies during the World War II with a service in Pushto language to counter the German Radio Blitzkrieg in the region and supplement the efforts by the BBC in this part of the world. At the dawn of Independence, ESD had to don a new avatar as the voice of an emerging nation, an old civilization, a tool for diplomacy and also effective propaganda machinery at the time of different crises. Since then the External Services Division of AIR has been a vital link between India and rest of the World, specially with those countries where the interest of India are intertwined because of Indian population staying in those countries.

ESD ranks high among the External Radio networks of the world both in reach and range covering about 100 countries in 27 languages. The languages in which AIR reaches its foreign audience are English, French, Russian, Swahili, Arabic, Persian, Tibetan, Chinese, Thai, Burmese, and Bhasha Indonesia. The services in Hindi, Bangla, Tamil, Telugu, Malayalam, Kannada and Gujarati are directed at overseas Indians, those in Urdu, Punjabi, Sindhi, Saraiki, Sinhala and Nepali are meant for listeners in the Indian sub-continent and immediate neighbourhood.

External Services Division's transmission directed to SAARC countries, West Asia, Gulf and South East Asian countries continue to carry the 9.00 p.m. National News bulletin in English originally meant for Home Services. This apart, External Services Division continues to beam all across the globe commentaries on contemporary and relevant issues and press reviews in all its transmissions.

Audience Research Unit

With the changing mass communication scenario, Audience Research has occupied the centre stage. World over, almost all the big media organizations have been doing in-house audience research in one form or the other or 'Market Research' in marketing parlance as no media organization can afford to put their scarce resource at stake without knowing the potential audience(consumers) and market for their media content.

All India Radio has been the pioneer in this field. It has a wide network of Audience Research Units across the country operational since 1946. It provides programme feedback to programme producers to plan, design, and modify the progrmmes according to the needs, tastes, and aspiration of the target audience.

o.w. http://www.allindiaradio.gov.in

Doordarshan

From an experimental service begun at Delhi in September 1959, Doordarshan (DD) over the years has grown tremendously to become one of the leading

TV organizations of the world. Over the years, it has not only expanded its network throughout length and breadth of the country but also kept pace with new technological developments in the field of TV broadcasting. Doordarshan is presently operating 33 satellite channels and has a vast network of 67 studios and 1,416 transmitters of varying power providing TV coverage to about 92 per cent population of the country. In addition, it is providing free-to-air DTH service.

DD National

DD National Channel, a Public Service Broadcaster is the largest terrestrial network in the world. It covers about 92.0 per cent population and 81.0 per cent land area of the country. Being a Public Service Broadcaster the channel continues to make significant contribution to accelerate socio-economic changes, promote national integration, inculcate a sense of unity and fraternity and stimulate scientific temperament among the people.It contributes to dissemination of knowledge/education and information for public awareness about means of population control, family welfare, preservation of environment, ecological balance and measures for women and children welfare. The channel lends a healthy mix of entertainment, information and education. The service is available in terrestrial mode from 05.30 a.m. till midnight. In the satellite mode it is available round-the-clock.

DD News

DD News is the only terrestrial cum satellite news channel of the country. The News Channel of India's Public Service Broadcaster has been successfully discharging its responsibility to give balanced, fair and accurate news without sensationalizing as well as by carrying different shades of opinion. DD-News channel was launched in November 2003 by converting DD-Metro into a 24-hours news channel. Its satellite footprint is available across the country. DD News terrestrial reach is 49 per cent area of the country. It is currently producing news content in Hindi, English, Urdu and Sanskrit languages. Over 17 hours of Live transmission include telecast of more than 30 news bulletins in these languages. The channel telecasts daily three sports bulletins, one business show, daily current affairs programme, special shows on health, youth issues, cinema, art & culture, flagship schemes, employment opportunities and market developments etc. DD News has launched India's first Sanskrit news magazine "Vaartaavali" in June 2015. DD News is also producing news content for its sister channels i.e. DD National, DD India, DD Urdu and DD Kisan. DD News is having 30 Regional News Units (RNUs) across the country which are broadcasting over 100 news bulletins in 22 languages/dialects. RNUs besides producing regional news also cater to DD News and provide inputs for news bulletins and programmes. DD News is also very active on the social media platforms. It is having English website www.ddinews.gov.in and Hindi website www.ddinews.gov.in/hindi .

DD India

Doordarshan opened its windows to the world by launching its international channel on March 14, 1995. The Channel, initially known as DD-World was renamed DD-India in 2002. The programming offers international viewers an update on the Indian social, cultural, political and economic scene. It is now reaching 38 countries which are within the footprint of INSAT-4B.

DD Bharati

DD Bharati Channel was launched in January 2002 as a niche channel for art and culture to preserve Indian culture and heritage with authenticity and to present it to the wider public. It is the only Channel dedicated to art and culture in India. DD Bharati has entered into partnerships with various national and international public institutions and NGOs to acquire premiere programmes available in their archives, after making very judicious selection keeping the profile and audience of the channel in view.

DD Urdu

DD Urdu came into existence in 2006 which, became 24x7 channel with effect from 2007. The transmission features a mix of repeat and non-repeat, acquired and in-house software, which encapsulates heritage, culture, literature, information, education and societal issues specific to the target audience apart from news, live events like Independence Day, Republic Day celebrations, messages of the President and Prime Minister, special programmes on the state leaders. Mandate/the theme that predominantly runs through the transmission relates to modernizing educational and social outlook of the target audience.

DD Sports

Sports Channel of Doordarshan was launched in 1999. The transmission of the channel was increased from 10 hours to 12 hours a day within a month and the transmission hours were extended to round the clock from June, 2000.

Doordarshan Commercial Service

Doordarshan Commercial Service is an independent wing to co-ordinate all the commercial activities being performed at the headquarters, Doordarshan Kendras, marketing divisions and DCD towards sale of airtime as well as collection of revenue from agencies/clients/ producers.It is responsible for framing of Commercial policies and updating of rate card as per inputs received from Marketing Divisions and regional Kendras, with the approval of Prasar Bharati Board.

DD Archives

From 1959 to 2003, DD Archives was more or less a storehouse and archiving was only a process of not erasing recordings which were deemed to be important by individuals. Doordarshan Archives reinvented itself in

2003 with a new approach and prepared itself to meet the challenges of Audio Visual Digital World.

Central Production Centre

Situated in Delhi, the Central Production Centre (CPC) is currently responsible for managing the transmission of channels, i.e. DD News, DD Sports, DD India and DD channels like DD National and DD Bharati. It also specializes in production of documentaries and other DD programmes.

Audience Research

The Audience Research unit of Doordarshan with its 19 field units located with Doordarshan Kendras all over the country, is involved in Research studies on various aspects of broadcasting since 1976. The field units are located at Ranchi, Jaipur, Delhi, Ahmedabad, Nagpur, Chennai, Bengaluru, Lucknow, Hyderabad, Bhubaneswar, Bhopal, Kolkata, Guwahati, Mumbai, Gorakhpur, Rajkot, Jalandhar, Thiruvananthapuram and Srinagar.

Developmental Activities

Digitisation

Projects of establishment of 40 digital High Power Transmitters (HPT) as part of continuing scheme of 11th Plan are being implemented in two phases. In first phase, 19 digital transmitters are under implementation. Installation has been completed for 16 digital HPTs and these are ready for commissioning and the remaining 03 digital HPTs are at advanced stage of completion. These 19 digital HPTs are expected to be commissioned during the current Plan period. Remaining 21 digital High Power Transmitters are to be set up along with 23 additional digital High Power Transmitters approved as part of 12th Plan new schemes. Action has been initiated for setting up of these 44 digital HPTs (21 DTTs as part of 11th Plan and 23 DTTs approved as part of 12th Plan). Specifications for transmitter equipment are under finalization. These 44 digital HPTs are expected to be setup, in phases, in about 2 years time. Locations of 40 digital HPTs approved in 11th Plan and 23 digital HPTs approved in 12th Plan.

New 24 hrs Satellite Channel

One new 24 hours Regional Satellite Channel has been launched from DDK Vijayawada.

DTH

Installation of equipment for upgradation of Doordarshan's DTH Platform "DD FREE DISH" from 59 to 112 channels has been completed. Commissioning of upgraded platform is dependent upon implementation of Conditional Access System (CAS). All the channels would be free and no subscription would be payable by the viewers. Presently, there are 64 channels on DTH Platform. Prasar Bharati Board, in its 129th meeting held on October 16, 2015, has approved engagement of Department of Elecronics and Information Technology)(DeitY) approved Indian CAS vendor, M/s By Design, for implementation of CAS on "DD Free Dish".

High Definition Television

HDTV refers to video having resolution 5 times higher than traditional television systems (Standard-Definition TV). Main features of HDTV are Crystal clear & noise free picture, more realistic colors, wide screen picture and more viewing realism. Following HDTV projects are presently under implementation: (i) HDTV transmitters at Delhi, Mumbai, Kolkata and Chennai (Installation of transmitters has been completed at all locations and ready for commissioning.); (ii) Multi-Camera mobile production facility at Delhi; and (iii) HDTV Studios at Kolkata & Chennai (Layout Plan & Specifications are under finalisation).

Modernisation, Augmentation and Replacement

It has been the constant endeavour of Doordarshan to modernise its network by replacing old equipment by state-of-art equipment and augment the existing facilities. At present, following major projects have been implemented /are under implementation for modernisation and augmentation of Doordarshan network.

Terrestrial Transmitters

a) Two old 100 W LPTs replaced with 500 W Automode (1+1) LPTs at Kankauli (Maharashtra) and Sheopur Kalan (MP) b) replacement of following 15 existing old analog High Power Transmitters.

o.w. http://www.ddindia.gov.in

Electronic Media Monitoring Centre

emmc.gov.in

Protecting the citizens from undesirable content being aired by television channels is a norm followed by almost all leading democracies in the world. In India, Electronic Media Monitoring Centre (EMMC) is entrusted with the task of monitoring the content being aired by TV channels. EMMC is among one of the premier organisations of the world that monitor the broadcasting sector and the content being aired by broadcasters. The Centre is also one of the youngest among the government-owned media units in the country.

It is worth recalling that the need to monitor content arises in response to grievances and complaints coming from different quarters against invasion of raunchy reality shows, talk shows, news, documentaries and soap operas into the television industry.

EMMC records and monitors the content of around 600 channels, beaming over the Indian Territory, so that any violations of codes framed under the Cable Television Network (Regulation) Act, 1995 could be checked. Cable Television Networks (Regulation) Act, 1995 identifies several codes which must be adhered to by all broadcasting entities. The revised up-linking guidelines and downlinking guidelines for channels beamed at

Indian viewers also require monitoring of content for possible violations and remedial measures thereto.

Electronic Media Monitoring Centre identifies topical matters of immense public importance and reports them to the Ministry for evaluation and for taking any action, if needed. EMMC also prepares and submits special reports to the Ministry on topics desired by the Government. Setting up examples of success, the EMMC has taken a big leap forward by starting Radio Monitoring since January 1, 2015. The newly started wing of EMMC is currently monitoring Community Radio Stations (CRS) for detection of possible violations. At present, 30 Community Radio Stations from across the country are being monitored to check whether they are airing any content that violates the 'General Agreement between Government of India and Community Radio Stations (GOPA)' and 'Programme and Advertisement Code of All India Radio'. In a very short span of time, several apparent violations have been detected in the content being broadcast by CRS and submitted before the Ministry by EMMC. These apparent violations not only include obscene and vulgar programmes but several other types of content too which violate general rules laid by the Ministry.

Because of the ever-increasing number of channels, there is a race among channels to attract as many eyeballs as possible, and this trend has resulted in most of the channels treading on a very thin line and often barging into grey area. The somewhat callous attitude of TV channels towards the regulatory guidelines is becoming a matter of concern, particularly when an average Indian family, increasingly finds itself sitting in front of the TV for a time longer than ever before. The change in trend of TV viewing is also due to the fact that television industry has grown immensely over the past few years. Television shows have evolved over the years as more and more TV shows resort to unwarranted content to capture their audience. It has been observed that some of the TV shows affect young viewers and it is becoming a problem. Television influences the lives of young children in a big way. Children are exposed to all sorts of violence and anomalous culture at home. Public Interest obligation is missed by mass media when they air programmes.

Advertisement sector is a key part of Indian television industry. With the rising influence of TV media on people, it has become a catalyst of consumerism. The scope of creativity is enormous in the field of advertising. People like advertisements because they provide information and create awareness about new products in the market. Our decisions, whether to buy a product or not, are often completely influenced by the promotional activities of the companies concerned. Therefore, due to unfair trade practices, deceptive advertisements and widespread adverse impact of the advertisements of unhealthy products like tobacco and liquor, the Government of India has always endeavoured to curb or at least restrict advertisements of such products by bringing in appropriate legislations, orders and directives.

As a reaction to the Government's directive to ban advertisements of products that are adverse to health, the major companies of liquor and tobacco have taken the route of "Surrogate Advertisements". These advertisements are bombarded on viewers lest they forget the liquor and tobacco brands as there is a ban on directly advertising them.

The advent of the "Era of Reality Shows", in the Indian TV industry, has generated fairly good TRP for many a TV channels. Nowadays, when every second TV channel is coming with its own version of the "reality programmes based on borrowed ideas and values", it is very much imperative for the Government to ensure that the 'Freedom of Expression' is not misused to play with the young minds of our country. Such shows have a greater impact on children than other regular TV programmes as they interpret real life situations. Reality shows are meant for adults, and without proper knowledge, understanding, and guidance, children can be misled by such programmes. Some reality shows have children as participants who are under tremendous pressure to perform. Also, children who are left to watch these shows on television can often be baffled at the display and can take them as behaviour expected out of everyone, especially themselves and their peers.

A large number of misleading advertisements make unsubstantiated claims about the impact of certain products. Ministry of I&B has cautioned that advertisements should not dwell on a product's seemingly miraculous properties that cannot be proven. This is in violation of the Advertising Code, particularly rule 7(5) contained in the Cable Television Networks Rules framed under the Cable Television Networks Regulation Act, 1995.

Press and Print Media

Registrar of Newspapers for India

rni.nic.in

The Office of the Registrar of Newspapers for India (RNI) is an attached Office of the Ministry of Information and Broadcasting. Under its Statutory and derivative functions, it verifies and approves titles of newspapers, registers them, checks and establishes circulation claims. It also submits to the Secretary, I & B by 31st December every year the "Press in India Report", highlighting the state of Print Media in the country; the report is subsequently published under the title "Press in India". Under its non-statutory functions, the RNI issues Eligibility Certificates for import of newsprint, to actual users which are registered with RNI as well as Essentiality Certificates for import of printing machinery, etc.

Title Verification

RNI receives applications of the intending publishers for title verification, duly forwarded by the DM concerned and processes them for title verification as per the proviso to Section 6 of the PRB Act. During 2015, RNI scrutinized 15,293 applications for verification of titles, of which 9,272 titles were verified. To facilitate the applicants RNI has started online application filling facility on its website. For further processing by the DM concerned, the applicant is required to take out a printout of the filled application and submit to DM concerned for forwarding to RNI. The applicants are intimated through SMS and e-mail at application receipt stage and title verification stage at RNI to facilitate the applicants and ensure transparency. The status of title applications can be checked on RNI website. Discrepancy letters and title verification letters can also be downloaded from RNI website.

De-Blocking of Titles

After getting the title verified, the publishers are required to get the title registered. If the documents for registration are not received in RNI in 2 years, the title gets de-blocked and is available for verification to any intending applicant.

Registration

After the title verification, publisher is required to submit a declaration duly authenticated by the District Magistrate concerned, along with a copy of the first issue published within specified days after authentication of declaration as per the Act and an affidavit for no-foreign tie-up. After ascertaining that the publication has been printed and published in conformity with the various provisions of the PRB Act and the rules made thereunder, a registration number is allotted to the newspaper/periodical and entries made in the Register of RNI. The Certificate of Registration (CR) is then issued to the publisher. During 2015, a total of 5,737 certificates of registration were issued, which includes 4,315 fresh cases and 1,422 revision cases.

Annual Statement

As per Section 19D of the PRB Act, an Annual Statement in Form-II prescribed in the Registration of Newspapers (Central) Rules 1956 is required to be submitted by the publishers of newspapers to the Press Registrar on or before the last day of May each year containing various information as prescribed under the rules. It is also obligatory on the part of every publisher to print in the publication, a statement indicating the ownership and other relevant particulars in Form IV in the first issue every year after the last day of February. Annual Statement is the basic document on the basis of which RNI undertakes compilation and analysis of the status of the Press, which is incorporated in its Annual Report, called "Press in India". Annual Statements were received cent percent online for the first time for 2013-14 and the number was 19755. For 2014-15, 23,394 annual statements were received.

Press Information Bureau

pib.gov.in

The Press Information Bureau (PIB) is the nodal agency of the Government of India to disseminate information to the print and electronic media on government policies, programmes, initiatives and achievements. It functions as an interface between the Government and the media and also provides feedback to the Government on people's reaction as reflected in the media.

Prime Minister's Unit

PIB has a dedicated unit for the publicity and media support to the Prime Minister's office. This unit functions all 365 days of the year on 24X7 basis. The PM Unit compiles a number of reports on all days including holidays for PMO, Cabinet Secretariat and other senior officials of PMO. It works in two shifts from 6.30 am in the morning till 8.00 pm in the night. Very often, additional working hours are required in the late evenings/holidays on account of late cabinet meetings/briefings or other engagements of the PM. The Unit reaches out extensively to regional/branch offices for ensuring nation-wide publicity efforts, and gathering feedback for perusal of PMO.

Social Media

With the opening up of the air waves, 24x7 news channels in English, Hindi and other languages have come up in the country. PIB is doing video releases which facilitate more effective projection of the Government's point of view through the electronic media.

PIB has also expanded its presence on social media, both in terms of engagement, followers and the number of platforms in a big way, despite extremely limited resources.

Twitter: On Twitter, PIB's handle, @PIB_India has nearly doubled its number of followers in the last one year, from 3.7 lakhs to nearly 6.8 lakhs by end of November. The average number of impressions generated by the handle is now approximately 12 milion per month.

New Platforms: PIB has also expanded its presence to three more platforms: Facebook, Instagram and Vine. On Facebook, within a year, PIB has attracted a reach of more than 50,000 followers per week on an average. Attractive news pictures are uploaded on PIB's Instagram gallery, www.instagram.com/pibindia, while the Vine platform is used for looping short news videos. PIB has also launched a blog – pibindia.wordpress.com – where soft stories and feature-like articles on Government programmes and policies are posted. On YouTube, in the last one year, PIB's YouTube Channel, www.youtube.com/pibindia has doubled the number of subscribers, to more than 6,800 while the number of page-views has tripled, to 3.6 lakh, and the number of videos has gone up five times, to more than 750.

Online Accreditation System

PIB provides accreditation to media representatives including foreign media at the Headquarters in New Delhi. A fully on-line system of accreditation has been operationalised from 2010 onwards to make the process prompt and efficient. PIB provides accreditation to media representatives including foreign media at the PIB Headquarters. The Bureau utilized the process of online accreditation during 2014-15 successfully. During 2015, 474 press accreditation cards have been issued by the Bureau.

Emergency Control Room

The PIB has a News Room/Control Room which is operational round the year to meet challenges emerging out of any eventuality during any time of the day or night. Arrangements for holding press conferences at short notices and simultaneous web-cast through PIB centres across the country are also kept in a state of readiness to handle any sudden development and unexpected situation even after 9.00 P.M. The Control Room functions on 24X7 basis during emergencies and time of crisis.

Journalists' Welfare Scheme

The Press Information Bureau has been implementing the scheme of 'Journalists' Welfare Fund'. The revised scheme provides one time ex gratia relief on urgent basis to journalists and their families suffering from hardship. Assistance of up to an amount of ₹ 5 lakh can be sanctioned to the journalist under this scheme. Relief can be given to the family under extreme hardship on account of death of the journalist or to the journalist in case of permanent disability. Assistance is also given towards the cost of treatment of major ailments like cancer, renal failure, heart ailment, brain haemorrhage etc. Financial assistance is also given in case of accidents causing serious injuries requiring hospitalization.

Press Tours

The media interactive sessions is the 'Media Outreach Programme' which is planned in selected state capitals on issues such as socio-economic development, infrastructure, development schemes etc. Under this initiative, important Union Ministers and senior officials of the concerned Ministries are invited to participate in the event for interaction with national and local media to highlight the important initiatives taken by the Government. Vartalaap is a programme organized for urban/rural journalists to keep them aware/updated about the various Central Government Flagship Schemes for the welfare of urban/rural populace. Booklets/pamphlets related to various programmes/projects of the Central Government were distributed during media interactive sessions. In 2015-16, 54 Vartalaaps were conducted up to November. Press Tours are conducted by the Regional and Branch offices of PIB with a view to showcase the success stories of the various schemes/projects being run by the Central Government in rural/urban areas throughout the country.

Feedback, Feature and Photo Services

One of the important functions of the Press Information Bureau is to keep the Government informed of public perception about government policies and programmes as reflected in media. The feedback reports prepared by the PIB include inputs from the national English and Hindi dailies published from the capital, inputs from regional language newspapers as sent by the

Regional/Branchoffices of the PIB, inputs from TV news channels, web media and magazines. PIB Officers provided feedback to their respective Ministries and Departments.

The PIB officers also provided inputs regarding media trends on important matters relating to their Ministries/ Departments. As part of the Special Services, the Feedback Cell in PIB prepared daily digests and special digests based on news stories and editorials from National as well as Regional dailies and periodicals for the use by Ministries. The Feature Unit of the Bureau issued Features, success stories backgrounders, info-nuggets, photo-features which were also sent to the Regional/Branch Offices for translation and circulation to the local media. The Feature Unit of PIB has been issuing on an average over 200 features annually.

137 features have been issued in 2015. The subjects covered include everything that comes under PIB's publicity purview. The contributions come from Union Ministers, secretaries, scientists, economists, specialized journalists and PIB officials at headquarters and in Regional and Branch Offices. The Unit releases special features during Republic Day and Independence Day highlighting the policies and programmes of the Government.

International Film Festival of India

The Press Information Bureau had set up and managed Media Centre at the venue of 46th International Film Festival of India (IFFI) – 2015, to facilitate dissemination of Festival related information to media at the venue in Goa. The Media Centre was made operational from November 18 and worked till November 30, 2015. It provided favourable and encouraging work environment and facilitated participation of the media persons in the festival. A total of 455 media persons were accredited through online registration process for the coverage of the Festival.

News Agencies

Press Trust of India

ptinews.com

India's largest news agency, Press Trust of India (PTI) is a non-profit sharing cooperative owned by the country's newspapers with a mandate to provide efficient and unbiased news to all subscribers. Founded in August, 1947, PTI began functioning from 1949. It offers its news services in English and Hindi languages. Bhasha is the Hindi language news service of the agency. PTI subscribers include 500 newspapers in India and scores abroad. All major TV and radio channels in India and several abroad, including BBC in London, receive its services. PTI now has its own satellite delivery system through a transponder on an INSAT satellite for reaching its services directly to subscribers anywhere in the country. Increasingly more and more subscribers are opting for satellite reception. Photo service is delivered by satellite as well as accessed by dial up.

PTI has also begun satellite transmission by Ku band which offers subscribers the option of receiving news through a cheaper and small size satellite receiver. The Agency is on the Internet too. The agency's news services have been showcased on its website http.//www.ptinews.com. Clients also have the option of taking any of PTI's services through Internet. PTI news is also available through World Space radio broadcast reception. The Photo service is delivered by satellite as well as accessed through dial-up. The agency is now engaged in archiving its photos. It employs more than 400 journalists and 500 stringers to cover almost every district and small town in India. Collectively, they put out more than 2,000 stories and 200 photographs a day.

Its correspondents are also based in leading capitals and important business and administrative centres around the world. It also has exchange arrangements with several foreign news agencies to magnify its global news footprint. Currently, PTI commands 90 per cent of news agency market share in India. Besides the news and photo services, the other services of the agency include mailer packages of feature, science service, economic service and Data India, and screen-based services as News-scan and stock scan. A television wing, PTI-TV, does features and undertakes corporate documentaries on assignment basis. The PTI has arrangements with the Associated Press (AP) and Agency France Press (AFP) for distribution of their news in India. AP's photo and international commercial information are also distributed in the country through PTI.

United News of India

uniindia.com

United News of India (UNI) was incorporated under the Companies Act, 1956 in December, 1959 and started functioning effectively from 1961. In the past five decades, UNI has grown into a major news organisation in India and, with its vibrant presence, provided the much-needed spirit of competition in the vital areas of news gathering and dissemination. It also has a full-fledged Hindi wire service 'UNIVARTA' since 1982 and a Photo Service and a Graphics Service in the same decade. In June 1992, it launched the firstever wire service in Urdu. UNI's Photo Service distributes about 200 pictures every day, including sixty international photographs from EPA, the European Pressphoto Agency and Reuters. Its Graphics Service distributes five or six graphics every day.

NAM News Network

namnewsnetwork.org

NAM News Network (NNN) is the internet-based news and photo exchange arrangement of the news agencies belonging to member countries of the nonaligned movement. News and photo contributions of NAM news agencies including Press Trust of India are uploaded onto the NNN website http:/

www.namnewsnetwork.org for online access by all. Malaysian news agency Bernama is at present handling the operation of the website from Kuala Lumpur.

Formally launched in April 2006, NNN replaces the Non-aligned News Agencies Pool (NANAP) which had acted as the news exchange mechanism among non-aligned countries for 30 years. With internet a cheap and reliable mode of communication, NNN contributes to sustained flow of information in the 116 member non-aligned world. NANAP, set up in 1976, was the first attempt of the non-aligned movement to provide for exchange of news among its member countries. At a time when communication costs were very high, NANAP provided for sharing of communication channels of member news agencies to ensure a common network for exchange of news among all countries of the non-aligned movement.

Press Council of India

presscouncil.nic.in

The Press Council of India is a statutory quasi-judicial autonomous authority mandated by the Parliament for the twin objective of preserving the freedom of the press and maintaining and improving the standards of newspapers and the news agencies in India exercising equal quasi-judicial functions over the authorities as well the press person. It comprises of a Chairman and 28 members. While the Chairman has, by convention, been a sitting or retired judge of the Supreme Court of India, of the 28 members, 20 represent various segments of the Press and eight overseeing the readers' interest, are representatives of the two Houses of Parliament (3 Lok Sabha and 2 Rajya Sabha) and premier literary and legal bodies of the country i.e. University Grants Commission, Bar Council of India and Sahitya Akademi. The Council has its own funds for performance of its functions under the Act that comprises of the fee collected by it from newspapers, other receipts and also Grants in-Aid by from the Central Government.

The Council is presently chaired by Mr. Justice Chandramauli Kumar Prasad. For the financial year 2015-16, the Council has a total sanctioned budget of ₹ 663 lakhs. The Council discharges its functions primarily through adjudications on complaint cases received by it, either against the Press for violation of journalistic ethics or by the Press for interference with its freedom. Where the Council is satisfied, after inquiry, that a newspaper or a news agency has offended against the standards of journalistic ethics or public taste or that an editor or working journalist has committed any professional misconduct, the Council may warn, admonish or censure them or disapprove of their conduct. The Council is also empowered to make such observations as it may think fit in respect of the conduct of any authority, including Government, for interfering with the freedom of the press. The decisions of the Council are final and cannot be questioned in any court of law except by way of writ under relevant article of the constitution.

Complaints before the Council

During 2015, Press Council of India received 677 complaints, of which 181 cases were filed by the press while 496 were filed against the press carrying over previous pendency, the cases totalled to 1938 cases. Of these the Council adjudicated 149 cases (including 4 matters placed directly before the Council), while 591 cases were closed at the threshold without oral inquiry. The Council thus disposed of 740 matters in 2015.

Press and Registration Appellate Board

Section 8C of the Press and Registration of Books Act,1867 entrusts to the Press Council of India, the Appellate Jurisdiction over the Magisterial Orders of non-authentication of a Declaration under Section 6 or its subsequent cancellation under Section 8B of the said Act. The Board consist of a Chairman and another member to be nominated by the Press Council of India among its members.

National Press Day 2015

The National Press Day celebrated annually centred on the subject "The Impact and Import of Cartooning and Caricature as a Medium of Expression of Opinion" to encourage debate and deliberations on the impact that cartoons and caricatures could have in the present day context. The National Awards for Excellence in Journalism were conferred on the Day in various categories. An exhibition on the illustrative of the President of India was also displayed on the occasion.

New Media Wing

Set up in the year 1945, the Research, Reference and Training Division now renamed as "New Media Wing" functions as information serving unit for the Ministry of Information & Broadcasting. It provides background, reference and research material for use of the Ministry, its media units and others engaged in mass communication.

Major Activities

Social Media

The New Media Wing is looking after the assignment of Monitoring of sending reports relating to media reports, content analysis, reports of EMMC, special report on PM's visit, floods and other national events of 24x7 working basis and sending these reports to various Senior bureaucrats and other VIPs on daily basis since June, 2014.

India-A Reference Annual

The Division compiles a reference book, 'India-A Reference Annual', on development and progress made by Central ministries/departments, states/ union territory administration and PSUs/autonomous bodies. It is simultaneously published in Hindi titled- 'Bharat'.

National Documentation Centre on Mass Communication

The National Documentation Centre on Mass Communication (NDCMC) was created in 1976 as a part of the Division on the recommendation of an Expert Committee set up by the Ministry for collecting, interpreting and disseminating information about the events and trends in mass media through its periodical services.

Photo Division

photodivision.gov.in

Photo Division, an independent media unit meant for the visual support of the varied activities of the Government of India, is a subordinate office of the Ministry of Information and Broadcasting and the biggest production unit of its kind in the country in the field of photography. Photo Division was established in late 1959 as a culmination of the government's decision for establishing a separate department keeping in view the importance of the medium, as the photograph gives the most authentic & truthful record as well as recognize the new medium for right projection, create the archival record under the professional experts. This was done with integrating the photo studios of the Publication Division and the Photo Unit of the Press Information Bureau and D.A.V.P. with a view of eliminating the duplication of the activities. The Division produces photographic visuals of achievements and activities of Government of India for internal and external publicity as well as other purposes. In its 50 years, the Division has a collection of nearly 10 lakhs images in its archive. On the occasion of completion of 50 years of its existence in 2010 the Division introduced National Photography Awards to promote nation's art, culture, development, heritage, history, life, people, society, traditions etc., and to encourage professional and amateur photographers from all corners of the country. The Division has its own official website for the photo publicity of the official assignments. The Division is in the process of selling the photographs through e-commerce gateway.

Synergy Between Media Units

To keep synergy between the other Media Units, the Division has taken up various measures. The Division has launched its official website to explore the global utility of around 8-10 lakh archival and current images. The Division is in progress of introducing E-commerce feature for the sell/buy of images through the official website. A high capacity server is installed for the on-line/off-line retrieval of archival images. The News Photo Network of the Division has been functioning on complete digital mode to avoid the delay in sending photographs to newspapers and Press Information Bureau. The official website of PIB is completely supported by the Division by supplying digital images and hard copies etc., of the Day-today assignments. On assignments of Vice President, Prime Minister and visiting VVIP's the digital camera equipment has been utilized with laptop and V-data cards to download and upload the digital images from venue itself in city as well as in local tours. The Division provides facility to DAVP for the supply of life size digital inkjet images for the exhibition purpose.

Publications Division

Publications Division (DPD) is among the premier publishing organisations of the Government of India involved in production, sale and distribution of popular books and journals on matters of national importance. Established in 1941, it is mandated to bring out books and journals highlighting subjects of national importance and India's rich cultural heritage including children's literature. The Division publishes books and journals on diverse aspects of Indian panorama, ranging from art and culture, land and people, flora and fauna, biographies of the Builders of Modern India, cultural leaders of India, life and works of other prominent Indian personalities from different walks of life, India's history and freedom struggle among many other subjects.

Books on the life and thoughts of Mahatma Gandhi hold a place of pride for the Division. DPD has published several books on Gandhian thoughts including the Collected Works of Mahatma Gandhi (CWMG) in 100 volumes, in English and Sampoorna Gandhi Vangmaya in Hindi which is considered to be the most comprehensive and authentic collection of Gandhiji's writings. The Division enjoys credibility among the publishers and is well recognised for the authenticity of content and affordable price of publications. Publications Division, in collaboration with Gujarat Vidyapith, and under supervision of prominent Gandhian scholars, has also prepared the e-version of the Collected Works of Mahatma Gandhi (e-CWMG), fully searchable Master copy, in the form of a well-designed set of DVDs. This monumental work is a lasting contribution to the national heritage by preserving Mahatma Gandhi's written words in permanent and tamper-proof electronic format. The e-CWMG is also hosted on the Gandhi Heritage Portal, a comprehensive repository of authentic Gandhian literature.

Since last year Publications Division is also engaged in publishing several high quality books which document the rich legacy of the Rashtrapati Bhavan (RB), as a series to preserve for posterity, various aspects of the office of the President of India. Another heritage value publication for Hon'ble Supreme Court of India has been recently brought out titled "Courts in India- Past to Present". The Division has also published a title for Election Commission of India presenting the diversity of experiences on conduct of elections.

Journals

Besides books, the Publications Division also publishes 18 monthly journals, which include *Yojana* in English, Hindi and 11 other languages, *Aajkal* (Hindi and Urdu), *Bal Bharati* (Hindi), *Kurukshetra* (English and Hindi) and a weekly journal *Employment News* (English, Hindi and Urdu). Its journals have a large readership and enjoy a high degree of credibility among the public. These journals reflect the initiatives of the Government and the country's progress in different areas covering a wide range of subjects such as economic development, rural reconstruction, community development, literature, culture, children's literature and information on employment and career opportunities.

Yojana, the flagship journal of the Division published since 1957, seeks to carry the message of planned development to all sections of society and serves as a forum to promote a healthy discussion representing a cross-section of views on socio-economic aspects of development. With a combined circulation of above 2 lakhs per month, the journal is counted among the largest circulated journals in the field of development journalism. The Journal, which is published in 13 languages, presents an all India perspective while highlighting regional development, innovations and initiatives.

Kurukshetra, published since 1952 in English and Hindi, is a unique monthly journal dedicated to rural development issues combined circulation nearly to 1,00,000 per month. It serves as a platform for exchange of ideas on policies, programmes and implementation status of development efforts in the field of rural development. Combined circulation of Kurukshetra (English and Hindi) is close to 1,00,000 per month.

Bal Bharati, the popular children's monthly in Hindi, is being published regularly since 1948. Its objective is to provide healthy entertainment to children and also inculcating in them human values and scientific temper through short stories, poems, picture stories and informative articles.

Ajkal, the prestigious literary magazine published since 1945 in Hindi and 1942 in Urdu, brings out a number of special issues and covers different aspects of Indian culture and literature.

Employment News/Rozgar Samachar, *Employment News* is a weekly journal, released every Saturday, and is published simultaneously in Hindi, English and Urdu. Launched in 1976, the weekly carries advertisements for job vacancies as advertised by Centre and state governments, public sector undertakings, autonomous bodies, universities, admission notices for professional courses, examination notices and results of organizations like UPSC, SSC and other general recruitment bodies. In addition, the paper carries an editorial segment, which carries articles on topical issues and career opportunities. With the average combined circulation of about over 2.2 lakhs per week, the Journal is popular among the job seekers. Both it's print and e-versions can be subscribed onlie at www.employmentnews.gov.in.

Creation of Digital Archives and e-Books

Publications Division has now undertaken an important task of digitization of its publications with a purpose to preserve and promote the same and is making e-books of saleable titles. A rich digital archive of over 1,000 publications is under preparation. The Digital archives of DPD is preserving for posterity, books brought out through the years since the establishment of the Publications Division. The e-books of select titles are also made available for sale through e-commerce platforms like Google Play, Kobo, and Amazon. Since 2015, the flagship publications - Reference Annual India and Bharat have been digitized and converted into fully searchable and downloadable e-books for use on a variety of platforms. Over 100 prominent books on a variety of subjects have already been uploaded on e-commerce platforms. The eBooks have a variety of features like highlighting, searching, bookmarking, noting, and text to speech which can cater to the reading habits of new age hybrid readers.

Online sale of books and journals: DPD has also developed a portal to sell its printed journals online through Bharatkosh payment gateway developed in collaboration with Controller General of Accounts (CGA), Ministry of Finance. The portal, unveiled in 2016, is being widely used for subscriptions of the journals. It has also launched the popular weekly journal 'Employment News' in a digital format (e-Employment News) using this portal. Selected books have also been made available for online sale through the CGA's portal for ease of purchase.

Computerisation of Inventory and other Business Operations: The entire business process of Publications Division including inventory management, payment of royalty, sales, accounts, subscribers management, networking with the Sales Emporia is being computerized. The websites are also under renovation. Once the project is completed, apart from increasing the efficiency of working, online sale through its website and other on-line operations of business processes will be possible.

Organisational Structure: The Directorate of Publications Division is headed by Additional Director General. The Divisions are headed by Directors responsible for Editorial, Production, Business and Administration. The work of General Manager, Employment News is looked after by a Director.

The Division has dedicated websites http://www.publications division.nic.in, www.yojana.gov.in for *Yojana* and http://employment news. gov.in for *Employment News*.

Publications Division also has presence on facebook at https://www. facebook.com/prakashan.vibhag and Twitter @DPD_India.

Business and Distribution Network

The sales and distribution of books and periodicals published by Publications Division is undertaken through its Head Quarters in Soochna Bhawan and offices at Delhi Secretariat, Mumbai, Chennai, Kolkata, Patna, Lucknow, Hyderabad, Thiruvananthapuram. Besides *Yojana* units, regional offices also undertake this work at Guwahati, Kolkata, Chennai, Ahmedabad, Mumbai, Thiruvananthapuram, Bengaluru and Hyderabad. The network of registered agents empanelled at the HQ and regional offices supplement the sales and Marketing. To improve the visibility and to bring its publications nearer to people, the Division participates in major book fairs across the country and pursues with the concerned ministries and departments, state governments and libraries to get bulk orders. Revenue earned through sales, advertisement and subscriptions is deposited in the Consolidated Fund of India. Business enquiries can be made by sending emails to dpd@sb.nic.in, businesswng@gmail.com, and pdjucir@gmail.com and also by visiting Publications Division's websites.

Films Division

filmsdivision.org

The story of the Films Division is synchronous with the eventful years of the country since Independence and over the last 67 years, the Division has been motivating the broadest spectrum of the Indian public with a view to enlisting their active participation in nation building activities. The aims and objectives of the Division, focused on national perspectives, are to educate and motivate people in the implementation of national programmes and to project the image of the land and the heritage of the country to Indian and foreign audiences. The Division also aims at fostering the growth of the documentary film movement, which is of immense significance for the country in the information, communication and integration. Films Division produces documentaries, short films, animation films and news magazines. It caters to nearly 4000 cinema theatres all over the country and also to the non-theatrical circuits like units of the Directorate of Field Publicity, Doordarshan, educational institutions, film societies and voluntary organizations. The documentaries and newsreels of state governments are also featured in the Division's release on the theatrical circuit. This Division also sells prints, stock shots, DVDs/ VCDs and distribution rights of documentaries and feature films in India and abroad. Apart from production of films, Films Division also gives on hire, its recording theatre, editing rooms and other cine equipment to film makers.

Archival Research Centre

Archival Research Centre (ARC), a multi station research facility by Films Division has been opened on October 26, 2013. The aim of this facility is to share the enormous wealth of visual history and visual documentation that Films Division has accumulated since its conception. The ARC makes the entire archive of Films Division available to the fifteen research stations presently routed to it. The Films Division archive will be available to these fifteen stations for viewing and research purposes.

National Museum of Indian Cinema

The concept of National Museum of Indian Cinema (NMIC) is a unique idea to be pursued for the first time in the history of Indian Cinema. In the last 100 years of Indian Cinema, lot of historical material suitable for the film museum has been destroyed, damaged or not taken care of properly due to lack of restoration and preservation facilities of this kind. The Film Museum will not only provide a store house of information to the laymen but it will also help film makers, film students, enthusiasts and critics to know the development of cinema as a medium of artistic expression not only in the country but in all parts of the world, as there is no Film Museum in India.

FD Zone

FD Zone is a collaborative effort of Films Division with independent film makers to organize regular curated screenings of documentaries, short films and animation films and avant-garde and meaningful cinema. For every screening, an independent film maker curates on voluntary basis a mixture of films of Films Division and independent film makers. The Director, cinematographer or editor, sound recordist and other main members of the crew of the independent films screened in the event are invited for interaction with the audience. The screenings are free and open to all.

National Film Development Corporation Limited

nfdcindia.com

The National Film Development Corporation Limited (NFDC), incorporated in 1975, (100 per cent owned GOI body) was formed by the Government of India with the primary objective of planning and promoting an organized, efficient, and integrated development of the Indian film industry. NFDC was reincorporated in the year 1980, by merging the Film Finance Corporation (FFC) and Indian Motion Picture Export Corporation (IMPEC) with NFDC.

The erstwhile Film Finance Corporation (FFC) was set up in 1964, with the primary objective of extending finance to young talented film makers for film production, whereas, the Indian Motion Picture Export Corporation (MPEC), an autonomous body, was set up to regulate the import and export of Films and canalization of new stock into the country. In recognition of the need for a body that could facilitate the growth of the Indian film industry, the Government of India merged the FFC and IMPEC and NFDC. The NFDC has so far funded/ produced over 200 films. These films, in various Indian languages, have been widely acclaimed and have won many national and international awards. The Corporation has its corporate office at Mumbai along with three regional offices situated at Chennai, Kolkata, and Delhi and a branch office at Thiruvananthapuram.

Directorate of Film Festivals

dff.nic.in

The Directorate of Film Festivals was set up in 1973 with the prime objective of promoting good cinema. This is undertaken by organizing a range of activities under these broad categories: (a) the International Film Festival of India; (b) the National Film Awards and the Dadasaheb Phalke Award; (c) cultural exchange programme and organizing screening of Indian films through the missions abroad; (d) the selection of Indian Panorama; (e) participation in international film festivals abroad; (f) special film expositions on behalf of the Government of India; and (g) print collection and documentation.

These activities provide a unique platform for exchange of ideas, culture and experiences between India and other countries in the field of cinema. It also provides a powerful platform for Indian cinema and fosters commercial opportunities for Indian films. Within the country, the latest trends in global cinema are made accessible to the general public, film industry and students.

International Film Festival of India

The 46th International Film Festival of India (IFFI), organized jointly by the Ministry of Information and Broadcasting and Government of Goa, successfully concluded on November 30, 2015, after ten days of film screenings, master classes, discussions and other events. 287 films in total from 95 countries were screened at 45th IFFI.

ICFT- UNESCO Fellini Medal

For the first time in India, the International Film Festival of India (IFFI) 2015 in collaboration with the International Council for Film, Television and Audiovisual Communication (ICFT), Paris, presented a special ICFT prize consisting of the UNESCO Fellini Medal awarded to a film which reflects the ideals promoted by UNESCO.

National Film Awards

The National Film Awards, the highest awards in the field of cinema continue to underline cinematic excellence. The National Awards along with cinema's highest honour, the Dadasaheb Phalke Award, are presented by the President of India. To commemorate the release of the first Indian Feature Film, Raja Harishchandra on 3rd May 1913, It has been decided to confer the National Film Awards on 3rd May of every year. Accordingly, 63rd National Film Awards were given away in 2015.

62nd National Film Awards

The Best Feature Film was bagged by 'Baahubali' directed by S.S. Rajamouli. The award for Best Popular Film Providing Wholesome Entertainment was given to 'Bajrangi Bhaijaan' (Hindi) directed by Kabir Khan. The Best Actor award was presented to Amitabh Bachchan for the film 'Piku' and Best Actress to Kangana Ranaut for the film 'Tanu weds Manu Returns' (Hindi). The film 'Amdavad Ma Famous' directed by Hardik Mehta was adjudged the Best Non-Feature Film. The Best Book on Cinema Award was given to 'Dr. Rajakumar Samagra Charithre' written by Doddahulluru Rukkoji, whereas Meghachandra Kongbam was awarded Best Film Critic. The prestigious Dadasaheb Phalke Award for the year 2015 was presented to renowned actor and producer Shri Manoj Kumar for his commendable contribution to Indian Cinema.

National Film Archive of India

nfaipune.gov.in

The importance of preserving cinema as an art and historical document has been recognized all over the world. The task of preserving cinema in all its varied expressions and forms is best entrusted to a national organization having a permanent set-up and the confidence of the film industry and adequate resources and expertise. Thus, the National Film Archive of India (NFAI) was established as a media unit in February, 1964 with the following aims and objectives : to trace, acquire and preserve for posterity the heritage of national cinema and build up a representative collection of world cinema; to classify and document data related to film, undertake and encourage research on cinema and publish and distribute them; to act as a centre for dissemination of films culture in the country and to ensure the cultural presence of Indian cinema abroad. During the 50 years of its existence NFAI has been making rapid strides in achieving its goals.

Film Storage/Preservation

NFAI houses, nearly 19 state-of-the-art, film preservation facilities/vaults with global standards and specifications. These vaults have the capacity of nearly 2 lakh film reels storage. There are 3 vaults in the Main building and 16 vaults at Phase-II facility in Pune. The film vaults are maintained with following temperatures for black and white films, colour films and nitrate based films:-

Type of films	Temperatures	Relative Humidity
Nitrate Films	140 C	40 per cent
Black & White films	140 C	40 to 50 per cent
Colour films	20 C +/- 10 C	24 per cent +/- 5 per cent

Film Appreciation Course

An important activity under dissemination of film culture is screen education scheme which includes long and short term film appreciation courses, conducted in collaboration with various educational and cultural institutions across India.

Supply of Films

NFAI's activities to disseminate film culture in the country are manifold. Its Distribution Library has about 25 active film club/ members throughout the country. The Archive supplies films for various screening programmes and film festivals across India.

Participation in Film Festivals

NFAI participates in various film festivals in India and abroad, showcasing its collection of classic films at vaious retrospectives and poster exhibitions on unique themes, curated for the festival.

National Film Heritage Mission

National Film Heritage Mission, a ₹ 597.41 crore project was set up in November, 2014 for restoring and preserving the film hertiage of India. This is a part of 12th Five Year Plan which will spill over to 13th Five Year Plan. This initiative will be greatly appreciated by the film industry. This new plan scheme has taken care of digitization/restoration of films available with NFAI.

Objectives of the National Film Heritage Mission include: (i) to undertake film condition assessment of the film collection and to ascertain the left over life of the film; (ii) preventive conservation of 1,32,000 film reels; (iii) 2k/4k picture and sound restoration of 1086 landmark feature films and 1152 shorts of Indian Cinema and recording of new picture and sound inter-negatives of each film; (iv) digitization of 1160 feature films and 1660 shorts; (v) construction of archival and preservation facilities for preservation of material restored under NFHM in dust free, low humidity, and low temperature conditions at NFAI campus, Pune; and (vi) training workshops and courses in field of conservation, preservation and archiving in co-ordination with international agencies that are experts in this field.

Children's Film Society of India

cfsindia.org

Children's Film Society India (CFSI) was established in 1955 to provide value based entertainment to children through the medium of films. CFSI is engaged in production, acquisition, distribution/exhibition and promotion of children's films. The head office of the CFSI is in Mumbai with branch offices at New Delhi and Chennai. The mission of CFSI is to facilitate promotion of children's films by encouraging, strengthening and spreading the children's film movement all over the country and abroad. Films produced/procured by society are exhibited through state/district level Children's Film Festivals as well as through theatrical, non- theatrical exhibition in schools through Distributors, NGOs etc.

During 2015, 7,502 shows were arranged by free screenings covering more than 21,24,054 children. CFSI also markets films on DVDs and VCDs. A total of 3,455 DVD/VCDs were sold resulting in revenue of ₹ 3,93,260. Fourteen CFSI films were telecast on National Network Programme of Chulbuli Filme, Chatpati Gap Shap for a royalty of ₹ 9.45 lakhs. The State level Children's Film Festivals were organized in 8 north east states. A package of 20 selected films was provided by CFSI and screened in theatres / auditoriums across all the states. A total number of 16 districts were covered through 54 shows viewed by 21,796 children.

A Children's Film Festival was conducted in Thiruvannamalai district during August 2016, 105 shows were conducted in 18 theatres. A record number of 55,740 children were benefited by these shows.

Directorate of Advertising and Visual Publicity

davp.nic.in

Directorate of Advertising and Visual Publicity (DAVP), established in 1955, is the nodal multi media advertising agency of the Government of India. Over the past 60 years it has been catering to the communication needs of almost all central ministries/departments, autonomous bodies and PSUs by providing them single window, cost effective service. It informs and educates people, both rural and urban, about the government's policies and programmes and motivates them to participate in developmental activities, through its various vehicles of communication viz., print media advertising, audio visual advertising, printed publicity, exhibitions, outdoor publicity, new media and mass mailing. The organizational set up of DAVP at the Headquarters consists of several wings like campaign, advertising, outdoor publicity, printed publicity, exhibition, mass mailing, audio visual wing, design studio, administration and accounts wings. It has two regional offices at Bengaluru and Guwahati to coordinate the Directorate's activities in the regions.

DAVP has a network of 32 Field Exhibition Units spread all over the country. The Field Exhibition Units act as a vital communication link between the government and the people. These Units mount multimedia exhibitions on social and developmental themes in far flung areas of the country to disseminate information about the policies and programmes of the central government on key national issues.

Directorate of Field Publicity

dfp.nic.in

Directorate of Field Publicity, (DFP), a media unit is the only Directorate under Government of India engaged in interpersonal communication. DFP undertakes well conceived communication programmes among the target and potential beneficiaries through inter-personal and micro level communication activities like briefings to opinion leaders, interactive sessions with target beneficiaries, group discussions, quiz and other competitions like Healthy Mother & Baby shows, photo exhibitions, rallies, film shows, and public meetings. In this process, DFP gets support from other implementing central and state departments/agencies.

There are 22 regional offices which are mostly located at state capitals and 207 Field Publicity Units which are spread all over the country and mostly located at district headquarters. Each regional office has 6 to 14 Field Units under its jurisdiction. The Field Publicity Units are equipped with vehicles and audio visual equipment for their field level activities. DFP's communication teams organized awareness generation programmes on Government schemes and policies among the masses, mainly in remote, rural and media shadow areas.

DFP has adopted ICT in a big way to facilitate functioning of its Regional Offices and Field Publicity Units in a more effective way. All the Regional Offices and Field Units have been equipped suitably to regularly report on programmes, financial and administrative matters 'online'. DFP has an informative website and 22 of its regions have their respective web pages. The Directorate has been using social media like YouTube, Facebook and Twitter for highlighting its outreach activities and promoting deliverable messages on the programmes and schemes of the government.

Song and Drama Division

The Song and Drama Division was set up in 1954 as a unit of All India Radio and was given the status of an Independent media unit in 1956 with the mandate of development communication. This is the largest organization in the country using performing arts as a medium of communication. The Division uses a wide range of art forms such as drama, ballets, operas, theatrical shows on national themes such as communal harmony, national integration, secularism, promotion of cultural heritage, health, environment, education, etc., through sound and light programmes.

Film and Television Institute of India

The Film and Television Institute of India (FTII) was set up in 1960. Following the addition of Television wing in 1974, the Institute was re-designated as Film and Television Institute of India. The Institute became a Society in October, 1974 under the Registration of Societies Act, 1860. The Society consists of eminent personalities connected with film, television, communication, culture, alumni of institute and ex-officio government members. The Institute is governed by a Governing Council, headed by a Chairman. The academic policies and plans of the Institute are formulated by the Academic Council. The matters involving finance are controlled by the Standing Finance Committee. The Institute consists of two Wings, The Film wing and the TV Wing, and offers courses in both Film and Television. The Three-year Diploma Courses lead to a Post Graduate Diploma in Film Direction, cinematography, Audiography and Film Editing. The Institute also offers a two-year post graduate diploma course in acting, a two-year post graduate course in art direction and production design, and one-year post graduate certificate course.

Film and Television Institute of India provides the latest education and technological experience in the art and technique of film making and television production. In-service training is provided to officers of all grades of the Doordarshan and others. It is equipped with the latest digital and broadcast grade production set-ups viz. Non Linear, beta cam and A/B roll editing setups, digital cameras viz. Sony BVP-500 P, Soft Chroma Keyer, digital special effect generator, silicon graphics 02 workstations with Alias software, modern movie cameras, rerecording equipment etc. which provide an excellent exposure to the faculty and students of Film and Television Institute.

Satyajit Ray Film and Television Institute

srfti.ac.in

Satyajit Ray Film and Television Institute (SRFTI), Kolkata was established as an autonomous educational institution and was registered under the West Bengal Societies Registration Act, 1961. Located at Kolkata and named after the legendary film maestro Satyajit Ray, SRFTI is the second national level film training institute to be established by the Government of India. The institute offers three-year post-graduate diploma courses in direction and screenplay writing, cinematography, editing and audiography. Apart from the basic diploma course, the institute also has the provision to conduct short and medium term courses on areas related to film and television. Research and explorative studies in sociology, culture and technology of film and television are the other areas of focus in SRFTI.

SRFTI is run by a Society constituted by the Government of India. The Society runs the Institute through a governing council that is constituted with select members of Society. The Governing Council is the supreme Body for all executive functions of the Institute. It also constitutes different committees/bodies as deemed necessary viz. Academic Council Standing Finance Committee etc.

Indian Institute of Mass Communication

iimc.nic.in

The Indian Institute of Mass Communication (IIMC), registered as a society under the Societies Registration Act, 1860 came into existence in 1965. The Institute, was established with the basic objective of undertaking teaching, training and research in the area of mass communication.

The Institute conducts a number of post-graduate diploma courses in print journalism, radio and TV journalism and advertising and public relations. Beginning in 1969, the Institute has organized a Post-Graduate Diploma Course in Development Journalism for middle level working journalists form Asian, African, Latin American and East European countries under the auspices of the Ministry of External Affairs, Government of India since 1969. A number of specialized short-term courses ranging from one week to twelve weeks are also organized to meet the ever-growing training needs of communication professionals working in various media/publicity outfits of Central/state governments and public sector organizations. The Institute also collaborates with different national and international agencies in conducting training programmes, seminars, workshops. etc. and in undertaking research projects.

The Institute endeavours to contribute towards the creation and strengthening of an information structure suitable not only for India requirements, but also those of other developing countries. It provides its expertise and consultancy services to other institutions/organs of the Central/state governments, public sector organizations, universities and other academic institutions. With the growing popularity of the Institute's training activities and with a view to meeting regional aspirations, the Institute opened a branch at Dhenkanal, Orissa in 1993 for catering to the demands of the eastern region.

At present, the Branch conducts two Post Graduate Diploma Courses—Journalism (English) and Journalism (Odia). The Government of India, through the Ministry of Information and Broadcasting makes financial support to the Institute available. The activities of the Institute are guided by its Executive Council, whose Chairman (Ex Officio) is the Secretary in the Ministry who is also the President of the Institute (Society). The other members of the Council include, *inter-alia,* representatives of the Institute's faculty and eminent personalities from the media. Through its continuous hard work over the last more than four decades of its existence and excellent delivery mechanism, the Institute has achieved the envious position of a "Centre of Excellence" in the area of communication teaching, training and research.

Teaching and Training Programme

The academic and training activities of the Institute can be divided into four programmes : (i.) Post-graduate Diploma programmes for students : These comprise four programmes in Journalism and one in Advertising and Public Relations; 1. Post-graduate Diploma Course in Journalism-English; 2. Post-graduate Diploma Course in Journalism-Hindi; 3. Post-graduate Diploma Course in Journalism-Oriya; 4. Post-graduate Diploma Course in Radio and TV Journalism-English and Hindi; and 5. Post-graduate Diploma Course in Advertising and Public Relations (English and Hindi).

This four month diploma course is highly sought after by mid career level working journalists in Africa, Asia and Latin America and other developing countries. The average intake of participants is 20-25 per batch. The Institute organizes two such courses each year.

Short-term Courses, Workshop, Seminars and Conferences

With a view to contributing towards better understanding of different issues pertaining to mass communication in the context of India and other developing countries and in order to increase awareness about the emerging techniques and sharpening their basic skills, the Institute has been organizing a variety of short- term courses, workshops, seminars and conferences in various areas of communication and media. The Institute runs regular short-term academic programmes for personnel of different media units of the Ministry of Information and Broadcasting. A number of specialized short-term courses, ranging from one week to 12 weeks' duration, are also conducted for meeting the professional training needs of defence officials and those working in various media/publicity organizations of the central/state governments and Public Sector Enterprises.

Apna Radio AR-I Community Radio : The Institute's community radio broadcasts on 96.9 MHz five days a week for two hours each day from 12.00

noon to 2.00 p.m. with a repeat broadcast from 3.00 p.m. to 5.00 p.m. Apna Radio has a range of 10-12 km around the Institute. The FM radio station has a broadcast studio, two recording studios and several sound editing workstations.

Broadcast Engineering Consultants India Limited

becil.com

Broadcast Engineering Consultants India Ltd. (BECIL), a profit making PSE was constituted in 1995 to provide the national broadcasters' expertise to the private broadcasters in the country. At present, BECIL is an established consultancy agency, system integrator and turnkey solution provider in all spheres of Broadcast Engineering. BECIL also undertakes operation and maintenance of various types of broadcast systems. Its clients include government, semi government, overseas and private organisations.

The area of specialisation of BECIL is as follows: establishment of radio and TV transmitting facility including frequency and coverage planning, prediction etc.; setting up state-of-the-art studio facilities for audio and video including ethernet connectivity capable of transmitting live content and data; establishment of cable TV systems and HITs (Head End In The Sky) and wireline broadcasting; turnkey Solution for establishing community radio stations; establishment from concept to commissioning of electronic media monitoring solutions (Radio and TV Terrestrial or Satellite), and security related Surveillance Set ups for GSM, CDMA and VSAT, sales and support for all type of broadcast engineering equipment/system, design and integration of outside broadcast vans (DSNG) with state-of-the- art technology. providing professionals for O&M of broadcast stations, TV studios, satellite earth stations, Electronic Media Monitoring Centre and supply and support for various type of monitoring, interception and encryption, decryption devices for forces and intelligence agencies.

BECIL client list includes Government, Semi Government, Overseas and Private organizations. It has many firsts to its credit like establishment of first teleport in India, first to establish infrastructure, first to set-up multi channel FM transmission in India combining up to 7 FM channels at Bengaluru, first to design and establish HDTV studio set-up for Presidential Secretariat and Lok Sabha TV, to name a few.

23 Planning

PLANNING in India derives its objectives and social premises from the Directive Principles of State Policy enshrined in the Constitution. Public and private sectors are viewed as complementary. The private sector covers, besides organized industry, small-scale industries, agriculture, trade and housing, construction and related areas. Individual efforts and private initiatives are considered necessary and desirable in the national endeavour for development with optimum voluntary cooperation.

NITI Aayog

The National Institution for Transforming India (NITI Aayog) came into existence in 2015 replacing the existing Planning Commission which was established in 1950. The NITI Aayog is the successor to the Planning Commission. The new institution is envisaged to be a catalyst to the developmental process; nurturing an overall enabling environment, through a holistic approach to development going beyond the limited sphere of the public sector and Government of India. This is to be built on the foundation of: an empowered role of states as equal partners in national development; underlying the principle of cooperative federalism. A knowledge hub of internal as well as external resources; serving as repository of good governance best practices, and a think tank offering domain knowledge as well as strategic expertise to all levels of government. A collaborative platform facilitating implementation; by monitoring progress, plugging gaps and bringing together the various ministries at the Centre and in states, in the joint pursuit of developmental goals.

Objectives

The Resolution setting up the NITI Aayog includes the following objectives: To evolve a shared vision of national development priorities, sectors and strategies with the active involvement of States in the light of national objectives. The vision of the NITI Aayog is to provide a framework 'national agenda' for the Prime Minister and the chief ministers to provide impetus to. To foster cooperative federalism through structured support initiatives and mechanisms with the states on a continuous basis, recognizing that strong states make a strong nation. To ensure, on areas that are specially referred to it, that the interests of national security are incorporated in economic strategy and policy. To pay special attention to the sections of our society that may be at risk of not benefitting adequately from economic progress. To design strategic and long term policy and programme frameworks and initiatives, and monitor their progress and their efficacy. The lessons learnt through monitoring and feedback will be used for making innovative improvements, including necessary mid course corrections. To create a knowledge, innovation and entrepreneurial support system through a collaborative community of national and international experts, practitioners and other partners. To offer a platform for resolution of inter-sectoral and inter-departmental issues in order to accelerate that implementation of the development agenda. To undertake other activities as may be necessary in order to further the execution of the national development agenda, and the objectives mentioned above.

Composition

The composition of the NITI Aayog is as follows:

(a) Prime Minister of India as the Chairperson

(b) The Governing Council comprising the Chief Ministers of all the States, Chief Ministers of Union Territories with Legislatures, viz., Delhi and Puducherry and Lt. Governors of other Union Territories.

(c) Regional Council will be formed to address specific issues and contingencies impacting more than one state or a region. These will be formed for a specified tenure. The Regional Councils will be convened by the Prime Minister and will comprise of the Chief Minister of States and Lt. Governors of Union Territories in the region. These will be chaired by the Chairperson of the NITI Aayog or his nominee.

(d) Experts, specialists and practitioners with relevant domain knowledge as special invitees nominated by the Prime Minister.

(e) The full time organizational framework will consist of, in addition to the Prime Minister as Chairperson.

  i. Vice-Chairperson: To be appointed by the Prime Minister,

  ii. Members. Full Time.

  iii. Part-time Members: Maximum of 2, from leading universities, research organizations and other relevant institutions in an ex-officio capacity. Part time members will be on a rotational basis.

  iv Ex officio Members: Maximum of 4 Members of the Union Council of Ministers to be nominated by the Prime Minister.

  v. Chief Executive Officer: To be appointed by the Prime Minister for a fixed tenure, in the rank of Secretary to the Government of India.

  vi. Secretariat as deemed necessary.

At present the approved constitution of the NITI Aayog is as under:

Chairperson: Shri Narendra Modi, Prime Minister

Vice Chairpersons: Dr. Arvind Panagariya, in the rank of Cabinet Minister.

Full Time Members:

(a) Dr. Bibek Debroy, in the rank of Minister of State

(b) Dr. V.K. Saraswat, former Secretary; Defence R & D, in the rank of Minister of State

(c) Prof. Ramesh Chand, Former Professor & Head, Institute of Economic Growth, Delhi University; and Professor at Punjab Agricultural University, Ludhiana.

Ex-Office Members:

(a) Shri Raj Nath Singh, Minister of Home Affairs

(b) Shri Arun Jaitley, Minister of Finance; Minister of Corporate Affairs.

(c) Shri Suresh Prabhu, Minister of Railways

(d) Shri Radha Mohan Singh, Minister of Agriculture

Special Invitees:

(a) Shri Nitin Jairam Gadkari, Minister of Road Transport and Highways, and Minister of Shipping

(b) Shri Thaawar Chand Gehlot, Minister of Social Justice and Empowerment

(c) Smt. Smriti Zubin Irani, Minister of Textiles.

Working of Governing Council of NITI Aayog

The first meeting of the Governing Council of NITI Aayog was held in 2015 in New Delhi. Its second meeting was held on July 15, 2015 where the Prime Minister reiterated the vision that states should be the focus of all development efforts. In order to work towards a federal structure, based on a two-way flow of priorities and cooperative action, a series of meetings were held in NITI Aayog with groups of States to develop a strategy of working together. This exercise culminated in the conference – 'Role of NITI Aayog: Consultation with the States' – held in November 2015.

The conference advocated the need for gradual shifting of the focus from Planning to Policy, in order to influence the behaviour of both public and private actors. This is important in the light of changed economic circumstances where the major share of investments today flow from the private sector. It was also observed that most states had achieved sizes of economy larger than many countries. As a result, they needed to interact a great deal not only with the Central Government but also with international government and non-governmental bodies.

Major Activities

NITI Aayog as a "Think Tank" of the Government is instrumental in providing a directional and policy dynamics for taking steps in liaison with states while fostering the spirit of cooperative federation. Major activities of NITI Aayog include : Appointments of Vice Chairman, Full Time Members and Chief Executive Officer of NITI Aayog have been made. A National Conference on the Role of NITI Aayog - Consultations with States was organized in New Delhi in

November, 2016. A Resource Book on Good Practices in Social Sector Service Delivery was published. Assisted Backward states, - Bihar, West Bengal and Odisha by granting Special Assistance of ₹ 1,887.53 crore, ₹ 536.77 crore and ₹ 132.07 crore respectively for their key development areas.

Fourteenth Finance Commission

Appointed every five years the Finance Commission is a constitutional body with the broad mandate to define centre - state federal relations. Its most important task is to recommend division of states' revenues collected by the Centre of the 'divisibility pool' between the Centre and the states and the share to be allocated to each state.

The Fourteenth Finance Commission (FCC) submitted its recommendations to the Government in December, 2014. Some of its important recommendations include the devolution of a significantly higher share of 42 per cent of the divisible pool to states compared with the 32 per cent share recommended by the 13th Finance Commission.

Accordingly the total devolution to the states in 2015-16 RE was ₹ 5.06 lakh crore which is about 50 per cent more than the previous year. The devolution in 2016-17 BE further increased to ₹ 5.70 lakh crore. This was in response to the demand by the states for increased flow of untied fiscal resources in place of tied resources that come with Centrally Sponsored Schemes. Similarly, the total grants-in-aid recommended by the FFC for its award period is ₹ 5.37 lakh crore as against ₹ 1.65 lakh crore.

Central Plan 2015-16 Revised Estimates & 2016-17 Budget Estimates

The Central Plan including Internal and Extra Budgetary Resources (IEBR) of Public Sector Enterprises (PSEs) 2016-17 BE stands at ₹ 7.06 lakh crores exceeding the RE 2015-16 by about ₹ 1.23 lakh crore. In 2014-15, Central Plan including IEBR stood at ₹ 4.21 lakh crore. In 2014-15, the IEBRs contribution to Central Plan was ₹ 2.29 lakh crore.

As a result of increased share in Central Taxes to the states, Central Assistance to State Plan (CASP) 2015-16 RE stands reduced to ₹ 2.16 lakh crore as compared to ₹ 2.70 lakh crore in 2014-15 Actual. In 2016-17, CASP is budgeted at ₹ 2.42 lakh crore.

Investment in Infrastructure

The Twelfth Plan had projected an investment of ₹ 55,74,663 crore at current prices with a share of 48 per cent from the private sector during the Plan period (2012-17). As against the annual Plan projection of ₹ 7,51,012 crore, the actual investment in 2012-13 was ₹ 5,52,431 crore, about 74 per cent. Similarly, against the annual Plan projection of ₹ 8,87,454 crore in 2013-14, the investment was ₹ 6,26,884 crore, implying an achievement of 71 per cent.

The investment anticipated in 2014-15 of ₹ 7,13,099 crore is somewhat higher than what was achieved during 2012-13 and 2013-14. However, investments anticipated in 2015-16 and 2016-17 of ₹ 8,92,085 crore and ₹ 10,38,324 crore respectively are significantly higher due to recent initiatives in many sectors like electricity, roads, railways, ports and telecommunications which are aimed at creating additional capacities and speed up project implementation. Further, higher budgetary allocations in the years 2015-16 and 2016-17 to infrastructure sectors have the potential to crowd in greater private investment. The total outlay for infrastructure in Budget Estimates 2016-17 stands at ₹ 2,21,246 crore.

Based on the lower investment received in the first two years of the Plan and the anticipated investment level in remaining three years of the Plan, the Twelfth Plan projections have been revised to ₹ 38,22,822 crore which is about 69 per cent of the original Plan projections of ₹ 55,74,663 crore. The revised projections of public investment (Centre & States) for the Twelfth Plan stands at 88 per cent of the target (revised from ₹ 28,90,823 crore to ₹ 25,41,599 crore), while the revision in private investment is estimated at 48 per cent of the target (revised from ₹ 26,83,840 crore to ₹ 12,81,223 crore). Thus, the shortfall in realizing the projected private sector investment largely accounts for the downward projections of the infrastructure investment in the Twelfth Plan. One of the principal reasons for shortfall in private investment across sectors relates to issues in financing of infrastructure projects.

The revised projected investment is still 1.6 times the investment of ₹ 23,77,746 crore achieved in the Eleventh Plan at current prices. The revised share of private investment in Twelfth Plan is projected at about 34 per cent compared to 48 per cent in the original projection and is less than the 37 per cent achieved in the Eleventh Plan. As per the revised projections, investment as a percentage of GDP for the Twelfth Plan as a whole would go down to 6.11 per cent against the original projection of 8.18 per cent and 7 per cent achieved in the Eleventh Plan.

The Twelfth Plan (2012-2017) was formulated in the backdrop of this remarkable performance of infrastructure sector during the Eleventh Plan. The Plan projected an investment of ₹ 55.75 lakh crore (at current prices) in infrastructure during the Plan period (2012-17), which is more than double the investment in infrastructure achieved in the Eleventh Plan period. Further, the Plan adopted a strategy of encouraging higher private investment in infrastructure, directly and through public private partnerships (PPPs). The share of private investment in infrastructure was projected to rise substantially from 37 per cent in Eleventh Plan to 48 per cent in the Twelfth Plan.

However, based on the lower investment received in the first two years of the 12th Plan and the anticipated investment level in remaining three years, the 12th Plan projected investment have been revised to ₹ 38.23 lakh crore, which is about 69 per cent of the original plan projections of ₹ 55.75 lakh crore. The revised projections of public investment (Centre & States) stands at 88 per cent of the target (revised from ₹ 26.91 lakh crore to ₹ 25.42 lakh crore), while the revision in private investment is estimated at 48 per cent of target (revised from

₹ 26.84 lakh crore to 12.81 lakh crore). Thus, the shortfall in realizing the projected private sector investment largely account for the downward projections of the Infrastructure investment in the Twelfth Plan.

First Plan

Keeping in view the large-scale import of food grains in 1951 and inflationary pressures on the economy, the First Plan (1951-56) accorded the highest priority to agriculture including irrigation and power projects. About 44.6 per cent of the total outlay of ₹ 2,069 crore in the public sector (later raised to ₹ 2,378 crore) was allocated for this purpose. The Plan aimed at increasing the rate of investment from five to about seven per cent of the national income.

Second Plan

The Second Five-Year Plan (1956-57 to 1960-61) sought to promote a pattern of development, which would ultimately lead to the establishment of a socialistic pattern of society in India. Its main aims were (i) an increase of 25 per cent in the national income; (ii) rapid industrialization with particular emphasis on the development of basic and heavy industries; (iii) large expansion of employment opportunities; and (iv) reduction of inequalities in income and wealth and a more even distribution of economic power. The Plan aimed at increasing the rate of investment from about seven percent of the national income to 11 per cent by 1960-61. It laid emphasis on industrialization, increased production of iron and steel, heavy chemicals including nitrogenous fertilizers and development of heavy engineering and machine building industry.

Third Plan

The Third Plan (1961-62 to 1965-66) aimed at securing a marked advance towards self-sustaining growth. Its immediate objectives were to : (i) secure an increase in the national income of over five per cent per annum and at the same time ensure a pattern of investment which could sustain this rate of growth in the subsequent Plan periods; (ii) achieve self-sufficiency in food grains and increase agricultural production to meet the requirements of industry and exports; (iii) expand basic industries like steel, chemicals, fuel and power and establish machine building capacity so that the requirements of further industrialization could be met within a period of about 10 years mainly from the country's own resources; (iv) fully utilize the manpower resources of the country and ensure a substantial expansion in employment opportunities; and (v) establish progressively greater equality of opportunity and bring about reduction in disparities of income and wealth and a more even distribution of economic power. The Plan aimed at increasing the national income by about 30 per cent from ₹ 14,500 crore in 1960-61 to about ₹ 19,000 crore by 1965-66 (at 1960-61 prices) and per capita income by about 17 per cent from ₹ 330 to ₹ 386 over the same period.

Annual Plans

The situation created by the Indo-Pakistan conflict in 1965, two successive years of severe drought, devaluation of the currency, general rise in prices and erosion of resources available for Plan purposes delayed the finalization of the Fourth Five Year Plan. Instead, between 1966 and 1969, three Annual Plans were formulated within the framework of the draft outline of the Fourth Plan.

Fourth Plan

The Fourth Plan (1969-74) aimed at accelerating the tempo of development of reducing fluctuations in agricultural production as well as the impact of uncertainties of foreign aid. It sought to raise the standard of living through programmes designed to promote equality and social justice. The Plan laid particular emphasis on improving the conditions of the less privileged and weaker sections especially through provision of employment and education. Efforts were directed towards reduction of concentration of wealth, income and economic power to promote equity. The Plan aimed at increasing the net domestic product (at 1968-69 factor cost) from ₹ 29,071 crore in 1969-70 to ₹ 38,306 crore in 1973-74. The average annual compound rate of growth envisaged was 5.7 per cent.

Fifth Plan

The Fifth Plan (1974-79) was formulated against the backdrop of severe inflationary pressures. The major objectives of the plan were to achieve self-reliance and adopt measures for raising the consumption standard of people living below the poverty line. This Plan also gave high priority to bring inflation under control and to achieve stability in the economic situation. It targeted an annual growth rate of 5.5 percent in the national income. Four Annual Plans pertaining to the Fifth Plan period were completed. It was subsequently decided to end the Fifth Plan period with the close of the Annual Plan 1978-79.

Sixth Plan

Removal of poverty was the foremost objective of the Sixth Plan (1980-85). The strategy adopted was to move simultaneously towards strengthening the infrastructure for both agriculture and industry. Stress was laid on tackling interrelated problems through a systematic approach with greater management, efficiency and intensive monitoring in all sectors and active involvement of people in formulating specific schemes of development at the local level and securing their speedy and effective implementation. The actual expenditure in the Sixth Plan stood at ₹ 1,09,291.7 crore (current price) as against the envisaged total public sector outlay of ₹ 97,500 crore (1979-80 prices) accounting for a 12 per cent increase in nominal terms. The average annual growth rate targeted for the Plan was 5.2 per cent.

Seventh Plan

The Seventh Plan (1985-90) emphasized policies and programmes, which aimed at rapid growth in food grains production, increased employment opportunities and productivity within the framework of basic tenets of planning, namely, growth, modernization, self reliance and social justice. Food grains production during the Seventh Plan grew by 3.23 per cent as compared to a long-term growth rate of 2.68 per cent between 1967-68 and 1988-89 and the growth rate of 2.55 per cent in the eighties due to overall favourable weather conditions, implementation of various thrust programmes and concerted efforts of the Government and the farmers. To reduce unemployment and consequently, the incidence of poverty, special programmes like Jawahar Rozgar Yojana were launched in addition to the existing programmes. Due recognition was accorded to the role, small-scale and food processing industries could play in this regard. The total expenditure during the entire Seventh Plan stood at ₹ 2,18,729.62 crore (current prices) as against the envisaged total public sector outlay of ₹ 1,80,000 crore, resulting in a 21.52 per cent increase in nominal terms. During this Plan period, the Gross Domestic Product (GDP) grew at an average rate of 5.8 per cent exceeding the targeted growth rate by 0.8 per cent.

Eighth Annual Plans

The Eighth Five-Year Plan (1990-95) could not take off due to the fast-changing political situation at the Centre. The Eighth five-Year Plan commence in 1992 and that 1990-91 and 1991-92 were treated as separate Annual Plans. Formulated within the framework of the Approach to the Eighth Five-Year Plan (1990-95), the basic thrust of these Annual Plans was on maximization of employment and social transformation.

Eighth Plan

The Eighth Five-Year Plan (1992-97) was launched immediately after the initiation of structural adjustment policies and macro stabilization policies, which were necessitated by the worsening Balance of Payments positions and the position of inflation during 1990-91. The various structural adjustment policies were introduced gradually so that the economy could be pushed to a higher growth path and improve its strength and thus prevent a crisis in Balance of Payments and inflation in the future. The Eighth Plan took note of some of these policy changes, which were to come about due to these reforms. The Plan aimed at an average annual growth rate of 5.6 per cent and an average industrial growth rate of about 7.5 per cent. These growth targets were planned to be achieved with relative price stability and substantial improvement in the country's Balance of Payments. Some of the salient features of economic performance during the Eighth Five-Year Plan indicate, among other things: (a) a faster economic growth, (b) a faster growth of the manufacturing sector and agriculture and allied sectors, (c) significant growth rates in exports and imports, improvement in trade and current account deficit and a significant reduction in the Central Government's fiscal deficit. However, a shortfall in expenditure in the Central sector due to inadequate mobilization of internal and extra budgetary resources by the PSUs and various departments was witnessed. In the States sector, there as on for the shortfall was lack of mobilization of adequate resources due to deterioration in the balance of current revenues, erosion in the contribution of state electricity boards and state road transport corporations, negative opening balance, mounting non-Plan expenditure and shortfalls in the collection of small savings, etc. The total expenditure during the entire Eighth Plan stood at

₹ 4,95,669 crore by taking 1996-97 (RE) as actual] at current prices as against envisaged total public sector outlay of ₹ 4,34,100 crore (1991-92 prices) resulting in a 14.2 per cent increase in nominal terms. The Eighth Plan envisaged an annual average growth rate of 5.6 per cent. Against this, an average annual growth rate of 6.8 per cent was achieved during this plan period.

Ninth Plan

The Ninth Plan (1997-2002) was launched in the fiftieth year of India's Independence. The Plan aimed at achieving a targeted GDP growth rate of seven per cent per annum and there was emphasis on the seven identified Basic Minimum Services (BMS) with additional Central Assistance earmarked for these services with a view to obtaining a complete coverage of the population in a time-bound manner. These included provision of safe drinking water, availability of primary health service facilities, universalization of primary education, public housing assistance to shelterless poor families, nutritional support to children, connectivity of all villages and habitations and streamlining of the public distribution system with a focus on the poor. The Plan also aimed at pursuing a policy of fiscal consolidation, whereby the focus was on sharp education in the revenue deficit of the Government, including the Centre, States and PSUs through a combination of improved revenue collections and control of inessential expenditures, particularly with regard to subsidies and through recovery of user charges and decentralization of planning and implementation through greater reliance on States and Panchayati Raj Institutions.

The specific objectives of the Ninth Plan included : (i) priority to agriculture and rural development with a view to generate adequate productive employment and eradication of poverty; (ii) accelerating the growth rate of the economy with stable prices; (iii) ensuring food and nutritional security for all, particularly the vulnerable sections of society; (iv) providing the basic minimum services of safe drinking water, primary health care facilities, universal primary education, shelter, and connectivity to all in a time-bound manner; (v) containing the growth rate of population; (vi) ensuring mobilization and participation of people at all levels; (vii) empowerment of women and socially disadvantaged groups such as Scheduled Castes, Scheduled Tribes and Other Backward Classes and minorities as agents of socio-economic change and development; (viii) promoting and developing people's participatory institutions like Panchayati Raj Institution, cooperatives and self-help groups; and (ix) strengthening efforts to build self-reliance. The Ninth Plan envisaged an average target growth rate of 6.5 per cent per annum in GDP as against the growth rate of 7 per cent approved earlier in the Approach Paper. The scaling down of the target was necessitated by the changes in the national as well as global economic situation in the first two years of the Ninth Plan. Against this, the achievement in the growth-rate on an average was to be 5.5 per cent per annum.

Tenth Plan

The Tenth Five-Year Plan (2002-07) was approved by the National Development Council (NDC) in December, 2002. The Plan has further developed the NDC mandate objectives, of doubling the per capita income in ten years and achieving a growth rate of eight per cent of GDP per annum. Since economic growth is not the only objective, the Plan aims at harnessing the benefits of growth to improve the quality of life of the people by setting of the following key targets : Reduction in the poverty ratio from 26 per cent to 21 per cent, by 2007; decadal population growth to reduce from 21.3 per cent in 1991-2001 to 16.2 per cent in 2001-11; growth in gainful employment, at least, to keep pace with addition to the labour force; all children to be in school by 2003 and all children to complete five years of schooling by 2007; reducing gender gaps in literacy and wage rates by 50 percent; literacy rate to increase from 65 per cent in 1999-2000, to 75 percent in 2007; Providing potable drinking water to all villages; increase in forest/tree cover from 19 per cent in 1999-2000, to 25 per cent in 2007; and cleaning of major polluted river stretches.

The Tenth Plan had a number of new features that include, among others, the following: Firstly, the Plan recognised the rapid growth in the labour force. At current rate of growth and labour intensity in production, India faces the possibility of rising unemployment, which could lead to social unrest. The Tenth Plan therefore aims at creating 50 million job opportunities during the period, by placing special emphasis on employment intensive sectors of agriculture, irrigation, agro-forestry, small and medium enterprises, information and communication technology and other services. Secondly, the Plan addresses the issue of poverty and the unacceptably low levels of social indicators. Although these have been the objectives in earlier Plans, in the current Plan there are specific monitorable targets, which will need to be attained along with the growth target.

The Incremental Capital Output Ratio (ICOR) of the economy was expected to come down to about 3.6 as against 4.5 during the Ninth Plan. This decline in ICOR was achieved mainly through better utilization of existing capacities and suitable sectorial allocation of capital and its efficient utilization. The growth target, therefore, would require an investment rate of 28.4 per cent of GDP. This requirement was to be met from domestic savings of 26.8 per cent of GDP and external savings of 1.6 per cent. The bulk of the additional domestic savings will have to come from reduction in Government dis-saving from -4.5 (2001-02) to -0.5 per cent (2006-07) of GDP. The average growth rate in the last four years of the 10th Plan (2003-04 to 2006-07) was little over 8 per cent, making the growth rate 7.7 per cent for the entire 10th Plan period. Though this was below the target of 8 per cent, it is the highest growth rate achieved in any Plan period.

Eleventh Plan

The Eleventh Five Year Plan (2007-12) provided a comprehensive strategy for inclusive development, building on the growing strength of the economy, while also addressing weaknesses that have surfaced. It set a target for 9 per cent growth in the five year period with acceleration during the period to reach 10 per cent by the end of the Plan.

Twelfth Plan

The Twelfth Plan fully recognizes that the objective of development is broad-based improvement in the economic and social conditions of our people. However, rapid growth of GDP is an essential requirement for achieving this objective.

The Approach Paper to the Twelfth Plan, had set a target of 9 per cent average growth of GDP over the Plan period (2012 to 2017). That was before the Euro-zone crisis in that year triggered a sharp downturn in global economic prospects, and also before the extent of the slowdown in the domestic economy was known. Twelfth Plan envisaged that the current slowdown in GDP growth can be reversed through strong corrective action, including especially an expansion in investment with a corresponding increase in savings to keep inflationary pressures under control. However, while our full growth potential remains around 9 per cent, acceleration to this level can only occur in a phased manner, especially since the global economy is expected to remain weak for the first half of the Plan period.

Inclusiveness as Poverty Reduction

The poverty estimates for 2011-12 was computed following the extant Tendulkar methodology and this was released in July 2013. The poverty ratio for 2011-12 was estimated as 21.9 at all India level, with 25.7 per cent in rural areas and 13.7 per cent in urban. The Task Force on Elimination of Poverty in India in its report has inter alia, stated that "a consensus in favour of either the Tendulkar or a higher poverty line did not emerge. Therefore, the Task Force has concluded that the matter be considered in greater depth by the country's top experts on poverty before a final decision is made. Accordingly, it is recommended that an expert committee be set up to arrive at an informed decision on the level at which the poverty line should be set".

Major Initiatives

Appraisal Document of Twelfth Plan

As a follow up of the decisions taken in the first meeting of the Governing Council the exercise of appraisal of the Twelfth Five Year Plan (2012-17) was undertaken. The appraisal broadly covered physical and financial targets vis-à-vis achievements for the first four financial years of the Plan (2012-16) and the financial targets (Budget Estimates) for the terminal year (2016-17) of the Plan. Breaking away from the past, the Appraisal document is based on the following nine broad themes: (i) economy and policies; (ii) macroeconomic factors; (iii) employment and skill development; (iv) governance; (v) human resource development; (vi) physical infrastructure; (vii) environmental sustainability; (viii) agriculture and rural transformation, and (ix) urban transformation.

The Twelfth Five Year Plan envisaged three scenarios termed as "strong inclusive growth", "insufficient action" and "policy logjam", pegging the average annual GDP growth rate under these at 8 per cent, 6 to 6.5 per cent, and 5 to 5.5 per cent, respectively. The performance in 2012-13 and 2013-14, in line with the projections based on the old GDP series, may be reasonably concluded as below the "policy logjam" scenario. In the later years, the economy recovered. The Appraisal of 12th Plan has provided an opportunity for incorporating the shared vision of national development and important initiatives taking by the Government.

The current financial year (2016-17) is the terminal year of the Twelfth Plan, NITI Aayog has initiated consultations with Union miniseries, state governments, experts in the domain and academia, to formulate strategies and draw action plans with differing time horizons.

Atal Innovation Mission

The Government has set up Atal Innovation Mission (AIM) in NITI Aayog with a view to promote a culture of innovation and entrepreneurship in the country. The key initiatives identified under the Mission include; (i) setting up of Atal Tinkering Laboratories (ATLs) in schools for fostering curiosity, creativity and imaginations in young minds, and inculcate skills such as design mindset, computational thinking, adaptive learning, physical computing etc. The Mission will provide one time grant-in-aid of ₹ 10 lakh towards establishment of ATLs in the first year and another grant of ₹ 10 lakh over a period of five years. During 2016-17, the Mission has selected 257 schools covering 31 states/UTs for this, (ii) setting up Atal Incubation Centres (AICs) for creating high class incubation facilities across India with suitable physical infrastructure in terms of capital equipment and operating facilities, coupled with the availability of sectoral experts for mentoring the start-ups, (iii) providing scale up support to Established Incubation Centres (EICs) in different parts of the country for upgrading their capacity. In addition the Mission will also launch Atal Grand Challenge (AGC) awards for developing novel disruptive technologies/ solutions for stubborn socio-economic problems of the country that are ultra-low cost, low maintenance, durable and customised to the local conditions of the country.

Pradhan Mantri Krishi Sinchai Yojana

Pradhan Mantri Krishi Sinchai Yojana (PMKSY) conceived in 2015 is an umbrella scheme for coverage of more and more area under assured irrigation as early as possible. Its major components are (i) Accelerated Irrigation Benefits Programme (AIBP) for major and medium irrigation including National; projects; (ii) *Har Khet Ko Pani* which includes command area development and water management (CAD&WM) works., surface minor irrigation, irrigation through groundwater and repair, renovation and restoration (RRR) of water bodies; (iii) per drop more crop for promotion of micro irrigation ; and (iv) watershed development for rain water harvesting, effective management of the run-off water, prevention of soil erosion, regeneration of natural vegetation and recharging of the ground water table.

Under AIBP component of PMKSY, 99 projects were prioritized for implementation which will provide additional irrigation coverage over 76 lakh hectare. Out of the 99 prioritized projects, 23 are targeted for completion during 2016-17, 31 projects during 2017-18 and the remaining 45 by December, 2019. All the 99 projects being taken up under AIBP would include CAD&WM works in order to ensure that the irrigation potential created gets utilized without any time lag. Under *Har Khet Ko Pani* (CAD&WM) component priority is for implementation of projects to fully utilize the irrigation potential, which has been created by implementing major, medium and minor irrigation projects in the country.

Soil Health Card

An outlay of ₹ 568.54 crore to assess the soil fertility status in respect of 1,400 lakh land holdings at 2 year interval was initiated. The states will be provided funds for strengthening of the soil testing labs, analysis of soil samples and distribution of the Soil Health Card. This would be continuous and dynamic exercise to be carried out periodically.

Agri-Tech Infrastructure Fund

Promotion of National Agricultural Market through Agri-Tech Infrastructure Fund (ATIF) with an outlay of ₹ 200 crore for 2015-16 to 2017-18 was formulated. ATIF is aimed at implementation of agricultural marketing reforms by initiating appropriate e-market platforms in states with a view to move towards a national market. It would also increase the farmers' access to markets through warehouse based sales and thus obviate the need to transport the produce to the mandi.

Public Financial Management System

Public Financial Management System (PFMS), earlier known as Central Plan Schemes Monitoring System (CPSMS), is a Central Sector Scheme of NITI Aayog started in April, 2008. It aims at establishing a suitable online Management Information System (MIS) and Decision Support System (DSS) for fund management of the Schemes of the Government of India. The system is envisaged to track the fund disbursement from Government of India under Schemes and ultimately report utilization under these Schemes at different levels of implementation in States/UTs on a real time basis. PFMS through its interface with banking networks, facilitates end-to-end beneficiary management and electronic payment system to the bank accounts/Aadhar linked bank accounts of the beneficiaries and provides an online-real time MIS to various stakeholders.

In December 2013, a total plan outlay of ₹1,080 crore for roll out of PFMS over a period of 4 years (2013-14 to 2016-17) during the 12th Five Year Plan was approved. A four tier dedicated organizational structure has been approved comprising Project Implementation Committee, Central Project Monitoring Unit (CPMU), State Project Monitoring Units (SPMUs) in all the states and District Project Monitoring Units (DPMUs).

PFMS has been fully implemented at Central level in all 98 ministries/departments. Sanction generation, bill generation and transfer of funds of Plan Schemes are through PFMS only. Complete MIS of sanctions, releases and allocations from Centre to states/UTs, implementing agencies and other recipients is available on PFMS

The application is integrated with COMPACT and e-Lekha, the core accounting applications and e-payment gateway of CGA, thereby linking the financial and accounting data for comprehensive MIS and DSS. It has developed an interface with Core Banking Solution (CBS) of 103 banks, including India Post, thereby bank balances/float and transactions details of implementing agencies receiving grants from Government is available on a real-time basis.

For monitoring the funds devolved to Consolidated Fund of states (and UTs with legislature) and obtaining real time expenditure information for schemes for which funds are transferred from the Central ministries, an interface for sharing data with state treasuries and state AGs has also been developed in PFMS. Since 2015, it was transferred to Department of Expenditure.

Housing for All

Housing for All has been proclaimed as a priority by the Government of India. Housing for All has two components: Housing for All (Rural) known as Pradhan Mantri Awas Yojana (Gramin) implemented by Ministry of Rural Development and Housing for All (Urban) known as Pradhan Mantri Awas Yojana (Urban) implemented by Ministry of Housing and Poverty Alleviation. To achieve the goal of Housing for All 2022, nearly 3 crore houses are to be built in rural areas and about 2 crore houses in the urban areas in the next 7 years.

Swachh Bharat Mission

The Swachh Bharat Mission (SBM) a joint mission of the Ministry of Urban Development and the Ministry of Drinking Water and Sanitation, emanates from the vision of the Government. Swachh Bharat Mission (SBM) was launched on October 2, 2014, with a target to make the country clean by October 2, 2019.

Smart Cities Mission

Smart Cities Mission (CSM), a Centrally Sponsored Scheme was launched in June 2015 as part of Urban Rejuvenation Mission for the development of 100 smart cities. The objective of the Mission is to promote cities that provide core infrastructure and give a decent quality of life to its citizens, a clean and sustainable environment and application of 'Smart' Solutions. The core infrastructure elements in a Smart City include (i) adequate water supply, (ii) assured electricity supply (iii) sanitation, including solid waste management (iv) efficient urban mobility and public transport (v) affordable housing, especially for the poor (vi) robust IT connectivity and digitalization (vii) good governance, especially e-Governance and citizen participation (viii) sustainable environment (ix) safety and security of citizens, particularly women, children and the elderly, and (x) health and education. The SCM outlay is to be ₹ 48,000 crores (Central Share) over five years @ ₹ 100 per smart city per year. During 2015-16 ₹ 1,475.38 crore have been released by the Centre. Budget allocation in BE 2016-17 for the Mission is ₹ 3,205 crore.

Smart City selection is through a nation-wide 2 stage challenge process. In August 2015, Centre selected 98 potential smart cities in Stage 1 of the challenge. 20 Smart Cities were selected in Stage 2 January 2016 viz., Bhubaneswar, Pune, Jaipur, Surat, Kochi, Ahmedabad, Jabalpur, Visakhapatnam, Solapur, Davanagere, Indore, New Delhi Municipal Corporation, Coimbatore, Kakinada, Belagavi, Udaipur, Guwahati, Chennai, Ludhiana and Bhopal. In 2016-17, 40 more cities are to be selected. Accordingly, 13 fast track cities selected in May, 2016 namely, Lucknow, Warangal, Dharmashala, Chandigarh, Raipur, New Town Kolkata, Bhagalpur, Panaji, Port Blair, Imphal, Ranchi, Agartala and Faridabad. Another 27 more smart cities selected in September, 2016 viz., Amritsar, Kalyan-Dombivili, Ujjain, Tirupati, Nagpur, Mangaluru, Vellore, Thane, Gwalior, Agra, Nashik, Rourkela, Kanpur, Madurai, Tumakuru, Kota, Thanjavur, Namachi, Jalandhar, Shivamogga, Salem, Ajmer, Varanasi, Kohima, Hubbali-Dharwad, Aurangabad, Vadodara. So far, 60 smart cities have been selected.

Additional Central Assistance for Left Wing Extremism Affected Districts

The Government initiated the scheme Integrated Action Plan (IAP) for selected tribal backward districts in 2010 in 60 districts which was subsequently extended to 82 districts of nine states namely, Andhra Pradesh, Bihar, Chhattisgarh, Jharkhand, Madhya Pradesh, Maharashtra, Odisha, Uttar Pradesh and West Bengal. This scheme was in operation up to March, 2013. In 2013-14, it was decided to continue the financial assistance to 88 districts including 82 districts covered under IAP through the scheme "Additional Central Assistance (ACA) for Left Wing Extremism (LWE) Affected Districts" for the remaining years of the Twelfth Plan. Under the scheme, each district has been allocated ₹ 30 crore per year for 2013-14 and 2014-15.

Backward Regions Grant Fund

The State Component of Backward Regions Grant Fund (BRGF) comprising the Special Plan for KBK districts of Odisha, special Plan for Bihar and West Bengal was being implemented by the erstwhile Planning Commission to address the issues of regional imbalances in development processes. During 2015-16, ₹ 132.07 crore under Special Plan for KBK districts of Odisha, ₹ 1,887.53 crore under Special Plan for Bihar and ₹ 836.77 crore for West Bengal was released as One Time Assistance.

Rural Development

Nearly 70 per cent of India's population is rural, 25 per cent of which lives in poverty. NITI Aayog oversees the Government's mega schemes which seek to ensure that benefits of growth reach rural India, and empower its inhabitants to rise above the poverty line. The schemes –the Mahatma Gandhi National Rural Employment Guarantee Act (MGNREGA), the Indira Awaas Yojana (IAY) now renamed as Pradhan Mantri Awas Yojana (PMAY-G), the National Rural Livelihoods Mission (NRLM) now renamed as Deendayal Antyodaya Yojana (DAY) and the National Social Assistance Programme (NSAP) - are implemented by the Ministry of Rural Development (MoRD). The Aayog also monitors the progress of rural drinking water and sanitation schemes of the Ministry of Drinking Water and Sanitation (MDWS).

The Plan and non-Plan provisions of the various schemes during 2016-17 are MGNREGA ₹ 38,500 crore, PMAY-'G' ₹ 5,000 crores, DAY ₹ 3000 and NSAP ₹ 9500 crore.

MGNREGA is a demand driven programme and the allocation made for it may vary according to the demand for the year end. Under it, by October 31, 2016, on expenditure of 38,190.23 crore have been incurred.

Saansad Adarsh Gram Yojana

Saansad Adarsh Gram Yojana (SAGY), a new initiative in rural development, was launched in 2014 with the objective that these Adarsh Grams (Model Villages) serve as the "nucleus of health, cleanliness, greenery and cordiality" within the village community. The scheme's Guidelines call upon Members of Parliament (MPs) to make one village of their choice in their constituency a Model Village by 2016, and another two villages by 2019. Unlike other Schemes, the SAGY does not look at the beneficiaries as receivers and the Government as the doer. Taking development to the doorstep of villages, the scheme aims to empower the villagers to make choices and provide them with opportunities to exercise these choices.

The Adarsh Gram will have a population of three to five thousand in plain areas and 1,000 to 3,000 in hilly, tribal and difficult areas. The Member of Parliament would be free to identify any village for the scheme, other than his own or that of his/her spouse. The scheme would utilize in a convergent manner resources available from existing schemes like IAY, PMGSY, MGNREGS, RKVY, NRLM, National Health Mission (NHM), Sarva Shiksha Abhiyan (SSA), Backward Regions Grant Fund (BRGF), Member of Parliament Local Area Development Scheme (MPLADS), schemes of MLAs and CSR funds, and no additional funding will be required. There will be evaluation mid-term and post project by competent independent agencies.

RURBAN Mission

The Government launched the Dr. Shayma Prasad Mukherji RURBAN Mission in 2014 to deliver integrated project based infrastructure in the rural areas. The RURBAN Mission aims at providing basic amenities in rural areas and check migration from there to cities. The scheme envisages development of economic activities and skill development and helping rural areas get efficient civic infrastructure and associate services. The preferred mode of delivery would be through PPPs, while using various scheme funds. The Mission will be linked with e-governance and achieve targets in a time bound manner. Best practices of cooperatives, NGOs and other sectors can also be dovetailed into the scheme. The scheme has an allocation of ₹ 300 crore during 2015-16 and the same amount has been allocated for mission in 2016-17.

Road Map for Poverty Elimination

Subsequent to the decision taken in the first meeting of the Governing Council of NITI Aayog, a Task Force on Elimination of Poverty in India was constituted in 2015. The background paper addressed two different aspects of the debate around poverty – how to measure, and how to combat poverty. The paper notes that the measurement of poverty, conventionally done through a poverty line, is used in India only for tracking the incidence of poverty across time and space. The other potential uses of a poverty line – identifying who the poor are, and allocation of anti-poverty expenditure across states – are fulfilled through other means. The paper also examines the question of the level at which the poverty line should be set. It recommends further deliberation informed by the idea that the objective behind an official poverty line is to track progress in combating extreme poverty and not identification of the poor for purposes of distribution of government benefits. On combating poverty, the paper recommends a two-pronged strategy – facilitating rapid and sustained employment intensive economic growth, and making anti-poverty programmes more effective.

24 Rural and Urban Development

INDIA has been a welfare state since independence and the primary objective of all governmental endeavours has been the welfare of its people. The policies and programmes have been designed with the aim of alleviation of rural poverty which has been one of the primary objectives of planned development in India. It was realized that a sustainable strategy of poverty alleviation has to be based on increasing the productive employment opportunities in the process of growth itself. Elimination of poverty, ignorance, diseases and inequality of opportunities and providing a better and higher quality of life were the basic premise upon which all the plans and blue-prints of development were built.

Rural development implies both the economic betterment of people as well as greater social transformation. In order to provide the rural people with better prospects for economic development, increased participation of people in the rural development programmes, decentralization of planning, better enforcement of land reforms and greater access to credit are envisaged. Initially, main thrust for development was laid on agriculture, industry, communication, education, health and allied sectors but later on it was realized that accelerated development can be provided only if governmental efforts were adequately supplemented by direct and indirect involvement of people at the grassroot level.

Accordingly, in 1952, an organization known as Community Projects Administration was set up under the Planning Commission to administer the programmes relating to community development. The Community Development Programme, inaugurated on October 2, 1952, was an important landmark in the history of rural development. This programme underwent many changes and was handled by different ministries. In October, 1974, the Department of Rural Development came into existence as a part of Ministry of Food and Agriculture. In August 1979, this Department was elevated to the status of a new Ministry of Rural Reconstruction. That ministry was renamed as Ministry of Rural Development and again converted into a Department under the Ministry of Agriculture and Rural Development. It was later rechristened as Ministry of Agriculture in September, 1985. In 1991 the Department was upgraded as Ministry of Rural Development. Another Department viz. Department of Wasteland Development was created under this ministry in 1992. In March, 1995, the ministry was renamed as the Ministry of Rural Areas and Employment with three departments namely Department of Rural Employment and Poverty Alleviation, Rural Development and Wasteland Development programmes which are aimed at poverty alleviation, employment generation, infrastructure development and social security. Integrated development of rural areas is one of the abiding tasks before the government.

Major Programmes for Rural Development

The following major programmes are being operated by the Ministry of Rural Development:

Mahatma Gandhi National Rural Employment Guarantee Act

Mahatma Gandhi National Rural Employment Guarantee Act (MGNREGA) is a rights based wage employment programme implemented in rural areas of the country. This programme aims at enhancing livelihood security by providing upto one hundred days of guaranteed wage employment in a financial year to every rural household whose adult members volunteer to do unskilled manual work.

Objectives of the Scheme are: providing upto one hundred days of unskilled manual work as a guaranteed employment in a financial year to every household in rural areas as per demand, resulting in creation of productive assets of prescribed quality and durability; strengthening the livelihood resource base of the poor; proactively ensuring social inclusion; and strengthening Panchayati Raj Institutions.

Outcome During 2015

The outcome of programme implementation in 2015 are as follows: employment generated: in 2015-16, 3.63 crore households were provided employment and 134.96 crore person-days of employment were generated; increasing outreach to the poor and marginalized: self targeting in nature, the programme had high work participation from marginalized groups like SC/ST women; strengthening natural resource base: in 2015-16, 102.32 lakh works were undertaken (spill over + new works), of which 32 per cent for water conservation, 28.33 per cent for the provision of irrigation facility on land owned by SC/ST/BPL and IAY beneficiaries, 12.56 per cent for rural connectivity and 6.47 per cent for land development.

National Rural Livelihoods Mission

The government launched National Rural Livelihoods Mission (NRLM), subsequently renamed as *Aajeevika* in 2011. It aims at mobilizing all rural poor household into Self Help Groups (SHGs) in a phased manner. The Mission provides them long term support to attain appreciable increase in incomes over a period of time to improve their quality of life and come out of abject poverty. NRLM also aims at supporting all women SHGs of the poor, including those promoted by other state agencies and Non-Governmental Organizations (NGOs). With a view to make Self Help Group movement more effective, NRLM was strengthened in May, 2013. The key features of the restructured NRLM include: (1) mobilization of at least one woman member from each rural poor household in the country into SHG network in a phased manner; (2) special focus on the mobilization of women from the Scheduled Castes (SCs) and the

Scheduled Tribes (STs), the Particularly Vulnerable Tribal Groups (PVTGs), the disabled and other vulnerable and marginalized household; (3) promotion of SHG federations at village and cluster levels—Village Level Self Help Group Federations (VLF) at village level and Cluster Federation (CF) at cluster (groups of villages) level; (4) provision of Revolving Fund (RF) support at the rate of ₹ 10,000-15,000 per eligible SHG to supplement own funds; (5) provision of Vulnerability Reduction Fund (VRF) as per norms to eligible VLF to meet community level food security, health and nutrition security and such other priority needs of the poor households; (6) intensive support to link each SHG to bank credit such that each SHG member would be able to leverage a cumulative bank credit of ₹ 1.00 lakh over a period of 5 to 8 years; (7) all women SHGs in selected 150 districts, which include all IAP districts, will be eligible to avail credit at 7 per cent interest upto the maximum credit outstanding of ₹ 3 lakh. Women SHGs who will repay in time will get an additional subvention of 3 per cent reducing the effective rate of interest to 4 per cent. It is proposed to extend this facility to additional 100 districts; (8) 25 per cent of NRLM allocation is earmarked for skill development and placement support component which seeks to build the skills of the rural youth and place them in relatively high wage employment sectors of the economy; and (9) so far 29 states (all states except Goa) union territory (Puducherry) have transited to NRLM. The implementation has started in 460 districts, 3,186 blocks of the country and so far 27,63,188 Self Help Groups have been promoted.

Statement each indicating the physical and financial progress under NRLM during the FY 2015-16 (including NRLP) and FY 2016-17 (upto June).

Rural Self Employment Training Institute

The government has decided to set up one Rural Self Employment Training Institute (RSETI) in each district of the country. RSETIs are bank lead initiative with the active support of state government. The Government of India provides one time infrastructure support of rupees one crore besides reimbursing the cost of training rural poor candidates, the state government provides land free of cost or at nominal charges and the banks are responsible for day to day functioning of the RSETI. The core strength of the RSETI lies in its short term training and long term handholding to the rural entrepreneurs for setting up micro enterprises. Currently 583 RSETIs are functioning in the country.

Mahila Kisan Sashaktikaran Pariyojana

Mahila Kisan Sashaktikaran Pariyojana (MKSP) is a sub-component of NRLM to meet the specific needs of women farmers and achieve their socio-economic and technical empowerment predominantly small and marginal. Under the programme, 34 lakh mahila kisans are being provided support in 16 states at a total outlay of ₹ 110 crore.

During 2015-16, a new scheme named Start-up Village Entrepreneurshiip Programme (SVEP) was included in NRLM. The SVEP is to provide the supported enterprises with business skills, exposure, loan for starting and business support during the first critical six months of the enterprises by using the NRLM SHGs and their federations.

Pradhan Mantri Gram Sadak Yojana

The government, in a bid to give better rural connectivity launched the Pradhan Mantri Gram Sadak Yojana (PMGSY) in December, 2000 as a centrally sponsored scheme to assist the states, though rural roads are in the state list as per the Constitution. The primary objective of the Yojana is to provide connectivity by way of an all-weather road (with necessary culverts and cross-drainage structures, which is operable throughout the year), to the reliable unconnected habitations as per core network with a population of 500 persons (as per 2001 census) and above in plan areas. In respect of 'Special Category States' (North-East, Sikkim, Himachal Pradesh, Jammu and Kashmir and Uttarakhand), the desert areas, the tribal (Schedule V) areas and 88 selected tribal and backward districts as indentified by the Ministry of Home Affairs/ Planning Commission, the objective is to connect eligible unconnected habitations as per core-network with a population of 250 persons and above (Census 2001). The programme envisages single all weather connectivity.

With a view to ensure full farm-to-market connectivity, the programme also provides for the upgradation of the existing "Through Routes" and major rural links to prescribed standards, though it is not central to the programme. Under PMGSY-II, the projects for upgradation of 11,234 km roads have been sanctioned against total target of 50,000 km of such roads.

Availability of funds since inception

Under PMGSY, the position of release of funds under the programme to the states is as given below in Table.

(₹ In crore)

S. No	Year(s)	Release for Programme	Release for Admin. Fund	Release under ADB assistance	Release Under WB assistance	Total Release
1	2000-01	2,435	0	-	-	2,435
2.	2001-02	2,493	7	-	-	2,500
3	2002-03	2,497	3	-	-	2,500
4	2003-04	2,299	26	-	-	2,325
5	2004-05	2,111	37	93	220	2,461
6	2005-06	3,770	40	193	218	4,221
7	2006-07	4,415	100	1,000	750	6,265
8	2007-08	3,834+ 4,500*	66	1,950	650	11,000
9	2008-09	5,380+ 7,500*	151	2,000	250	15,281

10	2009-10	10,390+ 6,500*	140	800	10	17,840
11	2010-11	21,325	185	800	90	22,400
12	2011-12	10,598	83	1,075	627	12,383
13	2012-13	3,272	125	425	575	4,397
14	2013-14	4,553	164	-	643	5,360
15	2014-15	6,475	95	1,182	2,208	9,960
16	2015-16	11,158**	341**	1,550**	2,126**	15,175**
	Total	1,15,505	1,563	11,068	8,367	1,36,503

** From NABARD as loan* *** Central allocation*

Indira Awaas Yojana

Rural Housing

Housing is universally recognized as a basic human need. Reducing rural housing shortage and improving the quality of housing especially for the poor is an important component of the poverty alleviation strategy of the government. The rural housing scheme Indira Awaas Yojana (IAY) implemented by Ministry of Rural Development, aimed at providing houses to families below the poverty line (BPL) in rural areas has since inception provided assistance for construction of 360 lakh houses, incurring a total expenditure of ₹ 1,06,789.93 crore by March, 2016.

In the context of Government's priority for "Housing for All" by 2022, the rural housing scheme IAY has been restructured to Pradhan Mantri Awaas Yojana-Gramin (PMAY-G), which came into effect from 2016-17. The main features of the scheme of PMAY-G include: a) providing assistance for construction of 1.00 crore houses in rural areas over the period of 3 years from 2016-17 to 2018-19; b) enhancement of unit assistance from ₹ 70,000 to ₹ 1.20 lakh in plain and from ₹ 75,000 to 1.30 lakh in hilly states, difficult areas and IAP districts; c) identification of beneficiaries based on the Socio-Economic and Caste Census (SECC 2011) data covering households that are houseless or living in houses with kutcha walls and kutcha roof with two rooms or less after excluding households falling under the automatic exclusion category; and d) in addition, the beneficiary will get ₹ 12,000/- as assistance for construction of toilet under Swachh Bharat Mission or any other dedicated source of funding including Swachh Bharat Kosh and Mahatma Gandhi National Rural Employment Guarantee Scheme (MGNREGS) and support of 90 person days in plain areas and 95 person days in hilly states, difficult areas and IAP districts under MGNREGS through convergence.

National Social Assistance Programme

The Directive Principles of State Policy in the Constitution of India enjoin upon the state to undertake within its means a number of welfare measures. In particular, Article 41 of the Constitution of India directs the State to provide public assistance to its citizens in case of unemployment, old age, sickness and disablement and in other cases of undeserved want within the limit of its economic capacity and development. It is in accordance with these noble principles that the Government of India in 1995 introduced the National Social Assistance Programme (NSAP).

NSAP is a social assistance programme for poor BPL households for the aged, widows, disable and also include provision for one time assistance in the case of death of the primary bread winner in a BPL family. Scheme under NSAP were under State Plan from 2002-03 to 2013-14. Allocation of funds for implementation of the scheme of NSAP was under the budget heads of Ministry of Finance and Ministry of Home Affairs till 2013-14. Funds were released in a combined manner for all the schemes under NSAP to the states and UTs by Ministry of Finance and Ministry of Home Affairs respectively from their budget heads. There is no provision of a state share. This is done to ensure that all the beneficiaries are provided with a uniform minimum assistance. States may contribute from their own resources to enhance the assistance. At present, NSAP comprises Indira Gandhi National Old Age Pension Scheme (IGNOAPS), Indira Gandhi National Widow Pension Scheme (IGNWPS), Indira Gandhi National Disability Pension Scheme (IGNDPS), National Family Benefit Scheme (NFBS) and Annapurna. The details of the eligibility and assistance provided is as follows:-

Indira Gandhi National Old age Pension Scheme (IGNOAPS): Pension / assistance of ₹ 200/- per month is provided to BPL person on fulfilling the eligibility criteria in the age group of 60-79 years and ₹ 500/- per month to those who are of the age of 80 years or above. Upto December 2015, 152 lakh beneficiaries have been covered under the scheme.

Indira Gandhi National Widow Pension Scheme (IGNWPS): This was introduced in 2009. Under this scheme, pension/assistance of ₹ 300/- per month is provided to widows belonging to BPL households in the age group of 40-79 years. After attaining the age of 80 years, the beneficiary is shifted to IGNOAPS for getting pension/assistance of ₹ 500/- per month. As per the latest report (upto December, 2015), 39 lakh beneficiaries have been covered under the scheme.

Indira Gandhi National Disability Pension Scheme (IGNDPS): Scheme was introduced in 2009. Under this scheme, assistance of ₹ 300/- per month is provided to persons with severe or multiple disabilities belonging to BPL households in the age group of 18-79 years. After attaining the age of 80 years, the beneficiary is shifted to IGNOAPS for getting pension/assistance of ₹ 500/- per month upto December, 2015, 5.53 lakh beneficiaries have been covered under the scheme.

National Family Benefit Scheme (NFBS): Under the scheme one time assistance of ₹ 20,000/- is provided to the bereaved BPL family in the case of death of primary breadwinner in the age group 18-59 years. Upto December 2015, 40 lakh beneficiaries have been benefited under the scheme

Annapurna: Under the scheme, 10 kgs. of foodgrains per month is provided free of cost to the beneficiaries who are though eligible but remain uncovered under the erstwhile National Old Age Pension Scheme.

Implementation

From 2002-03 to 2013-14, schemes under NSAP were under State Plan. Funds for these schemes were allocated by Planning Commission and funds were released as Additional Central Assistance (ACA) by the Ministry of Finance to states and by Ministry of Home Affairs to UTs in a combined manner for all the schemes together under NSAP. The recommendations were made by Ministry of Rural Development based on laid down principles. From the year 2014-15, NSAP has been converted into a Centrally Sponsored Scheme (CSS) and funds are released by the Ministry of Rural Development to states/UTs scheme-wise. NSAP is being implemented mainly by Social Welfare Department in the states. Since the scheme is meant for both the rural as well as urban BPL persons, the active involvement of Gram Panchayats and municipalities is recommended. States have also been instructed to conduct social audit, at least once a year, to verify and update their list of beneficiaries. The Gram Sabhas in rural area and Ward Committees in municipalities should be designated for this purpose. State/UTs have also been advised to utilize upto 3 per cent of funds released for administrative expenses.

Deen Dayal Upadhyaya - Grameen Kaushalya Yojana

The Deen Dayal Upadhyaya Grameen Kaushalya Yojana (DDU-GKY) is the flagship placement linked skill training programme under the Ministry. Announced in 2014, DDU-GKY is a critical component of the National Skill Development Policy, and has an ambitious agenda, to benchmark wage placement-linked skill programmes to global standards and requirements. The ultimate aim is to convert India's demographic surplus into a demographic dividend by developing rural India into a globally preferred source of skilled labour. As a result, the scheme will also benefit more than 55 million poor rural youth who are ready-to-be-skilled, by providing sustainable employment. In this way the scheme is expected to play a crucial role in generational poverty alleviation.

DDU-GKY is a pioneer in standards-led delivery of skilling in India, the first to notify standard operating procedures for training, and the first to introduce IT solutions for skilling, including mandatory tablets for trainees, Aadhar-linked biometric information on attendance, and geo-tagged time-stamped record of training centres and classes. DDU-GKY has its roots in the Swarnjayanti Gram Swarozgar Yojana (SGSY). SGSY was formed by the restructuring of the Integrated Rural Development Programme (IRDP) in 1999, with a 15 per cent allocation for special projects. In 2010, SGSY was restructured as the National Rural Livelihoods Mission (NRLM), also known as *Aajeevika*. The Ministry revised the guidelines for the programme in September 2013, as

Aajeevika Skills with a view to increase its reach. On Antyodaya Diwas, 25 September, Aajeevika Skills was announced as DDU-GKY with a focus on providing opportunities through skilling for rural poor youth in domestic and global jobs.

Its aims to ensure rural poor youth are skilled in market relevant trades and job-relevant competencies; b. to ensure regular and sustainable employment to its beneficiaries, and consistent career progression through upskilling; and c. to ensure independent assessment and globally acceptable certification of its beneficiaries.

Key Features

DDU-GKY follows a 3 tier implementation architecture in PPP mode, with the national unit responsible for policy, central investments and technical support, SRLMs/State Skills Missions are responsible for state investments, implementation and monitoring controls, and Project Implementing Agencies (PIAs), both public and private training partners with a legacy in skill training, responsible for mobilization, training and placements.

i. The focus of this programmes is on the rural youth from poor families, in the age group of 15 to 35 years, belonging to: (a) MGNREGA worker household in which household members have together completed 15 days of work; (b) RSBY household; (c) Antyodaya Anna Yojana card household; (d) BPL PDS card households; (e) NRLM-SHG household; and (f) Household covered under auto inclusion parameters of SECC 2011.

ii. Full social inclusion of candidates is ensured by the mandatory coverage of socially disadvantaged groups–50 per cent allocation to SC/ST groups, 15 per cent to minorities and 33 per cent for women and 3 per cent for persons with disabilities.

iii. Regional inclusion of candidates is enabled through, a special sub-scheme for the youth of Jammu & Kashmir, called *Himayat*; a special initiative for the rural youth of poor families in 27 most-affected Left-Wing Extremist (LWE) districts across nine states, called *Roshni* and 10 per cent of DDU-GKY's capital investment is reserved for projects from North-East region.

iv. Focus on quality is done through its framework of guidelines and Standard Operating Procedures (SOPs), curricula from NCVT or QP-NOS developed by SSCs of NSDC, rating/grading systems for projects and states implementing the projects.

v. Placement in wage employment is mandated for a minimum of 70 per cent of all successful candidates, with a minimum salary of ₹ 6,000 per month or the minimum wages, whichever is higher.

vi. Post-placement support is given to candidates to enable assimilation into workforce and society.

vii. Support for job retention, career progression and foreign placements are also given to PIAs.

viii. In allocation of skills projects, primacy is given to training partners who can train and support overseas placement and captive placements.

ix. The programme promotes *Make in India*, through pro-active partnership with industry through multi-pronged engagement - champion employer policy, captive employer policy and industrial internship policy.

x. Transparency and accountability through: a. geo-tagged time stamped biometric attendance based on unique ID for trainers and trainees; b. online check of inventory available for training in every training centre; c. CCTV and audio recording of all classroom and lab sessions; d. mapping of project implementing agencies on the public financial management system for tracking payments; e. reporting of performance on real time basis; f. concurrent monitoring process for reliability and validity of the monitoring process; g. independent mechanism for project appraisal and project monitoring apart from state level monitoring through designated technical support agencies i.e., the National Institute of Rural Development and the NABCONS.

During 2015, 12 projects have been sanctioned. Against the target of 1,77,986 candidates a total 1,90,330 lakh candidates were trained and 66,254 candidates placed till December 2015.

Saansad Adarsh Gram Yojana

Saansad Adarsh Gram Yojana (SAGY) and guidelines of the Scheme was launched in 2014, the birth anniversary of Loknayak Jayaprakash Narayan.

Mahatma Gandhi's concept of rural development revolves around creating model villages for transforming 'swaraj' into 'su-raj'. The goal of Saansad Adarsh Gram Yojana (SAGY) is to translate this comprehensive and organic vision of Mahatma Gandhi into reality, keeping in view the present context. Far beyond mere infrastructure development, SAGY aims at instilling certain values in the villages and their people so that they get transformed into models for other. These values include: adopting people's participating as an end in itself - ensuring the involvement of all sections of society in all aspects related to the life of village, especially in decision-making related to governance.

Salient Features of the Scheme: (i) aims to develop three Adarsh Grams chosen by MPs, by March 2019, of which one would be achieved by 2016. Thereafter, five such Adarsh Grams (one per year) will be selected and developed by 2024; (ii) focus on 'Jan Bhagidar' (community participation); (iii) members of parliament will guide and lead the initiative; (iv) not an infrastructure centered scheme; and (v) holistic development of the village. The programme is primarily about unleashing people's power, converging and implementing existing government schemes/programmes and adopting bottom-up approach in planning and execution. While the Members of Parliament will guide and lead the initiative leverage the leadership, capacity, commitment energy of the individual MPs develop model Gram Panchayats.

Under the Yojana a Village Development Plan would be prepared for every identified Gram Panchayat with special focus on enabling every poor household to come out of poverty, and villages which have achieved success as model villages, would be understood. Besides there would be convergence of the resources of various Centrally Sponsored and Central Sector Schemes.

Under the Scheme, 661 Gram Panchayats were identified by Members of Parliament till February 2015; each state has identified a State Nodal Officer (SNO) to coordinate all the activities of the programme at the state level; video conference was held twice with all district collectors/district magistrates and the state nodal officers explaining to them the Scheme and urging them to focus on the need to extend support to the Members of Parliament for identification of Adarsh GPs and subsequent implementation of Scheme.

A comprehensive capacity building plan has been formulated for all relevant stakeholders. Every state/UT has created a State Team of Trainers (STOT), who shall in-turn assist in the orientation of the MPs and the collectors of their states; 29 states/UTs have conducted the state orientation programme for Members of Parliament and district collectors; 10,000 copies of guidelines were printed and distributed. The SAGY guidelines were translated into seven regional languages (Gujarati, Kannada, Marathi, Punjabi, Tamil, Telugu and Urdu) and made available on the website http://www.saanjhi. gov.in under 'Guidelines' Section.

The outputs under each activity would be measured every quarter vis-a-vis the physical and financial targets set out in the Village Development Plans. Further, the core monitorable indicators of the 12th Five Year Plan would be utilised as appropriate. The outcomes will also be tracked from time to time to the extent possible. A mid-term evaluation of performance would be conducted through a competent independent agency. Also a post-project assessment of performance and outcomes would be similarly undertaken. 697 Gram Panchayats were adopted till 2015.

Watershed Programme

The Integrated Watershed Management Programme (IWMP) was one of the flagship programmes.

The Natural Land Reforms Modernization Programme

The Scheme of National Land Reforms Modernization Programme (NLRMP) has been renamed as Digital India Land Records Modernization Programme (DILRMP). Under DILRMP, 27 states/UTs have computerized the registration of Records (RoR) of land in their respective areas, 19 states/UTs have stopped manual issue of RoRs and 22 states/UTs have uploaded in their websites. Besides, 25 states/UTs have done computerization of Registration and 11 states/UTs have done integration of Land Records with Registration

As regards the training during this period, the NIRD & PR organized 864 training programmes with participation of 22, 032 trainees, including 400

NIRD&PR networking programmes in collaboration with 28 States Institutes of Rural Development in the country.

Ministry of Panchayati Raj

The Ministry of Panchayati Raj (MoPR) was created in 2004. It has the primary objective to ensure the compliance of the provisions of Part IX of the Constitution, provisions regarding the district Planning Committees as per Article 243 ZD and PESA.

Panchayats are local governments mandated in the Constitution of India. As per the Constitution, three tiers of Panchayats are to be constituted, through elections every five years, except in states with population less than 20 lakh, where Panchayats at two tiers may be created. The Constitution recognizes the Gram Sabha, i.e., all the electors in a Village Panchayat. The Constitution provides that seats and offices of chairpersons be reserved for the Scheduled Castes (SC) and Scheduled Tribes (ST) in proportion to their respective population, and not less than one third seats and offices of chairpersons be reserved for women, including within SC and ST reservations. Article 243 ZD of the Constitution mandates the setting up of District Planning Committees (DPCs) in every district, to consolidate the plans prepared by the Panchayats and Municipalities in the district and to prepare the draft development plan for the entire district.

The Constitution provides that State Election Commissions (SECs) be set up and vested with the superintendence, direction and control of the preparation of electoral rolls and the conduct of elections to the Panchayats. The Constitution further provides that State Finance Commissions (SFCs) be constituted every five years. SFCs are to make recommendations to the Governor regarding the distribution between the State and Panchayats of the net proceeds of taxes, duties, toll, fees, etc., the determination of taxes, duties, tolls and fees which may be assigned to, or appropriated by, the Panchayats, and grants-in-aid to the Panchayats from the Consolidated Fund of the State, as well as measures needed to improve the financial position of Panchayats.

Within this broad framework, as local government is a state subject, state legislatures have a critical role in determining various aspects of Panchayati Raj in their states. Panchayats are to function as institutions of local government and prepare plans and implement schemes for economic development and socials justice, but the precise devolution of powers and authority to Panchayats is left to the states. The state legislatures are to decide on the nature of devolution to the Panchayats, including the 29 matters illustratively set out in the Eleventh Schedule. Powers to impose taxes by the provision of funds to the Panchayats are determined by state. The powers of Gram Sabhas are also decided by states. Moreover, states play a critical role in building Panchayat capacities and in creating an appropriate framework for accountability and transparency.

Basic Details of Panchayats

The mandate of the Ministry is to oversee the implementation of Part IX of the Constitution (which is regarding Panchayats), the provisions regarding

District Planning Committee as per Article 243 ZD, and the provisions of the Panchayat Extension to Scheduled Areas Act (PESA) 1996. Today, there are more than 2.55 lakh Panchayats in the country, which include 2,48,263 Gram Panchayats, 6,618 Block Panchayats and 595 District Panchayats. There are more than 30 lakh Panchayat representatives which also include nearly 14.37 lakh Elected Women Representatives. 'Panchayat' is a State subject and MoPR promotes Panchayati Raj through its schemes, advocacy with states, and by creating and sharing knowledge about Panchayati Raj.

Rajiv Gandhi Panchayat Sashaktikaran Abhiyan

To improve the functioning of PRIs the MoPR has been implementing the Rajiv Gandhi Panchayat Sashaktikaran Abhiyaan (RGPSA) in the 12th Five Year Plan period. The RGPSA addresses the major constraints of inadequate devolution of powers, lack of manpower, inadequate infrastructure and limited capacity in the effective functioning of Panchayats by providing manpower, infrastructure, training and promotion of devolution of power to Panchayats and put in place structures of accountability. Substantial funds have been released to the states upto 2014-15 towards the above activities.

From 2015-16, the provision of funds to the states under the scheme was transferred to them. Funds to the tune of ₹ 191.00 crore were provided for RGPSA in 2015-16 for Central activities. These funds received under the Central Component were primarily meant for supporting states to meet their capacity building obligations under Fourteenth Finance Commission (FFC) Award particularly training support for Gram Panchayat Development Plan (GPDP). Support is provided for capacity building requirement for GPDP, training infrastructure and human resources (HR), HR for PESA and e-governance, and for programme management costs.

Rashtriya Gram Swaraj Abhiyan

The Constitutionally mandated Panchayati Raj system is in place across the country and there are nearly 2.55 lakh elected Panchayats and 30 lakh Elected Representatives (ERs).

The devolution of substantial resources to the Gram Panchayats - ₹ 2,00,292.20 crore for the period 2015-2020 under the Fourteenth Finance Commission award and the initiation of participatory local planning integrating Mahatma Gandhi National Rural Employment Guarantee Scheme (MGNREGS), have made available significant untied resources to strengthen Panchayati Raj especially at the grassroots levels. This opportunity needs to be supported by a massive capacity building effort. A new restructured scheme, namely, Rashtriya Gram Swaraj Abhiyan (RGSA) to help Panchayati Raj Institutions to develop governance capabilities to deliver on the Sustainable Development Goals (SDGs) was announced in 2016. RGSA will have the following sub-schemes:- a. capacity building; b. mission mode project on e-panchayat; c. ATM services in panchayat bhawans; and d. incentivization of panchayats.

Besides, the FFC award has created an opportunity for convergent plans at the local level and leadership by Panchayats in providing basic amenities and services to the people. The thrust of the new scheme will be on the lines of the *Gramoday se Bharat Uday* programme which focus on social empowerment, economic empowerment and enabled Gram Sabhas through convergence of resources at the Panchayat level. MoPR has supported states to develop state specific guidelines for Gram Panchayat Development Plans (GPDP) which converge all the resources over which the Panchayats have command including FFC funds, MGNREGS funds, Swachh Bharat funds, etc. Awareness building for Gram Panchayat Development Plans through a participatory process has resulted in 1.45 lakh Gram Panchayats preparing for this scheme. The challenge for capacity building has increased substantially, since all ERs and functionaries at GP level and all supporting structures at cluster, block and district levels need to be oriented on their roles in participatory planning. Therefore, under RGSA comprehensive efforts will be made to support and enhance the capacity building and training facilities for all stakeholders with particular thrust on the aspects of GPDP.

Initiatives undertaken by the Ministry for capacity building include: support for training of all stakeholders of local governance; support for building training capability – infrastructure and human resources for training; support for providing computers and e-governance tools for information capture and governance; support for strengthening governance in PESA villages; supporting material and guidelines have been prepared and disseminated to the states and training institutions: toolkit on GPDP, advisory on environment generation, central guidelines on GPDP, manual for grassroots planning, advisory on SHG – GP convergence, framework for participatory planning for GPDP, collaboration with National Institute of Rural Development & Panchayati Raj (NIRD&PR) as mentor institution for capacity building, reading materials for Gram Panchayats developed under "Strengthening Capacities of Panchayati Raj Institutions" (SCPRI) project supported by United Nations Development Programme.

e–Panchayat Initiatives

The Ministry is also working with the state governments towards automating internal workflow processes of nearly 2.5 lakh Panchayats across the country benefitting approximately 30 lakh elected members and about 10 lakh PRI functionaries and improve local governance and make democracy work effectively at grassroots level. In this regard, e-Panchayat is one of the Mission Mode Projects (MMPs) under the Digital India programme of Govt. of India. The project seeks to completely transform the functioning of Panchayati Raj Institutions, making them more transparent, accountable and effective as organs of decentralized self-governing institutions. This will make democracy truly decentralized. The states are also being provided financial support for manpower, computers and capacity building for the implementation of e-Panchayat through the Ministry's umbrella RGPSA scheme (Under restructuring to Rashtriya Gram Swaraj Abhiyan (RGSA). Under e-Panchayat MMP, a suite of Core Common Applications has been developed to address various aspects of Panchayats' functioning including planning, budgeting, implementation, accounting, monitoring, social audit and delivery of citizen services like issue of certificates, licenses, etc.

Recommendations of Fourteenth Finance Commission

Under the Fourteenth Finance Commission (FFC) award for the period 2015-20 grants to the tune of ₹ 2,00,292.20 crore are being devolved to Gram Panchayats in the country constituted under Part IX of the Constitution constituting an assistance of ₹ 488 per capita per annum at an aggregate level for 26 states to ensure stable flow of resources at regular intervals which will augment resources available with them to discharge their statutorily assigned functions. The FFC has not recommended grants to Non-Part IX areas under Schedule VI in Meghalaya, Mizoram, Tripura and Assam, the areas in the hill districts of Manipur, rural areas of Nagaland and Mizoram.

The grants are allocated and released to various states by Ministry of Finance (Department of Expenditure) in accordance with the guidelines issued by that Ministry. The guidelines are also available on that Ministry's website http://www.finmin.nic.in/FFC/guidelines.asp. The states are to distribute the grants to Gram Panchayats as per the approved formula recommended in the latest State Finance Commission (SFC) report. However, in the absence of SFC formula, grant should be distributed using population of 2011 Census with a weight of 90 per cent and area with a weight of 10 per cent. To facilitate better monitoring of the release and utilization of grants including FFC grants an online system (MIS) has been developed. PRIASoft (web based Panchayat accounting software) and Plan Plus (web based participatory planning software) are the two important Applications under e-Panchayat Mission Mode Project (MMP) that foster transparency and accountability in Panchayati Raj Institutions (PRIs) have been developed by the Ministry for adoption by the states.

Ministry of Drinking Water and Sanitation

The Department of Drinking Water Supply (DDWS) was created in the Ministry of Rural Development in 1999, which was subsequently renamed as the Department of Drinking Water and Sanitation in 2010. Keeping in view the significance of rural water supply and sanitation, the Government of India created and notified the Ministry of Drinking Water and Sanitation as a separate Ministry in 2011. The Ministry of Drinking Water and Sanitation is the nodal Ministry for the overall policy, planning, funding and coordination of the flagship programmes of the Government of India viz., the National Rural Drinking Water Programme (NRDWP) for rural drinking water supply and the Swachh Bharat Mission (Gramin) [SBM(G)] for sanitation in the country.

National Rural Drinking Water Programme

The National Rural Drinking Water Programme (NRDWP) is a Centrally sponsored scheme aimed at providing adequate and safe drinking water to the rural population of the country. The NRDWP is a component of Bharat Nirman which focuses on the creation of the infrastructure. This has resulted in the provision of significant additional resources to the sector and for creating an environment for the development of infrastructure and capacities for the successful operation of drinking water supply schemes in rural areas

Swachh Bharat Abhiyan

Swachh Bharat Abhiyan was launched on the birth anniversary of the Father of the Nation on October 2, 2014.The concept of Swachh Bharat Abhiyan is to pave access for every person to sanitation facilities including toilets, solid and liquid waste disposal systems, village cleanliness and safe and adequate drinking water supply. The programme is implemented by the Ministry of Drinking Water and Sanitation.

An Action Plan has been drawn up for a Swachh Bharat to become a reality by 2019, the 150th birth anniversary of Mahatma Gandhi. The Abhiyan aims to triple the growth percentage of toilets from present 3 per cent to 10 per cent by 2019. From the present level of construction of 14,000 toilets per day this Action Plan proposes to increase the construction to 48,000 toilets daily. The Action Plan calls for an Open Defecation Free (ODF) India in five years. To begin with, as part of Swachh Bharat, priority is being given to build toilets for boys and girls in all schools of the country. This is envisaged to be completed in one year. To strengthen delivery mechanism in sanitation in rural areas some of the important measures have been proposed: (a) signing MoU with states, on water and sanitation for implementation of both water and sanitation, with interchangeability of funds between water and sanitation so that idle funds do not lie in states and targets are not starved of funds in either of the two sectors; (b) release to states with 'Just in Time' concept, to be adopted by Centre to avoid extra cost of funds to Government of India; (c) enable a system of small loans through agencies like NABARD, SIDBI (or banks through priority sector lending without collateral) to those households for the construction of toilets which are eligible for incentives or need funds to construct better toilets maybe with bathing space; (d) developing a Block Level cadre of sanitation coordinators who shall be the main support to Gram Panchayats (GP) in disseminating information and strengthening capacity in sanitation activities; (e) identifying a Swachchata Doot (messenger) for each GP in the country, equipping him with skills on sanitation and giving him performance linked incentives; and (f) intensive monitoring at the household level shall be taken up through the MIS of the Ministry, as already name of each household has been collected by Ministry of Drinking Water Supply through baseline data recently. Besides senior officers of Centre and state should directly talk to the Sarpanches on telephone to get feedback.

Swachh Bharat Mission (Gramin)

Intervention in the rural sanitation sector in the country was initially started in 1954 as a part of the First Five Year Plan. The Government introduced a structured scheme in the form of the Central Rural Sanitation Programme

(CRSP) in 1986 primarily with the objective of improving the quality of life of the rural people and also to provide privacy and dignity to women. From 1999, a "demand driven" approach under the "Total Sanitation Campaign" (TSC) emphasizing more on Information, Education and Communication (IEC), Human Resource Development (HRD), capacity development activities to increase awareness among the rural people and generation of demand for sanitary facilities was started. The "Nirmal Bharat Abhiyan" (NBA), the successor programme of the TSC, was launched from 2012, aimed at creating Nirmal villages, provided increased incentives through convergence with MNREGS. Though these programmes had their successes, there still remained a large portion of the rural population which did not have access to toilets.

To significantly upscale the programme, and bring the focus on the issue of sanitation, the Swachh Bharat Mission (Gramin) was launched in 2014. The focus of the new strategy is to move towards a Swachh Bharat by providing flexibility to state governments (sanitation being a state subject), to decide on their implementation policy and mechanisms, taking into account state specific requirements. Rural drinking water supply is a state subject and is also included in the Eleventh Schedule of the Constitution amongst the subjects that may be entrusted to Panchayats by the states. Thus the participation of the Panchayati Raj Institutions in the rural drinking water supply sector is an important area of focus.

Government of India's major intervention in water sector started in 1972-73 through the Accelerated Rural Water Supply Programme (ARWSP) for assisting states/UTs to accelerate the coverage of drinking water supply in 'problem villages'. A Technology Mission with stress on water quality, appropriate technology intervention, human resource development support and other related activities was introduced in 1986 which was subsequently renamed as the Rajiv Gandhi National Drinking Water Mission (RGNDWM) in 1991. In 1999-2000, Sector Reform Projects were started to involve the community in planning, implementation and management of drinking water schemes which was in 2002 scaled up as the Swajaldhara programme. The programme was revised in 2009 and named as National Rural Drinking Water Programme (NRDWP).

The National Rural Drinking Water Programme (NRDWP) is a Centrally sponsored scheme aimed at providing adequate and safe drinking water to the rural population of the country. It is a component of Bharat Nirman which focuses on the creation of rural infrastructure. This has resulted in the provision of significant additional resources to the sector and for creating an environment for the development of infrastructure and capacities for the successful operation of drinking water supply schemes in rural areas.

Bharat Nirman

Bharat Nirman was launched by the Government of India in 2005 as a programme to build rural infrastructure. While phase-I of the programme was implemented in 2005-06 to 2008-09, the phase-II from 2009-10 to 2011-12. Rural drinking water is one of the six components of Bharat Nirman.

Urban Development

The Ministry of Urban Development has the responsibility of broad policy formulation and monitoring of programmes in the area of urban development. Urban Development is a state subject but the Government of India plays a co-ordinating and monitoring role and also supports urban development through Centrally sponsored schemes. The Ministry addresses various issues of urban sector through policy guidelines, legislative guidance and sectoral programmes.

Urbanization in India has become an important and irreversible process, and an important determinant of national economic growth and poverty reduction. The process of urbanization is characterized by a dramatic increase in the number of large cities, although India may be said to be in the midst of transition from a predominantly rural to a quasi urban society. At current rate of growth, urban population in India will reach a staggering total of 575 million by 2030 A.D. According to Census 2011, as many as 52 cities in India had population of a million plus.

National Heritage City Development and Augmentation Yojana

The National Heritage City Development and Augmentation Yojana (HRIDAY) was launched in 2015 with an initial coverage of 12 cities. The scheme is aimed at preserving and revitalizing the soul and unique character of the heritage cities in the country. The Mission is being operated as a Central Sector Scheme and is initially being implemented in 12 identified cities namely, Ajmer, Amaravati, Amritsar, Badami, Dwarka, Gaya, Kanchipuram, Mathura, Puri, Varanasi, Velankanni and Warangal.

Jawaharlal Nehru National Urban Renewal Mission

Jawaharlal Nehru National Urban Renewal Mission (JNNURM) was launched in 2005. It is a reform driven, fast track programme to ensure planned development of cities/towns with focus on efficiency in urban infrastructure/ service delivery mechanisms, and through community participation and enhanced accountability of ULBs/parastatal agencies towards citizens. It has attempted to trigger investments in the urban infrastructure sector and undertake reforms to sustain these investments. Priority has been accorded in sanctioning of projects for water supply, sewerage and drainage sectors. Also, projects have been sanctioned for urban transport sector which include construction of roads, flyovers, bus rapid transport system (BRTS). To support and develop public transport system, procurement of buses is also funded under this programme.

The programme focuses on higher level of resources and management attention to 65 select cities across the country. Out of the 65 cities, 35 cities are with million plus population and other 30 cities are either state capitals or cities of heritage and tourism importance totalling 55 Mission cities under Urban Infrastructure and Governance (UIG). The other towns of states/UTs are eligible for funding under the Urban Infrastructure Development for Small and Medium Towns Scheme (UIDSSMT).

Urban Infrastructure and Governance

The extended phase of Urban Infrastructure and Governance (UIG) sub-component of JNNURM concluded in 2014. In the Initial phase of project implementation under UIG sub-component, 538 projects at a total cost of ₹ 60,200.78 crore was sanctioned with an ACA commitment of ₹ 27,655.13 crore, of which an amount of ₹ 21,119.24 crore has already been released to the 65 Mission cities. Under stimulus package, 15,485 buses have been sanctioned at a total cost of ₹ 4,748.97crore with an ACA amount of ₹ 2,101.05 crore, of which an amount of ₹ 1,546.72 crore has already been released. In addition, ACA amount of ₹ 469. 86 crore has been committed for various capacity building activities under JNNURM of which SF188.62 crore has been released till date. Out of the total 538 projects sanctioned earlier under UIG Sub Mission, 243 projects have been completed till December, 2014 and 295 projects are reported to be in various stages of implementation.

Urban Infrastructure Development Scheme for Small and Medium Towns

The extended phase of Urban Infrastructure Development Scheme for Small and Medium Towns (UIDSSMT) sub-component of JNNURM concluded in 2014. Under the first phase of UIDSSMT, 801 projects at a total cost of ₹13,866.27 crore have been sanctioned with an ACA commitment of ₹ 11,197.20 crore, of which ₹ 9,968. 05 crore have already been released to 668 small and medium towns. Of 801 projects taken up under UIDSSMT Sub Mission, 454 projects have been physically completed till December, 2014 and 347 projects are under various stages of implementation.

Scheme for Urban Infrastructure Development in Satellite Towns around Seven Mega Cities

Ministry of Urban Development is implementing a pilot scheme for urban infrastructure development in satellite towns around seven mega cities. The objectives of this scheme are: i) to develop urban infrastructure facilities such as drinking water, sewerage and solid waste management, etc. at satellite towns around the seven megacities and to channelize their future growth so as to reduce pressure on the mega cities; ii) to implement reforms such as e-Governance, property tax, double entry accounting, creation of barrier free environment, structural safety norms in compliance with the national building code, water and energy audit of water and wastewater utilities and implementation of service level benchmarks; iii) strengthening implementation of reforms such as levy of reasonable user charges, earmarking of budgets for basic services and at least 10-15 per cent of housing sites for the urban poor, formulation of bye-laws to incorporate provisions for disaster management, water harvesting and reuse and recycle of waste water and implementation of Public Private Partnership (PPP) projects.

Atal Mission for Rejuvenation and Urban Transformation

The Atal Mission for Rejuvenation and Urban Transformation (AMRUT) was launched in 2015. The objective of the Mission is to improve basic urban infrastructure in 500 cities/ towns which would be known as Mission cities/ towns. The Mission is being operated as a Centrally Sponsored Scheme (CSS). It aims to cover all cities and towns with a population of over one lakh with notified Municipalities, including Cantonment Boards (Civilian areas) and certain other cities like capital towns, some cities on stem of main rivers and tourist and hill destinations.

The purpose of AMRUT is to (i) ensure that every household has access to a tap with assured supply of water and a sewerage connection; (ii) increase the amenity value of cities by developing greenery and well maintained open spaces (e.g. parks); and (iii) reduce pollution by switching to public transport or constructing facilities for non-motorized transport (e.g., walking and cycling). AMRUT makes states equal partners in planning and implementation of projects, thus actualizing the spirit of cooperative federalism. As of now, 497 cities/ towns have been selected under this Mission.

An advance of ₹ 25.00 lakh per city or as per eligibility wherever it comes below ₹ 25.00 lakh, has been released to states/UTs for preparation of Service Level Improvement Plans (SLIP) by ULBs. On the basis of SLIP, states will prepare the State Annual Action Plan (SAAP). As an advance of ₹ 123.38 crore has been released to states/UTs for preparation of SLIP under A&OE of this Mission.

Smart Cities Mission

This Mission was launched in 2015. Smart Cities Mission is based on the idea of developing the entire urban eco-system on the principles of complete and integrated planning. The focus is on sustainable and inclusive development and the idea is to look at compact areas, create a replicable model which will act like a light house to other aspiring cities. The Smart Cities Mission is meant to set examples that can be replicated both within and outside the Smart City, catalysing the creation of similar cities in various regions and parts of the country. The Mission is operated as a Centrally Sponsored Scheme (CSS). Subsequent to finalization of names of 98 potential Smart Cities and evaluation of their smart city proposals by a panel of national and international experts the government has announced the list of first 20 urban areas that will be developed as smart cities.

In the approach of the Smart Cities Mission, the objective is to promote cities that provide core infrastructure and give a decent quality of life to its citizens, a clean and sustainable environment and application of 'Smart' Solutions. The focus is on sustainable and inclusive development and the idea is to look at compact areas, create a replicable model which will act like a lighthouse to other aspiring cities. The core infrastructure elements in a smart city would include: (i) adequate water supply; (ii) assured electricity supply;

(iii) sanitation, including solid waste management; (iv) efficient urban mobility and public transport; (v) affordable housing, especially for the poor; (vi) robust IT connectivity and digitalization; (vii) good governance, especially e-Governance and citizen participation; (viii) sustainable environment; (ix) safety and security of citizens, particularly women, children and the elderly; and (x) health and education.

List of Cities Shortisted for Stage-2 of Smart Cities Mission

Sl. No.	Name of State/UT	No. of cities shortlisted	Name of Potential Cities shortlisted
1.	Andaman & Nicobar Islands	1	1 Port Blair
2	Andhra Pradesh	3	1. Vishakhapatnam 2. Tirupati 3. Kakinada
3.	Arunachal Pradesh	1	1. Pasighat
4.	Assam	1	1. Guwahati
5.	Bihar	3	1. Muzaffarpur 2. Bhagalpur 3. Biharsharif
6	Chandigarh	1	1. Chandigarh
7.	Chhatisgarh	2	1. Raipur 2. Bilaspur
8.	Daman & Diu	1	1. Diu
9.	Dadra & Nagar Haveli	1	1. Silvassa
10.	Delhi	1	1 New Delhi Muncipal Council
11.	Goa	1	1. Panaji
12.	Gujarat	6	1. Gandhinagar 2. Ahmedabad 3. Surat 4. Vadodara 5. Rajkot 6. Dahod
13.	Haryana	2	1. Karnal 2. Faridabad

14.	Himachal Pradesh	1	1. Dharamshala
15.	Jharkhand	1	1. Ranchi
16.	Karnataka	6	1. Mangaluru 2. Belagavi 3. Shivamogga 4. Hubli-Dharwad 5. Tumakuru 6. Davanegere
17.	Kerala	1	1. Kochi
18.	Lakshadweep	1	1. Kavaratti
19.	Madhya Pradesh	7	1. Bhopal 2. Indore 3. Jabalpur 4. Gwalior 5. Sagar 6. Satna 7. Ujjain
20.	Maharashtra	10	1. Navi Mumbai 2. Nashik 3. Thane 4. Greater Mumbai 5. Amravati 6. Solapur 7. Nagpur 8. Kalyan-Dombivali 9. Aurangabad 10. Pune
21.	Manipur	1	1. Imphal
22.	Meghalaya	1	1. Shillong
23.	Mizoram	1	1. Aizawl
24.	Nagaland	1	1. Kohima

25.	Odisha	2	1. Bhubaneshwar 2. Raurkela
26.	Puducherry	1	1. Oulgaret
27.	Punjab	3	1. Ludhiana 2. Jalandhar 3. Amritsar
28.	Rajasthan	4	1. Jaipur 2. Udaipur 3. Kota 4. Ajmer
29.	Sikkim	1	1. Namchi
30.	Tamil Nadu	12	1. Tiruchirapalli 2. Tirunelveli 3. Dindigul, 4. Thanjavur 5. Tiruppur 6. Salem 7. Vellore 8. Coimbatore 9. Madurai 10. Erode 11. Thoothukudi 12. Chennai
31.	Telangana	2	1. Greater Hyderabad 2. Greater Warangal
32.	Tripura	1	1. Agartala
33.	Uttar Pradesh	12	1. Moradabad 2. Aligarh 3. Saharanpur 4. Bareilly 5. Jhansi 6. Kanpur 7. Allahabad

			8. Lucknow
			9. Varanasi
			10. Ghaziabad
			11. Agra
			12. Rampur
34.	Uttarakhand	1	1. Dehradun
35.	West Bengal	4	1. New Town Kolkata
			2. Bidhannagar
			3. Durgapur
			4. Haldia
		Total	**98**

Urban Transport

Increasing urban population coupled with increased city size has led to a rapid growth in the urban travel demand. Rapid growth in the use of personal motor vehicle along with neglect of public transport, pedestrianisation and non-motorized modes has resulted in increased congestion, air pollution, higher incidence of accidents as well as an increasing consumption of petroleum products. Significant improvement in public transport, pedestrianisation and ion-motorized modes are a critical requirement for improving mobility in urban areas and hereby facilitating economic growth. Such improved mobility would also have a beneficial impact on the urban poor by improving their access to employment, education and health care. For urban planning it is necessary to give attention to an appropriate policy for integration of transportation and traffic plans with land use plans for every urban agglomeration.

A National Urban Transport Policy has been formulated by the Central Government. The focus of the policy is to "Move People Not Vehicles". This policy envisages integrated land use and transport planning, significant improvements in public transport, encouragement of non-motorised modes of travel, provision of adequate parking spaces as also a comprehensive set of measures for capacity building in urban transport planning.

i. Delhi Metro

Delhi Metro Phase-3 and extensions covers a length of 135.003 km at a cost of ₹ 41,078.79 crore. Extension of 4.373 km from Jahangirpuri to Samaypur Badli was operationalized and 13.875 km from Badarpur to YMCA Chowk, Faridabad was operationalized in 2015.

ii. Bengaluru Metro

Rail Project Bengaluru Metro Rail Corporation Ltd. (BMRCL) is a 50:50 joint venture company set up under Section 617 of the Companies Act, 1956 with equity participation of Central and Karnataka government in equal proportion. The 3.5 km stretch (Reach 3-B) between Peenya Industry and Nagasandra has become operational in 2015. Reach-2 from Magadi Road to Mysore Road, measuring 7 km has become operational later. Total 27 km of Phase-1 is operational as on date. Centre approved the Bengaluru Metro Rail Project Phase-2 in 2014 consisting of 61 stations and 72.095 km route length at a total cost of ₹ 26,405 crore.

iii. Mumbai Metro

Government of India has approved the Mumbai Metro Project in three corridors which are as under: a. Mumbai Metro Rail Line-1 (Versova-Andheri-Ghatkopar) covering a length of 11.40 km at a cost of ₹ 2,356 crore, b. Mumbai Metro Rail Line-2 (Charkop-Bandra-Mankhurd) covering a length of 31.871 km at a cost of ₹ 7,660 crore, and c. Mumbai Metro Rail Line-3 (Colaba-Bandra-SEEPZ) covering length of 32.5 km at a cost of ₹ 23,136 crore.

25 Scientific and Technological Developments

DEPARTMENT of Science and Technology, in its endeavour to strengthen national science and technology capacity and capability, kept its pace to implement several planned initiatives to enable Indian S&T community to increase scientific and technological outputs. Some of the important domains in which the Department devotes its attention are: strengthening the pool of scientists and technologists for carrying out globally competitive R&D in cutting edge areas of science; nurturing R&D institutions and building infrastructural facilities for enhancing global ranking of India in scientific research; support for the establishment of multi-stakeholder mechanisms for partnerships for promoting science; deploying technology through national missions; developing capacity of institutions and industry for technology commercialization for solving national challenges; providing S&T inputs to society for its socio-economic benefits; and policy formulation for S&T sector.

O.W.: http//www.dst.gov.in

Department of Science and Technology

Science, Technology and Innovation Policy

The new Science, Technology and Innovation (STI) Policy unveiled in 2013 includes a thrust for innovations in science and technology sector. STI policy reveals an aspiration to gain global competitiveness and link science sector to the developmental agenda of the country. Science, Research and Innovation System for High Technology led path for India (SRISHTI) is the main policy goal. Integration of science, research and innovation systems and emergence of India as one of the top five of six knowledge powers in science are expressed aspirations of the new STI policy. To translate this vision into action, the Department has already established a dedicated Policy Research Cell. Five Policy Research Centers in academic institutions have been established to develop and design new programmes and action plans for implementation in Science, Technology and Innovation sector in the country.

Science & Engineering Research

The research and development in frontier areas of science and engineering has received an overwhelming support with the establishment of the Science and Engineering Research Board (SERB). The multifaceted programmes of the Board have ensured its reach among various S&T stakeholders. Several new initiatives have been launched by the Board recently to reverse the brain drain at different stages of scientific careers such as Early Career Research Awards (ECRA) for young faculty for setting up laboratory facilities for quick launching of research by new faculty, around 300 candidates will be supported annually under ECRA. A National Postdoctoral Fellowship (N-PDF) scheme will allow the best of our 3000 scientists to stay in India to serve and strengthen our R&D institutions, industry and universities. To augment quality manpower in niche areas of research, Overseas Doctoral Fellowship has been launched in 2015-16. Under this programme, fellowship to Indian students graduating from Indian universities/ institutes to pursue PhD in select areas of science, technology, engineering and medicine in academic institutions of international repute abroad will be provided.

Attracting Young Talent to Science

Innovation in Science Pursuit for Inspired Research (INSPIRE) is an ongoing initiative for attraction of talent for science and research. More than 13 lakh students in the age group of 10-15 have been provided INSPIRE awards. About 3,40,000 INSPIRE awards have been given during the last two years to school students for their innovations. Science camps of five days duration are organised to provide opportunity to class XI students pursuing science to interact with the science icons from India and abroad including Nobel Laureates to experience the joy of innovations.

Opportunities for Women Scientists

Department of Science & Technology has launched several initiatives for women in science under its flagship scheme namely KIRAN (Knowledge Involvement in Research Advancement through Nurturing). Through this unique initiative, DST provides opportunity to women scientists who had break in their career, primarily due to family reasons, to pursue research in Physical & Mathematical Sciences, Chemical Sciences, Life Sciences, Earth & Atmospheric Sciences and Engineering Technology. More than 2,500 women scientists are beneficiaries of this scheme. During 2015-16, 139 new R&D projects were supported. The second component is focused on Science & Technology solutions at the grassroots level for social benefit. The third component provides one year internship in the domain of Intellectual Property Rights (IPRs) which includes theory as well as hands on training in different law firms.

International S&T Cooperation

International S&T Cooperation programme is being leveraged by the Department for enhancing S&T competitiveness of the country. Large number of joint R&D projects, multi-institutional Networked Research Projects and Applied R&D projects are under implementation through bilateral and multilateral S&T cooperation mechanisms indicative of trends in fostering international S&T cooperation and partnerships. Some recent initiatives are: New Africa and Neighbouring Country-centric programmes; Water and Cyber Security Agreements with Israel; Big Data, Artificial Intelligence and Internet of Things Agreements with Japan; Clean Energy programmes with USA and UK; Newton-Bhabha programme with UK in the areas of affordable healthcare, clean technologies and ICT; Joint R&D Centre on Robotics with South Korea; Grassroots Innovation with South Africa; and Young Scientist Forum and Innovation Circle with BRICS.

Nano Science and Technology

National Mission of Nano Science and Technology - an umbrella programme was launched in 2007 to promote R&D in this emerging area of research in a comprehensive fashion. The main objectives of the Nano Mission are - basic research promotion, research infrastructure development, nano application and technology development, human resource development, international collaboration and orchestrating national dialogues. India has secured third position amongst nations of the world in terms of scientific publications in this emerging area.

Climate Change

National Mission for Sustaining the Himalayan Ecosystem (NMSHE) and National Mission for Strategic Knowledge on Climate Change (NMSKCC) launched under National Action Plan for Climate Change (NAPCC) are under implementation by the Department. As part of deliverables of these national missions, six major research programmes have been initiated and supported. Himalayas Climate Change Portal (http://knowledgeportal-nmshe.in/) has been launched to make the knowledge on Himalayas readily available for the end users and community

New Initiatives Aligned with the National Agenda

National Supercomputing Mission was approved in March 2015. This is a visionary programme to enable India to leapfrog to the league of world class computing power nations. The Mission is under implementation jointly by the Department of Science and Technology (DST) and Department of Electronics and Information Technology (DeitY) at an estimated cost of ₹ 4,500 crore over a period of seven years.

DST has launched a new programme viz. **Science and Technology of Yoga and Meditation (SATYAM)** in 2015-16 to rejuvenate research in yoga and meditation. 15 R&D projects worth ₹ 6 crores have already been supported

Five **Technical Research Centres (TRCs)** in the existing autonomous institutions of the DST have been set-up to translate basic science to technology.

National Initiative for Developing and Harnessing Innovations (NIDHI) has been evolved as an umbrella scheme for a seamless innovation ecosystem booster. Major links of the innovation to market value chain would be supported and strengthened at various nodes (each node signifying a cluster of three neighbouring districts) across the country to attain the mission of nation building through innovation, entrepreneurship and incubation. Target is to scale up current 65 nodes to 125 nodes. The specific components of NIDHI are – Grand Challenge and Competitions for scouting innovations; Promotion and Acceleration of Young and Aspiring innovators & Startups (PRAYAS) - Support from Idea to Prototype; Entrepreneur in Residence (EIR) - Support system to reduce risk; Startup-NIDHI through Innovation and Entrepreneurship Development Centres (IEDCs) in academic institutions for encouraging students to promote start-ups; Start-up Centre in collaboration with MHRD—Inculcating a spirit of entrepreneurship in National Institutions of Higher Learning; Technology Business Incubator (TBI)—Converting Innovations to startups; Accelerator - Fast tracking a start-up through focused intervention; Seed Support System (SSS)—Providing early stage investment; Centres of Excellence (COE)—A world class facility to help startups go global and/or scale up.

MANAK (Million Minds Augmenting National Aspirations and Knowledge): To widen the base of the innovation pyramid by cultural intervention, ideas relevant to the national needs are to be invited from 10 lakh school students in any language. Top ideas will be supported for mentoring, prototype development, showcasing from the district to national levels and intellectual property protection.

With the objective to contribute towards Swachh Bharat, a new programme viz. **Technology Development for Waste Management** has been initiated to come up with technological solutions for the problems faced by the country in waste management. Areas under this include hospital waste, plastic waste, e-waste, etc. First call for proposals has received an overwhelming response.

Survey of India

O.W.: http//www.surveyofindia.gov.in

Survey of India (SOI), the national survey and mapping organisation under the Ministry of Science and Technology, was set up in 1767. In its assigned role as the National Principal Mapping Agency, Survey of India bears a special responsibility to ensure that the country's domain is explored and mapped suitably to provide base maps for expeditious and integrated development and ensure that all resources contribute their full measure to the progress, prosperity and security of India. The primary responsibility of SOI is to maintain topographical map coverage on 1:250K, 1:50K and l:25K scales. The topographical map coverage on l:250K, and 1:50K scales covering the entire country have been completed and the map sheets are being updated at regular intervals to depict latest spatial information. Surveys on 1:25K scale were taken up as national requirement keeping in view the priorities indicated by the central/ state governments and other user agencies. It has also been called upon extensively to deploy its expertise in the field of geodetic and geophysical surveys, study of seismicity and seismotectonics, glaciology, participation in Indian Scientific Expedition to Antarctica and projects related to digital cartography and digital photogrammetry, etc. to provide basic data to keep pace with Science and Technology Department.

SOI has undertaken creation of Digital Cartographic Data Base of Topographical maps on various scales. The digital data is being used by various agencies for planning and GIS applications. It also undertakes large scale surveys for various developmental projects including hydro-electric, irrigation, command area, canal area, cantt. area schemes, etc. The Department is responsible to fix the external boundary of India, their depiction on maps published in the country and also advise on the demarcation of inter-state boundaries. The Survey of India also provides support to other countries, e.g., Nigeria, Afghanistan, Kenya, Iraq, Nepal, Sri Lanka, Zimbabwe, Indonesia, Bhutan, Mauritius, etc., in the field of mapping, survey education, transfer of technology, and various other surveying technologies under bilateral arrangements. Under UN mandate, Survey of India also provides support to countries in Asia-Pacific region for capacity building in Spatial Data Infrastructures.

Survey Training Institute, Hyderabad established under UNDP assistance is a premier institution for training in various disciplines of surveying and mapping to the trainees sponsored by the Department, other state/central government organisations and neighbouring countries.

Keeping in view a new National Map Policy announced in May, 2005, Open Series Maps based on UTM projection and WGS-84 datum which is compatible with the coordinate system of GPS, used in all activities of surveying and mapping, are being published for users community. Defence Series Maps based on-Lambert Conformal Conic Projection and WGS-84 datum are being published for Defence Forces which are declared as classified. SOI is in the forefront of providing tidal information for the Indian Ocean by observing sea level data at various ports of India and other countries. These are crucial for scientific study in fields including climatology modelling, analysis of sea level changes, predicting tsunami, etc. Besides, this is also important input for sea navigation.

Geo-spatial data are being generated at various levels and by various agencies. These are being utilized for various application which need the integration of data from various sources. To enable this data integration, SOI has taken in its hand a herculean task of redefining the vertical datum of Geoids by establishing a network of well spread standard ground control points throughout the country. This will enable the state cadastral department besides other agencies and industries engaged in acquiring geo-spatial information to carryout their job in a national reference system.

While Survey of India meets the national needs in cartography, some specialised thematic maps required to meet the needs of the specific users are taken care of by the National Atlas and Thematic Mapping Organisation (NATMO) operating under the Department. It also concentrates its attention in a number of areas to integrate resource maps with other relevant socioeconomic data and represent them in spatial forms, useful for developmental planning. NATMO is trying to develop the technology of reverse printing for NATMO maps on experimental basis. It is also trying to introduce the technique of using metallic colours in map printing. These facilities are also being modernised.

Council of Scientific & Industrial Research (CSIR)

O.W.: http//www.csir.res.in

The Council of Scientific & Industrial Research, constituted in 1942 is an autonomous body which is known for its cutting edge R&D knowledge base in diverse S&T areas. Having pan-India presence, CSIR has a dynamic network of 38 national laboratories, 39 outreach centres, 3 innovation complexes and 5 units. Its R&D expertise and experience is embodied in about 4000 active scientists supported by about 7000 scientific and technical personnel. It covers a wide spectrum of science and technology—from radio and space physics, oceanography, earth sciences, geophysics, chemicals, drugs, genomics, biotechnology and nanotechnology to mining, aeronautics, instrumentation, environmental engineering and information technology. It provides significant technological intervention in many areas with regard to societal efforts which include environment, health, drinking water, food, housing, energy, leather, farm and non-farm sectors. CSIR is the nation's custodian for measurement standards of mass, distance, time, temperature, current, etc. CSIR has created and is the custodian of Traditional Knowledge Digital Library (TKDL) which is a powerful weapon against unethical commercial exploitation of Indian traditional knowledge. It maintains Microbial Type Culture Collection (MTCC) and Gene Bank. Pioneer of India's intellectual property movement, CSIR today is strengthening its patent portfolio to carve out global niches for the country in select technology domains.

Atomic Energy

O.W.: http//www.dae.nic.in

The Department of Atomic Energy (DAE), established in 1954 is engaged in the development of nuclear power technology, applications of radiation technologies in the fields of agriculture, medicine, industry, and basic research. Some of these are : (i) increasing the share of nuclear power through deployment of indigenous and other proven technologies and also developing fast breeder reactors and thorium reactors with associated fuel cycle facilities; (ii) building and operation of research reactors for production of radioisotopes and carrying out radiation technology applications in the field of medicine, agriculture and industry; (iii) developing advanced technologies such as accelerators, lasers and encourage transfer of technology to industry; (iv) support to basic research in nuclear energy and related frontier areas of science, interaction with universities and academic institutions, support to R&D projects having a bearing on DAE's programmes and international cooperation in related areas of research; and (v) contribution to national security. An integrated group of organizations, the Department comprises five research centres, three industrial organisations, five public sector undertakings and three service organisations. It has two boards for promoting and funding extramural research in nuclear and allied fields, and mathematics. It also supports seven institutes of international repute, engaged in research in basic sciences, astronomy, astrophysics, cancer research, education, etc. and a society that provides educational facilities to the children of DAE employees.

Following is the profile of DAE's achievements and activities under its major programmes.

Nuclear Power Programme: State 1

Pressurised Heavy Water Reactors & Light Water Reactors

The Nuclear Power Corporation of India Ltd. (NPCIL) is a dividend paying company with AAA credit rating by Crisil and CARE and is responsible for sitting, design, construction, commissioning and operation of nuclear power reactors.

Projects Under Commissioning

Kudankulam Nuclear Power Project (KKNPP) Unit-2 (1000 Mwe)

The reactor critically followed by connection to grid is expected in first quarter of 2016-17.

Project Under construction

1. Kakrapar Atomic Power Project (KAPP) Unit-3&4 (2x700 MWe)

2. Rajasthan Atomic Power Project (RAPP) Unit 7&8 (2x700 MWe)

Sanctioned Projects

1. Kudankulam Nuclear Power Project (KKNPP) Unit-3&4 (2x1000 MWe LWRs)

2. Gorakhpur Anu Vidyut Pariyojana Harayana (GHAVP) Units-1&2 (2x700 MWe PHWRs)

Quality Assurance

Quality Assurance (QA)/ surveillance activities are being carried out by NPCIL for projects and stations. Pre-Service/In-Service Inspections of KKNPP-1&2, TAPS-1&2, TAPS-3&4, KAPS-1&2, NAPS-1&2, RAPS-5&6, RAPS-3&4 and KGS 3&4 have been completed successfully. Corporate QA audits of projects, i.e. KAPP-3&4 and RAPP-7&8 have been completed in a planned way. Corporate reviews of operating stations have been conducted based on the World Association of Nuclear Operators (WANO) guidelines. NPCIL continued to provide QA consultancy services to BARC, BHAVINI and DRDO. Various Directorates at NPCIL HQ are ISO: 9001 certified. Surveillance/Re-certification audits of all these Directorates by the certifying body have been completed successfully.

Front End Fuel Cycle

Front End Fuel Cycle comprises operations such as mining, milling and processing of ore, and fabrication of fuel. In addition, production of heavy water, used as moderator and coolant in pressurized heavy water reactors, also constitutes a major programme segment of the Nuclear Power Programme.

DAE has wide ranging capabilities in uranium mining and mineral processing, and is self-sufficient in the production of heavy water, zirconium alloy components and other materials and supplies, for pressurised heavy water reactor. The Nuclear Fuel Complex at Hyderabad manufactures fuel assemblies for pressurised heavy water reactors, boiling water reactors and fast breeder reactor.

Heavy Water Board

The Heavy Water Board has contributed successfully to the first stage of Nuclear Power Programme by producing heavy water for all Pressurised Heavy Water Reactors in a cost effective manner enabling the department to provide nuclear power at an affordable cost to common man. Presently, Heavy Water Board is not only self-sufficient in meeting the domestic demand of heavy water, but is also geared up to supply heavy water for the future PHWRs and AHWRs as per the envisioned nuclear power programme of DAE. Over a period of time, HWB has emerged as the largest global producer and a trusted supplier of this strategic material. Realizing the large potential for non-nuclear applications of deuterium and heavy water in life sciences, pharmaceuticals and technology areas, HWB is also nurturing R&D activities in this area.

Performance of the Board during the period was excellent with respect to production, specific energy consumption, on stream factor and plant safety. As per the Annual Action Plan for the year 2015-16, HWPs at Manuguru, Kota, Hazira & Thai have carried out the Annual Turn Around jobs during the period.

The Heavy Water Board achieved more than 112 per cent of targeted production for the financial year 2015-16 and the specific energy consumption was 28.6 GJ/kg.

Diversification Activities

HWB has made major progress on its extended mandate in the field of development, demonstration and deployment of technologies for in-core and out of core material inputs for Indian Nuclear Power Programme, required at the Front-end as well as Back-end of nuclear fuel cycle mainly centering around three broad areas such as solvents for front and back end hydrometallurgical operations of nuclear fuel cycle; demonstrating solvent extraction technology for extraction of various rare materials and producing stable isotopes like ^{10}B for Fast Breeder Reactors and ^{18}O for societal applications.

Solvent Technology

In the area of solvents, both the industrial facilities at HWP, Baroda and Talcher for production of TBP (Tributyl Phosphate) and D2EHPA have performed very well enabling HWB to meet the entire requirement of NFC, NRB and all other units of DAE.

Developmental efforts have already been put in place at HWP, Tuticorin in the Versatile Solvent Synthesis Pilot Plant (VSSP) in campaign mode for special and futuristic solvents like D2EHPA-II, TiAP, DHOA and TAPO for collection of data for industrial level production of these solvents. HWB has initiated setting up of Solvent Production Plant (SPP) for industrial scale production of these solvents with an objective to achieve self-reliance. HWB is also planning to take up synthesis of some special solvents viz. DGA, Calixarene, etc. based on collaborative efforts with DAE units as requested by them.

Boron Enrichment

In consonance with the material input required for second stage of NPP based on FBRs, HWB, with its decades of experience of handling isotope separation process, took up development, demonstration and deployment of indigenous technologies for production of enriched Boron. HWB has now acquired comprehensive capability in this area achieving enrichment levels beyond 95 per cent in multiple chemical forms. To support the second stage of NPP, HWB has successfully delivered the entire quantity of enriched Boron for the 1st core of PFBR.

Sodium Metal

Sodium is another important input for FBRs, used as coolant in the reactor. Networking with the Indian R&D organizations, HWB has developed indigenous and safer closed electrolytic cell technology for production of nuclear grade sodium. Successively larger size cells are tested with the ultimate intent of an industrial scale set up.

Mineral Exploration and Mining

Atomic Minerals Directorate for Exploration and Research (AMD) continued the accelerated pace of exploration activities during the year by integrated, multi-disciplinary methodology and judicious utilisation of manpower with a focussed approach on augmentation of uranium, thorium and rare metals. This resulted in the augmentation of additional uranium oxide (U_3O_8) reserve of over 15,775 tonnes in the areas of Andhra Pradesh, Meghalaya, Rajasthan and Jharkhand. The country's uranium reserve has been updated to 2,29,936 tonnes of Uranium Oxide (U_3O_8) as of December 31, 2015.

Geochemical surveys (4,040 sq km) have been carried out in different parts of the country for delineating the target for detailed investigations. Ground geophysical surveys (about 560 sq km) have delineated conducting zones in Haryana and high chargeability zones in Karnataka and Jharkhand. Airborne survey and remote sensing survey has also been carried out over 42,559 line km in parts of Rajasthan and Karnataka.

Rare Metal and Rare Earth (RMRE) investigations resulted in location of significant concentrations of RMRE alongwith Chhattisgarh, Tamil Nadu and Karnataka.

Beach Sand and Offshore Investigations (BSOI) resulted in establishing potential heavy mineral zones mainly along the east coast. Significant zones of Total Heavy Mineral (THM) concentration have been located at Andhra Pradesh, Odisha and Tamil Nadu. Sonic drilling was initiated in beach sand investigations to evaluate deeper horizons.

Mining and processing of uranium ore in India is done by the Uranium Corporation of India Ltd. (UCIL). The Corporation operates in Jharkhand state with seven mines at Jaduguda, Bhatin, Narwapahar, Turamdih, Bagjata, Banduhurang, Mohuldih and two processing plants at Jaduguda and Turamdih. A new mine and a processing plant are also under construction at Tummalapalle, Andhra Pradesh. The Indian Rare Earths Limited (IREL) is a Mini Ratna (Category-1) company and it is engaged in mining and production of beach sand minerals and rare earth compounds.

Fuel Fabrication

Nuclear Fuel Complex (NFC) manufactures and supplies fuel bundles for Pressurised Heavy Water Reactors (PHWRs) and Boiling Water Reactors (BWRs) of NPCIL. Highest ever production of PHWR fuel bundles, PHWR fuel tubes, Niobium metal and SS tubes & job orders was achieved during the period.

Production of 202 nos. of pressure tubes for 700 MWe PHWRs through new route of two stage radial forging and single pilgering of billets were completed, thus meeting the complete requirement of forthcoming KAPP—3 & 4 and RAPP—7 & 8.

NFC launched 19 new projects during the XII Plan and 3 new projects during MTA. These projects were launched to meet the fuel and zircaloy requirements of forthcoming 700 MWe PHWRs and 300 MWe AHWR, in addition to augmentation and modernisation of the present production facilities, in line with the demand from M/s NPCIL.

Back End Fuel Cycle

Fuel Reprocessing and Waste Management

All the fuel reprocessing plants are operating at their design capacity. Warm commissioning of Power Reactor Fuel Reprocessing Plant-3A commenced. Power Reactor Thoria Reprocessing Facility (PRTRF) was hot commissioned to recover ^{233}U from irradiated Th. Demonstration of reprocessing of irradiated thoria bundle and quantitative separation/recovery of ^{233}U is an important milestone in the 3 stage nuclear power programme.

Advanced Vitrification System, Tarapur completed vitrification of radioactive liquid waste in joule melter. Centralized Waste Management Facility, Kalpakkam continued to provide uninterrupted radioactive waste management services & filter testing services to various units of DAE at Kalpakkam. Plutonium Plant, Trombay continued processing of the spent fuel from Dhruva to fissile and fertile material. An innovative method to partition the radio-elements from inactive salt constituents using indigenously developed solvents was employed for the management of radioactive waste.

R&D Support to Power Sector

The research and development support to the Nuclear Power Programme is provided by the research centers of DAE.

The fuel utilization in Indian Pressurised Water Reactor equilibrium configuration was enhanced to get a discharge burn-up of 45 GWd/T with a profiled fuel assembly of average ^{235}U content of 4.22 per cent. Numerical models were developed and validated for deflagration, flame acceleration and detonation using experimental data to understand different physical and chemical processes during hydrogen combustion. Fitness-for-Service and assessment of remaining life of hemispherical bottom head of second stage hot tower of HWP, Kota was carried out by finite element analyses and limit load calculations.

Health Safety & Environment

NPCIL has recorded about 430 reactors years of safe operation of reactors by the end of December 2015. Review of safety of operating stations was carried out on a regular basis. All safety significant proposals and documents were reviewed by a multidisciplinary Safety Review Committee (SRC) to meet the regulatory compliance. The individual and collective doses of radiation workers at various NPPs were maintained within the budget approved by Atomic Energy Regulatory Board by following the principles of ALARA (As Low as Reasonably Achievable) and maintaining the highest standards of safety within the Nuclear Power Plants (NPPs). The radioactive effluents discharged from NPPs to the environment were maintained well below the authorized limits specified by AERB.

NPCIL continued to maintain low radiation exposure in the public domain due to operation of nuclear power stations. At all operating stations of NPCIL, certified Environmental Management System (EMS) as per (SO-14001: 2004 and Occupational Health and Safety Management System (OHSMS) as per IS-18001: 2007 are maintained and regular audits (internal, external and management) were carried out for continual improvement.

An online thoron monitoring network was installed and made operational at PRTRF at Trombay to monitor the thoron gas concentration at various locations in the facility. Internal exposure assessment of occupational workers from various facilities of BARC at Mumbai and Tarapur was carried out by whole body/lung counting and bioassay (urine/fecal) sample analysis.

All the plants of Heavy Water Board are certified for ISO Quality Management System, Environmental Management System and OSHA System. The overall safety standards of Heavy Water Plants were far better than similar chemical industries in the country.

Nuclear Power Programme: Stage 2

Fast Breeder Reactors

For the second stage of the Nuclear Power Generation Programme, the Indira Gandhi Centre for Atomic Research (IGCAR) is pursuing development of sodium cooled fast breeder reactors and associated fuel cycle technologies. Breeder reactors produce more fuel than they consume.

The Fast Reactor Programme of IGCAR is supported by its research and development endeavour in a range of disciplines such as reactor engineering, metallurgy, materials science, instrumentation, safety, etc. The Fast Breeder Test Reactor (FBTR), operating at Kalpakkam for over 25 years, also caters to technology development related to fast reactors.

Based on the fast breeder reactor technology developed by IGCAR, a 500 MWe Prototype Fast Breeder Reactor (PFBR) is coming up at Kalpakkam. The project is being executed by the Bharatiya Nabhikiya Vidyut Nigam Limited (BHAVINI), a public sector undertaking of DAE.

BARC contributes to the research & development and manufacture of fuels for fast reactors, technology for reprocessing of fuels, waste management and health and safety of the work force.

Prototype Fast Breeder Reactor

PFBR is a pool type reactor using mixed oxide of uranium and plutonium as fuel. The coolant used is liquid sodium. The project is located 500 m south of the existing Madras Atomic Power Station.

The project has achieved an overall physical progress of 97.64 per cent at the end of January, 2016.

Fast Breeder Test Reactor

During 2015-16, Fast Breeder Test Reactor (FBTR), the flagship of the IGCAR, continued to play an important role in testing the fuel, structural materials and special neutron detectors for FBR programmes. On December 29, 2015, the reactor power was raised to 26.1 MWt for the first time with turbo generator generating a power of 5 MWe. Currently the 24th irradiation campaign has been started. About 122 number of thoria sub-assemblies were loaded in the reactor towards production of Uranium-233. Recommendations of SARCOP including post Fukushima and seismic retrofits were implemented.

FBR Fuels

The U-Pu mixed carbide fuel pins for FBTR at Kalpakkam and fuel pins for the full core of PFBR were supplied by BARC. Electro refining of U-Pu-Zr alloy in molten LiKCl-PuCl$_3$ electrolyte was demonstrated at IGCAR.

Fast Reactor Fuel Reprocessing

Towards reprocessing programme, the operation of CORAL (Compact Reprocessing facility for Advanced fuels in Lead cells) facility provided immense experience in the domain of remote handling & maintenance and in achieving product purity in addition to reprocessing the FBTR fuel. In the Fast Reactor Fuel Cycle Facility, civil construction of various buildings is progressing well.

FBR Related Technologies

Towards R&D related activities for the fast reactors and associated fuel cycle, various experimental facilities such as commissioning of a 100 tonne shake table, research facility for irradiation studies in sodium at high temperature, an innovative out of pile test loop and rupture and ballooning in tubes facility were completed.

Future FBRs

A 5/8th scale 90° sector model simulating the hot pool of future FBRs was commissioned for conducting hydraulic studies in water. A new facility was commissioned to study the flow induced vibration characteristics of a cluster of subassemblies of the core of FBR.

Health, Safety & Environment

Effective radiological surveillance and health physics services were provided for the radioactive facilities. TLD (Thermo Luminescence Dosimeters) personnel monitoring services, covering about 2,500 occupational workers of IGCAR and BARC facilities, whole body counting, routine and special monitoring procedures for about 800 occupational workers of various active labs of IGCAR, contract workers engaged by active facilities and bioassay services for over 150 occupational workers were also carried out.

Nuclear Power Programme: Stage 3

Thorium Based Reactors

Nuclear power employing closed fuel cycle is the only sustainable option for meeting a major part of the world energy demand. World resources of thorium are larger than those of uranium. Thorium, therefore is, widely viewed as the 'fuel of the future'. The Indian Nuclear Power Programme Stage-3 aims at using thorium as fuel for power generation on a commercial scale. In the thorium fuel cycle, thorium 232 is transmuted into the fissile isotope uranium 233 which is a nuclear fuel. As a part of this programme, BARC has been developing a 300 MWe Advanced Heavy Water Reactor (AHWR). Fuelled by thorium and using light water as coolant and heavy water as moderator, this reactor will have several advanced passive safety features.

Advanced Heavy Water Reactor

The Advanced Heavy Water Reactor (AHWR) equilibrium core cluster having (Th, Pu-U) MOX fuel was re-optimized for better performance. A Passive Auto Depressurization System was developed for fast depressurisation of main heat transport system to initiate timely injection of cooling water to ensure safety and integrity of the core. A mock-up facility was developed and installed in BARC to demonstrate all aspects of automatic and remote fabrication of (Th-$^{233}U)O_2$ fuel.

Other Thorium Reactor Systems

The refueling and removal of molten salt fuel from the 850 MWe Indian Molten Salt Breeder Reactor was computed for various burn-ups. A high temperature heat pipe was fabricated with sodium as the working fluid and tested. A process was developed to prepare high purity beryllium oxide and fabrication of rectangular shape high density sintered beryllia ceramic by vacuum hot pressing. A vitrification process was developed for safe disposal of solid waste generated during extraction of Be from its ore by immobilizing the Be value present in waste mud. Boron alloy composites $(TiCr)B_2+MoSi_2$ and B_4C+ZrO_2 for control rods of P-4 facility and shut-off rods of project B-3 were prepared. A carbon vapour deposition spray coating facility using induction heating to coat the internal and external surfaces of CHTR fuel tube with pyrolytic carbon and silicon carbide was commissioned.

Kalpakkam Mini (Kamini) Reactor

Kamini reactor was operated successfully for neutron radiography of various pyro devices for Department of Space. High temperature fission chambers required for neutron flux measurement of PFBR were successfully tested.

Research Reactors

Dhruva operated at rated power of 100 MWt at a high safety level and availability factor. A number of researchers from across the country utilized the neutron beam facility of the UGC-DAE Consortium for Scientific Research.

Advanced Technologies

The research centres of DAE are engaged in developing advanced technologies such as accelerators, lasers, advanced materials, robotics, supercomputers, instrumentation and others. BARC, RRCAT, VECC and BRIT are also engaged in the development of radiation technologies and their applications for better crop varieties, techniques for crops protection, radiation based post-harvest technologies, techniques for radio-diagnosis and radiotherapy of diseases particularly cancer, technologies for safe drinking water, better environment and industrial growth.

Accelerators

A facility for processing of multi-cell 1.3 GHz Superconducting Radio Frequency (SCRF) cavities has been set up at RRCAT. Using this facility a nine-cell 1.3 GHz SCRF cavity has been fabricated and electro-polished to remove an average of 50 micron material. A semi-automatic cavity tuning machine has been designed and developed indigenously for the RF resonating frequency and field flatness correction of a multi-cell 1.3 GHz SCRF cavity. A centrifugal barrel polishing machine has been indigenously designed and developed for polishing of the internal surface of multi-cell SCRF cavities.

Laser Technology Development and Applications

A fiber coupled pulsed Nd:YAG laser providing pulses of 20 kW peak power has been developed at RRCAT for laser welding of up to 4 mm thick niobium SCRF cavities. A pulsed Nd:YAG laser for remote dismantling of irradiated fuel subassemblies of the Prototype Fast Breeder Reactor (PFBR) has been developed. An Yb-doped Continuous Wave (CW) fiber laser of 400 W output power has been developed using a single oscillator. A diode side-pumped continuous wave (CW) Nd:YAG laser of output power 1 kW operating at 1060 nm wavelength has also been developed. An Er-doped fiber laser emitting at the eye-safe wavelength of 1600 nm which uses a large mode-area Er-doped fiber pumped by a 975 nm diode laser and having a CW output power of 25 W has been developed.

Electronics & Instrumentation

The Electronics Corporation of India Limited (ECIL) continued to remain engaged in the design, development, manufacture, supply, installation and commissioning of electronic equipment for the Atomic Energy, Defence, Aerospace, Security, Information Technology and e-Governance sectors. Some of the new products introduced during the year were Uranium Analyser; Solid State Digital Video Recorder System; Radar Target Echo Simulator; High Power Solid State Switches; TDM Signal Analyser and De-multiplexer and Linux based ECSCADA Server Software.

Robotics

A robot based frameless stereotactic system is developed at BARC for performing neurosurgery which has accuracy and patient comfort level comparable to frame based system. It automates the frameless stereotaxy using a high precision robot (Parallel Mechanism based Robot). A 4 DOF (Degrees of Freedom) Surgical Coordinate Measuring Mechanism (SCMM), a 6 DOF Parallel Kinematic Mechanism (6D-PKM) based robot and the visualization display to aid the surgeon during neurosurgery are the major components of the system.

Cryogenics

A cryogenic system consisting of cryogen distribution lines for liquid helium and liquid nitrogen, sub-atmospheric vacuum jacketed lines for helium, warm helium lines between the helium buffer tanks and compressors, and a 500 watt helium liquefier is being set-up for the superconducting electron and heavy-ion linacs at VECC. The design of the cryogenic system has been finalized.

Radioisotopes & Radiation Technology and their Applications

DAE has been playing a significant role in the development and applications of various radioisotopes in healthcare, industry, agriculture and research. India is one of the leading countries in the isotope technology today as a result of the consistent efforts of DAE.

Radioisotopes are produced in the Dhruva research reactor at Trombay, accelerator at Kolkata and the various nuclear power plants of NPCIL during the report period, a wide variety of radioisotopes for medical, industrial and research applications were produced and supplied by BARC. The Board of Radiation and Isotope Technology (BRIT) produced and supplied a wide range of radioisotope products, and radiation technology equipment for medical and industrial uses. BRIT's plants for radiation sterilization of medical products and radiation processing of spices and allied products continued to offer services to medical and agro-industry. Radiation technology based tools and techniques benefitted variety of industries and social sector.

Agriculture

Trombay Groundnut (TG) varieties TG 79 and TG 80 entered for evaluation in Indian Council of Agricultural Research trials all over the country. 340 quintals of breeder seed of TG varieties were produced in BARC, Gauribidanur and from contract farming and distributed to seed agencies in various states. Seed multiplication of black gram varieties TAU-1, TAU-2, TPU-4, TU94-2 and TU-40 was done. Protocol for the preparation of biomass for the uptake of U and suitable color reagent for its detection was established.

A gel-free protocol has been developed for rapid assessment of single band DMA markers and to expedite selection of desired traits in wheat plants. 148 new indigenous and exotic germplasm lines of sorghum were evaluated for their synchronous flowering, seed set and potential to be used in the hybrid development. A purely organic, seed dressing biofungicide formulation of an improved Trichoderma virens mutant strain was developed.

Food Technology

The potential of using irradiated onion scales as a source of natural food additive was evaluated. Methods were standardized for the preparation of ready to eat (RTE), shelf stable mutton masala using gamma radiation. A procedure was standardized for ready to bake chapattis by radiation processing at 1 kGy dose and heating at 800°C for 15 minutes in water bath. Silver nanoparticles synthesized using mint extract were found to be bactericidal against E. coli, S. aureus, B. cereus and P. aeruginosa. Copper nanoparticles were incorporated in PVA films to develop active antimicrobial films. Improvement and modification of litchi preservation technology was effected by replacing hydrochloric acid treatment with tartaric acid doing away with the ascorbic acid treatment making the process more cost effective. The effect of allylisothiocyanate (AITC) in combination with low temperature (10 °C) storage on post harvest quality of minimally processed shredded cabbage was investigated. Technology for preparation of radiation processed guar gum as a dietary fiber is ready for transfer to the prospective entrepreneurs.

Nuclear Medicine and Healthcare

More than 12,000 patients were benefitted from nuclear medicine diagnosis and therapy for various ailments such as thyroid, heart, etc. The Scintigraphy and PET-CT Section performed nearly 12,000 diagnostic scans. Facility for indigenous sourcing of expensive and clinically relevant peptides such as DOTA-TATE, HYNIC-TOC, cyclic-RGD, etc., using solid phase peptide synthesis has been developed. A two-vial kit for the preparation of ^{188}ReN-DEDTC/lipiodol (DEDTC-diethyl dithiocarbamates) for inoperable liver cancer as a cost-effective alternative to imported ^{90}Y-based products was developed.

More than 20,000 consignments of ready to use Radiopharmaceuticals of Sodium Iodide (Na^{131}l) in the form of both solution and capsules for diagnosis and therapy of thyroid disorders, ^{131}l-meta lodo Benzyl Guanidine (mlBG) for neuroendocrine tumor detection & therapy, ^{32}P, ^{153}Sm and ^{177}Lu for bone pain palliation were supplied to various nuclear medicine centres and hospitals all over India in the form of ready-to-use injectables.

For societal applications of radio-technology, VECC has collaborated with BRIT, Kolkata to install and evaluate the TCM-AUTOSOLEX generator for preparation and use of [^{99m}Tc] pertechnetate in hospital. Irradiation of Enriched ^{100}Mo for ^{99m}Tc production in VEC cyclotron and determination of radionuclidic purity of the cyclotron produced ^{99m}Tc, as part of the IAEA Coordinate Research Project (CRP) on direct production of ^{99m}Tc in cyclotron, production feasibility of ^{89}Zr from ^{nat}Y and subsequent radiochemical separation of ^{89}Zr from the target matrix, evaluation of ^{68}Ge/^{68}Ga generator and synthesis of cross linked Chitosan for preparation of ^{99}Mo-^{99m}Tc Generator have also been performed.

Alternative Applications of Heavy Water

Realizing the potential requirements of Oxygen-18 (^{18}O) having application in nuclear medicine and bio-chemical research, HWB has successfully accomplished technology development for enrichment of ^{18}O at H WP, Tuticorin. The industrial scale facility for ^{18}O production plant has been commissioned at HWP, Manuguru. All columns have been successfully operated with DM water. Nuclear grade heavy water was charged and is under enrichment in coupled condition since July 2015.

Considering the immense potential of application of Deuterium and heavy water in life sciences, pharmaceuticals and technology areas, HWB has put in place an action plan to facilitate and nurture R&D activities in this area. Many Indian companies and government institutions like Indian Council of Agricultural Research (ICAR), Indian Veterinary Research Institute (IVRI), Institute of Plasma Research (IPR), Tata Institute of Fundamental Research (TIFR), etc., have shown their interest in this area and HWB has supplied small quantities of heavy water to support their R&D jobs.

As part of developmental activities on non-nuclear uses of heavy water, methods for synthesizing deuterated NMR solvents have been developed at HWP Baroda in laboratory scale. Process optimization has also been done to minimize the consumption of heavy water used for synthesizing these molecules. As part of MoU signed between HWB & BRIT, BRIT has already started marketing these solvents to various reputed research institutes in the country.

Cancer Diagnostics & Treatment Services

During the period, TMC acquired around 140 equipments. Installation of major equipments like Surface Plasmon Resonance System, Refrigerated Shaker Incubators, Tabletop Centrifuges, Inverted Microscope, Thermal Cycler, Water Purification System, Micro Plate Reader, Gel Documentation System, Real Time PCR Machine, etc. has been done. Household survey was continued for screening of eligible women for breast, uterine, cervix and oral cavity cancers.

Construction work has commenced for the establishment of cancer hospital in Andhra Pradesh. For the cancer hospital in Chandigarh, work order has been issued. Clinical Research Secretariat (CRS) and Department of Atomic Energy Clinical Trials unit (DAE-CTC) has continued to play a key role in facilitating research in the field of oncology at the hospital. The number of patients referred to and registered at ACTREC has increased over the years. A new state-of-the-art linear accelerator (Varian True Beam) was installed and commissioned for clinical use towards the year-end. The indigenously developed Multi Leaf Collimator (MLC) system installed on the Bhabhatron-ll telecobalt unit received regulatory approval for clinical use. About 2000 major surgical procedures were performed in ACTREC. The achievement of clinical pharmacology lab involved in drug development included the encouraging preclinical findings of chlorophyllin as a radio protective agent and its technology transfer to an industry partner.

Radiation Processing

About 5116 cubic meters of healthcare products were processed using radiation for terminal sterilization at ISOMED, BRIT upto December 2015.

Gamma Radiation Indicator Buttons were developed indigenously as an import substitute (Made in India) for qualitative indication of low and medium range gamma radiation dose delivery to the products.

About 2,933 tonnes of spices and other products like nutraceuticals and colour pigments were processed during the report period.

NABL accreditation for dosimeter calibration laboratory of Radiation Processing Plant (RPP), Vashi was obtained during the period.

Radiation Technology Based Equipment and Services

About 81 radiography cameras, ROLI-2 and ROLI-3, were supplied by BRIT to various NDT users within India. One Blood Irradiator containing 800 Ci of ^{60}Co was supplied to Ruby Hospital, Pune. First ^{137}Cs based Blood Irradiator was manufactured during the period.

During the year, six units of 'Bhabhatron' have been commissioned at BARC, taking the total number of operating units to 36. One unit at ACTREC has been integrated with multi-leaf collimator, which is aimed at superior conformity. Six units of Radiotherapy Simulator 'Imagin' have been installed taking the total number of operating units of 'Imagin' to 10. One unit of 'Bhabhatron' and 'Imagin' were gifted to Mongolia during the honorable Prime Minister's visit. Postal Dosimetry Audit Phantom and methods for intensity modulated radiotherapy was developed.

Water Purification, Water Desalination & Isotope Hydrology

A 250 m^2/hr capacity ultra-filtration plant was commissioned at BARC for conventional pre-treatment of SWRO (Sea Water Reverse Osmosis) process.

A simple and low cost method based on an innovative chemical agent was developed for removal of fluoride from contaminated water. BARC has designed a solar photo-bioreactor capable of treating domestic waste water and simultaneously generating biomass for biofuel generation.

Isotope hydrological investigation was carried out in Goa to investigate the impact of iron ore mining to groundwater and surface water quality in downstream of the mine pits. Isotope techniques in aquifer mapping at a model project site in Patna district of Bihar state was carried out to understand recharge mechanism.

Basic & Applied Research

Basic and applied researches relevant to DAE's programme are carried out in the research centres of the Department and the autonomous research institutes are supported by the grant-in-aid. Following were the notable developments in the fields of basic and applied research carried out during the report period, by these research institutes.

Mathematics & Computational Sciences

Extraordinary fast fluid transport through carbon nanotubes was established at BARC using two phase thermodynamic method.

At SINP, a challenging integrable defect problem is solved with an innovative application of space-time duality, hidden in integrable systems. A novel class of exactly solvable spin Calogero models, associated with the D_N root system has been constructed by using the polarized spin reversal operators.

At HRI, new results have been obtained in the area of zero-sum problems with weights. A conjecture of Zagier regarding the asymptotic behavior of the inverse Mellin transform of the symmetric square L-function associated with the Ramanujan tau function has been generalized. All finite groups whose non-linear irreducible characters of the same degree are Galois conjugates have been classified. An optimal Hardy-Sobolev inequality has been proven for the twisted Laplacian.

The Institute of Mathematical Sciences (IMSc) remained involved in joint projects with national and international institutes for many projects on Mathematics.

Physics

At BARC, Neutron induced cross-sections for fusion technology application were determined for the first time for ^{55}Fe radio-nuclei by surrogate ratio method. TeV Atmospheric Cerenkov Telescope with Imaging Camera at Mt. Abu, Rajasthan continued to study extragalactic very high energy gamma-ray sources having low red shift, flaring history and hard gamma-ray emission spectra. The setting up of the Major Atmospheric Cerenkov Experiment Telescope at Hanle in Ladakh is in progress. A Collimator housing assembly and its supporting platform designed for neutron radiography was installed in VSSC, Trivandraum under a MoU between BARC and VSSC.

In astronomy at TIFR, ASTROSAT, India's first astronomy satellite was launched and placed into orbit. Three of the payloads were designed and fabricated at TIFR. All instruments on board are functioning according to specifications. At the National Centre for Radio Astrophysics, a giant radio galaxy was discovered by the Giant Metrewave Radio telescope, and good progress was made on the upgrade of the GMRT.

In the area of experimental physics at TIFR significant advances were made in the fields of condensed matter, materials science, nuclear and atomic physics. Advances were made in the research of superconducting circuits, and in semiconductor research, synthesis of single crystals and the study of their properties was conducted.

Significant advances were made at SINP in the research activities in various areas of Condensed Matter Physics, Surface Physics, Nuclear Physics, Applied Nuclear Physics, Theoretical Physics and Astrophysical Sciences and Plasma Physics.

At VECC, a Total Absorption Gamma Spectroscopy (TAGS) set up using BaF_2 detectors was designed and tested for accurate beta-decay feeding measurements, which has application in the reactor decay heat calculations. A method has been developed to calculate microscopically mass and charge distributions of spontaneous fission yields.

NISER continued to carryout research in the areas of Cosmology and Galaxy formation, Black holes and String theory, Particle Physics and Quark-gluon Plasma, Hadron Spectroscopy, Statistical Mechanics and Soft matter, Quantum Optics and Non-linear dynamics, Magnetism and Superconductivity and several other areas of Condensed Matter Physics.

Synchrotrons and their Applications

The Raja Ramanna Centre for Advanced Technology (RRCAT) has set up Synchrotron Radiation Sources Indus-1 &2 for carrying out advanced basic research.

During the year, both the synchrotron radiation sources, Indus-1 and Indus-2, were operated round-the-clock. Indus-2 was operated at beam current up to 200 mA and 2.5 GeV energy while Indus-1 was operated at 100 mA current and 450 MeV energy. The Indus-2 storage ring is operating with a highly stable electron beam. The improved performance of the Indus synchrotron radiation sources is reflected in a substantial increase in the number of users. The user experiments have doubled from 190 in 2013 to 390 in 2015. The availability of 13 beamlines in Indus-2 for user experiments was about 4370 hours.

Two planar undulators U1 and U2, one for Atomic, Molecular and Optical Science (AMOS) beamline and another for Angle Resolved Photoelectron Spectroscopy (ARPES) beamline, installed last year in the Indus-2 storage ring, were commissioned. Images of the synchrotron radiation beam emitted from the undulator and its neighboring bending magnet were recorded using a fluorescent screen beam viewer.

An APPLE-2 (Advanced Planar Polarized Light Emitter-2) type undulator made of permanent magnet blocks was installed in the long straight section, LS-5, of Indus-2, after carrying out offline tests.

Using the X-ray lithography beamline (BL-7) of Indus-2, X-ray lenses for use in the hard X-ray regime have been fabricated in a new antimony free material, code named SUEX. A focal beam diameter with Full Width at Half Maximum (FWHM) of 0.8 micron was obtained when this lens was used at the Diamond Light Source, UK. Next, Fresnel Zone Plates (FZP) with a focal length of 25 mm have been fabricated in Polymethyl Methacrylate (PMMA) on ultra-thin titanium film using 30 keV electron-beam lithography. These have been designed for focusing of capillary discharge based argon X-ray laser (wavelength: 46.9 nm).

Work on the installation and vacuum testing of various components for beamlines and frontends has also been carried out. A compact two stage differential pumping system (length 415 mm) has been developed, tested and installed on the BL-3 of Indus-2 to provide a windowless transition between high and low vacuum regions of the beamline.

At BARC, crystal structures of various important proteins were determined using Protein Crystallography beamline PXBL21 of Indus-2 and the structure data were deposited in Protein Data Bank database. An in-situ low temperature liquid nitrogen (77 K) & liquid helium (4.2 K)) infrared absorption/reflection facility has been set up at the IR beamline at Indus-1 SRS.

Fusion and other Plasma Technologies

At the Institute of Plasma Research (IPR), the Steady-state Superconducting Tokamak-1 (SST-1) has completed the 1st phase of upgradation with successful installation and integration of all its First Wall components.

At BARC, a novel technique has been developed for preparation of specific composition of Dysprosium titanate material for high temperature application. An innovative space saving online fabrication facility has been set up for the fabrication of long length Cable in Conduit Conductors (CICC). 200 m long CICC on a bobbin has been fabricated in the facility.

Chemistry

BARC has developed the material technology for the anode (nano lithium titanate) and cathode (nano lithium iron phosphate carbon composite) materials of lithium ion battery. BARC in collaboration with National Physical Laboratory, New Delhi has prepared the first quartz certified reference material of the country following the international guidelines.

A high end two-dimensional infrared spectrometer for advanced studies in Chemistry and Biology was developed. NCCCM, Hyderabad has been validated as a supplier by European Commission for homogeneity, stability and characterization of major element content in food and trace element content. Time resolved laser induced fluorescence spectrometer, for studying speciation of lanthanides and actinides, with different complexing agents, sorbents and host matrices, has been installed and commissioned. A new type of biocompatible and task-specific hydrogel beads were synthesized for controlled and sustained delivery of the anti-cancer drug doxorubicin.

At TIFR, a technique was developed to determine the conformation of membrane proteins in physiological conditions using Surface Enhanced Raman Spectroscopy.

Different architecture of nanomaterials have been developed at SINP which include tunable gold nano-flowers, silver nano-wires, selenium nano-spheres, etc and successfully used in effective drug delivery and bioanalytical detection.

NISER continued to impart high quality undergraduate and postgraduate level of knowledge to students coupled with cutting edge research activity in the School of Chemical Sciences.

Biology

An advanced and economic Clustered Regularly Interspaced Short Palindromic Repeats (CRISPR) cascade based tool was developed at BARC and used for genome editing and gene silencing in Mycobacterium tuberculosis (Mtb).

Advances were made at TIFR in the field of malaria research with the identification of a protein that could be a candidate for a malaria vaccine. At the National Centre for Biological Sciences, advances were made in understanding cellular organization and signaling, genetics and development and in understanding ecological processes across multiple scales.

A two color single molecule FRET imaging set up for real time monitoring of complex macromolecular systems has been developed at SINP. Research in the area of Disease Biology continued to focus on two major disorders, the haematological and neurological. New initiatives were taken to study epigenetic regulator proteins and nuclear lamins and their involvements in disease processes.

Materials Science

Several functional and energy conversion ceramics such as beta-alumina, BeO and Solid Oxide Fuel Cell (SOFC) ceramics have been fabricated at BARC. Ni-Cr based alloys were indigenously developed for high burn up clad applications. Composite fibres have been prepared by dispersing Carbon Nanotubes (CNTs), developed in-house, in polymeric fibres with improved toughness. Aluminide coating on Ni-Cr-Fe based super alloys was developed for high temperature application. A methodology for joining stainless steel 304L to Zircaloy-4, based on a novel Ga-assisted diffusion bonding technique was developed using Ni and Ti inter-layers.

Different samples of indigenously developed (with collaboration of BARC and NFC) Ni-Cr alloy have been irradiated with proton beam from the Variable Energy Cyclotron. A comparative study has been done with the imported alloy to assess the radiation resistant capability. Microstructural characterisations of different deformed and irradiated alloys were carried out using X-ray Diffraction and Field Emission Scanning Electron Microscopy.

At RRCAT, a new indigenous process has been developed to produce Nb pipe/316 G stainless steel flange joints suitable for use in low-beta SCRF cavities. An experimental facility based on the resonant ultrasound spectroscopy technique was designed and developed for the measurement of the elastic constants materials at low temperatures (2-300 K) and in high magnetic fields (up to 70 kOe). Several high-quality crystals have been grown by different techniques for various photonic applications. These include Er and Cr co-doped YVO_4 for lasers, Cr doped Strontium Barium Niobate (SBN) crystals for pyroelectric infrared sensors and transstilbene for scintillation detectors.

A key achievement in materials research at TIFR was the engineering and assembly of atomically thin layers of grapheme allowing them to be used for novel energy and sensing applications through doping. Also, an ammonia sensor-which can detect both ionized and un-ionized ammonia in sub-pico molar level, was developed using fluorinated grapheme.

Cancer Research

ACTREC, located at Navi Mumbai, comprises of two sub-units the Clinical Research Centre (CRC), 111 bed research hospital that focuses on research and treatment of cancer patients and the Cancer Research Institute (CRI) that focuses on basic and applied research on cancer. During the year, the CRI's 20 principal investigator led laboratories remained engaged in a large number of basic and applied research projects.

A non-toxic herbal radioprotector BRM was developed at BARC for enhancing the radio-sensitivity of human breast cancer cells. Radio-protecting technology for lungs and other organs was transferred to the private domain for clinical trials as a prophylactic/therapeutic radioprotector and an adjuvant in radiotherapy. An indigenous synthesis of the precursor of ^{18}F-FLT, a tumor imaging agent has been developed for making the PET tracer at a cheaper cost for assessing tumor proliferation, its staging and identifying the treatment outcome of patients.

International Research Collaborations

The experimental data on piping components and systems generated by BARC has been selected by Organization for Economic Cooperation and Development—Nuclear Energy Agency for the benchmark exercise on Metallic Component Margins under High Seismic Loads. Corrosion Loop Experiment is designed to study the phenomenon of Irradiation Assisted Stress Corrosion Cracking in LWR operating conditions for installation in Jules Horowitz Reactor, France as a part of Indian in-kind contribution in the JHR programme.

Two large-size advanced types of gaseous detectors i.e., Gas Electron Multiplier (GEM) and Resistive Plate Chamber (RPC) have been built and tested successfully at VECC during 2015. The GEM chamber of trapezoidal shape (length 80 cm and larger width of 40 cm) is a real-size prototype module built for the Compressed Baryonic Matter (CBM) experiment in the upcoming FAIR facility at Darmstadt, Germany.

For the Large Hadron Collider and Compact Muon Solenoid (CMS) Experiment, TIFR has participated in data collection, data quality monitor and data analysis. Also, several analyses based on Run 1 data are being collated. The CMS collaboration also pursued a comprehensive programme of Phase I detector upgrades. An important milestone in building an electrically working prototype for the Belle II Silicon Vertex Detector (SVD), was achieved. For the International Centre for Theoretical Sciences, the new campus at Shivakote, Hesaraghatta Hobli in north Bangalore was inaugurated in June 2015. The in-house research areas at the Centre grew successfully in various disciplines.

International collaborations were continued at SINP with CERN in ALICE and CMS experiments and with SNOLAB in PICASSO experiment. The two experiments, ALICE and CMS collected data with a very high efficiency and members of SINP took active parts in the data collection, data analysis and extracting important physics results from these experiments.

IMSc continued the joint projects with International Institutes on India based Neutrino Observatory (INO) and DINO (Darkmatter at INO), EU-FP7 Indo-European Network on Mathematics in Health and Disease and Belle & Belle II Collaboration.

ITER-Project

Institute of Plasma Research (IPR), Bhabha Atomic Research Centre (BARC) and Indira Gandhi Centre for Atomic Research (IGCAR) are involved in the design, material development, thermo fluid MHD analysis and various aspects of Lead Lithium Cooled Ceramic Breeder (LLCB) Test Blanket Module (TBM) for lTER necessary are being done at the (TER-lndia laboratory, which will then be transferred to the vendor site after due process and approval. Good progress has been achieved and other various R&D activities.

Other Activities

Research Education Linkages

The Department of Atomic Energy supports the research education linkages mainly through grants-in-aid to institutes of national eminence, funding of extra-mural research, DAE-UGC consortium for scientific research and others.

Research reactor Dhruva at BARC continued to serve as a national facility for neutron beam research. A number of research scholars from various academic institutions in the country utilized the reactor under the aegis of the UGC-DAE Consortium for Scientific Research. The Variable Energy Cyclotron were utilized by in-house experimental groups of VECC, as well as by experimentalists from several national laboratories and academic institutions for conducting experiments in the various fields of research. Nuclear counting and calibration facilities of IGCAR were extended to various institutions involved in BRNS projects, researchers and industries in the southern region. The Indus synchrotron radiation sources, a national facility, was used by scientists and students from various universities, national institutes and research laboratories all over the country.

Human Resource Development and Knowledge Management

Homi Bhabha National Institute

The Homi Bhabha National Institute (HBNI) accredited as a deemed university by Ministry of Human Resource and Development (MHRD) completed ten years of its existence. HBNI continued its academic programmes by offering various courses with its eight Boards of Studies namely as Chemical Sciences, Engineering Sciences, Health Sciences, Life Sciences, Mathematical Sciences, Physical Sciences, Strategic Studies and Undergraduate Studies. Degrees and diplomas including Ph.D were awarded to students. HBNI continued to strengthen its linkages with premier research and academic institutes in the country and abroad.

Training

Selection of trainees under Orientation Course for Engineering Graduates & Science Post-Graduates (OCES) and DAE Graduate Fellowship Schemes (DGFS) at BARC were pursued with high standards.

At IGCAR the training programmes for Trainee Scientific Officers (TSOs) and doctoral programmes in the frontier areas of engineering & basic sciences for the inducted research scholars were continued.

BARC Training School, AMD Campus, Hyderabad continued its activity in the sixth year by imparting induction training to Trainee Scientific Officers (TSO) in Geology and Geophysics.

Human Resource Development activities at RRCAT were continued to be enhanced by extending the available research facilities for training of university students in the areas of accelerators, lasers and their applications.

The Administrative Training Institute (ATI), with the motto "Prashikshaneshu Dakshprayate—Training Empowers" made its presence at national level by bagging the National Award for Excellence in Training, 2015 in the Management of Training category from Department of Personnel and Training, Government of India and UNDP. During the year, ATI offered wide range of programmes starting from induction to post retirement and periodic in-service programmes, subject specific workshops ensuring depth and range.

All the aided institutions such as SINP, TMC, IOP, HRI and IMSc of DAE continued to provide training by conducting various training programmes for the students and the research scholars.

Sponsored Research

Promotion of Extra-mural Research in Nuclear Science

The Board of Research in Nuclear Sciences (BRNS) continued to award projects to young scientists to initiate them in a career of research and Dr. K. S. Krishnan Research Associateship to identify and encourage highly talented young scientists and technologists. The DAE Graduate Fellowship Scheme (DGFS) for inducting Graduate Level students doing M.Tech at the IITs, Visiting Scientists programme for promoting short term in-house interactions amongst senior level experts and the Raja Ramanna Fellowship for reasonably long-term involvement of the eminent scientists and engineers in the various on-going programmes of the Department were continued. The Homi Bhabha Chair was instituted to avail the honourable services of scientists and technologists who have distinguished themselves at national and international levels.

During the year 2015-16, 214 new research projects were sanctioned till December, 2015.

Under DAE Graduate Fellowship Scheme (DGFS), fellowship was offered/awarded to M.Tech students studying in different IITs. New students were inducted under DGFS-Ph.D programme.

Promotion of Mathematics

The National Board for Higher Mathematics (NBHM) continued to provide grants for promotion of activities in pure and applied Mathematics, under several schemes, including support to research projects, travel grants for participation in workshops, conferences, and undertaking collaborative research, funds for organizing conferences, etc.

NBHM continued to be in-charge of the Mathematics Olympiad activity for talented young students at higher secondary (the plus two) level. This year six-member team secured 1 silver medal and two bronze medals and three Honourable Mentions at the 56th International Mathematical Olympiad held at Chiang Mai, Thailand.

This year NBHM has sponsored 51 delegates for participation in the prestigious International Congress of Industrial and Applied Mathematics (ICIAM) - 2015 event, held in Beijing, China during August 10-14, 2015.

Grants-in-AID

Grants to Aided Institutions

The aided institutions of the DAE are an integral part of the Department. The Department has nine aided institutions fully funded in terms of their recurring and non-recurring expenditure. These institutions are growing at a faster pace in terms of the projects undertaken by them. University of Mumbai & Department of Atomic Energy Centre for Excellence in Basic Sciences (UM-DAE-CBS) has been recently granted the status of aided institution of the Department of Atomic Energy w.e.f. January 01, 2016.

Grants to Cancer Hospitals

The Department of Atomic Energy (DAE) is releasing grant to Dr. B. Barooah Cancer Institute (BBCI), Guwahati through Tripartite Agreement (which was signed among DAE, the North Eastern Council (NEC) and the Government of Assam.

Olympiad Programme

The Homi Bhabha Centre for Science Education (HBCSE) successfully hosted the International Physics Olympiad.

Information Technology Application Development

The highlights of the Information Technology Application Development at IGCAR included Integration, Testing & Commissioning of BHEL steam water system / turbo generator Simulator; Deployment of Wireless Sensor Network for Radiation Monitoring; 3D Modeling and Animation of Power Manipulator and Containment Box of Pyroprocessing R&D facility; Advanced IT Enabled Customizable Knowledge Management Portal for IGCAR and development of continuous air monitoring system.

Collaborative Programmes

Collaboration with industry under incubation included Incubation of Development of a Radioprotector Drug technology, Development of Diamond Waste Powder (Uniform Size Particles) Processing Methodology and Development of Fluoride Removal Reagent.

In order to promote technologies developed by BARC for rural populace, establishment of DAE Technology Display & Dissemination Facility (DTDDF) centres all over India are proposed under XII Plan in collaboration with educational institutes. Out of 24 proposals received from all over India, preliminary meetings and site visits to 7 institutes have already been concluded. Further, MoUs with two institutes have been finalized.

Societal Initiatives

Four agreements were approved for signing with companies/organisations and individuals to promote rural entrepreneurship with BARC technologies under Advanced Knowledge & Rural Technology Implementation (AKRUTI) Tech Pack. The agreements provide a perpetual license for exclusive rural deployment of the technologies like Foldable Solar Dryer, Domestic Water Purifier, Soil Organic Carbon Detection and Testing Kit, Nisargruna, Vibrothermal disinfestor, Solar BWRO, Dip N Drink Membrane Pouch, Litchi Preservation and Banana Tissue Culture.

Intellectual Property Rights

During the calendar year 2015, ten new inventions and one national phase entry were reviewed for the patentability. DAE filed eight new patent applications which includes two applications under PCT (Patent Co-operation Treaty), five Indian and one application in USA.

Seven of the previously filed patents have been granted to the Department during the year. These includes two each in India & USA and one each in Canada, Europe & South Africa.

Apart from patents, DAE has also filed 200 trademarks applications during the period. These applications were filed under various classes and consists of 49 logos, 31 word marks which include the acronyms of DAE and its 29 units and the DAE slogan "Atoms in the Service of the Nation".

Public Sector Undertakings

Financial performance of DAE's public sector undertakings namely, the Nuclear Power Corporation of India Ltd., Uranium Corporation of India Ltd., Indian Rare Earth Ltd. and Electronics Corporation of India Ltd. are given below (BHAVINI is yet to commence commercial operations).

Nuclear Power Corporation of India Ltd.

The expected net profit after tax (PAT) for the year 2015-16 is about ₹ 2,300 crore. The net profit after tax for previous FY 2014-15 was ₹ 2,201 crore. NPCIL bonds continued to be rated at AAA (Highest Safety) by CRISIL and CARE.

Uranium Corporation of India Ltd.

The overall performance of the company during the year 2014-15 was satisfying. The total income of the company during the year 2014-15 was ₹ 890.24 crore (Previous year ₹ 814.30 crore). The profit before tax during the year 2014-15 was ₹ 11.34 crore. Performance of the company in terms of MoU signed with DAE is expected to be "Good".

Indian Rare Earths Ltd.

During the year 2015-16, the Gross Sales Turnover anticipated is ₹ 434.64 crore (provisional) against ₹ 420.97 crore of previous year. Anticipated loss in 2015-16 is ₹ 22.67 crore (provisional) compared to profit before tax of ₹ 3.15 crore in 2014-15.

Electronics Corporation of India Ltd.

Against the MoU target of ₹ 1,620 crore each for production and net sales, the Company achieved a production of ₹ 721 crore and a net sale of ₹ 690 crore upto December, 2015.

Indian Space Programme

O.W.: http//www.isro.org

Space activities in the country were initiated with the setting up of Indian National Committee for Space Research (INCOSPAR) in 1962. In the same year, work on Thumba Equatorial Rocket Launching Station (TERLS) near Thiruvananthapuram was also started. Indian Space Research Organisation (ISRO) was established in August, 1969. The Space Commission was constituted and established the Department of Space (DOS) in June, 1972 and brought

ISRO under DOS in 1972. Space Commission formulates the policies and oversees the implementation of the Indian space programme to promote the development and application of space science and technology for the socio-economic benefit of the country. DOS implements these programmes through, mainly, Indian Space Research Organisation (ISRO), Physical Research Laboratory (PRL), National Atmospheric Research Laboratory (NARL), North Eastern-Space Applications Centre (NE-SAC) and Semi-Conductor Laboratory (SCL). Antrix Corporation, established in 1992 as a government owned company, markets the space products and services. The establishment of space systems and their applications are coordinated by the national level committees, namely, INSAT Coordination Committee (ICC), Planning Committee on National Natural Resources Management System (PCNNRMS) and Advisory Committee for Space Sciences (ADCOS).

The year 2015 witnessed many significant achievements of the Indian Space programme which caught the attention of the country as well as the outside world. With the successful completion of the intended six month period by Mars Orbiter Spacecraft in its orbit around Planet Mars, India became the first country to achieve total success in its maiden attempt to explore Mars. Besides, the second consecutively successful launch of GSLV-MkII carrying the indigenous Cryogenic Upper Stage (CUS) underscored ISRO's capability in cryogenic rocket propulsion. The year also saw the launch of India's multi wavelength Space Observatory ASTROSAT and its successful operationalisation. Additionally, launch of IRNSS-1D and IRNSS-1E - the fourth and fifth satellites of the Indian Regional Navigation Satellite System (IRNSS) —by PSLV-C27 and PSLV-C31 respectively into the required sub-Geosynchronous Transfer Orbits (sub-GTO), also occurred during the year 2015-16. The year also witnessed the launch of India's latest communication satellite GSAT-15 carrying communication transponders and GAGAN payload. And, the launch by the workhorse PSLV of 17 foreign satellites, 11 of them in two dedicated commercial PSLV missions, is yet another highlight of the Indian space programme during the reporting period. The significant events of the Indian space programme during 2015-16 in chronological order are:

- On March 24, 2015, India's Mars Orbiter Spacecraft, which had earlier successfully entered into the scheduled orbit around planet Mars, completed the intended six month period in Mars orbit. As of February 2016 end, the spacecraft had completed seventeen months of operation in Mars orbit.
- IRNSS-1D, the fourth of the seven satellites constituting the IRNSS Constellation, was successfully launched by PSLV-C27 into a sub GTO on March 28, 2015. It was the 29th launch of PSLV as well as its 28th consecutively successful mission. IRNSS constellation will enable introduction of satellite based position, timing and velocity services to a spectrum of users in the country and to the neighbouring regions.

- PSLV-C28, the 30th flight of PSLV, was conducted on July 10, 2015, in which the vehicle placed United Kingdom's three DMC3 satellites, each weighing 447 kg, along with two auxiliary payloads, also from United Kingdom, into the required Sun Synchronous Orbit of 647 km height.
- GSLV-D6, the ninth flight of GSLV as well as the third flight of GSLV carrying indigenously developed Cryogenic Upper Stage (CUS), conducted on August 27, 2015, successfully launched 2117 kg GSAT-6 communication satellite into a Geosynchronous Transfer Orbit (GTO). It was the second consecutive success for GSLV carrying indigenous Cryogenic Upper Stage (GSLV-MkII).
- ASTROSAT, India's first multi wavelength astronomy mission, was successfully launched by PSLV-C30 along with six co-passenger satellites from abroad, into a 650 km orbit of 6 degree inclination on September 28, 2015.
- GSAT-15, India's latest communication satellite carrying communication transponders as well as GPS Aided Geo Augmented Navigation (GAGAN) payload was launched into GTO by the European Ariane-5 from Kourou, French Guiana on November 11, 2015.
- PSLV-C29, the thirty second flight of PSLV carrying six customer satellites from abroad including the 400 kg TeLEOS-1 of Singapore, successfully placed them in an orbit of 550 km height on December 16, 2015. This was the thirty first consecutive success of PSLV.
- IRNSS-1E, fifth of the seven satellites constituting IRNSS Constellation, was successfully launched on-board PSLV-C31 on January 20, 2016 into a sub Geosynchronous Transfer Orbit (sub GTO).

By February 2016 end, ISRO had a constellation of several commercial communication satellites, exclusive Meteorological satellites, Earth Observation satellites, Navigation satellites, a multi wavelength astronomical observatory and a spacecraft orbiting planet Mars.

Launch Vehicle Programme

During the year under review, ISRO's workhorse Launch Vehicle PSLV, in its 'XL" version, placed two Navigation Satellites IRNSS-1D and 1E in the required sub Geosynchronous Transfer Orbits in two separate flights—PSLV-C27 and PSLV-C31. Besides, the 'XL' version of PSLV launched five satellites from United Kingdom successfully into a 647 km Sun Synchronous Orbit in its 30th flight (PSLV-C28). PSLV-XL also launched India's first multi-wavelength space observatory ASTROSAT along with six customer satellites from abroad, in its thirty first flight (PSLV-30). In its 'Core Alone' version, PSLV placed six satellites from Singapore including the 400 kg Satellite TeLeos-1 into a 550 km orbit, further proving its reliability and versatility. Another prominent development in the Indian launch vehicle programme was the second consecutively successful flight (GSLV-D6) of GSLV-MkII on August 27, 2015, which was equipped with indigenous cryogenic upper stage. This flight further highlighted ISRO's strength in cryogenic propulsion technologies.

Activities pertaining to LVM3 (GSLV-MkIII) launch vehicle, capable of launching four tonne satellites into a Geosynchronous Transfer Orbit (GTO), progressed well during the year with the successful ground test of its S200 booster to validate the changes in its head end segment as well as the flight and the extended duration hot (ground) tests of CE-20 cryogenic engine of its third stage. This apart, research and development activities in semi-cryogenic propulsion engine, air breathing propulsion and re-usable launch vehicle technology are also being pursued in earnest in an effort towards reducing the cost of access to space. Development of critical technologies for undertaking human spaceflight has also made additional progress.

Satellite Programme

IRNSS-1D and 1E, the fourth and fifth satellites of the IRNSS Constellation, were successfully launched on board PSLV-C27 and PSLV-C31 on March 28, 2015 and January 20, 2016 respectively. IRNSS satellites employ the standard I-1K structure with a power handling capability of around 1660 W and a lift-off mass of about 1,425 kg. Like their three predecessors, IRNSS-1D and IE carry a navigation payload as well as a C-band ranging payload. The satellites also carry Corner Cube Retro Reflectors for laser ranging. In Orbit Tests (IOT) of Navigation Payload, Ranging Payload and TT&C transponder of IRNSS-1D and 1E have been successfully completed during the year and the satellites have been cleared for Navigation activities. The 2117 kg GSAT-6, an advanced communication satellite providing services through five spot beams in S-band and a national beam in C-band, was successfully launched by GSLV-D6 on August 27, 2015 into GTO. Later, the satellite was placed in its geostationary orbital slot with the help of its own propulsion system. GSAT-15, India's latest communication satellite carrying Ku-band communication transponders, launched on-board European Ariane-5 VA227 on November 11, 2015, was later successfully taken to its geostationary orbital slot by firing its Liquid Apogee Motor in steps from MCF, Hassan.

The new satellites being built for meeting the country's future requirements include IRNSS-1F, and 1G which are planned to be launched on-board PSLV, and GSAT-9 and GSAT-6A communication satellites to be launched by GSLV-MkII, GSAT-19 by GSLV-MkIII (LVM3), GSAT-17, GSAT-18 and GSAT-11 communication satellites planned to be launched through procured launch. In the domain of earth observation satellites, it is planned to design, develop and build Cartosat-2E and Cartosat-3 in the Cartosat series of satellites, Resourcesat-2A in the Resourcesat series, Oceansat-3 and Scatsat-1 in the Oceansat series, INSAT-3DR and GISAT-1 in the INSAT series for meteorological applications during the 12th Five Year Plan.

Space Science Programme

Mars Orbiter Mission is India's first interplanetary spacecraft mission as well as the first Indian spacecraft mission to planet Mars. With a lift-off mass of 1340 kg, the Mars Orbiter Spacecraft carries five payloads – Mars Colour Camera, Thermal infrared Imaging Spectrometer, Methane Sensor for Mars, Lyman Alpha Photometer and Mars Exospheric Neutral Composition Analyser. Mars Orbiter Mission primarily envisaged to demonstrate the technologies for building, launching and navigating an unmanned spacecraft to Mars as well as to explore the planet by placing it in an orbit around that planet.

The spacecraft, which was launched by PSLV-C25 on November 05, 2013 from SDSC, Sriharikota into an elliptical earth parking orbit, was successfully placed in orbit around Mars on September 24, 2014. Mars Orbiter Mission is primarily a technological mission, which enabled ISRO to achieve critical mission operations with enhanced autonomy functions and stringent capabilities of propulsion and other spacecraft systems.

Another prominent highlight of the year was yet another space science mission – ASTROSAT – which was successfully launched on September 28, 2015 by India's workhorse launch vehicle PSLV. ASTROSAT is India's first multi wavelength observatory capable of simultaneously viewing the universe in the visible, ultra violet and X-ray regions of the electromagnetic spectrum. After its launch into the planned orbit, ASTROSAT became operational following extensive in orbit test of its five payloads. The future space science missions of ISRO include Chandrayaan-2, a follow-on mission to Chandrayaan-1 with an Orbiter, Lander and Rover to explore the moon, is to be launched onboard GSLV and Aditya-1, a scientific mission for solar studies carrying five scientific payloads including a Coronagraph. ADITYA is planned to be placed in a halo orbit around the L1 Legrangian point.

Space Applications and Disaster Management

Support Remote Sensing applications projects at national, state and local levels are being carried out through well-established multi-pronged implementation architecture of National Natural Resources Management System (NNRMS) in the country. During the year, Indian Remote Sensing Satellite constellation helped in Agricultural Crops Inventory, Agricultural Drought, Forest Fire, Landslides and Earthquakes Monitoring, Groundwater Prospects Mapping, Inventory; Monitoring of Glacial Lakes/Water Bodies, Sericulture Development and Satellite Aided Search and Rescue. The hallmark of Indian space programme has been the application-oriented efforts and the benefits that have accrued to the country. The societal services offered by INSAT/GSAT satellites in the area of tele-education and telemedicine were continued during the year. Today, tele-education network has about 60,000 classrooms connected to various academic institutions and universities. ISRO telemedicine network facilities now cover 380 hospitals connecting 302 rural hospitals and 18 mobile vans to 60 superspecialty hospitals for providing healthcare to citizens, especially in rural areas.

The Disaster Management Support (DMS) Programme of ISRO continues to provide space based information and services to the State and Central Government Departments to strengthen the disaster management activities. The major activities during the year were monitoring all the flood events, supporting the disaster management during the Nepal earthquake and monitoring the landslide dammed Phutkal river in Jammu and Kashmir. In 2015, flood monitoring and mapping was carried out for floods in 10 states and more than 105 flood maps were disseminated to the concerned State and Central officers, in addition to making it available to users on the web through Bhuvan and NDEM web portals. LIDAR based experimental flood depth maps for part of Lakhimpur district of Assam were generated and disseminated to the state agencies for severe floods during August 23 and 25 and September 4, 2015.

Space Commerce

Antrix Corporation, the commercial arm of the Department of Space, has been marketing the Indian space products and services in the global market. Under commercial contract with Antrix, 57 international customer satellites have been successfully launched by PSLV since 1999. During 2015, PSLV successfully launched 17 satellites from abroad. Many proposals from international customers for the launch of their satellites onboard PSLV are under discussion and active consideration.

Indian Space Industry

Involvement of Indian space industry continued during the year. In the past, it has made significant contribution towards the realisation of subsystems required for Indian space programme. Department of Space has associated more than 500 small, medium and large scale industries while implementing various programmes. So far, the Department of Space has transferred about 300 technologies to Indian industries for commercialisation and undertaken technical consultancies in various fields.

International Cooperation

International cooperation is an integral part of Indian space activities, and ISRO continues to lay importance on bilateral and multilateral relations with space agencies and space related bodies with the aim of taking up new scientific and technological challenges, defining international frameworks for exploitation and utilisation of outer space for peaceful purposes, refining space policies and building and strengthening existing ties between the countries. During the year, ISRO signed cooperative agreements with the French, Canadian, Russian and Chinese space agencies as well the US Geological Survey, Jet Propulsion Laboratory and Kuwait Institute of Scientific Research.

Indian Institute of Space Science and Technology

Towards capacity building in human resources and to meet the growing demands of the Indian Space Programme, the Indian Institute of Space Science and Technology (IIST), a deemed university, was established at Thiruvananthapuram in 2007. Towards the fulfillment of its primary objective of providing quality manpower to ISRO, 99 students of 2011 batch of B. Tech graduates were placed as Scientists/ Engineers at various centres of ISRO in 2015.

Ministry of Earth Sciences

Ministry of Earth Sciences has been striving to address a wide range of issues relating to earth system science with a view to study the complex interactions among various components of the system namely, atmosphere, oceans, cryosphere, geosphere and biosphere. The objective of this endeavor is to improve our understanding of the earth system and its components leading to improvement of the services for socio-environment benefits of the country. In 2015, several major milestones have been accomplished and it has been overall a productive year. The important achievements include (i)International Indian Ocean Expedition (IIOE); (ii)International Ocean Drilling Programme; (iii)Strengthening of the Polar Observations; (iv)Ocean Mixing Monsoon Experiments; (v) Improved Weather Forecasts and the Seasonal Monsoon Forecast for the year 2015; (vi) Winter Fog Campaign 2015-16; (vii) Borehole Geophysical Research Laboratory (BRGL); (viii) Nepal Earthquake Monitoring; and (ix) Ocean State Forecasts. The salient features of the activities carried out under the various schemes are summarized as under.

Atmospheric and Climate Research, Observations Science Services (ACROSS)

2015 Southwest Monsoon Forecast vis-à-vis Actual Precipitation: The seasonal forecasts for monsoon rainfall were provided with good accuracy. For the first time, deficient monsoon rainfall during the 2015 season was predicted accurately. The forecast of the monsoon season for the country as a whole was 88 per cent with a model error of ±4per cent of Long Period Average (LPA) against the actual rainfall of 86per cent of LPA. The predictability of active and break cycles has been improved. Quantitative Precipitation Forecast (QPF) for different river basins is provided for flood forecasting. Dynamic models were employed on experimental basis to predict quantitative precipitation associated with the monsoon. Out of the total 36 meteorological subdivisions, 18 subdivisions constituting 55 per cent of the total area of the country received normal seasonal rainfall and 17 subdivisions (39per cent of the total area of the country) received deficient seasonal rainfall. One subdivision (West Rajasthan) constituting 6 per cent of the total area of the country received excess rainfall. Monthly rainfall over the country as a whole was 116 per cent of LPA in June, 84 per cent of LPA in July, 78 per cent of LPA in August, and 76 per cent of LPA in September. The monsoon onset over Kerala for this year was on 5th June against the forecast of 30th May.

Agro-Meteorological Advisory Services (AAS)

The AAS services have been extended to district level from the agro-climatic zone level (cluster of 4-6 districts) and now covers 608 districts of the country.

Currently, over 11.54 million farmers are receiving crop specific advisories under the AAS services in regional languages. Block level forecast for 37 districts (342 blocks) has been initiated in pilot mode.

Winter Fog Campaign 2015-16

Recognizing the importance of fog forecasting for Aviation sector, an observational campaign was launched to understand different physical features of fog and factors responsible for its genesis, intensity and duration. For the first time, an observational campaign was conducted at the Indira Gandhi International Airport (IGIA) and at ICAR Institute at Pusa during this winter season (2015-16) in pilot mode.

Ocean Services, Technology, Observations, Resources, Modeling and Science (O-STORMS)

Autonomous Coring System (ACS) sea trials were conducted and drilling qualification trial was conducted at 1057 m water depth in KG basin, Bay of Bengal with drilling up to 24 m below the sea floor. Similar trial was conducted at 816 m water depth, offshore Chennai with drilling up to 40 m below the sea floor. The Corner Stone Laying function of ESSO—National Institute of Ocean Technology (NIOT), Nellore was held in 2015. A baseline survey for analysis of physico-chemical and biological parameters of the water from Buckingham canal, Swarnamukhi river and open sea of Pamanji coast at the newly inaugurated seafront facility near Nellore, Andhra Pradesh has been successfully completed.

As part of marine algal biotechnology, biodiesel was extracted and with this fuel, ESSO-NIOT vehicle was successfully operated from Nellore to Chennai on April 25, 2015.

Ocean Science and Services

The Indian Tsunami Early Warning Centre (ITEWC) kept the watch of all tsunamigenic earthquakes in and around the Indian Ocean and issued appropriate messages in the event of any threats from potential tsunamis. The early warnings by the Ministry on the wind-waves and storm surges during the occurrence of cyclone 'Ashoba' (during 8-10 June, 2015) helped the authorities to reduce the damages to the property and loss of life. The Coast Guard appreciated the timely assistance that helped in the search of missing Coast Guard aircraft off-the coast of Karaikal on June 11, 2015. MoES extended the ocean forecast services to two other Indian Ocean Rim countries, Sri Lanka and Seychelles. The Ocean State Forecast services for neighbouring countries, Seychelles and Sri Lanka was inaugurated on July 10, 2015 by the Union Minister for Earth Sciences, Dr. Harsh Vardhan in New Delhi.

The potential fishing zone (PFZ) advisories and specific advisories (Tuna) to fishermen were also continued. An atlas of the PFZ advisories was prepared for ready reference. The observational network was augmented by installing 11 additional Automated Weather Stations (AWS) in the vessels operated by Shipping Corporation of India and deploying 20 additional Argo floats in the Indian Ocean. Periodic maintenance were carried out to the observational platforms—RAMA moored buoy array, Wave rider buoy network, coastal and equatorial ADCPs, Tsunami buoy network and tide gauge network. A cruise onboard ORV Sagar Nidhi organized during 21st August – September 15, 2015 in the northern Bay of Bengal as part of the Ocean Mixing and Monsoon (OMM) programme collected very high resolution data to study the upper ocean mixing processes.

Several state-of-the art instruments, including Sea Glider, underway CTD (uCTD) and Inherent Optical Profiler (IOP) were used in this observational campaign. The second very high-resolution operational ocean forecasting system was setup for the south-eastern Arabian Sea, now covering for the entire west coast of India, as part of the ongoing High-resolution Operational Ocean Forecast and Reanalysis System (HOOFS) project. This system is capable of accurately forecasting the three dimensional structure of ocean at a spatial resolution of approximately 2.25 km x 2.25 km. R&D efforts are progressing well to setup the HOOFS for the Bay of Bengal.

Large scale fish production through mariculture is the viable alternative to cope up with the ever increasing demand for fish proteins. Towards this, an open sea cage culture mooring system was designed and developed for commercially important marine fishes in different sea conditions with the available marine engineering and biological expertise. The open sea cage culture technology seems to be an ideal alternate livelihood option for the coastal fisherfolk, generating a considerable employment opportunity in the country and pave way to achieve the fish food production targets of the nation.

A Wave Atlas for the Indian coast has been published which acts as a reference for basic wave related information, viz. design wave height, wave approach, period, etc. in the public domain, hitherto not readily available. It presents the statistics derived from past information using simulated wave data. The simulation domain covers major portion of the Indian Ocean including the Bay of Bengal and the Arabian Sea. Towards commemorating the 50th Anniversary of IIOE, the Ministry has taken a lead in launching the IIOE-2 in the Indian Ocean in coordination with Intergovernmental Oceanographic Commission of UNESCO.

Polar and Cryosphere Research (PACER)

The Indian Arctic observatory deployed in July 2014 was successfully retrieved on 15th July 2015. The observatory that is designed and deployed by NIOT-OOS has functioned well and recorded one year data continuously which is a major achievement in the area of in-situ observation. New Arctic observatory (Ind ARC II) with additional biogeochemical and acoustic sensors was deployed successfully by NIOT-OOS/OA team along with NCAOR on July 19, 2015 in the Arctic. The next generation Tsunami surface buoy which was indigenously designed, developed and deployed as a part of Sagar Bhoomi buoy system in Bay of Bengal, was retrieved after successful functioning for more than a year and found to be in order.

The technology for the demonstration in the Polar regions has been achieved with the development of Polar Remotely Operable Vehicle (PROVe). PROVe was deployed on 9th and 10th of February 2015 at Priydarshini Lake, Antarctica. System functionality was successfully tested and it recorded the lake bed videography by black & white, color and HD camera showing the abundance of algal mats.

Seismology and Geoscience Research (SAGE)

In May 2015, two sites (U 1456 and U 1457) were drilled in Laxmi Basin in the eastern Arabian Sea to document the co-evolution of mountain building, weathering, erosion, and climate over a range of timescales. A set of two sediment cores were recovered from Sites U 1456 and U 1457 in the Laxmi Basin, penetrating 1109.4 and 1108.6 m below seafloor (mbsf), respectively. The National Centre for Seismology with the help of its nationwide network of seismographs reported the occurrence of the 25th April 2015 Nepal earthquake (M 7.9) which occurred 80 km northwest of Kathmandu.

This event was also felt in all northern, eastern and some parts of central India. The main shock produced lots of seismological and geodetic data. The strong motion accelerograph network in India has produced remarkable data which provides constraints on the attenuation relations, site response and source dynamics.

A Borehole Geophysics Research Laboratory (BGRL) has been set up at Karad, Maharashtra to carry out Scientific Deep Drilling Investigation in Koyna-Warna region of Maharashtra. The Koyna region located close to the west coast of India is the most outstanding example of Reservoir Triggered Seismicity (RTS). A major national project, "Scientific Deep Drilling in the Koyna Intra-plate Seismic zone of Maharashtra", has been undertaken for directly measuring the in-situ physical properties of rocks, porefluid pressure, hydrological parameters, temperature and other parameters of an intraplate, active fault zone in the near-field of earthquakes – before, during and after their occurrence.

The National Center for Seismology (NCS) was established as an attached office of the Ministry, with the objectives of inter-alia (i) provide earthquake related information to all user agencies in the shortest possible time (ii)earthquake hazard and risk related products of specific regions required by various agencies as mitigative measures (iii) carryout research in pure and applied seismology and earthquake precursory phenomena, earthquake processes and modeling. A project of upgradation of 44 existing seismological observatories and establishment of 34 new seismological observatories has been initiated. A total of 23 seismological observatories have been upgraded and one new observatory has been established. NCS is also involved in the microzonation studies and has just completed the seismic hazard microzonation analysis of NCT Delhi on 1:10,000 scale. NCS has taken an initiative to carry out the seismic microzonation studies for additional 30 Indian cities having population more than half a million and lying in seismic zone III, IV and V.

Reachout

The Regional Integrated Multi-Hazard Early Warning System (RIMES) was established for cooperation for exchanging information to deal with natural, technological and human-induced disasters particularly to minimize the loss of life and property. Twenty three countries of the Indian Ocean are currently members of RIMES viz., Afghanistan, Armenia, Bangladesh, Bhutan, Comoros, India, Lao PDR, Maldives, Mongolia, Mozambique, Myanmar, Nepal, Papua New Guinea, Pakistan, Philippines, Seychelles, Sri Lanka, Tanzania, Thailand, Timor-Leste, Uzbekistan, and Vietnam.

National Facility

The dedicated Accelerator Mass Spectrometry (AMS) Measurement Facility for 14Carbon has been established at IUAC, New Delhi in March 2015 with Ministry support. The facility will be used for the measurement of 14 Carbon and to measure ultra-low concentrations of the isotopes of Carbon for applications in radiocarbon dating and earth sciences. The facility has been named as MoES-IUAC AMS facility. The facility will enable researchers in India to analyze their samples for 14 Carbon and radiocarbon dating.

High Performance Computing System (HPC)

The HPC system Bhaskara at ESSO-NCMRWF with a peak computing power of 350 Teraflops and 67 Terabytes of memory was dedicated to the nation by the Minister for Science and Technology and Earth Sciences on 2nd June 2015. With the commissioning of Bhaskara, the overall ESSO HPC facility has increased to a peak computing power of 1.1 Petaflops. 1.7 International Interface: During the last one year, a total of six MoUs have been signed with USA, China, State of Qatar, Germany, Sweden and Bangladesh, respectively for cooperation in the field of marine scientific research and other earth system science related subjects. Several actions have been taken for implementation of programmes under the respective MoUs.

Autonomous Institutions

The Department has established a number of autonomous institutions for basic, applied and translational research in the field of life sciences and biotechnology.

National Institute of Immunology (NII), New Delhi

NII's research efforts continued on frontier areas of modern biology pertaining to disease processes with an aim to provide understanding of the basis of disease pathology to enable better diagnosis and treatment. The innovative research at the institute has resulted in substantial intellectual property and transfer of several technologies to the industry.

National Centre for Cell Sciences (NCCS), Pune

NCCS's research focus on cell organization and function, genome architecture and regulation, regulatory RNAs and gene expression, macromolecular structure and cell function, stem cell and regeneration, biology of cancer and other diseases, pathogenesis and cellular response and microbial ecology have continued.

Centre for DNA Fingerprinting and Diagnostics (CDFD), Hyderabad

CDFD has excelled in its diverse activities that include DNA based services, in human DNA profiling to law enforcement agencies and other authorities of the nation, toward diagnostics and counselling of genetic disorders and for certification of basmati rice for export along with undertaking molecular biology research in other areas. The Centre has achieved an impressive record of publication in international peer reviewed journals and of patents.

National Brain Research Centre (NBRC), Manesar

NBRC's research efforts are focused to understand brain function in health and disease, generate trained human resources with the capability to carry out interdisciplinary research in neurosciences along with promoting neuroscience in India through networking among institutions across the country. As a part of centre for Epilepsy research, the Magneto- Encephalogram has become fully functional during the year. This is now being used for accurate source localization in epilepsy surgery and also for basic and translational research on brain mapping.

Institute of Life Sciences (ILS), Bhubaneshwar

Research activities in ILS are centered around infectious disease biology, various aspects of gene function as well as regulation and translational research through technology development.

National Institute of Biomedical Genomics (NIBMG), Kalyani

NIBMG has continued its research efforts to unravel the genomic basis of various cancers, chronic diseases (such as, chronic pancreatitis and non-alcoholic fatty liver disease) and infectious diseases (such as Tuberculosis, Hepatitis C, Sepsis). Biomedical Genomics Centre's flagship project on non-alcoholic fatty liver disease gained momentum this year and exome sequencing of DNA of several patients were undertaken.

Regional Centre for Biotechnology (RCB), Gurgaon

RCB was set up for education, training and research in biotechnology under the auspices of UNESCO as a Category II Centre. The Centre undertakes contemporary research at the interface of disciplines with integration of science, engineering and medicine with emphasis on relevance to the regional needs.

Institute of Stem Cell Science and Regenerative Medicine (InStem), Bangalore

InStem, Bangalore houses six scientific themes and a clinical translational unit. These include: Centre for Inflammation and Tissue Homeostasis, Centre for Brain Development and Repair, Centre for Cardiovascular Biology and Disease, Centre for Chemical Biology and Therapeutics, Technology Team and Regulation of Cell Fate. Clinical translational possibilities are being attempted in Clinical Translational Unit located at Christian Medical College, Vellore.

26 Transport

A WELL-KNIT and coordinated system of transport plays an important role in the sustained economic growth of country. The present transport system of the country comprises several modes including rail, road, coastal shipping, air transport, etc. Transport has recorded a substantial growth over the years both in spread of network and in output of the system. The Ministry of Shipping and the Ministry of Road Transport and Highways are responsible for the formation and implementation of policies and programmes for the development of various modes of transport save the railways and the civil aviation.

Railways

The Railways in India provide the principal mode of transportation for freight and passengers. It brings together people from the farthest corners of the country and makes possible the conduct of business, sightseeing, pilgrimage and education. The Indian Railways have been a great integrating force during the last more than 163 years. It has bound the economic life of the country and helped in accelerating the development of industry and agriculture. From a very modest beginning in 1853, when the first train steamed off from Mumbai to Thane, a distance of 34 kms, Indian Railways have grown into a vast network of 7,137 stations spread over a route length of 66,030 km with a fleet of 10,773 locomotives, 51,798 passenger service vehicles, 7,000 other coaching vehicles and 2,54,006 wagons. The growth of Indian Railways in the 163 years of its existence is thus phenomenal. It has played a vital role in the economic industrial and social development of the country. The network runs multi-gauge operations extending over 66,030 route kilometers. Some important efficiency indices for 2014-15, compared to 2013-14 are as follows:

Efficiency Index	Broad Gauge				Metre Gauge			
	2011-12	2012-13	2013-14	2014-15	2011-12	2012-13	2013-14	2014-15
Net tonnes Kms: per wagon per day	9,261	8,453	8,068*	8,113*	632	907	1245	1029
Speed (kmph) of all goods trains (all traction)	25.0	25.5	25.9	23.8*	14.1	14.0	14.5	16.5
Percentage of loaded to total wagon (kms)	66.1	65.4	65.1	65.2	51.5	52.3	52.4	50.9

Net Load per goods train (tonnes)	1,711	1732	1592*	1703	443	455	565	902
Net tonnes kms per engine hour	20,466	19468	18804*	18586	2151	2386	3453*	5467
Passenger vehicle per kms per day	550	558	565*	581*	203	191	138	89

(* Revised)

About 36.66 per cent of the route kilometre and 45.19 per cent of running track kilometre and 46.84 per cent of total track kilometre is electrified. The network is divided into 17 Zones. Divisions are the basic operating units. The 17 zones and their respective headquarters are given below:

Zonal Railways	Headquarters
Central	Mumbai
Eastern	Kolkata
East Coast	Bhubaneshwar
East Central	Hajipur
Northern	New Delhi
North Central	Allahabad
North Eastern	Gorakhpur
Northeast Frontier	Maligaon (Guwahati)
North Western	Jaipur
Southern	Chennai
South Central	Secunderabad
South Eastern	Kolkata
South East Central Railway	Bilaspur
South Western Railway	Hubli
Western	Mumbai
West Central Railway	Jabalpur
Metro Railway	Kolkata

The rolling stock fleet of Indian Railways in services in 2015 comprised 43 steam, 5,714 diesel and 5,016 electric locomotives. Currently, the Railways are in process of inducting new designs of fuel-efficient locomotives of higher horse power, high-speed coaches and modern bogies for freight traffic. Modern signalling like panel inter-locking, route relay inter-locking, centralized traffic control, automatic signalling and multi-aspect colour light signalling, are being progressively introduced. Railways have made impressive progress regarding indigenous production of rolling stock and variety of other equipment over the years and is now self-sufficient in most of the items.

The main objectives of railways have been to develop the transport infrastructure to carry the projected quantum of traffic and meet the developmental needs of the economy. Since the inception of the planned era in 1950-51, Indian Railways have implemented nine five-year plans, apart from annual plans in some years. During the Plans, emphasis was laid on a comprehensive programme of system modernization. With capacity being, stretched to its limits, investments of cost-effective technological changes become inescapable in order to meet the ever-increasing demand for rail transport. Along with the major thrust directed towards rehabilitation of assets, technological changes and upgradation of standards were initiated in important areas of track, locomotives, passenger coaches, wagon bogie designs, signalling and telecommunication.

Public Undertakings

There are thirteen undertakings under the administrative control of the Ministry of Railways, viz. (i) Rail India Technical & Economic Services Limited (RITES), (ii) Indian Railway Construction (IRCON) International Limited, (iii) Indian Railway Finance Corporation Limited (IRFC), (iv) Container Corporation of India Limited (CONCOR), (v) Konkan Railway Corporation Limited (KRCL), (vi) Mumbai Railway Vikas Corporation Limited (MRVC) (vii) Indian Railway Catering & Tourism Corporation Ltd. (IRCTC), (viii) Railtel Corporation of India Ltd. (Rail Tel), (xi) Rail Vikas Nigam Ltd. (RVNL) (ix) Mumbai Rail Vikas Nigam Ltd. (MRVNL), (x) Dedicated Freight Corridor Corporation of India Limited (DFCCIL), (xi) Bharat Wagon and Engineering Co. Ltd. (BWEL, (xii) Burn Standard Company Limited (BSCL) and (xiii) Braithwaite and Company Limited (BCL).

Research and Development

The Research Design and Standards Organization (RDSO) at Lucknow is the R&D wing of Indian Railways. It functions as a consultant to the Indian Railways in technical matters. It also provides consultancy to other organizations connected with railway manufacture and design.

Railway Finance

Since 1924-25, railway finances remained separated from general revenues. They have their own funds and accounts and the Railway Budget is presented separately to Parliament. However, the Railways contribute to the general revenue a dividend on the capital invested. Quantum of contribution is reviewed periodically by a Parliamentary Convention Committee.

Freight Traffic

Rapid progress in industrial and agricultural sectors has generated a higher level of demand for rail transport, particularly in core sectors like coal, iron and steel ores, petroleum products and essential commodities such as food grains, fertilizers, cement, sugar, salt, edible oils etc. Revenue from freight traffic increased from 73.2 million tonnes in 1950-51 to 969.05 million tonnes in 2011-2012. In 2014-15, IR loaded 1,101.09 million tonnes of which 1,095.26 million tonnes was revenue-earning and 5.83 million tonnes non-revenue-earning, and achieved total net tonne kilometres (NTKMs) of 683 billion as against 666 billion in 2013-14. The freight earnings went up from 91,570.85 crore in 2013-14 to 1,03,100.15 crore in 2014-15, registering a growth of 12.59 per cent.

Achievements

I. Passenger Amenities

Railways launched three social media platforms on Facebook, Twitter and You Tube with the handle @railminindia. It employed first of its kind, a real time 24x7 public grievance system through Twitter and provided medical, security and other emergency assistance to travelling passengers. All India Security Helpline 182 was set up to report any untoward incident and seek emergency help during travel. The All India Passenger Helpline '138' provided for all other query/complaints during travel. E-catering facility launched at 100 stations. 408 railway stations are designated for it. Reservation quota of two lower berths per coach in sleeper class enhanced to four lower berths per coach for senior citizens and women. Tatkal reservation timings have been staggered to serve dual purpose of providing convenience to the passengers and for staggering traffic on the e-ticket portal.All agents are debarred from booking tickets during first thirty minutes of opening of booking. Automatic refund of Confirmed /RAC e-tickets on cancellation of trains similar to waitlisted e-tickets is granted without filing of TDR. Time limit for booking reserved tickets was increased to 120 days from April 2015. E-ticketing facility launched for disabled persons and for accredited journalist on concession pass. Out of 1252 stations identified for upgradation to Adarsh stations, 986 stations have so far been developed. 160 developed in last two years. New generation system put in place which can book 7200 online tickets instead of 2000 tickets per minute and can attend 2,00,000 enquiries instead of 50000 per minute. Rationalization of Computerized Passenger Reservation System (PRS) done to enable passengers to buy tickets even after the preparation of reservation charts. E-booking of disposable linen started on trains at New Delhi Railway Station and Nizamuddin Railway Station, Mumbai Central (BCT), Chattarpati Shivaji Terminus (CSTM), Southern Railway. Currency coin cum card operated automatic ticket vending machines installed at select stations. Launched one of the largest free public wifi systems in the world. 26 stations with a plan to extend it to 100 stations. Cancellation of confirmed, RAC and Waitlisted PRS counter tickets made easy using IRCTC website or phone No. 139. Provision made for acceptance of international debit and credit cards for payment of e-ticket through IRCTC website. Yatri Ticket/Sewa Kendra (YTSK) Scheme launched to allow private agents to operate ticketing terminals for selling reserved as well as unreserved tickets. Number of berths available for physically challenged has been increased from 2 to 4. 'Vikalp', Alternative Train Accommodation System (ATAS) launched with a view to provide confirmed accommodation to waitlisted passengers and also to ensure optimal utilization of available accommodation. This facility is now available on New Delhi –

Jammu, New Delhi – Lucknow, Delhi-Howrah, Delhi-Chennai, Delhi-Mumbai and Delhi-Secunderabad Circuits, Commencement of provision of Braille signage on 3000 coaches has been given in order to facilitate travel to visually impaired passengers. Provision of foldable ladder in First AC coaches launched. Provision of Bio degradable garbage bags to passengers started on pilot basis. Security helpline 182 activated and real time complaint resolution through Twitter employed with a high priority to women security issues.

II. Infrastructure Creation

The Ministry has initiated process for procuring high speed train sets which will improve average speed of passenger carrying trains thereby reducing journey time. MoU between India and Japan signed for Mumbai–Ahmedabad High Speed Rail Project using Shinkansen Technology covering a total of 508 kms. Railways launched Gatimaan Express, country's first semi high speed train with a maximum speed of 160 kmph between Delhi and Agra heralding a new era of high speed rail travel in the country. Railways commissioned 2828 km of Broad Gauge lines, highest ever in 2015-16 against an average of 1528 km from 2009-14. One of the most challenging railway projects, conversion of 1500 V DC to 25000 V AC traction system has been successfully completed over the entire Mumbai division of Central Railway.

III. Reforms

Powers delegated and decentralized for improving efficiency and transparency. Measures for e-tendering, e-auctioning, e-ticketing, e-governance, e-freight demand, e-catering, e-wheelchair, e-concierge, etc., taken for efficiency and transparency. Four centres of railways research set up in premier educational institutions. Development of an online system initiated for grievance redressal of both serving as well as retired railwaymen.

IV. Green Initiatives

Commissioned 26 MW wind mill power plant at Jaisalmer. Railways provided 27,000 bio-toilets in trains in the last two years. First 'Green' DEMU train introduced on Northern Railway to run between Rewari-Rohtak section. A hybrid toilet system, combining best features of a vacuum toilet system and indigenous bio-toilet system was installed for trial in a First Class air conditioned coach of Dibrugarh Rajdhani which is running well since September 2015. The system does not require any waste handling facilities for evacuation and processing of waste. This system uses significantly less quantity of water for flushing. A new separate Environment Management Directorate formed to address all environment related issues in a focused and integrated manner. Indian Railways has started a massive exercise of planting trees alongside Railway Track with the signing agreement with Haryana and Punjab Government in the first phase.

Cleanliness

Railways joined the Swacch Bharat Abhiyan in a big way. It formulated an integrated policy on cleanliness. 27 Charitable Institutions/Social Organizations invited to take part in 'Swachh Rail, Swachh Bharat Abhiyan' through Shramdaan campaign

"Clean My Coach" service launched for any cleaning requirement in the coach. A passenger can send an SMS on a mobile number 58888 or book through app and his request is attended to. Cleaning of 50 major stations has been outsourced to professional agencies. Cleanliness audit through third party started for railway stations institutionalised. Ranking of stations based on cleanliness would be generated periodically.

Connectivity in North East and J&K

Railways completed Udhampur-Katra Broad gauge line in Jammu and Kashmir bringing Katra on broad gauge railway map.

Fast passenger carrying train namely Banihal-Baramulla Fast Passenger (DEMU) and Budgam-Baramulla DEMU was started in Jammu and Kashmir. Lumding-Silchar Broad gauge section inaugurated giving seamless BG connectivity to Barak Valley of Assam. Meghalaya came on the rail map with the flagging off the first ever train from Guwahati to Medipathar in Meghalaya. The Prime Minister laid the foundation for a new line to take rail connectivity to Mizoram's capital Aizwal. Tripura's capital Agartala came on the broad gauge rail map. Meter gauge is to be fully eliminated in North-East in near future.

PPP in Projects

In 2015-16, Indian Railways generated an investment of ₹15,000 cr through PPP.

Freight

Massive rationalization of freight policies initiated. Merry-Go-Round system introduced to capture short lead traffic near steel plants and thermal power house. Roll on – Roll off scheme launched on Digha Rail Bridge over Ganges near Patna. Under this scheme loaded trucks would be moved on the flat wagons to avoid congested roads across Ganges. Busy season charge withdrawn. Automatic freight rebate scheme for traffic loaded in traditional empty flow direction introduced.

Safety in Rail Operations

Working towards 'Zero Accident' Mission. TPWS is a safety Automatic Train Protection (ATP) system conforming to European Train Control System (ETCS) Level-1. TPWS trials at 160 Kmph were successfully conducted.

Miscellaneous

Railways made successful arrangements to transport drinking water to drought-affected areas of Latur district in Maharashtra. Railways lent helping hand during the Nepal earthquake by providing 'Rail Neer' bottles and by transporting Nepali evacuees. Railways also helped during the J&K floods.

Railways were in the forefront in extending help to the Indian nationals returning from Yemen. Railway weightlifters (5 women and 1 Men) represented India in the Commonwealth Youth; junior and senior weightlifting championship held at Pune where railway players won medals.

Roads

Road as a mode of transport is a critical infrastructure for economic development of a country. It influences the pace, structure and pattern of development. The Ministry of Road Transport and Highways was formed in 2009 by bifurcating the erstwhile Ministry of Shipping, Road Transport and Highways into two independent ministries. The Ministry of Road Transport and Highways encompasses construction and maintenance of National Highways (NHs), administration of Motor Vehicles Act, 1988 and Central Motor Vehicles Rules 1989, formulation of broad policies relating to road transport, environmental issues, automotive norms, fixation of user fee rate for use of National Highways etc. besides making arrangements for cross-border movement of vehicular traffic with neighboring countries.

The capacity of national highways in term of handling traffic (passenger and goods) needs to keep pace with industrial growth. India has one of the largest road networks of over 52.32 lakh km. It comprises national highways, expressways, state highways, major district roads, other district roads and village roads with following length distribution:

National Highways / Expressway	1,00,475 km
State Highways	1,48,256km
Other Roads	49,83,579km

Development and Maintenance of National Highways

The Government is implementing National Highways Development Project (NHDP), the largest highways project ever undertaken in the country since 2000. The NHDP is mainly being implemented by National Highways Authority of India.

National Highways Authority of India

National Highways Authority of India (NHAI) was constituted to develop, maintain and manage the national highways vested or entrusted to it by the Central Government. It became operational in 1995 with the appointment of the first Chairman. Presently, NHAI is headed by a Chairman with six full time members and four part time (ex-officio) members. The Authority has its field offices in the form of zonal offices, regional offices, project implementation units (PIUs) and corridor management units (CMU) spread all over the country.

Border Road Development Board

Border Road Development Board (BRDB) was set up in 1960 to co-ordinate the development of road communication in the border areas of the country, as inadequate communication facilities were seriously hampering defence preparedness and economic development of these areas. The Board has financial and other powers of a Department of Government and functions under over all control of Chairman. All sanctions of the Board are processed by the secretariat of the Board. MoRT&H provides fund to BRDB. Border Road Organisation (BRO) is the executive arm of the Secretariat, BRDB.

An amount of ₹ 4207.56 crore was allocated during current year 2015-16, for the NH entrusted to state PWDs and nil amount for NHs entrusted to BRO. In addition to ₹ 4207.56 crore an amount of ₹ 50.00 crore from permanent bridge fee fund (PBFF) has been allocated for NHs entrusted to state PWD.

Road Transport

Road transport is considered to be one of the most cost effective and preferred modes of transport, both for freight and passengers, keeping in view its level of penetration in populated areas. Thus, it is vital to the economic development and social integration of the country. Road transport has emerged as the dominant segment in India's transportation sector with a share of 4.8 per cent in India's Gross Domestic Product (GDP) in 2011-12. Although national highways constituted 1.58 per cent of the total road network in 2012, they carried 40 per cent of the total road traffic. Easy availability, adaptability to individual needs and cost savings are some of the factors which go in favour of road transport. Road transport also acts as a feeder service to railway, shipping and air traffic. The total number of registered motor vehicles has been growing at 10.5 per cent per annum during the period 2002 to 2012. The share of road traffic in total traffic movement by roads and railways has grown from 13.8 per cent of freight traffic and 15.4 per cent of passenger traffic in 1950-51 to an estimated 64.5 per cent of freight and 85.9 per cent of passenger traffic respectively in 2011-12.

Road Safety

The National Road Safety Policy places emphasis on awareness regarding road safety issues, establishment of road safety information database, strengthening of driving licence system and training, better enforcement of road safety laws, etc. The important schemes on road safety operated by the Ministry include publicity measures and awareness campaign on road safety, scheme for setting up institutes for driving training, refresher training of drivers in unorganized sector and human resource development, national highways accident relief service scheme (NHARSS), setting up of inspection and certification centres and road safety and pollution testing equipment and so on.

National Highway Accident Relief Service Scheme

National Highway Accident Relief Service Scheme (NHARSS) entails providing cranes and ambulances to states/ UTs/NGOs for relief and rescue measures in the aftermath of accidents by way of evacuating road accident victims to the nearest medical aid centre and for clearing the accident site. So far, 347 ten tonnes cranes and 106 small/medium size cranes have been provided under the scheme. 509 ambulances have been provided to states/UTs/NGOs under the scheme.

Further, the Ministry has also provided 140 advanced life support ambulances to 140 identified hospitals upgraded under the Ministry of Health and Family Welfare's Scheme 'establishment of an integrated network of Trauma Centres' along the golden quadrilateral, north-south and east-west corridors of the National highways by upgrading the trauma care facilities in 140 identified state government hospitals.

Indian Academy of Highway Engineers

Indian Academy of Highway Engineers (IAHE) is a registered Society under the administrative control of the Ministry. It is a collaborative body of both central and state governments and was set up in 1983 with the objective of fulfilling the long felt need for training of highway engineers in the country, both at the entry level and during the service period.

Bharatmala Project

The Ministry has taken up detailed review of national highways network with a view to improving road connectivity to coastal/border areas, backward areas, religious places, tourist places, construction/ rehabilitation/widening of about 1,500 major bridges and 200 railway over bridges (ROBs)/railway under bridges (RUBs) on NHs, improvement of newly declared NHs providing connectivity to district head quarters, connectivity improvement programme for Char-Dham (Kedarnath, Badrinath, Yamunotri and Gongotri in Uttarakhand) under proposed Bharatmala Pariyojana.

Setu Bharatam Programme

The Setu Bharatam programme for building bridges for safe and seamless travel on national highways was launched in 2016. The Setu Bharatam programme is to make all national highways free of railway level crossings by 2019. This is being done to prevent the frequent accidents and loss of lives at level crossings. The Minister informed that 208 railway over bridges (ROB) railway under bridges (RUB) are to be built at the level crossings at a cost ₹20,800 crore as part of the programme. The details of 208 ROBs are as : Andhra Pradesh-33, Assam-12, Bihar-20, Chattisgarh-5, Gujarat-8, Haryana-10, Himachal Pradesh-5, Jharkhand-11, Karnataka-17, Kerala-4, Madhya Pradesh-6, Maharashtra-12, Odisha-4, Punjab-10, Rajasthan-9, Tamil Nadu-9, Utarakhand-2, Uttar Pradesh-9, West Bengal-22.

In addition to this, about 1,500 old and worn down bridges are also to be improved by replacement/widening/strengthening in a phased manner at a cost of about ₹ 30,000 crore. The Ministry of Road Transport and Highways has also established an Indian Bridge Management System (IBMS) at the Indian Academy for Highway Engineer in Noida, U.P. The aim is to carry out conditions survey and inventorization of all bridges on national highways by using mobile inspection units. 11 consultancy firms have been appointed for this purpose. Inventorization of 50,000 bridges had already been done.

Shipping

Ministry of Shipping was formed in 2009 by bifurcating the erstwhile Ministry of Shipping, Road Transport and Highways into two independent ministries. Maritime transport is a critical infrastructure for the economic development of a country. It influences the pace, structure and pattern of development. The Ministry of Shipping encompasses within its fold shipping and port sectors which also include ship building and ship repair, major ports and inland water transport. The Ministry has been entrusted with the responsibility to formulate policies and programmes on these sectors and their implementation.

Maritime Development

The maritime sector in India comprises ports, shipping, ship building and ship repair and inland water transport systems. India has 12 major ports and about 200 non major ports. Indian shipping industry has over the years played a crucial role in the transport sector of India's economy. Approximately 95 per cent of the country's trade by volume and 68 per cent by value is moved through maritime transport. Therefore, shipping and ocean resources, ship design and construction, ports and harbours, issues relating to human resource development, finance, ancillaries and new technologies need to be developed in the light of the emerging scenario. Shipping continues to remain unchallenged as the world's most efficient means of transportation and we need to do all, we can, to recognize, reward and promote quality within the industry.

India has a long coastline of about 7517 km, spread on the western and eastern shelves of the mainland and also along the Islands. It is an important natural resource for the country's trade.

Maritime Agenda

In the Maritime Agenda 2010-20, a target of 3,130 MT port capacity has been set for the year 2020. More than 50 per cent of this capacity is to be created in the non-major ports as the traffic handling by these ports is expected to increase to 1,280 MT. The objective of the Maritime Agenda is not only creating more capacity but augmenting port performance. This enlarged scale of operation is expected to reduce transaction costs considerably and make Indian ports globally competitive. The proposed investment in major and non-major ports by 2020 is expected to be around ₹ 2,77,380 crore. Most of this investment has to come from the private sector including foreign direct investment (FDI). FDI up to 100 per cent under the automatic route is permitted for construction and maintenance of ports. Private-sector participation will not only increase investment in the ports infrastructure, but also efficiencies in ports through induction of latest technology and better management practices. Public funds will be mainly deployed for common use infrastructure facilities like deepening of port channels, rail and road connectivity from ports to hinterland etc.

Port Sector

During 2015, major and non-major ports in the country handled a total cargo throughput of around 786 million tonnes (MT). The traffic grew by 1.4 per cent over the corresponding period of previous year. The 12 major ports handled a traffic of 447.05 MT during April – December 2015, representing an increase of about 3.18 per cent over the corresponding period of previous year. During 2015-16 upto December 2015, 12 major ports handled 447.05 MT of traffic as against 433.27 MT over the corresponding period of previous year. The composition of the cargo is given here:

(in Million Tonnes)

Table : Cargo

Year	POL	Iron Ore	F & RM	Coal	Container (in Million (TEUs)	Other	Total
2005-06	142.09	79.17	12.19	58.76	61.98 (4.61)	69.38	423.57
2006-07	154.34	80.58	14.13	59.98	73.44 (5.54)	81.31	463.78
2007-08	168.75	91.80	16.63	64.93	92.27 (6.71)	84.94	519.31
2008-09	176.14	94.04	18.23	70.40	93.14 (6.59)	78.59	530.53
2009-10	175.09	100.33	17.72	71.71	101.24 (6.90)	95.00	561.09
2010-11	179.17	87.06	19.99	72.73	113.93 (7.52)	96.97	570.03
2011-12	179.10	60.40	20.39	78.78	120.10 (7.78)	101.36	560.14
2012-13	185.98	28.47	14.74	86.66	119.82 (7.70)	110.12	545.79
2013-14	187.31	24.66	13.74	104.73	114.64 (7.46)	110.42	555.50
2014-15	188.77	17.91	16.20	117.86	119.44 (7.96)	121.16	581.34
April-Dec 2015	144.28	7.86	13.18	95.12	91.20 (6.09)	95.41	447.05

Major Ports

Kolkata Port

Kolkata Port is the only riverine major port in the country having been in existence for about 138 years. It has a vast hinterland comprising the entire Eastern India including West Bengal, Bihar, Jharkhand, U.P., M.P., Assam, North East hill states and the two landlocked neighbouring countries namely, Nepal and Bhutan. The port has twin dock systems viz., Kolkata Dock System (KDS) on the eastern bank and Haldia Dock Complex (HDC) on the western bank of river Hooghly.

Paradip Port

Paradip Port is one of the major ports in the country. Pandit Jawaharlal Nehru, the first Prime Minister of India, laid the foundation stone of the port in 1962 near the confluence of river Mahanadi on the east coast of Bay of Bengal in Odisha. Government of India took over the management of the port from the state government in1965. The construction of iron ore berth was completed and INS "Investigator" had the privilege of maiden berthing in the port in March, 1966. The Government of India declared Paradip Port Trust (PPT) as the eighth major port in India in 1966 making it the first major port in the east coast commissioned in independent India. Paradip Port is situated 210 nautical miles south of Kolkata and 260 nautical miles north of Vishakhapatnam at Latitude 20^0-15'—55.44" N and Longitude 86^0-40'—27.34" E.

New Mangalore Port

New Mangalore port was declared as the ninth major port in May, 1974 inaugurated in 1975. The provisions of Major Port Trusts Act, 1963 were extended to the new Mangalore port and a Port Trust Board was formed in 1980. Over the years, the port has grown from the level of handling less than a lakh tonnes of cargo to 39.37 million tonnes in 2013-14. The major commodities imported through the port are POL crude for Mangalore Refinery and Petrochemicals Limited (MRPL), coal, iron ore, LPG, fertilizer, edible oil, limestone, wooden logs, cement, liquid chemicals, containerized cargo etc., and the major export cargo are POL products, iron ore pellets, granite stone, maize, wheat, containerized cargo like coffee, cashew kernels, etc.

Cochin Port

The modern port of Cochin was developed during 1920-1940 due to the untiring efforts of Sir Robert Bristow. By 1930-31 it was formally opened for vessels up to 30 feet draught. Cochin was given the status of a major port in 1936. The administration of the port got vested in a Board of Trustees in 1964 under the Major Port Trusts Act, 1963. The port of Cochin is located on the Willington island at latitude 9^0 58' north and 76^0 14' east on the south-west coast of India about 930 km south of Mumbai and 320 km North of Kanyakumari. With its strategic location on 'he south-west Coast of India and at a commanding position at the cross-roads of the east-west Ocean trade, it is a natural gateway to the vast industrial and agricultural produce markets of the south-west India. The hinterland of the port includes the whole of Kerala and parts of Tamil Nadu and Karnataka. A study carried out on the traffic flow in the hinterland of the port indicates that about 97 per cent of the total volume of traffic is accounted for by Kerala. The hinterland of Cochin port has further spread over to different areas with the growth of containerization in the country and establishment of inland container depots of different load centres in the country. Cochin with its proximity to the international sea route between Europe and the Far East and Australia can attract a large number of container lines offering immense business opportunities. Cochin port has handled 20.89 mt of traffic during 2013-14 compared to 19.85 mt during the previous year.

Jawaharlal Nehru Port

Constructed in the mid 1980's and commissioned in 1989, Jawaharlal Nehru Port has come a long way by becoming a world-class international container handling port. The port is a trendsetter in the matter of port development in India through new initiatives like private sector participation. It is situated in between 18^0 56′43" north and 72^0 56′24" east along the eastern shore of Mumbai harbour off Elephanta Island. Port handles vessels having draught up to 12.50 metres.

Mumbai Port

Mumbai port is a fully integrated multi-purpose port handling container, dry bulk, liquid bulk and break bulk cargo. The port has extensive wet and dry dock facilities to meet the normal needs of ships using the port. There are three enclosed wet docks namely, Prince, Victoria and Indira Docks, having a total area of 46.30 hectares and quayage of 7,776 meters inside the wet basin and 853 meters along the harbour wall. Oldest of the three was Prince's Dock, a semi- tidal dock, commissioned in 1880. It has 8 berths, each with a designed draft of 6.4 meters. The Victoria dock, commissioned in 1888, was also a semi-tidal dock. It has 14 berths each with a designed draft of 6.7 meters. The Prince's and Victoria Dock basins are now being filled up and will be used as Container Storage Yard under the Offshore Container Terminal Project. The same have been decommissioned for Shipping.

Shipping Corporation of India

The Shipping Corporation of India Ltd. (SCI) was formed in 1961. Presently, the authorised capital of the company is ₹ 450.00 crore and the paid up capital is ₹ 423.45 crore. The status of SCI has been changed from a private limited company to public limited company from 1992. The SCI was conferred the "Navratna" status by the Government of India in August, 2009. Presently, the Government is holding 80.12 per cent of the share capital and the balance is held by financial institutions, public and others (NRIs, corporate bodies etc.)

Cochin Shipyard

Situated in the south western coast of India in Kochi, Kerala, Cochin Shipyard is the largest shipyard in the country. Incorporated in 1972, Cochin Shipyard can build ships upto 1,10,000 DWT and repair upto 1,25,000 DWT. The yard has built varied types of ships including tankers, bulk carriers, port crafts, offshore vessels, tugs and passenger vessels. The orders executed by CSL in recent past include bulk carriers for M/s Clipper Group, Bahamas; Firefighting tugs for M/s ATCO, Saudi Arabia and Platform Supply vessels for M/s Deep Sea Supplies, Norway; M/s Tidewalter, USA and M/s Vroon Offshore AS, Netherlands.

The yard's ship building order book position as in 2010 includes platform supply vessels for shipping companies of Norway, USA, Netherlands and India and anchor handling tugs for shipping companies of Cyprus and India. The yard is also a leading ship-repairer of the country and has repaired more than 1,200 ships of all types. These include upgradation of vessels and jack up rigs belonging to ONGC, periodical lay up repairs and life extension of ships including aircract carrier of navy and coast guard. The yard had been consistently achieving profits for the last several years. Considering its achievement, the Government granted it Miniratna status in 2008.

Hooghly Dock and Port Engineers Ltd

Hooghly Dock and Port Engineers Limited (HDPEL), Kolkata became a Central Public Sector undertaking in 1984. The Company has two working units in Howrah District of West Bengal, one at Saikia and another at Nazirgunge. The installed capacity in shipbuilding is 1,100 tonnes per annum and in ship-repairs 125 ships per annum. Apart from a dry dock and a jetty, it has six slipways. The yard is capable of constructing various types of ships (including passenger ships) and other vessels such as dredgers, tugs, floating dry docks, fishing trawlers, supply-cum-support vessels, multipurpose harbour, vessels, light house tender vessels, barges, mooring launches, etc., and undertaking repairs of different types of vessels.

Shipping Sector

Shipping plays an important role in the economic development of the country, especially in India's international trade. The shipping industry also plays an important role in the energy security of the country, as energy resources, such as coal, crude oil and natural gas are mainly transported by ships. Further, during crisis situation, Indian shipping contributes to the uninterrupted supply of essentials and can serve as second line of defence. Approximately, 95 per cent of the country's trade by volume and 68 per cent in terms of value is being transported by sea.

Shipping is an important indicator of both commodity and services trade of any country. As on December 31, 2015, India had a fleet strength of 1247 ships with Gross Tonnage (GT) of 10.51 million, with the public-sector Shipping Corporation of India having the largest share of 38 per cent. Of this, 373 ships with 9.00 million GT cater to India's overseas trade and the rest to coastal trade.

As of January 1, 2015, Panama, Liberia and the Marshall Islands are the largest vessel registries. Together, they account for 41.81 per cent share of world tonnage. Marshall Islands recorded an impressive growth of over 13.32 per cent year on year. More than three quarters of world fleet is registered in developing countries including many open registries. Open registries are those where the owner does not need to be of the same nationality as the country where the ship is registered. The tonnage registered under a foreign flag (where the nationality of the owner is different from the flag flown by the vessel) is 71 per cent of the world total.

Greece continues to be the largest ship owning country, accounting for 16.11 per cent of the world, followed by Japan, China, Germany and Singapore. Together, the top five shipowning countries control more than half of the world tonnage (DWT). Five of the top ten ship-owning countries are from Asia, four are European and one is from the United States.

Coastal Shipping

The share of coastal shipping in domestic cargo movement is around 7 per cent including just 0.5 per cent through inland waterways. The contiguous coastline of India covers 5400 kms and 2100 kms of shores on more than 1190 islands. Therefore, there is huge potential for coastal shipping in the country. Coastal shipping is best suited for bulk cargo. This transportation at present is regulated through a policy on cabotage enshrined in the Merchant Shipping Act, 1958. As an intermediate measure, a scheme of green channel clearance of coastal cargo and priority berthing for coastal vessels has been operationalized. Coastal vessels are exempted from lighthouses dues. 40 per cent rebates on coastal related charges are provided to all coastal vessels at major ports.

Inland Water Transport

Various projects for development and maintenance of national waterways 1, 2, 3, 4 & 5 (The Ganga river, the Brahmaputra river, the west coast canal, Krishna – Godavari rivers alongwith canal system between Kakinada and Puducherry and Brahmani river - east coast canal, Matai river and Mahanadi delta rivers) were implemented by Inland Waterways Authority of India (IWAI) for providing / upgrading / maintaining Inland Water Transport (IWT) infrastructure as per requirement. Transportation of imported coal from Sandheads in Bay of Bengal to Farakka power plant of NTPC started in October 2013 is going on. A similar project for NTPC's power plant at Barh is being pursued for finalization. Implementation of Jal Marg Vikas Project for capacity augmentation on NW-1 from Haldia to Allahabad (1620 km) has commenced with estimated cost of ₹ 4200 crore.

Dredging Corporation of India

Dredging Corporation of India Limited (DCI) was established in 1976 to provide integrated dredging service to the major ports of the country. DCI is a Miniratna Category-I Public Sector Undertaking under the administrative control of Ministry of Shipping. The Company is a Schedule "B" Company. Clients include major ports, non-major ports, Indian navy, state government etc. The Company has 10 trailer suction hopper dredgers (ISHDs) and 3 cutter suction dredgers. The paid-up capital of the company is ₹ 28.00 crores divided into equity shares of ₹10/- each of which 78.56 per cent i.e., 2,19,97,700 shares are held by President of India.The Company is listed in Mumbai, National, Delhi and Kolkata Stock Exchanges. The number of shareholders is about 53000. The Company has adopted a Corporate Social Responsibility Policy for fulfilling its obligation to the society at large.

Sagarmala Project

The National Perspective Plan for the Sagarmala programme was put in place in 2016. In all 173 projects have been initially identified under four projects archetypes of Sagarmala. The Project archetype and the number of projects identified are given as:

1	Port Modernisation	53
2	Port Connectivity	83
3	Port Led Industrialisation	29
4	Coastal Community development	8

26 Port rail connectivity projects were identified of which 2 have been completed and 18 are under implementation by Ministry of Railways. Most of these projects will be completed by 2019-20. For 1 project, Indian Port Corporation Limited has awarded the PMC work and 1 project is being implemented by the port itself. The implementation of the projects identified under the National Perspective Plan, at an estimated investment of ₹ 41 crore, will be taken up starting FY 16-17 by the relevant ports, state governments/ maritime boards, central ministries, mainly through private or PPP mode. Sagarmala Development Company (SDC) is to be set up by the Ministry of Shipping to provide support to the project SPVs and funding support for the residual projects under Sagarmala. The Sagarmala Consultants have projected that the identified industrial cluster projects will enable creation of approximately 1 crore new jobs, including 40 lakh direct jobs in the next 10 years.

Civil Aviation

The Ministry of Civil Aviation is responsible for the formulation of national policies and programmes for development and regulation of civil aviation and for devising and implementing schemes for orderly growth and expansion of civil air transport. Its functions also extend to overseeing the provision of airport facilities, air traffic services, carriage of passengers and goods by air, safeguarding civil aviation operations, regulation of air transport services, licensing of aerodromes, air carriers, pilots and aircraft maintenance engineers. The Ministry also administratively controls the institution of Commission of Railway Safety, which is responsible for the safety in rail travel and operations in terms of the provisions of the Railways Act.

India has been a member of the International Civil Aviation Organisation (ICAO) and is also on the Council of ICAO since its inception. The civil aviation sector has three main functional divisions-regulatory, infrastructural and operational. This sector has seen an unprecedented growth in the recent years. There are a large number of companies providing passenger transport and cargo handling services in the country. The Air Transport Companies are both in the public and the private sector. In the public sector, there are National Aviation Company of India Limited (Air India) and its subsidiaries viz., Alliance Air, Air India Charters Ltd, (Air India Express), etc.

Apart from Air India, Indian Airlines, Alliance Air and Air India Charters Ltd., there are at present six private scheduled operators, viz., Jet Airways (India) Ltd., Jetlite Airlines, Go Airlines (India) Pvt. Ltd., Spicejet Ltd., Paramount Airways Pvt. Ltd., and Inter Globe Aviation Ltd. (IndiGO) operating on the domestic sector providing a wide choice of flights and connectivity to various parts of India. Besides these, a new category of scheduled airlines i.e. Scheduled Air Transport (Regional) services has been introduced to enhance connectivity to smaller cities and within a region. MDLR airlines is operating as regional scheduled airlines in northern region. Three cargo airlines viz., Blue Aviation Pvt Ltd., Deccan Cargo and Express Logistics (Pvt.) Ltd. and Aryan Cargo Express Pvt. Ltd. are operating scheduled cargo services in the country.

Bureau of Civil Aviation

The Bureau of Civil Aviation Security (BCAS) was initially set up as a cell in the DGCA in January, 1978. The role of the cell was to coordinate, monitor, inspect and train personnel in Civil Aviation Security matters. It was reorganized into an independent Department in April, 1987 under the Ministry of Civil Aviation following the Kanishka Tragedy in June, 1985. The main responsibility of BCAS is to lay down standards and measures in respect of security of civil flights at international and domestic airports in India and Indian aircraft operators at foreign airports. It is the regulator for civil aviation security in the country and is responsible for laying down the standards for pre-embarkation security and anti-sabotage measures in respect of civil flights and ensuring their compliance through regular inspections and security audits. The aim of BCAS is to safeguard civil aviation operations against acts of unlawful interference and it is the regulatory authority for discharging all relevant national and international obligations in respect of training of personnel in aviation security responsibilities which include, inter alia, planning and co-ordination of all aviation security related activities, operational emergencies and crisis management.

BCAS is headed by Commissioner of Security (Civil Aviation) who is the appropriate authority to ensure development, maintenance, updating and implementation of National Civil Aviation Security programme for India and fulfill all international obligations in this context. The BCAS has its headquarters in New Delhi and at present has four regional offices located in Delhi, Mumbai, Kolkata and Chennai airport. Its four new regional offices are to be created, in pursuance of the approval of the proposal for restructuring and strengthening the BCAS. A post of Joint Commissioner of Security (CA) has also been created to strengthen the senior management level at the BCAS headquarters.

Indira Gandhi Rashtriya Uran Akademi

The Indira Gandhi Rashtriya Uran Akademi (IGRUA) was set up at Fursatganj, Raebareli (Uttar Pradesh) to bring about a quantum improvement in the standards of flying and ground training of commercial pilots in the country. The Akademi is equipped with most modern and sophisticated trainer aircraft, up-to-date audio-visual training aids and other facilities for effective ground training. It employs qualified flying and ground instructors, with long experience in the field of aviation and flying training. The aim at IGRUA is not only to train to make a pilot but also to make one an effective systems manager in aeronautics. The flying trainees of the Akademi acquire the standards required for their transit with ease into the cockpits of the airlines. It is an Autonomous Body under the control of the Ministry.

The Akademi has made remarkable expansion of its existing infrastructure, viz., doubling the capacity of hostel from 72 fully furnished rooms to 144 including a 20 room girls' hostel. Construction of three 'D' type officers residential quarters, store/class room buildings, re-carpeting of roads, installation of solar water heating system in hostels, installation of air-conditioning plant having capacity of 60 TR x 3, laying of new water supply lines, renovations of sports complex, recreation centre, mess kitchen, etc., are the other major infrastructure upgradations carried out in the institutional area. In the airport side, runway re-carpeting, construction of a new hangar, expansion of Apron, installation of high mast lighting, etc., have been carried out. The Akademi's infrastructure, such as exclusive runway and ATC, night flying facilities including navigation aids like Instrument Landing System (ILS) and Precision Approach Path Indicator (PAPI) are the hallmarks of a flying training institution that matches contemporary international standards.

Airports Authority of India

Airports Authority of India (AAI) is a leader in building airport infrastructure along the length and breadth of the country, including remote and far flung areas. Airports Authority of India came into being in April, 1995. AAI manages 115 airports including 23 civil enclaves. In addition, AAI provides CNS-ATM facilities at 11 other airports. About 2.8 million nautical square mile area of the national airspace covering the Bay of Bengal and the Arabian Sea has been assigned to AAI for provision of Air Traffic Services.

As part of modernization, passenger New Terminal Buildings have been constructed/commissioned at Dehradun, Jaipur, Kullu, Udaipur, Gaya, Cooch Behar, Dibrugarh, Lilabari, Ahmedabad (New Departure Block for Domestic Terminal Building), Aurangabad, Bhuj, Gondia, Porbandar, Mysore, Mangalore, Trichy, Vizag, Srinagar, Trivandrum, Varanasi, Barapani (Shillong), Ahmedabad (New International Terminal Building) and Madurai. These terminals have modern passenger facilities besides comfortable lounges/user friendly amenities and good ambience. State-of-the-art technology has been used in these terminals.

National Flying Training Institute

Airport Authority of India (AAI) in collaboration with CAE, Canada has set up a Joint Venture Company in the name of National Flying Training Institute Private Limited (NFTIPL). This Institute is located at Gondia in Maharashtra. AAI holds 49 per cent equity share capital while CAE holds 51 per cent share capital in this joint venture company.

Rajiv Gandhi National Flying Training Institute

Rajiv Gandhi National Flying Training Institute (RGNFTI) became operational in September, 2008. The objective of setting up this Institute is to provide qualified and well trained pilots. The Institute, spread over an area of 12 acres has state-of-the-art-simulator, administration block, class rooms, hostels for boys and girls, sports complex and a wi-fi enabled cafeteria. Training is imparted on simulator and through a fleet of seven single engine aircraft (DA-42).

Gagan Project

GPS Aided Geo Augmented Navigation (GAGAN) is an augmentation system to enhance the accuracy and integrity of GPS signals to meet precision approach requirements in civil aviation and it is being implemented jointly by AAI and ISRO in three phases. Technology demonstration system is to be upgraded to a full operational capability system in the second and third phase. GSAT IV being fabricated by ISRO will carry GAGAN payload. The footprint of this satellite will cover a vast geographical area from Africa to Australia and hence would facilitate expansion of the service area of 'GAGAN' far beyond Indian airspace. When implemented, this would replace most of the ground based navigational aids and it would be possible to provide precision approach and landing guidance up to category 1, to aircraft hitherto not available due to terrain conditions precluding the provision of Instrument Landing System.

AAI is undertaking upgradation and modernization of 35 non-metro airports in the country in a time bound manner as per government's decision.

Greenfield Airports

A Greenfield airport project at Devanahalli near Bengaluru has been implemented on a Build Own Operate and Transfer (BOOT) basis for 30 years with Public Private Participation (PPP) at a revised cost of ₹ 2,068 crore. Government of Karnataka and AAI together hold 26 per cent equity and the strategic joint venture partners hold the balance 74 per cent. AAI's investment in the equity is capped at ₹ 50 crore. A consortium led by Siemens, Germany with Unique Zurich, Switzerland and Larsen and Toubro, India Limited, as other members has been chosen as the strategic Joint Venture Partners. The airport was commissioned in 2008. Rajiv Gandhi International Airport, a Greenfield airport has been developed in Shamshabad, near Hyderabad on Build Own Operate and Transfer (BOOT) basis with Public Private Participation (PPP) by the Government of Andhra Pradesh. The approximate cost of the

Project is ₹ 2,920 crore. AAI and Government of Andhra Pradesh together hold 26 per cent equity with AAI's equity being capped at ₹50 crore. The balance 74 per cent is held by the strategic partner, a consortium consisting of M/s GMR Enterprises and Malaysian Airports Holdings Berhand (MAHB). The airport was also commissioned in 2008.

Greenfield Policy for Airports

The Government promulgated the policy for Greenfield Airports in 2008. This policy aims to streamline the approval process to facilitate strengthening and augmenting of airports infrastructure in the country. It also attempts to make the approval process more transparent and perdictable.

Air India

Air India and Indian Airlines merger attained its official status on the formation of National Aviation Company of India Ltd. (Air India) in 2007. Post merger the new entity is known as Air India while its mascot is retained as 'Maharajah'.

The Hotel Corporation of India Limited (HCI) is a public limited company wholly owned by Air India Limited and was incorporated in 1971 under the Companies Act, 1956 when Air India decided to enter the hotel industry in keeping with the then prevalent trend among world airlines. The objective was to offer to the passengers a better product, both at the international airports and at other places of tourist interest, thereby also increasing tourism to India. However, in 2002-03, three properties of HCI, viz, Indo-Hokke Hotel Limited (Centaur Hotel, Rajgir), Centaur Hotel, Juhu Beach and Centaur Hotel, Mumbai airport were sold off. The remaining units of HCI are Centaur Hotel, Delhi Airport, Centaur Hotel Lakeview, Srinagar and Flight Kitchens at Delhi and Mumbai.

Air India Express has a fleet of seven leased and six owned B 737-800 aircrafts. Commencing with 26 Kerala/Gulf flights, Air India Express operations have grown and new routes have been added to the network. Currently, 57 international flights are operated on different routes. In addition, Air India Express operates five weekly flights on the Chennai/Kuala Lumpur sector on behalf of Air India. Effective from, 2007, Air India flights between India and Bahrain/Doha are being operated by Air India Express. Effective from 2007, with the fleet expansion, it is anticipated that Air India Express would operate approximately 130 flights per week. New cities such as Tiruchirapally, Jaipur, Lucknow, Hyderabad and Kolkata are to be added to the network. In addition, frequencies on some of the existing routes may be increased in response to market requirements.

Historically, Alliance Air was set up in 1996 as a separate company envisioned to function as profit centre of erstwhile Indian Airlines Limited to effectively utilize the Boeing 737 aircraft fleet and to improve productivity and profitability of Indian Airlines Ltd. At present, Alliance Air has taken on lease 4 ATR-42 aircraft and commenced scheduled operations in the north-east region from 2003.

As a part of improvement of the infrastructure, Air India is in the process of creation of bases for new aircraft. As a part of setting up a base of B 737 aircraft, a MRO facility is being set up at Thiruvananthapuram. The hangar facility for the same is nearing completion. As a part of setting up the additional base at Delhi for B 777 and B 787 aircraft, a wide body hangar facility is being set up at Delhi for these aircraft.

With the growing increase in the usage of the web, Air India offers its passengers the facility of booking and purchasing the tickets through the internet. Currently around 90 per cent of the domestic tickets issued are e-tickets. For round-the-clock access to NACIL reservations, a toll free number has been arranged to enable passengers to get the services of booking of seats/ obtaining information regarding flight arrivals/departures, etc., from Call Centres that have been established at Belapur in Mumbai and Gurgaon in New Delhi to meet the needs of the passengers.

Pawan Hans Helicopters

Pawan Hans Helicopters Limited (PHHL) was incorporated in 1985 and commenced its operations within one year, to provide helicopter services to the oil sector, operate in hilly and inaccessible areas and make available charter flights for promotion of travel and tourism. The present authorized capital of PHHL is ₹120 crore and its paid-up capital is ₹113.76 crore. Out of this the Government of India holds 78.5 per cent shares and the balance is held by ONGC. Its corporate office is located in Delhi with regional offices in Delhi and Mumbai. The Company at present has a fleet of 35 helicopters comprising 18 SA- 365N Dauphin, 8 Dauphin AS365N3, 3 Bell 206 L4, 4 Bell 407 and 2 Mi-172 helicopters. The Company achieved flying of more than 4 lakh hours and 15 lakh landings on its fleet since its formation.

Since October, 1986 Pawan Hans has been providing helicopter support for offshore operation for ONGC for carrying its men and vital supplies round-the-clock to drilling rigs situated in Bombay off-shore platforms. PHHL operates at ONGCs Rigs (mother platforms and drilling rigs) and production platforms (wells) within a radius of 130 km from the main land at Mumbai. At present 12 Dauphin N and N3 helicopters are on contract with ONGC. The Company has been successful in providing all the 12 Dauphin N and N3 helicopters fully compliant with AS-4 as per the new contract with ONGC.

PHHL provides helicopter support services to several state governments namely, Arunachal Pradesh, Punjab, Meghalaya, Tripura, Sikkim, Jharkhand, Lakshadweep and Andman and Nicobar Islands. It is also providing helicopter services to Ministry of Home Affairs at Guwahati and GAIL, PHHL runs the helicopter services from Phata to the Holy Shrine of Kedarnath during the May- June and September-October seasons, after construction of helipad at the location. The Company has succeeded in obtaining award of contract for two light single engine helicopters for a period of 3 years at Mata Vaishno Devi from Katra to Sanjhichat under competitive bidding and the services commenced in 2008. The Company has undertaken a pilot project for M/s Power Grid Corporation of India Ltd. for hotline washing of insulation of the power transmission lines for five months. These operations were successfully carried out for the first time in India. The Company has also got Operation and Maintenance Contract of a Dauphin N3 helicopter of Government of Gujarat, 2 Dhruv helicopters of ONGC with M/s HAL and 4 Dhruv helicopters owned by MHA with M/s HAL. Pawan Hans operates flights from 39 destinations covering 64 sectors by 148 weekly flights under the aegis of the state governments of Meghalaya, Tripura, Sikkim and Arunachal Pradesh.

27 Water Resources

THE Ministry of Water Resources, River Development and Ganga Rejuvenation lays down policies and programmes for development and regulation of the water resources of the country. It covers sectoral planning, coordination, policy guidelines, technical examination and techno-economic appraisal of projects, providing central assistance to specific projects, facilitation of external assistance and assistance in the resolution of inter-state water disputes, policy formulation, planning and guidance in respect of major, medium & minor irrigation, ground water management, command area development, flood management, dam safety and river development and Ganga rejuvenation (including its tributaries rejuvenation), regulation and development of inter-state rivers, implementation of awards of Tribunals, water quality assessment, bilateral/external assistance and matters relating to rivers common to India and neighbouring countries.

National Water Mission

With a view to address Climate Change and the related issues, the National Action Plan on Climate Change (NAPCC) has been prepared by the Government of India, which laid down the principles and has identified the approach to be adopted to meet the challenges of impact of climate change through eight National Missions. National Water Mission is one of the missions under NAPCC. The main objective of the National Water Mission is "conservation of water, minimizing wastage and ensuring its more equitable distribution both across and within States through integrated water resources development and management". The five identified goals of the Mission are: (a) comprehensive water data base in public domain and assessment of impact of climate change on water resource; (b) promotion of citizen and state action for water conservation, augmentation and preservation; (c) focused attention to vulnerable areas including over-exploited areas; (d) increasing water use efficiency by 20 per cent, and (e) promotion of basin level integrated water resources management. Various strategies for achieving the goals have been identified which lead to integrated planning for sustainable development and efficient management with active participation of the stakeholders.

Main Activities undertaken by the National Water Mission: *1. Comprehensive water data base in public domain*: India-WRIS (Water Resource Information System), a portal for providing information on water resources has been developed by Central Water Commission. All the data pertaining to surface water and ground water are made available at India-WRIS. GIS data pertaining to surface water resources and ground water resources are displayed on the site of India-WRIS. 2. *NWM web portal:* - An independent Web Portal of NWM has been launched. The portal aims at providing all the information relating to water resources, organisations and their activities on different aspects of water resources at one point. 3. *Assessment of Impact of Climate Change on water resources*: NWM has identified eight river basins (Mahanadi, Mahi, Luni, Tapi, Sutlej, Sabarmati, Subarnarekha and western flowing rivers from Tadri to Kanyakumari) for study of impact of climate change in association with research institutes like IITs, NITs, IISc. and NIH under the R and D scheme of the Ministry. 4. *Convention on Participatory Irrigation Management (PIM)*:- The National Convention of Water Users Associations (WUA) was held at CSMRS, New Delhi in 2014. Two Regional Convention covering WUAs and officials from northern States J&K, HP, Uttrakhand, Punjab, Rajasthan and Haryana and western Maharashtra, M.P., Gujarat, Chattishgrah and Goa regions were organized at Punjab Agricultural University, in August 2015 and Aurangabad in 2016. The main objective of PIM regional conventions was to promote equitable distribution of water, creating awareness about conservation of water, minimizing wastage, depletion of ground water table and adopting on-farm water efficient techniques etc. in the command areas.

National Water Policy

The National Water Policy, 2012 was adopted by the National Water Resources Council. The National Water Policy, 2012 made several recommendations for conservation, development and improved management of water resources in the country. Emphasis on the need for a National Water Framework Law; comprehensive legislation for optimum development of inter-state rivers and river valleys; evolving a system of benchmarks for water uses for different purposes to ensure efficient use of water; setting up of Water Regulatory Authority by each state; and incentivizing recycle and reuse of water are some of the important recommendations in the Policy. The Policy also lays emphasis on community participation in management of water resources projects and services; incentivizing water saving in irrigation through methods like aligning cropping pattern with natural resource endowments, micro irrigation, automated irrigation operation, evaporation-transpiration reduction etc; undertaking conservation of rivers, river corridors, water bodies and infrastructure in a scientifically planned manner through community participation; and arresting declining ground water levels in over-exploited areas.

National Water Resources Council

The National Water Resources Council (NWRC) was set up by the Government of India in March, 1983. The Prime Minister is the Chairman and Union Minister of Water Resources, River Development and Ganga Rejuvenation is the Vice-Chairman of the Council. The Union Minister of State for Water Resources, concerned Union Ministers/Ministers of State, and Chief Ministers of all States & Lieutenant Governors/Administrators of the Union Territories are the Members. Secretary, Ministry of Water Resources, River Development & Ganga Rejuvenation, is the Secretary of the Council.

National Water Board

The Government of India constituted a National Water Board in September, 1990 to review the progress achieved in implementation of the National Water Policy and to report the progress to the National Water Resources Council from time to time. The Secretaries of the concerned Union Ministries, Chairman, Central Water Commission, Chief Secretaries of all states/union territories are its Members and Member (Water Planning & Projects), Central Water Commission is the Member Secretary of the Board.

A National Forum of Water Resources and Irrigation Ministers of states was constituted by the Ministry with the following terms of reference; (i) to deliberate on various reforms needed in the water resources sector from time to time and attempt towards evolving consensus at the national level; and (ii) to provide appropriate platform for sharing of ideas and facilitating support to new and innovative ideas and initiatives for better water governance proposed by the Central and/or state governments. It is a permanent forum of twelve Members with the provision that half of its Members would retire after every two years and would be replaced by the Ministers from states / union territories from similar regions in the country. Thus, a member shall have a tenure of four years except for six members from the initial constitution who would have a tenure of only two years.

National Mission for Clean Ganga

"Namami Gange" Programme integrates the efforts to clean and protect the river Ganga in a comprehensive manner with a budget outlay of ₹ 20,000 crores for next 5 years. In order to speed up progress, the Centre has decided to take over 100 per cent funding of various activities/projects and plans to provide for operation and maintenance of the assets for a minimum 10 year period. The primary focus of the programme is on pollution abatement and by 2020, the gap in treatment capacity for 118 priority towns located along Ganga will be addressed. In order to address the problem of open defecation, complete sanitation coverage of 1657 Gram Panchayats located along Ganga will be taken up. Identified grossly polluting Industries have been directed to move towards implementing zero liquid discharge and installing real-time effluent monitoring stations. Comprehensive river surface and ghat cleaning programme has been initiated for major urban centres of Haridwar, Rishikesh, Gharmukteshwar, Mathura-Vrindavan, Kanpur, Allahabad, Varanasi, Patna, Sahibganj, Kolkata and Nabadwip. This programme will include solid waste management and environmental monitoring/ surveillance of drains. Intensive afforestation drive has also been initiated along the banks of the river with focus on regeneration of native/medicinal species and providing comprehensive intervention that leads to the overall objective of cleaning river Ganga by reducing sediment load, recharging ground water and reducing non-point source pollution.

Jal Kranti Abhiyan

The Ministry celebrated Jal Kranti Abhiyan during the year 2015-16 to consolidate water conservation and management in the country through a holistic approach involving all stakeholders, making it a mass movement. The objectives of Jal Kranti Abhiyan are as follows: Strengthening grass root involvement of all stakeholders including Panchayati Raj Institutions and local bodies in the water security and development schemes; encouraging the adoption/utilization of traditional knowledge in water resources conservation and its management; utilizing sector level expertise from different levels in government, NGO's, citizens etc; and enhancing livelihood security through water security in rural areas.

The activities under Jal Kranti Abhiyan are as: Jal Gram Yojana; development of model command area; pollution abatement; mass awareness programme and other activities

Water Resources Potential

The average annual water availability of the country is assessed as 1869 billion cubic meters (BCM). Of this, total utilizable water resource is assessed as 1123 BCM out of which 690 BCM is surface water and 433 BCM replenish able ground water resources.

Accelerated Irrigation Benefits Programme

The Accelerated Irrigation Benefits Programme (AIBP) was launched in 1996-97 to provide central assistance to major/medium irrigation projects in the country, with the objective to accelerate implementation of such projects which were beyond resource capability of the states or were in advanced stage of completion. Priority was given to those projects which were started in pre-Fifth and Fifth Plan period and also to those which were benefiting tribal and drought prone areas. From the year 1999-2000 onwards, Central Loan Assistance under AIBP was also extended to surface mining irrigation projects (SMI) of special category States (N.E. States and Hilly States of H.P., Sikkim, J&K, Uttaranchal and projects benefiting KBK districts of Odisha). Since its inception, 297 Irrigation/Multi Purpose Projects have been included for funding under AIBP. Out of this 143 projects have been completed and 5 projects were foreclosed. An irrigation potential of 24.39 lakh ha has been created through the completed projects. The cumulative Central loan assistance/grant provided to states under AIBP to all of These projects till March 2015 was ₹ 67,539.52 crore. Twenty five states got benefited from the programme.

Pradhan Mantri Krishi Sinchayee Yojana

During 2015-16, Pradhan Mantri Krishi Sinchayee Yojana (PMKSY) was launched with an aim to enhance physical access of water on farm and expand cultivable area under assured irrigation, improve on farm water use efficiency, introduce sustainable water conservation practices etc. The main objective of the scheme are as: a) achieve convergence of investments in irrigation at the field level (preparation of district level and, if required, sub district level water use plans); b) enhance the physical access of water on the farm and expand cultivable area under assured irrigation (Har Khet Ko Pani); c) enhance the adoption of precision-irrigation and other water saving technologies (more crop per drop); d) enhance recharge of aquifers and introduce sustainable water conservation practices; e) ensure the integrated development of rainfed areas using the watershed approach towards soil and water conservation, regeneration of ground water, arresting runoff, providing livelihood options and other NRM activities. f) promote extension activities relating to water harvesting, water management and crop alignment for farmers and grass root level field functionaries; g) explore the feasibility of reusing treated municipal water for peri-urban agriculture, and h) attract greater private investments in precision irrigation.

Ministry of WR, RD & GR has been entrusted with two main components of PMKSY e.g. AIBP and PMKSY-HKKP. Major and medium irrigation/ multipurpose irrigation (MMI) projects are being funded under PMKSY-AIBP and repair, renovation and restoration (RRR) of water bodies, surface minor irrigation (SMI) projects and command area development and water management (CADWM) projects are being funded under PMKSY-Har Khet Ko Pani (HKKP).

Targets under PMKSY and achievements during 2015-16 are given here:

Schemes	2015-16 to 2019-20		2015-16	
	Outlay (Crore)	Benefit (L. ha.)	CA (Crore)	Benefit/Target (L. ha.)
a. AIBP	11060	7.5	2327.82	1.2
b. PMKSY(HKKP)				
Surface Minor Irrigation	9050	2.0	601.92	0.3
CAD&WM		15.0	1142.71	2.0
Ground Water		2.5	0.0	0.3
RRR of Water Bodies		1.5	161.18	0.2
Total:	20110	28.5	4233.63	4.0*

* *As per preliminary information targets of 4 lakh ha. are likely to exceed.*

Prioritization of Projects & Innovative Funding Mechanism

Further, 99 projects have been prioritized for completion upto 2019-20. 23 projects (Priority-I) have been identified to be completed by 2016-17 and another 31 projects (Priority-II) have been identified to be completed by 2017-18. The balance 45 projects (Priority-III) have been identified to be completed by Dec., 2019. Total funds required for completion of all the 99 identified projects have been estimated at ₹ 77595 crore (₹ 48546 crore for project works and ₹ 29049 crore for CAD works) with estimated CA of ₹ 31342 crore. Likely potential utilisation through these projects is estimated to be 76.03 lakh hectare (lakh ha).

The Government has approved establishment of a mission and arrangement to fund central as well state share through NABARD for time bound completion of these projects.

Command Area Development and Water Management

Objective: - The Centrally Sponsored Command Area Development (CAD) Programme was launched in 1974-75 for development of adequate delivery system of irrigation water up to farmers' field with an objective to enhance water use efficiency and production and productivity of crops per unit of land and water for improving socio-economic condition of farmers. The Programme envisages integration of all activities relating to irrigated agriculture in a coordinated manner with multi-disciplinary team under a Command Area Development Authority.

Coverage:- Initially, 60 major and medium irrigation projects were taken up under the CAD Programme, covering a Culturable Command Area (CCA) of about 15 million hectare. The Programme was restructured and renamed as Command Area Development and Water Management (CAD&WM) Programme from 2004. After inclusion of new projects, deletion of 219 completed projects and clubbing of some projects, there are now 142 projects under implementation. Completion reports of 29 projects are awaited or to be re-included under the programme as per XII Plan guidelines. The Programme is being implemented under Pradhan Mantri Krishi Sinchai Yojana (PMKSY) – Har Khet Ko Pani - from 2015-16.

Programme Components: - The components of the CAD&WM Programme are as follows: a) survey, planning and designing of on-farm developments (OFD) works; b) on farm development (OFD) works comprising construction of field channels, land leveling and micro-irrigation; c) construction of field, intermediate and link drains for letting out surplus water; d) correction of system deficiencies above the outlet up to distributaries of 4.25 cumec (150 cusec) capacity; e) reclamation of waterlogged area including use of location specific biodrainage techniques to supplement conventional techniques for reclamation of waterlogged area; f) one time functional and infrastructure grants to Water Users' Associations; g) trainings/adaptive trials/ demonstrations through Water and Land Management Institutes (WALMIs)/

Irrigation Management and Training Institutes (IMTIs) and other Central/state institutions and monitoring & evaluation of the programme with 75 per cent funding from Government of India; h) one time infrastructure grants to WALMIs/IMTIs; and i) establishment cost - 10 per cent of the total Central Assistance on items (b), (c), (d) and (e).

The following broad provisions have been made in the Programme during XII Five Year Plan: (i) to promote water use efficiency in irrigation, financial assistance is provided to the states for development of infrastructure for micro-irrigation to facilitate use of sprinkler/drip irrigation as an alternative to construction of field channels. At least 10 per cent CCA of each project is to be covered under micro-irrigation without any restriction on upper limit. The assistance under this item is not admissible for sprinkler and drip irrigation systems (assistance for drip and sprinkler irrigation systems is available under the schemes of Ministry of Agriculture) but limited to construction of stilling tank, pump house and laying conveyance pipes up to farmer's fields; ii) Inclusion of any new project/command is to be governed as per the approved District Irrigation Plan (DIP)/State Irrigation Plan (SIP), except for the year 2015-16. Lift irrigation schemes, surface minor irrigation/cluster of surface minor irrigation schemes along with conjunctive use of ground water, may also be included under the programme. For the year 2015-16, existing procedure of the programme would continue subject to an undertaking of the state government that the project would be included under DIP/SIP. Ongoing CAD&WM projects should also be part of DIP/SIP.

Under the Programme, there is a thrust on Participatory Irrigation Management (PIM) and, therefore, following features have been made mandatory for its implementation: i) Central assistance to states has been linked to enactment of PIM legislation. Till this is done, alternative arrangements have to be in place for formation and empowerment of Water Users' Associations (WUAs); ii) WUAs have to be in position before Project Components are taken up so that beneficiaries are involved in the implementation of Programme activities since inception; iii) Central assistance for correction of system deficiencies up to distributaries of 4.25 cumec (150 cusec) capacity has been linked to formation of Distributaries Committees and handing over of the distributaries to such Committees for maintenance in future.

Programme Implementation

The Command Area Development and water management wing of the Ministry of Water Resources coordinate and monitor the implementation of the Command Area Development Programme at the national level. Progress of the projects is monitored through physical and financial progress reports of the Programme received from the states and six monthly monitoring by field units of Central Water Commission. The quality of works is ensured through monitoring, including field visits. Technical guidelines and manuals have been circulated to the States in this regard. Functionaries are trained on specific subjects from time to time, besides holding various meetings, workshops and seminars on different technical and managerial aspects. The convergence with the MGNREGA is also to be explored for the components of correction of system deficiencies, reclamation of water logged areas and construction of field, intermediate and link drains, in case of earth works.

Financing Pattern

The funding pattern for all the programme components is on 50:50 sharing basis between the Centre and the state except for state sponsored software components such as training of farmers and field functionaries and officials, adaptive trials and demonstrations, seminars/conferences/ workshops, monitoring and evaluation of the programme, etc., and one time financial assistance to WALMIs/IMTIs for strengthening & upgradation of infrastructure and infrastructure grant to WUAs for which the funding pattern is 75:25 basis between the Centre and the states. There is also provision of one time functional grants at the rate of ₹ 1,200/- per hectare (45:45:10 as Centre: State: Farmers) to the registered water users' associations. The interest accrued from this fund is utilized to upgrade the irrigation system and infrastructure developed under this Programme.

Progress under Command Area Development

The approved outlay for Command Area Development and Water Management Programme during the XI Five Year Plan (2008-09 to 2011-12) was ₹1600 crore and physical target was 1.32 Mha. The outlay for the XII Five Year Plan is ₹15000 crore and physical target is 7.6 Mha. In the mid-term appraisal, the total target has been reduced to 3.6 Mha.

The core components of physical works are construction of field channels. Since its inception in 1974-75 up to March, 2015, CCA of about 20.8 Mha has been covered. The progress of works on this component under the scheme during XI and XII Plan is given in Table-27.1.

Table-27.1

Physical Progress for Construction of Field Channels in XI & XII Plan

(million hectare)

XI Plan		
Duration	Targets	Achievements
2008-09 to 2011-12	1.32	1.686
XII Plan		
2012-13	0.35	0.361
2013-14	0.50	0.308
2014-15	0.50	0.146*

* *As per reports received from the States till December, 2014.*

Delay in approval of Cabinet for continuation of the scheme and subsequent delay in issuance of guidelines have adversely affected the progress.

Financial Achievements

Central Assistance of about ₹ 5,953 crore has been released to States under the CAD Programme since its inception in 1974-75 up to March, 2015. An amount of ₹ 283 crore has been released during 2015-16 (upto September, 2015). The details of Central Assistance released under State Sector Scheme during XI and XII Plan are as in Table-27.2.

Table-27.2

Central Assistance Released under CAD&WM in XI & XII Plan

XI Plan Period	(₹ crore) XI Plan Outlay by Planning Commission	BE Allocation	Release	% Releases w.r.t. BE Allocation
2008-09 to 2011-12	1833	1833	1680.12	92%
XII Plan				
2012-13	811	811	365.18.	45%
2013-14	1766	1766	179.98	10%
2014-15	1077	1077	199.99*	18.6%

* *Budget allocation of fund reduced to ₹ 200 crore in RE.*

Reclamation of Water Logged Areas

Although development of irrigation has increased agriculture production, it has also caused adverse effect in the form of water logging and associated problem of soil salinity/alkalinity in many irrigation commands. The problem of water logging can be mitigated to a large extent by efficient water management and by adopting suitable preventive measures. However, in spite of best efforts, the problem of water logging has surfaced in many irrigation commands and thus, it is essential to reclaim such areas so as to have optimum agricultural production from them. Ministry of Water Resources, introduced a component of Reclamation of Water Logged Areas under the Centrally Sponsored Command Area Development Programme from 1996. Under PMKSY (Har Khet Ko Pani), convergence is also to be explored in case of earth works. So far 823 schemes of 9 states, namely, Bihar, Gujarat, Madhya Pradesh, Jammu & Kashmir, Karnataka, Kerala, Maharashtra, Odisha and Uttar Pradesh have been approved for reclamation of 122.53 thousand hectare (th. ha) water logged area.

Participatory Irrigation Management

National Water Policy stresses participatory approach in water resources management. It has been recognized that participation of beneficiaries will help greatly in the optimal upkeep of irrigation system and effective utilization of irrigation water. The participation of farmers in the management of irrigation would include transfer responsibility for operation and maintenance and also collection of water charges to the Water Users' Association in their respective jurisdiction from 2008-09. One time functional grant @ ₹1200/- per hectare to be shared by the Centre, state and farmers in the ratio of 45:45:10 respectively is being paid to outlet level Water Users Associations' as incentive, the interest from which is to be used for maintenance.

16 states viz., Andhra Pradesh, Assam, Bihar, Chhattisgarh, Goa, Gujarat, Karnataka, Kerala, Madhya Pradesh, Maharashtra, Nagaland, Odisha, Rajasthan, Sikkim, Tamil Nadu and Uttar Pradesh have either enacted exclusive legislation or amended their Irrigation Acts for involvement of farmers in irrigation management. Other States are also taking steps in this direction. So far 84,779 Water Users' Associations have been formed in various states covering an area of 17.84 million hectare under various commands of irrigation projects.

Flood Management

Devastation by floods is a recurrent annual phenomenon in India. Almost every year, some or the other part of the country is affected by floods. Floods cause enormous damage to life, property—public and private, and disruptions to infrastructure, besides psychological and emotional instability amongst the people. Rashtriya Barh Ayog (RBA) had estimated in 1980, total flood-prone area in the country as 40 million hectare (mha) which was revised further to 45.64 mha by the Working Group on Flood Management set up by the Planning Commission for the 11th Five-Year Plan, based upon the information furnished by the state governments. Proper management of floods constitutes an important element in national development activities. In order to protect human life, land and property from flood fury in the country; the state governments had been engaged in flood management works for last 5 decades and a total of 18.22 million ha area has been provided a reasonable degree of protection by the end of 10th Plan. The Working Group on Water Resources constituted by Planning Commission has set a target to protect an additional area of 2.18 million hectare during the XI Plan.

Government of India has also been assisting the flood prone states in flood management and anti-erosion works for critical reaches, by providing financial assistance to the state governments through a number of centrally sponsored schemes.

Central Ground Water Board

Central Ground Water Board (CGWB), under the Ministry of Water Resources, River Development and Ganga Rejuvenation is a multidisciplinary scientific organization with a mandate to: "Develop and disseminate technologies, monitor and implement national policies for the scientific and sustainable development and management of India's ground water resources including their exploration, assessment, conservation, augmentation, protection from pollution and distribution based on principles of economic and ecological efficiency and equity".

Major Activities

Major activities of the Board include management of ground water, exploratory drilling, monitoring of ground water levels and water quality through a network of ground water observation wells, implementation of demonstrative schemes for artificial recharge and rainwater harvesting for recharge augmentation, periodic assessment of ground water resources of the country, etc. The Board also takes up special studies on various aspects of ground water such as ground water depletion, sea water ingress, ground water contamination, conjunctive use of surface & ground water, water balance etc. CGWB also organizes various campaigns and training programmes with an objective to create awareness regarding water conservation, rainwater harvesting, artificial recharge, etc.

Brief details of the major activities are as follows:-

1. Aquifer Mapping and Formulation of Aquifer Management Plan:

Aquifers are natural rock formations which can store and economically yield water. In XII Plan CGWB has taken up the National Project on Aquifer Management (NAQUIM) to facilitate identification, delineation, characterization and effective management of aquifers to ensure sustainability of ground water resources. The project is proposed to span over XII & XIII Plan periods and it is proposed to cover around 23.25 Lakh Km^2 mappable areas of the country. During the XII Plan (2012-17) an area of 8.89 lakh Km^2 is proposed to be covered under this project and remaining will be taken up during 2017-22. Major objectives of the project are i) delineation of aquifers in 3D on 1:50,000 scale in priority areas (Over- Exploited, Critical and Semi-critical categories of assessment units as well as water quality and other problem/ vulnerable areas); ii) detailed characterization of aquifers including quality of ground water; and iii) formulation of aquifer management plans. The project also envisages a participatory approach involving stakeholders at grassroots level for ground water management at local levels. The preparation of Aquifer Map and Aquifer management has been plan completed for an area 2.28 lakh.sq.km till March2016.

2. Water Supply Investigations:

The Board carries out short-term water supply investigations for Government Agencies to help them in augmenting their water supply. Normally minimum financial implications are charged from all other departments except Defense. The Board has carried out 221 investigations up to March, 2016.

3. Demonstrative Projects on "Artificial Recharge to Groundwater and Rainwater Harvesting:

CGWB has implemented demonstrative projects on artificial recharge to groundwater and rain water harvesting in Andhra Pradesh, Arunachal Pradesh, Bihar, Chhattisgarh, Delhi, Gujarat, Himachal Pradesh, Jammu & Kashmir, Jharkhand, Karnataka, Kerala, Madhya Pradesh, Maharastra, Nagaland, Odisha, Punjab, Rajasthan, Tamil Nadu, Telangana, Uttar Pradesh, West Bengal and Chandigarh, during XI Plan. Another 133 projects amounting to ₹ 99.87 crore envisaging construction of 1661 recharge structures were approved and funds of ₹ 92.69 crore were released till March, 2015. A total of 43 artificial recharge structures were constructed during 2015-16 and total structures constructed under the scheme are 1434.

4. Central Ground Water Authority:

Central Ground Water Board was constituted as Central Ground Water Authority (CGWA) under sub-Section (3) of Section 3 of the Environment (Protection) Act, 1986 for the purpose of regulation and control of ground water management and development in the country. As part of streamlining the regulatory function of Central Ground Water Authority (CGWA), district magistrates/deputy commissioners of revenue districts have been appointed as authorized officers for grant of permission for extraction of ground water for drinking/domestic uses in notified areas. They have been advised to process requests for grant of permission for extraction of ground water for drinking/domestic purposes in notified areas as per guidelines issued by CGWA. Central Ground Water Authority has also framed revised guidelines for grant of No for ground water abstraction by industries/projects in the country.

5. Ground Water Development:

There is a considerable variation in ground water potential in different parts of the country. While some areas like Indo-Gangetic alluvium have huge ground water potential, many hard rock areas have limited ground water resources. Similarly, the development of ground water resources in different areas of the country has not been uniform. Highly intensive development of ground water in certain areas in the country has resulted in over-exploitation leading to decline in ground water levels, whereas in some other areas ground water is still sub-optimally developed, leaving scope for future extraction.

CGWB carries out periodic assessment of ground water resources jointly with the state ground water departments. As per the latest assessment carried out with 2011 as base year, estimated total Annual Replenishable Ground Water Resources of the country is 433 billion cubic metres (bcm). Keeping 35 bcm for natural discharge, the net annual ground water availability is estimated as 398 bcm. Annual ground water draft for the entire country for 2011 is estimated as 245 bcm per year. The overall stage of ground water development is 62 per cent. Out of 6,607 assessment units in the country, 1,071 units have been categorized as 'over-exploited', 217 units as 'critical', 697 units as 'semi-critical', 92 assessment units as 'saline' and the remaining have been categorized as safe from ground water development point of view.

6. Rajiv Gandhi National Ground Water Training and Research Institute

The Rajiv Gandhi National Ground Water Training and Research Institute (RGNGWTRI) located at Raipur, Chhattisgarh caters to the training requirements of Central Ground Water Board and other Central and state organizations, academic institutes, NGOs, etc.

7. Hydrology Project-II

Under the World Bank funded Hydrology Project-II, pilot projects on aquifer mapping were taken up in Six different Hydrogeological terrains in the country covering parts of Bihar, Rajasthan, Maharashtra, Karnataka and Tamil Nadu. CSIR-National Geophysical Research Institute, Hyderabad was engaged as a consultant for aquifer characterization using advanced geophysical techniques and to establish the efficacy of various geophysical techniques for different Hydrogeological terrains. By integrating the data generated from hydrogeological studies including exploration and geophysical studies, the aquifer system was delineated and its characteristics established in each area. Aquifer maps have been prepared and aquifer management plans formulated using the aquifer response modeling techniques

Central Water Commission

Central Water Commission is headed by a Chairman, with the status of an Ex-Officio Secretary to the Government of India. The work of the Commission is divided among 3 wings namely, Designs and Research Wing (D&R), Water Planning and Projects Wing (WP&P) and River Management Wing (RM). Allied functions are grouped under respective wings and each wing is placed under the charge of a full-time Member with the status of an ex-Officio Additional Secretary to the Government of India. Each wing comprises of a number of units/organizations and is responsible for the disposal of tasks and duties falling within the scope of functions assigned to it. There is a separate human resources management Unit headed by a Chief Engineer, to deal with human resources management and development, financial management, training and administrative matters of the Central Water Commission.

In order to achieve better management in the water resources sector and have better coordination with the state departments, CWC has established 13 regional offices, each headed by a Chief Engineer. The offices are located at Bangalore, Bhopal, Bhubaneshwar, Chandigarh, Coimbatore, Delhi, Hyderabad, Lucknow, Nagpur, Patna, Shillong, Siliguri and Gandhi Nagar.

National Water Academy, the training institute of CWC, is located at Pune for training of Central and state in-service engineers, NGO's etc and functions directly under the guidance of the Chairman.

Functions

CWC is charged with the general responsibility of initiating, coordinating and furthering in consultation with the State Governments concerned, schemes for the control, conservation and utilization of water resources in the respective state for the purpose of flood management, irrigation, drinking water supply and water power generation. The Commission, if so required, can undertake the construction and execution of any such scheme.

In exercise of these responsibilities the functions of CWC include: to carry out techno-economic appraisal of irrigation, flood control and multipurpose projects proposed by the state governments; to collect, compile, publish and analyse the hydrological and hydro-meteorological data relating to major rivers in the country, consisting of rainfall, runoff and temperature, etc; to collect, maintain and publish statistical data relating to water resources and its utilization including quality of water throughout the country; to provide flood forecasting services to all major flood prone inter-state river basins of the country; monitoring of selected major and medium irrigation projects, to ensure the achievement of physical and financial targets. Monitoring of projects under Accelerated Irrigation Benefit Program (AIBP), and Command Area Development (CAD) programme, RRR and FMP has also been included in its field of activities; to undertake construction work of any river valley development scheme on behalf of the Government of India or state government concerned; to conduct and coordinate research on the various aspects of river valley development schemes such as flood management, irrigation, navigation, water power development, etc., and the connected structural and design features; to conduct studies on dam safety aspects for the existing dams and standardize related instrumentation for dam safety measures; to carry out morphological studies to assess river behaviour, bank erosion/coastal erosion problems and advise the Central and state governments on all such matters.

Major Activities

Hydrological Observations

Central Water Commission is operating a network of 954 hydro-meteorological observation stations throughout the country on all major river basins to observe (i) water level (gauge), (ii) discharge, (iii) water quality, (iv) silt besides (v) selected meteorological parameters including snow observations at key stations. The data so collected is utilized for planning and development of water resources projects, climate change studies, water availability studies, flood / inflow forecasting, examination of international and inter-state issues, river morphological studies, inland waterway development, reservoir siltation studies and research related activities, etc.

Water Quality Monitoring

Central Water Commission is monitoring water quality at 396 key locations covering all the major river basins of India. CWC is maintaining a three tier laboratory system for analysis of the physico-chemical parameters of the water. The level- I laboratories are located at 370 field water quality monitoring stations on major rivers of India where physical parameters such as temperature, colour, odour specific conductivity, electrical conductivity, total dissolved solids, pH and dissolved oxygen of river water are observed. There are 18 level–II laboratories located at selected division offices throughout India to analyze 25 physico-chemical characteristics and bacteriological parameters of water. 5 level-III / II+ laboratories are functioning at Varanasi, Delhi, Hyderabad, Coimbatore and Guwahati where 41 parameters including heavy metals / toxic parameters and pesticides are analyzed. The water quality data is used by different agencies for planning of water resources project, research purposes etc. The water quality data being so collected are put in various uses related to planning and development of water resources projects.

Flood Forecasting

There are 187 flood forecasting stations, of which 150 are level forecasting and 37 are inflow forecasting stations on major dams/barrages. It covers 11 major river systems in the country including 72 river sub-basins. They pertain to 20 states viz., Andhra Pradesh, Arunachal Pradesh, Assam, Bihar, Chattisgarh, Gujarat, Haryana, Jharkhand, Jammu & Kashmir, Karnataka, Madhya Pradesh, Maharashtra, Odisha, Rajasthan, Tamilnadu,Telangana, Tripura, Uttaranchal, Uttar Pradesh and West Bengal and one Union Territory Dadra and Nagar Haveli and National Capital Territory of Delhi. On an average, about 6000 forecasts are being issued during flood season every year by the Central Water Commission. Normally, these forecasts are issued 12 to 48 hours in advance, depending upon the river terrain, the locations of the flood forecasting sites and base stations.The methodology based on mathematical model using windows based Mike-11 software is progressively being used for flood forecasting.

Survey and Investigation

CWC is carrying out surveys and investigations for preparation of detailed project reports (DPRs) in the NE region, Sikkim, Uttrakhand, Bihar and J&K on the request of the respective states for development of water resources potential for irrigation, hydropower and other uses. The projects which are presently under investigation are KalezKhola HE Project (Sikkim), Rukni and Sonai Irrigation Project (Assam), Kali Khola HE Project (Sikkim), Tarum Chu HE Project(Sikkim), Twalang HE Project(Mizoram).

Project Appraisal

One of the important activities assigned to Central Water Commission is techno-economic appraisal of irrigation, flood control and multipurpose projects proposed by state governments. This task is performed and coordinated by Project Appraisal Organisation (PAO). Besides these, the Hydro-power projects proposed by state power corporations / electricity boards / private sector organisations for techno-economic clearance by Central Electricity Authority (CEA) are also scrutinised in CWC from the view point of hydrology, civil design, inter-state issues and cost aspects of civil components. Technical aspects of water supply schemes and cost aspects of Flood Control Schemes (except projects for Ganga Basinand Brahmaputra Basin) are also appraised as and when referred by state governments.

Project Monitoring

A three tier system of monitoring at Centre, state and project level was introduced in 1975. At the Central level, this work was entrusted to CWC. The main objective of monitoring is to ensure the achievement of physical and financial targets and achieve the targets of creation of irrigation potential. Monitoring system is also expected to contribute in identification of the inputs required, analysis of the reasons for any shortfalls/bottlenecks and suggest remedial measures etc., with a view to complete the projects in a time bound manner. The field inspection is also being supplemented with satellite based online monitoring using processed Cartosat imageries available on BHUVAN web services (SatAIBP).

Monitoring of Glacial Lakes

CWC is monitoring glacial lakes/water bodies in the Himalayan Region of Indian river basins on monthly basis during monsoon season from 2011 onwards. As per the monitoring report of October, 2015, cloud free data of 437 GL/WBs was available. Amongst these, 234 GL/WBs have shown decrease in water spread area, 55 have shown increase, 145 have not shown any significant charge (+/-5%) while one glacial lake and two water bodies have dried up. 9 out of 234 have decreased by more than 30 per cent and 6 out of 55 water bodies have shown increase in area by more than 30 per cent.

Hydrological Studies

Hydrological studies form the backbone of a water resources project. The success of a project is largely governed by the hydrological inputs. The inputs at Detailed Project Report (DPR) or Pre-Feasibility (PFR) stage are made available in the form of: (i) water availability/yield studies; (ii) design flood estimation; (iii) sedimentation studies; and (iv) diversion flood studies.

In addition to above, special studies in respect of review of flood hydrology for existing projects as per dam safety guidelines is also carried out.

Design Consultancy

Central water Commission is actively associated with design of majority of the mega water resources projects in India and neighbouring countries viz.

Nepal, Bhutan, Afghanistan, Myanmar, Sri Lanka and African countries by way of design consultancy or in the technical appraisal of the projects. Four design units are functioning to cater to specific requirements and to attend to special design related problems of different regions. These units have specialized directorates for hydel civil design, concrete and masonry dam design, embankment design, gates design and barrage and canal design.

Dam Rehabilitation & Improvement Project

Dam Rehabilitation and Improvement Project (DRIP) is the World Bank assisted project with the provision of rehabilitation of about 225 large dams in the seven participating states (namely Jharkhand, Karnataka, Kerala, Madhya Pradesh, Odisha, Tamil Nadu and Uttarakhand) alongwith institutional strengthening component for participating states and Central Water Commission. It had become effective from 2012 for implementation over a period of six-years. The Dam Safety Organisation, CWC has received ISO 9001: 2008 certification for its quality management systems from the Bureau of Indian Standards during the year 2015. Central Water Commission also received "CBIP Award 2016" for promoting health and safety of large dams under DRIP.

National Register of Large Dams

As per the latest information compiled under the National Register of Large Dams (NRLD) maintained by CWC, there are 5174 large dams in the country. Out of this, 4861 large dams have been completed and 313 large dams are under construction. The NRLD is available on CWC website.

Water Resource Information System

CWC and ISRO has jointly developed Water Resources Information System (India-WRIS) in 2010. Subsequently, four versions of the website of India-WRIS have been launched. The version 4.1 was launched in July, 2015 and is available in public domain at 1:250000 scale. The information system contains several GIS layers on water resources projects, thematic layers like major water bodies, land use/land cover, wastelands, land degradation etc., environmental layers as well as infrastructure and other administrative layers. The information system has all the basic map viewing and navigation capabilities like zoom, overview, bookmark, table of contents, etc. As per provision of Hydro-Meteorological Data Dissemination Policy 2013 (MoWR), all unclassified data of CWC G&D stations has been made available on India-WRIS website.

Training and Capacity Building

Central Water Commission offers training to water sector professionals every year. These training are organised at National Water Academy (NWA), CWC Headquarter and field offices of CWC. The National Water Academy, CWC is a centre of excellence for imparting training on all facets of Water Resources Development and Management covering the different areas of planning, design, evaluation, construction, operation and monitoring of water resources projects, and also the application of high-end technology in water sector. The programs at NWA are open to all stakeholders of water sector including those from NGOs, media, private sector organisations, academic institutions, PSUs, individuals and foreign nationals also.

National Water Academy

National Water Academy (NWA) is an institute established by the Ministry under Central Water Commission at Khadakwasla, Pune. The objective of NWA is to function as 'Centre of Excellence' in training and capacity building for all stakeholders on various aspects of water resources planning, development and management and to develop institutional capability at the national level for imparting training in new emerging technologies in water resources sector on continued basis. NWA conducts training programmes on whole gamut of water resources development and management comprising both technical and non-technical areas. Technical area comprises topics like designs, project planning, hydrological sciences, irrigation management and agriculture, hydropower, information technology, river basin management and basin planning etc. Non-technical area comprises environmental science, social science, economic aspects, management development, legal issues and policy issues, etc. NWA has been recognised as Regional Training Centre (RTC) of the World Meteorological Organisation (WMO), and is conducting distance learning programmes on the topics of hydraulics, hydrological sciences and hydrometeorology in association with WMO for Asian countries. In the recent past, many new areas have been added to the NWA's portfolio like e-SWIS (Surface Water Information System); e-Water; preparation of probable maximum precipitation (PMP) atlases; monitoring irrigation projects using BHUVAN software; modernization and capacity enhancement of hydropower projects etc.

Since its inception in 1988, NWA has contributed immensely in the capacity building and training in water resources sector for all stakeholders including cadre training programmes for Central Water Engineering Services Officers, Capacity Building for state and Central organizations; Programmes under PMKSY; programme for all other stakeholders like teachers, non-governmental organisations (NGOs), Panchayat Raj Institutions (PRIs), media personnel, youth representatives etc. NWA also conducts programme for foreign nationals.

Central Soil and Materials Research Station

Central Soil and Materials Research Station (CSMRS), New Delhi, is a premier organization in the country that deals with the field explorations, laboratory investigations, and research in the field of geotechnical engineering and civil engineering materials, particularly for construction of river valley projects, and safety evaluation of existing dams. The Research Station primarily functions as an adviser and consultant to various departments of Government of India, state governments and Government of India Undertakings. The Research Station has excellent facilities and highly qualified officers and has acquired some unique capabilities in the country in the field of geotechnical engineering and construction materials' characterisation. The Research Station is involved in the safety evaluation of existing hydraulic structures and quality control of construction for various river valley projects including those in neighboring Bhutan.

The sphere of activities of the Research Station is covered under the following main areas: soil mechanics including studies on expansive soils, dispersive soils, organic soils, and quality control of structures comprising soil; rockfill, soil dynamics, geosynthetics, numerical modelling and quality control of rockfill dams. Concrete Technology including construction materials survey and characterisation, design of concrete mixes, roller compacted concrete, substitution of sand with bottom ash, thermal studies and quality control of concrete structures; concrete diagnostics including investigation/monitoring, material for repair and rehabilitation, petrography, durability of concrete, mineralogy, water quality, alkali aggregate reaction, new material such as polymer, grout, etc., SSC/SFRC/HPC/HSC/CFRD; rock mechanics (I) including foundation rock characterisation, in-situ assessment such as evaluation of in-situ stresses, shear stresses and deformability characteristics and geophysical investigations; and rock mechanics (II) including rock mechanics laboratory investigations, workshop instrumentation, and electronics

Central Water and Power Research Station

Central Water and Power Research Station (CWPRS) under MoWR, RD & GR has been serving nation since the year 1916 rendering its services to the national needs through basic and applied research on dam construction, river engineering projects, flood control and energy dissipation, coastal harbors and ports, nuclear power plants, and infrastructure foundations. CWPRS is recognized as the Regional Laboratory for Economic and Social Committee for Asia and Pacific (ESCAP) since 1971. From its inception in the year 1916, CWPRS has been unstintingly working to establish an impetus for improvements in the integrated basic, applied & result-oriented research and development programs, for achieving greater competence and efficacy.

As a premier hydraulic research institute in the country, CWPRS is mandated to provide R&D and consultancy support to a variety of projects using physical hydraulic models, mathematical models and field and laboratory experiments. Basic research is carried out pertaining to water resources and related sciences, for optimization, safety, design and testing of different components of the river training measures and dams and appurtenant structures. With the expertise of seven major civil engineering disciplines under one umbrella, CWPRS has distinct advantage in providing single window solutions to problems involving multiple disciplines.

The main functions of CWPRS include: undertaking applied research in hydraulics and allied disciplines to provide comprehensive R&D inputs for optimizing the designs of river, coastal, water storage and conveyance hydraulic structures; conducting basic and fundamental research for providing innovative and world-class R&D solutions to specific problems; disseminating research findings amongst hydraulic research fraternity by way of publications and training programmes; offering advisory services to various ministries and departments within the sphere of its activities; and evolving and updating standards (ISO & BIS) and advising the apex regulatory agencies to ascertain compliance to required stipulations.

The research at CWPRS is based on sound engineering practice and many of its projects have a national and international perspective. It institutes in-depth relations with its clientele, by learning their environments and challenges, to enable it to offer tangible solutions with a sincere perspective. Advisory services are also offered to the government within the sphere of its activities by participation in various expert committees. Disseminating the research findings amongst hydraulic research fraternity, and promoting research activities at other institutions by imparting training to their research manpower, are also undertaken. Considering the infrastructure and expertise available, CWPRS has been identified under World Bank aided national hydrology project as a nodal agency for providing overall guidance on hydro-meteorological and water quality equipments selection, commission and quality control to all states/ union territories.

Farakka Barrage Project

Farakka Barrage Project with headquarters at Farakka in Murshidabad district of West Bengal is a subordinate office under the Union Ministry of Water Resources, River Development & Ganga Rejuvenation. The Farakka Barrage Project Authority was set up in 1961 with the mandate to execute and thereafter operate and maintain the Farakka Barrage Project Complex comprising of Farakka Barrage, Jangipur Barrage, Feeder Canal, Navigation Lock and associated structures. The Barrage comprises 112 Gates (108 Nos. main Gates and 4 Nos. Fish Lock Gates) and 11 Nos. Head Regulator Gates for diversion of approximately 40,000 cusec (1035 cumec) of discharge into the Feeder Canal. The project construction commenced in 1961 and the project was commissioned and dedicated to the Nation in May 1975.

Main objective of the Farakka Barrage Project complex is to divert adequate quantity of Ganga waters to Bhagirathi-Hoogly river system through 38.38 km long feeder canal for preservation and maintenance of Kolkata Port by improving the regime and navigability of the Bhagirathi-Hoogly river system. The increased upland supply from Ganga at Farakka into Bhagirathi reduces salinity and ensures sweet water supply to Kolkata and surrounding areas. The rail-cum-road bridge built across the river Ganga at Farakka establishes direct road and rail communication link to the North-Eastern Region with rest of the country. The Hoogly-Bhagirathi river system, the Feeder Canal and the Navigation Lock at Farakka form part of the Haldia-

Allahabad Inland Waterway (National Waterway No:1). The Feeder Canal also supplies water to 2,100 MW Farakka Super Thermal Power Project (FSTPP) of NTPC Ltd. at Farakka.

Ganga Flood Control Commission

Ganga Flood Control Commission (GFCC), a subordinate office of Ministry of Water Resources, River Development and Ganga Rejuvenation with its headquarte at Patna, was created in 1972 to deal with floods and its management in Ganga Basin states as secretariat and executive wing of Ganga Flood Control Board. Headed by Union Minister of Water Resources, chief ministers of basin states or their representatives and members, Planning Commission, Chairman, GFCC acts as the Member-Secretary of the Board.

Ganga Flood Control Commission (GFCC) carries out several activities as outlined here: preparation and updating of comprehensive plan of flood management; techno-economic appraisal of flood management schemes; assessment of adequacy of waterways under road and rail bridges; framing of guidelines for quality control and maintenance; and monitoring of all flood management schemes funded by Central Govt. and important flood management schemes funded by state governments.

Bansagar Control Board

Bansagar Control Board is a subordinate office of the Union Ministry of Water Resources. The Board was set up in 1976. This was in accordance with the Bansagar Agreement reached between the Governments of Madhya Pradesh, Uttar Pradesh and Bihar for sharing the waters of river Sone and the cost of the Bansagar dam. The main features of the resolution are as below: in consultation with the Governments of Madhya Pradesh, Bihar and Uttar Pradesh, it has been decided to set up the Bansagar Control Board with a view to ensuring the efficient, economical and early execution of Bansagar dam including all connected works in Madhya Pradesh, but excluding the canal systems which will be executed by respective states namely, Madhya Pradesh, Uttar Pradesh and Bihar. The Control Board is in overall charge of the project including its technical and financial aspects. The actual work of construction will be carried out under the direction of the Control Board by the Chief Engineer concerned of the Madhya Pradesh Government. The three state governments agree to delegate powers to the Chief Engineer, Madhya Pradesh, to contract for works, supplies and services under the direction of the Board. The contract in respect of all works will be executed in the name of the Governor of Madhya Pradesh.

Betwa River Board

A decision to harness the available water resources of Betwa river was taken in by Uttar Pradesh and Madhya Pradesh. Further, the two states agreed for setting up of a tripartite Control Board for the speedy, smooth and efficient execution of the various inter-state projects of both the states. Betwa River Board (B.R.B) was constituted in 1976 under the Chairmanship of Union

Minister of Water Resources by an Act of Parliament to execute the Rajghat Dam Project and Power House. The project authority started construction of the project under the overall guidance of Betwa River Board Act, 1976. The benefits and cost of the above project are shared equally by both the State Governments.

Construction of dam upto top level was completed with installation of Radial Gates. Since then the impounding of water is being done regularly for generation of power and irrigation in both the states. Impounding of water during monsoon 2015 was done upto FRL. 371.00 and 369 lakh units of power were generated during the year 2015-16. The reservoir created by the Rajghat Dam has been renamed as "Rani Laxmibai Sagar."

Sardar Sarovar Construction Advisory Committee

The Sardar Sarovar Construction Advisory Committee (SSCAC) was constituted by the Government of India in accordance with the directives of the Narmada Water Disputes Tribunal (NWDT)in September 1980 with the Secretary Ministry of Water Resources as its Chairman. The Tribunal considered that the said Construction Advisory Committee is desirable and necessary for ensuring efficient, economical and timely execution of Unit-I (dam and appurtenant works) and unit-III (power complex) of the project. The principal composition of the SSCAC includes senior most officers from Govt of India and of the states of Gujarat, Madhya Pradesh, Maharashtra and Rajasthan.

Functions of SSCAC

The functions of the Committee include: scrutinize the project estimates of dam and powerhouse works and recommend for the administrative approval; examine and make recommendations on all proposals pertaining to technical features and designs; examine the requirement of funds for the construction of works and other purposes according to the approved programme; examine and recommend delegation of powers - both technical and financial - to the officers engaged in the execution of the project. examine and recommend specifications for various classes of work; and review progress reports, both for works and expenditure.

Tungabhadra Board

The Tungabhadra Board was constituted by the President of India in exercise of the powers vested under Sub-section (4), Section 66 of Andhra State Act 1953 for completion of the Tungabhadra project and for its operation and maintenance. The Board consists of a Chairman, appointed by the Government of India, and four Members, one each representing the states of Andhra Pradesh, Karnataka, Telangana and Government of India. The Board appoints a full time Secretary to look after its works. In the discharge of its assigned functions, the Board exercises powers of a state government. It makes rules for the conduct of its own business. The Government of Andhra Pradesh, Government of Telangana and the Government of Karnataka provide funds in agreed proportions and also depute staff to man the various specified posts, as per an agreed proportion.

Upper Yamuna River Board

Upper Yamuna refers to the reach of Yamuna from its origin at Yamunotri to Okhla Barrage at Delhi. A Memorandum of Understanding (MOU) was signed by Uttar Pradesh, Haryana, Rajasthan, Himachal Pradesh and NCT of Delhi in 1994 regarding allocation of utilizable surface flow of Yamuna up to Okhla among the co-basin states. Government of India constituted the Upper Yamuna River Board in 1995 for regulation and supply of water to the basin states. The newly formed state of Uttaranchal (now Uttrakhand) was also subsequently inducted to the Board. Upper Yamuna River Board is a subordinate office under Ministry of Water Resources, Government of India.

Brahmaputra Board

Brahmaputra Board, an autonomous statutory body was set up under an Act of Parliament called Brahmaputra Board Act (46 of 1980) for planning and implementation of measures for the management of flood and bank erosion in the Brahmaputra Valley for the matter connected therewith. The Board stated functioning with its headquarters at Guwahati from 1982. The jurisdiction of Brahmaputra Board includes both Brahmaputra and Barak valley and covers all the states of North Eastern Region, Sikkim and Northern part of West Bengal falling under Brahmaputra basin. The major functions of the Board are to carry out survey and investigation and to prepare Master Plan for control of flood, bank erosion and improvement of drainage congestion, development and utilization of water resources of the Brahmaputra and Barak River system for irrigation, hydro power, navigation and for other beneficial purposes.

Brahmaputra Board has altogether formulated 57 Master Plans and additional 11 Master Plans (nine of Meghalaya, one of Tripura and one of Manipur) have been taken up for formulation during the XII Plan. The Board had taken up survey and investigation of Multipurpose River Valley Projects in Brahmaputra and Barak Basin and in the South flowing rivers of Meghalaya. Presently 5 DPRs of multipurpose of River Valley Projects (Simsang in Meghalaya, Noa-Dehing in Arunachal Pradesh, Jiadhal in Assam-Arunachal Border, Kulisi and Killing in Assam-Meghalaya Border) are under preparation by Brahmaputra board.

In addition to above, 41 drainage congested areas in Brahmaputra and Barak basins have been identified based upon findings of 49 approved Master Plans. Out of which, 2 Drainage Development Schemes (DDS) have been completed (Harang and East of Berpeta, both in Assam) and handed over to Government of Assam. 5 DDS are under execution. Rest DDS are under various stages of appraisal/ modification/ investigation.

The Board had taken up construction of Pagladia Project across Pagladia river in Assam for flood moderation to benefit an area of 40,000 ha, irrigation to 54,160 ha of agricultural land and incidental power generation of 3MW. The Board has set up North Eastern Hydraulic & Allied Research Institute (NEHARI) at Rudreswar in North Guwahati with the facilities of Hydraulic Laboratory with 4 model trays and 1 flume besides Material Testing Laboratories (soil, concrete, construction material and foundation rock).

National Water Development Agency

The National Water Development Agency (NWDA) was established in July, 1982 by the Government of India as a registered Society under the Societies Registration Act, 1860 under the Ministry of Water Resources, River Development and Ganga Rejuvenation to study the feasibility of the links under peninsular component of National Perspective Plan. The NWDA is fully funded by the Government of India through grant-in-aid. Subsequently in 1990-91, NWDA Society resolved to take up the studies of the Himalayan Component also.

The Agency functions with the following main objectives: (a) to carry out detailed surveys and investigations of possible reservoir sites and inter-connecting links in order to establish feasibility of the proposal of Peninsular Rivers Development and Himalayan Rivers Development Components forming part of the National Perspective for Water Resources Development prepared by the then Ministry of Irrigation (now Ministry of Water Resources) and Central Water Commission; (b) to carry out detailed surveys about the quantum of water in various Peninsular River Systems and Himalayan River Systems which can be transferred to other basins/states after meeting the reasonable needs of the basin/states in the foreseeable future; (c) to prepare pre-feasibility / feasibility / detailed project reports of the intra-State links as may be proposed by the states. The concurrence of the concerned co-basin States for such proposals may be obtained before taking up their FRs / DPRs ; and (d) to do all such other things the Society may consider necessary, incidental, supplementary or conducive to the attainment of above objectives.

Narmada Control Authority

In pursuance of the decision of the Narmada Water Disputes Tribunal (NWDT) under Clause-XIV of its final orders, the Government of India framed the Narmada Water Scheme, which, interalia, constituted the Narmada Control Authority and Review Committee in 1980 for proper implementation of the decisions and directions of the Tribunal.The Narmada Control Authority (NCA) has been vested with powers for the implementation of the orders of the Tribunal with respect to the storage, apportionment regulation and control of the Narmada water, sharing of power benefits from SardarSarovar Project (SSP), regulated release of water by Madhya Pradesh, acquisition of land likely to be submerged under the SardarSarovar Project by the concerned States, compensation, resettlement/rehabilitation of the oustees, sharing of costs and implementation of the environmental safe guard measures.

The Authority is headed by the Secretary, Ministry of Water Resources, as its Chairman, with Secretaries of the Union Ministries of Power, Environment and Forests, Social Justice and Empowerment and Tribal Welfare, Chief Secretaries of the four party states, one full time Executive Member and three full time independent Members appointed by the Central Government and four part time Members nominated by party states as Members.

National Institute of Hydrology

The National Institute of Hydrology (NIH), established in 1978 as an autonomous organization under Ministry of Water Resources, River Development & Ganga Rejuvenation (Government of India), is a premier R&D institute in the country to undertake, aid, promote and coordinate basic, applied and strategic research on all aspects of hydrology and water resources development. The Institute has its headquarters at Roorkee (Uttarakhand). To carry out field related research covering different regions of the country, the Institute has four regional centres located at Belgaum, Jammu, Kakinada and Bhopal, and two centres for flood management studies at Guwahati and Patna.

The objectives of the Institute include: (a) to undertake, aid, promote and coordinate systematic and scientific work on all aspects of hydrology; (b) to cooperate and collaborate with other national foreign and international organizations in the field of hydrology; (c) to establish and maintain a research and reference library in pursuance of the objectives of the society and equip the same with books, reviews, magazines and other relevant publications; and (d) to do all other such things as the Society may consider necessary, incidental or conducive to the attainment of the objectives for which the Institute has been established. To fulfil these objectives, the Institute has established state-of-art laboratory facilities in the area of nuclear applications in hydrology, water quality, soil water, remote sensing and GIS applications, snow and glacier, numerical groundwater modelling and hydrological instrumentation.

The Institute acts as a center of excellence for transfer of technology, human resources development and institutional development in specialized areas of hydrology, and conducts user defined, demand-driven research through collaboration with relevant national and international organizations. The Institute vigorously pursues capacity development activities by organizing training programmes for field engineers, scientists and researchers, NGOs. The Institute has undertaken a number of internationally funded projects, including those from UNDP, USAID, UNESCO, the World Bank, the Netherlands, Sweden, and European Union. As an agency of the Ministry the Institute is now participating in the National Hydrology Project (NHP). Some of the significant contributions of NIH include studies for solution of real-life problems related to augmentation of water supply and water management in cities, river-bank filtration, glacier contribution in stream flow of Himalayan rivers for hydro-electric power projects, watershed development, water availability studies for lakes, coastal groundwater dynamics and management, watershed development, storm water drainage network in cities, flood inundation mapping and flood risk zoning, drought assessment, and water quality assessment in major cities.

National Projects Construction Corporation Limited

National Projects Construction Corporation Limited (NPCC) was established in 1957 as a premier construction company to create necessary infrastructure for economic development of the country. NPCC ltd comply with Quality management requirements of ISO 9001-2008 for execution of civil works for thermal & hydro electric projects', river valley projects, industrial structures, project management consultancy services for buildings, housings, roads, bridges and infrastructure projects. In its 59 years of existence the Corporation has successfully associated itself with completion of several National Projects from concept to commissioning stage. Some of them are in remote and hazardous location over the country. The corporation is making profit for the last five years. National Project Construction Corporation Ltd. has been conferred with "Udyog Ratan Award 2015" to CMD and "Excellence Award 2015" by Institute of Economic Studies. It has also been assigned a credit rating of A+ by ICRA. Today as a Team, NPCC is gearing up to achieve greater heights for "Mini Ratna" status.

WAPCOS Limited

WAPCOS Limited is a "MINI RATNA-I" Public Sector Enterprise under the aegis of the Union Ministry of Water Resources, Ganga Rejuvenation and River Development. Incorporated in 1969 under the Companies Act, 1956; WAPCOS has been providing consultancy services in all facets of water resources, power and infrastructure sectors in India and abroad. The quality management systems of WAPCOS comply with the Quality Assurance requirements of ISO 9001:2008 for consultancy services in water resources, power and infrastructure development projects.

28 Welfare

IN 1985-86, the erstwhile Ministry of Welfare was bifurcated into the Department of Women and Child Development and the Department of Welfare. Simultaneously, the Scheduled Castes Development Division, Tribal Development Division and the Minorities and Backward Classes Welfare Division were shifted from the Ministry of Home Affairs and also the Wakf Division from the Ministry of Law to form the then Ministry of Welfare. Subsequently, the name of the Ministry was changed to the Ministry of Social Justice & Empowerment in May, 1998. In October, 1999, the Tribal Development Division moved out to form a separate Ministry of Tribal Affairs. In January, 2007 the Minorities Division along with Wakf Unit also shifted away from the Ministry and was formed as separate Ministry. The Ministry of Social Justice & Empowerment (SJ&E) was bifurcated into two Departments which are, Department of Social Justice and Empowerment and Department for Empowerment of Persons with Disabilities.

Welfare of Scheduled Castes

Statutory Framework

The Constitution contains several provisions in the nature of safeguards for the Scheduled Castes. The following two Acts specifically aim at curbing (i) untouchability and (ii) atrocities against SCs and STs, and are therefore very important for the Scheduled Castes:- (i) The Protection of Civil Rights Act, 1955, and (ii) The Scheduled Castes and the Scheduled Tribes (Preventions of Atrocities) Act, 1989.

Protection of Civil Rights

In pursuance of Article 17 of the Constitution of India, The Untouchability (Offences) Act, 1955 was enacted and notified in May, 1955. Subsequently, it was amended and renamed in the year 1976 as The Protection of Civil Rights Act, 1955. Rules under this Act, viz., The Protection of Civil Rights Rules, 1977 were notified in 1977. The Act extends to the whole of India and provides punishment for the practice of untouchability. It is implemented by the respective state governments and union territory administrations.

Scheduled Castes and the Scheduled Tribes (Preventions of Atrocities) Act

The Scheduled Castes and the Scheduled Tribes (Prevention of Atrocities) Act, 1989 (The PoA Act) came into force with effect from 1990. This legislation aims at preventing commission of offences by persons other than Scheduled Castes and Scheduled Tribes against Scheduled Castes and Scheduled Tribes.

Comprehensive Rules under this Act, titled "Scheduled Castes and the Scheduled Tribes (Prevention of Atrocities) Rules, 1995 were notified in the year 1995, which, inter-alia, provide norms for relief and rehabilitation. These Rules had not been amended thereafter.

Scheduled Castes and Scheduled Tribes (Prevention of Atrocities) Amendment Act, 2015

Despite the deterrent provisions made in the PoA Act, continuing atrocities against the members of Scheduled Castes (SCs) and Scheduled Tribes (STs) had been a cause of concern. High incidence of occurrences of offences against members of SCs and STs also indicated that the deterrent effect of the PoA Act was not adequately felt by the accused. It was, therefore, considered appropriate to strengthen the Act and make the relevant provisions of the Act more effective. Based on the consultation process with all the stakeholders, amendments in the PoA Act were proposed to broadly cover five areas.

National Commission for Scheduled Castes

The National Commission for Scheduled Castes and Scheduled Tribes which was set up under Article 383 of the Constitution in 1990 was bifurcated into two Commissions namely, National Commission for Scheduled Castes and National Commission for Scheduled Tribes after the 89th Constitutional (Amendment) Act, 2003. The National Commission for Scheduled Castes is responsible for monitoring the safeguards provided for Scheduled Castes and also to review issues concerning their welfare.

Functions of the NCSC as enumerated in the Article 338(5) of the Constitution are:- (a) to investigate and monitor all matters relating to the safeguards provided for the Scheduled Castes under the Constitution or under any other law for the time being in force or under any order of the Government and to evaluate the working of such safeguards; (b) to inquire into specific complaints with respect to the deprivation of rights and safeguards of the scheduled castes; (c) to participate and advise on the planning process of socio-economic development of the Scheduled Castes and to evaluate the progress of their development under the Union and any State; (d) to present to the President, annually and at such other times as the Commission may deem fit, reports upon the working of those safeguards; (e) to make in such reports, recommendations as to the measures that should be taken by the Union or any State for the effective implementation of those safeguards and other measures for the protection, welfare and socio-economic development of the scheduled castes; and (f) to discharge such other functions in relation to the protection, welfare and development and advancement of the scheduled castes as the President may, subject to the provisions of any law made by Parliament, by rule specify.

O. W.: http://www.ncsc.nic.in

Educational Empowerment

Pre-Matric Scholarship to the Children

This is also a centrally sponsored scheme, which is implemented by the state governments and union territory administrations, which receive 100 per cent central assistance for Government of India for the total expenditure under the scheme, over and above their respective committed liability. The level of committed liability of respective state Governments/union territory administrations for a year is equivalent to the level of actual expenditure incurred by them under the scheme during the terminal year of the last Five Year Plan.

Pre-Matric Scholarship for SC Students

The scheme has been introduced in 2012. The Scheme is centrally sponsored scheme and implemented by the state governments and union territory administrations, which will 100 per cent assistance from Government of India for expenditure under the Scheme, over and above their committed liability. The level of committed liability of a state government/union territory administration for a year will be equivalent to the level of actual expenditure incurred by them under the Scheme during the terminal year of the previous Five Year Plan Period, and will be required to be borne by them by making provision in their own budget.

National Overseas Scholarship for SCs

The scheme provides for fees charged by institutions as per actual, monthly maintenance allowance, passage visa fee and insurance premium etc. annual contingency allowance, incidental journey allowance. Only two children of the same parents/guardians are eligible to get under the benefit. The second child of the same parents/guardian will be considered only if the slots are still available for that year. The prospective awardees should not be more than 35 years of age. The total number of awards to be given is 100 in 2014-15 for women candidates. Financial assistance under the scheme is provided maximum period of 4 years for Ph.D and 3 years for Master's programme. The income ceiling from all sources of the employed candidate or his/her parents/ guardians should not be more than ₹ 50,000/- per month.

Babu Jagjivan Ram Chhatrawas Yojana

The objective of the Scheme is to provide hostel facilities to SC boys and girls studying in middle schools, higher secondary schools, colleges and universities. The state governments/union territory administrations and the Central and state universities/institutions are eligible for central assistance, both for fresh construction of hostel buildings and for expansion of the existing hostel facilities while NGOs and deemed Universities in the private sector can avail the benefit only for expansion of their existing hostel facilities.

Rajiv Gandhi National Fellowship for SC Students

The scheme provides financial assistance to Scheduled Caste students for pursuing research studies leading to M. Phil, Ph.D, and equivalent research degree in universities, research institutions and scientific institutions. University Grants Commission (UGC) is the nodal agency for implementing the scheme. About 2000 Junior Research Fellowships (JRF) per year are awarded to Scheduled Caste students. Number of fellowships were increased from 1333 in 2010 to 2000 in 2011. In case of non-availability of adequate number of Scheduled Caste candidates, the number of fellowships not availed during a year will be carried forward to the next academic session. In case, the number of candidates exceeds the number of available awards, the UGC selects the candidates based on the percentage of marks obtained by the candidates in their Post Graduation examination. There is no income ceiling prescribed under the Scheme.

Economic Empowerment

Special Central Assistance

Special Central Assistance (SCA) to Scheduled Castes Sub Plan (SCSP) is a central sector scheme, started in 1980, under which 100 per cent grant is given to the states/UTs, as an additive to their Scheduled Castes Sub Plan (SCSP). The main objective is to give a thrust to family oriented schemes of economic development of SCs below the poverty line.

Assistance to State Scheduled Castes Development Corporation

The Centrally Sponsored Scheme for participating in the equity share of the Scheduled Castes Development Corporation (SCDC) in the ratio of 49:51 (Central State) was introduced in 1979. At present, SCDCs are functioning in 27 states/UTs. The main functions of SCDCs are identification of eligible SC families and motivating them to undertake economic development schemes, sponsoring the schemes to financial institutions for credit support, providing financial assistance in the form of margin money at low rate of interest and subsidy in order to reduce the repayment liability and providing necessary tie up with other poverty alleviation programmes. The SCDCs are playing an important role in providing credit and inputs by way of margin money loans and subsidy to the target group.

National Scheduled Castes Finance and Development Corporation

The National Scheduled Castes Finance and Development Corporation (NSFDC) was set up in February, 1989 under Section 8 of the Companies Act, 2013 (formerly Section 25 of the Companies Act, 1956). The broad objective of NSFDC is to provide financial assistance in the form of concessional loans to scheduled castes families, and skill-cum-entrepreneurial training to the youth of the target group, living below double the poverty line [presently ₹ 98,000/- per annum for rural areas and ₹1,20,000/- per annum for urban areas] for their economic development. National Safai Karamcharis Finance and Development Corporation (NSKFDC) was incorporated in January, 1997 as a company not for profit under Section 25 of the Companies Act, 1956. NSKFDC is an Apex Corporation under the Ministry of Social Justice and Empowerment, Government of India. The target group of the Corporation are "Scavengers",

"Manual Scavenger" means a person engaged or employed by an individual or a local authority or a public or private agency, for manually cleaning, carrying, disposing of, or otherwise handling in any manner, human excreta in an insanitary latrine or in an open drain or pit into which the human excreta from insanitary latrines is disposed of, or on a railway track or in such other spaces or premises, as the Central Government or a State Government may notify, before the excreta fully decomposes, and the expression "manual scavenging" shall be interpreted accordingly.

O. W.: http://www.ncsk.nic.in

Welfare of Persons with Disabilities

In order to give focused attention to different policy issues and meaningful thrust to the activities aimed at welfare and empowerment of the Persons with Disabilities, a separate Department of Disability Affairs was carved out of the Ministry of Social Justice and Empowerment in May, 2012. The Department acts as a Nodal Agency for matters pertaining to disability and Persons with Disabilities including effecting closer coordination among different stakeholders : related Central ministries, state/UT governments, NGOs etc. in matters pertaining to disability.

According to Census 2011, there are 2.68 crore persons with disabilities in the country (who constitute 2.21 percent of the total population). Out of the total population of persons with disabilities, about 1.50 crore are men and 1.18 crore are women. These include persons with visual, hearing, speech and locomotor disabilities, mental illness, mental retardation, multiple disabilities and other disabilities.

Relevant Constitutional Provisions

The Constitution of India through its Preamble, inter-alia seeks to secure to all its citizens; justice, social, economic and political; liberty of thought, expression, belief, faith and worship; equality of status and of opportunity. Part-III of the Constitution provides for a set of six Fundamental Rights to all the citizens (and in a few cases to non citizens also). These include - Right to Equality; Right to Freedom; Right against Exploitation; Right to Freedom of Religion; Cultural and Educational Rights and Right to Constitutional Remedies. All these rights are also available to the Persons with Disabilities even though no specific mention of such persons appear in this Part of the Constitution.

The Directive Principles of State Policy have been incorporated in Part- IV of the Constitution. Even though non-justiciable, these have been declared as fundamental in the governance of the country. These principles are intended to be the imperative basis of State policy. These are really in the nature of instructions issued to future legislatures and executives for their guidance. Article 41: Right to work, to education and to public assistance in certain cases, provides: "The State shall, within the limits of its economic capacity and development, make effective provision for securing the right to work, to education and to public assistance in case of unemployment, old age, sickness and disablement and in other cases of undeserved want. Besides, Eleventh Schedule to Article 243-G and Twelfth Schedule to Article 243-W, which pertain to the powers and responsibilities of the Panchayats and Municipalities respectively with respect to implementation of schemes for economic development and social justice, include welfare and safeguarding the interests of Persons with Disabilities among other weaker sections of the society. The relevant extracts of the said schedules are reproduced below: Eleventh Schedule to Article 243-G : "Social welfare, including welfare of the handicapped and mentally retarded." (Entry No. 26). Twelfth Schedule to Article 243-W: "Safeguarding the interests of weaker sections of society, including the handicapped and mentally retarded." (Entry No. 9)

The Department deals with the following Legislations governing different aspects of disability and welfare & empowerment of the Persons with Disabilities:-

1. The Rehabilitation Council of India Act, 1992.
2. The Persons with Disabilities (Equal Opportunities, Protection of Rights and Full Participation) Act, 1995; and
3. The National Trust for the Welfare of Persons with Autism, Cerebral Palsy, Mental Retardation and Multiple Disabilities Act, 1999.

Department of Empowerment of Persons with Disabilities (DEPwD), has formulated the accessible India Campaign (Sugamya Bharat Abhiyan), as a nation-wide campaign for achieving universal accessibility for PwDs. The campaign targets three separate verticals for achieving universal accessibilities namely the built up environment, transportation eco-system and information and communication eco-system. The campaign has ambitious targets with defined timelines and will use IT and social media for spreading awareness about the campaign and seeking commitment/engagement of various stakeholders. The Department has asked various state to identify about 50 to 100 public buildings in big cities and also identify citizen centric public websites, which if made fully accessible would have the highest impact on the lives of PwDs. Once identified "Access Audit" of these buildings and websities will be conducted by professional agencies. As per the audit findings, retrofitting and conversion of buildings, transport and websites would be undertaken by various government departments. This will be supported by the Scheme of Implementation of Persons with Disabilities Act (SIPDA), an umbrella scheme run by the Department of Empowerment of Persons with Disabilities (DEPwD) for implementing various initiatives for social and economic empowerment of PwDs.

Department of Empowerment of Persons with Disabilities is collaborating with Ministry of Home, Ministry of Health and Family Welfare and Ministry of Tourism for creating "Accessible police station', "Accessible hospitals and 'Accessible tourism' respectively across the country. The Department is also coordinating with the Ministry of Information and Broadcasting for enhancing accessibility of Television programmes by incorporating features like captioning, text to speech and audio description.

DEPwD is also in the process of creating a mobile app, along with a web portal for crowd sourcing the request regarding inaccessible places. With the app, downloaded on his/her mobile phone, any person would be able to click a photograph or video of an inaccessible public place (like a school, hospital, government office etc.) and upload the same to the Accessible India portal. The portal will process the request for access audit, financial sanction and find retrofitting of the building to make it completely accessible. The mobile app and portal will also seek engagement of big corporates and PSUs to partner in the campaign by offering their help to conduct access audit and for accessibility conversion of the buildings/transport and websites.

Tribals Affairs

Development of Scheduled Tribes

The Ministry of Tribal Affairs was set up in 1999 after the bifurcation of Ministry of Social Justice and Empowerment with the objective of providing more focused approach on the integrated socio-economic development of the Scheduled Tribes (STs), the most underprivileged of the society, in a coordinated and planned manner.

Scheduled Areas and Tribal Areas

Scheduled Tribes live in contiguous areas unlike other communities. It is, therefore, much simpler to have an area approach for development activities and also regulatory provisions to protect their interests. In order to protect the interests of Scheduled Tribes with regard to land alienation and other social factors, provisions of the "Fifth Schedule" and "Sixth Schedule" have been enshrined in the Constitution.

The Fifth Schedule under Article 244 (1) of Constitution defines "Scheduled Areas" as such areas as the President may by Order declare to be Scheduled Areas after consultation with the Governor of the state. The Sixth Schedule under Article 244 (2) of the Constitution relates to those areas in the states of Assam, Meghalaya, Tripura and Mizoram which are declared as "Tribal Areas" and provides for District Councils and/or Regional Councils for such Areas. These Councils have been conferred with wide ranging legislative, judicial and executive powers. The Fifth Schedule Areas: The criteria for declaring any area as a "Scheduled Area" under the Fifth Schedule are: (a) preponderance of tribal population, (b) compactness and reasonable size of the area, (c) a viable administrative entity such as a district, block or taluk, and (d) economic backwardness of the area as compared to neighbouring areas. The specification of "Scheduled Areas" in relation to a State is done by a notified Order of the President, after consultation with the State Governments concerned. The same applies for altering, increasing, decreasing, incorporating new areas, or rescinding any orders relating to "Scheduled Areas".

The advantages of Scheduled Areas are that: (a) the Governor of a state, which has Scheduled Areas, is empowered to make regulations in respect of the following: (i) prohibit or restrict transfer of land from tribal people; (ii) regulate the business of money lending to the members of Scheduled Tribes. In making any such regulation, the Governor may repeal or amend any Act of Parliament or of the Legislature of the State which is applicable to the area in question. (b) The Governor may be through public notification direct that any particular Act of Parliament or of the Legislature of the state, shall not apply to a Scheduled Areas or any part thereof in the state or shall apply to such area subject to such exceptions and modifications as he may specify. (c) the Governor of a state having Scheduled Areas therein, shall annually, or whenever so required by the President of India, make a report to the President regarding the administration of the Scheduled Areas in that State and the executive power of the Union shall extend to the giving of directions to the State as to the administration of the said area. (d) Tribes Advisory Council (TAC) shall be established in States having Scheduled Areas. The role of TAC is to advise the State Government on matters pertaining to the welfare and advancement of the Scheduled Tribes in the State as may be referred to it by the Governor. The TAC will consist of not more than twenty members of whom about 3/4 are from ST-MLAs. The TAC may also be established in any State having Scheduled Tribes but not Scheduled Areas on the direction of the President of India (e) The Provisions of the Panchayats (Extension to Scheduled Areas) Act, 1996 (PESA), vide which the provisions of Panchayats, contained in Part IX of the Constitution, were extended to Scheduled Areas, also contain special provisions for the benefit of Scheduled Tribes. The Sixth Schedule - Tribal Areas: The Sixth Schedule under Article 244 of the Constitution identifies Autonomous districts in the tribal areas in Assam, Meghalaya, Tripura and Mizoram. It also makes provisions for recognition of Autonomous Regions within these Autonomous Districts. These have been specified in Parts I, II, II A & III of the table appended to paragraph 20 of the Sixth Schedule. In other words, areas where provisions of Sixth Schedule are applicable are known as Tribal Areas. The state-wise details of Tribal Areas are as under:-

Part-I Assam 1. The North Cachar Hills District; 2. The Karbi-Anglong District; and 3. The Bodo Land Territorial Area Districts

Part II Meghalaya 1. Khasi Hills District; 2. Jaintia Hills District; and 3. The Garo Hills District

Part II Tripura

Tripura Tribal Areas District

Part III Mizoram 1. The Chakma District 2. The Mara District; and 3. The Lai District

The district or regional councils are empowered to make rules with the approval of the Governor with regard to matters like establishment, construction or management of primary schools, dispensaries, markets, cattle ponds, ferries, fisheries, roads, road transport and waterways in the district. The Autonomous Councils of the North Cachar Hills and Karbi Anglong have been granted additional powers to make laws with respect to other matters like secondary education, agriculture, social security and social insurance, public health and sanitation, minor irrigation etc. The Councils have also been conferred powers under the Civil Procedure Code and Criminal Procedure Code for trial of certain suits and offences, as also the powers of a revenue authority for their area for collection of revenue and taxes and other powers for the regulation and management of natural resources.

Procedure for Declaration as ST

The term Scheduled Tribes is defined in the Constitution of India under Article 366(25) as such tribes or tribal communities or parts of groups within such tribes or tribal communities as are deemed under Article 342 to be Scheduled Tribes for the purposes of this Constitution. Article 342 prescribes the procedure to be followed in the matter of specification of Scheduled Tribes. In terms of Article 342(1), the President may, with respect to any State or Union Territory, and where it is a State, after consultation with the Governor thereof, notify tribes or tribal communities or parts thereof as Scheduled Tribes. This confers on the tribe or part of it a constitutional status invoking the safeguards provided for in the Constitution, to these communities, in their respective States/UTs. Thus, in terms of Article 342(1), only those communities who have been declared as such by the President through an initial public notification will be considered as Scheduled Tribes. Any further amendment in the list is to be done through an Act of Parliament (Article 342(2)). Parliament may, by law, include in or exclude from the list of Scheduled Tribes, any tribe or tribal community or parts thereof. The list of Scheduled Tribes is State-specific. In other words, a community declared as Scheduled Tribe in one State need not be so in another State.

Scheduling and De-Scheduling of Tribes

Thus, the first specification of Scheduled Tribes in relation to a particular state/ union territory is by a notified order of the President, after consultation with the state governments concerned. The criteria generally adopted for specification of a community as a Scheduled Tribe are : (a) indications of primitive traits; (b) distinctive culture; (c) shyness of contact with the community at large; and(d) geographical isolation i.e. backwardness.

These are not spelt out in the Constitution but have become well established. They take into account the definitions in the 1931 Census, the reports of the first Backward Classes Commission (Kalelkar Committee), 1955, the Advisory Committee on Revision of SC/ ST lists (Lokur Committee), 1965 and the Joint Committee of Parliament on the Scheduled Castes and Scheduled Tribes Orders (Amendment) Bill, 1967 (Chanda Committee), 1969. There are over 700 tribes (with many of them overlapping in more than one State) as notified under

Article 342 of the Constitution of India, spread over different States and Union Territories of the country. It is worth noting that no community has been specified as a Scheduled Tribe in relation to the States of Haryana and Punjab and the Union Territories of Chandigarh, Delhi and Puducherry.

Ascertaining ST Status

Where a person claims to belong to a Scheduled Tribe by birth, it should be verified: (a) that the person and his parents actually belong to the community claimed; (b) that the community is included in the Presidential Order specifying the Scheduled Tribes in relation to the concerned State; (c) that the person belongs to that State and the area within that State in respect of which the community has been scheduled; (d) he may profess any religion; (e) that he or his parents/grandparents, etc., should be permanent resident of the State/UT on the date of notification of the Presidential Order applicable in his case; (f) a person who is temporarily away from his permanent place of residence at the time of the notification of the Presidential Order—applicable in his case, say for example to earn a living or seek education, etc. can also be regarded as a Scheduled Tribe, if his tribe has been specified in that order in relation to his home State/Union Territory; (g) but he cannot be treated as such in relation to the place of his temporary residence notwithstanding the fact that the name of his tribe has been scheduled in respect of that State where he is temporarily settled, in any Presidential Order; (h) in the case of persons born after the date of notification of the relevant Presidential Order, the place of residence for the purpose of acquiring Scheduled Tribe status, is the place of permanent abode of their parents at the time of the notification of the Presidential Order under which they claim to belong to such a tribe. This does not apply to the STs of the Lakshadweep Islands for whom there is a requirement of being born in the Union Territories in order to be eligible for ST status.

Scheduled Tribe claims on migration

i) Where a person migrates from the portion of the State in which his/her community is scheduled, to another part of the same State in respect of which his/her community is not scheduled, the person will continue to be deemed to be a member of the Scheduled Tribe, in relation to that State

ii) Where a person migrates from one State to another, he can claim to belong to a Scheduled Tribe only in relation to the State to which he originally belonged and not in respect of the State to which he has migrated.

Scheduled Tribe claims through Marriages

The guiding principle is that no person who is not a Scheduled Tribe by birth will be deemed to be a member of Scheduled Tribe merely because he or she has married a person belonging to a Scheduled Tribe. Similarly, a person who is a member of a Scheduled Tribe will continue to be a member of that Scheduled Tribe, even after his or her marriage with a person who does not belong to a Scheduled Tribe.

Issue of Scheduled Tribe certificates

The candidates belonging to Scheduled Tribes may get Scheduled Tribe certificates, in the prescribed form, from any one of the following authorities:

(i) District Magistrate/Additional District Magistrate/Collector/Deputy Commissioner/Additional Deputy Commissioner/Deputy Collector/1st Class Stipendiary Magistrate/City Magistrate/Sub Divisional Magistrate/ Taluka Magistrate/Executive Magistrate/Extra Assistant Commissioner [not below the rank of 1st Class Stipendiary Magistrate]; (ii) Chief Presidency Magistrate/ Additional Chief Presidency Magistrate/Presidency Magistrate; (iii) Revenue Officers not below the rank of Tehsildar; (iv) Sub-Divisional Officer of the Area where the candidate and/or his family normally resides; (v) Administrator/ Secretary to the Administrator/Development Officer (Lakshadweep Islands).

Punishments for officials issuing Scheduled Tribe Certificates without proper verification action is to be taken under the relevant provisions of the Indian Penal Code if any official is found to have issued a Scheduled Tribe certificate carelessly and without proper verification. This will be in addition to other action to which they are liable under the appropriate disciplinary rules applicable to them.

Migrants from other states/union territories persons belonging to a Scheduled Tribe who have migrated from one State to another for the purpose of employment, education etc. experience great difficulty in obtaining ST certificates from the State from which they have migrated. In order to remove this difficulty, it has been decided that the prescribed authority of a State Government/Union Territory Administration may issue a Scheduled Tribe certificate to a person who migrated from another state, on the production of the genuine certificate issued to his father/mother by the prescribed authority of the State of the father/mother's origin except where the prescribed authority feels that a detailed enquiry is necessary through the state of origin before issue of the certificate. The certificate will be issued irrespective of whether the tribe in question is scheduled or not in relation to the state/union territory to which the person has migrated to.

National Commission for Scheduled Tribes

In addition to the Office of the Commissioner for Scheduled Caste and Scheduled Tribes created in 1950 for effective implementation of various safeguards provided in the Constitution for the SCs & STs and various other protective legislations, a multi-member Commission for SCs and STs was set up in 1978. In 1992 these two organizations were replaced by a statutory multi-member National Commission for Scheduled Castes and Scheduled Tribes. However, since the needs and problems of Scheduled Tribes and the solutions required were quite different from those of Scheduled Castes, a special approach for tribal development and independent machinery to safeguard the rights of Scheduled Tribes was considered necessary. Accordingly, a separate National Commission for Scheduled Tribes (NCST) was set up with effect from 19th

February, 2004 by amending Article 338 and inserting a new Article 338A in the Constitution, through the Constitution (Eighty-ninth Amendment) Act, 2003.

Tribal Sub Plan

The present Tribal Sub Plan (TSP) strategy was initially developed by an Expert Committee set up by the Ministry of Education and Social Welfare in 1972 for rapid socio-economic development of tribal people and was adopted for the first time in the Fifth Five Year Plan. The TSP strategy, with some modifications, continues till this day and the salient features with respect to TSP for States, are given below:

i) The funds provided under the Tribal Sub Plan of the State have to be at least equal in proportion to the ST population of each State or UT;

ii) Tribals and tribal areas of a State or UNION TERRITORIES are given benefits under the TSP, in addition to what percolates from the overall Plan of a state/UT;

iii) The Sub-Plan should; a) identify the problems and need of tribal people and critical gaps in their development; b) identify all available resources for TSP; c) prepare a broad policy framework for development; e) define a suitable administrative strategy for its implementation; and f) specify the mechanism for monitoring and evaluation.

National Scheduled Tribes Finance and Development Corporation

With a view to pay a focused attention and accelerate the pace of economic development of Scheduled Tribes, the erstwhile National Scheduled Castes and Scheduled Tribes Financial Development Corporation was bifurcated and National Scheduled Tribes Finance and Development Corporation (NSTFDC) was set up in April, 2001 under the Ministry of Tribal Affairs. The NSTFDC has been granted license under Section 25 of the Companies Act (A Company not for profit). The Authorized Share Capital of the NSTFDC is ₹ 500.00 crore and paid up capital is ₹ 230.50 crore as on date. In order to achieve the mandate set for the NSTFDC, (for undertaking selfemployment ventures/activities) financial assistance is extended by NSTFDC to the Scheduled Tribes, who are having annual family income upto double the poverty line. NSTFDC also provides financial assistance as grant for skill and entrepreneurial development of the target group. The financial assistance is channelized through Government owned agencies nominated by the respective ministries/state governments and union territories administrations. NSTFDC also provides financial assistance for procurement and marketing minor forest produce so as to avoid the distress sale of produce/ products by the Scheduled Tribes.

Eligibility Criteria for the Beneficiary

The beneficiary (ies) should belong to ST community and annual family income of the beneficiary (ies) should not exceed double the poverty line (DPL) income limit (presently DPL is ₹ 39,500/- per annum for the rural areas and

₹ 54,500/- per annum for the urban areas) In the case of Self Help Groups (SHGs), all the members of the SHG should belong to the ST community having annual family income upto Double the Poverty line (DPL). Similarly for Cooperative Society, loan is extended to the eligible STs through co-operative Society having minimum 80 per cent or more STs as member of the said cooperative society. NSTFDC is implementing following programmes for the economic development of STs.

Term loan is provided for income generating activities. Marketing Support Assistance is provided for financial support for meeting the working capital requirement of the Central/State Government owned agencies and national level federations for undertaking procurement and/or marketing of minor forest produce/agricultural produce collected/ grown by the STs and /or related product/services. Marketing Support Assistance extended to the beneficiaries through the SCAs, the interest is at par with rates of interest for long term loan and the assistance is extended to the Central/ State/UT owned organizations, national level federations directly involved in procurement, the interest rate is 7 per cent per annum. Assistance by way of grant is also given.

Special Schemes

(a) Adivasi Mahila Sashaktikaran Yojana (AMSY) is an exclusive scheme for the economic development of ST women, at a highly concessional rate of interest. Under the scheme NSTFDC provides Term Loan for scheme(s)/ project(s) costing upto ₹ 50,000/- per individual unit/profit centre. Financial assistance up to 99 per cent of the cost of the scheme(s)/project(s) is provided by the NSTFDC. The SCAs may charge a maximum interest @ 4 per cent per annum from the ultimate women beneficiaries.

(b) Micro-credit scheme is meant to provide financial assistance for undertaking small self-employment ventures/activities by the eligible STs through existing profit making SHGs. SCAs shall provide eligible amount of subsidy or margin money as per their scheme(s) for the target group and remaining amount may be provided as term loan by NSTFDC. In case of no subsidy and or no share of SCAs/banks as SCAs, NSTFDC may provide 100 per cent of the funds required as term loan subject to maximum of ₹ 15,000/- per member.

Tribal Cooperative Marketing Development Federation of India Ltd.

O. W.: http://www.trifed.in

The Tribal Cooperative Marketing Development Federation of India Limited (TRIFED), was set up in 1987 as a national level apex body under the Multi State Cooperative Societies Act, 1984 (MSCS Act, 1984) After the enactment of the Multi-State Cooperative Societies Act, 2002 (MSCS Act, 2002) TRIFED is deemed to be registered under the latter Act and is also listed in the Second Schedule to the Act as a National Cooperative Society.

The Bye-laws of TRIFED were revised in April, 2003 in tune with the new Multi State Cooperative Societies Act, 2002 read with the Multi State Cooperative Societies Rules, 2002. Under its revised mandate TRIFED has stopped bulk procurement in Minor Forest Produce (MFP) and surplus Agricultural Produce (SAP) from Tribals. (This procurement is now done by the State-level Tribal Cooperatives Societies/Federations). TRIFED now functions as a 'market developer' for tribal products and as 'service provider' to its member federations.

TRIFED is now engaged in the marketing development of tribal products (natural and organic products, handicrafts, ratification etc.) through its own shops (TRIBES India) and shops selling its products on consignment basis.

Recognition of Forest Rights of STs

The Scheduled Tribes and Other Traditional Forest Dwellers (Recognition of Forest Rights) Act, 2006 seeks to recognize and vest the forest rights and occupation in forest land in forest dwelling Scheduled Tribes and other traditional forest dwellers who have been residing in such forests for generations but chose rights on ancestral lands and their habitat were not adequately recognized in the consolidation of State forests during the colonial period as well as in independent India resulting in historical injustice to them. The Act has been notified for operation with effect from December 31, 2007.

Rules, for implementing the provisions of the Act, were notified in January, 2008 and they envisage the constitution of various Committees under the Act, viz, the sub divisional level committee, district level committee and the state level monitoring committee, by the state governments; All the states have been requested to nominate the nodal officer for implementing the provisions of the Act. The state governments were also requested to take necessary steps to ensure that awareness is created about the objectives, provisions and procedures of the Act and the Rules through various measures including awareness programmes and printed material such as posters in the regional languages; ensure the translation and publication of the Act and the Rules in all the regional languages and arrange to distribute to all Gram Sabhas, Forest Right Committees and all Departments of the Government including Panchayati Raj, Rural Development, Tribal and Social Welfare and Forest Departments; undertake the orientation of officials, civilian representative and non-Governmental organizations in the State, who can then be called upon to assist as resource persons in the awareness programmes; and sensitize the sub-divisional and district level committees on the objectives, provisions and procedures of the Act and the Rules.

As per the Act, the responsibility for recognition and vesting of forest rights and distribution of land rights rests with the State Government, as per the Rules notified for implementation of the Act. All the state governments have been directed that the entire process of vesting of forest rights as per the Scheduled Tribes and Other Traditional Forest Dwellers (Recognition of Forest Rights) Act, 2006 should be completed at the earliest. Web-based MIS for online monitoring of the implementation of the Act has been made operational with effect from 4th June, 2008 for testing purposes on website http://www.tribal.gov.in. However, final website would be operational which is at present under process of getting security-audit clearance.

Vanbandhu Kalyan Yojana

Major activities approved under VanbhanduKalyan Yojana (VKY) Scheme during 2015-16 are: education/infrastructure/toilets in hostel and schools; health/sports/safe drinking water; self employment/skill development / fruit farming/livelihood/dairy/fishery; irrigation; culture/tourism; monitoring cell/institution; and connectivity/market/electricity/solar energy.

Umbrella Scheme for Education of ST Children

The Ministry is re-engineering its educational schemes with the objective of providing adequate educational infrastructure for STs and incentive for education for ST children through scholarships. This is intended to be achieved through convergence of schemes of line ministries along with simplification of process for availing scholarships and also through technological aids in improving learning activities. As needs vary from state to state, the proposed new scheme is expected to give flexibility to each states/UTs. In the proposed Umbrella Scheme, the following schemes have been merged: (a) Establishing and strengthening of Ashram Schools; (b) Establishing and strengthening of Hostels; (c) Vocational training in tribal areas; (d) Post-Matric Scholarship; and (e) Pre-Matric Scholarship.

Overseas Scholarships (NOS) for ST students

The Ministry of Tribal Affairs has approved the revised Scheme of National Overseas Scholarships (NOS) for ST students. The scheme is providing scholarship to students selected for pursuing higher studies abroad for Post-Graduation, Ph. D and Post-Doctoral research programmes. The Ministry has revised some of its provisions to make it more beneficial for ST students.

To expand the scope of field of study, the number of awards has been increased from existing 15 to 20. In order to make the scheme more inclusive, out of total 20 awards, 3 awards have been earmarked for Particularly Vulnerable Tribal Groups (PVTGs) and 30 per cent awards have been earmarked for girl candidates. Now with the inclusion of more subjects into the scheme and reorganizing field of study by grouping various subjects under broadbased fields, more ST students would be benefited as the number of subjects has increased from 35 to 52. Earlier the eligibility criteria was 60 per cent marks, now it has been reduced to 55 per cent so as to enable a larger number of ST students to become eligible to apply for the scholarships under NOS. The maximum income ceiling has been increased to ₹ 6 lakhs per annum. However, all other parameters being same, preference is given to students with lower income. Similarly, financial assistance, equipment allowance and Incidental Journey expenses have been increased to 10 per cent keeping in view the inflation rates.

Forest Rights Act

The Forest Rights Act, (FRA)2006 was reviewed under PRAGATI initiative In order to take up FRA on a campaign mode, the Ministry has taken several steps to review the status of implementation with state governments. Odisha has the distinction of issuing highest number of titles which is 3,54,404 (3,49,400 individual titles and 5,004 community titles). Madhya Pradesh has the distinction of having highest forest area over which titles have been issued under this Act. The total forest area over which title has been issued in Maharashtra is 20,36,382.10acres. During the year, National Resource Centre at TRI Campus, Odisha, set up by the Ministry conducts training programmes to train master trainers on FRA not only for Odisha but also for other States who are implementing FRA. Many states have translated the Forest Right Act and Rules in local and tribal languages.

Welfare of other Backward Classes

The Second Backward Classes Commission (commonly known as Mandal Commission), constituted under Article 340, submitted its Report in 1980. In the light of this report, the Government of India provided 27 per cent reservation in Central Government posts for persons belonging to the Socially and Economically Backward Classes, (also referred to as "Other Backward Classes" or OBCs). Several writ petitions were disposed of by the Supreme Court in 1992, commonly known as the Indra Sawhney case. In this judgement, the Court upheld 27 per cent reservation for OBCs in civil posts and services under the Union of India, subject to exclusion of the "Creamy Layer". The Government of India in 1993 reserved 27 per cent of vacancies in civil posts and services under the Central Government, to be filled through direct recruitment in favour of the Other Backward Classes (OBCs). With the amendment of Article 15 of the Constitution in January, 2006 and the enactment of the Central Educational Institutions (Reservation in Admissions) Act in January, 2007, listing of other backward classes has become relevant for admission in Central Educational Institutions also. Under this Act, OBC students are entitled to 27 per cent reservation in Central Educational Institutions in a phased manner, over a period of three years commencing from the academic session 2008-09. The National Commission for Backward Classes (NCBC) was set up in August, 1993 as per the provision of the National Commission for Backward Classes Act, 1993.

O. W.: http://www.ncbc.nic.in

Persons with Disability

Section 2 (t) of The Persons with Disabilities (Equal Opportunities, Protection of Rights and Full Participation) Act, 1995, *(also referred to as PwD Act, 1995)* defines *"Person with Disability"* as a person suffering from not less than 40 per cent of any disability as certified by a medical authority. The disability being (a) blindness (b) low vision (c) leprosy cured (d) hearing impairment (e) locomotor disability (f) mental illness (g) mental retardation (h) autism (i) cerebral palsy or (j) a combination of any two or more of (g), (h) and (i) (Section 2 (i) of the PwD Act, 1995 read alongwith Section 2(j) of The National Trust for Welfare of Persons with Autism, Cerebral Palsy, Mental Retardation and Multiple Disabilities Act, 1999).

Mental Health Act

Mental illness has been recognized as one of the disabilities under The Persons with Disabilities (Equal Opportunities, Protection of Rights and Full Participation) Act, 1995. The treatment and care of the mentally ill persons are governed by The Mental Health Act, 1987. The Act is administered by the Ministry of Health and Family Welfare.

Persons with Disabilities Act

A comprehensive law, namely, The Persons with Disabilities (Equal Opportunities, Protection of Rights and Full Participation) Act, 1995 was enacted and enforced in February, 1996. The law deals with both prevention and promotion aspects of the rehabilitation such as education, employment and vocational training, creation of barrier-free environment, provision of rehabilitation services for persons with disabilities, institutional services and supportive social security measures like unemployment allowance and grievance redressal machinery both at the Central and state Level. National Trust for the Welfare of Persons with Autism, Cerebral Palsy, Mental Retardation and Multiple Disabilities: The National Trust is a statutory body under "The National Trust for the Welfare of Persons with Autism, Cerebral Palsy, Mental Retardation and Multiple Disabilities Act, 1999". The main objectives of the Trust are to enable and empower persons with these disabilities to live independently as fully as possible, to extend support to registered organisations providing need-based services and to evolve procedure for appointment of legal guardians for persons with disabilities requiring such protection.

Office of the Chief Commissioner for Persons with Disabilities

The Chief Commissioner is an important statutory functionary, appointed under Section 57 of The Persons with Disabilities (Equal Opportunities, Protection of Rights and Full Participation) Act, 1995. The functions and duties of the Chief Commissioner include coordinating the work of State Commissioners for persons with disabilities, monitoring of utilisation of funds disbursed by the Central Government, taking steps to safeguard rights and facilities made available to persons with disabiliteis and also to look into complaints with respect to deprivation of rights of persons with disabilities. The Chief Commissioner can also take suo motu notice of non-implementation of any rule, law, etc. meant for persons with disabilities and is vested with the powers of a civil court relating to summoning of witness, discovery, requistioning and production of any document, etc.

Rehabilitation Council

The Rehabilitation Council of India is a statutory body set up under the Rehabilitation Council of India Act, 1992. The Council is responsible for regulating the training policies and programmes for various categories of professionals in the area of rehabilitation and special education. Its functions include: (i) standardisation and regulation of training courses at different levels in all the training institutions throughout the country, (ii) recognition of institutions/universities running training courses in the area of rehabilitation of the disabled within and outside the country on a reciprocal basis, (iii) promotion of research in rehabilitation and special education (iv) maintenance of a Central Rehabilitation Register for professionals possessing the recognised rehabilitation qualifications in the area of rehabilitation and (v) encouragement of Continuing Rehabilitation Education Programmes in collaboration with organisations working in the area of disability.

O. W.: http://www.rehabcouncil.nic.in

National Institutes

In order to effectively deal with the multi-dimensional problem of the disabled population, the following National Institutes/apex level Institutes have been set-up in each major area of disability; (i) National Institute for the Visually Handicapped, Dehradun, (ii) National Institute for Orthopedically Handicapped, Kolkata, (iii) Ali Yavar Jung National Institute for the Hearing Handicapped, Mumbai, (iv) National Institute for the Mentally Handicapped, Secunderabad, (v) National Institute of Rehabilitaion Training and Research, Cuttack, (vi), Institute for the Physically Handicapped, New Delhi, (vii) National Institute for Empowerment of Persons with Multiple Disabilities, Chennai. These institutes are mainly responsible for conducting innovative researches, organise training programmes for manpower development and deliver services in the country. Artificial Limbs Manufacturing Corporation of India: The Artificial Limbs Manufacturing Corporation of India (ALIMCO), Kanpur is a public sector body, engaged in manufacturing of aids and appliances for persons with disabilities. The products manufactured by the Corporation conform to ISI standards approved by the Bureau of Indian Standards. Marketing of products is done through Regional Marketing Centres at Kolkata, Mumbai, Chennai, Bhubaneshwar and Delhi and also through National Institutes, voluntary organisations.

Five Composite Regional Centres (CRCs) for the Persons with Disabilities are located at Srinagar, Lucknow, Bhopal, Sundernagar and Guwahati. These centres conduct training programmes to prepare professionals in the field of rehabilitation as well as provide rehabilitation services to the disabled. Four Regional Rehabilitation Centres for Spinal Injuries and other Orthopaedic Disabilities at Mohali, Cuttack, Jabalpur and Bareilly are providing services for basic management and follow-up of the spinally injured so as to make the affected persons functionally independent.

Economic Development

The National Handicapped Finance and Development Corporation (NHFDC) is an apex-level financial institution for extending credit facilities to persons with disabilities for their economic development. Funds assistance is disbursed through the channelising agencies authorized by the State Governments/UT Administrations and Non-Governmental Organisations. It also extends loans for pursuing education at graduate and higher levels. Besides, it assists in the upgradation of technical and entrepreneurial skills to enable beneficiaries to manage their production units efficiently.

O. W.: http://www.nhfdc.nic.in

Under the scheme for Assistance to Disabled Persons for Purchase/Fitting of AIDs and Appliances assistance is given for procuring durable, sophisticated and scientifically manufactured, standard aids and appliances that can promote their physical, social and psychological rehabilitation by reducing the impact of disability and enhance their economic potential. The scheme is implemented through agencies like voluntary organisations, National Institutes under the Ministry, ALIMCO, Zilla Panchayats, DRDAs, etc. The implementing agencies are provided grant-in-aid for purchase, fabrication and distribution of aids and appliances. The scheme also includes under its ambit medical/surgical correction and intervention that may be essential prior to fitment of aids and appliances.

Social Defence

In the areas of Social Defence the Ministry is committed towards welfare of Older Persons and rehabilitation of Drug Addicts. The programmes for the targeted groups are as follows:

National Policy for Older Persons

The National Policy for Older Persons (NPOP) was announced in January, 1999, with the primary objective viz., to encourage individuals to make provision for their own as well as their spouse's old age; to encourage families to take care of their older family members; to enable and support voluntary and non-governmental organisations to supplement the care provided by the family; to provide care and protection to the vulnerable elderly people, to provide health care facility to the elderly; to promote research and training facilities to train geriatric care givers and organisers of services for the elderly; and to create awareness regarding elderly persons to develop them into fully independent citizens.

National Council for Older Persons

The Government has reconstituted National Council for Older Persons (NCOP) to advise and aid the Government on developing policies and programmes for older persons. It provides feedback to the Government on the implementation of the National Policy on Older Persons and the specific initiatives for older persons. The NCOP is the highest body to advise and coordinate with the Government in the formulation and implementation of policy and programmes for the welfare of the aged. Under Integrated Programme for Older Persons financial assistance upto 90 per cent of the project cost is provided to NGOs for establishing and maintaining old age homes, day care centers, Mobile Medicare Units and to provide non-institutional services to older persons.

Prevention and Rehabilitation of Drug Addicts/Alcoholics

Under the Scheme, grant-in-aid to the extent of 90 per cent (95 per cent in North East States, J & K and Sikkim) of the expenditure is provided to voluntary organisations for rehabilitation of drug addicts and alcoholics. Assistance to Voluntary Organisation for Social Defence Services provides for undertaking programmes for the rehabilitation of various social segments at risk, not currently covered under the existing schemes of the Ministry. In particular, the scheme provides for Pilot Projects in unchartered areas in which the Ministry may like to formulate independent programmes in due course. A number of programmes are being supported for rehabilitation of children of sex workers. Initiatives have also been taken to support projects for rehabilitation of widows and for providing counselling and support to traumatised children and women particularly those who have been victims of physical violence and sexual abuse.

Welfare Measures for the Minorities

Six religious communities viz., Muslims, Christians, Sikhs, Buddhists, Zoroastrians (Parsis) and Jains have been notified as minorities as per provisions under the National Commission for Minorities (NCM) Act, 1992. The Government has taken the following measures for the welfare of Minorities: The Ministry of Minority Affairs was created in January 2006 to ensure a focused approach to the issues relating to the minorities and to play a pivotal role in the overall policy planning, coordination, evaluation and review of the regulatory and development programme for the benefit of the minority communities. The Ministry is also responsible for the administration and implementation of the: (i) National Commission for Minorities Act, 1992; (ii) Wakf Act, 1995 and (iii) Durgah Khwaja Saheb Act, 1955. In a short period of time, not only the Ministry has been made fully functional but concerted efforts have been made to streamline the ongoing programmes/schemes and to launch innovative and effective schemes/ programmes for the welfare of minority communities. The details/ developments pertaining to scheme run by the Ministry as well as its subordinate organizations are as under:

O. W.: http://www.ncm.nic.in

O. W.: http://www.minorityaffairs.gov.in

15-Point Programme for the Welfare of Minorities

The Prime Minister's New 15-Point Programme for the Welfare of Minorities was announced in June, 2006. The objectives of the programme are: (a) enhancing opportunities for education, (b) ensuring an equitable share for minorities in economic activities and employment, through existing and new schemes, enhanced credit support for self-employment and recruitment to State and Central Government jobs, (c) improving the conditions of living of minorities by ensuring an appropriate share for them in infrastructure development schemes, (d) prevention and control of communal disharmony and violence. An important aim of the new programme is to ensure that the benefits of various government schemes for the underprivileged reach the disadvantaged sections of the minority communities. In order to ensure that the benefits of these schemes flow equitably to the minorities, the new programme envisages location of a certain proportion of development projects in minority concentration areas. It also provides that, wherever possible, 15 per cent of physical targets and financial outlays under various schemes should be earmarked for minorities.

Exclusive Scholarship Schemes for Minority Students

Three Centrally sponsored scholarship schemes for students belonging to the minority communities have been launched. To ensure that girl students get a fair share, all three schemes have 30 per cent scholarships earmarked for them. These schemes are :

(i) Merit-cum-Means scholarship scheme: The Merit-cum-Means Scholarship Scheme is a Centrally sponsored scheme launched in 2007. It is being implemented through state governments/union territory administrations. The entire expenditure is being borne by the Central Government.

(ii) Post-Matric Scholarships scheme: The scheme of Post-matric scholarship for students belonging to the minority communities was launched in November, 2007 as a Centrally Sponsored Scheme (CSS) with 100 per cent central funding and is implemented through the state government/union territory administrations. Post-matric Scholarship Scheme is awarded for studies in India in a government higher secondary school/college including residential government higher secondary school/college and eligible private institutes selected and notified in a transparent manner by the state government/union territory administration concerned. Students with not less than 50 per cent marks in the previous year's final examination, whose parents'/ guardians' annual income does not exceed ₹ 2.00 lakh are eligible for award of scholarship. 30 per cent of scholarships have been earmarked for girl students. In case sufficient numbers of girl students are not available, then eligible boy students are to be given these scholarships.

(iii) Pre-Matric Scholarship: The Pre-matric scholarship scheme for students belonging to the minority communities was approved in January, 2008. This scheme was launched as a Centrally Sponsored Scheme (CSS) on a 75:25 fund sharing ratio between the Centre and states/union territories. The Scheme is with 100 per cent Central funding. It is implemented through the state governments/ union territory administrations. Students with not less than 50 per cent marks in the previous final examination, whose parents'/ guardians' annual income does not exceed ₹ 1.00 lakh, are eligible for award of the Pre-matric scholarship under the scheme. An outlay of ₹ 5,000 crore has been provided in the Twelfth Five Year Plan to award 414.50 Lakh scholarships and

renewals during the plan period (2012-17). 30 per cent of scholarships have been earmarked for girl students. An amount of ₹ 1,040.11 crore was released and 64.73 lakh scholarships were awarded. Out of this 51.03 per cent scholarships were catered to girl students.

National Commission for Minorities

The Minorities Commission which was set up in January, 1978 by a Resolution issued by Ministry of Home Affairs became a statutory body with the enactment of The National Commission for Minorities Act, 1992 and renamed as the National Commission for Minorities. The first statutory National Commission was set up on May 17, 1993. The NCM Act, 1992 was amended in 1995 which provided for a Vice Chairperson in the Commission. With the 1995 amendment, the Commission's composition was expanded to 7 members (including a Chairperson and a Vice Chairperson). The provision under Section 3(2) of the Act stipulates that five members including the Chairpersons shall be from amongst the minority communities.

O. W.: http://www.ncm.nic.in

State Commission for Minorities

Thirteen state governments namely Andhra Pradesh, Assam, Bihar, Chhattisgarh, Government of NCT of Delhi, Jharkhand, Karnataka, Maharashtra, Madhya Pradesh, Rajasthan, Uttar Pradesh, Tamil Nadu and West Bengal have set up statutory commissions for minorities. Manipur and Uttarakhand have set up non-statutory commissions.

National Commission for Religious and Linguistic Minorities

The Government of India has been seized of the welfare needs of socially and economically backward sections among religious and linguistic minorities. For having a detailed examination to determine the criteria for identification of socially and economically backward sections among religious and linguistic minorities and to suggest measures for their welfare, the Government constituted a National Commission for Religious and Linguistic Minorities, with the following terms of reference: (a) to suggest criteria for identification of socially and economically backward sections among religious and linguistic minorities; (b) to recommend measures for welfare of socially and economically backward sections among religious and linguistic minorities, including reservation in education and government employment; (c) to suggest the necessary constitutional, legal and administrative modalities, as required for the implementation of their recommendations, and to present a report of their deliberations and recommendations. The Office of the Special Officer for Linguistic Minorities (commonly known as the Commissioner for Linguistic Minorities (CLM) was created in July, 1957, in pursuance of the provision of Article 350-B of the Constitution. The CLM takes up all the matters pertaining to the grievances arising out of the non-implementation of the constitutional and nationally agreed scheme of safeguards provided to linguistic minorities that come to its notice are brought to its knowledge by the linguistic minority individuals, groups, associations or organisations at the highest political and administrative levels of the state governments and UT administrations and recommends remedial actions to be taken.

Central WAKF Council

A Wakf is a permanent dedication of movable or immovable properties for purposes recognised by the Muslim Law as religious, pious or charitable. Apart from these religious aspects, the Wakfs are also instruments of social and economic upliftment. Administration of Central Legislation for Wakfs is the responsibility of the Ministry of Social Justice and Empowerment. For the purpose of advising the Central Government on matters relating to working of the State Wakf Boards and the proper administration of the Wakfs in the country, the Central Wakf Council was established as a statutory body by the Central Government in December, 1964, under Section 8A of the Wakf Act, 1954 (now read as Sub-Sec(1) of the Section 9 of Wakf Act, 1995). The present Council has been reconstituted in March, 2005. The Union Minister in charge of Wakf is the Chairperson of the Council. The Central Wakf Council is also playing a vital role in the development of the society by way of implementing Development of Urban Wakf Properties and Educational Development Programmes.

O. W.: http://www.centralwakfcouncil.org

Durgah Khwaja Saheb Act

It is an Act to make provision for the proper administration of Dargah and Endowment of the Dargah Khwaja Moin-ud-din Chishty (R.A.). Under this Central Act, the administration, control and management of the Dargah endowment has been vested in a representative committee known as the Dargah Committee appointed by the Central Government. The Dargah of Khwaja Moin-ud-din Chishti at Ajmer in Rajasthan is a Waqf of international fame. The Dargah is being administered under the Dargah Khwaja Saheb Act, 1955. With the help of the Government of India, the Ministry of Urban Development and with the active involvement of the Government of Rajasthan through local administration, the Dargah Committee is implementing a scheme of providing lodging facilities for lakhs of pilgrims who visit the holy Dargah during the annual Urs. The facility was earlier named "Vishram Sthali" and has been renamed "Gharib Nawaz Mehmankhana". The infrastructure is meant to provide facilities/amenities to the zaireen of Dargah Khwaja Sahab.

Ministry of Women and Child Development

The development of women and children is of paramount importance and sets the pace for overall development. A separate Ministry of Women and Child Development came into existence from January, 2006 with the prime intention of addressing gaps in state action for women and children and for promoting inter ministerial and inter-sectoral convergence to create gender equitable and child centred legislation, policies and programmes. The Ministry has the main responsibility to advance the rights and concerns of women and children and to promote their survival, protection, development and participation in a holistic manner. The Ministry has a vision of empowered women living with dignity and contributing as equal partners in development in an environment free from violence and discrimination and well nurtured children with full opportunities for growth and development in a safe and protective environment. Its mission for children is to ensure development, care and protection through cross-cutting policies and programmes, spread awareness about their rights, facilitate access to learning, nutrition, institutional and legislative support for enabling them to grow and develop to their full potential.

Acts relating to Women and Children

The Ministry is in charge of the administration of the following Acts relating to women and children: (a) The Immoral Traffic (Prevention) Act, 1956 (as amended in 1986), (b) The Indecent Representation of Women (Prevention) Act, 1986 (60 of 1986), (c) The Dowry Prohibition Act, 1961 as amended in 1986, (d) The Commission of Sati (Prevention) Act, 1987 (3 of 1988), (e) The Prohibition of Child Marriage Act 2006 (notified in January 2007), (f) Protection of Women from Domestic Violence Act, 2005, (g) National Commission for Women Act, 1990, (h) Infant Milk Substitutes, Feeding Bottles and Infant food (Regulation of Production, Supply and Distribution) Act, 1992 (41 of 1992),(i) Commission for Protection of Child Rights Act, 2005, and (j) Juvenile Justice (Care and Protection of Children) Act 2000. (k) The Protection of Children from Sexual Offences (POCSO) Act and POCSO Rules, 2012 and (l) Sexual Harassment of Women at Workplace (Prevention, Prohibition and Redressal), 2012. The Juvenile Justice (Care & Protection of Children), Amendment Bill was passed in Parliament in August, 2011. The Ministry's mandate primarily includes formulation of plans, policies and programmes for women and children; enactment and amendment of legislations related to them; and overall guidance and coordination of efforts of governmental and non-governmental organizations working in the field of women and child development. The Ministry's schemes and programmes play a supplementary and complementary role to the development programmes of the Ministry.

Policy and Schemes

National Policy for Empowerment of Women

In 2001, the National Policy for Empowerment of Women (NPRW) was formulated as the blueprint for the future, with the goal of bringing about the advancement, development and empowerment of women. The NPEW laid down detailed prescriptions to address discrimination against women, strengthen existing institutions which includes the legal system, provide better access to health care and other services, equal opportunities for women's participation in decision-making, and mainstreaming gender concerns in the development process, etc. The policies/programmes of the Government are all directed towards achieving inclusive growth with special focus on women in line with the objective of the National Policy for Empowerment of Women.

O. W.: http://www.wcd.nic.in

Schemes for Women

Rajiv Gandhi Scheme for Empowerment of Adolescent Girls - (RGSEAG)-Sabla: Sabla was introduced in the year 2010-11 and is operational in 205 selected districts on a pilot basis. It aims at all-round development of adolescent girls (AGs) of 11-18 years (with a focus on all out-of-school AGs). Sabla is being implemented through the state governments/UTs with 100 per cent financial assistance from the Central Government for all inputs other than nutrition provision for which 50 per cent Central assistance to states is provided. Anganwadi Centre (AWC) is the focal point for the delivery of the services. The scheme has two major components nutrition and non-nutrition. Nutrition is being given in the form of take home ration or hot cooked meal for 11-14 years out of school girls and 14-18 years all AGs (out of school and in school girls). Each adolescent girl is given 600 calories and 18-20 grams of protein and micronutrients (which is approx. 1/3 of recommended dietary allowance) per day for 300 days in a year. The out of school adolescent girls (11-14 years) attending AWCs and all girls (14-18 years) are provided supplementary nutrition in the form of take home ration/hot cooked meal. The nutrition provided is as per the norms for Pregnant & Lactating (P&L) mothers. While the nutrition component aims at improving the health and nutrition status of the adolescent girls, the non-nutrition component addresses the developmental needs. In the non-nutrition component, out of school adolescent girls of 11-18 years are being provided IFA supplementation, health check-up and referral services, nutrition and health education, Adolescent Reproductive Sexual Health (ARSH) counselling /guidance on family welfare, life skill education, guidance on accessing public services and vocational training (only 16-18 year old adolescent girls).

Indira Gandhi Matritva Sahyog Yojana (IGMSY): A Conditional Cash Transfer Scheme for pregnant and lactating women was introduced in October, 2010 to contribute to better enabling environment by providing cash incentives for improved health and nutrition to pregnant and nursing mothers. The scheme attempts to partly compensate for wage loss to pregnant and lactating women both prior to and after delivery of the child. The beneficiaries are paid ₹ 4,000/- in three instalments per P & L woman between the second trimester and till the child attains the age of 6 months on fulfilling specific conditions related to maternal and child health. Being implemented on pilot basis in 53 selected districts using the platform of ICDS, 12.5 lakh P & L women are expected to be covered every year under IGMSY. Pregnant women of 19 years of age and above for first two live births are eligible under the scheme. All organized sector employees are excluded from the Scheme as they are entitled for paid maternity leave. Under IGMSY scheme, transfer of amount to the beneficiary is done through bank/post office only. The modalities of cash transfer are decided by the state governments/union territories. The modes of cash transfer include – nationalized bank, post office, cooperative bank, business correspondent model of bank, etc. IGMSY is a Centrally Sponsored Scheme under which amount is given as grant-in-aid to state governments/union territories. The scheme is covered under Direct Benefit Transfer (DBT) programme.

Women Empowerment and Livelihood Programme in Mid-Gangetic Plains - "Priyadarshini" : The Ministry is administering a pilot project titled Women's Empowerment and Livelihood Programme in the Mid Gangetic Plains "Priyadarshini' in 13 blocks spread over five districts in Uttar Pradesh and two in Bihar. The project is assisted by IFAD. It aims at holistic empowerment (economic and social) of vulnerable groups of women and adolescent girls in the project area through formation of women's Self Help Groups (SHGs) and promotion of improved livelihood opportunities. Over 1,00,000 households are to be covered under the project and 7200 SHGs will be formed during the project period ending 2016-17. Though the focus of the project is on livelihood enhancement, the beneficiaries will be empowered to address their political, legal and health problems through rigorous capacity building.

National Bank for Agriculture and Rural Development (NABARD) is the lead programme agency for the implementation. Field Non-Governmental Organisations (NGOs) will carry out all field level activities, whereas Resource NGO has been involved to undertake activities on specialized capacity building and provide other technical support to the field level project functionaries. The Programme involves giving training to SHG members on topics such as income generation and allied activities, marketing of products and social issues, etc.

Swadhar

The Swadhar Scheme was launched in 2001-2002 as a Central Sector Scheme for providing holistic and integrated services to women in difficult circumstances and without any family, social and economic support, such as destitute widows deserted by their families in religious places like Vrindaban and Kashi, women prisoners released from jails; women surivors of natural disasters who have been rendered homeless, trafficked women/girls rescued or runaway from brothels, women victims of terrorist violence without any means for survival, mentally challenged women and women with HIV/AIDS deserted by their family, etc. The package or services made available under the Scheme include provision for food, clothing, shelter, health care counselling and legal support, social and economic rehabilitation through education, awareness generation, skill upgradation and behavioural training. The Scheme also supports a helpline for women in distress. The Scheme is implemented through Social Welfare/Women and Child Development Department, Women's Development Corporation, urban local bodies, reputed public/private trust or voluntary organisations, etc., provided they have the needed experience and expertise in the rehabilitation of such women on a project to project basis.

Short Stay Homes

The Scheme of Short Stay Homes provides temporary accommodation, maintenance and rehabilitative services through voluntary organizations to homeless women and girls. Under the scheme, temporary shelter to the needy women and girls is provided for 6 months to 3 years. Children accompanying the mother or born in the home are permitted to stay in the home upto age of 7 years, after which they may be referred to children's institutes. Rehabilitation of residents is provided with vocational training and skill development to make them economically independent and self-reliant. Working Womens' Hostel : In order to promote greater mobility of women in the employment market and to provide suitable, safe and inexpensive accommodation to women residing away from their hometowns to be able to work, working womens' hostels exist.

Ujjawala

Launched in 2009, 'Ujjawala' is a Comprehensive Scheme for Prevention of trafficking, with five specific components; (i) prevention, which includes formation of community vigilance groups/ adolescents groups, awareness and sensitization of important functionaries like policy, community leaders and preparation of awareness generation materials, holding workshops, etc.; (ii) rescue, for safe withdrawal of the victim from the place of exploitation.; (iii) rehabilitation, which includes providing safe shelter for victims with basic amenities such as food, clothing, counselling, medical care, legal aid, vocational training and income generation activities, etc.; (iv) reintegration, for restoring the victim into the family/community (if she so desires) and the accompanying costs; (v) repatriation, to provide support to cross - border victims for their safe repatriation to their country of origin.

Gender Budgeting Initiatives

Gender budgeting is a powerful tool for achieving gender mainstreaming so as to ensure that benefits of development reach women as much as men. It is not an accounting exercise but an ongoing process of keeping a gender perspective in policy/programme formulation, its implementation and review. To institutionalize gender budgeting in the country, the setting up of Gender Budgeting Cells (GBCs) in all ministries/departments was mandated by the Ministry of Finance in 2005. The Ministry of Women and Child Development (MWCD) as the nodal agency for gender budgeting has been undertaking several initiatives for taking it forward at the national and state levels. One of the key areas has been advocating for setting up of GBCs in all ministries/ departments, strengthening internal and external capacities and building expertise of GBCs to undertake gender mainstreaming of policies/ schemes/ programmes. Till date, GBCs have been set up in 56 ministries which are expected to serve as focal point for coordinating gender budgeting initiatives, both intra and inter-ministerial.

National Mission for Empowerment of Women

O. W.: http://www.nmew.gov.in

National Mission for Empowerment of Women (NMEW), a Centrally Sponsored Scheme (CSS), was launched by the government in 2010 with a view to empower women holistically. The Mission aims to achieve empowerment of women by securing inter sectoral convergence of schemes/programmes of different ministries/ departments of Government of India as well as state governments. It has the mandate to strengthen and facilitate the process of coordinating all the women's welfare and socio-economic development programmes. The Mission has an executive director and experts in the fields of poverty alleviation, social empowerment, health and nutrition, gender budgeting, gender rights & law enforcement, empowerment of vulnerable and marginalized women, media, awareness generation, advocacy and mass communication and information technology services.

The Central Monitoring Committee and Inter-Ministerial Coordination Committee have been set up to monitor and facilitate covergence across Ministries.

The convergence model is aimed at convergent implementation of programmes intended for welfare and development of women. The model would include introduction of convergence cum facilitation centres at the district (few urban agglomerations), tehsil/ward and village/area levels. The women centre at the village level, the first point of contact for women will be known as the Poorna Shakti Kendras (PSK), an unique model of 'convergence centres' for women, dedicated to helping women access the benefits made available to them through various government programmes. The Poorna Shakti Kendra is the focal point for action on ground through which the services to grassroots women would be facilitated.

Child Sex Ratio

NMEW is the nodal agency for addressing the issue of declining child sex ratio. A National Action Plan is now being drafted by the NMEW in consultation with all relevant stakeholders. A national consultation was organised in January, 2013, to bring various stakeholders including government officials, civil society organizations (CSO) members, medical practitioners and legal experts together to identify ways to address the issues of declining CSR.

Beti Bachao, Beti Padhao

In the backdrop of a trend of declining sex ratio in the age group upto five years ,the Government has introduced a new scheme called Beti Bachao, Beti Padhao with the twin aim of not only improving the adverse sex ratio but also to ensure that girls are educated. With an initial corpus of ₹ 100 crore, it will help in generating awareness and improve the efficiency of delivery of welfare services meant for women. With the government's emphasis on gender mainstreaming, the school curriculum will have a separate chapter on gender mainstreaming. This will sensitize students, teachers and the community at large to be more sensitive to the needs of a girl child and women and will promote growth of a more harmonious society. The important activities that would be undertaken under the Beti Padhao Abhiyan are as under: activate SMCs to ensure universal enrolment of girls; balika Manch in schools; construction of girl's toilets; make dysfunctional toilets functional; completion of Kasturba Gandhi Bal Vidyalayas; sustained campaign to re-enroll drop-out girls in secondary schools; and construction of girls hostels for secondary and senior secondary level.

The overall goal of the Beti Bachao, Beti Padhao(BBBP) Scheme is to celebrate the girl child and enable her education . The objectives of the Scheme are as under :- prevent gender biased sex selective elimination ensure survival and protection of the girl child Ensure education of the girl child. Mass Communication Campaign on Beti Bachao Beti Padhao aims at ensuring girls are born, nurtured and educated without discrimination to become empowered citizens of this country. The campaign interlinks national, state and district level interventions with community level action in 100 districts, bringing together different stakeholders for accelerated impact.

Social Media Presence:

YouTube: www.youtube.com/user/BetiBachaoBetiPadhao

- MyGov: www.mygov.in/group_info/beti-bachao-beti-padhao
- Vikaspedia:www.vikaspedia.in/social-welfare/women-and-child-development/betibachao-beti-padhao

Scheme of Central Social Welfare Board

Family Counselling Centre (FCC): Through these Centres, counselling, referral and rehabilitative services are provided to the women who are victims of atrocities, family maladjustment and social ostracism and services are also provided for crisis intervention and trauma counselling in case of natural and manmade disasters. The Centres also create awareness and mobilize public opinion on social issues affecting status of women. The FCCs work in close collaboration with the local administration, police, courts, legal aid cells, medical and psychiatric institutions, vocational training centres, short stay homes etc. to provide referral and rehabilitative services. The FCCs provide professional counselling to the clients through counsellors, in many states, the respective state governments have declared the FCC centres as service providers and counsellors as protection officer under the Protection of Women from Domestic Violence Act 2005.

Condensed Courses of Education for Women: The Condensed Courses of Education was initiated by Central Social Welfare Board to cater to the needs of adult girls/women who could not join mainstream education and who were drop-outs from formal schools. Under the Scheme, priority is being given to tribal, hilly and backward areas. The scheme aims to provide educational opportunities to girls/women above the age of 15 years along with additional inputs of skill development/vocational training at different levels - primary, middle/high school and matric/secondary levels. The main focus of the Scheme is to ensure that contents of the course are need-based and modified according to local requirement and simultaneously targeted towards various stages of educational levels in order to make them empowered.

Awareness Generation Programme

The Scheme aims to identify the needs of rural and poor women and to increase women's active participation in development and other allied programmes. Issues such as the status of women, women and law, women and health, community health and hygeine, technology for women, environment and economy are being taken up in the camps with special focus on local issues. This Scheme aims at empowering women by providing knowledge through organizing Awareness Generation Camps and to enhance their participation in development process and decision making.

'Stree Shakti Puraskar

As a recognition of achievements of individual women in the field of social development, the government has instituted six national awards known as 'Stree Shakti Puraskar'. These awards carrying a cash prize of ₹ 3 lakh and a citation are in the name of eminent women personalities from Indian history, who are famous for their personal courage and integrity: Devi Ahilya Bai Holkar, Kannagi, Mata Jijabai, Rani Gaidenliou Zeliang, Rani Lakshmi Bai and Rani Rudramma Devi.

Policies and Schemes

National Policy for Children

The Government adopted a new National Policy for Children (NPC) in April, 2013. The new Policy reaffirms the government's commitment to the realization of the rights of all children in the country. It recognizes every person below the age of eighteen years as a child. The Policy recognizes childhood as an integral part of life with a value of its own, and a long term, sustainable, multi-sectoral, integrated and inclusive approach is necessary for the harmonious development and protection of children. The Policy lays down the guiding principles that must be respected by the national, state and local government in their actions and initiatives affecting children. Some of the key guiding principles are the right of every child to life, survival, development, education, protection and participation, equal rights for all children without discrimination; the best interest of the child as a primary concern in all actions and decisions affecting children; and family environment as the most conducive for the all-round development of children.

The Policy has identified survival, health, nutrition, education, development, protection and participation as the undeniable rights of every child, and has also declared these as key priority areas. As children's needs are multisectoral, interconnected and require collective action, the Policy aims at purposeful convergence and strong coordination across different sectors and levels of governance; active engagement and partnerships with all stakeholders; setting up of a comprehensive and reliable knowledge base, provision of adequate resources; and sensitization and capacity development of all those who work for and with children. The Protection of Children from Sexual

Offences Act, 2012: To deal with child abuse cases, the Government has brought in a special law "The Protection of Children from Sexual Offences Act, 2012". The Act has come into force with effect from November 14, 2012 along with the rules framed thereunder.

The Act defines a 'child' as any person below eighteen years of age. Being gender neutral, this definition provides equal protection to both the male and the female child. The Act provides for stringent punishments, which have been graded as per the gravity of the offence. The punishments range from simple to rigorous imprisonment of varying periods. There is also a provision for fine, which is to be decided by the Court. An offence is treated as 'aggravated' when committed by a person in a position of trust or authority of child such as a member of security forces, police officer, public servant, etc. The Act provides for the establishment of special courts for trial of offences under the Act, keeping the best interest of the child as of paramount importance at every stage of the judicial process.

The National Commission for the Protection of Child Rights (NCPCR)and State Commissions for the Protections of Child Rights (SCPCRs) have been made the designated authority to monitor the implementation of the Act.

Food and Nutrition Board

Food and Nutrition Board in the Ministry of Women and Child Development is involved in policy making, strategy development as well as identifying innovative measures for the improvement of the nutritional status of the people of our country. It also focuses on improving the dietary habits of the people through nutrition eduction and extension; promotion of low cost, locally available foods; conservation of fruits and vegetables through home-scale processing; and training of health functionaries in nutrition. The FNB operates through a technical wing at the Centre, four regional offices, quality control laboratories in Delhi, Mumbai, Kolkata and Chennai and 43 Community Food and Nutrition Extension Units (CFNEUs) located in 29 states/UTs.

The National Nutrition Policy was formulated in 1993, and as a followup the National Plan of Action was developed in 1995. The National Plan of Action identified the different sectors in the government for taking up coordinated action to combat malnutrition. Programmes are undertaken to train master trainers such as medical officers/nursing officers, child development project officers/supervisors., principals of schools implementing mid-day meal scheme as well as the field level functionaries. Nutrition awareness programmes for the community, home-scale preservation of fruits and vegetables which also promotes skill development in the adolescent girls and women are organized. Demonstrations for promotion of low cost nutritious recipies are held to facilitate adoption of means to achieve better nutrition. Linkages with ICDS for better quality of supplementary nutrition, health and nutrition education are maintained. For promotion of infant and young child feeding practices, focus on appropriate feeding and implementation of IMS Act are undertaken.

Rajiv Gandhi National Creche Scheme

Rajiv Gandhi National Creche Scheme provides day care facilities to the children in the age group of 0-6 years from families with monthly income of less than ₹ 12,000/-. In addition to being a safe space for the children, the creches provide services as supplementary nutrition, pre-school education and emergency health care, etc. The scheme is presently being implemented through the Central Social Welfare Board (CSWB), Indian Council for Child Welfare (ICCW). The scheme provides a grant of ₹ 3,532/- per month for a creche, limited to 90 per cent of the schematic pattern or actual expenditure whichever is less and the remaining expenditure is borne by the implementing agencies. Every crèche is required to be inspected at least once in a period of two years. The scheme is being structurally revamped with revised cost-norms and additional models.

Integrated Child Protection Scheme (ICPS)

Ministry of Women and Child Development is implementing this comprehensive Centrally sponsored scheme since 2009-10 through the state government/UT administrations on a predefined cost sharing financial pattern. The objectives of the Scheme are to contribute to the improvement in the well being of children in difficult circumstances, as well as reduction of vulnerabilities to situation and actions that lead to abuse, neglect, exploitation, abandonment and separation of children from parents. ICPS provides preventive, statutory care and rehabilitation services to children who are in need of care and protection and children in conflict with law as defined under The Juvenile Justice (Care and Protection of Children) Act, 2000 and its Amendment Act, 2006 and any other vulnerable child. It provides financial support to state governments/UT administrations for running services for children either themselves or through suitable NGOs. These services include (a) homes of various types for children (b) emergency outreach service through childline; (c) open shelters for children in need of care and protection in urban and semi urban areas; (d) family based non institutional care through sponsorship, foster care and adoptions. Financial assistance under this Scheme is also provided for setting up of statutory bodies under the JJ Act Child Welfare Committees (CWCs) and Juvenile Justice Boards (JJBs). As reported by the state governments/UT administrations, 619 CWCs and 608 JJBs have so far been set up across the country to ensure effective implementation of the scheme and provide quality services to children. ICPS also provides financial assistance to set up service delivery structures with dedicated staff at state and district levels.

Childline Services

Childline is a 24 hour toll free emergency outreach telephone service (1098) for children in distress. At present, Childline is functioning in 276 cities/ districts. The basic objectives of Childline are to: (i) respond to the emergency needs of the children in difficulty and refer him/ her to such services as he/ she is in need of; (ii) provide a forum for networking among government agencies and non-government agencies dedicated to the network of services in child care and protection; (iii) sensitize hospitals, medical personnel , police municipal corporations etc. towards needs of children, (iv) ensure protection of rights of the child, and (v) provide an opportunity to communities to respond to the needs of children in difficult circumstances. Childline operations are coordinated, monitored and expanded by Childline India Foundation, which is a society substantially funded by the Government of India.

Scheme for Welfare of Working Children in Need of Care and Protection

The scheme is being implemented since January, 2005 with the objective of providing non-formal education, vocational training, etc., to working children to facilitate their entry/re-entry into mainstream education in cases where they have either not attended, any learning system or where, for some reason, their education has been discontinued, with a view to prevent their future exploitation. Financial assistance is provided under this scheme to Non-Governmental Organizations (NGOs) for setting up of composite centres of working children exclusively in those areas which have not already been covered by the Ministry of Labour and Employment under their schemes, namely, National Child Labour Project and Indo-US Project. At present, Ministry is assisting 116 projects of 100 children each under this scheme in 14 states/UTs. The Scheme is being implemented in 11 blocks across seven states of Andhra Pradesh, Chhattisgarh, Odisha, Jharkhand, Bihar, Uttar Pradesh and Punjab.

Child Awards

The National Child Award for exceptional Achievement was instituted in 1996 to give recognition to children with exceptional abilities who have achieved outstanding status in various fields including academics, arts, culture and sports etc. Children between the age of 4 -15 years who have shown an exceptional achievement in any field are eligible for this award. One gold medal and 35 silver medals (one for each state/UT) are given annually. National Award for Child Welfare was instituted in 1979 to honour five institutions and three individuals for their outstanding performance in the field of child welfare.

International Cooperation

Convention on Elimination of Discrimination against Women

India signed the Convention of Elimination of Discrimination against Women (CEDAW) in 1980 and ratified it in 1993 with one reservation and two declaratory statements. The Convention obligates the State parties to undertake appropriate legislative and other measures to eliminate discrimination against women and for guaranteeing them the exercise and enjoyment of human rights and fundamental freedom on the basis of equality with men.

Statutory and Autonomous Organisations

National Commission for Women

O. W.: http://www.ncw.nic.in

The National Commission for Women (NCW) was constituted in January, 1991 as a statutory body at the national level in pursuance of The National Commission for Women Act, 1990 to safeguard the interests of women. It has a wide mandate covering almost all aspects of women's development, viz., to investigate and examine the legal safeguards provided for women under the Constitution and other laws and recommend to Government measures for their effective implementation; review the existing provisions of the Constitution and other laws affecting women and recommended amendments to meet any lacunae, inadequacies or shortcomings in such laws; look into complaints and take suo motu notice of matters relating to deprivation of women's rights etc., and take up the issues with appropriate authorities; take up studies/research on issues of relevance to women, participate and advise in the planning process for socio-economic development of women, evaluate the progress made thereof, inspect jails, remand homes etc where women are kept under custody and seek remedial action wherever necessary. National Commission for women had taken up the review of the MTP Act, 1971 and Immoral trafficking (Prevention) Act, 1956 with a view to examine whether the existing provisions of the Act require any amendments. The recommendations have been forwarded to the Government. The Commission was designated as the coordinating agency at the National Level for dealing with issues pertaining to NRI marriages. NRI Cell of NCW deals with complaints received from deserted women in India and abroad due to cross country marriages wherein there is any deprivation of women's rights or any issue involving grave injustice to women. The Commission is implementing a project called "Violence Free Home- A Women's Right' with Delhi Police to Safeguard the interests of girls and women in Delhi and NCR region. The objective of the project is to train and sensitize police personnel in dealing with the cases of atrocities against women and provide counsellors for effecting reconciliation in cases of marital dispute. A memorandum of Understanding (MOU) was signed between NCW and Delhi Police and Tata Institute of Social Sciences, Mumbai for the purpose. The Commission has taken initiatives to honour outstanding women achievers in their respective fields.

National Commission for Protection of Child Rights

The National Commission for Protection of Child Rights Act (NCPCR), 2005 was notified in January, 2006. A National Commission for Protection of Child Rights was set up in March, 2007 in accordance with the provisions of the Act for proper enforcement of children's rights and effective implementation of laws and programmes relating to children. Its mission is to protect, promote and defend child rights in India. Its mandate is to ensure that all laws, policies, programmes, practices and administrative structure in the country are in consonance with the child rights perspective as enshrined in the Constitution of India and also the UN Convention on the Rights of the Child (CRC). Under the provisions of the Act, state commissions have been set up in Assam, Bihar, Chhattisgarh, Delhi, Goa, Karnataka, Madhya Pradesh, Maharashtra, Manipur, Odisha, Punjab, Rajasthan, Sikkim, Tamil Nadu, Uttarakhand, West Bengal and Nagaland. The Rights of Child to Free and Compulsory Education Act, 2009 came into force in April, 2010. The NCPCR along with the state commissions have a specific role for the implementation of the Act. The Protection of Children from Sexual Offences Act, 2012 (POCSO) came into force on November 14, 2012. This comprehensive piece of legislation provides protection to all children under the age of 18 years from offences of sexual assault, sexual harassment and pornography and overcomes the lacunae in the different sections of the IPC and more important, does not distinguish between adult and child victims. The SCPCRs have also been entrusted with the task of monitoring the implementation of the Protection of Children from Sexual offences (POCSO) Rules, 2012.

O. W.: http://www.ncpcr.gov.in

Rashtriya Mahila Kosh

Rashtriya Mahila Kosh (RMK) extends micro-finance to the needy and poor women in the informal sector through a client-friendly, without collateral and in a hassle-free manner for livelihood activities, housing, micro-enterprises, etc., for their socio-economic upliftment. RMK has pioneered an alternate credit delivery mechanism in the country by advancing micro-credit to the Self- Help Groups (SHGs) of poor women through a diverse range of intermediary organizations working at the grass-root level such as NGOs, women federations, co-operatives, urban women cooperative banks. Government autonomous bodies, not-for-profit Section 25 Companies registered under the Companies Act, etc. RMK took a number of promotional measures to popularize the concept of micro financing, thrift and credit, formation and stabilization of SHGs and also enterprise development for poor women through these intermediaries. To be eligible for loan from RMK the Intermediary Micro-financing Organisations (IMOs) should have experience in thrift and credit management of 3 years or more and must not work for profit. While loans to IMOs are given at 8 per cent p.a., IMOs are allowed to charge women beneficiary maximum up to 18 per cent p.a. on reducing balance method. In order to remove the uneven presence of micro-credit in the country which is witnessed mostly in North-Eastern region due to the poor presence of banking network, lack of infrastructure and awareness, RMK has formulated a client-friendly credit package for the North-East region by relaxing it's credit norms to meet the needs of the women. RMK believes in the women empowerment through micro financing. The partner organizations that take loans from RMK are instructed to impart literacy, education, awareness on health, hygiene, nutrition, HIV/AIDS, legal rights etc. to the women SHG members. RMK has extended micro-credit across 27 states and UTs including the Andaman & Nicobar Islands and Jammu and Kashmir.

O. W.: http://www.rmk.nic.in

National Institute of Public Cooperation and Child Development

National Institute of Public Cooperation and Child Development (NIPCCD), an autonomous organization under the aegis of the Ministry of Women and

Child Development, is a premier organisation devoted to promotion of voluntary action and research, training and documentation in the overall domain of women and child development. The objectives of the institute are to: develop and promote voluntary action in social development; take a comprehensive view of child development and to promote relevant need-based programmes in pursuance of the National Policy for Children; national policy for empowerment of coordination between governmental and voluntary action in social development; evolve framework and perspective for organizing programmes related to women and children through governmental and voluntary efforts; and establish liaison with international and regional agencies, research institutions, universities and technical bodies engaged in activities similar to those of the Institute.

Integrated Child Development Services

Integrated Child Development Services (ICDS) Scheme is one of the flagship programmes of the Government and represents one of the world's largest and unique programmes for early childhood development. The programme aims at addressing health, nutrition and the development needs of young children, pregnant and nursing mothers. NIPCCD has been functioning as an apex institution for training of the ICDS functionaries since 1975. As a nodal resource agency, the Institute has also been entrusted with the responsibility of training and capacity building of functionaries at the national and regional level, under the Integrated Child Protection Scheme (ICPS). The Institute, had finalized syllabi for functionaries under ICPS in collaboration with UNICEF and training manuals have been prepared for various stakeholders for effective child protection, as envisaged under the legal framework. The current thrust areas relate to child development are maternal and child health and nutrition, early childhood care and education, childhood disability, positive mental health in children and child care support service. Several programmes have been designed for various groups of clientele, namely, representatives of NGOs, parents, teachers, and officers of various government departments.

Since 2005-06 the Institute runs one year regular Advanced Diploma in Child Guidance and Counselling with a vision to bridge the gap of trained professionals for undertaking guidance and counselling intervention with children and their families in different settings. It is currently focusing on gender planning and mainstreaming, gender budgeting, economic and political empowerment of women, prevention of sexual harassment at work place, prevention of gender related violence such as female foeticide, female infanticide, trafficking of women and children, child marriage, etc. The major initiatives during 2013-14 include Capacity Building Programmes on Protection of Children from Sexual Offences (POCSO) Act & Rules, 2012 for stakeholders; consultation with stakeholders on experiences in service delivery under IGMSY in the implementing districts, workshop on strengthening and restructuring of ICDS programme under 12th Five Year Plan, cross learning workshop on innovation and potential best practices in (ICDS; sensitization of ICDS functionaries on management of severe acute malnourished (SAM) children and their follow-up; and prevention of malnutrition on women & children. In addition to these, the Institute has embarked upon newer areas concerning women & children in its research initiatives as well. The Institute provides technical advice and consultancy to government and Voluntary Agencies in promoting and implementing policies and programmes for women and child development and voluntary action.

O. W.: http://www.nipccd.nic.in

Central Social Welfare Board

The Central Social Welfare Board (CSWB) was set-up in August, 1953 with the objective of promoting social welfare activities and implementing welfare programmes for women and children through voluntary organizations. Thirty-three state social welfare boards were set up with jurisdiction over all states and union territories to work together with Central Social Welfare Board in implementing the programmes of the Board across the country. It is functioning as an interface between the government and the voluntary sector. The Board has been making concerted efforts for empowerment of women through family counselling programmes, short stay homes, awareness generation projects, condensed Course of Education Programmes and other support services. The Board was registered as a Charitable Company in 1969. The Board has been revamping and redesigning its programmes that best fulfil emerging requirements. As the Central Board is committed for implementation of developmental schemes in a transparent manner, a webbased online application system i.e., e-Awedan (Electronic Application for Women Empowerment and Development Action by NGOs) has been evolved with the objective to provide transparency, better monitoring and effective implementation of Board's programmes.

O. W.: http://www.cswb.gov.in

Central Adoption Resource Authority

The Central Adoption Resource Authority (CARA) is an autonomous body under the Ministry of Women and Child Development. It functions as the nodal body for adoption of Indian children and is mandated to monitor and regulate in-country and inter-country adoptions. CARA is designated as the central authority to deal with inter-country adoptions in accordance with the provisions of the Hague Convention on Inter-country Adoption, 1993, ratified by Government of India in 2003. The objectives of CARA are to : (i) function as a nodal body on non institutional child care services in the country; (ii) act as a Central Authority as envisaged under the Hague Convention on Inter-country Adoption; (iii) facilitate and promote adoption of orphan, abandoned and surrendered children; and (iv) streamline adoption procedures and delivery systems. Details about adoption procedures are available at www.adoptionindia.nic.in CARINGS (Child Adoption Resource Information & Guidance System), an IT application for greater transparency in adoption system: CARINGS is an online platform, building bridges and creating links through a robust webbased management system. It facilitates expeditious adoption, ensures transparency in the adoption process, increases accountability of implementing agencies, creates a network of stakeholders towards improved synergy, and maintains a National Database to enable effective policy making and research.

Sukanya Samriddhi Account

Along with the Beti Bachao, Beti Padhao scheme, the government also launched the "Sukanya Samriddhi Account" programme. Despite being a small savings scheme, the Sukanya Samriddhi Account has the potential to have a phenomenal impact on the lives and self esteem of young girls in the country. The scheme aims to ensure a bright future for the girl children by facilitating their education and marriage expenses.

Under the scheme, a parent or legal guardian can open an account in the name of the girl child until she attains the age of ten years. As per the government notification on the Scheme, the account can be opened in any post office branch and designated public sector banks. The rate of interest for the scheme is an attractive 9.2 per cent which will be compounded annually. This rate, however, will be revised every year by the government and will be announced at the time of the Union budget. The minimum deposit that needs to be made every year in ₹ 1,000 and the maximum amount that can be deposited in a year is ₹ 1,50,000. There is no limit on the number of deposits either in a month or in a financial year.

The account will be valid for 21 years from the date of opening, after which it will mature and the money will be paid to the girl child in whose name the account had been opened. If the account is not closed after maturity, the balance amount will continue to earn interest as specified for the scheme from time to time. The account will also automatically close if the girl child gets married before the completion of the tenure of 21 years. Deposits can be made up to 14 years from the date of opening of the account. After this period the account will only earn interest as per applicable rates. In case the required minimum annual deposit of ₹ 1,000 is not made by a parent or a guardian, the account will cease to be active. In such a situation, the account can be easily reactivated by paying a penalty of ₹ 50 per year along with the minimum amount required for deposit for that year. Premature withdrawal-withdrawing money before the completion of the maturity period of 21 years - can only be made by the girl child in whose name the account has been opened after she attains the age of 18 years. This withdrawal will also be limited to 50 per cent of the balance standing at the end of the preceding financial year, and will only be allowed for the purpose of higher education or if the girl intends to get married. It is also worthy to note that in order to make a withdrawal, the account should have a deposit of at least 14 years or more. A parent or guardian can open only one account per girl child, and a maximum of two such bank accounts in the name of two girl children. In case of twin girls as second birth, or if the first birth itself results in the birth of three girl children, three bank accounts can be opened in the name of three girl children.

29 Youth Affairs and Sports

THE Ministry of Youth Affairs and Sports functions under the overall guidance of the Minister of State (Independent Charge) for Youth Affairs and Sports. In April, 2008, two separate Departments, namely, Department of Youth Affairs and Department of Sports, were created under the Ministry, each Department under the charge of a Secretary to the Government of India.

Youth Affairs

The youth represent the most dynamic and vibrant segment of the population. India is one of the youngest nations in the world, with about 65 per cent of the population being under 35 years of age. The youth in the age group of 15-29 years comprise 27.5 per cent of the population. India is expected to become the 4th largest economy by 2025, only after the United States, China and Japan, contributing about 5.5-6 per cent to the world GDP. While most of these developed countries face the risk of an ageing workforce, India is expected to have a very favourable demographic profile. It is estimated that by the year 2020, the population of India would have a median age of 28 years only as against 38 years for United States, 42 years for China and 48 years for Japan. This 'demographic dividend' offers a great opportunity. However, in order to tap this demographic dividend, it is essential that the economy has the ability to support the increase in the labour force and the youth have the appropriate education, skills, health awareness and other enablers to productively contribute to the economy. The Government of India currently invests more than ₹ 90,000 crore per annum on youth development programmes, i.e., approximately ₹ 2,710 per young individual per year. In addition, the state governments and a number of other stakeholders are also working to support youth development and to enable productive youth participation. However, there is a need for a more focused and coordinated effort to empower the youth to achieve their full potential.

National Youth Policy

The National Youth Policy, 2014 (NYP-2014) reiterates the commitment of the entire nation to the all-round development of the youth, so that they can realise their full potential and contribute productively to the nation-building process. The Policy defines 'youth' as persons in the age-group of 15-29 years. Its vision, objectives and priority areas proposes a holistic 'vision' for the youth of India, which is "To empower youth of the country to achieve their full potential, and through them enable India to find its rightful place in the community of nations". In order to realise this, it identifies five clearly defined 'objectives' which need to be pursued and the 'Priority Areas' under each of the objectives.

The objectives and priority areas identified under the Policy are summarised here:

Objectives	Priority Areas
1. Create a productive workforce that can make a sustainable contribution to India's economic development	1. Education 2. Employment and skill development 3. Entrepreneurship
2. Develop a strong and healthy generation equipped to take on future challenges	1. Health and healthy lifestyle 2. Sports
3. Instil social values and promote community service to build national ownership	1. Promotion of social values 2. Community engagement
4. Facilitate participation and civic engagement at all levels of governance	1. Participation in politics and governance 2. Youth engagement
5. Support youth at risk and create equitable opportunity for all disadvantaged and marginalised youth	1. Inclusion 2. Social justice

National Young Leaders Programme

National Young Leaders Programme (NYLP) aims at developing leadership qualities among the youth to enable them to realise their full potential and in the process, to contribute to the nation-building process. The Programme aims at motivating the youth to strive for excellence in their respective fields and to bring them to the forefront of the development process. It seeks to harness the immense youth energy for nation building. The Programme beneficiaries shall be the youth in the age-group of 15-29 years, in line with the definition of 'youth' in the National Youth Policy, 2014.

Programme Components

The National Young Leaders Programme is proposed as a Central Sector Scheme. It has the following components: Neighbourhood Youth Parliament (NYP); Youth for Development Programme (YFDP); National Young Leaders Awards (NYLA); National Youth Advisory Council (NYAC); and National Youth Development Fund (NYDF).

Nehru Yuva Kendra Sangathan

Nehru Yuva Kendra Sangathan (NYKS), launched in 1972, is one of the largest youth organisations in the world. NYKS currently has about 81 lakh youth enrolled through 2.85 lakh youth clubs/ mahila mandals. NYKS has presence in 623 districts through NYKS. Its objective is to develop the personality and leadership qualities of the youth and to engage them in nation-building activities. The areas of focus of the activities include literacy and education, health and family welfare, sanitation and cleanliness, environment conservation, awareness on social issues, women empowerment, rural development, skill development and self-employment, entrepreneurship development, civic education, disaster relief and rehabilitation, etc. The youth associated with the Kendras are not only socially aware and motivated but are also inclined towards social development work through voluntary efforts.

Activities of NYKS

The programmes/activities carried out can be broadly classified in the following categories, namely: (a) core programmes implemented with its own budgetary resources (block grants released by the Department), (b) programmes organised with funding from NPYAD (National Programme for Youth and Adolescent Development), (c) programmes organised in collaboration with/ funding from other ministries/organisations, (d) programmes/activities in coordination with various development departments/agencies. All the programmes of NYKS are implemented in close coordination with active involvement of state governments, elected local bodies and various development departments/ agencies.

National Youth Corps

The Scheme of National Youth Corps (NYC) was launched in the country during 2010-11. The earlier schemes, namely, National Service Volunteer Scheme (NSVS) and Rashtriya Sadbhavana Yojana (RSY) were subsumed in the National Youth Corps (NYC) Scheme. The NYC Scheme is being implemented through NYKS. Under the Scheme, youth in the age-group of 18-25 years are engaged as volunteers to serve upto maximum two years in nation-building activities. The minimum qualification for NYC volunteers is Class-X and they are paid honorarium @ ₹ 2,500/- per month. The selection of NYC volunteers is done by a Selection Committee, headed by District Collector/ Deputy Commissioner of the concerned district. The volunteers are given 15-day induction training at the time of joining and seven-day refresher training in the second year of their tenure. During the training, NYKS provides them skill development training so that they can get some employment after their term with NYKS ends. After two years, another set of NYC volunteers are recruited. Normally, two NYC volunteers are deployed in every block. They act as an extended arm of NYKS in the block and play an active role in implementation of various programmes and initiatives of NYKS. During 2014-15, 5,008 new NYC volunteers have been selected to replace those volunteers completing their tenure and the same have been deployed in blocks after induction training.

National Service Scheme

National Service Scheme (NSS) was introduced in 1969 with the primary objective of developing the personality and character of the student through voluntary community service. 'Education through Service' is the purpose of the NSS. The ideological orientation of the NSS is inspired by the ideals of Mahatma Gandhi. Very appropriately, the motto of NSS is *"Not Me, But You"*. An NSS volunteer places the 'community' before 'self'.

NSS aims at developing the following qualities/competencies among the volunteers: (a) to understand the community in which the NSS volunteers work and to understand themselves in relation to their community; (b) to identify the needs and problems of the community and involve themselves in problem-solving exercise; (c) to develop among themselves a sense of social and civic responsibility; (d) to utilize their knowledge in finding practical solutions to individual and community problems; (e) to gain skills in mobilizing community participation; (f) to acquire leadership qualities and democratic values; (g) to develop capacity to meet emergencies and natural disasters; and (h) to practice national integration and social harmony.

NSS was launched in 1969 in 37 universities involving about 40,000 volunteers. NSS has about 36.42 lakh volunteers on its rolls spread over 351 universities, 16,056 colleges/ technical institutions and 12,004 senior secondary schools. Since inception, over 4.60 crore students have benefited from NSS.

Rajiv Gandhi National Institute of Youth Development

Rajiv Gandhi National Institute of Youth Development (RGNIYD), Sriperumbudur, Tamil Nadu, is an 'Institute of National Importance' under the Ministry of Youth Affairs and Sports, Government of India, by virtue of enactment of RGNIYD Act, 2012. The RGNIYD was set up in 1993 as a Society under the Societies Registration Act, 1975 and was conferred the status of 'Deemed to be University' under *'De-novo'* category in 2008, by the Ministry of Human Resources Development. RGNIYD functions as a vital resource centre with its multi-faceted functions of offering academic programmes at post-graduate level encompassing various dimensions of youth development, engaging in seminal research in the vital areas of youth development and coordinating training programmes for state agencies and the officials of youth organisations, besides the extension and outreach initiatives across the country.

The Institute functions as a think-tank of the Ministry and premier organization of youth-related activities in the country. As the apex institute at the national level, it works in close cooperation with the NSS, NYKS and other youth organisations in the implementation of training programmes. It is a nodal agency for training youth as a facilitator of youth development activities in rural, urban as well as tribal areas. The RGNIYD serves as a youth observatory and depositary in the country thereby embarking on youth surveillance on youth-related issues. It has a wide network with various organizations working for the welfare and development of young people and serves as a mentor. The vision of RGNIYD is to be a globally recognised and acclaimed centre of academic excellence in the field of youth development.

Punarjagaran (Rejuvenation) Programme

The year-long Punarjagaran programme and Yatra which was started from 2014 on the birth anniversary of Mahatma Gandhi, from four corners of the country viz., Leh (J&K), Kanyakumari (Tamil Nadu), Roing (Arunachal Pradesh) and Okha (Gujarat), culminated at Deen Dayal Upadhyay Dham, Nagla Chandrabhan, Mathura marking the birth centenary of Pandit Deen Dayal Upadhyay, the proponent of integral humanism.

National Programme for Youth and Adolescent Development

National Programme for Youth and Adolescent Development (NPYAD) is an "Umbrella Scheme" of the Ministry under which financial assistance is provided to government/non-government organisations for taking up activities for youth and adolescent development. The Scheme is operational since 2008. The assistance under NPYAD is provided under five major components : (a) youth leadership and personality development training; (b) promotion of national integration programmes, youth festivals, multi-cultural activities, etc.; (c) promotion of adventure; Tenzing Norgay National Adventure Awards; (d) development and empowerment of adolescents life skills education, counselling, career guidance, etc.; and (e) technical and resource development research and studies on youth issues, documentation, seminars/ workshops.

National Youth Awards

National Youth Awards are conferred every year on young individuals and NGOs for excellent work done for nation-building/ community service. A cash award of ₹ 40,000/-, a medal and a certificate of honour is given to each individual awardee. The award to voluntary youth organisations comprises a certificate, a medal and an amount of ₹ 2,00,000/-. National Youth Awards for 2016 were conferred on 25 youths and 2 organizations from different states/ UTs.

Youth Hostels

Youth hostels are built to promote youth travel and to enable the young people to experience the rich cultural heritage of the country. The construction of the youth hostels is a joint venture of the central and state governments. While the Central government bears the cost of construction, the state governments provide fully developed land free-of-cost, with water supply, electricity connection and approach roads. Youth hostels are located in areas of historical and cultural value, in educational centres, in tourist destinations, etc. Youth hostels provide good accommodation for the youth at reasonable rates.

These hostels are looked after by managers, appointed by the Central government. The Ministry selects managers for the youth hostels from amongst the retired defence personnel, preferably from the catchment area of the youth hostel and those having command over Hindi, English and local languages. Under the new appointment policy, a graduate preferably having a degree in

Hotel Management/ Youth Development/ MBA/ LSW/ MSW and having at least three years' working experience in the field of hostel/hotel Industry or running boarding schools/ guest houses or retired government officers of central/ state government having working experience of youth activities, are also eligible for appointment as managers in youth hostels. The age limit for the appointment for the post is between 35 years to 62 years and will be counted from the date of the contract. So far, 83 youth hostels have been constructed across the country and one more youth hostel, at Roing (Arunachal Pradesh), is in advanced stage of completion. Out of 83 youth hostels, 11 have been transferred to Nehru Yuva Kendra Sangathan/ Sports Authority of India (SAI)/ concerned state governments for optimum use for youth and sports development and the remaining 72 hostels are under direct control of the Department. Four youth hostels, namely, Dalhousie (Himachal Pradesh), Jodhpur (Rajasthan), Mysore (Karnataka) and Puducherry have got the ISO 9001:2008 Certification. Two more youth hostels, namely, Agra (Uttar Pradesh) and Panaji (Goa) have been identified for obtaining ISO 9001:2008 Certification.

Scouting and Guiding

The Department provides assistance to the scouting and guiding organisations, with a view to promoting the scouts and guides movement in the country. This is an international movement aimed at building character, confidence, idealism and spirit of patriotism and service among young boys and girls. Scouting and guiding also seeks to promote balanced physical and mental development among the boys and girls. The financial assistance is provided to scouting and guiding organisations for various programmes such as organization of training camps, skill development programmes, holding of jamborees, etc. The activities, inter alia, include programmes related to adult literacy, environment conservation, community service, health awareness and promotion of hygiene and sanitation. During the year 2015-16, the Department has sanctioned total grants of ₹1.50 crore @ ₹ 75.00 lakh each to (i) Bharat Scouts and Guides and (ii) Hindustan Scouts and Guides, for various scouting and guiding activities.

Sports

Sports and games have always been seen as an integral component in all round development of human personality. Apart from being means of entertainment and physical fitness, sports have also played a great role in generation of spirit of healthy competition and bonding within the community. Achievements in sports have always been a source of national pride and prestige. With modern sports being highly competitive, the use of modern infrastructure, equipment and advanced scientific support has changed the scenario of sports at the international level. Keeping in line with the growing demands for advanced infrastructure, equipment and scientific support, Government of India has taken several initiatives and is providing the necessary assistance to sportspersons by way of training and exposure in international competitions backed up with scientific and equipment support.

Rio Olympics

India's star P. V. Sindhu won silver in the women's singles event Badminton category in the Rio Olympics. Sakshi Malik won the bronze in the 58 kg category, becoming the first Indian women wrestler to win a medal at the Olympics and the fourth female Olympic medalist from the country.

National Sports Policy

National Sports Policy, 2001 envisages mainly broad basing and promotion of excellence in sports. The salient features of this Policy are: (i) broad basing of sports and achievement of excellence; (ii) upgradation and development of infrastructure; (iii) support to national sports federations and other appropriate bodies; (iv) strengthening of scientific and coaching support to sports; (v) incentives to promote sports; (vi) enhanced participation of women, scheduled tribes and rural youth; (vii) involvement of corporate sector in sports promotion; and (viii) promotion of sports mindedness among the public at large.

Rajiv Gandhi Khel Abhiyan

Rajiv Gandhi Khel Abhiyan (RGKA), a centrally sponsored plan scheme was launched in 2014 in place of Panchayat Yuva Krida aur Khel Abhiyan (PYKKA). The new scheme will involve an estimated outlay of about ₹ 9,000 crore spread over the remaining three years of the 12th Five Year Plan and the 13th Five Year Plan. The key objectives of the scheme are promotion of sports as a way of life among the youth, increased access to sports facilities throughout the country, conduct of sports competitions across the country to identify sports talent and achieving excellence in sports. Under the scheme, integrated sports complexes are to be constructed in every rural block panchayat of the country. Each sports complex will cost ₹ 1,765 crore and have eleven outdoor and five indoor games with flexibility to choose three local games within the limit of 16 games. The outdoor disciplines are athletics, archery, badminton, basketball, football, handball, hockey, kabaddi, kho-kho, tennis and volleyball. The indoor disciplines are boxing, wrestling, table tennis, weightlifting and also provision of a multi-gym. Three sports trainers, preferably one female, is to be made available at each integrated sports complex. Under the scheme, assistance will be provided for sports equipment and a Youth Resource Centre. Provision for self defence training, especially for women has also been made. Funds are also to be provided to conduct competition to identify talent as well as for the conduct of special category games namely women competition, northeast area games, and special area games.

Promotion of Urban Sports

The Government introduced a scheme titled 'Scheme of Assistance for the Creation of Urban Sports Infrastructure' on pilot basis in 2010-11 for creating/ upgrading sports facilities and for training of coaches. Further, financial assistance is provided under the scheme to the state governments and the National Playing Field Association for protection and preservation of playing spaces across the country. Under the scheme, state governments, local civic bodies, schools, colleges, universities and sports control boards are eligible for assistance.

Promotion of Excellence in Sports

The Sports Authority of India (SAI) was established by the Government of India in year 1984 as a registered society primarily to ensure effective maintenance and optimum utilization of the sports infrastructure that was built in Delhi during ASIAD, 1982. It is now the nodal agency in the country for broad basing sports and for training of sportspersons to achieve excellence in national and international sports. The Society for National Institute of Physical Education and Sports (SNIPES) was merged with SAI in 1987. Subsequently Netaji Subhash National Institute of Sports (NSNIS), Patiala and its allied centres at Bengaluru, Kolkata and Gandhinagar, and Lakshmibai National College of Physical Education at Thiruvananthapuram came under SAI. It has now regional centers at Bengaluru, Gandhinagar, Kolkata, Sonepat, Bhopal, Imphal, Chandigarh and Lucknow. SAI also operates a High Altitude Training Center (HATC) at Shillaroo (HP).

SAI operates various schemes at sub-junior, junior and senior levels, namely, national sports talent contest (NSTC), army boys sports company (ABSC), SAI training centres (STC) and special area games to achieve excellence at national and international level. SAI has also set up centres of excellence for elite sportspersons at each of its regional centres and one at the National Institute of Sports, Patiala.

Lakshmibai National Institute of Physical Education (LNIPE)

The Institute was established initially as a College on August 17, 1957, the centenary year of the first war of India's Independence. The University is located at Gwalior, where Rani Lakshmibai of Jhansi had laid down her life for the country's freedom struggle. In recognition of the services rendered in the field of physical education and sports by the Institute, it was upgraded to a "Deemed University" in 1995. The LNIPE is fully funded by the Government of India.

The Institute offers the following full time courses: (1) Bachelor of Physical Education (BPE) (4 year degree course), (2) Master of Physical Education (MPE) (2 year course), (3) M. Phil in Physical Education (1 year course) and (4) Ph.D in Physical Education. Apart from these, following certificate, diploma and post-graduate courses are also being conducted by the Institute: (a) adventure sports, (b) special sports, (c) youth affairs, (d) information technology, (e) sports coaching, (f) yoga and alternate therapies, (g) sports management, and (h) sports journalism.

The Institute also conducts in-service training programmes in physical education for ex-army personnel, refresher/orientation course for physical education teachers in universities, colleges and schools. The Institute attracts students from abroad also. A North East Campus of LNIPE has been established at Guwahati (Assam) and has started functioning since 2010-11.

Promotion of Sports

Government of India provides assistance to National Sports Federations (NSFs) for conducting national championships and international tournaments, participation in international tournaments abroad, organizing coaching camps, procuring sports equipment, engagement of foreign coaches, etc.

The Ministry of Youth Affairs and Sports has revised the existing 'Scheme relating to Talent Search and Training' in 2014 and renamed it as 'Scheme of Human Resources Development in Sports'. Under the revised Scheme, the Government intends to focus on developing human resources in sports sciences and sports medicine, sports coaching/umpires for the overall development of sports and games in the country. This will help the country be self reliant in these fields over a period of time in general and meet the requirements of the proposed National Institute of Sports Sciences and Medicine in particular.

National Sports Development Fund

The National Sports Development Fund (NSDF) was instituted by the Central Government with a view to mobilizing resources from the Government as well as non-governmental sources, including the private/corporate sector and non-resident Indians, for promotion of sports and games in the country. To make contributions to the fund attractive, 100 per cent exemption from income tax is available on all contributions. To begin with, the Government made a contribution of ₹ 2 crore in 1998-99. Further, Government contribution is on matching basis to the contributions received from other sources. The funds available under NSDF are used for promotion of sports in general and specific sports disciplines and individual sportspersons for achieving excellence at the national and international level in particular; imparting special training and coaching in relevant sport disciplines to sportspersons, coaches and sports specialists; to construct and maintain infrastructure as may be required for promotion of excellence in sports; to supply equipment to governmental and non-governmental organizations and individuals with a view to promoting excellence in sports; to identify problems and take up research and development studies for providing support to excellence in sports, etc.

Incentive Schemes for Sportspersons

The Ministry of Youth Affairs and Sports also implements various schemes to give incentives to sportspersons to take up sports as given here:

Rajiv Gandhi Khel Ratna Award

The scheme was launched in the year 1991-92 with the objective of honouring sportspersons to enhance their general status and to give them greater dignity and place of honour in society. Under this scheme, an amount of ₹ 7.5 lakh is given as award for the most spectacular and outstanding performance by a sportsperson over a period of four years immediately preceding the year in which award is to be given.

Arjuna Award

The award was instituted in 1961. To be eligible for the award, a sportsperson should have not only good performance consistently for the previous four years at the international level with excellence for the year for which award is recommended, but should have also shown qualities of leadership, sportsmanship and a sense of discipline. The awardee is given a statuette, a certificate, ceremonial dress and a cash award of ₹ five lakh. Not more than fifteen awards are given every year.

Dhyan Chand Award for Life Time Achievements

This award was instituted in 2002. This award is given to honour those sportspersons who have contributed to sports by their performance and continue to contribute to promotion of sports even after their retirement from active sporting career. The awardee is given a statuette, a certificate, ceremonial dress and a cash award of ₹ five lakh. Not more than three awards are given every year.

Dronacharya Award

This award was instituted in 1985 to honour eminent coaches who have successfully trained sportspersons or teams and enabled them to achieve outstanding results in international competitions. The awardee is given a statuette of Guru Dronacharya, a certificate, ceremonial dress and a cash award of ₹ five lakh. Not more than five awards are given every year.

Maulana Abul Kalam Azad Trophy

This trophy was instituted in 1956-57. The top overall performing university in the inter-university tournaments is given the Maulana Abul Kalam Azad (MAKA) Trophy, which is a rolling trophy. A small replica of the MAKA Trophy is also awarded for retention by the university. In addition, the university also gets a cash prize of ₹10 lakh. The second and third best universities also receive cash awards amounting to ₹ five lakh and ₹ three lakh respectively.

Rashtriya Khel Protsahan Puruskar

With a view to recognizing the contribution made to sports development by entities other than sportspersons and coaches, Government has instituted a new award titled 'Rashtriya Khel Protsahan Puruskar' from 2009, which has four categories, namely, identification and nurturing of budding/young talent, Encouragement to sports through Corporate Social Responsibility, Employment of sportspersons and Sports Welfare Measures and Sports for Development. The award consists of a citation and a trophy in each of the above mentioned categories. There is no cash award.

Special Awards to Winners in International Sports Events and their Coaches

This scheme was introduced in 1986 to encourage and motivate outstanding sportspersons for higher achievements and to attract the younger generation to take up sports as a career. Under the scheme, special awards are given to sportspersons and their coaches for winning medals in recognized international sports events held in a year at the following rates:

(a) Category :- Open Category Sports

S. No.	Name of Event	Amount of Award Money (in Rupees)		
		Gold Medal	Silver Medal	Bronze Medal
1	Olympic Games (Summer & Winter)	75 lakh	50 lakh	30 lakh
2	Asian Games	30 lakh	20 lakh	10 lakh
3	Commonwealth Games	30 lakh	20 lakh	10 lakh
4	World Championships or World Cup (conducted in Four Year Cycle)/All England Championship of Badminton	40 lakh	25 lakh	15 lakh
5	World Championships/ World Cup (Held once in two years)	20 lakh	14 lakh	8 lakh
6	World Championships/World Cup (Held annually)	10 lakh	7 lakh	4 lakh
7	Asian Championships (Held once in 4 years)	15 lakh	10 lakh	5 lakh
8	Asian Championships (Held once in 2 years)	7.5 lakh	5 lakh	2.5 lakh
9	Asian Championships (Held annually)	3.75 lakh	2.5 lakh	1.25 lakh
10	Commonwealth Championships (Held once in 4 years)	15 lakh	10 lakh	5 lakh
11	Commonwealth Championships (Held once in 2 years)	7.5 lakh	5 lakh	2.5 lakh
12	Commonwealth Championships (Held once in 1 year)	3.75 lakh	2.5 lakh	1.25 lakh
13	World University Games	3.75 lakh	2.5 lakh	1.25 lakh

(b) Category :- Para - Sports

S. No.	Name of Event	Amount of Award Money (in Rupees)		
		Gold Medal	Silver Medal	Bronze Medal
1	Paralympic Games (Summer & Winter)	75 lakh	50 lakh	30 lakh
2	Para Asian Games	30 lakh	20 lakh	10 lakh
3	Commonwealth Games (Para Athletes)	30 lakh	20 lakh	10 lakh
4	IPC World Cup/ Championship (Held biennially)	20 lakh	14 lakh	8 lakh
5	IPC World Cup/ Championship (Held biennially)	10 lakh	7 lakh	4 lakh

(c) Category:- Blind-Sports

S. No.	Name of Event	Amount of Award Money (in Rupees)		
		Gold Medal	Silver Medal	Bronze Medal
1	IBSA World Championship	10 lakh	7 lakh	4 lakh

Deaf-Sports

S. No.	Name of Event	Amount of Award Money (in Rupees)		
		Gold Medal	Silver Medal	Bronze Medal
1	Deaflympics	15 lakh	10 lakh	5 lakh

(d) Category:- Special Olympics-Sports

S. No.	Name of Event	Amount of Award Money (in Rupees)		
		Gold Medal	Silver Medal	Bronze Medal
1	Special Olympics (Summer/Winter)	5 lakh	3 lakh	1 lakh

Cash award is also given to coaches who have trained the medal winners for at least 180 days immediately preceding the tournament. Award money to a coach is 50 per cent of the award money given to the sportsperson coached. In case, there is more than one coach, the award money is distributed among them equally.

Scheme of Sports Fund for Pension to Meritorious Sportspersons

This scheme was launched in 1994. Those sportspersons, who are Indian citizens and have won gold, silver and bronze medals in olympic games, world cup/world cha pionships, asian games, commonwealth games and paralympic games, have attained the age of 30 years and have retired from active sports career are eligible for life pension under this scheme at the following enhanced rates, which are effective from 2008:

(a)	Medalists at the Olympic Games	₹ 10,000/- p.m.
(b)	Gold medalists at the World Cups/ World Championships in Olympic and Asian Games disciplines	₹ 8,000/- p.m.
(c)	Silver or Bronze medalists of the World Cups/World Championships in Olympic and Asian Games disciplines	₹ 7,000/- p.m.
(d)	Gold medalists of the Asian/ Commonwealth Games	₹ 7,000/- p.m.
(e)	Silver and Bronze medalists of Asian/ Commonwealth Games	₹ 6,000/- p.m.
(f)	Gold medalists of Paralympic Games	₹ 5,000/- p.m.
(g)	Silver medalists of Paralympic Games	₹ 4,000/- p.m.
(h)	Bronze medalists of Paralympic Games	₹ 3,000/- p.m.

National Welfare Fund for Sportspersons

The National Welfare Fund for sportspersons was set up in 1982 with a view to assisting outstanding sportspersons of yesteryears, living in indigent circumstances who had won glory for the country in sports. Assistance from the Fund is given in the form of lumpsum financial assistance, *ex-gratia* to sportspersons or their families in case of sustaining a fatal injury during training for, or participation in, an international competition; sportsperson sustaining injury other than a fatal injury, families of sportspersons living in indigent circumstances, for medical treatment of sportspersons, and for sports promoters (referees, coaches and umpires) living in indigent circumstances. Assistance is provided to those whose monthly income from all sources is less than ₹ 2,00,000/- per annum. The fund is managed and operated by a Committee with the Minister for Youth Affairs and Sports as the Chairperson.

Other Initiatives

Scheme for Promotion of Sports among Persons with Disabilities

The Ministry formulated a scheme for promotion of sports and games among disabled during 2009. The objective of the Scheme is broad-basing participative sports among the disabled. The Scheme has the following components:- (i) grant for sports coaching and purchase of consumables and non-consumable sports equipment for schools; (ii) grant for training of coaches; and (iii) grant for holding district, state and national level competitions for the disabled. The successful implementation of the Scheme will go a long way in integration of the disabled in the mainstream of the society.

Scheme of Assistance for Anti-Doping Activities

Doping is the deliberate or inadvertent use by sportspersons of a substance or method banned by Medical Commission of International Olympic Committee/ World Anti Doping Agency (WADA). In pursuit of gold and glory, large numbers of sportspersons all over the world are tempted to use performance enhancing substances in an effort to gain a competitive edge over others. India is no exception to this malaise. Recognizing the urgent need for embarking upon a concerted effort to check doping in collaboration with the global anti doping community, the Government of India became one of the members of the Foundation Board of WADA, set up with the initiative of the International Olympic Committee.

National Anti Doping Agency

This agency is the national organization responsible for promoting, coordinating, and monitoring the doping control programme in sports in the country. The Anti Doping rules of NADA are compliant with the Anti Doping Code of WADA.

National Dope Testing Laboratory

This is responsible for testing dope samples and conducting advance research on the subject by maintaining close association with the WADA and WADA accredited laboratories. National Dope Testing Laboratory (NDTL) achieved WADA accreditation in September 2008 after undergoing probation from October, 2006. The NDTL has now become the 35th WADA accredited laboratory in the world and 6th in the Asian region.

Come and Play Scheme

For optimum utilization of its five stadia which were renovated at substantial cost for Commonwealth Games, 2010, Sports Authority of India has introduced 'Come and Play Scheme' in 2011. The designated areas in the SAI stadia viz., Jawaharlal Nehru Stadium, Dr. Karni Singh Shooting Ranges, Dr. SPM Swimming Pool Complex, Major Dhyan Chand Hockey Stadium and Indira Gandhi Indoor Stadium (Gymnastics, Wrestling and Cycling Velodrome) were thrown open in 2011 for both imparting professional training to establish sportspersons and also to beginners with the objective of encouraging participation in sports and for optimum utilization of stadia. 'Come and Play Scheme' received a very enthusiastic response and more than 10,000 trainees enrolled for using the sports facilities for practice and training in disciplines such as badminton, boxing, basketball, cricket, cycling, football, hockey, gymnastics, judo, shooting, swimming, table tennis, volleyball, weightlifting and wrestling.

After the successful launch of the Scheme in Delhi, SAI launched the 'Come and Play Scheme' in all its centres spread across the country from 2011 with the objective of encouraging the local youth to use the sports facilities available at these centres and to impart coaching, primarily to the beginners, to encourage participation in sports. This would result in optimal utilization of the sports facilities. The Scheme would also lead to talent scouting. Meritorious talent emerging from this Scheme will also form a pool and entry link for induction into regular residential sports promotional schemes of STC and SAG. Talent emerging from this Scheme can also be financed under various other schemes of the Ministry and SAI.

National Sports Talent Search Scheme

A new scheme, namely, National Sports Talent Search Scheme (NSTSS) has been formulated by the Ministry of Youth Affairs and Sports for talent identification in the age group of 8-12 years and nurturing of identified talented sportspersons. The objectives of the scheme are: (a) identification of sporting talent among students in the age-group of 8–12 years (for admission in class IV to class VI) who possess inborn qualities such as anthropometric, physical and physiological capabilities without any anatomical infirmities; and (b) nurturing of the sporting potential/talent in district level sports schools/central sports schools/national sports academies, etc., to make them excel at the national and international sports competitions.

30 States and Union Territories

ANDHRA PRADESH

Area	:	1,60,200 sq. km	*Population*	:	4.9 crore (as per prov. census 2011)
Capital	:	Hyderabad	*Principal Languages*	:	Telugu, Urdu, Hindi, Banjara

THE earliest mention of the Andhras is said to be in *Aitereya Brahmana* (2000 BC). It indicates that the Andhras, originally an Aryan race living in north India migrated to south of the Vindhyas and later mixed with non-Aryans. Regular history of *Andhra Desa*, according to historians, begins with 236 BC, the year of Ashoka's death. During the following centuries, *Satavahanas, Sakas, Ikshvakus,* Eastern *Chalukyas,* and *Kakatiyas* ruled the Telugu country. Other dynasties that ruled over the area in succession were the kingdoms of Vijayanagar and Qutub Shahi followed by Mir Qumruddin and his successors, known as the Nizams. Gradually, from the 17th century onwards, the British annexed territories of the Nizam and constituted the single province of Madras. After Independence, Telugu-speaking areas were separated from the composite Madras Presidency and a new Andhra State came into being on 1st October 1953. With the passing of the States Reorganisation Act, 1956, there was a merger of Hyderabad State and Andhra State, and consequently Andhra Pradesh came into being on 1 November 1956.

Andhra Pradesh is situated on the country's southeastern coast. It is the eighth largest state in the country covering an area of 160,205 sq. km. According to 2011 census, the state is tenth largest by population, with 49,386,799 inhabitants.

The state has the second longest coastline of 974 km (605mi) among all the states of India, second only to Gujarat. It borders Telangana in the north west, Chhattisgarh in the north, Odisha in the north-east, Karnataka in the west, Tamil Nadu in the south and water body of Bay of Bengal in the east. A small enclave of 30 sq. km of a district of Puducherry, lies in the Godavari delta to the north east of the State.

Andhra Pradesh Reorganisation Act, 2014

Andhra Pradesh Reorganisation Act, 2014 commonly called Telangana Act is an Act of Indian Parliament proclaiming the bifurcation of the Andhra Pradesh state into two states, Telangana and residuary Andhra Pradesh. The Act consists of all aspects of division of assets and liabilities, finalize the boundaries of the proposed new states and status of Hyderabad.

Agriculture

Agriculture is the main occupation of about 62 per cent of the people in the state. Rice is a major food crop and staple food contributing about 77 per cent of the foodgrain production. Other important crops are jowar, bajra, maize, ragi, small millets, pulses, castor, tobacco, cotton and sugarcane. Forests cover 23 per cent of the state's area. Important forest products are teak, eucalyptus, cashew, casuarina, bamboo, softwood, etc.

The Government is working with a mission of "Sustainable agriculture production with minimum cost of cultivation, eventually enhancing the return on income to the farmer". In the process of making the mission a reality, the Government is implementing schemes for the welfare of farmers like 9 hours free power supply, subsidized seeds, subsidized interest rate on crop loans, subsidized and quality agricultural inputs, etc. Andhra Pradesh occupies the first position in respect of agricultural loans from commercial and cooperative banks.

The debt waiver scheme of Central Government and the incentive scheme of the state government have helped about one crore farmers in the state to the tune of ₹16,000 crore.

Irrigation

A total of 86 projects (44 major+30 medium+4 flood banks+8 modernisation) have been taken up under *Jalayagnam* programme. The programme aims at completing the ongoing and new projects in a record time to provide immediate irrigation to water starved areas on top priority by mobilizing funds from all possible sources.

Power

Important power projects in the state are the Nagarjunasagar and Neelam Sanjiva Reddy Sagar (Srisailam Hydel Project), Upper Sileru, Lower Sileru, Tungabhadra Hydel projects and Nellore, Ramagundam, Kothagudem, Vijayawada and Mudanur Thermal Power Projects. The Srisailam Hydro Electric Project (Right Bank) with an installed capacity of 770 MW and the Srisailam Left Bank HES capacity of 900 MW and the Nagarjunasagar complex with 960 MW are the principal sources of hydel generation. Vijayawada Thermal Power Station with an installed capacity of 1,260 MW and Kothagudem Thermal Power Station with an installed capacity of 1,220 MW are the main sources of thermal power generation. The 1,000 MW coal-based Simhadri Thermal Power Station aims at supplying the entire energy generated to the state.

Industries

The state government is extending various incentives for SSI and tiny sector and large and medium scale industries. The state government has been promoting the manufacturing sector in a big way by providing concessions in power tariff, allotting land and relaxing labour laws in Special Economic Zones (SEZs). The state has recommended to the centre for setting up 59 IT/ITES SEZs, with active private sector participation.

Mines and Geology

Andhra Pradesh is well known globally for its variety of rocks and minerals and is called Ratna Garbha. The state has the largest deposits of quality chrysotile asbestos in the country. Other important minerals found in the state are copper ore, manganese, mica, coal and limestone. The Singareni Coal Mines supply coal to the entire south India. The mineral consumption is increasing due to promotion of various industries and manufacture of mineral based products. The state produces about 100 to 110 million tonnes of industrial minerals and 200 million cubic metres of stone and building material. AP stands first in barytes and limestone production in the country. The state stands first in value of minor mineral production and second in total value of mineral production in the country contributing about 9 to 10 per cent to the country's mineral value production. The state stands first in mineral revenue among the important mineral producing states of the country.

Housing

The government has introduced an innovative, unique, self financed housing scheme "Rajiv Swagruha" for the moderate income group in the state with an objective that every person with moderate income in the state having no house of his/her own must have a house at affordable cost in the urban/municipal areas in the state. The houses/flats have to be made available to them at prices 25 per cent less than the existing market rates on similar specifications. The construction of housing programme under "Rajiv Swagruha" is under progress.

Health

'Rajiv Arogyasri' is a unique health insurance scheme being implemented in Andhra Pradesh. The scheme enables the poor, suffering from chronic diseases, to undergo treatment costing upto ₹ 2 lakh. All white cardholders can undergo treatment for about 942 diseases. Medical and surgical treatment is provided in 344 corporate, private and government hospitals free of cost to patients. Arogyasri scheme is unique in its applicability, since no other state/government agency has provided universal health coverage to the poor for major ailments. The choice of hospital for treatment is with the patient. The entire process from the time of conduct of health camps to the screening, testing, treatment, follow-up and claim for payment is made transparent through online web-based processing to prevent any misuse and fraud.

Information Technology

Andhra Pradesh has been forging ahead in the sphere of Information Technology. It is ahead of other states in exploiting the opportunities to the hilt. The state government has introduced many schemes to utilize the maximum number of skilled human resources in the IT Sector.

Transport

Roads : The total R&B road network in the state is 69,051 km of which, the national highways passing through the state constitute 4,472 km and the state highways constitute 10,519 km. Major district roads constitute 32,170 km and rural roads 21,714 km. The density with reference to R&B road network in the state is 0.23 km per one sq.km. and 0.86 km per 1000 persons.

Railways : Of the railways route covering 5,107 km in Andhra Pradesh, 4,633 km is broad-gauge, 437 km is metre-gauge and 37 km is narrow gauge.

Aviation : Important airports in the state are located at Shamshabad, Tirupathi and Visakhapatnam. International flights are operated from Shamshabad.

Ports : There is one major port at Visakhapatnam under Government of India and 13 non-major ports under state government. Ports offer tremendous potential for development and for the growth of a wide spectrum of maritime activities such as international shipping, coastal shipping, ship repairs, fishing, captive ports for specific industries, all weather ports, tourism and sports, etc.

Tourist Centres

Andhra Pradesh Tourism Development Corporation continues to strive for promotion of new tourism products such as eco-tourism, beach-tourism and cruise-tourism. The Corporation currently runs a chain of 52 hotels with 1043 rooms and 2222 beds in prime locations fostering homely ambience. An impressive fleet of 144 buses cater to varied tour packages connecting important tourism locations within and outside the state.

Charminar, Salarjung Museum, Golconda Fort in Hyderabad, Thousand Pillar Temple and Fort in Warangal, Sri Lakshmi Narasimha Swamy Temple at Yadagirigutta, Buddha Stupa at Nagarjunakonda, Nagarjuna Sagar, Sri Venkateswara Temple at Tirumala-Tirupathi, Sri Mallikarjunaswamy Temple at Srisailam, Kanaka Durga Temple at Vijayawada, Sri Satyanarayana Swamy Temple at Annavaram, Sri Varaha Narasimha Swamy Temple at Simhachalam, Sri Sita Rama Temple at Bhadrachalam, Araku Valley, Horsley Hills, Nelapattu, etc. are the major tourist attractions in Andhra Pradesh.

O. W.: http//www.ap.gov.in

GOVERNMENT

Governor	: Shri E.S.L. Narasimhan	*Chief Secretary*	: Shri S.P. Tucker
Chief Minister	: Shri N. Chandra Babu Naidu	*Jurisdiction of High Court*	: Andhra Pradesh and Telangana

ARUNACHAL PRADESH

Area	: 83,743 sq. km	*Population*	: 13.84 lakh (as per prov. census 2011)
Capital	: Itanagar	*Speakers of Major Languages*	: Monpa, Miji, Aka, Sherdukpen, Nyishi, Apatani, Tagin, Hill Miri, Adi, Digaru-Mishmi, Idu-Mishmi, Khamti, Miju-Mishmi, Nocte, Tangsa and Wancho

History and Geography

Arunachal Pradesh became a full-fledged state on February 20 1987. Till 1972, it was known as the North-East Frontier Agency (NEFA). It gained the Union Territory status on 20 January 1972 and renamed as Arunachal Pradesh. On August 15 1975, an elected Legislative Assembly was constituted and the first Council of Ministers assumed office. The first general election to the Assembly was held in February 1978. Administratively, the state is divided into sixteen districts. The capital of the state is Itanagar in Papum Pare district. Itanagar is named after Ita fort, meaning fort of bricks, built in the 14th century AD. Arunachal Pradesh finds mention in the literature of *Kalika Purana* and *Mahabharata*. This place is the Prabhu Mountains of the *Puranas*.

The widely scattered archaeological remains at different places in Arunachal Pradesh bear testimony to its rich cultural heritage.

Agriculture and Horticulture

Agriculture is the mainstay of the people of the state and mainly depends on *jhum* cultivation. Encouragement is being given to the cultivation of cash crops like potatoes and horticulture crops like apples, oranges and pineapples.

Industries and Minerals

For conservation and exploration of the vast minerals the Arunachal Pradesh Mineral Development and Trading Corporation Limited (APMDTCL) was set up in 1991. Namchik-Namphuk coal fields are taken up by APMDTCL. To provide training to craftsmen in different trades there are two industrial training institutes at Roing and Daporijo.

Festivals

Some of the important festivals of the state are *Mopin* and *Solung* of the Adis, *Lossar* of the Monpas, *Boori-boot* of the Hill Miris, *Sherdukpens, Dree* of the Apatanis, *Si-Donyi* of the Tagins, *Reh* of the ldu-Mishmis, *Nyokum* of the Nyishis, etc. Animal sacrifice is a common ritual in most festivals.

Tourist Centres

Places of tourist interest are Tawang, Dirang, Bomdila, Tipi, Itanagar Malinithan, Likabali, Pasighat, Along, Tezu, Miao, Roing, Daporijo Namdapha, Bhismaknagar, Prashuram Kund and Khonsa.

O. W.: http://www.arunachalpradesh.gov.in

GOVERNMENT

Governor	: Shri V. Shanmuganathan (Add. Charge)	*Chief Secretary*	: Ms Shakuntala Gamlin
Chief Minister	: Shri Pema Khandu	*Jurisdiction of High Court*	: Falls under Guwahati High Court

ASSAM

Area	: 78,438 sq. km	*Population*	: 3.12 crore (census 2011)
Capital	: Dispur	*Principal Language*	: Asamiya, Bodo

History and Geography

Assam is situated in the north-east corner of the country between 89° 42' E to 96° E longitude and 24° 8' N to 28° 2' N latitude. For centuries, people and communities have been attracted to the fertile environs of Assam and its abundant natural resources. Streams of people have met and mingled, cultures and customs have merged and in this process a rich and composite culture has been evolved.

Assam, also known as a "Land of Red River and Blue Hills", is one of the most attractive and beautiful states of the country. The mighty river Brahmaputra flows through it, serving as a lifeline for its people settled on both sides of its banks. The word 'Assam' is believed to have derived from the Sanskrit word Asoma meaning peerless or unparalleled. Another academic interpretation claims that the word came from the Ahoms, who ruled the land for about six hundred years prior to its annexation by the British. The influence of several races like Austric, Mongolian, Dravidian and Aryan that came to this land long long ago; have contributed to its rich composite culture.

Assam was known as Pragjyotisha or the place of eastern astronomy during the epic period and later named as Kamrupa. The earlier epigraphic reference to the kingdom of Kamrupa is found in the Allahabad pillar inscription of King Samudragupta. Kamrupa is mentioned as a *pratyanta* or Frontier state outside the Gupta Empire, but with friendly and subordinate relation to it. Hiuen Tsang, the Chinese scholar pilgrim who visited Kamrupa in about 743 AD on an invitation of its monarch, Kumar Bhaskar Varman, left a record of the kingdom he called Kamolupa. Kamrupa also figured in the writings of the Arabian historian Alberuni in the eleventh century. Thus, from the epic period down to the twelfth century AD, the eastern frontier kingdom was known as Pragjyotisha and Kamrupa and kings called themselves ' Lords of Pragjyotisha'.

The advent of the Ahoms across the eastern hills in 1228 AD was the turning point in Assam history. They ruled Assam nearly for six centuries. The Burmese entered through the eastern borders and over-ran the territory at a time when court intrigues and dissensions were sapping the vitality of the Ahom royalty. It became a British protectorate in 1826 when the Burmese ceded Assam to the British under the provision of the Treaty of Yandaboo.

Assam covers an area of 78,438 sq. km, which represents 2.39 per cent of the total land area of the country. International boundaries that extend up to nearly 3,200 km, surround the state. Assam - the gateway to the north-eastern states is surrounded by Bhutan and Arunachal Pradesh on the north, Manipur, Nagaland and Arunachal Pradesh on the east and Meghalaya, Tripura and Mizoram on the south and Bangladesh, Meghalaya and West Bengal on the west.

Physiography

A significant geographical aspect of Assam is that it contains three of six physiographic divisions of India—The Northern Himalayas (eastern Hills) The Northern Plains (Brahmaputra Plain) and Deccan Plateau (Karbi Anglong). As the Brahmaputra flows in Assam the climate here is cold and there is widespread rainfall. The hills of Karbi Anglong, North Cachar and those in and close to Guwahati (also Khasi-Garo Hills) now eroded and dissected are originally parts of the South Indian Plateau system. In the south, the Barak originating in the Barail Range (Assam-Nagaland border) flows through the Cachar district with a 25-30 miles (40-50 km) wide valley and enters Bangladesh with the name Surma river. The almond shaped valley is built mostly by aggregation work of the Brahmaputra and its tributaries. Most of the prominent towns and cities of Assam are situated in this valley whose length and breadth are 725 kms and 80-100 kms respectively. Running through a narrow passage at the Meghalaya plateau and Bhutan-Arunachal-Himalayas, the valley finally opens out into the North Bengal Plains.

The second natural division of Assam is the Barak or Surma Valley which is surrounded by north Cachar, Manipur and Mizoram. This valley is dominated by the Barak river. It flows through the valley and finally empties itself to the old bed of Brahmaputra in Bangladesh. This valley has hills and 'Beels' or lakes in plenty. Flood is a common feature lending the quality of fertility to the valley.

The two valleys are separated by long range of hills. The Karbi Hills and the N.C. Hills are located in the south of the Brahmaputra valley. Karbi Hills are a part of the Meghalaya plateau. These hills are dotted with plain areas. The average height of this plateau is 600 metres with occasional peaks like Chenghehision (1,359 m) and Dunbukso (1,361 m). Greenery is the hallmark of these hills, slowly reaching their full height towards the middle of the Dima Hasao district, merging with the Barail range, which is the highest hill range in Assam. The elevation of the Barail range varies from 1,000 to 1,200 metres above sea level. The south side of the Barail range is very steep. It attains a maximum height of 1,953 metres in Mahadeo peak to the east of Haflong. This valley is full of dense forest and rare wild lives.

Economy

The State finances have improved considerably. Over the years with industry and businesses picking up.

Agriculture

Assam is endowed with abundant fertile land and water resources with a total geographical area of 78438 sq. km. the mighty river Brahmaputra and the Barak with their 121 small and tiny tributaries and branches flow through the two valleys keeping the state fertile and cool all along.

Assam has achieved 40 per cent increase in the contribution of agriculture to state GDP. Rice production has increased to 54.40 lakh MT. Likewise, production of foodgrains has also increased from 41.72 lakh MT to 57.22 lakh MT.

Forest & Wildlife

Assam has a total 29,282 sq. km. area of forest and tree cover which covers 37.33 per cent of total geographical area of the state. It has 13,870 sq. km of Reserved Forests; 3103 sq. km. of Proposed Reserved Forests; 5,850 sq. km of Unclassed State forests; and 3,925 sq. km of Protected Area Network. (Source: FSI Data-2009 and "Assam 2011", page-152).

About 180 species of mammals are found in the state which includes globally threatened species such as Golden Langoor, Hoolock Gibbon, Pigmy Hog, Hispid Hare, White-winged Wood Duck, Tiger, Clouded Leopard, Elephant, Swamp Deer, Gangetic Dolphin, etc. More than 800 species of birds and about 195 species of reptiles are found in the State. Strong enforcement of wildlife conservation measures have resulted increase in the tiger population of the State. The tiger population has risen to 167 in 2014 from 143 during 2010-11. The rhino population in Assam stands at 2,624 as per 2015 census. Efforts are also being taken to provide sustainable livelihood to the forest communities.

Industry

Today's Assam embarks on the new charter in the path of development, laying emphasis on new capital formation through the creation of ecologically compliant assets in a sustainable manner. The focus of the growing investment climate today is to build the economy on the core strengths of this region so that the resources can be managed efficiently. The recognized core strengths of the state today are its nature, water, agriculture, human resources and geographical location.

Loans are extended for small industries and service sector under PMRY scheme (till 2008) and under PMEGP. Under these schemes, 2,76,022 unemployed youths have been offered self-employment opportunities between 2001 and 2014. Under Mukhyamantrir Karmajyoti Achoni (MMKA), tools, equipment and raw materials worth ₹ 3,946.11 lakh were distributed among the beneficiaries of various SHGs till 2014. The state government has launched Angel Fund in 2010-11 to extend loans up to ₹ 5.0 lakh at a nominal rate of interest to the entrepreneurs for setting up of small scale industries. So far 506 beneficiaries took advantage of the scheme. Plan is afoot to broaden the scheme in the coming days.

The results of the industrial policies undertaken by the state government are 41,573 industries have been set up in 2014, investment made was ₹ 34,255.74 crore besides providing direct employment to 1,92,504 persons.

Power

The state's power generationin 2014-15 was 1,894.7 MU as against 935 MU in 2001. Number of consumers accordingly has increased to 33 lakh as compared to 9 lakh in 2001. Similarly, per capita availability of electricity has also increased to 232 units as against 83 units in 2001. This has become possible due to timely execution of renovation and modernization works in all areas of power generation, distribution and transmission. Under the Rajiv Gandhi Grameen Vidyutikaran Yojana, the state government has provided free electricity connections to nearly 12 lakh BPL families.

Transport & Communication

The state government has been placing great priority on expanding and improving the rural road network and construction of RCC bridges by replacing old timber bridges. Since 2001, more than 23,000 km of all-weather roads and about 3800 RCC bridges have been constructed. Moreover, construction of about 5,000 km all-weather road including construction of 1,250 numbers of RCC bridges is in progress. Chief Minister's special package has also been taken up for improvement of road network in the Barak Valley and Dhemaji and Lakhimpur districts.

Festivals

Assam, being an inseparable part of this great country, shares all the religious festivals observed elsewhere in India, the state also has an exclusive range of festivals which have enriched the cultural mosaic of the land. *Bihu* is by far the most important festival of Assam. While *Rongali Bihu* or *Bohag Bihu*, coinciding with the Assamese New Year, is the principal *Bihu*, the harvest festival, known as the *Bhogali Bihu* or *Magh Bihu* is also equally important. There is a third *Bihu* called the *Kangali Bihu* or *Kati Bihu*, which is solemnly observed to prey of love and yearning, sometimes having distinct erotic overtones, with characteristically catchy and earthy tunes. The Bodos, the largest tribal group, perform *Kherai* puja as a festival, which assumes the shape of a fair in most places. The *Kherai puja* is accompanied by shamanistic dance performed by female artists who get into a trance, other with vigorous movements of the head, tossing and swinging the dishevelled hair. Bathow is another important puja of the Bodos.

Tourism

Over the years, Assam, the "Gateway of the North-East" has emerged as a popular tourist destination. The natural beauty and bounty, the environment, rich topography, the unique flora and fauna, the bio-diversity, virgin forest, proud hills and green valleys all contribute in making Assam a major hub for wildlife and echo-tourism. Assam is located about 79.5 m above sea level. The five national parks, nineteen wildlife sanctuaries and three bird sanctuaries are treasure houses of rare flora and fauna.

Important places of tourism are Kamakhya temple, Umananda (Peacock Island), Navagraha (temple of nine planets), Basistha Ashram, Dolgobinda, State Zoo, State Museum, Madan Karndev temple—a magnificent archeological place of interest, Saraighat Bridge, Srimata Sankaradeva Kalakshetra Science Museum, Kaziranga Park, etc.

O. W.: http//www.assam.gov.in

GOVERNMENT

Governor	: Shri Banwarilal Purohit	*Chief Secretary*	: Shri Vinod Kumar Pipersenia
Chief Minister	: Shri Sarbananda Sonowal		
		Jurisdiction of High Court	: Guwahati High Court

BIHAR

Area	: 94,163 sq km	*Population*	: 10.41 crore (2011 census)
Capital	: Patna	*Principal Language*	: Hindi

History and Geography

Bihar finds mention in the *Vedas, Puranas*, epics, etc., and was the main scene of activities of Buddha and the 24 Jain Tirthankars. Great rulers of the state before the Christian era were Bimbisar, Udayin, who founded the city of Pataliputra, Chandragupta Maurya and Emperor Ashoka of Maurya dynasty, the Sungas and the Kanvas. Then came the Kushan rulers followed by Chandragupta Vikramaditya of the Gupta dynasty. Muslim rulers made inroads into the territory during the medieval period. The first conqueror of Bihar was Mohammed- bin-Bakhtiar Khalji. The Tughluqs and then the Mughals followed the Khaljis.

One of the major states of the Indian Union, Bihar is bound on the north by Nepal, on the east by West Bengal, on the west by Uttar Pradesh and on the south by Jharkhand. Bihar has a number of rivers, the most important of which is the Ganga. The other rivers are the Sone, Poonpoon, Falgu, Karmanasa, Durgawati, Kosi, Gandak, Ghaghara, etc.

Agriculture

Bihar has a total geographical area of about 93.60 lakh hectares, out of which only 55.54 lakh hectares is the net cultivated area with a gross cultivated area of 72.95 lakh hectares. The principal food crops are paddy, wheat, maize and pulses. Main cash crops are sugarcane, potato, tobacco, oilseeds, onion, chillies, jute and mesta. Bihar has a notified forest area of 6.22 lakh hectare, which is 6.65 per cent of its geographical area. About 30.64 thousand hectares net area and 44.33 thousand hectare gross area had received irrigation from different sources.

Irrigation

Bihar has an irrigation potential of 28.73 lakh hectares created through major and medium irrigation schemes and 6.63 lakh hectares through minor irrigation schemes.

O. W.: http://www.gov.bih.nic.in

GOVERNMENT

Governor	: Shri Ram Nath Kovind	*Chief Secretary*	: Shri Anjani Kumar Singh
Chief Minister	: Shri Nitish Kumar	*Jurisdiction of High Court*	: Patna High Court

CHHATTISGARH

Area	: 1,35,192 sq km	*Population*	: 2.56 crore (census 2011)
Capital	: Raipur	*Principal Language*	: Hindi

History and Geography

Chhattisgarh, carved out of Madhya Pradesh came into being in November 2000 as the 26th state of the Union. It fulfils the long-cherished demand of the people. In ancient times the region was known as Dakshin-Kausal. This finds mention in *Ramayana* and *Mahabharata* also. Between the sixth and twelfth centuries Sarabhpurias, Panduavanshi, Somvanshi, Kalchuri and Nagvanshi rulers dominated this region. Kalchuris ruled in Chhattisgarh from 980 to 1791 AD. With the advent of the British in 1845, Raipur gained prominence instead of capital Ratanpur. In 1904 Sambalpur was transferred to Orissa and estates of Sarguja were transferred from Bengal to Chhattisgarh.

Chhattisgarh is bounded by southern Jharkhand and Odisha in the east, Madhya Pradesh and Maharashtra in the west, Uttar Pradesh and western Jharkhand in the north and Andhra Pradesh in the south. Are-wise, Chhattisgarh is the ninth largest state and population-wise it is seventeenth populous state of the nation.

Agriculture

Total geographical area of Chhattisgarh is 137.90 lakh ha. out of which arable land is about 47.70 lakh ha. Area under kharif crop is around 47.60 lakh ha. and rabi is 16.61 lakh ha. At present due to various irrigation sources, area in kharif season is 13.55 lakh ha. which is about 29 per cent of arable area.

In Chhattisgarh, out of 34.61 lakh farm families, 77 per cent belongs to small and marginal farmers. Here, 33 per cent of farm families belong to Scheduled Tribe and 12 per cent belong to Scheduled Caste. The agro climate zones of Chhattisgarh are three viz., Northern Hill Zone, Chhattisgarh Plain and Plateau of Baster. The average annual rainfall of this area is about 1307.3 mm.

The main kharif crop of this region is paddy which is about 76 per cent of total kharif crops. Apart from it other main crops grown here are maize, soyabean, groundnut, urdbean and pigeon pea. Similarly main rabi crops grown here are wheat, gram, lathyrus, mustard and linseed.

Irrigation and Power

When the state came into being, the total irrigation capacity was 13.28 lakh hectares which has 23 per cent of total sown area which has now increased to 18.44 lakh hectares which is 33.15 per cent of total sown area.

Major completed projects are Mahanadi Reservoir Projects, Hasdeo Bango Project, Tandula, Kodar, Jonk D/S, Kharung, Maniyari Tank and Pairy (Sikasar) Project, Jonk Project, Kharang Project, Mariyani Project. The capacity of State Electricity Production Company is 1924.70 MW of which 1786 MW in thermal and 138.7 MW in hydel electricity.

Mineral Resources

Chhattisgarh has the perfect geological set up to host a number of economically crucial minerals. Large deposits of coal, iron ore, limestone, bauxite and dolomite are found in various parts of the state. Districts of north Chhattisgarh such as Surguja, Raigarh, Koriya and Bilaspur are known for huge coal deposits. The state has 50846 million tonnes reserve in coal as on 1.4.2012 in 12 coal fields. Mineral activities contribute approximately 13.63 per cent to the State G.S.D.P. against the national figure of 2.5 per cent.

Industry

The economy of Chhattisgarh is largely natural resource driven and it leverages the state's rich mineral resources. The key sectors where Chhattisgarh has a competitive advantage include cement, mining, steel, aluminium and power. One of the most mineral-rich states in India, Chhattisgarh provides a lucrative opportunity for cement production at the most competitive prices. Along with vast natural resources, industries also find ample skilled human resources.

Transport

Roads: The total length of the roads in the state under PWD is 31803 km. The length of National Highway is 2226 km; State highways 5240 kms; 10,539.80 km; main district roads; and 13798 kms other district and rural roads. The length of roads in Chhattisgarh has increased from 17.75 km to 21.40 km per 100 km.

19,718 km of roads have been constructed under Pradhan Mantri Grameen Sadak Yojna. To connect interior areas of state, not covered under PMGSY, state government started Mukhya Mantri Gram Sadak Yojna and 4000 km of roads worth ₹ 2000 crores will be constructed within two years.

Railways : Raipur, Bilaspur, Durg, Rajnandgaon, Raigarh and Korba are important railway stations.

Tourist Centres

Chhattisgarh situated in the heart of India, is endowed with a rich cultural heritage and attractive natural diversity. The state is full of ancient monuments, rare wildlife species, carved temples, Buddhist sites, palaces, water falls, caves, rock paintings and geographical formations.

O. W.: http://www.cgstate.gov.in

GOVERNMENT

Governor	: Shri Balramji Das Tandon	*Chief Secretary*	: Shri Vivek Kumar Dhand
Chief Minister	: Dr. Raman Singh	*Jurisdiction of High Court*	: Chhattisgarh

GOA

Area	: 3,702 sq km	*Population*	: 14.59 lakh (prov. census 2011)
Capital	: Panaji	*Principal Languages*	: Konkani (Official Language); other languages: Marathi, Hindi, English, Kannada

History and Geography

Goa, known in the bygone days as Gomanchala, Gopakapattam, Gopakapuri, Govapuri, Gomantak, etc., abounds in a rich historical heritage. Early history of Goa is obscure. In the first century of the Christian era, Goa was a part of the Satavahana empire, followed by the Kadamba, the Rashtrakutas of Malkhed, the Chalukyas and the Silharas. The empire of the Yadavas by the end of the 14th century was displaced by the Khiljis of Delhi and thus Muslim rule came to Goa. After the discovery of the sea route to India by Vasco-da-Gama in 1498, many Portuguese expeditions came to India. In 1510, Alfonso de Albuquerque with the help of the emperor of Vijayanagar attacked and captured Goa. With the arrival of the Jesuit priest Francis Xavier in 1542 proselytisation began in Goa. However, the Portuguese continued to rule over the territory except for an interlude during the latter half of the 17th century when Shivaji conquered a few areas in and around Goa.

Even after India's independence, Goa continued to be in the hands of the Portuguese. However, they could not fulfil the aspirations of the Goan people and ultimately on 19 December 1961, Goa was liberated and made a composite Union Territory with Daman and Diu. In May 1987, Goa was conferred statehood and Daman and Diu was made a separate Union Territory. It is situated on the western coast of the Indian peninsula. On its north runs the Terekhol river which separates Goa from Maharashtra and on the south lies north Canara district of Karnataka. On the east lie the Western Ghats and in the west the Arabian Sea. Panaji, Margao, Vasco, Mapusa and Ponda are the main towns of Goa.

Agriculture

The total cultivated area in Goa is 160,320 hectares while the total production is 108,333 tonnes. Several schemes have also been launched by the Government to promote farming and attract youth towards this activity. Farmers can avail the benefit of up to 90 per cent on solar power battery fencing scheme. A subsidy of upto 90 per cent is also provided for construction of polyhouses and green houses. Similar subsidies are provided for drip irrigation and for construction of biogas plants. In order to enhance the yield of sugarcane it is proposed to provide 90 per cent subsidy on drip irrigation. The Government has also taken steps to recognize the contribution from biogas to contribution of progressive farmers to the states economy by awarding them three state level awards of ₹ 2.00 lakhs, ₹ 1.00 lakh and ₹ 50,000 called Krishi Ratna, Krishi Vibhushan and Krishi Bhushan, respectively.

Water Resources

The Tillari Irrigation Project, an ambitious joint venture project under major and medium irrigation aimed at creating an irrigation potential of 21,056 hectares and 117.03 MCM of water for domestic and industrial has been taken-up. For better and efficient utilization of the potential so created, apart from the irrigation purpose it is proposed to supply the raw water to domestic and industrial units in the state and augment its supply to PWD. The Water Resources Department apart from supplying raw water for irrigation has also augmented raw water supply to the PWD. Assonora Water Works has been augmented with a 25 MLD raw water from Chapora river at Sal and 10 MLD from Amthane tank. Opa Water Works has been augmented with a 50 MLD raw water to Kalay river. 35 MLD raw water is fed from Madei river at Gunjem to Khandepur river.

Social Welfare

It is proposed to provide a insurance cover through an insurance policy scheme to be called as 'Swaranjayanti Aarogya Bima' to the entire resident population of the state similar on the lines of Central Government's health insurance scheme for BPL families called 'Rashtriya Bima Swasthya Yojana.

Industries

All schemes under the State Industrial Policy as well as the State Biotech Policy will continue to be in force and are to be popularized further. To provide encouragement to artisans of Goan handicrafts, it is proposed to develop Goa Haat-cum-shilpagram, new emporia in Goa and outside Goa and develop e-portal for the sale of handicraft items across the globe.

Art and Culture

The Government desires to give thrust on library movement in Goa in order to make the libraries as information and knowledge centres. It intends to document all forms of folk art, folk festivals, other cultural traditions and intangible heritage of Goa, through audio-video documentation, for which adequate budgetary provision has been provided within the existing scheme for art and culture.

Transport

Roads: Of the motorable roads, national highway constitutes 264 km, state highways 279.4 km and other roads MDR/RR/4501.18 km.

Railways : Goa is linked with Mumbai, Mangalore and Thiruvananthapuram through the Konkan Railway, which has introduced several fast trains on these lines. Vasco da Gama is connected with Bengaluru and Belgaum on the South Central Railway, presently for goods traffic only.

Aviation : Mumbai, Delhi, Thiruvananthapuram, Cochin, Chennai, Agati and Bengaluru are linked with Dabolim through regular airline services.

Ports : Mormugao is the major port in the state. Mormugao handles cargo vessels. Minor ports are located at Panaji, Tiracol, Chapora Betul and Talpona, out of which Panaji is the main operative port. One off-shore berth at Panaji has also been commissioned.

Tourist Centres

Important tourist centres are Colva, Calangute, Vagator, Baga, Harmal, Anjuna and Miramar beaches; Basilica of Bom Jesus and St. Cathedral churches at Old Goa; Kavlem, Mardol, Mangeshi, Bandora temples; Aguada, Terekhol, Chapora and Cabo de Rama Forts; Dudhsagar and Harvalem waterfalls and Mayem lake resort. The state has rich wildlife sanctuaries, viz., Bondla, Cotigao, Molem and Dr Salim Ali Bird Sanctuary at Chorao covering an area of 354 sq km.

Forest

Goa has a good forest cover of 34 per cent against the national requirement of 33 per cent and nearly 62 per cent tree cover. During the year 6 lakh seedlings were planted and nearly one lakh seedlings distributed to various institutions and industries to make tree planting a people's movement.

Health

Goa became the first state in the country to launch diabetic registry. The new district hospital at Margao, new district hospital at Mapusa and the new 170 bedded ID hospital at Ponda are important hospitals. Other new hospitals at Sanqulim, Bicholim and Valpoi are under construction.

O. W.: http://www.goa.gov.in

GOVERNMENT

Governor	:	Smt. Mridula Sinha	*Chief Secretary*	:	Shri R. K. Srivastava
Chief Minister	:	Shri Laxmikant Parsekar	*Jurisdiction of High Court*	:	Goa Bench of Bombay

GUJARAT

Area	:	1,96,024 sq km	*Population*	:	60,439,692 (prov. census 2011)
Capital	:	Gandhinagar	*Principal Language*	:	Gujarati

History and Geography

The history of Gujarat goes back to 2000 BC. It is believed that Lord Krishna left Mathura to settle in the west coast of Saurashtra which later came to be known as Dwarka. Later it witnessed various kingdoms as Mauryas, Guptas and others. It was during the rule of Chalukya's (Solankis) that Gujarat witnessed progress and prosperity. In spite of the plundering of Mahmud Ghazni, the Chalukya kings were able to maintain general prosperity and well-being. After this glorious respite, Gujarat faced troubled times under the Muslims, Marathas and the British rule. Before independence, the present territories of Gujarat used to be in two parts - the British and the Princely territories. With the re-organization of the states, the Union of the States of Saurashtra and the Union Territory of Kachchh along with the former British Gujarat became a part of the biggest bilingual State of Bombay. Gujarat officially formed as a state in May 1960. It is situated on the west coast of India. The State is bounded by the Arabian Sea on the west, Pakistan and Rajasthan in the north and north-east respectively, Madhya Pradesh in the south-east and Maharashtra in the south.

Mahatma Gandhi Swachhata Mission

The nationwide cleanliness campaign was launched in 2014 with a call to free India of filth by the 150th birth anniversary of Gandhiji on October 2, 2019. Gujarat is the most active state in implementing 'Swatchh Bharat' campaign and launched statewide *'Swatchh Gujarat, Swasth Gujarat'* campaign to free the state of open defecation.

Urban Mission

Grant sanctioned to undertake development works for basic facilities such as underground sewerage, road and potable water supply in towns and cities.

Special thrust has been incurred for potable water supply. 30 schemes for potable water supply were completed and 68 more are in progress. Seven sewerage related schemes were completed and 143 are in progress. Around 27 sewerage treatment plants for waste water treatment are in progress.

U-WIN Card Shramev Jayate

A scheme for securing rights of labours was launched under *Shramev Jayate* programme. The state government has brought labours of unorganized sector on a platform and made registration of more than 4 lakh labours through *Shramyogi Kalyan Mela.* Also, kits worth ₹ 12.40 crore were distributed among 18,519 beneficiaries. The government has planned to issue *U-WIN (Unorganised Worker Identification Number)* Cards to the unorganized sector workers with a view to recognise their work. In Gujarat 82 per cent workers belong to the unorganized sector. So far, around 7 lakh unorganized workers have been registered. Under the scheme, unorganized sector workers will get access to benefits of provident fund, employment injury benefits, housing, education schemes for children, skill upgradation for workers, old age homes, etc.

Swavlamban Abhiyan

Under *Pandit Deen Dayal Upadhyaya Yuva Sahsik Yojna* 12,653 youth were provided interest assistance against the target of 7,000 youth. *Pandit Deen Dayal Upadhyaya Young Entrepreneurship Scheme* was put in place for interest subsidy on self-employment loans for ITI trainees. Certificates were provided to 50,443 physically handicapped persons.

Agriculture

In order to boost agricultural growth and to further improve it, government celebrated 2014-15 as *krishi vikas varsh*. The government is giving high priority to water conservation and water management activities in order to provide rain water to the arid areas of the state. 'Krishi Mahotsav' is being organized every year to make farmers aware of modern technologies and methods of scientific farming.

Gujarat is the major producer of cotton, groundnut and tobacco and provides inputs for important industries like textiles, oil and soap. Other important cash crops are paddy, wheat and bajra.

Electricity

Gujarat has become the first state in the country to come with a solar policy in 2009, with a view to give boost to the solar energy sector. Installed capacity of this project is about 400 MW. World's first solar photovoltaic project set up in Mehsana district near Chandarsan village canal produce 16 lakh unit electricity.

Roads

Road network plays a crucial role in the development of the state. As a novel approach, the state government has involved private sector in the building of a sound road network. With a view to meet up the needs of increasing population, BRTS facility has been started in Ahmedabad for speedy commuting.

Ports

During the last decade, Gujarat has acquired a status of an important maritime state of the country. Nearly 80 per cent of the total traffic on the non-major ports and about 48 per cent of the total traffic on all the ports of the country is being recorded on the ports of Gujarat, which is a matter of pride for the state. There are 41 minor and intermediate and one major port—Kandla Port.

Festivals

Tarnetar fair is held at village Tarnetar of Surendranagar district in the honour.of Lord Shiva. This fair is held every year in the month of *Bhadrapada* (August/ September). *Madhavrai fair* at Madhavpur near Porbandar is held on the ninth day of the bright half of the month of *Chaitra* (March/April). *Ambaji* fair dedicated to *Amba* mother goddess is held in *Banaskantha* district. The biggest annual fair, *Janmashtami,* the birthday of Lord Krishna, is celebrated at *Dwarka* and *Dakor* with great enthusiasm. Navratri - world's longest dance festival, *Jagannath Rath Yatra* famous chariot festival, *Modhera Dance Festival-Utrardh Mhotsav* in the backdrop of famous Sun Temple in north Gujarat, *Rann Utsav*—basking in moonlit nights in the vast stretches of Rann of Kutchh and other festivals are *Makar-Sankranti, Dang Darbar, Shamlaji fair,* and *Bhavnath fair.*

Tourist Centres

Religious spots like Dwarka, Somnath, Palitana, Pavagadh, Ambaji, Bhadreshwar, Shamlaji, Taronga and Girnar; Porbandar, birth place of Mahatma Gandhi, monuments of architectural and archaeological surprises like Patan, Siddhpur, Ghurali, Dabhoi; Vadnagar, Modhera, Lothal and Ahmedabad; beaches like Ahmadpur-Mandvi, Chorvad, Ubharat, and Tithal; the hill station Saputara lion sanctuary of Gir forest and wild ass sanctuary in small desert of Kachchh area are major tourist attractions in the state. Moreover Sabarmati Riverfront: Displays development level and tourism potential. Sursagar lake in Vadodara, centre of tourists' attraction, Nal Sarovar Bird Sanctuary—Home for migrant birds from across the globe.

O. W.: http://www.gujaratindia.com

GOVERNMENT

Governor	: Shri Om Parkash Kohli	*Chief Secretary*	: Shri J.N. Singh
Chief Minister	: Sh. Vijay Rupani	*Jurisdiction of High Court*	: Gujarat High Court

HARYANA

Area	:	44,212 sq km	*Population*	:	2.54 crore (2011 census)
Capital	:	Chandigarh	*Principal Language*	:	Hindi

History and Geography

Haryana has a proud history dating back to the Vedic Age. The state was home to the legendary Bharata dynasty, after which the country was named Bharat. The land of Haryana has been the cradle of Indian culture and civilization. Archaeological findings by Guy E. Pilgrim in 1915 established that 15 million years ago, the early man lived in the Shivaliks. *Vamana Purana* states that King Kuru ploughed the field of Kurukshetra with a golden plough, drawn by the Nandi of Lord Shiva, and reclaimed an area of seven 'kosas'.

Replete with myths, legends and Vedic references, Haryana's past is steeped in glory. It was on the soil of Haryana that Saint Ved Vyas wrote *Mahabharata*. It was here that Lord Krishna preached the gospel of duty to Arjuna about 5,000 years ago. It was here that the epic battle of Mahabharata was fought. Being the gateway to north India, the region has been the battleground of many a war. The Huns, the Turks and the Tughlaqs invaded India and decisive battles were fought on this land. At the end of the 14th century, Taimur led an army through this area to Delhi. Later, the Mughals defeated the Lodhis in the historic battle of Panipat in 1526. Another decisive battle was fought in 1556 at this very site, establishing the supremacy of the Mughals up to the advent of the British rule, and the rise of Delhi as the imperial capital of India.

An adjunct to Delhi, Haryana practically remained anonymous until the uprising in 1857. After the British crushed the rebellion, they deprived the Nawabs of Jhajjar and Bahadurgarh, the Raja of Ballabharh and Rao Tula Ram of Rewari in Haryana region, of their territories. These were either merged with British territories or handed over to the rulers of Patiala, Nabha and Jind, making Haryana a part of the Punjab province. With the reorganization of Punjab in November 1956, Haryana was born as a full-fledged state.

Strategically located, Haryana is bounded by Uttar Pradesh in the east, Punjab in the west, Himachal Pradesh in the north, and Rajasthan in the south. The National Capital of Delhi juts into Haryana. With just 1.37 per cent of the total geographical area and less than two per cent of India's population, Haryana has carved a place of distinction for itself. Whether it is agriculture or industry, canal irrigation or rural electrification, Haryana keeps marching towards modernity. The state enjoys the unique distinction of being among the first to provide electricity, metalled roads and potable drinking water to all its villages. Ranked among the most prosperous states in the country, Haryana has the second highest per capita income in India, after Goa.

Agriculture

Agriculture is the mainstay of more than 65 per cent population in Haryana with the second largest contribution to the food bowl of the country. The production of foodgrains which aggregated 25.92 lakh tonnes at the time of inception of the state, touched 162.25 lakh tonnes. This is mainly due to the holistic approach to the growth of agriculture, adopted by successive state governments in Haryana, and the slew of measures taken to boost both production and productivity. Under the diversification of crops, more and more area is being brought under cash crops like sugarcane, cotton and oilseeds, vegetable and fruits. Sustainable agriculture is being promoted through the propagation of resource conserving technologies and organic farming.

Irrigation

The 1,429-strong network of canals constitutes the bedrock of the irrigation system in Haryana with 6.83 lakh tubewells and pumpsets playing no mean role. 38.09 lakh hectare of land is under agriculture in the state. The major irrigation projects in the state are Western Yamuna Canal System, Bhakra Canal System and Gurgaon Canal System. Giving practical shape to the lift irrigation system for the first time in India, Haryana has raised water from lower levels to higher and drier slopes through the Jawaharlal Nehru Canal Project. Haryana is among the beneficiaries of the multipurpose Sutlej-Beas project, sharing benefits with Punjab and Rajasthan.

Power

The first state in the country to have achieved hundred per cent rural electrification way back in 1970, Haryana is well on way to becoming power surplus from a power deficit state. The total installed generation capacity available with Haryana is 5801.82 MW. Out of this, the Haryana Power Generation Corporation Limited has an installed generation capacity of 3230.5 MW, comprising 1367.8 MW Panipat Thermal Power Station, Panipat; 1200MW Rajiv Gandhi Thermal Power Project, Hisar; 600 MW Deen Bandhu Chhotu Ram Thermal Power Project, Hisar; and 62.7 MW WYC Hydro Electric Station, Yamuna Nagar. The balance comes from Haryana's share in the central sector generating stations and from long-term power contracts.

Education

Haryana is emerging as an education hub and shaping into a modern-day Takshila and Nalanda. Making elementary education available at reachable distance to all children and opening a large number of institutes of higher learning, offering global standard education, the state is moving fast on the road to becoming a modern hub of education. According to 2011 census, the literacy rate in Haryana is 76.64 per cent against the all-India literacy rate of 74.04 per cent. Haryana's female literacy rate is 66.77 per cent and male literacy rate is 85.38 per cent. The rural population is served by primary schools within a radius of 1.01 km, middle schools within a radius of 1.17 km, high schools within a radius of 1.45 km, and senior secondary schools within a radius of 2.10 km.

Industry

The investment and industry-friendly policies pursued by the state government have made Haryana the cynosure of all investing eyes and put the state on threshold of industrial revolution. Small wonder then, that there are more than 1,354 large and medium and 80,000 small-scale units dotting the industrial landscape of the State. Haryana today is the largest producer of passenger cars, tractors, motorcycles, bicycles, refrigerators, scientific instruments, etc. Besides, it is the largest exporter of basmati rice. Panipat handlooms and carpets are known all over the world besides its tasty panchranga pickle.

Health

Healthcare has been made both affordable and reachable by setting up a state-wide network of district and sub-divisional hospitals. These are being beefed up with staff and equipment and deficiencies in referral services are being removed. The state-wide network of health centres includes 56 hospitals, 109 community health centres, 467 primary health centres, 2,630 sub-centres, 15 district TB centres, 639 ayurvedic, homeopathy and unani centres, 90 urban RCH centres are functioning.

Information Technology

Out of the 85 proposals for setting up IT/cyber parks in the state, recommended by the committee constituted for the purpose, 35 companies have been granted licences by the Town and Country Planning Department. The building plan of 13 proposals and zoning plan of eight proposals have been approved by the Department and the remaining are being processed. In addition, 28 SEZ proposals in IT and ITEs sectors have also been recommended and approved by the government. Out of these, four SEZs are functioning and the remaining are under process. These projects are expected to provide employment to about 13 lakh persons in the next five years in IT sector.

Transport

Road and rail transport are the main carriers of passenger traffic in Haryana with aviation too playing a small role. Haryana is one state where all villages are linked with metalled roads. The length of the roads in the state is more than 35,303 km.

Railways also play an important role in carrying both interstate and intra-state passengers. Kalka, Ambala, Kurukshetra, Panipat, Rohtak, Jind, Hisar and Jakhal are important railway stations. There is a railway workshop at Jagadhari. Aviation too plays its role. There are civil aerodromes at Pinjore, Karnal, Hisar, Bhiwani and Narnaul.

Tourist Centres

A pioneer in highway tourism, Haryana has set up a vast network of 43 tourist complexes all over the state. Having 846-roomed accommodation in them, Haryana Tourism attracts 70 lakh tourists every year. The state government has adopted a multi-pronged strategy to promote tourism. Tourist complexes have been set at strategic points along the highways and tourist complexes have been developed around Delhi with the intent of promoting leisure tourism and conference tourism.

Besides, tourist facilities have been set up at the district headquarters, and in important towns, to cater to the needs of tourists and local people. Some of the important tourist complexes are Surajkund and Baddhkal Lake near Delhi; Sultanpur Birds Sanctuary (Sultanpur); Sohna and Damdama in Gurgaon; and the fascinating pocket of pines in the Morni Hills. The other important resorts are Ethnic India Rai, Blue Jay (Samalkha), Skylark (Panipat), Karna Lake and Oasis (Uchana), Parakeet (Pipli), Kingfisher (Ambala), Magpie (Faridabad), Dabchick (Hodal), Shama (Gurgaon), Jungle Babbler (Dharuhera), Gaurriyya (Bahadurgarh), Myna (Rohtak), Blue Bird (Hisar), Red Bishop (Panchkula), and Pinjore Gardens (Pinjore).

O. W.: http://www.haryana.gov.in

GOVERNMENT

Governor	:	Prof. Kaptan Singh Solanki	*Chief Secretary*	:	Shri Depinder Singh Dhesi
Chief Minister	:	Shri Manohar Lal Khattar	*Jurisdiction of High Court*	:	Punjab and Haryana

HIMACHAL PRADESH

Area	:	55,673 sq km	*Population*	:	68.65 lakh (census 2011)
Capital	:	Shimla	*Principal Languages*	:	Hindi and Pahari

History and Geography

Himachal situated in the heart of the Western Himalaya, identified as "Dev Bhumi" is believed to be the abode of Gods and Goddesses. The entire state is punctuated with stone as well as wood temples. The rich culture and traditions have made Himachal unique in itself. The shadowy valleys, rugged crags, glaciers and gigantic pines and roaring rivers and exquisite flora and fauna compose the symphony that is forever Himachal.

Himachal Pradesh came into being as a Union Territory in April 1948 as a result of integration of 30 princely states spread over 27,000 sq.km. In 1954, when another "C" class state of Bilaspur merged in Himachal Pradesh, its area increased to 28,241 sq.km. The position remained unchanged till 1966. On reorganisation of the state, the hilly areas of Punjab were merged with the state, increasing its size to 55,673 sq.km. Himachal Pradesh today is quoted as a successful model of not only hill area development but also for having realised development in education, health and social services.

Agriculture

Agriculture being the main occupation of the people of Himachal Pradesh has an important role in the economy of the state. It provides direct employment to about 69 per cent of the main working population. Income from agriculture and allied sectors accounts for nearly 22.1 per cent of the total State Domestic Product. Out of the total geographical area of 55,673 sq. km., area of operational holding is about 9.79 lakh hectare owned by 9.14 lakh farmers. The marginal and small farmers possess 86.4 per cent of the total land holdings.

Horticulture

Nature has endowed Himachal Pradesh with a wide range of agro-climatic conditions which have helped the farmers to cultivate large varieties of fruits ranging from temperate to sub-tropical. The main fruits under cultivation are apple, pear, peach, plum, apricot and citrus fruits like mango, litchi, guava and strawberry.

The Horticulture Technology Mission for the integrated development of horticulture is being implemented. This Mission is based on the "end to end approach" taking into account the entire gamut of horticulture development with all backward and forward linkages in a holistic manner. Under this scheme, four centres of excellence are being created in different Agro-Climatic Zones with common facilities like water harvesting, vermicompost, greenhouses, organic farming and farm mechanisation.

Roads

Roads are the lifeline and major means of communication in the predominantly hilly state of Himachal Pradesh. Out of its 55,673 sq. km area, 36,700 sq. km is inhabited out of which 16,807 inhabited villages are scattered over slopes of numerous hill ranges and valleys. When the Pradesh came into existence in 1948 there were 288 km of roads. There are 14 National Highways with a total length of 1752.830 km.

Hydro-Power Generation

Himachal Pradesh has immense hydro-potential in its five river basins. Chenab, Rabi, Beas, Satluj and Yamuna which emanate from the western Himalayas pass through the state. The strategy of development in the power sector comprises expeditious actualisation of the Hydro Electric Potential and introduction of power sector reforms to bring efficiency in the sector and provide high quality power to the consumers at reasonable rates besides availability of abundant power to industrial and tourism sectors. The total identified potential in the state stands at 23,230 MW which is one fourth of India's total hydro-power potential. Presently out of this 6,480 MW has already been harnessed by various agencies. Projects aggregating to 7,602 MW are under execution.

There is no denying this fact in view of the way the Government has embarked upon an accelerated Power Development Programme, the state is speedily moving towards becoming a "Power State" of the country. All the census villages in the state have been electrified.

Industrial Growth

Industrial development has been given big boost in the state. Pollution free environment, abundant availability of power and rapidly developing infrastructure, peaceful atmosphere and responsive and transparent administration are some of the added attractions and advantages that the entrepreneurs get in Himachal Pradesh. 349 large and medium and about 33,284 small-scale industrial units with an investment of about ₹ 4,822.54 crore have been set up in the state generating employment for 2 lakh persons. The sector is contributing 17 per cent to the State Domestic Product and the annual turnover on this account is about ₹ 6,000 crore.

Information Technology

The Government of Himachal Pradesh has developed an IT Vision-2010 in collaboration with NASSCOM to make the state an IT destination. Under this, it has been decided to accord the status of industry to all IT projects including related services and educational institutions. As such, all the incentives available for industrial units are also being given to all IT units, and related services.

Bio-technology

Keeping in view the importance of bio-technology, special emphasis is being laid on exploiting the vast bio-technology potential available in the state. A separate Department of Bio-technology has been set up in the state. State's own bio-technology policy has been formulated. All bio-technological units are entitled for incentives which have been allowed for industrial units. The state government proposes to set up a Bio-Technology Park in Solan district.

Irrigation and Water Supply

Villages have been provided with drinking water. Over 15,000 hand pumps have been installed in the state so far. For better reform in water supply and irrigation sector, the state government has taken up a project with the total cost of ₹ 339 crore for irrigation as well as for drinking water supply schemes with Gesellschaft for Technische Zusammenarbeit (GTZ).

Forestry

The total geographical area of the state is 55,673 sq km. As per record, the total forest area is 37,033 sq. km. Out of this, 16,376 sq. km. area is not fit for tree growth comprising alpine pastures, area under permanent snow, etc. The cultivable recorded forest area is only 20,657 sq. km.

Efforts are being taken to bring maximum area under green cover by implementing state's projects, Government of India's projects and also under external aided projects. The World Bank has sanctioned a ₹ 365 crore Integrated Watershed Development Project for the Mid Himalayas under which all panchayats of 42 developmental blocks in 10 districts would be covered during the next five years. There are 2 National Parks and 32 wildlife sanctuaries in the state. Total area under wildlife sanctuaries is 5562 sq. km; area under National Parks is 1440 sq. km and total area of Protected Area Network is 7002 sq. km.

Education

Himachal Pradesh has emerged as the third best state in terms of over-all development and performance. Himachal Pradesh has been adjudged number one in primary education and teacher-student ratio. The state has witnessed literacy revolution as it is second only to Kerala in literacy. It has about 17,000 educational institutes, including three universities, two medical colleges, one engineering college in the government sector and a number of technical, professional and other educational institutions. Now the state government's emphasis is to ensure qualitative improvement in the education besides need based expansion.

Tourism

Tourism industry in the state has been given very high priority and the government has developed an appropriate infrastructure for its devlopment which includes provision of public utility services, roads, communication network, airports, transport facilities, water supply and civic amenities, etc. The state government is poised to transform it into "A Destination for All Seasons and All Reasons". The State Tourism Development Corporation contributes 10 per cent to the state exchequer. The Corporation contributes more than ₹ 200 crore per annum by way of sales tax, luxury tax and passenger tax.

The state has a rich treasure of places of pilgrimage and of anthropological value. The state has also the pride of being the home to rishis like Vyas, Parashar, Vashist, Markandey and Lamas. Hot water springs, historic fort, natural and man-made lakes are in attractions for its tourists.

The state government is aiming at promoting sustainable tourism, encouraging private sector to develop tourism-related infrastructure without disturbing the existing ecology and environment. The main thrust is on employment generation and promoting new concepts of tourism in the State.

For the promotion and development of the State from the tourism point of view, the government is focusing on the following areas : (1) history related tourism, (2) identification of new areas/tourist destinations and promotion of village tourism, (3) improvement of infrastructure, (4) pilgrimage tourism, (5) tribal tourism, (6) eco-tourism, (7) health tourism. (8) promotion of adventure tourism, (9) wildlife tourism, and (10) cultural tourism.

O. W.: http://www.himachal.gov.in

GOVERNMENT

Governor	:	Acharya Devvrat	*Chief Secretary*	:	Shri V.C. Pharka
Chief Minister	:	Shri Virbhadra Singh	*Jurisdiction of High Court*	:	Himachal Pradesh

JAMMU AND KASHMIR

Area	:	*2,22,236 sq km	*Population*	:	1.25 crore (2011 census)
Capital	:	Srinagar (Summer) Jammu (Winter)	*Principal Languages*	:	Urdu, Dogri, Kashmiri, Pahari, Punjabi, Ladakhi, Balti, Gojri and Dadri

* includes 78,114 sq km under illegal occupation of Pakistan, 5,180 sq km illegally handed over by Pakistan to China and 37,555 sq km under illegal occupation of China. The population figures exclude population of areas under unlawful occupation of Pakistan and China where census could not be taken.

History and Geography

According to the most popular legend that is also recorded in *Rajtarangani* and *Nilmat Purana*, two most authoritative books, Kashmir was once a large lake and it was Kashyap Rishi who drained off the water, making it a beautiful abode. But geologists have their own theory, which says that geographical changes made way for the outflow of water by subsidence of the mountain at Khadianayar, Baramulla and thus emerged the Valley of Kashmir, the paradise on earth. Ashoka introduced Buddhism to Kashmir in the 3rd century B.C. which was later strengthened by Kanishka. Huns got the control of the valley in the early 6th century. The valley regained freedom in 530 AD but soon came under the rule of the Ujjain empire. After the decline of the Vikramaditya dynasty, the valley had its own rulers. There was a synthesis of Hindu and Buddhist cultures. Lalitaditya (697-738 AD) extended his rule up to Bengal in the east, Konkan in the south, Turkistan in the north-west and Tibet in the north-east. Considered as the most famous Hindu ruler, he was known for constructing beautiful buildings. Islam came to Kashmir during 13th and 14th centuries AD. Zain-ul-Abedin (1420-70) was the most famous Muslim ruler, who came to Kashmir when the Hindu King Sinha Dev fled before the Tatar invasion. Later Chaks over-ran Haider Shah, son of Zain-ul-Abedin. They continued to rule till 1586 when Akbar conquered Kashmir. In 1752, Kashmir passed on from the control of the Mughal emperor to Ahmed Shah Abdali of Afghanistan. The valley was ruled by the Pathans for 67 years.

Name of Jammu figures in the *Mahabharata*. The finds of Harappan remains and artefacts of Mauryan, Kushan and Gupta periods at Akhnoor have added new dimensions to its ancient character. The land of Jammu was divided into 22 hill principalities. Raja Maldev, one of the Dogra rulers, conquered many territories to consolidate his kingdom. Raja Ranjit Dev ruled over Jammu from

1733 to 1782. His successors were weak and thus Maharaja Ranjit Singh annexed the territory to Punjab. He later handed over Jammu to Raja Gulab Singh, a scion of the old Dogra ruling family, who had grown powerful among Ranjit Singh's governors and had annexed almost the whole of Jammu region. The state was governed by Dogra rulers till 1947 when Maharaja Hari Singh signed the *Instrument of Accession* in favour of the Indian Union on 26 October 1947.

Transport

Roads : The State is connected to the rest of the country through just one highway (NH 1A), 400 km stretch (approx.) maintained by Border Roads Organization (BRO). As railway network is still in infancy stage, this has rendered the state totally dependent on road connectivity which provides links to the remote areas of the state. The Jammu-Srinagar National Highway (NH1A) is considered to be the most expensive road for maintenance in the world.

Railways : Because of the difficult terrain railway network has not developed as in other parts of the country. At present Jammu is the rail head of the State and the line has been extended upto District Udhampur only (53 km). The work on Udhampur-Banihal rail line is under progress and intra-rail link between Quzigund to Baramulla is complete. In July, 2014 the first Katra-Udhampur train was flagged off.

Aviation : There are three major airports in the state providing aerial transport among three regions of the state and the country. Out of the three Srinagar airport has been upgraded as international airport (named as Sheikh-ul-Alam Airport), while the facilities at Jammu and Leh airports have also been upgraded. One more airport at Kargil headquarters is connected by Dakota service.

Agriculture

Agriculture constitutes an important sector of the state economy as around 70 per cent of the population derive greater part of their income directly or indirectly from this sector. Economy continues to be predominantly agrarian as 49 per cent (2011) of the total working force with 42 per cent as cultivators and 7 per cent as agriculture labourers depend directly on agriculture for their livelihood. Apart from direct impact of agriculture growth on generation of rural employment and incomes, its significant secondary linkages with development of rural non-farm sectors are more crucial. Agriculture has a significant contribution in the export of rare produce like saffron, honey and basmati and remains an important source of raw material demanded by many industries.

Irrigation

Irrigation is an essential input of agriculture and is practiced in all parts of the world where rainfall does not provide enough ground moisture. In areas of irregular rainfall, irrigation is used during dry spells to ensure harvests and to increase crop yields. A major constraint to the development of agriculture is the fact that only 50 per cent of the ultimate irrigation potential of the state has been harnessed. The ultimate irrigation potential has been assessed at 1,358 thousand hectare, which includes 250 thousand hectare to be developed through major and medium irrigation and 1,108 thousand hectare through minor irrigation.

Horticulture

Jammu and Kashmir is well known for its horticulture produce both in India and abroad. The state offers good scope for cultivation of all types of horticulture crops covering a variety of temperate fruits like apple, pear, peach, plum, apricot, almonds, cherry and sub-tropical fruits like mango, guava, citrus, litchi, etc. Apart from this, well-known spices like saffron and *zeera* are cultivated in some parts of the state. Horticulture is emerging as a fast growing sector in the state. Its importance is visualised by its contribution to the state's economy which is estimated to be 7-8 per cent. Almost 45 per cent economic returns in agriculture sector is accounted for by horticulture produce. 6 lakh families comprising 30 lakh people are involved in horticulture trade.

Industry

In order to achieve a self sustaining economy with continued higher levels of investment, rapid rate of increase on income and employment there is no option but to go for industrialisation.

To usher in new era of industrialization comprehensive industrial policy came into being in 2004 to be lasted till 2015 under which planned incentives are being taken to raise the state which is predominantly known as consumer state for most of its requirements to a level of self sufficiency and in the near future to a producer state. The incentives provided in the policy are ahead of other states of the country.

Handloom

It is also labour intensive cottage industry having considerable potential for generation of employment opportunities. To give boost to this industry the state government is laying focus on products design and diversification, providing credit facilities, enhancing weavers' productivity through upgradation of skills and use of efficient looms, market access to handloom products is being extended through marketing incentives and wide publicity.

Tourism

Jammu and Kashmir is an important tourist destination and has been a place of attraction for tourists since centuries. The lush green forests, sweet springs, perennial rivers, picturesque alpine scenery and pleasant climate of Kashmir valley—the paradise on earth has remained an internationally acclaimed tourist destination, whereas Jammu region—the land of temples is attracting a large number of pilgrim tourists and the important destination has been the Shri Mata Vaishno Devi Shrine. Ladakh region—the moon land has been a much sought after destination especially for the foreign tourists and is famous for adventure tourism.

Power

The estimated hydro power potential is 20,000 megawatts (MWs), of which 16,480 MWs have been identified. Out of the identified potential, only, 2457.96 MWs or 15 per cent have been exploited so far, consisting of 760.46 MWs in state sector from 21 power projects and 1680 MWs from three power projects under central sector i.e., 690 MWs (Salal Hydro Electric Project) and 480 MWs (Uri-I Hydro Electric Project) and Dulhasti 390 MWs and 120 MW (Sewa III) and 17.5 MW from two private sector projects. 450 MW of Baglihar Phase-I constructed at a cost of ₹ 5,827 crore by the J&K State Power Development Corporation.

Fairs and Festivals

The fairs and festivals are a reflection of diverse cultural and social heritage of the state. All Hindu, Muslim and Sikh fairs and festivals are celebrated with full vigour and enthusiasm regardless of the religion. Like all parts of India, Jammu and Kashmir also celebrates Diwali, Holi, Eid-ul-Fitr, Eid-ul-Azha, Milad-un-Nabi.

O. W.: http://www.jk.gov.in

GOVERNMENT

Governor	: Shri N.N. Vohra	*Chief Secretary*	: Shri Braj Raj Sharma
Chief Minister	: Smt. Mehbooba Mufti Sayeed	*Jurisdiction of High Court*	: Jammu, Kashmir & Ladakh

JHARKHAND

Area	: 79,716 sq km	*Population*	: 3,29,88,134 (as per 2011 census)
Capital	: Ranchi	*Principal Language*	: Hindi

History and Geography

Jharkhand which came into being in November 2000 as the 28th state of the Union is the homeland of the tribals who had dreamed of a separate state for a long time. According to legend, Raja Jai Singh Deo of Odisha had declared himself the ruler of Jharkhand in the 13th century. It largely comprises forest tracks of Chhotanagpur plateau and Santhal Pargana and has distinct cultural traditions. In post-Independence era, the Jharkhand Mukti Morcha started a regular agitation which impelled the Government to establish the Jharkhand Area Autonomous Council in 1995 and finally a full-fledged state.

Jharkhand is bounded by West Bengal in the east, Uttar Pradesh and Chhattisgarh in the west, Bihar in the north and Odisha in the south.

Agriculture

The state has an area of 79,714 sq km of which 18,423 sq km is forest land. Agriculture and allied activities are the major source of Jharkhand's economy. The total cultivable land is only 38 lakh hectare.

Irrigation and Power

Damodar, Maurakshi, Barakar, North Koyel, South Koyel, Sankh, Subarnarekha, Kharkai, and Ajay are major water resources in the State. The net sown area is 1.8 million hectare of which 8 per cent is irrigated.

The installed capacity of power in the state is 2,590 MW. This includes 420 MW (Tenughat Thermal Power Station), 840 MW (Patratu Thermal Power Station), 130 MW (Sikkidiri Hydel Project) and 1,200 MW (Damodar Valley Corporation Thermal/Hydel Project). The prospect of capacity, addition in both the thermal and hydel sectors of various power stations is 4,736 MW. This includes 686 MW hydel generation.

Industry and Minerals

Some of Jharkhand's major industries are Bokaro Steel Plant in the public sector, Tata Iron and Steel Company (TISCO) in Jamshedpur in the private sector. Other important industries are Tata Engineering and Locomotive Company (TELCO), Timken India Limited (Jamshedpur), Bharat Coking Coal Limited (Dhanbad), Khilari Cement Factory (Palamu), Indian Aluminum (Muri), ACC Cement (Chaibasa), Central Coalfields Limited (Ranchi), Usha Martin, Usha Beltron, Uranium Corporation (I) Limited (Jadugora), Hindustan Copper Limited (Mussabani), Tin Plate Company of India Limited (Jamshedpur), Indian Explosive Limited (Gomia), Hindalco Bauxite (Lohardaga), etc.

The state is rich in mineral resources. The important available minerals are coal, iron ore, limestone, copper ore, bauxite, pyrite, china clay, kyanite, fine clay, dolomite, graphite, bentonite, soap stone, quartz sand and silica sand. The nascent state of Jharkhand has the enormous potential for exploitation of coal, mica and other minerals particularly in Singhbhum, Bokaro, Hazaribagh, Ranchi, Koderma and Dhanbad.

Transport

Roads : The total length of roads is 4,311 km. This includes 1,500 km national highways and 2,711 km state highways.

Railways : The state has a well-developed railway system. Ranchi, Bokaro, Dhanbad, Jamshedpur are some of the major railway stations.

Aviation : Ranchi is connected with Delhi, Patna and Mumbai. Cities which have our strips are Jamshedpur, Bokaro, Giridih, Deoghar, Hazaribagh, Daltonganj and Noamundi.

Tourist Centres

There are many scenic attractions in the state, namely, Ichagarh Bird Sanctuary, Udhava Bird Sanctuary-Sahibganj (Pathara Lake), Chachro Crocodile Breeding Centre–Koderma (Tilaya Dam), Chandrapura Bird Sanctuary, Jawaharlal Nehru Zoological Garden (Bokaro), Tenughat Bird Sanctuary, Dalma WildLife Sanctuary (Jamshedpur), Tata Steel Zoological Park (Jamshedpur), Palkote Wildlife Sanctuary (Gumla), Bhagwan Birsa Zoological Gardens (Ranchi), Birsa Deer Sanctuary (Kalmati Ranchi), Betla National Park (Palamau), Ranchi Aquarium (Ranchi), Hazaribagh National Park, Tatoloi Hot Water Stream (Dumka) and Saranda Forest.

Apart from this, Jharkhand has some famous temples like, Jharkhand Dham, Lagnta Baba Temple/Majar, Bindhvashini Temple, Masanjore Dam, etc.

O. W.: http://www.jharkhand.gov.in

GOVERNMENT

Governor	: Smt. Draupadi Murmu	*Chief Secretary*	:	Shri Raj Bala Verma
Chief Minister	: Shri Raghubar Das	*Jurisdiction of High Court*	:	Jharkhand

KARNATAKA

Area	:	1,91,791 sq km	*Population*	:	6.11 crore (prov. census 2011)
Capital	:	Bengaluru	*Principal Language*	:	Kannada

History and Geography

Karnataka has a recorded history of more than 2,000 years. Apart from its subjection to the rule of Nandas, Mauryas and the Satavahanas, Karnataka came to have indigenous dynasties like the Kadambas of Banavasi and the Gangas from the middle of the 4th century AD. The world renowned Gomateshwara monolith at Shravanabelagola was installed by a Ganga minister Chavundaraya. The colossal rock cut image of Sri Gomateshwara is the most magnificent among all Jaina works of art. Numerous visitors arrive at Shravanabelagola to gaze at this and other monuments. The Chalukyas of Badami (500-735 AD) reigned over a wider area, from Narmada to the Kaveri from the days of Pulikeshi II (609-642 AD) who even defeated the mighty Harshavardhana of Kanauj. This dynasty created fine, everlasting and the most beautiful monuments at Badami, Aihole and Pattadakal, both structural and rock-cut. Aihole has been one of the cradles of temple architecture in the country. The Rashtrakutas (753-973 AD) of Malkhed who succeeded them heaped tributes on the rulers of Kanauj successively in the so-called 'Age of Imperial Kanauj'. Kannada literature developed during this period. Outstanding Jain scholars of

India lived in their court. The Chalukyas of Kalyana (973 to 1189 AD) and their feudatories, the Hoysalas of Halebidu built exquisite temples, encouraged literature and various fine arts. Noted jurist Vijnaneshwara (work: *Mitakshara*) lived at Kalyana. The great religious leader Basaveshwara was a minister at Kalyana. Vijayanagar empire (1336-1646) patronised and fostered indigenous traditions and encouraged arts, religion and literature in Sanskrit, Kannada, Telugu and Tamil. Overseas trade flourished. The Bahamani Sultans (Capital: Gulbarga, later Bidar) and the Bijapur Adilshahis raised fine Indo-Saracenic buildings and encouraged Urdu and Persian literature. Advent of the Portuguese resulted in the introduction of new crops (tobacco, maize, chillies, groundnut, potato, etc.). After the fall of the Peshwa (1818) and Tipu (1799), Karnataka came under British rule. Christian missionaries introduced English education and printing during the 19th century. Revolution in transport, communication and industries was ushered in. The urban middle-class emerged. Mysore dynasty initiated and helped industrialisation and cultural growth.

Freedom movement was followed by the movement for the unification of Karnataka. After Independence, the Mysore State was created in 1953, wherein all the Kannada dominant areas under different dispensations were unified and the enlarged Mysore state carved in 1956 and was renamed Karnataka in 1973.

Karnataka is situated between 11°31' and 18°14' north latitudes and 74°12' and 78°10' east longitudes. It is bounded by Goa and Maharashtra on the north; Telangana and Andhra Pradesh on the east; Tamil Nadu on the south east and Kerala on the South.

Forestry and Wildlife

The forest department manages about 20.15 per cent of the geographical area of the state. Forests have been classified as reserved forests, protected forests, unclassified forests, villages forests, and private forests. There are 5 national parks and 23 wildlife sanctuaries. To overcome shortage of fuel wood, fodder and timber, degraded forests and waste lands are being developed. Emphasis is also being laid on the conservation, protection and development of the fragile ecosystem of the Western Ghats. Several wildlife protection schemes such as Project Tiger and Project Elephant are being implemented with the Central assistance. The concept of Joint Forest Planning and Management applied to the two externally aided projects viz. Western Ghats Forestry and Environment Project (DFID) and Forestry and Environment Project for Eastern Plains (JBIS) has resulted in village forest planning and management through establishment of Village Forest Committees.

Agriculture

The state has 66 per cent rural population and 55.60 per cent of workers are agricultural labourers. The state has 60 per cent (114 lakh ha) cultivable land and 72 per cent of the cultivable area is rainfed; only 28 per cent is under irrigation. The state has 10 Agro Climatic Zones. The red soil constitutes major soil type, followed by black soil. The net sown area of the state constituted 51.7 per cent of the total land.

Dairy

Karnataka is one of the major milk producers and the Karnataka Milk Federation has 21 dairy processing plants with a capacity of 26.45 lakh litres a day and 42 chilling centres having 14.60 lakh litres of chilling capacity.

Horticulture

Horticulture crops are grown in an area of 16.80 lakhs hectare and the produces amount to 101 lakh tonnes. The Union Government earmarked ₹ 171.29 crore for Karnataka under National Horticulture Mission.

Power Generation

Karnataka was the pioneer in establishing hydroelectric projects in the country. Karnataka has 7222.91 power generation installed capacity and 31,229 million units of electricity was generated.

Biotechnology

Karnataka State and Bengaluru city in particular have become the largest bio-clusters in the country.

Transport

Roads : Total road length has increased from 83,749 km to 2,15,849 km. The Karnataka Highways Improvement Project with World Bank assistance will improve 2,375 km of road, i.e. upgradation of 900 km and rehabilitation of 1,475 km comprising state highways and major district roads at an estimated cost of ₹ 2402.51 crore. Assistance is being provided under the Rural Infrastructure Development Fund for the construction and improvement of roads and bridges in the state.

Ports : The state has a maritime coastline of 155 nautical mile (300 kilometres) and has only one major port at Mangalore, i.e., New Mangalore Port and studded with ten minor ports—Karwar, Belekeri, Tadria, Honnavar, Bhatkala, Kundapur, Hangarkatta, Malpe, Padubidri and Old Mangalore. Out of ten ports, Karwar is the only all weather port while the other nine are the riverine anchorage lighterage ports.

Aviation : The Civil Aviation Sector has seen tremendous growth with international air passenger traffic growth of 50 per cent and domestic air passenger growth at 44 per cent.

Tourism

Karnataka "One State Many Worlds" is becoming a hub of tourist attraction of south India. The IT and BT Centre Bengaluru has received more tourists in the recent past. The state is known for its heritage monuments and eco-tourism destinations. The Golden Chariot named after the famous Stone Chariot in

Hampi, a world heritage site, in southern India will travel through timeless historical heritage sites, resplendent palaces, wildlife and golden beaches. Its 7 nights/8 days colourful journey begins every Monday from Bengaluru and traverses through Mysore, visiting Srirangapatna, Mysore Palace, the Nagarhole National Park (Kabini) and continuing to the historical sites of Shravanabelagola, Belur—the 11th century cradle of Hoysala architecture and a world heritage site, Halebidu, Hampi and thereafter entering into the triangular heritage sites of Badami, Pattadakal, Aihole and finally the Golden Beaches of Goa before ending in Bengaluru.

Karnataka has a blend of heritage places, thick dense forests and holy places. The new concept of 'Homestay' has added a new dimension to tourism in the state. Hampi and Pattadakal have been declared as world heritage sites.

O. W.: https://www.karnataka.gov.in

GOVERNMENT

Governor	: Shri Vajubhai Rudabhai Vala	*Chief Secretary*	: Shri Arvind Jadhav
Chief Minister	: Shri Siddaramaiah	*Jurisdiction of High Court*	: Karnataka

KERALA

Area	: 38,852 sq km	*Population*	: 3,34 crore (as per census 2011)
Capital	: Thiruvananthapuram	*Principal Language*	: Malayalam

History and Geography

Kerala is in the extreme south-west of the Indian subcontinent. When independent India amalgamated small states together Travancore and Cochin states were integrated to form Travancore-Cochin state in July 1949. However, Malabar remained under the Madras province. Under the State's Re-organisation Act, 1956, Travancore-Cochin state and Malabar were united to form Kerala state in November, 1956.

In between the high Western Ghats on the east and the Arabian Sea on the west, the width of the state varies from 35 km to 120 km. According to the geographical features, the state can be divided into hills, valleys, midland plains and coastal belt. 44 rivers (41 west flowing and 3 east flowing) cut across Kerala with their innumerable tributaries and branches. The backwaters form an attractive and economically valuable feature of Kerala.

Agriculture

Kerala, the land of lush green paddy fields, cool coconut groves, fragrant spice garden, dubbed as "God's own country" is nestled in the southern tip of India. Fertile soil and warm humid tropical climate make Kerala an ideal place for cultivation of a wide variety of crops which included coconut, rice, rubber, banana, spices, fruits, vegetables, cashew nut, tubers, coffee, tea, medicinal plants, are ca nut, etc.

Industry

Kerala, India's most emerging industrial destination beckons with an endless listing of opportunities in varied sectors. To transform Kerala into a vibrant entrepreneurial society with faster, inclusive and sutainable economic growth in order to achieve global standards in every domain, the government has taken steps to implement investor friendly industrial policy to enable constructive investment in all sectors.

Irrigation

The surface irrigation constitutes major chunk of irrigation infrastructure. There are 18 dams intended for irrigation. Irrigation development is mainly centered on the developement of surface water resources mainly on the developoment of major and medium irrigation projects. In each plan, priority in allocation was given for the development of major and medium irrigation projects. Rice is the major crop benefited through irrigation infrastructure. With the fast changes taking place in the farm front with notable reduction in the area under rice cultivation, even the distribution system already developed for gravity irrigation to service rice cultivation now require realignment.

Drinking Water Supply

Demand for water is increasing due to multitude of human activities in the country. The primary responsibility of providing drinking water facilities in the country rests with the respective state governments. In urban and rural areas of the state, 29 per cent and 71 per cent of the population were covered. The total number of urban and rural people covered by water supply schemes was 70.41 lakh and 169.30 lakh respectively.

Power

Power sector plays a vital role in all developmental activities in Kerala. Obviously power crisis is the prime obstacle to start new initiatives in the industrial field. The need for power is increasing and the production of power should also increase accordingly. Monsoon is essential to sustain the hydropower base in the state and the shortage in rainfall usually creates power crisis. Kerala is a power deficit state which imports 60 per cent of power from other states. A major achievement is that it has achieved full electrification in all villages. The need for power is increasing and the production of power should be increased accordingly. Monsoon is essential to sustain the hydropower base in the state. Hydel energy is the most reliable and dependable source.

Transport

Transport sector plays a pivotal role in the overall development of the country which enables social, cultural and trade development between countries. Transport infrastructure consists of fixed installations, roads, railways, airways, waterways, canals, pipelines and terminals. Kerala holds a good transport system. The roads in Kerala are maintained by National Highway Authority,

Public Works Department, local bodies, Department of Irrigation, Kerala State Electricity Board, Department of Forest, Railways, etc.

In Kerala the Public Works Department has a total road length of 318116 km of state roads and 1542 kms of national highways. The state roads include 4341.65 km of major district roads. Road improvements, repair and maintenance of existing roads, development and upgradation are the major activities taken up in the sector during the year.

Port Sector : Kerala lies in the south west corner of the Indian peninsula. It has a coastal length of 585 km and has an average width of about 60 km with one major port at Kochi and 17 minor ports. The geographical location of the state is very close to international shipping route. There are 17 minor ports, out of which 3 are considered as intrermediate ports based on berthing, cargo handling and storage facilities available in them. These have contributed much to the development of industry, trade, commerce and agriculture in the country.

Railways : Railways are essentially the cause for industrial upsurge in the nation and it still remained the largest employment provider for the huge population of the country. The total railway route in Kerala has a length of 1257 km and covers 13 railway route. The Railway Division at Thiruvananthapuram, Palakkad and Madurai jointly carry out railway operations.

Air Transport : Kerala has three airports at Thiruvananthapuram, Kochi and Kozhikode handling both international and domestic flights. Thiruvananthapuram and Kozhikode airports are owned by Government of India and Kochi airport is owned by Kochi International Airport Ltd., a company set up by Government of Kerala with public private participation.

Festivals

Kerala is the home of many colourful festivals. *Onam* is the most typical of festivals which coincides with the harvest season. It is now celebrated on astronomical New Year Day. Navarathri is celebrated as Saraswathi Pooja. Maha Shivarathri is celebrated on the banks of Periyar river as a spectacular festival which is compared to Kumbhamela. The 41-day festival, which coincides with Makaravilakku in Sabarimala Ayyappan Temple, attracts lakhs of people from India and abroad. The Vallamkali or boat race is typical of Kerala. All the boat festivals have a religious origin except Nehru Trophy Boat Race conducted in the Punnamada Lake. Thrissur celebrates *Pooram* festival in April - May every year with an impressive procession of caparisoned elephants and display of unparalleled pyrotechnics. Main Christian festivals are Christmas and Easter. Mormon Convention held every year on the Pumba riverbed is the biggest gathering of Christians in Asia. The Muslims celebrate *Milade Shareef, Ramzan* fasting, *Id-ul-Fitr* and *Bakrid*.

Tourism

Kerala, located on the south western tip of India, enjoys unique geographical features that have made it one of the most sought after tourist destinations in the world. Fondly referred to as "God's Own Country", Kerala was selected by the

National Geographic Traveller as one of the 50 destinations of a lifetime and one of the thirteen paradises in the world. Its unique eco tourism initiatives, culture and traditions coupled with its varied demography has made Kerala one of the most popular tourist destinations in the world. An equable climate, serene beaches, tranquil stretches of back waters; lush hill stations and exotic wildlife are the major attractions of this land. A unique advantage of Kerala is that the most of the destinations here are only a two-four hour drive from the other. Kerala has fascinated people from all over the world with her secularism and culture.

O. W.: http://www.kerala.gov.in

GOVERNMENT

Governor	: Justice P. Sathasivam	*Chief Secretary*	: Shri S.M. Vijayanand
Chief Minister	:Shri Pinarayi Vijayan	*Jurisdiction of High Court*	: Kerala and Lakshadweep

MADHYA PRADESH

Area	3,08,252 sq km	Population :	7.27 crore (prov. census 2011)
Capital :	Bhopal	Principal Language : Hindi	

History and Geography

Madhya Pradesh is the second largest Indian state in size with an area of 3,08,000 sq.km. Geographically it occupies a pivotal position in the country. King Ashoka, first of all, ruled over Ujjain. A sizeable portion of Central India was part of the Gupta empire (300-500 A.D.). The Muslims here in the beginning of 11th century. First of all, Mahmud Ghazni came over here and then Mohammad Gouri, who incorporated some parts of Central India into the ruling territory of Delhi. This part was also part of the Mughal empire. During the period between the beginning of the influence of Marathas and the death of Madhoji Scindia in 1794, Marathas were on the ascendant in Central India but later on the small states started coming into existence. These small states became the cause of perpetuation of British power in the country.

Queen Ahilyabai Holkar of Indore, the Gond Maharani Kamalapati and Queen Durgawati, etc., were women rulers whose names have left an indelible imprint on Indian history for their outstanding rule. Madhya Pradesh came into being in November 1956. It was reorganised in November 2000 to create a new Chhattisgarh state. The successive state, now, is bounded in north by Uttar Pradesh, east by Chhattisgarh, south by Maharashtra and west by Gujarat and Rajasthan.

Economy

Madhya Pradesh has gone from strength to strength in economic growth that has emerged as a study of success all over the country. Its GSDP has gone up from more ₹ 1 lakh crore to a whopping ₹ 5 lakh crore over the decade.

Agriculture

Madhya Pradesh has posted country's highest agricultural growth rate which had averaged above 20 per cent over last four years. For its excellent performance in farm sector, the state has received Government of India's prestigious. Krishi Karman Award, for last four years in a row. The state leads the country in production of pulses, oilseeds, soybean, gram, pea, garlic, guava and medicinal and aromatic herbs. Horticulture is being promoted in a big way in the state. The area under it has been extended three fold from 5 lakh hectare to 15 lakh hectare. After identifying fruit and vegetable routes, about 600 clusters are going to be developed where 50 thousand hectare will be covered under horticulture crops.

Irrigation

Top priority has been given to irrigation following which the area under irrigation has increased from more 7.5 lakh hectare ten years back to 40 lakh hectare now. Narmada-Kshipra Link Project has been successfully implemented. Three major, five medium and over 700 minor irrigation projects have been completed over last five years, thereby increasing the canal irrigation capacity by over 2.5. times.

Power

Madhya Pradesh has witnessed a total turnaround in power sector. Twelve years ago the state was reeling under acute electricity shortage and now it is power surplus. Power availability has increased from just 4500 MW twelve years ago to 17,169 MW now. Last five years have seen about 64 per cent increases in power supply. Country's largest 130 MW solar energy plant has been established in Neemuch and world's largest one with 750 MW capacity is coming up in Rewa district.

Industry

In order to promote micro, small and medium industries a separate MSME department has been set up. Following implementation of MSME Promotion Policy of State Government 50,000 units were registered under industry based memorandum. With an investment of over ₹ 5 thousand crore these units have provided jobs to over 2 lakh people. A target has been set to register 1 lakh MSME units.

Department of Happiness

A Department of Happiness has been set up in the state as part of efforts to create an enabling atmosphere for people to live a happy and blissful life. The concept of happiness that Madhya Pradesh aspires to pursue is primarily based on time tested Indian wisdom besides taking into account the indices that determine national growth as also the experiences of other countries in our strategies and action plans.

Transport

Roads : The total length of roads in the state is 58,423 km. The length of national highway in the state is 4,709 km while state highway extends to 10,501 km. The state government has taken up the construction and upgradation of roads in a big way and about 70 thousand kilometer of roads will be constructed and upgraded.

Railways : The main rail route linking northern with southern India passes through the state. Main junctions are Bhopal, Bina, Gwalior, Indore, Itarsi, Jabalpur, Katni, Ratlam and Ujjain. The divisional railways headquarters are at Bhopal, Ratlam and Jabalpur.

Festivals

A number of festivals are celebrated in the state. An important tribal festival is *Bhagoriya* marked by traditional gaiety and enthusiasm. *Shivratri* is celebrated in Khajuraho, Bhojpur, Pachmarhi and Ujjain and has its own local flavour while *Ramnavami* festival at Chitrakoot and Orchha has a unique sense of devotion imbued with tradition. Festivals of Orchha, Malwa, Pachmarhi bring to the fore repertoire of culture and art of the people. Tansen Music Festival, Gwalior; Ustad Allauddin Khan Music Festival are; Maihar; Kalidas Samaroh, Ujjain; and Festival of Dances at Khajuraho was some of the well-known art festivals of Madhya Pradesh. An annual Narmada festival has been started from this year at Bedhaghat in Jabalpur, famous for its marble rocks. A Shivpuri festival has been started at Shivpuri. Betwa festival has also been started at Vidisha.

Tourist Centres

Perfectly preserved medieval cities, refreshing and enchanting wildlife sanctuaries and some of the holiest and most revered pilgrim centres offer to the tourist the most fulfilling experience. Tranquil beauty of Pachmarhi, glittering splendour of marble rocks and roaring sound of Dhuandhar Fall at Bedaghat, Kanha National Park, with its unique Barasingha, and Bandhavgarh National Park with its prehistoric caves and wildlife are some of the major attractions of the state. Gwalior, Mandu, Datia, Chanderi, Jabalpur, Orchha, Raisen, Sanchi, Vidisha, Udaygiri, Bhimbetika, Indore and Bhopal are the places well-known for their historical monuments. Maheshwar, Omkareshwar, Ujjain, Chitrakoot and Amarkantak are major centres of pilgrimage. Unique temples of Khajuraho are famous all over the world. The temples of Orchha, Bhojpur and Udaypur attract large number of tourists as well as pilgrims. Archaeological treasures are preserved in the museums at Satna, Sanchi, Vidisha, Gwalior, Indore, Mandsaur, Ujjain, Rajgarh, Bhopal, Jabalpur, Rewa and many other places. Omkareshwar, Maheshwar and Amarkantak have been declared as holy cities for their integrated development in accordance with their religious significance. Burhanpur is being developed as a new tourist destination.

GOVERNMENT

Governor	: Shri Om Prakash Kohli (Add. Charge)	*Chief Secretary*	: Shri Basant Pratap Singh
Chief Minister	: Shri Shivraj Singh Chouhan	*Jurisdiction of High Court*	: Madhya Pradesh

MAHARASHTRA

Area	: 3,07,713 sq km	*Population*	: 11.24 crore (census 2011)
Capital	: Mumbai	*Principal Language*	: Marathi

History and Geography

The first well-known rulers of Maharashtra were the Satavahanas (230 BC to 225 AD), who were practically the founders of Maharashtra, and have left a plethora of literary, epigraphic, artistic, and archaeological evidence. Then came the Vakatakas, who established a pan-Indian empire. Under them, this area witnessed an all-sided development in the fields of learning, arts and religion. Some of the Ajanta Caves and Fresco Paintings reached their pinnacle during their rule. After the Vakatakas and after a brief interlude of the Kalachuri dynasty, the most important rulers were the Chalukyas followed by the Rashtrakutas and the Yadavas apart from the Shilaharas on the coast. The Yadavas, with Marathi as their court language extended their authority over large parts of the Deccan.

While the Bahamani rule brought a degree of cohesion to the land and its culture, a uniquely homogeneous evolution of Maharashtra as an entity became a reality under the able leadership of Shivaji. A new sense of Swaraj and nationalism was evolved by Shivaji. His noble and glorious power stalled the Mughal advances into this part of India. The Peshwas established the Maratha supremacy from the Deccan Plateau to attack in Punjab.

Maharashtra was in the forefront during freedom struggle and it was here that the Indian National Congress was born. A galaxy of leaders from Mumbai and other cities in Maharashtra led the Congress movement under the guidance of Tilak and then Mahatma Gandhi. Maharashtra was the home of Gandhiji's movement, while Sevagram was the capital of nationalistic India during the Gandhian era.

The administrative evolution of Maharashtra is the outcome of the linguistic reorganisation of the states of India, effected in May, 1960. The state was formed by bringing together all contiguous Marathi-speaking areas, which previously belonged to four different administrative hegemonies. They were the districts between Daman and Goa that formed part of the original British Bombay Province; five districts of the Nizam's dominion of Hyderabad; eight districts in the south of the Central provinces (Madhya Pradesh) and a sizeable number of petty native-ruled state enclaves lying enclosed within the above areas, were later merged with adjoining districts. Located in the north centre of Peninsular India, with the command of the Arabian Sea through its Port of Mumbai, Maharashtra has a remarkable physical homogeneity, enforced by its underlying geology. The dominant physical trait of the state is its plateau character. Maharashtra is a plateau of plateaus, its western upturned rims rising to form the Sahyadri Range parallel to the sea-coast and its slopes gently descending towards the east and south-east. Satpura ranges cover the northern part, while Ajanta and Satmala ranges run through central part. Arabian Sea guards the western boundary of the state, while Gujarat and Madhya Pradesh are on the northern side. Chhattisgarh and Telangana cover the eastern boundary of the state. Karnataka and Andhra Pradesh are on its southern side.

Agriculture

About 65 per cent of the total workers in the state depend on agriculture and allied activities. Principal crops grown are rice, jowar, bajra, wheat, tur, mung, urad, gram and other pulses. The state is a major producer of oilseeds. Groundnut, sunflower, soyabean are major oilseed crops. Important cash crops are cotton, sugarcane, turmeric and vegetables.

Industry

The state has been identified as the country's powerhouse and Mumbai, its capital as the centre point of India's financial and commercial markets. Industrial sector occupies a prominent position in the economy of Maharashtra. Food products, breweries, tobacco and related products, textiles and textile products, paper and paper products, printing and publishing, rubber, plastic, chemical and chemical products, machinery, electrical machinery, apparatus and appliances, and transport equipment and parts contribute substantially to the industrial production.

Transport

Roads : Total length of roads in the state is 2.43 lakh km consisting of 4,376 km of national highways, 34,157 km of state highways, 50,256 km of major district roads, 46,817 km of other district roads, and 1,06,601 km of village roads.

Railways: Maharashtra has 5,983 km of railway routes which is 9.2 per cent of total railway route in the country.

Aviation : There are 3 international and 5 domestic airports in the state. To reduce congestion in Mumbai International Airport, an additional airport has been proposed at Navi Mumbai.

Ports : Mumbai is a major port. There are two major and 48 notified minor ports in the state.

Tourist Centres

Some important tourist centres are Ajanta, Ellora, Elephanta, Kanheri and Karla caves, Mahabaleshwar, Matheran and Panchgani, Jowhar, Malshej ghat, Amboli,

Chikaldara, Panhala hill stations and religious places at Pandharpur, Nashik, Shirdi, Nanded, Aundha Nagnath, Trimbakeshwar, Tuljapur, Ganpatipule, Bhimashanker, Harihareshwar, Shegaon, Kolhapur, Jejuri and Ambajogai.

O. W.: http://www.maharashtra.gov.in

GOVERNMENT

Governor	: Shri Chennamaneni Vidyasagar Rao	*Chief Secretary*	: Shri Swadhin Kshatriya
Chief Minister	: Shri Devendra Fadnavis	*Jurisdiction of High Court*	: Maharashtra, Goa, Daman and Diu, Dadra and Nagar Haveli

MANIPUR

Area	: 22,327 sq km	*Population*	: 28.56 lakh (2011 census)
Capital	: Imphal	*Principal Language*	: Manipuri

History and Geography

Manipur has a long and glorious history from before the beginning of the Christian era. The political history of Manipur could be traced back to 33 A.D. with the coronation of Nongda Lairen Pakhangba. After Pakhangba a number of kings ruled over the kingdom of Manipur. The independence and sovereignty remained uninterrupted until the Burmese invasion and occupation for around seven years in the first quarter of the 19th century (1819-1826). Then, Manipur came under British Rule in 1891. Manipur regained its independence in 1947 and merged into Indian Union in 1950. Thus, it became a Part C State under the purview of Chief Commissioner. During 1950-51, an advisory form of Government was introduced and in 1957 this was replaced by a Territorial Council of 30 elected and 2 nominated members. Later, in 1963 a Territorial Assembly of 30 elected and 3 nominated members was set up under the Government of Union Territories Act, 1963. The status of administrator was raised from that of a Chief Commissioner to that of a Lt. Governor in December, 1969. Manipur became a full-fledged state in 1972 with a Legislative Assembly of 60 members of whom 19 are reserved for Scheduled Tribes and one for Scheduled Castes. The state is represented in the Lok Sabha by two members and by one member in the Rajya Sabha.

The state is situated in the extreme north-eastern border of India. It is bound on the east by upper Myanmar, on the north by Nagaland, on the west by Cachar district of Assam and on the south by Chin Hills of Myanmar and Mizoram. Manipur has a total border line of about 854 km of which about 352 km are international boundary line with Myanmar on the east and south-east. This state is in a geographically unique position, since it virtually is the meeting point between India and South-East Asia. Manipur lies between 23.80^0 N and 25.68^0 N latitude and between 93.03^0 E and 94.78^0 E longitude.

The state has a total area of 22,327 sq. km. There is a small oval shaped plain in the central part. This central plain known as Imphal Valley is at a height of about 790 metres above Mean Sea Level (MSL). This valley is surrounded by hills on all sides. The hill covers about 9/10 of the total area of the state. The hill ranges are higher on the north and gradually diminish in height towards the south. The valley itself slopes down towards the south.

Agriculture

Agriculture and allied activities are the only mainstay of the state's economy where about 70 per cent of the population depends on it. The state has two topographical zones — valley and hills. The valley is known as the 'Rice Bowl' of the state. The valley has sub-tropical to tropical to sub-temperate climates. The hills have sub-temperate to temperate climate with an average altitude of 3000 metres above MSL. It has distinct winter, warm, humid and rainy summer. The average rainfall during the last ten years has been recorded 1482.20 mm, with heavy precipitation during the month of June, July and August. The growth of agriculture in the state has been quite uneven for the reason that its production still depends on seasonal rainfall.

During the 12th Five Year Plan thrust was given to get self-security in foodgrains, oilseeds, sugarcane and potato.

Forest

In terms of forest canopy density classes, it has 701 sq. km of very dense forests, 5474 sq. km. moderately dense forests and 11,105 sq. kms open forests. An overall increase in forest cover of 328 sq. km was seen from 2005 to 2007. This overall increase in forest cover is mainly due to regeneration in abandoned jhum areas.

Irrigation

Major and medium irrigation projects had been introduced in the state since 1980. So far 8 (eight) major and medium irrigation and multipurpose projects have been taken up of which 5 projects viz. Loktak Lift Irrigation Project, Khoupum Dam Project, Imphal Barrage Project, Sekmai Barrage Project and Singda Multipurpose Project have been completed.

Commerce and Industries

The handloom industry is by far the largest and most important cottage industry. It improves the socio-economic conditions of handloom weavers and has attained high degree of excellence. As per the 3rd National Handloom Census of Weavers and Allied Workers 2010 conducted by the National Council of Applied Economic Research (NCAER), Manipur topped in distribution of handloom workers. There are 218,753 handloom workers (200,607 weavers, 18, 146 workers) which is 4th position among the top states of the country, 1,90,634 looms which is 3rd position and consuming 186,703 kg of yarn in 2009-10 which is 3rd in the country. About 91 per cent of the total handloom workers are independent weavers outside the co-operative/master weavers/corporation/

KVIC/private owners. Manipur is, therefore, among the top four states of the country promoting and nurturing the handloom industry for generating employment to a large section of the state's population.

Power

Power supply in Manipur is fully dependent on the Central Generating Stations situated in the North Eastern Region (NER). As the generating stations in the NER are mainly of hydel in nature, during lean period there is a shortfall in generation and therefore the available share of Manipur reduces drastically.

Transport

Roads: Road transport is the only means of communication in the state and there are no inland waterways, railways or ropeways. All development activities depend entirely on the road transport facilities.

The total length of roads in Manipur (including national highways, NEC, BRTF and roads under Rural Development) was 12,618 km.

Three national highways : i) NH-39, ii) NH-53 and iii) NH-150 criss-cross the state connecting all districts. Imphal, the capital is connected by NH-39 with Nagaland on the north and Myanmar on the east, on the west with Assam by NH-53 and Mizoram on the south by NH-150.

Aviation : Imphal airport is the second largest airport in the north eastern region, which is connected to Agartala, Aizwal, Dimapur, Guwahati, Kolkata, Pune, Silchar, Bengaluru and New Delhi.

The airport is being upgraded to international status. The construction of infrastructure for Night Landing Facility at Imphal airport has been completed and Night Flights have started.

Railways: The state was included in the railway map of India with the opening of a rail head at Jiribam in May 1990. It is 225 km from Imphal. Dimapur (Nagaland), 215 km from Imphal is the nearest rail-head. The Jiribam - Tupul - Imphal railway line has been declared as a national project. Construction of the line is in good progress and is targeted for completion by 2014 (upto Tupul) and 2016 (upto Imphal).

Festivals

A year in Manipur represents a cycle of festivals. Hardly a month passes by without a festival which to the Manipuris is a symbol of their social, cultural and religious aspirations. Important festivals of the state are Lai Haraoba, Rasa Leela, Cheiraoba, Ningol Chak-Kouba, Rath-Jatra, Idul Fitr, Imoinu Iratpa, Gaan-Ngai, Lui-Ngai-Ni, Idul Zuha. Yaoshang (Holi), Durga Puja, Mera Houchongba, Diwali, Kut, Christmas, etc.

Tourist Centres

Manipur is not only the gateway of the north eastern region but is also a fascinating destination for discerning tourists. Blessed with a salubrious climate, natural beauty and scenic splendour, the state extends to the tourists a warm welcome. Some important tourist centres in the state are Kangla, Shree Shree Govindajee Temple, Khwalramband Bazar (Ima Keithel), War Cemeteries, Shaheed Minar, Nupi Lan (Women's War) Memorial Complex, Khonghampat Orchidarium, INA Memorial (Moirang), Loktak Lake, Keibul Lamjao National Park, Sendra, Moreh, Siroy Hills, Dzuko Valley, State Museum, Kaina Tourist Home, Khongjom War Memorial Complex, India Peace Memorial (Red Hill), etc. O. W.: http://www.manipur.gov.in

GOVERNMENT

Governor	: Dr. Najma A. Heptulla	*Chief Secretary*	:	Shri O. Nabakishore Singh
Chief Minister	: Shri O. Ibobi Singh	*Jurisdiction of High Court*	:	A permanent Bench of the Guwahati High Court, Imphal Bench started functioning from14th March 1992.

MEGHALAYA

Area	: 22,429 sq km	*Population*	:	29.67 lakh (prov. 2011 census)
Capital	: Shillong	*Principal Languages*	:	Khasi, Pnar, Garo & English

History and Geography

Meghalaya was created as an autonomous state within the state of Assam in 1970. The full-fledged state of Meghalaya came into existence in 1972. It is bound on the north and east by Assam and on the south and west by Bangladesh. Meghalaya literally means the 'Abode of Clouds' and is essentially a hilly state. It is predominately inhabited by the tribal Khasis, Jaintias and Garos population. The Khasi Hills and Jaintia Hills which form the central and eastern part of the state form an imposing plateau with rolling grassland, hills and river valleys. The southern face of the plateau is marked by deep gorges and abrupt slopes, at the foot of which, a narrow strip of plain runs along the international border with Bangladesh.

Carved from the erstwhile state of Assam, Meghalaya became a full fledged State on January 21, 1972. Bounded on the north and east by Assam and on the south and west by Bangladesh, Meghalaya is spread over an area of 22, 429 square kilometers, and lies between 24^0 57′ and $26^0$10 north latitude and 89^0 46′ and 92^0 53′ east longitudes.

Agriculture

Meghalaya is basically an agricultural state with about 81 per cent of its total population depending entirely on it for their livelihood. The hilly terrain and land conditions of the state do not offer much scope in bringing additional area under wet condition, but the state has a vast potential for developing horticulture. The agro-climatic variations offer much scope for cultivation of temperate as well as tropical fruits and vegetables. Besides the major food crops of rice and maize, the state is also renowned for its horticultural crops like orange. lemon, pineapple, guava, litchi, banana, jackfruits and temperate fruits such as plum, pear, peach, etc. Potato, ginger, turmeric, black pepper, arecanut, tezpata, betel, short- staple cotton, jute, mesta, mustard and rapeseed etc., are some of the important cash crops. Apart from these, the state has achieved success in the cultivation of non-traditional crops like tea, cashew nut, oilseeds, tomato, mushroom, wheat, etc.

Forest

The total forest area is 9,49,56,000 hectares which includes reserved forest, protected forest, national park and unclassed forest. The principal timber species are sal, teak, titachap, gomari, bol, pine, birch and makri-sal. The principal forest products include timber, bamboo, reed, broomstick, cane, ipecac, medicinal herbs and plants, cinnamon and thatch grass. Azaleas and rhododendrons grow wild in the forests of Khasi Hills and Jaintia Hills forest and many kinds of wild and rare orchids are also found in many parts of the state. Pitcher plants, the insect-eating plants of botanical wonder is found in plenty in the Jaintia Hills, West Khasi Hills and South Garo Hills and it is said that such a plant is found nowhere else in the world. Many rare and interesting plants like wild citrus and pygmy lily are also found.

Wildlife

The state is also rich in wildlife. There are elephants, tigers, bears, wild-boars, leopards, golden cats, leopard cats and jungle cats, deers of various kinds, binturongs, slow loris, monkeys of different types including capped-langurs, golden langurs and hoolock, flying squirrels and giant squirrels. There are also many rare and interesting birds including the hornbills, partridges, pheasants, teals, snipes, geese, ducks and quails. The state has two national parks, viz, Nokrek and Balpakram and two wildlife sanctuaries, viz, Nongkhyllem and Siju.

Industry

The most important non-agro based industry is cement. Because of its rich limestone deposits, the state has a number of cement plants operating in different parts. The number of small scale industrial units covering service industry, bakeries, furniture making, iron and steel fabrication, tyre retreading etc., are increasing. The Meghalaya Industrial Development Corporation encourages private entrepreneurs to register themselves so that they may benefit from support and training to set up industries in small and tiny sectors by way of financing and equity participation.

Places of Interest

Meghalaya is dotted with a number of lovely tourist spots. Shillong, the capital city, has a number of beautiful spots. They are the Ward's Lake, the Phan

Nonglait Park, the expensive Polo Grounds, the Elephant Falls, the Shillong Peak over looking the city. Umiam, lies 17 km away from Shillong and has been developed into a popular tourist centre in the state. Shillong Peak, an ideal picnic spot rises 1960 metres above the sea level and is 10 km from the city. Sohra, 56 km from Shillong, is noted for its heavy rainfall. It is 1,300 metres above sea-level. Mawsynram, is situated on the South West of Shillong by the side of Shillong-Mawphlang-Balat road. It closely rivals Sohra in annual rainfall. Jakrem, 64 km from Shillong, is a popular health resort with hot springs of sulphur water which is believed to have medicinal properties. Ranikor, 140 km from Shillong. It is also a place of scenic beauty. Dawki, 96 km from Shillong. It is an excellent picnic spot with silver streams and deep waters with magnificient views of the Khasi Hills on one side and Bangladesh on the other.

Transport

Being a hilly state, with 4/5th of the population living in the rural areas, the necessity of proper road network is of utmost importance. The state is not served by railways and river transportation is not feasible. Hence roads are the only means of bulk transportation here.

Roads: Six national highways pass through the state. The state has 9350 km of road length with road density of 41.69 km per 100 sq.kms.

Aviation: the only airport in the state at Umroi, 35 km from Shillong is functional.

O. W.: http://www.meghalaya.gov.in

GOVERNMENT

Governor	: Shri V. Shanmuganathan	*Chief Secretary*	: Shri K.S. Kropha
Chief Minister	: Dr. Mukul Sangma	*Jurisdiction of High Court*	: Falls under the jurisdiction of Guwahati High Court. There is a High Court Bench at Shillong.

MIZORAM

Area	: 21,081 sq km	*Population*	: 10.97 lakh (Prov. 2011 census)
Capital	: Aizawl	*Principal Languages*	: Mizo and English, Lushai

History and Geography

Mizoram is a mountainous region which became the 23rd state of the Indian Union in February 1987. It was one of the districts of Assam till 1972 when it became a Union Territory. After being annexed by the British in 1891, for the first few years, Lushai Hills in the north remained under Assam while the southern half remained under Bengal. Both the parts were amalgamated in 1898 into one district called Lushai Hills District under the Chief Commissioner of Assam. With the implementation of North-Eastern Reorganization Act in 1972, Mizoram became a Union Territory and as a sequel to the signing of the historic memorandum of settlement between the Government of India and the Mizo National Front in 1986, it was granted statehood in 1987. Sandwiched between Myanmar in the east and the south and Bangladesh in the west, the state occupies an area of great strategic importance in the north-eastern corner of India. Mizoram has a great natural beauty and an endless variety of landscape rich in flora and fauna.

The Mizos came under the influence of the British Missionaries in the 19th century. Now most of the Mizos are Christians. Mizo language has no script of its own. The missionaries introduced the Roman script for the Mizo language and formal education.

Agriculture

About 60 per cent of the people of the state are engaged in agricultural and allied activities. The main pattern of the agriculture followed is jhum or shifting cultivation. Of the total 21 per cent is put on paddy/seasonal crops. About 63 per cent of the total crop area is under jhum cultivation. To replace the destructive and unproductive jhum cultivation with sustainable means of occupation, the state government has launched an innovative programme called the New Land Use Policy covering all the districts. The area under Jhum cultivation has decreased from 44,947 hectare at the beginning of 11th Plan to 20,064 hectare during 2014-15 which account for above 55.36 per cent reduction. The significant reduction in jhum area is mainly due to the implementation of NLUP, oil palm development programme, sugarcane cultivation programme, RKVY, and RAD.

Horticulture

Owing to the fact that more than 60 per cent of the population depends on land based activities for their livelihoods, horticulture plays a vital role and occupies very important place in the economy of Mizoram. Because of its advantageous agro-climatic condition, hilly terrain nature of the landscape and well distributed rainfall during monsoon season horticulture is a sustainable land based activities for development of the economy. Out of the estimated total of 21 lakh hectare of land 6.30 lakh hectare is available for cultivation of horticulture crops. The main horticulture crops are mandarin orange, banana, passion fruit, grapes, hatkora, pineapple, papaya, etc. and flowers like anthurium, bird of paradise, orchid, chrysanthemum, rose and other subsidiary seasonal flowers. Spices like ginger, turmeric, black pepper, bird's eye chillies are also grown. A multi-purpose packaging house has been set up at the Horticulture Centre, Chite in collaboration with M/s Argos (Agri Projects) Ltd., Israel.

Floriculture was a growing occupation in Mizoram. Cultivation of anthurium was introduced in 2002 and today anthurium cut flowers are exported outside the state and overseas market. Commercial cultivation of rose under hi-tech green house was introduced in 2006 and about 10,000 rose cut flowers are being harvested everyday.

Forest

Mizoram has one of the highest forest cover among the states of India. India State of Forest Report-2015 indicated that about 91.47 per cent of the state's total geographical area is under forests cover. Tropical semi evergreen, tropical moist deciduous, subtropical broadleaved hill and subtropical pine forests are the common vegetation types found. Bamboo resources covers around 31per cent (about 6446 Sq.km) of its geographical area and as many as 35 species of bamboo have been identified in the state of which Melocanna baccifera (mautak) contributes about 77 per cent of the total bamboo coverage.

Jhum cultivation, or slash-and-burn practice, was a historic tradition and a threat to its forest cover. This practice is reduced in recent decades from a government supported initiative particularly New Land Use Policy of the state.

The popular and effective Green Mizoram Programme has been continuing with stress on the survival of the trees planted under which mass afforestation and maintenance activities have been taken up every year. 4700 hectares of plantation have also been created under the National Afforestation Programme.

Irrigation

Due to hilly nature of the state, all irrigation projects are confined to minor irrigation. As per estimation of Mizoram Remote Sensing Application Centre, the total Wet Rice Cultivation potential area is 74,644 ha. So far, 439 minor irrigation projects covering 18,228 ha command area have been completed. 25 new minor irrigation projects are proposed to be cover during 2016-17 which will cover an area of 1,117.90 ha. and create an irrigation potential of 1656 ha. The proposed projects will benefit 791 of farmers covering different parts of the state.

Industry

Due to its topographical and geographical disadvantages coupled with underdeveloped infrastructure and transport bottleneck, growth in industry is very modest. However, with the opening up of border trade with Myanmar and Bangladesh, the 'Look/Act East Policy' of the Government of India and the peaceful condition of the state, industrialization is gaining momentum.

Small industries dominate the industrial scenario acquiring prominent place in the socio-economic development of the state. With the objectives of promoting industries in rural areas, the state government has been running two commonly facility centre and one Regional Industrial Development Corporation (RIDC) with an intake of 35 trainers.

Scientific cultivation of tea has also been taken up. Establishment of apparel training and design centre, gems cutting and polishing are in the pipeline to encourage setting up of Export Oriented Units (EOUs). Of the cottage industries, handloom and handicraft are given high priority and the two sectors are nourishing to meet consumers' demand in the state and in neighboring states of Maghalaya, Nagaland, etc.

Power

As per the 18th Power Survey of India, the bulk power requirement of Mizoram is 201 MW and the allocated share is 103.09 MW (real time power availability is normally 60 MW). Per capita consumption is 280kWh. The present peak demand is 102MW but the state generates only about 15MW from the installed capacity of 29.35MW. The rest of the requirement has to be imported from various sources like Loktak, Ranganadi, etc from Central Sector Utilities like NEEPCO, NHPC, NTPC, etc.

Transport

Road: Road serves as the most important means of communication, transportation of goods and passengers within the state, interstate and with international borders. Total road length in the state is 6349.60 km and road density is 300012 km/100 sq km approximately. There are six national highways passing through the length and breadth of Mizoram. NH 54 connects Aizawl with the rest of the country through Silchar, Assam. Aizawl is also accessible by road from Shillong and Guwahati.

Railways: Broad gauge rail link has been established in Bairabi, Mizoram near Assam border.

Aviation: The airport at Lengpui is connected by flights to and from Kolkata, Imphal and Guwahati. Internal helicopter service also connects Aizawl with Lunglei, Lawngtlai, Saiha,Chawngte, Serchhip, Champhai, Kolasib, Khawzawl, Mamit and Hnahthial.

Festival

Being predominantly an agricultural community all the activities of the Mizo centre around jhum cultivation. 'Kut' is the Mizo term for festival. Among the various cultural festivals, only three, viz., Chapchar Kut, Mim Kut and Thalfavang Kut are being observed now a days.

Tourist Centres

Mizoram is a place with flora and fauna rich landscape and pleasant climate. Aizawl, the capital city is located at 3715 ft above sea level, is a religious and cultural centre. Champhai is a beautiful resort on the Myanmar border. Tam Dil, a natural lake with virgin forest, is 76km from Aizawl and 10 km from tourist resort of Saitual. Vantawng Falls, 5 km from the town of Thenzawl is the highest and most beautiful waterfall in the state. 2 km from Vantawng one can find a quaint and beautiful fall known as Tuirihiau. Thenzawl is also the main centre for handlooms. Phawngpui is the highest peak at an elevation of 2157 m and a trekkers delight. Just 30 km from Aizawl is beautiful Reiek Peak. A typical Mizo village which is a recreation of an old Mizo village is located at Falkawn, 24 km from Aizawl. Hmuifang Tlang about 50 km and Sialsuk Tlang about 66 km from Aizawl respectively are popular tourist destination. The Department of Tourism has opened tourist lodges in all the bigger towns all over the state and highway restaurants and travellers inns in other township. There is also a recreational centre at Beraw Tlang, Aizawl and Alpine Picnic Hut at district park near Zobawk. Reiek Tlang, where the Tourism Department created a typical Mizo village, modern Mizo village, resort.

GOVERNMENT

Governor	:	Lt. General Nirbhay Sharma (Retd.)	*Chief Secretary*	:	Shri Lalmalsawma
Chief Minister	:	Shri Lalthanhawla	*Jurisdiction of High Court*	:	Falls under the jurisdiction of Guwahati High Court. There is a Bench at Mizoram.

O. W.: http://www.mizoram.gov.in

NAGALAND

Area	: 16,579 sq km	*Population*	:	19.79 lakh (Prov. census 2011)
Capital	: Kohima	*Principal Languages*	:	English, Hindi and 16 tribal dialects, Nagamese

History and Geography

Nagaland became the 16th state of the Indian Union in 1963. It is bordered by Myanmar on the east, Arunachal on the north, Assam on the west and Manipur on the south. It lies between the parallels of 98 degree and 96 degree east longitude and 26.6 degree and 27.4 degree latitude north of the equator.

The Naga people belong to the Indo-Mongoloid group of people living in a contiguous areas of the north-eastern hills of India and the upper portion of western Myanmar. The major recognised tribes of Nagaland are Angami, Ao, Chakhesang, Chang, Khiamniungan, Kuki, Konyak, Kachari, Lotha, Phom, Pochury, Rengma, Sangtam, Sumi, Yimchungrii and Zeliang. The Naga languages differ from tribe to tribe and sometimes even from one village to another. They are, however, under the Tibeto-Burman family.

In the 12th and 13th centuries, gradual contacts with the Ahoms of present day Assam was established but this did not have any significant impact on the traditional Naga way of life. However, in the 19th century the British appeared on the scene and ultimately the area was brought under British administration. After Independence this territory was made a centrally administered area in 1957, administered by the Governor of Assam. It was known as the Naga Hills Tuensang Area. This failed to quell popular aspirations and polilical unrest began. Hence, in 1961, the area was renamed as Nagaland and given the status of state of the Indian Union, which was formally inaugurated in December 1963.

Agriculture

Nagaland is basically a land of agriculture with about 70 per cent of the population depending on agriculture. The contribution of agricultural sector in the state is very significant. Rice is the staple food. It occupies about 70 per cent of the total area under cultivation and constitutes about 75 per cent of the total food production in the state. The major land use pattern is slash and burn cultivation locally known as *jhum*. Total cultivable area is 7,21,924 hectares.

Forest

Out of the total land area of 16,579 sq.km, forest area occupies approximately 8,62,9.30 sq.km. There are Rangapahar wildlife sanctuaries in Dimapur district, Fakim wildlife sanctuaries in Tuensang district and Singphan wildlife sanctuaries in Mon district, Intanki National Park in Peren district and Zoological Park in Dimapur district.

Power

The state has an installed generation capacity of 27.84 MW only from Small Hydro Electric Power Projects against the requirement of 95 MW. The main source of power is from the Central Sector Power allocation. The total number of consumer is 1,80,000 (approximately) 90 per cent of which is domestic.

Irrigation

The state has so far been constructing minor irrigations to divert small hill streams to the valleys and terraced field for rice cultivation covering an area of 82,150 hectares. The state is implementing Themezie M.I Project at Chiechama village under Kohima district.

Transport

The state is connected to the rest of the country with airport and railway stations at Dimapur and National Highway-39 which passes through the state from Dimapur via Kohima to Manipur. This NH-39 is soon to be an international route under the Look East Policy of the GOI. The rest of the state is connected only with roads covering about 24,709 kms, this includes the NH-61 and state highways. The state is also inter-connected with postal services in all district hqrs, telephone line and mobile services.

Tourism

With the opening of the state to the International tourist by relaxation of Restricted Area Permit (RAP), a good number of foreign tourists as well as domestic tourists visit Nagaland every year.

The Hornbill festival conceived by the Tourist Department and held in the first week of December is an annual event where all tribes of the state come together to celebrate, exhibit and sell their traditional wares, foodstuffs and crafts. Three traditional festivals, namely *Sekrenyi* at Touphema in Kohima district (Feb), *Monyu* at Pongo in Longleng Sub-division (April) and *Moatsu* at

Chuchuyimlang in Mokokchung district (May) have been identified as festival destinations.

Music and dances are an intrinsic part of Naga life. Folk songs and ballads eulogizing bravery, beauty, love, generosity, etc, are transmitted from generation to generation. Likewise dancing is an important part of every festive occasion. Feasting, singing, dancing and merry-making invariably accompany festivals. Name of the tribes and their festivals are Angami-Sekrenyi, Ao-Moatsu, Chakhesang-Sukhrunye and Tsukhenye, Chang-Naknyulem, Khiamniungan-Tsokum, Kuki-Mimkut, Konyak-Aoleang Monyu, Kachari-Bushu, Lotha-Tokhu Emong, Phom-Monyu, Pochury-Yemshe, Rengma-Ngada, Sumi-Tuluni, Sangtam-Amongmong, Yimchungru-Metemneo, and Zeliang-Meileingi/Hega Langsimngi/Chegagadi.

Industries

The process of industrialisation in the state is in its infancy, but the need to have more industries has been well recognised. Under the 'Year of Entrepreneur 2010' Entrepreneur Awareness Programme was held in all the (11) eleven districts of Nagaland. The state has set up 17 Citronella Demonstration Farms (i.e. called as 'Economic Plant') all over the state. The Nagaland Handloom and Handicrafts Development Cooperation Ltd, Dimapur is the state owned corporation, which is responsible for the promotion and marketing of handloom and handicraft products. An Industrial Growth Centre has been established at Ganeshnagar, Dimapur to facilitate entrepreneurs and educated unemployed youth to promote industries.

The Nagaland Industrial Development Corporation is the premier promotional organisation in providing guidance and capital assistance to entrepreneurs.

O. W.: http://www.nagaland.gov.in

GOVERNMENT

Governor	:	Shri P. B. Acharya	*Chief Secretary*	:	Shri Pankaj Kumar
Chief Minister	:	Shri T. R. Zeliang	*Jurisdiction of High Court*	:	Falls under Guwahati High Court. There is a Bench at Kohima.

ODISHA

Area	:	1,55,707 sq km	*Population*	:	4.2 crore (2011 census)
Capital	:	Bhubaneswar	*Principal Language*	:	Odia

History and Geography

The history of Odisha dates back to antiquity, its most famous old names being Kalinga, Utkal and Odra. By the time of Mahavir and Buddha, the Kalinga Utkal region on the entire east coast of India acquired recognition and fame. Mauryan

Emperor, Ashoka's invasion of Kalinga was an epoch-making event of ancient times of far reaching consequences. Kalinga was conquered but the conquest changed the heart of the conqueror. The change in Ashoka changed the course of religion and cultural history not only of India but also of the whole of Asia. The next great era of Odisha's history commenced during the reign of Mahameghavahana Kharavela who ruled in the 1st half of the second century B.C. During Kharavela's reign the empire of Kalinga extended upto the river Ganga in the north and the river Godavari in the south. Subsequently the great dynasties such as the Shailodvabas, Bhoumakaras, Somavamsis, Gangas were not only great empire builders, but also promoters of art, literature and culture. The world famous Sun Temple at Konark was built in the thirteenth century by Narasimha Deva, the famous Jagannath temple at Puri in the twelfth century by Anangabhima Deva and the Lingaraj temple, Bhubaneshwar in the eleventh century by Jajati-II. From mid-16th century, Odisha was ruled successively by five Muslim kings till 1592, when Akbar annexed and included it into the Mughal empire. With the decline of the Mughal empire, Marathas occupied Odisha. They continued to hold it till the British took over in 1803.

Modern Odisha took birth in1936. After Independence, princely states in and around Odisha surrendered their sovereignty to the Government of India. By the States' Merger Order 1949 the rest of the princely states of Odisha were completely merged with the state of Odisha in January 1949.

Odisha situated on the shores of Bay of Bengal is surrounded by West Bengal on the north-east, Jharkhand on the north, Chhattisgarh and Telangana on the west and Andhra Pradesh on the south. Its diverse landscape comprises coastal plains, mountainous terrain, plateaus, verdant river valleys and slopes dotted with watersheds, springs, lakes and forest cover of varying density.

Change of Name

British Government occupied Odisha in the year 1803. British administrators felt difficulty in uttering the name of Odisha and its language Odia. So they changed the name as Orissa and its language as Oriya. However, the use of the name of Odisha deriving from "Odra" can be dated back to AD 1435. In independent India after 74 years, people of Orissa and the state government made endeavour to change the name from Orissa to Odisha and its language Oriya to Odia. After a long exercise and as a result of the legitimate demand of the people of Orissa and consistent efforts of the state government, the Bill relating to change of the name of the state from "Orissa" to "Odisha" and its language "Oriya" to "Odia" was passed in the Rajya Sabha in 2011.

Agriculture

Agriculture continues to be the backbone of the state's economy. About 65 per cent of the population of the state is dependant on it. Government has been giving priority to the development of agriculture sector through a number of pro-active measures. As seed is the most important input for boosting productivity of crops, effective steps are taken to increase seed replacement rate of various crops. Besides, six mobile soil testing laboratories have been engaged to expedite the soil analysis process in rural areas.

Irrigation and Power

Irrigation is the most important input for agriculture. Private Lift Irrigation Points under Jalanidhi scheme are being promoted by providing 50 per cent subsidy to farmers. Due emphasis has also been given on judicious utilization of water for crop production through promotion of micro irrigation system over 4,564 hect. under drip and sprinkler irrigation. The state has a cultivable land of 61.65 lakh hectare, out of which 49 per cent was provided irrigation facilities. For accelerated irrigation development, Government is implementing various farmer centric schemes such as Biju Krushak Vikash Yojana, Deep Bore Well Construction Programme, Megalift and Check Dam Construction. Construction activities of major and medium irrigation projects have been increased to complete the ongoing projects in the 12th Plan period.

Industry

On the strength of good governance and industry friendly atmosphere, Odisha is on its way to becoming the premier manufacturing hub for companies. This has enabled the state to sign MoU with 93 reputed investors across various sectors such as steel, aluminium, power, cement, auto component, oil refinery, titanium dioxide and four ancillary and downstream industries with an investment of ₹ 4,62,768.74 crore. Such industrialization is creating opportunities for broad-basing the growth of ancillary and downstream industries in the state.

Transport

Roads: Government made significant efforts for building roads and bridges with a view to strengthen road infrastructural facilities in the state with special focus on backward regions. Eight road projects out of nine have been completed under Economic Importance Scheme.

Railways: Odisha is well connected with the national rail network. It has rail lines of 2339 km including 91 km. narrow gauge. The Odisha railway network is a part of the East Coast Railways, which is the largest carrier of commercial load in both freight as well as passenger traffic in the country.

Aviation: The expansion and modernization of Bhubaneswar airport is in progress. Direct link is available from Bhubaneswar to places like Delhi, Kolkata, Mumbai, Bengaluru and Hyderabad. There are 13 airstrips and 16 helipads at different places in the state.

Ports: Government is taking steps to develop modern all weather deep sea ports at the potential port sites to give impetus to maritime trade and port based industries. Dhamra Port, which has been developed in PPP mode has started its commercial operation during this year.

Tourism : A new tourism policy is being formulated by the government aiming at strengthening the tourism prospects of Odisha, increasing private sector participation, augmenting tourism infrastructure and improving marketing and promotion of tourism. To further enhance the security of the tourists, government has created a separate wing called tourist police and deployed them at Sea Beach at Puri, Konark and Gopalpur. Tourist police cells have also been created in Golden Triangle and Diamond Triangle.

Considering the tourism potential of Odisha, Government has identified tourism as one of the focused areas of development. 320 places have so far been identified as tourist centres. Steps have been taken to make Odisha a most preferred tourist destination and placing it prominently on the national and international tourist map.

O. W.: http://www.odisha.gov.in

GOVERNMENT

Governor	:	Dr. S.C. Jamir	*Chief Secretary*	:	Shri Aditya Prasad Padhi
Chief Minister	:	Shri Naveen Patnaik	*Jurisdiction of High Court*	:	Odisha

PUNJAB

Area	*: 50,362 sq km*	***Population***	*: 2,77,43,338*
Capital	*: Chandigarh*	*Principal Language*	*: Punjabi*

History and Geography

Ancient Punjab formed part of the vast Indo-Iranian region. In later years it saw the rise and fall of the Mauryas, Bactrians, Greeks, Sakas, Kushans and Guptas. Medieval Punjab saw a supremacy of the Muslims. Ghaznavi was followed by the Ghoris, the slaves, the Khiljis, the Tughlaks, the Lodhis and the Mughals. Fifteenth and sixteenth centuries marked a period of watershed in the history of Punjab. Through teachings of Guru Nanak, Bhakti movement received a great impetus. Sikhism began as a socio religious movement, which was more interested in fighting evils in religion and society. It was Guru Gobind Singh, the tenth Guru, who transformed the Sikhs into the Khalsa. They rose to challenge tyranny and after centuries of servitude, established a Punjabi Raj based on secularism and patriotism. Maharaja Ranjit Singh, in the works of a Persian writer, changed Punjab from Madam-Kada to Bagh-Bahist (from the abode of sorrow to the garden of paradise). But soon after his death the entire edifice collapsed due to internal intrigues and British machinations. After two abortive Anglo-Sikh wars, Punjab was finally annexed to the British Empire in 1849.

The fight against the British rule had begun long before Mahatma Gandhi's arrival on the scene. The revolt found expression through the movement of a revivalist or reformist character. It was Lala Lajpat Rai who played a leading role in the freedom movement. Punjab was in the vanguard of India's freedom struggle on all fronts in India and abroad. Punjab's hardships did not end with Independence. It had to face the misery of partition with large-scale blood shed and migration. Besides their rehabilitation, there was the task of re -organization of the state.

Eight princely states of East Punjab were grouped together to form a single state called PEPSU—Patiala and the East Punjab States Union—with Patiala as its capital. PEPSU state was merged with Punjab in 1956 with its capital at Chandigarh. Later in 1966, Haryana was carved out of Punjab. Situated in the north-western corner of the country, Punjab is bound on the west by Pakistan, on the north by Jammu and Kashmir, on the north-east by Himachal Pradesh and on the south by Haryana and Rajasthan. There are 13 Members of Parliament from Punjab and 117 Members of Legislature.

Agriculture

Punjab has achieved an extraordinary growth in the field of agriculture. The state has about 4.2 million hectares of cultivable area, which is 3 per cent of the net area sown in the country. It produces about 18.4 per cent of India's wheat and 10.4 per cent of rice from 11.3 per cent and 6.6 per cent of the total area under wheat and rice; it has contributed 25-50 per cent of rice and 38-75 per cent of wheat to the Central pool of food-grains over the last four decades. Punjab ranks seventh as gross producer of wheat in the world. It generates third largest marketable surplus after Canada and Australia which is about one tenth of the global trade in wheat. In the case of rice, its marketable surplus is second only to Thailand.

A comprehensive Crop Diversification Plan with emphasis on increasing area under maize, cotton and other alternative crops is being implemented. The area under maize cultivation increased from 1.5 to 1.72 lac hectares in the Kharif season. In addition, the Department has facilitated the setting-up of two maize drying units at Saila Khurd (Hoshiarpur) and SBS Nagar, with a view to ensuring proper marketing of the crop. Besides, Punjab has fixed a target to bring 2 lac hectares under maize cultivation in 2016-17.

Under National Horticulture Mission, Centres of Excellence have been established at Kartarpur (Jalandhar) and Khanaura (Hoshiarpur). Centres of Excellence for potato and flowers are being established under Indo-Dutch agreement. Litchi and pear estates with ultramodern laboratory and state of art nursery would also be set up. The state government has ensured the full payment of arrears to the cane growers in the state and for this purpose, ₹ 331 crore was disbursed during 2015-16. An amount of ₹ 350 crore was provided for 2016-17.

Industry

There are 1.59 lakh small-scale and 454 (project) large and medium units in the state of Punjab as by 2015.These units produce bicycle parts, sewing machines, hand tolls, machine tools, auto parts, electrical items, sports goods, surgical instruments, leather goods, hosiery, knitwear, nuts and bolts, textile goods, textile, sugar, vegetable oil, etc., giving employment to about 13.85 lakh persons. Separately, 46 clusters have been proposed to GoI under its different schemes namely Micro & Small Enterprises Cluster Development Programme for development in the state. Out of these proposals, 28 proposals have been approved by Government of India for conducting Diagnostic Study Report which is at different stages of implementation under the programme.

Irrigation

The total geographical area of the state is 50.36 lakh hectares out of which about 42.90 lakh hectares area is under cultivation. After partition of the country in 1947, Indus water treaty of 1960 between India and Pakistan restricted India right to usage to only three eastern rivers Satluj,Beas and Ravi. The state has three dams namely Bhakra Dam with storage capacity of 5.60 MAF constructed on river Satluj, Pong Dam with storage capacity 5.91 MAF constructed on river Beas and a diversion Dam at Pandoh Upstream of Pong Dam for Diversion of 3.82 MAF of waters of river.

Beas into Bhakra reservoir and Ranjit Sagar Dam with a storage capacity of 1.90 MAF construct on river Ravi. At present the area under irrigation is 30.88 lakh hectares, which is 71.98 per cent of the area under cultivation. The canal surface water distribution system consists of 14500 km of canals / distributaries covering six major systems in the state.

Power

Punjab has achieved the status of power surplus state in the country with inauguration of two new thermal power plants at Rajpura (1400 MW) and Talwandi Sabo (1980 MW) in 2013.

PEDA

Punjab Government's department of New and Renewable Energy with its nodal agency Punjab Energy Agency (PEDA) have installed 1100 MW capacity NRSE power plants out of which 491 MW capcity solar power plants with the investment of ₹ 8,000 crores which are equivalent to planting 4.30 crore trees. This initiative had also provided direct and indirect jobs to 5,000 youth. Punjab has set up a target of installation of 2,550 MW capacity solar power plants by or before the year 2022.

Roads

The total road network length is 71742 km, consisting of 2630 km national highways 1133 km state highways, 1826 km major district roads and 5119 km of other district roads(ODRs) and 61034 km rural link roads. Out of the link roads PWD B&R looks after 31696 km and Punjab Mandi Board looks after 29338 km of link roads.

Aviation

Punjab has two international airports at Amritsar (Rajasansi) and Mohali. First phase of the terminal building at Mohali airport is complete and awaiting commissioning.

Fairs and Festivals

Besides festivals of Dussehra, Diwali, Holi, other important festivals/fairs/melas are Maghi Mela at Mukatsar, Rural Sports at Kila Raipur, Basant at Patiala, Holla Mohalla at Anandpur Sahib, Baisakhi at Talwandi Saboo, Urs at Rauza Sharif at Sirhind, Chappar Mela at Chappar, Skeikh Farid Aagman Purb at Faridkot, Ram Tirath at Village Ram Tirath, Shaheedi Jor Mela at Sirhind, Harballab Sangeet Sammelan Baba Sodal at Jalandhar. In addition to these, three heritage festivals at Amritsar, Patiala, Kapurthala are also celebrated every year and are very popular among the tourists.

GOVERNMENT

Governor	: Shri V.P. Singh Badnore	*Chief Secretary*	: Shri Sarvesh Kaushal
Chief Minister	: Shri Parkash Singh Badal	*Jurisdiction of High Court*	: Punjab, Haryana & Chandigarh

RAJASTHAN

Area	: 3,42,239 sq km	*Population*	: 6.86 crore
Capital	: Jaipur	*Principal Languages*	: Hindi and Rajasthani

History and Geography

Rajasthan is the largest state in India area-wise. Prior to Independence was known as Rajputana or Rajputs-a martial community who ruled over this area for centuries. The history of Rajasthan dates back to the pre-historic times. Around 3,000 and 1,000 BC, it had a culture akin to that of the Indus Valley civilization. It were the Chauhans who dominated Rajput affairs from seventh century and by 12th century they had become an imperial power. After the Chauhans, it were the Guhilots of Mewar who controlled the destiny of the warring tribes. Besides Mewar, the other historically prominent states were Marwar, Jaipur, Bundi, Kota, Bharatpur and Alwar. Other states were only offshoots of these. All these states accepted the British Treaty of Subordinate Alliance in 1818 protecting the interest of the princes. This naturally left the people discontented.

After the revolt of 1857, the people united themselves under the leadership of Mahatma Gandhi to contribute to the freedom movement with the introduction of provincial autonomy in 1935 in British India agitation for civil liberties and political rights became stronger in Rajasthan. The process of uniting scattered states commenced from 1948 to 1956 when the States Reorganization Act was promulgated, first came Matsya Union (1948) consisting of a fraction of states, slowly and gradually other states merged with this Union. By 1949, Major states like Bikaner, Jaipur, Jodhpur. and Jaisalmer joined this Union making it the United State of Greater Rajasthan. Ultimately in 1958, the present state of Rajasthan formally came into being, with Ajmer state, the Abu Road Taluka and Sunel Tappa joining it.

The entire western flank of the state borders with Pakistan, while Punjab in north, Haryana in north-east, Uttar Pradesh in east and Madhya Pradesh in south-east and Gujarat in south-west of the state.

Agriculture

Estimated total sown area in the state is 241.21 lakh hectare and estimated foodgrain production for 182.76 lakh m. tonnes in the year 2014-2015. Principal crops in the state are wheat, barley, jowar, millet, maize, gram, oilseeds, kharif pulses and cotton. Cultivation of vegetable and citrus fruits such as orange and malta have also picked up over last few years. Red chilies, mustard, cumin seeds and methi are commercial crops.

Industry

Endowed with a rich culture, Rajasthan is also rich in minerals and is fast emerging on the industrial scenario of the country. Some of the important Central undertaking are Hindustan Zinc Smelter Plant at Devari (Udaipur), Chanderia (Chittorgarh), Hindustan Copper Plant at Khetri Nagar (Jhunjhunu), Hindustan Salt Ltd. at Sambhar (Jaipur), HMT Ltd. at Ajmer and Precision Instrument Factory at Kota. Small-scale industrial units numbering 4.16 lakh with a capital investment of ₹ 23,302 crore provides employment potential to about 18.74 lakh people as on March 2015. Major industries are textiles and woollens, engineering goods, electronic items, automobile, food processing, gems and jewellery, cement, marble slabs and tiles, glass & ceramics, oxygen, zink, fertilizers, railway wagons, ball bearings, water and electricity metres, sulphuric acid, handicraft items, television sets, synthetic yarn, insulators, stainless steel, re-rolling, steel-foundry and insulting bricks. Besides precious and semi-precious stones, caustic soda, calcium carbide, nylon and tyers, etc. are other important industries.

Rajasthan has rich deposits of zinc concentrates, emerald, garnet, gypsum, silver, asbestos, felspar and mica. The state also abounds in exports, so Exports Promotion Industrial Park of the state has been established and made operational at Sitapura (Jaipur), Boranada (Jodhpur). Inland Container Depots have been established at Jaipur, Bhilwara, Jodhpur, and Bhiwadi (Alwar) to promote the exporters. Special Economic Zone for gems and jewellery at Sitapura (Jaipur) and Special Economic Zone for handicraft at Boranada (Jodhpur) have been established and Multipurpose Special Economic Zone "Mahendra World City" has been established in PPP model at Jaipur.

Minerals

The state is one of the leading mineral producing states in India. The state has a glorious heritage in the field of mining and is second only to Jharkhand as regards to mineral wealth. The state is conferred as museum of minerals; having resources of both metallic and non-metallic minerals including building stones and also resources of radioactive minerals, lignite, petroleum and natural gas. Important minerals with which the name of state is associated are non-ferrous metals such as lead-zinc, copper, ferromagnesian metals such as tungsten, a number of industrial minerals and different varieties of dimensional and decorative stones. There are 79 varieties of minerals available out of which 57 are produced commercially. Presently it is the sole producer of lead-zinc, wollastonite, calcite and selenite and leading producer of silver, gypsum, marble, ochre, ball clay, rock phosphate, cadmium and feldspar in the country. Different varieties of marble, granite, sandstone and Kota stone of the state has a large demand not only in the country but also world over. With the discovery of oil and natural gas in western Rajasthan the state has become the second highest producer of crude oil after Bombay High.

More than 85 per cent of the country's potash, lead-zinc, silver and wollastonite resources are located in the state. The state possess substantial share of the total resources of potash (94 per cent), lead-zinc ore (89 per cent), wollastonite (88 per cent), silver ore (87 per cent), gypsum (82 per cent), fuller's earth (74 per cent), diatomite (72 per cent), feldspar (66 per cent), marble (64 per cent), asbestos (61 per cent), copper ore (50 per cent), calcite (50 per cent), talc-soapstone-steatite (49 per cent), granite (42 per cent), ball clay (38 per cent), rock phosphate (30 per cent), fluorite (29 per cent), tungsten ore (27 per cent), laterite (26 per cent), gold ore (primary) (23 per cent), mica (21 per cent) and china clay (16 per cent).

Irrigation

By the end of March, 2015 irrigation potential of 38.22 lakh hectares was created in the state through major, medium and minor irrigation projects. During the year 2014-15 additional irrigation potential of 10969 hectares (including Indira Gandhi Nahar Project) were created.

Power

The installed power capacity in the state has become 15,986.87 MW upto March, 2015 in which 5,357.35 MW is produced from state owned projects, 853.44 MW from collaboration projects, 2,803.47 MW from the allocation from central power generating stations, 3,916.61 MW from wind, solar and biomass projects and 3,056.00 MW from private sector projects.

Mahatma Gandhi National Rural Employment Guarantee Scheme

In first phase Mahatma Gandhi National Rural Employment Guarantee Scheme was initiated in 2006 by Government of India in six districts—Banswara, Dungarpur, Jhalawar, Karouli, Sirohi and Udaipur. In second phase this scheme was initiated in 2007 in other six districts Barmer, Chittorgarh, Jaisalmer, Jalore, Sawai Madhopur and Tonk. In third phase this scheme was initiated in 2008 in rest of the districts of the state.

Transport

Roads : The estimated total length of roads was 2,07,019 km.

Railways : Jodhpur, Jaipur, Bikaner, Sawai Madhopur, Kota, Bharatpur and Udaipur are main railway junctions of the state. Total length of railway line is 5,871.65 km (4801.18 km broad gaze, 983.71 km gaze and 86.76 km narrow gaze) in the state.

Jaipur Metro : Phase I-A. The metro track work has been completed from Mansarovar to Jaipur Railway Station with total route length 9.72 km. Phase I-B. Metro track work from Chandpole to Badi Chaupar is in progress with total route length of 2.35 km.

Aviation : All eminent cities are regular connected with Jaipur airport under domestic air services in which Delhi, Mumbai, Ahemdabad, Kolkata, Chennai. Hyderabad, Bengaluru, Pune and Guwahati are important domestic air services. International air services are also available for Dubai, Mascutt and Sharjah from Jaipur airport.

Festivals

Rajasthan is a land of festivals and fairs, besides that national festivals of Holi, Deepawali, Vijayadashmi, Christmas, etc., auspicious days related to deities of gods and goddesses, saintly figures, folk heroes and heroines are celebrated. Important fairs are Teej, Gangaur, Holi-Dhulandi, Kite and Rajasthan Divas (Jaipur), annual Urs of Ajmer Sherif and Galiakot Pushkar Fair (Ajmer), Ramdevji Cattel Fair (Nagaur), Camel Festival (Bikaner), Desert Festival (Jaisalmer), Beneshwar Fair (Dungarpur), Braj-Holi Festival (Bharatpur), Kailadevi Fair, Shri Mahaveer fair (Karouli), Ranakpur Festival, Godwar Festival (Pali), Mewar Festival (Udaipur), Summer and Winter Festival Mount Abu (Sirohi), Kajli Teej and Bundi Festival (Bundi), Dussehra Festival and Adventure Festival (Kota), Matsya Festival (Alwar), Marwar Festival (Jodhpur), Chandrabhaga Fair (Jhalawar), Jambheshwar Fair and Koloyat Fair (Nokha Bikaner) and Khatu Shyamji Fair (Khatu-Sikar), etc.

Tourists Centres

Jaipur, Jodhpur, Udaipur, Bikaner, Mount Abu (Sirohi), Ranthambhore National Park (Tiger Reserve)-(Sawai Madhopur), Sariska Tiger National Park (Alwar), Keoladeo National Park (Bharatpur), Ajmer, Jaisalmer, Pali, Bundi, Kota, Jhalawar, Shekhawati (Sikar) and Chittorgarh are important places of tourists interest in the state.

O. W.: http://www.rajasthan.gov.in

GOVERNMENT

Governor	: Shri Kalyan Singh	*Chief Secretary*	: Shri O. P. Meena
Chief Minister	: Smt. Vasundhara Raje	*Jurisdiction of High Court*	: Rajasthan

SIKKIM

Area	: 7,096 sq km	*Population*	: 6.11 lakh (provisional census 2011)
Capital	: Gangtok	*Principal Languages*	: Lepcha, Bhutia, Nepali, Limboo, Sikkimese

History and Geography

The early history of Sikkim starts in the 13th century with the signing of a blood-brotherhood treaty between the Lepcha Chieftain Thekong Tek and Bhutia Chieftain Khye-Bumsa at Kabi Lungtsok in North Sikkim. This follows the historic visit of three revered Lamas to Yuksam in 1641 in West Sikkim where they consecrated Phuntsog Namgyal, a sixth generation descendant of Khye-Bumsa as the first Chogyal of Sikkim, thus heralding the beginning of the Namgyal dynasty in Sikkim. With the march of history, events in Sikkim saw the process of democratisation and became an integral part of the Indian Union in 1975. Sikkim, the land blessed by Guru Padmasambhava during his sojourn to Tibet in 8th century, are inhabited by people from different communities and live in total harmony. Sikkim is perhaps the most peaceful state of the Indian Union to promote communal harmony, a feat which is much to be expected in a plural society like India.

The world's third highest mountain, Khangchendzonga, is regarded as the guardian deity of Sikkim. Sikkim is one of the 18 biodiversity hotspots in the world. More than 5000 species of angiosperms are found in the state, nearly one third of the total species of angiosperms are found in the country. There are over 4,500 species of flowering plants, 362 species of ferns and allies, over 550 species of wild orchids, atleast 36 species of rhododendrons besides many variations and wild natural hybrids, 11 species of oaks, 30 species of primulas, 28 bamboos, over 700 species of butterflies, probably thrice as many moths, at least 48 species of freshwater fish, around 50 species of amphibians, over 80 reptiles, 600 species of birds and around 150 species of mammals in the state.

Rare and globally threatened snow leopard, Tibetan argali sheep, red panda, as well as highest altitude domesticated bovid, the yak, black-necked crane and fairrieanum orchid are some of the important species found here.

Tourism

Situated in the eastern Himalayas, Sikkim is one of the most beautiful states of the Indian Union. It is home to the third highest mountain in the world, Mt. Khangchendzonga which is also worshipped as the guardian deity. Sikkim is adorned with snowy mountains, luxuriant forests with exotic flora and fauna, pristine waterfalls, sacred lakes, holy caves, medicinal hot-springs, cascading rivers and gentle streams making it a tourist destination for all seasons. An interlace of mixed culture of various communities residing here, the state celebrates festivals and activities of each other with grand fervour. There are tours for everyone, from those seeking solitude for meditation to the adventurous or those seeking leisure holiday. For the more adventurous there is trekking in the mountains, river rafting, bird watching, mountain biking, rock climbing, paragliding and angling as well as the mountain flights for experiencing the snow clad mountains.

Agriculture

In the agriculture sector, the state has made immense breakthrough with the introduction of crops like baby corn, sweet corn, etc., bringing manifold increase in income to the farming community. Focus is on crops which can grow under moisture stress conditions and which have high global demands of the likes of buckwheat, millet and such other cereals.

Horticulture

The production of fruits has increased from 5250 tonnes to 22240 recording to growth of 323 per cent. Vegetable production has increased from 22130 tonnes to 78820 tonnes registering 256 per cent growth. In floriculture a record growth of 200 ha with production of over 230 lakh numbers of cut flowers and planting materials.

Irrigation and Power

The Department of Irrigation and Flood Control has covered 3866.68 hectares of agricultural land in eleventh five year plan. 225 numbers of schemes were sanctioned under the accelerated irrigation.

Power

The total hydro power potential of Sikkim as assessed by Central Water Commission, is around 8,000 MW. With the view to harness the immense hydro power potential of the state, the Government of Sikkim in the year 2004 constituted the Hydro Committee to examine the various aspects related to hydro power development and make recommendations for early implementation of the hydro power projects.

Transport

Roads : Gangtok is connected by roads with Darjeeling district of West Bengal and also with all the district headquarters within Sikkim. The total road length of the state is 3,672.32 km and 216 bridges, which includes 873.40 km road maintained by the Border Roads Organisation.

Railways and Aviation : The closest railway stations are Siliguri (113 km) and New Jalpaiguri (125 km) connecting Kolkata, Delhi and other important cities and Bagdogra airport. Greenfield airport is being constructed at Pakyong in East Sikkim. There is a regular helicopter service between Gangtok and Bagdogra.

Information Technology

The state government has made encouraging steps to improve the lives of common people through several IT-oriented projects. To meet the objectives various initiatives have been taken like the establishment of 45 community service centres and state-wide area network all across even in remote areas as a step to bring IT to the grassroot level of people. This has greatly increased the government's interface with the public and enhanced the quality of some state services. CSC in Sherethang which is an achievement for the state government and its citizens, is declared as the highest cyber cafe in the world by the Limca Book of Records.

O. W.: http://www.sikkim.gov.in

GOVERNMENT

Governor	:	Shri Shrinivas Patil	*Chief Secretary*	:	Dr A.K. Srivastava
Chief Minister	:	Shri Pawan Chamling	*Jurisdiction of High Court*	:	Sikkim

TAMIL NADU

Area	:	1,30,060 sq km	*Population*	:	7.21 crore (census 2011)
Capital	:	Chennai	*Principal Language*	:	Tamil

History and Geography

Tamil Nadu has a hoary antiquity. Though early *Sangam* classics throw historical references it is only from the Pallavas we pass to recorded history. South India had remained under the hegemony of the Cholas, the Cheras and the Pandyas for centuries. The Pallavas held supremacy from about the second quarter of the fourth century AD. They were the originators of the famous Dravidian style of temple architecture. The last Pallava ruler was Aparajita in whose reign the later Cholas under Vijayalaya and Aditya asserted themselves by about the 10th century. At the end of the 11th century, Tamil Nadu was ruled by several dynasties like the Chalukyas, Cholas and Pandyas. In the two centuries that followed, the imperial Cholas gained paramountcy over South India.

Muslims gradually strengthened their position, which led to the establishment of the Bahamani Sultanate, by the middle of the 14th century. At the same time, the Vijayanagar Kingdom quickly consolidated itself and extended its sway over the whole of South India and at the close of the century, Vijayanagar became the supreme power in South. However, it crumbled at the battle of Talikota in 1564 to the confederate forces of the Deccan Sultans.

Even during the period of the tumultuous confusion that followed the battle of Talikota, European commercial interest had appeared as rivals in the area of South India. The Portuguese, the Dutch, the French and the English came in quick succession and established trading centres known as 'Factories'. East India Company which had established their factory at Masulipatnam, now in Andhra Pradesh, in 1611 gradually annexed territories by encouraging enmity among the native rulers. Tamil Nadu was one of the first of British settlements in India. The state is the successor to the old Madras Presidency which in 1901 covered the bulk of the southern peninsula. The composite Madras state was later reorganised and the present Tamil Nadu was formed.

Tamil Nadu is bound on north by Andhra Pradesh and Karnataka, on west by Kerala, on east by the Bay of Bengal and on south by the Indian Ocean.

Agriculture

The Mettur Dam was opened in 2011 bringing an additional paddy area of 1,80,000 acres. Around 1,22,230 farmers are benefited. To reduce the burden of the farmers, 4 per cent VAT exemption to agricultural inputs and farm machineries. 63.40 lakh farmers are benefited.

Tourism

As a veritable treasure trove of art and culture, the state has always been a great attraction to offer to the tourists. It is the consummate expression of art and culture of past period than elsewhere in the country. The state possesses the glorious sculptures, frescoes and murals adorning walls and pillars, giant temple towers (gopurams). Tamil Nadu has multifarious tourist attractions which include 1076 kms of pristine coastline, more than 30,000 temples and places of worship date back beyond the beginning of the Christian era, waterfalls, wildlife sanctuaries, hill stations, dam sites, arts, exotic culture, beautifully made handicrafts and handlooms, heritage, cuisine, business opportunities, etc.

To facilitate the visiting tourists, Tamil Nadu Tourism is making a concerted effort in improving the basic infrastructure and services in a big way in all important tourist centres. Alternate demand through promotion of medical tourism, educational tourism, adventure tourism, rural tourism and business tourism also enabled a quantum leap in tourist arrivals.

Geology and Mining

Minerals form the basic resources for several important industries and contribute substantially to the Gross State Domestic Product and Industrial Growth. Minerals are considered to be the backbone for the economic growth and deemed to be the wealth of the country. The developmental activities of the state and its economic prosperity are reflected by the availability of mineral, wealth and its prudent exploitation.

The state is endowed with several industrial minerals like lignite, limestone, garnet sand, silica sand, quartz and feldspar, graphite, oil and natural gas, magnesite, iron ore, etc., and also common use minor mineral deposits including world famous black granite and multi colour granite deposits which enabled in setting up of cement, refractory, glass, ceramic and granite polishing industries.

Transport

Roads: The length of road network under the control of Highway Department is 62,294 km.

Southern Railway : (1) Total length of route km 3846 km

(2) Running Track kms as on March 2015 : 4943 km

The major stations are: Chennai Central, Tiruchirappalli, Madurai, Tirunelveli, Nagarkoil, Coimbatore , Erode, Salem, Jolarpettai, Katpadi and Arakkonam.

Ports: Major ports are Chennai, Ennore and Thoothukudi. There are 23 declared minor ports including 7 government. Minor ports namely Cuddalore, Nagapattinam, Rameswaram, Pamban, Colachel Kanniyakumari and Valinokkam. There are 16 declared captive minor ports including Kattupalli, Ennore Minor Port, PY-3 Oilfield and Thirukkadaiyur which are operational and others are at various stages of obtaining statutory clearances and development.

O. W.: http://www.tn.gov.in

GOVERNMENT

Governor	: Shri. Ch. Vidyasagar Rao	*Chief Secretary*	: Dr. P. Rama Mohana Rao
Chief Minister	: Shri O. Panneerselvam	*Jurisdiction of High Court*	: Madras High Court

TELANGANA

Area	: 114840 sq. km	*Population*	: 3,51,93,978 (as per 2011 census)
Capital	: Hyderabad	*Principal Languages*	: Telugu and Urdu

In 2014 Telangana was formed as 29th state of India with Hyderabad as its capital. Earlier Telangana was part of Andhra State as per the linguistic re-organisation of states in 1956. Telangana state has 10 districts including Hyderabad, Adilabad, Khammam, Karimnagar, Mahbubnagar, Medak, Nalgonda, Nizamabad, Rangareddy and Warangal.

History of Telangana

The name Telangana refers to the word Trilinga Desa, earned due to the presence of three ancient Shiva temples at Kaleswaram, Srisailam and Draksharamam. A more historical reason is that during the reign of Nizams the region was known as Telugu Angana to differentiate it from the areas where Marathi was spoken. The region has been ruled by great dynasties such as Sathavahanas, Kakatiyas, Chalukyas, Mughals, Qutubshahis, Asafjahis. The Kakatiyas contributions to architecture are considered very impressive. Among Kakatiyas, Prataparudra was a great ruler who ruled till AD 1323. The Satavahanas ruled Telangana region for about 400 years right from the 2nd century BC to beyond the 2nd century AD.

There have been several movements to revoke the merger of Telangana and Andhra, major ones occurred in 1969, 1972 and 2009. The movement for a new state of Telangana gained momentum over the decades. In 2009 the Government of India announced the process of formation of the Telangana. Violent protests led by people in the Coastal Andhra and Rayalaseema regions occurred immediately after the announcement, and the decision was put on hold in December, 2009. The movement continued in Hyderabad and other districts of Telangana. There have been large scale strikes, protests and demonstrations coupled with many suicides also demanding separate statehood.

In July, 2013 the process of formation of a separate state gained momentum. After various stages, the Bill was placed in the Parliament and in February, 2014 Andhra Pradesh Reorganization Act, 2014 Bill was passed by the Parliament for the formation of Telangana state comprising ten districts from north-western Andhra Pradesh.

Geography

Telangana is situated on the Deccan plateau in the central stretch of the eastern seaboard of the Indian Peninsula. It covers 114,800 sq km (44,300 sq miles). The region is drained by two major rivers, with about 79 per cent of the Godavari river catchment area and about 69 per cent of the Krishna river catchment area, but most of the land is arid due to higher elevation of most of the state compared to rivers. Telangana is also drained by several minor rivers such as the Bhima, the Manjeera and the Musi. The state is surrounded by Maharashtra on north and north-west; Karnataka on the west; Chhattisgarh on the north-east and Odisha lies on its west.

Agriculture

Rice is the major food crop of the state. Other important crops are tobacco, mango, cotton and sugarcane. The major Kharif coarse cereals maize, jowar, bajra, ragi are produced in the State. Out of the total geographical area 40.5 per cent is under net area sown, 23.9 per cent is under forests, 10.5 per cent is under current fallow lands, 7.7 per cent is under non-agricultural uses and 5.4 per cent is under barren and uncultivable land. Net cropped area is 46.54 lakh hectares. Agriculture production depends upon the distribution of rainfall. The influence of south-west monsoon is predominant.

Arts and Crafts

Handicrafts have been an integral part of the state. The region offers many astounding handicrafts like bidri crafts, banjara needle crafts, dokra metal crafts, nirmal arts, bronze castings, lacquer ware, etc. Be it an intricate needle craft or the surprising bronze castings, metal craft or the classic stone craft, Telangana has a wide assortment of handicrafts.

Festivals

'Bathukamma' is a colourful and vibrant festival and this unique festival of flowers stands as a symbol of cultural identity. "Bonalu" is an annual Hindu festival celebrated in the state in which Goddess Mahakali is worshipped. Dussehra, Samakka Saarakka Jaathara, Peerla Panduga, Ramzan are also largely celebrated in Telangana.

O. W.: http://www.telangana.gov.in

GOVERNMENT

Governor	:	Shri E.S.L. Narasimhan	*Chief Secretary*	:	Dr. Rajiv Sharma
Chief Minister	:	Shri Kalvakuntla Chandrashekar Rao	*Jurisdiction of High Court*	:	Hyderabad High Court

TRIPURA

Area	:	10,486 sq km	*Population*	:	36.74 lakh (prov. census 2011)
Capital	:	Agartala	*Principal Languages*	:	Bengali and Kokborok

History

Tripura has its unique tribal culture and a fascinating folklore. The history of Tripura can be learnt from *Rajmala* chronicles of King Tripura and writings of historians. There are references of Tripura even in the *Mahabharata* and the *Puranas*. According to *Rajmala*, the rulers were known by the surname *Fa* meaning *father*. There is a reference to rulers of Bengal helping Tripura kings in the 14th century. Kings of Tripura had to face frequent Mughal invasions with varying successes. They defeated the Sultans of Bengal in several battles. Nineteenth century marked the beginning of the modern era in Tripura when King Maharaja Bir Chandra Kishore Manikya Bahadur modelled his administrative set-up on the British India pattern and brought in various reforms. His successors ruled Tripura till 15 October 1949 when the state merged with the Indian Union. Initially, a part 'C' State, it became a centrally administered territory with the Reorganisation of States in 1956. In 1972, Tripura attained the status of a full-fledged state.

Tripura is strategically situated between the river valleys of Myanmar and Bangladesh. Encircled almost on three sides by Bangladesh, it is linked with Assam and Mizoram in the north-east.

Agriculture

The economy of Tripura is primarily dependent on agriculture. 24 per cent land is being utilized by this sector, and 51 per cent population is dependent on agriculture for their livelihood.

Irrigation

Tripura is predominantly a hilly state having geographical area of 10,49,169 hectare. Amid the undulating terrain the recently assessed land under cultivation is 2,55,241 hectares. Presently assessed irrigable land is 1,17,00 hectares.

Tourism

Tripura is a small but picturesque state in the north eastern region of the country. The area is about 10,491,69 sq km. to its north, south and south east it has an international boundary with Bangladesh while to its east; it shares a common boundary with two states of Assam and Mizoram. There are 19 ethnic tribes, Bengali, Manipuri and others, inhabiti g this panoramic tiny state.

The scenic beauty of Tripura, its rich and varied culture, archaeology and architecture, its handloom and handicraft which is exquisite in colour, excellent in design and craftsmanship, its verdant forests, and lakes, its excellent bracing climatic conditions, its enhancing and abounding floral treasures and panoramic view points and above all its very hospitable ethnic population are so attractive that anyone who visits the state once cannot resist his temptation to come oftener.

O. W.: http://www.tripura.gov.in

GOVERNMENT

Governor :	Shri Tathagata Roy	*Chief Secretary*:	Shri Yashpal Singh
Chief Minister :	Shri Manik Sarkar	*Jurisdiction of High Court* :	High Court of Tripura

UTTARAKHAND

Area :	53,483 sq km	*Population* :	1.01 crore (census 2011)
Capital :	Dehradun	*Principal Languages* :	Hindi, English, Garhwali, Kumauni

History

Uttarakhand finds mention in the ancient Hindu scriptures as Kedarkhand, Manaskhand and Himavant. The Kushanas, Kunindas, Kanishka, Samudra Gupta, Pauravas, Katuris, Palas, Chandras and Panwars and the British have ruled it in turns. It is often called the Land of the Gods *(Dev Bhoomi)* because of its various holy places and abundant shrines. The hilly regions of Uttarakhand offer pristine landscapes to the tourists. Uttarakhand was earlier a part of the United Province of Agra and Awadh which came into existence in 1902. In 1935, the name of state was shortened to the United Province. In January 1950, the United Province was renamed as Uttar Pradesh and Uttaranchal remained a part of Uttar Pradesh before it was carved out in 2000. It is incepted as the 27th state of India.

Located in the foothills of the Himalayas, the state has international boundaries with China (Tibet) in the north and Nepal in the east. On its north-west lies Himachal Pradesh while on the south is Uttar Pradesh.

Agriculture

About 90 per cent of the population depends on agriculture. The total cultivated area in the state is 7,67,459 hectare.

Industry and Minerals

The state is rich in mineral deposits like limestone, marble, rock phosphate, dolomite, magnesite, copper greyphyte, gypsum, etc. The number of small-scale industries is 37,928 providing employment to 162453 persons, with an investment of ₹ 6280.48 crore.

Irrigation and Energy

Agricultural land under irrigation is 5,61,733 hectare. The state has excellent potential for hydropower generation. There are a number of hydroelectric projects on the rivers Yamuna, Bhagirathi, Bhilangana, Alaknanda, Mandakini, Saryu Gauri, Kosi and Kali generating electricity. Total hydropower potential is approx. 25,450 MW. Projects allotted to various agencies are 13,667 MW. Out of 15,761 villages, 15,298 villages have been electrified.

Transport

Roads : The total length of metalled roads is 33,914 km. The length of PWD roads is 25,665 km. The length of roads built by local bodies is 2674 km.

Railways : The main railway stations are Dehradun, Haridwar, Roorkee, Kotdwar, Kashipur, Udhamsingh Nagar, Haldwani, Ramnagar and Kathgodam.

Aviation : There are air strips at Jolly Grant (Dehradun) and Pantnagar (Udham Singh Nagar). Air strips at Naini-Seni (Pithoragarh), Gauchar (Chamoli) and Chinyalisaur (Uttarkashi) are under construction. Pawan Hans Ltd. is also operating helicopter service from Rudraprayag to Kedarnath for pilgrims.

Festivals

The world-famous *Kumbh Mela/Ardh Kumbh Mela* is held at Haridwar at every twelfth/sixth year interval. Other prominent fairs/festivals are Devidhura Mela (Champawat), Purnagiri Mela (Champawat), Nanda Devi Mela (Almora), Gauchar Mela (Chamoli), Baisakhi (Uttarkashi), Magha Mela (Uttarkashi), Uttaraini Mela (Bageshwar), Vishu Mela (Jaunsar Bhabar), Peerane-Kaliyar (Roorkee), and Nanda Devi Raj Jat Yatra held every twelfth year.

Tourist Centres

Prominent places of pilgrimage/tourist interests are Gangotri, Yamunotri Badrinath, Kedarnath, Haridwar, Rishikesh, Hemkund Sahib, Nanakmatta, etc. Kailash Mansarovar Yatra can be performed through Kumaon region. The world-famous Valley of Flowers, Pindari Glacier, Roop Kund, Dayara Bugyal, Auli and hill stations like Mussoorie, Dehradun, Chakrata, Nainital, Ranikhet, Bageshwar, Bhimtal, Kausani, Lansdowne, etc. are the other tourist destinations.

O. W.: http://www.uk.gov.in

GOVERNMENT

Governor	: Dr. K. K. Paul	*Chief Secretary*	: Shri Shatrughna Singh
Chief Minister	: Shri Harish Rawat	*Jurisdiction of High Court*	: Uttarakhand

UTTAR PRADESH

Area	: 2,36,286 sq km	*Population*	: 19.98 crore (prov. census 2011)
Capital	: Lucknow	*Principal Languages*	: Hindi and Urdu

History

The history of Uttar Pradesh is very ancient and interesting. It is recognised in the later Vedic Age as Brahmarshi Desha or Madhya Desha. Many great sages of the Vedic times like Bhardwaja, Gautam, Yagyavalkaya, Vashishtha, Vishwamitra and Valmiki flourished in this state. Several sacred books of the Aryans were also composed here. In the sixth century BC Uttar Pradesh was associated with two new religions—Jainism and Buddhism. It was at Sarnath that Buddha preached his first sermon and laid the foundations of his order and it was in Kushinagar in Uttar Pradesh where Buddha breathed his last. Several centres in Uttar Pradesh like Ayodhya, Prayag, Varanasi and Mathura became reputed centres of learning. In the medieval period Uttar Pradesh passed under Muslim rule and led the way to new synthesis of Hindu and Islamic cultures. Ramananda and his Muslim disciple Kabir, Tulsidas, Surdas and many other intellectuals contributed to the growth of Hindi and other languages.

Uttar Pradesh preserved its intellectual excellence even under the British administration. The British combined Agra and Oudh into one province and called it United Provinces of Agra and Oudh. The name was shortened to the United Provinces in 1935. In January 1950, the United Provinces was renamed as Uttar Pradesh. The state is bounded by Uttarakhand and Himachal Pradesh in the north, Haryana in the west, Madhya Pradesh in the south and Bihar in the east. Uttar Pradesh can be divided into two distinct regions (i) Southern Hills and (ii) Gangetic Plains.

Agriculture

Agriculture is the main occupation of 66 per cent of the population. The net cultivated area is 164.17 lakh hectare.

Industry and Minerals

There were 6,12,338 small scale industries involving a total investment of 7172 crores. Under the public sector, mining of limestone, magnesite, coal, rock phosphate, dolomite and silicon-sand is carried out. The bulk production of minor and some of the major minerals like limestone, silica-sand, magnesite, pyrophyllite and diaspora is mostly with the private sector. Important mineral based industries include large cement plants in Sonebhadra.

Irrigation and Power

UP Power Corporation, UP State Power Generation and UP Hydel Power Corporation had been formed by reorganising UP State Electricity Board. The total installed capacity has now been raised upto 5077 MW. Power is an important input to accelerate the process of economic growth. At the time of inception the total installed capacity of UPSEB, including thermal and hydro, was 2,635 MW which has now been raised to 5414 MW (derated 5,885.75 MW).

Transport

Roads : The total road length of PWD is 146728 km. This includes 3820 km of national highways, 8391 km of state highways, 119726 of other district roads and 134517 km of rural roads.

Railways : Lucknow is the main junction of the northern network. Other important railway junctions are Agra, Kanpur, Allahabad, Mughalsarai, Jhansi, Moradabad, Varanasi, Tundla, Gorakhpur, Gonda, Faizabad, Bareilly and Sitapur.

Aviation : There are airports at Lucknow, Kanpur, Varanasi, Allahabad, Agra, Jhansi, Bareilly, Hindon (Ghaziabad), Gorakhpur, Sarsawa (Saharanpur) and Fursatganj (Raebarelli).

Festivals

The biggest congregation, perhaps of the world, Kumbha Mela is held at Allahabad every twelfth year and Ardh Kumbh Mela every sixth year. Magh Mela is also held at Allahabad in January when the people come in large numbers to have a dip in the holy Sangam. Among other fairs is the fortnight long Jhoola fair of Mathura, Vrindavan and Ayodhya, when dolls are placed in gold and silver jhoolas or cradles. A dip in the Ganga on Kartik Poornamasi is supposed to be the holiest and there are big congregations at Garhmukteshwar, Soran, Rajghat, Kakora, Bithur, Kanpur, Allahabad, Varanasi and Ayodhya. A famous cattle fair is held at Bateswar in Agra district. Dewa in Barabanki district has become famous because of the Muslim saint Waris Ali Shah. Besides, important festivals of the Hindus, Muslims, etc. are widely celebrated in the state.

Tourist Centres

Besides ancient places of pilgrimage like Varanasi, Vindhyachal, Ayodhya, Chitrakoot, Prayag, Naimisharanya, Mathura, Vrindavan, Dewa Sharief, Dargah of Sheikh Saleem Chisti in Fatehpur Sikri, Sarnath, Shravasti, Kushinagar, Sankisa, Kampil, Piprahwa and Kaushambi, places like Agra, Ayodhya, Sarnath, Varanasi, Lucknow, Jhansi, Gorakhpur, Jaunpur, Kannauj, Mahoba, Devgarh, Bithur, and Vindhyachal have rich treasures of Hindu and Islamic architecture and culture.

O. W.: http://www.up.gov.in

GOVERNMENT

Governor	:	Shri Ram Naik	*Chief Secretary*	:	Shri Rahul Prasad Bhatnagar
Chief Minister	:	Shri Akhilesh Yadav	*Jurisdiction of High Court*	:	Allahabad High Court

WEST BENGAL

Area	:	88,752 sq km	*Population*	:	9.13 crore (prov. census 2011)
Capital	:	Kolkata	*Principal Language*	:	Bangla

History

The name of Bengal or *Bangla* is derived from the ancient kingdom of Vanga, or Banga. However, Stone Age tools dating back 20,000 years have been excavated in the state. The region was settled by Dravidian, Tibet-Burman, and Austro-Asiatic peoples and was a part of the Vanga kingdom of ancient India. It was a part of Magadha empire. It was one of the four main kingdoms of India during the times of Mahaveera and Buddha, and consisted of several *Janapadas*. Bengal was referred to as Gangaridai by the ancient Greeks around 100 BC, meaning, speculatively, a land with the river Ganga in its heart. The first recorded independent King of Bengal was Shashanka, reigning around the early 7th century. After a period of anarchy, the Buddhist Pala dynasty ruled the region for four hundred years, followed by a shorter region of the Hindu Sena dynasty.

Islam came to Bengal in 12th century by Sufi missionaries. Later, occasional Muslim raiders reinforced the process of conversion by building mosques, madrassas and Sufi Khanqahh. Bengal was ruled by various Muslim rulers and governors till the Mughal period in the 16th century.

History of modern Bengal begins with the advent of Europeans, more precisely, with the English trading companies. The Battle of Plassey in 1757 changed the course of history when the English first gained a strong foothold in Bengal and India as well. Bengal was partitioned in 1905 to achieve some political returns. The land frontiers touch Bangladesh in the east and are separated from Nepal in the west, Bhutan lies in the north-east, while Sikkim is on the north. On the west are the states of Bihar and Jharkhand, while in the south lies Odisha and the Bay of Bengal washes its southern frontiers.

Agriculture

Agriculture is the main source of income for about 70 per cent of the population. Jute and rice are the principal crops grown in the state, along with tea, maize, tobacco and sugarcane. The state government is concerned with activities relating to policy decisions on agricultural production and productivity, and its extension through technology generation, transfer of technology, ensuring availability and timely distribution of agriculture inputs specially seeds, fertilizers, subsidy, credit, etc., along with support service through soil testing, soil conservations, water conservations, seed testing, seed certification, plant production, quality control of fertilizers and pesticides, etc.

Industry

The state policy on industrial promotion and economic development welcomes foreign technology and investment, private sector investment in power generation, improvement and upgradation of industrial infrastructure. The thrust areas are petrochemicals and downstream industries, electronics and information technology, iron and steel, metallurgical and engineering, textile, leather and leather products, food processing, medicinal plants, edible oil, vegetable processing and aquaculture.

Power and Irrigation

Provision of electricity is vital for the socio-economic development as it accelerates economic growth, generates employment, eliminates poverty and is an essential input for human development. The power sector in West Bengal is predominantly thermal in view of the easy and cheaper availability of cost; the state has an adverse hydel-thermal power mix of 3:97. Significant ground has been broken in the renewable energy sector. WBREDA, the nodal agency for implementation of technology demonstration projects in the state, have benefited a large number of remote villages in the Sundarbans, parts of West Midnapur and Bankura and areas of Malda, Murshidabad.

Transport

Transport Department is primarily responsible for providing better transportation facilities both for passengers and goods by way of formulation and implementation of policies and creation of transport oriented infrastructures. The state transport undertakings are playing a pivotal role in social commitment. The Department has taken some initiatives to improve the scenario like, computerization of motor vehicles department, road safety schemes, bus stand schemes, TOIP schemes, pollution control, replacement of existing 2-stroke auto rickshaws by 4-stroke auto rickshaws to reduce automobile pollution, replacement of buses more than 15 years old, etc.

O. W.: http://www.westbengal.gov.in

GOVERNMENT

Governor	: Shri Keshari Nath Tripathi	*Chief Secretary* :	Shri Basudeb Banerjee
Chief Minister	: Km. Mamata Banerjee	*Jurisdiction of High Court* :	Calcutta High Court

ANDAMAN AND NICOBAR ISLANDS

Area	: 8,249 sq km	*Population* :	3,79,944 (2001 census)
Capital	: Port Blair	*Principal Languages* :	Hindi, Nicobarese, Bengali, Tamil, Malayalam, Telugu

History and Geography

The union territory of the Andaman and Nicobar Islands is situated between 6° and 14° latitude and 92° and 94° longitude. The Islands located north of 10° north latitude are known as Andaman Group of Islands while islands located south of 10° north latitude are called Nicobar Group of Islands. The climate of the Islands can be defined as humid, tropical coastal climate. The Islands receive rainfall from both the south-west and north-east monsoons and maximum precipitation is between May and December.

The original inhabitants of Islands lived in the forests on hunting and fishing. There are four Negrito tribes, viz., Great Andamanese, Onge, Jarawa and Sentinalese in the Andaman Group of Islands and two Mongoloid tribes, viz. Nicobarese and Shompens in the Nicobar Group of Islands.

Agriculture

Out of the geographical area of 8249 sq.km only 6 per cent i.e., around 50,000 ha which has been reduced to 47,000 ha (of the Tsunami 2004) is at present under agriculture. Paddy, the main food crop, is mostly cultivated in Andaman Group of Islands, whereas coconut and arecanut are the cash crops of Nicobar Group of Islands. Field crops, namely, pulses, oilseeds and vegetables are grown followed by paddy during rabi season. Different kinds of fruits such as mango, sapota, orange, banana, papaya, pineapple and root crops are grown on hilly land. Spices, viz. pepper, clove, nutmeg and cinnamon are grown under multitier cropping system. Rubber, red oil, palm and cashew are grown on a limited scale in these Islands.

Forests

Recorded forest is 7,171 sq km of the total geographical area of the Islands. Many types of forests are found, such as tropical wet evergreen, tropical semi-evergreen, moist deciduous, littoral mangrove and swamp forests. A large variety of timbers are also found. The most valuable timbers are padauk and gurjan. These species are not found in Nicobar.

Wildlife

There are 96 wildlife sanctuaries, 9 national parks and 1 biosphere reserve in these Islands. Mammals—out of 55 terrestrial and 7 marine mammal species reported so far, 32 species are endemic. Birds—as many as 246 species and sub -species of birds are reported to inhabit these Islands and of these 99 species and sub-species are endemic. Reptiles - there are 76 terrestrial reptiles found here, of these, 24 species are endemic. Marine Life - Islands harbour more than 1,200 species of fish, 359 species of echinoderms, 1067 species of molusscs and many more lower forms of life. Among vertebrates dugongs, dolphins, whales, salt water crocodiles, sea turtles, sea snakes, etc., are common. So far, 424 reef species of corals belonging to 61 genus have been reported. Reefs are mostly fringing type on eastern coast and barrier type on the western coast.

Industry

There are 1833 registered MSMEs and handicrafts units. Two units are 100 per cent export oriented in the line of fish/prawn processing activity. Apart from this, there are shells and wood based handicraft units. SSI units are engaged in the production of paints and varnishes, mini flour mills, soft drinks and beverages, steel furniture and fixtures, readymade garments, steel gate grills and structures. MSMEs handicraft units are also engaged in shell crafts, bakery products, rice-milling, furniture-making, etc. The Andaman and Nicobar Islands Integrated Development Corporation in the public sector has spread its wings in the field of tourism, fisheries, industries and industrial financing and functions as authorized agents.

Transport

The Motor Transport Department operates from 14 stations in northern and southern Islands. The Department has a fleet of 264 buses in operation mainly in rural area. Computerized advanced ticketing for ATR express service is in operation since 2007 where advance tickets can be obtained.

Tourism

Andaman and Nicobar Islands have been recognised as an eco-friendly tourist's destination. As a tourist paradise, these Islands have something very special to offer like historic Cellular Jail, Ross and Havelock Islands. The Andaman tropical evergreen rain forests, beautiful silver sandy beaches, serpentine mangrove-lined creeks, marine life abounding in rare species of plants, animals, corals, etc. provide a memorable experience to the tourists. There is a tremendous scope for enjoying nature in the beach resorts, water sports and adventure water sports, adventure tourism like trekking, island camping, nature trail, scuba diving, etc.

Tourism Department runs guest houses in various parts for comfortable accommodation. The important places of tourist interest are Anthropological Museum, Marine Museum, Water Sports Complex, Gandhi Park, North Bay, Viper Island, Ross Island, Chidiyatapu, (Bird watching), Red Skin Island, Corbyn's Cove Beach, Islands like Neil Island, Havelock Island, Cinque, Little Andaman, Diglipur (Ross and Smith), etc.

The Islands are well connected to the mainland by air and sea. Air Deccan, Jetlite, Air India operate to Port Blair from Kolkata and Chennai. There are regular passengership services from Chennai, Kolkata and Vishakhapatnam.

O. W.: http://www.and.nic.in

GOVERNMENT

Lt. Governor	:	Prof. Jagdish Mukhi	*Chief Secretary*	:	Shri Anindo Majumdar
			Jurisdiction of High Court	:	Falls under the jurisdiction of Calcutta High Court

CHANDIGARH

Area	:	114 sq km	*Population*	:	10.55 lakh (census 2011)
Capital	:	Chandigarh	*Languages*	:	Hindi, Punjabi

History and Geography

Chandigarh is a fully grown town of most modern architectural splendour. The city nestles in a picturesque setting in the foothills of Shivalik hills and enjoys the popular epithet the "City Beautiful". Representative of modern architecture and town planning, the city is a creation of the French architect, Le Corbusier. Chandigarh and the area surrounding it, were constituted as a Union Territory on 1 November 1966. It serves as the joint capital of both Punjab and Haryana states. It shares its boundary on north and west by Punjab and on the east and south by Haryana.

Administration

Chandigarh Administration is moving on four broad fronts. First, it is its aim to provide, with the help of information technology, an accessible and transparent administration. Chandigarh was among the earliest to implement the provisions of the Right to Information Act. A number of services, for which citizens earlier had to go to government offices, are now available on computer and mobile phones. All rules are being reviewed to see what simplification can be carried out to make them user-friendly. The purpose is to minimise the exercise of discretion, and minimise the leg-work of the citizen in dealing with the administration.

Secondly, the administration is working towards a higher rate of economic growth by encouraging economic activities which provide greater value addition, such as knowledge based industries, high-end commercial activity, etc. Chandigarh already has the highest per capita income in the country.

Thirdly, the administration is seeking to provide infrastructural services such as electricity supply, water supply, health and educational services and public transport. Fourthly, the administration is all too conscious of the fact that the benefits of development do not reach everyone equally. Hence, there is a special emphasis on reaching out to those whom development has by-passed.

Transport

Chandigarh administration comprehending the need for a user-friendly transport system has decided to launch a Mass Rapid Transport System shortly. The UT administration and the state governments of Punjab and Haryana have come together for implementation of the project.

CTU has computerized 70 per cent of its working and is in the process of further computerization. The undertaking will also install a Global Positioning System to monitor its fleet in a phased manner.

Rural Development

In order to sensitize the poor and weaker sections of the society about the rights and different benefits being extended to them by the State Legal Services Authority, 14 legal awareness seminars have already been organized in different villages of the UT.

Cement concrete paving and underground drains in village Kajheri and Palsora have been completed. 70 per cent work in village Mauli Jagran has been completed.

Information Technology

Construction work of Chandigarh Administration's visionary project Rajiv Gandhi Chandigarh Technology Park is in full swing. Completion of Phase III will provide direct employment to 35,000 professionals, thereby increasing the direct employment of RGCTP to 67,000 and would create 2,00,000 indirect jobs in Chandigarh. The Entrepreneur Development Centre at the RGCTP is being set up over an area of 1.5 acre approximately.

Chandigarh has become a role model in using Information Technology to provide fast and user friendly services to the masses. Under the e-Governance initiatives of the Department, seven more Gram Sampark Centres have been set up in the villages of Dhanas, Khudda Jassu, Kaimbwala, Raipur Khurd, Raipur Kalan, Makhan Majra and Bahlana. Gram Sampark Centres in villages Palsora, Dadu Majra, Hallo Majra, Khuda Alisher, Daria, Mauli Jagran and Maloya are operative. The administration is working on energy conservation. A work order has been issued to the Tata BP Solar Ltd. for commissioning the Energy Park at the Botanical Garden. Under the solar lighting initiative, all street lights in the villages would be replaced with solar based street lights.

Social Welfare

Social Welfare has been a major focus of the administration. Many people-friendly and innovative schemes for them have been launched by the administration. To wipe out the menace of casteism and encourage the people for inter-caste marriage, a sum of ₹ 5,000 was granted to the married couples provided that one of the spouses belongs to SC community. The administration has enhanced the amount to ₹ 50,000.

Under the Balika Samridhi Yojana, a sum of ₹ 500 is being given to the newly born girl child in the BPL families. The Chandigarh administration has decided to set up a Preparatory School for Children with Special Needs (for 50 children) which will run in the premises of PRAYAS Building, Sector 38. The Vocational Training Centre for Street Children in Maloya with the capacity to provide training for 900 children is under construction. The administration has set up a child helpline.

Health

Telemedicine Project has been launched with the state-of-the art facilities at Government Medical College and Hospital, Sector 32, Chandigarh aiming to help needy patients to avail the expert advice of the doctors of specialized fields in PGI and ensuring them high-quality medical services. The Government Multi Speciality Hospital, Sector 16 has been upgraded by adding a Trauma Unit having 28 beds with emergency operation theatres. The administration has launched the project for improving the Monitorable Indicators of Reproductive and Child Health at a cost of ₹ 5,273 per mother and her child.

Seven more "state-of-the-art" operation theatres including pre-anesthesia, post- anesthesia rooms and a post-operative ward have been commissioned in Government Medical College and Hospital, Chandigarh. "SAMARTH", a residential house for mentally retarded individuals had also been set up in Sector 15, Chandigarh.

Industries

The administration is developing the Phase-III of the industrial area at the revenue estate of village Mauli Jagran.

Education

Chandigarh administration is coming up with its World Class Project, the multi institutional 'Chandigarh Education City' at Sarangpur with a total area of 130 acres. Administration has enhanced the attendance scholarship being given to girl students of general category from ₹ 30 per month to ₹ 250 per month for a period for classes 1st to 5th. For ensuring enrolment and education among scheduled caste boys and girls, administration has also decided to increase the attendance scholarship being given to the Scheduled Castes students studying in class 1st to 8th from ₹ 30 to ₹ 250 per month in the age group of 6 to 14 years.

It has been decided to increase the scholarship to the meritorious SC/ST students of Classes 9th to 12th; it has been now increased to ₹ 300 per month whereas it was ₹ 20 and ₹ 25 earlier.

Chandigarh administration has also decided to exempt the tuition fees of Muslims, Christians, Other Backward Classes, handicapped, ward of freedom fighters, ex-servicemen, widows and divorcees having family income below ₹ 1.5 lakh per year. For the children belonging to low income groups and slum based families, it has decided to give an incentive of ₹ 250 per month to rope in the children presently not enrolled in any school on their fresh enrolment.

Tourism

Administration has taken many innovative and novel measures like Wedding Tourism. With the focus on extending efficient medical, educational and entertainment oriented facilities, Administration is promoting cinematic tourism, sports tourism and medical tourism in a big way.

Power

Provision of sufficient electricity to all the residents is also getting attention of the administration. To improve the voltage profile and to reduce the load on the power distribution network of UT, the Electricity Wing had planned to add 80 MVAR Automatic Capacitor Banks at various existing 66 KV Grid Sub-Stations located at different points in the periphery of UT. Use of CFL is mandatory in all government buildings. Similarly, all institutional buildings will have to provide solar lighting in their parking spaces within their complexes.

O. W.: http://www.chandigarh.gov.in

GOVERNMENT

Administrator :	Shri.V.P. Singh Badnore	*Jurisdiction of High Court* :	Falls under jurisdiction of Punjab and Haryana High Court
Advisor to the Administrator :	Shri Parimal Rai		

DADRA AND NAGAR HAVELI

Area :	491 sq km	*Population* :	3. 44 lakh
Capital :	Silvassa	*Principal Languages* :	Gujarati, Hindi, English

History and Geography

The Portuguese ruled this territory until its liberation by the people in 1954. From 1954 till 1961 the territory functioned almost independently by what was known as "Free Dadra and Nagar Haveli administration". However, the territory was merged with the Indian Union in 1961 and since then is being administered by the Government of India as a Union Territory. After liberation from the Portuguese rule, a *Varishtha Panchayat* was working as an advisory body of the Administration. This was dissolved in August 1989 and a Pradesh Council for Dadra and Nagar Haveli District Panchayat and 11 Village Panchayats were constituted as per constitutional amendments. Dadra and Nagar Haveli has an area of 491 sq km and it is surrounded by Gujarat and Maharashtra. It consists of two pockets, namely, Dadra and Nagar Haveli. The nearest railway station is at Vapi which is 18 km from Silvassa, which is also the capital of this UT. Silvassa Municipal Council came in existence in 2006 and is formed of two towns namely– Silvassa and Amli. Another five villages viz. Dadra, Naroli, Samarvani, Mast and Rakholi are treated as non-statutory census towns in population census 2011.

Agriculture

Dadra and Nagar Haveli is a predominantly rural area with about 79 per cent tribal population. It has about 21,115 hectare under cultivation. Major crop is paddy (*Kharif*) while Nagli and hill millets are the other crops of the area. Among fruits mango, chiku, banana, etc. are also produced. Forests cover 40 per cent of the total geographical area. Sugarcane cultivation has also been taken up in a big way in the UT. Efforts are afoot to adopt a multiple cropping system in assured irrigated areas. The Wadi Development programme in the tribal area of both Dadra and Nagar Haveli is being implemented by the Bhartiya Agro Industries Foundation (BAIF) an NGO with the financial allocation from NABARD.

Industry

Prior to 1965-66 there was no industry. There were a few traditional craftsmen who used to make pots, leather items, viz. chappals, shoes and some other items of bamboo. Industrial development started on a low-key during 1967-68 with the establishment of an industrial estate under the cooperative sector by Dan Udyog Sahakari Sangh Ltd. Thereafter, three Government industrial estates were developed at Silvassa, Masat and Khadoli. With the inception of the economic liberalization policy, a real boost in industrial development was seen. There are 1863 small sector industrial units and 430 MSI/LSI units functioning in the Union Territory providing gainful employment to over 46,000 people.

Irrigation and Power

Prior to liberation of the territory, there was no irrigation facility and cultivators had to fully depend upon rainfall. After the merger of the territory with the Indian Union, adequate steps were taken under minor irrigation sector. So far 128 lift irrigation schemes have been completed creating an additional irrigation potential of 1,851 hectare. Under medium irrigation project viz. Damanganga Reservoir Project, about 115 km of minor canals and distributaries are falling in the union territory. Development works have been completed in field channels in all respects in 4,300 hectare and testing is done in 4,049 hectare.

After liberation, the administration commenced rural electrification work with the co-operation of the neighbouring state of Gujarat. The power demand is met by Gujarat Electricity Board through a single circuit from Vapi-Silvassa and distributed amongst limited number of consumers. The first 66 KV Sub-Station was established at Amli in 1979. With the commissioning of a new project all the villages are electrified.

Transport

The Union Territory depends heavily on Maharashtra and Gujarat road network as the territory can be accessed only after crossing these two states from Mumbai. At present road length is about 635 km out of which 570 km is surfaced. Almost all villages are connected with all-weather roads. The rail route from Mumbai to Ahmedabad links Vapi also. Mumbai is the nearest airport. Recently, the work of widening of roads has been taken up to meet the requirement of increasing vehicular traffic. To meet the need of rapid industrialisation, four-lane work has been taken up in Silvassa and adjoining areas, besides other spillover works.

Tourism

Tourism sector has been assigned high priority, keeping in view the dense forest area and favourable climate.

The prominent places of tourist interest are Tadekeshwar Shiva Mandir, Bindrabin, Deer Park at Khanvel, Vanganga Lake and Island Garden, Dadra, and Vanvihar Udhyan Mini Zoo, Bal Udhyan, Tribal Museum and Hirvavan Garden at Silvassa. To attract tourists, annual celebration of festivals like Tarpa and World Tourism Day is a regular event.

Festivals

Normally all festivals of Hindus, Muslims and Christians are celebrated in the territory, while tribals celebrate their own festivals. Diwaso is celebrated by Dhodia and Varli tribes and Raksha Bandhan is celebrated by Dhodia tribe.

Other festivals include Bhawada amongst Varlis, Koli tribes and Khali Puja by all tribes after harvesting of crops and Gram Devi before harvesting of crops.

O. W.: http://www.dnh.nic.in

GOVERNMENT

Administrator	:	Shri Vikram Dev Dutt
Jurisdiction of High Court	:	Falls under Bombay High Court

DAMAN AND DIU

Area	:	111 sq km	*Population*	:	2,42,911 (prov. census 2011)
Capital	:	Daman	*Principal Language*	:	Gujarati

History and Geography

Daman and Diu along with Goa was a colony held by the Portuguese even after Independence. In 1961, it was made an integral part of India. After Goa was conferred statehood on 30 May 1987, Daman and Diu was made a separate Union Territory. Daman lies about 193 km away from Mumbai. It is bound on the east by Gujarat, on the west by the Arabian Sea, on the north by the Kolak river and on the south by Kalai river. The neighbouring district of Daman is Valsad in Gujarat. Diu is an island connected by two bridges. The neighbouring district of Diu is Junagadh of Gujarat.

Agriculture and Irrigation

Total irrigated area is 393.93 ha and unirrigated is 3304.73 ha. Important field and garden crops are paddy, ragi, bajra, jowar, groundnut, pulses and beans, wheat, banana, sapota, mango, coconut and sugarcane. There are no major forests in the territory.

Industry and Power

There are 2930 small-scale and medium-scale industries in Daman and Diu. Two industrial areas have been developed by Omnibus Industrial Development Corporation at Daman. The other industrial areas are Dabhel, Bhimpore, Kachigam and Kadaiya.

All villages have been electrified. Daman and Diu have got adequate power allocation from Central sector power stations in western region.

Transport

Roads : The total length of roads is 191 km and 78 km respectively.

Railways : There is no railway link with Daman and Diu. The nearest railway station from Daman is Vapi on western railway on Mumbai-Delhi route. The nearest railway station from Diu is Delvada on metre-gauge.

Aviation : There are airports both in Daman and Diu. Diu is connected by air and there is regular air service from Mumbai.

Tourist Places

Important tourist places in Daman are Bom Jesus Church; Our Lady of Sea Church; Our Lady of Remedios Church; Forts of Moti Daman and Nani Daman; Jampore and Devka Beaches; Public Garden at Nani Daman and Moti Daman Jetty, Pargola Garden. Moti Daman; Amusement Park; Devka; Damanganga Tourist Complex, Kachigam; Satya Sagar Udyan; Mirasol Garden; Mirasol Water Park.

In Diu, St. Paul's Church; Diu Fort and Panikota Fort; Nagoa and Chakratirth and Children's Park at Ghoghla and Summer House are worth seeing.

O. W.: http://www.daman.nic.in

GOVERNMENT

Administrator	:	Shri Praful Patel
Jurisdiction of High Court	:	Falls under Bombay High Court

DELHI

Area	: 1,483 sq km	*Population*	:	1.68 crore (as per census 2011)
Capital	: Delhi	*Principal Languages*	:	Hindi, Punjabi, Urdu and English

History and Geography

Delhi finds prominent reference right from the times of the epic *Mahabharata*. Its control passed from one ruler/dynasty to another, beginning with the Mauryas, Pallavas, Guptas of Central India and then going on to the Turks of Afghan during the 13th to 15th centuries, and finally to the Mughals in the 16th century. In the latter half of the 18th century and early 19th century, British rule was established in Delhi. In 1911, Delhi became the centre of all activities after the capital was shifted from Kolkata (Calcutta). It was made a Union Territory in 1956. Lying in the northern part of the country, Delhi is surrounded by Haryana on all sides except the east where it borders with Uttar Pradesh. The 69th constitutional amendment is a milestone in Delhi's history as it got a Legislative Assembly with the enactment of the National Capital Territory Act, 1991.

Agriculture

The principal food crops are wheat, bajra, jowar, gram and maize. However, emphasis has now shifted from food crops to vegetables and fruit crops, dairy and poultry farming, floriculture, etc., as these are more remunerative than food crops in the territory.

Industry

Delhi is not only the largest commercial centre in northern India, but also the largest centre of small industries. These units manufacture a wide variety of items like television, tape recorders, light engineering machines and automobile parts, sports goods, bicycles and PVC goods including footwear, textiles, fertilizers, medicines, hosiery, leather goods, software, etc.

Delhi's new millennium industrial policy emphasizes setting up of high-tech and sophisticated industries in electronics, telecommunications, software industries, IT enabling services, etc. The industries, which are non-polluting and encourage high value addition and depend largely on skilled manpower are being promoted.

For the purpose of relocating industrial units functioning in residential non-conforming areas, the Government of NCT of Delhi took possession of 1900 acres of land at village Bawana, Holambi Kalan and Holambi Khurd for developing new industrial estates. Bawana industrial area developed by DSIDC is the largest in Asia and is spread over 1900 acres of land.

Irrigation and Power

Due to fast urbanisation of the rural areas of Delhi, cultivable command area under irrigation is getting reduced day by day. Two schemes, namely, "Keshopur Effluent Irrigation Scheme Phase-III" and "Improvement and Extension of Effluent Irrigation System from Coronation Treatment Plant" are under execution. Irrigation of about 350 hectare with state tube-wells and 1,376 hectare from effluent water is being provided in the rural area of NCT of Delhi. In addition about 4,900 hectare of land is being irrigated from western Yamuna Canal network.

The availability of power for Delhi from its own generating units at Rajghat Power Houses, IP Station and Gas Turbines including Badarpur Thermal Station is of the order of 850-900 MW. The remaining power is drawn from Northern Regional Grid. Delhi has also envisaged a number of generating projects to be taken up. Pragati Combined Cycle Power Project has been established at Indraprastha Estate. A 330 MW Pragati Power Project under construction is scheduled to be commissioned soon. To streamline the distribution of power, DVB has been privatised and Delhi is now served by two of the best electric utilities in India, BSES and Tata Power (NDPL).

Transport

Delhi is well connected by roads, rail and air with all parts of India. It has three airports—Indira Gandhi International Airport for the international flights, Palam Airport for domestic air services and Safdarjung Airport for training purposes. It has three important railway stations — Delhi Junction, New Delhi Railway Station and Nizamuddin Railway Station. Delhi has three interstate bus terminals at Kashmere Gate, Sarai Kale Khan and Anand Vihar.

Keeping in view the rising vehicular pollution and chaotic traffic condition in the city of Delhi, it has been decided to start Mass Rapid Transit System (MRTS) in Delhi. The project is under implementation and it uses the state-of-the-art modern technology. The metro rail project runs in Delhi. Now Delhi Metro comprises six lines with a total length of around 190 km.

Festivals

Being a cosmopolitan city, all major festivals of India are celebrated here. Moreover, some tourism festivals have become regular annual events of Delhi. Delhi Tourism and Transportation Development Corporation organises Roshnara Festival, Shalimar Festival, Qutab Festival, Winter Carnival, Garden Tourism Festival, Jahan-e-Khusrao Festival and Mango Festival every year.

Tourist Places

Important tourist places are Lal Quila (Red Fort), Jama Masjid, Qutab Minar, India Gate, Laxmi Narain Mandir (Birla Mandir), Humayun's Tomb, Lotus Temple, Akshardham, etc. Delhi Tourism and Transportation Development Corporation Limited conducts city sight-seeing and excursion tours. The Corporation has also introduced adventure tourism activities such as para-sailing, rock-climbing and boating in Delhi. The Corporation has also developed two Delhi Haats where beverages and food items of different states are available at one place. More such Haats are planned in different parts of Delhi. The Corporation is also running Coffee Homes in different parts of Delhi. The "Garden of Five Senses" has also been opened in the South District of Delhi, which attracts a lot of tourists visiting Delhi.

O. W.: http://www.delhi.gov.in

GOVERNMENT

Lt. Governor	: Shri Najeeb Jung	*Chief Secretary*	:	Dr M. M. Kutty
Chief Minister	: Shri Arvind Kejriwal	*Jurisdiction of High Court*	:	Delhi

LAKSHADWEEP

Area	: 30 sq km	*Population*	:	64 thousand (census 2011)
Capital	: Kavaratti	*Principal Languages*	:	Malyalam, Dhivehi (language of Maldives)

History and Geography

Not much is known of the early history of these Islands. The Islands supposed to have been inhabited first by Amini, Andrott, Kavaratti and Agatti. It was earlier believed that the islanders were originally Hindus and later converted to Islam under the influence of Arab traders sometime in the 14th century. But archaeological evidences unearthed indicate that there were Buddhist settlements around the 6th or 7th century. Earliest Muslim converts or settlers pre-date the year 139 AH of the Hijri year (eighth century) of which period grave stones have recently been discovered in Agatti. This would tend to bear out the traditional belief that Islam was brought to the Island by Arab Saint, Ubaidulla in 41 AH.

Probably independent till 16th century the Islands were driven to seek the assistance of Raja of Chirakal to help them avert establishment of Portuguese domination. This enabled him to establish his authority and, later, the Islands were transferred in jaggeer to Ali Raja, head of Moplah community in Cannanore, who later became an independent ruler himself. The Arakkal rule was not popular and in 1787, Tipu Sultan acceded to the petitions of the Northern Islands to annex these Islands. After the fall of Tipu Sultan, the Islands were passed to East India Company but continued to be ruled de facto by the rulers of Cannanore till their ultimate annexation by the British in the early 20th century. In 1956, the Islands were constituted into a single territory and since then, have been directly administered by the Union Government through an administrator. The Laccadives, Minicoy and Amindivi Group of Islands were renamed Lakshadweep in 1973. Lakshadweep, a Group of Coral Islands, consists of 11 inhabited Islands, 16 uninhabited Islands, three reefs and six submerged sand banks. These lie scattered in the Arabian Sea about 280 km off Kerala coast between 8° and 12° 3′ North Latitude and 71° and 74° East Longitude.

Agriculture

Coconut is the only major crop with a production of 60 million nuts per year. The area under cultivation is about 2,689 hectare. Lakshadweep coconut is branded as an organic product. In India, Lakshadweep stands first in coconut production and productivity per hectare is 20,600 and average yield per palm per year is 82 coconuts. The Lakshadweep coconuts are the highest oil content nuts in the world (82 per cent).

Fisheries

Fishing is another major activity. The sea around the Islands is highly productive. The Islands stand first in the country in per capita availability of fish.

Industries

Coconut fibre extraction and conversion into fibre products is the main industry in the Islands. Under Government Sector, there are seven coir fibre factories, 5 coir production-cum-demonstration centres and 7 fibre curling units, functioning under coir sector. These units produced coir fibre and coir yarn in addition to other coir products like curled fibre, corridor mat, mat and mattings. A few coir twisting units also function in private sector.

Transport

At present M.V. Kavaratti, M.V. Arabian Sea, M.V. Lakshadweep Sea, M.V. Bharat Seema, M.V. Amindivi and M.V. Minicoy accommodate the passenger traffic in mainland-islands and inter-island sector. Further three 150 Passenger High Speed Vessels (HSC Parali, HSC Valiyapani and HSC Cheryapani), three 50 Passenger High Speed Vessels (HSC Skip Jack, Hsc Blue Marlin and HSC Black Marlin), one 15 Passenger High Speed Vessel HSC Viringili and two 100 passenger Ferry Vessels (M.V. Kadeeja Beevi and M.V. Hameedath Bee) provides connectivity between inter-island sectors. Moreover three 150 Passenger HSCs also connect island and mainland depending upon the requirements. The cargo transportation from mainland to islands are handled with four cargo barges, MV Ubaidulla, M.V. Thinnakara, MV. Laccadives and M.V. Cheriyam.

The administration operates two Pawan Hans helicopters on charter for the inter-Island service and evacuation of patients from Islands to Kavaratti/ Agatti and mainland. Besides connectivity is maintained by Indian Airlines between Agatti and Kochi except on Sundays.

Tourist Centres

Tourism is developing into an important industry. Important tourist places are Agatti, Bangaram, Kalpeni, Kadmat, Kavaratti and Minicoy, etc.

O. W.: http://www.lakshadweep.gov.in

GOVERNMENT

Administrator	:	Shri Farooq Khan
Collector and Development Commissioner	:	Shri J. Ashok Kumar
Jurisdiction of High Court	:	Falls under Jurisdiction of Kerala High Court

PUDUCHERRY

Area	:	490 sq km	*Population*	:	12.48 lakh (prov. census 2011)
Capital	:	Puducherry	*Principal Languages*	:	Tamil, Telugu, Malayalam, English and French

History and Geography

The territory of Puducherry comprises the former French establishment of Puducherry, Karaikal, Mahe and Yanam, which lie scattered in South India. Puducherry, the capital of the territory was once the original headquarters of the French in India. It was under the French rule for 138 years and merged with the Indian Union in 1954. It is bound on the east by the Bay of Bengal and on the three sides by Tamil Nadu. About 150 km south of Puducherry on the east-coast lies Karaikal. Mahe is situated on the Malabar coast on the Western Ghats surrounded by Kerala. It can be reached from Calicut Airport, which is 70 km from Mahe. Yanam is situated adjoining the East Godavari district of Andhra Pradesh and is about 200 km from Visakhapatnam Airport.

Agriculture

Nearly Department of Agriculture is committed to support the farming community to uplift them by increasing their net income level through strategic intervention by technology dissemination and technological inputs. In spite of the decrease in the cultivable area the UT administration has always been optimistic in carrying forward the task of increasing the productivity of crops with the available resources and technological intervention based on the location specific needs. Promotion of complete mechanization in respect of paddy and sugarcane has always been the priority area in view of the scarcity of the agricultural labour and for timely completion of agricultural operations Paddy Transplantors are hired out at reasonable cost to the farmers through the Krishi Vigyan Kendra.

Industry

Puducherry has a total area of 479 sq.kms with a total population of 12.44 lakh as per last census. It comprises four coastal enclaves in South India. It is situated 170 km south of Chennai, Karaikal 150 km South of Puducherry while Yanam is about 900 kms away in the lap of Kakinada district of Andhra Pradesh and Mahe in Kerala is 650 km away in the west coast. Keeping in view the need for the investment of investable surplus, the administration has taken a number of major initiatives to upgrade the infrastructure to boost economic growth in this region.

With its reputation of being an investor-friendly, the Union Territory having proven track record of attracting surplus investment and has witnessed vibrant industrial growth over the years. Even though there was some industrial slow down for a few years because of the general down turn in the economy, the growth continues. Puducherry as nearly 77 large and 8,955 micro, small and medium enterprises and with an investment of ₹ 2843 cores, these industries are deemed to be the life blood of economy providing employment to about one lakh persons.

Irrigation

Under the assistance from the European Union many water tanks were revived. 8 bed dams have been constructed across the river Sankaraparani and Pennar at various places. In addition to the above, necessary proposal to construct bed dams for groundwater recharges at Aratchikuppam, Pambaiyar confluence point at Sellipet, across Malatar in Vadukuppam at Puducherry and across Mullaiyar.

Power

The power requirements of the union territory are met by availing share of power from the central generating stations and by purchasing power from the neighbouring State Electricity Boards viz., Tamil Nadu Electricity Board, Kerala State Electricity Board and from the Puducherry Power Corporation Limited. The total power available is 396.58 MW.

Transport

Roads: Nearly 677.525 km of various category are being maintained by Roads Division of PWD. Construction of bridges and improvement of roads are under progress.

Tourism

It has an interesting cross-cultural history and its built form lends a unique identity to the town. The old part of the UT is known as Boulevard Town since it is bounded by four boulevards that once constituted the outer limits of the city's fortification. The Boulevard Town presents two distinct architectural styles in the Tamil and French Quarters, which are separated by a canal and unified by a rectilinear grid plan. In the French Town the buildings are in European style adapted to a tropical climate, whereas in the Tamil Town area they are in the local vernacular. While maintaining their individual identities, the two styles have streetscapes so distinctive. Some must-see sights include Arikanmedu, a famous historical site that was discovered by the Romans in 200 B.C. and is being excavated, influenced one another, evolving into a synthesis: Franco-Tamil architecture. There are few monumental buildings in Pondicherry, and the architectural character of the town is the result of hundreds of traditional-style houses (both in Tamil and French Quarters) that form the unique Aayi Mandapam, a monument built during the reign of Napoleon III, Eglise De Sacre Coeur De Jesus or Church of Sacred Heart of Jesus, known for its Gothic architecture and the Mansion of Ananda Rangapillai, a fine specimen of Indo-French architecture that was built in 1773.

Otheman's Fort is believed to have been built by Thatcholi Othenan, a widely known folklore hero who became the Robin Hood of North Malabar (Mahe). Only the remnants of this castle can be seen by the public now.

O. W.: http://www.py.gov.in

GOVERNMENT

Lieutenant Governor	:	Dr. Kiran Bedi I.P.S. (Retd.)
Chief Minister	:	Shri V. Narayanasamy
Chief Secretary	:	Shri Manoj Parida
Jurisdiction of High Court	:	Fall under jurisdiction of Madras High Court

31 Diary of National Events

(December 2015—December 15, 2016)

- Union Cabinet, approves setting up of six new Indian Institutes of Technology (IITs) in Andhra Pradesh, Chhattisgarh , Goa, Jammu, Kerala and Karnataka.
- "Accessible India Campaign"(*Sugamya Bharat Abhiyan*), a nationwide campaign launched, that will enable persons with disabilities to gain universal access, equal opportunity for development, independent living and participation in all aspects of life in an inclusive society.
- A 'Handbook on Sexual Harassment of Women at Workplace (Prevention, Prohibition and Redressal) Act, 2013 released by Ministry of Women and Child in New Delhi.
- A Memorandum of Understanding (MoU) for skill development in the manufacturing sector, with focus on capital goods and automotive sector signed between Ministry of Skill Development and Entrepreneurship (MSDE) and the Department of Heavy Industry (DHI).
- Real Estate (Regulation and Development) Bill, 2015, approved by the Select Committee of Rajya Sabha.
- India and the United Kingdom launch a joint initiative "2016: UK-INDIA Year of Education, Research and Innovation".
- Central Government signs a Memorandum of Understanding and documentation, for establishing three Indian Institute of Information Technology (IIITs) at Ranchi, Nagpur and Pune to be operated on a Public-Private-Partnership (PPP) mode with participation of State Government and Industry, apart from the Central Government.
- Lok Sabha passes the landmark "Atomic Energy (Amendment) Bill, 2015" which seeks to amend the Atomic Energy Act of 1962, thus paving the way for Atomic Energy Units, including Nuclear Power Corporation of India Limited (NPCIL) to enter into joint-ventures with other Public Sector Undertakings (PSUs) and government sector companies.
- ISRO's Polar Satellite Launch Vehicle PSLV-C29 successfully launches six satellites from Sriharikota, Andhra Pradesh.
- Cabinet approves a policy framework for development of Underground Coal Gasification (UCG) in coal and lignite bearing areas in the country.
- Sixth All India Survey on Higher Education (AISHE) launched in New Delhi.

- Cabinet approves the Lucknow Metro Rail Project Phase - 1 A, which will cover a length of 22.878 km with 22 stations.
- A Committee on Revisiting and Revitalising the PPP model of Infrastructure Development has been set-up.
- Prime Minister, Shri Narendra Modi, inaugurates the National Conference of Dalit Entrepreneurs at Vigyan Bhawan, in New Delhi.

January, 2016

- The River Information System (RIS) inaugurated, the first of its kind, RIS will facilitate safe and accurate navigation on National Waterway – 1 on the Ganges River.
- Ministry of Petroleum & Natural Gas (MoPNG) launches an online initiative to engage the LPG Consumers and Citizens of India, in providing efficient and citizen friendly services in LPG distribution.
- A system of aerosol monitoring and research and user-friendly website of India Meteorological Department dedicated.
- Mobile Health Services– Mobile Academy, Kilkari, M-Cessation and TB Missed Call initiative launched to Strengthen Public Health Infrastructure.
- Prime Minister, Shri Narendra Modi, launches the Start-up India Initiative in New Delhi.
- ISRO's Polar Satellite Launch Vehicle, PSLV-C31, successfully launches the 1,425 kg IRNSS-1E, the fifth satellite in the Indian Regional Navigation Satellite System (IRNSS).
- A scheme 'Nai Manzil' aimed at empowering the minorities launched in Jammu and Kashmir

February, 2016

- President Shri Pranab Mukherjee inaugurates the Counter-Terrorism Conference- 2016 at Jaipur, Rajasthan.
- Council for Scientific and Industrial Research (CSIR) launches the country's first anti-diabetic ayurvedic drug, known as 'BGR-342, for type two Diabetes mellitus.
- Official Youtube Channel of the Ministry of Finance launched.
- Prime Minister, Shri Narendra Modi dedicates to the nation Brahmaputra Cracker and Polymer Limited, a petrochemical complex, at Lepetkata, near Dibrugarh in Assam.
- Prime Minister Shri Narendra Modi inaugurates the 12th South Asian Games, 2016 at the Sarusajai Sports Complex in Guwahati.
- Directorate General of Civil Aviation (DGCA) of India and United States Technical Development Agency (USTDA) sign the Grant Agreement for India Aviation Safety Technical Assistance Phase II ,in New Delhi.
- Global Network Operations Centre (g-NOC) of Employees Provident Fund Organisation (EPFO) inaugurated at Dwarka, New Delhi.

- National Deworming Day launched at a function in Hyderabad.
- National Framework for Elimination of Malaria launched.
- Integrated website of 'India Handloom' Brand "www.indiahandloombrand.gov.in" launched.
- Twenty fourth National Homoeopathic Congress 'Homeo-Vision 2016' inaugurated in Nagpur.
- Prime Minister inaugurates "Make in India Week" in Mumbai.
- Government identifies 150 critical projects to augment infrastructure in coastal areas under its Sagarmala project.
- Non-Tax Receipt Portal (NTRP), developed by the Office of Controller General of Accounts (CGA) inaugurated.
- Government unveiles the National Capital Goods Policy.
- Fifteen cities from across the country felicitated by the central government for their good work in different areas of sanitation.
- India test-fires its indigenously developed Prithvi-II missile, which is capable of carrying 500 kg to 1,000 kg of warheads, as part of a user trial by the army from a test range at Chandipur, Odisha.
- Cabinet approves the proposal for Notification of Commitments under the Trade Facilitation Agreement (TFA) of World Trade Organization (WTO), ratification and acceptance of the Instrument of Acceptance of Protocol of TFA to the WTO Secretariat and constitution of the National Committee on Trade Facilitation (NCTF).
- Cabinet approves the Agreement for collaborative activities to be signed in the area of Traditional Medicine between Ministry of AYUSH and the World Health Organization, Geneva.
- Prime Minister, Shri Narendra Modi, unveiles the operational guidelines for the Pradhan Mantri Fasal Bima Yojana.
- The print and digital versions of Reference Annual -India 2016 and *Bharat* 2016 released in New Delhi.
- "Swachh Parayatan Mobile App" launched.
- Railway Budget presented; no hike in passenger and freight rates, over 65,000 additional berths, wi-fi services at 100 stations, improvement in passenger amenities including cleanliness and making the Railways a safer means of travel are the highlights.
- Economic Survey 2015-16 presented in the Parliament .
- Government announces the constitution of Banks Board Bureau with a view to improve the governance of Public Sector Banks.
- Union Budget 2016-17 presented in Parliament.

March, 2016

- Government approves the proposal for laying down the procedure and mechanism for strategic disinvestment of Central Public Sector Enterprises (CPSEs).
- Prime Minister constitutes a task force to rationalise central government staff.
- The Aadhaar (Targeted Delivery of Financial and Other Subsidies, Benefits and Services) Bill, 2016, introduced in Lok Sabha.
- "Setu Bharatam" – an ambitious programme with an investment of ₹ 50,000 crore to build bridges for safe and seamless travel on National Highways launched.
- Government releases a new categorization of industries based on their pollution load.
- Online marketing platform *Mahila E-HAAT* launched to facilitate women entrepreneurs to sell their products.
- Rajya Sabha passes the Real Estate (Regulation and Development) Bill, 2015 which seeks to set up a regulatory authority for the sector.
- Cabinet approves 8,000-crore rupee Pradhan Mantri Ujwala Yojna for providing LPG connections to BPL families.
- Indian Space Research Organization (ISRO) puts the nation's sixth exclusive navigation satellite IRNSS 1F into space using the rocket PSLV C32.
- Parliament passes the Real Estate (Regulation and Development) Bill, 2015 which aims at protecting the interests of the aspiring house buyers while at the same time enhancing the credibility of real estate sector by ensuring transparency and accountability.
- Parliament passes the Aadhaar (Targeted Delivery of Financial and Other Subsidies, Benefits and Services) Bill, 2016 .
- A Web Portal for distribution of coal by State Nominated Agencies (SNA) launched.
- Government launches Depot Online System of Food Corporation of India (FCI) as a part of Digital India Initiative to bring transparency and for minimizing storage losses of foodgrains.
- Prime Minister, Shri Narendra Modi inaugurates 'Krishi Unnati Mela'- the National Level Agriculture Fair-cum-Exhibition in New Delhi.
- Prime Minister lays the foundation stone for the Dr. Ambedkar National Memorial, to be built at Alipur Road in Delhi.
- Winners of the 5th National Photography Awards felicitated.
- New Environment Standards for gensets running on Liquid Petroleum Gas (LPG) / Natural Gas (NG), Diesel with LPG / NG and Petrol with LPG / NG, operated in various cities / towns in the country notified.

- Atal Pension Yojana (APY) amended to give an option to the spouse to continue to contribute for balance period, on premature death of the subscriber.
- Cabinet approves 1,500 million dollar World Bank Support to Swachh Bharat Mission (Gramin) [(SBM(G)].
- Cabinet approves the implementation of the rural housing scheme of Pradhan Mantri Awaas Yojana – Gramin.
- Cabinet approves that India should accede to the Ashgabat Agreement, an international transport and transit corridor facilitating transportation of goods between Central Asia and the Persian Gulf.
- E-Waste Management Rules, 2016 notified in supersession of the e-waste (Management & Handling) Rules, 2011.
- Rotavirus vaccine launched as part of Universal Immunization Programme.
- 63rd National Film Awards, 2015 announced. 'Bahubali' awarded Best Feature Film and 'Bajrangi Bhaijaan' declared Best Popular Film providing wholesome entertainment.
- Defexpo India, inaugurated at Goa.
- Construction and Demolition Waste Management Rules, 2016 notified to effectively tackle the issues of pollution and waste management.
- Government releases Indian Intellectual Property Panorama -a single window interface for information on Intellectual Property and guidance on leveraging it for competitive advantage.

April, 2016

- Low Cost and Environment-friendly solar lighting device launched.
- Cabinet approves implementation of the National Hydrology Project.
- 'Swasth Bharat Mobile application' and 'ANM Online application-ANMOL' launched on World Health Day.
- 'Make in India Action Plan' and 'State Level Business Reform Action Plan' Dashboards launched in the Capital to monitor progress made on the two action plans.
- Prime Minister, Shri Narendra Modi, launches the pilot of e-NAM - the e-trading platform for the National Agriculture Market.
- National Monuments Authority (NMA)'s Web Portal called "NOC Online Application and Processing System (NOAPS), launched.
- Railways sign a Memorandum of Understanding (MoU) with Indian Space Research Organisation (ISRO) for developing applications in the field of Remote Sensing and Geographic Information System.
- National LED programme - Unnat Jyoti by Affordable LEDs for All (UJALA), launched.

May, 2016

- Prime Minister, Shri Narendra Modi, launches the Pradhan Mantri Ujjwala Yojana at Ballia, Uttar Pradesh which aims to provide cooking gas connections to five crore below-poverty-line beneficiaries.
- Prime Minister launches a scheme for environment-friendly solar-powered 'e-boats' at the Assi Ghat in Varanasi.
- Railways launch one E-enabled project, namely, Project Management & Information System (PMIS).
- Veteran actor Manoj Kumar conferred the prestigious Dadasaheb Phalke award by President Pranab Mukherjee, at the 63rd National Film Awards ceremony for his contribution to the film industry.
- Harmukh Khadi Gram Udyog Sansthan, a spinning and weaving centre and marketing plaza for khadi goods inaugurated in Srinagar, Jammu & Kashmir.
- A web-based application on Integrated Waste Management System (IWMS) – www.iwms.nic.in, for better management of waste launched.
- Nine projects for rural sanitation initiatives under Namami Gange Programme for conservation of river Ganga in Sahibganj, Jharkhand, launched.
- Indigenously developed fecal incontinence management system 'Qora' launched.
- Common Application Software (ICDS-CAS) and Information and Communication Technology enabled Real Time Monitoring (ICT-RTM) of ICDS launched.

June, 2016

- Asia's first 'Gyps Vulture Reintroduction Programme' launched.
- Tiger Express train launched on the World Environment Day.
- Ministry of New and Renewable Energy (MNRE) launches a scheme for setting up of 1000 MW Wind Power Project connected to transmission network of Central Transmission Utility (CTU) with an objective to facilitate supply of wind power to the non-windy states.
- PSLV-C34 successfully launches 20 satellites in a single flight.
- Prime Minister, Shri Narendra Modi launches the flagship Smart City Mission into implementation mode with the launch of 14 projects.
- The fourth in the series of Follow-on Water Jet Fast Attack Craft (FO-WJFAC) of the Indian Navy launched.

July, 2016

- "National Mineral Exploration Policy" launched.
- Election Commission of India Launches"National Electoral Roll

Purification" (NERP) 2016, to improve Electoral Rolls and optimize the polling station location and area.

- Ministry of Tourism sanctions 25 projects worth ₹ 2,048 crore in 21 States and UTs under Swadesh Darshan scheme.
- Indian Space Research Organisation (ISRO) successfully launches an earth observation satellite namely CARTOSAT-2.

August, 2016

- Swachh Survekshan of 500 cities launched.
- AMRIT outlet inaugurated at NEIGRIHMS-Shillong, RIMS -Imphal and AIIMS-Jodhpur to dispense affordable drugs for cancer, heart diseases and other lifestyle diseases.
- An online complaint box for reporting child sexual abuse, the POCSO e-Box launched by the Ministry of Women and Child Development,
- ISRO's Scramjet Engine Technology Demonstrator, successfully flight tested.
- Border Roads Organisation (BRO), under Ministry of Defence launches a massive tree plantation drive in the Northern and Eastern states of the country.
- Sakshi Malik wins Bronze medal in wrestling at 2016 Rio Olympics.
- P. V. Sindhu wins Silver Medal in badminton at 2016 Rio Olympics.

September, 2016

- President Shri Pranab Mukherjee congratulates the Indian Space Research Organisation (ISRO) on the successful launch of the tenth flight of India's Geosynchronous Satellite Launch Vehicle GSLV-F05, carrying an advanced weather satellite 'INSAT – 3DR'.
- Indian Coast Guard Ship 'Sarathi', third ship in the series of six Offshore Patrol Vessels (OPV) commissioned.
- Prime Minister, Shri Narendra Modi congratulates ISRO on successful launch of PSLV-C35, advanced weather satellite SCATSAT-1 and 7 other co-passenger satellites.

October, 2016

- President Shri Pranab Mukherjee presents 'Vayoshreshtha Samman' to Older Persons and Institutions on 1st October , International Day of Older Persons (IDOP).
- Ministry of Tourism organises the "5th International Buddhist Conclave" in Varanasi-Sarnath in collaboration with the State Governments of Uttar Pradesh and Bihar.
- Prime Minister, Shri Narendra Modi, inaugurates the Pravasi Bharatiya Kendra in New Delhi.

- India ratifies the Paris Agreement on Climate Change.
- Gujarat and Andhra Pradesh become first States to be Open Defecation Free (ODF) in urban areas; Porbandar becomes the first district to be ODF on the 147th Birth Anniversary of Mahatma Gandhi.
- Jharkhand becomes the first state in the country to implement Direct Benefit Transfer (DBT) in kerosene, in four identified districts.
- Ministry of Road Transport & Highways and Shipping launches the Indian Bridge Management System (IBMS) .which will create an inventory of all bridges in the country and rate their structural condition, so that timely repair and rehabilitation work can be carried out.
- India hosts 8th BRICS Summit in Goa.
- First BRICS U – 17 Football Tournament kicks off in Goa .
- President Shri Pranab Mukherjee inaugurates the first edition of the World Sustainable Development Summit on the theme 'Beyond 2015: People, Planet and Progress' organized by The Energy and Resources Institute (TERI) in New Delhi.
- All ASI Protected Historical Monuments and Archaeological Sites Declared Polythene Free Zones.
- India's communication satellite GSAT-18 was launched successfully by the European Ariane 5 VA-231 launch Vehicle.
- HIMANSH, India's Remote, High-Altitude Station opens in the Himalayas.
- Cabinet approves MoU between Export-Import Bank of India (Exim Bank) on General Cooperation with the New Development Bank (NDB), along with other Development Financial Institutions of BRICS nations.
- India joins the nations of the world in lauding the Hydroflurocarbon (HFC) Amendment to the Montreal Protocol, agreed to at the 28th Meeting of Parties at Kigali, Rwanda. .
- Brazil lifts the 1st BRICS U-17 Football Tournament 2016, held at Goa.
- The 1st BRICS Trade Fair organized at Pragati Maidan in New Delhi from 12-14 October 2016.
- Indian Navy commissions the highly manoeuvrable fast attack craft INS Tihayu at the Eastern Naval Command.
- Ministry of Civil Aviation launches regional connectivity scheme "UDAN",the first-of-its-kind globally, which will create affordable yet economically viable and profitable flights on regional routes .
- Indian Coast Guard Ship *Aryaman* and *Atulya* Commissioned into the force.

- India Signs Guarantee Agreement with the World Bank For IBRD direct lending of US$ 650 million to the Dedicated Freight Corridor Corporation of India Ltd. (DFCCIL) for Eastern Dedicated Freight Corridor-III (EDFC-III) Project.
- India beat Iran 38-29 to win the Kabaddi World Cup 2016.
- Prime Minister, Shri Narendra Modi inaugurates the first National Tribal Carnival in New Delhi.
- Government issues Notification amending rule 23 of the Conduct of Elections Rules, 1961 enabling service voters, including armed forces personnel, to cast their vote in elections through e-postal ballot.
- Cabinet approves establishment of National Academic Depository. Union Cabinet approves an Agreement on Trade, Commerce and Transit between India and Bhutan.
- Union Cabinet approves MoU between India and European Union on water cooperation.
- Prime Minister, Shri Narendra Modi launches National SC/ST hub and Zero Defect – Zero Effect scheme for Micro, Small and Medium Enterprises (MSMEs).
- NITI Aayog launches the first ever Agricultural Marketing and Farm Friendly Reforms Index. Maharashtra ranks first.

November, 2016

- Kerala becomes the third State overall and the largest State so far to be declared Open Defecation Free (ODF) under the Swachh Bharat Mission (SBM) (Gramin).
- Kerala and Tamil Nadu roll out the National Food Security Act (NFSA). With this, the Act has been now implemented in all the States and Union Territories
- Ministry of Environment, Forest and Climate Change constitutes a four-member team for conservation and management of Loktak Lake in Manipur.
- Pradhan Mantri Surakshit Matritva Abhiyan, (PMSMA) launched which aims at reducing maternal and infant mortality rates through safe pregnancies and safe deliveries.
- India and the United Nations Office for Disaster Risk Reduction sign a Statement of Cooperation during the Asian Ministerial Conference on Disaster Risk Reduction (AMCDRR) 2016, in New Delhi.

- Election Commission of India conducts pilot of Electronic Transmitted Postal Ballot for service voters in Nellithope Assembly by–election in Puducherry.
- First-ever International Agro-biodiversity Congress held in New Delhi , which would initiate and encourage a dialogue among relevant stakeholders – including farmers – to better understand everyone's role in agro-biodiversity management and conservation of genetic resources.
- India hosts Seventh Session of the Conference of the Parties, to the WHO Framework Convention on Tobacco Control (FCTC) which will review the implementation of the WHO Framework Convention on Tobacco Control (FCTC) and the protocol to eliminate the illicit trade in tobacco products.
- Indian Navy Sailing Vessel Mhadei with an all-women crew flagged off from Goa to Cape Town, South Africa .
- Protocol amending the Double Taxation Amending Convention (DTAC) between India and Japan comes into force.
- Ministry of Health and Family Welfare launches "Healthy India Initiative" magazine and "No More Tension" Mobile app.
- Ministry of Skill Development and Entrepreneurship announces the launch of Pradhan Mantri Yuva Yojana to scale up an ecosystem of entrepreneurship for youngsters .
- With a view to curb financing of terrorism through the proceeds of Fake Indian Currency Notes (FICN) and use of such funds for subversive activities, and for eliminating black money ,Government decides to cancel the legal tender character of the High Denomination bank notes of ₹ 500 and ₹1,000 from the expiry of the 8th November, 2016.
- National Skill Development Agency and the British Council sign an MoU to collaborate for undertaking joint research projects in the area of skill development.
- Government approves the establishment of National Institute of Sowa Rigpa (The Tibetan Medicine system) at Leh, Jammu & Kashmir. Sowa Rigpa has been recognized by Government of India by amending the Indian Medicine Central Council (IMCC) Act, 2010.
- "Qaumi Ekta Week" (National Integration Week) observed all over the country, from November 19 to 25, 2016.
- The 47th International Film Festival of India held at Panaji, Goa from 20th to 28th November 2016. Iranian film *Daughter* directed by Reza Mirkarimi wins the **Golden Peacock Award for the Best Film**.

32 General Information

The Table, with respect to the rank and precedence of the persons named therein as approved by the President, is given as under :

1. President
2. Vice-President
3. Prime Minister
4. Governors of States within their respective States
5. Former Presidents

5A. Deputy Prime Minister

6. Chief Justice of India
   Speaker of Lok Sabha
7. Cabinet Ministers of the Union
   Chief Ministers of States within their respective States
   Deputy Chairman, NITI Aayog
   Former Prime Ministers
   Leaders of Opposition in Rajya Sabha and Lok Sabha

7A. Holders of Bharat Ratna Decoration

8. Ambassadors Extraordinary and Plenipotentiary and High Commissioners of Commonwealth Countries accredited to India
   Chief Ministers of States outside their respective States
   Governors of States outside their respective States
9. Judges of Supreme Court

9A. Chairperson, Union Public Service Commission
   Chief Election Commissioner
   Comptroller & Auditor General of India

10. Deputy Chairman, Rajya Sabha
    Deputy Chief Ministers of States
    Deputy Speaker, Lok Sabha
    Members of the NITI Aayog
    Ministers of State of the Union (and any other Minister in the Ministry of Defence for defence matters).
11. Attorney General of India
    Cabinet Secretary
    Lieutenant Governors within their respective Union Territories
12. Chiefs of Staff holding the rank of full General or equivalent rank.
13. Envoys Extraordinary and Ministers Plenipotentiary accredited to India.
14. Chairmen and Speakers of State Legislatures within their respective States.
    Chief Justices of High Courts within their respective jurisdictions

15. Cabinet Ministers in States within their respective States

    Chief Ministers of Union Territories and Chief Executive Councillor, Delhi within their respective Union Territories

    Deputy Ministers of the Union

16. Officiating Chiefs of Staff holding the rank of Lieutenant General or equivalent rank

17. Chairman, Central Administrative Tribunal

    Chairman, Minorities Commission

    Chairperson, National Commission for Scheduled Castes

    Chairperson, National Commission for Scheduled Tribes

    Chief Justices of High Courts outside their respective jurisdictions

    Puisne Judges of High Courts within their respective jurisdictions

18. Cabinet Ministers in States outside their respective States

    Chairmen and Speakers of State Legislatures outside their respective States

    Chairman, Monopolies and Restrictive Trade Practices Commission

    Deputy Chairmen and Deputy Speakers of State Legislatures within their respective States

    Ministers of State in States within their respective States

    Ministers of Union Territories and Executive Councillors, Delhi, within their respective Union Territories

    Speakers of Legislative Assemblies in Union Territories and Chairman of Delhi Metropolitan Council within their respective Union Territories

19. Chief Commissioners of Union Territories not having Councils of Ministers, within their respective Union Territories

    Deputy Ministers in States within their respective States

    Deputy Speakers of Legislative Assemblies in Union Territories and Deputy Chairman of Metropolitan Council Delhi, within their respective Union Territories

20. Deputy Chairman and Deputy Speakers of State Legislatures, outside their respective States.

    Ministers of State in States outside their respective States

    Puisne Judges of High Courts outside their respective jurisdictions

21. Members of Parliament

22. Deputy Ministers in States outside their respective States

23. Army Commanders/Vice-Chief of the Army Staff or equivalent in other services

    Chief Secretaries to State governments within their respective States

    Commissioner for Linguistic Minorities

    Commissioner for Scheduled Castes and Scheduled Tribes

    Members, Minorities Commission

    Members, National Commission for Scheduled Castes and Scheduled Tribes

Officers of the rank of full General or equivalent rank
Secretaries to the Government of India (including officers holding this office ex-officio)
Secretary, Minorities Commission
Secretary, Scheduled Castes and Scheduled Tribes Commission
Secretary to the President
Secretary to the Prime Minister
Secretary, Rajya Sabha/Lok Sabha
Solicitor General
Vice-Chairman, Central Administrative Tribunal

24. Officers of the rank of Lieutenant General or equivalent rank

25. Additional Secretaries to the Government of India
Additional Solicitor General
Advocate Generals of States
Chairman, Tariff Commission
Chargê d'affaires and Acting High Commissioners *en-pied* and *ad interim*
Chief Ministers of Union Territories and Chief Executive Councillor, Delhi outside their respective Union Territories
Chief Secretaries of State governments outside their respective States.
Deputy Comptroller and Auditor General, Deputy Speakers of Legislative Assemblies in Union Territories and Deputy Chairman, Delhi Metropolitan Council, outside their respective Union Territories.
Director, Central Bureau of Investigation
Director General, Border Security Force
Director General, Central Reserve Police Force
Director, Intelligence Bureau
Lieutenant Governors outside their respective Union Territories
Members, Central Administrative Tribunal
Members, Monopolies and Restrictive Trade Practices Commission
Members, Union Public Service Commission
Ministers of Union Territories and Executive Councillors, Delhi, outside their respective Union Territories
Principal Staff Officers of the Armed Forces of the rank of Major General or equivalent rank
Speakers of Legislative Assemblies in Union Territories and Chairman of Delhi Metropolitan Council, outside their respective Union Territories

26. Joint Secretaries to the Government of India and officers of equivalent rank
Officers of the rank of Major-General or equivalent rank

NOTES

Note 1 The order in this Table of Precedence is meant for State and Ceremonial occasions and has no application in the day-to-day business of Government.

Note 2 Persons in the Table of Precedence will take rank in order of the number of the articles. The entries in the same article are arranged alphabetically. Those included in the same article will take precedence *inter se* according to date of entry into that article. However, where the dignitaries of different States and Union Territories included in the same article are present at a function outside their States or Union Territories and there is difficulty in ascertaining their dates of entry, they may be assigned precedence *inter se* in the alphabetical order of the name of States and Union Territories concerned after those whose precedence is determined according to date of entry into that article.

Note 3 In Article 7, former Prime Ministers will take precedence over the Cabinet Ministers of the Union and the Leaders of Opposition in the Rajya Sabha and the Lok Sabha. The Chief Ministers of States within their respective States will take precedence over the Cabinet Ministers of the Union in official functions held in the respective States.

Note 4 In Article 8 :

(a) Ambassadors Extraordinary and Plenipotentiary and High Commissioners of Commonwealth countries accredited to India will *en bloc* rank above Governors of States outside their respective States.

(b) Governors of States outside their respective States will en bloc rank above Chief Ministers of States outside their respective States.

Note 5 The Ministry of External Affairs may assign appropriate ranks to foreign dignitaries and Indian Ambassadors, High Commissioners and Ministers Plenipotentiary during their visit to India.

Note 6 Notwithstanding the procedure laid down in Note 2, the rank *inter se* and precedence of the persons in Article 10 shall be assigned in the following order :

(1) Deputy Chairman, Rajya Sabha

(2) Deputy Speaker, Lok Sabha

(3) Ministers of State of the Union and any other Minister in the Ministry of Defence for defence matters

(4) Deputy Chief Ministers of States

(5) Members of NITI Aayog.

However, the Deputy Chief Ministers of States outside their respective States will always rank below all other dignitaries figuring in this article.

Note 7 The Chairman of State Legislative Councils will rank above the Speakers of Legislative Assemblies in cases where they were elected on the same date.

Note 8 When Members of Parliament are invited *en bloc* to major State functions, the enclosures reserved for them should be next to the Chief Justice, Speaker of the Lok Sabha, Ambassadors, etc.

Note 9 Speakers of Legislative Assemblies in Union Territories and Chairman of the Delhi Metropolitan Council, Delhi, will take precedence over Ministers and Executive Councillors, included in the same article.

Note 10 In Article 23 :

(a) Secretaries in the Ministry of External Affairs other than the Foreign Secretary, between themselves, will take precedence in the order to their seniority in Grade-I of the Indian Foreign Service and both of them will take precedence after the Foreign Secretary.

(b) Members of the Minorities Commission and the Scheduled Castes and Schedule Tribes Commission will always take precedence over the Secretaries of these Commissioners.

(c) In official functions held at Delhi/New Delhi, Army Commanders/Vice Chief of the Army Staff or equivalent in other Services will always rank after Secretaries to the Government of India.

Note 11 In Article 25 :

(a) Additional Secretaries in the Ministry of External Affairs, among themselves, will take procedence in the order of their seniority in Grade-II of the Indian Foreign Service;

(b) Additional Solicitor General will take precedence above the Advocate General of States;

(c) Lieutenant Governors will take precedence over the Chief Ministers and Chief Executive Councillor, Delhi, and the latter will take precedence over Speakers of Legislative Assemblies and Chairman, Metropolitan Council, Delhi;

(d) Deputy Speakers of Legislative Assemblies of Union Territories and Deputy Chairman of Delhi Metropolitan Council will take precedence after Ministers of Union Territories and Executive Councillors, Delhi.

Note 12 For the purpose of Article 26, the posts equivalent to the posts of Joint Secretaries to the Government of India will be determined by the Ministry of Home Affairs.

PRESIDENTS OF INDIA[1]

Name	Tenure
Dr Rajendra Prasad (1884-1963)	January 26, 1950-May 13, 1962
Dr Sarvepalli Radhakrishnan (1888-1975)	May 13, 1962-May 13, 1967
Dr Zakir Husain (1897-1969)	May 13, 1967-May 03, 1969
Varahagiri Venkata Giri (1894-1980)	May 03, 1969-July 20, 1969 (Acting)
Justice Muhammad Hidayatullah (1905-1992)	July 20, 1969-August 24, 1969 (Acting)
Varahagiri Venkata Giri (1894-1980)	August 24, 1969-August 24, 1974
Dr. Fakhruddin Ali Ahmed (1905-1977)	August 24, 1974-February 11, 1977
B.D. Jatti (1912-2002)	February 11, 1977-July 25, 1977 (Acting)
Neelam Sanjiva Reddy (1913-1996)	July 25, 1977-July 25, 1982
Giani Zail Singh (1916-1994)	July 25, 1982-July 25, 1987
R. Venkataraman (1910-2009)	July 25, 1987-July 25, 1992
Dr Shankar Dayal Sharma (1918-1999)	July 25, 1992-July 25, 1997
K.R. Narayanan (1920-2005)	July 25, 1997-July 25, 2002
Dr. A.P.J. Abdul Kalam (1931-2015)	July 25, 2002-July 25, 2007
Smt. Pratibha Devisingh Patil (b-1934)	July 25, 2007-July 25, 2012
Shri Pranab Mukherjee (b-1935)	July 25, 2012-till date

VICE-PRESIDENTS OF INDIA[2]

Name	Tenure
Dr Sarvepalli Radhakrishnan (1888-1975)	May 13, 1952-May 12, 1962
Dr Zakir Hussain (1897-1969)	May 13, 1962-May 12, 1967
Varahagiri Venkata Giri (1894-1980)	May 13, 1967-May 03, 1969

1. Source : President of India website http://presidentofindia.nic.in
2. Source : Vice President of India website http://vicepresidentofindia.nic.in

Gopal Swarup Pathak (1896-1982)	August 31, 1969-August 30, 1974
B.D. Jatti (1912-2002)	August 31, 1974-August 30, 1979
Justice Muhammad Hidayatullah (1905-1992)	August 31, 1979-August 30, 1984
R. Venkataraman (1910-2009)	August 31, 1984-July 24, 1987
Dr. Shankar Dayal Sharma (1918-1999)	September 03, 1987-July 24, 1992
K.R. Narayanan (1920-2005)	August 21, 1992-July 24, 1997
Krishan Kant (1927-2002)	August 21, 1997-July 21, 2002
Bhairon Singh Shekhawat (1923-2010)	August 19, 2002-July 21, 2007
Mohammad Hamid Ansari (b-1937)	August 11, 2007-till date

PRIME MINISTERS OF INDIA[3]

Name	Tenure
Jawaharlal Nehru (1889-1964)	August 15, 1947-May 27, 1964
Gulzari Lal Nanda (1898-1998)	May 27, 1964-June 09, 1964 (Acting)
Lal Bahadur Shastri (1904-1966)	June 09, 1964-January 11, 1966
Gulzari Lal Nanda (1898-1998)	January 11, 1966-January 24, 1966 (Acting)
Indira Gandhi (1917-1984)	January 24, 1966-March 24, 1977
Morarji Desai (1896-1995)	March 24, 1977-July 28, 1979
Charan Singh (1902-1987)	July 28, 1979-January 14, 1980
Indira Gandhi (1917-1984)	January 14, 1980-October 31, 1984
Rajiv Gandhi (1944-1991)	October 31, 1984-December 02, 1989
Vishwanath Pratap Singh (1931-2008)	December 02, 1989-November 10, 1990
Chandra Shekhar (1927-2007)	November 10, 1990-June 21, 1991
P.V. Narasimha Rao (1921-2004)	June 21, 1991-May 16, 1996
Atal Bihari Vajpayee (b-1924)	May 16, 1996-June 01, 1996
H.D. Deve Gowda (b-1933)	June 01, 1996-April 21, 1997
I.K. Gujral (1919-2012)	April 21, 1997-March 19, 1998
Atal Bihari Vajpayee (b-1924)	March 19, 1998 -May 22, 2004
Dr. Manmohan Singh (b-1932)	May 22, 2004-May 26, 2014
Narendra Modi (b-1950)	May 26, 2014 - till date

CHIEF JUSTICES OF INDIA[4]

Name	Tenure
Harilal J. Kania	January 26, 1950—November 06, 1951
M. Patanjali Sastri	November 07, 1951—January 03, 1954
Mehr Chand Mahajan	January 04, 1954—December 22, 1954

3. Source : Prime Minister's office website http://pmindia.nic.in
4. Source : Supreme Court of of India website http://www.supremecourtofindia.nic.in.

B.K. Mukherjea .... December 23, 1954—January 31, 1956
S.R. Das .... February 01, 1956—September 30, 1959
Bhuvneshwar Prasad Sinha .... October 01, 1959—January 31, 1964
P.B. Gajendragadkar .... February 01, 1964—March 15, 1966
A.K. Sarkar .... March 16, 1966—June 29, 1966
K. Subba Rao .... June 30, 1966—April 11, 1967
K.N. Wanchoo .... April 12, 1967—February 24, 1968
M. Hidayatullah .... February 25, 1968—December 16, 1970
J.C. Shah .... December 17, 1970—January 21, 1971
S.M. Sikri .... January 22, 1971—April 25, 1973
A.N. Ray .... April 26, 1973—January 28, 1977
M.H. Beg .... January 29, 1977—February 21, 1978
Y.V. Chandrachud .... February 22, 1978—July 11, 1985
P .N. Bhagwati .... July 12, 1985—December 20, 1986
R.S. Pathak .... December 21, 1986—June 18, 1989
E.S. Venkataramiah .... June 19, 1989—December 17, 1989
S. Mukherjee .... December 18, 1989—September 25, 1990
Ranganath Misra .... September 25, 1990—November 24, 1991
K.N. Singh .... November 25, 1991—December 12, 1991
M.H. Kania .... December 13, 1991—November 17, 1992
L.M. Sharma .... November 18, 1992—February 11, 1993
M.N. Venkatachaliah .... February 12, 1993—October 24, 1994
A.M. Ahmadi .... October 25, 1994—March 24, 1997
J.S. Verma .... March 25, 1997—January 17, 1998
M.M. Punchhi .... January 18, 1998—October 09, 1998
A.S. Anand .... October 10, 1998—October 31, 2001
S.P. Bharucha .... November 01, 2001—May 05, 2002
B.N. Kirpal .... May 06, 2002—November 07, 2002
G.B. Pattanaik .... November 08, 2002—December 18, 2002
V. N. Khare .... December 19, 2002—May 01, 2004
S. Rajendra Babu .... May 02, 2004—May 31, 2004
R.C. Lahoti .... June 01, 2004—October 31, 2005
Y.K. Sabharwal .... November 01, 2005—January 13, 2007
K.G. Balakrishnan .... January 14, 2007—May 11, 2010
S.H. Kapadia .... May 12, 2010—September 28, 2012
Altamas Kabir .... September 29, 2012—July 18, 2013
P. Sathasivam .... July 19, 2013—April 26, 2014
R.M. Lodha .... April 27, 2014—September 27, 2014
H.L. Dattu .... September 28, 2014—December 02, 2015
T.S. Thakur .... December 03, 2015—till date

CHIEF ELECTION COMMISSIONERS OF INDIA[5]

Name	Tenure
Sukumar Sen	March 21, 1950—December 19, 1958
K.V. K. Sundaram	December 20, 1958—September 30, 1967
S.P. Sen Verma	October 01, 1967—September 30, 1972

5. Source : Website of Election Commission of India http://eci.nic.in

Dr Nagendra Singh .... October 01, 1972—February 06, 1973
T. Swaminathan .... February 07, 1973—June 17, 1977
S.L. Shakdhar .... June 18, 1977—June 17, 1982
R.K. Trivedi .... June 18, 1982—December 31, 1985
R.V. S. Peri Sastri .... January 01, 1986—November 25, 1990
Smt V. S. Ramadevi .... November 26, 1990—December 11, 1990
T.N. Seshan .... December 12, 1990—December 11, 1996
M.S. Gill .... December 12, 1996—June 13, 2001
J.M. Lyngdoh .... June 14, 2001—February 07, 2004
T.S. Krishna Murthy .... February 08, 2004—May 15, 2005
B.B. Tandon .... May 16, 2005—June 29, 2006
N. Gopalaswami .... June 30, 2006—April 20, 2009
Navin B. Chawla .... April 21, 2009—July 29, 2010
S.Y. Quraishi .... July 30, 2010—June 10, 2012
V.S. Sampath .... June 11, 2012—January 15, 2015
H.S. Brahma .... January 16, 2015—April 18, 2015
Nasim Zaidi .... April 19, 2015—till date

CABINET SECRETARIES[6]

Cabinet Secretary	From	To
Shri N.R. Pillai	06-02-1950	13-05-1953
Shri Y.N. Sukthankar	14-05-1953	31-07-1957
Shri M.K. Vellodi	01-08-1957	04-06-1958
Shri Vishnu Sahay	01-07-1958	10-11-1960
Shri B.N. Jha	10-11-1960	08-03-1961
Shri Vishnu Sahay	09-03-1961	15-04-1962
Shri S.S. Khera	15-04-1962	18-11-1964
Shri Dharam Vira	18-11-1964	27-06-1966
Shri D.S. Joshi	27-06-1966	31-12-1968
Shri B. Sivaraman	01-01-1969	30-11-1970
Shri T. Swaminathan	01-12-1970	02-11-1972
Shri B.D. Pande	02-11-1972	31-03-1977
Shri N.K. Mukarji	31-03-1977	31-03-1980
Shri S.S. Grewal	02-04-1980	30-04-1981
Shri C.R. Krishnaswamy Rao	30-04-1981	08-02-1985
Shri P.K. Kaul	08-02-1985	22-08-1986
Shri B.G. Deshmukh	23-08-1986	27-03-1989
Shri T.N. Seshan	27-03-1989	23-12-1989
Shri V.C. Pande	23-12-1989	11-12-1990
Shri Naresh Chandra	11-12-1990	31-07-1992

6. Source : Cabinet Secretariat Website http://cabsec.nic.in

Shri S. Rajgopal	01-08-1992	31-07-1993
Shri Zafar Saifullah	31-07-1993	31-07-1994
Shri Surendra Singh	01-08-1994	31-07-1996
Shri T.S.R. Subramanian	01-08-1996	31-03-1998
Shri Prabhat Kumar	01-04-1998	31-10-2000
Shri T.R. Prasad	01-11-2000	31-10-2002
Shri Kamal Pande	01-11-2002	14-06-2004
Shri B.K. Chaturvedi	14-06-2004	13-06-2007
Shri K.M. Chandrasekhar	14-06-2007	13-06-2011
Shri Ajit Kumar Seth	14-06-2011	13-06.2015
Shri Pradeep Kumar Sinha	13-06-2015	till date

CHAIRMEN OF UPSC[7]

Name	Tenure
Sir Ross Barker	October 1926-August 1932
Sir David Petrie	August 1932-1936
Sir Eyre Gorden	1937-1942
Sir F.W. Robertson	1942-1947
Shri H.K. Kripalani	April 01, 1947-January 13, 1949
Shri R.N. Banerjee	January 14, 1949 - May 09, 1955
Shri N. Govindarajan	May 10, 1955 - December 09, 1955
Shri V.S. Hejmadi	December 10, 1955-December 09, 1961
Shri B.N. Jha	December 11, 1961-February 22, 1967
Shri K.R. Damle	April 18, 1967-March 02, 1971
Shri R.C.S. Sarkar	May 11, 1971-February 01, 1973
Dr. A.R. Kidwai	February 05, 1973-February 04, 1979
Dr. M.L. Shahare	February 16, 1979-February 16, 1985
Shri H.K.L. Capoor	February 18, 1985-March 05, 1990
Shri J.P. Gupta	March 05, 1990 -June 02, 1992
Smt. R.M. Bathew (Kharbuli)	September 23, 1992-August 23, 1996
Shri S.J.S. Chhatwal	August 23, 1996-September 30, 1996
Shri J.M. Qureshi	September 30, 1996-December 11, 1998
Lt. Gen. (Retd.) Surinder Nath	December 11, 1998-June 25, 2002
Shri P.C. Hota	June 25, 2002-September 08, 2003
Shri Mata Prasad	September 08, 2003-January 04, 2005
Dr. S.R. Hashim	January 04, 2005-April 01, 2006
Shri Gurbachan Jagat	April 01, 2006-June 30, 2007
Shri Subir Dutta	June 30, 2007-August 16, 2008

7. Source : Annual Report UPSC 2009-10, Appendix-44

Prof. D.P. Agrawal	August 16, 2008-August 16, 2014
Smt. Rajni Razdan	August 16, 2014 -November 22, 2014
Shri Deepak Gupta	November 22, 2014-September 20, 2016
Smt. Alka Sirohi	September 20, 2016 - till date

CIVILIAN AWARDS

RECIPIENTS OF BHARAT RATNA

S. No.	Name	Awarded in
1.	Shri Chakravarti Rajagopalachari (1878-1972)	1954
2.	Dr Sarvepalli Radhakrishnan (1888-1975)	1954
3.	Dr Chandrasekhara Venkata Raman (1888-1970)	1954
4.	Dr Bhagwan Das (1869-1958)	1955
5.	Dr Mokshagundam Visvesvaraya (1861-1962)	1955
6.	Pt. Jawaharlal Nehru (1889-1964)	1955
7.	Pt. Govind Ballabh Pant (1887-1961)	1957
8.	Dr Dhondo Keshav Karve (1858-1962)	1958
9.	Dr Bidhan Chandra Roy (1882-1962)	1961
10.	Shri Purushottam Das Tandon (1882-1962)	1961
11.	Dr Rajendra Prasad (1884-1963)	1962
12.	Dr Zakir Hussain (1897-1969)	1963
13.	Dr Pandurang Vaman Kane (1880-1972)	1963
14.	Shri Lal Bahadur Shastri (Posthumous) (1904-1966)	1966
15.	Smt. Indira Gandhi (1917-1984)	1971
16.	Shri Varahagiri Venkata Giri (1894-1980)	1975
17.	Shri Kumaraswamy Kamraj (Posthumous) (1903-1975)	1976
18.	Mother Mary Teresa Bojaxhiu (Mother Teresa) (1910-1997)	1980
19.	Acharya Vinoba Bhave (Posthumous) (1895-1982)	1983
20.	Khan Abdul Ghaffar Khan (1890-1988)	1987
21.	Shri Marudur Gopalan Ramachandran (Posthumous) (1917-1987)	1988
22.	Dr Bhimrao Ramji Ambedkar (Posthumous) (1891-1956)	1990
23.	Dr Nelson Rolihlahla Mandela (1918-2013)	1990
24.	Shri Rajiv Gandhi (Posthumous) (1944-1991)	1991
25.	Sardar Vallabhbhai Patel (Posthumous) (1875-1950)	1991
26.	Shri Morarji Ranchhodji Desai (1896-1995)	1991
27.	Maulana Abul Kalam Azad (Posthumous) (1888-1958)	1992
28.	Shri Jehangir Ratanji Dadabhai Tata (1904-1993)	1992

29.	Shri Satyajit Ray (Posthumous) (1922-1992)	1992
30.	Shri Gulzari Lal Nanda (Posthumous) (1898-1998)	1997
31.	Smt. Aruna Asaf Ali (Posthumous) (1909-1996)	1997
32.	Dr A.P.J. Abdul Kalam (1931-2015)	1997
33.	Smt. Madurai Shanmukhavadivu Subbulakshmi (1916-2005)	1998
34.	Shri Chidambaram Subramaniam (1910-2000)	1998
35.	Loknayak Jayaprakash Narayan (Posthumous) (1902-1979)	1999
36.	Professor Amartya Sen (b-1933)	1999
37.	Lokpriya Gopinath Bordoloi (Posthumous) (1890-1950)	1999
38.	Pandit Ravi Shankar (1920-2012)	1999
39.	Sushil Lata Dinanath Mangeshkar (b-1929)	2001
40.	Ustad Bismillah Khan (1916-2006)	2001
41.	Pandit Bhimsen Gururaj Joshi (1922-2011)	2009
42.	Prof. C.N.R. Rao (1934)	2014
43.	Shri. Sachin Ramesh Tendulkar (1973)	2014
44.	Pandit Madan Mohan Malaviya (Posthumous) (1861-1946)	2015
45.	Shri Atal Bihari Vajpayee (b. 1924)	2015

PADMA AWARDS ANNOUNCED ON REPUBLIC DAY 2016

Padma Vibhushan Recipients	:	Ms. Yamini Krishnamurthi
	:	Shri Rajinikanth
	:	Smt. Girija Devi
	:	Shri Ramoji Rao
	:	Dr. Viswanathan Shanta
	:	Shri Shri Ravi Shankar
	:	Shri Jagmohan
	:	Dr. Vasudev Kalkante Antre
	:	Shri Avinash Dixit (Foreigner)
	:	Late Dhiru Bhai Ambani (Posthumous)
Padma Bhushan Recipients	:	Sh. Anupam Kher
	:	Sh. Udit Narayan Jha
	:	Sh. Ram V. Sutar
	:	Sh. Heisnam Kanhailal
	:	Sh. Vinod Rai
	:	Dr. Yarigadda Lakshmi Prasad
	:	Prof. N.S. Ramanuja Tatacharya
	:	Dr. Barjinder Singh Hamdard

	:	Prof. D. Nageshwar Reddy
	:	Swami Tejomayananda
	:	Shri Hafeez Contractor
	:	Shri Ravindra Chandra Bhargava
	:	Dr. Venkata Rama Rao Alla
	:	Ms. Saina Nehwal
	:	Ms Sania Mirza
	:	Ms. Indu Jain
	:	Late Swami Dayanand Sarawasati (Posthumous)
	:	Shri Robert Blakwill (Foreigner)
	:	Shri Pallonji Shapoorji Mistry (NRI/PIO)
Padma Shri Recipients	:	Smt. Prathibha Prahlad
	:	Sh. Bhikhudan Gadhvi
	:	Shri Sribhas Chandra Supakar
	:	Shri Ajay Devgan
	:	Ms. Priyanka Chopra
	:	Pt. Tulsidas Borkar
	:	Dr. Soma Ghosh
	:	Shri Nila Madhab Panda
	:	Shri S.S. Rajamouli
	:	Shri Madhur Bhandarkar
	:	Prof. M. Venkatesh Kumar
	:	Ms. Gulabi Sapera
	:	Smt. Mamta Chandrakar
	:	Ms. Malini Awasthi
	:	Shri Jai Prakash Lekhiwal
	:	Shri K. Laxma Goud
	:	Shri Bhalchandra Dattatray Mondhe
	:	Shri Naresh Chander Lal
	:	Shri Dhirendra Nath Bezbaruah

: Shri Prahlad Chandra Tasa

: Dr. Ravindra Nagar

: Sh. Dahyabhai Shastri

: Dr. Santeshivara Bhyrappa

: Shri Haldar Nag

: Shri Kameshwaram Brahma

: Prof. Pushpesh Pant

: Shri Jawaharlal Kaul

: Sh. Ashok Malik

: Dr. Mannam Gopi Chand

: Prof. Ravi Kant

: Prof. Ram Harsh Singh

: Prof. Shiv Narain Kureel

: Dr. Sabya Sachi Sarkar

: Dr. Alla Gopala Krishna Gokhale

: Prof. T.K. Lahiri

: Dr. Praveen Chandra

: Prof. (Dr.) Daljeet Singh Gambhir

: Dr. Chandrasekar Shesadri Thoguluva

: Dr. (Mrs.) Anil Kumari Malhotra

: Prof. M.V. Padma Srivastava

: Dr. Sudhir V. Shah

: Dr. M. M. Joshi

: Prof. (Dr.) John Ebnezar

: Dr. Nayudamma Yarlagadda

: Shri Simon Oraon

: Shri Imitiaz Qureshi

: Sh. Piyush Pandey

: Sh. Subhash Palekar

: Sh. Ravinder Kumar Sinha

: Dr. H.R. Nagendra
: Sh. M.C. Mehta
: Sh. M.N. Krishna Mani
: Sh. Ujjwal Nikam
: Sh. Tokheho Sema
: Dr. Satish Kumar
: Dr. Mylswamy Annadurai
: Prof. Dipankar Chatterji
: Prof. (Dr.) Ganapati Dadasaheb Yadav
: Smt. (Prof.) Veena Tandon
: Sh. Onkar Nath Srivastava
: Ms. Sunita Krishnan
: Sh. Ajoy Kumar Datta
: Shri M. Pandit Dasa
: Sh. P.P. Gopinathan Nair
: Smt. Madeleine Herman de Blic
: Shri Srinivasan Damal Kandalai
: Shri Sudhakar Olwe
: Dr. T.V. Narayana
: Shri Arunachalam Murugantham
: Ms. Deepika Kumari
: Sh. Sushil Doshi
: Sh. Mahesh Sharma
: Sh. Saurabh Srivastava
: Sh. Dilip Sanghvi
: Dr. Keki Hormusji Gharda
: Sh. Prakash Chand Surana (Posthumous)
: Sh. Saeed Jaffrey (NRI/PIO/Posthumous)
: Shri Michael Postel (Foreigner)
: Sh. Salman Amin Sal Khan (NRI/PIO)
: Smt. Hui Lan Zhang (Foreigner)

	:	Shri Predrag K. Nikic (Foreigner)
	:	Dr. Sundar Aditya Menon (NRI/PIO)
	:	Sh. Ajaypal Singh Banga (NRI/PIO)

Sources: http:/mha.nic.in

JEEVAN RAKSHAK PADAK SERIES OF AWARDS

Sarvottam Jeevan Raksha Padak (3)

1. Shri Ullas Unnikrishnan (Posthumous), Kerala
2. Shri Munna Alias Ramdars Sisodiya (Posthumous), Madhya Pradesh
3. Shri Ankit Kumar Mishra (Posthumous), Uttar Pradesh

Uttam Jeevan Raksha Padak (9)

1. Shri Shivakumar R., Karnataka
2. Shri Laldinpuia, Mizoram
3. Shri Shaitan Singh (Posthumous), Rajasthan
4. Dr. Jitendra Kumar Soni, Rajasthan
5. Master Shourya Veer Singh (Posthumous), Madhya Pradesh
6. Kumari Riya Chaudhary (Posthumous), Uttar Pradesh
7. Kumari Monika alias Manisha (Posthumous), Uttarakhand
8. Master Gaurav Kumari Bharti (Posthumous), Uttar Pradesh
9. Shri Ravindra Pal Singh (Posthumous), Uttar Pradesh

Jeevan Raksha Padak (38)

1. Shri Vikas Kumar Singh, Chhattisgarh
2. Shri Amar Singh Gond, Chhattisgarh
3. Master Abhishek P.V., Kerala
4. Shri Tomy Thomas, Kerala
5. Shri Praveen P.K., Kerala
6. Shri Jineesh, Kerala
7. Shri Rabeesh, Kerala
8. Shri Vipin, Kerala
9. Shri Kiran Das, Kerala
10. Shri Pradeep, M.V., Kerala
11. Shri Harish Kumar Bhil, Rajasthan

12. Shri Satish Vaijanathrao Bolegave, Maharashtra
13. Miss. Podo Soba, Mizoram
14. Shri Syamol Kanty Chakma, Mizoram
15. Master Lalduhawma, Mizoram
16. Smt. R. Zoengmawi, Mizoram
17. Shri R. Rothantluanga, Mizoram
18. Shri Kuldeep Singh Kumpawat, Rajasthan
19. Shri Rishipal Singh Kumpawat, Rajasthan
20. Shri Jawahar Singh Yadav, Uttar Pradesh
21. Shri Narender Singh, Uttarakhand
22. Shri Shree Prakash, Uttar Pradesh
23. Shri Kesav Kumar Yadav, Uttar Pradesh
24. Shri Amit Kumar, Haryana
25. Master Aditya Raj Aanjaneya, Rajasthan
26. Kumari Abhiruchi Shrivastava, Madhya Pradesh
27. Master Muhammed Vahid P, Kerala
28. Master Romario Johnson, Kerala
29. Master Akshay Anand Tambe, Maharashtra
30. Shri Mohit Kumar Mongare, Chhatisgarh
31. Shri Kanhaiya Gadiya, Chhattisgarh
32. Shri Avinash Pandey, Uttar Pradesh
33. Md. Javed Hussain, Bihar
34. Shri Onkar Singh, Jammu & Kashmir
35. Shri Rizen Wanchok, Jammu & Kashmir
36. Shri Manjeet Singh, Punjab
37. Shri Yogesh Kumar, Haryana
38. Shri Narendra Singh, Uttarakhand

SAHITYA AKADEMI AWARDS 2015

Language	Title and Genre	Author
Assamese	Akashar Chhabi Aru Anyanya Galpa (Short Stories)	Kula Saikia
Bodo	Baidi Dengkhw Baidi Gab (Poetry)	Brajendra Kumar Brahma
Dogri	Parchhamen Di Lo (Poetry)	Dhian Singh
English	Chronicle of a Corpse Bearer (Novel)	Cyrus Mistry
Gujarati	Antey Aarambh (Part I & II) (Essays)	Rasik Shah
Hindi	Aag Ki Hansi (Poetry)	Ramdarash Mishra
Kannada	Akshaya Kavya (Poetry)	K.V. Tirumalesh

Kashmiri	Jamis Ta Kasheeri Manz Kashir Natia Adabuk Tawareekh (Criticism)	Bashir Bhadarwahi
Konkani	Karna Parva (Play)	Uday Bhembre
Maithili	Khissa (Short Stories)	Man Mohan Jha
Malayalam	Aarachar (Novel)	K.R. Meera
Manipuri	Ahingna Yekshilliba Mang (Poetry)	Kshetri Rajen
Marathi	Chalat-Chitravyooh (Memoirs)	Arun Khopkar
Nepali	Samayaka Prativimbaharu (Short Stories)	Gupta Pradhan
Odia	Mahishasurara Muhan (Short Stories)	Bibhuti Pattanaik
Punjabi	Maat Lok (Novel)	Jaswinder Singh
Rajasthani	Gawaad (Novel)	Madhu Acharya 'Ashawadi'
Sanskrit	Vanadevi (Epic)	Ram Shankar Awasthi
Santali	Paarsi Khatir (Play)	Rabilal Tudu
Sindhi	Mahengi Murk (Short Stories)	Maya Rahi
Tamil	Ilakkiya Suvadugal (Essays)	A. Madhavan
Telugu	Vimuktha (Short Stories)	Volga
Urdu	Tasawwuf Aur Bakti (Tanqeedi Aur Taqabuli Mutalea) (Criticism)	Shamim Tariq

Award for Bengali language to be declared later

NOBEL LAUREATES

KAILASH SATYARTHI (b. 1954): The Nobel Peace Prize of 2014 was awarded to Kailash Satyarthi for struggle against the suppression of children and young people and for the right of all children to education. Satyarthi was born in Vidisha, Madhya Pradesh. He completed his degree in electrical engineering and a post-graduate degree in high voltage engineering. In 1980, he left his career as an electrical engineer to set up Bachpan Bachao Andolan (Save Childhood Movement). He also heads the Global March Against Child Labour, a movement to mobilise worldwise efforts to protect and promote the rights of all children.

VENKATRAMAN RAMAKRISHNAN (b. 1952) : Venkatraman Ramakrishnan was awarded the Nobel Prize for Chemistry in 2009 for studies of the structure and function of the ribosome, molecular machine that makes protein. He was born in Chidambaram, Tamil Nadu. Dr. Ramakrishnan earned his B.Sc. in Physics (1971) from M. S. University in Baroda, Gujarat and Ph.D. (1976) in Physics from Ohio University in the USA. Making a transition from physics to biology, he studied a molecule called rhodopsin, as a graduate student in biology at the University of California, San Diego, from 1976 to 1978.

AMARTYA SEN (b-1933) : Prof. Amartya Sen is the recipient of the Nobel Prize for Economics for the year 1998, becoming the first Asian to have been honoured with the award. The Santiniketan-born economist who is a pioneer in Welfare Economics has to his credit several books and papers on aspects of welfare and development. An economist with a difference, Prof. Sen is a humanist. He has distinguished himself with his outstanding writings on famine, poverty, democracy, gender and social issues. The 'impossibility theorem' suggested earlier by Kenneth Arrow states that it was not possible to aggregate individual choices into a satisfactory choice for society as a whole. Prof. Sen showed mathematically that societies could find ways to alleviate such a poor outcome.

SUBRAMANIAN CHANDRASHEKHAR (1910-1995) : The Nobel Prize for Physics in 1983 was awarded to Dr S. Chandrashekhar, an Indian-born astrophysicist. Educated in Presidency College, Chennai, Dr Chandrashekhar happened to be the nephew of his Nobel forbear, Sir C.V. Raman. He later migrated to the United States where he authored several books on Astrophysics and Stellar Dynamics. He developed a theory on white dwarf stars which posts a limit of mass of dwarf stars known also as Chandrashekhar Limit. His theory explains the final stages of stellar evolution.

MOTHER TERESA (1910-1997) : The Nobel Peace Prize was awarded to Mother Teresa in 1979. Of Albanian parentage, Agnes Gonxha Bojaxhiu was born at Skopje, now in Yogoslavia. She joined the Irish order of the Sisters of Loretto at Dublin in 1928 and came to Kolkata in 1929 as a missionary, only to find the misery of the abandoned and the destitute. Concern for the poor and the sick prompted her to found a new congregation, Missionaries of Charity. Having become an Indian citizen, Mother Teresa served the cause of dying destitutes, lepers and drug addicts, through *Nirmal Hriday* (meaning Pure Heart), the main centre of her activity. Her selfless service and unique devotion, not only to helpless fellow-Indians but also to the cause of world peace, earned her and India the first Nobel Peace Prize.

HARGOBIND KHORANA (b. 1922-2011) : Hargobind Khorana was awarded the Nobel Prize for Medicine in 1968. Of Indian origin, Dr Khorana was born in Raipur, Punjab (now in Pakistan). He took his doctoral degree in Chemistry from Liverpool University and joined the University of Wisconsin as a Faculty Member in 1960. His major breakthrough in the field of Medicine — interpreting the genetic code and analysing its function in protein synthesis — fetched him the Nobel Prize.

CHANDRASEKHARA VENKATA RAMAN (1888-1970) : India's first Nobel Prize for Physics was claimed in 1930 by the renowned physicist Sir C.V. Raman. Born at Thiruvanaikkaval near Tiruchirapalli in Tamilnadu, Raman studied at Presidency College, Chennai. Later, he served as Professor of Physics at Calcutta University. Recipient of many honours and awards, including the title of 'Sir', Sir C.V. Raman received the Nobel Prize for an important optics research, in which he discovered that diffused light contained rays of other wavelengths—what is now popularly known as Raman Effect. His theory discovered in 1928 explains the change in the frequency of light passing through a transparent medium.

RABINDRANATH TAGORE (1861-1941) : Rabindranath Tagore was the first Indian ever to receive a Nobel Prize. Popularly known as *Gurudev,* India's Poet Laureate Tagore was born on May 07, 1861 in Kolkata. He was awarded the Nobel Prize for Literature in recognition of his work *Geetanjali,* a collection of poems, in 1913. Tagore wrote many love lyrics. *Geetanjali* and *Sadhana* are among his important works. The poet, dramatist and novelist is also the author of India's National Anthem. In 1901, he founded the famous Santiniketan which later came to be known as Vishwabharati University.

COMMANDERS-IN-CHIEF

Name	Tenure
General Sir Rob Lockhart	August 15, 1947-December 31, 1947
General Sir Roy Bucher	January 01, 1948-January 14, 1949
General (Late Field Marshal) K.M. Cariappa	January 15, 1949-January 14, 1953
General Maharaj Rajendra Sinhji	January 15, 1953-March 31, 1955

CHIEFS OF ARMY STAFF

Name	Tenure
General Maharaj Rajendra Sinhji	January 15, 1953-May 14, 1955
General S.M. Srinagesh	May 15, 1955-May 07, 1957
General K.S. Thimayya	May 08, 1957-May 07, 1961
General P.N. Thapar	May 08, 1961-November 19, 1962
General J.N. Choudhuri	November 20, 1962-June 07, 1966
General P.P. Kumaramangalam	June 08, 1966-June 07, 1969
Field Marshal S.H.F.J. Manekshaw	08 June 1969-15 January 1973
General G.G. Bewoor	January 16, 1973-May 31, 1975
General T.N. Raina	June 01, 1975-May 31, 1978
General O.P. Malhotra	June 01, 1978-May 31, 1981
General K.V. Krishna Rao	June 01, 1981-July 31, 1983
General A.S. Vaidya	August 01, 1983-January 31, 1985
General K. Sundarji	February 01, 1985-May 31, 1988
General V.N. Sharma	June 01, 1988-June 30, 1990
General S.F. Rodrigues	July 01, 1990-June 30, 1993
General B.C. Joshi	July 01, 1993-November 19, 1994
General S. Roychowdhury	November 20, 1994-September 30, 1997
General V.P. Malik	01 October 1997-30 September 2000
General S. Padmanabhan	October 01, 2000-December 30, 2002
General N.C. Vij	December 31, 2002-January 31, 2005
General J.J. Singh	February 01, 2005 -September 30, 2007
General Deepak Kapoor	September 30, 2007-March 30, 2010
General V.K. Singh	March 31, 2010 - May 31, 2012
General Bikram Singh	June 01, 2012 - July 31, 2014
General Dalbir Singh	August 01, 2014 - till date

Source : indianarmy.nic.in

CHIEFS OF NAVAL STAFF

Name	Tenure
Rear Admiral J.T.S. Hall	August 15, 1947-August 14, 1948
Admiral Sir Edward Parry	August 14, 1948-October 13, 1951
Admiral Sir Mark Pizey	October 13, 1951-July 21, 1955
Vice Admiral Sir Stephen Carlill	July 21, 1955-April 21, 1958
Vice Admiral R.D. Katari	April 22, 1958-June 04, 1962
Vice Admiral B.S. Soman	June 04, 1962-March 03, 1966
Admiral A.K. Chatterjee	March 03, 1966-February 27, 1970
Admiral S.M. Nanda	February 28, 1970-February 28, 1973
Admiral S.N. Kohli	February 28, 1973-February 28, 1976
Admiral J.L. Cursetji	February 29, 1976-February 28, 1979
Admiral R.L. Pereira	February 28, 1979-February 28, 1982
Admiral O.S. Dawson	February 28, 1982-November 30, 1984
Admiral R.H. Tahiliani	November 30, 1984-November 30, 1987
Admiral J.G. Nadkarni	November 30, 1987-November 30, 1990
Admiral L. Ramdas	November 30, 1990-September 30, 1993
Admiral V.S. Shekhawat	September 30, 1993-September 30, 1996
Admiral Vishnu Bhagwat	September 30, 1996-December 30, 1998
Admiral Sushil Kumar	December 30, 1998 -December 29, 2001
Admiral Madhvendra Singh	December 29, 2001 -July 31, 2004
Admiral Arun Prakash	July 31, 2004 -October 30, 2006
Admiral Sureesh Mehta	October 31, 2006 -August 31, 2009
Admiral Nirmal Verma	August 31, 2009 -August 31, 2012
Admiral D.K. Joshi	August 31, 2012 - April 16, 2014
Admiral Robin K. Dhawan	April 17, 2014 -May 31, 2014
Admiral Sunil Lanba	May 31, 2016 - till date

Source : india.gov.in

CHIEFS OF AIR STAFF

Name	Tenure
Air Marshal Sir Thomas W. Elmhirst	August 15, 1947-February 21, 1950
Air Marshal Sir Ronald I. Chapman	February 22, 1950-December 09, 1951
Air Marshal Sir Gerald E. Gibbs	December 10, 1951-March 31, 1954
Air Marshal S. Mukherjee	April 01, 1954-November 08, 1960
Air Marshal A.M. Engineer	December 01, 1960-July 31, 1964

Air Chief Marshal Arjan Singh	August 01, 1964- July 15, 1969
Air Chief Marshal P.C. Lal	July 16, 1969-January 15, 1973
Air Chief Marshal O.P. Mehra	January 16, 1973-January 31, 1976
Air Chief Marshal H. Moolgavkar	February 01, 1976-August 31, 1978
Air Chief Marshal I.H. Latif	September 01, 1978-August 31, 1981
Air Chief Marshal Dilbagh Singh	September 01, 1981-September 03, 1984
Air Chief Marshal L.M. Katre	September 04, 1984-July 01, 1985
Air Chief Marshal D.A. La Fontaine	July 03, 1985-July 31, 1988
Air Chief Marshal S.K. Mehra	August 01, 1988-July 31, 1991
Air Chief Marshal N.C. Suri	July 31, 1991-July 31, 1993
Air Chief Marshal S.K. Kaul	August 01, 1993- December 31, 1995
Air Chief Marshal S.K. Sareen	December 31, 1995-December 31, 1998
Air Chief Marshal A.Y. Tipnis	December 31, 1998-December 31, 2001
Air Chief Marshal S. Krishnaswamy	December 31, 2001-December 31, 2004
Air Chief Marshal S. P. Tyagi	December 31, 2004-March 31, 2007
Air Chief Marshal F. H. Major	March 31, 2007-May 31, 2009
Air Chief Marshal P. V. Naik	May 31, 2009-July 31, 2011
Air Chief Marshal N.A.K. Browne	July 31, 2011-December 31, 2013
Air Chief Marshal Aroop Raha	December 31, 2013-till date

Source : indianairforce.nic.in

WINNERS OF PARAM VIR CHAKRA

Major Som Nath Sharma, Kumaon Regiment
Posthumous-November 1947 (Kashmir Operations 1947-48)

2nd Lt. R.R. Rane, Corps of Engineers
April 1948 (Kashmir Operations 1947-48)

Company Havaldar Major Piru Singh, Rajputana Rifles
Posthumous-July 1948 (Kashmir Operations 1947-48)

L/NK Karam Singh, Sikh Regiment
October 1948 (Kashmir Operations 1947-48)

Naik Jadu Nath Singh, Rajput Regiment
Posthumous-February 1948 (Kashmir Operations 1947-48)

Captain Gurbachan Singh Salaria, Gorkha Rifles
Posthumous-December 1961 (Congo)

Major Dhan Singh Thapa, Gorkha Rifles
October 1962 (Ladakh)

Subedar Joginder Singh, Sikh Regiment
Posthumous-October 1962 (NEFA)

Major Shaitan Singh, Kumaon Regiment
Posthumous-November 1962 (Ladakh)

CQMH Abdul Hamid, Grenadiers
Posthumous-September 1965 (Operation against Pakistan)

Lt. Col. A.B. Tarapore, Poona Horse
Posthumous-October 1965 (Operation against Pakistan)

Flg. Officer Nirmal Jit Singh Sekhon, Flg. Pilot
Posthumous-December 1971 (Indo-Pakistan conflict)

Major Hoshiar Singh, Grenadiers
December 1971 (Indo-Pakistan conflict)

2nd Lt. Arun Khetarpal, 17 Poona Horse
Posthumous-December 1971 (Indo-Pakistan conflict)

L/NK Albert Ekka, Brigade of Guards
Posthumous-December 1971 (Indo-Pakistan conflict)

Naib Subedar Bana Singh, J & K Light Infantry
June 1987 (Operations in Siachen Glacier)

Major Ramaswamy Parameswaran, Mahar Regiment,
Posthumous-November 1987 (IPKF Operations in Sri Lanka)

Capt Vikram Batra, 13 J & K Rifles
Posthumous-June 1999 (OP Vijay in Kargil)

Lt Manoj Kumar Pandey, 11th Gorkha Rifles
Posthumous-July 1999 (OP Vijay in Kargil)

Rifleman Sanjay Kumar, 13 J&K Rifles
July1999 (OP Vijay in Kargil)

Cdr Yogender Singh Yadav, 18 Grenadiers
July 1999 (OP Vijay in Kargil)

GALLANTRY AWARDS

The following Gallantry Awards were announced on Republic Day, 2016:

Award	Total	Posthumous
Gallantry Award		
Ashoka Chakra	1	1
Kirti Chakra	2	1
Shaurya Chakra	8	3
Bar to Sena Medal	1	-
Sena Medal/Nao Sena Medal/Vayu Sena Medal (Gallantry)	48	7
Distinguished Awards		
Param Vishisht Seva Medal	20	-

Uttam Yudh Seva Medal	5	-
Bar to Ati Vishisht Seva Medal	3	-
Ati Vishisht Seva Medal	29	-
Yudh Seva Medal	14	-
Bar to Sena Medal/Nao Sena Medal (Devotion to Duty)	3	-
Sena Medal/Nao Sena Medal/Vayu Sena Medal (Devotion to duty)	37	-
Bar to Vishisht Seva Medal	5	-
Vishisht Seva Medal	71	-

The following Gallantry Awards were announced on Independence Day, 2016 :

Award	**Total**	**Posthumous**
Ashoka Chakra	1	1
Kirti Chakra	-	-
Shaurya Chakra	14	7
Bar to Sena Medal (Gallantry)	-	-
Sena Medal (Gallantry)	63	12
Nao Sena Medal (Gallantry)	2	-
Vayu Sena Medal (Gallantry)	2	-

Source: http://pib.nic.in

LIST OF STATE-WISE NATIONAL HIGHWAYS IN THE COUNTRY[8]

Sl. No.	Name of State	National Highway No.	Total Length (in km)
1	Andhra Pradesh (Seemandhra)	4, 5, 7, 9, 16, 18, 18A, 42 New, 43, 63, 67 Ext. New, 150 New, 167 New, 202, 205, 214, 214A, 216, 219, 221, 222, 234, 326, 326A, 67 New, 71 New, 161 New, 340 New, 340C New, 353 New, 363 New, 365 New, 544D New, 565 New, 765 New	5231.74
2	Arunachal Pradesh	52, 52A, 153, 229, 52B Ext., 37 Ext., 315A, 713 New, 513 New, 313 New, & 713A New	2513.05
3	Assam	6 New, 31, 31B, 31C, 36, 37, 37A, 37E, 38, 39, 44, 51, 52, 52A, 52B, 53, 54, 61, 62, 117A New, 127B New, 127E New, 151, 152, 153, 154, 315A New, 127C New, & 127D New, 329 New, 427 New, 627 New, 702 New, 702B New, 702C New, 702D & 715A New	3811.67

4	Bihar	2, 2C, 19, 28, 28A, 28B, 30, 30A, 31, 57, 57A, 77, 80, 81, 82, 83, 84, 85, 98, 99, 101, 102, 103, 104, 105, 106, 107, 110, 122A New, 131A New, 133 New, 133B New, 219 New, 227A New, 327A New, 327 Ext. New, 333 New, 333A New, 333B New, 527A New, 527C New, 727 A New & 766C	4678.79
5	Chandigarh	21	15.28
6	Chhattisgarh	6, 12A, 16, 43, 78, 111, 130A New, 130B New, 130C New, 130D New, 149B New, 163A New, 200, 202, 216, 217, 221, 343 New, 930 New	3078.40
7	Delhi	1, 2, 8, 10, 24 & 236	80.00
8	Goa	4A, 17, 17A & 17B	262.00
9	Gujarat	NE-I, 6, 8, 8A, 8B, 8D, 8E, 14, 15, 56, 58 New, 58 Ext. New, 59, 113, 228, 251 New, 753B New, 848 & 848A New, 848B New, 341 New, 68 Ext., New, 147A New, 168 New, 68A New, 351 New, 927D New & 953 New	4970.90
10	Haryana	1, 2, 8, 10, 11 New, 21A, 22, 54 New, 64, 65, 71, 71A, 72, 73, 73A, 71B, 148B New, 236, 248 A New, 254 New, 334B New, 352A, 444A New, 703 New, 709 Ext. New, 709A New & NE-II	2622.48
11	Himachal Pradesh	1A, 3 New, 20, 20A, 21, 21A, 22, 70, 72, 72B, 88, 73A, 154A New, 305 New, 503 New, 503A New, 503 Ext. New, 505 New, 705 New, 907 A New	2622.48
12	Jammu & Kashmir	1A, 1B, 1C, 1D, 3 New, 144 New, 144A New, 301 New, 444 New, 501 New, 701 New, 244 New	2593.00
13	Jharkhand	2, 6, 23, 31, 32, 33, 43 New, 75, 78, 80, 98, 99, 100, 114A New, 133 New, 133A New, 133B, 143 New, 143A New, 220 New, 333 New, 333A New, 343 New & 419 New	2653.64
14	Karnataka	4, 4A, 7, 9, 13, 17, 48, 50 New, 63, 67, 67 New, 150, 150 Ext. New, 150A New, 167 New, 169A New, 173 New, 206, 207, 209, 212, 218, 234, 275 New, 367 New, 766C	6502.29
15	Kerala	17, 47, 47A, 47C, 49, 183A New, 185 New, 208, 212, 213, & 220	1811.52
16	Madhya Pradesh	3, 7, 12, 12A, 25, 26, 26A, 26B, 27, 56 New, 59, 59A, 69, 69A, 75, 76, 78, 86, 92, 927A New & 339B	5193.57
17	Maharashtra	3, 4, 4C, 6, 7, 8, 9, 13, 16, 17, 26B, 50, 50 New, 69, 150 Ext. New, 161 New, 204, 211,222, 348 New, 848 New, 160 New, 166 New, 166A New, 348 New, 348A New, 353C New, 353D New, 353E New, 361 New, 363 New, 547E New, 548 New, 753 New, 753 A New, 150, 166A, 753B New, 848A, 930 New & 953 New, 965New	7434.79
18	Manipur	39, 53, 102 New,102A New, 102B New, 102C New, 129A New, 108A New, 129 New, 137 New, 137A New, 150, 155, 702A New	1745.74
19	Meghalaya	40, 44, 51, 62 & 127B New	1204.36

20	Mizoram	6 New, 44A, 54, 54A, 54B, 102B New,150, 154, 302 New, 306A New, & 502A New	1381.00
21	Nagaland	36, 39, 61, 129 New, 150, 155, 702 New, 702A New & 702B New,702 D	1150.09
22	Odisha	5, 5A, 6, 23, 42, 43, 60, 75, 130 C New, 153B New, 157 New, 200, 201, 203, 203A, 215, 217, 220 New, 224, 326 New, & 326A New	4644.52
23	Puducherry	45A & 66	64.03
24	Punjab	1, 1A, 10, 15, 20, 21, 22, 64, 70, 71, 72, 95, 103 A New, 154A, 205A New, 254 New, 344A New, 344B New, 503 Ext. New, 503A New, 703 New, 703A New, 754 New &148B New	2769.15
25	Rajasthan	3, 11 New, 123 New (3A Old), 8, 11, 11A, 11B, 11C, 12, 14, 15, 25 Ext. New, 54 New, 65, 458 New& 65A Old, 71B 76, 58 Extn. New &76A Old, 758 New & 76B Old, 79, 79A New, 89, 90, 113, 112, 114, 116, 148B New, 148D New & 116A Old. 158 New, 162A New, 162 Extn. New, 168 New, 168A New, 248A New, 325 New, 709 Ext. New, 927A New	7906.20
26	Sikkim	31A, 310, 310A New, 510 New, 710 New	309.00
27	Tamil Nadu	4, 5, 7, 7A, 45, 45A, 45B, 45C, 46, 47, 47B, 49, 66, 67, 68, 205, 207, 208, 209, 210, 219, 220, 226, 226 Ext., 227, 230, 234, 381 New, & 532 New	5006.14
28	Tripura	44, 44A, 108A & 208 New	577.00
29	Telangana	7, 9, 16, 202, 221, 222, 223, 326 New, 167 New, 150 New, 363 New, 365 New, 565 New, 161, 765 New, 50 New, 563 New, & 365 A New	2635.84
30	Uttarakhand	9 New, 58, 72, 72A, 72B, 73, 74, 87, 94, 107A New, 108, 109, 123, 119, 121,125, 309A New, 309B New, 334A & 707A New	2841.92
31	Uttar Pradesh	2, 2A, 3, 123 New (3A Old), 7, 11, 12A, 19, 24, 24A, 24B, 25, 25A, 26, 27, 28, 28B, 28C, 29, 56, 56A, 56B, 58, 72A, 73, 74, 75, 76, 86, 87, 91, 91A, 92, 93 ,96, 97, 119, 219 New, 227 A New, 231, 232, 232A, 233, 235, 330, 330A New, 330 B New, 334B New, 709 A, 727 A New, 730 New, 730 A New, 731 A New, 931 New, 931A New & NE-II	8483.00
32	West Bengal	2, 2B, 6, 10, 31, 31A, 31C, 31D, 32, 34, 35, 41, 55, 60, 60A, 80, 81, 114A New, 116B New, 117, 131A, 133A New, 317A, 327B, 419 New, 512 New & 717,	2909.80
33	Andaman & Nicobar	223	330.70
34	Dadra & Nagar Haveli	848A New	31.00
35	Daman and Diu	848B New & 251 New	22.00
		Total	100087.08

Sources: Ministry of Road Transport & Highways http://morth.nic.in

AMENDMENTS TO THE CONSTITUTION

1. *The Constitution (First Amendment) Act, 1950*—This amendment provided for several new grounds of restrictions to the right to freedom of speech and expression and the right to practise any profession or to carry on any trade or business as contained in Article 19 of the Constitution. These restrictions related to public order, friendly relations with foreign States or incitement to an offence in relation to the right to freedom of speech, and to the prescribing of professional or technical qualifications or the carrying on by the State, etc., of any trade, business, industry or service in relation to the right to carry on any trade or business. The amendment also inserted two new Articles, 31A and 31B and the Ninth Schedule to give protection from challenge to land reform laws.

2. *The Constitution (Second Amendment) Act, 1952*—By this amendment, the scale or representation for election to the Lok Sabha was readjusted.

3. *The Constitution (Third Amendment) Act, 1954*—This amendment substituted entry 33 of List III (Concurrent List) of the Seventh Schedule to make it correspond to Article 369.

4. *The Constitution (Fourth Amendment) Act, 1955*—Article 31 (2) of the Constitution was amended to re-state more precisely the State's power of compulsory acquisition and requisitioning of private property and distinguish it from cases where the operation of regulatory or prohibitory laws of the States results in "deprivation of property". Article 31A of the Constitution was also amended to extend its scope to cover categories of essential welfare legislation like abolition of zamindaris, proper planning of urban and rural areas and for effecting a full control over the mineral and oil resources of the country, etc. Six Acts were also included in the Ninth Schedule. Article 305 was also amended to save certain laws providing of State Monopolies.

5. *The Constitution (Fifth Amendment) Act, 1955*—This amendment made a change in Article 3 so as to empower President to specify a time limit for state legislatures to convey their views on the proposed Central laws affecting areas, boundaries, etc., of their states.

6. *The Constitution (Sixth Amendment) Act, 1956*—This amendment made some changes in Articles 269 and 286 relating to taxes on sale and purchase of goods in the course of inter-state trade and commerce. A new entry 92 A was added to the Union List of the Seventh Schedule to the Constitution.

7. *The Constitution (Seventh Amendment) Act, 1956*—This amendment purported to give effect to the recommendations of the State Reorganisation Commission and the necessary consequential changes. Broadly, the then existing states and territories were changed to have two-fold classification of states and union territories. The amendment also provided for composition of the House of the People, re-adjustment after every census, provisions regarding the establishment of new High Courts, High Court Judges, etc.

8. *The Constitution (Eighth Amendment) Act, 1960*—Article 334 was amended with a view to extending the period of reservation of seats for Scheduled Castes and Scheduled Tribes and to the Anglo-Indian community by nomination in Parliament and in the State Legislatures for a further period of ten years.

9. *The Constitution (Ninth Amendment) Act, 1960*—The purpose of this amendment is to give effect to the transfer of certain territories to Pakistan in pursuance of the agreement entered into between Governments of India and Pakistan. This amendment was necessitated in view of the Judgement of Supreme Court in *In Re Berubari Union* by which it was held that any agreement to cede a territory to another country could not be implemented by a law made under Article 3 but would only be implemented by an amendment of the Constitution.

10. *The Constitution (Tenth Amendment) Act, 1961*—This Act amended Article 240 and the First Schedule in order to include areas of Dadra and Nagar Haveli as a Union Territory and to provide for its administration under the regulation making powers of President.

11. *The Constitution (Eleventh Amendment) Act, 1961*—The purpose of this amendment was to amend Articles 66 and 71 of the Constitution to provide that the election of President or Vice President could not be challenged on the ground of any vacancy in the appropriate electoral college.

12. *The Constitution (Twelfth Amendment) Act, 1962*—This amendment sought to include Goa, Daman and Diu as a Union Territory and to amend Article 240 for the purpose.

13. *The Constitution (Thirteenth Amendment) Act, 1962*—By this amendment, a new Article 371A was added to make special provisions with respect to state of Nagaland in pursuance of an agreement between Government of India and Naga People's Convention.

14. *The Constitution (Fourteenth Amendment) Act, 1962*—By this Act, Pondicherry was included in the First Schedule as a Union Territory, and this Act has also enabled the creation of Legislature by Parliamentary law for Himachal Pradesh, Manipur, Tripura, Goa, Daman and Diu and Pondicherry.

15. *The Constitution (Fifteenth Amendment) Act, 1963*—This amendment provided for increase in the age of retirement of High Court Judges and for the provision of compensatory allowance to judges who are transferred from one High Court to another. The Act also provided for appointment of retired judges to act as judges of High Court. Article 226 was also enlarged to empower High Court to issue direction, orders or writs to any Government authority, etc., if the cause of action for the exercise of such power arose in the territories wherein the High Court exercise jurisdiction notwithstanding that seat of such Government authority is not within those territories. The Act also provided for the exercise of powers of Chairman of the Service Commissions, in their absence, by one of their Members.

16. *The Constitution (Sixteenth Amendment) Act, 1963*—Article 19 was amended by this Act to impose further restriction on the rights to freedom of speech and expression, to assemble peaceably and without arms and to form associations in the interests of sovereignty and integrity of India. The oath of affirmation to be subscribed by candidates seeking election to Parliament and State Legislatures have been amended to include as one of the conditions that they will uphold the sovereignty and integrity of India. The amendments are intended to promote national integration.

17. *The Constitution (Seventeenth Amendment) Act, 1964*—Article 31A was further amended to prohibit the acquisition of land under personal cultivation unless the market value of the land is paid as compensation and the definition of "estate" as contained in that Article had also been enlarged with retrospective effect. The Ninth Schedule had also been amended to include 44 more Acts.

18. *The Constitution (Eighteenth Amendment) Act, 1966*—Article 3 was amended by this Act to specify that the expression "State" will include a union territory also and to make it clear that the power to form a new state under this Article includes a power to form a new state or union territory by uniting a part of a state or a union territory to another state or union territory.

19. *The Constitution (Nineteenth Amendment) Act, 1966*—Article 324 was amended to effect a consequential change as a result of the decision to abolish Election Tribunals and to hear election petitions by High Courts.

20. *The Constitution (Twentieth Amendment) Act, 1966*—This amendment was necessitated by the decision of the Supreme Courts in Chandramohan vs. State of Uttar Pradesh in which certain appointments of District Judges in State of Uttar Pradesh were declared void by Supreme Court. A new Article 233A was added and the appointments made by Governor were validated.

21. *The Constitution (Twenty-first Amendment) Act, 1967*—By this amendment, Sindhi Language was included in the Eighth Schedule.

22. *The Constitution (Twenty-second Amendment) Act, 1969*—This act was enacted to facilitate the formation of a new autonomous state of Meghalaya within state of Assam.

23. *The Constitution (Twenty-third Amendment) Act, 1969*—Article 334 was amended so as to extend the safeguards in respect of reservation of seats in Parliament and State Legislatures for Schedules Castes and Scheduled Tribes as well as for Anglo-Indians for a further period of ten years.

24. *The Constitution (Twenty-fourth Amendment) Act, 1971*—This amendment was passed in the context of a situation that emerged with the verdict in Golaknath's case by Supreme Court. Accordingly, this Act amended Article 13 and Article 368 to remove all doubts regarding the power of Parliament to amend the Constitution including the Fundamental Rights.

25. *The Constitution (Twenty-fifth Amendment) Act, 1971*—This amendment further amended Article 31 in the wake of the Bank Nationalisation case. The word 'amount' was substituted in place of 'compensation' in the light of the judicial interpretation of the word 'compensation' meaning 'adequate compensation'.

26. *The Constitution (Twenty-sixth Amendment) Act, 1971*—By this amendment, the privy and privileges of the former rulers of Indian states were abolished. This amendment was passed as a result of Supreme Court decision in Madhav Rao's case.

27. *The Constitution (Twenty-seventh Amendment) Act, 1971*—This amendment was passed to provide for certain matters necessitated by the reorganisation of north-eastern states. A new Article 239B was inserted which enabled the promulgation of Ordinances by Administrators of certain union territories.

28. *The Constitution (Twenty-eighth Amendment) Act, 1972*—The amendment was enacted to abolish the special privileges of the members of Indian Civil Services in matters of leave, pension and rights as regard to disciplinary matters.

29. *The Constitution (Twenty-ninth Amendment) Act, 1972*—The Ninth Schedule to the Constitution was amended to include therein two Kerala Acts on land reforms.

30. *The Constitution (Thirtieth Amendment) Act, 1972*—The purpose of the amendment was to amend Article 133 in order to do away with the valuation test of Rs 20,000 as fixed therein, and to provide instead for an appeal to Supreme Court in Civil proceedings only on a certificate issued by High Court that the case involves a substantial question of law of general importance and that in opinion of High Court, the question needs to be decided by Supreme Court.

31. *The Constitution (Thirty-first Amendment) Act, 1973*—This Act *inter alia* raises the upper limit for the representation of states in the Lok Sabha from 500 to 525 and reducing the upper limit for the representation of union territories from 25 members to 20.

32. *The Constitution (Thirty-second Amendment) Act, 1973*—This Act provided the necessary constitutional authority for giving effect to the provision of equal opportunities to different areas of the State of Andhra Pradesh and for the constitution of an Administrative Tribunal with jurisdiction to deal with grievances relating to public services. It also empowered Parliament to legislate for the establishment of a Central University in the State.

33. *The Constitution (Thirty-third Amendment) Act, 1974*—By this amendment, Articles 101 and 190 were amended in order to streamline the procedure for resignation of Members of Parliament and State Legislatures.

34. *The Constitution (Thirty-fourth Amendment) Act, 1974*—By this Act, twenty more land tenure and land reforms laws enacted by various State Legislatures were included in the Ninth Schedule.

35. *The Constitution (Thirty-fifth Amendment) Act, 1974*—By this Act a new Article 2A was added thereby conferring on Sikkim the status of an associate State of Indian Union. Consequent amendments were made to Articles 80 and 81. A new schedule, *i.e.*, Tenth Schedule, was added laying down terms and conditions of association of Sikkim with the Union.

36. *The Constitution (Thirty-sixth Amendment) Act, 1975*—This was enacted to make Sikkim a full-fledged State of Indian Union and to include it in the First Schedule to the Constitution and to allot to Sikkim one seat each in the Council of States and in the House of the People. Article 2A and the Tenth Schedule inserted by the Constitution (Thirty-fifth Amendment) Act were omitted and Articles 80 and 81 were suitably amended.

37. *The Constitution (Thirty-seventh Amendment) Act, 1975*—By this Act, Union Territory of Arunachal Pradesh was provided with a Legislative Assembly. Article 240 of the Constitution was also amended to provide that as in the case of other union territories with Legislatures, the power of President to make regulations for the Union Territory of Arunachal Pradesh may be exercised only when the assembly is either dissolved or its functions remain suspended.

38. *The Constitution (Thirty-eighth Amendment) Act, 1975*—This Act amended Articles 123, 213 and 352 of the Constitution to provide that the satisfaction of President or Governor contained in these Articles would be called in question in any court of law.

39. *The Constitution (Thirty-ninth Amendment)* Act, 1975—By this Act, disputes relating to the election of President, Vice-President, Prime Minister and Speaker are to be determined by such

authority as may be determined by Parliamentary Law. Certain Central enactments were also included in the Ninth Schedule by this Act.

40. *The Constitution (Fortieth Amendment) Act, 1976*—This act provided for vesting in the Union of all mines, minerals and other things of value lying in the ocean within the territorial waters or the continental shelf or the exclusive economic zone of India. It further provided that all other resources of the exclusive economic zone of India shall also vest in the Union. This act also provided that the limits of the territorial waters, the continental shelf, the exclusive economic zone and the maritime zones of India shall be as specified from time to time by or under any law made by Parliament. Also some more Acts were added to the Ninth Scheme.

41. *The Constitution (Forty-first Amendment) Act, 1976*—By this Act, Article 316 was amended to raise the retirement age of Members of State Public Service Commissions and Joint Public Service Commissions from 60 to 62 years.

42. *The Constitution (Forty-second Amendment) Act, 1976*—This act made a number of important amendments in the Constitution. These amendments were mainly for purpose of giving effect to the recommendations of Swaran Singh Committee.

Some of the important amendments made are for the purpose of spelling out expressly the high ideals of socialism, secularism and the integrity of the nation, to make the Directive Principles more comprehensive and giving them precedence over those Fundamental Rights which have been allowed to be relied upon to frustrate socio-economic reforms. The amendment Act also inserted a new chapter on the Fundamental Duties of citizens and made special provisions for dealing with anti-national activities, whether by individuals or by associations. The judiciary provisions were also amended by providing for a requirement as to the minimum number of judges for determining question as to the constitutional validity of law and for a special majority of not less than two-third for declaring any law to be constitutionally invalid.

To reduce the mounting arrears in High Courts and to secure the speedy disposal of service matters, revenue matters and certain other matters of special importance in the context of socio-economic development and progress, this amendment Act provided for the creation of Administrative and other tribunals for dealing with such matters while preserving the jurisdiction of the Supreme Court in regard to such matters under Article 136 of the Constitution. Certain modifications in the writ jurisdiction of High Courts under Article 226 were also made.

43. *The Constitution (Forty-third Amendment) Act, 1977*—This Act *inter alia* provided for the restoration of the jurisdiction of the Supreme Court and High Courts, curtailed by the enactment of the Constitution (Forty-second Amendment) Act, 1976 and accordingly Articles 32A, 131A, 144A, 226A and 228A included in the Constitution by the said amendment, were omitted by this Act. The Act also provided for the omission of Article 31 which conferred special powers on Parliament to enact certain laws in respect of anti-national activities.

44. *The Constitution (Forty-fourth Amendment) Act, 1978*—The right to property which had been the occasion for more than one amendment of Constitution was omitted as a Fundamental Right and it was made only as a legal right. It was, however, ensured that the removal of the right to property from the list of Fundamental Rights would not affect the right of minorities to establish and administer educational institutions of their choice. Article 352 of the Constitution was amended to provide "armed rebellion" as one of the circumstances for declaration of emergency. Internal disturbance not amounting to armed rebellion would not be a ground for the issuance of a Proclamation. The right to personal liberty as contained in Articles 21 and 22 is further strengthened by the provision that a law for preventive detention cannot authorise, in any case, detention for a longer period than two months unless an Advisory Board has reported that there is sufficient cause for such detention. The additional safeguard has also been provided by the requirements that Chairman of an Advisory Board shall be a serving Judge of the appropriate High Court and that the Board shall be constituted in accordance with the recommendations of the Chief Justice of that High Court.

With a view to avoid delays, Articles 132 and 134 were amended and a new Article 134A was inserted to provide that a High Court should consider the question of granting a certificate for appeal to Supreme Court immediately after the delivery of the judgement, final order or sentence concerned on the basis of an oral application by a party or, if the High Court deems it so to do, on its own. The other amendments made by the Act are mainly for removing or correcting the distortions which came into the Constitution by reason of the amendment initiated during the period of internal emergency.

45. *The Constitution (Forty-fifth Amendment) Act, 1980*—This was passed to extend safeguards in respect of reservation of seats in Parliament and State Assemblies for Scheduled Castes, Scheduled Tribes as well as for Anglo-Indians for a further period of ten years.

46. *The Constitution (Forty-sixth Amendment) Act, 1982*—Article 269 was amended so that the tax levied on the consignment of goods in the course of inter-state or commerce shall be assigned to the states. This Article was also amended to enable Parliament to formulate by law principle for determining when a consignment of goods takes place in the course of inter-state trade or commerce. A new entry 92B was also inserted in the Union List to enable the levy of tax on the consignment of goods where such consignment takes place in the course of inter-state trade or commerce.

Clause (3) of Article 286 was amended to enable Parliament to specify, by law, restrictions and conditions in regard to the system of levy rates and other incidence of tax on the transfer of goods involved in the execution of a works contract, on the delivery of goods on hire-purchase or any system of payment of instalments, etc.

Article 366 was also suitably amended to insert a definition of "tax on the sale or purchase of goods" to include transfer for consideration of controlled commodities, transfer of property in goods involved in the execution of a works contract, delivery of goods on hire-purchase or any system of payment by instalments, etc.

47. *The Constitution (Forty-seventh Amendment) Act, 1984*—This amendment is intended to provide for the inclusion of certain land Reforms Acts in the Ninth Schedule to the Constitution with a view to obviating the scope of litigation hampering the implementation process of those Acts.

48. *The Constitution (Forty-eighth Amendment) Act, 1984*—The Proclamation issued by President under Article 356 of the Constitution with respect to the State of Punjab cannot be continued in force for more than one year unless the special conditions mentioned in clause (5) of the said Article are satisfied. As it is felt that the continued force of the said Proclamation is necessary, therefore, the present amendment had been effected so as to make the conditions mentioned in clause (5) of Article 356 inapplicable in the instant case.

49. *The Constitution (Forty-ninth Amendment) Act, 1984*—Tripura Government recommended that the provisions of the Sixth Schedule to the Constitution may be made applicable to tribal areas of that State. The amendment involved in this Act is intended to give a constitutional security to the autonomous District Council functioning in the State.

50. *The Constitution (Fiftieth Amendment) Act, 1984*—by Article 33 of the constitution, Parliament is empowered to enact laws determining to what extent any of the rights conferred by Part III of the constitution shall, in their application to the members of the armed forces or the forces charged with the maintenance of public order, be restricted or abrogated so as to ensure proper discharge of their duties and maintenance of discipline among them.

It was proposed to amend Article 33 so as to bring within its ambit:

(i) the members of the Force charged with the protection of property belonging to or in the charge or possession of the state; or

(ii) persons employed in any bureau or other organisation established by the state for purposes of intelligence or counter-intelligence; or

(iii) persons employed in or in connection with the telecommunication systems set up for the purposes of any Force, bureau or organisation.

Experience has revealed that the need for ensuring proper discharge of their duties and maintenance of discipline among them is of paramount importance in the national interest.

51. *The Constitution (Fifty-first Amendment) Act, 1984*—Article 330 has been amended by this Act for providing reservation of seats for Scheduled Tribes in Meghalaya, Nagaland, Arunachal Pradesh and Mizoram in Parliament and Article 332 has been amended to provide similar reservation in the Legislative Assemblies of Nagaland and Meghalaya to meet the aspirations of local tribal population.

52. *The Constitution (Fifty-second Amendment) Act, 1985*—It amends the Constitution to provide that a Member of Parliament or a State Legislature who defects or is expelled from the party which set him up as a candidate in the election or if an independent member of the House joins a political party after expiry of six months from the date on which he takes seat in the House shall be disqualified to remain a member of the House. The Act also makes suitable provisions with respect to splits in and merger of political parties.

53. *The Constitution (Fifty-third Amendment) Act, 1986*—This has been enacted to give effect to the Memorandum of Settlement of Mizoram which was signed by Government of India and Mizoram Government with Mizoram National Front on 30th June 1986. For this purpose, a new Article 371G has been inserted in the Constitution *inter alia* preventing application of any Act of Parliament in Mizoram in respect of religious or social practices of Mizos, Mizos' customary law and procedure, administration of civil and criminal practice involving decisions according to Mizos' customary law and ownership and transfer of land unless a resolution is passed in the Legislative Assembly to that effect. This, however, will not apply to any Central Act already in force in Mizoram before the commencement of this amendment. The new Article also provides that the Legislative Assembly of Mizoram shall consist of not less than 40 members.

54. *The Constitution (Fifty-fourth Amendment) Act, 1986*—This Act increases the salaries of Supreme Court and High Court judges as follows :

Chief Justice of India	₹ 10,000 per month
Judges of Supreme Court	₹ 9,000 per month
Chief Justice of High Court	₹ 9,000 per month
Judges of High Court	₹ 8,000 per month

This Act amended Part 'D' of the Second Schedule to the Constitution to give effect to the above increases in the salaries of judges and to make an enabling provision in Articles 125 and 221 to provide for changes in the salaries of judges in future by Parliament by law.

55. *The Constitution (Fifty-fifth Amendment) Act, 1986*—This Act seeks to give effect to the proposal of Government of India to confer statehood on the Union Territory of Arunachal Pradesh and for this purpose, a new Article 371H has been inserted which, *inter alia,* confers, having regard to the sensitive location of Arunachal Pradesh to vest special responsibility on Governor of the new State of Arunachal Pradesh with respect to law and order in the State and in the discharge of his functions, the Governor shall after consulting the Council of Ministers, exercise his individual judgement, as to the action to be taken and this responsibility shall cease when President so directs. The new Article also provides that the new Legislative Assembly of the new State of Arunachal Pradesh, shall consist of not less than thirty members.

56. *The Constitution (Fifty-sixth Amendment) Act, 1987*—Government of India has proposed to constitute the territories comprised in Goa District of the Union Territory of Goa, Daman and Diu as the State of Goa and the territories comprised in Daman and Diu districts of that Union Territory as a new Union Territory of Daman and Diu. In this context, it was proposed that the Legislative Assembly of the new State of Goa shall consist of 40 members. The existing Legislative Assembly of the Union Territory of Goa, Daman and Diu has 30 elected members and three nominated members. It was intended to make this Assembly with the exclusion of two members representing Daman and Diu districts the provisional Legislative Assembly for the new State of Goa until elections are held on the expiry of the five year terms of the existing Assembly. It was, therefore, decided to provide that the Legislative Assembly of the new State of Goa shall consist of not less than 30 members. The special provision required to be made to give effect to this proposal is carried out by this amendment.

57. *The Constitution (Fifty-seventh amendment) Act, 1987*—The Constitution (Fifty-first Amendment) Act, 1984 was enacted to provide for reservation of seats in the house of the people for scheduled tribes in Nagaland, Meghalaya, Mizoram and Arunachal Pradesh and also for reservation of seats for scheduled tribes in the legislative assemblies of Nagaland and Meghalaya by suitably amending articles 330 and 332. Even though these states are predominantly tribal, the underlying objective of the aforesaid act was to ensure that the members of scheduled tribes in these areas do not fail to secure a minimal representation because of their inability to compete with the advanced sections of the people. The Constitution (fifty-first amendment) act, though formally enforced, could not be fully implemented unless parallel action is taken to determine the seats which are to be reserved for Scheduled tribes in these areas. The number of seats reserved for Schedule Castes and Schedule Tribes in the Legislative Assembly of any State under article 332 of the constitution will have to be determined having regard to the provisions of article 332 (3) of the Constitution. However, in view of the historical background with respect to the areas comprised in north-eastern states, the circumstances obtaining in these areas in the State of development of Scheduled Tribes and other relevant considerations, it was considered necessary to provide for special arrangements with regard to the reservation for Scheduled Tribes in these areas for a temporary period so as to facilitate easy transition of these areas to the normal arrangements as envisaged in the Constitution. Article 332 of the Constitution was further amended for making a temporary provision, until the re-adjustment of seats on the basis of first census after the year 2000 under article 170 of the Constitution for these states, for the determination of the number of seats reserved for Scheduled Tribes. This amendment seeks to provide that if all the seats in the Legislative Assembly of such States in existence on the date of coming into force of this constitution amendment act are held by the members of Scheduled Tribes, all the seats except one shall be reserved for scheduled tribes and in any other case such number of seats as bears to the total number of seats a proportion not less than the number of members belonging to Scheduled Tribes in the existing assembly bears to the total number of seats in the existing assembly. The act achieves these objectives.

58. *The Constitution (Fifty-eighth Amendment) Act, 1987*—There has been general demand for the publication of authoritative text of the Constitution in Hindi. It is imperative to have an authoritative text of the Constitution for facilitating its use in the legal process. Any Hindi version of the Constitution should not only conform to the Hindi translation published by the Constituent Assembly, but should be in conformity, with the language style and terminology adopted in the authoritative texts of Central Acts in Hindi. The Constitution has been amended to empower President of India to publish under his authority the translation of the Constitution in Hindi signed by the Members of the Constituent Assembly with such modification as may be necessary to bring it in conformity with the language, style and terminology adopted in the authoritative texts of Central Acts in Hindi language. President has also been authorised to publish the translation in Hindi of every amendment of the Constitution made in English.

59. *The Constitution (Fifty-ninth Amendment) Act, 1988*—The Act amends Article 365 (5) of the Constitution so as to facilitate the extension of a Presidential Proclamation issued under clause (1) of Article 356 beyond a period of one year, if necessary upto a period of three years, as permissible under clause (4) of Article 356 with respect to the State of Punjab because of the continued disturbed situation there. The Act also amends Article 352 of the Constitution pertaining to the Proclamation of Emergency in its application to the State of Punjab and includes internal disturbance as one of the grounds for making a Proclamation in respect of the State of Punjab only. As a consequence of amendment in Article 352, Articles 358 and 359 in relation to the State of Punjab will be operative only for a period of two years from 30 March 1988, which is the date of commencement of the amendment.

60. *The Constitution (Sixtieth Amendment) Act, 1988*—The Act amends clause (2) of Article 276 of the Constitution so as to increase the ceiling of taxes on professions, trades, callings and employment from Rs 250 per annum to Rs 2,500 per annum. The upward revision of this tax will help state governments in raising additional resources. The proviso to clause (2) has been omitted.

61. *The Constitution (Sixty-first Amendment) Act, 1989*—The Act provides for reducing voting age from 21 to 18 years by amending Article 326 of the Constitution to provide to the unrepresented youth of the country an opportunity to give vent to their feelings and help them become a part of political process.

62. *The Constitution (Sixty-second Amendment) Act, 1989*—Article 334 of the Constitution lays down that the provisions of the Constitution relating to the reservation of seats for the Scheduled Castes and the Scheduled Tribes and the representation of the Anglo-Indian community by nomination in the Lok Sabha and in the Legislative Assemblies of the States shall cease to have effect on the expiry of a period of 40 years from the commencement of the Constitution. Although the Scheduled Castes and the Scheduled Tribes have made considerable progress in the last 40 years, the reasons which weighed with the Constituent Assembly in making provisions with regard to the aforesaid reservation of seats and nomination of members, have not ceased to exist. The Act amends Article 334 of the Constitution to continue the reservation for the Scheduled Castes and the Scheduled Tribes and the representation of the Anglo-Indians by nomination for a further period of 10 years.

63. *The Constitution (Sixty-third Amendment) Act, 1989*—The Constitution (Fifty-ninth Amendment) Act, 1988 was enacted in March 1988 making certain changes in regard to making a Proclamation of Emergency in Punjab and to the duration of President's rule in State. On reconsideration, the Government decided that the special powers in regard to the Proclamation of Emergency in Punjab as envisaged in the said amendment is no longer required. Accordingly the provision to clause (5) of Article 356 and Article 359A of the Constitution have been omitted.

64. *The Constitution (Sixty-fourth Amendment) Act, 1990*—This Act amends clauses (4) and (5) of Article 356 of the Constitution with a view to facilitate the extension of the proclamation issued under clause (1) of Article 356 of the Constitution on 11th May 1987 upto a total period of three years and six months in relation to the State of Punjab.

65. *The Constitution (Sixty-fifth Amendment) Act, 1990*—Article 338 of the Constitution provides for a Special Officer for the Scheduled Castes and Scheduled Tribes to investigate all matters relating to the safeguards provided for the Scheduled Castes and Scheduled Tribes under the Constitution and to report to the President on their working. The Article has been amended for the constitution of a National Commission for Scheduled Castes and Scheduled Tribes consisting of a Chairperson, Vice Chairperson and five other Members who shall be appointed by the President by warrant under his hand and seal. The amended Article elaborates the duties of the said Commission and covers measures that should be taken by the Union or any state for the effective implementation of the reports presented by the Commission. It also provides that the Commission shall, while investigating any matter or inquiring into any complaint have all the powers of a Civil Court trying a suit and the reports of the said Commission shall be laid before Parliament and the Legislature of the states.

66. *The Constitution (Sixty-sixth Amendment) Act, 1990*—The Act protects 55 State Acts relating to land reforms and ceiling on agricultural land holdings enacted by States of Andhra Pradesh, Bihar, Gujarat, Himachal Pradesh, Karnataka, Kerala, Madhya Pradesh, Maharashtra, Orissa, Rajasthan,Tamilnadu, Uttar Pradesh, West Bengal and administration of the Union Territory of Puducherry, from challenge in courts, by including them in the Ninth Schedule to the Constitution.

67. *The Constitution (Sixty-seventh Amendment) Act, 1990*—The three year period in the case of proclamation issued on 11th May 1987 with respect to the State of Punjab was extended to three years and six months by the Constitution (Sixty-fourth Amendment) Act, 1990. This Act further amends clause (4) of Article 356 so as to further extend the period upto a total period of four years.

68. *The Constitution (Sixty-eighth Amendment) Act, 1991*—The three year period in the case of proclamation issued on 17th May 1987 with respect to the State of Punjab was earlier extended to four years by the Constitution (sixty-seventh Amendment) Act, 1990. This Act further amends clause (4) of Article 356 so as to further extend the period upto a total period of five years.

69. *The Constitution (Sixty-ninth Amendment) Act, 1991*—The Government of India appointed on 24th December 1987 a Committee to go into various issues connected with the administration of Delhi and to recommend measures, *inter alia* for the streamlining of the administrative set up. After detailed inquiry and examination, it recommended that Delhi should continue to be a union territory and may be provided with a Legislative Assembly and a Council of Ministers responsible

to such assembly with appropriate powers to deal with matters of concern to the common man. The Committee also recommended that with a view to ensuring stability and permanence, arrangements should be incorporated in the constitution to give the national capital a special status among the union territories. This act has been passed to give effect to the above recommendations.

70. *The Constitution (Seventieth Amendment) Act, 1992*—While considering the (Seventy-fourth Amendment) Bill, 1991 and the Government of National Capital Territory Bill, 1991 views were expressed in both the Houses of Parliament in favour of including also the elected members of the legislative assemblies of union territories in the electoral college for the election of the President under Article 54 of the Constitution.

At present Article 54 relating to the election of the President provides for an electoral college consisting of only the elected Members of Parliament as well as the legislative assemblies of the states (not of union territories). Similarly, Article 55 providing for the manner of such election also speaks of legislative assemblies of states.

Accordingly, an Explanation was inserted in Article 54 to provide that reference to 'State' in Article 54 and 55 would include the National Capital Territory of Delhi and the Union Territory of Puducherry for constituting the electoral college for election of the President. This would enable the elected members of the Legislative Assembly created for the Union Territory of Puducherry under the provisions of Article 239A and of the proposed Legislative Assembly of the National Capital Territory of Delhi under Article 239AA to be included in the electoral college.

71. *The Constitution (Seventy-first Amendment) Act, 1992*—There have been demands for inclusion of certain languages in the Eighth Schedule to the Constitution. This Act amends the Eighth Schedule to the Constitution to include Konkani, Manipuri and Nepali languages in the Eighth Schedule to the Constitution.

72. *The Constitution (Seventy-second Amendment) Act, 1992*—For restoring peace and harmony in the areas of the State of Tripura where disturbed conditions prevailed, a Memorandum of Settlement was signed by the Government of India with Tripura National Volunteers on 12 August 1988.

In order to implement the said Memorandum, Article 332 of the Constitution has been amended by the Constitution (Seventy-second Amendment) Act, 1992 for making a temporary provision for the determination of the number of seats reserved for the Scheduled Tribes in the State Assembly of Tripura, until the re-adjustment of seats is made on the basis of the first Census after the year 2000 under Article 170 of the Constitution.

73. *The Constitution (Seventy-third Amendment) Act, 1993*—Article 40 of the Constitution which enshrines one of the Directive Principles of State Policy lays down that the State shall take steps to organise village *panchayats* and endow them with such powers and authority as may be necessary to enable them to function as units of self-government.

In the light of the above, a new Part IX relating to the Panchayats has been inserted in the Constitution to provide for among other things, *Gram Sabha* in a village or group of villages; constitution of *Panchayats* at village and other level or levels; direct elections to all seats in Panchayats at the village and intermediate level, if any and to the offices of Chairpersons of Panchayats at such levels; reservation of seats for the Scheduled Castes and Scheduled Tribes in proportion to their population for membership of Panchayats and office of Chairpersons in Panchayats at each level; reservation of not less than one-third of the seats for women; fixing tenure of five years for Panchayats and holding elections within a period of six months in the event of supersession of any Panchayat.

74. *The Constitution (Seventy-fourth Amendment) Act, 1993*—In many states local bodies have become weak and ineffective on account of a variety of reasons, including the failure to hold regular elections, prolonged supersession and inadequate devolutions of powers and functions. As a result, Urban Local Bodies are not able to perform effectively as vibrant democratic units of self-government.

Having regard to these inadequacies a new part IX-A relating to the Municipalities has been incorporated in the Constitution to provide for among other things, constitution of three types of Municipalities, *i.e., Nagar Panchayats* for areas in transition from a rural area to urban area, Municipal Councils for smaller urban areas and Municipal Corporations for larger urban areas.

75. *The Constitution (Seventy-fifth Amendment) Act, 1994*—The operation of the Rent Control Legislations, as are today in various states, suffers from major weaknesses and has led to various unintended consequences. Some of the deleterious legal consequences include mounting and mending litigation, inability of the courts to provide timely justice, evolution of practices and systems to bypass the operations of rent legislations and steady shrinkage of rental housing market.

The Supreme Court taking note of the precarious state of rent litigation in the country in case of Prabhakaran Nair and others vs. State of Tamilnadu (Civil Writ Petition 506 of 1986) and other writs observed that the Supreme Court and the High Courts should be relieved of the heavy burden of rent litigation. Tiers of appeals should be curtailed. Laws should be simple, rational and clear, litigations must come to end quickly.

Therefore, this Act amends Article 323B in Part XIVA of the Constitution so as to give timely relief to the rent litigants by providing for setting up of state-level Rent Tribunals in order to reduce the tiers of appeals and to exclude the jurisdiction of all courts, except that of the Supreme Court, under Article 136 of the Constitution.

76. *The Constitution (Seventy-sixth Amendment) Act, 1994*—The policy of reservation of seats in educational institutions and reservation of appointments or posts in public services for Backward Classes, Scheduled Castes and Scheduled Tribes has had a long history in Tamilnadu dating back to the year 1921. The extent of reservation has been increased by the State Government from time to time, consistent with the needs of the majority of the people and it has now reached the level of 69 per cent (18 per cent Scheduled Castes, one per cent Scheduled Tribes and 50 per cent Other Backward Classes).

The Supreme Court in Indira Sawhney and others vs. Union of India and others (AIR, 1993 SC 477) on 16th November 1992 ruled that the total reservations under Article 16(4) should not exceed 50 per cent.

The Tamilnadu Government enacted a legislation, namely, Tamilnadu Backward Classes, Scheduled Castes and Scheduled Tribes (Reservation of Seats in Educational Institution and of appointments or posts in the Services under the State) Bill, 1993 and forwarded it to the Government of India for consideration of the President of India in terms of Article 31-C of the Constitution. The Government of India supported the provision of the State legislation by giving the President's assent to the Tamilnadu Bill. As a corollary to this decision, it was necessary that the Tamilnadu Act 45 of 1994 was brought within the purview of the Ninth Schedule to the Constitution so that it could get protection under Article 31B of the Constitution with regard to the judicial review.

77. *The Constitution (Seventy-seventh Amendment) Act, 1995*—The Schedule Castes and the scheduled tribes have been enjoying the facility of reservation in promotion since 1955. The Supreme Court in its judgment dated 16th November 1992 in the case of Indira Sawhney and others vs. Union of India and others, however, observed that reservation of appointments or posts under Article 16(4) of the Constitution is confined to initial appointment and cannot extend to reservation in the matter of promotion. This ruling of the Supreme Court will adversely affect the interests of the Scheduled Castes and the Scheduled Tribes. Since the representation of the Scheduled Castes and the Scheduled Tribes in services in the States have not reached the required level, it is necessary to continue the existing dispensation of providing reservation in promotion in the case of the Scheduled Castes and the Scheduled Tribes. In view of the commitment of the Government to protect the interests of the Scheduled Castes and the Scheduled Tribes, the Government have decided to continue the existing policy of reservation in promotion for the Scheduled Castes and the Scheduled Tribes. To carry out this, it was necessary to amend Article 16 of the Constitution by inserting a new clause (4A) in the said Article to provide for reservation in promotion for the Scheduled Castes and the Scheduled Tribes.

78. *The Constitution (Seventy-eighth Amendment) Act, 1995*—Article 31B of the Constitution confers on the enactments included in the Ninth Schedule to the Constitution immunity from

legal challenge on the ground that they violate the fundamental rights enshrined in Part III of the Constitution. The Schedule consists of list of laws enacted by various State Governments and Central Government which *inter alia* affect rights and interest in property including land.

In the past, whenever, it was found that progressive legislation conceived in the interest of the public was imperilled by litigation, recourse was taken to the Ninth Schedule. Accordingly, several State enactments relating to land reforms and ceiling on agricultural land holdings have already been included in the Ninth Schedule. Since, the Government is committed to give importance to land reforms, it was decided to include land reform laws in the Ninth Schedule so that they are not challenged before the courts. The State Governments of Bihar, Karnataka, Kerala, Orissa, Rajasthan, Tamilnadu and West Bengal had suggested the inclusion of some of their Acts relating to land reforms in the Ninth Schedule.

Since the amendment to Acts which are already placed in the Ninth Schedule are not automatically immunised from legal challenge, a number of amending Acts along with a few principal Acts have been included in the Ninth Schedule so as to ensure that implementation of these Acts is not adversely affected by litigation.

79. *The Constitution (Seventy-ninth Amendment) Act, 1999*—By this Act the Government has extended the reservations of seats for the Scheduled Castes and the Scheduled Tribes as well as for the Anglo-Indians in the House of the People and in the Legislative Assemblies of the States for another ten years.

80. *The Constitution (Eightieth Amendment) Act, 2000*—Based on the recommendations of the Tenth Finance Commission, an alternative scheme for sharing taxes between the Union and the States has been enacted by the Constitution (Eightieth Amendment) Act 2000. Under the new scheme of devolution of revenue between Union and the States, 26 per cent out of gross proceeds of Union taxes and duties is to be assigned to the States in lieu of their existing share in the income-tax, excise duties, special excise duties and grants in lieu of tax on railway passenger fares.

81. *The Constitution (Eighty-first Amendment) Act, 2000*—By this amendment the unfilled vacancies of a year which were reserved for the Scheduled Castes and the Scheduled Tribes for being filled up in that year in accordance with any provision for reservations made under Article 16 of the Constitution, shall be considered as a separate class of vacancies to be filled up in any succeeding year or years, and such class of vacancies shall not be considered together with the vacancies of the year in which they were filled up for determining the ceiling of fifty per cent reservation against total number of vacancies of that year.

82. *The Constitution (Eighty-second Amendment) Act, 2000*—The amendment provides that nothing in Article 335 shall prevent the State from making any provision in favour of the members of the Scheduled Castes and the Scheduled Tribes for relaxation in qualifying marks in any examination or lowering the standards of evaluation for reservation in matters of promotion to any class or classes of services or posts in connection with affairs of the Union or of a State.

83. *The Constitution (Eighty-third Amendment) Act, 2000*—The Act amended Acticle 243M of the Constitution to provide that no reservation in Panchayats need be made in favour of the Scheduled Castes in Arunachal Pradesh wholly inhabited by tribal population.

84. *The Constitution (Eighty-fourth Amendment) Act, 2001*—The Act amended provisos to articles 82 and 170(3) of the Constitution to readjust and rationalise the territorial constitutencies in the States, without altering the number of seats allotted to each State in House of People and Legislative Assemblies of the States, including the Scheduled Castes and Scheduled Tribes constituencies, on the basis of the population ascertained at the census for the year 1991 so as to remove the imbalance caused due to uneven growth of population/electorate in different constituencies. It is also to refix the number of seats reserved for the Scheduled Castes and the Scheduled Tribes in the House of the People and the Legislative Assemblies of the States on the basis of the population ascertained at the census for the year 1991 so as to remove the imbalance caused due to uneven growth of population/electorate in different constituencies. It is also to refix the number of seats reserved for Scheduled Castes and the Scheduled Tribes in the House of

the People and the Legislative Assemblies of the States on the basis of the population ascertained at the census for the year 1991.

85. *The Constitution (Eighty-fifth Amendment) Act, 2001*—This Act amended article 16(4A) of the Constitution to provide for consequential seniority in the case of promotion by virtue of rule of reservation for the Government servants belonging to the Scheduled Castes and the Scheduled Tribes. It also provides retrospective effect from 17th day of June 1995.

86. *The Constitution (Eighty-sixth Amendment) Act, 2002*—The Act deals with insertion of a new article 21A after article 21. The new article 21A deals with Right to Education—"The State shall provide free and compulsory education to all children of the age of six to fourteen years in such manner as the State may, by law, determine".

Substitution of new Article for Article 45. For Article 45 of the Constitution, the following article shall be substituted, namely, Provision for early childhood care and education to children below the age of six years. Article 45: "The State shall endeavour to provide early childhood care and education for all children until they complete the age of six years."

Article 51A of the Constitution was amended and a new clause (k) was added after clause (j), namely, "(k) who is a parent or guardian to provide opportunities for education to his child or, as the case may be, ward between the age of six and fourteen years."

87. *The Constitution (Eighty-seventh Amendment) Act, 2003* - In Article 81 of the Constitution, in clause (3), in the proviso, in clause (ii), for the figures "1991", the figures "2001" shall be substituted.

In Article 82 of the Constitution, in the third proviso, in clause (ii), for the figures "1991", the figures "2001" shall be substituted.

In Article 170 of the Constitution, - (i) in clause (2), in the Explanation, in the proviso, for the figures "1991", the figures "2001" shall be substituted; (ii) in clause (3), in the Explanation, in the third proviso, for the figures "1991", the figures "2001" shall be substituted.

In Article 330 of the Constitution, in the Explanation, in the proviso, for the figures "1991", the figures "2001" shall be substituted.

88. *The Constitution (Eighty-eighth Amendment) Act, 2003* - It shall come into force on such date as the Central Government may, by notification in the Official Gazette, appoint.

After Article 268 of the Constitution, the following article shall be inserted, namely :

"268A. (1) Taxes on services shall be levied by the Government of India and such tax shall be collected and appropriated by the Government of India and the States in the manner provided in clause (2).

(2) The proceeds in any financial year of any such tax levied in accordance with the provisions of clause (1) shall be - (a) collected by the Government of India and the States; (b) appropriated by the Government of India and the States, in accordance with such principles of collection and appropriation as may be formulated by Parliament by law".

In Article 270 of the constitution, in clause(1), for the words and figures "Article 268 and 269", the words, figures and letter "Articles 268, 268A and 269" shall be substituted.

In the Seventh Schedule to the Constitution, in **List I-Union List,** after entry 9.2B, the following entry shall be inserted, namely : "92C. Taxes on services".

89 *The Constitution (Eighty-ninth Amendment) Act, 2003*-It shall come into force on such date as the Central Government may, by notification in the Official Gazette, appoint.

In Article 338 of the Constitution, - (a) for the marginal heading, the following marginal heading shall be substituted, namely :

"National Commission for : Scheduled Castes";

(b) for clauses (1) and (2), the following clauses shall be substituted, namely:

"(1) There shall be a Commission for the Scheduled Castes to be known as the National Commission for the Scheduled Castes.

(2) Subject to the provisions of any law made in this behalf by Parliament, the Commission shall consist of a Chairperson, Vice-Chairperson and three other Members and the conditions of service and tenure of office of the Chairperson, Vice-Chairperson and other Members so appointed shall be such as the President may by rule determine";

(c) in clauses (5), (9) and (10), the words "and Scheduled Tribes", wherever they occur, shall be omitted.

After Article 338 of the Constitution, the following article shall be inserted, namely:

"338A. (1) There shall be a Commission for the Scheduled Tribes to be known as the National Commission for the Scheduled Tribes.

(2) Subject to the provisions of any law made in this behalf by Parliament, the Commission shall consist of a Chairperson, Vice-Chairperson and three other Members and the conditions of service and tenure of office of the Chairperson, Vice-Chairperson and other Members so appointed shall be such as the President may by rule determine.

(3) The Chairperson, Vice-Chairperson and other Members of the Commission shall be appointed by the President by warrant under his hand and seal.

(4) The Commission shall have the power to regulate its own procedure.

(5) It shall be the duty of the Commission - (a) to investigate and monitor all matters relating to the safeguards provided for the Scheduled Tribes under this Constitution or under any other law for the time being in force or under any order of the Government and to evaluate the working of such safeguards; (b) to inquire into specific complaints with respect to the deprivation of rights and safeguards of the Scheduled Tribes; (c) to participate and advise on the planning process of socio-economic development of the Scheduled Tribes and to evaluate the progress of their development under the Union and any State; (d) to present to the President, annually and at such other times as the Commission may deem fit, reports upon the working of those safeguards; (e) to make in such reports recommendations as to the measures that should be taken by the Union or any State for the effective implementation of those safeguards and other measures for the protection, welfare and socio-economic development of the Scheduled Tribes; and (f) to discharge such other functions in relation to the protection, welfare and development and advancement of the Scheduled Tribes as the President may, subject to the provisions of any law made by Parliament, by rule specify.

(6) The President shall cause all such reports to be laid before each House of Parliament along with a memorandum explaining the action taken or proposed to be taken on the recommendations relating to the Union and the reasons for the non-acceptance, if any, of any of such recommendations.

(7) Where any such report, or any part thereof, relates to any matter with which any State Government is concerned, a copy of such report shall be forwarded to the Governor of the State who shall cause it to be laid before the Legislature of the State along with a memorandum explaining the action taken or proposed to be taken on the recommendations relating to the State and reasons for the non-acceptance, if any, of any of such recommendations.

(8) The Commission shall, while investigating any matter referred to in sub-clause(a) or inquiring into any complaint referred to in sub-clause (b) of clause (5), have all the powers of a civil court trying a suit and in particular in respect of the following matters, namely:

(a) summoning and enforcing the attendance of any person from any part of India and examining him on oath; (b) requiring the discovery and production of any document; (c) receiving evidence on affidavits; (d) requisitioning any public record or copy thereof from any court or office; (e) issuing commissions for the examination of witnesses and documents; (f) any other matter which the President may, by rule, determine.

(9) The Union and every State Government shall consult the Commission on all major policy matters affecting Scheduled Tribes".

90. *The Constitution (Ninetieth Amendment) Act, 2003*-In Article 332 of the Consitution, in clause (6), the following proviso shall be inserted, namely :

"Provided that for elections to the Legislative Assembly of the State of Assam, the representation of the Scheduled Tribes and non-Scheduled Tribes in the constituencies included in the Bodoland Territorial Areas District, so notified, and existing prior to the constitution of the Bodoland Territorial Areas District, shall be maintained".

91. *The Constitution (Ninety-first Amendment), Act, 2003* - In Article 75 of the Constitution, after clause (1), the following clauses shall be inserted, namely :

"(1A) The total number of Ministers, including the Prime Minister, in the Council of Ministers shall not exceed fifteen per cent of the total number of members of the House of the People.

(1B) A member of either House of Parliament belonging to any political party who is disqualified for being a member of that House under paragraph 2 of the Tenth Schedule shall also be disqualified to be appointed as a Minister under clause (1) for duration of the period commencing from the date of his disqualification till the date on which the term of his office as such member would expire or where he contests any election to either House of Parliament before the expiry of such period, till the date on which he is declared elected, whichever is earlier"

In Article 164 of the Constitution, after clause (i), the following clauses shall be inserted, namely:

"(1A) the total number of Ministers, including the Chief Minister, in the Council of Ministers in a State sall not exceed fifteen per cent of the total number of members of the Legislative Assembly of that State :

Provided that the number of Ministers, including the Chief Minister, in a State shall not be less than twelve:

Provided further that where the total number of Ministers, including the Chief Minister, in the Council of Ministers in any State at the commencement of the Constitution (Ninety-first Amendment) Act, 2003 exceeds the said fifteen per cent or the number specified in the first proviso, as the case may be, then, the total number of Ministers in that State shall be brought in conformity with the provisions of this clause within six months from such date as the President may by public notification appoint.

(1B) A member of the Legislative Assembly of a State or either House of the Legislature of a State having Legislative Council beloging to any poitical party who is disqualified for being a member of that House under paragraph 2 of the Tenth Schedule shall also be disqualified to be appointed as a Minister under clause (1) for duration of the period commencing from the date of his disqualification till the date on which the term of his office as such member would expire or where he contests any election to the Legislative Assembly of a State or either House of the Legislature of a State having Legislative Council, as the case may be, before the expiry of such period, till the date on which he is declared elected, whichever is earlier"

After Article 361A of the Constitution, the following article shall be inserted, namely :

316B. A member of a House belonging to any political party who is disqualified for being a member of the House under paragraph 2 of the Tenth Schedule shall also be disqualified to hold any remunerative political post for duration of the period commencing from the date of his disqualification till the date on which the term of his office as such member would expire or till the date on which he contests an election to a House and is declared elected, whichever is earlier.

Explanation : For the purposes of this Article,—

(a) the expression "House" has the meaning assigned to it in clause (a) of paragraph 1 of the Tenth Schedule :

(b) the expression "remunerative political post" means any office—(i) under the Government of India or the Government of a State where the salary or remuneration for such office is paid out of the public revenue of the Government of India or the Government of the State, as the case may be, or (ii) under a body, whether incorporated or not, which is wholly or partially owned by the Government of India or the Government of a State and the salary or remuneration for such office is paid by such body, except where such salary or remuneration paid is compensatory in nature'.

In the Tenth Schedule to the Constitution,—(a) in paragraph, 1, in clause (b), the words and figure "paragraph 3 or, as the case may be," shall be omitted; (b) in paragraph 2, in sub-paragraph (1), for the words and figures "paragraphs 3, 4 and 5", the words and figures "paragraphs 4 and 5" shall be substituted; (c) paragraph 3 shall be omitted.

92. *The Constitution (Ninety-second Amendment) Act, 2003*—In the Eighth Schedule to the Constitution,—(a) existing entry 3 shall be re-numbered as entry 5, and before entry 5 as so re-numbered, the following entries shall be inserted, namely:

"3. Bodo;

4. Dogri".

(b) existing 4 to 7 shall respectively be re-numbered as entries 6 to 9; (c) existing entry 8 shall be re-numbered as entry 11 and before entry 11 as so renumbered, the following entry shall be inserted, namely:

"10. Maithili".

(d) existing entries 9 to 14 shall respectively be re-numbered as entries 12 to 17;

(e) existing entry 15 shall be re-numbered as entry 19 and before entry 19 as so re-numbered, the following entry shall be inserted, namely :

"18. Santhali".

(f) existing entries 16 to 18 shall respectively be re-numbered as entries 20 to 22.

93. *The Constitution (Ninety-third amendment) Act, 2006*—Greater access to higher education including professional education, is of great importance to a large number of students belonging to the Scheduled Castes, the Scheduled Tribes and other socially and educationally backward classes of citizens. The reservation of seats for the Scheduled Castes, the Scheduled Tribes and the Other Backward Classes of citizens in admission to educational institution is derived from the provisions of clause (4) of articles 15 of the constitution. At present, the number of seats available in aided or State maintained institutions, particularly in respect of professional education, is limited, in comparison to those in private unaided institutions.

Clause (i) of article 30 of the Constitution provides the right to all minorities to establish and administer educational institutions of their choice. It is essential that the rights available to minorities are protected in regard to institutions established and administered by them. Accordingly, institutions declared by the State to be minority institutions under clause (1) of article 30 are excluded from the operation of this enactment.

To promote the educational advancement of the socially and educationally backward classes of citizens, i.e., the Other Backward Classes or of the Scheduled Castes and the Scheduled Tribes in matters of admission of students belonging to these categories in unaided educational institutions, other than the minority educational institutions referred to in clause (1) of article 30, the provisions of article 15 were amplified. The new clause (5) of said article 15 shall enable the Parliament as well as the State Legislatures to make appropriate laws for the above mentioned purpose.

94. *The Constitution (Ninety-fourth amendment) Act, 2006*—In Article 164 of the Constitution, in Clause (I), in the proviso, for the word "Bihar", the words "Chhattisgarh, Jharkhand" shall be substituted.

95. *The Constitution (Ninety-fifth amendment) Act, 2009*—In Article 334, Extended the reservation of the seats for SCs and STs in the Lok Sabha and State Assemblies from Sixty Years to Seventy Years.

96. *The Constitution (Ninety-Sixth Amendment) Act, 2011*—In Schedule 8 of the Constitution, Substituted "Odia" for "Oriya".

97. *The Constitutions (Ninety-Seventh Amendment) Act, 2011*—Added the words "Or Co-operative Societies" after the world "Or Unions" in Article 19(i)(c) and insertion of article 43B, i.e., Promotion of Co-operative Societies and added Part 1x8, i.e. The Co-operative Societies.

98. *The Constitution (Ninety-Eighth Amendment) Act, 2012*—Inserted Article 371J in the constitution. The objective was to empower the Governor of Karnataka to take steps to develop the Hyderabad-Karnataka region.

99. The Constitution (*Ninety-Ninth Amendment*) Act, 2014–Inserted new articles-124 A, 124B and 124C after article 124 of the constitution. The Act also provided for the composition and the functions of the proposed National Judicial Appointments Commission.

100. The Constitution (*One Hundredth Amendment*) Act, 2015—amended the First Schedule of the Constitution, for the purpose of giving effect to the acquiring of territories by India and transfer of territories to Bangladesh through retaining of adverse possession and exchange of enclaves, in pursuance of the Agreement between India and Bangladesh concerning the demarcation of the land boundary, signed on 16th May 1974 and its Protocal, signed on 6th September, 2011.

101. The Constitution (*One Hundred and First Amendment*) Act, 2016—The act amends the constitution to introduce "The Goods and Services Tax (GST)". It amended the articles 248, 249, 250, 268, 269, 270, 271, 286, 366 & 368. Amended the Sixth & Seventh Schedules. Omitted article 268A. Inserted new articles 246A (Special provision with respect to goods and services tax), 269A (Levy and collection of goods and services tax in course of inter-State trade or commerce) and 279A (Goods and Services Tax Council). The act also provided for compensation to States for loss of revenue on account of introduction of goods and services tax.

Source : http/indiacode.nic.in

Appendices

GOVERNMENT OF INDIA

Shri Pranab Mukherjee—President
Mohammad Hamid Ansari—Vice-President

COUNCIL OF MINISTERS
(As on December 15, 2016)[1]

Shri Narendra Modi	Prime Minister and also in-charge of: Ministry of Personnel, Public Grievances and Pensions; Department of Atomic Energy; Department of Space; and All important policy issues and all other portfolios not allocated to any Minister

CABINET MINISTERS

Shri Raj Nath Singh	Minister of Home Affairs
Smt. Sushma Swaraj	Minister of External Affairs;
Shri Arun Jaitley	Minister of Finance; and Minister of Corporate Affairs;
Shri M. Venkaiah Naidu	Minister of Urban Development; Minister of Housing and Urban Poverty Alleviation; and Minister of Information and Broadcasting
Shri Nitin Jairam Gadkari	Minister of Road Transport and Highways and Minister of Shipping
Shri Manohar Parrikar	Minister of Defence
Shri Suresh Prabhu	Minister of Railways
Shri D.V. Sadananda Gowda	Minister of Statistics and Programme Implementation
Sushri Uma Bharati	Minister of Water Resources, River Development and Ganga Rejuvenation
Shri Ramvilas Paswan	Minister of Consumer Affairs, Food and Public Distribution
Shri Kalraj Mishra	Minister of Micro, Small and Medium Enterprises

1. Source : Cabinet Secretariat website http://cabsec.nic.in/council_ministerofstate.php

Smt. Maneka Sanjay Gandhi	Minister of Women and Child Development
Shri Ananthkumar	Minister of Chemicals and Fertilizers; and Ministry of Parliamentary Affairs
Shri Ravi Shankar Prasad	Minister of Law and Justice; and Minister of Electronics and Information Technology
Shri Jagat Prakash Nadda	Minister of Health and Family Welfare
Shri Ashok Gajapathi Raju Pusapati	Minister of Civil Aviation
Shri Anant Geete	Minister of Heavy Industries and Public Enterprises
Smt. Harsimrat Kaur Badal	Minister of Food Processing Industries
Shri Narendra Singh Tomar	Minister of Rural Development; Minister of Panchayati Raj; and Minister of Drinking Water and Sanitation
Shri Chaudhary Birender Singh	Minister of Steel
Shri Jual Oram	Minister of Tribal Affairs
Shri Radha Mohan Singh	Minister of Agriculture and Farmers Welfare
Shri Thaawar Chand Gehlot	Minister of Social Justice and Empowerment
Smt. Smriti Zubin Irani	Minister of Textiles
Dr. Harsh Vardhan	Minister of Science and Technology; and Minister of Earth Sciences
Shri Prakash Javadekar	Minister of Human Resource Development

MINISTERS OF STATE (Independent Charge)

Rao Inderjit Singh	Minister of State (Independent Charge) of the Ministry of Planning; and Minister of State in the Ministry of Urban Development; and Minister of State in the Ministry of Housing and Urban Poverty Alleviation
Shri Bandaru Dattatreya	Minister of State (Independent Charge) of the Ministry of Labour and Employment
Shri Rajiv Pratap Rudy	Minister of State (Independent Charge) of the Ministry of Skill Development and Entrepreneurship
Shri Vijay Goel	Minister of State (Independent Charge) of the Ministry of Youth Affairs and Sports; and Minister of State in the Ministry of Water Resources, River Development and Ganga Rejuvenation

2. Source : Cabinet Secretariat website http://cabsec.nic.in/Council_Cabinet_independent.php

Shri Shripad Yesso Naik	Minister of State (Independent Charge) of the Ministry of Ayurveda, Yoga & Naturopathy, Unani, Siddha and Homoeopathy (AYUSH)
Shri Dharmendra Pradhan	Minister of State (Independent Charge) of the Ministry of Petroleum and Natural Gas
Shri Piyush Goyal	Minister of State (Independent Charge) of the Ministry of Power; Minister of State (Independent Charge) of the Ministry of Coal; Minister of State (Independent Charge) of the Ministry of New and Renewable Energy; and Minister of State (Independent Charge) of the Ministry of Mines
Dr. Jitendra Singh	Minister of State (Independent Charge) of the Ministry of Development of North Eastern Region; Minister of State in the Prime Minister's Office; Minister of State in the Ministry of Personnel, Public Grievances and Pensions; Minister of State in the Department of Atomic Energy; and Minister of State in the Department of Space
Smt. Nirmala Sitharaman	Minister of State (Independent Charge) of the Ministry of Commerce and Industry
Dr. Mahesh Sharma	Minister of State (Independent Charge) of the Ministry of Culture; and Minister of State (Independent Charge) of the Ministry of Tourism;
Shri Manoj Sinha	Minister of State (Independent Charge) of the Ministry of Communications; and Minister of State in the Ministry of Railways
Shri Anil Madhav Dave	Minister of State (Independent Charge) of the Ministry of Environment, Forest and Climate Change
Shri Mukhtar Abbas Naqvi	Minister of State (Independent Charge) of the Ministry of Minority Affairs; and Minister of State in the Ministry of Parliamentary Affairs

MINISTERS OF STATE

General(Retd.) V.K. Singh	Minister of State in the Ministry of External Affairs
Shri Santosh Kumar Gangwar	Minister of State in the Ministry of Finance
Shri Faggan Singh Kulaste	Minister of State in the Ministry of Health and Family Welfare
Shri S. S. Ahluwalia	Minister of State in the Ministry of Agriculture and Farmers Welfare; and Minister of State in the Ministry of Parliamentary Affairrs
Shri Ramdas Athawale	Minister of State in the Ministry of Social Justice and Empowement
Shri Ram Kripal Yadav	Minister of State in the Ministry of Rural Development
Shri Haribhai Parthibhai Chaudhary	Minister of State in the Ministry of Micro, Small and Medium Enterprises
Shri Giriraj Singh	Minister of State in the Ministry of Micro, Small and Medium Enterprises
Shri Hansraj Gangaram Ahir	Minister of State in the Ministry of Home Affairs
Shri Ramesh Chandappa Jigajinagi	Minister of State in the Ministry of Drinking Water and Sanitation
Shri Rajen Gohain	Minister of State in the Ministry of Railways
Shri Parshottam Rupala	Minister of State in the Ministry of Agriculture and Farmers Welfare; and Minister of State in the Ministry of Panchayati Raj
Shri M. J. Akbar	Minister of State in the Ministry of External Affairs
Shri Upendra Kushwaha	Minister of State in the Ministry of Human Resource Development
Shri Radhakrishnan P.	Minister of State in the Ministry of Road Transport and Highways; and Minister of State in the Ministry of Shipping
Shri Kiren Rijiju	Minister of State in the Ministry of Home Affairs

3. Source : Cabinet Secretariat website http://cabsec.nic.in/council_ministers_of_state.php

Shri Krishan Pal	Minister of State in the Ministry of Social Justice and Empowerment
Shri Jaswantsinh Sumanbhai Bhabhor	Minister of State in the Ministry of Tribal Affairs
Dr. Sanjeev Kumar Balyan	Minister of State in the Ministry of Water Resources, River Development and Ganga Rejuvenation
Shri Vishnu Deo Sai	Minister of State in the Ministry of Steel
Shri Sudarshan Bhagat	Minister of State in the Ministry of Agriculture and Farmers Welfare
Shri Y.S. Chowdary	Minister of State in the Ministry of Science and Technology; and Minister of State in the Ministry of Earth Sciences
Shri Jayant Sinha	Minister of State in the Ministry of Civil Aviation
Col. Rajyavardhan Singh Rathore	Minister of State in the Ministry of Information and Broadcasting
Shri Babul Supriyo	Minister of State in the Ministry of Heavy Industries and Public Enterprises
Sadhvi Niranjan Jyoti	Minister of State in the Ministry of Food Processing Industries
Shri Vijay Sampla	Minister of State in the Ministry of Social Justice and Empowerment
Shri Arjun Ram Meghwal	Minister of State in the Ministry of Finance; and Minister of State in the Ministry of Corporate Affairs
Dr Mahendra Nath Pandey	Minister of State in the Ministry of Human Resource Development
Shri Ajay Tamta	Minister of State in the Ministry of Textiles
Smt. Krishna Raj	Minister of State in the Ministry of Women and Child Development
Shri Mansukh L. Mandaviya	Minister of State in the Ministry of Road Transport and Highways; Minister of State in the Ministry of Shipping; and Minister of State in the Ministry of Chemicals and Fertilizers
Smt. Anupriya Patel	Minister of State in the Ministry of Health and Family Welfare

Source : Rajya Sabha Website http://rajyasabha.nic.in

Shri C. R. Chaudhary	Minister of State in the Ministry of Consumer Affairs, Food and Public Distribution
Shri P. P. Chaudhary	Minister of State in the Ministry of Law and Justice; and Minister of State in the Ministry of Electronics and Information Technology
Dr Subhash Ramrao Bhamre	Minister of State in the Ministry of Defence

Note: Incorporates changes in the council of Ministers as on July 12, 2016

MEMBERS OF PARLIAMENT

RAJYA SABHA (State Wise List as on December 15, 2016)

Chairman	**Shri Mohammad Hamid Ansari**
Deputy Chairman	**Prof. P.J. Kurien**

Name	Party/Group
STATES	
ANDHRA PRADESH (11)	
1. Chiranjeevi, Dr. K.	INC
2. Chowdary, Shri Y. S.	TDP
3. Chowdhury, Smt. Renuka	INC
4. Goud T., Shri Devender	TDP
5. Khan, Shri Mohd. Ali	INC
6. Prabhu, Shri Suresh	BJP
7. Rao, Dr. K. Keshava	TRS
8. Reddy, Dr. T. Subbarami	INC
9. Reddy, Shri V. Vijayasai	YSRCP
10. Seetharama Lakshmi, Smt. Thota	TDP
11. Venkatesh, Shri T.G.	TDP
ARUNACHAL PRADESH (1)	
12. Mukut Mithi, Shri	INC
ASSAM (7)	
13. Bora, Shri Ripun	INC
14. Daimary, Shri Biswajit	BPF
15. Kalita, Shri Bhubaneswar	INC

16. Kujur, Shri Santiuse	INC
17. Narah, Smt. Ranee	INC
18. Singh, Dr. Manmohan	INC
19. Sinh, Dr. Sanjay	INC

BIHAR (16)

20. Ansari, Shri Ali Anwar	JD(U)
21. Bharti, Smt. Misha	RJD
22. Harivansh, Shri	JD(U)
23. Jethmalani, Shri Ram	RJD
24. Mahendra Prasad, Dr.	JD(U)
25. Perween, Smt. Kahkashan	JD(U)
26. Pradhan, Shri Dharmendra	BJP
27. Prasad, Shri Ravi Shankar	BJP
28. Sahani, Dr. Anil Kumar	JD(U)
29. Singh, Shri Bashistha Narain	JD(U)
30. Singh, Shri Gopal Narayan	BJP
31. Singh, Shri Ram Chandra Prasad	JD(U)
32. Sinha, Shri R. K.	BJP
33. Thakur, Dr. C.P.	BJP
34. Thakur, Shri Ram Nath	JD(U)
35. Yadav, Shri Sharad	JD(U)

CHHATTISGARH (5)

36. Jangde, Dr. Bhushan Lal	BJP
37. Judev, Shri Ranvijay Singh	BJP
38. Netam, Shri Ram Vichar	BJP
39. Verma, Smt. Chhaya	INC
40. Vora, Shri Motilal	INC

GOA (1)

41. Naik, Shri Shantaram	INC

GUJARAT (11)

42. Gohel, Shri Chunibhai Kanjibhai	BJP
43. Irani, Smt. Smriti Zubin	BJP
44. Jaitley, Shri Arun	BJP
45. Mandaviya, Shri Mansukh L.	BJP

46.	Mistry, Shri Madhusudan	INC
47.	Pandya, Shri Dilipbhai	BJP
48.	Patel, Shri Ahmed	INC
49.	Rupala, Shri Parshottam	BJP
50.	Tundiya, Mahant Shambhuprasadji	BJP
51.	Vadodia, Shri Lal Sinh	BJP
52.	Vegad, Shri Shankarbhai N.	BJP

HARYANA (5)

53.	Batra, Shri Shadi Lal	INC
54.	Kashyap, Shri Ram Kumar	INLD
55.	Selja, Kumari	INC
56.	Singh, Chaudhary Birender	BJP
57.	Subhash Chandra, Dr.	IND

HIMACHAL PRADESH (3)

58.	Anand Sharma, Shri	INC
59.	Nadda, Shri Jagat Prakash	BJP
60.	Thakur, Smt. Viplove	INC

JAMMU AND KASHMIR (4)

61.	Azad, Shri Ghulam Nabi	INC
62.	Fayaz, Mir Mohammad	J&K PDP
63.	Laway, Shri Nazir Ahmed	J&K PDP
64.	Manhas, Shri Shamsher Singh	BJP

JHARKHAND (6)

65.	Balmuchu, Dr. Pradeep Kumar	INC
66.	Gupta, Shri Prem Chand	RJD
67.	Naqui, Shri Mukhtar Abbas	BJP
68.	Nathwani, Shri Parimal	IND
69.	Poddar, Shri Mahesh	BJP
70.	Sanjiv Kumar, Shri	JMM

KARNATAKA (12)

71.	Chandrasekhar, Shri Rajeev	IND
72.	Fernandes, Shri Oscar	INC
73.	Gowda, Prof. M.V. Rajeev	INC
74.	Hariprasad, Shri B.K.	INC

75. Khan, Shri K. Rahman	INC
76. Kore, Dr. Prabhakar	BJP
77. Nirmala Sitharaman, Smt.	BJP
78. Patil, Shri Basawaraj	BJP
79. Ramamurthy, Shri K. C.	INC
80. Ramesh,Shri Jairam	INC
81. Rangasayee Ramakrishna, Shri	BJP
82. Reddy, Shri D. Kupendra	JD(S)

KERALA (9)

83. Abdul Wahab, Shri	IUML
84. Abraham, Shri Joy	KC(M)
85. Antony, Shri A.K.	INC
86. Kurien, Prof. P.J.	INC
87. Narayanan, Shri C.P.	CPI(M)
88. Ragesh, Shri K.K.	CPI(M)
89. Ravi, Shri Vayalar	INC
90. Somaprasad, Shri K.	CPI(M)
91. Veerendra Kumar, Shri M.P.	JD(U)

MADHYA PRADESH (11)

92. Akbar, Shri M. J.	BJP
93. Chaturvedi, Shri Satyavrat	INC
94. Dave, Shri Anil Madhav	BJP
95. Ganesan, Shri La.	BJP
96. Gehlot, Shri Thaawar Chand	BJP
97. Jain, Shri Meghraj	BJP
98. Jatiya, Dr. Satyanarayan	BJP
99. Javadekar, Shri Prakash	BJP
100. Jha, Shri Prabhat	BJP
101. Singh, Shri Digvijaya	INC
102. Tankha, Shri Vivek K.	INC

MAHARASHTRA (19)

103. Athawale, Shri Ramdas	RPI(A)
104. Chavan, Smt. Vandana	NCP
105. Chidambaram, Shri P.	INC

106. Dalwai, Shri Husain INC
107. Desai, Shri Anil SS
108. Dhoot, Shri Rajkumar SS
109. Goyal, Shri Piyush BJP
110. Kakade, Shri Sanjay Dattatraya IND.
111. Mahatme, Dr. Vikas BJP
112. Memon, Shri Majeed NCP
113. Patel, Shri Praful NCP
114. Patil, Smt. Rajani INC
115. Pawar, Shri Sharad NCP
116. Raut, Shri Sanjay SS
117. Sable, Shri Amar Shankar BJP
118. Sahasrabuddhe, Dr. Vinay P. BJP
119. Sancheti, Shri Ajay BJP
120. Shukla, Shri Rajeev INC
121. Tripathi, Shri D.P. NCP

MANIPUR (1)

122 Salam, Haji Abdul INC

MEGHALAYA (1)

123. Syiem, Smt. Wansuk INC

MIZORAM (1)

124. Tlau, Shri Ronald Sapa INC

NAGALAND (1)

125. Kenye, Shri K. G. NPF

NATIONAL CAPITAL TERRITORY OF DELHI (3)

126. Dwivedi, Shri Janardan INC
127. Hashmi, Shri Parvez INC
128. Karan Singh, Dr. INC

ODISHA (10)

129. Acharya, Shri Prasanna BJD
130. Biswal, Shri Ranjib INC
131. Das, Shri Bishnu Charan BJD

132. Deo, Shri A.U. Singh	BJD
133. Hembram, Smt. Sarojini	BJD
134. Mohanty, Shri Anubhav	BJD
135. Nekkanti, Shri Bhaskar Rao	BJD
136. Swain, Shri Narendra Kumar	BJD
137. Swamy, Shri A.V.	IND.
138. Tirkey, Shri Dilip Kumar	BJD

PUDUCHERRY (1)

139. Gokulakrishnan, Shri N.	AIADMK

PUNJAB (7)

140. Bajwa, Shri Pratap Singh	INC
141. Bhunder, Shri Balwinder Singh	SAD
142. Dhindsa, Sardar Sukhdev Singh	SAD
143. Dullo, Shri Shamsher Singh	INC
144. Gujral, Shri Naresh	SAD
145. Malik, Shri Shwait	BJP
146. Soni, Smt. Ambika	INC

RAJASTHAN (10)

147. Budania, Shri Narendra	INC
148. Dudi, Shri Ram Narain	BJP
149. Dungarpur, Shri Harshvardhan Singh	BJP
150. Goel, Shri Vijay	BJP
151. Mathur, Shri Om Prakash	BJP
152. Naidu, Shri M. Venkaiah	BJP
153. Panchariya, Shri Narayan Lal	BJP
154. Singhvi, Dr. Abhishek Manu	INC
155. Verma, Shri Ramkumar	BJP
155. Yadav, Shri Bhupender	BJP

SIKKIM (1)

157. Lachungpa, Shri Hishey	SDF

TAMIL NADU (18)

158. Arjunan, Shri K. R.	AIADMK
159. Balasubramoniyan, Shri S.R.	AIADMK

160.	Bharathi, Shri R.S.	DMK
161.	Elangovan, Shri T.K.S.	DMK
162.	Kanimozhi, Smt.	DMK
163.	Lakshmanan, Dr. R.	AIADMK
164.	Maitreyan, Dr. V.	AIADMK
165.	Muthukaruppan, Shri S.	AIADMK
166.	Navaneethakrishnan, Shri A.	AIADMK
167.	Raja, Shri D.	CPI
168.	Rangarajan, Shri T.K.	CPI(M)
169.	Rathinavel, Shri T.	AIADMK
170.	Sasikala Pushpa, Smt.	AIADMK
171.	Selvaraj, Shri A. K.	AIADMK
172.	Siva, Shri Tiruchi	DMK
173.	Vaithilingam, Shri R.	AIADMK
174.	Vijayakumar, Shri A.	AIADMK
175.	Vijila Sathyananth, Smt.	AIADMK

TELANGANA (7)

176.	Ramesh, Shri C.M.	TDP
177.	Rao, Shri Garikapati Mohan	TDP
178.	Rao, Dr. K.V.P. Ramachandra	INC
179.	Rao, Shri V. Lakshmikantha	TRS
180.	Rapolu, Shri Ananda Bhaskar	INC
181.	Reddy, Shri Palvai Govardhan	INC
182.	Srinivas, Shri Dharmapuri	TRS

TRIPURA (1)

183.	Baidya, Smt. Jharna Das	CPI(M)

UTTAR PRADESH (31)

184.	Agrawal, Shri Naresh	SP
185.	Ali, Shri Munquad	BSP
186.	Ashok Siddharth, Shri	BSP
187.	Bachchan, Smt. Jaya	SP
188.	Katiyar, Shri Vinay	BJP
189.	Khan, Shri Javed Ali	SP

190.	Mayawati, Km.	BSP
191.	Misra, Shri Satish Chandra	BSP
192.	Nagar, Shri Surendra Singh	SP
193.	Nanda, Shri Kiranmay	SP
194.	Nishad, Shri Vishambhar Prasad	SP
195.	Parrikar, Shri Manohar	BJP
196.	Punia, Shri P.L.	INC
197.	Rajaram, Shri	BSP
198.	Saleem, Chaudhary Munvvar	SP
199.	Seth, Shri Sanjay	SP
200.	Shekhar, Shri Neeraj	SP
201.	Shukla, Shri Shiv Pratap	BJP
202.	Sibal, Shri Kapil	INC
203.	Singh, Shri Amar	SP
204.	Singh, Shri Rewati Raman	SP
205.	Singh, Shri Veer	BSP
206.	Tazeen Fatma, Dr.	SP
207.	Tiwari, Shri Alok	SP
208.	Tiwari, Shri Pramod	INC
209.	Verma, Shri Beni Prasad	SP
210.	Verma, Shri Ravi Prakash	SP
211.	Yadav, Dr. Chandrapal Singh	SP
212.	Yadav, Shri Darshan Singh	SP
213.	Yadav, Prof. Ram Gopal	SP
214.	Yadav, Ch. Sukhram Singh	SP

UTTARAKHAND (3)

215.	Babbar, Shri Raj	INC
216.	Mahra, Shri Mahendra Singh	INC
217.	Tamta, Shri Pradeep	INC

WEST BENGAL (16)

218.	Bandyopadhyay, Shri D.	AITC
219.	Banerjee, Shri Ritabrata	CPI(M)
220.	Bhattacharya, Shri P.	INC
221.	Chakraborty, Shri Mithun	AITC
222.	Chowdhury, Prof. Jogen	AITC
223.	Ghosh, Shri Kunal Kumar	AITC
224.	Gupta, Shri Vivek	AITC
225.	Haque, Shri Md. Nadimul	AITC
226.	Hassan, Shri Ahamed	AITC
227.	O Brien, Shri Derek	AITC
228.	Roy, Shri Mukul	AITC
229.	Roy, Shri Sukhendu Sekhar	AITC
230.	Sen, Ms. Dola	AITC
231.	Sen, Shri Tapan Kumar	CPI(M)
232.	Singh, Dr. Kanwar Deep	AITC
233.	Yechury, Shri Sitaram	CPI(M)

NOMINATED (12)

234.	Aga, Ms. Anu	NOM.
235.	Chhatrapati, Shri Sambhaji	NOM.
236.	Dasgupta, Shri Swapan	NOM.
237.	Ganguly, Smt. Roopa	BJP
238.	Jadhav, Dr. Narendra	NOM.
239.	Kom, Smt. M.C. Mary	NOM.
240.	Parasaran, Shri K.	NOM.
241.	Rekha, Ms.	NOM.
242.	Suresh Gopi, Shri	BJP
240.	Swamy, Dr. Subramanian	BJP
243.	Tendulkar, Shri Sachin Ramesh	NOM.
244.	Tulsi, Shri K.T.S.	NOM.

LOK SABHA (State Wise List as on December 15, 2016)

Speaker : **Smt. Sumitra Mahajan**

Deputy Speaker : **Dr M. Thambi Durai**

Secretary-General : **Shri Anoop Mishra**

S. No.	State/Constituency	Name of the Member	Party/ Group
ANDHRA PRADESH (25)			
1	Amalapuram (SC)	Pandula, Dr. Ravindra Babu	TDP
2	Anakapalle	Rao (Avanthi), Shri Muthamsetti Srinivasa	TDP
3	Anantapur	Reddy, Shri J.C. Divakar	TDP
4	Araku (ST)	Kothapalli, Smt. Geetha	YSR (CP)
5	Bapatla (SC)	Malyadri, Shri Sriram	TDP
6	Chittoor (SC)	Sivaprasad, Dr. Naramalli	TDP
7	Eluru	Magantti, Shri Venkateswara Rao (Babu)	TDP
8	Guntur	Galla, Shri Jayadev	TDP
9	Hindupur	Nimmala, Shri Kristappa	TDP
10	Kadapa	Reddy, Shri Y. S. Avinash	YSR (CP)
11	Kakinada	Thota, Shri Narasimham	TDP
12	Kurnool	Butta, Smt. Renuka	YSR (CP)
13	Machilipatnam	Rao, Shri Konakalla Narayana	TDP
14	Nandyal	Reddy, Shri S.P.Y.	YSR (CP)
15	Narasaraopet	Rao, Shri Rayapati Sambasiva	TDP
16	Narsapuram	Raju, Shri Gokaraju Ganga	BJP
17	Nellore	Reddy, Shri Mekapati Rajamohan	YSR (CP)
18	Ongole	Subba Reddy, Shri Yerram Venkata	YSR (CP)
19	Rajahmundry	Maganti, Shri Murali Mohan	TDP
20	Rajampet	Reddy, Shri Midhun	YSR (CP)
21	Srikakulam	Ram Mohan Naidu, Shri Kinjarapu	TDP
22	Tirupati (SC)	Velagapalli, Dr. Vara Prasadarao	YSR (CP)
23	Vijayawada	Kesineni, Shri Srinivas	TDP
24	Visakhapatnam	Kambhampati,Dr. Hari Babu	BJP
25	Vizianagaram	Pusapati, Shri Ashok Gajapathi Raju	TDP
ARUNACHAL PRADESH (2)			
26	Arunachal East	Ering, Shri Ninong	INC
27	Arunachal West	Rijiju, Shri Kiren	BJP

Source : Lok Sabha Website http://loksabha.nic.in

ASSAM (13)

28	Autonomous District (ST)	Engti, Shri Biren Singh	INC
29	Barpeta	Ajmal, Shri Sirajuddin	AIUDF
30	Dhubri	Ajmal, Maulana Badruddin	AIUDF
31	Dibrugarh	Teli, Shri Rameswar	BJP
32	Gauhati	Chakravarty, Smt. Bijoya	BJP
33	Jorhat	Tasa, Shri Kamakhya Prasad	BJP
34	Kaliabor	Gogoi, Shri Gaurav	INC
35	Karimganj (SC)	Biswas, Shri Radheshyam	AIUDF
36	Kokrajhar	Sarania, Shri Naba (Hira) Kumar	Ind.
37	Mangaldoi	Deka, Shri Ramen	BJP
38	Nawgong	Gohain, Shri Rajen	BJP
39	Silchar	Dev, Km. Sushmita	INC
40	Tezpur	Sarmah, Shri Ram Prasad	BJP

BIHAR (40)

41	Araria	Taslim Uddin, Shri	RJD
42	Arrah	Singh, Shri Raj Kumar	BJP
43	Aurangabad	Singh, Shri Sushil Kumar	BJP
44	Banka	Yadav, Shri Jay Prakash Narayan	RJD
45	Begusarai	Singh, Dr. Bhola	BJP
46	Bhagalpur	Kumar, Shri Shailesh (Bulo Mandal)	RJD
47	Buxar	Choubey, Shri Ashwini Kumar	BJP
48	Darbhanga	Azad, Shri Kirti (JHA)	BJP
49	Gaya (SC)	Manjhi, Shri Hari	BJP
50	Gopalganj (SC)	Ram, Shri Janak	BJP
51	Hajipur (SC)	Paswan, Shri Ram Vilas	LJSP
52	Jahanabad	Kumar, Dr. Arun	RLSP
53	Jamui (SC)	Paswan, Shri Chirag	LJSP
54	Jhanjharpur	Chaudhary, Shri Birendra Kumar	BJP
55	Karakat	Kushwaha, Shri Upendra	RLSP
56	Katihar	Anwar, Shri Tariq	NCP
57	Khagaria	Kaiser, Choudhary Mehboob Ali	LJSP
58	Kishanganj	Mohammad, Shri Asrarul Haque	INC
59	Madhepura	Ranjan (Pappu Yadav), Shri Rajesh	RJD
60	Madhubani	Yadav, Shri Hukmdev Narayan	BJP
61	Maharajganj	Sigriwal, Shri Janardan Singh	BJP
62	Munger	Devi, Smt. Veena	LJSP

63	Muzaffarpur	Nishad, Shri Ajay	BJP
64	Nalanda	Kumar, Shri Kaushalendra	JD(U)
65	Nawada	Singh, Shri Giriraj	BJP
66	Paschim Champaran	Jaiswal, Dr. Sanjay	BJP
67	Pataliputra	Yadav, Shri Ram Kripal	BJP
68	Patna Sahib	Sinha, Shri Shatrughan Prasad	BJP
69	Purnia	Kumar, Shri Santosh	JD(U)
70	Purvi Champaran	Singh,Shri Radha Mohan	BJP
71	Samastipur (SC)	Paswan, Shri Ramchandra	LJSP
72	Saran	Rudy, Shri Rajiv Pratap	BJP
73	Sasaram (SC)	Paswan, Shri Chhedi	BJP
74	Sheohar	Devi, Smt. Rama	BJP
75	Sitamarhi	Sharma, Shri Ram Kumar	RLSP
76	Siwan	Yadav,Shri Om Prakash	BJP
77	Supaul	Ranjan, Smt. Ranjeet	INC
78	Ujiarpur	Rai, Shri Nityanand	BJP
79	Vaishali	Singh, Shri Rama Kishore	LJSP
80	Valmiki Nagar	Dubey, Shri Satish Chandra	BJP

CHHATTISGARH (11)

81	Bastar (ST)	Kashyap, Shri Dinesh	BJP
82	Bilaspur	Sahu, Shri Lakhan Lal	BJP
83	Durg	Sahu, Shri Tamradhwaj	INC
84	Janjgir-Champa (SC)	Patle, Smt. Kamla Devi	BJP
85	Kanker(ST)	Usendi, Shri Vikram	BJP
86	Korba	Mahto, Dr. Banshilal	BJP
87	Mahasamund	Sahu, Shri Chandu Lal	BJP
88	Raigarh (ST)	Sai, Shri Vishnu Deo	BJP
89	Raipur	Bais, Shri Ramesh	BJP
90	Rajnandgaon	Singh, Shri Abhishek	BJP
91	Surguja (ST)	Marabi, Shri Kamalbhan Singh	BJP

GOA (2)

92	North Goa	Naik, Shri Shripad Yesso	BJP
93	South Goa	Sawaikar, Shri Advocate Narendra Keshav	BJP

GUJARAT (26)

94	Ahmedabad East	Rawal, Shri Paresh	BJP
95	Ahmedabad West	Solanki, Dr. (Prof.) Kirit Premjibhai	BJP

96	Amreli	Kachhadiya, Shri Naranbhai Bhikhabhai	BJP
97	Anand	Patel, Shri Dilip M.	BJP
98	Banaskantha	Chaudhary, Shri Haribhai Parthibhai	BJP
99	Bardoli	Vasava, Shri Parbhubhai Nagarbhai	BJP
100	Bharuch	Vasava, Shri Mansukhbhai Dhanjibhai	BJP
101	Bhavnagar	Shyal, Dr. Bharati Dhirubhai	BJP
102	Chhota Udaipur	Rathwa, Shri Ramsinh Pataliyabhai	BJP
103	Dahod	Bhabhor, Shri Jaswantsinh Sumanbhai	BJP
104	Gandhinagar	Advani, Shri Lal Krishna	BJP
105	Jamnagar	Maadam, Smt. Poonamben Hematbhai	BJP
106	Junagadh	Chudasama,Shri Rajeshbhai Naranbhai	BJP
107	Kachchh (SC)	Chavda, Shri Vinod	BJP
108	Kheda	Chauhan, Shri Devusinh Jesingbhai	BJP
109	Mehsana	Patel, Smt. Jayshreeben	BJP
110	Navsari	Patil, Shri C. R.	BJP
111	Panchmahal	Chauhan, Shri Prabhatsinh Pratapsinh	BJP
112	Patan	Vaghela, Shri Liladharbhai Khodaji	BJP
113	Porbandar	Radadiya,Shri Vitthalbhai Hansrajbhai	BJP
114	Rajkot	Kundariya, Shri Mohanbhai Kalyanji	BJP
115	Sabarkantha	Rathod, Shri Dipsinh Shankarsinh	BJP
116	Surat	Jardosh, Smt. Darshana Vikram	BJP
117	Surendranagar	Fatepara, Shri Devajibhai Govindbhai	BJP
118	Vadodara	Bhatt, Smt. Ranjanben Dhananjay	BJP
119	Valsad(ST)	Patel, Dr. K. C.	BJP

HARYANA (10)

120	Ambala (SC)	Kataria, Shri Rattan Lal	BJP
121	Bhiwani-Mahendragarh	Dharambir Singh, Shri	BJP
122	Faridabad	Gurjar, Shri Krishan Pal	BJP
123	Gurgaon	Rao Inderjit Singh,	BJP
124	Hisar	Chautala,Shri Dushyant	INLD
125	Karnal	Ashwini Kumar, Shri	BJP
126	Kurukshetra	Saini, Shri Raj Kumar	BJP
127	Rohtak	Hooda, Shri Deepender Singh	INC
128	Sirsa (SC)	Rori, Shri Charanjeet Singh	INLD
129	Sonipat	Kaushik, Shri Ramesh Chander	BJP

HIMACHAL PRADESH (4)

130	Hamirpur	Thakur, Shri Anurag Singh	BJP

131 Kangra	Kumar, Shri Shanta	BJP
132 Mandi	Sharma, Shri Ram Swaroop	BJP
133 Shimla (SC)	Kashyap, Shri Virender	BJP

JAMMU AND KASHMIR (4)

134 Baramulla	Baig, Shri Muzaffar Hussain	J&KPDP
135 Jammu	Sharma, Shri Jugal Kishore	BJP
136 Ladakh	Chhewang, Shri Thupstan	BJP
137 Udhampur	Singh, Dr. Jitendra	BJP

JHARKHAND (14)

138 Chatra	Singh, Shri Sunil Kumar	BJP
139 Dhanbad	Singh, Shri Pashupati Nath	BJP
140 Dumka (ST)	Soren, Shri Shibu	JMM
141 Giridih	Pandey, Shri Ravindra Kumar	BJP
142 Godda	Dubey, Shri Nishikant	BJP
143 Hazaribagh	Sinha,Shri Jayant	BJP
144 Jamshedpur	Mahato, Shri Bidyut Baran	BJP
145 Khunti (ST)	Munda, Shri Kariya	BJP
146 Kodarma	Ray, Dr. Ravindra Kumar	BJP
147 Lohardaga (ST)	Bhagat, Shri Sudarshan	BJP
148 Palamu (SC)	Ram, Shri Vishnu Dayal	BJP
149 Rajmahal (ST)	Hansdak, Shri Vijay Kumar	JMM
150 Ranchi	Choudhary, Shri Ram Tahal	BJP
151 Singhbhum (ST)	Giluwa, Shri Laxman	BJP

KARNATAKA (28)

152 Bagalkot	Gaddigoudar, Shri Parvatagouda Chandanagouda	BJP
153 Bangalore Central	Mohan, Shri P. C.	BJP
154 Bangalore North	Gowda, Shri D.V. Sadananda	BJP
155 Bangalore Rural	Suresh, Shri Doddaalahalli Kempegowda	INC
156 Bangalore South	Ananth Kumar, Shri	BJP
157 Belgaum	Angadi, Shri Suresh Chanabasappa	BJP
158 Bellary (ST)	Sreeramulu, Shri B.	BJP
159 Bidar	Khuba, Shri Bhagwanth	BJP
160 Bijapur (SC)	Jigajinagi, Shri Ramesh Chandappa	BJP
161 Chamrajanagar	Dhruvanarayana, Shri R.	INC
162 Chikkballapur	Moily, Dr. M. Veerappa	INC

163 Chikkodi	Hukkeri, Shri Prakash Babanna	INC
164 Chitradurga (SC)	Chandrappa, Shri B.N.	INC
165 Dakshina Kannada	Kateel, Shri Nalin Kumar	BJP
166 Davanagere	Siddeshwara, Shri Gowdar Mallikarjunappa	BJP
167 Dharwad	Joshi, Shri Pralhad Venkatesh	BJP
168 Gulbarga (SC)	Kharge, Shri Mallikarjun	INC
169 Hassan	Devegowda, Shri H.D.	JD(S)
170 Haveri	Udasi, Shri Shivkumar Chanabasappa	BJP
171 Kolar	Muniyappa, Dr. K.H.	INC
172 Koppal	Karadi, Shri Sanganna Amarappa	BJP
173 Mandya	Puttaraju, Shri C.S.	JD(S)
174 Mysore	Simha, Shri Prathap	BJP
175 Raichur	Naik,Shri B.V.	INC
176 Shimoga	Yeddyurappa, Shri B. S.	BJP
177 Tumkur	Muddahanumegowda, Shri S.P.	INC
178 Udupi Chikmagalur	Karandlaje, Km. Shobha	BJP
179 Uttara Kannada	Hegde, Shri Anantkumar	BJP

KERALA (20)

180 Alappuzha	Venugopal, Shri K. C.	INC
181 Alathur (SC)	Biju, Shri Parayamparambil Kuttappan	CPI(M)
182 Attingal	Sampath, Dr. Anirudhan	CPI(M)
183 Chalakudy	Innocent, Shri	Ind.
184 Ernakulam	Thomas, Prof. Kuruppassery Varkey	INC
185 Idukki	George, Shri (Adv.) Joice	Ind.
186 Kannur	Teacher, Smt. P.K. Sreemathi	CPI(M)
187 Kasaragod	Karunakaran, Shri P.	CPI(M)
188 Kollam	Premachandran, Shri N.K.	RSP
189 Kottayam	Mani,Shri Jose K.	KC(M)
190 Kozhikodé	Raghavan, Shri M. K.	INC
191 Malappuram	Ahamed, Shri E.	IUML
192 Mavelikkara (SC)	Kodikunnil, Shri Suresh	INC
193 Palakkad	Rajesh, Shri M. B.	CPI(M)
194 Pathanamthitta	Antony, Shri Anto	INC
195 Ponnani	Basheer, Shri E. T. Mohammed	IUML
196 Thiruvananthapuram	Tharoor, Dr. Shashi	INC
197 Thrissur	Jayadevan, Shri C. N.	CPI
198 Vadakara	Mullappally, Shri Ramachandran	INC
199 Wayanad	Shanavas, Shri M. I.	INC

MADHYA PRADESH (29)

200 Balaghat	Bhagat, Shri Bodhsingh	BJP
201 Betul (ST)	Dhurve, Smt. Jyoti	BJP
202 Bhind (SC)	Prasad, Dr. Bhagirath	BJP
203 Bhopal	Sanjar, Shri Alok	BJP
204 Chhindwara	Kamal Nath,Shri	INC
205 Damoh	Patel, Shri Prahlad Singh	BJP
206 Dewas	Utawal, Shri Manohar	BJP
207 Dhar (ST)	Thakur, Smt. Savitri	BJP
208 Guna	Scindia, Shri Jyotiraditya Madhavrao	INC
209 Gwalior	Tomar, Shri Narendra Singh	BJP
210 Hoshangabad	Singh, Shri Uday Pratap	BJP
211 Indore	Sumitra Mahajan (Tai),	BJP
212 Jabalpur	Singh, Shri Rakesh	BJP
213 Khajuraho	Singh, Shri Nagendra	BJP
214 Khandwa	Chauhan, Shri Nand Kumar Singh	BJP
215 Khargone (ST)	Patel, Shri Subhash	BJP
216 Mandla (ST)	Kulaste, Shri Faggan Singh	BJP
217 Mandsour	Gupta, Shri Sudheer	BJP
218 Morena	Mishra, Shri Anoop	BJP
219 Rajgarh	Nagar, Shri Rodmal	BJP
220 Ratlam (ST)	Bhuria, Shri Kantilal	INC
221 Rewa	Mishra, Shri Janardan	BJP
222 Sagar	Yadav, Shri Laxmi Narayan	BJP
223 Satna	Singh, Shri Ganesh	BJP
224 Shahdol (ST)	Singh, Shri Gyan	BJP
225 Sidhi	Pathak, Smt. Riti	BJP
226 Tikamgarh (SC)	Kumar, Dr. Virendra	BJP
227 Ujjain (SC)	Malviya, Prof. Chintamani	BJP
228 Vidisha	Swaraj, Smt. Sushma	BJP

MAHARASHTRA (48)

229 Ahmednagar	Gandhi, Shri Dilip Kumar Mansukhlal	BJP
230 Akola	Dhotre, Shri Sanjay Shamrao	BJP
231 Amravati	Adsul, Shri Anandrao	SS
232 Aurangabad	Khaire, Shri Chandrakant Bhaurao	SS
233 Baramati	Sule, Smt. Supriya Sadanand	NCP
234 Beed	Munde, Dr. Pritam Gopinath	BJP

235	Bhandara-Gondiya	Patole, Shri Nanabhau Falgunrao	BJP
236	Bhiwandi	Patil, Shri Kapil Moreshwar	BJP
237	Buldhana	Jadhav, Shri Prataprao	SS
238	Chandrapur	Ahir, Shri Hansraj Gangaram	BJP
239	Dhule	Bhamre, Dr. Subhash Ramrao	BJP
240	Dindori (ST)	Chavan, Shri Harishchandra Deoram	BJP
241	Gadchiroli-Chimur (ST)	Nete, Shri Ashok Mahadeorao	BJP
242	Hatkanangle	Shetti,Shri Raju alias Devappa Anna	SWP
243	Hingoli	Satav, Shri Rajeev Shankarrao	INC
244	Jalgaon	Patil, Shri A.T. (Nana)	BJP
245	Jalna	Danve, Shri Raosaheb Patil	BJP
246	Kalyan	Shinde, Dr. Shrikant Eknath	SS
247	Kolhapur	Mahadik, Shri Dhananjay Bhimrao	NCP
248	Latur (SC)	Gaikwad, Dr. Sunil Baliram	BJP
249	Madha	Patil, Shri Vijaysinh Mohite	NCP
250	Maval	Barne, Shri Shrirang Appa	SS
251	Mumbai South-Central	Shewale, Shri Rahul Ramesh	SS
252	Mumbai-North	Shetty,Shri Gopal Chinayya	BJP
253	Mumbai-North-Central	Mahajan, Smt. Poonam	BJP
254	Mumbai-North-East	Dr. Kirit Somaiya	BJP
255	Mumbai-North-West	Kirtikar, Shri Gajanan Chandrakant	SS
256	Mumbai-South	Sawant, Shri Arvind Ganpat	SS
257	Nagpur	Gadkari, Shri Nitin Jairam	BJP
258	Nanded	Chavan, Shri Ashok Shankarrao	INC
259	Nandurbar (ST)	Gavit, Dr. Heena Vijaykumar	BJP
260	Nashik	Godse, Shri Hemant Tukaram	SS
261	Osmanabad	Gaikwad, Prof. Ravindra Vishwanath	SS
262	Palghar (ST)	Wanaga, Shri Chintaman Navsha	BJP
263	Parbhani	Jadhav, Shri Sanjay Haribhau	SS
264	Pune	Anil (alias Padmakar) Gulabrao, Shirole, Shri	BJP
265	Raigad	Geete, Shri Anant Gangaram	SS
266	Ramtek (SC)	Tumane, Shri Krupal Balaji	SS
267	Ratnagiri-Sindhudurg	Raut,Shri Vinayak Bhaurao	SS
268	Raver	Khadse, Smt. Raksha Nikhil	BJP
269	Sangli	Patil, Shri Sanjay(Kaka) Ramchandra	BJP
270	Satara	Bhonsle, Shri Udayanraje Pratapsingh	NCP
271	Shirdi (SC)	Lokhande, Shri Sadashiv Kisan	SS
272	Shirur	Adhalrao Patil, Shri Shivaji	SS

273 Solapur (SC)	Bansode, Shri Sharadkumar Maruti	BJP
274 Thane	Vichare, Shri Rajan Baburao	SS
275 Wardha	Tadas, Shri Ramdas Chandrabhanji	BJP
276 Yavatmal-Washim	Bhawana Gawali (Patil), Ms.	SS

MANIPUR (2)

277 Inner Manipur	Meinya, Dr. Thokchom	INC
278 Outer Manipur (ST)	Baite, Shri Thangso	INC

MEGHALAYA (2)

279 Shillong (ST)	Pala, Shri Vincent H	INC
280 Tura (ST)	Sangma, Shri Conrad Kongkal	NPP

MIZORAM (1)

281 Mizoram (ST)	Ruala, Shri C. L.	INC

NAGALAND (1)

282 Nagaland	Rio, Shri Neiphiu	NPF

ODISHA (21)

283 Aska	Swain, Shri Ladu Kishore	BJD
284 Balasore	Jena, Shri Rabindra Kumar	BJD
285 Bargarh	Singh, Dr. Prabhas Kumar	BJD
286 Berhampur	Mohapatra, Shri Sidhant	BJD
287 Bhadrak (SC)	Sethi, Shri Arjun Charan	BJD
288 Bhubaneswar	Patasani, Dr. (Prof.) Prasanna Kumar	BJD
289 Bolangir	Singh Deo, Shri Kalikesh Narayan	BJD
290 Cuttack	Mahtab, Shri Bhartruhari	BJD
291 Dhenkanal	Satpathy, Shri Tathagata	BJD
292 Jagatsinghpur (SC)	Samal, Dr. Kulamani	BJD
293 Jajpur (SC)	Tarai, Smt. Rita	BJD
294 Kalahandi	Deo, Shri Arka Keshari	BJD
295 Kandhamal	Singh, Smt. Pratyusha Rajeshwari	BJD
296 Kendrapara	Panda, Shri Baijayant "Jay"	BJD
297 Keonjhar (ST)	Laguri, Smt. Sakuntala	BJD
298 Koraput (ST)	Hikaka, Shri Jhina	BJD
299 Mayurbhanj (ST)	Hansdah, Shri Rama Chandra	BJD
300 Nabarangpur (ST)	Majhi, Shri Balabhadra	BJD
301 Puri	Misra, Shri Pinaki	BJD
302 Sambalpur	Pradhan, Shri Nagendra Kumar	BJD

303 Sundargarh (ST)	Oram, Shri Jual	BJP

PUNJAB (13)

304 Amritsar	Singh, Captain Amarinder	INC
305 Anandpur Sahib	Chandumajra, Shri Prem Singh	SAD
306 Bathinda	Badal, Smt. Harsimrat Kaur	SAD
307 Faridkot (SC)	Singh, Prof. Sadhu	AAP
308 Fatehgarh Sahib (SC)	Khalsa, Shri Harinder Singh	AAP
309 Ferozpur	Ghubaya, Shri Sher Singh	SAD
310 Gurdaspur	Khanna, Shri Vinod	BJP
311 Hoshiarpur (SC)	Sampla, Shri Vijay	BJP
312 Jalandhar	Chaudhary, Shri Santokh Singh	INC
313 Khadoor Sahib	Brahmpura, Shri Ranjit Singh	SAD
314 Ludhiana	Singh, Shri Ravneet	INC
315 Patiala	Gandhi, Dr. Dharam Vira	AAP
316 Sangrur	Mann, Shri Bhagwant	AAP

Rajasthan (25)

317 Ajmer	Jat, Prof. Sanwar Lal	BJP
318 Alwar	Yogi, Shri Chand Nath	BJP
319 Banswara (ST)	Ninama, Shri Manshankar	BJP
320 Barmer	Col. Choudhary, Sona Ram, VSM (Retd.)	BJP
321 Bharatpur (SC)	Koli, Shri Bahadur Singh	BJP
322 Bhilwara	Baheria, Shri Subhash Chandra	BJP
323 Bikaner (SC)	Meghwal, Shri Arjun Ram	BJP
324 Chittorgarh	Joshi, Shri C. P.	BJP
325 Churu	Kaswan, Shri Rahul	BJP
326 Dausa (ST)	Meena, Shri Harish Chandra	BJP
327 Ganganagar (SC)	Chauhan, Shri Nihal Chand	BJP
328 Jaipur	Bohra, Shri Ramcharan	BJP
329 Jaipur Rural	Rathore, Col. Rajyavardhan Singh	BJP
330 Jalore	Patel, Shri Devji Mansingram	BJP
331 Jhalawar-Baran	Singh, Shri Dushyant	BJP
332 Jhunjhunu	Ahlawat, Smt. Santosh	BJP
333 Jodhpur	Shekhawat, Shri Gajendra Singh	BJP
334 Karauli-Dholpur (SC)	Rajoria, Dr. Manoj	BJP
335 Kota	Birla, Shri Om	BJP
336 Nagaur	Chaudhary, Shri C.R.	BJP
337 Pali	Chaudhary, Shri P.P.	BJP

338 Rajsamand	Rathore, Shri Hariom Singh	BJP
339 Sikar	Saraswati, Shri Sumedhanand	BJP
340 Tonk-Sawai Madhopur	Jaunapuria, Shri Sukhbir Singh	BJP
341 Udaipur	Meena,Shri Arjunlal	BJP

SIKKIM (1)

342 Sikkim	Rai, Shri Prem Das	SDF

TAMIL NADU (39)

343 Arakkonam	Hari, Shri G.	AIADMK
344 Arani	V., Shri Elumalai	AIADMK
345 Chennai Central	S.R., Shri Vijayakumar	AIADMK
346 Chennai North	Venkatesh Babu, Shri T.G.	AIADMK
347 Chennai South	Jayavardhan, Dr. Jayakumar	AIADMK
348 Chidambaram (SC)	Chandrakasi, Shri M.	AIADMK
349 Coimbatore	P., Shri Nagarajan	AIADMK
350 Cuddalore	Arunmozhithevan, Shri A.	AIADMK
351 Dharmapuri	Ramadoss, Dr. Anbumani	PMK
352 Dindigul	Udhayakumar, Shri M.	AIADMK
353 Erode	Selvakumarachinnayan,Shri S.	AIADMK
354 Kallakurichi	Kamaraj, Dr. K.	AIADMK
355 Kancheepuram(SC)	Maragatham, Smt. K.	AIADMK
356 Kanniyakumari	Radhakrishnan, Shri Pon	BJP
357 Karur	Thambi Durai, Dr. M.	AIADMK
358 Krishnagiri	Ashokkumar, Shri K.	AIADMK
359 Madurai	Gopalakrishnan, Shri R.	AIADMK
360 Mayiladuthurai	Bharathimohan, Shri R.K.	AIADMK
361 Nagapattinam (SC)	Gopal, Dr. K.	AIADMK
362 Namakkal	Sundaram, Shri P.R.	AIADMK
363 Nilgiris (SC)	Chinnaraj, Shri Gopalakrishnan	AIADMK
364 Perambalur	Marutharajaa, Shri R.P.	AIADMK
365 Pollachi	Mahendran, Shri C.	AIADMK
366 Ramanathapuram	Raajhaa, Shri A. Anwhar	AIADMK
367 Salem	Selvam, Shri V. Panneer	AIADMK
368 Sivaganga	Senthilnathan, Shri P.R.	AIADMK
369 Sriperumbudur	Ramachandran, Shri Krishnan Narayanasamy	AIADMK
370 Tenkasi (SC)	M., Smt. Vasanthi	AIADMK
371 Thanjavur	K., Shri Parasuraman	AIADMK
372 Theni	Parthipan, Shri R.	AIADMK

373 Thoothukkudi	Natterjee, Advocate Jayasingh Thiyagaraj	AIADMK
374 Tiruchirappalli	Kumar, Shri P.	AIADMK
375 Tirunelveli	Prabakaran, Shri K.R.P.	AIADMK
376 Tiruppur	Sathyabama, Smt. V.	AIADMK
377 Tiruvallur (SC)	Venugopal, Dr. Ponnusamy	AIADMK
378 Tiruvannamalai	Vanaroja, Smt. R.	AIADMK
379 Vellore	Senguttuvan, Shri B.	AIADMK
380 Viluppuram (SC)	Rajendran, Shri S.	AIADMK
381 Virudhunagar	Radhakrishnan, Shri T.	AIADMK

TELANGANA (17)

382 Adilabad (ST)	Godam, Shri Nagesh	TRS
383 Bhongir	Goud, Dr. Boora Narsaiah	TRS
384 Chevella	Reddy, Shri Konda Vishweshwar	TRS
385 Hyderabad	Owaisi, Shri Asaduddin	AIMIM
386 Karimnagar	Boianapalli, Shri Vinod Kumar	TRS
387 Khammam	Reddy, Shri Ponguleti Srinivasa	YSR (C P)
388 Mahabubabad	Naik, Dr. (Prof.) Azmeera Seetaram	TRS
389 Mahabubnagar	Reddy, Shri A.P. Jithender	TRS
390 Malkajgiri	Reddy, Shri Ch. Malla	TDP
391 Medak	Reddy, Shri Kotha Prabhakar	TRS
392 Nagarkurnool (SC)	Yellaiah, Shri Nandi	INC
393 Nalgonda	Gutha, Shri Sukender Reddy	INC
394 Nizamabad	Kalvakuntla, Smt. Kavitha	TRS
395 Peddapalle (SC)	Suman, Shri Balka	TRS
396 Secunderabad	Dattatreya, Shri Bandaru	BJP
397 Warangal	Pasunoori, Shri Dayakar	TRS
398 Zahirabad	Patil, Shri Bheemrao Baswanthrao	TRS

TRIPURA (2)

399 Tripura East (ST)	Chaudhury, Shri Jitendra	CPI(M)
400 Tripura West	Datta, Shri Sankar Prasad	CPI(M)

UTTAR PRADESH (80)

401 Agra	Ram Shankar, Prof. (Dr.)	BJP
402 Akbarpur	Singh, Shri Devendra (Alias) Bhole Singh	BJP
403 Aligarh	Gautam, Shri Satish Kumar	BJP
404 Allahabad	Gupta, Shri Shyama Charan	BJP
405 Ambedkar Nagar	Pandey, Shri Hari Om	BJP

406 Amethi	Gandhi, Shri Rahul	INC
407 Amroha	Tanwar, Shri Kanwar Singh	BJP
408 Aonla	Kumar, Shri Dharmendra	BJP
409 Azamgarh	Yadav, Shri Mulayam Singh	SP
410 Badaun	Yadav, Shri Dharmendra	SP
411 Baghpat	Singh, Dr. Satya Pal	BJP
412 Bahraich (SC)	Phoole, Sushree Sadhvi Savitri Bai	BJP
413 Ballia	Singh, Shri Bharat	BJP
414 Banda	Mishra, Shri Bhairon Prasad	BJP
415 Bansgaon (SC)	Paswan, Shri Kamlesh	BJP
416 Barabanki (SC)	Rawat, Smt. Priyanka Singh	BJP
417 Bareilly	Gangwar, Shri Santosh Kumar	BJP
418 Basti	Dwivedi, Shri Harish	BJP
419 Bhadohi	Singh, Shri Virendra	BJP
420 Bijnor	Singh, Kunwar Bharatendra	BJP
421 Bulandshahr	Singh, Shri Bhola	BJP
422 Chandauli	Pandey, Dr. Mahendra Nath	BJP
423 Deoria	Mishra, Shri Kalraj	BJP
424 Dhaurahra	Verma, Smt. Rekha Arun	BJP
425 Domariyaganj	Pal , Shri Jagdambika	BJP
426 Etah	Singh, Shri Rajveer (Raju Bhaiya)	BJP
427 Etawah (SC)	Dohrey, Shri Ashok Kumar	BJP
428 Faizabad	Singh, Shri Lallu	BJP
429 Farrukhabad	Rajput, Shri Mukesh	BJP
430 Fatehpur	Jyoti, Sadhvi Niranjan	BJP
431 Fatehpur Sikri	Chaudhary, Shri Babulal	BJP
432 Firozabad	Yadav, Shri Akshay	SP
433 Gautam Buddha Nagar	Sharma, Dr. Mahesh	BJP
434 Ghaziabad	General (Dr.) , Vijay Kumar Singh (Retd.)	BJP
435 Ghazipur	Sinha, Shri Manoj Kumar	BJP
436 Ghosi	Rajbhar, Shri Hari Narayan	BJP
437 Gonda	Singh,Shri Kirti Vardhan	BJP
438 Gorakhpur	Adityanath, Shri Yogi	BJP
439 Hamirpur	Chandel, Kunwar Pushpendra Singh	BJP
440 Hardoi (SC)	Verma, Shri Anshul	BJP
441 Hathras (SC)	Diwakar, Shri Rajesh Kumar	BJP
442 Jalaun (SC)	Verma, Shri Bhanu Pratap Singh	BJP
443 Jaunpur	Singh, Dr. Krishna Pratap	BJP

444 Jhansi	Sushree, Uma Bharati	BJP
445 Kairana	Singh, Shri Hukum	BJP
446 Kaiserganj	Singh, Shri Brijbhushan Sharan	BJP
447 Kannauj	Yadav, Smt. Dimple	SP
448 Kanpur	Joshi, Dr. Murli Manohar	BJP
449 Kaushambi (SC)	Sonkar, Shri Vinod Kumar	BJP
450 Kheri	Misra, Shri Ajay (Teni)	BJP
451 Kushi Nagar	Pandey, Shri Rajesh	BJP
452 Lalganj (SC)	Sonker, Smt. Neelam	BJP
453 Lucknow	Singh, Shri Rajnath	BJP
454 Machhlishahr	Ram Charitra Nishad,Shri	BJP
455 Maharajganj	Chowdhary, Shri Pankaj	BJP
456 Mainpuri	Yadav, Shri Tejpratap Singh	SP
457 Mathura	Hema Malini,Smt.	BJP
458 Meerut	Agrawal, Shri Rajendra	BJP
459 Mirzapur	Patel, Smt. Anupriya	Apna Dal
460 Misrikh (SC)	Bala, Smt. Anju	BJP
461 Mohanlalganj (SC)	Kishore, Shri Kaushal	BJP
462 Moradabad	Kumar, Shri Kunwar Sarvesh	BJP
463 Muzaffarnagar	Balyan, Dr. Sanjeev Kumar	BJP
464 Nagina (SC)	Singh, Dr. Yashwant	BJP
465 Phulpur	Maurya, Shri Keshav Prasad (Kushwaha)	BJP
466 Pilibhit	Gandhi, Smt. Maneka Sanjay	BJP
467 Pratapgarh	Singh, Shri Kunwar Haribansh	Apna Dal
468 Rae Bareli	Gandhi, Smt. Sonia	INC
469 Rampur	Singh, Dr. Nepal	BJP
470 Robertsganj (SC)	Chhotelal, Shri	BJP
471 Saharanpur	Lakhanpal, Shri Raghav	BJP
472 Salempur	Kushawaha, Shri Ravindra	BJP
473 Sambhal	Singh, Shri Satya Pal	BJP
474 Sant Kabir Nagar	Tripathi, Shri Sharad	BJP
475 Shahjahanpur (SC)	Raj, Smt. Krishna	BJP
476 Shrawasti	Mishra, Shri Daddan	BJP
477 Sitapur	Verma, Shri Rajesh	BJP
478 Sultanpur	Gandhi, Shri Feroze Varun	BJP

479 Unnao	Swami Maharaj, Dr. Sakshi Ji	BJP
480 Varanasi	Modi, Shri Narendra	BJP

UTTARAKHAND (5)

481 Almora(SC)	Tamta, Shri Ajay	BJP
482 Garhwal	Khanduri, Maj Gen Bhuwan Chandra AVSM (Retd.)	BJP
483 Hardwar	Nishank, Dr. Ramesh Pokhriyal	BJP
484 Nainital-Udhamsingh Nagar	Koshyari, Shri Bhagat Singh	BJP
485 Tehri Garhwal	Shah, Smt. Mala Rajya Laxmi	BJP

WEST BENGAL (42)

486 Alipurduars (ST)	Tirkey, Shri Dasrath	AITC
487 Arambagh (SC)	Poddar, Smt. Aparupa	AITC
488 Asansol	Babul Supriyo,Shri	BJP
489 Baharampur	Chowdhury, Shri Adhir Ranjan	INC
490 Balurghat	Ghosh, Ms. Arpita	AITC
491 Bangaon (SC)	Thakur, Smt. Mamata	AITC
492 Bankura	Varma, Smt. Dev (Moon Moon Sen)	AITC
493 Barasat	Dastidar, Dr. (Smt.) Kakoli Ghosh	AITC
494 Bardhaman Purba (SC)	Mondal, Shri Sunil Kumar	AITC
495 Bardhaman-Durgapur	Sanghamita, Prof. (Dr.) Mamtaz	AITC
496 Barrackpur	Trivedi, Shri Dinesh	AITC
497 Basirhat	Ali, Shri Idris	AITC
498 Birbhum	Roy (Banerjee), Smt. Satabdi	AITC
499 Bishnupur (SC)	Saumitra, Shri Khan	AITC
500 Bolpur (SC)	Hazra, Dr. Anupam	AITC
501 Coochbehar (SC)	Ray, Shri Partha Pratim	AITC
502 Darjeeling	Ahluwalia, Shri S.S.	BJP
503 Diamond Harbour	Banerjee, Shri Abhishek	AITC
504 Dum Dum	Roy,Prof. Saugata	AITC
505 Ghatal	Adhikari, Shri Deepak (Dev)	AITC
506 Hooghly	De (Nag), Dr. (Smt.) Ratna	AITC
507 Howrah	Banerjee, Shri Prasun	AITC
508 Jadavpur	Bose, Prof. (Dr.) Sugata	AITC
509 Jalpaiguri (SC)	Barman, Shri Bijoy Chandra	AITC

510 Jangipur	Mukherjee, Dr. Abhijit	INC
511 Jaynagar (SC)	Mondal, Smt. Pratima	AITC
512 Jhargram (ST)	Saren, Dr. Uma	AITC
513 Kanthi	Adhikari, Shri Sisir Kumar	AITC
514 Kolkata Dakshin	Bakshi, Shri Subrata	AITC
515 Kolkata Uttar	Bandyopadhyay, Shri Sudip	AITC
516 Krishnanagar	Paul, Shri Tapas	AITC
517 Maldaha Dakshin	Choudhury, Shri Abu Hasem Khan	INC
518 Maldaha Uttar	Noor, Smt. Mausam	INC
519 Mathurapur (SC)	Jatua, Shri Choudhury Mohan	AITC
520 Medinipur	Roy, Smt. Sandhya	AITC
521 Murshidabad	Khan, Shri Md. Badaruddoza	CPI(M)
522 Purulia	Mahato, Dr. Mriganka	AITC
523 Raiganj	Salim, Shri Mohammad	CPI(M)
524 Ranaghat (SC)	Mandal, Dr. Tapas	AITC
525 Serampore	Banerjee, Shri Kalyan	AITC
526 Tamluk	Adhikari, Shri Dibyendu	AITC
527 Uluberia	Ahmed, Shri Sultan	AITC

ANDAMAN AND NICOBAR ISLANDS (1)

528 Andaman and Nicobar Islands	Ray, Shri Bishnu Pada	BJP

CHANDIGARH (1)

529 Chandigarh	Kher, Smt. Kirron Anupam	BJP

DADRA AND NAGAR HAVELI (1)

530 Dadra and Nagar Haveli (ST)	Patel, Shri Natubhai Gomanbhai	BJP

DAMAN AND DIU (1)

531 Daman and Diu	Patel, Shri Lalubhai Babubhai	BJP

NATIONAL CAPITAL TERRITORY OF DELHI (7)

532 Chandni Chowk	Harsh Vardhan, Dr.	BJP
533 East Delhi	Girri, Shri Maheish	BJP
534 New Delhi	Lekhi, Smt. Meenakashi	BJP

535 North East Delhi	Tiwari, Shri Manoj Kumar	BJP
536 North West Delhi (SC)	Raj, Dr. Udit	BJP
537 South Delhi	Bidhuri, Shri Ramesh	BJP
538 West Delhi	Singh, Shri Parvesh Sahib	BJP

LAKSHADWEEP (1)

539 Lakshadweep (ST)	Mohammed, Shri Faizal P. P.	NCP

PUDUCHERRY (1)

540 Puducherry	Radhakrishnan, Shri R.	AINRC

NOMINATED (2)

541 Baker, Shri George	Nominated Anglo-Indian (West Bengal)
542 Hay, Prof. Richard	Nominated Anglo-Indian (Kerala)

VACANT SEATS (3)

Abbreviations used for Parties : All India Forward Bloc - AIFB; All India Majlis-e-Ittehadul Muslimeen - AIMEIM; All India Namathu Rajiyam (Our Kingdom Congress - AINR Congress; All India Trinamool Congress -AITC; Asom Gana Parishad - AGP; Bahujan Samaj Party - BSP; Bharatiya Janata Party- BJP; Bharatiya Navshakti Party - BNP; Biju Janata Dal - BJD; Communist Party of India - CPI; Communist Party of India (Marxist) - CPI(M); Dravida Munnetra Kazhagam - DMK; Indian National Congress - INC; Jammu & Kashmir National Conference - J&KNC; Janata Dal (Secular) - JD (S); Janata Dal (United JD (U); Jharkhand Mukti Morcha - JMM; Kerala Congress - KC; Lok Jan Shakti Party - LJSP; Marumalarchi Dravida Munnetra Kazhagam - MDMK; Mizo National Front - MNF; Muslim League - ML; Nagaland Peoples Front - NPF; Nationalist Congress Party - NCP; Pattali Makkal Katchi - PMK; Jammu and Kashmir Peoples Democratic Party - J&K PDP; Rashtriya Janata Dal - RJD; Rashtriya Lok Dal - RLD; Republican Party of India (A) - RPI (A); Revolutionary Socialist Party - RSP; Samajwadi Janata Party (Rashtriya) - SJP (R); Samajwadi Party - SP; Shiromani Akali Dal - SAD; Shiv Sena - SS; Sikkim Democratic Front - SDF; Swabhimani Raksha Party-SWP; Telangana Rashtra Samithi - TRS; Telugu Desam Party - TDP; Viduthalai Chiruthaigal Katchi - VCK; Independent-IND.

Source : http://loksabha.nic.in

IND-05/2017

IND-09/2017

IND-14/2017